MACMILLAN
ENCYCLOPEDIA
OF
WORLD SLAVERY

MACMILLAN ENCYCLOPEDIA OF WORLD SLAVERY

VOLUME 1

Edited by

Paul Finkelman
Joseph C. Miller

MACMILLAN REFERENCE USA
SIMON & SCHUSTER MACMILLAN
NEW YORK

SIMON & SCHUSTER AND PRENTICE HALL INTERNATIONAL
LONDON   MEXICO CITY   NEW DELHI   SINGAPORE   SYDNEY   TORONTO

Simon & Schuster Macmillan
1633 Broadway
New York, NY 10019-6785

PRINTED IN THE UNITED STATES OF AMERICA

1 2 3 4 5 6 7 8 9 10

LIBRARY OF CONGRESS CATALOGING-IN-PUBLICATION DATA

Macmillan encyclopedia of world slavery / edited by Paul Finkelman,
   Joseph C. Miller.
      p.   cm.
   Includes bibliographical references (p.   ) and index.
   ISBN 0-02-864607-X (set : lib. bdg. : alk. paper). — ISBN
0-02-864780-7 (Vol. 1 : lib. bdg. : alk. paper). — ISBN 0-02-864781-5
(Vol. 2 : lib. bdg. : alk. paper).
   1. Slavery—Encyclopedias.   I. Finkelman, Paul, 1949– .
II. Miller, Joseph Calder.   III. Macmillan Reference USA (Firm)
HT861.M24   1998
306.3′62′03—dc21   98-30610
                                                              CIP

This paper meets the requirements of ANSI/NISO Z39.48-1992 (Permanence of Paper)

Contents

Editorial and Production Staff

Project Editor
Thomas McCarthy

Editorial Assistant
Anthony Coloneri

Production Editor
Evangeline Legones

Manuscript Editors
Susan Gamer
Nancy E. Gratton
Richard P. Larkin
Ingrid Sterner

Proofreaders
Al McDermid
Edward G. McLeroy

Illustrations Editor
Brian Kinsey

Cartographer
Donald S. Frazier

Indexer
AEIOU, Inc.

Production Manager
Dabney Smith

MACMILLAN REFERENCE
Elly Dickason, *Publisher*
Toni Ann Scaramuzzo, *Managing Editor*

Preface

For most Americans "slavery" evokes an image of black bondsmen, white masters, and cotton fields. The image is simultaneously accurate and misleading. In the United States and throughout most of the Western Hemisphere, slavery was indeed tied to race and field labor. Although Spanish conquistadors also enslaved Native Americans in the first years of contact, as did some early British colonists, by the seventeenth century most slaves in the Americas were Africans or of African ancestry. On the other hand, while cotton was the predominant crop in the nineteenth-century United States, more New World slaves were involved in the production of sugar than of any other product. Slaves in mainland North America and elsewhere in the New World were also used in the cultivation of tobacco, rice, indigo, wheat, and coffee. Many thousands toiled in mines. Others hawked foods on the streets of colonial cities or cut trees in American forests; still others were among the first industrial workers in Virginia or were cowboys in Brazil or South Carolina.

Even this wide range of tasks, however, does not approach the diversity of employments to which slaves have been put in the history of the world. While the customs of slavery in the Americas usually put "black" Africans and their descendants at the beck and call of European or European-descended "whites," at most places and times race has not been central among the distinctions observed between masters and slaves. Most slaves in the ancient Mediterranean came from other cultures, cultures that Greeks and Romans viewed as "barbarian." But there were Greek slaves in Greece and Italian slaves in Rome. In Asia particularly, ethnicity seems not to have prohibited captivity, and there were Chinese slaves in China, Javanese in Java, Japanese in Japan, and Korean in Korea. Africans regarded themselves as members of many distinct groups, and those who were Muslims regarded those who were not as *kaffirs*—unbelievers—and thus enslavable. Similarly, to group all the native inhabitants of the Americas as "Indians" or to see the diverse peoples of India and the surrounding regions as "South Asians" is to impose a perspective unknown to the peoples themselves, who saw no immorality in enslaving individuals from other groups in the area. The Aztec in Mexico enslaved the neighboring meso-American populations they conquered in the fifteenth century, and Pacific peoples in Hawaii and New Zealand held slaves from their own islands. In the Middle Ages European Christians enslaved pagans, in the sixteenth century Russian nobles enslaved other Slavs, and in the 1930s Communist authorities in the Soviet Union created totalitarian state power so overwhelming that thousands of political prisoners endured conditions strongly akin to slavery. At the same time, Nazi theorists in Germany developed standards of racial purity so narrow that they condemned Russians, Poles, and other Europeans beyond the Jews—as well as their own countrymen—to toil in slave labor camps.

In *Slavery and Social Death* Orlando Patterson, the leading sociologist of slavery, wrote, "There is nothing notably peculiar about the institution of slavery. It has existed from before the dawn of human history right down to the twentieth century, in the most primitive of human societies and in the most civilized." He concluded, "Probably there is no group of people whose ancestors were not at one time slaves or slaveholders." With the exceptions of marriage, the family, and religion, slavery is perhaps the most ubiquitous social institution in human history. A central event of Judeo-Christian theology is the Exodus of Hebrew slaves from Egypt in the thirteenth century B.C.E. Slaves in Babylonia, Assyria, Greece, and Rome built the great stone monuments that we now admire in those ancient civilizations. They also worked the farmlands of wealthy nobles, excavated mines, rowed galleys, and performed all manner of other menial tasks that we associate with the burdens of modern slaves. But others practiced respected professions such as medicine and pharmacy, entertained as gladiators, educated the children of prominent families, fought as soldiers for their masters, and wielded power as agents of political figures, including even the Roman emperors themselves. Chinese dynasties, rulers throughout southeast Asia, Muslim political authorities, and kings almost everywhere in Africa surrounded themselves with slave soldiers, often eunuchs, and showered them with privileges and comforts.

In the late fifteenth century slavery of this domestic sort thrived everywhere in the Muslim world and in most of southern Europe, including Spain and Portugal, where it was primarily a source of domestic servants and urban workers for the growing cities of the Renaissance. The Portuguese introduced Africans, brought back from their early explorations of the coast of West Africa, to these markets. Columbus returned from America in 1495 with captive Carib Indians whom he meant to sell as slaves in Spain. Within a few years Spaniards were enslaving large numbers of New World natives to work in the mines and fields of their American colonies, until Amerindian populations died out from overwork and exposure to Old World diseases. The Spaniards also brought Africans to the Americas, mostly skilled slaves from the cities of Iberia, as domestics and artisans to staff the households of the cities they built there.

In Brazil in the sixteenth century the Portuguese similarly enslaved natives, but in the 1570s, when they developed sugar as the New World's first major plantation crop and needed workers for the cane fields, they turned to Africa for forced laborers in much greater numbers. Over the next two centuries, as sugar spread to the Caribbean and the English developed tobacco, rice, and then cotton in North America, Africans and their descendants labored throughout the hemisphere as slaves. But the spread of trade across the world, much of it centered on Europe, prompted the Dutch and many local planters to put people to work as slaves in Southeast Asia, in India, and

throughout the Arab world. Russian landholders subjected their peasants to a serfdom much like slavery. Africans, although sending millions of captives—mostly men—to the New World, kept millions more—many of them women—as wives and as workers to support the networks they had built to supply slaves to Europeans. By the nineteenth century, as Western Europe celebrated the ideals of freedom and human dignity, nearly everywhere else more people than ever before toiled in bondage, subject to the most degrading humiliation and physical abuse.

This Encyclopedia, centered on slavery, summarizes current knowledge about all forms of human bondage throughout the world, in its full diversity and ubiquity. The complex and differing characters of the various manifestations of slavery have led us to accept several definitions of it, according to the ways that masters in other times and places have incorporated outsiders in their midst. In some cultures slaves served for a limited term of years, while in others they served for life. In many, slave status passed from parents to children, according to varying rules of descent; in others children with slave parentage could gain a degree of acceptance as free persons. In some times and places, slaves serving for life toiled side by side with others condemned only for a given number of years. However a society declared some within its bounds to have been slaves, their experiences fall within the scope of this work.

We have also acknowledged other forms of forced labor—including serfdom, peonage, coolie status, and conscription under government corvée—usually where they replaced slavery but occasionally where they existed simultaneously. These pages also cover the full array of antislavery movements that emerged in Europe and the Americas at the end of the eighteenth century, movements dedicated to suppression of the maritime trade in enslaved Africans and then to emancipation of the people held as slaves in the Americas. We follow these abolition movements on through their modern and contemporary successors, dedicated to eradicating the lingering and revived forms of slavery in the world today. We have extended the subject as far as knowledge permits, beyond its familiar context in the nineteenth-century United States, to the world as a whole.

The root of all forms of forced labor has been the exploitation of the laborer for the benefit of the master; but slavery is distinguished from all the others by the element of exclusive, total control and dependency, combined with its tendency to originate in violence. Other than in Rome and the Americas, this totality of control made the sense of ownership and entitlement that came with the status of master often as important as the control of the slave's labor or of what the slave produced. Masters in societies as diverse as parts of the Arab world, the Tlingit cultures of the Pacific Northwest, and the Aztec of Mexico used slaves prominently for prestige, for satisfaction of personal obsessions, and in other uneconomical ways that suggest a logic of consumption—a consumption of human beings. Even in the Americas, where industrial-style production of commodities set the dominant tone of slavery, English West Indian sugar barons and U.S. rice and cotton planters kept house slaves in numbers far in excess of what they needed for comfort or convenience to demonstrate to their slaveholding neighbors, and their competitors, how truly wealthy they were.

The conventional definition of slaves as "persons owned by someone else" applies principally to ancient Greece and Rome, to southern Europe in the Middle Ages, and, in recent centuries, to places where commercial practices and the rule of law make "property" the principal method of control and advantage. Slavery in these circumstances extended the familiar legal rights of ownership from objects and animals to human beings. Thus, in Rome and in modern western societies, the difference between a contract laborer and slave was clear: the former sold his or her labor to a purchaser, and the employer could command the laborer's time and effort for the term of the contract, but no longer. The owner of a slave, on the other hand, owned the body of the slave for his or her lifetime, as well as (in most American legal systems) owning the children that female slaves produced. Such ownership, because of the involuntary element vital to it, was very unlike modern "trading" in employment rights. In non-American cultures the idea of ownership has assumed less legalistic and commercial forms, forms less likely to involve "sale"; though they may often not appear so, such forms of personal dependency are often just as onerous for those enslaved.

Another hallmark of slavery is the diminished rights and capacities allowed the slaves. In most western colonies and nations, slaves could own no property, could not sign a binding contract, and had no political rights. In the United States slaves could not testify at the trial of a free person. In ancient Rome a slave's testimony was acceptable in courts of law, but only when preceded by torture, since honor and responsibility to the law, presumed for Roman citizens or subjects, could not be taken for granted with slaves. Among Muslims, slaves were excluded from the blessings of membership in the religious community, or *umma,* and manumission or—for concubines—the birth of a master's child entailed conversion as well as freedom. Among those Africans who emphasized the communal solidarity of kinship, the knowledge that one belonged *to,* rather than *in,* the network of family and in-laws left a slave humiliated and despised, regardless of any incidental similarities of garb or labor between master and slave.

Most students of slavery today also define their subject in terms of what Patterson has called "natal alienation." Thus understood, slaves were deracinated people, denied a place in the society in which they were forced to live. In the ancient world slaves were often men defeated in battle or men, women, and children taken when cities fell to an invader. Under the rules of war at that time, these captives might have been legitimately killed by their captors. Instead, enslaved, they were, in Patterson's terminology, socially dead, having no kin, no protectors, and no reputable place in the society in which they lived.

The vulnerability and dishonor of slave status also assumed extremely personal forms. In almost every society masters have been free to make claims on their slaves' sexuality. In Africa, the Middle East, and Asia, where descent and claims over progeny constituted major components of wealth and power, the sexual aspect of slavery involved more than physical gratification. Slaves lacked kin of their own, and so no one could compete with their masters for rights over the children they bore. Under Islamic law, which limited a man to four legitimate marriages, masters could fill out their harems with as many slave concubines as their resources allowed or could gratify other desires with enslaved boys. In the modern West, slaves' lack of rights to their own bodies left women, particularly, open to the private passions, sometimes abusive and twisted, of their owners. In the antebellum South and throughout Latin America, masters and their sons commonly pursued liaisons—sometime casual, sometimes long-lasting, sometimes open, sometimes hidden—with female slaves, relatively free of the social condemnation that would have followed the same behavior with free, "respectable" women. During World War II both Germany and Japan coerced civilian women into "service" of the men they conscripted as soldiers, thus hoping to deflect the notorious sexual aggressiveness among armies of men. The Japanese euphemistically referred to these captive females as "comfort women."

Just as masters claimed the bodies of slaves, men as well as women, for their sexual use and abuse, in most societies they also claimed the products of that contact—the children of slaves—as additions to their property. In such societies, slave women lived in isolation from one another as members of their masters' households and produced children as dependent contributions to the households. The laws of slavery in ancient Rome recognized family rights for slaves primarily through the mechanisms provided for manumission; "slave families," as such, barely existed in law, whatever informal domestic arrangements may have arisen within wealthy Roman households staffed by numerous slaves. So unlikely were slaves to live in conditions adequate to support themselves, much less their children or aged parents, that slave families seemed an impossibility.

Nonetheless, with the rise of large communities of slaves of both sexes, slave families, segregated by growing racial distinctions and built up to tend the agricultural commodity exports of Europe's colonies, became common in certain areas of the Americas. Similar large-scale agriculture, often for export, also promoted the assemblage of villages of slave families in nineteenth-century Africa; in a few locations— notably in the Sokoto caliphate and in Zanzibar— these assemblages approached a scale that resembled American plantations. In most parts of the Americas, particularly the colonies of the northern Europeans, exclusive racial rules tended to deny the children of master-slave liaisons recognition as offspring of their free fathers, thus leaving them to their maternal slave families. This tendency was less pronounced in colonies where European wives were scarce, notably Brazil, where fathers of Portuguese backgrounds tended to recognize, and sometimes to free, their children by slave women. Such recognition assumed greatest significance where circumstances hindered the formation of families among the slaves.

Although slavery is generally seen as a historical phenomenon, a disturbing, extreme form of human cruelty and domination that we would like to consign to the oblivion of a distant past, it still exists in some parts of Africa and Asia today. Humans still force others to labor against their will in conditions reminiscent of slavery, even in the world of cybertechnology and the United Nations Charter of Human Rights. This persistence of slavery, and the universality of the institution throughout world history, may illustrate the profound roots of domination and uncontrollable greed in the human psyche.

The memories of slaveries past are also fundamental parts of modern culture. A hundred million North and South Americans descend from Africans brought to the New World as slaves, and from southern Brazil to southern Canada they are challenging inequalities that they ascribe to the racial legacy of their slave progenitors' subordination to their masters. Citizens of contemporary African nations, equal before the laws of their countries, privately regard one another in terms of their descent from ancestors known to have been masters or slaves. Asian women who survived their wartime enslavement for the "comfort" of Japanese soldiers are demanding compensation and, what is at least as important to them, an apology from a Japanese nation reluctant to admit

the horrors of its past. Contemporary Europeans are haunted by the enslavement and murder of millions of their neighbors under Nazism and Communism. Europeans, as well as Americans, contemplate the social and moral costs of the massive system of slavery from which their shippers and purchasers profited. Africans, meanwhile, debate how to assess the roles of their ancestors in selling their neighbors into foreign bondage, how to memorialize those who left the continent in chains, and also how to regard the American descendants of the enslaved who return from the diaspora seeking identities as "Africans."

The legacy of slavery haunts the United States, a nation dedicated to human equality, with particular profundity. Until the middle of the nineteenth century, the economy of the new nation depended heavily on racially based slavery, and its political institutions accommodated and protected this form of bondage in a myriad of ways. The most wrenching moment in U.S. history, the Civil War that killed and maimed many of its youth and ultimately transformed its political institutions, arose from the contradiction of what was, in Lincoln's words, a nation "half slave and half free." That war ended slavery but opened the way to generations of virulent racism and discrimination and to a continuing racial divide.

As this Encyclopedia goes to press, a presidential commission contemplates racism as a problem besetting the tranquillity of the nation. Its chairman, Dr. John Hope Franklin, is a historian whose scholarship is central to the understanding of slavery in the United States. As the existence of the commission makes clear, debates still rage around the consequences of slavery and how the United States should come to terms with them. We, the editors, hope that the coverage of world slavery in this Encyclopedia sets these debates in their full global context.

Acknowledgments

This Encyclopedia would not have been possible without the collegiality and dedication of the numerous scholars who have written for it and who gracefully accepted editorial suggestions, as well as the constrictions of space and style that the encyclopedia format necessarily imposes. We are also extremely grateful to our Advisory Board, whose advice was essential throughout the project. Elly Dickason, publisher of Macmillan Reference, was a key player in this project from the first meeting of the board to the last detail of publication. Her support and enthusiasm for the project were essential to its success. Also important in the early planning and development was the late Charlie Smith, who, with Paul Bernabeo, initiated the project and then placed it in the superbly able hands of Stephen Wagley, who now sits across the hall at Scribner Reference. We also thank Ed Ayers, Jack McKivigan, and Peter Wallenstein, who served as consultants. We owe special thanks to Donald Frazier for the production of the superb maps that grace these volumes and to Brian Kinsey, who tracked down photographs and illustrations with persistence and skill.

Finally, we are supremely grateful to our project editor, Thomas McCarthy. Tom's wit, charm, good humor, great intelligence, and demanding E-mails kept the project on track in the face of impossible deadlines and mountains of paperwork. We sincerely thank him for his enormous effort and his first-class professionalism.

Paul Finkelman
Joseph C. Miller

Alphabetical List of Entries

Directory of Contributors

A

Sean Adams
University of Wisconsin–Madison
Miners: U.S. Mines

Virginia H. Aksan
McMaster University
Egypt: Ottoman Egypt
Islam: Islamic Caliphates
Janissaries

Richard B. Allen
Worcester, MA
Mauritius and Réunion

Robert J. Allison
Suffolk University
Barbary Wars
Equiano, Olaudah

Douglas Ambrose
Hamilton College
Bible: Jewish and Christian Interpretations
Christianity: An Overview
Christianity: Protestantism
Perspectives on Slavery: Defenses of Slavery

David H. Anthony III
University of California, Santa Cruz
Arts: Verbal Arts
Dance
Freedmen: Brazil and the United States
Missionaries
Music about Slavery
Urban Slavery: The World

B

Edwin T. Bacon
University of Birmingham (UK)
Gulag

Edward E. Baptist
University of Miami
Florida

Diane Barnes
West Virginia University
Industrial Slaves

Barbara C. Batson
Library of Virginia
Arts: Visual Arts

Edna G. Bay
Emory University
Literature of Slavery: African Literature

Hilary McD. Beckles
University of the West Indies
Abolition and Antislavery Movements:
    Caribbean Region
Caribbean Region: English Colonies
Labor Systems: Indentured Labor
    (Seventeenth-Century)

Malcolm Bell, Jr.
Hendersonville, NC
Butler, Pierce Mease

Ira Berlin
University of Maryland
MANUMISSION: UNITED STATES

Carol Bleser
Clemson University
HAMMOND, JAMES HENRY

David Booth
University of Hawaii at Manoa
COMFORT WOMEN IN WORLD WAR II
LABOR SYSTEMS: CORVÉE
MAORI

James F. Brooks
University of Maryland
AMERINDIAN SOCIETIES: PRECONTACT
AMERINDIAN SOCIETIES: POSTCONTACT

Henry Bucher Jr.
Austin College
LIBREVILLE

C

Edward D. C. Campbell Jr.
Library of Virginia
FILM AND TELEVISION, SLAVERY IN

Gwyn Campbell
University of Avignon
EAST AFRICA: MADAGASCAR

Charles W. Carey Jr.
Central Virginia Community College
BURNS, ANTHONY
CIVIL RIGHTS ACT OF 1866 (U.S.)
CIVIL RIGHTS ACT OF 1875 (U.S.)
COMPROMISE OF 1850
DRED SCOTT V. SANDFORD (1857)
ELKINS THESIS
HURD, JOHN CODMAN
INTERNATIONAL LABOR ORGANIZATION
LAY, BENJAMIN AND SARAH
LUNDY, BENJAMIN
MILL, JOHN STUART
MISSOURI COMPROMISE
MUSIC BY SLAVES
NABUCO DE ARAUJO, JOAQUIM
ONESIMUS
RAMSEY, JAMES
RAYNAL, G.-T.-F. DE, ABBÉ
SHARP, GRANVILLE
STOWE, HARRIET BEECHER
TANEY, ROGER B.
TRUTH, SOJOURNER
TUBMAN, HARRIET
WALKER, DAVID
WARD, SAMUEL RINGGOLD
WELD, THEODORE

WHEATLEY, PHILLIS
WHITNEY, ELI
WILBERFORCE, WILLIAM
WRIGHT, HENRY CLARKE

Calum Carmichael
Cornell University
BIBLE: AN OVERVIEW
BIBLE: BIBLICAL LAW
CHRISTIANITY: EARLY CHURCH
EXODUS

David A. Chappell
University of Hawaii at Manoa
BLACKBIRDING IN THE PACIFIC ISLANDS
PACIFIC ISLAND SOCIETIES

Indrani Chatterjee
Azad Institute for Asian Studies, Calcutta
INDIAN SUBCONTINENT

Gabriel J. Chin
University of Cincinnati College of Law
LABOR SYSTEMS: COOLIES

Catherine Clinton
Wofford College
CIVIL WAR, U.S.
JACOBS, HARRIET
KEMBLE, FRANCES ANNE ("FANNY")
SEXUAL EXPLOITATION
STEWART, MARIA W.

David M. Cobin
Hamline University School of Law
JEWS
JUDAISM
LAW: ANCIENT ISRAEL

Peter Cohee
Ohio University
TEMPLE SLAVES IN ANCIENT GREECE AND ROME

Thomas M. Cohen
Catholic University of America
VIEIRA, ANTÓNIO

Ronald G. Coleman
University of Utah
UTAH

Robert E. Conrad
Beaver, PA
ABOLITION AND ANTISLAVERY MOVEMENTS: BRAZIL
BRAZIL: CENTRAL AND SOUTHERN BRAZIL
BRAZILIAN ANTISLAVERY SOCIETY
SLAVE TRADE: UNITED STATES

Edward Countryman
Southern Methodist University

CLARKSON, THOMAS
DOUGLAS, STEPHEN A.
LINCOLN, ABRAHAM
UNITED STATES: COLONIAL PERIOD
WASHINGTON, GEORGE

John J. Crocitti
University of Miami
COMTE, AUGUSTE
FREYRE, GILBERTO
LAS CASAS, BARTOLOMÉ DE
NÓBREGA, MANUEL DA
PORTUGAL: ATLANTIC ISLANDS SLAVERY

Valerie Cunningham
African American Resource Center, Portsmouth, NH
NEW HAMPSHIRE

R. Emmett Curran
Georgetown University
CHRISTIANITY: ROMAN CATHOLICISM

D

Davison M. Douglas
William and Mary School of Law
BADGES OF SLAVERY

Katherine Fischer Drew
Rice University
CRUSADES
LAW: GERMANIC LAW AND PEOPLES
MEDIEVAL EUROPE, SLAVERY AND SERFDOM IN

Melvyn Dubofsky
State University of New York at Binghamton
LABOR SYSTEMS: CONTRACT LABOR

Stephen L. Dyson
University of Buffalo
PLANTATIONS: ANCIENT ROME

E

Douglas R. Egerton
Le Moyne College
AMERICAN COLONIZATION SOCIETY
GABRIEL
GABRIEL'S REBELLION (1800)
REBELLIONS AND VIOLENT RESISTANCE
VESEY REBELLION (1822)

Ivana Elbl
Trent University
PORTUGAL: SLAVERY IN PORTUGAL
PORTUGAL: COLONIES AND EMPIRE

Elizabeth A. Eldredge
Michigan State University
SOUTHERN AFRICA: SOTHO/NGUNI

Kirk Endicott
Dartmouth College
MALAYA

William McKee Evans
Pomona, CA
PERSPECTIVES ON SLAVERY: ETYMOLOGY AND SEMANTICS
PERSPECTIVES ON SLAVERY: SOCIOLOGY OF SLAVERY
RECONSTRUCTION, U.S.

Janet J. Ewald
Duke University
NORTHEAST AFRICA: UPPER NILE REGION
NORTHEAST AFRICA: ETHIOPIA

F

Geneviève Fabre
Université Denis Diderot
HOLIDAYS
MEMORY AND HISTORY

Robert Fahs
University of Hawaii at Manoa
EPICTETUS

Andrew T. Fede
Montclair State University
SLAVE CODES

Paul Finkelman
University of Akron School of Law
ABOLITION AND ANTISLAVERY MOVEMENTS:
    MEANING OF THE TERMS
BIRNEY, JAMES G.
CONFLICT OF LAWS
CONSTITUTION, U.S.
FUGITIVE SLAVE LAWS, U.S.
GRADUAL EMANCIPATION STATUTES
HENSON, JOSIAH
HISTORICAL APPROACHES TO SLAVERY: UNITED STATES
HUMAN SACRIFICE: THE NEW WORLD AND PACIFIC
    CULTURES
ILLINOIS
INDIANA
IOWA
LAW: LAW AND LEGAL SYSTEMS
LAW: ANCIENT ISRAEL
LAW: U.S. NORTH
MASSACHUSETTS
NORTHWEST ORDINANCE
OHIO
PLEASANTS V. PLEASANTS (VA., 1799)
PRIGG V. PENNSYLVANIA (1842)
SMITH, GERRIT
STATE V. MANN (N.C., 1829)

Alan Fisher
Michigan State University
OTTOMAN EMPIRE

PALACE SLAVES IN THE MIDDLE EAST
SLAVS
ZANJ SLAVES

Harold S. Forsythe
Fairfield University
CHURCHES, AFRICAN-AMERICAN
FREEDMEN'S BUREAU
PEONAGE: UNITED STATES
SPIRITUALS

Bruce Fort
University of Virginia
EDUCATION OF SLAVES: UNITED STATES

David F. Forte
Cleveland-Marshall College of Law
LAW: ISLAMIC LAW

G

Larry Gara
Wilmington College (emeritus)
UNDERGROUND RAILROAD

Eugene Garver
Saint John's University
ARISTOTLE
PHILOSOPHY: AN OVERVIEW
PHILOSOPHY: GREEK AND HELLENISTIC PHILOSOPHY
PLATO
ROUSSEAU, JEAN-JACQUES

David Geggus
University of Florida
CARIBBEAN REGION: AN OVERVIEW
CARIBBEAN REGION: FRENCH COLONIES
CODE NOIR
CONCUBINAGE: CARIBBEAN REGION
ENLIGHTENMENT
MONTESQUIEU, CHARLES-LOUIS DE SECONDAT DE
TOUSSAINT-LOUVERTURE

Louis S. Gerteis
University of Missouri, Saint Louis
CONTRABAND

Michael A. Gomez
University of Georgia
ISLAM: MUSLIMS IN AMERICA
SIERRA LEONE
SOLOMON, JOB BEN
WEST AFRICA: MEDIEVAL WESTERN SUDAN

Lawrence B. Goodheart
University of Connecticut
CONNECTICUT

Virginia Meacham Gould
Atlanta, GA
CONCUBINAGE: UNITED STATES

Kenneth S. Greenberg
Suffolk University
TURNER, NAT

David Grimsted
University of Maryland, College Park
INSURRECTIONS

H

David T. Haberly
University of Virginia
LITERATURE OF SLAVERY: BRAZILIAN AND
    PORTUGUESE LITERATURE

Sally Hadden
Florida State University
TRIALS OF SLAVES

Ian Hancock
International Romani Union
ROMA

Richard Hellie
University of Chicago
BYZANTIUM
RUSSIA

Per Hernæs
Norwegian University of Science and Technology
CARIBBEAN REGION: DANISH COLONIES

B. W. Higman
Australian National University
SLAVE SOCIETIES

Steven L. Hoch
University of Iowa
RUSSIA, SERFDOM IN

Graham Hodges
Colgate University
GRÉGOIRE, HENRI, BISHOP
NEW JERSEY
NEW YORK
NEW YORK MANUMISSION SOCIETY
SEWALL, SAMUEL
TAPPAN BROTHERS

Wim Hoogbergen
Universiteit Utrecht
BRAZIL: DUTCH BRAZIL
CARIBBEAN REGION: DUTCH COLONIES
SURINAME

Reginald Horsman
University of Wisconsin, Milwaukee
NOTT, JOSIAH CLARK

Timothy S. Huebner
Rhodes College
COBB, THOMAS R. R.
CONFEDERATE STATES OF AMERICA

Peter Hunt
Davidson College
CONCUBINAGE: ANCIENT ROME
FAMILIA CAESARIS
FREEDMEN: ANCIENT ROME
MANUMISSION: ANCIENT ROME
MINERS: GREEK AND ROMAN MINES
PECULIUM
SPARTACUS

I

John C. Inscoe
University of Georgia
NAMES AND NAMING

Charles F. Irons
University of Virginia
SLAVE RELIGION: UNITED STATES

J

Karl Jacoby
Oberlin College
PREHISTORIC SOCIETIES

M. H. A. Jaschok
Oxford University
CONCUBINAGE: CHINA

Lawrence C. Jennings
University of Ottawa
ABOLITION AND ANTISLAVERY MOVEMENTS: FRANCE

Douglas H. Johnson
Oxford University
MILITARY SLAVES: MUSLIM MILITARY SLAVERY

Michael P. Johnson
Johns Hopkins University
ELLISON, WILLIAM
FREE PEOPLE OF COLOR

Howard Jones
University of Alabama
AFRICA SQUADRON
AMISTAD
CINQUÉ
CREOLE INCIDENT (1841)
WEBSTER-ASHBURTON TREATY

K

Doris Y. Kadish
University of Georgia
LITERATURE OF SLAVERY: FRENCH LITERATURE

Gerald E. Kadish
State University of New York at Binghamton
ANCIENT GREECE
LAW: ANCIENT GREECE

Mary Karasch
Oakland University
BRAZIL: AN OVERVIEW

Ruth Mazo Karras
Temple University
SCANDINAVIA
THRALLDOM

Ray A. Kea
University of California, Riverside
WEST AFRICA: FOREST AREAS

Ralph Ketcham
Syracuse University
COLES, EDWARD

Hyong-In Kim
Seoul, South Korea
KOREA

Gregg D. Kimball
Library of Virginia
CHAINS AND RESTRAINTS
MEMORIALS
MUSEUMS AND HISTORIC SITES

Pauline N. King
University of Hawaii at Manoa
HAWAII

Kenneth F. Kiple
Bowling Green State University
FOOD AND COOKING
HEALTH: NUTRITION
SEASONING

Herbert S. Klein
Columbia University
SLAVE TRADE: BRAZIL

Martin A. Klein
University of Toronto
HISTORIOGRAPHY OF SLAVERY: WORLD SLAVERY
WEST AFRICA: SENEGAMBIA

Igor Kopytoff
University of Pennsylvania
ANTHROPOLOGY OF SLAVERY
PERSPECTIVES ON SLAVERY: DEFINITIONS

Perry L. Kyles Jr.
West Virginia University
LABOR SYSTEMS: CONVICT LABOR IN AUSTRALIA
REPARATIONS

L

George Michael La Rue
Clarion University
EGYPT: MODERN EGYPT

Jane G. Landers
Vanderbilt University
COARTACIÓN
CONCUBINAGE: LATIN AMERICA
MANUMISSION: LATIN AMERICA
PEONAGE: LATIN AMERICA

Michael L. Lanza
Washington, DC
BUTLER, BENJAMIN

Richard W. Lariviere
University of Texas
HINDUISM

Robin Law
University of Stirling
BARRACOONS

Ronald J. Leprohon
University of Toronto
EGYPT: ANCIENT EGYPT

Daniel C. Littlefield
University of Illinois, Urbana-Champaign
DOUGLASS, FREDERICK
OKLAHOMA
SEMINOLE WAR
SOUTH CAROLINA

Timothy J. Lockley
University of Warwick
GENDER RELATIONS

Claude-Anne Lopez
Yale University
FRANKLIN, BENJAMIN, AND THE MARQUIS DE CONDORCET

Paul E. Lovejoy
York University
PLANTATIONS: SOKOTO CALIPHATE AND WESTERN SUDAN
WEST AFRICA: SOKOTO CALIPHATE

Bobby L. Lovett
Tennessee State University
KENTUCKY
MISSISSIPPI
MISSOURI
NORTH CAROLINA

TENNESSEE
TEXAS
WEST VIRGINIA

Steven Luckert
Washington, DC
NAZI SLAVE LABOR

M

Ian W. Mabbett
Monash University
CAMBODIA

Beverly B. Mack
University of Kansas
CONCUBINAGE: ISLAMIC WORLD
EUNUCHS
HAREM

Matthew J. Mancini
Southwest Missouri State University
LABOR SYSTEMS: CONVICT LEASING IN THE
    UNITED STATES

Patrick Manning
Northeastern University
DEMOGRAPHIC ANALYSIS OF SLAVES AND SLAVERY

John Edwin Mason
University of Virginia
PLANTATIONS: CAPE COLONY
SOUTHERN AFRICA: CAPE OF GOOD HOPE

David McBride
Pennsylvania State University
HEALTH: DISEASES AND EPIDEMIOLOGY
HEALTH: MEDICINE AND MEDICAL CARE

Jennifer Davis McDaid
Library of Virginia
HEADRIGHT SYSTEM
SOCIETY FOR THE PROPAGATION OF THE GOSPEL
WET NURSES

Al McDermid
New York, NY
BUDDHISM
CONFISCATION ACTS, U.S.
JAPAN
OVERSEERS
PANICS

Roderick A. McDonald
Rider University
LONG, EDWARD
PLANTATIONS: CARIBBEAN REGION

E. Ann McDougall
University of Alberta

ISLAM: AN OVERVIEW
NORTH AFRICA: MOROCCO
NORTH AFRICA: SAHARA REGION

Robert E. McGlone
University of Hawaii at Manoa
BROWN, JOHN
POLITICS

John R. McKivigan
West Virginia University
BAPTIST CHRISTIANITY
GODWYN, MORGAN
IRISH ANTI-SLAVERY SOCIETY
MASSACHUSETTS ANTI-SLAVERY SOCIETY
METHODISM

Elizabeth A. Meyer
University of Virginia
ARCHAEOLOGY OF SLAVERY: ANCIENT WORLD

Stephen Middleton
North Carolina State University
NORTHWEST ORDINANCE
OHIO

Suzanne Miers
Ohio University
PROSTITUTION
SLAVERY, CONTEMPORARY FORMS OF
SLAVE TRADE: TWENTIETH-CENTURY TRADE
WHITE SLAVERY

Joseph C. Miller
University of Virginia
AFRICA: A THEMATIC AND SYNOPTIC OVERVIEW
AFRICA: POLITICAL AND HISTORICAL EFFECTS OF
   THE ATLANTIC SLAVE TRADE
CENTRAL AFRICA
FREEDOM
HISTORICAL APPROACHES TO SLAVERY: AN OVERVIEW
HISTORICAL APPROACHES TO SLAVERY:
   BIBLIOGRAPHY OF SLAVERY
HUMAN SACRIFICE: THE OLD WORLD
MIDDLE PASSAGE
ROYAL AFRICAN COMPANY
SLAVE TRADE: AN OVERVIEW
SPAIN: AFRICAN SLAVERY
A SELECT BIBLIOGRAPHY OF SLAVERY

Randall M. Miller
Saint Joseph's University
RELIGIOUS GROUPS, SLAVE OWNERSHIP BY

Gary B. Mills
University of Alabama
ALABAMA
LOUISIANA

Murray Milner, Jr.
University of Virginia

CASTE SYSTEMS
PATTERSON THESIS

Carl H. Moneyhon
University of Arkansas at Little Rock
ARKANSAS

David Moon
University of Newcastle upon Tyne
ABOLITION AND ANTISLAVERY MOVEMENTS: RUSSIA

Philip D. Morgan
Omohundro Institute of Early American History and Culture
ARTISANS
PLANTATIONS: UNITED STATES
SLAVE TRADE: TRANSATLANTIC

Fred Morton
Loras College
EAST AFRICA: SWAHILI REGION

L. D. Mouer
Virginia Commonwealth University
ARCHAEOLOGY OF SLAVERY: MODERN WORLD

Patricia A. Mulvey
Bluefield State College
SLAVE RELIGION: LATIN AMERICA

Doug Munro
University of the South Pacific
LABOR SYSTEMS: INDENTURED LABOR (1834–1960)

Amy E. Murrell
University of Virginia
CLOTHING, U.S.
MINNESOTA

N

Sharleen N. Nakamoto
University of Hawaii at Manoa
GARNET, HENRY

Nancy Priscilla Naro
University of London
PLANTATIONS: BRAZIL

Mieko Nishida
University of Maryland at College Park
BRAZIL: NORTHEASTERN BRAZIL
DEMERARA SLAVE REVOLT (1823)

O

Greg O'Brien
University of Kentucky
NATIVE AMERICANS: ENSLAVEMENT OF NATIVE
   AMERICANS

NATIVE AMERICANS: SLAVEHOLDING BY NATIVE
  AMERICANS

Joseph F. O'Callaghan
Fordham University
TORDESILLAS, TREATY OF

Patrick M. O'Neil
Broome Community College/SUNY
ANGLICANISM
ANTIPEONAGE LAWS, U.S.
CALIFORNIA
CHRISTIANA SLAVE REVOLT (1851)
CHRISTIANITY: MEDIEVAL WEST
DEBT SLAVERY
DRACO, CODE OF
EMANCIPATION
ENGELS, FRIEDRICH
EPICTETUS
GENOCIDE, SLAVERY AS
HEGEL, G. W. F.
HOBBES, THOMAS
KANT, IMMANUEL
LABOR SYSTEMS: FORCED LABOR
LABOR SYSTEMS: PENAL SERVITUDE
LAW: SLAVERY CASES IN ENGLISH COMMON LAW
LAW: ENGLISH COMMON LAW IN ENGLAND AND
  THE AMERICAN COLONIES
LAW: OVERVIEW OF U.S. LAW
LOCKE, JOHN
MAINE
MARXISM: THEORY OF SLAVERY
MURDER OF SLAVES
PHILO OF ALEXANDRIA
PHILOSOPHY: ROMAN PHILOSOPHY
PUBLIC WORKS
RIGHTS OF MAN
SCIENCE FICTION AND FANTASY, SLAVERY IN
SLAVE GRACE
STEREOTYPES, SLAVISH
THOMAS AQUINAS
TRIBUTE, SLAVES AS
UTOPIAS AND SLAVERY
VERMONT
WISCONSIN
WITNESSES, SLAVES AS

James Oldham
Georgetown University
SOMERSET V. STEWART (1772)

Peter S. Onuf
University of Virginia
JEFFERSON, THOMAS

P

Stephan Palmié
University of Maryland
SLAVE RELIGION: CARIBBEAN REGION

Eric Robert Papenfuse
Yale University
BELLON DE SAINT-QUENTIN, JEAN
DE BOW, JAMES D. B.
FITZHUGH, GEORGE
HARPER, ROBERT GOODLOE
HOLMES, GEORGE FREDERICK
HUGHES, HENRY
MELON, JEAN-FRANÇOIS
THORNWELL, JAMES HENLEY
TURNBULL, GORDON

Robert L. Paquette
Hamilton College
CUBA
DISCIPLINE AND PUNISHMENT
ENSLAVEMENT, METHODS OF
RESISTANCE, DAY-TO-DAY

Nerys Thomas Patterson
University of Wales, Bangor
IRELAND

James W. Paxton
Virginia Polytechnic Institute
HONOR
HOUSEHOLD SLAVES

Gustavo Pellon
University of Virginia
LITERATURE OF SLAVERY: SPANISH LITERATURE

Carl F. Petry
Northwestern University
EGYPT: MEDIEVAL EGYPT

William D. Phillips, Jr.
University of Minnesota
ASIENTO
COLUMBUS, CHRISTOPHER
MEDITERRANEAN BASIN
SIETE PARTIDAS (THE SEVEN DIVISIONS)
SLAVE TRADE: MEDIEVAL EUROPE
SPAIN: SLAVERY IN SPAIN

Johannes Postma
Mankato State University
NETHERLANDS AND THE DUTCH EMPIRE

Richard Price
College of William and Mary
LITERATURE OF SLAVERY: DUTCH LITERATURE
MAROONS
SLAVE REPUBLICS

R

James A. Rawley
University of Nebraska (emeritus)

Kansas
Kansas-Nebraska Act (1854)

James H. Read
College of Saint Benedict
Natural Law

Renee C. Redman
Hughes Hubbard & Reed, LLP
Abolition and Antislavery Movements:
    International Perspective, 1770 to the Present
Berlin Conference (1885)
Brussels Act (1890)
League of Nations
Liberia
Slavery Convention (1926)
Universal Declaration of Human Rights (1948)

David A. Reichard
Albuquerque, NM
Birney, James G.
Lovejoy, Elijah P.
New Mexico

Jacqueline S. Reinier
California State University, Sacramento
Slavery and Childhood

João José Reis
Universidade Federal da Bahia
Palmares

David Richardson
University of Hull
Africa: Economic and Demographic Effects
    of the Atlantic Slave Trade
Slave Trade: Africa

Thomas M. Ricks
Villanova University
Ancient Middle East: Mesopotamia
Ancient Middle East: Persia
Modern Middle East
Slave Trade: Islamic World

James L. Roark
Emory University
Ellison, William

Richard Roberts
Stanford University
Africa: A Brief Historical Overview
Africa: The End of Slavery

O. F. Robinson
University of Glasgow
Ancient Rome
Education of Slaves: Ancient Rome
Elite Slaves
Gladiators

Law: Ancient Rome and Byzantium
Torture in Ancient Rome

Joshua D. Rothman
University of Virginia
Miscegenation

David Ryden
Brunel University
Marxism: Historiography of Slavery

S

Francisco A. Scarano
University of Wisconsin–Madison
Caribbean Region: Spanish Colonies
Montejo, Esteban
Spain: Colonies and Empire

Walter Scheidel
Cambridge University
Finley, Moses I.
Galley Slaves
Slave Trade: Ancient Mediterranean

Philip J. Schwarz
Virginia Commonwealth University
Virginia
Virginia Society for the Abolition of Slavery

Otey M. Scruggs
Syracuse University (emeritus)
Repatriation to Africa

O. Semikhnenko
University of Toronto
Central Asia

John David Smith
North Carolina State University
Du Bois, W. E. B.
Historiography of Slavery: Slavery in
    North America, 1865–1920
Historiography of Slavery: Slavery in
    North America, 1920–1997
Perspectives on Slavery: African-American
    Perspectives, 1865–1965

Daniel C. Snell
University of Oklahoma
Ancient Middle East: Assyria and Babylonia
Ancient Middle East: Israel
Hammurabi's Code
Law: Ancient Middle East

Jean R. Soderlund
Lehigh University
Hepburn, John
Pennsylvania
Pennsylvania Society for the Abolition of Slavery

QUAKERS
SANDIFORD, RALPH
WOOLMAN, JOHN

Barbara L. Solow
Boston, MA
CAPITALISM AND SLAVERY
WILLIAMS THESIS

Lucia C. Stanton
Thomas Jefferson Memorial Foundation
HEMINGS, SALLY
JEFFERSON, ISAAC

Richard H. Steckel
Ohio State University
DEMOGRAPHY OF SLAVES IN THE UNITED STATES
MORTALITY IN THE NEW WORLD
UNITED STATES: BREEDING OF SLAVES

Peter G. Stein
Cambridge University (emeritus)
SMITH, ADAM

James B. Stewart
Macalester College
ABOLITION AND ANTISLAVERY MOVEMENTS:
    UNITED STATES
PHILLIPS, WENDELL

Jean A. Straus
University of Liège
EGYPT: GRECO-ROMAN EGYPT

Jonathan Swainger
University of Northern British Columbia
ANTI-SLAVERY SOCIETY OF CANADA
CANADA

T

Vijaya Teelock
Mahatma Gandhi Institute
SLAVE TRADE: INDIAN OCEAN

Howard R. Temperley
University of East Anglia
ABOLITION AND ANTISLAVERY MOVEMENTS:
    GREAT BRITAIN
ANTI-SLAVERY INTERNATIONAL
BRITISH AND FOREIGN ANTI-SLAVERY SOCIETY
    (1839–1909)
EMANCIPATION ACT, BRITISH (1833)
SCOTTISH ANTISLAVERY MOVEMENT

Barend Jan Terwiel
Hamburg University
THAILAND

Gordon C. Thomasson
Broome Community College/SUNY
LATTER-DAY SAINTS, CHURCH OF JESUS CHRIST OF

Phillip D. Troutman
University of Virginia
FAMILY, U.S.

V

Deborah Bingham Van Broekhoven
Ohio Wesleyan University
AMERICAN AND FOREIGN ANTI-SLAVERY SOCIETY
AMERICAN ANTI-SLAVERY SOCIETY
PERSPECTIVES ON SLAVERY: OPPOSITION TO SLAVERY
RHODE ISLAND

William L. Van Deburg
University of Wisconsin–Madison
DRIVERS

Wendy Hamand Venet
Georgia State University
CHILD, LYDIA MARIA
GARRISON, WILLIAM LLOYD
GRIMKÉ, ANGELINA AND SARAH
WOMEN IN THE ANTISLAVERY MOVEMENT

John Michael Vlach
George Washington University
HOUSING
MATERIAL CULTURE IN THE UNITED STATES

Peter M. Voelz
Eastern Illinois University
MILITARY SLAVES: AFRICAN MILITARY SLAVES IN
    THE AMERICAS

W

Stephen Wagley
Institute of Religious Studies, New York
CLAVER, PEDRO
REDEMPTION OF CAPTIVES

Jenny Bourne Wahl
Carleton College
CHATTEL SLAVERY
ECONOMIC INTERPRETATION OF SLAVERY
ECONOMICS OF SLAVERY
LAW: U.S. SOUTH
LITERATURE OF SLAVERY: BRITISH LITERATURE
PRICES OF SLAVES

Peter Wallenstein
Virginia Polytechnic Institute
CHENG HO
FIELD LABOR
GEORGIA
SLAVE NARRATIVES
TANNENBAUM, FRANK
UNITED STATES: THE SOUTH
URBAN SLAVERY: UNITED STATES

Andrew F. Walls
University of Edinburgh
BUXTON, THOMAS FOWELL

Eric H. Walther
University of Houston
BLEDSOE, ALBERT TAYLOR
DEW, THOMAS RODERICK

James Walvin
University of York
ABOLITION AND ANTISLAVERY MOVEMENTS:
    INTRODUCTION AND OVERVIEW
GREAT BRITAIN, AFRICAN SLAVERY IN

Xi Wang
Indiana University of Pennsylvania
CHINA
ENFORCEMENT ACTS, U.S.

Kerry Ward
University of Michigan
INDONESIA
PHILIPPINES
SLAVE TRADE: SOUTHEAST ASIA
SOUTHEAST ASIA

Alan Watson
Athens, GA
LAW: ROMAN LAW IN THE NEW WORLD

Matthew C. Whitaker
Michigan State University
MICHIGAN
OREGON

T. Stephen Whitman
Mount Saint Mary's College
ALBORNOZ, BARTOLOMÉ DE
AMBAR, MALIK
AMERICAN REVOLUTION
BAXTER, RICHARD
DEBT PEONAGE
DELAWARE
DISABILITY, LEGAL
DORT, SYNOD OF
ÉPAONE, COUNCIL OF
ÉPHÉMÉRIDES DU CITOYEN
ESCAPE
GRAY, SIMON
LITERATURE OF SLAVERY: U.S. LITERATURE
MARYLAND
MERCADO, TOMÁS DE
NORRIS, ROBERT
PURITANS
SANDOVAL, ALONSO DE
SELF-PURCHASE

SLAVES, SALE OF
TRYON, THOMAS
UNITED STATES: THE NORTH

Charles E. Williams
Arlington, VA
ENCYCLOPÉDIE
SOCIÉTÉ DES AMIS DES NOIRS

Justin Willis
Cambridge University
PLANTATIONS: ZANZIBAR AND THE SWAHILI COAST

Peter H. Wood
Duke University
STONO REBELLION (1739)

C. Vann Woodward
Yale University
CHESNUT, MARY

Nigel Worden
University of Cape Town
INDONESIA
PHILIPPINES
SLAVE TRADE: SOUTHEAST ASIA
SOUTHEAST ASIA

Marcia Wright
Columbia University
AFRICA: WOMEN AS SLAVES IN AFRICA

Bertram Wyatt-Brown
University of Florida
PSYCHOLOGY

X

Han Xiaorong
University of Hawaii at Manoa
HISTORIOGRAPHY OF SLAVERY: CHINA AND THE
    ANCIENT MEDITERRANEAN
SLAVE TRADE: CHINA
SLAVE TRADE: COOLIE TRADE

Z

Arthur Zilversmit
Lake Forest College
EMANCIPATION IN THE UNITED STATES:
    THE NORTHERN EXPERIENCE
EMANCIPATION IN THE UNITED STATES: CIVIL WAR

Clarisse Zimra
Southern Illinois University at Carbondale
LITERATURE OF SLAVERY: CARIBBEAN LITERATURE

Maps

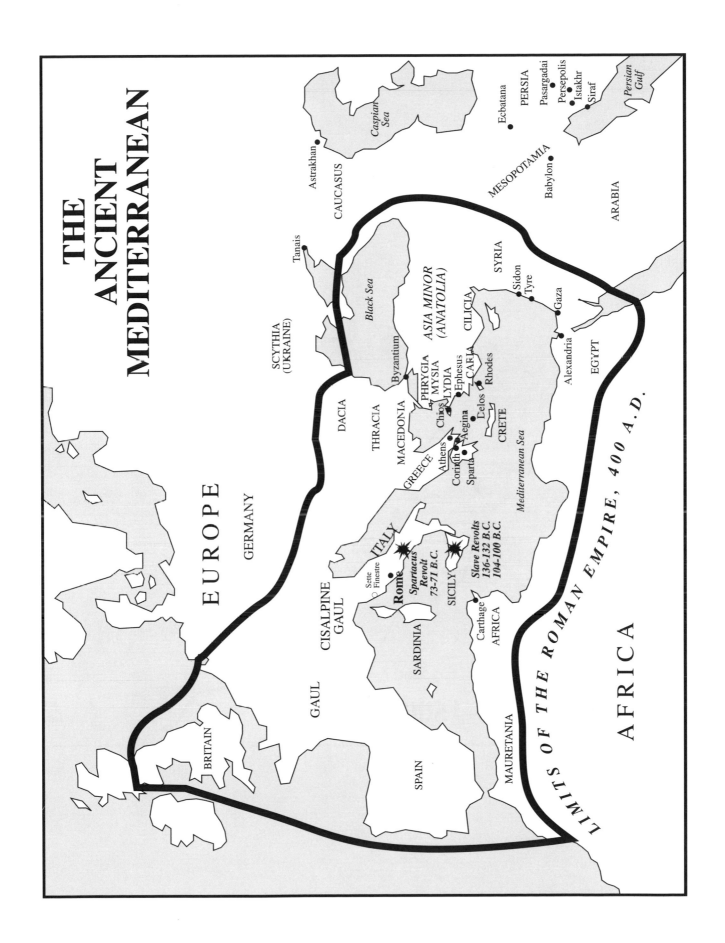

THE ANCIENT MEDITERRANEAN

EUROPE 500-1500

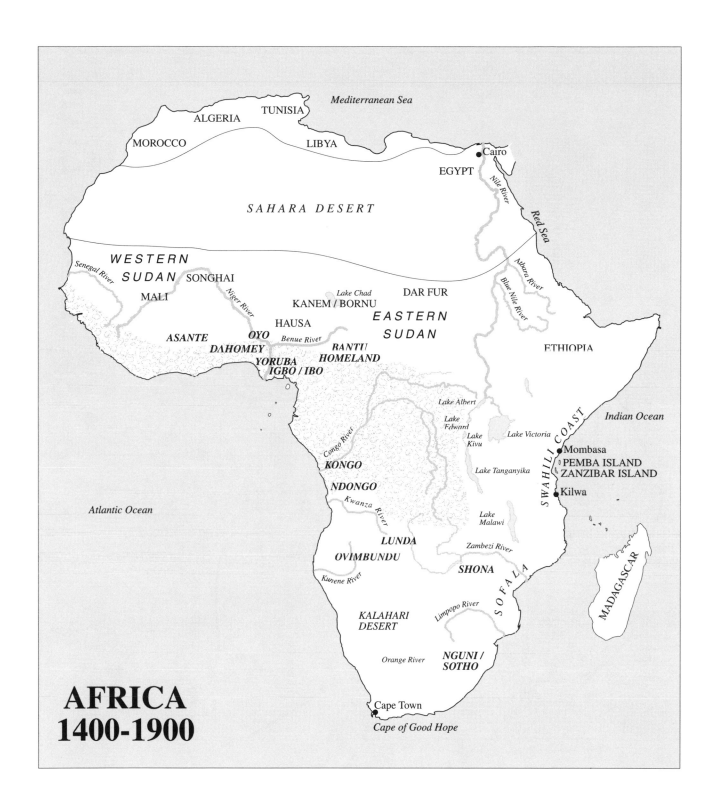

**AFRICA
1400-1900**

Mediterranean Sea

MOROCCO ALGERIA TUNISIA

LIBYA

Cairo

EGYPT

Nile River

Red Sea

SAHARA DESERT

Athara River

Senegal River

WESTERN
SUDAN

SONGHAI

MALI

Niger River

Lake Chad

KANEM / BORNU

DAR FUR

EASTERN
SUDAN

Blue Nile River

HAUSA

ASANTE

OYO

DAHOMEY

Benue River

*BANTU
HOMELAND*

YORUBA

IGBO / IBO

ETHIOPIA

Lake Albert

Lake
Edward

Lake
Kivu

Lake Victoria

SWAHILI COAST

Indian Ocean

Congo River

Mombasa

PEMBA ISLAND
ZANZIBAR ISLAND

Kilwa

KONGO

NDONGO

Lake Tanganyika

Kwanza River

Atlantic Ocean

LUNDA

Lake
Malawi

OVIMBUNDU

Zambezi River

SHONA

SOFALA

MADAGASCAR

Kunene River

KALAHARI
DESERT

Limpopo River

Orange River

*NGUNI /
SOTHO*

Cape Town

Cape of Good Hope

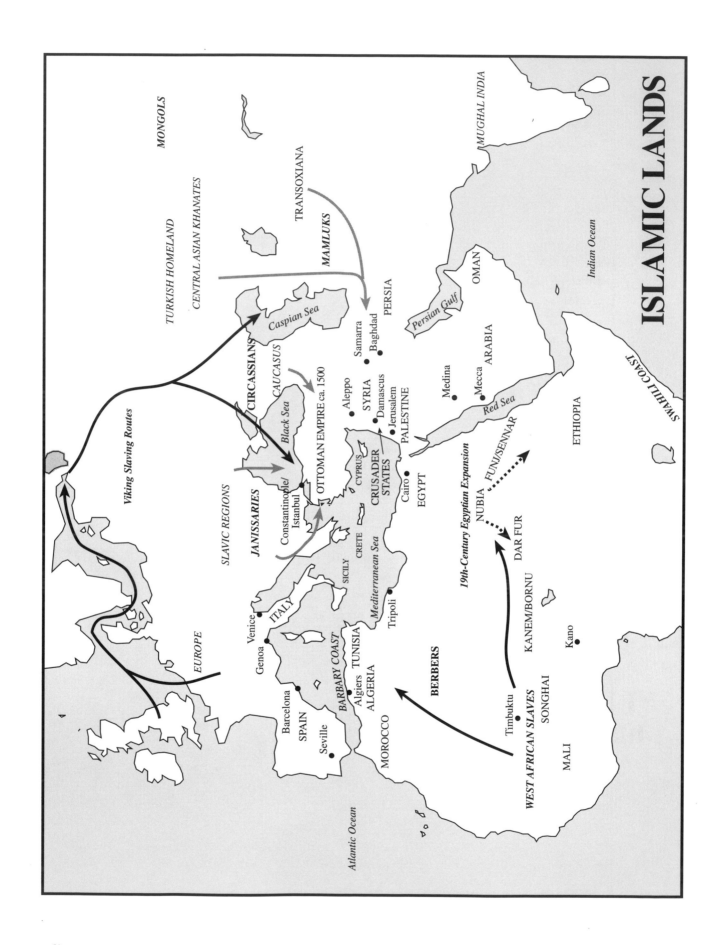

ISLAMIC LANDS

MUGHAL INDIA

MONGOLS

TURKISH HOMELAND

CENTRAL ASIAN KHANATES

TRANSOXIANA

MAMLUKS

Caspian Sea

Indian Ocean

OMAN

Persian Gulf

Samarra
Baghdad

PERSIA

CIRCASSIANS

CAUCASUS

Black Sea

Medina
Mecca

ARABIA

OTTOMAN EMPIRE ca. 1500

Aleppo

SYRIA

Damascus

Jerusalem

PALESTINE

Red Sea

SWAHILI COAST

Viking Slaving Routes

SLAVIC REGIONS

JANISSARIES

Constantinople/
Istanbul

CYPRUS

CRUSADER
STATES

Cairo

EGYPT

ETHIOPIA

19th-Century Egyptian Expansion

NUBIA

FUNJ/SENNAR

CRETE

SICILY

Mediterranean Sea

DAR FUR

EUROPE

Venice

ITALY

Genoa

Tripoli

KANEM/BORNU

Kano

Barcelona

SPAIN

Seville

BARBARY COAST

TUNISIA

Algiers

ALGERIA

MOROCCO

BERBERS

Timbuktu

SONGHAI

Atlantic Ocean

WEST AFRICAN SLAVES

MALI

xliv

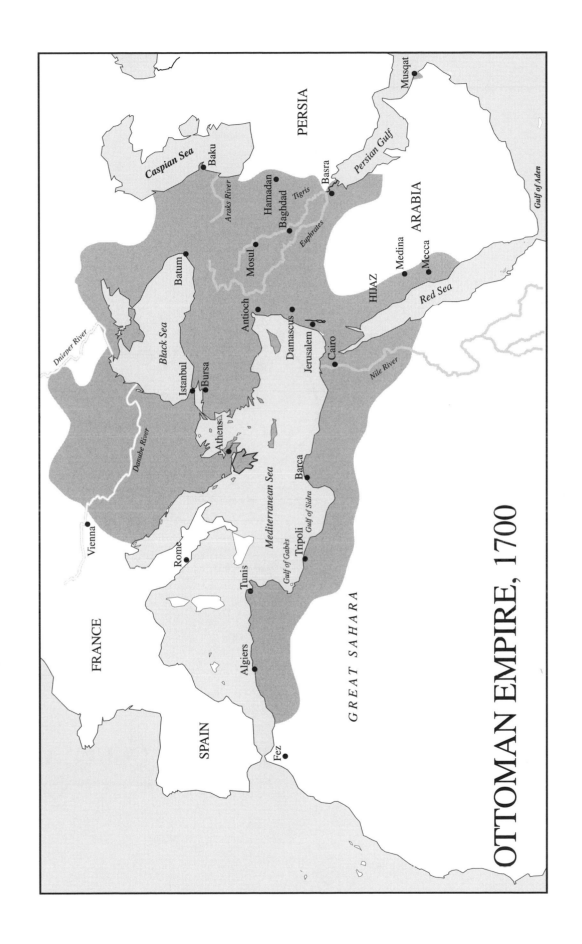

OTTOMAN EMPIRE, 1700

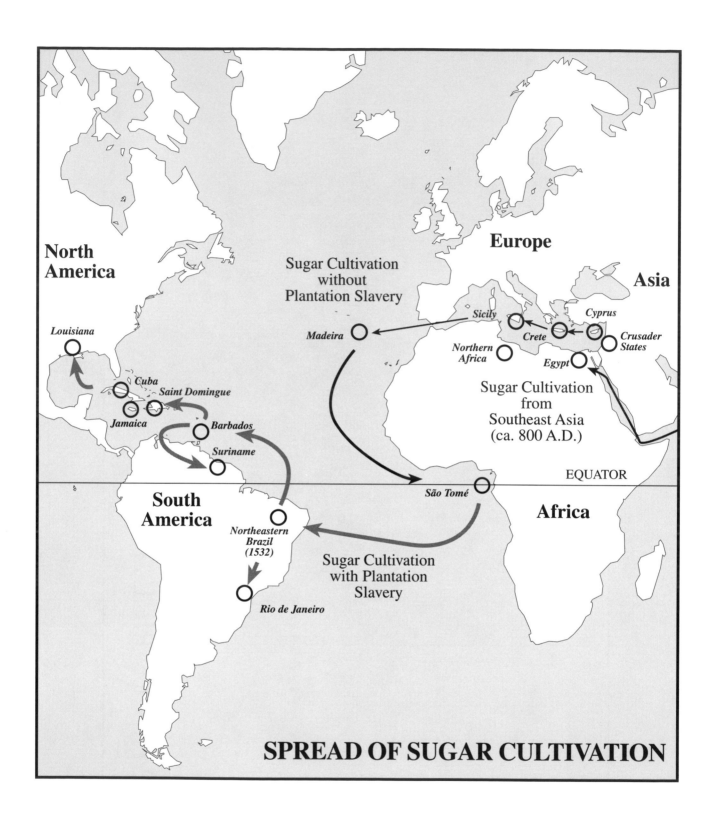

North America

Louisiana

Cuba

Saint Domingue

Jamaica

Europe

Sugar Cultivation
without
Plantation Slavery

Madeira

Sicily

Crete

Cyprus

Northern Africa

Egypt

Asia

Crusader States

Sugar Cultivation
from
Southeast Asia
(ca. 800 A.D.)

Barbados

Suriname

South America

Northeastern Brazil (1532)

EQUATOR

São Tomé

Africa

Sugar Cultivation
with Plantation
Slavery

Rio de Janeiro

SPREAD OF SUGAR CULTIVATION

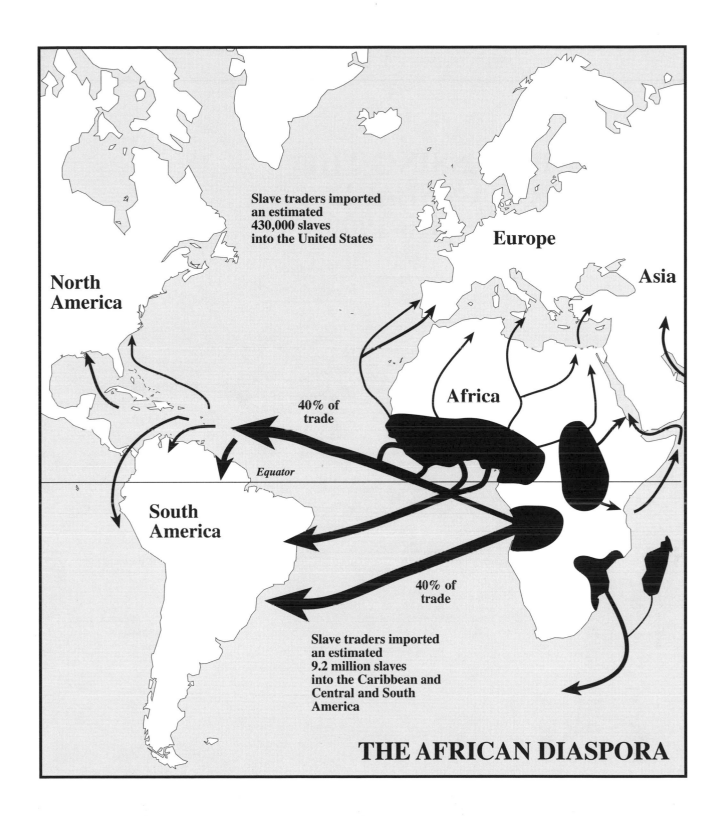

Slave traders imported an estimated 430,000 slaves into the United States

Europe

Asia

North America

Africa

40% of trade

Equator

South America

40% of trade

Slave traders imported an estimated 9.2 million slaves into the Caribbean and Central and South America

THE AFRICAN DIASPORA

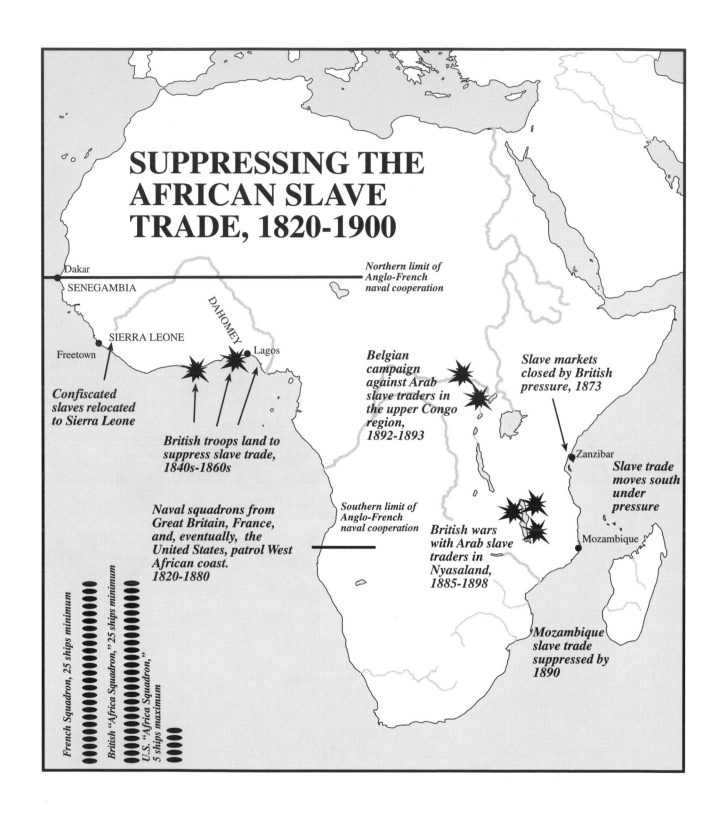

SUPPRESSING THE AFRICAN SLAVE TRADE, 1820-1900

Dakar

SENEGAMBIA

Northern limit of Anglo-French naval cooperation

DAHOMEY

SIERRA LEONE

Freetown

Lagos

Confiscated slaves relocated to Sierra Leone

British troops land to suppress slave trade, 1840s-1860s

Belgian campaign against Arab slave traders in the upper Congo region, 1892-1893

Slave markets closed by British pressure, 1873

Zanzibar

Slave trade moves south under pressure

Naval squadrons from Great Britain, France, and, eventually, the United States, patrol West African coast. 1820-1880

Southern limit of Anglo-French naval cooperation

British wars with Arab slave traders in Nyasaland, 1885-1898

Mozambique

Mozambique slave trade suppressed by 1890

French Squadron, 25 ships minimum

British "Africa Squadron," 25 ships minimum

U.S. "Africa Squadron," 5 ships maximum

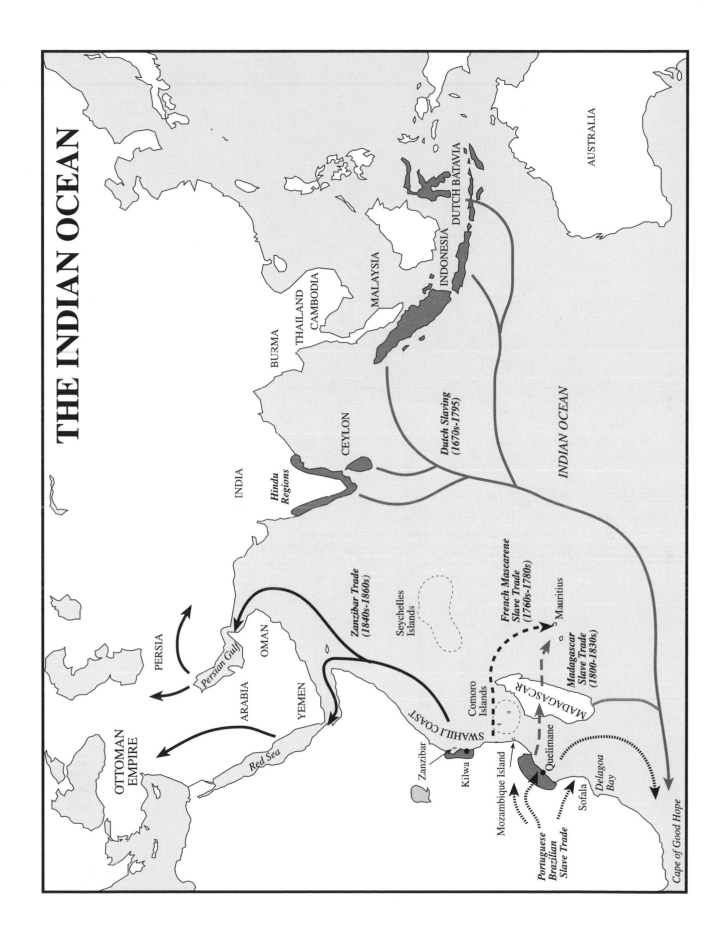

THE INDIAN OCEAN

AUSTRALIA

DUTCH BATAVIA

INDONESIA

MALAYSIA

BURMA

THAILAND

CAMBODIA

Dutch Slaving
(1670s-1795)

CEYLON

INDIA

Hindu Regions

INDIAN OCEAN

Zanzibar Trade (1840s-1860s)

Seychelles Islands

French Mascarene Slave Trade (1760s-1780s)

Mauritius

PERSIA

Persian Gulf

OMAN

ARABIA

YEMEN

Madagascar Slave Trade (1800-1830s)

OTTOMAN EMPIRE

Red Sea

SWAHILI COAST

Comoro Islands

MADAGASCAR

Quelimane

Zanzibar

Kilwa

Mozambique Island

Delagoa Bay

Sofala

Portuguese Brazilian Slave Trade

Cape of Good Hope

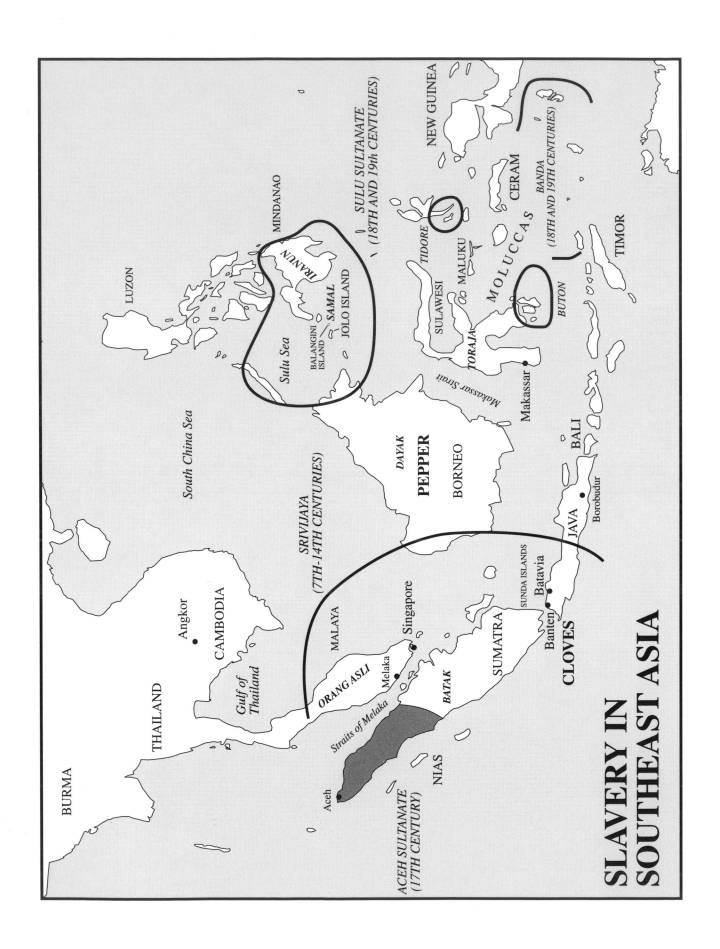

SLAVERY IN SOUTHEAST ASIA

BURMA

THAILAND

CAMBODIA

Angkor

Gulf of
Thailand

South China Sea

LUZON

MINDANAO

IRANUN

SULU SULTANATE
(18TH AND 19th CENTURIES)

Sulu Sea

SAMAL

BALANGINI
ISLAND

JOLO ISLAND

NEW GUINEA

CERAM

BANDA
(18TH AND 19TH CENTURIES)

TIDORE

MALUKU

MOLUCCAS

SULAWESI

TORAJA

BUTON

TIMOR

Makassar

Makassar Strait

SRIVIJAYA
(7TH-14TH CENTURIES)

DAYAK

PEPPER

BORNEO

BALI

Borobudur

JAVA

MALAYA

Singapore

ORANG ASLI

Melaka

Straits of Melaka

SUNDA ISLANDS

Batavia

Banten

SUMATRA

BATAK

CLOVES

Aceh

NIAS

ACEH SULTANATE
(17TH CENTURY)

1

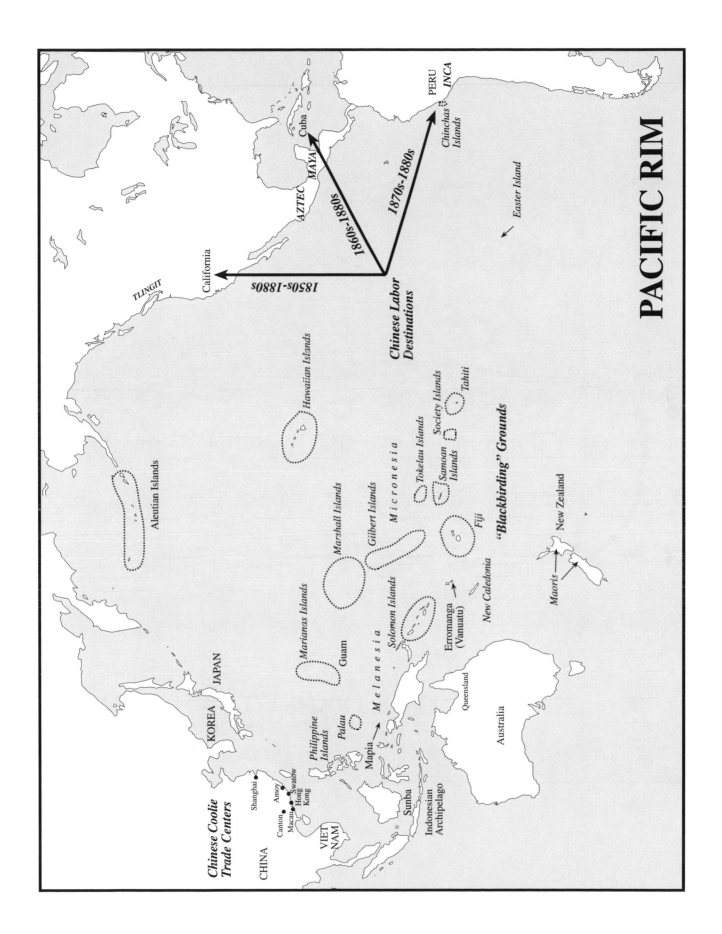

PACIFIC RIM

Chinese Coolie
Trade Centers

CHINA

KOREA

JAPAN

VIET
NAM

Shanghai
Amoy
Swatow
Canton
Macau
Hong
Kong

Philippine
Islands

Palau

Mapia

Sunba

Indonesian
Archipelago

Marianas Islands

Guam

Melanesia

Solomon Islands

Marshall Islands

Gilbert Islands

Micronesia

Queensland

Australia

New Caledonia

Erromanga
(Vanuatu)

Fiji

"Blackbirding" Grounds

Tokelau Islands

Samoan
Islands

Society Islands

Tahiti

New Zealand

Maoris

Aleutian Islands

Hawaiian Islands

Chinese Labor
Destinations

1850s-1880s

1860s-1880s

1870s-1880s

California

TLINGIT

AZTEC

MAYA

Cuba

PERU

INCA

Chinchas
Islands

Easter Island

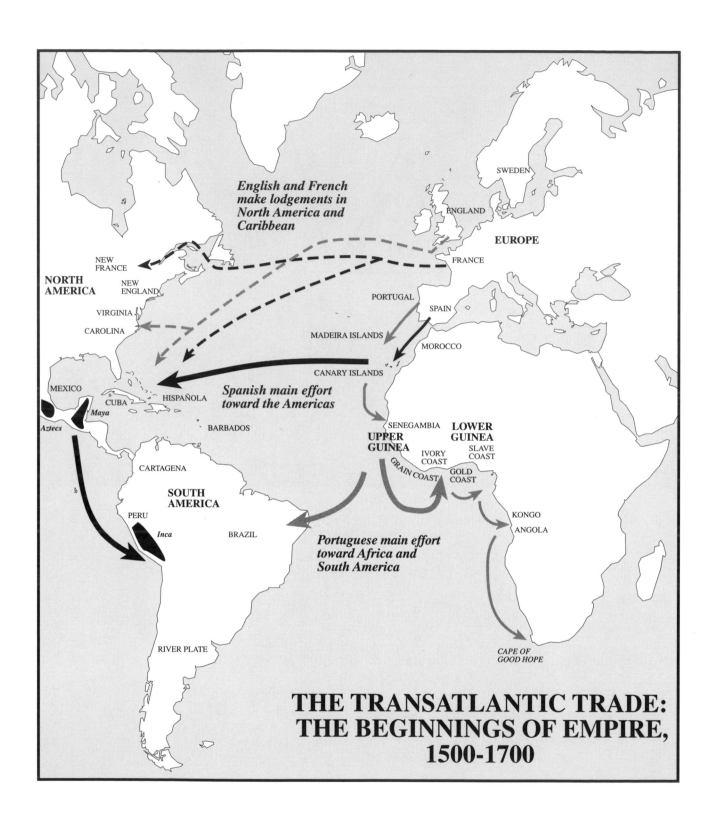

English and French
make lodgements in
North America and
Caribbean

SWEDEN

ENGLAND

EUROPE

FRANCE

NEW
FRANCE

**NORTH
AMERICA**

NEW
ENGLAND

PORTUGAL

SPAIN

VIRGINIA

MADEIRA ISLANDS

MOROCCO

CAROLINA

CANARY ISLANDS

MEXICO

CUBA

Maya

HISPAÑOLA

*Spanish main effort
toward the Americas*

Aztecs

BARBADOS

SENEGAMBIA

**LOWER
GUINEA**

**UPPER
GUINEA**

SLAVE
COAST

CARTAGENA

IVORY
COAST

GRAIN COAST

GOLD
COAST

**SOUTH
AMERICA**

KONGO

PERU

Inca

BRAZIL

ANGOLA

*Portuguese main effort
toward Africa and
South America*

RIVER PLATE

*CAPE OF
GOOD HOPE*

**THE TRANSATLANTIC TRADE:
THE BEGINNINGS OF EMPIRE,
1500-1700**

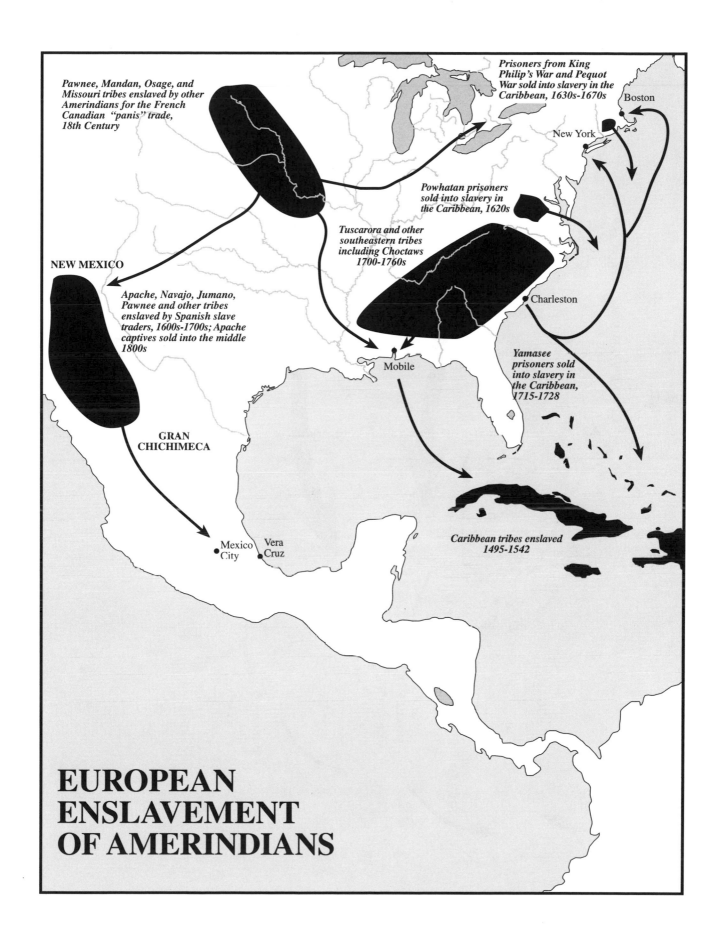

Pawnee, Mandan, Osage, and
Missouri tribes enslaved by other
Amerindians for the French
Canadian "panis" trade,
18th Century

Prisoners from King
Philip's War and Pequot
War sold into slavery in the
Caribbean, 1630s-1670s

Boston

New York

Powhatan prisoners
sold into slavery in
the Caribbean, 1620s

Tuscarora and other
southeastern tribes
including Choctaws
1700-1760s

NEW MEXICO

Apache, Navajo, Jumano,
Pawnee and other tribes
enslaved by Spanish slave
traders, 1600s-1700s; Apache
captives sold into the middle
1800s

Charleston

Yamasee
prisoners sold
into slavery
in the Caribbean,
1715-1728

GRAN
CHICHIMECA

Mobile

Mexico
City

Vera
Cruz

Caribbean tribes enslaved
1495-1542

EUROPEAN
ENSLAVEMENT
OF AMERINDIANS

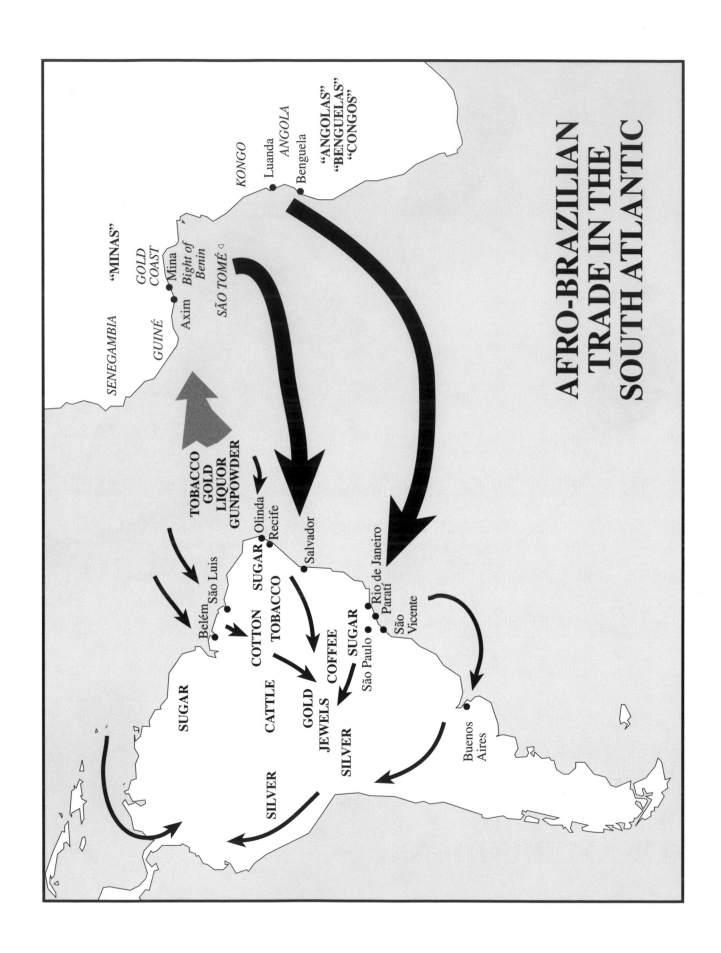

AFRO-BRAZILIAN TRADE IN THE SOUTH ATLANTIC

SENEGAMBIA

GUINÉ

"MINAS"

GOLD COAST

Mina

Axim

Bight of Benin

SÃO TOMÉ

KONGO

Luanda

ANGOLA

Benguela

"ANGOLAS"
"BENGUELAS"
"CONGOS"

TOBACCO
GOLD
LIQUOR
GUNPOWDER

Olinda
Recife

Salvador

Rio de Janeiro
Paratí
São Vicente

São Luis
Belém

São Paulo

Buenos Aires

SUGAR

COTTON
TOBACCO

CATTLE

GOLD
JEWELS
SILVER

SUGAR

COFFEE

SUGAR

SILVER

SILVER

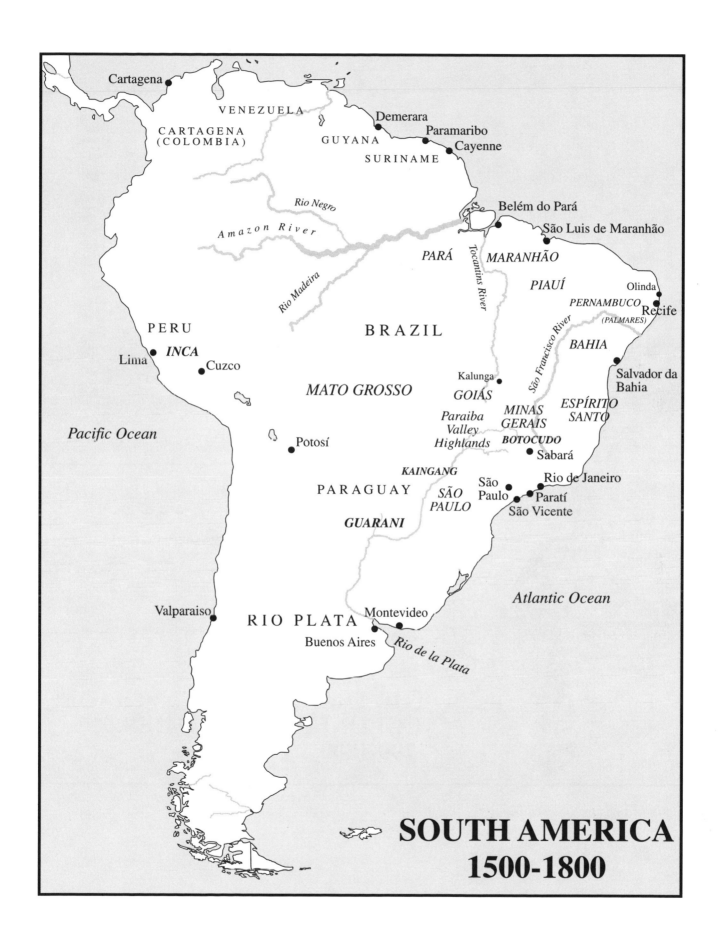

Cartagena

VENEZUELA

CARTAGENA
(COLOMBIA)

Demerara

GUYANA

Paramaribo
Cayenne

SURINAME

Rio Negro

Amazon River

Belém do Pará

São Luis de Maranhão

PARÁ

MARANHÃO

Tocantins River

Rio Madeira

PIAUÍ

Olinda

PERNAMBUCO
(PALMARES)

Recife

BRAZIL

São Francisco River

BAHIA

PERU

INCA

Lima

Cuzco

Kalunga

MATO GROSSO

GOIÁS

Salvador da
Bahia

*ESPÍRITO
SANTO*

*MINAS
GERAIS*

*Paraiba
Valley
Highlands*

BOTOCUDO

Pacific Ocean

Potosí

Sabará

KAINGANG

Rio de Janeiro

PARAGUAY

*SÃO
PAULO*

São
Paulo

Paratí

São Vicente

GUARANI

Atlantic Ocean

Valparaiso

RIO PLATA

Montevideo

Buenos Aires

Rio de la Plata

SOUTH AMERICA
1500-1800

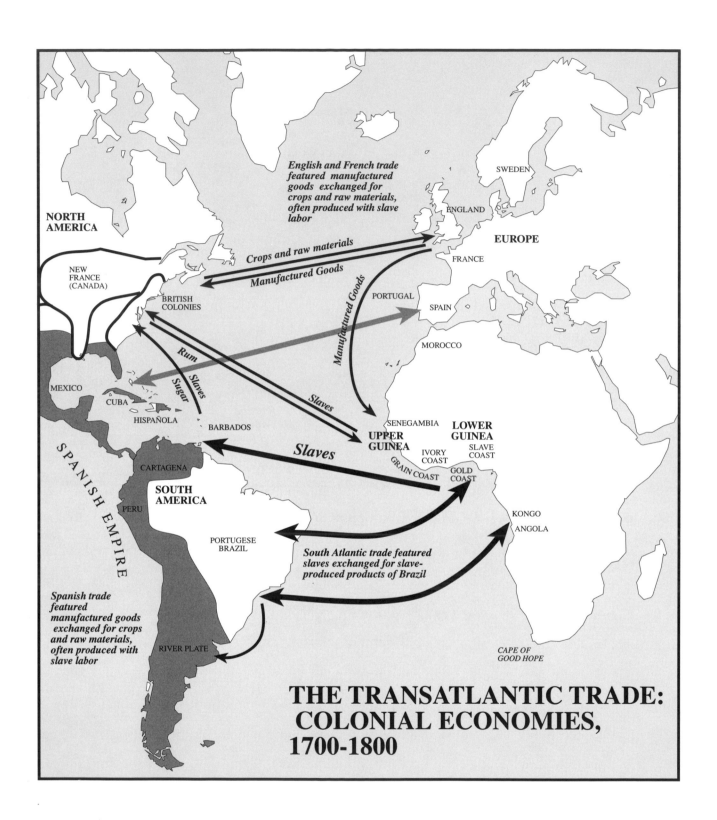

THE TRANSATLANTIC TRADE: COLONIAL ECONOMIES, 1700-1800

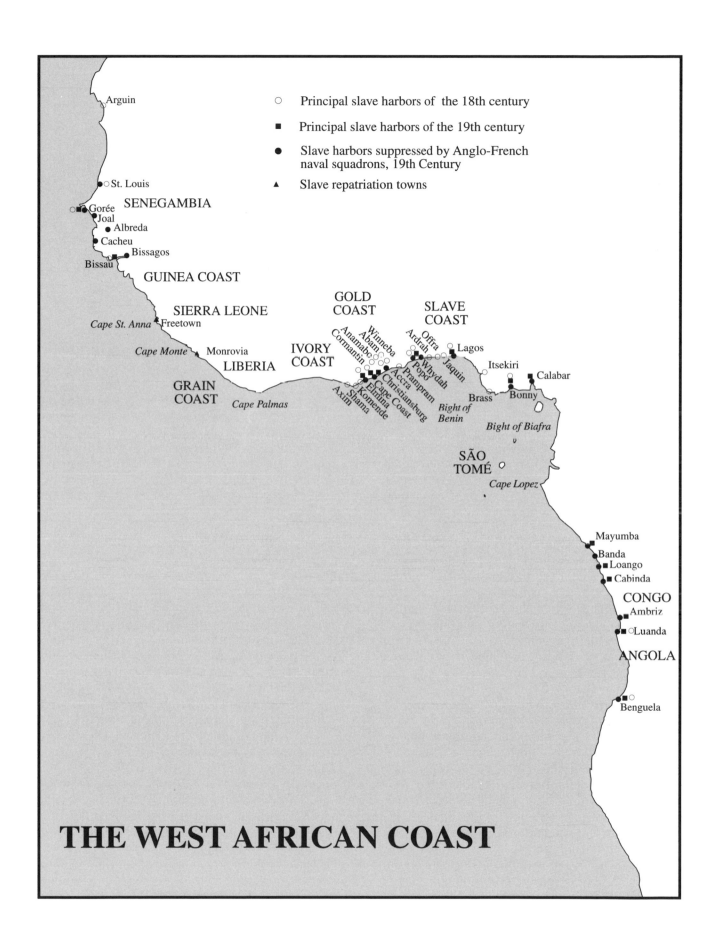

Principal slave harbors of the 18th century

Principal slave harbors of the 19th century

Slave harbors suppressed by Anglo-French
naval squadrons, 19th Century

Slave repatriation towns

Arguin

St. Louis

SENEGAMBIA

Gorée
Joal
Albreda
Cacheu
Bissagos
Bissau

GUINEA COAST

SIERRA LEONE

Cape St. Anna Freetown

Cape Monte Monrovia

LIBERIA

GRAIN
COAST

Cape Palmas

IVORY
COAST

GOLD
COAST

Cormantin
Anamabo
Abam
Winneba
Accra
Prampram
Christiansburg
Cape Coast
Elmina
Komende
Shama
Axim

SLAVE
COAST

Ardrah
Offra
Whydah
Popo
Jaquin

Lagos

Itsekiri

Brass

Bight of
Benin

Bight of Biafra

SÃO
TOMÉ

Cape Lopez

Calabar

Bonny

Mayumba
Banda
Loango
Cabinda

CONGO

Ambriz

Luanda

ANGOLA

Benguela

THE WEST AFRICAN COAST

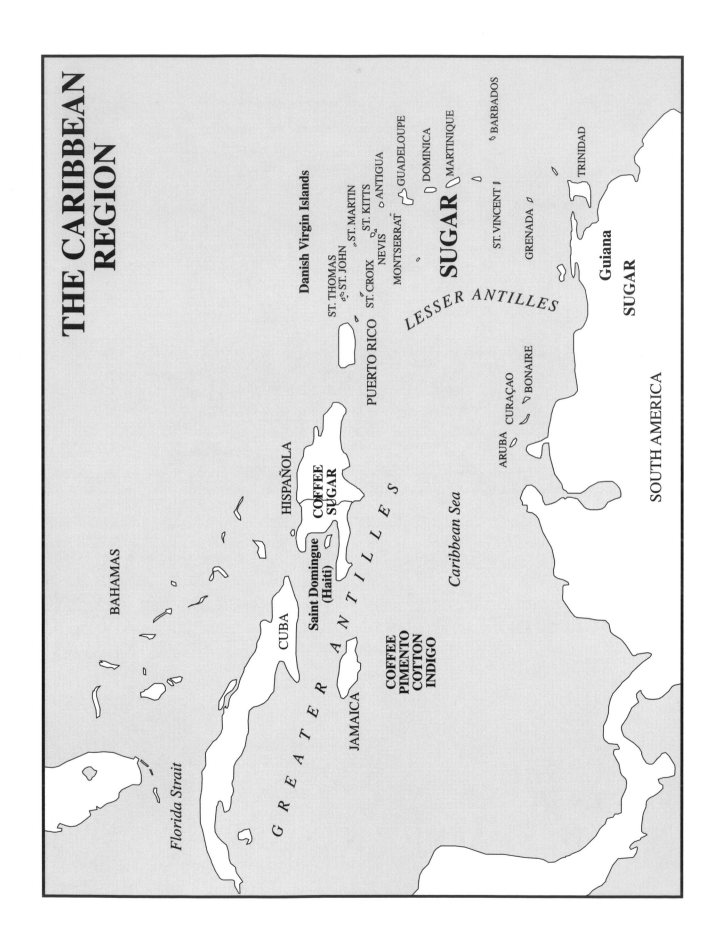

THE CARIBBEAN REGION

Florida Strait

BAHAMAS

CUBA

G R E A T E R A N T I L L E S

JAMAICA

**COFFEE
PIMENTO
COTTON
INDIGO**

**Saint Domingue
(Haiti)**

HISPAÑOLA

**COFFEE
SUGAR**

Danish Virgin Islands

ST. THOMAS
ST. JOHN

ST. MARTIN

ST. KITTS
NEVIS
ST. CROIX

MONTSERRAT
ANTIGUA

GUADELOUPE

DOMINICA

MARTINIQUE

SUGAR

LESSER ANTILLES

BARBADOS

ST. VINCENT

GRENADA

TRINIDAD

PUERTO RICO

Caribbean Sea

ARUBA
CURAÇAO
BONAIRE

Guiana
SUGAR

SOUTH AMERICA

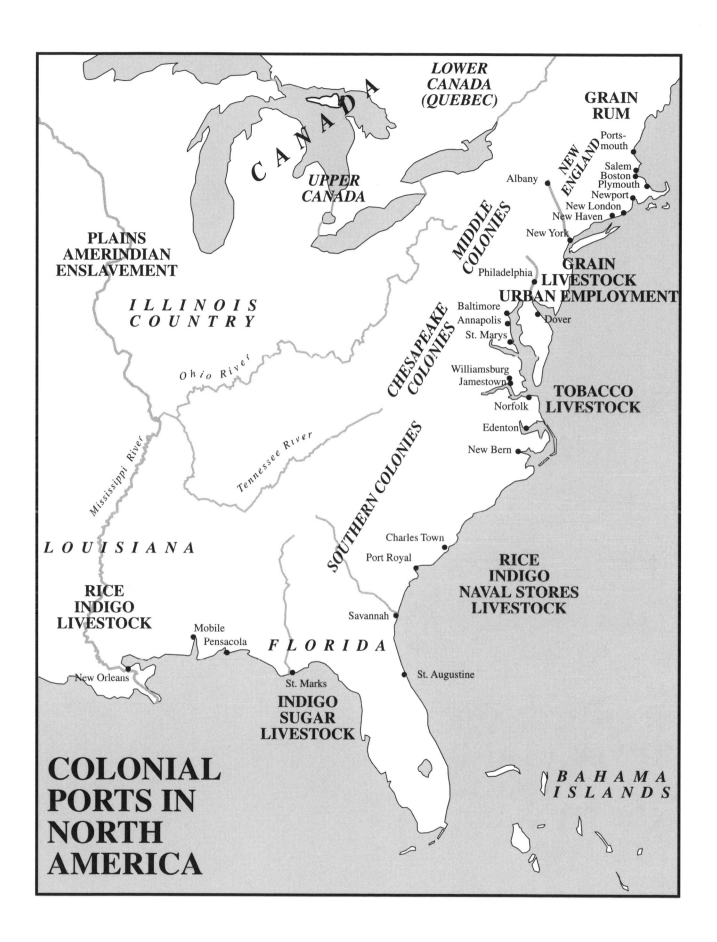

LOWER
CANADA
(QUEBEC)

CANADA

UPPER
CANADA

GRAIN
RUM

NEW ENGLAND

Ports-
mouth
Salem
Boston
Plymouth
Newport
New London
New Haven

Albany

PLAINS
AMERINDIAN
ENSLAVEMENT

ILLINOIS
COUNTRY

MIDDLE
COLONIES

New York

Philadelphia

GRAIN
LIVESTOCK
URBAN EMPLOYMENT

Ohio River

Baltimore
Annapolis
St. Marys

Dover

CHESAPEAKE
COLONIES

Williamsburg
Jamestown

Tennessee River

TOBACCO
LIVESTOCK

Norfolk

Mississippi River

Edenton

New Bern

SOUTHERN COLONIES

LOUISIANA

Charles Town

RICE
INDIGO
LIVESTOCK

Port Royal

RICE
INDIGO
NAVAL STORES
LIVESTOCK

Mobile
Pensacola

Savannah

FLORIDA

New Orleans

St. Marks

St. Augustine

INDIGO
SUGAR
LIVESTOCK

BAHAMA
ISLANDS

COLONIAL
PORTS IN
NORTH
AMERICA

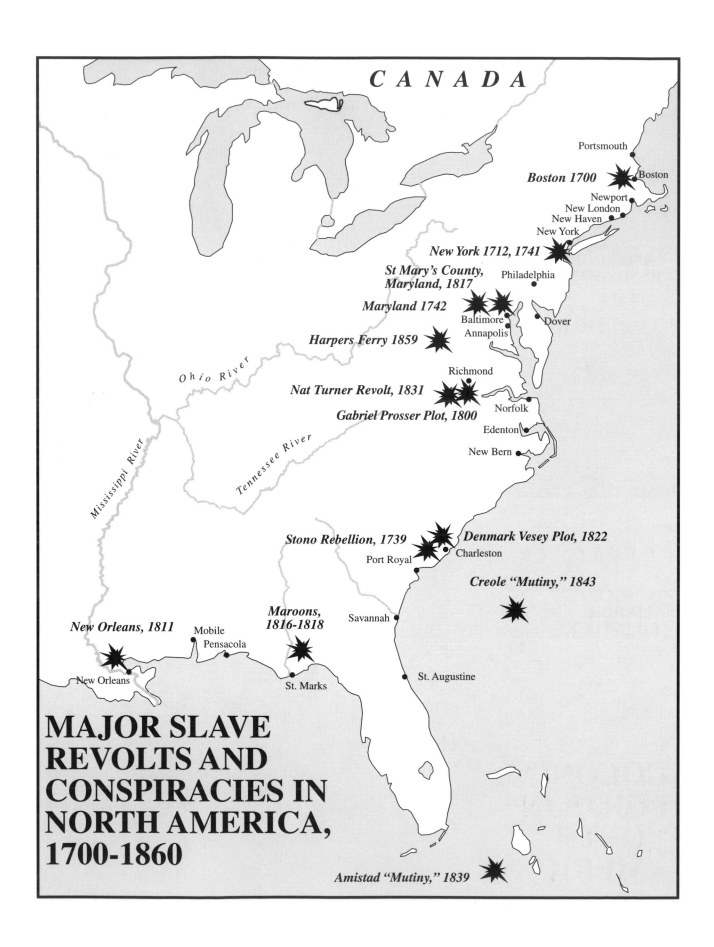

MAJOR SLAVE REVOLTS AND CONSPIRACIES IN NORTH AMERICA, 1700-1860

CANADA

Portsmouth

Boston 1700 Boston

Newport
New London
New Haven
New York

New York 1712, 1741

St Mary's County, Maryland, 1817 Philadelphia

Maryland 1742
Baltimore Dover
Annapolis

Harpers Ferry 1859

Ohio River

Richmond

Nat Turner Revolt, 1831
Norfolk
Gabriel Prosser Plot, 1800
Edenton
New Bern

Tennessee River

Mississippi River

Stono Rebellion, 1739 *Denmark Vesey Plot, 1822*
Port Royal Charleston

Creole "Mutiny," 1843

New Orleans, 1811 Mobile *Maroons, 1816-1818* Savannah
Pensacola
New Orleans St. Marks St. Augustine

Amistad "Mutiny," 1839

lx

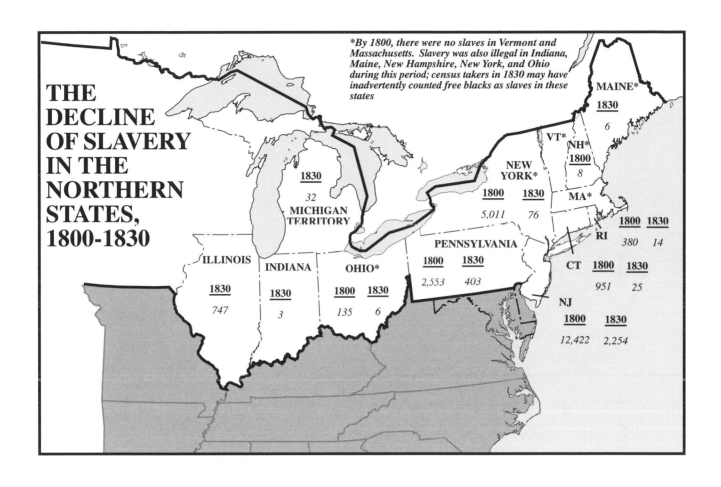

THE DECLINE OF SLAVERY IN THE NORTHERN STATES, 1800-1830

*By 1800, there were no slaves in Vermont and Massachusetts. Slavery was also illegal in Indiana, Maine, New Hampshire, New York, and Ohio during this period; census takers in 1830 may have inadvertently counted free blacks as slaves in these states

MICHIGAN TERRITORY
1830
32

MAINE*
1830
6

VT*

NH*
1800
8

NEW YORK*
1800 **1830**
5,011 *76*

MA*

RI **1800** **1830**
380 *14*

ILLINOIS
1830
747

INDIANA
1830
3

OHIO*
1800 **1830**
135 *6*

PENNSYLVANIA
1800 **1830**
2,553 *403*

CT **1800** **1830**
951 *25*

NJ
1800 **1830**
12,422 *2,254*

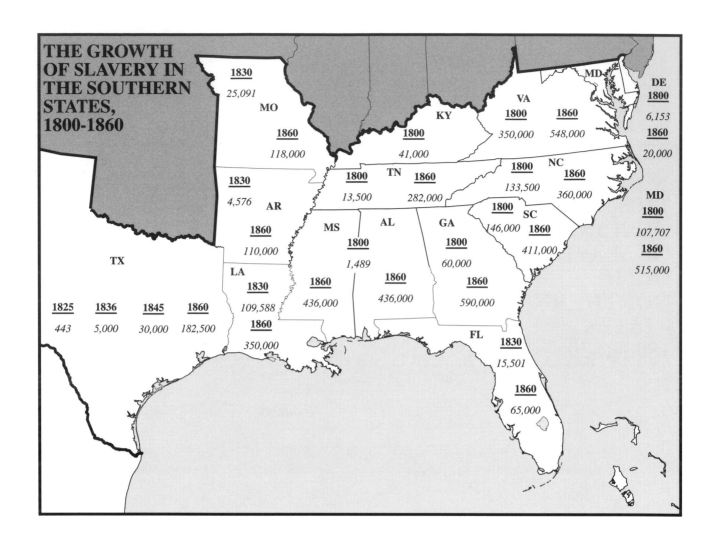

THE GROWTH OF SLAVERY IN THE SOUTHERN STATES, 1800-1860

MO
1830
25,091
1860
118,000

KY
1800
41,000

VA
1800
350,000
1860
548,000

MD

DE
1800
6,153
1860
20,000

AR
1830
4,576
1860
110,000

TN
1800
13,500
1860
282,000

NC
1800
133,500
1860
360,000

MD
1800
107,707
1860
515,000

MS
1800
1,489
1860
436,000

AL
1860
436,000

GA
1800
60,000
1860
590,000

SC
1800
146,000
1860
411,000

TX
1825
443
1836
5,000
1845
30,000
1860
182,500

LA
1830
109,588
1860
350,000

FL
1830
15,501
1860
65,000

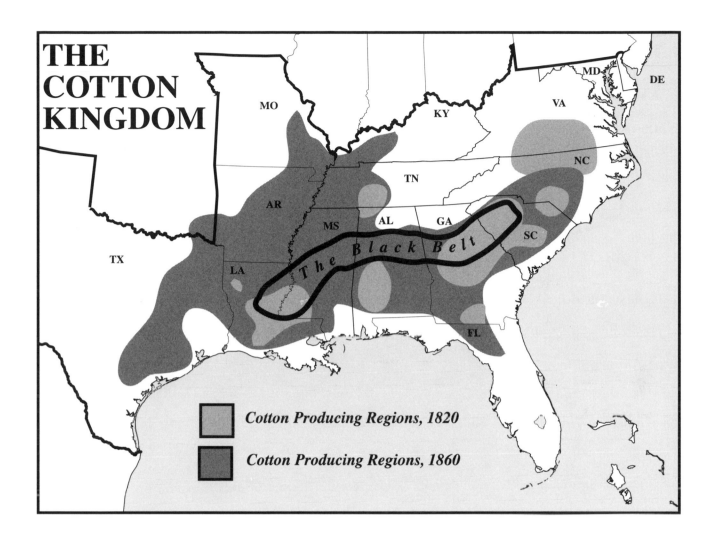

THE COTTON KINGDOM

TX
MO
AR
MS
AL
GA
SC
NC
VA
MD
DE
KY
TN
LA
FL

The Black Belt

Cotton Producing Regions, 1820

Cotton Producing Regions, 1860

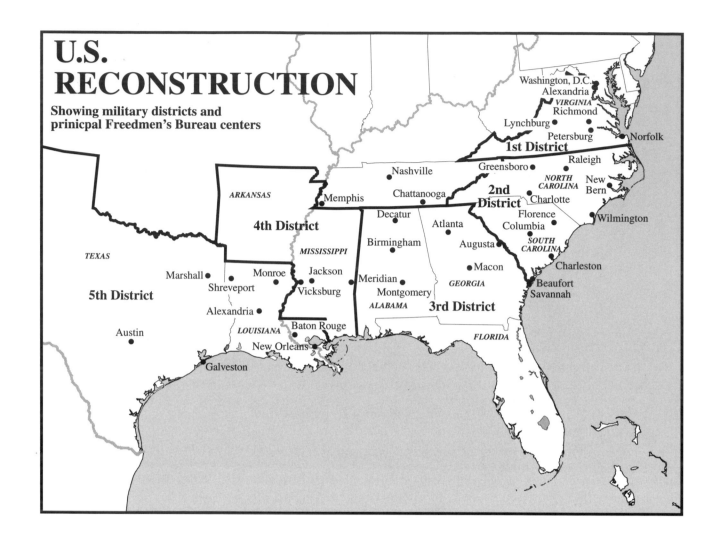

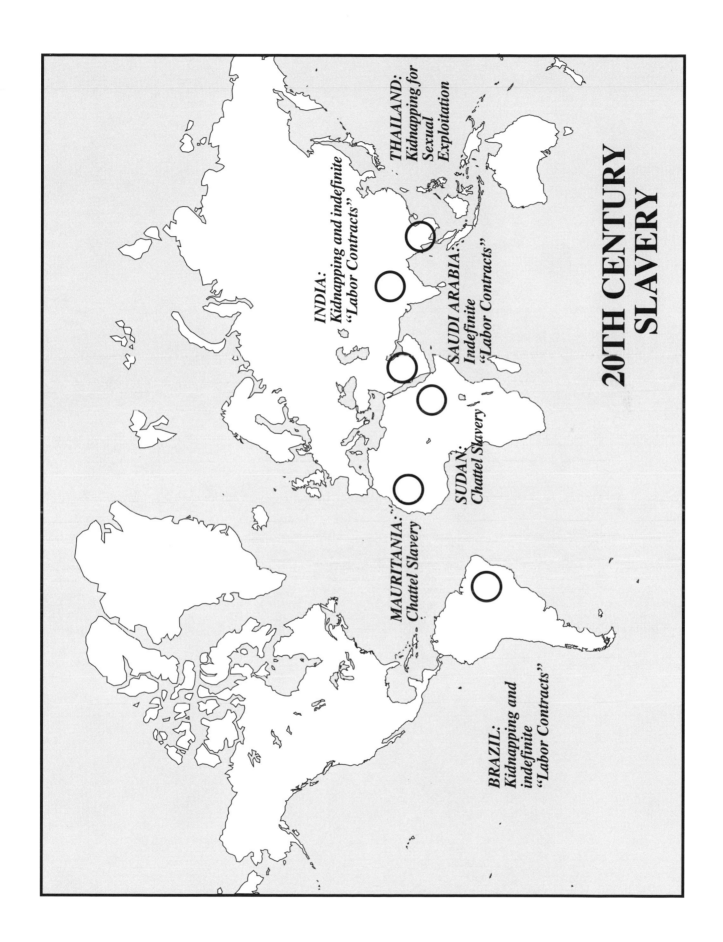

20TH CENTURY SLAVERY

THAILAND: *Kidnapping for Sexual Exploitation*

INDIA: *Kidnapping and indefinite "Labor Contracts"*

SAUDI ARABIA: *Indefinite "Labor Contracts"*

SUDAN: *Chattel Slavery*

MAURITANIA: *Chattel Slavery*

BRAZIL: *Kidnapping and indefinite "Labor Contracts"*

Abolition and Antislavery Movements

This entry includes the following articles: Meaning of the Terms; Introduction and Overview; International Perspective, 1770 to the Present; Great Britain; United States; France; Brazil; Russia; Caribbean Region.

Meaning of the Terms

The meanings of the terms *abolition, antislavery, emancipation,* and *manumission* varied and changed from the 1770s to the end of slavery in the United States.

Technically, *manumission* referred to the voluntary freeing of a slave by a master. However, some organizations opposed to slavery, such as the New York Manumission Society, used this term to describe larger efforts, such as building schools and orphanages for former slaves. This was not incorrect because when the society was organized in the 1780s, slavery was legal in New York State; thus, besides working for a change in the law, the society also lobbied masters to voluntarily manumit their slaves. In the nineteenth century this term almost always applied to the actions of individual southern masters who voluntarily manumitted their slaves.

From the 1770s to 1808, the terms *abolition* and *abolitionist* in Great Britain referred to reformers who wanted to abolish the African slave trade—the members of the London Society for the Abolition of the Slave Trade, for example. In Britain during this period, *abolition* did not refer to an ending of slavery in the American and Caribbean colonies. British reformers turned to ending slavery in the Caribbean and other overseas colonies only after Britain closed the African trade in 1808. These reformers usually adopted the term *antislavery* to describe activities focused on ending slavery throughout the empire.

During and immediately after the American Revolution, abolition societies dedicated to the end of slavery in particular states emerged throughout the North, as well as in Virginia, Maryland, Delaware, and Kentucky. These abolition societies, often dominated by Quakers, were gradualist in approach and conservative in their opposition to slavery. In 1775 Pennsylvanians organized the Society for the Relief of Free Negroes Unlawfully Held in Bondage, and for Improving the Condition of the African Race. However, other organizations used different terminology; one example is the New York Manumission Society, which initially focused on encouraging private manumission and building schools and other institutions for blacks already free as well as those recently manumitted through the society's efforts. Between 1780 and 1808 the abolition societies were instrumental in gaining the passage of gradual emancipation statutes in Pennsylvania (1780), Connecticut (1784), Rhode Island (1784), New York (1799), and New Jersey (1804), and a ban on the slave trade in the United States and England in 1807–1808. By 1820 the first wave of abolition societies had become moribund. After the 1820s emancipation and emancipationists in the United States came to be associated with gradualism, individual acts, and a conservative approach to ending slavery.

Under the leadership of William Lloyd Garrison, a new movement opposed to slavery arose in the United

1

A political cartoon depicts the controversy surrounding the issue of "immediate abolition" by showing William Lloyd Garrison being mobbed and dragged through the streets with a rope around his neck. [Corbis-Bettmann]

States in 1831. Garrison called his organization the American Anti-Slavery Society, while he was seen throughout the nation as the leading apostle of radical abolitionism. In the early 1830s these terms—*antislavery* and *abolitionist*—were often used interchangeably. Members of antislavery societies were "abolitionists," as opposed to the members of the "abolition societies" of the 1790s, who were known as "emancipationists." Garrison distinguished his movement from the earlier abolition societies by asserting that he was in favor of immediate abolition rather than the gradual process adopted in most of the northern states. Acknowledging the impracticality of immediate abolition in the South, he adopted the oxymoronic slogan Immediate Abolition, Gradually Achieved. By this slogan he meant that his followers should demand that immediate steps be taken to end slavery, with the understanding that the social transition might take a few years. This was in fact the tactic that England adopted in 1833 to end slavery in its American colonies, a goal that was achieved in 1838.

In the United States, from the end of the 1830s until the Civil War, the term *abolition* was tied to the most radical opponents of slavery, who ironically were members of numerous organizations that called themselves antislavery societies. Garrison and his followers

at first hoped to convert slaveholders to abolition through "moral suasion." Garrison's tactics initially included petitioning Congress and sending antislavery literature to southern politicians, lawyers, ministers, and other leading citizens. By 1840 Garrison had personally concluded that the Constitution was proslavery, calling it a "covenant with death and an agreement in hell." After that, Garrison and his followers rejected all electoral politics and, under the slogan No Union with Slaveholders, in fact argued that the North should secede from the Union.

By the 1840s the American abolitionists had divided into Garrisonian and non-Garrisonian wings. The term *antislavery* came to be associated with the non-Garrisonians, many of whom pursued their strategies through electoral politics as well as through agitation, petition, and propaganda wars. Modern historians tend to separate "abolitionists" from "antislavery activists" by the nature of their tactics and programs rather than by their ultimate goal. Both groups wanted to end slavery, but the abolitionists were often more confrontational and less likely to participate in traditional party politics or to compromise on issues.

By the 1850s the distinctions between political and nonpolitical and between antislavery and abolition were disappearing except on the extremes. Although the Garrisonian abolitionists rejected all political activity, other abolitionists—that is, advocates of an immediate and unconditional end to slavery, such as Gerrit Smith and Frederick Douglass, the nation's most famous black opponent of slavery—participated in the Liberty Party and other political movements. In addition, mainstream antislavery politicians, like Salmon P. Chase of Ohio and Charles Sumner of Massachusetts, were called "political abolitionists," an appellation they rarely rejected. After 1855 the Republican Party had a distinct antislavery wing made up of "political abolitionists" like Chase, Sumner, William H. Seward of New York, and Hannibal Hamlin of Maine, who would serve as Abraham Lincoln's first vice president.

During the Civil War the term *emancipation* re-emerged—this time as a radical term—when President Lincoln issued his preliminary Emancipation Proclamation in September 1862 and his final Emancipation Proclamation one hundred days later, on 1 January 1863. Lincoln chose his language quite carefully. He was emancipating millions of slaves who were owned by rebel masters, but he was not abolishing slavery, which continued to exist in some states until the ratification of the Thirteenth Amendment. Significantly, that amendment avoided all of these controversial terms, simply declaring, "Neither slavery nor involuntary servitude . . . shall exist within the United States, or any place subject to their jurisdiction."

See also DOUGLASS, FREDERICK; EMANCIPATION; GARRISON, WILLIAM LLOYD; NEW YORK MANUMISSION SOCIETY; PERSPECTIVES ON SLAVERY; PHILLIPS, WENDELL.

BIBLIOGRAPHY

BARNES, GILBERT HOBBES. *The Antislavery Impulse: 1830–1844*. 1933.
DAVIS, DAVID BRION. *The Problem of Slavery in the Age of Revolution, 1770–1823*. 1974.
DUMOND, DWIGHT L. *Antislavery: The Crusade for Freedom in America*. 1961.
STEWART, JAMES BREWER. *Holy Warriors: The Abolitionists and American Slavery*. Rev. ed. 1996.

Paul Finkelman

Introduction and Overview

The economic benefits of black slavery overwhelmed its early critics. Yet, by the late eighteenth century Britain, the pre-eminent slave-trading nation and key beneficiary of the Atlantic trade, spawned a pioneering and highly effective abolition campaign. Though Quakers had objected to slavery from the late seventeenth century, theirs had been a voice in the wilderness. From the 1760s, however, an intellectual groundswell of abolitionist sentiment began to emerge among Quakers, initially in Philadelphia and London. Their voices joined a critique of slavery from a number of Enlightenment writers and benefited from the broader debate about social and political rights. This was given added force and direction in the debate culminating in American independence (1776) and the creation of the new American Republic (1787). At the same time the critical philosophy launched by Adam Smith's *Wealth of Nations* (1776), with its emphasis on the benefits of freedom of trade (and freedom of labor), raised doubts about the economic wisdom of Britain's highly protected imperial slave system.

Quakers led the British campaign launched in 1787 against the Atlantic slave trade, and their national networks proved crucial in providing the early organizational framework across Britain. They also suffused the movement with a sense of outraged religious sensibility. Thanks to Thomas Clarkson's indefatigable campaigns in the country and the political machinations of William Wilberforce in Parliament a popular and a parliamentary opposition to the slave trade were quickly put in place. But the shadow of the French Revolution and its bloody consequences in Saint Domingue (now Haiti) halted abolition by 1793. However, by then—a mere six years after its launch—there was no doubt that abolition had seized the moral high ground in Britain. And there were ever more people willing to believe that a free trade to and from Africa would bring greater economic benefits to Britain than the previously unchallenged benefits of the slave trade. Helped by the proliferation of dissenting churches, the abolition movement became popular in plebeian communities, allowing more middle-class women to engage in politics. Petitions, tracts, and public meetings sustained the campaign. But the parliamentary climate was not ready until 1806. The slave trade was outlawed in 1807.

Slavery itself continued to thrive both in the British Caribbean islands and in the expansive American cotton states. West Indian slaves showed their own hatred of their bondage in major slave revolts in Barbados (1816), Demerara (1823), and Jamaica (1831–1832). Missionaries made major inroads among the slaves, and thus the repression of black Christians by plantation owners and the colonial government seemed doubly outrageous. British opinion swung more firmly against slavery, driven forward from the mid-1820s by an increasingly powerful abolitionist movement using the old tactics—tracts, rallies, petitions, and political lobbying—which could now rally support as never before. The economics of free trade also offered a powerful argument against slavery. But it was the Reform Act passed by Parliament in 1832 that, by changing the composition and tone of Parliament itself—new groups of MPs who favored abolition were subsequently elected—made emancipation possible. Temporary freedom (apprenticeship) lasted from 1834 to 1838, and final freedom, bought through compensation to the planters, totaling a massive twenty million pounds, came to Britain's 750,000 slaves in August of 1838.

Slavery continued to thrive in North America, however, on the back of the expansive cotton industry. The 697,897 slaves of 1790 had increased to 3,953,760 in 1860 and had spread to new states along the expanding frontier, fed by an internal, not transatlantic, slave trade. Though slavery in the Old South had faded in economic importance, in the cotton states, notably Mississippi, Alabama, Louisiana, Arkansas, and Texas, it took on a new and major importance that transcended economics. It also created a slaveholding culture that became bitterly opposed to ideas of black freedom, ideas which flowed from the North and from aggressive British abolitionists. Moreover, slave owning was a feature of early American politics; five of the first seven presidents were slaveholders. Under attack, the South turned in on itself, resistant to the idea of progress as defined by Northerners and Europeans and preferring instead to maintain its addiction to a slave-based economy and culture. North American slavery stood in sharp contrast to the broader American attachment to freedom at all levels. There was a social and political tension about slavery throughout the United States that was not resolved until slavery was abolished by passage of the Thirteenth Amendment in 1865.

To many people slavery in the South seemed to be a religious outrage as well as an economic relic. Southern slavery drew the fire of diverse church groups and sects, which saw slavery as a sin. The vernacular imagery and institutional bases of American abolitionism—influenced initially by the successful British campaign—was religious. The South, however, had its own distinctive defenses, including religious ones. The proslavery case was reinforced by the rise of racial arguments that, though rooted in new social sciences, were ultimately populist in inspiration and strength. Furthermore, Southerners pointed to the economic virtues of slavery and to the fact that there were worse labor systems—the fate of the Irish peasantry in 1846 was an obvious case in point. Slavery was, in effect, not so much a separate Southern institution as Southern life itself.

In the 1830s and 1840s American abolition evolved differently from the British prototype. It was inevitably deeply influenced by the ideals of the American Revolution, but it was also sustained by separate waves of powerful religious sentiment and organization, often of a local nature. Campaigns to boycott slave-made products and to encourage black migration were tried and failed. From the 1830s onward, a new wave of American abolitionist sentiment emerged, partly a function of the Second Great Awakening, and like its British counterpart, it took the form of a crusade. It swiftly developed a popular organization with paid agents, massive petitioning, and large-scale meetings. But it faced firm, sometimes violent opposition. It was also a movement seriously and periodically divided in itself. It prompted a fierce and organized proslavery movement to arise in the South in reaction.

By the 1850s a siege mentality had developed in the South, and the threats to secede from the Union were not merely idle. It became increasingly clear that the South was prepared to fight to defend its economic attachment not only to slavery but to the broader Southern culture of which slavery was the heart and rationale. The election of Abraham Lincoln to the presidency in 1860 and the secession of the South in 1861 brought on the Civil War, which ensured that slavery would indeed be ended. Although the war was not "about" slavery, it offered the North cause and occasion to rally support and recruits. The slaves' general refusal to join the Southern cause was a serious flaw at the heart of the Confederacy. Slavery collapsed wherever the Union armies drew near; slaves crossed the lines, dropped their tools, and simply ran away. Slave owners, who had long claimed a special understanding of their slaves, were generally confounded. Like slave owners everywhere, they were ignorant of what had motivated their slaves. As the war and bloodletting dragged on, Northern demands inevitably became more severe. In January of 1863, Lincoln issued the Emancipation Proclamation. Two years later the Thirteenth Amendment to the U.S. Constitution confirmed black freedom throughout the United States. Abolitionists were left to ponder the fate of the freed slaves in the United States and the West Indies and to consider how best to tackle the surviving slave systems in Cuba and Brazil.

See also EMANCIPATION; ENLIGHTENMENT; MANUMISSION; QUAKERS.

BIBLIOGRAPHY

DAVIS, DAVID BRION. *Slavery and Human Progress.* 1985.
TURLEY, DAVID. *The Culture of English Antislavery, 1780–1860.* 1991.
WALVIN, JAMES. *Questioning Slavery.* 1996.

James Walvin

International Perspective, 1770 to the Present

The underpinnings of the abolition and antislavery movements in the United States and England were in a religious movement that was primarily led by Quakers. Since at least the mid-1600s individual Quakers preached against the ownership of and trade in slaves. In 1761 the Society of Friends in England approved a resolution disowning those who refused to stop trading in slaves. In 1763 the annual meeting of the Society of Friends in Philadelphia condemned all who invested in or supplied cargos for the slave trade. Quakers also began to work to abolish slavery and the slave trade in the rest of the world.

The first abolition society in the United States was formed in Pennsylvania in 1775. Most of its members were Quakers, and its only purpose was to provide relief to free blacks who were unlawfully held in bondage. The society suspended its work during the American Revolution but regrouped in 1784. In 1787 it changed its name to The Pennsylvania Society for Promoting the Abolition of Slavery, the Relief of Free Negroes Unlawfully Held in Bondage, and for Improving the Condition of the African Race. Benjamin Franklin was the president. Similar organizations were formed in other states. By 1791 twelve states in both the North and the South had such organizations. In 1794 delegates from all the abolition societies met in Philadelphia and instituted a series of annual meetings. Although this American Convention sought to support the individual societies in their efforts, its primary focus was the national agenda. Similarly, in England, the movement was largely confined to Quakers until 1787, when the Committee for Affecting the Abolition of the Slave Trade was formed by Thomas Clarkson and Quakers.

Abolitionists in both countries sought to further their goals by influencing public opinion and their respective legislative bodies. They distributed pamphlets written by their members as well as reprints of foreign tracts, corresponded with each other, lectured, commissioned studies, addressed state and federal legislatures, and sent letters and petitions to legislatures. In 1787 the Pennsylvania Society sent a memorial to the Federal Convention. In 1790 it addressed the United States Congress with a memorial advocating federal abolition of slavery.

Antislavery societies initiated court action aimed at preventing the kidnapping and sale of blacks from free states to slave states and the enforcement of state manumission and emancipation acts. They also initiated prosecutions to enforce state and federal laws that restricted or prohibited the slave trade. Many societies worked to improve the welfare of free blacks through education and employment.

These organizations and their members generally advocated the gradual abolition of slavery and the slave trade through moral and religious persuasion. In England they concentrated on abolishing the slave trade out of their belief that slaveowners would treat their slaves better if there was no source of new slaves. They hoped that eventually slaveowners would realize that free workers were better workers. The issue was regularly debated in the House of Commons until, in 1804, England outlawed the importation of slaves into its colonies on a gradual basis until 1807, when the trade would be banned.

Abolitionists in the United States also sought to abolish the slave trade in the hopes that such actions would lead to the eventual disappearance of the institution of slavery and were instrumental in obtaining the passage of the United States Trade Act of 1807, which prohibited the importation of slaves. However, in the United States there was also a strong movement which sought to remove free blacks from the country because of fears that having large numbers of them in the population would lead to unrest. The American Colonization Society was formed in 1817 to encourage such emigration. Similar societies existed in all states except South Carolina. In 1819, with the encouragement of the colonization societies, Congress passed the Anti-Slave-Trade Act, which was ostensibly intended to suppress the slave trade by returning Africans from captured slavers to Africa. It also paved the way for the emigration of free blacks. In 1820 the first shipload of freed slaves left for the west coast of Africa under the auspices of the federal government. Several thousand freed slaves from the United States and Africans from slave ships captured by U.S. vessels off the African coast were eventually settled in several colonies that later became Liberia.

The British and American antislavery societies were models for the *Société des Amis des Noirs,* which was founded in 1788 in France. The *Société* argued that the slave trade was bad for Africans and the French and urged that Africans remain in Africa and be converted to consumers.

By 1803 the abolitionists in the United States South had stopped their work in the face of increasing hostility, and many of the Northern societies did not feel much urgency in the cause due to the lack of slaves within their territories and the apparent difficulties in interfering with slavery in the South. In 1806 the American Convention began to hold triennial meetings.

However, in about 1817, new abolition societies began to form, and old societies were revived. By 1827 there were approximately 130 antislavery societies in the United States. Although it is unknown exactly how many societies were members of the American Anti-Slavery Society, by 1838 it claimed a membership of 1,350.

These societies were more radical than the earlier societies and advocated immediate abolition as well as racial equality. In 1819 the Pennsylvania Society for the Abolition of Slavery approved a declaration that slavery should be "immediately abandoned." On 1 January 1831 William Lloyd Garrison began publishing the *Liberator,* a newspaper that advocated "immediatism." The New England Antislavery Society, formed on 1 January 1832, stated that its goals were the elimination of slavery and racial prejudice. In 1833 the Declaration of Sentiments, written by Garrison and adopted by the American Anti-Slavery Society, aimed uncompromisingly for immediatism. The British Anti-Slavery Society, which was formed in 1823, was officially gradualist only until 1831, when it reor-

ganized and began focusing its efforts on swaying public opinion against the institution of slavery.

There were probably several forces that led to this change. On one level, the change was simply a shift in strategy: if the public could be convinced that slavery was evil, it would pressure the politicians to outlaw it. In addition, in the United States there was concern about uprisings by slaves and free blacks. Groups of free blacks vehemently criticized the colonization movement, and threats of violent slave revolts increased. In 1831 the slave Nat Turner led a revolt in Southampton, Virginia, during which nearly one hundred whites were killed. Slaveholders were partly responsible for the rise of immediatism due to their uncompromising criticisms of the more moderate gradualist positions. British slave owners in the Caribbean had reacted violently to relatively benign reforms aimed at improving the conditions of slaves. Lastly, the shift might have reflected a fundamental

A speech is delivered at the 1840 convention of an antislavery society in London. [Corbis-Bettmann]

change in outlook from a detached and rational view of human progress to one in which a compromise with sin was unacceptable.

Initially, the new abolition societies declared their opposition to the use of violent means to liberate slaves. The Massachusetts Anti-Slavery Society encouraged slaves to endure slavery until they were freed by peaceful means. In 1840 a faction that believed in political action broke with Garrison and formed the American and Foreign Anti-Slavery Society. Many members of this group also supported the Liberty Party. Thus, antislavery thought split into two factions: the supporters of "political action" and the "disunionist" Garrisonians who rejected politics.

By the 1850s the movement for peaceful abolition was waning. The New England Non-Resistance Society suspended publication of *The Non-Resistant* in 1842. Several abolitionists who had been at the forefront of the peaceful-means movement began to acknowledge that violence might be necessary, especially to resist enforcement of the Fugitive Slave Law of 1850. John Brown's violent actions in Kansas and his bloody assault at Harpers Ferry, Virginia, led many abolitionists to reconsider their rejection of violence.

During the Civil War abolitionists formed societies to aid slaves who had escaped by establishing relief centers as well as schools. After the Civil War these societies sent teachers and missionaries to the South.

In 1865 a second group broke with Garrison over the future of antislavery societies after slavery had been abolished in the United States. Garrison believed the societies should be disbanded, as their purpose, the abolition of slavery, had been accomplished. Others believed that the societies should continue to work to end racial discrimination. In 1863 the Massachusetts Anti-Slavery Society rejected a resolution put forward by Garrison and pledged to work towards a congressional act that made the readmission of the Southern states into the Union conditional upon full emancipation, including the right to vote.

The crusade to end slavery and the slave trade internationally continued in the twentieth century. During the last two decades of the nineteenth century, the British and Foreign Anti-Slavery Society, the descendant of the British Anti-Slavery Society that was founded in 1839, continued to work toward arousing public opinion against slavery and pressuring the British government to enter into treaties for the eradication of slavery and the slave trade in Africa and the Middle East. The society, as well as similar committees in France, Belgium, Holland, Italy, and Spain, instigated the conference that was held in Brussels in 1889 to reach agreement on enforcement procedures in an effort to eradicate the slave trade in Africa.

At the end of World War I, the issue was still of significant enough concern that it was one of the first issues addressed by the League of Nations. First the Temporary Slavery Commission and later the Advisory Committee on Slavery compiled reports of slavery and the slave trade that were submitted to the Assembly up until 1938.

In the late twentieth century human rights organizations and the United Nations continued to investigate and compile influential reports on slavery, the slave trade, and slavery-like practices. One organization, Anti-Slavery International (ASI), has been concerned with abolition of slavery and similar practices. ASI was the result of a merger in 1909 between the British and Foreign Anti-Slavery Society and the Aborigines Protection Society. ASI is concerned not only with old forms of slavery but also with newer slavery-like practices, such as exploitation of women and children, sham adoption, forced labor, and the protection of indigenous peoples. It collects information and data and compiles reports that are then sent to the governments concerned. If an adequate response is not received, ASI often engages in either diplomacy or publicity. It also brings the practices to the attention of the United Nations Working Group of Experts on Slavery, with which it is affiliated.

See also AMERICAN ANTI-SLAVERY SOCIETY; LIBERIA; QUAKERS; SOCIÉTÉ DES AMIS DES NOIRS.

BIBLIOGRAPHY

DAVIS, DAVID BRION. "The Emergence of Immediatism in British and American Antislavery Thought." *Mississippi Valley Historical Review* 69 (1962): 209–230.

FILLER, LOUIS. *The Crusade against Slavery 1830–1860.* 1960.

FLADELAND, BETTY. *Men and Brothers: Anglo-American Antislavery Cooperation.* 1972.

LOCKE, MARY STOUGHTON. *Anti-Slavery in America from the Introduction of African Slaves to the Prohibition of the Slave Trade (1619–1808).* 1901.

MCPHERSON, JAMES M. *The Struggle for Equality.* 1964.

Renee C. Redman

Great Britain

The public agitation over the slavery issue that began in Britain in the 1780s was the first large-scale attempt in modern times to mobilize national opinion in support of a humanitarian cause. It proved so successful that in 1807 the British government outlawed the slave trade and, in 1833, abolished chattel slavery throughout the empire. It also provided a model for antislavery activists in the United States and elsewhere who looked to Britain for inspiration and guidance. Thus, from the 1830s onwards, Britons saw themselves as being in the forefront of a worldwide movement dedicated to the promotion of human freedom. One consequence of this was that antislavery became part of the national ideology, finding expression in, among other things, Britain's continuing endeavors to suppress the foreign slave trade and, ironically, the imperial drive that extended British rule over large parts of Africa and Asia.

Origins

These developments, representing as they did a dramatic reversal in national attitudes, are all the more remarkable in that Britain had up to that time been the principal purveyor of slaves to the New World as well as a major slaveholding power in its own right. These were profitable activities, which contributed significantly to the nation's wealth and prestige as a world power. Nevertheless, from the beginning of the eighteenth century onward, voices were heard expressing unease at the country's involvement in such undertakings. Among the earliest were those of settlers in Pennsylvania and Massachusetts. Many were those of religious groups pointing out the extent to which such behavior contravened Christian ethics. More often than not these were the views of Quakers, Methodists, and others who, rejecting traditional authorities, looked to their individual consciences for moral guidance. Adding to the chorus of dissent, spokesmen of the Enlightenment argued that slavery was both anachronistic and contrary to natural rights. More broadly, however, there was a growing awareness of the contradiction between those principles of political liberty that the British had adopted at home and on which they prided themselves and the behavior of their nationals abroad. This contradiction, on other than empirical grounds, was becoming increasingly difficult to justify.

Slavery had never possessed more than a vestigial presence in Britain itself. Its legal status, always ambiguous, received a mortal blow in 1772 when, in a test case brought by Granville Sharp, Lord Justice Mansfield ruled that James Somerset, a former Virginia slave, was not property under English law and so could not be returned to America against his will.

But it was not until the 1780s that anything worth calling an antislavery *movement* emerged. One significant watershed was the loss of the North American colonies, which not only helped to popularize libertarian ideas of the kind espoused by the defenders of the colonial cause but, more important, removed an obstacle that would have made action virtually unthinkable. Inept as Parliament had been with regard to colonial taxation, it is hard to believe that it would

have been so foolhardy as to provoke its North American colonists over the slavery issue.

The Attack on the Slave Trade

The first campaign began, significantly enough, in 1783, the year peace with the colonies was achieved. Thus it was in the immediate aftermath of the American War of Independence that the British Quakers, responding to the urgings of their Philadelphia brethren, established what was effectively the first British antislavery society. This small body was entirely Quaker in membership. Quakers, however, already had considerable experience in political lobbying, initially undertaken in their own defense from persecution, and controlled a well-established national network of regional and local bodies on which they could rely for support. Even so, it is unlikely that they would ever have been able to achieve much on their own. The major breakthrough came four years later with the establishment of the Society for the Abolition of the Slave Trade (1787–1807), a more broadly-based body that included, besides the original members of the Quaker committee, a number of talented non-Quakers. Among them were Thomas Clarkson, who took on the task of gathering information and organizing provincial support, and William Wilberforce, who became the movement's principal parliamentary spokesman.

The organizational arrangements made in 1787 created a structure that remained largely unchanged for the next forty years even though the movement waxed and waned and, more than once, underwent significant changes of direction. At its center stood the London-based national committee and its parliamentary spokesmen, jointly responsible for formulating policy and coordinating action. Around the periphery were the auxiliaries, whose number fluctuated according to circumstance. Some, like those in Manchester and Bristol, were large and sufficiently well funded to contribute significantly to the movement's coffers. Others represented little more than local church groups that could, when required, be pressed into service to circulate petitions or obtain undertakings from prospective parliamentary candidates. The result was a nationwide movement responsive to central direction and dedicated to bringing popular pressure to bear on Parliament and the government, yet with the capacity, as events were to show, of remaining dormant for long periods.

Initially, many people in the movement were uncertain as to the object of the campaign. Should its aim be to get rid of slavery as well as the slave trade? Although opposed to both, the movement's leaders agreed that, for the time being, they should confine their attention to ending the slave trade. To have attacked slavery would have involved interfering with property, a subject on which Parliament was notoriously sensitive, whereas the regulation of trade had always been accepted as one of Parliament's functions. Moreover, of the two, the slave trade was plainly the more replete with horrors.

There was never any question, however, as to where to look for redress or any doubt that, once Parliament had passed the necessary legislation, the government had the powers necessary to ensure that it was enforced. It soon became evident, too, that there was little support for the trade in the country at large. The problem was the patronage and tight control over parliamentary procedures exercised by the West India lobby. Nevertheless, abolitionists were heartened by the enthusiastic response they received from people of all ranks. As one contemporary noted, it was as if the necessary tinder had already been collected and were merely waiting to be ignited.

The massive petition campaign of 1792, involving some 400,000 individuals, persuaded the House of Commons to agree to a motion providing for Britain's gradual withdrawal from the trade. Although the measure was subsequently overturned in the House of Lords, it looked for a moment as if victory were assured. The moment, however, soon passed, less because of the opposition of the West India lobby than on account of the revolution in France and the fear of domestic insurrection, which made challenges to existing practices appear to be a reflection of Jacobinical tendencies. Thus, finding the times inopportune,

the movement effectively went into hibernation for a decade.

The final overthrow of the British slave trade was accomplished without significant popular pressure and largely by subterfuge. Capitalizing on the recent turn of events in Britain's struggles with France, Parliament was prevailed upon in 1806 to forbid the export of slaves from Africa to newly conquered colonies on the grounds that this would, when peace returned and these colonies were restored to their original owners, be to Britain's disadvantage. The following year, on learning to its surprise that it had already abolished the greater part of the country's trade in slaves, Parliament was duly persuaded to put an end to that portion which remained.

Encouraged by this success, the movement's leaders now turned their attention to what they saw as the linked issues of making amends to Africa for Britain's past misdeeds and combating the slave trade carried on in foreign vessels, using as their instrument the African Institution (1807–1827). The great fear was that, as their opponents had argued from the first, Britain's withdrawal would simply create a gap for other nations to fill. This proved to be largely the case despite the representations of British diplomats, spurred on, as at the time of the Treaty of Vienna in 1815, by a fresh wave of petitions.

The other disappointment of these years was the realization that, contrary to what many had hoped, the ending of the trade to Britain's own possessions had had no discernible effect on the treatment of the slaves held there. To remedy this situation a new organization, the Anti-Slavery Society (1823–1839), was formed. By and large its membership was the same as that of its two predecessors, although the role of titular leader and parliamentary spokesman now passed from the aging Wilberforce to Thomas Fowell Buxton. Once again, however, Clarkson was on the road drumming up support and, as before, Quakers played a prominent part at both the national and the regional level.

The Attack on Slavery

The campaign against slavery was, initially at least, largely a replay of the earlier campaign against the trade. Its declared aim was to secure, first, the amelioration of slavery and then, in the fullness of time, its abolition. This gradualist approach appeared the one most likely to win the support of Parliament, and bills were accordingly introduced, speeches delivered, petitions presented, and pamphlets published. What had not been counted on was the intransigence of the colonial planters, who showed themselves willing to fight tooth and nail for their interests in Parliament

An illustration from the early 1830s shows children presenting a petition for abolition of the slave trade. [Corbis-Bettmann]

and who were prepared to defy the government by refusing to implement its instructions.

Observing these developments, the movement's younger and more radical members found themselves in a quandary. Hitherto they had shown a notable willingness to follow the lead of the London-based committee and its parliamentary spokesmen. Finding, however, that neither had a solution to the current impasse, a group of younger abolitionists broke ranks by establishing an Agency Committee (1831–1834) for the purpose of breaking this deadlock through popular agitation. The method adopted was to employ salaried lecturers, itinerant antislavery preachers, to go from town to town appealing to peoples' moral instincts by insisting upon the immediate and unconditional emancipation of all the slaves in Britain's overseas possession.

The resulting upsurge of popular feeling, coinciding as it did with the agitation over parliamentary reform, finally provoked the government to action, although the promotion of the issue in Parliament itself remained firmly in the hands of Buxton and his colleagues. In practice, the Emancipation Act of 1833 did not give abolitionists all that they hoped for and left behind a legacy of bitterness. Supporters of the Agency Committee claimed that Buxton and his group had sold out by agreeing to consign the slaves to a period of so-called apprenticeship and to compensate their owners to the tune of £20,000,000. Buxton's group, in turn, argued that no better terms had been on offer and that the alternative would have been to delay emancipation indefinitely.

Later Developments

With its initial goals achieved, the antislavery movement became increasingly fragmented. Supporters of the Agency Committee reconstituted themselves under the leadership of Joseph Sturge to form the Central Negro Emancipation Committee (1837–1840) for the purpose of ending apprenticeship. When apprenticeship was finally done away with in 1838, members of this same group went on to form the British and Foreign Anti-Slavery Society. Meanwhile, Buxton had grown alarmed at what he took to be the growing number of slaves being carried in foreign vessels to the Americas, particularly Cuba and Brazil, and conceived the notion that the only effective way to combat this traffic was to "civilize" Africa. The result was the famous Niger Expedition of 1841, which ended in disaster when virtually all its members succumbed to malaria.

During the 1840s and 1850s the situation grew ever more complicated with the arrival of emissaries from rival branches of the newly burgeoning American antislavery movement and the establishment of local British organizations devoted to their support. British people found these rivalries confusing. There was no longer any doubt, however, concerning Britain's commitment to antislavery principles, as was revealed by the government's continuing commitment to suppressing the Atlantic slave trade by means of a combination of diplomacy and naval power. These efforts continued into the 1860s when, with U.S. assistance, the traffic was finally ended. Antislavery matters remained a British concern up to the end of the century and beyond when, as earlier noted, a belief that it was Britain's destiny to rid the world of slavery became an important factor in determining both official and popular attitudes toward imperial expansion in Africa and Asia.

Important as this was from the point of view of Britain's self-image, it brought with it practical difficulties. Indigenous slavery was very different from chattel slavery of the type found in the New World. British authority depended to a large extent on the sufferance of those over whom it was exercised. It was thus hardly consistent with imperial interests for officials to intrude any more than was essential into the domestic lives of those over whom they ruled. In the case of India, where slavery in many forms had long existed, a compromise of sorts was achieved with the adoption of Act V of 1843, which provided that under Indian law there would be no recognition of slavery. Officials were thereby freed from the charge of supporting slavery while being relieved from the obligation of doing anything much about it.

See also BRITISH AND FOREIGN ANTI-SLAVERY SOCIETY (1839–1909); BUXTON, THOMAS FOWELL; CLARKSON, THOMAS; EMANCIPATION ACT, BRITISH (1833); QUAKERS; SLAVE TRADE; WILBERFORCE, WILLIAM.

BIBLIOGRAPHY

ANSTEY, ROGER. *The Atlantic Slave Trade and British Abolition.* 1975.

BLACKBURN, ROBIN. *The Overthrow of Colonial Slavery, 1776–1848.* 1988.

COUPLAND, REGINALD. *The British Anti-Slavery Movement.* 1933.

DAVIS, DAVID B. *The Problem of Slavery in the Age of Revolution, 1770–1823.* 1975.

DRESCHER, SEYMOUR. *Capitalism and Antislavery: British Mobilisation in Comparative Perspective.* 1986.

———. *Econocide: British Slavery in the Era of Abolition.* 1977.

LLOYD, CHRISTOPHER. *The Navy and the Slave Trade: The Suppression of the Slave Trade in the Nineteenth Century.* 1949.

OLDFIELD, J. R. *Popular Politics and British Anti-Slavery: The Mobilisation of Public Opinion against the Slave Trade, 1787–1807.* 1995.

TEMPERLEY, HOWARD. *British Antislavery, 1833–1870.* 1972.

———. *White Dreams, Black Africa: The Antislavery Expedition to the Niger, 1841–1842.* 1991.

WILSON, ELLEN GIBSON. *Thomas Clarkson: A Biography.* 1989.

Howard R. Temperley

United States

When American abolitionism first took form in the late eighteenth century, the institution of slavery possessed enormous power and legitimacy, as it had for centuries. From the time of ancient Athens, the exploitation of unfree labor had shaped the economies of Western Europe, and by the seventeenth century it was fueling their expansion into the Western Hemisphere. Slaves by the tens of thousands had built the civilizations of classical Egypt, Greece, and Rome. Throughout the Middle Ages and the Renaissance and well into the eighteenth century, landed aristocrats had commanded the labor of ordinary people who passed their unfree lives as villeins and serfs. By the seventeenth century Spain, Portugal, Holland, France, and England were developing immense empires throughout the Western Hemisphere, relying on the forced relocation of millions of enslaved Africans to produce extraordinary wealth and transform the global economy. In 1776, when Thomas Jefferson's *Declaration of Independence* first asserted a revolutionary claim of equality, it did so in a world in which slavery and other forms of unfree labor were deeply entrenched and extraordinarily productive.

Though in general rural New Englanders had little interest in slave labor, leading citizens asserted their high status by owning slaves for personal use. In Rhode Island, New York, New Jersey, Delaware, and Pennsylvania, by contrast, slavery proved a profitable way to farm on a large scale. In major northern cities slavery was commonly applied to manufacturing and artisan enterprises. Though the total number of African-Americans living in the North, free or enslaved, was only 4 percent of the total population, slavery clearly contributed to the development of an expansive economy. In the southern colonies, meanwhile, slavery exercised an infinitely more pervasive influence, causing that region to develop a distinctive political culture and economy which contrasted sharply with that of the North.

Every southern colony prior to the Revolution was led by elite groups of slaveholders who dominated politics, controlled the economy, and defined social norms. From the rice-growing coasts of South Carolina and Georgia to the tobacco plantations of Virginia and Maryland, these distinguished "first families" derived their obvious power from their numerous slaves and presided over a region which, in 1776, had thirty-five African-Americans for every hundred inhabitants. The majority of the South's whites—small slaveholders and middling subsistence farmers—often resented these aristocratic "betters" but usually deferred to them, for this slavery-dominated society required a clear ordering of unequals—proud over humble, rich over poor, male over female, and above all white over black.

For this reason, southern whites of all social classes generally concurred with Jefferson, their fellow slaveholder, that "unalienable rights" and claims of equality did not apply to people of African ancestry. From the beginning some English settlers harbored certain prejudices against dark-skinned Africans, while almost all thought them inferior because they were heathens. Indeed, it was their status as heathens that justified their enslavement, and, once they were enslaved, helped create a climate of racism. By 1776 such attitudes were becoming deeply ingrained as an almost instinctive white supremacism. The strength of such biases ensured that many white Northerners agreed with their southern counterparts that the Declaration of Independence should apply exclusively to their own white race. For all these reasons, by 1776 slave owning and white prejudice had come to pose an enormous challenge to those who linked independence with abolitionism. Nevertheless, the colonists' revolt against Great Britain inaugurated what was to become the American crusade against slavery.

Several factors account for this development, many of which involved the colonists' revolutionary beliefs. Some prominent figures like James Otis, Benjamin Franklin, Thomas Paine, and Benjamin Rush found strong abolitionist imperatives in the Enlightenment philosophy of rationalism that also underlay their hatred of monarchy and aristocracy. Believing that environmental conditions—not color or inherited status—determined the intellectual and moral development of all human beings, such leaders concluded that the contradictions between patriots' demands for liberty and their oppression of black slaves were too obvious to ignore. According to this logic, emancipation would relieve African-Americans of their "degraded" circumstances and allow them to "rise," even as white Americans cast off their own corrupting attachments to the slaveholding "aristocracy." Other patriotic spokesmen drew their abolitionism from evangelical religion. Calvinist revivalists such as Samuel Hopkins and Jonathan Mayhew joined with Quaker evangelicals such as John Woolman and Anthony Benezet and Methodists such as Francis Asbury to condemn slavery as the foulest transgression of God's will, and the principal obstacle to the achievement of independence. Some prominent planter politicians in the upper South, such as Peyton Randolph, even began gradually emancipating their own slaves, calling on others to follow their example. In all these respects, the ideology of the Revolution challenged slavery's moral legitimacy as never before.

Just as important, the Revolution led African-Americans themselves to cast off their enslavement, turning the struggle for independence into what the

Though Peyton Randolph, first president of the Continental Congress, favored gradual emancipation, he owned twenty-seven slaves at his death in 1775. His will identified six slaves by name as bequests. [Library of Congress/Corbis]

historian Benjamin Quarles has characterized as North America's largest single slave insurrection. In both North and South, many slaves fought on both sides in the revolutionary struggle in exchange for the promise of freedom. Others took advantage of the disruptions of war to escape to cities. In the North slaves petitioned state legislatures to enact bills of emancipation, bargained with their masters to purchase their freedom, and filed emancipation suits. In all these ways, African-Americans not only secured their individual liberty but also established in every northern city communities of color that supported church and civic organizations, offered economic opportunities, and provided leadership in the struggle against discrimination and slavery.

In the North, the combined force of this black and white activism yielded notable results. By 1804 every state north of Maryland, Delaware, and Virginia had either ended slavery outright or passed a gradual emancipation act that would put slavery on the road to extinction. Liberation itself was often a painfully slow and partial process, since some slaves—those born before the passage of gradual emancipation statutes—remained in bondage long after most blacks were free. Also, the gradual emancipation acts required the children of slaves to serve long terms as apprentices or in-dentured servants, usually controlled by the same white person who had owned their mothers. Nevertheless, by 1830 slavery had ceased to exist in most of the North. A few slaves remained in Pennsylvania, Connecticut, and Illinois until the 1840s. In 1848 New Jersey changed the status of its last remaining slaves to that of indentured servants, although their involuntary bondage continued until the end of the Civil War. But throughout the North freedom did not bring full citizenship. In most cases African-Americans found their political and civil rights being strictly limited in this new regime, while harsh patterns of segregation and discrimination emerged to blight their daily lives. Throughout the antebellum years, as abolitionists always knew, "freedom" for African-Americans in the North had little to do with equality.

Meantime, the new federal constitution of 1787 also worked in conservative directions by guaranteeing powerful protections for slavery in the southern states, where voluntary emancipation ultimately made no permanent headway. Constitutional features such as counting a slave as three-fifths of a full person when apportioning representation, guaranteeing the use of federal power to quell slave insurrection, and providing for a federally enforced fugitive slave law all indicated that slavery had been granted formidable legitimacy by the founding fathers, who had seen their task as creating a strong national government, not promoting sectionally divisive abolitionism.

For all these reasons, as Eli Whitney's cotton gin stimulated an explosive westward expansion of the cotton-growing frontier in the early nineteenth century, the Revolution's abolitionist legacy all but expired. As several new slave states such as Kentucky, Tennessee, and Alabama entered the Union, the domestic slave trade was thriving, and abolitionist voices had been reduced to a quiet few—mostly isolated Quakers such as Benjamin Lundy and energetic free black leaders living in northern cities such as Philadelphia's James Forten and Richard Allen or New York City's John Teasman.

Abortive insurrections in Virginia led by the slave Gabriel Prosser (1800) and in South Carolina by the free black Denmark Vesey (1820), as well as the violent black revolution which succeeded in Haiti in the 1790s, had extinguished slaveholders' interest in private manumission. Such frightening developments had also heightened their fears of local slave revolts and increased their interest in the American Colonization Society, which proposed the voluntary repatriation to Liberia of free blacks and emancipated slaves. Benevolent northern whites also joined this organization, regarding it as a moderate way to address their moral concerns about slavery in an age of ideological conservatism. Most free blacks in the free states, however, denounced colonization as a gross denial of their right to full citizenship in the United States. Though strong political disagreements split northern and southern congressmen over the admission of the slave state Missouri (1819–1821), such sectional tension did nothing to revive the flagging spirit of grassroots abolitionism.

Instead, throughout the North, the 1820s witnessed an unprecedented spread of antiblack bigotry. Massive immigration from the British Isles suddenly put economically vulnerable English, Scottish, and Irish workers into competition with northern free blacks, stimulating fears about "white slavery" and creating deeper prejudice in the white working class. Among respectable middle-class whites, the belief grew that free blacks represented a "naturally degraded race" which needed stringent policing rather than benevolent assistance. Free African-Americans grew understandably defensive as antiblack riots erupted for the first time in major cities, and as state and local governments passed harsh new discriminatory legislation, even while broadening the franchise to include all adult white males. In newly admitted western "free" states such as Illinois and Ohio, for example, specific constitutional provisions hindered blacks from immigrating and explicitly denied them most civil rights. In 1822 New York's new constitution continued to restrict black suffrage to males possessing more than $200 in taxable property, while removing that restriction for white males. In 1829 the white residents of Cincinnati rioted so viciously that many local blacks sought permanent residence elsewhere. In response, besieged black leaders throughout the North gathered their collective strength by founding their own newspaper, *Freedom's Journal,* and their own organization, the Colored Convention Movement (1830)—vehicles for protesting against discrimination, denouncing colonization, and debating the possibility of voluntary emigration to Haiti or lower Canada. In 1829, when Boston's David Walker first published his extraordinary pamphlet, *An Appeal to the Colored Citizens of the World, and Most Particularly to Those of the United States,* his beleaguered black readers understandably embraced his revolutionary call for defensive violence, his scathing criticism of black Americans' apathy and ignorance, and his wholesale condemnation of the American Colonization Society. Clearly, as free blacks in the North understood it, the 1820s were closing on a note of heightening racial crisis.

By 1831 this crisis exploded as four nearly simultaneous events set off fundamental struggles over slavery and racial equality unprecedented in the nation's history, conflicts that ultimately pointed toward the coming of the Civil War. In addition to the discovery that Walker's *Appeal* was circulating among slaves in the coastal South, 1831 brought Nat Turner's bloody insurrection in Southampton County, Virginia; another slave revolt of unprecedented size in British Jamaica; threats of secession from South Carolinian "nullifers" who feared that the federal government would deny their right to hold slaves; and, most portentous of all, the publication by the Bostonian William Lloyd Garrison of a new abolitionist newspaper, the *Liberator,* which espoused a radical new doctrine—"immediate emancipation." To slaveholders and free northern blacks, to white reformers of all persuasions, and to politicians everywhere, it was suddenly clear that slavery constituted a moral question of unprecedented proportions.

The demand for immediate emancipation, above all, foreordained this result. The imperative that the "God-defying sin" of owning humans be expunged from the earth as rapidly as possible originated in Great Britain's militant abolitionist movement. Soon after Garrison adopted immediatism, dozens of influential white reformers throughout New England joined him. They formed the nucleus of a vibrantly radical white-led crusade that was to continue in one form or another for at least four decades, even after Civil War. They openly invited the participation of northern African-Americans, who initially joined in with great enthusiasm, thereby creating the nation's first biracial social movement. In the atmosphere of mounting racial intolerance so prevalent in the 1820s and 1830s, this was undoubtedly the most radical and disruptive feature of immediate abolitionism.

Historians who have examined the motives of white immediatists have usually emphasized the importance of religious revivalism. During the 1820s a popular resurgence of evangelical Protestantism known as the Second Great Awakening swept across the nation, and to certain New Englanders it had deep implications for abolitionism. Powerful revivalist preachers such as Lyman Beecher and Charles G. Finney propounded doctrines that stressed the individual's free-will choice to renounce sin, to strive for personal holiness, and then, once "saved," to bring God's truth to the "unredeemed" and to combat the social evils that sin inevitably perpetuated—drunkenness, impiety, sexual licence, and the exploitation of the weak and defenseless. To certain of Beecher's and Finney's devotees, such as Arthur and Lewis Tappan, Theodore Dwight Weld, and Elizur Wright Jr., to evangelical Baptists like Garrison, to neo-Calvinists like Samuel Sewall Jr. and William Jay, or to radical Quakers like Lucretia Mott or John Greenleaf Whittier, these doctrines made it clear that slavery was the most God-defying of all sins. What other social practice exploited the weak and defenseless more brazenly? Where was sexual wantonness more rampant than in a master's debauchery of his female slaves? Where was impiety more openly encouraged than in the masters' refusal to permit their slaves freedom of religious expression? Where was brutality more evident than in the masters' use of the whip, or their callous disregard for their slaves' ties of family and community? Who besides the slaveholders needed more desperately to respond to the challenge to repent and begin immediately to emancipate those whom they abused so vilely? The answer to all these urgent questions, of course, required preaching immediate emancipation by means of what was called "moral suasion," that is, by making peaceful Christian appeals which would awaken the slumbering conscience of southern slaveholders and their unwitting northern abettors.

The immediatist cause, though always unpopular, did make some dramatic gains at first, as it multiplied its activities during the early 1830s. Leaders like the Tappans, the Motts, and Garrison helped to establish hundreds of antislavery societies in towns and cities in New England, New York State, and Pennsylvania. Further west, particularly in Ohio, Theodore Weld, Elizur Wright Jr., Beriah Green, and their many coworkers also established an extensive network of abolitionist organizations. The denunciatory appeals of Garrison's *Liberator* were quickly amplified by dozens of immediatist pamphlets and newspapers—with titles such as *The Slaves' Friend, The Emancipator,* and *Human Rights*—that circulated widely throughout the free states. Salaried agents crisscrossed the North, organizing meetings and denouncing the sins of slaveholding in public speeches. The American Anti-Slavery Society, founded in 1833, underwrote these myriad activities; in addition, in 1835 it developed a "great postal campaign" which used the United States Mail Service to awaken the conscience of slaveholders by flooding the South with abolitionist literature. It also set in motion a "great petition campaign," presenting the United States Congress with thousands of petitions, accompanied by tens of thousands of signatures, each praying that the representatives consider enacting specific pieces of antislavery legislation. In cities across the North, meanwhile, white abolitionists joined with local African-American activists in daring efforts to "uplift the black race" by founding schools, moral reform societies, manual labor academies, and Sunday school groups. The most enduring of these, Oberlin College, established in 1835, was the nation's first example of multiracial coeducation.

As this example and many others made clear, immediatism was from its inception a racially amalgamated enterprise that also included both genders. Prominent black leaders such as James Forten and James Barbadoes visibly involved themselves in the American Anti-Slavery Society; Garrison and the

Tappans, in turn, entered into the deliberations of the National Colored Convention. The presence of women of both races in the immediatist ranks, such as Lydia Maria Child (who was white) or Sarah Forten (who was black), further reinforced the impression, among the ever multiplying opponents of abolitionism, that the movement sought to undermine all traditional relationships—particularly those which placed masters over slaves, men over women, and whites over blacks. Considering their extraordinary range and their radicalism, it is hardly surprising that the abolitionists' peaceful "moral suasion" provoked unprecedented political repression and organized violence.

In the South, the "great postal campaign" soon ended in mayhem as mobs organized by angry slaveholders broke into post offices, burned "incendiary" pamphlets, and hanged leading abolitionists in effigy—all with the approval of President Andrew Jackson. In Congress, the petition campaign initially fared no better; in fact, it resulted in a controversial "gag rule" that prevented antislavery requests from being debated at all. Meanwhile, in the free states, between 1834 and 1838, cities exploded in racial violence as white mobs attacked African-American communities and abolitionist meetings in Boston, Philadelphia, Utica, New York City, Hartford, Pittsburgh, and Cincinnati. Encouraging the mobs were commercial and business elites—"gentlemen of property and standing," as the abolitionists sneeringly called them—powerful men who sensed in immediatism a threat to their traditional moral authority. Leading the attacks on black churches and abolitionist meeting halls were ordinary day laborers, often recent immigrants, who deeply feared that black emancipation would cause their own social and economic enslavement. Condoning the violence and blaming the abolitionists for causing it were spokesmen for the nation's two great political parties, the Whigs and Democrats, whose national organizations both required support from southern slaveholders as well as from antiblack voters in the free states. By the late 1830s both political parties, nearly all the nation's leading business and church figures, the vast bulk of the northern working class, and the entire white population of the South had arrayed themselves as one against the abolitionists. "Immediate abolition" had plainly failed.

To be sure, repression did bring abolitionism some gains, particularly new leaders such as the magnificent orator Wendell Phillips and the millionaire philanthropist Gerrit Smith, who were impelled toward immediatism by their disgust with proslavery mobs. The suppression of civil liberties like the right to petition and assemble peacefully also began leading northerners in increasing numbers to suspect that

EMANCIPATOR—*EXTRA*.

NEW-YORK, SEPTEMBER 2, 1839.

American Anti-Slavery Almanac for 1840.

The seven cuts following, are selected from thirteen, which may be found in the Anti-Slavery Almanac for 1840. They represent well-authenticated facts, and illustrate in various ways, the cruelties daily inflicted upon three millions of native born Americans, by their fellow-countrymen! A brief explanation follows each cut.

The peculiar "Domestic Institutions of our Southern brethren."

Selling a Mother from her Child.

Mothers with young Children at work in the field.

A Woman chained to a Girl, and a Man in irons at work in the field.

"They can't take care of themselves"; explained in an interesting article.

Hunting Slaves with dogs and guns. A Slave drowned by the dogs.

Servility of the Northern States in arresting and returning fugitive Slaves.

The illustrated front page of the 2 September 1830 issue of the Emancipator.
[Corbis-Bettmann]

The defeat of "immediate abolition" in the United States is depicted in a political cartoon first published in 1839. [Library of Congress/Corbis]

slaveholders and their free-state allies were conspiring against white people's constitutional freedoms and political interests. But at the same time, the impact of repression shattered the immediatist movement, as warring factions drew conflicting meanings from their trials by violence. For the abolitionists who followed William Lloyd Garrison—such as Phillips, Henry C. Wright, and Sarah and Angelina Grimké—repression by church, state, and the political process alienated them from all such institutions and evoked a deepening reverence for the sanctity of noncoercive relationships and a belief in the possibility of human perfectibility. Thus most Garrisonians rejected church and state authority, endorsed radical pacifism, embraced women's rights, and demanded the dissolution of a presumably proslavery union. These were creeds that most Garrisonians maintained until the eve of the Civil War and that also directly inspired the first woman's rights movement, founded by feminist abolitionists in Seneca Falls, New York, in 1848. Garrison's opponents vehemently rejected these novel doctrines, but they were divided among themselves. Some, following Lewis Tappan, attempted to persevere with "moral suasion" by founding the American and For-

eign Anti-Slavery Society, designed to compete with the American Anti-Slavery Society, which was dominated by Garrison. Others, following Joshua Leavitt and Henry B. Stanton, noted that northern voters increasingly resented the South because of such issues as the "gag rule" and the possible annexation of new frontier slave territories (for example, Texas). To these anti-Garrisonians, abolitionism meant plunging into politics; they founded an emancipationist third party, the Liberty Party, which, in one form or another, campaigned in presidential contests from 1840 through Lincoln's election in 1860.

For the next two decades, from 1840 until 1861, these competing abolitionists pursued their preferred political strategies with few measurable results. The focus of the national conflict over slavery shifted to Congress, where Whigs and Democrats struggled with growing sectional discord over slavery's westward expansion. In the complex electoral process of sectional estrangement that began with the annexation of Texas and the Mexican War (1845–1848) and exploded after the Kansas-Nebraska Act and the Dred Scott decision (1854–1857), immediate abolitionists played a peripheral role. They did, however, exert considerable influence in more limited spheres as the Civil War drew closer.

On the state and local level, for example, white and black abolitionists sometimes formed significant alliances to challenge segregation and political disenfranchisement. Boston in particular witnessed successful biracial efforts by Garrisonians to desegregate public education; in New York state, white and black members of the Liberty Party campaigned (though unsuccessfully) to repeal unequal suffrage restrictions against black men. During these struggles, African-American activists undertook their own independent crusades against slavery and discrimination, partly in reaction to expressions of racially tinged superiority on the part of white abolitionists. Impressive new leaders, some escaped slaves, others free northerners—such as Frederick Douglass, Henry Highland Garnet, James McCune Smith, and Sojourner Truth—came to the fore in the 1840s and 1850s to testify eloquently against slavery and white supremacy and to infuse black abolitionism with a rich new ideology and vision.

This new vision sharpened after Congress passed a stringent new Fugitive Slave Law in 1850 that threatened not only escapees but even free northern blacks with reenslavement. In response, black and white abolitionists united in acts of defiance which sometimes turned to violence, as in Christiana, Pennsylvania, in 1851, where a slaveholder was shot and killed when attempting to recapture a fugitive. Syracuse, Boston, Oberlin, and Detroit also witnessed such confrontations in the 1850s. The risk of bloodshed was always high.

By becoming confrontational, abolitionists of both races did exert surprising political influence among slaveholders during the decade before the Civil War. Because of resistance to the Fugitive Slave Law southern planters saw the North in the 1850s as overrun with lawbreaking abolitionists that the authorities could or would not put down. When protracted guerrilla warfare between southern and northern settlers broke out in Kansas in the mid-1850s over the possible introduction of slavery there, these suspicions became fears, which were amply substantiated. Leading immediatists such as Wendell Phillips, Thomas Wentworth Higginson, and Frederick Douglass were glad to be implicated in the frontier bloodshed, especially when supporting the abolitionists most responsible for spilling it—John Brown and his sons, who captured and killed several proslavery settlers during the Kansas "wars" of 1855–1856. In this, however, such immediatists were hardly alone, since prominent members of the North's emerging Republican party also proved eager to "save" Kansas from slavery by sending arms to free-staters. Though Republicans denied any intention to dismantle slavery in the South, their plat-

"Bleeding Kansas" was the site of fierce struggles between abolitionists and slavery advocates in the 1850s. [Corbis-Bettmann]

forms were consistently opposed to letting slavery expand westward, a position that won them the sympathy of the abolitionists, northern majorities in the elections of 1856, and a victorious national plurality for Abraham Lincoln in 1860. By this time Brown had been hanged for his incendiary attempt (which had been secretly financed by six prominent immediatists) to provoke a slave insurrection by attacking Harpers Ferry, Virginia; and slaveholders were now well satisfied that Lincoln and his party were fundamentally no different from Brown, Douglass, and Garrison—"black Republican abolitionists" all. Although (as noted earlier) three decades of immediatist crusading had produced few measurable results, the abolitionists' influence on the slaveholders' decision to begin the Civil War was unmistakable.

A few principled pacifists opposed the war, but the vast majority of abolitionists enthusiastically supported it. Until late 1862, President Lincoln, like most Republicans, understood the war as an effort to restore the Union, not to abolish slavery—a view that the abolitionists hotly contested. Their thirty-year crusade against slavery now gave them the status of vindicated prophets in the eyes of many northerners, and they exploited this to mold public opinion in favor of emancipation. Douglass, Phillips, and Garrison suddenly became the North's most sought-after public speakers, and in their orations they castigated Lincoln for his failure to emancipate and urged the mobilization of African-American fighting units. In private, they cultivated political alliances with abolitionist-minded Republican congressmen and senators. And when large numbers of slaves took advantage of the chaos of war by abandoning their masters and following the Union armies, they also advanced the abolitionists' cause, indeed as no congressman, senator, or immediatist could.

For the Republican Party, it was politically unthinkable to force these refugees to return to their masters, traitorous slaveholders who had taken up arms against the Union. The logic of emancipation thus became impossible to deny. But as soon as President Lincoln's Emancipation Proclamation came into force, on 1 January 1863, Phillips, Douglass, and the rest next began demanding constitutional amendments which would outlaw slaveholding permanently and give full citizenship to the emancipated slaves. Abolitionists also took advantage of Union victories in coastal South Carolina by sending into that region ministers, schoolteachers, and businessmen whose task it became to prepare the former slaves for political and social equality. Thanks to the combined efforts of northern abolitionists, black soldiers, and self-liberated slaves, when the war ended in 1865, it had initiated a social revolution in the South.

This was, however, a revolution that many southern whites immediately attempted to suppress, violently if necessary. In 1865–1866, following Lincoln's assassination, the former Confederate states recognized the permanence of emancipation by ratifying the Thirteenth Amendment; but they then imposed so many harsh restrictions on the rights of blacks as to suggest that they were reinstating slavery in another form. Actually, such intransigence played into the hands of abolitionists such as Phillips and Douglass and radical Republicans such as Thaddeus Stevens, who truly wished to reconstruct the nation as a biracial democracy by granting freed people farmlands confiscated from leading Confederates. Since many northerners feared that their hard-won victory would be lost if the former Confederates were allowed to return themselves to power, the idea of enfranchising blacks and protecting them as free laborers seemed not only just but politically imperative. Thus, most Republicans finally threw their support behind the idea of black enfranchisement.

Although Garrison and some of his supporters argued that the abolitionists' mission had been achieved with the passage of the Thirteenth Amendment, Phillips, Douglass, Elizabeth Cady Stanton, and many other veterans adamantly disagreed, insisting that the real struggle was only beginning. Until 1870, when Congress and two-thirds of the states had ratified the Fourteenth and Fifteenth Amendments, these aging radicals kept up an incessant agitation for complete, federally enforced equality for blacks, dividing among themselves only on the question of extending the vote to women of both races. They led the unsuccessful battle in 1867 to impeach Lincoln's successor, President Andrew Johnson, because of his intransigent opposition to radical Reconstruction. But when the Fifteenth Amendment did become a reality, the abolitionists concluded that they had at last redeemed their commitment—made decades earlier—to sweep away the tyranny of slaveholding and to construct a society secured by just, uniform principles of racial equality.

In retrospect, the abolitionists' legacy seems far less hopeful. By the 1890s, white counterinsurgents had overturned Reconstruction governments throughout the South. Disenfranchisement, terrorism, sharecropping, and segregation, inflicted in the name of "white supremacy," characterized the new order. So it can hardly be claimed that the abolitionists, for all their idealism and persistence, actually inspired the nation to surmount its racial tragedy. Yet it must be emphasized that the abolitionists did discover terrible truths about racial injustice and laid them bare before their fellow citizens. Among themselves they nurtured rich discussions—unprecedented in their time—about the meaning of race, gender, and equality. They engaged the world and one another honestly, fearlessly exploring their movement's deeper tensions while indicting the larger society for its deeper injustices. Theirs is, in short, a legacy from which more recent struggles for justice—the modern civil rights and feminist movements—have drawn significant inspiration.

See also: AMERICAN REVOLUTION; CIVIL WAR; CONSTITUTION, U.S.; ENLIGHTENMENT; FUGITIVE SLAVE LAWS, U.S.; KANSAS-NEBRASKA ACT; MANUMISSION; REBELLIONS AND VIOLENT RESISTANCE; RECONSTRUCTION, U.S.

BIBLIOGRAPHY

ABZUG, ROBERT A. *Cosmos Crumbling: American Reform and the Religious Imagination.* 1994.

BLIGHT, DAVID. *Frederick Douglass's Civil War: Keeping Faith in the Jubilee.* 1989.

DAVIS, DAVID BRION. *The Problem of Slavery in the Age of Revolution.* 1974.

———. *The Problem of Slavery in Western Culture.* 1966.

DILLON, MERTON. *Slavery Attacked: Southern Slaves and Their Allies, 1619–1865.* 1990.

FINKLEMAN, PAUL. *An Imperfect Union: Slavery, Federalism and Comity.* 1981.

FONER, ERIC. *Free Soil, Free Labor, Free Men: The Ideology of the Republican Party before the Civil War.* 1970.

———. *Reconstruction: America's Unfinished Revolution, 1863–1877.* 1990.

FRIEDMAN, LAWRENCE J. *Gregarious Saints: Self and Community in American Abolitionism, 1830–1870.* 1982.

MCPHERSON, JAMES M. *The Struggle for Equality: The Abolitionists and the Negro in the Civil War and Reconstruction.* 1964.

NASH, GARY B. *Forging Freedom: The Formation of Philadelphia's Black Community, 1720–1840.* 1988.
———. *Race and Revolution.* 1990.
OATES, STEVEN. *To Purge This Land with Blood: A Biography of John Brown.* 1970.
PEASE, JANE, and PEASE, WILLIAM H. *They Who Would Be Free: Blacks' Search for Freedom, 1831–1861.* 1974.
RICHARDS, LEONARD. *"Gentlemen of Property and Standing": Antiabolitionist Mobs in Jacksonian America.* 1970.
ROEDIGER, DAVID. *The Wages of Whiteness: Race and the American Working Class.* 1991.
ROSE, WILLIE LEE. *Rehearsal for Reconstruction: The Port Royal Experiment.* 1965.
STEWART, JAMES BREWER. *Holy Warriors: The Abolitionists and American Slavery.* 1997.
———. *Wendell Phillips: Liberty's Hero.* 1986.
———. *William Lloyd Garrison and the Challenge of Emancipation.* 1992.
YELLIN, JEAN FAGAN. *Women and Sisters: The Antislavery Feminists and American Culture.* 1989.

James B. Stewart

France

Inspired by Enlightenment thought and influenced by the British antislavery movement, the first French abolitionist formation, the Société des Amis des Noirs (Society of Friends of the Blacks), was founded in early 1788 by Jacques Pierre Brissot. Other prominent members were Abbé Henri Grégoire, Antoine de Condorcet, Marquis de Lafayette, Count Honoré de Mirabeau, and Abbé Emmanuel Sieyès. It was elitist in nature, avoiding appeals to public opinion except through publications, and never having more than 150 adherents. The society followed the British strategy of attacking primarily the slave trade, something it did on the basis of humanitarian principles. Its membership was so closely tied to Brissot and his faction that when this group was proscribed by the Robespierrists in 1793, the society was dealt a mortal blow. It played no significant role in the emancipation of France's 650,000 colonial slaves in 1794, an

French colonial emancipation is celebrated in The Abolition of Slavery Proclaimed at the Convention of 16 Pluviôse, II Year of the Republic (*4 February 1794*) *by Nicola A. Monsiau.* [Gianni Dagli Orti/Corbis]

action forced upon France by the slave revolt in Saint Domingue (now Haiti). The French Revolution also declared free any slave brought to metropolitan France by a colonial master. However, the society's activities had prepared the terrain by raising the slave trade and slavery questions in the legislature, and it had influenced the granting of voting rights to free colonial blacks in 1791. Revived briefly in the period from 1796 to 1799 as the Société des Amis des Noirs et des Colonies, the group was a mere shadow of its former self. The society was stifled definitively by the coming power of Napoleon, who reintroduced colonial slavery and the slave trade in 1802.

French abolitionism languished under Napoleonic repression. Only in 1821 was a new abolitionist-oriented philanthropic organization formed. Encouraged once again by the British, a group of French Protestants founded the Société de la Morale Chrétienne (Society of Christian Morality), an ecumenical organization which addressed charitable issues of all kinds. Its limited abolitionist activities concentrated more on the slave trade than on slavery, as was true of its predecessor's. Influenced by Enlightenment and Christian humanitarianism, it probably never exceeded a membership of 388, drawn from the political and religious elite. Most of its officers and about two-thirds of its identifiable members were Catholic, often prominent liberals opposed to the Restoration governments of Louis XVIII and Charles X: Marquis Gaetan de La Rochefoucauld-Liancourt, Duke Victor de Broglie, Charles de Rémusat, Benjamin Constant, Alexandre Delaborde, Adolphe Thiers, and the Duke d'Orléans, the future King Louis Philippe. François Guizot, Auguste de Staël-Holstein (son of Madame de Staël), and Benjamin Delessert led a strong contingent of Protestants. In the legislature de Broglie spearheaded the society's attack on the illicit slave trade, while de Staël-Holstein headed the group's committee on the slave trade and slavery. In the society's journal this committee attacked particularly the slave trade, but it also encouraged the preparation of slaves for eventual freedom. After the death of de Staël-Holstein in 1827, the committee's activities floundered. The society, diminished considerably after the Revolution of 1830, continued in a truncated form until 1861. In the early 1830s, however, it yielded the abolitionist initiative to a new group.

With the repression of the illegal French slave trade by 1831, emancipation became the primary objective of the Société Française pour l'Abolition de l'Esclavage (French Society for the Abolition of Slavery), founded right after the British promulgation of slave liberation in 1834. It too was strongly encouraged and inspired by the British. Its president was de Broglie, but its influential secretary, François Isambert, dominated the organization. Some of the society's leading members came from the Société de la Morale Chrétienne: Delaborde, La Rochefoucauld-Liancourt, and Rémusat. It also attracted to its ranks such influential politicians as Hippolyte Passy, Victor Destutt de Tracy, Alphonse de Lamartine, Alexis de Tocqueville, and Gustave de Beaumont. With an elitist membership that probably never exceeded one hundred, it operated principally through corridors of power, the printed media, and the Chamber of Deputies. Its interventions in the latter from 1835 on forced the government to confront the slavery problem and form commissions to consider emancipation. Without the society's pressure on successive cabinets it is doubtful whether antislavery would have made any progress under a status quo–oriented July Monarchy (the regime of Louis Philippe, 1830–1848), which was highly receptive to colonial lobbying. The society's program was gradualist until 1847, attacking slavery in principle but agreeing that slaves had to be prepared for liberty. Besides, French abolitionism suffered from disunity. The radical black abolitionist Cyrille Bissette acted apart from the society, though with some free black support. The immediatist Victor Schoelcher also never belonged to the society and was at loggerheads with Bissette. The Protestant Guillaume de Félice was not a society member, but he cooperated with Bissette; both were subsidized by British abolitionists who favored their immediatism. Because of its close ties with the British, French abolitionism suffered a setback with the revival of anglophobia after the Egyptian crisis of 1840 and the right-of-search controversy of 1842–1845. Moreover, the society was prevented by the government and its own elitism from appealing to the masses. Concerted attempts at petitioning began only in the mid-1840s; the society did not accept immediatism until 1847. The abolitionist movement had nevertheless paved the way for emancipation, which came suddenly in 1848 after the Revolution of February overthrew the July Monarchy, established a republic, brought Schoelcher to power, and afforded him the opportunity to decree emancipation. After the Second Republic freed the approximately 235,000 slaves in the French colonies of Guadeloupe, Martinque, Réunion, and Bourbon, the French abolition society disintegrated. Without the political upheaval of 1848, French colonial slavery would probably have endured for many more years.

See also CARIBBEAN REGION; FRANKLIN, BENJAMIN, AND THE MARQUIS DE CORDOCET; SOCIÉTÉ DES AMIS DES NOIRS.

BIBLIOGRAPHY

BÉNOT, YVES. *La Révolution française et la fin des colonies.* 1988.

DRESCHER, SEYMOUR. "British Way, French Way: Opinion Building and Revolution in the Second French Slave Emancipation." *American Historical Review* 96 (1991): 707–734.

GEGGUS, DAVID. "Racial Equality, Slavery, and Colonial Secession during the Constituent Assembly." *American Historical Review* 94 (1989): 1290–1308.

JENNINGS, LAWRENCE C. "Cyrille Bissette, Radical Black French Abolitionist." *French History* 9 (1985): 48–66.

———. "French Anti-Slavery under the Restoration: The Société de la Morale Chrétienne." *Revue française d'histoire d'outre-mer* 81 (1994): 321–331.

———. *French Reaction to British Slave Emancipation.* 1988.

RESNICK, DANIEL P. "The Société des Amis des Noirs and the Abolition of Slavery." *French Historical Studies* 7 (1972): 558–569.

SCHMIDT, NELLY. *Victor Schoelcher.* 1994.

TARRADE, JEAN. "Les colonies et les principes de 1789. Les assemblées révolutionnaires face au problème de l'esclavage." *Revue française d'histoire d'outre-mer* 76 (1989): 9–34.

Lawrence C. Jennings

Brazil

Compared with the United States and most Latin American countries, Brazil was slow to develop a full-fledged antislavery movement. In 1810, in fact, Great Britain, for complex economic and humanitarian reasons, initiated the long process leading to Brazilian abolition, forcing a reluctant Portugal, and then an independent Brazil, to agree to a series of treaties restricting and finally outlawing the importation of African slaves. Thus, on 7 November 1831 after two decades of persistent resistance to British policies, a Brazilian legislature passed a law banning the importation of African slaves and freeing all those illegally introduced from that date on. Brazilian slaveholders, however, aware that ending the traffic would result in a rapid decline of the slave population, flagrantly violated the law for the next twenty years, and so more than half a million Africans entered Brazil illegally, most remaining slaves for the rest of their lives.

Unlike most Conservative regimes, Liberal governments tried at times to stop the illegal traffic, notably in the 1830s and again in 1848. In the latter year, as sentiment against the African trade was beginning to mount, a Liberal regime tried but failed to halt the importation of slaves. In that same year several newspapers in Rio allegedly financed by Great Britain—notably *O Philantropo*, the journal of a short-lived Anti-Slavery Society—began a propaganda campaign against the trade. More important, however, was the direct role of Great Britain, which in 1850 launched a determined diplomatic and naval campaign against the trade and continued "meddling" for some years

thereafter, forcing Brazil to take the steps required to bring it to an end.

Although the traffic was thus terminated, not until after the U. S. Civil War did Brazil take further steps to end slavery. Prior to the 1860s, the poor example set by the United States had given proslavery Brazilians a powerful line of defense, but the sudden loss of this advantage convinced many of the need for cautious steps leading toward eventual abolition. The reform recommended by a prominent lawyer, Agostinho Marques Perdigão Malheiro, and sanctioned by Emperor Pedro II, was the "Law of the Free Womb," intended to free newborn children of slave women and so eliminate Brazil's last remaining source of slaves. A long war with Paraguay delayed the reform, but by 1865 activists had begun to call for a considerable list of fundamental changes, including an end to the internal slave trade and to separation of slave families, prohibition of public slave sales, and a specific date for total abolition.

In 1868 the reformist movement was vitalized by the emperor's unexpected appointment of a Conservative cabinet, a step which in the view of opponents

Emperor Dom Pedro II sanctioned movements toward abolition, but his political opponents overthrew him soon after the end of legal servitude in Brazil was declared. [Corbis-Bettmann]

of slavery was designed to delay a bold reform. Led by José Tomás Nabuco de Araujo, a senator from Pernambuco, an influential political club was established in Rio de Janeiro with serious reform of slavery high on its agenda. Emancipationist organizations also appeared at the law faculties of Recife and São Paulo, led by, among others, Joaquim Nabuco de Araujo, son of Senator Nabuco; the brilliant Rui Barbosa, a statesman from Bahia; and the poet, lawyer, and ex-slave Luiz Gama.

Fearful of the growing agitation against slavery, with the end of the Paraguayan war the government at last introduced its reform bill, which, after a long and acrimonious debate, was passed on 28 September 1871. The bill provided mainly for the liberation of the newborn, who previously had had to work for masters until the age of twenty-one. An emancipation fund was also set up to free children. This complex legislation, like the ending of the Atlantic traffic, was a major stride toward abolition but was nevertheless followed by a long period of near-silence on the question of slavery.

In 1879, however, Joaquim Nabuco, now a national legislator, renewed the campaign in the General Assembly, and the following year he proposed a program of radical reforms intended to end slavery by 1890. Rebuked by the Assembly, in late 1880 Nabuco and fellow reformers established the Brazilian Anti-Slavery Society to combat slavery through propaganda. This new campaign ignited a dynamic movement in Rio de Janeiro, bringing prominence to two black leaders—the engineer and teacher André Reboucas and the poet and journalist José do Patrocinio, both authors of antislavery articles and organizers of fervent public meetings.

In those same months abolitionism spread to distant parts of the country. The most effective campaign was in the northeastern province of Ceará, where a devastating drought had ravaged the agricultural economy and thus greatly diminished the value of slaves while swelling the volume of the regional slave trade. As in Rio, a newly established antislavery society, the Sociedade Cearense Libertadora, sponsored public meetings and published a journal, *O Libertador*, activities encouraging popular demonstrations that culminated in the closing of the local port to the slave traders and a virtual halt to the exodus of slaves from the region. With these successes, antislavery action grew into a mass movement in Ceará, in turn revitalizing the abolitionists in Rio and inspiring similar efforts in the provinces of Rio Grande do Sul and Amazonas. By 1884 slavery had practically ceased to exist in Ceará and Amazonas, and in Rio Grande do Sul a popular campaign to liberate slaves reduced the provincial slave population from sixty thousand in 1884 to twenty-seven thousand in 1885, though most

freed persons were required to grant their owners five additional years of unpaid labor.

Events quickened in the last years of slavery. Antislavery activists helped liberate many slaves through purchase or by putting masters to shame. In 1884 a Liberal government proposed a "Sexagenarian Law" to free slaves sixty years of age and older; but, after a bitter debate, the General Assembly passed the far less progressive Saraiva-Cotegipe Law, freeing elderly slaves but requiring them to grant their owners as much as three additional years of unpaid labor. After the three years a slave might choose to continue to work for his master.

This backward-looking legislation, in Nabuco's words, eclipsed the abolitionist movement, but the eclipse was partial and brief. Near the end of 1886, reacting to the death of two brutally punished slaves, the assembly voted to ban the whipping of slaves in public establishments—masters often took their slaves to jails for punishment—despite opponents' warnings that suspending the threat of physical punishment would render slavery unworkable. Soon after passage of the law, in fact, a massive runaway movement aided by radical abolitionists erupted in the province of São Paulo and spread to nearby coffee zones and then to other regions of the country. (At the same time, and for the first and only time, some in the antislavery movement advocated the use of violence.) The first response to the runaways was to use armed force, but some slaveholders, witnessing a wholesale loss of workers needed to harvest the ripening coffee crop, began to offer conditional freedom to their slaves, and when this halfway measure failed to stop the growing exodus of slaves, even many die-hard slaveholders recognized that the institution was collapsing. On 13 May 1888 the General Assembly voted overwhelmingly to end slavery in Brazil, and thus ended legal servitude in the Americas. The antislavery organizations disbanded soon afterward. In the following months there was a powerful political reaction: the empire was overthrown in November 1889 and a conservative republic was created.

See also BRAZIL; BRAZILIAN ANTISLAVERY SOCIETY; NABUCA DE ARAUJO, JOAQUIM; SLAVE TRADE.

BIBLIOGRAPHY

BETHELL, LESLIE. *The Abolition of the Brazilian Slave Trade.* 1970.

CONRAD, ROBERT. *The Destruction of Brazilian Slavery, 1850–1888.* 1972.

GORENDER, JACOB. *O escravismo colonial.* 5th. ed. 1988.

TOPLIN, ROBERT BRENT. *The Abolition of Slavery in Brazil.* 1972.

VIOTTI DA COSTA, EMÍLIA. *Da senzala à colônia.* 1966.

Robert E. Conrad

Russia

Serfdom, rather than slavery, existed in Russia from the late sixteenth century until 1861. A substantial part of the peasantry was bound to the estates of nobles, to whom they owed obligations in cash, kind, or labor. Nobles secured additional rights, including the right to buy and sell their serfs. By the eighteenth century, Russian serfdom was similar to slavery.

There were no organized movements aimed primarily at the abolition of serfdom in Russia. The autocracy, backed by secret police and censorship, did not tolerate political activity independent of the state. Nevertheless there was opposition to serfdom.

Some serfs resisted the conditions imposed upon them. In most cases their actions were limited and isolated. Serfs usually protested not against serfdom itself, but against harsh and exploitative landowners. A few serfs initiated lawsuits to prove that they had been illegally enserfed or were entitled to be freed on other grounds. Not many succeeded. The most dramatic open resistance occurred in the summer of 1774. A revolt that had broken out on the southeastern frontier spread to the Volga basin, where there was a large serf population. The rebel leader, the cossack Pugachev, claimed to be the late Tsar Peter III. In this guise he issued "proclamations" abolishing serfdom and calling on serfs to slaughter their landowners. Thousands rose up and over a thousand nobles were killed. The "freedom" the rebels seized was short-lived, however, as they were soon crushed by armed force.

Some educated Russians opposed serfdom. In the late eighteenth century, under the influence of the Enlightenment, some intellectuals were critical of serfdom on the grounds that a system of forced labor, in which some people were the property of others, was incompatible with such ideas as free labor, equality before the law, and "natural justice." In 1765, with the support of Catherine the Great (r. 1762–1796), the Free Economic Society was formed. It publicized free-market economic ideas, but did not openly attack serfdom. The first open assault in print came in 1790, when Alexander Radishchev (1749–1802) published *A Journey from St. Petersburg to Moscow*. Using the device of a traveler's account, Radishchev attacked serfdom on humanitarian grounds. As a result he was banished to Siberia. His book had little immediate impact.

Opposition to serfdom among educated Russians was linked with hostility to the autocracy. In December of 1825 a group of aristocratic army officers (the Decembrists) staged an abortive revolt in Saint Petersburg. If they had succeeded in overthrowing the autocracy, they intended to abolish serfdom. During the subsequent reign of Nicholas I (1825–1855) strict censorship compelled critics of serfdom to voice their views in private, obliquely, or from abroad. Ivan Turgenev (1818–1883) drew attention to the inhumanity of serfdom in a series of "Sportman's Sketches" published in the periodical *The Contemporary* between 1847 and 1851. Turgenev portrayed serfs as people with feelings rather than human property. He was one of several literary figures and polemicists who expressed veiled criticism of the existing order, including serfdom. Most outspoken was Alexander Herzen (1812–1870), who ran a propaganda campaign from exile in London. From the mid-1850s he published a series of periodicals (*The Polar Star, Voices from Russia*, and *The Bell*) which were smuggled into Russia.

The views of these educated Russians influenced some "enlightened bureaucrats," for example the brothers Dmitrii (1816–1912) and Nicholas Miliutin (1818–1872), and members of the imperial family, in particular the Grand Duchess Elena Pavlovna (1806–1873). Opposition to serfdom inside the government was based less on humanitarian grounds than fears that resistance by serfs threatened social stability, and that serfdom retarded economic development and was a barrier to reforms in other areas, especially military recruitment. Russia's defeat in the Crimean War (1853–1856) spurred the new tsar, Alexander II (1855–1881), to abolish serfdom in 1861.

See also ENLIGHTENMENT; RUSSIA, SERFDOM IN.

BIBLIOGRAPHY

BLUM, J. *Lord and Peasant in Russia from the Ninth to the Nineteenth Century.* 1961.
FIELD, D. *The End of Serfdom, Nobility and Bureaucracy in Russia, 1855–1861.* 1976.
KOLCHIN, P. *Unfree Labor: American Slavery and Russian Serfdom.* 1987.
MOON, D. *Russian Peasants and Tsarist Legislation on the Eve of Reform, 1825–1855.* 1992.
RIASANOVSKY, N. V. *A Parting of the Ways: Government and the Educated Public in Russia, 1801–1855.* 1976.
SEMEVSKII, V. I. *Krest'yanskii vopros v Rossii v XVIII i pervoi polovine XIX veka.* 2 vols. 1888.

David Moon

Caribbean Region

By the end of the Seven Years' War in 1763, Britain, France, Spain, Holland, and Denmark possessed flourishing slave colonies scattered across the Caribbean Sea. A century later only the Spanish in Cuba had any such colonies, and by the mid-1880s the Caribbean world had been rid of slavery. Slave revolution, imperial legislation, and market forces made the contradictory aspects of slavery apparent and undermined it economically and politically. In Britain between 1788 and 1793, and in France from 1789 to 1794 and in the 1840s, influential antislavery opinion developed into a political movement that played a critical role in the overthrow of Caribbean slavery. Spain, Denmark, and the Netherlands lagged considerably behind Britain and France in this regard, but their colonies were no less turbulent, given the conflicts inherent in the social relations of slavery.

The literature on antislavery movements has emphasized the transatlantic dimension. This perspective has shown that across imperial lines, political linkages, real or imaginary, were fashioned between plantation-based resistance and the European antislavery ethos. The French abolitionist Société des Amis des Noirs was established in Paris in 1788, but three years later the slaves in France's principal colony, St. Domingue, had taken to arms in an act of self-liberation. The blacks, then, did not wait for aristocratic philanthropists, radical intellectuals, and self-proclaimed Christian moralists to secure their freedom. By 1794, when the convention abolished slavery in French colonies, the slaves had already effectively done so themselves. Napoleon's subsequent attempt to reestablish slavery in the colonies met with considerable armed resistance, and finally with a major revolt at Martinique in 1848, which prompted the final surrender of proslavery forces.

Developments were similar with the English. The establishment of the Society for Effecting the Abolition of the Slave Trade in London in 1787, by the Quaker Granville Sharp and other evangelical Christians, found in place a long established tradition of antislavery rebellion and negotiation in the Caribbean. Rebellions had preceded it and would follow it with regularity in the British colonies, and the 10,000 signatures its members gathered in November 1787 for submission to Parliament may have matched the number of blacks in the colonies who in that year lost life or limb in the quest for freedom. The abolition of slavery by the English in 1838, by the French and Danish in 1848, and by the Spanish in 1886 was therefore part of a wider political context—a persistent antislavery ethos in the colonies.

At first glance the immediate goals of the Caribbean and European antislavery movements seem ideologically at variance—indeed, polarized. The metropolitan movement was essentially philosophical and respectably radical in character. It relied initially on a strong moral perspective, though increasingly on economic arguments in its latter years. The Caribbean movement, led by enslaved blacks with some support from Amerindians and free people of color, was also generally nonviolent, but it occasionally erupted into revolutionary warfare. The metropolitan movement depended upon popular mobilization and parliamentary lobbying—a legislative approach to emancipation. The slaves' approach, it may be said, was more complex; they wanted freedom by any means necessary or possible, and they engaged in activities which ranged from self-purchase to violent armed struggle for territory and political sovereignty.

There is some fragmentary evidence that the more informed slaves saw their antislavery actions as linked to those of metropolitan lobbyists, though they were not prepared to lose the initiative—they wanted to strike for freedom when circumstances, local or foreign, dictated autonomous action. Some slaves, whether in revolutionary St. Domingue or rebellious Barbados and Jamaica in 1816 and 1831 respectively, had knowledge (considered crude and inaccurate by most historians) of developments in metropolitan antislavery ideas and strategies. This information base, it has been argued, partly shaped their own costly movement for liberation (measured in human life) and thus illustrates the internationalism of their political consciousness.

Ideally, it could be said that rebel slaves and metropolitan antislavery lobbyists shared the same goals, and hence their respective movements ought to be considered as different levels of a general process. This position is attractive but oversimplified, and it does not stand up under the weight of empirical evidence. It may very well be suggested that slaves wanted more than legal freedom on many occasions—that they also wanted political power and economic autonomy. These were certainly objectives that most "humanitarians" preferred blacks not to have. The records of slave rebellion also show, it is true, that in some instances slaves might well have wanted only the right to reasonable wages and conditions of work under their old masters. But rebellions in St. Domingue between 1791 and 1804 and in Barbados in 1816 also suggest that blacks understood that meaningful freedom could be guaranteed only by seizing the organs of law and government and then imposing a revolutionary constitutionalism to enforce the reality of freedom.

William Wilberforce, for instance, had no time for slaves' revolutionary approach to emancipation in the English colonies, and considered such actions, in spite of his friendship with King Henry of Haiti, as detrimental to the survival of English authority in America—not only in terms of economic and political leverage, but also in terms of the hegemony of western civilization. The prospect of black revolution, the formation of Afro-Caribbean republics of monarchies, and the freezing of "things European" did not excite English antislavery lobbyists. From this point of view, then, it may be suggested that the two segments of the transatlantic antislavery movement were heading in different directions most of the time. It was a

The watchtowers of Barbados were used both as lookout posts for enemy ships and as a means of sounding the alarm in the event of a slave revolt. [Dave G. Houser/Corbis]

matter not simply of procedure but also of what kind of world was to be created in the aftermath.

A simple statistical analysis might show that, given some 400,000 blacks who gained freedom by revolution in St. Domingue, together with the large numbers who freed themselves by means of marronage and otherwise, there is no basis for the claim that European legislative emancipation should be the first consideration. Numerical analysis may not necessarily be the best way to proceed, but it at least imposes some demographic constraints on the argument that, by and large, freedom was brought to the blacks and self-attained freedom was of marginal significance. In addition, it would illustrate more clearly the impressive record of achievement of slave communities as sponsors of libertarian ideology.

Such an analysis is relevant partly because recent historiography has found a dichotomy between the core and the periphery in the transatlantic antislavery movement. Eric Williams was perhaps the first to suggest this dichotomy, when he argued that while metropolitan antislavery lobbyists intensified their campaign during the early nineteenth century, the slaves did likewise. By 1833, he said, "the alternatives were clear"—"emancipation from above or emancipation from below, but Emancipation." He does not

detract from the achievements of Wilberforce, Thomas Clarkson, Victor Schoelcher, and others; but he does suggest that the world created, even if temporarily, by Toussaint-Louverture and other slave leaders seemed comparatively more "hell-bent" on destroying Caribbean slavery.

English and French abolitionist leaders, of course, saw themselves as the vanguard of antislavery thought and practice, a vision which historians have continued to perpetuate. This perception, not surprisingly, managed to survive long after the 1790s, when blacks in St. Domingue overthrew the slave regime to establish (in 1804) the state of Haiti, which had an antislavery constitution and an aggressively antislavery foreign policy. Haiti emerged regionally and internationally as the real symbol and manifestation of antislavery, and Toussaint eclipsed Wilberforce in the watchful eyes of the Western world as the prime antislavery leader. For the hardworking and determined English abolitionists, however, Haiti was in general more of a hindrance to their crusade than an asset, and they continued to see antislavery as being endangered by Caribbean slaves' impatient tendency to resort to arms. This is why abolitionists tended to favor a strong police force, an independent magistracy, draconian vagrancy laws, and increased missionary activity.

Persistent antiblack prejudice in western discourse accounts for the tensions between European abolitionists and Caribbean rebels. The Europeans' rejection of the slaves' revolutionary approach suggests that they conceived of liberation strictly in legal and sociological terms. That is, they did not support the slaves' attempts to undermine the hegemony of the planter elite and the supportive Christian missions. They wanted slaves to be legally free and to some extent recognized as social and biological equals to whites. But they did argue that blacks should be economically dependent on and politically subordinate to whites, for the sake of the blacks' own advancement as well as for the continued growth of the Caribbean. Blacks, they generally believed, had nothing of superior merit to offer the New World in advancing its civilization, and therefore blacks were to play a submissive role in the expansion of Eurocentric culture by the white-controlled economic regime, the plantations.

The racism implied by this idea of black liberation was entrenched in the abolitionists' thought. Emancipation was not seen in terms of liberation from Europeans' power, values, and domination. From this point of view, then, it was only when Toussaint showed himself, like King Christophe at a later date, to be receptive to the European educational religious mission, and its cultural and linguistic baggage, that he received some measure of ideological acceptance by English statesmen and humanitarians. Furthermore, the abolitionists' tendency to conceive of slaves as unfortunate children to be liberated from tyrannical parents, with the moral outrage which that implied for the reasonable mind, served to deepen the racist perceptions of their audience and enhanced fear among them that blacks seeking independence, economic autonomy, and political power were irresponsible, rash, ungrateful, and naive.

It cannot be shown, then, that slaves existed in an atheoretical world, devoid of ideas, political concepts, or an alternative sociopolitical vision. Their tradition of antislavery activity had more impact on the social culture and polity of the Caribbean world than antislavery lobbyists had on metropolitan societies. Indeed, the entire Caribbean reality was shaped and informed by the persistent forces of slavery and antislavery as long as the slave regimes lasted. From a Caribbean perspective, slaves' struggle for freedom should not be diminished when placed alongside the legislative interventions of European parliaments. These metropolitan actions were part of the final episode in an epic struggle—initiated and propelled by its greatest sufferers, the slave population. Only in Haiti were blacks able to overthrow the slave regime and achieve their freedom. Yet slaves throughout the region consistently rebelled, and over time they used a wide range of political tools and methods in their struggle.

See also CARIBBEAN REGION; CLARKSON, THOMAS; HISTORIOGRAPHY OF SLAVERY; SOCIÉTÉ DES AMIS DES NOIRS; TOUSSAINT-LOUVERTURE; WILBERFORCE, WILLIAM.

BIBLIOGRAPHY

ANSTEY, ROGER. *The Atlantic Slave Trade and British Abolition, 1769–1810.* 1975.

BECKLES, HILARY. *Black Rebellion in Barbados: The Struggle against Slavery, 1627–1838.* 1984.

BLACKBURN, ROBIN. *The Overthrow of Colonial Slavery, 1776–1848.* 1988.

CRATON, MICHAEL. "The Passion to Exist: Slave Rebellion in the British West Indies, 1650–1832." *Journal of Caribbean History* 13, no. 1 (1980).

———. *Testing the Chains: Resistance to Slavery in the British West Indies.* 1982.

DAVIS, DAVID BRION. In *The Problem of Slavery in the Age of Revolution, 1770–1823.* 1975.

DIRKS, ROBERT. *The Black Saturnalia: Conflict and Its Ritual Expression on British West Indian Slave Plantations.* 1987.

DRESCHER, SEYMOUR. *Capitalism and Antislavery: British Mobilisation in Comparative Perspective.* 1986.

GASPAR, BARRY. *Bondsmen and Rebels: A Study of Master-Slave Relations in Antigua (with Implications for Colonial British America).* 1985.

GEGGUS, DAVID. "British Opinion and the Emergence of Haiti, 1791–1805." In *Slavery and British Society, 1776–1846,* edited by James Walvin. 1982.

JAMES, C. L. *Black Jacobins: Toussaint L'Ouverture and the San Domingo Revolution.* Paperback, 1963.

KOPYTOFF, BARBARA. "The Early Political Development of Jamaican Maroon Societies." *William and Mary Quarterly* 35, no. 2 (1978).

RECORD-TURNER, MARY. "The Jamaican Slave Rebellion of 1831." *Past and Present* 40 (July 1968).

RICHARDSON, DAVID, ed. *Abolition and Its Aftermath: The Historical Context, 1790–1916.* 1985.

SCHULER, MONICA. "Akan Slave Rebellion in the British Caribbean." *Savacou* 1, no. 1 (1970).

WALVIN, JAMES, ed. *Slavery and British Society, 1776–1846.* 1982.

WILLIAMS, ERIC. *Capitalism and Slavery. 1944,* 1964.

Hilary McD. Beckles

Adoption

See Manumission.

Africa

This entry includes the following articles: A Brief Historical Overview; A Thematic and Synoptic Overview; Economic and Demographic Effects of the Atlantic

Slave Trade; Political and Historical Effects of the Atlantic Slave Trade; The End of Slavery; Women as Slaves in Africa. *These articles are intended to provide an overarching historical perspective on the impact that slavery and the slave trade had on the African continent as a whole. Related articles—which treat individual geographical areas and historical topics in greater detail—may be found at the entries* Central Africa; East Africa; North Africa; Northeast Africa; Plantations; Slave Trade; Southern Africa; West Africa.

A Brief Historical Overview

Scholars have generally laid to rest the fundamental debate between Walter Rodney and John Fage regarding whether European demand for African slaves stimulated slavery in African societies. Most now agree that slavery existed in a variety of different forms in Africa before Europeans arrived in the mid-fifteenth century and that demand for slaves to feed the markets for labor in the New World nonetheless stimulated political consolidation and the military expression of state power. Slaves were by-products of warfare associated with political centralization, although kidnapping and judicial punishments also yielded slaves.

Africans' participation in the slave trade had contradictory consequences for Africa. Though it strengthened polities, the warfare this fostered created conditions for political dissolution. The slave trade stimulated commerce, since imported goods found their way into internal circuits of trade, but the export of millions of human beings reduced the size of the domestic market. Warfare and enslavement discouraged long-term investment in agriculture, mining, and industry. Not all slaves captured were exported from Africa, but the slave trade left more people who lived and worked in Africa in slavery.

Historians estimate that over time and among regions, 60 to 70 percent of those entering the transatlantic slave trade were males. But warfare, kidnapping, and other forms of enslavement probably netted more females than males, since more males were likely to have been killed while resisting or defending, or because they were more intransigent. The female slaves who were not exported were retained in Africa because they were more valued than male slaves. The retention of female slaves in Africa hints at subtle changes in gender roles and contributed both to polygyny and patriarchy and to the expansion of female farming systems. Male slaves retained in Africa were used as menial farm laborers, craftsmen, miners, soldiers, traders, high government officials, and surrogate kin.

The nature of slavery in Africa has been the subject of considerable debate. Suzanne Miers and Igor Kopytoff argued that slavery in Africa resembled mar-

A young Ethiopian slave. [Hulton-Deutsch Collection/Corbis]

riage because it involved exchanges in "rights in persons." Like marriage, slavery in Africa led to the absorption of the outsider into the master's kin group. In contrast, Claude Meillassoux argued that slavery in Africa rested upon violence associated with enslavement, which made the slave subject to the master's harsh and arbitrary treatment. Meillassoux also argued that slave status was not inherited generationally, since children of slaves were akin to serfs, and that maintenance of slave populations rested upon constant infusions of new captives.

Scholars now consider both interpretations limited. Miers and Kopytoff modeled their arguments on small-scale, less differentiated societies, drawn largely from colonial-era ethnography when slavery was in decline. Meillassoux, in turn, drew his information from a pastiche of hierarchical, market-oriented West African societies at the end of the nineteenth century. Neither model covered the full range of slave systems in Africa or accounted for changes in them over time.

Students of comparative slavery often differentiate slave systems according to whether slaves were treated mildly or harshly. However, treatment of slaves itself depended on the interplay of market forces and political power in slaveowning societies. Where market forces were not well developed, masters may not have exploited the labor power of their slaves. Similarly, where state power was not well developed, masters may not have been able to exploit the labor of their slaves regardless of market forces. Thus, the ideology of slavery as well as the treatment of slaves was related to the interplay of political and economic circumstances.

Just as the expansion of the transatlantic slave trade had contradictory consequences for African systems of slavery, so too did the European efforts to end the slave trade. The trade was abolished first by the Danes in 1792. The British took the initiative in 1807, and actively suppressed it after the Napoleonic wars. The abolition of the slave trade coincided with the expansion of European industrial capitalism, which required massive inputs of tropical raw materials, including vegetable oils and cotton, that African producers hastened to provide.

European prohibition of the slave trade thus forced change on African political economies, in which capturing and exporting slaves were well established activities. But the decline in demand for African slaves in the Americas was gradual, and there was a coincident increase in the demand for slaves in Africa itself. Africans increasingly turned to slave labor to expand production for both international and domestic trade. By limiting demand and thus reducing the export price of slaves, the abolition of the transatlantic slave trade paradoxically encouraged reliance on slavery in Africa.

Thus, when European colonial powers moved to end slavery in Africa in the late nineteenth and early twentieth centuries, they confronted a variety of slave systems, mostly in stages of expansion. The end of slavery in Africa is a complex story of contradictory metropolitan directives, deeply ambivalent colonial administrators, slaves' initiatives, masters' resistance to colonial policies, and slaves' efforts to change their conditions. Although colonial states eventually prohibited all new enslavement, slave raiding continued on a small scale well into the twentieth century. By the late 1920s and 1930s, slavery had become a vestige of what it had been forty years earlier.

Although slavery ceased to be a major factor in African societies, various other forms of unfree labor persisted during the colonial period and into the present. In particular, the pawning of dependents, who worked without pay for the creditors of their patrons, increased during the Depression of the 1930s. As a result of government demand for unpaid labor, Africans in many parts of Africa considered themselves to be the slaves of European colonial officials. Slave status persists to this day as an element in the ordering of many African societies. For example, the ritual slave category *osu* among the Igbo figures prominently in the novels of contemporary Nigeria, and young girls are still given as slaves to religious leaders among the Ewe of Ghana.

Civil wars in postcolonial Africa provided fertile ground for the enslavement and impressment of boys and young men to serve in competing armies. In the Sudan, where civil war raged in the late twentieth century, girls and women were also enslaved, taken far from their homes and made to toil in the fields and in domestic service. In Mauritania, where slavery was again abolished in 1980, a journalist in 1997 recorded the sale of children for as little as fifteen dollars and complaints of adult slaves that they had no control over their lives and that their possessions were inherited by their masters.

The persistence of slavery in modern Africa has its roots in the economic and social patterns that developed during the precolonial period, and in pressures to restrict the development of free labor during the colonial period. Demand for unfree labor persists in Africa today because it feeds on the inequities of power based on gender, age, and class and on continued barriers to economic resources and legal safeguards.

See also CENTRAL AFRICA; EAST AFRICA; NORTHEAST AFRICA; SLAVERY, CONTEMPORARY FORMS OF; SLAVE TRADE; SOUTHERN AFRICA; WEST AFRICA.

BIBLIOGRAPHY

ACHEBE, CHINUA. *No Longer at Ease*. 1960.
COOPER, FREDERICK. "The Problem of Slavery in African Studies." *Journal of African History* 20, no. 1 (1979).
FAGE, JOHN. "Slavery and the Slave Trade in the History of West Africa." *Journal of African History* 10, no. 3 (1969).
FRENCH, HOWARD. "The Ritual Slaves of Ghana: Young and Female." *New York Times*, 20 January 1997.
HECHT, DAVID. "Where African Slavery Still Exists in the Eyes of Many." *Christian Science Monitor*, 13 February 1997.
LOVEJOY, PAUL E. *Transformations in Slavery: A History of Slavery in Africa*. 1983.
MEILLASSOUX, CLAUDE, ed. *L'Esclavage en Afrique précoloniale*. 1975.
MIERS, SUZANNE, and RICHARD ROBERTS, eds. *The End of Slavery in Africa*. 1988.
———. *Slavery in Africa*. 1977.
RODNEY, WALTER. "Slavery and Other Forms of Social Oppression on the Upper Guinea Coast in the Context of the Atlantic Slave Trade." *Journal of African History* 7, no. 4 (1966).

Richard Roberts

A Thematic and Synoptic Overview

Slavery in Africa, as in most other regions before the twentieth century, provided a critical means of achieving political and economic growth, as well as a path to personal advancement for those able to control enslaved people. To describe slavery as having these "progressive" characteristics sounds paradoxical in the context of Mediterranean-European-American history, where progress is associated with personal "freedom." But no such paradox applied in most of Africa before the nineteenth century. There, a communal ethos saw personal autonomy, for most individuals, as vulnerability and found security in subordination within communities integrated around hierarchies of many sorts—patriarchal control of women, patronage of clients by the wealthy, and ranking by age. The quality that defined slaves was isolation from these networks of protectors, through whatever circumstances; thus, slaves survived as dependents of whoever took them in. Slaves' dependence on a single individual in an otherwise communal environment created a totality of control that exposed them to personal domination in Africa as extreme as what characterized slavery anywhere in the world.

Slavery in some parts of Africa also fell under Islamic law, in varying degrees, from as early as the eighth or ninth century. Islam did not challenge the prevailing communal or hierarchical loyalties but merely incorporated slaves within complex patriarchal households comparable to those of senior males in non-Muslim areas. But Islam also provided a commercial legal environment that permitted owners to assemble large numbers of slaves as laborers on commodity-producing plantations in some regions, settling them in villages separate from nonfarming populations.

Since no one in Africa enjoyed the "impersonal" civil protections modern Europeans and Americans defined as "freedom" after the seventeenth and eighteenth centuries, slaves there were vulnerable, not because they lacked "rights," but because they had lost access to anyone morally obligated to defend them. Honor in Africa derived from ancestry, and slaves were dishonored because they utterly lacked recognized parentage and kin. As in other parts of the world, slaves were disdained because they were "different"; but they were seen as such because they were not descended from the shared progenitors believed to impose reciprocal loyalties on kin, rather than for reasons perceived or describable as racial. In a continent divided into numerous language communities, slaves often few in number, usually arrived unable to communicate with their patrons or masters. Alone and unable to protect themselves, they suffered accordingly. For slaves, the loss of the intense bond of community that prevailed in Africa was as traumatic as their uprooting itself. Even a few miles seemed very far from home, and even neighbors seemed much unlike the home community. Slavery in Africa thus possessed

all the disabilities accepted as defining the institution elsewhere, though in ways that reflected distinctively communal, local African values of self and status.

It has nonetheless often been conventional to describe African slavery as somehow "mild" in contrast to eighteenth- and nineteenth-century slavery in the Americas. This comparison fails because it applies modern standards of racial difference, intensity of labor, and material comfort to a generally false image of slavery in Africa. This image typically contrasts the relatively unexacting life of enslaved Africans hoeing alongside their "masters" in village fields with the brutal work regimens found on New World plantations. The tendency of small African communities to incorporate those they took in as slaves seems humanely assimilative against the background of modern European and American racial exclusivity. And African slaves sometimes had access to imports that Europeans regarded as material comforts.

The roots of this stereotype—beyond a tendency among descendants of Africans in the American diaspora to romanticize a distant ancestral homeland—lie in rural colonial societies of the 1930s and 1940s reduced by then to an impoverished uniformity that left little differentiation in material welfare for anyone. It also reflects slave-and-master distinctions muted by a full generation of ambivalent government antislavery policies. European efforts to end slavery in Africa had rendered the subject too sensitive for Africans to acknowledge to outsiders, particularly to ethnographers associated with the colonial government whose descriptions became the source of the stereotype's currency. These anthropologists also often emphasized consensus more than conflict and ideals more than practice. The historical experience of most Africans with slavery was more diverse, humiliating, and disabling.

Domestic Slavery

The notion of a single generic "African slavery" cannot survive confrontation with thousands of communities' distinctive historical experiences, through several millennia and across sharp geographical contrasts, in a landmass three times the size of the United States. Slavery had never been common among Africans living in the drier northern, eastern, and southern margins of the continent, who have supported themselves in relatively modest numbers in unforgiving environments since about the fifth millennium B.C.E. by the management of livestock, especially cattle. Herders have favored their animals as their key capital investment, and ambitious men seeking followers tended to lend beasts to neighbors to assemble clienteles and to negotiate marriages aimed at increasing the number of people beholden to them. Cattle lords generally confined violence to rustling animals from their enemies' herds—to give for wives and to lend to clients—rather than seizing dependents directly as slaves. Other factors also discouraged enslavement as a strategy among herders: pastoral populations usually lived (or moved) far apart, defended themselves effectively, or maintained alliances underwritten by their far-reaching networks of cattle loans. Only where pastoralists controlled caravan routes carrying slaves from more populous regions destined for distant markets, and where they exploited agricultural oases that they preferred not to work for themselves, have desert dwellers held significant numbers of slaves, always imported from far away.

Slaves figured more prominently in populous agricultural lands, particularly the grassy savannas south of the Sahara Desert, the rich, moist highlands around the great eastern African lakes, and the woodlands south of the equatorial forest and along the valleys of the Zambezi River system. Because most regions sufficiently moist for farming also harbored insect populations that transmitted diseases lethal to horses and cattle, their inhabitants, lacking animal power for plowing and for overland transport of basic foodstuffs, relied on hoe cultivation. These conditions had preserved high labor demands—particularly on women—ever since the third or second millennium B.C.E., when Africans first domesticated crops along the southern margins of the Sahara. By the fifth century C.E. settlers speaking Bantu languages had spread hoe cultivation east to the coast of the Indian Ocean and south to the margins of the Kalahari Desert.

In these labor-intensive agricultural systems landholding neighbors intermarried to produce children who would contribute to the prosperity of both groups. They focused on fertility—of their lands, and of their women—and on the rains, from which abundance flowed. Competitive advantage went to men who could bypass the biological limits of human reproduction in pursuit of aspirations not likely to be realized soon through the usual slow advancement in seniority. They made use of women and children captured in wars, refugees from drought, unwanted kin expelled by their families, condemned criminals from neighboring communities, and the occasional vulnerable stranger. All of these lacked relatives (ties to potential competitors) and all were available to individual patrons as slaves.

Masters would protect such dependents as much as they exploited them—to retain their personal loyalty against the communal ethos of sharing—or would marry the dependent women to their clients. Thus,

although the dependency of such people, at least when they arrived, approached the total control of a master over a slave, those who lived tended to overcome that incapacity in time. Few masters could accumulate significant numbers of slave wards without access to resources from outside their local communities' otherwise balanced networks of reciprocity.

In the extensive, mostly wet forests in the center of the continent drained by thousands of miles of navigable tributaries of the Zaire (or Congo) River system, the Bantu-speaking immigrants who settled this area during the millennium from 500 B.C.E. to 500 C.E. made less extensive use of slaves. They hacked out clearings for fields and built villages along the riverbanks, where they found canoe transport along the rivers easy and inexpensive. They thus structured their economic and social systems around communities of male artisans producing for distribution to neighbors, teams of fishermen, fifty- or sixty-man crews for canoes for transportation, and war. These essentially commercial groups recruited new members by exchanging the material wealth they produced to attract skilled males rather than by acquiring women for childbearing. The merchant "big men" at the heads of these residential commercial firms tended to buy, rather than capture, the few slaves they might need for unspecialized menial chores to supplement their retinues of trained clients. But there, too, younger men, junior clients, or other individuals marginal to local networks of wealth and prestige must have seen slave wives and retainers as a means to overcome the obstacles that the elders in power placed athwart their ambitions.

Military and Merchant Slavery

In societies where only the possession of dependents could confer power, ambitious men used whatever resources they could obtain from outside their home communities to acquire people as slaves. These opportunities increased south of the Sahara in the eighth and ninth centuries, after the Arab conquest of North Africa. Muslim merchants followed the trade routes across the Sahara Desert in search of gold from the headwaters of the Niger River. The commercial capital they brought back stimulated trade in the agricultural grasslands—which they termed the Sudan—and hence demand for labor beyond that needed to support the existing exchanges of desert salt and livestock products for grain and for products from the forests. The Muslim merchants also introduced large North African horses suited to cavalry warfare, and Africans used them to raid populous surrounding areas for captives. They sold some of the captives to pay for their imported mounts and kept others to staff the retinues they assembled in military camps.

During the following five or six hundred years, the most successful African rulers built their war camps into courts at the heart of extensive, kingdom-like networks of military control. The result was the well-known succession of "Sudanic" slave-raiding cavalry states—Ghana, Kanem, Mali, and Songhai. These grew increasingly military in character over time, and their rulers came ever more to rely on the sale of slaves to replenish their cavalry forces and to sustain the towns and armies of their realms. Warlords tasting individual power and wanting to extend it claimed independence from their relatives and patrons by employing slaves—isolated individuals utterly bereft of personal or social obligations other than to their master—to cultivate fields to feed the court retinues they assembled, to act as trustworthy emissaries, and to fight as armed loyal soldiers. Slaves thus constituted the core of the state bureaucracy in the larger African kingdoms, and like the *familia caesaris* of the Roman Empire, they were reliably distinct from the competing aristocratic clans, landholding communities, and commercial families of the realm. In Songhai, which flourished in the sixteenth century (by which time Islamic law prevailed and facilitated commercial production), the aristocracy and merchants employed slaves in groups distinguishable from the mass of the population.

Slaves sometimes supported existing power, sometimes served as means to challenge it. The credit terms of which Muslim merchants sold their goods allowed people who were otherwise marginal to the established aristocracies based on land and kinship to use their own resources to challenge the establishment with trade goods and slaves. Berber herders in the Sahara prospered by managing the trade routes to North Africa that ran through their desert domains. They kept many of these slaves to tend commercial date palm groves in the oases they controlled or toiled as domestic servants or as miners of rock salt and other minerals they sent to the Sudan.

During these same centuries other Muslim merchants ventured southward along Africa's Indian Ocean coasts in search of gold and ivory from the highlands south of the Zambezi River. Africans who profited from their commerce had no possibility of buying horses; so rather than import weapons, they invested in herding and agriculture. They used imported textiles, shells, and other wares to supplement their cattle as means to indebt clients and mobilize trained regiments of young warriors. In the area of late-twentieth-century Zimbabwe they employed labor to build the large stone structures (*madzimbabwe*) for which the region subsequently was famed. Gold and ivory evidently paid for this enterprise, and so these Africans did not turn significantly to either slavery or dealing in slaves.

Towns grew up along the Indian Ocean coast from the Muslim maritime trade, and their prosperous inhabitants exchanged Asian textiles, porcelain, and seashells for food, wives, and slaves from neighboring farming communities. These women—mothers and slave domestics from Bantu-speaking backgrounds—taught their language to the children of the Arab and Persian merchants of these towns. The distinctive blend of Arabic and Persian with native Bantu speech became modern Swahili.

The Portuguese sailed along Africa's Atlantic coast in the fifteenth century and initiated exchanges of manufactures for people in the western and central parts of the continent. Unlike the Muslim commerce of the Indian Ocean, this trade stimulated massive sales of slaves, especially after Dutch (then English and French) merchants introduced, in the seventeenth and eighteenth centuries, vastly greater quantities of commercial capital and added cheap muskets to their offerings. In the sixteenth century established authorities in Africa had generally welcomed the first Europeans as providers of valuable commercial credit and imports with which to strengthen their networks of patronage and their holdings of slaves. Rulers thus consolidated independent cores of more centralized power within previously balanced political systems. But by the seventeenth century their gains provoked their rivals to resistance. Other Europeans provided goods and muskets that they used to escalate the conflicts. The growing violence produced captives both for retinues to support the emerging opponents in Africa and for sale to Europeans, who bought them as slaves to work the mines and plantations then taking shape in the New World. Droughts in both western and central Africa intensified the violence every ten years or so, and about once each century a decade-long climatic disaster would change community identities and revolutionize the political order by forcing people to flee, thus exposing many to enslavement.

The African victors in these struggles tended to keep slave women as wives, to bear children and to work the fields. This African preference for reproductive females complemented the European quest for young males suited to heavy lifting on the plantations and in the mines of the Americas and produced the well-known idealization of the African youth as the "prime" slave in the Atlantic trade. In Africa, the children of the resettled women captives grew up in slave-descended retinues that surrounded ambitious newcomers who seized the advantage in the severely disrupted conditions that followed initial scrambles for European goods. The most successful of these new men became domineering war leaders; by the eighteenth century some had established dynasties in the powerful military kingdoms that grew up between the populous regions in the interior, where their raiding parties preyed, and the coast, where their agents sold a portion of the captives as slaves.

The rulers of the African states of this era—from Segu on the upper Niger River; through Asante, Dahomey, and Oyo near the forested regions of western Africa; to the numerous broker states inland of the Portuguese slaving ports in central Africa—maintained their dominion by selling captives to Europeans for imports that they distributed to indebted followers. They retained other captives at their courts and in their armies—which were often equipped with imported muskets—and bestowed still others on clients to consolidate their realms. As African dependency on imports grew, the merchant groups who handled the transactions—whether as agents of governing authorities, as independent operatives acting by royal favor in one of the big kingdoms, or as merchant princes in their own right—also took their profits in captives, often males whom they trained as members of trading houses in coastal towns and commercial settlements throughout the interior. Favorable terms of exchange allowed successful Africans to resettle many slaves—perhaps as many as or more than they sold—to labor for the political gain of kings and merchants. The slaves were mostly women, and the sexual and reproductive services demanded of them maintained the old tendencies of African domestic slavery to assimilate their children to the personal retinues of the profiteers. Merchants and kings controlled male slaves, whom they assembled in potentially dangerously large numbers, by giving them access to the plunder of military expansion and the profits of commercial growth—never by admitting them to the respect their masters enjoyed by virtue of descent from long lines of local ancestors. By 1800 the profits of slavery had brought the western parts of the continent firmly within the Atlantic economy.

Slaves in Production

By the time of British suppression of slave trading in the Atlantic (between 1810 and the 1860s), the successors of these African entrepreneurs controlled enough descendants of these slaves and managed sources of new captives so efficiently that they were able to use their labor to produce the commodities—palm and peanut oils in western Africa, wax and ivory in central Africa—that then replaced people as western and central Africa's principal exports. At the same time, the growing European commercial stimulus extended to the Indian Ocean, where it set off similar violence, occasional political consolidation, and mercantile development in eastern Africa and Madagascar. As in the Atlantic, the victors sold some of their captives abroad and resettled many others as workers in the towns, trading networks, and kingdoms they established.

Northeastern Africa entered the same violent transition to slave-based strategies of political and economic development after about 1850. Muslim raiders from the Nile Valley and from the Swahili coast virtually invaded the upper Nile watershed and inland beyond the Great Lakes of eastern Africa. Their use of modern rifles made the process even more destructive. As Britain consolidated its control in India after 1750 and Egypt struggled to recover from Napoleon's invasion (1798), Egyptian Muslim interests and Omanis from the Persian Gulf turned to Africa, first for ivory and then for slaves. Both sold their commodities in central Ottoman markets then growing from trade with industrializing Europe. After about 1840, when British naval patrols restricted maritime slaving in the Indian Ocean, Omani sultans settled on the island of Zanzibar (just off the Swahili coast of East Africa) put the slaves they no longer dared export to work on clove plantations there. Swahili landowners on the adjoining mainland brought other slaves to produce grain to feed the large captive populations on the islands.

In West Africa the last phases of the internal African slaving wars stimulated by the Atlantic trade had reached inland to the Sudan by the end of the eighteenth century. There resistance to the upswing of violence took the form of Islamic *jihads,* or holy wars, after 1805. Throughout the nineteenth century several markets for slave labor encouraged these raids for captives, which took on increasingly commercial overtones. The coastal regions of West Africa needed labor to grow and process palm and peanut products. The exigencies of Saharan transport and the demand in the Ottoman domains multiplied the volume of the desert trade. In addition, many local victors in these wars had moved to towns employing large rural slaveholdings for plantation agriculture. They luxuriated in slave-staffed households and royal courts in the style of the prosperous Islamic piety to which they aspired. Millions of captives on agricultural estates in the Hausa region made the Sokoto caliphate and its numerous emirates one of the largest slave societies in the world.

Only southern Africa remained largely outside the intensified slave production that entrepreneurs built to trade with the commercial economies of the Atlantic and Indian Oceans. Dutch settlement at the temperate Cape of Good Hope (1652) had led in the eighteenth century to imports of East Africans and

Asians as slaves, who were set to work on European commercial wheat and wine farms. But the British suppression of maritime slaving in the nineteenth century and their emancipation of the Dutch slaves at the Cape in 1838 deflected the European farmers' continuing search for labor into local raiding. Their activities expanded steadily north until their seizures of people blended with the slaving then spreading southward from the Indian Ocean. The southern African counterpart of trade-induced slaving violence characterisitic of western Africa started in the 1820s among Nguni-speakers in latter-day Natal, whose successful wars captured the women and cattle at the center of the "Zulu" nation thus assembled. These wars continued into the 1860s largely independently of the import-export trade with the consolidation of new "Ngoni" kingdoms as far north as the Swahili trading sphere in eastern Africa.

The Ending of Slavery

Africans—west, central, south, and east—had mobilized through enslavement to become players on the mercantilist fringes of European capitalism by the onset of European colonial rule at the end of the nineteenth century. Slavery in Africa—as elsewhere in the world—offered the most efficient path to development for states and commerical networks in economies rich in labor but lacking the financial institutions and the industrial technologies that were by then making Europe the center of a capitalist global economy. Europeans attempted to justify the colonial rule they imposed on Africa in the 1890s as a humanitarian effort to eradicate the slavery they had been instrumental in stimulating throughout the continent. Until after World War I the colonial authorities' fiscal and military weakness forced them to collaborate with the wealthy, influential African slaveholders who controlled most of the people, whether slaves or their descendants, living in the new domains.

Late-nineteenth-century Africans had positioned more and more slaves—particularly the men no longer sold off to the Americas—as commodity producers; excluded them from the society of their masters, often on plantations and in segregated villages; and exposed them to brutal treatment quite unlike the small-scale, relatively assimilative, family-based control of women in earliest times. The change from ancient African communal values to the assertive individualism of masters surrounded by slave dependents had begun much earlier in isolated instances, and it had become common in some Muslim areas during the five centuries before 1500 as Islamic merchants stimulated commerce in western and eastern Africa. Beginning in the seventeenth century, Europeans had provided commercial credit and manufactures, including ever more powerful weapons, in quantities that grew at unprecedented rates. The military and mercantile uses of slaves spread so widely that Britain's nineteenth-century suppression of Atlantic and then Indian Ocean slaving forced African masters to use slaves to produce export commodities to maintain the supplies of imports, on which power and wealth then depended. Productivity in Africa had grown with slavery, in a kind of labor-intensive economic development, but at enormous costs in human life and investment in security measures against the violence associated with the maintenance of slavery. The architects of twentieth-century European empires, intent on appropriating the productive capacity that Africans had built on modern, productive slavery, used abolition as the basis of their claims to colonial legitimacy. At the same time, they deprived their colonies of the currency and technology that alone could have reduced reliance on slavery and on successor forms of coerced labor.

See also ISLAM; MILITARY SLAVES.

BIBLIOGRAPHY

CAMPBELL, GWYN R. "Slavery and Fanompoana: The Structure of Forced Labour in Imerina (Madagascar), 1790–1861." *Journal of African History* 29, no. 3 (1988): 463–486.

COOPER, FREDERICK. *Plantation Slavery on the East Coast of Africa.* 1977.

CURTIN, PHILIP C. *Economic Change in Pre-colonial Africa: Senegambia in the Era of the Slave Trade.* 2 vols. 1975.

ELDREDGE, ELIZABETH A., and FRED MORTON, eds. *Slavery in South Africa: Captive Labor on the Dutch Frontier.* 1994.

GLASSMAN, JONATHAN. "The Bondsman's New Clothes: The Contradictory Consciousness of Slave Resistance on the Swahili Coast." *Journal of African History* 32, no. 2 (1991): 277–312.

INIKORI, JOSEPH E. "Slavery in Africa and the Transatlantic Slave Trade." In *The African Diaspora* edited by Alusine Jalloh and Stephen E. Maizlish. 1996; pp. 39–72.

————, ed. *Forced Migration: The Impact of the Export Slave Trade on African Societies.* 1981.

KLEIN, MARTIN A. *Slavery and Colonial Rule in French West Africa.* 1998.

LOVEJOY, PAUL E. *Transformations in Slavery: A History of Slavery in Africa.* 1983.

LOVEJOY, PAUL E., and JAN S. HOGENDORN. *Slow Death for Slavery: The Course of Abolition in Northern Nigeria, 1897–1936.* 1993.

MANNING, PATRICK. *Slavery and African Life: Occidental, Oriental and African Slave Trades.* 1990.

MASON, JOHN EDWIN. "The Slaves and Their Protectors: Reforming Resistance in a Slave Society, 1826–1834." *Journal of Southern African Studies* 17, no. 1 (1991): 103–128.

MEILLASSOUX, CLAUDE. *Anthropologie de l'esclavage: le ventre de fer et d'argent.* 1986. Translated by Alide Dasnois as *The Anthropology of Slavery: The Womb of Iron and Gold* (foreword by Paul E. Lovejoy). 1991.

———, ed. *L'esclavage en Afrique précoloniale.* 1975.

———. "The Role of Slavery in the Economic and Social History of Sahelo-Sudanic Africa." In *Forced Migration,* edited by Joseph E. Inikori, pp. 74–99. 1981.

Joseph C. Miller

Economic and Demographic Effects of the Atlantic Slave Trade

The impact on Africa of the estimated 12 million Africans forcibly shipped from their homeland to the Americas and of the associated injuries and death suffered by countless others during the enslavement process has been the subject of much controversy. Even at the time when abolition of the Atlantic slave trade was being debated, contemporaries were divided over the consequences of the slave trade for Africa. Opponents of the trade frequently reminded their listeners of the damage inflicted on Africa's social fabric by the wars and violence that were seen as natural corollaries of slaving activities. By comparison, apologists for the trade tended to overlook such effects of slaving and to focus instead on the capacity of African societies to supply some 50,000 to 100,000 slaves a year in the late eighteenth century, a feat that they ascribed to high levels of natural reproduction on the continent.

Two centuries after the initial moves in Europe to abolish the slave trade, there are no defenders of the traffic in humans. But the impact of the slave trade on Africa is still the subject of very divergent historical interpretations. For instance, some historians, notably David Eltis, have argued that the export of slaves to the Americas was a relatively marginal activity outside the coastal littoral of Africa, while others, including John Fage, have sought to remind us that in some respects European contact with western Africa, whether in the form of the slave trade or other trades, may have stimulated commercialization and thus brought some benefits to the regions in Africa associated with such activities. Echoes of Fage's claims are to be found in the writings of some other historians. In his *Trade without Rulers,* David Northrup, for instance, suggests that, "though cruelly exploitative," the slave trade of southeastern Nigeria laid the foundations for "even more profitable, yet unexploitative" trades in the nineteenth century. Joseph Miller, in *Way of Death,* argues that contact with Europeans brought the introduction of new food crops such as manioc and maize, thereby helping to support modest population growth in West Central Africa.

These suggestions that the slave trade, marginal or other, may have brought some benefits to Africa stand in stark contrast to the belief of Walter Rodney that the Atlantic slave trade had only catastrophic consequences for Africa and its peoples. In one of many graphic passages in his *History of the Upper Guinea Coast,* Rodney argues that, in the case of the slave trade, European capitalism "paraded without even a loincloth to hide its nakedness." For Rodney, Africans were the "weaker party" in dealing with Europeans, and the economic dislocation and social upheaval that arose from slave trafficking were in his view directly responsible for the continent's subsequent "underdevelopment" relative to the West. Since Rodney's death, his message has continued to be articulated in various forms by other scholars, most notably by Joseph Inikori. Thus, for instance, Inikori reminds us that incomes and population in Western Europe and North America experienced relatively sustained growth in the century or so after 1750 while Africa stagnated. Indeed, there are claims that in West and West Central Africa population may even have declined between 1750 and 1850.

Evaluating radically different interpretations of any set of historical events often poses problems, but this is especially so where the impact of the slave trade on Africa is concerned, since reliable data on precolonial African populations and outputs are rare. The problem is compounded by modern evidence that the level and incidence of slave shipments from Africa varied greatly between regions and over through time. Although Rodney wrote extensively on Upper Guinea, that region supplied only a small proportion of the slaves shipped to the Americas compared with Angola, the Bight of Benin (or Slave Coast), and the Bight of Biafra. Modern research suggests, in fact, that only in the second half of the eighteenth century—when the Atlantic slave trade was at its height—did slave shipments from Upper Guinea begin to approximate the levels reached in any of the other three regions mentioned. Whether the marginality of some regions as suppliers of enslaved Africans to the Americas means that the "collateral damage" arising from slaving activities varied similarly between supply regions is an open question. But given that population densities within Africa were also uneven and that political and institutional structures varied across regions, it would be surprising to find that the export slave trade affected the social history of all African regions in the same way.

On one issue, at least, most modern scholarship seems to have reached a consensus: that while Europeans may have occasionally seized Africans, the vast majority of those shipped to the Americas were prisoners of war, victims of kidnapping, criminals, or debtors whom African dealers sold to European traders. The

Slave traders purchase captured African villagers to be sold into slavery in the Americas in the nineteenth century. [Library of Congress/Corbis]

dealers were often drawn from local political elites who sought to enrich themselves through control of trade routes to the coast and regulation of commercial negotiations with Europeans. Rodney may have been correct in thinking that in Upper Guinea African sellers were the weaker parties in negotiating slave transactions, but this too remains a debatable issue. More recent research suggests that, on balance, the advantage in negotiations tended to lie, if anywhere, with African slave dealers, thereby allowing those in control of them to accumulate sizable fortunes. Often these were embodied in ownership of slave retinues. As a result, political competition for control of the slave trade became in some regions an important source of interstate conflict, demonstrated perhaps most clearly by Dahomey's conquest of the coastal powers of Ardrah and Whydah in the Bight of Benin in the early eighteenth century and, later, in Asante's efforts to extend its influence over the Gold Coast.

The complicity of prosperous African elites in the export slave trade does not, of course, diminish the broader social and human costs to Africa. As noted above, however, any attempt to measure such costs faces acute problems regarding data. For example, while our knowledge of the age and gender composition of slave shipments through time and by African region of embarkation has improved sharply during the last few decades, historians still disagree, largely because of a paucity of background data on the African population, about the demographic implications of these slave exports for African societies. Occasionally, evidence is uncovered that sustained exports of slaves, most of whom were adult males, could severely distort local population structures. One notable example is census material for parts of Angola in 1777, which shows that there were up to twice as many adult females as males. Similar gender imbalances have been found in other regions heavily plundered by slavers. In addition, there are signs that in the hinterlands of some regions, population displacement or even depopulation occurred as a result of sustained slaving activities either because too many captives were taken or because people fled to more defensible sites. There seems little doubt, therefore, that the export trade in slaves had a discernible and, in some areas, a genuinely dramatic impact on local population structures and distributions.

Despite these insights any assessment of the general impact on population levels, whether regionally or throughout West Africa and West Central Africa, must still depend on what assumptions are made about several other key variables. These include total populations and their natural growth rates, the extent of the slaving hinterland, and the mortality rates of slaves—not to mention fatalities and injuries experienced by others—during the enslavement process and the movement of slaves to the coast. Although we now know from evidence on slave ethnicities that slaving "frontiers" tended to extend further inland over time, especially during the eighteenth century, hard evidence on each of these variables is, frankly, very patchy and in some cases nonexistent.

In these circumstances, therefore, there must inevitably be a "credibility gap" in any calculation of the demographic impact on Africa of the Atlantic slave trade. Those who have nonetheless attempted such calculations have painted three scenarios of the demographic effects of the trade. One scenario suggests that overall population growth may have been slowed by slave exports, with the export of slaves being accommodated within the natural growth rate of African populations. A second scenario indicates that, at least in the century after 1750, slave exports absorbed all potential demographic growth in West Africa, thereby causing the subcontinent's population to stagnate. A third, and conceptually more sophisticated, scenario embodying demographic simulations, associated with Patrick Manning and William Griffiths, has suggested that the export of slaves caused a fall of total populations in West Africa and West Central Africa between 1750 and 1850, and probably also in regions such as the Bight of Benin in earlier years. The first of these scenarios seems to rely on highly optimistic, if not highly implausible, assumptions about natural growth rates of population, and the weight of scholarly opinion at present appears to favor more pessimistic assessments of the effect of the Atlantic slave trade on population levels in both West Africa and West Central Africa.

However, even if population levels in Africa fell as a result of the Atlantic slave trade, it is still not certain that such losses of population were wholly damaging to the economies of West and West Central Africa. It is true that most of those shipped to the Americas were young adults, mainly male, arguably in the prime working years of their lives. But the loss to Africa of such people may not have been totally detrimental to the economic performance of African societies if there was, as some historians have suggested, either chronic underemployment of labor in such societies or a high level of employment of women in African agriculture. In effect, unproductive, arguably largely male labor could conceivably have been seized and shipped abroad from a given locality without lowering total output there. Moreover, the feeding of those enslaved on their way to the coast as well as the provisioning of slave ships before their Atlantic crossing may well have given an impetus to agriculture in some, mainly coastal, locations. It would be unwise, therefore, simply to assume that, even if the Atlantic slave trade caused African population levels to fall, this had universally harmful effects in terms of output or productivity throughout West and West Central Africa.

That said, there seems little doubt that, in cost-benefit terms, the economic and social costs of the slave trade to Africa probably outweighed the private profits accruing to the local commercial and political elites who supplied slaves for export to the Americas. It is easy to overlook the fact, for example, that, insofar as slaves were victims of war, raids, or kidnappers, any gains accruing to enslavers ought perhaps to be counterbalanced by the costs borne by those who had nurtured those enslaved during their childhood. Also, one cannot ignore the lost or forgone production associated with the social and political disruption arising from slave raiding or from wars induced by political contests over the spoils of the slave traffic. Nor should one ignore the fact that, as slaving frontiers reached farther inland from the coast, the social costs or "externalities" related to slave trafficking would appear to have become more widespread throughout West Africa and West Central Africa. Given the paucity of statistics on precolonial Africa, any attempt to produce an overall balance sheet must, of course, be regarded as speculative. But at least one calculation made for West Africa by Henry Gemery and Jan Hogendorn suggests that, even if only private economic costs and benefits are taken into account, it is highly unlikely that the economic gains of the slave trade in West Africa exceeded its costs. This conclusion, they remind us, is reached "without any reference to the massive intangible costs of the trade." On balance, therefore, it is difficult to believe that those who privately gained from slave trafficking in Africa outnumbered the others who carried the burden of the indirect costs. On the contrary, the likelihood is that, in numerical terms at least, the latter far exceeded the former. In this respect at least, the Atlantic slave trade may be regarded as having been regressive in its impact on West and West Central African societies.

See also DEMOGRAPHIC ANALYSIS OF SLAVES AND SLAVERY; ECONOMICS OF SLAVERY; SLAVE TRADE.

BIBLIOGRAPHY

ELTIS, DAVID. *Economic Growth and the Ending of the Transatlantic Slave Trade.* 1987.

EVANS, E. W., and DAVID RICHARDSON. "Hunting for Rents: The Economics of Slaving in Pre-Colonial Africa." *Economic History Review* 48, no. 4 (1995): 665–686.

FAGE, JOHN D. "Slavery and the Slave Trade in the Context of West African History." *Journal of African History* 10 (1969): 393–404.

GEMERY, HENRY A., and JAN S. HOGENDORN. "The Economic Costs of West African Participation in the Atlantic Slave Trade: A Preliminary Sampling of the Evidence." In *The Uncommon Market: Essays in the Economic History of the Atlantic Slave Trade,* edited by Henry A. Gemery and Jan S. Hogendorn. 1979.

INIKORI, JOSEPH E., ed. *Forced Migration: The Impact of the Export Slave Trade on African Societies.* 1982.

LAW, ROBIN. *The Slave Coast of West Africa, 1550–1750: The Impact of the Atlantic Slave Trade on an African Society.* 1991.

LOVEJOY, PAUL E., and DAVID RICHARDSON. "British Abolition and Its Impact on Slave Prices along the Atlantic Coast of Africa, 1783–1850." *Journal of Economic History* 55, no. 1 (1995): 98–119.

MANNING, PATRICK, and WILLIAM S. GRIFFITH. "Divining the Unprovable: Simulating the Demography of African Slavery." *Journal of Interdisciplinary History* 19, no. 2 (1988): 177–201.

MILLER, JOSEPH C. *Way of Death: Merchant Capitalism and the Angolan Slave Trade, 1730–1830.* 1988.

NORTHRUP, DAVID. *Trade without Rulers: Pre-Colonial Economic Development in South-Eastern Nigeria.* 1978.

RODNEY, WALTER. *A History of the Upper Guinea Coast, 1545–1800,* 1970.

David Richardson

Political and Historical Effects of the Atlantic Slave Trade

Since the late eighteenth century, abolitionists and defenders of slavery have debated how European slaving influenced Africa's history as its exchanges with the Atlantic economy grew from 1450 to 1850. Both abolitionists and proponents of the trade claimed to defend its victims' welfare by attributing radically different consequences to it. The issue remained politically charged as subsequent generations of well-meaning but partisan outsiders assessed the trade's "effects" in Africa in terms of current concerns of their own, largely without systematic historical research. Professional historians of Africa are currently abandoning such depersonalized abstractions as "the slave trade" as explanations and are instead attempting to understand the motivations of the many different sorts of people—Africans as well as Europeans—who were, in fact, engaged in slaving.

Self-proclaimed abolitionist defenders of slavery's victims alleged that European muskets sold in Africa generated war captives whom African captors sold, thus spreading violence throughout an otherwise peaceful continent. The idea of European responsibility for disrupting an Eden-like continent implicit in these charges later thrived in the context of modern racial tensions, to underlie popular, though false, impressions that Europeans had themselves gone ashore to kidnap Africa's people. Eighteenth-century defenders of the trade had countered the abolitionists' idyllic Africa by depicting a barbarous place, dominated by tyrannical kings who kept their own people in slavery more abject than bondage on the mines and plantations of the Americas. This self-serving rationalization exaggerated both the authoritarianism of politics in Africa and the paternalism of slavery in the Americas, but hardly more so than the countervailing myth of Africa as Eden romanticized them.

Professional historians translated these questions into academic debates in the 1960s. Although European slavers had known that Africans enslaved other Africans, colonial ethnographers tended to overlook all differences in rank or status in African societies, and the historians who first reconstructed eighteenth-century kingdoms emphasized participation more than domination. Modern scholars thus looked beyond the evidence that slavery had existed in Africa and understood the slavery they noticed as marginal and benign compared with the hardships that Africans endured as slaves in the Americas. But they also meant to refute stereotypes of Africans as passive victims of European aggression and so emphasized that Africans had themselves captured and sold nearly all the people that Europeans had bought as slaves along the coast.

This initial round of systematic research also began to discern the pervasiveness of slavery in nineteenth-century Africa, if not also long before. But since the existence of slavery—no less in Africa than in the Americas—connoted brutality and backwardness so strongly, some historians, led by Walter Rodney, perceived this fact as potentially damaging in the hands of racist detractors and sought to explain it by attributing responsibility for it to Europeans, in a version of the abolitionist myth of Atlantic slaving expelling Africa from its Garden of Eden, updated to use the history then being revealed to show *How Europe Underdeveloped Africa* (Rodney, 1972/1982) by the standards of the ideology of economic "development" of the 1960s. This hypothesis, which also reflected disillusionment in the late 1960s with self-serving African nationalist politicians, asserted that Africans had been progressing toward modern prosperity along lines similar to Europe's, until the violence associated with slaving allowed opportunistic collaborating rulers to thrive by exploiting their own subjects.

Parallel indictments of Europe, capitalism, and racism explained the slave trade's damage to Africa in relation to other economic and demographic models. According to one, the population lost to European slaving had shrunk African consumer markets below levels that might sustain the tendencies toward industrialism previously under way. Some nonspecialists perceived the demographic losses in much stronger terms: exports of people and deaths attending the violence of their capture had "depopulated" the continent in genocidal proportions comparable to the Jewish Holocaust. In economic terms, cheap European manufactures had overwhelmed African production in all but the subsistence underdeveloped agriculture then thought to characterize colonial rural Africa. Exile of Africa's male youth as slaves had deprived a labor-intensive economy of its strongest, most productive forces. Other scholars calculated the numbers of guns sold to Africans and debated whether buyers had fired them in violent pursuit of captives or to hunt game and, when they discovered that Europeans had actually offered mostly cheap trade muskets, whether these weapons were accurate or reliable enough to do either effectively. Most saw other European goods that Africans had received as being of little economic value, emphasizing beads, old military uniforms, alcohol, and other trinkets.

But other lines of research sought explanations internal to Africa by exploring the social and ethical values of seventeenth- and eighteenth-century Africans, personal ambitions, political tensions, economic trade-offs, environmental pressures, consumption preferences, and how the tragic long-run consequences that later Europeans and Americans saw as "the slave trade" might have emerged, unintended, from short-term strategies motivated by more immediate concerns. These scholars asked why rational people in Africa, as much masters of their own fate as the human condition allowed, might have given up people in trade with the Atlantic economy. They looked beyond the stereotypes of what Africans had received as guns and worthless junk and rejected the search for "effects of the slave trade on Africa" as overly abstract and structural, as reflecting preoccupations with

European initiative, post facto neoabolitionist moralities, subsequent economic outcomes in Africa, and false racial dichotomies in constructing the story as a conflict between white European slavers and black African victims.

On the assumption that the Africans involved knew what they were doing and got something that they desired out of doing it, research turned to the delicate balances and intense rivalries of African political systems and the strength that the powerful gained from depleting the followings of their rivals by selling them as slaves. Political strategies in an environment of low-energy technologies (or labor-intensive production) rested on the axiom "People are power" or "People are wealth." Further, the interchangeability in Africa of material things with wealth in people allowed transactions across two domains that modern thought holds entirely separate. Sale of captured adversaries enhanced political gains for the captor, who could distribute the imports received in exchange to indebt new clients, buy women slaves as wives, and enlarge personal retinues in other ways. If "people were wealth," a powerful African's prospects rose and fell depending on whether he had to distribute fewer goods acquiring the people he sold than he could indebt or influence with the imports he received for them. The marginal cost of corrupting political institutions to seize and exile opponents as well as criminals was low, and ambitious politicians often thus abused the power they held. The advantage of this move from people to goods to people varied with the ratios of material to vulnerable human assets, and since supply and demand altered these ratios from time to time and place to place, Africans resorted to the Atlantic trade to get ahead in different parts of the continent at different times over the four hundred years of the trade.

Economic historians viewed Africans primarily as merchants, who, they argued, largely set the terms on which Europeans traded at the coast, and as consumers. One economist estimated Africa's foreign trade as never more than about 2 percent of total production and wondered if any significant "effect" at all could stem from so small an economic sector. Upon close examination of the goods African consumers had received, the stereotypical alcohol (about 20 percent) and muskets and powder (together only about 10 percent) amounted to less than a third of imports by European currency values; the largest general category was textiles (in the range of 55 percent), many of those not European luxury fabrics but rather mass-consumption cottons from India. The cliché of "trinkets" ignored the significance of African's uses of beads, metalwares made of copper or its alloys (brass and bronze), cowry shells from the Indian Ocean, and at least some of the textiles—in fact, Africans used these as money. Imported iron replaced the production of local smelters, who were running out of hardwoods suitable for charcoal to fire their draft furnaces, and semifinished imported goods became tools and materials for domestic African cottage industries. The volume of the imports received for each person sold increased throughout the trade, perhaps enough to cover growing costs of transporting goods and herding people through trading areas that expanded continuously into the interior. Uses of these sorts revealed a largely domestic economy importing currencies to expand its commercial sectors, maintaining its primary capacity to manufacture its own iron agricultural implements, dressing and adorning many, if not a majority, of the people counted as its wealth, and investing imports in converting more and more of them from relatives or clients of rivals to slaves of one's own. Africans thus increased productivity by labor-intensive strategies to achieve a tragic sort of economic development based on slavery.

In an economy that measured productivity in terms of the number and variety of personal services on which the wealthy could draw, those in control could only have gained from the coercion they could apply to the slaves who thus replaced subordinate relatives and clients. Since they concentrated on building personal retinues, they would have preferred young women able to bear children; the fact that Africans sold Europeans almost twice as many males as females would have left a preponderance of women among the captives retained as trading "profits" and would have increased reproduction rates in areas able to retain them. The men remaining would have controlled these women through polygynous marriages. They would have intensified agriculture by setting many women to work in fields, growing New World crops also obtained from Atlantic merchants—notably maize (corn) and manioc (or cassava), which added calories to the diet, though at the cost of nutrients and variety; thus more people could be fed, but less nutritiously.

The apparent emphasis on fertility, human and agricultural, was a response to broader environmental pressures that also predisposed African populations to seek imports from the Atlantic in the prevailing labor-intensive economy. Deforestation was advancing as smelters cut wood for charcoal and as farmers burned timber to clear and fertilize fields with ash. Repeated decade-long droughts—their effects no doubt intensified by slaving wars—forced farmers intruding on the margins of the Sahara and southern African deserts to abandon their fields and disperse to survive; refugees subjugated themselves to anyone with

food to offer, isolated individuals were vulnerable to capture, and parents found themselves compelled to abandon some children to save others. Many of these farmers, refugees, and abandoned children became slaves, and some were marched off toward the coast for sale to Europeans; export volumes tended to surge during the droughts. African polities fell under the control of military warlords, particularly along the desert edge and where violent slaving forced people to organize to protect themselves, and the deprivations of drought escalated underlying tensions into active hostilities that more and more involved firearms and yielded captives, and slaves, on both sides.

Although conflicts of these sorts long antedated the appearance of Europeans on the Atlantic coast, the vast material wealth from the expanding world economy that capitalist merchants poured into African economies intensified, prolonged, and extended them to continual regional population displacements, resettlement—often in less fertile lands—of the displaced as slaves, banditry and warlordism, and indebtedness and seizure of debtors and their entire families for default, through the ambition, greed, and competitiveness of the numerous participants in the trade. Profits from converting others' followers to subordinates of one's own also financed the well-known large, centralized political systems of the era—notably Asante in modern Ghana, Dahomey in present-day Bénin, Oyo in what is now southwestern Nigeria, and numerous others. Warlords typically began by sheltering subjects from the worst slaving but then altered their strategies to protect merchants conveying goods inland and driving slaves coastward. Localities were deserted for a few years and then repopulated with slaves; on a regional scale, populations probably could not have grown beyond the environmental limits they had already reached, but they may have declined in the areas of greatest violence—mostly in western Central Africa—for as long as a generation or two late in the eighteenth century and early in the nineteenth. With such extensive relocations of people, old languages and cultures expanded or disappeared, and many of the modern ethnic communities of Africa emerged. It has recently been argued that the immorality, psychological trauma, and betrayal of trust that characterized those times left enduring patterns of hostility and lack of self-assurance among the survivors' descendants.

These profound transformations, and others, make modern Africa very much a product of the era of Atlantic slaving—though not only that, since nineteenth-century commodity exporting and accelerating population growth and colonial rule in the first half of the twentieth century added more immediate legacies as well. The human costs of bringing growing portions of the continent into the Atlantic economy—as a supplier of labor funded by European capital—to bring the lands of the Americas into slave-worked productivity thus fell on the captives, mostly women, who remained in Africa. These women were displaced from their families, were less well fed, were subject to patriarchal as well as political domination, and worked harder to grow the food consumed by merchants, porters, guards, and others who left agriculture to join new commercial firms. But the costs also fell on the slaves, mostly men, sold into the Atlantic trade. Africans' reactions to the commercial stimulus, even the opportunities, of the emerging Atlantic economy surely arose as much from human greed, African as well as European, and from tensions in African societies under growing environmental pressures as from external "effects of the Atlantic slave trade." Viewed in the longer term of Africa's history, these processes became more widespread and more intense but differed little in kind from earlier Africans' reactions to commercial contacts with Muslims from across the Sahara. Other Muslim slavers, from the lower Nile and the Indian Ocean coast, invaded eastern and northeastern Africa after the 1860s with modern firearms; they captured people, sent some as slaves to the coast, and kept others for themselves in patterns involving greater violence and less commercial debt. Such patterns recalled the early, poorly financed years of the Atlantic trade.

See also SLAVE TRADE.

BIBLIOGRAPHY

CURTIN, PHILIP D. *Economic Change in Precolonial Africa: Senegambia in the Era of the Slave Trade.* 1975.
ELTIS, DAVID, and LAWRENCE C. JENNINGS. "Trade between Western Africa and the Atlantic World in the Pre-Colonial Era." *American Historical Review* 93, no. 4 (1988): 936–359.
FAGE, JOHN D. "Slavery and the Slave Trade in the Context of West African History." *Journal of African History* 10, no. 3 (1969): 393–404.
INIKORI, JOSEPH E., ed. *Forced Migration: The Impact of the Export Slave Trade on African Societies.* 1981.
JOHNSON, MARION. "The Atlantic Slave Trade and the Economy of West Africa." In *Liverpool, the African Slave Trade and Abolition,* edited by Roger T. Anstey and P. E. H. Hair. 1977.
Journal of African History. 12, nos. 2 and 4 (1971). Special issues devoted to the gun trade.
LOVEJOY, PAUL E. *Transformations in Slavery: A History of Slavery in Africa.* 1983.
MANNING, PATRICK. *Slavery and African Life: Occidental, Oriental, and African Slave Trades.* 1990.
MILLER, JOSEPH C. *Way of Death: Merchant Capitalism and the Angolan Slave Trade, 1730–1830.* 1988.
RODNEY, WALTER. *How Europe Underdeveloped Africa.* 1972. Revised 1982.
SHAW, ROSALIND. *The Dangers of Temne Divination: Ritual Memories of the Slave Trade in West Africa.* 1997.
THORNTON, JOHN K. *Africa and Africans in the Making of the Atlantic World, 1400–1680.* 1992.

Joseph C. Miller

The End of Slavery

Manumission in Africa was a selective, individualized, and limited process, which strengthened the authority of the master and the ideology of slavery. Many African societies practiced some form of gradual, multigenerational incorporation of slaves into the masters' lineage or community. When a female slave gave birth to a child fathered by her master or another free male, the birth often freed the mother and the child. Other societies practiced deathbed manumission, and in some societies slaves could ransom themselves, or their kin could buy them back. Among the Bambara in West Africa, slaves who had accumulated some wealth often preferred to buy their own slaves rather than purchase freedom for themselves.

Wholesale emancipation of slaves was a European concept born of the wrenching political, ideological, and economic struggles associated with the emergence of industrial capitalism. European antislavery initially focused on the slave trade. It was first prohibited by the Danes in 1792, and the movement to end it achieved a major success in Great Britain in 1807. The United States followed suit in 1808. Following the Napoleonic wars, Britain engaged in diplomacy, backed by naval patrols at sea, designed to persuade or force other nations' carriers to prohibit the trade. Despite the efforts of the British, slaves continued to reach the plantation economies of Brazil and Cuba until the 1860s, and to reach the Indian Ocean islands. In other parts of the Caribbean, later in the Indian Ocean, and on West African plantation islands, a slave trade disguised as "contract" labor persisted into the twentieth century.

European efforts to end the slave export trade confronted expanded reliance on slavery in Africa that had been stimulated by the demand for slaves in the Americas as well as North Africa, the Middle East, and the Indian Ocean. The potential crisis facing African rulers and warriors—loss of their principal sources of revenue—was eased by the gradualness of the decline in demand for slaves in the Americas and the coincident expansion of demand in Europe for African tropical commodities, such as vegetable oils, cotton, and cloves, to feed the growing industries and consumer markets there. Africans had long used slaves as menial agricultural laborers, miners, soldiers, high government officials, surrogate kin, and wives. When suppression of slave exports reduced the price of slaves, Africans increased their own slaveholding.

Increased slaveholding in Africa coincided with vigorous European and American campaigns against slavery itself. France was the first nation to outlaw slavery, in 1794; but Napoleon reinstated slavery in 1802 as part of a failed effort to restore order in the empire. In 1833 the British Parliament abolished slavery in its colonies but required emancipated slaves to serve as apprentices for up to four years. Thus emancipation did not apply to British colonies in South Asia, where slavery was a widespread institution and where Britain depended upon the local slave-owning classes as intermediaries and local officials. Humanitarians maintained their pressure, and by 1843 Parliament declared that slavery had no legal status in areas administered directly by the British. This approach was designed to accommodate their Indian allies while ending slavery gradually. It became the model for European efforts to end slavery in Africa.

Abolitionist movements were more diffuse and weaker in France, Portugal, and Germany than in Britain. In 1848 France again, and finally, abolished slavery in all its possessions, including its tiny outposts in West Africa. Because African traders in adjoining regions feared that their slaves would gain freedom simply by entering the French colony, they refused to trade there, causing commercial and political crises. Fugitive slaves often sought refuge in these European coastal enclaves. In order to minimize the effects of abolition, local French officials disannexed territories, turning them into protectorates where local laws prevailed. The Portuguese took a more gradual approach, beginning to dismantle colonial slavery in 1854, but requiring slaves to remain in unpaid services as apprentices until 1878. Even then, enforcement of the rights of the people nominally "freed" was limited.

As the pace of the European colonial expansion accelerated in the late 1870s, Europeans took responsibility for African societies in which slavery and the slave trade were important economic and social institutions. Activist Protestant and Catholic missionaries maintained pressure on metropolitan and colonial governments to suppress the slave trade and slavery there. European governments publicly expressed antislavery sentiments and justified colonial conquest as a means to end the slave trade and slavery in Africa. But, paradoxically, European colonial expansion in Africa actually led to a brief explosion of enslavement of the victims of the widespread political and economic instability that accompanied conquest. By the end of the century, though, the vast supply of slaves generated by these precolonial warrior states ended. Still, a small but steady stream of new slaves, fed by kidnapping, persisted well into the twentieth century.

A decree for liberation of a slave under German rule in East Africa. [Bojan Brecelj/Corbis]

In many areas of Africa, increased personal security stimulated regional economies. Booming economies increased demand for more slaves and often led to harsher working conditions. Pacification also contributed to increased flight by slaves during the first decade of the century, as some slaves sought to return to their former homelands or simply to move away from their masters. Under pressure from missionaries and from the actions of the slaves themselves, European colonial powers moved to end slavery.

But European colonial powers understood slavery in Africa to be a "domestic" institution (both masters and slaves were African), and they sought to avoid disrupting the social, economic, and political fabric of African societies. The British had already applied a variant of their Indian indirect antislavery legislation in the Gold Coast, when they annexed the region in 1874. Thereafter, no colonial or indigenous court could recognize slavery as a legal category, and so masters could not enforce claims over slaves who managed to appear before a court. Laws were enacted to end dealing in slaves and to declare all children born to slaves free. Although this British legislation did not abolish slavery as an institution, it accelerated the end of slavery by prohibiting new enslavement and liberating children born into slavery. In northern Nigeria and their other African colonies, the British applied a variant of this gradualist model.

The French pursued a similarly legalistic and gradual antislavery strategy. Legal cases involving the status of slaves were not admissible in any of the tribunals created under the native legal code of 1903. And in 1905, faced with what they called an "exodus" of slaves abandoning their masters, the French formally prohibited alienation of any person's liberty, thus ending new enslavement. The Germans and the Belgians abolished slave trading in their colonies in the 1890s but often took no action to enforce these restrictions. Missionaries maintained pressure on colonial and metropolitan governments to put their antislavery legislation into practice.

In many regions of Africa, slaves themselves took the action that led to the end of slavery. What actions slaves actually took depended upon the political, economic, and ecological history of their regions. In parts of West Africa, when market forces encouraged harsher forms of slavery during the first two decades of the twentieth century, as many as half of the total slave population began to flee their masters in a period of one or several years. Many sought to return to their homelands, some moved to the new colonial centers of commerce and administration, others sought refuge in the new missionary settlements, and some merely moved away from their masters but stayed within the same districts. In areas where plantations fed international commerce, such as Zanzibar and along the Zambezi River, colonial officials and African chiefs collaborated to prevent former slaves from gaining access to property in order to encourage transitional forms of sharecropping. Along the edge of the desert, slaves often remained with their former masters because they feared that they would be deprived of their livelihood if they attempted to live alone in that region's very harsh environment.

In most regions of Africa, neither chiefs nor colonial officials had sufficient economic and political power to coerce former slaves into remaining as they were. Neighboring chiefs often welcomed fugitives, letting them settle on vacant land in return for respect and token payments of rent. Where former slaves chose to remain close to their former masters, the latter were forced to renegotiate the nature of the dependency. These new relationships often took the form of fictive kinship, although the stigma of former slave status often persisted into the present. In other regions, particularly where they fled to mission stations or to the new urban settlements associated with European colonialism, former slaves took on more independent identities of their own. By the 1930s, slavery in Africa was a mere vestige of what it had once been.

Despite the formal end to slavery, many Africans continued to rely on unpaid dependent labor for economic and social goals. Chiefs often used "customary law" to restrict access to economic resources, thus forcing former slaves into persistent unfree labor relations. Pawning of people also expanded during the bleak years of the 1930s, as indebted people found themselves desperate to raise cash for taxes and other obligations. Neither the decline of slavery nor colonial suppression of the legal category resulted in the wholesale disappearance of slave status. In many parts of Africa, former slave status is remembered and utilized to maintain social hierarchies, even when the economic benefits of control have disappeared.

Explaining the impact of the end of slavery on African societies has given rise to considerable debate about interpretation and evidence. Some scholars have argued that the end of slavery had a negligible impact on African economies and cultures. These scholars argue that the number of slaves who actually left their masters was small relative to the number of those who remained and that those slaves who left were probably the most incorrigible and least integrated. Thus, their departure served only to reinforce assimilationist African slave systems. Other scholars argue that the number of slaves who left their masters was sufficiently large to force masters to renegotiate their relationships with the slaves who remained. They argue that the end of slavery also led to subtle and sometimes profound changes in relations between husbands and wives and between generations.

See also ABOLITION AND ANTISLAVERY MOVEMENTS; ECONOMICS OF SLAVERY; EMANCIPATION; SLAVE TRADE.

BIBLIOGRAPHY

COOPER, FREDERICK. *From Slaves to Squatters: Plantation Labor and Agriculture in Zanzibar and Coastal Kenya, 1890–1925.* 1980.

FALOLA, TOYIN, and PAUL E. LOVEJOY, eds. *Pawnship in Africa: Debt Bondage in Historical Perspective.* 1994.

HOGENDORN, JAN, and PAUL E. LOVEJOY. *Slow Death to Slavery: The Course of Abolition in Northern Nigeria.* 1993.

KLEIN, MARTIN, ed. *Breaking the Chains: Slavery, Bondage, and Emancipation in Modern Africa and Asia.* 1993.

MIERS, SUZANNE, and RICHARD ROBERTS, eds. *The End of Slavery in Africa.* 1988.

MORTON, FRED. *Children of Ham: Freed Slaves and Fugitive Slaves on the Kenya Coast.* 1990.

WRIGHT, MARCIA. *Strategies of Slaves and Women.* 1993.

Richard Roberts

Women as Slaves in Africa

The slavery of women in Africa can be seen as a result dependent on the trade in slaves and in particular the export of men, leaving behind a demographically skewed population. Or it can be dismissed as inconsequential because it conformed relatively rarely to the patterns of social exclusion typical of institutionalized slavery. To say that Africa has been everywhere and always the site of female farming is an exaggeration, but women assigned to farming through arranged marriages have continually been responsible for subsistence food production. As women became the majority of slaves in Africa, their burdens increased and norms were reshaped. Precisely because of such institutional and ideological fluidity, questions of the status and consciousness of female slaves are not peripheral but rather test the boundaries of received understanding and may call for reevaluations beyond, as well as within, Africa.

The most important generalization about women slaves in Africa is that their value resided in versatility: as workers in the fields and homes of their owners, as potential mothers of highly dependent progeny, and as sexual objects. Male slaves were more likely to become specialized in some productive capacity, often achieving status through their crafts, offices of trust, or ability, in the later nineteenth century, and to join a labor market and share their earnings with their masters. Women slaves, on the other hand, improved their condition most often by concubinage, bearing children who could assume a standing in the free families of their fathers. By the 1880s the overseas trade in slaves had been largely suppressed, and yet the internal demand, if anything, increased, owing to the production of commodities for continental or world trade. The exchange value of female slaves continued to exceed that of males by a factor of between 10 percent and 50 percent. Age and physical attributes affected individual cases, but the gender disparity remains pervasive in recorded prices.

The newly enslaved females who had the best chances of survival were young (probably prepubescent) and hardy enough to travel by foot. They came

A nineteenth-century photograph of a group of female slaves held in chains on the island of Zanzibar. [Bojan Brecelj/ Corbis]

into the possession of traders in a number of ways: as a result of violence, dislocation, and the indebtedness of male relatives. The trauma of initial slavery was registered by their being witnesses to the murder and abandonment of older women and infants. Sexual advances could not be refused, although narratives of slavery do not stress this kind of violation. The chances for greater security depended upon the social setting to which the slave girl became attached.

A considerable but unmeasurable number of female slaves became absorbed into small-scale household units of production and were assimilated to the status of wife, a category that contained a greater degree of inequality and potentially arbitrary treatment than the society openly acknowledged. In fact, a deterioration of the normative security of wives was noted in the advantages men found in acquiring slave wives who were unequivocally dependent on them. The case of the Bakongo of West Central Africa suggests that, whereas this matrilineal society honored sisters, wives came increasingly to be treated as slaves, whether purchased as such or not.

A further analysis of slavery and polygyny is overdue. In the nineteenth century, the logic of polygyny was reenforced by the availability of slave women in areas not earlier subject to commercial trade. The attendant influx of caravans required provisioning and other services provided by broker chiefs. Women supplied most of the labor thus entailed. Outsiders observed very swollen households of female dependents, yet only the women themselves could have testified to their degree of servility or vulnerability to arbitrary sale or transfer as a gift.

The benefits of slave women's services did not all go to the men. Female slave servants permitted women as owners or relatives of the owners to enjoy greater leisure, withdrawing from the drudgery of daily life. Two consequences were interrelated, for as a differentiated stratum of high-status women enjoyed the life of self-conscious civilization marked by housing, clothing, and elite associations, they became interdependent with a subculture of slave women, who for their part could form associations which became public performance groups, as well as being identified as servants to the upper class in a variety of reproductive functions. Muslim women in Mombasa, East Africa, have been most closely studied for such slave-free interrelations among women. Women of inherited slave status belonging to aristocratic families in Mali banded together to sing publicly of their collective superiority to women owned by commoners. Bearing in mind the priority given here to the newly incorporated slave, the questions of socialization into such collectivities within structurally unequal, frequently Muslim society become ever more vital to pursue.

As western Africa after midcentury adjusted to the ending of transatlantic slave trade, the internal slave trade persisted, with prices supported by the labor demands of producers of legitimate export commodities and the vibrancy of the desert-side economy. Artisanal production flourished. Non-Muslim slave women as agriculturalists provided the food for specialist producers. Women slaves also performed such female tasks as preparing thread for weavers. On the East African coast and islands, plantation economies favored slave family reproduction. Women nevertheless bore a full share of plantation labor. It has yet to be resolved whether the low birthrate of many slave women was a result of choice, their physical hardships, or the priority given to their labor over childbearing.

In one exceptional case sex was a defining factor in the potential elevation of female slave status: the Kingdom of Dahomey. Kings there employed women slaves as warriors and functionaries and rewarded their distinguished service.

The slavery of women in Africa remains a significant issue because it sharpens the questions that must be asked about the status and condition of nominally free wives. The evidence of women as slaves and former slaves in the period after the abolition of overt trade in Africa provides a wealth of information exposing either the extreme difficulties and vulnerability of poor women or the arbitrariness still to be found in their continuing dependence upon the families of owners. What is lost in later former-slave narratives is the rawness of extraction from a familial setting, the discovery by girls that they were sold and might be resold, and the threatening object lessons as they witnessed the death of women and children whom it became inexpedient for traders to preserve. Many did not acquiesce and took advantage of institutional ambiguity where slavery had not yet become an economic system. In nineteenth-century conditions, women as slaves were important above all in production, of various types, yet their consciousness and exploitability were nevertheless grounded in their being female and in their cultural definition within the spheres of reproduction.

See also HOUSEHOLD SLAVES; SEXUAL EXPLOITATION.

BIBLIOGRAPHY

Falola, Toyin, and Paul E. Lovejoy, eds. *Pawnship in Africa: Debt Bondage in Historical Perspective.* 1994.

Lovejoy, Paul, and Jan S. Hogendorn. *Slow Death for Slavery: The Course of Abolition in Northern Nigeria, 1897–1936.* 1993.

Miers, Suzanne, and Igor Kopytoff, eds. *Slavery in Africa.* 1977.

Miers, Suzanne, and Richard Roberts, eds. *The Ending of Slavery in Africa.* 1988.

ROBERTSON, CLAIRE, and MARTIN KLEIN, eds. *Women and Slavery in Africa.* 1983.

TWADDLE, MICHAEL, ed. *The Wages of Slavery: From Chattel Slavery to Wage Labour in Africa, the Caribbean and England.* 1993.

WRIGHT, MARCIA. *Strategies of Slaves and Women: Life Stories from East-Central Africa.* 1993.

Marcia Wright

African-American Perspectives on Slavery

See Perspectives on Slavery.

African Methodist Episcopal Church

See Churches, African-American.

Africa Squadron

In 1842, as part of the Webster-Ashburton Treaty, the United States and England approved a joint squadron plan intended to resolve their longtime disagreements over mutual searches on the high seas and put an end to the African slave trade. Following an idea

Daniel Webster. [The National Archives/Corbis]

first propounded by Secretary of State John Quincy Adams in the 1820s, Daniel Webster (holding the same position) in 1841 proposed a joint cruising arrangement whereby the two nations would assign pairs of vessels to work together patrolling the waters along the West African coast.

But the "African squadron clause" proved a failure. Article 8 stipulated that each nation assign a naval force of at least eighty guns along the West African coast. Each remained responsible for only its own laws, although the two could cooperate when necessary. The United States, however, did not fulfill its part of the agreement—primarily because of southerners in the Congress who were concerned that Britain's assault on the African slave trade might turn to an attack on the institution of slavery itself. Admittedly, part of the United States' failure was attributable to the fact that from 1843 to the outbreak of the Civil War in 1861, its small navy focused less on squelching the slave trade than on safeguarding other types of commerce along the West African coast. But during this same period, six of nine secretaries of the navy were from the South and two others openly supported southern interests. Whereas the United States after 1847 seldom had more than five ships in African waters, Britain and France maintained at least twenty-five.

In 1853, southern congressmen succeeded in cutting the annual appropriation for the joint squadron by more than fifty percent. Indeed, they even tried to abrogate the treaty provision and to replace the death penalty for slaving with life imprisonment. Although they failed in both efforts, the United States government only authorized one American slave trader for execution, in 1862. That same year, the United States and England agreed to the Seward-Lyons Treaty, which permitted mutual searches in peacetime and marked a major step toward the eradication of the African slave trade. Effective American action against the illegal practice did not begin until 1863, when President Abraham Lincoln announced the Emancipation Proclamation.

See also CREOLE INCIDENT; SLAVE TRADE; WEBSTER-ASHBURTON TREATY.

BIBLIOGRAPHY

JONES, HOWARD. *To the Webster-Ashburton Treaty: A Study in Anglo-American Relations, 1783–1843.* 1977.

JONES, HOWARD, and DONALD A. RAKESTRAW. *Prologue to Manifest Destiny: Anglo-American Relations in the 1840s.* 1997.

Howard Jones

Agricultural Slavery

See Plantations

Alabama

The War of 1812 marked the turning point in Alabama slavery. Anglo-America seized Spanish Mobile, giving itself a port through which it could ship produce; it wrested millions of acres from the Indians, on which to expand its plantation system; and it had a crop compatible with the soil and climate, cotton. Agricultural slavery, which the French, English, and Spanish had toyed with unsuccessfully for nearly a century, became the linchpin of a new regime.

The growth of slavery reflected the nineteenth century's symbiotic relationship between agriculture, industry, and labor. Eli Whitney's gin made cotton a profitable market crop, but manufacturing that fiber required new industrial technology. It took improvements in transportation to speed delivery of raw materials to textile mills in the northern United States and Europe. It took the harnessing of steam to power both ships and plants. It took a worldwide public hunger for consumer goods. And it took land—lots of land—which Alabama and other new territories supplied. Slaves were just another factor of production within runaway industrial development, but international economic growth rested upon their shoulders.

The humans who bore this burden were primarily African; Indian slavery in Alabama never amounted to more than a few dozen domestic workers in colonial Mobile. The 1800 census of the new Mississippi Territory (including Alabama above Mobile) counted only 494 blacks—virtually all slaves. By 1860 that population had exploded a thousandfold, to 435,080 slaves.

Alabama's post-1815 development means that it played a scant role in the African slave trade. Illegal trade is documented only in the 1859 *Clotilde* incident, wherein contraband cargo was freed and settled on the outskirts of Mobile ("Africky Town"). The 1870 census tally of only 237 blacks listing Africa as a

An 1861 woodcut depicts an auction at a slave market in Montgomery, Alabama. [Corbis-Bettmann]

birthplace supports the assumption of minimal slave importation in Alabama.

Slavery in Alabama was concentrated in two alluvial crescents. The primary zone, the fabled Black Belt—named for the soil, not the population as commonly believed—lay in the south between the Tombigbee and Alabama Rivers, which flowed into Mobile Bay. The second area was the Tennessee River Valley of northern Alabama. In both regions it was soil and market accessibility that lured planters, but those magnets drew even larger numbers of merchants, craftsmen, and yeomen.

Cotton-rich though Alabama was, slave owners were a definite minority, and the super-rich were exceedingly rare. Through the 1840s Alabama was a frontier in flux; even in the 1850s it was far from a fully developed slave economy. By 1860 only a third of the state's households included even one slave, and planters with at least fifty slaves and five hundred acres constituted only three-tenths of one percent of the population. Some aristocratic planters from the seaboard South relocated in Alabama, but most slave owners were nouveau riche, and some of the largest planting operations were owned by men of northern birth.

Many unanswered questions remain about slavery in Alabama. The study of wealthy Alabama slave owners in both New England and the Mid-Atlantic is yet in its nascence. Their attitudes and their political impact—upon race relations, secession, and the war—remain undefined. The small but steady growth of the free Negro class (from 571 in 1820 to 2,690 in 1860) belies the cliché that free Negroes were systematically driven from the South. The contradictions between

Table 1. Alabama Slavery, 1810–1860.

Year	Free White	Free Colored	Slave	Total
1820	85,461	571	41,879	127,901
1830	190,406	1,572	117,549	309,527
1840	335,185	2,039	253,532	590,756
1850	426,514[1]	2,265[1]	342,844	771,623
1860	526,271[2]	2,690[2]	435,080	964,201

1. Dwellings of whites and free colored = 73,070.
2. Dwellings of white and free colored = 96,682.

antimanumission laws and the indulgent social attitudes, which generated this population's growth, remain unsettled.

See also the individual entries on the other states of the United States.

BIBLIOGRAPHY

MILLS, GARY B. "Miscegenation and the Free Negro in Antebellum 'Anglo' Alabama: A Reexamination of Southern Relations." *Journal of American History* 68 (1981): 16–34. Reprinted in *Free Blacks in a Slave Society*, edited by Paul Finkelman. 1989. Volume 17 of *Articles on American Slavery.*
SELLARS, JAMES B. *Slavery in Alabama.* 1950.

Gary B. Mills

Albornoz, Bartolomé de   [fl. 1550–1575]

Spanish critic of the slave trade.

Bartolomé de Albornoz was a scholar associated with the University of Mexico at its founding in 1551; he was its first professor of law. His major work, *Arte de los contratos*, published in Valencia in 1573, contained a treatise entitled "De la esclavitud," a sharp attack on the Atlantic slave trade.

Albornoz questioned the legality of holding slaves as persons ostensibly justly captured in war. He pointed out that slave purchasers generally were ignorant of whether such circumstances applied to those they bought, and that such logic could in no case apply to noncombatants, such as women and children. He likewise disputed the contention that the Christianization of Africans justified their enslavement, noting that no proof existed for the claim that slavery was necessary to produce conversions, and decrying the unwillingness of the clergy to go to Africa and seek conversation there. While Albornoz did not call for the emancipation of slaves, he strongly affirmed Africans' right to natural liberty, and he urged merchants to avoid investing in the sinful slave trade.

Albornoz commented on and sharpened the critique of slavery offered in *Suma de Tratos y Contratos* (1569) by Tomás de Mercado, another Spaniard who had lived in Mexico. Both men may have been moved by the growth of a slave trade to Mexico, carried on by officially sanctioned Portuguese traders, as well as by English and Dutch interlopers. Albornoz's stern condemnation of the slave trade did not reach a wide European audience: his work was not translated, and it was banned by the Inquisition.

See also MERCADO, TOMÁS DE; PERSPECTIVES ON SLAVERY; SLAVE TRADE; SPAIN.

BIBLIOGRAPHY

BLACKBURN, ROBIN. *The Making of Colonial Slavery, 1492–1800.* 1997.

DAVIS, DAVID BRION. *The Problem of Slavery in Western Culture.* 1966.

T. Stephen Whitman

Ambar, Malik   [ca. 1550–1626]

African ruler in India.

Malik Ambar was born free in the Ethiopian region of Harar around 1550 under the name Shambu. Sold into slavery in the Arab world, he converted to Islam while living at the Yemeni port of Mocha, where he received an education in finance and public affairs. He was taken to India by a slave dealer in the 1570s and sold to a minister of the king of Ahmadnagar. While remaining legally a slave, by 1590 Ambar had risen to prominence in several central Indian kingdoms as a leader of mercenary soldiers, a life path that had been open to African slave-soldiers in Islamic-ruled areas of India from as early as the 1200s.

In the 1590s Ambar established himself as an independent army leader and shed his slave status. By 1602 he had returned to Ahmadnagar, where he staged a coup, imprisoned the king, and named himself regent. Malik Ambar used his power to resist Mughal expansion, defeating armies of Akbar, Jahangir, and Shah Jahan over the next twenty years. He cemented his rule by reforming tax and land-use policies; by spreading administrative appointments among Brahmins, Arabs, and Persians; and by purchasing Afro-Indian slaves, who served as his personal guard.

Ambar left a mark on Ahmadnagar, constructing mosques and his own tomb of black stone and as a patron of literary and cultural revival. While some of his Indian contemporaries detested his blackness, most regarded him as an exemplary leader and lauded his rise to power as unique for a former African slave.

See also INDIAN SUBCONTINENT.

BIBLIOGRAPHY

HARRIS, JOSEPH E. *The African Presence in Asia.* 1971.

T. Stephen Whitman

American and Foreign Anti-Slavery Society

Founded by the evangelicals Amos Phelps, Joshua Leavitt, James G. Birney, and Lewis and Arthur Tappan, the American and Foreign Anti-Slavery Society formed when these men walked out of the 1840 annual meeting of the American Anti-Slavery Society to protest both "ultra" denunciations of churches as proslavery and the old organization's endorsement of women's rights. While managing to attract transatlantic support for a protracted court battle to return the survivors of the *Amistad* slave ship to their African homes, the new organization never developed the wide network of antislavery auxiliaries that had provided grassroots support for the American Anti-Slavery Society. Their headquarters remained in New York, where meetings were held until 1854. Members like Birney and Henry Stanton gave more time to Liberty Party politics than to the new society, and efforts to build female auxiliaries as active as those in the old organization failed. Their official, though sporadic, publications included the *American and Foreign Anti-Slavery Reporter* and the *Liberty Almanac*.

These evangelicals did continue to press for antislavery policies at denominational meetings, particularly in the decade prior to the Civil War. After failing to gain concessions from any mainline churches, the Tappans in 1846 organized the American Missionary Association (AMA) for the purpose of providing "Bibles for slaves" and support for antislavery ministers. The longest-lasting of U.S. antislavery organizations, the AMA worked after the Civil War to recruit teachers and fund schools for freedmen. The records of these efforts and those of many associated black colleges are held in the AMA collection, Amistad Center, Tulane University.

See also ABOLITION AND ANTISLAVERY MOVEMENTS; AMISTAD; AMERICAN ANTI-SLAVERY SOCIETY.

BIBLIOGRAPHY

JOHNSON, CLIFTON H. *The American Missionary Association, 1846–1861: A Study of Christian Abolitionism.* 1958.
WYATT-BROWN, BERTRAM. *Lewis Tappan and the Evangelical War against Slavery.* 1969.

Deborah Bingham Van Broekhoven

American Anti-Slavery Society

Founded on 4 December 1833 in Philadelphia, the American Anti-Slavery Society brought together abolitionists who until this point had worked through an uncoordinated network of local and state organizations. Guided chiefly by New York businessmen Arthur and Lewis Tappan and by William Lloyd Garrison, editor of *The Liberator*, delegates adopted a constitution and commissioned Garrison to write a "Declaration of Sentiments," which pledged them to work toward ending slavery immediately and gaining "rights and privileges" for free blacks. They also promised to circulate missionary agents and tracts; to help organize local auxiliaries "in every city, town, and village"; and to enlist churches in their moral campaign.

Between 1834 and 1838 the society circulated thousands of tracts, and several antislavery newspaper and periodicals, employing one hundred agents. Their official organ was the *National Anti-Slavery Standard*, but many copies of the *Liberator* were also distributed. The burning of abolitionist mail sent to Charleston, South Carolina, in 1835, followed by postal restrictions on the free distribution of controversial literature, led the leaders to refocus on petitioning Congress, which they argued had the power to abolish slavery in the District of Columbia and the territories. By 1836 congressmen were annoyed, especially with the hundreds of women who were circulating and signing thousands of petitions. The result was a series of infamous gag rules, not lifted until 1844, which automatically tabled any petition mentioning slavery. Inadvertently, this gag popularized the idea that Southerners were determined to suppress the free speech of whites, not just antislavery activity.

In 1840 disagreements about both the role of women and that of politics resulted in schism and a second impromptu organization, the American and Foreign Anti-Slavery Organization. While losing some financial, most church, and much black support, the American Anti-Slavery Society continued to circulate agents like the popular Abby Kelley and Wendell Phillips right up to the Civil War.

See also ABOLITION AND ANTISLAVERY MOVEMENTS; AMERICAN AND FOREIGN ANTI-SLAVERY SOCIETY; GARRISON, WILLIAM LLOYD; PHILLIPS, WENDELL; TAPPAN BROTHERS.

BIBLIOGRAPHY

KRADITOR, AILEEN. *Means and Ends in American Abolitionism: Garrison and His Critics on Strategy and Tactics, 1834–1850.* 1969.
STEWART, JAMES BREWER. *William Lloyd Garrison and the Challenge of Emancipation.* 1992.

Deborah Bingham Van Broekhoven

American Colonization Society

Founded by a coalition of former Federalists, evangelicals, and upper-South cosmopolitans in December 1816, the American Society for Colonizing the Free People of Color was for a brief time a politically powerful organization that promoted the removal of free blacks to western Africa. Supreme Court Justice Bushrod Washington served as its first president, while the then House Speaker Henry Clay and (society founder) Congressman Charles Fenton Mercer of Virginia ran the Board of Managers, the governing

An 1838 broadside issued by the American Anti-Slavery Society in its fight to abolish slavery. [Library of Congress/Corbis]

body of the society. On January 1819, at the request of the society, Congress allocated one hundred thousand dollars to facilitate removal and pay the salary of a colonial agent in Africa; Eli Ayers later purchased most of Liberia at gunpoint for less than three hundred dollars.

Because many northern black leaders had for several decades considered the notion of a mass return to Africa, several influential freemen, including Paul Cuffe, a successful merchant with commercial ties to Africa, initially made overtures to northern philanthropists connected with the society. In the South, former slaves who concluded that they would never be allowed to prosper in a country that guaranteed equality only to whites often proved willing to accept the society's assistance in starting anew in a foreign land. But once it became clear that no African-Americans would be allowed to hold leadership posts in the society, the free black community began to separate from the organization. Most of the society's leaders were petty slaveholders who resorted to crudely racist arguments to justify the removal of free blacks, and because the organization hoped that all freedpersons could be prodded into leaving the United States, society spokesmen refused to fight the segregation emerging in the North.

Philadelphia's energetic free community took the lead in denouncing the society. On 15 January 1817, just days after the society was founded, Richard Allen organized a meeting of over one thousand blacks at his Bethel church to condemn the ACS and announce their determination to remain in the land of their birth. *Freedom's Journal,* the United States' first national black newspaper, was initially an anticolonization publication; the *Journal* lost its readership shortly after editor John Russworm altered his stance and began to write editorials in support of the ACS. Ensuing black newspapers and pamphlets, including David Walker's 1829 *Appeal to the Colored Citizens of the World,* were consistently hostile to any plan for emigration directed by a white-run organization.

The ACS, however, was never the planter-run society that Walker and its abolitionist critics depicted it to be, and modern assertions that proslavery theorists backed the ACS in hopes of removing dangerous free blacks are largely without foundation. In Virginia, proslavery politicians like John Tyler and Abel Upshur hoped to use the organization to rid their state of free blacks. But despite the racist tone of their rhetoric, many white colonizationists harbored progressive views of black activities. Society spokesmen argued that southern poverty was not the result of alleged African-American incompetence, but rather that the institution of slavery deprived blacks of both

Edward Everett, a renowned orator of the nineteenth century, delivers an address to a meeting of the American Colonization Society. [Corbis-Bettmann]

the incentives and the education that made northern workers so productive. Because many border state colonizationists boldly advocated the elimination of the entire African-American labor force, bond and free, in the name of regional prosperity, planter politicians like Robert Turnbull of South Carolina bitterly castigated the organization as an "Abolition Society."

In response to Lower South demands, President Andrew Jackson ceased all federal aid to the society in 1830, after which the organization ceased to be a viable part of the antislavery movement. In 1832, Maryland's legislature seceded from the parent body and incorporated a state society. The following year, William Jay and James G. Birney publicly abandoned the organization. (William Lloyd Garrison had ended his brief flirtation with the society in 1829.) In hopes of regaining its northern support, the ACS unsuccessfully tried to appease the American Anti-Slavery Society by firing five southern board members. The ACS continued to exist formally until 1899, but over the course of the nineteenth century only 15,386 free blacks and former slaves migrated to Liberia.

See also ABOLITION AND ANTISLAVERY MOVEMENTS; AMERICAN ANTI-SLAVERY SOCIETY; BIRNEY, JAMES G.; GARRISON, WILLIAM LLOYD; LIBERIA; REPATRIATION TO AFRICA.

BIBLIOGRAPHY

EGERTON, DOUGLAS. "Averting a *Crisis*: The Proslavery Critique of the American Colonization Society." *Civil War History* 43 (1997): 141–155.

———. *Charles Fenton Mercer and the Trial of National Conservatism.* 1989.

STAUDENRAUS, PHILIP. *The African Colonization Movement, 1816–1865.* 1961.

TYLER-McGRAW, MARIE. "Richmond Free Blacks and African Colonization." *Journal of American Studies* 21 (1987): 210–217.

Douglas R. Egerton

American Indians

See Amerindian Societies; Native Americans.

American Revolution

The Revolutionary War posed a severe challenge to slavery: thousands of blacks escaped from bondage while thousands more gained greater autonomy within slavery. But in the longer term, the Revolution strengthened slavery and sped its growth in the new United States.

In the late colonial era, disputes over regulating the slave trade helped bring forth the Revolution. British vetoes of colonial proposals to tax slave imports led the Continental Congress to urge the nonimportation of slaves. Calls for resistance to British policies were fueled by metaphorical references to slavery as the fate awaiting colonists if they submitted to British power. Virginia's Governor Dunmore's recruitment of slaves in 1775 and his formation of an "Ethiopian Regiment," intended to cow rebellious planters, would be categorized in the Declaration of Independence as "exciting domestic insurrections," and listed as a justification for revolution.

During the war, both sides enlisted slaves as soldiers. In 1779 General Clinton's Philipsburg Proclamation offered to arm and free slaves who fought for Britain. The Continental Army and individual state regiments, especially in New England, recruited slaves. Some blacks gained freedom; others remained slaves but earned bounties or service exemption for their masters.

Blacks served as infantrymen, cooks, sailors, and pilots. One ex-slave, styled "Colonel Tye," led raids on New Jersey slaveholders and helped slaves escape to the British until his death in action. All together,

approximately twenty thousand blacks fought in the Revolution, about two-thirds for the British.

British strategy acknowledged slavery's importance: the 1778 decision to shift the war south stressed regaining control of revenue from slave-grown tobacco, rice, and indigo, as well as the belief that southerners' fears of slave insurrections would weaken resistance. But General Clinton's appeal to slaves alarmed slaveholders, pushing many into supporting the Revolution. Ultimately, the strategy may thus have contributed to the defeat of the British. After the war, the British evacuated more than ten thousand blacks to England, Nova Scotia, Jamaica, and Sierra Leone.

Besides those who enlisted, thousands more blacks sought freedom as civilians behind British lines, passed for free in American territory, or set up as maroons (communities of runaways that evaded or resisted white control) in the southern backcountry. Those who remained with masters used the threat of flight to bargain for better lives: dramatic increases in slaves learning trades, hiring themselves out, and obtaining freedom by self-purchase or manumission all date from the revolutionary era, and all contributed to the weakening of masters' control.

Some masters took slaves to Kentucky, Tennessee, and the western Carolinas to avoid wartime losses. After independence was gained, the absence of British restraint on occupying Indian lands in the old Southwest cleared the path for a rapid expansion of slavery: as early as 1790, the slave population of 698,000 considerably exceeded that of the 1770s. In the northern states, slavery was put on the road to extinction, beginning during the war years, by constitutional provisions and gradual emancipation laws inspired partly by black pressure for freedom, and partly by white endorsement of revolutionary principles. But in both the North and the South, whites reconciled support for individual liberty with the continuation of slavery by stigmatizing blacks as racially inferior beings unworthy of freedom. The Revolution thus indirectly contributed to strengthening racist concepts of human nature and freedom in the nineteenth century.

See also MAROONS; MILITARY SLAVES; UNITED STATES.

BIBLIOGRAPHY

DAVIS, DAVID BRION. *The Problem of Slavery in the Age of Revolution.* 1975.

FINKLEMAN, PAUL. *Slavery and the Founders: Race and Liberty in the Age of Jefferson.* 1996.

FREY, SYLVIA R. *Water from the Rock: Black Resistance in a Revolutionary Age.* 1991.

QUARLES, BENJAMIN. *The Negro in the American Revolution.* 1961.

T. Stephen Whitman

Americans, Pre-Columbian

See Amerindian Societies; Native Americans.

Amerindian Societies

This entry includes the following articles: Precontact; Postcontact.

Precontact

While never practicing the widespread, market-based chattel slavery of classical antiquity or the early modern European world, many Amerindian societies did use various war-captive systems. These may be analyzed with the tools that students of slavery usually bring to their task. In most cases, the war-captive complexes did contain familiar elements: often permanent and violent domination, natal alienation (removal from society of birth), and, if captives were not subject to ritualized retributive death, social assimilation within categories beneath those of the "host" society. In some complex cultures like the classical Maya, the Zapotec, and the Mexica (Aztec), the war-captive complex was so central to the functioning of the society that it can be considered an ideological and hierarchical keystone. As social units, however, rather than labor units, war-captive "slaves" would have differing experiences, depending upon sex, age, and the socio-ritualistic framework of assimilation. Women and children more often than not would become members of the capturing society through marriage and adoption rituals, while adult men would more likely become subjects of sacrificial rituals.

Judging from the prevalence of mixed-descent motifs and "outsider" clan ancestresses in indigenous origin narratives, the cultural assimilation of captured women and children seems ubiquitous throughout the Americas. This phenomenon often takes on cosmological significance for specific groups. The Zunis of present-day New Mexico enact one aspect of their origins in the kan'a:kwe ("enemy ancestors") ceremony, which features three Sacred Lake *kachinas* (sacred dancers) held captive and ultimately integrated through ritual practice in the emergence of Zunis onto the earth, and through which Zunis acquire the mixed farming and hunting skills necessary for their survival. Skidi Pawnees of the Plains Village culture area ritually sacrificed captives in their "Morning Star" ceremony, in which the (male, Pawnee) Morning Star pursues and subdues the (female, captive, non-Pawnee) Evening Star and thereby infuses Pawnee society with new life. Regarding an even more widespread pattern of incorporating outsiders, nineteenth-century American ethnographers estimated that as many as one-

third of Diné (Navajo) clans traced themselves back to non-Diné clan ancestresses, at least some of whom fit into the Diné linguistic category *naalté*, "slave."

Raiding for and assimilating women and children probably occurred throughout the Americas, if traditions as widely dispersed as those of the Yanomami of Brazil and the Tlingit and Haida of northwestern North America may serve as representative examples. But it took organized warfare between complex societies to elevate the scale and numbers of capture to the point where we might consider the term "slave system" applicable, insofar as the phenomenon was central to the everyday functioning of society. The ritual decapitation of male war captives was widespread in Mesoamerica, beginning perhaps as early as the Archaic period (5,000–1,500 B.C.), with the hunters and gatherers of the central valley of Mexico.

But with more complex societies—for example, among the Zapotec of Monte Albán (Oaxaca state)—for example, in the sixth century B.C.—iconographic

The figures from the Temple of the Danzantes in Oaxaca, Mexico. Many believe that they represent captives as victims of human sacrifice. [Charles and Josette Lenars/ Corbis]

representations show that such practices had become part of the ritual structure—the famous stone tableau of *danzantes* ("dancers") at Monte Albán almost certainly shows war captives in various stages of bondage, torture, and sacrifice. So too with the classic Maya (A.D. 250–800) of southern Mexico and Guatemala, where rulers of city-states like Tikal, Bonampak, and Copan made the humiliation and sacrifice of captives a prominent part of their claim to martial prestige and nobility. With hieroglyphs including the noun *bac* ("bone, captive") and verbs like *chuc-ah* ("capture"), legendary figures like Pacal of Palenque used honorific phrases like "he of twenty captives" in their monumental stelae and frescoes, a clear indication that the ability to subjugate, humiliate, and sacrifice prominent men from warring city-states figured significantly in their status as rulers. Although scholars have generally thought such captive-systems were restricted to relatively small-scale seizure of elite warlords, whose subordination brought symbolic honor to the victor, some suggest today that the numbers may have been much larger and may have included rank-and-file fighters who were spared death if needed as labor in the construction of Maya monumental architecture.

A massive increase in the numerical scale of capture certainly accompanied the emergence of the Mexica (Aztec) Empire (ca. A.D. 1400–1520) in the central valley of Mexico. Descended from a relatively small group of Chichimec nomadic fighters and mercenaries who merged both diplomatically and through lineage marriages with earlier residents of the valley, the Mexica brought the captive system associated with human sacrifice to its fullest expression in the New World. If archaeological evidence, Aztec chronicles, and Spanish observers can be believed (each contains pitfalls), by the early sixteenth century the empire required thousands of war captives each year for sacrifice in what some scholars have described as a "unified imperialist cult." Through their "flowery wars" with other city-states they obtained male captives who were killed to meet the need of the pantheon of Aztec gods for blood. This demand grew so great as the century progressed that a class of slave-merchants seem to have emerged, to discover and expand market alternatives to ritualized warfare. By 1520 the need for captives began to interfere with another imperial requirement, tributary payments from subjugated states—a contradiction that some analysts see as central to the fragile condition of Aztec society as the moment of its contact with Spanish colonialism.

Slavery could occur within Aztec society as well, however. The most famous case is that of Malantzin, or "La Malinche," a Nahua-speaking Aztec girl sold into slavery with the coastal Maya by her own family to simplify an inheritance. Given as a gift to Hernando Cortés, "Doña Marina" served as an interpreter for the conquest, a consort to Cortés, and a symbolic mother to mestizo Mexicans. Her life and her ambiguous place in the narrative of Mexican racial politics serve as perhaps the best example of the tenuous position from which Amerindian slavery encountered the slave systems of the Atlantic world.

See also ENSLAVEMENT, METHODS OF; NATIVE AMERICANS.

BIBLIOGRAPHY

CLENDINNEN, INGA. *Aztecs: An Interpretation.* 1991.
CONRAD, GEOFFREY W., and ARTHUR A. DEMAREST. *Religion and Empire: The Dynamics of Aztec and Inca Expansion.* 1984.
COE, MICHAEL D. *Breaking the Maya Code.* 1994.
———. *The Maya.* 1956.
CYPESS, SANDRA MESSINGER. *La Malinche in Mexican Literature: From History to Myth.* 1991.
DEL CHAMBERLAIN, VON. *When Stars Came Down to Earth: Cosmology of the Skidi Pawnee Indians of North America.* 1982.
MOSER, CHRISTOPHER L. *Human Decapitation in Ancient Mesoamerica.* 1973.
SCHELE, LINDA, with DAVID FREIDEL. *Forest of Kings: The Untold Story of the Ancient Maya.* 1990.

James F. Brooks

Postcontact

European colonization dramatically transformed the systems of inequality and subjugation that had existed in the Americas before 1492. In some cases the initial mesh went easily, but in others the chattel nature of European slavery challenged and corrupted the Amerindian slave systems that had been mitigated by their association with indigenous kinship systems. In some cases, however, Amerindian slavery proved remarkably durable, and ended only with application of a combination of moral and military force similar to what brought an end to the enslavement of Africans in the Americas.

In central Mexico, Spanish conquest eliminated the practice of sacrificing war captives, but a continuing desire for Indian slaves as laborers actually extended slave-raiding in networks vaster than those of the Aztec empire. Working with Indian military allies like the Tlaxcalans, Spanish raiders utilized the doctrine of "just war" to enslave peripheral Indian peoples both north and south of the central valley. The practice was especially brutal in the northern territories of the Gran Chichimeca, where conquest and enslavement were the principal means of subduing nomadic peoples, only slightly touched by continuous injunctions from the church (especially after the sixteenth-century Las Casas-Sepulveda debates) to treat Indians humanely and release them from bondage once they were "settled and civilized." Even after Indian slavery was abolished in the 1550s, the practice persisted in the hinterlands, most notably with the creation of "slave militaries" like the *nijoras* of Sonora and the *genízaros* of New Mexico. Although driven by Spanish colonialism, much of the actual capture and sale of Indian slaves occurred at the hands of neighboring Indian groups.

The colony of New Mexico had biennial trade fairs called *rescates* ("ransoms") at which equestrian nomads like the Comanches and Kiowas would bring captive Apaches, Pawnees, and Jumanos for sale to Spanish administrators and priests. These "ransoms" were ostensibly for the purpose of rescuing the captives from the horrors of barbarian slavery, and the ransom price was understood to be retirable by service of the ransomed to their rescuers. In practice, however, few such slaves ever experienced freedom.

Indians were not the only target of enslavement. Throughout the eighteenth and nineteenth centuries Spanish subjects living in hinterland villages also became vulnerable to Indian slave raids, and several thousand found themselves seized and assimilated into Comanche, Kiowa, and Navajo societies through the mixed system of violent capture, adoption, or marriage. So damaging to Mexican settlements were these dynamics that the Treaty of Guadelupe-Hidalgo (1848) included a clause in which the United States agreed to inderdict Indian raiders and to undertake the ransom of Mexican citizens from Plains tribes. The pattern ended only with the military subjugation of the Plains in the 1870s.

Euroamerican colonization influenced Amerindian slavery elsewhere in North America. Iroquoian peoples in the Northeast had long sacrificed war captives or assimilated them (or both) in their "Mourning Wars," but with the Fur Wars of the seventeenth century this relatively small-scale pattern intensified and extended deep into the interior. Huron villagers linked in alliance to the French through Jesuit missions and fur trading found themselves nearly obliterated by Iroquois raiders, and those who survived did so through large-scale adoptions into the Iroquois League. By the early years of the eighteenth century this slaving network extended onto the Great Plains. "Panis" (Pawnees) became a generic term for Plains village slaves taken from locations along the Platte and Missouri rivers and traded through networks as far east as French Canada, where they were used as substitutes in diplomatic exchanges between rival Indian groups—some allied with the British and others with the French. Some Plains Indian captive women found themselves traded down the Mississippi and as far distant as Cuba, where they were exchanged for Christianized (and marriageable) Cuban women.

In the Southeast, Indian traditions of assimilating war captives met and merged over time with the introduction of African slaves into the region. Groups like the Cherokees had maintained a social category, *atsi nahas'i*, into which captives were incorporated, a status outside Cherokee kin and clan systems, but with mitigating relations of reciprocity between owner and captive. European colonization first stimulated widespread slaving wars between Indian groups for captives to sell to settlers, but by the later years of the seventeenth century planters deemed importation of African slaves a more reliable method of maintaining a permanent labor force on the landscape. This did not relieve Indian groups from the effects of slavery, however, for peoples like the Cherokees, Choctaws, and Creeks served variously as slave-catchers for coastal plantations, or occasionally as a refuge for fugitive Africans. In time each of these groups had to make choices regarding the adoption of chattel African slavery themselves. In most cases, prominent mixed-blood (white-Indian) families introduced African slavery into Indian societies. The legacy was ongoing factional fighting and in some cases all-out civil war between slaveholding and nonslaveholding members of these "civilized tribes."

It was in the Pacific northwest that Amerindian slavery emerged in the most elaborate form, through contact with Euroamericans. Native coastal peoples like the Tlingits, Haislas, Haidas, and Tsimshains all held war captives as slaves. In these affluent, stratified cultures, slaves served as a widely recognized symbol of wealth. With the advent of a Euroamerican maritime trade in fish and furs after 1780, the indigenous slave system became interlocked with the world economy. Indian slaves were now both social units of wealth and prestige, and also valuable laborers in the nascent commercial economy. Slaving depots and networks were now concentrated at the mouth of the Columbia River among the Chinooks, who pursued new slaves as far inland as the Columbia Plateau. The Dalles of the Columbia became a central slave market. As new wealth poured into the Pacific Northwest, long-term customs of reciprocal gift-giving (potlatching) became increasingly competitive and ostentatious, to the point that the execution of slaves was one way a potlatcher could demonstrate his inexhaustible wealth. American and British reformers seized upon this striking, though minor, aspect of the potlatch to justify its general suppression after 1900.

Perhaps one of the most painful ironies of Amerindian slavery is the question of African slavery among the Five Tribes of Indian Territory (Oklahoma) after 1865. Slaveholding Indians had sided with the Confederacy and in their defeat had a unique sanction imposed upon them. The Union required that these

Sacagawea, a member of the Lemhi Shoshones, was captured by Hidatsa raiders who sold her to a French Canadian trader. Sacagawea later served as a translator for the expedition of Meriwether Lewis and William Clark. [Corbis-Bettmann]

tribes adopt their former slaves as tribal members, with full rights of citizenship. Although this was accomplished on paper, continuing social and racial prejudice blocked many Indian freedmen from actual tribal citizenship. Where adoption had once been an Indian method of voluntarily assimilating war captives, it now stands as an unwelcome and unresolved source of friction within these Indian nations today.

See also CHATTEL SLAVERY; ENSLAVEMENT, METHODS OF; NATIVE AMERICANS.

BIBLIOGRAPHY

BROOKS, JAMES F. "'This Evil Extends Especially to the Feminine Sex': Negotiating Captivity in the New Mexico Borderlands." *Feminist Studies* 22, no. 2. (Summer 1996).

DEMOS, JOHN. *The Unredeemed Captive: A Family Story from Early America.* 1994.

FORBES, JACK D. *Apache, Navaho, and Spaniard.* 1960.

MERRELL, JAMES H. *The Indians' New World: Catawbas and Their Neighbors from European Contact through the Era of Removal.* 1989.

PERDUE, THEDA. *Slavery and the Evolution of Cherokee Society, 1540–1866.* 1979.

RICHTER, DANIEL K. *The Ordeal of the Longhouse: The Peoples of the Iroquois League in the Era of European Colonization.* 1992.

RUBY, ROBERT H., and JOHN A. BROWN. *Indian Slavery in the Pacific Northwest.* 1993.

ZAVALA, SILVIO. *Los esclavos indios en Nueva España.* 1968.

James F. Brooks

Amistad

Just north of Cuba on the night of 1–2 July 1839, Joseph Cinqué, a West African from Mende, led fifty-three slaves in a mutiny on the coastal schooner *Amistad* that culminated in a historic court battle in the United States between human and property rights. The episode marked the only instance in history in which a group of blacks captured in Africa and brought to the New World for the purpose of enslavement made it back to their homeland. The arguments that erupted over the relationship of race and slavery to liberty severely challenged the republic.

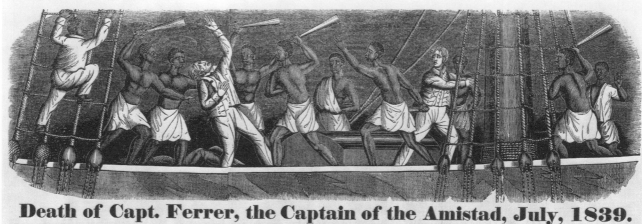

Death of Capt. Ferrer, the Captain of the Amistad, July, 1839.

Don Jose Ruiz and Don Pedro Montez, of the Island of Cuba, having purchased fifty-three slaves at Havana, recently imported from Africa, put them on board the Amistad, Capt. Ferrer, in order to transport them to Principe, another port on the Island of Cuba. After being out from Havana about four days, the African captives on board, in order to obtain their freedom, and return to Africa, armed themselves with cane knives, and rose upon the Captain and crew of the vessel. Capt. Ferrer and the cook of the vessel were killed; two of the crew escaped; Ruiz and Montez were made prisoners.

An illustration depicting the death of Captain Ramon Ferrer aboard the Amistad *is accompanied by a description of the revolt.* [Library of Congress/Corbis]

After the mutineers seized the *Amistad,* they ordered the two Spanish slave owners aboard, José Ruiz and Pedro Montes, to navigate the vessel to Africa. But the two Spaniards zigzagged through Cuban waters, hoping for rescue by a British anti–slave trade patrol. This ploy did not work, and the *Amistad* soon crept northward, where—after a sixty-day odyssey—it entered the waters off Long Island, New York, with only forty-three survivors (thirty-nine men and four children, three of them girls under age nine).

At this point, the slave revolt began to draw national attention. Lieutenant Thomas Gedney of the USS *Washington* spotted the *Amistad* and seized the vessel and cargo as salvage. Abolitionists, however, took the matter before the courts, hoping to expose the evils of the slave trade and slavery itself. Lewis Tappan, a wealthy New York businessman and evangelical abolitionist, underwrote the "*Amistad* Committee," which enlisted the Connecticut attorney Roger Baldwin to defend the blacks as "kidnapped Africans" entitled to freedom. Baldwin first sought a writ of habeas corpus intended to designate the captives as human beings, not property, and allow them to charge the Spaniards with piracy. According to Baldwin, the Africans were not, as the Spaniards claimed, slaves born in Cuba. An Anglo-Spanish treaty had outlawed the African slave trade in 1820, but slavery itself remained legal in Cuba.

The Spanish government meanwhile demanded the blacks' return to Cuba. Under Pinckney's Treaty of 1795, Spain and the United States had agreed to return any vessel from one nation driven into the port of the other for reasons beyond its control. President Martin Van Buren opted to comply, largely because the issue of slavery would split his Democratic Party and cost him reelection in 1840. Further, he feared that the British might accuse Spain of violating their anti–slave trade treaty and use this as a pretext to intervene in Cuba. Van Buren authorized federal interference with the judicial process, blocking an appeal by the blacks after the expected ruling against them.

Baldwin failed to win a writ of habeas corpus in the lower court, but he later secured a district court ruling that the blacks were kidnapped Africans who must return to Africa. The president ordered an appeal to the U.S. Supreme Court, where five of the nine justices were southerners who had been or still were slaveowners.

The abolitionists had achieved a monumental success in taking their case before the highest public forum in the land. Further, they had the services of a former president, John Quincy Adams. Even though he was seventy-three years of age and nearly deaf and had been absent from the courtroom for three decades, Adams nonetheless delivered a long, impassioned speech that called for the blacks' freedom, arguing from the principle of natural right in the Declaration of Independence.

On 9 March 1841, Justice Joseph Story declared the captives free on the basis of the "eternal principles of justice." The abolitionists assumed that the decision rested on the immorality of slavery, but Story explained that although slavery was repugnant, it was legal in the United States. The blacks were free because their ownership papers were fraudulent and they had never been slaves in Cuba. As kidnapped Africans, they had the inherent right of self-defense to win their freedom. Story's decision, however, left the impression that he had acted out of morality: in freeing the captives, he cited eternal principles.

Thirty-five of the original fifty-three blacks on the *Amistad* returned to Africa in January 1842. President John Tyler, a Virginia slaveholder, had rejected their pleas for assistance on the ground that no law provided him with such authority. But the *Amistad* Committee worked with church groups and the former captives, raising enough money through public exhibitions and other enterprises to charter a ship.

The *Amistad* Committee soon became the basis of the American Missionary Association, which was the first Christian mission in Africa. There is no conclusive evidence that Cinqué was reunited with his wife and three children; and—also because of lack of evidence—there is no justification for the frequent assertion that he himself engaged in the slave trade on his return home. The period following his arrival in Africa in early 1842 remains a matter of speculation.

See also CINQUÉ; TAPPAN BROTHERS.

BIBLIOGRAPHY

JONES, HOWARD. *Mutiny on the Amistad: The Saga of a Slave Revolt and Its Impact on American Abolition, Law, and Diplomacy.* 1987; revised and expanded edition, 1997.
WYATT-BROWN, BERTRAM. *Lewis Tappan and the Evangelical War against Slavery.* 1969.

Howard Jones

Ancient Greece

The origin of slavery among the ancient Greeks is no longer recoverable. If the Greeks did not bring slavery with them when they erupted into the Balkan peninsula around the beginning of the second millennium B.C.E., they probably soon acquired slaves and worked out conventions of slavery, partly in response to the question of what to do with the survivors of the populations they dispossessed, and partly, as their experience of the Mediterranean world expanded, under the influence of neighboring cultures, notably the Minoans of Crete, the Egyptians, and the inhabitants of the Near East and Anatolia. Whatever the case, fully developed Mycenaean Greek culture (ca. 1600–1100 B.C.E.) included, as is evident in the Linear B tablets from Crete and the Greek mainland, the exploitation of slaves, men and women acquired to some extent as a result of warfare and perhaps to a greater extent by means of the two favorite forms of Mycenaean economic activity, trade and piracy. The institution of slavery remained henceforth an intrinsic component of Greek social and economic life. So far as we can tell, no Greek polis forswore slavery; indeed, it was regarded as normal and was widely practiced long after Hellas had lost its freedom to the Roman imperium.

Knowing about Ancient Greek Slavery

The surviving evidence from which we learn about the nature and extent of slavery in ancient Greece poses a number of problems. For one thing, the amount of such evidence varies considerably, both chronologically and geographically. Although there is a modest amount of evidence from the classical age of Greece in the fifth century B.C.E., the bulk of the documentation comes from the period beginning with the fourth century B.C.E. and continuing into the Hellenistic period (from the late fourth century to the late first century B.C.E.). Moreover, the overwhelming majority of what we know comes from places like Athens, Sparta, the island of Chios, and, for the era of the Hellenistic monarchies, principally from Egypt, always something of an anomaly. It is usually difficult at best to say just how typical the Athenian situation was of the rest of the Greek world, but Athens nonetheless affords the clearest picture. In addition, there are significant differences between the world of the polis and, later, the more cosmopolitan environment of the Hellenistic world.

A second difficulty is the impressionistic and unquantifiable nature of the evidence. Comparatively few legal or "accounting" documents remain recording such things as purchases, manumission, utilization, or numbers of slaves; it is not even clear to what extent such documentation was thought necessary. Consequently, for most issues statistics can only occasionally be adduced. For Athens, much of our information comes from such quasi-juridical sources as orations commissioned by litigants and prepared by professional speechwriters (logographers); these works are often tendentious and designed to plead a case, rather than to present an accurate account of the circumstances of slavery. Some of the speeches, mainly those from fourth-century Athens, are deeply political and reflect a personal animus or rivalry that raises more doubt than certainty. Thus only the embedded citations of specific legislation or customs pertaining to slavery are likely to be entirely trustworthy. The result of these limitations is that we have hardly any reliable statistics at all; those we do get generally prove to be preserved in much later documents and represent unreliable, even patently erroneous, traditions. For instance, a claim made in the second century C.E. that Athens had 400,000 slaves at its peak is surely far-fetched.

Another source of information on slavery is literature, particularly tragedy, comedy, and epic and lyric poetry; such works may contain useful insights on attitudes or values but rarely provide any hard evidence on the details of the everyday lives of slaves or, for that matter, slave owners. While their social settings may reflect contemporary usage, they may also represent a conscious effort to create a sense of the archaic. This is the case with Homer and the Athenian tragedies. In comedy in particular, whether the Old Comedy of Aristophanes or the New Comedy of the fourth and third centuries, slaves often are stock figures of social manners, not infrequently portraying a reality turned upside down for comic effect. One literary genre that is a bit difficult to classify consists of one or two manuals on the subject of household and estate management. In the early fourth century, the Athenian general and writer Xenophon wrote one such essay for his new wife; it included instructions on how to handle slaves by means of a system of rewards and punishments.

Last, there is the evidence of the philosophers, mainly—but not exclusively—Plato and Aristotle, whose interests center on the moral questions: whether slavery is natural or accidental, what the nature of slaves is, the relationship between the distinction between body and soul and that between slave and free, and so forth. These discussions are, of course, of interest, but they are generally placed at some remove from the realities of slaves' lives. In any event, apart from some of the Sophists and isolated musings from a very few other philosophers, none of the discussions proceeds from the point of view that slavery is in any sense wrong; indeed the Greeks on the whole took slavery as a normal part of life, albeit one marked by misfortune. Among the wide range of Greek philosophical speculation and systematic discussion, no treatise on slavery has come down to us.

One other problem merits some mention: the Greek lexicon of slavery. The terms are varied, sometimes overlapping, rather vague, and for the most part decidedly nontechnical. The most common Greek term for slavery was *douleia* (in contrast to *eleutheria*, "freedom"); thus the *doulos* (feminine, *doulē*) was contrasted with the *eleutheros*, or free man. This term is sometimes generic and might not even distinguish between a chattel slave and a communal slave, of which the Spartan helots are perhaps the best-known example; it was sometimes applied to both. To make matters worse, the term could also describe free people

The funerary stele of a Greek youth includes a relief of a slave. [Wolfgang Kaehler/Corbis]

living under some sort of political domination, despotic or imperial. Some Greeks noted that the Great King of Persia regarded all his subjects as his *douloi*, translating the Persian usage with their own word for the concept. The Greeks also used such words as *oiketes*, a "houseboy"; a variety of words meaning "attendant," "member of an entourage," or "follower"; the generic term for human being (*anthropos*); or simply a "body" (*soma*). Not surprisingly, the derogatory term "child" (*pais*)—boy or girl—was used of slaves, regardless of age. Even an elderly male slave might be called "boy." Oddest of all, but revealing, is the term *andrapodon*, a neuter noun that means "a creature with human feet," a usage that fits neatly with Aristotle's characterization of a slave as "motile property."

Varieties of Slavery and Sources of Slaves

With the formation of the characteristic Greek poleis during the eighth and seventh centuries B.C.E. and the nearly universal disappearance in Greece of the institution of monarchy, the inhabitants of most Greek cities came to regard two questions about status as fundamental: (1) whether one was a citizen or an alien, that is, someone from some other polis (a Greek) or culture (a "barbarian"); and (2) whether a person was free or a slave. All other issues, such as wealth, gender, or age, were of lesser importance, even if they were subsets of the main issues. The ability to function as a full member of these societies depended on the answer to these questions; that only males could so function was simply assumed. The philosopher Heraclitus (fl. ca. 500 B.C.E.) held that war made people slaves. This is certainly the case in the Homeric epics of the eighth century B.C.E. During the ten years at Troy, Achilles, for example, took time to raid other nearby settlements, acquiring slaves along with other forms of booty.

In the period from the eighth through the sixth centuries, the Greeks began a wave of colonization and established new settlements in the western Mediterranean (Sicily, southern Italy, southern France, and eastern Spain); to the long-established Greek settlements in the Aegean and along the coast of Asia Minor were added new colonies in the Black Sea area. Such new centers of Greek life accelerated Greek trade and increased the range and quantity of commodities available, including slaves. War among the various poleis certainly continued to provide slaves to the victors. During the Peloponnesian War (431–403), the Athenians killed all the men who survived their attack on the Greek island of Melos and sold all the women and children into slavery. As the Greeks came more and more into contact with various non-Greek populations north of Greece or along the Mediterranean littoral, the numbers of non-Hellenic slaves inevitably increased. Over time non-Greeks came to form by far the largest segment of the Greek slave population. In the Hellenistic period, there was an increase in the number of black Africans being sold in the Greek slave markets. For a long time there seems to have been no disinclination to enslave fellow Greeks, although in Athens in particular and Hellas generally, enslaving one's own free citizens was done only in exceptional circumstances. Clearly, Cassander's restoration (316 B.C.E.) of the previously enslaved population of the Greek city of Thebes was at least in part an index of the discomfort some Greeks had come to feel by this time over enslaving other Greeks, but no general movement in this direction followed. Selling Greeks to barbarians was doubtless seen as reprehensible but was nonetheless sometimes done.

Prior to the sixth century B.C.E., Athenians could pledge their bodies against repayment of a loan; were they to default, they—and in some instances, their families—would become the permanent property of the person to whom they had made the pledge. Among the provisions of Solon's reform of the Athenian constitution and legal system in or about 594 B.C.E. was the elimination of such "debt slavery"; to this welcome change, the Athenians applied the term *seisachtheia*, "the shrugging off of the yoke." Henceforth, while one might still, for a time at least, enter into a contractual commitment of one's services (a form of servitude not to be confused with a freely negotiated work agreement) for a specific term, it was no longer possible to be enslaved in lieu of repaying a debt. Even this form of bond-servanthood seems to have disappeared from the Athenian scene by the fifth century.

The most common form of slavery in the Greek world saw the slave as chattel, something susceptible to sale or purchase at the whim of the owner, much like real property, movable or not, or farm animals. Such slavery was absolute, with every expectation that it would be permanent. Manumission was possible, but that was generally at the discretion of the owner. Buying one's freedom is attested to, but it was apparently a less common procedure. We know of a former slave-courtesan in the later fourth century B.C.E. whose lovers, formerly her joint owners, had offered to help defray the cost of her manumission. We learn that war captives might be ransomed, thereby being spared the humiliation of permanent slavery. By and large, such chattel slaves were privately owned, but there were a number of slaves owned directly by the Athenian state (public slaves) or slaves owned by companies that then leased their human property to the state. This latter arrangement came to be the more typical one for the Athenian state silver mining operations at Laureion in southern Attica and for public construction projects. This practice was probably followed in other Greek cities as well.

Rather atypical, but apparently a form of enslavement that harked back to an earlier era, was the form of communal slavery best known from Sparta (although it was also known in Thessaly in a similar form). In the seventh century B.C.E., after several wars, the Spartans converted the formerly free non-Spartan inhabitants of Laconia and Messenia into helots ("captives"), wholly dependent "serfs" who were the property of the Spartan state, but, in effect, under the immediate control and supervision of the free Spartan holders of land allotments. This state captivity may well have emulated earlier Bronze Age practices, although that cannot be demonstrated. Helots were allocated to free Spartans along with the plots of land and bound to that land. The prospect of manumission was vanishingly small (although it did increase in later periods) because Sparta needed to keep these populations under control—the helots outnumbered the Spartans by a considerable amount. Indeed, each year the five ephors, or chief magistrates, of Sparta declared war on these helots, so that, should the Spartan equivalent of a secret police (actually called the *krupteia*, the "secret group") come to regard any helot as a plotter or in any way dangerous, that helot could be "disappeared" and his death would not incur blood pollution, for it could then be seen not as murder but rather as an act of war. The Spartan helots had the distinct, albeit limited, advantage of retaining their social connections. In general, they continued their familial, religious, and cultural life unaffected by Spartan domination, maintaining their sense of communal identity, even if they lacked any freedom of action on most levels.

Chattel slaves, on the other hand, suffered a quite different fate. For those who were ethnic Greeks, there was a keen sense of dishonor, not to mention a sense of being cut off from free participation in civic life, such as it might have been, in their home city or region. They underwent what Orlando Patterson has called "social death," a transformation from self-determining human beings into pieces of property stripped of the identity into which they had been born (assuming that they were not "homegrown" slaves who had never experienced a status other than servility). For foreign slaves, the situation was similar but even worse, in that they were cut off from their homes and countries, and obliged to learn a new language, receive new names, acquire new customs, wear new and unfamiliar (sometimes demeaning) clothes, and generally, as a result of these changes, lose their identity. Slaves might get a new name that indicated their place of origin, but more often the new appellation was that of their owner. All the social associations of name and family indicators were stripped away, so that for modern scholars the ethnicity of particular slaves has been obscured, although it would have been evident, in the case of barbarians, to their contemporaries. Some slaves, recalcitrants or escapees, were chained, distinctively tattooed, and branded. In the new culture, their ability to participate in the civic life of the community was nil; even participation in religious activities was sharply limited, and then largely a question of whether the owner permitted it.

In addition to the sources of slaves noted above, it is clear that some slaves simply begot more slaves. In the helot system, this was probably a rather normal process; if the Spartans did anything to limit the helot birthrate, it is not clear in the evidence before us. But the maintenance of family life among the helots almost certainly sustained their numbers, without the Spartans' having to avail themselves of other sources.

Slave breeding among holders of chattel slaves was not common, at least not in the sense of a deliberate breeding program. No doubt chattel slaves had children, but this seems to have been strictly controlled by owners. Women constantly available for the sexual use of their masters are more than likely to have had children at a greater rate. Whether infanticide was widely practiced to deal with unwanted children is not at all certain. The possibility of taking a mate and having children was one reward held out to slaves in exchange for good behavior and service.

It is nearly impossible to estimate the numbers of slaves in the Greek world. That helots outnumbered Spartans seems quite certain (as noted above)—hence the extreme violence directed against these people by the Spartans. Just how great the population disparity was is another matter, but the helots may, in earlier times, have outnumbered the Spartans by about five to one, and some ancient authorities estimate seven to one. The disparity actually got worse, not so much because the helot population increased as because of a long-term decline in the numbers of adult male Spartans. By 362 B.C.E., the Spartan army could not field more than 1,500 actual Spartiates, and it had become necessary on several occasions to arm helot units for combat. There was some desertion, but there were no massive uprisings.

To determine the number of slaves in Athens is equally difficult. We are not even well informed as to the total number of Athenian male citizens; estimates range from 20,000 to about 75,000 for the peak years in the fifth century. Moderate modern estimates tend toward 40,000 or 45,000. It is little more than an educated guess, but this would place the figure for slaves at about 100,000, perhaps as many as 125,000. The evidence does not allow better estimates.

Uses of Slaves

The helots, whether in Spartan-controlled territory or in Thessaly, were used almost entirely to work the land to which they were attached. Some manpower was no doubt used for state construction projects, but remarkably few helots became craftsmen of any sort, except perhaps within the framework of the farm. On the other hand, the extent to which slaves were used in agriculture in Athens is somewhat less certain. It is often held that, since most Athenians probably owned some farmland, even if they dwelt in the city proper, agriculture was the principal sphere of employment for Athenian slaves. However, several considerations suggest that a more moderate position might well be in order.

The history of Athenian agriculture from the early sixth century on involved a significant shift from an emphasis on cereal grain production to the raising of grapevines and olive trees, cash crops which would make the importation of grain feasible. Neither of these was a labor-intensive form of agriculture; nor was the herding of sheep, goats, pigs, and cattle. Large plantations like those in Roman Italy were unknown in Athenian territory. It is clear that a significant number of urban Athenians continued to maintain small farms or even plots of land; these rarely required the efforts of more than a handful of slaves at most, although the gentry who had remained essentially rooted in the old landholding value system of the hoplite class no doubt had more slaves. In general, however, it seems unlikely that massive numbers of slaves were engaged in Athenian agriculture.

In general, agricultural slaves were used to tend the crops, the work and food animals, and the vineyards and orchards. They were responsible for bringing harvests and by-products to market; their supervisors, even when themselves servile, probably used stern methods to enforce discipline and prevent escape.

There can be no doubt that the growth of Athenian imperial hegemony after the Persian wars (492–479 B.C.E.) made large numbers of slaves available, at lower prices (although they were still not very cheap). It is equally clear that the largest number of these found their way into domestic service, an urban sphere that even in relatively modest urban households offered opportunity as much for ostentation as for useful labor. The work to be done, in addition to attending to the personal needs of their owners (hairdressing, barbering, etc.), included baking, cooking, and, for the women slaves in particular, wool-working. Many households continued to make their own clothes. Slaves also attended to basic chores such as cleaning, washing, and the management of food preparation and serving. In some households, slaves served as wet nurses, attendants for children (the pedagogus was such an attendant), and doorkeepers. The general distaste for wage labor—which looked suspiciously like servitude, even to poor Athenians—meant that there was very little competition for domestic slave labor. As the supply of domestic slaves increased and perhaps exceeded the capacity of households to absorb them, short of bankruptcy, it became economically desirable to set up the supernumerary slaves in small businesses and to allow them to live apart from the owner's household. A percentage of their income would then go to the owner. Both domestic slaves seen in public and those living on their own came to be attired in more respectable fashion; the cantankerous conservative known to us as "the Old Oligarch" (late

fifth to early fourth century) complained that it was no longer possible to distinguish slaves from free citizens. He was particularly grumpy because these well-dressed slaves would not even step aside to let their betters pass by.

Slaves staffed some manufacturing shops, in some cases working side by side with free laborers. Here, owners might be fortunate enough to acquire slaves with certain manual skills; otherwise, they would have to train their slaves. Such slaves were engaged in the manufacture of weapons, pottery, some specialty clothing, musical instruments, jewelry, and so on. Most of these shops would have been comparatively small, but we know of some that employed as many as 120 slaves. There were slaves employed in trade as well, and some in what, for want of a better term, might be called banking.

Publicly owned and contract slaves labored in the several phases of the construction of temples, civic buildings, theaters, and so forth. In addition to serving as carpenters and stoneworkers, they provided the principal labor force for the quarrying and transport of stone, as well as in the logistics supporting the shipbuilding industry. Mention has already been made of the use of slaves in the silver mines at Laureion. This was regarded as the worst imaginable destination for slaves; the work was hard and unrelenting, and the life expectancy notoriously short. It is likely that the majority of the slaves so assigned were problem cases: resistant to discipline; criminally, even violently inclined; habitual escapees; and the like.

In Athens, a somewhat unexpected use of slaves was in maintaining public order. A small body of men—referred to as "Scythian bowmen," though some were probably just brawny rather than actually of Scythian origin—were posted in public areas and buildings and at public meetings. They show up in some Athenian plays (e.g., Aristophanes' *Thesmophoriazusai*), where they are depicted as somewhat stolid and stupid and speak Greek in a way designed to show that they are barbarians.

Prostitution—from the lowliest streetwalker to the denizen of a brothel to the high-priced, cultivated courtesan—might be practiced by individuals who were not slaves (including metics, or resident aliens); but many of these girls and women (and some men and boys as well) were in fact someone's slave. These slaves kept some of their money for maintenance after their owners had taken a cut. A courtesan might accumulate enough money to purchase her freedom in due course, presumably most easily after she became older and her potential earnings decreased. The profession also required the services of musicians, dancers, and other servants to enhance the pleasure of the clientele.

Slave labor was often used in the construction of temples in ancient Greece. [Corbis-Bettmann]

Treatment of Slaves

Slaves in Greece were subjected to the same range of treatment one expects in any slaveholding society. Some masters were inclined to be benign, even caring toward their slaves, regarding them as members of the household (*oikos*). Such slaves generally fared well and, in the long run, stood the best chance of manumission, either during the lifetime of the owner or in the deceased owner's will. Indeed, we find isolated cases of a man manumitting slaves in his will, sometimes stipulating that the slave will get a wife as well—in one case, the wife of the owner. Other slaves, though, were subject to brutal treatment that included severe beatings, physical restraint, and even torture. (Under Athenian law, torture was almost routinely applied to slaves whose testimony was required in a lawsuit. The theory was that slaves would not otherwise tell the truth.) In theory, a master was not free to murder a slave, but in practice it was unlikely that any penalty would ensue from destruction of one's own property—even human property. Between these extremes was a spectrum of treatment that depended almost entirely on the personality and moods of the owner. The power to reward (with privileges, better food or living conditions, etc.) or to punish is stressed in essays on home and estate management as the best way to control one's slaves.

While male slaves were used sexually by their owners, female slaves had to endure such use to a far greater extent. Modern misunderstanding of the nature and extent of male homosexuality in Greece often obscures the fact that many men had strong heterosexual impulses that they satisfied with household slaves or with prostitutes. In general, there was a distinction between sex with one's wife, which was essentially reproductive, and recreational sex with slaves. Many wives chose to ignore this reality, although some disapproved of it. Some men with the resources to manage it had slave mistresses living outside the home. Distinguishing such women from prostitutes is not always easy.

Slave Resistance and Rebellion

Helots—serfs—were rather more likely than other slaves to engage in organized rebellion, mainly because even after centuries they had retained a good deal of their earlier communal consciousness and were therefore likely to be able to collaborate in self-defense. The fact that they were treated so brutally also contributed to the potential for uprisings; that uprisings did not happen more often is surprising. Chattel slaves in the Greek world, on the other hand, seem only rarely to have been involved in such revolts. For one thing, they generally came from such diverse geographic, ethnic, and social backgrounds that they had no sense of community or shared goals. Since there were no large slave-run plantations like those that bedeviled the Romans during the slave rebellions in Sicily (135–131 B.C.E.) and in Italy (early first century B.C.E.), the concentration of slaves in the rural areas was not great. Likewise, even though slaves may well have had some of the rudiments of class consciousness, they found new opportunities to articulate them or take advantage of would-be leaders within the slave community.

Justifications for Slavery

It appears that early Greek thinking about slavery took it to be an acquired status, which anyone might at some point have to face. It was owing to the weakness of defeated people at a given point in time; and, since chance was a considerable factor in life, things might well have turned out differently under other circumstances. Over time, however, the idea emerged that slavery was a natural phenomenon for some people—individual Greeks are probably the subject here—by nature too weak or too cowardly to maintain their freedom. As barbarian slaves became progressively more common, the notion was extended to whole groups of people who, again by nature, were inherently servile. Aristotle, in the *Politics*, expresses this idea, emphasizing especially those barbarians who were ruled by kings. This construction depends on the Greeks' notion of their inherent superiority over barbarians as far as institutions and culture were concerned. People who were ruled by kings were clearly natural slaves. In the Hellenistic era, a few dreamers caught up in a cosmopolitan, vaguely egalitarian vision speculated about the possibility of a slaveless society. This was a tiny group, joined by a small group of Sophists and Stoics who came to see a moral objection to slavery.

See also CHATTEL SLAVERY; ENSLAVEMENT, METHODS OF; LAW; MINERS; PATTERSON THESIS; PERSPECTIVES ON SLAVERY; PHILOSOPHY.

BIBLIOGRAPHY

ARCHER, L., ed. *Slavery and Other Forms of Unfree Labour*. 1988.
FINLEY, M. I. *Ancient Slavery and Modern Ideology*. 1980.
———. *Economy and Society in Ancient Greece*. 1981.
———. *Slavery in Classical Antiquity*. 1968.
FISHER, N. R. E. *Slavery in Classical Greece*. 1993.
LEFKOWITZ, MARY, and MAUREEN FANT. *Women's Life in Greece and Rome*. 1992.
PATTERSON, O. *Slavery and Social Death*. 1982.
POMEROY, SARAH B. *Goddesses, Whores, Wives, and Slaves*. 1975.
POWELL, C. A., ed. *Classical Sparta: Techniques behind Her Success*. 1989.
SINCLAIR, R. M. *Democracy and Participation in Athens*. 1988.
STE. CROIX, G. E. M. DE. *The Class Struggle in the Ancient Greek World*. 1981.

Gerald E. Kadish

Ancient Middle East

This entry includes the following articles: Assyria and Babylonia; Israel; Mesopotamia; Persia.

Assyria and Babylonia

Slavery was a permanent but usually minor feature of the societies of ancient Iraq, both in the south, Babylonia, and in the north, Assyria. Those enslaved included foreigners caught in war and used in domestic service and household production. Natives were enslaved for debt, and others served because the heads of their families had committed a crime.

The earliest attested slaves were the blinded slaves, called "not opening the eyes," who may have been prisoners of war. They were sold as individuals in the late Early Dynastic Period, around 2400 B.C.E.

The Assyrian state deported defeated populations from their homeland at least as early as 1245 B.C.E., and the persons deported were assigned new lands, sometimes in the Assyrian heartland. Not free to leave, they were treated almost as chattel slaves, but they may have retained some rights. They were sold with the land they farmed.

In the south there were royal slaves and temple slaves. Perhaps the temple slaves came to their status by having been donated by family members who could no longer afford to support them. Royal slaves may have become slaves as punishment for offenses to the king.

We know much more about slaves of persons who did not work for temples and palaces. Slaves were allowed to marry and have families, and some had property, which they could buy and sell as if they were free persons. They had to pay their owners a yearly fee for the privilege of economic independence.

Some slaves in Babylonia became fabulously rich under the auspices of well-placed masters, and owned slaves of their own. Here we see a discontinuity between the slaves' legal status and their economic status. Rich slaves still could be sold, along with their families, for enormous sums of silver. One family was sold for 1,440 shekels of silver (about a quarter of an ounce or 8.33 grams); a single man would fetch 60.

Slave prices, like the prices for most goods and services, rose from earliest times to the end of the cuneiform record, at the end of the first millennium B.C.E. In the third millennium B.C.E., slaves cost 10 to

15 shekels of silver. In the old Babylonian period from 2000 to 1600 B.C.E. they cost around 20 shekels. By the middle of the first millennium prices had climbed to 50 to 60 shekels for men and 40 for women. In the Persian period, from 539 to 333 B.C.E., prices usually ranged from 75 to 90 shekels. All these prices seem high, since a lower-class worker received the grain equivalent of a shekel of silver per month in most periods.

Children born of the union of a slave woman and her master were free, as were those of a male slave and a free woman. Manumission was possible, if not common, as early as 2050 B.C.E. In the Neo-Babylonian period before 539 B.C.E., manumission was used as a reward for slaves who cared for an aging master. Except for the Assyrian peasants, almost all slaves were employed in domestic labor within households, and they were not used in large gangs in agricultural work.

See also ARCHAEOLOGY OF SLAVERY.

BIBLIOGRAPHY

DANDAMAEV, MUHAMMAD A. *Slavery in Babylonia.* 1984.
MENDELSOHN, ISAAC. *Slavery in the Ancient Near East.* 1949.

Daniel C. Snell

Eliezer, the servant of Abraham, meets Rebecca, the future wife of Isaac, at the well. [Chris Hellier/Corbis]

Israel

Slaves are attested to in all periods of ancient Israelite history. They were usually few in number, except in the late periods, and they sometimes attained significant positions of power within households. Most appear to have been of foreign origin, though debt bondage, self-sale, and child sale seem to have been common within the Israelite groups in times of economic hardship.

In the Genesis stories, the patriarchs' slaves play minor but valued roles. Eliezer of Damascus was to inherit from Abraham, his master, but then was sent to find a spouse for Abraham's son (Gn 15: 2; 24: 1–67). The Egyptian slave Hagar bore the patriarch his first-born son, who was rejected in favor of the son of the favored free wife (Gn 16: 1–16, 21: 1–2). Slaves worked in agriculture (2 Sm 9: 10; perhaps Ru 2: 5), building (Neh 4: 16–23), and sheep-herding (Gn 32: 16; 1 Sm 21: 7).

The legal material, which derives from groups critical of kings and is associated with the prophets in the first millennium B.C.E., assumed that a term of slavery for an Israelite man would be for seven years, but women and non-Israelite slaves would have to serve in perpetuity (Ex 21: 2–7; compare Dt 15: 12–18). In Leviticus 25: 39–43 the liberation of the Hebrew slave was said to be linked with the utopian Jubilee year in the fiftieth year, when both the slave and his children were to go free. Stories about slaves do not indicate that such "term slavery" was ever practiced.

Before the exile of the southern kingdom to Babylon (587–539 B.C.E.) slaves served in small numbers in great households. The largest number noted was twenty, the slaves of King Saul's son (2 Kgs 9: 10). Escapees fled and were caught (1 Kgs 2: 39–40). And yet in Deuteronomy 23: 15–16 there was the feeling that escapees ought not to be returned to their owner—a sentiment that, had it been widely implemented, would certainly have destroyed slavery as an institution. Therefore the verse probably has to be interpreted either as a pious wish or as referring only to Israelite slaves sold abroad who managed to return home. Another stipulation that might in itself have decreed abolition if applied broadly was the prohibition against stealing people (Ex 21: 16; Dt 24: 7).

Some Israelite thinkers recommended humane treatment of slaves. There was supposed to be punishment for striking a slave (Ex 21: 20–22, 26–27). And the free person was advised not to criticize a slave to his master, for fear of inducing punishment (Prv 30: 10). But the rules about the goring ox show that the death of a free person was to be fully compensated, while a slave's life was worth only 30 shekels of silver (Ex 21: 28–32). There was a feeling that slaves were lazy and untrustworthy (Prv 29: 19, 21; Sir 33: 24–28) and disastrous in positions of authority (Prv 19: 10).

Slave prices included 20 shekels of silver for Joseph (Gn 37: 28). Hosea 3: 2 records that 15 shekels of silver, along with some barley, were paid for an adulteress. Leviticus 27: 3–7 implies an average cost of 50 shekels for men and 30 for women, and less for younger or aged slaves. Such prices are within the range known from the rest of the ancient Near East. Deuteronomy 15: 18 says that a slave cost half a hireling's wage, so owning a slave was seen as a good investment.

Debt slavery is attested to in Nehemiah 5: 4–5, where the Israelites complained to the Persian governor that they had to sell their children to pay taxes (also 2 Kgs 4: 1; Am 2: 6; and Is 50: 1). Other texts imply that thieves were to be sold into slavery, but the context is a story about events in Egypt and so may not reflect Israelite practice (Gn 43: 18, 44: 9–10, 17).

Manumission was possible through purchase (Lv 25: 47–50). Jeremiah 34: 8–22 criticizes a wartime mass manumission, which the slave owners reversed when the crisis passed. Jacob 3: 19 and 31: 13–15 recognizes the basic equality of human beings, slave and free.

After the exile to Babylon as many as a fifth of the returnees from exile were slaves, as one sees from the lists (Ezr 2: 64–65; Neh 7: 66–67, with 42,360 returnees and 7,337 slaves). This proportion may represent a Babylonian practice that was mirrored among the Israelites. There may have also been temple slaves, called "those given (to the temple)," linked to the descendants of Solomon's slaves, though it is possible that these persons were free officials of the temple (1 Chr 9: 2; Ezr 2: 58; 8: 20). Earlier, the Gibeonites who tricked Israelites into sparing their lives may have had a collective and serflike obligation imposed on them (Jos 9: 23).

See also Bible; Law.

BIBLIOGRAPHY

CARDELLINI, INNOCENZO. *Die biblischen "Sklaven": Gesetze im Lichte des Heilschriftlichen "Sklavenrechts."* 1981.
DANDAMAEV, MUHAMMAD A. "Slavery in the Old Testament." In *Anchor Bible Dictionary,* edited by David N. Freedman. 1992.
MENDELSOHN, ISAAC. *Slavery in the Ancient Near East.* 1949.
VAUX, ROLAND DE. *Ancient Israel.* Vol. 1, *Social Institutions.* 1965.

Daniel C. Snell

Mesopotamia

Between 3500 and 500 B.C., four impressive river-valley civilizations dominated the economy, society, and politics of the Tigris and Euphrates alluvial plains of present-day Iraq; that is, the region of ancient Mesopotamia. The southern Mesopotamian civilization was Sumer (3500–1400 B.C.), the central civilizations were Akkad (2350–1350 B.C.) and Babylon (1350–539 B.C.), and the northern civilization was Assyria (1250–520 B.C.). Rising up between the rivers, the river-valley empires relied heavily on the labor of the commoners of the city-states and the cultivators of the surrounding villages for their survival and prosperity. Pastoralists from the western Syrian desert cooperated with as well as threatened the Mesopotamian village and town communities. The use of slave labor began to be documented after 2700 B.C., when war prisoners, kidnapped free men and women, and impoverished citizens were listed as slaves laboring in the king's household, in the temple, and on the princely estates. By the time of the Achaemenian conquest in 520 B.C., markets existed in some of the major Mesopotamian towns for slaves, who worked in their fields, markets, and households.

The southern Mesopotamian region had the oldest permanent human settlements of ancient Mesopotamia. The highly literate, city-building Sumerian and Akkadian empires (3500–1350 B.C.) controlled the fields, waterways, and urban settlements from the central plains around present-day Baghdad to the headwaters of the Persian Gulf, creating unparalleled wealth, military prowess, and artistic production. In the later northern and central Mesopotamian regions, the Babylonians (1350–539 B.C.) in the central plains and the Assyrians (1250–520 B.C.) in the northern piedmont and mountain region achieved even greater wealth and military power than their southern Mesopotamian predecessors. Underlying the social, political, and military successes of the Assyrians and particularly the Babylonians were the captive foreign slaves, who formed an integral part of the merchants' activities.

Sumer and Akkad

Records show that by 2700 B.C., the Sumerian city-state of Uruk had temple slaves assisting the priests in rituals and ceremonies, and the palace had others, probably females, as domestic servants. In the succeeding years, the Sumerian city-states that dotted the Euphrates river basin from the central plains near Babylon to the present-day Kut al-'Amara in southern Iraq increasingly relied on the labor of prisoners of war, town captives, and self-enslaved citizens, who survived by selling themselves. The self-enslaved were undoubtedly the pastoralists and villagers of the countryside whose homes surrounded the burnt-brick walled Sumerian city-states. Though prosperous and independent in the earlier period, the Sumerian city-states appear to have dwindled between 2700 and 2200 B.C. In the waning years of the independence of the southern Sumerian city-state, both male and female slaves are recorded as not only prisoners of war, defeated townspeople, or impoverished citizens but also laborers from the foreign lands to the east (the Persian Gulf and the Iranian plateau) and to the west (the Egyptian Nile region and the Red Sea area). Although there appear to have been no slave markets or long-distance trade in slaves during the earlier Sumerian period, the traffic in foreign captives in the later years of Sumer indicates very active slave markets and a well-developed long-distance merchant slave trade. The decline in the urban and rural Sumerian population as well as increased defensive needs explains the rise in foreign slaves as replacement labor for the declining Sumerian city-states. Overall, the tripartite Sumerian social structure of aristocracy (king, landholders, and priests), commoners (artisans, traders and merchants, and skilled laborers), and slaves (domestic servants, musicians, soldiers, and occasional cultivators) remained intact over the long period of Sumerian history, each element protected by Sumerian social customs, traditions, and laws.

The rapid rise and fall of the Akkad civilization in central Mesopotamia belies its overall contributions to the civilizations of the river-basin. Known for its linguistic and cultural influences on Sumer and its peoples, Akkad reached its period of highest military and cultural prominence during the reign of Sargon the Great (2330 to 2200 B.C.). Using temporary forced labor recruited from free villagers and from war prisoners, Sargon constructed the elegant city of Agade near present-day Baghdad. With the use of expert archers, mule-driven chariots, and skilled infantry, Sargon quickly seized a number of Sumerian cities to the south before turning to Syria and Palestine and reaching the Egyptian delta within the first decade of his reign. The conquests yielded thousands of war prisoners and kidnapped citizens; the former were pressed into service in the temples and in canal and roadway construction as well as in farming the temple and royal estates, while the latter were enslaved as domestic servants, concubines, and palace guards in the households of the king and notables.

In 2200 B.C., an invasion of western Iranian mountaineer horsemen known as Gutians ravaged Akkad and so effectively leveled the city-fortress of Agade that its exact location remains unknown to this day. The Guti continued southward, destroying Sumerian fields, canals, villages, and towns, except for the Sumerian city of Lagash, whose cooperative and compliant governor spared that city the fate of other Sumer settlements. Akkad and Akkadian society, including the semislaves, domestic servants, and palace guards, managed to remain intact in the central Mesopotamian plains, though in a much diminished and impoverished state compared with previous decades.

Assyria and Babylon

In northern Mesopotamia, the Assyrian Empire (1250–520 B.C.) adopted many of the social, economic, and political features of Sumer and Akkad, such as their market and temple networks, their small craft and intensive farming techniques, their laws of social conduct, and their city-state concepts of self-rule. On the other hand, the Assyrians also incorporated the military tactics and technology of the Anatolian and Egyptian kingdoms, gathering large numbers of armed infantry along with expert archers and charioteers in flanking strategies and surprise assaults. The great Assyrian kings, such as Assurnasirpal II (884–859 B.C.), Sargon II (722–705 B.C.), and Assurbanipal (668–631 B.C.), constructed the royal palaces and cities of Nineveh and Nimrod. The documentation of the palace construction projects as well as of the massive irrigation systems in the northern Mesopotamian plains shows extensive use of slave labor taken both from the rural population and from military conquests of the eastern Mediterranean (Syrians and Palestinians) and the Anatolian mountains and plains.

From the mid-700s to the eve of the Achaemenian conquest in 520 B.C., slave labor was increasingly essential to the diversely skilled Assyrian society of charioteers and groomers of the famed Assyrian horses, temple workers and keepers of the palace libraries, and domestic servants, musicians, entertainers, and market tradesmen. The frequent wars of Assyria and Babylon produced most of the slave labor for the river-valley empires of northern Mesopotamia. In the last decades of Assyrian rule, several major cities held slave markets and engaged in a long-distance slave trade with the markets and port towns of the eastern Mediterranean, northern Anatolia, the Caucasus, and the Persian Gulf. These avenues of slave trading were the major routes for the import and export of the Mesopotamian basin's goods and products, such as wool and cotton, carpets and tools, and a wide variety of grains and tree crops.

Following the reign of King Assurbanipal in 631 B.C., Scythian raids from the west and north followed by the breakaway of the Babylonians in central Mesopotamia began a period of Assyrian imperial decline and transition. The passion for walled cities, palaces, and gardens gave way to a Babylonian renaissance of culture and art—a neo-Babylonian era—from the mid-600s to the Achaemenian conquests of 520 B.C. The prominent role of war prisoners, kidnapped citizens,

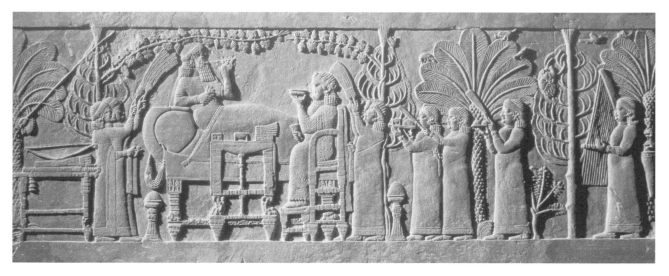

King Assurbanipal and his queen are waited upon by their royal slaves. [Gianni Dagli Orti/Corbis]

and debt slaves in the creation of the Babylonian monuments of grandeur is well documented. It is also clear from the existing records that, as in other ancient Mesopotamian civilizations, slaves and slave labor were essential to the royal households, temple activities, and building industries of the urban economy. Slaves were primarily an urban force, while free tenant farmers worked the agricultural lands both for themselves and for the nobility. Even in the marketplace, slave labor was unusual, since free artisans and skilled craftsmen were the major sources of labor for the town "industries." At best, Babylonian "slave labor was only one of several types of forced labor and not always the most significant" to the Babylonian economy of ancient Mesopotamia (Dandamaev, 1984).

The period of greatest use of slaves occurred under King Nebuchadnezzar (605–562 B.C.), with increasing documentary evidence in artifacts, cylinder seals, and bas-relief portrayals of slaves engaged in various professional occupations, such as medicine, law, and scholarship, as well as in domestic service and military training and as laborers on construction projects. The numbers of slaves engaged in building and irrigation canal construction ran into the thousands. The chronicles and archaeological evidence also reveal that the number of runaway slaves and slave uprisings against Babylonian rule and, in particular, against King Nebuchadnezzar were on the rise by 550 B.C. Protected by the older social codes and laws from Akkadian and Sumerian times, the slaves were generally treated well and, on occasion, given freedom or manumitted for faithful service or heroic or unusual deeds.

The subsequent Achaemenian (Persian) period briefly increased the exchanges of slaves over the long-distance routes as the demand for larger military forces and greater numbers of skilled construction laborers and the increased need for domestic slaves accompanied the Persian imperial expansion from India and Transoxiana to the shores of the eastern Mediterranean, the Egyptian Nile, and Ethiopia.

See also ARCHAEOLOGY OF SLAVERY.

BIBLIOGRAPHY

DANDAMAEV, MUHAMMAD A. *Slavery in Babylonia from Nabopolassar to Alexander the Great (626–331 B.C.).* Rev. ed. 1984.
DU RAY, CAREL J. *Art of the Ancient Near and Middle East.* 1969.
Epic of Gilgamesh. English version with introduction by N. K. Sandars. Rev. ed. 1972.
KRAMER, SAMUEL NOAH. *Cradle of Civilization.* 1967.
MALLOWAN, M. E. L. *Early Mesopotamia and Iran.* 1965.
MENDELSOHN, ISSAC. *Slavery in the Ancient Near East.* 1949.

Thomas M. Ricks

Persia

Extending from the northern Caucasus Mountains and the Caspian Sea littoral to the southern Zagros Mountains and the Persian Gulf, ancient Persia was the fertile plateau between the lower Central Asian steppes to the north and the river-basin kingdoms of Mesopotamia and the Indus Valley to the west and east. Slavery existed in this region by the eighth century B.C. under the kings of southwestern Iran. While the cuneiform and chronicle evidence is weak for that early period of Persian history, rock carvings, coins, urban bas-reliefs, fire-temples, and enameled-brick sculptures support the presence of slaves and slavery in both urban and rural environments. Typically, the

Persian slave (*garda*) of the eighth century was either an agricultural worker on one of the aristocratic estates surrounding the towns or a servant in the household of the Persian king or a noble household. The slaves were people captured as war prisoners, born as slaves, or (in a few cases) bought in Mesopotamian markets to the west. Little evidence appears of slave-artisans, debt bondage, slave markets, or a slave trade in ancient Persia prior to the eighth century B.C.

Between the eighth and sixth centuries B.C., a slow migration brought Iranian-speaking peoples into northwestern Iran. As new arrivals moved on to southern and southwestern Iran, they reoccupied abandoned villages, constructed new towns, and engaged in intensive agricultural production and animal husbandry. The Iranians also brought their military technologies: horsemanship, archery, and the chariot. The peopling of ancient Persia with groups having similar cultural, political, and economic characteristics laid the foundation for the emergence of the Achaemenian Empire.

The earlier forms of slavery associated with aristocratic wealth gave way to a more diverse system of slave labor. Evidence from coinage, language, and pottery indicates that eighth- to sixth-century Iranians, including the Persians of Parsa, practiced a kind of "patriarchal" slavery, in which heads of families behaved as if they were slaveholders in respect to the members of their own families. In time, this absolute authority came to characterize merchants' control over their artisans, landlords' power over rural laborers, and the king's command over his subjects. The origin of the practice is evident from the Old Persian term for slave (*garda*), which meant "household slave" or "domestic slave." The Iranian-speakers subjugated descendants of the pre-eighth-century population of the Iranian plateau as captives and kidnapped skilled laborers to augment their predominantly agricultural economy. These two hundred years of transformation in ancient Persia ended with the emergence of a number of petty Iranian kingdoms throughout the north (Parthians), northwest (Medes), and south (Persians) around 600 B.C.

In the patriarchal households of royalty, nobles, and priests, slave labor increased production of goods and services, while semifree slaves were utilized as servants and guards in the temples, as craftsmen and artisans in the royal workshops, or as farm laborers on the royal household agricultural estates of the petty kings surrounding the towns. Even with these more diverse uses of slaves, the majority of laborers in urban crafts and agriculture remained free men and women.

In 600 B.C., the Median kingdom controlled the northern and central Iranian plains, forcing other kingdoms—including the Persians—to pay taxes and serve as vassals. The petty Iranian kingdoms of ancient Persia then began to contest the Medes' power, and in 558 the Persian king Cyrus II began a series of military and political campaigns that weakened first the Median kingdom and then the remaining Iranian petty states, resulting in establishment of the Achaemenian Empire by 548. This date marked the beginning of imperial unification of ancient Persia under one dynasty. The Achaemenian era on the Iranian plateau also marked a sharp qualitative transformation from primitive patriarchal slavery to the intensive use of the labor of foreign workers in agriculture and also partly in crafts; some of these foreign workers were held as slaves, while the rest were exploited as semifree people settled on royal lands.

Combining the equestrian and chariot technology of the Medes with its own cavalry, infantry, and expert archery units, the Achaemenian Empire soon conquered the Iranian plateau, the lands of the southern Caucasus and Tranoxiana to the east as well as all the Mesopotamian lands of Babylon from the Tigris-Euphrates basin to the eastern Mediterranean coasts of Syria, Phoenicia, and Palestine. By 512 B.C. the Achaemenian Empire extended westward to the Egyptian delta and eastward to northwestern India. With imperial expansion came increased slaving and a nascent long-distance trade with the Mediterranean lands and as far as Ethiopia to the south and Transoxiana, the Persian Gulf, and the Indus Valley to the east. The steady trade, including slaves, contributed enormously to the rise of the "silk route" between Iran and China in the east and the trade from the Persian Gulf to the Indian Ocean in the west.

Centered in the old Median capital city of Ecbatana (present-day Hamadan in western Iran), Darius I reorganized the older Iranian, Mesopotamian, and Egyptian administrations into an unprecedented imperial network of satrapies, roads, canals, and urban centers. Key provincial administrative towns, with palaces and temples, were first at Parsa or Persepolis in southern Iran (520 to 450 B.C.) and then in the old Elamite city of Susa (518 to 512 B.C.). Darius relied on the labor of thousands of war prisoners and kidnapped free men to build the palaces, towns, roadways, station houses, and canals that allowed the Achaemenian Empire to prosper. It is reported that 4,000 craftsmen, millers, masons, and carpenters were used in the construction of Persepolis alone. The Achaemenian social structure—bound by Zoroastrianism and comprising priests, warriors, scribes, and commoners including artisans, traders, peasants, and slaves of the towns and countryside—remained stable over the subsequent 150 years. Unlike some other Mediterranean empires, the Achaemenian was not heavily dependent upon slave labor in the marketplace, in workshops, or in agricultural production; and for the most part it needed skilled laborers in the construction industries and military affairs only temporarily. Indeed, one of the principal weaknesses of the Achaemenian rulers, beyond their refusal to adopt new military techniques, was their failure to expand slavery.

The Achaemenian Empire recognized slavery but protected slaves with rules of fairness, including possible manumission upon rendering good services to the master. Generally, war prisoners were taken to the estates of temple priests and aristocratic households to work in the fields, while kidnapped free men and women were employed in the households and temples as domestic servants, prostitutes, or guards. In both cases, from the sixth to fourth centuries B.C. manual and unskilled labor was increasingly relegated to slaves. Overall, Achaemenian slaves were war prisoners and kidnapped citizenry largely set to work on temporary labor-intensive projects such as building monuments and temples or extending irrigation systems. With consolidation of the empire, Achaemenian slaves became regular military troops and domestic servants in royal and aristocratic households.

The Achaemenian slave was considered a person, not a thing, and both social custom and religious laws

A servant (probably a slave) in the Achaemenian court. [Gianni Dagli Orti/Corbis]

forbade mistreatment and allowed inheritance and manumission; masters were expected to treat slaves with reasonable care, and many slaves were taught artisan and musical skills to be practiced in the household or the marketplace. There are only scattered references to indebtedness as a reason for enslavement, and even fewer sources refer to a long-distance trade in slaves of the sort characteristic of other Mediterranean societies of the sixth to fourth centuries B.C. Among the slaves traded, Achaemenian sources distinguish between black slaves from the southern lands of the Persian Gulf, Arabia, or Egypt and white slaves from the northern lands of Anatolia, the Caucasus, or Transoxiana.

In 520 B.C. Darius I moved Cyrus's capital out of the Zagros Mountains to Persepolis in the Marvdasht plains of central Persia, creating the Achaemenian summer capital of Pasargadai. He did so in order to relocate the Achaemenian Empire securely away from the Mediterranean in the west and from nomadic raids from the north, both regions that had rebelled and engaged in external raiding. Darius thus also moved closer to the Persian Gulf trade routes, revitalizing the Achaemenian empire and its markets and emphasizing the "Persian" character of his rule. Subsequent Achaemenian warfare, particularly against the Egyptians and Greeks, necessitated larger military forces, longer supply lines, and a more extensive imperial administrative system. According to Herodotus, Darius established twenty provinces throughout the empire, with each province ruled by a *satrap*, a "protector of the empire." The satraps recruited large regular and irregular military forces from the various minorities and ethnic groups under their authority to maintain the security of towns, markets, and roads; collect taxes; and protect the empire's borders. The subsequent revitalization of the Achaemenian Empire from 520 to 350 B.C. depended on the skilled labor of war prisoners for military duty and on kidnapped citizens for imperial services.

Sitting astride both the principal north-south and east-west trade routes of the eastern Mediterranean and southwest Asia, the Persian Empire applied the skills of captive warriors, scribes, artisans, and tradesmen to reap the riches of river-irrigated and coastal rain-fed agriculture and other resources. Thousands of Greeks, Anatolians, Egyptians, Syrian-Palestinians, and Mesopotamians constituted the slave labor force that facilitated trade, built monuments and religious centers of great magnificence, expanded agricultural production through canals and extensive irrigation systems, and accelerated the marketing of cheap goods toward Rome to the west and India to the east. With increased reliance on slave labor, the Achaemenians became concerned about the legal boundaries of enslavement, manumission, and slaves' rights. Slaves replaced women in the pottery and textile industries and became bakers, barbers, and tradesmen and, in time, owners of land. The aristocracy, the priestly class, and warriors utilized the expanding domestic slave labor force as concubines, as domestic servants, and occasionally as artisans. Slave markets appeared in the principal imperial towns throughout the empire within a hundred years after the reign of Darius I. By 420 B.C., increased protection for slaves against punitive measures by masters, and even freedom as a reward for honorable service, lessened the social and political distance between slaves and the freedmen and serfs; the latter were found more often on estates on the frontiers, while the former soon found that their skills were less needed and migrated increasingly to Rome and other Mediterranean capitals.

In fall of 331 B.C., the Achaemenian Empire came under a new threat when Alexander the Macedonian and his powerful Greek forces reached Persepolis, sacking the Achaemenian capital nearly beyond recognition, slaying all men without mercy, and enslaving the women. A five-hundred-year hiatus in the political unity of ancient Persia followed, ending only with the emergence of the Sasanian Empire (224 B.C.–A.D. 652). The Sasanians were as inclined toward warfare as their predecessor, and they reconquered the Mesopotamian and Syrian-Palestinian mountains, rivers, and plains, including Egypt and southern Arabia. In a latter-day sequel to the Achaemenians' wars on Greece, the Sasanians carried out continuous assaults on Constantinople and Byzantium, once more producing large numbers of war prisoners and kidnapped citizens. The Sasanians expanded their household servants to include domestic slaves while using the war prisoners more often than not as craft and agricultural labor. Their major interest was creating increasing numbers of slave administrators to supervise the imperial roadways and soldiers to control the rural and urban populations and to collect the growing variety of imperial taxes.

Less inclined to foster an expansive slave raiding system, but interested in long-distance trade and overseas markets, the Sasanians devoted more time than their predecessor to the northern trade of the Caspian Sea through Astrakhan and to the maritime trade of the Persian Gulf and the Indian Ocean at Hormuz, seeking minerals, spices, foods, and slaves in Egypt, Ethiopia, East Africa, South and Southeast Asia, and China. They thus sought seasoned sailors and sea captains in addition to the stonecutters and masons of previous times. In time, the slaves and merchandise were destined less for Persian or Sasanian households than for transshipment to Central Asia, to India, and to China. With the more developed trade of the Sasanian period, the Persians elaborated currency, credit and banking systems, shipbuilding and port administration, overseas agencies and trading houses, and more sophisticated forms of diplomacy and communication.

By A.D. 652, Arab Muslims overthrew the last of the Sasanian kings, leaving medieval Persia once more a mosaic of petty Iranian rulers, most of them preserving the heritage of the Sasanian and Achaemenian eras, including slaves, slavery, and long-distance slave trading.

See also ENSLAVEMENT, METHODS OF; LABOR SYSTEMS; SLAVE TRADE.

BIBLIOGRAPHY

ARBERRY, A. J., ed. *The Legacy of Persia.* 1953.
BAUSANI, ALESSANDRO. *The Persians: From Earliest Days to the Twentieth Century.* Translated from Italian by J. B. Donne. 1971.
DANDAMAEV, MUHAMMAD A., and VLADIMIR G. LUKONIN. *The Culture and Social Institutions of Ancient Iran.* 1989.
FERDOWSI. *The Epic of the Kings: Shah-Nama, the National Epic of Persia.* Translated from Persian by Reuben Levy. 1967.
FRYE, RICHARD N. *The Heritage of Persia.* 1966.
GHIRSHAM, R. *Iran: From the Earliest Times to the Islamic Conquest.* 1954.
HERODOTUS. *The Histories,* translated by Aubrey de Selincourt, revised with notes by A. R. Burn. 1972.
OLMSTEAD, A. T. *History of the Persian Empire.* 1948.
XENOPHON. *The Persian Expedition.* Translated by Rex Warner; new introduction and notes by George Cawkwell. 1972.

Thomas M. Ricks

Ancient Rome

According to tradition the city of Rome was founded in 753 B.C.; the emperor Justinian (A.D. 518–565) is considered both the last Roman and the first Byzantine emperor. (The Roman Empire in the West had collapsed in the late fifth century.) Throughout these twelve centuries, or certainly from very early on, Rome was a slave-owning society. This was normal for the place and the period; no country in the ancient Mediterranean world did without slaves. From around 200 B.C. Rome came to dominate this world. For roughly the next four hundred years, Rome and Roman Italy were, however, unusual—compared with either the ancient or the modern world—in having a slave economy, in the sense that a substantial part of productive labor in Italy was servile. However, in Rome, unlike the modern slave economies of Brazil, the Caribbean islands, and the southern United States, the motive for slave-owning was not exclusively economic. This is not to deny that making a profit was extremely important, but slaves were also an expression of their owners' social status and power. This aspect of Roman slavery seems to have become predominant in the later empire, by perhaps the fifth century A.D., when there had come to be many employed persons who were imperfectly free.

There are many theories about early Rome, but our knowledge for the first hundred and fifty years, the period of the kings, is all inferential. It does seem likely that Rome became a republic in 510 B.C., or within the next fifty years. Until the third century B.C., Rome's external history was one of slowly consolidating its power, at first as the dominant state in central Italy and then in the peninsula as a whole. At home, however, around the middle of the fifth century—in 453 and then 451—the Romans codified some of their legal customs in what are known as the Twelve Tables—twelve tablets, presumably of stone, with laws written on them for all who could to read. The actual tablets seem to have been destroyed when the Gauls sacked Rome in 390 B.C., and their replacements may have been somewhat modernized. But their content was still known in the late republic, the last century before the turn of the era. We can observe a small city-state, essentially agricultural, often at war with its neighbors—with whom, nevertheless, it shared gods and their worship.

Slaves appear in the Twelve Tables, not surprisingly, but several of the provisions concerning them are surprising. We learn that freed slaves would be citizens whose inheritance, however, went to their patron—their former owner—if they died without heirs. We learn that slaves conditionally freed in a will could be understood to buy their own freedom although they were technically incapable of owning anything (less surprising is the fact that, in such circumstances, the heir could expect compensation for his loss of an expectation). When somebody's status—whether free or slave—was questioned, the court procedure (which required a sum to be staked) required only the smaller of the two possible sums. Again, it is hardly surprising that slaves should be more heavily punished for manifest theft than free men and that injury to slaves was valued lower. But when a slave committed a tort, the owner had the alternative of paying damages or offering a slave in surrender to the victim of the tort—just as a father had with a son. Although the Twelve Tables do not explicitly classify slaves—along with land and animals working the land, such as horses or oxen—as property that must be conveyed formally (by emancipation) for ownership to pass, it is likely that custom treated them as such. Thus, in the mid-fifth century B.C. slaves were clearly chattels, yet they could become citizens.

Slaves came from captives taken in the early Italian wars—the etymology given by Gaius, a jurist of the second century A.D., is that the word *servus* (slave) came from *servare* (to spare) because in defeat the captives' lives were spared. Slaves were thus men (and women) very like the Romans themselves in their customs and their cults. Slaves could not marry with rights such as the law granted to citizens, but they could enter a factual reflection of marriage, with no legal consequences, known as a *contubernium*. It is not very surprising that there was no very clear distinction between the powers of owners over their slaves and of the head of a family (*paterfamilias*) over his children. A son could own nothing, nor could a slave; but both alike were normally given a personal fund (*peculium*), which they could deal with almost as if they owned it. A slave could be put to death by an owner, at the owner's discretion, but so could a son by his father. What the slave acquired, physically or through some form of obligation, was acquired for the owner, and the same was the case with a son and his father. The pervasive nature of paternal power, which was lifelong—that is, even an adult son remained under paternal power until his father died—meant therefore that, with regard to purely legal rights, a slave was not so very much worse off than a child. This, of course, ignores the natural human love of kin and the certainty of a son's reaching independent status with his father's death. A slave was a chattel, which became the property of the heir; he could be sold at a moment's notice, and his chance of freedom was contingent on the will of the owner, not (normally) a right.

What was unique about the Roman form of slavery, although one can perhaps explain it by the habit of enslaving captive neighbors, was that freed slaves became Roman citizens; they took their former owner's civic status. (Presumably, some went back home.) Rules were in time developed about the formalities required to turn a slave into a citizen. Slaves informally freed (relieved of duties) did not become citizens, but clearly citizenship was the norm. This was achieved by manumission (the technical term for release from slavery) in three formal ways: the owner could present a slave to the censors at the quinquennial enrollment of citizens; a collusive claim to liberty could be made before the praetor (the magistrate with jurisdiction in matters of private law), which is known as manumission *vindicat,* "by the rod"; and an owner could free a slave in a will. The understanding of slavery as an unfortunate accident resulting from defeat in war must also explain why Romans who were taken prisoner were themselves understood to have become slaves. There were rules here too about their right of rehabilitation (*postliminium*) if they returned from captivity, but it was not denied that they had been enslaved. In early Rome, then, slavery was seen as due to the fortunes of war, not to any innate inferiority in the enslaved individual.

Once Rome had consolidated its power in Italy during the middle of the third century B.C., it began to expand into the wider world of the Mediterranean. War with the Carthaginians to protect its commerce led to the annexation of Sicily as Rome's first province in 241 B.C. The annexation of Sardinia followed in 239. The Second Punic War (218–202 B.C.) nearly brought Rome to its knees but then led to its conquest of southern and eastern Spain. Rome had entered the war as the leader of a confederacy of allies but ended by ruling subject peoples; the war also led to Roman rule over Cisalpine Gaul—Italy south of the Alps but north of the River Po. It is in this context that we find distant peoples seeking alliances with Rome against more immediately threatening neighbors (as *Maccabees* tells us happened with the Jews in 161 and 143 B.C.). Strife between Antiochus of Syria and the Greek cities led the Romans, through a series of wars, to make Macedonia a province in 146 B.C., when they also sacked the great and highly civilized Greek city of Corinth. Further, in the same year Carthage was captured and destroyed, and Africa became a province. After various difficult wars in Spain, the greater part of the Iberian peninsula was brought under Roman rule in 133 B.C., and in the same year Pergamum became Rome's province of Asia (Minor) as a bequest from the dying king Attalus. Eleven years later the province of Gallia Narbonensis was created in the southern strip of modern France to be the land link between Italy and Spain. Deliberately or not, Rome had become the great power of the Mediterranean world.

From then on, prisoners of war were no longer neighbors speaking the same language and sharing the same cults, and their numbers swelled enormously. All statistics for the ancient world are dubious, but most historians accept that perhaps a third of the population of Italy—well over two million people—were servile by the time of the emperor Augustus (27 B.C.–A.D. 14). The numbers were such that control became an obvious problem. Slave revolts in Sicily in 136–132 and 104–100 B.C. had heightened apprehension about the threat posed by the presence of slaves. One solution was to herd captives into chain gangs and set them to work on farms or in mines, treating them rather as though they were dangerous wild animals. At the same time, another solution was to make use of their skills—and this applied particularly to educated Greeks—while emphasizing their moral inferiority. Although it was still the fortunes of war that were most likely to reduce someone to slavery, by this period the Romans were expecting to be victo-

A captured barbarian (soon to be enslaved) adorns the Porta Bojano within the Roman ruins at Sepino, Italy. [Enzo and Paolo Ragazzini/Corbis]

rious; they were "better" than other peoples, and attitudes toward slaves changed to reflect this.

The origins of the use of slaves as personal servants and as bodies available to do the heavy or dirty work around the house or farm are lost in the mists of antiquity. But the development of an economy dependent on servile labor does seem linked to the expansion of Roman interests in the third and second centuries B.C., with military successes making huge numbers of slaves available. These same wars had also led to a decline in the numbers of independent peasant farmers—many of whom were conscripted into the legions—and a concentration of land ownership in the hands of an elite. To many people in Rome the most attractive policy of the later second century was embodied in the populist agrarian laws of the Gracchi brothers, Tiberius and Caius (killed by their political enemies in 133 and 121, respectively), which aimed at redistributing land in Italy to the dispossessed. At the same time the population of Rome was growing, and at the end of the second century Marius created a standing army, building on the already semipermanent legions. The urban and military populations created an expanded market for grain, oil, and wine, enough to explain the growth of latifundia farming—the cultivation of huge estates with predominantly slave labor. In the south of Italy great numbers of sheep were raised. Industrial enterprises also grew, producing clay amphorae (pottery) to contain wine and oil, bricks and tiles for new buildings, presumably cloth for uniforms, and so on.

In the late Republic the miserable state of many slaves—particularly those on the latifundia, who sometimes worked chained and were not even treated as the valuable animals the were—led to several major slave revolts, of which Spartacus's was the most alarming because it took place closest to Rome. Spartacus held out for nearly three years (73–71 B.C.) against the best generals of the republic, but his rebellion was not against society or slavery as an institution; it was rather a doomed attempt to find his way home to Thrace. The period of slave revolts did not last long, although its impact may have remained in senators' memories and colored later legislation.

Nevertheless, although the social distance between owner and slave had changed so radically, slaves who were formally freed continued to become citizens. Freed citizens might have some public disabilities, apart from the duties they owed their former owners (patrons), but their freeborn children had none. And citizenship was acquired whether a slave was Italian-born; or from the Danube; or a German captured on the Rhine, a Spanish Celt, a Moor, a Persian, or a Syrian. The Roman state—not yet constitutionally an empire, but imperialistic as regards the colonies it controlled—was based on the Mediterranean; there were huge differences between the urbanized Greek-speaking east and the rustic west where Latin became the lingua franca, but there was still a measure of common culture. So the Romans were content to continue with their uniquely generous policy of assimilating even foreign slaves into the citizen body. However, this policy had become less generous than before in that fewer slaves could hope to benefit from it. We have no figures, but it does not seem impossible that in the fifth century B.C. eventual freedom had been a realistic expectation for almost all slaves, if they lived long enough. In the flood of slaves from the wars of Rome's expansion, only a minority must have been freed.

Military conquests, and with them supplies of new slaves, began to taper off in the late first century B.C., with the end of the republic under the first emperor, Augustus. In Rome and Italy, for fifty years before his victory over Mark Antony at Actium in 31 B.C., there had been either civil war or at least civil disorder, proscriptions, and extralegal activity, as revealed, for example, in Cicero's speech on behalf of Cluentius. Warlords had followed each other; Marius, Sulla, Pompey, and Julius Caesar were the most prominent among them. Yet Rome's power abroad was not diminished: Augustus's empire was bounded only by the Atlantic, the Rhine, and the Danube to the west and north; it included northern Africa and Egypt to the south and Judaea, Syria, and Asia Minor in the east. Southern Britain was to be added—and the corner between the Danube and the Rhine—but the frontiers had stabilized. There were to be no more great influxes of prisoners of war.

At home, Augustus's empire seems to have been welcomed by a considerable proportion of the politically interested population, not only his friends and allies among the senatorial order, but also the bulk of the better-off ranks of society. One may presume that the lower orders were for the most part simply relieved that the fighting was over. Augustus promised, and provided, stability. And with this stability the urban poor and not-so-poor had a patron they could approach for help, someone who was reliably there, who would not necessarily grant what they wanted but often could. The bulk of the Roman population became the emperor's clients and for the most part were content; only among the senatorial order did men continue to feel that they had lost privileges and that they might have been sitting on the throne had things only been different.

Rome had never been a democracy. True, every adult male citizen had had a vote in the various assemblies that elected magistrates, passed legislation, or sat as criminal courts. But the assembly court had fallen out of use decades before Augustus; the election of magistrates had become a farce, or at best a matter of squabbles among ambitious clans; and legislation had not been generally important to most of the population since Sulla. Under Augustus's adopted son and successor, Tiberius, the election of magistrates was transferred to the senate without a whimper from anyone as far as we can tell. Augustus and his stepgrandson Claudius made use of assembly legislation, particularly to suggest ancient custom while disguising fundamental changes, but the senate was more apt for the purpose. and by the end of the first century A.D. it had taken over this function. The old republican constitution had been designed for a small city-state; it was irrelevant to a huge empire. Augustus's rule was autocratic—if mostly shrouded in legality—but it is totally inappropriate to mourn as a loss of liberty the decline of the close-knit senatorial oligarchy that had previously ruled Rome.

In the new atmosphere of hope it made sense for Augustus to consider to what degree the servile population could join the stable element in society. Among other legislation, Augustus arranged the enactment of a package of laws on manumission of which the overall effect was to make citizenship more easily achievable for the increasingly locally born slave population. The *lex Junia* should almost certainly be ascribed to this package, since it is presupposed in acts that were certainly owing to him. It created a specific legal status for informally freed slaves, who had hitherto been under the protection of the praetor but not in strict

Various aspects of Roman life are illustrated in The Age of Augustus, *from an original painting by George Hiltensperger.* [Corbis-Bettmann]

law free at all. They now became Junian Latins, holding a new legal status inferior to citizenship; as time went by Latin status was given to other categories, such as a female slave prostituted against a condition of her acquisition. However, various ways were created by which Junian Latins could achieve citizenship. One way was a repetition of the manumission when there had been some flaw in the original procedure. Another, deriving from the *lex Aelia Sentia* (see below), was to marry another Latin or a citizen in the presence of seven citizen witnesses and to have a baby in due course; when the baby was a year old, the couple could appear before the praetor and claim citizenship for themselves and the child. Another way that appeared was by public service of some sort, such as service in the fire brigade (the *vigiles*) or building a ship for importing corn to Rome.

Augustus's *lex Aelia Sentia* of A.D. 4 laid down a new status category, the *dediticii*—slaves who had been put in chains as a punishment (not just for restraint) by their owners or who had been interrogated under torture concerning some wrongdoing and convicted. They could never be allowed to become citizens, or even to live within a hundred miles of Rome. More importantly, the *lex Aelia Sentia* put restrictions on manumission by owners under twenty or of slaves under thirty years of age, and also manumission in fraud of creditors. Manumission by one too young was totally void, unless the young person had received the approval of a council in Rome, consisting of five senators and five members of the equestrian order (next in rank to senators), sitting with the praetor. Approval was at their discretion, but they seem regularly to have considered both blood and foster relationships as well as the relationship of nurse or *paedagogus,* and also intention to marry. This last case would almost always—particularly for women owners—have applied to someone freed who wished to bring a partner in a *contubernium* into a lawful citizen marriage. Manumission of a slave under thirty was not normally void, but it created a Junian Latin, again unless the manumission had been approved by the council; grounds similar to those for owners under twenty might justify the council approving citizenship for a slave under thirty. The provision that manumission in fraud of creditors was void was the only case applying to a manumission performed by a foreigner (*peregrinus*); this and the requirement that an owner must be twenty (except for freedom granted by will) were the only real restrictions preserved by the emperor Justinian.

The *lex Fufia Caninia* of 2 B.C. restricted the number of slaves who could be freed by will: an owner with only two slaves could free both, but for larger numbers of slaves only a proportion could be freed, up to a maximum of one hundred. The act put no limit, however, on the number who could be freed while an owner was alive. Many scholars have seen Augustus's package as restricting manumission and as preventing the citizen body from being diluted by alien blood. But a consideration of the actual measures laid down suggests rather that, while Augustus was certainly trying to restrict irresponsible manumission by owners careless of the interests of their families or creditors, he also intended to make it easier for virtuous freed persons to achieve citizenship, to give them, as we might say nowadays, a stake in society. Slaves were a very substantial group in society, to be controlled by the carrot as well as the stick.

Since captives were no longer being brought to Rome in huge numbers, the major source of slaves must have become the institution itself: those born into slavery. There were, of course, other sources, but the vast extent of Rome's empire meant that relatively few slaves were imported from beyond its boundaries; slave dealers were in general concerned with trade within the empire. Kidnapping and piracy cannot have brought significant numbers of apparent slaves onto the market, although literary romances made use of the device. Slavery was sometimes a criminal penalty, but penal slaves usually either were sent to the arena or worked in the state's mines and other enterprises; they were not a commercial source of supply. Another source of new slaves was the exposure of newborn children and babies. Someone who took in a foundling had the choice as to whether the child should be brought up free or slave; one guesses that the latter choice was more common. The law said that nobody freeborn could ever lose this status— even being made a penal slave did not affect the birthright—but for most foundlings it must have been impossible to prove.

Easily the simplest and most useful source of supply was from within the existing slave population. The rule that the Romans understood as applying to all peoples was that children took their mother's status at birth (although for Roman citizens there was a special rule that children born of a citizen marriage took

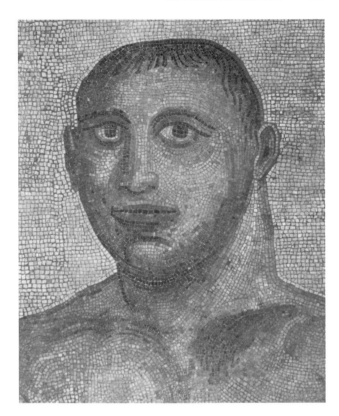

A mosaic of a gladiator (probably a slave), from the floor of the Caracalla Spa in Rome, demonstrates the type of skilled work some Roman slaves were capable of producing. [Christel Gerstenberg/Corbis]

their status from their father); so, by the ordinary operation of the law, children born to a female slave were themselves slaves. These slaves (sometimes known as *vernae*) who were born in the household, or at least on the farm, were of known quality. It became easier to trust slaves again—at least to some degree. This was important, since slavery continued despite the decline of the latifundia as the economic basis of society, at least in Italy, although maybe not in the majority of provinces. There is really no economic activity where we do not find slaves. They were bailiffs and farm managers as well as agricultural laborers; some were also small tenant farmers, hardly distinguishable from their free neighbors. Among craftsmen, slaves, freed, and freeborn seem to have worked alongside each other, as is widely evidenced by inscriptions and makers' marks. We find silversmiths and jewelers; specialists in enameling, glass, bronze, and pewter; workers in iron, wood, leather, textiles, stucco, and marble; makers of mosaics; painters; shopkeepers; managers of bars or brothels; and attendants at the baths. Slaves were the principal employees of the industries producing pottery, bricks, and tiles; in the imperial mints; and in the mines. This was the state of affairs during the two hundred and fifty years or so of the principate, the earlier empire from Augustus to the mid-third century after Christ.

There is relatively little information about female slaves; the man was the norm in Rome, even within slavery. Most women slaves were probably in domestic service, as remained true of wage-earning women into the twentieth century. But female slaves also worked on farms and in some crafts. They worked in what we might call the service industry, as shopkeepers, tavern keepers, waitresses, and prostitutes. Women too became citizens if freed with due formality, and they were subject then to the same disabilities or disadvantages as freeborn women, or a little bit worse. A freedwoman needed four, not three, live births to gain the privilege of children (*ius liberorum*), which through the first and second centuries A.D. exempted her from the need for a guardian; a female slave freed specifically so that her former owner could marry her could not refuse to become his wife—but if she had remained his slave, she could not have refused sexual relations anyway. A freedwoman could not be required to work as a prostitute by her patron; she had, if she wished, joined the respectable classes by the act of being freed.

In the course of the third century after Christ, turmoil—in internal politics, from invaders, from plague, and from a collapse of certainty—meant that free labor again became dominant in agriculture and industry. This may have happened because it was not difficult for discontented slaves to run away or because it was easier to turn to hired labor than to feed slaves or even because so many had died in a particular district that there was no longer any social organization. The distinction, already visible in outline between the privileged upper ranks of society (the *honestiores*) and the rest of the free population (the *humiliores*) became sharper. Free workers on the land might become tied to the land, whether as tenants or as employees, like medieval serfs; thus the clear distinction between free and slave was eroded by the growth of half-free categories. Slavery in this period and for the rest of the empire became primarily domestic slavery, as much a matter of flaunting one's wealth as anything else. Great households survived with their huge array of carefully differentiated slave servants, with separate titles in the dressing room for the slave in charge of pins and the slave in charge of pearls and with separate titles in the pantry for the slave in charge of silver, the slave in charge of jeweled objects, and the slave in charge of crystal. Apart from bodyguards, perhaps the slave hairdresser really was as useful as any.

The third century saw the beginning of the slow collapse of Rome's frontiers as migrating Germans pressed westward and southward. In many provinces the population dropped sharply, and land went out of cultivation. Taxes became harder to collect. The tone of central government became more shrill. The emperor Constantine (A.D. 312–337) became a Christian and founded a new Rome at a small city on the Bosphorus called Byzantium, to be renamed Constantinople. The division between the western and eastern halves of the empire, between Latin and Greek as the common language, became more marked. The insignia and habits of the emperors increasingly reflected Hellenistic rather than Italian influence. But in all this ferment the legal status of slaves seems to have changed very little. Christianity seems to have made little difference; Christian slaves could hope for their reward in the next world. Slavery might be against natural law—this view had already been expressed by Aristotle and echoed by pagan jurists in the early empire—and common humanity was recognized in theory by Cicero, Seneca, and Pliny the Younger. But slavery remained part of the *jus gentium,* the law of all peoples; it was a fact of life. There was never a discernible movement for its abolition in the ancient world, either among rebels or among philosophers.

Legally, it is interesting that there was virtually no distinct "slave law" in ancient Rome. Slaves as human beings occupied a legal position very close to that of sons; slaves as possessions were treated exactly like other valuable animate property, such as horses. Special rules did apply occasionally—for example, enforcing the services owed by a freed person to a patron through an oath sworn by slave to owner. In taking oaths, as in most religious activities, no line was drawn between free and slave. Slaves could be in a suspended state of freedom—*statuliberi*—freed under a condition, with their liberty guaranteed for the future but not yet enjoying it. From the time of the emperor Antoninus Pius (A.D. 138–161), slaves who were treated with excessive cruelty could seek asylum at a temple or a statue of the emperor, or later in a church; if their plea was found justified, by a slave-owning magistrate, they were to be sold away, with a condition that they should never return to the ownership from which they had fled. It must have been a very risky business and of little practical help; the very existence of asylum did, however, send out a message that cruelty was against the conventions of good Roman life and against the discipline of the times. It was the same emperor who laid down that owners who killed their own slaves without cause should be liable for homicide; again though, this theoretical protection cannot have been very meaningful in practice. In criminal law slaves sometimes received different penalties from those imposed on the humbler sort of free persons (*humiliores*), although more often they shared the tougher penalties in contrast to the lighter ones imposed on the upper classes (*honestiores*).

The *Senatusconsultum* (resolution of the Senate) *Silanianum* of A.D. 10 (and its extensions) was the one law aimed exclusively and pejoratively at slaves. Tacitus says, and Cicero implies, that custom held the slaves of a household collectively responsible for the mysterious death of their owner and allowed for the execution of all of them. This resolution of the senate laid down that all the slaves of the household should, in such circumstances, be tortured in order to discover the cause and the murderer; meanwhile, the dead person's will was not to be opened, and thus its provisions would remain unknown. In this way no *statuliberi* would get their freedom until the investigation was finished and their names were cleared, but equally, no overeager heirs would be able to benefit from an inheritance of slaves that they might have hastened. Because of the ban on opening the will, the compilers of the *Digest*, and doubtless the upper classes generally, thought of this state of affairs primarily in the context of succession. The resolution of the senate must have seemed very different to the slaves it exposed to torture or execution. It seems indisputable that one purpose of the law was to remind slaves that their lives were of no account when balanced against the lives of their owners and that in all circumstances their first duty was to protect the owner no matter at what cost.

The emperor Justinian, as well as codifying the law of Rome (in the *Corpus Iuris Civilis*), was also himself a law reformer in many fields, such as family law and the status of women. Although a devout Christian, he never questioned the existence of slavery, but he did, as elsewhere, attempt to simplify the law and return it to its classical elegance. Nevertheless, he did not have the *Senatusconsultum Silanianum* repealed, although he abolished the category of *dediticii*—those slaves who because of some crime could never achieve citizenship even if they were freed—and he also abolished penal slavery, the slavery imposed on a freeborn person as well as a slave condemned to death or in perpetuity to the mines. Further, he ruled that interpretation of any ambiguous terms in a will was always to favor liberty. And in his simplifying reforms, he abolished the status of Junian Latin and made a return to the most extraordinary feature—the unique feature—of Roman slavery: that manumission, any manumission other than one in fraud of creditors, made the former slave a full citizen. The medieval and modern worlds were not to know such generosity, but then true slavery, chattel slavery, was not to be a significant feature in later European society. The economic importance of slavery had already diminished greatly long before the Roman Empire came to an end, and after the fall of the Roman Empire there was no longer any economy that could sustain slavery as ostentatious display.

See also EDUCATION OF SLAVES; LAW; MINERS.

BIBLIOGRAPHY

BRADLEY, K. R. *Slavery and Society at Rome*. 1994.
———. *Slaves and Masters in the Roman Empire*. 1987.
BUCKLAND, W. W. *The Roman Law of Slavery*. 1908.
DUMONT, J. C. *Servus: Rome et l'esclavage sous la république*. 1987.
FINLEY, M. *Ancient Slavery and Modern Ideology*. 1980.
GARNSEY, P. *Ideas of Slavery from Aristotle to Augustine*. 1996.
GRANT, M. *History of Rome*. 1978.
HOPKINS, K. *Conquerors and Slaves*. 1978.
VOGT, J. *Ancient Slavery and the Ideal of Man*. 1975.
WATSON, A. *Roman Slave Law*. 1987.
WEAVER, R. R. C. *Familia Caesaris*. 1972.
WIEDEMANN, T. *Greek and Roman Slavery*. 1981.
YAVETZ, Z. *Slaves and Slavery in Ancient Rome*. 1988.

O. F. Robinson

Anglicanism

The Anglican church, which was created, in effect, by the Act of Supremacy in the reign of Henry VIII, is a worldwide Christian communion which has the British monarch as its temporal governor and the archbishop of Canterbury as its ranking cleric. It includes the established Church of England, the formerly established Church of Ireland, the international Anglican denomination, and the Episcopalian church in the United States.

Like the Catholic church—which high-church Anglicanism most resembles in theology, liturgy, and discipline—Anglicanism never endorsed slavery, holding it to be (at best) the lesser of evils, but active Anglican opposition to slavery developed slowly. An early struggle took place over the baptism and instruction of slaves held in English colonies, since masters feared that the law might free Christianized slaves. The Society for the Propagation of the Gospel was an Anglican organization intimately involved in that dispute.

It was with the rise of the so-called Evangelical group within Anglicanism that antislavery activism truly got under way. The intellectual center of Evangelicalism was Cambridge University, and the movement combined elements of high- and low-church Anglicanism, favoring greater personal devotion to private prayer and reflection, greater devotion to the sacraments and ceremonies of the church, greater emphasis on conversion and moral reformation at home and abroad, and greater support for social reforms.

Societies were formed to promote specific reforms, including the Church Missionary Society, the Society for the Bettering of Conditions of the Poor, the Religious Tract Society, and the British and Foreign Missions Society. The Anti-Slavery Society was founded as a collaboration of Evangelicals and dissenter Protestants.

Groups of lay Evangelicals were formed on the basis of shared interests and friendships, and to pursue specific social goals. The Clapham Sect, one of the most famous of these, contributed important leadership to the antislavery cause. William Wilberforce, who went on to become a member of Parliament, was the most famous of the Claphamites.

Under the influence of Wilberforce and an alliance of Anglicans and Dissenters, Parliament was pushed to enact its two great antislavery ordinances—the outlawing of the international slave trade (1806) and the abolition of slavery in the British Empire (1833).

In the southern United States, both in colonial times and under the republic, the record of the Anglican church and its post-Revolution offspring, the Episcopal church, was uneven. Some Anglican clergy owned slaves, as did a few Anglican churches. Only in regard to the right and duty of the clergy to preach to and baptize slaves was the church fully united in outlook.

One of the most inspiring antislavery stories to arise out of the Anglican communion was that concerning the spiritual awakening of John Newton, who went from command of a slave ship to repentance and, ultimately, to a curacy in the Church of England. An inspiration to the whole Evangelical movement within that church, he is best remembered for having composed the moving hymn "Amazing Grace," which was the direct result of his conversion and his reflection upon his former life.

See also CHRISTIANITY; SLAVE TRADE; SOCIETY FOR THE PROPAGATION OF THE GOSPEL; WILBERFORCE, WILLIAM.

BIBLIOGRAPHY

HYLSON-SMITH, K. *Evangelicals in the Church of England, 1734–1984.* 1989.
NEILL, STEPHEN. *Anglicanism.* 1958.
WILBERFORCE, WILLIAM ISAAC, and SAMUEL WILBERFORCE. *The Life of William Wilberforce.* 5 vols. 1838.

Patrick M. O'Neil

Anthropology of Slavery

Regarding the relationship of early anthropology to slavery, a distinction must be made between the precursors of physical anthropology and those of cultural anthropology. Many nineteenth-century physical anthropologists were polygenists, convinced that the different human "races" were independent creations or at least stable and very ancient entities with distinctive biological and behavioral characteristics, existing within a natural hierarchy of superior Caucasoids at the apex and inferior "colored" races below them. It is not surprising that these theories of race could be and were used by some of them to explain or justify the contemporaneous enslavement of Africans.

By contrast, within cultural and social anthropology, slavery was seen as a cultural-historical problem, and its theoretical treatment reflected current approaches to the study and explanation of behavioral differences. The treatment of slavery corresponds roughly to three stages of the discipline's history. In its formative period (mid-nineteenth century to early twentieth), cultural anthropology gave slavery a distinct place in its theories; in its classic period (turn of the century to 1960), it largely ignored slavery; and in the modern period (since 1960), it has given slavery a restrained recognition.

The precursors of cultural and social anthropology were almost universally monogenists, insisting that all existing "races" had a common origin, shared a common psychological makeup, and were therefore subject to the same laws of historical development and progress. These were unitary evolutionary laws on a grand scale, accounting for the origins of human institutions—laws that the emerging discipline had set out to discover. Most of these early scholars were trained in the law, well-versed in the classics and ancient history, and aware of the ubiquity of slavery in history. Slavery was thus a historical problem: like all institutions, slavery was to be fitted into the broad progressive movement of history, its origins and various forms emerging out of particular historical contexts. To this scheme, contemporaneous slavery was of little relevance; slavery in the modern period was seen either as a survival from earlier cultural stages or as an evolutionary anomaly.

The prevailing evolutionary theories saw slavery as absent in early hunting-fishing stages and as coming into its own with agriculture. A benign domestic institution at the outset, it developed into a variety of types in which slaves were used for many different purposes in addition to production—e.g., as wives and kinfolk, retainers, clerks, warriors, and bureaucrats. As society developed, slavery took on an increasingly economic cast as a labor institution, finally maturing into the dominant chattel form characteristic of the ancient and medieval Mediterranean and Middle East. Within this evolutionary perspective, a considerable body of theoretical argument arose, largely hypothetical at first but from early in the twentieth century increasingly grounded in ethnographic data from around the world. For example, Nieboer (1910) surveyed a great number of societies to arrive at his theory that slavery was a response to the need for labor when labor could not be secured by hire. He was in turn criticized, from an equally broad ethnographic perspective, by Westermarck (1924) and Sumner and Keller (1927) for ignoring the political factor—the ability to obtain and control slaves—and by MacLeod (1925) for oversimplifying the data on North American Indians to fit his overly economic thesis.

With the onset of the twentieth century, anthropology began to emphasize the need for fieldwork in "primitive" societies as a way of gathering data firsthand: it also emphasized sociological at the expense of historical theorizing. As a result, the data of anthropology became increasingly contemporary and nonhistorical, largely drawn from societies under colonial control: this meant that fieldworkers could not observe slavery as a fully functioning institution, since it was prohibited, dead, or dying. In descriptive monographs, there were few or no references to slavery, and slavery virtually disappeared from anthropological consciousness as a subject for theoretical discussion.

Moreover, it was at this time that anthropology began to see, as one of its missions, a battle against the cultural prejudice that was so widespread in Western popular culture. This quasi public-relations goal encouraged anthropologists to deny, ignore, explain away, or rationalize nonwestern customs that were particularly offensive to current Western sensibilities—customs like cannibalism, human sacrifice, mutilation, and slavery. In the case of slavery, its harsher forms in "primitive" societies were glossed over or ignored while its benign familial attributes were emphasized. The decline of classical education (which had informed previous generations of anthropologists about ancient slavery) contributed to confining the image of slavery to its New World forms: African-American slavery thus furnished the overriding model of slavery in general, making the varieties existing in other societies relatively invisible. During this period, studies of slavery by a Russian scholar (Averkieva, 1941/1966) and an American scholar (Siegel, 1945) stood virtually alone, and they found no response. This neglect of slavery was evident in the overwhelming majority of textbooks in anthropology; although these books were meant to introduce the student to the range of human social arrangements, most of them ignored slavery and the historical and cross-cultural prevalence of servile institutions.

The situation began to change in the 1960s. Partly as a result of the civil rights movement, much scholarly at-

In 1934 an expedition happened upon a troop of slaves and slave traders in northern Ethiopia, allowing its members to observe twentieth-century African slavery firsthand. [UPI/Corbis-Bettmann]

tention began to be given to African-American history and therefore to slavery. At the same time, a blossoming of African history encouraged study of the transatlantic slave trade and of African indigenous slavery. In the latter case, historians had to turn to anthropology while anthropology itself was increasingly turning to history and becoming more aware of slavery as an important indigenous African institution. This rising anthropological interest was exemplified by Cohen (1967) and several collaborative works (Meillassoux, 1975; Miers and Kopytoff, 1977; Watson, 1980).

While modern anthropology has rediscovered slavery, it has done so rather hesitantly. The work in anthropology is generally done in dialogue with historians and in the context of theoretical debates of which historians are an integral part. Articles on the subject scarcely ever appear in the main anthropological journals. This closeness of anthropology and history reflects an overlap in the work of the two disciplines. Historians of slavery have predominantly dealt with the United States, the Caribbean, and Latin America, with a more recent surge in interest in Africa. Similarly—as the most authoritative bibliography on slavery (Miller, 1993) shows—about two-thirds of the anthropological publications on slavery have been evenly divided between Africa and the African-American New World.

Within anthropology itself, general theoretical discussions of slavery are few (Kopytoff, 1982; Meillassoux, 1991) and generate no controversy. Studies of slavery continue to represent a truly minute proportion of total anthropological output. Slavery continues to be almost entirely ignored in anthropology textbooks, which reflect the consensus on the main interests of the discipline. There is also a paucity of anthropological attention to servile institutions outside of Africa and the African-American New World, and this means a lack of the kind of cross-cultural perspective on which anthropological theory thrives. For most anthropologists, then (as indeed for most historians), the dominant image of slavery continues to be shaped by its least representative forms—the slave systems of the New World.

See also CHATTEL SLAVERY; ECONOMIC INTERPRETATION OF SLAVERY; ECONOMICS OF SLAVERY; ENSLAVEMENT, METHODS OF; HISTORICAL APPROACHES TO SLAVERY; LABOR SYSTEMS; PERSPECTIVES ON SLAVERY.

BIBLIOGRAPHY

AVERKIEVA, IU. P. *Slavery among the Indians of North America,* translated by G. R. Elliot. 1966. Originally published 1941.

COHEN, RONALD. "Slavery in Africa: Special Supplement." *Trans-Action* 4 (1967): 44–56.

KOPYTOFF, IGOR. "Slavery." *Annual Review of Anthropology* 11 (1982): 207–230.

MACLEOD, W. C. "Debtor and Chattel Slavery in Aboriginal North America." *American Anthropologist* 27 (1925): 370–380.

MEILLASSOUX, CLAUDE. *The Anthropology of Slavery: The Womb of Iron and Gold.* 1991.

———, ed. *L'esclavage en Afrique precoloniale.* 1975.

MIERS, SUZANNE, and IGOR KOPYTOFF, eds. *Slavery in Africa: Historical and Anthropological Perspectives.* 1977.

MILLER, JOSEPH C. *Slavery and Slaving in World History: A Bibliography, 1900–1991.* 1993.

NIEBOER, H. J. *Slavery as an Industrial System,* 2nd ed. 1910.

SIEGEL, BERNARD J. "Some Methodological Considerations for a Comparative Study of Slavery." *American Anthropologist* 47 (1945): 357–392.

SUMNER, W. G., and A. G. KELLER. *The Science of Society,* vol. 1. 1927.

WATSON, JAMES L., ed. *Asian and African Systems of Slavery.* 1980.

WESTERMARCK, EDVARD A. *The Origin and Development of Moral Ideas,* 2nd ed., vol. 1. 1924.

Igor Kopytoff

Antipeonage Laws, U.S.

Peonage, from the Spanish *peon,* meaning a foot soldier, has come to indicate a system of debt servitude or slavery. In theory, persons held in peonage might be otherwise free persons who were bound to labor only because they owed money to their employers. In practice, they were kept in such a condition as to be unable to satisfy their debts, since their only source of money was their pay and their only source of the necessities of life was their employer—a terrible combination of monopsony and monopoly.

In 1867, Congress passed an antipeonage law aimed at the system of peonage that the New Mexican Territory had inherited from its former Mexican rulers, who had received it from Spanish law. In the aftermath of defeat in the Civil War and the disruption of its traditional labor system, the South developed alternative arrangements, utilizing sharecropping, tenant farming, and peonage—although peonage could be used in combination with either of those alternatives.

The laws of most southern states allowed the arrest of employees who attempted to leave the service of an employer to whom they were in debt. The laws of many states allowed the auctioning off of the labor of those incarcerated, so that persons imprisoned often found themselves working for private employers under compulsion. Most often, of course, employers engaged in peonage simply bypassed judicial proceedings; they used such means as holding or retaking workers by force or threat and compelling labor by beatings or starvation, and they sometimes even resorted to murder to make an example of an escapee.

After the passage of the antipeonage law of 1867, there was little federal intervention in this matter until 1901. In that year, Fred Cubberly, a U.S. commissioner in Florida, witnessed a violent recapture without law officers or warrant of a fugitive from a turpentine farm. With permission of the U.S. attorney general, Cubberly moved to test the constitutionality of the antipeonage statute and its applicability to southern practice by pursuing a case against Samuel M. Clyatt, who had seized men in Florida and forcibly returned them to his farm in Georgia.

The trial took place on 24 March 1902, and Clyatt was convicted, receiving a sentence of four years. This was eventually appealed to the U.S. Supreme Court. Simultaneously, Robert W. Lewis was charged with peonage for his kidnapping of George Walker, an indebted black worker. Lewis's claim of an absence of federal jurisdiction was denied in a hearing on a writ of habeas corpus in *In re Lewis.* Although the Supreme Court ordered a retrial of Clyatt on technicalities, the government was successful in upholding the constitutionality of the antipeonage statute.

In *U.S. v. Reynolds* (1914), the Supreme Court held that the Alabama law which permitted continuing re-arrest on a labor contract imposed for fines and court costs in criminal proceedings effectively violated the Thirteenth Amendment. In a federal court in Montgomery, Alabama, meanwhile, Judge Thomas Goode Jones presided over a block of cases known as the *Peonage Cases* (1903), involving ninety-nine indictments against eighteen individuals with several resulting convictions.

In 1903, Alabama amended its "false pretenses" statute, which provided for the punishment of laborers who received advances on a labor contract and wilfully failed to complete the contract, so that failure to fulfill a labor contract was prima facie evidence of an attempt to defraud. A 1907 amendment to the law eliminated testimony by the laborer.

In 1908, Alonzo Bailey, a black agricultural worker, petitioned on a writ of habeas corpus, claiming that the Alabama "false pretenses" law under which he was tried was unconstitutional. The case was remanded to the trial court for rehearing; but on an appeal, the U.S. Supreme Court in *Bailey v. Alabama* (1911) voided the Alabama law because it contravened the 1867 antipeonage statute.

In *Taylor v. Georgia* (1942), the Supreme Court struck down Georgia's contract-labor statute, and in *Pollock v. Williams* (1944), Florida's statute fell; but South Carolina's was restored in *Taylor v. U.S.* (1917), after having been suppressed in *Ex parte Drayton* (1907).

In 1921, national attention to the abuses of peonage centered upon a sensational murder trial, *Manning v. Georgia,* wherein Clyde Manning, the black foreman of a farm, was convicted of killing eleven workers to destroy evidence of ongoing peonage. In 1924, in *David v. U.S.,* four whites were convicted of peonage that had taken place on a turpentine farm in rural Florida.

The Depression and war years saw an increase in prosecutions for peonage, with cases such as *U.S. v. Thomas Jefferson Blair* (1938) and *U.S. v. Skrobarcek* (1942); but it was the great Mississippi Basin flood of 1927 that made the American public aware of the extent and conditions of peonage in the South, as the inhabitants of innumerable backcountry farms and camps were forced to flee the rising waters. Groups such as the National Association for the Advancement of Colored People (NAACP), the American Civil Liberties Union (ACLU), and the Workers Defense League (WDL) campaigned for more effective laws, better enforcement of existing laws, and greater public awareness of the problem.

In 1948, a recodification of federal law regarding peonage and related abuses produced laws with greater flexibility—covering peonage (1581 USC), slave kidnapping (1583 USC), and sale into involuntary servitude (1584 USC).

From the late 1940s on, there seems to have been no widespread peonage, but sporadic cases have been discovered and prosecuted.

See also LAW.

BIBLIOGRAPHY

Bailey v. Alabama, 219 U.S. 231 (1911).
Clyatt v. United States, 197 U.S. 209 (1905).
DANIEL, PETE. *The Shadow of Slavery: Peonage in the South, 1901–1969.* 1973.
Davis v. United States, 12 Fed. 2nd 254-55 (1925).
Ex parte Drayton, 153 F. 986 (1907).
In re Lewis, 114 F. 963 (c.c. Fla., 1902).
Manning v. Georgia, 153 Ga. 190 (1922).
Peonage Cases, 123 F. 678-81 (M.D. Ala., 1903).
Pollock v. Williams, 322 U.S. 4 (1944).
Taylor v. Georgia, 315 U.S. 25 (1942).
Taylor v. United States, 244 F. 321 (1917).
United States v. Reynolds, 235 U.S. 150 (1914).

Patrick M. O'Neil

Anti-Slavery International

Anti-Slavery International assumed its present form as a result of the amalgamation in 1909 of the British and Foreign Anti-Slavery Society with the Aborigines Protection Society (1838–1909). It was thereafter known as the Anti-Slavery Society for the Protection of Human Rights, and its principal concern was to draw attention to the mistreatment and exploitation of native peoples. One of the first cases it took up involved the British-registered Peruvian Amazon Rubber Company, which routinely employed torture and murder to punish Indians who failed to produce their allotted quotas. It was also able to show that the Portuguese in West Africa, under the guise of recruiting contract laborers, were carrying on what amounted to a slave trade in order to keep their cocoa plantations supplied with workers.

Following the First World War, the society looked to the League of Nations as a means of suppressing such practices. It was largely responsible for the establishment in 1932 of the league's Standing Committee of Experts on Slavery. The United Nations has no such body, although the society has continually pressed for one. It has, however, been granted consultative status by the United Nations, which has enabled members to participate in the Economic and Social Council's discussions. Anti-Slavery International maintains offices in London, publishes books and pamphlets on issues of the day, and actively campaigns against bonded labor, child labor, and other forms of modern slavery.

See also ABOLITION AND ANTISLAVERY MOVEMENTS; BRITISH AND FOREIGN ANTI-SLAVERY SOCIETY (1839–1909); LEAGUE OF NATIONS.

BIBLIOGRAPHY

SAWYER, ROGER. *Slavery in the Twentieth Century.* 1986.
UNITED NATIONS. *Slavery: A Report.* Prepared by Benjamin Whittaker. 1984.

Howard R. Temperley

Antislavery Movement

See Abolition and Antislavery Movements. *See also the entries on specific antislavery societies.*

Anti-Slavery Society of Canada

The Anti-Slavery Society of Canada came into existence during a public meeting at Toronto's city hall on 26 February 1851. Formed in response to the Fugitive Slave Law in the United States, the society dedicated itself to fighting racial intolerance in Canada West, while also orchestrating moral and vocal support for the more expansive efforts of like-minded organizations south of the border. Led and championed by influential individuals such as George Brown, owner and editor of the *Toronto Globe* newspaper, and future

Ontario premier Oliver Mowat, the society suffered from a weak financial base, its removal from the mainstream battle against slavery, the fractiousness which beset the abolitionist movement generally, and the sense that more immediate and local reform concerns, unconnected to abolition, deserved equal if not greater attention. As a result, membership never exceeded two hundred individuals, and the society's core numbered approximately twenty.

The society's activities included providing money and clothes for fugitives fleeing the United States, as well as operating a small night school for adults. In time, it organized the appearance, in Canada West, of prominent abolitionist speakers such as Frederick Douglass and John Brown. Opportunities to act on a broader international state were limited until it fought the attempt, beginning in March 1860, to extradite fugitive John Anderson back to Missouri, where, in effecting his escape, he had killed Seneca P. Digges. Not only did George Brown ensure that the Anderson case remained a prominent news story, but the society organized rallies in support of Anderson against extradition. The extradition request was eventually denied. Although it elected a new slate of officers during a gathering in February 1863 celebrating Abraham Lincoln's Emancipation Proclamation, the Anti-Slavery Society of Canada never met again.

See also BROWN, JOHN; CANADA; DOUGLASS, FREDERICK; FUGITIVE SLAVE LAWS, U.S.

BIBLIOGRAPHY

LANDON, FRED. "The Anti-Slavery Society of Canada." *Ontario History* 48 (1956): 125–131.
STOUFFER, ALLEN P. *The Light of Nature and the Law of God: Antislavery in Ontario, 1833–1877.* 1992.
WINKS, ROBIN W. *The Blacks in Canada: A History.* 1971.

Jonathan Swainger

Aquinas, Thomas

See Thomas Aquinas.

Archaeology of Slavery

This entry includes the following articles: Ancient World; Modern World.

Ancient World

Archaeology, the study of human artifacts, can never demonstrate conclusively—in the absence of other evidence, like writing—the existence of slavery. Despite archaeologists' increasing ability to map patterns in the distribution of artifacts over time, and thus to present a fuller picture of past human settlement and habits of production than the extant written sources might yield alone, the legal status of the agents of that production, whether slave, free, or in between, cannot be identified directly from archaeological evidence. The what and the how, archaeology's strengths, cannot tell us the who or the why.

This strong caution aside, archaeology can support or illuminate other, more forthright evidence—usually from written sources—about slavery. Three groups of artifacts make particularly useful contributions. Objects recovered through archaeological excavation, if written on themselves (like late Roman slave collars or the numerous and varied Greek and Latin inscriptions) can directly attest the existence of

The Law Code of Gortyn, the earliest known law code in Greek, deals in detail with property and social issues, including the treatment of slaves. The code is written boustrophedon (literally, "as the ox plows"); one line is read left to right, the next, right to left. [Jack Fields/Corbis]

slavery and manumission, as well as some of the conditions under which both were practiced. Inscriptions in particular can reveal the kinds of work slaves could do, from being skilled workmen on an Athenian temple in the fifth century B.C. to being hairdressers or mirror-holders in the great Roman noble houses of the first century A.D.; from being nurses and child minders, everywhere, to estate managers and city archivists and accountants in the great cities of the Roman East. The social and economic valuation of slaves can be elicited from inscribed legal codifications like the Gortyn Code in mid-fifth-century-B.C. Crete, where crimes committed against slaves were punished with considerably less rigor than those against free men, or from the Roman emperor Diocletian's Price Edict of A.D. 301, which lists adult males between the ages of sixteen and forty as the most expensive slaves, females over sixty as the least. Prices, names, ages, and sometimes origins of slaves, along with legal warranties stating that they were healthy and not fugitives, are conveyed by contracts of slave sale that survive on papyrus and wood from the eastern half of the Roman Empire. From mainland Greece, the Aegean islands, and Asia Minor, between the third century B.C. and the fourth century A.D., numerous inscriptions have been found that preserve the terms under which slaves were freed by their owners. These terms sometimes stipulated a money price for freedom, a requirement to stay and serve the master for a fixed period of time, or the handing over of future children to the former master. Although these manumission inscriptions have, with some controversy, become the basis of larger studies of the long-term health of a slave system, the contribution of most inscribed archaeological evidence relating to slaves remains anecdotal or serves to establish possibilities rather than demonstrate patterns.

Art objects recovered through excavation, such as Attic vases or Roman funerary monuments, constitute the second category of artifact. These contribute images of men and women who can be identified as slaves or freedmen with greater or lesser certainty depending, again, on writing. The significance of these figures lies less in their attestation to the fact of slavery and some of its conditions and variety, and more in what their depictions can imply about how slaves were viewed or how freedmen viewed themselves. In Attic vase painting, slaves are depicted as smaller than their citizen masters—even when the masters are children—and often costumed in barbarian garb. Both representations convey nothing truly factual about slaves but reflect on the importance and centrality of citizens (and the citizen's role in the city-state) by contrasting them with deliberately insignificant or quintessentially marginal figures. Roman freedmen, by contrast, eagerly represented themselves (if only on their gravestones) as the Roman citizens they became at the time of their manumission—dressed in togas and surrounded by the families and property that they were not allowed under slavery. Archaeological evidence of this sort beckons the interpreter into the world of *mentalités,* into how slavery and freedom could be conceived, and does so in subtle ways that literary or documentary evidence cannot always establish.

Large archaeological sites, such as the Athenian silver mines in southeast Attica and the *Settefinestre* villa in first-century-B.C. Roman Tuscany, provide the third type of evidence. As complexes of artifacts, they can be used as the foundation of larger arguments about the role of slaves and slave labor in the ancient economy. To be sure, these sites can be identified as establishments that used slaves only by a close reading of literary sources (e.g., the works of ancient historians and agronomists), and even so, the extent to which they used slaves remains conjectural. But scholars have nonetheless based far-reaching interpretations on them. At Athens, the mining of silver was contracted out by the state to its citizens, who in turn used slaves to perform this economically necessary, physically unpleasant, and often life-threatening work.

Archaeological excavations of the ancient city of Pompeii, which was destroyed by the eruption of Mount Vesuvius in 79 C.E., unearthed the preserved bodies of many of the city's inhabitants. This find was important because it made possible the study of bones for the classification of slaves. [UPI/Corbis Bettmann]

An important segment of the Athenian economy (and one of the most labor-intensive and wealth-producing of its industries) was thereby put in the hands of slaves. This qualitative contribution is one major reason why M. I. Finley categorized Athens as a "slave society." Similarly, the *Settefinestre* villa, a large estate that raised pigs and produced wine, has been interpreted by its Marxist excavator, A. Carandini, as a slave-powered "agribusiness": the visible economic consequence of two centuries of Roman slave-taking in foreign wars and a predictable indicator of the development of a full-fledged slave economy, which was itself a proximate cause of the fall of the Roman Republic. In both conclusions archaeological evidence plausibly interpreted as slave-related is crucial to the construction of larger important theses. Yet in both cases, the theoretical biases that interpreters or excavators bring to bear on the data—whether these biases derived from Anglo-American common sense or Italian Marxism—are as determinative of the conclusions as the archaeological evidence itself. This subjective contribution is present in the interpretation of all objective archaeological evidence, and exercises a particularly powerful influence when archaeology and slavery are conjoined.

See also ANCIENT GREECE; ANCIENT MIDDLE EAST; ANCIENT ROME; FINLEY, MOSES I.; MINERS.

BIBLIOGRAPHY

CARANDINI, A., ed. *Settefinestre: Una villa schiavistica nell'Etruria romana.* 1985.

FINLEY, M. I. *The Ancient Economy.* 1973.

HIMMELMANN, N. *Archäologisches zum Problem der griechischen Sklaverei.* 1971.

HOPKINS, K., and P. J. ROSCOE. "Between Slavery and Freedom: On Freeing Slaves at Delphi." In *Conquerors and Slaves,* edited by Keith Hopkins. 1978.

ZANKER, P. "Grabreliefs römischer Freigelassener." *Jahrbuch des Deutschen Archäologischen Instituts* 90 (1975): 267–315.

Elizabeth A. Meyer

Modern World

There are some written sources useful for helping in understanding the culture and history of enslaved people in the nineteenth century. Those who seek original source materials pertaining to slaves in the sixteenth, seventeenth, and eighteenth centuries, however, learn that there is very little to be found. Slave owners, from their peculiar perspective and for their particular purposes, produced nearly all of those documents. Unbiased, reliable written evidence of the culture, beliefs, and patterns of everyday life of those who lived in slave quarters, kitchens, and garrets is virtually nonexistent.

Archaeology is the science that seeks to understand human culture and history through examination of the material evidence that people have left behind. By carefully excavating and studying the sites where enslaved persons lived, worked, and were buried, archaeologists have begun to shed light on the lives of enslaved Africans in the Americas. This field of study, sometimes called "slave archaeology" or "African-American archaeology," emerged in the 1960s and has grown to encompass the many and varied sites and artifacts of the African diaspora. Excavated sites run the gamut from slave-trading forts on Africa's Atlantic coast to humble plantation slave huts throughout the American South and the West Indies to the substantial homes of free African-American merchants and physicians in cities and port towns. Even the resting places of the ancestors of modern African-Americans have been uncovered, by design and by accident, and their study by archaeologists and physical anthropologists has led to controversy, political struggle, and discovery.

The archaeologists of slavery generally recognize the late Professor Charles Fairbanks of the University of Florida as the founder of this discipline. By the mid-1970s a number of important studies on plantations had been completed or were under way. The best of these early studies compared the material remains of planters, tenants, merchants, overseers, and slaves (e.g., Otto, 1984; Kelso, 1984). These studies tended to approach plantations as communities of unequal statuses. Among their primary goals was a greater understanding of the economic, cultural, and status relationships that bound these complex communities together. Material remains quickly revealed that there was no single "norm." The lives of slaves varied tremendously across time, space, and social conditions.

Kelso first reported finding small storage pits that apparently had been hidden beneath the floors of seventeenth- and eighteenth-century slave quarters in Virginia. These "root cellars," as he called them, contained a variety of surprising finds, including remains of some very fine porcelain dishes. Some archaeologists quickly began to speculate that slaves had pilfered fine china from the "big house," an activity sometimes lauded as a form of resistance to slavery. Another suggestion was that planters handed chinaware down to slaves once it had become outdated and old-fashioned. While there is some evidence to support both scenarios, more recent thought is that dishes were a small luxury purchased by slaves with cash earned in a variety of ways.

The "trash" found in these small cellars, and in other areas in or around slaves' houses, often suggests that the occupants raised chickens, tended groves of fruit and nut trees, made and used fishing gear, and owned or borrowed firearms for hunting. Rather than viewing the enslaved only in terms of their slavery, archaeology has helped us view slaves as creating their own social and economic lives. A combination of evidence now suggests that many—perhaps most—supplemented the rations granted them by their masters with provisions grown in their own gardens, with game and fish taken in the woods and waters near their quarters, and through trade in markets using money earned by the sale of goods and services.

Along with archaeological and documentary evidence for the production of crafts by slaves, these remains all suggest that the plantation quarters served as a locus of production, and that enslaved people often participated directly in local economies through means other than their forced labor. None of this suggests that life in the slave quarters was somehow easier than we might once have imagined. After all, these various subsistence and economic activities took place on top of a grueling schedule of backbreaking, mind-numbing work. However, it does humanize the quarters and illustrate the responsibility that enslaved men and women took for their own lives and communities, despite intolerable conditions.

One important pioneering study from the 1970s stands out. Excavations of a large eighteenth-century slave cemetery in Barbados by Jerome Handler and Frederick Lange (1978) revealed important expressions of West African culture in a New World setting. Cowry-shell, glass, and dog-tooth beads, metal bangles, and other artifacts are strong evidence that the horrors of the Middle Passage had not managed to erase African habits, customs, or memories from the minds and practices of blacks in the New World, even under the oppressive conditions of a Barbadian sugar estate. Handler and his colleagues have continued to publish important findings from their excavation of the Newton plantation cemetery, and the evidence continues to underscore the persistence of some African lifeways in the slave quarters. Treatment of some individuals in the Newton cemetery suggests they had a special status. One may have been a healer or someone similar to an "obeah" practitioner, for instance.

By the mid-1980s sufficient excavations had been completed to permit Theresa Singleton to edit a landmark volume of critical early studies: *The Archaeology of Slavery and Plantation Life* (1985). These studies surveyed and summarized the approaches, problems, and findings that had emerged in the archaeology of slavery, and the initial results were impressive. The search for African-influenced practices and beliefs remained important for many researchers. Clear parallels were sought and found, for instance, in the techniques and forms of earthenware pottery made in West Africa, in Jamaica, and in the South Carolina low country.

The re-created slave quarters at the Carters Grove Plantation in Williamsburg, Virginia. [Lee Snider/Corbis]

"Africanisms"—a term introduced by the anthropologist Melville Herskovits—were also sought and were found in the preparation of foods, in the architecture of slave houses, in some burial practices, and in traditions of making and using earthenware pottery and other crafts. Work has progressed substantially over the years, and as a result, Singleton edited another volume of new contributions called *I, Too, Am America.* This book, to be published (probably in 1999) by University Press of Virginia, will be a valuable extension of her earlier book.

The Newton plantation cemetery mentioned above has become a sort of national shrine for the people of Barbados, but the archaeological excavation of graves is often a sensitive and controversial subject. While scientists seek in their own ways to revere the dead by trying to understand and celebrate their lives, modern descendants may sometimes be mortified at the desecration of their ancestors' graves. As a result, very few slave cemeteries have been excavated. Occasionally a construction project will reveal the presence of a cemetery, as happened in the case of the "African burial ground," an eighteenth-century slave graveyard uncovered in the financial district of Lower Manhat-

tan. Once it became apparent that hundreds of graves were being threatened by a construction project, archaeologists were brought in, first to identify and evaluate the site, then to begin the removal and study of human remains. Some African-American scientists quickly pointed out that the team assembled to study the site was headed entirely by white scientists. Eventually a new team was assembled, headed by William Blakely of Howard University. Blakely and his team of physical anthropologists are still at work studying the remains of the African burial ground, and in the process they are training a new generation of African-Americans in the art and science of anthropology and archaeology.

Although archaeologists occasionally make a spectacular discovery that changes our view of the past nearly overnight, such discoveries are rare. More typically, archaeology advances at a glacial pace as numerous sites are excavated and painstakingly analyzed and the data are made available through publication or other forms of interpretation. For instance, the recent re-creation of slave quarters at Carters Grove plantation, a museum site operated by the Colonial Williamsburg Foundation in Virginia, is the result of many years of study by archaeologists, architectural historians, historians, folklorists, and others. The archaeology of slavery is still very young, but it has already begun to help reshape the way historians, anthropologists, and the public at large think about slaves, the daily conditions of their lives, and the vast contributions they made to New World cultures.

See also ARTISANS; HOUSING; PLANTATIONS; SLAVE TRADE.

BIBLIOGRAPHY

HANDLER, JEROME, and FREDERICK LANGE. *Plantation Slavery in Barbados: An Archaeological and Historical Investigation.* 1978.

KELSO, WILLIAM M. *Kingsmill Plantations, 1619–1800: The Archaeology of Country Life in Colonial Virginia.* 1984.

OTTO, J. S. *Cannon's Point Plantation, 1794–1860: Living Conditions and Status Patterns in the Old South.* 1984.

SINGLETON, THERESA A., ed., *The Archaeology of Slavery and Plantation Life.* 1985.

SINGLETON, THERESA A., and MARK D. BOGRAD, eds., "The Archaeology of the African Diaspora in the Americas." *Guides to Historical Archaeological Literature,* no. 2. 1995. The most up-to-date summary of the major work in this field.

L. D. Mouer

Archives

See Museums and Historic Sites.

Aristotle [384–322 B.C.]

Greek philosopher.

Aristotle discusses slavery and slaves at two points in the *Politics.* The first and longer discussion occurs in Book I, his treatment of household economy. The master-slave relationship, along with the relations of husband and wife and parent and child, constitutes the household. Those who work for the state, in mines, and on ships are not slaves because they are not private property.

> A slave by nature is an individual who, being a man, is by his nature not his own but belongs to another, and a man is said to belong to another if, being a man, he is a thing possessed; and as a possession he is an instrument which, existing separately, can be used for action (*praxis*). (I.4.1254a15–18)

A slave is a living tool, a being without purposes of his own and adept at fulfilling the desires and policies of his owner.

It is only after Aristotle has proved the need for slaves, from the master's point of view, that he then goes on to ask whether there are any people naturally fit to be slaves. Slaves are those who have incomplete natures and require something outside themselves to fulfill their own natures. Who is naturally suited to be a slave will not coincide automatically with who is a slave, because the people who are fit for the slavish life do not seek out masters. If they did, they wouldn't have slavish natures.

In *Politics,* Book VII, Aristotle asserts a moral geography that shows which people are generally suited for slavery. There are three kinds: "The peoples of cold countries generally, and particularly those of Europe, are full of spirit, but deficient in skill and intelligence." These people are so wild that they cannot form a community.

> The peoples of Asia are endowed with skill and intelligence, but are deficient in spirit; and this is why they continue to be peoples of subjects or slaves. The Greek stock, intermediate in geographical position, unites the qualities of both sets of peoples. It possesses both spirit and intelligence: the one quality makes it continue free; the other enables it to attain the highest political development, and to show a capacity for governing every other people. (VII.7.1327b24–33)

See also ANCIENT GREECE; PHILOSOPHY.

BIBLIOGRAPHY

FORTENBAUGH, WILLIAM. "Aristotle on Slaves and Women." In *Articles on Aristotle II: Ethics and Politics,* edited by J. Barnes, Malcolm Schofield, and Richard Sorabji. 1977; pp. 135–139.

GARVER, EUGENE. "Aristotle's Natural Slaves: Incomplete *Praexis* and Incomplete Human Beings." *Journal of the History of Philosophy* 32 (1994): 1–22.

SCHOFIELD, MALCOLM. "Ideology and Philosophy in Aristotle's Theory of Slavery." In *Aristoteles' "Politike": Akten des XI Symposium Aristotelicum.* 1990; pp. 1–27.

SMITH, NICHOLAS D. "Aristotle's Theory of Natural Slavery." *Phoenix* 37 (1982): 109–122.

Eugene Garver

Arkansas

Slavery was introduced into the area that would become Arkansas in 1723, arriving with the first settlers in the French speculator John Law's colony along the Arkansas River at Arkansas Post. Subsequent French and Spanish censuses indicated a continuing, although small, slave population thereafter. Probably at

Table 1.	Slavery in Arkansas, 1810–1860.		
Year	Slaves	Slave Owners	Whites
1810	138		924
1820	1,617		12,597
1830	4,516		25,671
1835	9,938		42,302
1840	19,935		77,174
1850	47,100	5,999	162,189
1860	111,115	11,481	324,143

Source: Orville Taylor, *Negro Slavery in Arkansas*, 1959.

no time before American development of the area, however, were more than sixty slaves present.

During the territorial period between 1803 and 1835 the slave population grew steadily and dispersed throughout the territory. Initially, the area's economy was based mostly on trapping and trade, and slaves worked at many different occupations connected with these endeavors. As late as 1840, as many slaves lived in the state's upland countries as lived in the counties that were part of the broad Mississippi River delta in the east and the numerous river valleys, all containing potentially rich agricultural lands.

During the 1840s the number of slaves in Arkansas continued to grow, but most of them came to live in the areas that were being opened to cotton cultivation. By 1850, 70 percent of the slave population lived in the state's lowland counties. By 1860, the proportion of slaves in these counties had risen to 74 percent. While slaves continued to live in areas of the state that lacked significant commercial agriculture and a few resided in the state's towns and cities (3,799 in 1860), in the 1840s and 1850s the vast majority of slaves were involved in some aspect of the development of cotton growing.

The dominant trend in cotton agriculture, thus important for the lives of the slaves, was the development of the plantation system. Most whites did not own slaves—slave owners represented only 3.7 percent of the total white population in 1850 and 3.5 percent in 1860—but those who did steadily increased the size of their holdings. In 1850 the average slave owner had 7.8 slaves. By 1860 that average had increased to 9.6 slaves. In many lowland counties slaveholdings were larger. By 1860, Chicot County, which showed the most striking progress toward the development of plantations, had the largest average slaveholding, with 33.3 slaves per owner.

The developing plantations had the largest average slaveholding, with 33.3 slaves per owner. Precise numbers are not known, but many of the new plantations that opened in the 1850s reflected the growing interest of large planters in the older southern states in acquiring western lands. New plantations often were in the hands of the children or relatives of these established plantation families. Few, however, were run by overseers. In 1860, while only 27 percent of slave owners held ten or more slaves, 74 percent of slaves were part of holdings of ten or more. By the Civil War, Arkansas had sixty-one slave owners who possessed more than one hundred slaves, and one of these held over five hundred. In its slaveholding patterns, the state had begun to look like the older slaveholding states to the east.

While slavery as a system matured later in Arkansas, little about it marks it as different from the system as it existed elsewhere. The state's slave code, most of its provisions adopted in 1837, simply incorporated legislation from the territorial period. These laws and provisions in turn had been copied from already existing slave states. The developing nature of the Arkansas economy may have made life harder for the slaves, since many hands were engaged in clearing new grounds, and perhaps it destabilized slave family and community patterns. For the most part, however, the day-to-day life of slaves seems to have been similar to that of slaves throughout the South.

See also PLANTATIONS; UNITED STATES.

BIBLIOGRAPHY

TAYLOR, ORVILLE W. *Negro Slavery in Arkansas.* 1958.
———. "Slavery: The Manners and Mores of a Southern Institution in a Frontier Community." In *Arkansas Odyssey,* edited by Michael Dougan. 1989.
———. "Slavery and Slaves." In *Persistence in the Midst of Ruin: The Impact of the Civil War and Reconstruction on Arkansas,* edited by Carl H. Moneyhon. 1993.

Carl H. Moneyhon

Artisans

Although most slaves, particularly in the Americas, were field hands, a significant minority made objects, worked at a craft, or practiced a skilled trade. Slavery, renowned for its menial, forced, and brutal labor, also had a place for skilled work, for social differentiation, and for an occupational hierarchy. Artisans were close to the top of that hierarchy, and they had a reputation for being proud and independent— the antithesis of a slave.

Defining a skilled slave is not always easy. Carpenters, blacksmiths, and shoemakers obviously fit the category, but sailors, wagonners, and carters—those engaged in transportation—generally do not. Seamstresses, weavers, and knitters, yes, but most laundrywomen, dairy maids, and gardeners, no. Indigo makers, sugar boilers, and distillers, yes, but most drivers and foremen—those in supervisory positions—no. In fact, sugar boilers and rum distillers were specialists only for the duration of the harvest; they, like some other artisans, then spent time in the fields. Some woodworkers, notably sawyers and logcutters, were often viewed as little more than field workers; plowmen, conventionally termed agricultural hands, were often highly skilled. Some slaves were employed full-time as potters, basketmakers, and tailors and clearly were artisans; but many others made pots, crafted baskets, carved wood, repaired their clothing, built and rebuilt their cabins, and made musical instruments in their own time and might be considered part-time artisans. A core group of artisans can be readily identified, but artisanship was also a fluid category.

The number and functions of artisans varied markedly over time and across space. In frontier settings, few slaves had the chance to practice a trade; as plantation labor forces grew, the opportunities for skilled labor widened. Small plantations generally could not afford full-time artisans; large plantations often boasted a variety of skilled slaves. Competition from indigenous or imported free or servant craftsmen or from the products of economies based on free labor often inhibited the ability of slaves to become artisans. The nature of a staple economy—how much processing and servicing was necessary—was also a major determinant of artisanal opportunities. Sugar, for example, required intensive factory labor; tobacco could be processed with minimal skills. Cotton stood between sugar and tobacco in its processing requirements; many slaves in the U.S. South became cotton gin operators and mechanics. The proportion of slave men who were artisans could be one in ten in some sugar plantation economies but was rarely more than one in twenty in tobacco plantation economies. Some staple economies encouraged specialization; others, diversification. Thus, although specialized economies like sugar and rice gave rise to a large number of skilled slaves, they generally worked in just a few trades; whereas diversified economies such as cotton and tobacco restricted overall opportunities for skilled slaves but generated a wide range of skills that they might practice. Artisans were most numerous and practiced the widest range of crafts in towns and cities. In the Caribbean, towns contained roughly twice as many tradespeople as rural slave populations. Urban artisans performed highly skilled tasks such as goldsmithing, silversmithing, gunsmithing, harness-making, printing, watchmaking, and chairmaking.

In many slave societies, a majority of slave tradesmen were woodworkers. A hierarchy of skills quickly emerged within the woodworking fraternity: master carpenters ran workshops; some slaves developed highly specialized skills as coachmakers, housewrights, wheelwrights, shipwrights, and cabinetmakers; coopers, although crucial to plantation enterprises, generally ranked below carpenters in value; and sawyers were the lowest-valued woodworkers. Leatherworking, metalworking, brickmaking, brickmasonry, and textile production were other important trades involving slaves.

Artisanal opportunities followed a sharp sexual division of labor. Almost all artisans were male; few were female. On some slaveholding units, as many as a fifth to a quarter of the men were craftsmen. The only real, albeit extremely limited, opportunity for slave women to escape the fields was to work as domestics. But few household jobs, except cooking and spinning, involved making things—and even cooking was not a female preserve. However, some slave women fashioned baskets, pots, and cloth, most often in their spare time. Physical strength no doubt accounted for part of this sexual division of labor; the interruptions of childbearing too may have been thought to disqualify women from learning craft skills; but conventional male prerogatives and discrimination against women were probably most important.

Although some slaves became apprentice craftsmen at about age sixteen or seventeen—the typical pattern among skilled free labor—most slaves seem to have entered the nonfield labor force either earlier or later than free persons. Some slave boys were put to trades as early as nine or ten years of age. But most slaves became artisans as adults, learning their trades either from free white craftsmen or, more often, from fellow slaves. Why did most slaves become artisans somewhat late in life? First, if a master placed an African in a nonfield position, that African was almost always an adult. Second, masters most often used native-born slaves for nonfield work, but few had the resources to train such individuals from an early age. They either purchased trained slaves from neighbors or brought in from the fields an experienced slave of their own—and in both cases the slave was a mature adult. Third, masters used craft jobs as a reward to encourage productivity among field hands. The aging of an artisan rarely led to a reversion or conversion to field labor; rather, many skilled slaves mastered more than one trade during their lives. Versatility was the hallmark of the skilled slave.

Artisans enjoyed special privileges, although at some cost. The artisans' clothes, food, and shelter were superior to those of field hands, and they also tended to live longer, healthier lives. They could earn money in their spare time, thus expanding their chances of buying their way out of bondage. They were often itinerant—that is, hired out to do jobs for neighbors. Some artisans, most notably those in towns, hired themselves out. They sought their own jobs and paid their masters either a lump sum or a percentage of their wages. Despite these privileges artisans figured prominently among runaway slaves and often were leaders in slave rebellions.

Artisans gained a measure of self-esteem from their craft skills. They often created artifacts within a framework that owed much to their native culture but that also innovatively engaged with their new environment. For example, the coiled rush baskets made by low-country slaves were remarkably similar in design and shape to certain regional baskets in Africa, although made of New World materials and influenced by Native American coiled designs and European wickerware. Colono ware shows African influence both in vessel form and in decoration, and even the nineteenth-century slave potters of Edgefield County, South Carolina, who produced conventional Anglo-American stoneware, also drew on African aesthetic ideas for some of their products. Thus, South Carolinian slave basketmakers and potters created distinctive craft traditions. Although they enjoyed a measure of freedom, artisans also had to learn to cope with the constraints of their status as slaves and to deal with feelings of isolation and resentment. This inner personal turmoil, along with uneasiness in dealing with authority, may help to account for certain disorders—stuttering, stammering, and uncontrollable hand or facial movements—that some of these artisans were said to have exhibited.

See also PLANTATIONS.

BIBLIOGRAPHY

BERLIN, IRA, and PHILIP D. MORGAN, eds. *Cultivation and Culture: Labor and the Shaping of Slave Life in the Americas.* 1993.

FOGEL, ROBERT WILLIAM. *Without Consent or Contract: The Rise and Fall of American Slavery.* 1989.

GASPAR, DAVID BARRY, and DARLENE CLARK HINE, eds. *More Than Chattel: Black Women and Slavery in the Americas.* 1996.

GENOVESE, EUGENE D. *Roll, Jordan, Roll: The World the Slaves Made.* 1974.

HIGMAN, B. W. *Slave Populations of the British Caribbean, 1807–1834.* 1984.

MORGAN, PHILIP D. *Slave Counterpoint: Black Culture in the Eighteenth-Century Chesapeake and Lowcountry.* 1998.

SCHWARTZ, STUART B. *Sugar Plantations and the Formation of Brazilian Society.* 1985.

WARD, J. R. *British West Indian Slavery, 1750–1834: The Process of Amelioration.* 1988.

Philip D. Morgan

Arts

This entry includes the following articles: Verbal Arts; Visual Arts.

Verbal Arts

Among the richest cultural legacies of global slavery have been the provocative, ironic, and innovative achievements of men and women of words. Slave wordsmiths in the Americas often satirized their circumstances and those of their putative owners through indirect means using double-entendres, hyperbole, and verbal jousting. This habit has been traced to Old World antecedents, most notably the histrionic pyrotechnics of *griots*, the village bards who served as court historians and social commentators, mainly, though by no means exclusively, in western Africa. With the forced migration of Africans across the Atlantic, much of the impetus for chronicling the exploits of states and empires that vanquished their enemies was transformed into relating the personal travails of women and men who worked at physical, spiritual, and cultural survival. Thus, the exigencies of resistance gave rise to oral insurgents, men and women of words, whose prose, poetry, and lyrics functioned to create texts that James C. Scott has designated "hidden transcripts." In song and story they sought to transcend their anguish through spiritual release by appeals to the deity and by means of humor, satire, and parody.

Verbal insurrectionaries were especially adept at transforming folklore and folktales into instruments of combat, metaphorically using the master's tools to subtly undermine his authority. Thus "Brer Rabbit," the American version of the hare of African fables, became an archetype for cunning and with "Aunt Nancy," a New World transmutation of Ghana's spider trickster Ananse, stood as a proxy for daily battles waged by the powerful against the ostensibly powerless. These contests operated on several levels. First, through linguistic survivals Africans often managed to maintain control over key words that eluded the language police on slave ships, at the auction block, and on the plantation. In this way English was enriched by borrowings from a panoply of West African languages, ranging from "tote" to "goober" and "banjo" to "yeti" or "I hear tell." Many such Africanisms were especially evident in relatively isolated areas such as the Sea Islands off the coasts of Georgia and South Carolina, or on populous plantations and in quarters close to major seaports where slave imports proved voluminous. Each of these areas has been examined by folklorists, anthropologists, and musicologists.

A second arena of controversy was in Christianity itself. The initial battle was one of interpretation: Was Jesus the savior of the owners, or of the owned? Was the gospel to be seen as a mandate for minions to obey their masters, or for Pharaoh to "let my people go"? Although many masters taught their slaves that it was God's will to follow their lead, slave exhorters and preachers often had other ideas, and these made their way into their sermons. Through carefully disguised double messages, no less sophisticated than the subtlety of the spirituals, slave sermonizers subverted the teachings of those telling their flocks to submit. In spite of the fear and contempt shown by the white clergy toward many "primitive" slave pastors, their finely honed approach to speech and their effective folk renditions of Scripture became legendary. In their honor James Weldon Johnson wrote his evocative epic poem, *God's Trombones.* It was out

James Weldon Johnson, in addition to writing the poem "God's Trombones," edited the two-volume Book of American Negro Spirituals *(1925, 1926) with his brother, J. Rosamond Johnson.* [Library of Congress/ Corbis]

of this tradition that so many of the great African-American orators would come.

Third was the growth of a spoken subculture that seemed to transcend geography. In urban as well as rural areas, in the West and Midwest as well as the North and South, slavery and the separation it both demanded and symbolized imparted a uniqueness to black talk. Ethnomusicologist Alan Lomax has written, "Negro folklore grew behind the barbed-wire fence of segregation." From slavery to a freedom limited by discriminatory Jim Crow policies, verbal art forms continued to bear traces of the plantation. Thus, even though slavery ended formally in 1865, slave narratives persisted long after the fact.

Moreover, the circumstances that pertained in American society during Reconstruction and thereafter continued to reinforce notions of social and cultural difference, strengthening perceptions of African-American distinctiveness. This became as clear in the argot of the shacks and shanties of "tobacco road" as in the slums and ghettoes of the urban North and Midwest. As migrants fled the Mississippi delta for Chicago, they found new challenges awaiting them—residential segregation, occupational discrimination, and wage inequality—leading them to find strength in numbers in their own churches, fraternal orders, clubs, and bars. In these settings African-American verbal arts also flourished, from tall tales to "the devil's music," and in the imponderable distance between Saturday night and Sunday morning.

Scores of students of African-American letters have been moved to comment upon the innovations of aural artists. Apart from J. W. Johnson, W. E. B. Du Bois, and Carter G. Woodson, several generations of poets, essayists, novelists, historians, and social scientists have sought to capture the seductive spirit of the black voice on the written page. Langston Hughes, Arna Bontemps, Amiri Baraka, Toni Morrison, and Alice Walker are only a few whose writings beg to be read aloud, and this is a part of the verbal-art legacy. Its talented practitioners link prose with poetry, lyrics with libretti, and the ear with the eye. The author and playwright James Baldwin fused all of these elements in his autobiographical drama "The Amen Corner." "Standard" black verbal arts formed the core of the "ebonics" controversy.

Finally, black language has continued to make its mark on American, New World, and international culture and society. The rap tradition, so prominent in contemporary music, is in fact itself related to the innovations of countless generations of what James Weldon Johnson called "Oh Black and Unknown Bards." From the field hollers and work songs to the spirituals, in sacred and secular life, to the rise of new musical forms such as blues and jazz and gospel and the migrations of waves of refugees from racism, African-American verbiage, rooted in slavery, has continued to inspire all speakers, readers, and hearers of the spoken, sung, and written word, ranging far beyond the Anglophone arena.

See also LITERATURE OF SLAVERY.

BIBLIOGRAPHY

BAKER, HOUSTON A. *Black Studies, Rap, and the Academy.* 1993.

BALDWIN, JAMES. *The Amen Corner: A Play.* 1968.

BRASCH, WALTER M. *Black English and the Mass Media.* 1981.

DILLARD, J. L. *Black English: Its History and Usage in the United States.* 1972.

DU BOIS, W. E. B. *The Souls of Black Folk.* 1903.

HUGHES, LANGSTON, and ARNA BONTEMPS, eds. *The Book of Negro Folklore.* 1958.

JOHNSON, JAMES WELDON. *God's Trombones: Seven Negro Sermons in Verse.* 1961.

SCOTT, JAMES C. *Domination and the Arts of Resistance: Hidden Transcripts.* 1990.

———. *Talkin and Testifyin: The Language of Black America.* 1977.

SMITHERMAN, GENEVA. *Black Talk: Words and Phrases from the Hood to the Amen Corner.* 1994.

WOODSON, CARTER G. *Negro Orators and Their Orations.* 1925.

David H. Anthony III

Visual Arts

Representations of slavery in American art before the American Civil War are most varied where enslaved blacks moved from the periphery of the picture to the central focus as artists supported calls for the abolition of slavery or maintained the myth of slavery as a benevolent institution. Generally, artistic representations of slaves from ancient cultures to the nineteenth century included slaves as a fact of life. Occasionally carvings or paintings include symbols of bondage, such as chains or collars, but most early images of slaves lack such visual indicators of slave status. With the increased trade in African slaves, artists used the blackness of the slaves' skin and exaggerated their facial features to underscore the perceived inferiority of slaves to masters.

In many ancient societies slaves included both native-born people sold into servitude because of debts or criminal behavior and foreigners captured during war. Slavery was a basic condition of life in ancient societies, and artists generally used no technique or convention, such as differences in clothing, to indicate slaves. The laborers pulling a monument to the palace of Sennacherib, depicted on a carved slab from As-

syria (British Museum) may be slaves. Another limestone carving from the tomb of Harmhab, Dynasty XVIII (ca. 1350 B.C.E., Museo Civico Archeologico, Bologna), depicts registration of African captives who may then become enslaved laborers. Egyptian tombs included *ushabati*—figures in clay, wood, or faience that were meant to serve the deceased in the afterlife—and these figures may also indicate slaves. Relief carvings marking gravesites from ancient Greece occasionally include slave figures, such as the fourth-century-B.C. relief from Atticus (National Museum, Athens) and the marker for Silenis (Staatsliche Museum, Berlin). Roman carvings of shop interiors include figures of slaves as well as assistants. War captives wearing chains and with arms bound appear on the Column of Trajan and the Arch of Septimius Severus. Islamic societies participated in the African slave trade, although Islamic law eventually defined slaves as war captives or as debtors. Images of slaves in Islamic societies appear as miniature illustrations, such as *The Slave Market in Zabid,* in Yemen (1237, Bibliothèque Nationale, Paris) and *An Ottoman Prince and Grand Vizier with Black Attendants* (1597, Topkapi Saray Museum, Istanbul); the artists show the slaves as domestic servants and courtiers. Serfs, bound to the lands owned by feudal lords, are included in illuminated manuscripts, such as the *Très Riches Heures de Duc de Berry* (Limbourg Brothers, 1412–1416, Musée Condé, Chantilly.) The serfs labor in the fields and live outside the precincts of the castle that protects the nobles; in these illustrations, unlike earlier depictions of slaves and servants, feudal serfs are differentiated from the nobility by clothing and occupation. Artists in western Europe, drawing from biblical texts, also included scenes of Joseph bound and thrown in the well by his brothers, and Joseph being sold into bondage, in cycles detailing Joseph's life in Egypt (mosaic by Cimabue, Baptistry, Florence; James Northcote; Hippolyte Flandrin). Andrea del Sarto maintained the tradition of continuous narrative in his painting of Joseph (ca. 1520, Pitti Palace, Florence), which contains scenes of Joseph interpreting his father Jacob's dream, Joseph's brothers throwing him in the well, and Joseph being sold into bondage.

Western European artists reflected the growing African slave trade beginning in the fifteenth century. Despite the numbers imported into Europe, African slaves appear as exotic subjects, usually in conjunction with their owners. For example, a slave holds the music score for the musicians to read in *A Rich Man's Feast* by Paul Veronese, and six slave musicians play at the *Marriage of Saint Ursula* (ca. 1520, Museu National de Arts Antiga, Lisbon). Albrecht Dürer's sensitive portrait of *The Moorish Woman Katharina* (1521, Uffizi

Odalisque with Slave *by Jean-Auguste-Dominique Ingres.* [Corbis-Bettmann]

Gallery, Florence) is a rare portrait of a slave, although there is nothing to indicate her status as a slave. Attitudes of slavery as a metaphor for spiritual imprisonment occupied Michelangelo di Buonarotti, who sculpted two figures—*Dying Slave* and *Rebellious Slave*— in marble in the 1510s for the tomb of Julius II (ca. 1513, Louvre, Paris) and another four figures, which, at Michelangelo's death in 1564, remained in his studio (1530–1534, Galleria dell'Accademia, Florence).

Slaves in English painting are included in the portraits of their noble masters as symbols of wealth and as indicators of colonial interests. In his portraits of *Charles, Third Earl of Harrington* (1783), *George IV When Prince of Wales* (1787), and *Lady Elizabeth Keppel, Marchioness of Tavistock,* Sir Joshua Reynolds included portraits of their servants. Enslaved African servants appear in the fourth painting of William Hogarth's *Marriage à la Mode* (National Gallery, London) and in the etching *Taste in High Life* (1746, Colonial Williamsburg Foundation). Slaves are included in their role of servants in Johann Zoffany's *The Family of Sir William Young* (ca. 1766, oil on canvas, Walker Art Gallery, Liverpool). Slaves in paintings such as these are in-

variably dressed in livery and assume postures of service—for example, by holding the master's horse or carrying a tray. In *Captain Thomas Lucy* by Godfrey Kneller (1680, Charlecote Park, England), the slave not only holds the captain's horse but also wears a silver collar indicating his bondage. A rare portrait is *Ignatius Sancho* (1768, National Gallery of Art, Ottawa) by Thomas Gainsborough. In this portrait, Gainsborough shows Sancho, born on a slave ship in the West Indies and later brought to England, as the educated and freed man he became. As late as the 1830s, the French painter Jean-Auguste-Dominique Ingres included a black slave as a background figure in his *Odalisque with Slave* (1839, Fogg Art Museum, Cambridge, Massachusetts). In European art generally, slaves are uncommon, almost exotic, subjects and more often seen only in relation to their masters or relegated to the edge of the painting.

As European nations established colonies in the Americas, colonial painters rarely addressed the enslavement of the native peoples. More often, the paintings were scenes of imported African slaves, especially in the Caribbean colonies. Artistic representations of enslaved Africans created a visual fiction of benevolent slavery. In his *Black People Making Merry in Surinam* (1706–1708, Royal Museum of Fine Arts, Copenhagen), Dirk Valkenburg painted a rare scene of the Jonas Witsen plantation slaves at leisure and seemingly happy. The earliest portraits of southern planters in North America occasionally included their slaves, following the European tendency. The slaves and servants depicted in these portraits are clearly in positions of servitude despite their generally plain and neat clothing. In the earliest known portrait of an African-American subject and the earliest representation of a domestic servant in American art, the artist Justus Engelhardt Kuhn shows a slave child with Henry Darnall III, a planter's child, who is standing with a bow and arrow (ca. 1710, Maryland Historical Society). Kuhn indicated the slave child's status not only by placing him behind a balustrade and portraying him in a servile position but also by noting his metal collar, a symbol of servitude. Fifty years later, another Maryland artist, John Hesselius, included a

black slave in his portrait of the child Charles Calvert (1761, Maryland Historical Society). The slave wears an elaborate livery with a broad black band at his neck suggesting his status as a slave. In both these paintings, the slave's body is cropped within the picture frame as the master fills the center. In their posture and their position, both slave figures are linked visually by ownership and supplication to their white masters. Ralph Earl included a slave in the *Portrait of an Unidentified Man* (ca. 1795–1796, New Britain Museum of American Art); the young attendant submissively holds a letter out to his master, who, for the moment, ignores him. In a group portrait of the Payne children (ca. 1791, Virginia Museum of Fine Arts), the unidentified artist offers a rare glimpse of an African-American slave companion whose clothing reinforces his unequal status; whereas the white children are dressed neatly in plain clothes, the slave child wears a tunic or dress, a common outfit for slave children regardless of sex.

In the early years of the American republic, representations of African-American slaves reflected the

George Washington at Mount Vernon by Junius Brutus Stearns. [Library of Congress/Corbis]

fiction of benevolent slavery. Images of George Washington by Edward Savage, Louis Mignot, and Thomas Rossiter showed the Washington slaves in faithful and respectful attendance on the family (Edward Savage, *The Washington Family*, 1789–1796, National Gallery of Art, Washington, D.C.; and Louis Mignot and Thomas Rositer, *Lafayette and Washington at Mount Vernon*, ca. 1859, Metropolitan Museum of Art). Washington is the benevolent master in a painting by Junius Brutus Stearns (1851, Virginia Museum of Fine Arts); the slaves are on a break from haying as Washington converses with an overseer. Slaves appear most often as domestic servants in American paintings, including *Quilting Frolic* (John Lewis Krimmel, 1813, Henry Francis du Pont Winterthur Museum) and *The Chess Players* (George W. Flagg, ca. 1836, New-York Historical Society). The anonymous *Old Plantation* (ca. 1800, Abby Aldrich Rockefeller Folk Art Center) shows slaves playing banjos and beating drums in what may be a wedding ritual—jumping over a broom. Christian Mayr painted an African-American wedding celebration in *Kitchen Ball at White Sulphur Springs* (1838, North Carolina Museum of Art), which shows the bride and groom surrounded by fashionably dressed domestic slaves who accompanied their owners to the Virginia resort. An unusual depiction of African-American spiritual life is *A Plantation Burial* by John Antrobus (1860, Historic New Orleans Collection), in which the central figures are slaves who mourn the death of another slave, their white master and mistress barely visible through the trees.

As the eighteenth century progressed, debate over the legality and morality of slavery grew. The ugly side of slavery—the buying and selling of human beings—caught artists' imaginations. Accompanying John Gabriel Stedman's *Narrative of a Five Years' Expedition, against the Revolted Negroes of Surinam* (1796), illustrations composed by William Blake based on Stedman's drawings show the abject cruelty used to suppress the revolt. In 1791 George Morland exhibited *The Slave Trade* (1788) and its companion *African Hospitality* (1789) to bolster arguments that Africans were humans capable of compassion and love of family and country. In *The Slave Trade* white traders cruelly and maliciously beat and bind captive Africans, tearing them from their homes and families. In the companion painting, Africans supply whites with food and drink. The entrepreneur Josiah Wedgwood created a cameo for the Society for the Suppression of the Slave Trade, founded in 1787, in which an African slave in chains asks, "Am I not a man and a brother?" In an early American example of abolitionist sentiment, Samuel Jennings suggested the intellectual and moral equality of slaves in *Liberty Displaying the Arts and Sciences* (1792, Library Company of Phila-

delphia), in which the figure of Liberty offers the fruits of freedom—education and economic advancement—to freed slaves. The French artist Auguste-François Biard painted a number of scenes of the slave trade between 1835 and 1861, two of which visually argued for the end of the trade. *The Slave Trade* (1835, Kingston-upon-Hull Museum and Art Galleries, Wilberforce House) contrasted the indifference of both black and white traders to the cruelties and humiliations suffered by slaves. Biard depicted a happier moment with *Proclamation of the Abolition of Slavery in the French Colonies* (1849, Musée Nationale du Château de Versailles) in which slaves on the French Caribbean colonies rejoice at their liberation. The English artist Joseph William Turner depicted a ruthless act in his *Slavers Throwing Overboard the Dead and Dying: Typhoon Coming On (Slave Ship)*; 1840, Museum of Fine Arts, Boston). In a wildly swirling scene of color, light, and shadow, Turner conveys the terror of the slaves as the captain of the ship *Zong* had dead and dying slaves thrown overboard so that he could claim them as "lost at sea" and so receive insurance payable for such losses.

Scenes of slave sales and escapes interested artists before the American Civil War. The British artist Eyre Crowe accompanied the writer William Thackeray on a tour of the United States, including Richmond, Virginia. Crowe witnessed a slave auction and in three memorable paintings memorialized the silent resignation and anguish of slaves as they were sold to the Deep South's cotton kingdoms (*Slaves Waiting for Sale*, Richmond, 1853–1861, Jay P. Altmayer; *The Slave Auction*, 1852, private collection; and *Slaves Sold South*, 1852, Chicago Historical Society). Crowe included single male slaves and slave mothers with children in his paintings, but *Slaves Sold South* clearly shows that slave families were separated by masters who sold husbands or wives and children, disregarding family ties because the law denied slaves the right to marry. Eastman Johnson's *Old Kentucky Home* (*Negro Life in the South*; 1859, New-York Historical Society) shows a group of blacks, both free and slave, behind a house in the District of Columbia. Johnson's *Ride for Liberty—The Fugitive Slaves* (ca. 1862, Brooklyn Museum of Art) and *The Slave Hunt* by Thomas Moran dramatize the risks taken by slaves in their harrowing attempts to escape to freedom. Nor did images of slavery cease with the end of the American Civil War. Late representations of slaves include *Near Andersonville* (1865, Newark Museum) and *Visit from the Old Mistress* (1876, National Museum of American Art), both by Winslow Homer. In *Near Andersonville*, Homer shows a slave woman standing in the doorway of a house watching southern troops march captured federal prisoners to the notorious prison. *Visit from the Old Mistress*, painted after the Civil

Old Kentucky Home *by Eastman Johnson*. [Corbis-Bettmann]

War, suggests the tension between former slaves and their former owner. In 1939 the artist Hale Woodruff painted a vibrant mural outlining the story of the *Amistad,* a Spanish slave ship on which the Africans, led by Cinqué, mutinied (Talladega College, Talladega, Alabama). In the mural Woodruff showed the Africans with their supporters and the final arguments before the United States Supreme Court.

Three-dimensional works showing slaves are uncommon, although some pieces carved by American sculptors included blacks and whites. *The Greek Slave* by Hiram Powers (1843, Corcoran Gallery of Art) was intended to plead for support for Greece's claim to liberation from Turkey. Nevertheless, critics used the statue as a metaphor for the cruelty of chattel slavery and praised Powers for creating an enduring image of a naked slave in chains who manages to retain her human dignity. Erastus Palmer's *White Captive* (1857–1859, Metropolitan Museum of Art) depicts the nude figure of a white pioneer girl bound with bark thongs. Like Powers's Greek girl, Palmer's captive at-

tempts to retain her dignity and modesty. John Rogers sculpted a series of plaster narrative scenes intended for popular consumption. His series included *The Slave Auction* (1859, New-York Historical Society) and *The Fugitive's Story* (1869, New-York Historical Society), which show a young woman with a child as the focus of the scene. Thomas Ball designed *Emancipation Group* (1865, Montclair Museum) to commemorate the Emancipation Proclamation; as Abraham Lincoln declares the end to slavery in the southern states in rebellion, a slave begins to stand as his chains break. Chains are broken in *Forever Free,* composed by Edmonia Lewis (1867, Howard University Art Gallery), as a man stands and raises his arm upward and a woman kneels at his side to offer thanks for their freedom. Broken chains also indicate freedom in *The Freedman* by John Quincy Adams Ward (1863, Cincinnati Art Museum), as a seminude male figure begins to rise from his seat. Artists quickly adopted daguerreotype photography after its introduction to the United States by Samuel F. B. Morse in 1839. The photographic image captured black nurses, both free and slave, as well as slave artisans (*Gilbert Hunt, Blacksmith,* ca. 1855, Valentine Museum; *Sally Gladman, Nurse to Edward V. Valentine,* ca. 1850, Valentine Museum; *Nurse of the Minor Family,* ca. 1850s, Alderman Library of the University of Virginia). An unidentified daguerreotypist took the image of Caesar, the last slave owned in New York, around 1850 (New-York Historical Society). The geologist Louis Agassiz commissioned a series of daguerreotypes of slaves. The series included an image of Jack, a driver, from Columbia, South Carolina, taken in profile; Jack is shirtless and there are glimpses of scars on his back (ca. 1850, Peabody Museum, Harvard University). A more horrifying image was *The Scourged Back,* taken in Louisiana in 1863 and sent to the surgeon general of Massachusetts as an example of scars left by whipping.

See also DANCE; LITERATURE OF SLAVERY; MUSIC ABOUT SLAVERY; MUSIC BY SLAVES; SLAVE NARRATIVES; SPIRITUALS.

BIBLIOGRAPHY

BOIME, ALBERT. *The Art of Exclusion: Representing Blacks in the Nineteenth Century.* 1990.
CRAVEN, WAYNE. *Colonial American Portraiture.* 1986.
MCELROY, GUY C. *Facing History: The Black Image in American Art 1710–1940.* 1990.
THE MENIL FOUNDATION, INC. *The Image of the Black in Western Art.* 4 volumes. 1976.
MELTZER, MILTON. *Slavery: From the Rise of Western Civilization to the Renaissance.* 1971.
O'LEARY, ELIZABETH L. *At Beck and Call: The Representation of Domestic Servants in Nineteenth-Century American Painting.* 1996.
WALVIN, JAMES. *Slavery and the Slave Trade: A Short Illustrated History.* 1983.
WOOD, PETER H., and KAREN C. C. DALTON. *Winslow Homer's Images of Blacks: The Civil War and Reconstruction Years.* 1988.

Barbara C. Batson

Asia

See Cambodia; Central Asia; China; Indian Subcontinent; Indonesia; Japan; Korea; Malaya; Philippines; Slave Trade; Southeast Asia; Thailand.

Asiento

The *asiento* (exclusive contract) system of slave trading was a part of the Spanish government's effort to regulate colonial development and administration. From 1493 to 1513, only a few slaves crossed the Atlantic, as the Spanish crown wished to exclude them from its colonies. Thereafter, when the colonial demand for slaves could no longer be denied, the crown granted licenses to various foreign merchants, often Genoese, Flemish, or Portuguese, to deliver slaves to the American colonies.

By the 1580s the Portuguese dealers had attained a near monopoly on the trade, as Portugal controlled the slaving stations in sub-Saharan Africa. In 1595, the complete *asiento* system, with a single contractor (*asentista*) receiving an exclusive contract, replaced the open licensing system. The *asentista* subsequently resold his licenses in batches to shippers operating Iberian-built ships (until the later seventeenth century).

The shippers proceeded first to Seville, where their licenses, ships, and provisions were carefully inspected. Then they went to Africa to collect their human cargoes. The transatlantic passage was harsh, and on virtually every voyage a substantial percentage of the slaves perished before they could be delivered to specified American ports.

The Portuguese held the *asiento* until 1640. From then until 1675, either the system was in disuse or no nation held a monopoly. The Dutch received the *asiento* in 1675. The Portuguese held it from 1694 to 1701, when it passed to the French. The English got it in 1713 and retained it until 1750. Thereafter, the system was in disarray, and the Spanish finally abolished it, along with other anachronistic government controls, in 1789.

See also PORTUGAL; SLAVE TRADE; SPAIN.

BIBLIOGRAPHY

PALMER, COLIN. *Human Cargoes: The British Slave Trade to Spanish America, 1700–1739.* 1981.
VILA VILLAR, ENRIQUETA. *Hispanoamérica y el comercio de esclavos.* 1977.

William D. Phillips, Jr.

Assyria

See Ancient Middle East.

Australia

See Labor Systems.

Aztecs

See Amerindian Societies.

B

Babylonia

See Ancient Middle East.

Badges of Slavery

The Thirteenth Amendment to the United States Constitution, ratified in 1865, abolished slavery and gave Congress the power to enforce the amendment through appropriate legislation. In response, Congress enacted legislation granting the newly freed slaves various civil rights. Supporters of this legislation argued that Congress had the authority to eliminate not just slavery but also "badges of slavery"—those civil constraints imposed on slaves such as the inability to enter contracts or buy land.

The U.S. Supreme Court, however, adopted a restrictive view of Congress's authority to prohibit badges of slavery. In the *Civil Rights Cases* (1883), the Court conceded that the Thirteenth Amendment "clothes Congress with power to pass all laws necessary and proper for abolishing all badges and incidents of slavery," but concluded that "mere discriminations on account of race or color," such as the exclusion of African-Americans from public accommodations, did not constitute badges of slavery that Congress could prohibit. The Court went further in *Plessy v. Ferguson* (1896) and *Hodges v. United States* (1906), interpreting the Thirteenth Amendment to reach only compulsory labor. In the wake of these decisions, African-Americans had no protection from racial discrimina-tion by private parties and limited protection from state-imposed discriminatory treatment under the Fourteenth Amendment.

In 1968 in *Jones v. Alfred H. Mayer Co.*, the Court reversed its earlier precedents, concluding that Congress has the power under the Thirteenth Amendment "to determine what are the badges and the incidents of slavery, and the authority to translate that determination into effective legislation." The Court in *Jones* held that Congress had properly found racial discrimination in the sale of real estate to be an unlawful badge of slavery. Since *Jones*, the Court has found other types of private racial discrimination to constitute badges of slavery that Congress may prohibit. For example, the Court in *Runyon v. McCrary* (1976) found that the Civil Rights Act of 1866, now known as Sections 1981 and 1982, prohibits racial discrimination in private schools. The Court has also found that Sections 1981 and 1982, though enacted to implement the Thirteenth Amendment, prohibit racial discrimination against whites.

See also CIVIL RIGHTS ACT OF 1866; CONSTITUTION, U.S.; LAW.

BIBLIOGRAPHY

COLBERT, DOUGLAS L. "Liberating the Thirteenth Amendment." *Harvard Civil Rights–Civil Liberties Law Review* 30 (1995): 1–55.

TEN BROEK, JACOBUS. "Thirteenth Amendment to the Constitution of the United States." *California Law Review* 39 (1951): 171–263.

Davison M. Douglas

Bahamas

See Caribbean Region; Plantations.

Baptist Christianity

The Baptist church had been a small dissenting sect in the colonial era, but its effective evangelical techniques enabled it to grow into the country's largest denomination by the 1830s. Thanks to their evangelical techniques, Baptists attracted tens of thousands of members from both slaves and free blacks. A loose confederation of autonomous congregations, the Baptist denomination possessed no central governing structure to establish or enforce antislavery doctrine. During and soon after the Revolutionary War, however, many local associations of Baptist congregations in the Northeast condemned slavery. Various "Friends of Humanity" associations of Baptists in Kentucky and the Midwest also battled against the introduction of slavery into their locale in the early nineteenth century.

By the 1830s, however, the powerful influence of slaveholding members in the denomination and the traditional Baptist hesitancy to involve the church in civil action had quieted nearly all antislavery forces. In addition, bitter disputes within the denomination over questions of mission policy and theology in the early nineteenth century produced a strong sentiment among Baptists against raising another disruptive issue.

Still, thousands of individual Baptists and their local congregations cooperated in voluntary societies for the support of missions and religious publications. Abolitionist efforts among the Baptists therefore concentrated upon demanding that those societies repudiate all ties with slaveowners by refusing their contributions and barring them from any office or appointment. The abolitionists' American Baptist Anti-Slavery Convention, founded in 1840, created a "provisional committee" to collect and distribute funds for missionary activities from those no longer willing to cooperate with slaveholders in the regular societies.

By the early 1840s, abolitionist agitation produced a crisis in the Baptist denomination. In both the Baptist Triennial Convention (which oversaw foreign missions) and the American Baptist Home Missionary Society (which sponsored domestic missions), conservative northerners had to cope with growing pressure from both abolitionists and southerners. In an attempt to quell the southerners' fears, the mission societies dismissed abolitionists from all leadership posts. Both societies also issued public circulars affirming their neutrality toward slavery.

In November 1844, apparently dissatisfied with this position of official neutrality, Baptists in Alabama wrote to the Board of Foreign Missions asking for a "distinct, explicit, avowal that slaveholders are eligible . . . to receive any agency, mission, or other appointment." The board replied that it could not appoint slaveholding missionaries because "we can never be a party to any arrangement which would imply approbation of slavery." In an effort to retain southern support, though, the board reassured slave owners that the society nevertheless still welcomed their membership and contributions. This reply so infuriated southern Baptists that they promptly seceded and launched their own foreign missionary projects.

The American Baptist Home Missionary Society similarly debated the question of supporting slaveholding missionaries. A "select committee" studied the problem and reported back in 1845, advocating that neutrality toward slavery be continued. This report was tabled as unsatisfactory and the society agreed to a sectional division of its resources "upon amicable, honourable, and liberal principles."

The sectional separation of northern and southern Baptists was never as complete in the denomination's publishing enterprises as in its missionary operations. The Baptist General Tract Society and its successor, the American Baptist Publication Society, had never printed an antislavery work. Southerners nevertheless founded their own printing house in 1847, and the American Baptist Publication Society voluntarily withdrew from the slave states. After schisms developed in the missionary societies, the managers of the Baptists' American and Foreign Bible Society announced their determination to continue welcoming all Baptists "on terms of perfect equality." Despite the launching of a Southern Baptist Bible Board in 1851, the American and Foreign Bible Society continued to elect slaveholding officers and to receive substantial contributions from southerners during the entire pre–Civil War period.

Many Baptist abolitionists resolved to remain outside the regular denominational mission societies until the constitutions of those bodies "have been so defined that their antislavery character shall be distinctively marked." This "come-outer" group launched its own antislavery missionary enterprise, the American Baptist Free Mission Society.

Other abolitionists continued to agitate inside the main denominational societies after 1845. But only years later did the Baptist societies finally follow up their antislavery sentiments with action. The Home Mission Society reduced the number of its missionaries in slaveholding states from fourteen in 1846 to only three in 1850. The Missionary Union finally withdrew its missionaries from the Indian stations after the Indians repeated rejected calls to manumit their slaves. The publication and Bible societies, however, adamantly refused to make even minor concessions to their antislavery critics.

Besides the behavior of the mission societies, the practices of individual northern Baptist congregations and local associations reveal an inconsistent record regarding breaking fellowship with slaveholders. In the years after the Baptists divided in 1845, some northern Baptist associations passed strongly worded antislavery resolutions and ceased fraternizing with slaveowners. In the Midwest and in some eastern cities, however, many Baptist churches continued to welcome southerners to their pulpits and communion tables even during the Civil War.

During the sectionally divisive political controversies of the late 1840s and 1850s, many northern churchmen issued strong public condemnations of slavery. Among Baptists, some local associations and congregations spoke out against governmental policies favoring slavery such as the Fugitive Slave Law of 1850 and the Kansas-Nebraska Act. During the same years, northern Baptist newspapers editorialized on political events with an increasingly antislavery bias. Even as prominent a conservative spokesman as Francis Wayland joined the moderate antislavery Republican party.

In the slave states the Southern Baptist Convention was formed in 1845. Blacks composed approximately one-quarter of its congregations, but their status was clearly subordinate. Although southern white Baptists included many prominent apologists for slavery, local and state church associations often endorsed programs for amelioration of its worst abuses.

The Civil War severed the remaining ties between northern and southern Baptists. Southern contributions to northern-based Baptist benevolent associations had been dwindling during the 1850s and nearly disappeared after 1861. By the war's end, both the home and the foreign mission societies had endorsed immediate emancipation and begun programs to aid freedmen. Even northern local associations that had consistently clung to neutrality regarding slavery finally denounced it during the war. The southern Baptists' strong identification with the Confederate cause was a principal reason that postwar efforts at denominational reconciliation failed.

See also ABOLITION AND ANTISLAVERY MOVEMENTS; CHRISTIANITY; FUGITIVE SLAVE LAWS, U.S.; MISSIONARIES; NATIVE AMERICANS.

BIBLIOGRAPHY

CARWARDINE, RICHARD J. *Evangelicals and Politics in Antebellum America*, 1993.

MATHEWS, DONALD G. *Religion in the Old South*. 1977.

McKIVIGAN, JOHN R. *The War against Proslavery Religion: Abolitionism and the Northern Churches, 1830–1865*. 1984.

John R. McKivigan

Barbary Wars

After Britain encouraged Algiers to declare war on the United States in 1785, Algiers captured two U.S. merchant ships and detained the men aboard them. The United States could not redeem the crews, who remained in Algiers until 1797. In 1793 England encouraged Algiers to take a dozen more U.S. ships. With 120 Americans captive, in 1795 the United States agreed to send an annual tribute of naval supplies to Algiers and signed similar concessions with Tunis and

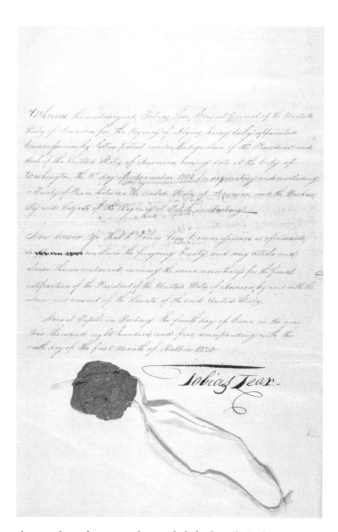

A page from the treaty that ended the hostilities between Tripoli and the United States. [The National Archives/Corbis]

Tripoli. In 1801 Tripoli declared war on the United States, which by then had a navy to patrol the Mediterranean and to blockade Tripoli. In 1803 the U.S. frigate *Philadelphia* ran aground off Tripoli, and over three hundred men were taken prisoner. The United States used greater military force and negotiation to end the war in 1805, ransoming the *Philadelphia's* crew. Algiers again declared war on the United States in 1807; finally, in 1815 the U.S. fleet forced Algiers to agree not to take its ships. Later that year, England forced Algiers to renounce the taking of Christian hostages. Although textbooks typically refer to these naval engagements as clashes with Barbary pirates, the term *pirates* is a misnomer. Pirates by definition operate without a state commission. But every vessel involved bore a commission from the ruler of Algiers, Tunis, or Tripoli, and these rulers received a share of every prize brought to port. In fact, vessels from Algiers and the other North African (Barbary) states had raided European commerce since the Crusades, and during subsequent Muslim-Christian conflicts around the Mediterranean.

Spanish novelist Miguel de Cervantes wrote of his experience as a captive in Algiers in *Don Quixote*. Susannah Rowson in 1795 adapted Cervantes's story as "Slaves in Algiers," a popular play on the U.S. stage. Benjamin Franklin and others questioned the commitment of the United States to liberty, noting the irony of white U.S. citizens being "enslaved" in Africa. Fictional captivity narratives (Royall Tyler, *The Algerine Captive*, 1797; *History of the Captivity and Suffering of Mrs. Maria Martin*, 1806) as well as genuine accounts (*Authentic Narrative of the Loss of the American Brig Commerce*, 1816) remained popular up to the Civil War and formed a link between Puritan captivity narratives and fugitive slave narratives.

See also LITERATURE OF SLAVERY; MEDITERRANEAN BASIN.

BIBLIOGRAPHY

ALLISON, ROBERT J. *The Crescent Obscured: The United States and the Muslim World, 1776–1815*. 1995.
FIELD, JAMES A., JR. *America and the Mediterranean World, 1776–1882*. 1969.
FOLAYAN, KOLA. *Tripoli during the Reign of Yusuf Pasha Karamanli*. 1979.
IRWIN, ROY WATKINS. *The Diplomatic Relations of the United States with the Barbary Powers, 1776–1816*. 1931.

Robert J. Allison

Barracoons

Barracoons were buildings in which slaves were held. The word is in origin Spanish (*barracón*; cf. also Por-

On 8 June 1850 the British navy attacked the town of Keonga, on the Zambezi River near the Mozambique Channel, and set fire to the barracoons in an attempt to suppress the slave trade in the area. [*Illustrated London News*/Corbis]

tuguese *barracão*), meaning a large shed or booth (*barraca*; whence also English "barracks"). Originally applied to slaves' quarters on plantations in Spanish America, the term was subsequently applied to the huts in which slaves were held on the coast of Africa prior to embarkation in ships for carriage across the Atlantic. Although a cognate French word (*barraques*) was already used in the eighteenth century for such slave pens, the word *barracoon* seems to have entered the English language only in the nineteenth century; earlier, the quarters in which slaves were temporarily housed while awaiting export were called in English "trunks" (also French *troncs*; Dutch *troncken*) or "prisons." The adoption of the term *barracoon* into English clearly reflected the pre-eminence of Spanish (and Portuguese/Brazilian) traders in the Atlantic slave trade following its legal abolition in the early nineteenth century. The stockpiling of slaves at the coast in advance of shipment, although done earlier to some extent, became a more regular practice in the illegal trade, because of the need to speed up the dispatch of slave ships to minimize the risk of interception. Barracoons on the West African coast were normally constructed from wooden piles and roofed with thatch, and the slaves in them were chained to prevent escape. The physical destruction, by burning, of barracoons—most notoriously at the River Gallinas

(Sierra Leone) in 1840 and again in 1849—was a prominent symbolic and practical feature of the British navy's campaign against the illegal slave trade. Treaties negotiated by the British with African rulers for the abolition of slave exports—as at Lagos (Nigeria) in 1851—also regularly stipulated the destruction of barracoons.

See also SLAVE TRADE.

BIBLIOGRAPHY

FORBES, LIEUTENANT [F. E.]. *Six Months' Service in the African Blockade.* 1849.

Robin Law

Baxter, Richard [1615–1691]

English theologian and prolific writer.

Born in Shropshire and largely self-educated, Richard Baxter was a prominent preacher and author of popular Christian literature in Caroline England. He wrote over one hundred books stressing the importance of faith and piety in personal life, exemplified by *Saint's Everlasting Rest* (1650). Baxter supported the cause of Parliament in the English civil war, but opposed the regicides and welcomed the restoration of Charles II. As a nonconformist, he was imprisoned in 1658, and later supported the Glorious Revolution. Through-

Richard Baxter. [Library of Congress/Corbis]

out his life, his religious thought was that of a moderate independent, supportive of limited forms of episcopacy but suspicious of ritual that smacked of Roman Catholicism.

Baxter's principal treatment of slavery appeared in *A Christian Directory* (1665) and *Chapters from a Christian Directory, or a Summ of Practical Theology and Cases of Conscience* (1673). In these works he accepted the legitimacy of slavery as a consequence of war or crime, but also urged masters to use their power over slaves to bring them to Christianity. Failure to do so, in Baxter's view, constituted an act of rebellion against God.

Baxter condemned the violence of the slave trade and the cruelty with which Barbadian masters treated their slaves as instances of unchristian greed and covetousness. In contrast, Baxter praised New England colonists for attempting to convert the Indians, unaware of the Puritans' enslavement of them. His only counsel for slaves was to accept their lot as God's calling and to "know your mercies, and be thankful for them."

See also CHRISTIANITY; PERSPECTIVES ON SLAVERY.

BIBLIOGRAPHY

DAVIS, DAVID BRION. *The Problem of Slavery in Western Culture.* 1966.
STEPHEN, SIR LESLIE, ed. *Dictionary of National Biography.* 1855–1901.

T. Stephen Whitman

Belize (British Honduras)

See Caribbean Region; Plantations.

Bellon de Saint-Quentin, Jean [fl. 1732–1764]

French theologian.

Though an influential theologian and writer in mid-eighteenth-century France, Jean Bellon de Saint-Quentin is known to modern scholars only as the editor of Pierre Le Brun's four-volume *Histoire critique des practiques superstitieuses* (1732–1737) and as the author of *Dissertation sur la traite et le commerce des négres* (1764). The latter of these works consists of an eighty-two page essay arguing that slavery is divinely ordained, with three supporting letters, penned between 17 January and 15 May 1764, to an unnamed trader who had expressed doubts about the moral legitimacy of buying and selling slaves.

According to Bellon, the doctrine that in Jesus Christ there is "neither slave nor free" cannot be applied to the temporal world. All individuals, he admits, are "one body" in Christ, but some are destined to be "the feet." Since Jesus came into the world to serve others, His message is chiefly one of "subordination, submission, and obedience." Citing authorities from Justinian to Grotius, Bellon further concludes that human bondage is in full accordance with the laws of nature. Harsh treatment of slaves in "the new parts of the world" is rare, he argues. More important, without African laborers, European settlers would never be able to endure the harsh climate of the Americas. At times Bellon's logic seems tortured, as when he insists that the "service" of slaves rather than their "humanity" is being bought and sold. Yet, in general, the pamphlet's highly accessible prose and straightforward, question-and-answer format succinctly and effectively convey the author's strident, proslavery message.

See also PERSPECTIVES ON SLAVERY.

BIBLIOGRAPHY

BELLON DE SAINT-QUENTIN, JEAN. *Dissertation sur la traite et le commerce des négres.* 1764.
PEABODY, SUE. *"There Are No Slaves in France": The Political Culture of Race and Slavery in the Ancien Régime.* 1996.
STEIN, ROBERT LOUIS. *The French Slave Trade in the Eighteenth Century: An Old Regime Business.* 1979.

Eric Robert Papenfuse

Berlin Conference (1885)

In November 1884 a conference was held in Berlin in an effort to reach agreement among European nations regarding the distribution of and free trade in Central African territories. The resulting General Act of the Berlin African Conference, subsequently the Berlin Act, was signed on 26 February 1885 by Austria, Belgium, Denmark, France, Germany, Italy, the Netherlands, Portugal, Spain, Sweden, Norway, Turkey, Great Britain, the United States, and Russia. All signatories subsequently ratified the Berlin Act, except the United States which, because of the Monroe Doctrine, chose not to involve itself in territories in which it had no interests. The act entered into force on 19 April 1886 and remained in force until it was abrogated by the signatories to the St.-Germain-en-Laye Convention at the end of World War I.

Although the Berlin Act was largely concerned with free trade, especially in liquor, between the European nations, it is generally recognized as the first time the European nations formally recognized any sort of duty to Africans. Although the Atlantic slave trade was virtually nonexistent, slaves continued to be traded in Africa and exported to Arabia. The parties bound themselves "to watch over the preservation of the native tribes, and to care for the improvement of the conditions of their moral and material well-being, and to help in suppressing slavery, especially the Slave Trade." The Berlin Act provided that "trading in slaves is forbidden in conformity with the principles of international law as recognized by the Signatory Powers." However, it did not contain any provisions for enforcement and therefore had little or no effect on the slave trade in Africa.

See also BRUSSELS ACT; SLAVE TRADE.

BIBLIOGRAPHY

CROWE, SYBIL ERE. *The Berlin West African Conference, 1884–1885.* Reprint, 1970.
PAKENHAM, THOMAS. *The Scramble for Africa: White Man's Conquest of the Dark Continent from 1876 to 1912.* 1991.

Renee C. Redman

Bermuda

See Caribbean Region; Plantations.

Bible

This entry includes the following articles: An Overview; Jewish and Christian Interpretations; Biblical Law. *Related articles may be found at the entries* Christianity; Judaism; Law.

An Overview

We first confront the issue of slavery in the Bible in a curious way. Ham looks on the nakedness of his drunken father Noah and informs his two brothers Shem and Japheth, who walk backward and cover their father. When Noah hears about Ham's wrongful act of looking, he curses Ham's descendants, saying that they shall be slaves to the descendants of Shem and Japheth (Gn. 9: 20–27). The precise nature of Ham's misdeed is elusive, and it is not clear why slavery should be the punishment. Later Christian religionists saw in this passage from Genesis a justification for discriminating against, as descendants of Ham/Canaan, native Africans and African-Americans.

The narrators of biblical history present it to show that the experience of one generation repeats itself in the next. The father of the nation, Jacob/Israel, himself experiences a form of slavery when a resident in the Aramean Laban's household. Eventually Jacob flees his oppressive service. Under his deity's guidance Jacob comes to his brother Esau, the ancestor of the nation Edom, as a slave in flight from a foreign master. Esau receives him well and lets Jacob dwell where he pleases. Jacob's own sons, in turn, experience

Joseph, who was sold into slavery in Egypt by his brothers, interprets Pharaoh's dreams and is made ruler of all Egypt, second only to Pharaoh himself. [Historical Picture Archive/Corbis]

enslavement, but they bring it on themselves. First, Joseph, at the instigation of his brother Judah, is sold and ends up as a slave in Egypt. There, again under providential guidance, he becomes the pharaoh's top official who deals with the problem of famine in Egypt. During his reign as vizier, Joseph so arranges matters for his own brothers that when they come from Canaan for food, they end up acknowledging him as a slave does a master.

The brothers reconcile and with their father settle in Egypt, where Joseph carries out a policy of enslavement of the entire Egyptian population. In return for food he arranges for the Egyptians to sell first their money, then their livestock, and finally themselves and their portions of land to the pharaoh (Gn 47: 13–26). The quid pro quo furnishes the earliest account of how a government in return for conferring a benefit takes away a people's freedom. The Israelites are exempt from slavery at this point, but a later generation experiences slavery in Egypt that lasts until Moses becomes its liberator and leads the Israelites out of Egypt. Their deliverance becomes a defining moment in the history of the nation and a source of profound reflection in both the Hebrew scriptures and the New Testament.

Israel's Understanding of Its Deliverance

The experience of the Exodus includes the giving of the law at Sinai, so there is deliverance in both a physical and a spiritual sense. Whenever the writers of the Hebrew Bible represent God as redeemer, they think of redemption not just in its original sense of ransoming people from slavery but also as freeing them from impurity, error, evil, and ultimately death. The prophet Hosea declares that the God who will redeem his people from death is the same God who redeemed them from Egypt (Hos 13: 4, 14). Job has both aspects in mind when he declares, "I know that my redeemer liveth, and that he shall stand up at the latter day upon the earth" (Jb 19: 25). Some passages in the Hebrew Bible in fact show a tendency to consider the entire religion as designed to commemorate the Exodus.

Theological reflection about the history of the Israelites' experience of slavery already shows up in the books of Genesis and Exodus. As Jacob prepares to meet a murderous Esau intent on avenging his brother's theft of his birthright, Jacob encounters a divine being who, threatening his life, ends up blessing him. Jacob's survival of this encounter is set down as anticipating and influencing Esau's astonishing change of heart from murderous hostility to a helpful, welcoming attitude when he declines to treat Jacob as a slave upon Jacob's return from Laban's household. Joseph's story, in turn, also illustrates the notion that good comes out of evil. He assures his brothers that God caused their terrible treatment of him to save the lives of many people.

God and Slavery

The role ascribed to God in biblical history influenced the substance of biblical laws on slavery. Near Eastern rules require, often with a severe penalty for noncompliance, that anyone who receives a fugitive slave return him to his master. By contrast, the one biblical rule about a runaway slave is remarkably liberal (Dt 23: 15, 16). It allows a slave who has run away from a foreign master to dwell where he pleases. The idiosyncratic model for the rule comes when God first directs Jacob to flee from his service under Laban with the many possessions he acquired despite being oppressed and then causes his brother Esau to receive him well. As a result, Esau allows Jacob to go where he pleases. The narrative about how God directs the first Israelite ever to flee from one situation of servitude to another anticipated one explains all the puzzles about the biblical rule: why there is a reference to receiving the slave as a brother Israelite, why the slave does not return to dwell with his own family but can decide to go wherever he wishes, and why the rule seems oblivious to a slave's not having the means to settle in a place of his own choosing.

Using rather enlightened notions from his own culture, the narrator of the Exodus story views God as a relative who is duty-bound to ransom from slavery his firstborn son, Israel. Moses acts the part of an emissary who, in line with international practice of the time, is sent by a powerful person to a foreign master, Pharaoh, to request his son's release. This master, however, abuses standards of decency that should apply even to slaves, and so God, sometimes at Moses's direction, uses force to prompt Pharaoh to act. Blow upon blow reigns down upon him and his people until, despite fierce resistance, he eventually relents and lets his slaves go. As is his right according to prevailing rules about the redemption of slaves, God becomes Israel's new master. Thus is born the powerful religious notion of redemption in later Judaism and Christianity.

Exodus and Redemption

The Exodus story profoundly influenced the biblical notion of salvation. God upheld laws and customs pertaining to the proper treatment of slaves and other oppressed groups. He condemned to destruction, according to the prophet Jeremiah, the slaveholders of the southern kingdom of Judah because they acted treacherously in dealing with their Hebrew slaves. They first released and then enslaved them again, contrary to Mosaic law (Jer 34: 15–22). Job states that if his slaves complain against him and he does not respond to their protest, God's judgment awaits him (Jb 31: 13, 14). When no human aid was available and Israel in particular was in distress, God would repeatedly act as redeemer. The prophet Isaiah proclaims how God will cause a new exodus that will deliver the people of Israel from all their woes (Is 40: 1–5, 63: 11ff.). So powerful is his language that it exerted enormous influence on outpourings of later Western cultural and artistic expression about the hopes of people seeking relief from oppression.

Like Jewish writers before them—Ben Sira, for example (Sir 36: 6)—New Testament writers think of final redemption in terms of the Exodus. According to Acts Jesus is a second Moses who, by signs and wonders that recall those of the Exodus from Egypt, delivers his people a second time from their oppression (Acts 2: 19, 22). The Passover eve liturgy current in New Testament times recalled, interpreted, and celebrated Israel's redemption from the Egyptian slavery and anticipated final redemption. The liturgy had pervasive influence on the composition of the Gospels. Their authors used it to shape their material and interpret Jesus as effecting a new exodus and a final deliverance of humankind from oppression and evil. The Virgin Birth, the Massacre of the Innocents, Jesus's use of bread and wine at the Last Supper, and the sleeping disciples at Gethsemane are among episodes that reveal the influence of the Passover eve liturgy.

The Israelites who are redeemed from slavery in Egypt become slaves to God. The idea underlies Paul's view about the nature of the Christian life. Christian freedom rests not on escape from service but on a change of master. The view contains teaching, taken over from Judaism, that separates Christianity from the pagan religions and philosophies surrounding it. The Christian is free, not to do evil, but to be a slave of God (Rom 6: 17, 18). Those bought to be slaves of Jesus, in the sense of having been redeemed by his death, are free from men, just as those free in their civil status are yet slaves of Jesus (1 Cor 7: 20ff.). A person's release by Jesus from the Law and sin involves his enslavement to his fellow in love (Gal 5: 1, 13ff.). The fourth Gospel claims that the truth brings freedom to those who are slaves to sin (Jn 8: 32ff.). Whatever their worldly position may be, Christians are free from men but only to be slaves of God (1 Pte). There is perennial tension—and harmony—between being God's son and being his slave. The term *to serve* has different shades of meaning: slave, son, free laborer, and worshiper.

See also ANCIENT MIDDLE EAST; CHRISTIANITY; EXODUS; FREEDOM; JEWS; JUDAISM; LAW.

BIBLIOGRAPHY

ALLISON, DALE C. *The New Moses: A Matthean Typology.* 1993.
CARMICHAEL, CALUM. *Law and Narrative in the Bible.* 1985.
DAUBE, DAVID. "The Earliest Structure of the Gospels." *New Testament Studies* 5 (1959): 174–187.
———.*The Exodus Pattern in the Bible.* 1963.

Calum Carmichael

Jewish and Christian Interpretations

Until the eighteenth century, most Jews and Christians believed that both the Old and the New Testament allowed slaveholding. Scholars and laymen often noted that the Bible implored masters to recognize the humanity of their slaves, and few interpreted the many references to slavery as an attack on slavery itself. With the rise of the modern antislavery movement some Jews and Christians developed an alternative reading of the scriptures, attempting to deny the biblical basis of slavery in the New World. As with so many older debates centered on the Bible, the competing interpretations of proslavery and antislavery forces revealed the difficulties inherent in scriptural analysis and in the attempt to make the word of God settle a clash between hostile social systems.

For most Jewish students of the Hebrew scriptures, at least until the rise of modern antislavery, the crucial questions of interpretation concerned the distinctions between Hebrew and non-Hebrew slaves and the regulation of their treatment. The great medieval scholar Moses Maimonides provided perhaps the best summary of premodern Jewish interpretations in Book XII of his *Code of Maimonides.* Building upon numerous Jewish sources, including the Mishnah and the Babylonian and Palestinian Talmuds, Maimonides devoted an entire treatise of Book XII to "Laws Concerning Slaves." He made no attempt to question either the existence of slavery among the ancient Israelites or its divine sanction. Instead, he focused extensively on the biblical references, especially Exodus 21, Leviticus 25, and Deuteronomy 15, that establish the laws regarding the acquisition, treatment, and manumission of Hebrew and Gentile slaves. A Hebrew became a slave only through self-sale due to extreme poverty or as punishment for theft. But as a "brother" (Leviticus 25: 39; Deuteronomy 15: 12), the Hebrew slave enjoyed privileges that the Gentile slave, acquired through war or purchase, did not. Surely part of this

Moses Maimonides. [Corbis-Bettmann]

distinction arose from the Hebrews' memory of their own enslavement and their desire not to subject their own people to harsh treatment. Hebrew slaves, unlike Gentile slaves, were not to be worked "rigorously." The duration of enslavement also differed. A master was to free his Hebrew slave after six years and "not let him go away empty," but "furnish him liberally" (Deuteronomy 15: 13–14), but the Gentile slaves and their children "shall be your bondmen forever" (Leviticus 25: 46). Although Maimonides' code recognized the legitimacy of slavery and the strong scriptural support for it in ways that subsequent defenders of slavery would continually return to, he concluded his discussion with a call for humane treatment of all slaves, Hebrew and Gentile alike. Urging that it "is the quality of piety and the way of wisdom that a man be merciful and pursue justice and not make his yoke heavy upon the slave or distress him," he left the books of the Pentateuch and turned to Job's query: "Did not He that made me in the womb make him [his slave]? And did not One fashion us in the womb?" (Job 31: 15). With this conclusion, Maimonides foreshadowed the ways that future antislavery Jewish and Christian interpretations of the Hebrew scriptures would attempt to minimize the law and focus instead on the spirit of passages such as the one he cited from Job.

Antislavery Jews and Christians in the generation before the U.S. Civil War attempted to deny that the Old Testament allowed slavery in the New World. Some denied that the ancient Israelites had held slaves. "Servants there were, but no slaves," wrote a New Yorker, William Hosmer, who argued that the regulations of treatment effectively "placed masters and servants on much the same terms that prevail in free countries, where labor is hired." Others accepted that slavery had existed among the Hebrews but asserted that it differed substantially, even qualitatively, from chattel slavery in the Americas. Some, such as Jewish scholar Moses Mielziner, concluded that of all "the religions and legislations of antiquity none could exhibit a spirit so decidedly averse to slavery as the religion and legislation of Moses." Antislavery advocates echoed Mielziner's emphasis on the spirit of the Old Testament, and of Judaism in general, by appealing to passages that spoke of mercy and justice. One of the most widely cited was Isaiah 58: 6: "Is not this the fast that I have chosen? to loose the bands of wickedness, to undo the heavy burdens, and to let the oppressed go free, and that ye break every yoke?" Finally, many Christian opponents of slavery argued that regardless of whether Mosaic law recognized and allowed slavery among the ancient Hebrews, the coming of Jesus Christ rendered the old law, or at least parts of it, obsolete. God, they reasoned, may have permitted certain practices under the old dispensation, but those practices were "no longer necessary now when we were to be guided by the superior doctrines of the New [Testament] in the moral instruction of the race."

Defenders of slavery responded to these interpretations of the Hebrew scriptures not only by reiterating familiar readings, such as those of Maimonides, but also by advancing new ones. Both Jews, such as Rabbi Morris J. Raphall of New York, and Christians, such as the Presbyterian minister Robert L. Dabney of Virginia, drew upon the Old Testament to support southern slavery. Raphall, in a fast-day sermon in January 1861, ridiculed the idea that the Old and New Testaments differed in terms of moral instruction; he could find no evidence that the New Testament contradicted the Mosaic laws regarding slaves. Proslavery Christians cited Jesus's own words to demonstrate that his coming did not render the old dispensation "no longer necessary": "Think not that I am come to destroy the law, or the prophets: I am not come to destroy, but to fulfil" (Matthew 5: 17). Some Jews, such as Raphall, and countless Protestant ministers in the South, and a few in the North, pointed out that Abraham, Isaac, Jacob, and Job were all slaveholders, strong evidence that slaveholding was not sinful. Dabney was only one of many who disputed the notion

that Hebrew slavery differed in kind from American slavery. "If it were true" he wrote in 1867, "that Hebrew slavery was milder, it might show that we were wrong in the way in which we treated our slaves; but it could not prove that slaveholding was wrong." The Hebrews' Gentile slaves, Dabney contended, "showed the essential features of slavery among us." But it is revealing of modern proslavery interpretations of the Old Testament that Raphall, and many of his colleagues, devoted more attention to the so-called "curse of Ham" than to traditional defenses of the legality of slaveholding.

The "curse of Ham," found in Genesis 9: 20–27, was actually a curse by Noah on Ham's son Canaan. As Noah lay drunk in his tent, his son Ham had looked on his naked body; it was for this that Noah issued the curse. But rather than punish Ham, Noah declared, "Cursed be Canaan; a servant of servants shall he be unto his brethren." As the modern scholar Ephraim Isaac and others have persuasively demonstrated, the curse on Canaan helped justify Hebrew enslavement of the Canaanites, but not until the medieval era did some use the curse to defend the enslavement of Africans. Before that time, most scholars of the Hebrew scriptures had believed that Africans were descended from another of Noah's son's, Cush, to whom the curse did not apply. However, as more slaves came from Africa, the interpretation of the curse slowly changed, and by the early modern era Africans increasingly were associated with the "curse of Ham." In the nineteenth century the association of Africans with the curse was a staple of the proslavery argument, although some southern divines, notably Dabney and fellow Presbyterian minister James Henley Thornwell of South Carolina, believed that the curse "authorized domestic slavery" but denied that it applied to a specific race. Most defenders of slavery, however, embraced the notion that the curse fell upon Africans. Raphall, for example, casually (and erroneously) claimed that Noah "uttered a bitter curse against [Ham's] descendants, and to this day it remains a fact which cannot be gainsaid that . . . the unfortunate negro is indeed the meanest of slaves." And the Presbyterian minister N. L. Rice of Cincinnati similarly asserted that "Canaan, from whom the Africans descended, was not only cursed of God, but expressly doomed, to be 'servant of servants,'" which justified "men in making slaves of the Africans." Antislavery Jews and Christians, such as the Presbyterian John Rankin, acknowledged the curse, but insisted that "Africans did not descend from [Canaan], and therefore were not consigned to servitude." They furthermore contended that the "Canaanites have mingled with other nations, and so do now not exist as a distinct people, and consequently the term of their servitude must be terminated."

The New Testament, like the Old, proved to be hotly contested ground in the battle between proslavery and antislavery forces in the eighteenth and nineteenth centuries, although prior to that era scholars differed little in their interpretations of the New Testament with regard to slavery. Jesus and his apostles lived in a world with slavery and, as proslavery commentators never tired of pointing out, neither he nor they evinced any displeasure with its presence. Indeed, proslavery writers usually noted Jesus's silence toward slavery as an affirmation of it. As the Baptist minister Thornton Stringfellow of Virginia suggested, "It is . . . strange, that . . . Jesus should fail to prohibit its further existence, if it was his intention to abolish it." But more often than not, defenders of slavery turned to the epistles, especially those of Paul, to make their case that the New Testament, like the Old, allowed slavery.

Supporters of slavery cited numerous passages from the epistles. Timothy 6: 1–2 urged slaves to "not despise" "believing masters," but "rather do them service." Ephesians 6: 5 demanded "servants, be obedient to them that are your masters according to the flesh, with fear and trembling, in singleness of your heart, as unto Christ." Titus 2: 9 called upon Christians to "exhort servants to be obedient unto their own masters, and to please them well in all things." And Colossians 3: 22 echoed Ephesians and implored, "servants, obey in all things your masters according to the flesh; not with eyeservice, as menpleasers; but in singleness of heart, fearing God." These passages proved especially popular among southern ministers in America, for they spelled out the duties and obligations of various members of a household. For these Christians, the Bible called upon individuals to recognize and accept their particular station in life and fulfill its duties. Wives, children, and slaves were to serve and obey; husbands, parents, and masters were to love and lead, but to do so justly, "knowing that [they] have a master in heaven." Although Paul's frequently cited letter to Philemon, in which he sends the slave Onesimus back to his master, offered defenders of slavery an explicit apostolic endorsement of slavery, it was the other epistles and their messages about a divinely ordained, hierarchical slaveholding household that provided the core of the proslavery interpretation of the New Testament. Antislavery interpretations of the New Testament focused considerably attention on language, particularly the Greek word *doulos*. Both proslavery and antislavery students understood *doulos* to mean servant, but proslavery interpreters (and modern biblical scholars) maintained that it referred to several types of servants, including slaves. Antislav-ery advocates insisted—erroneously—that the definition of *doulos* specifically excluded slaves. The King James Version of the New Testament, for instance, never uses the word "slave" for *doulos,* and some antislavery writers contended that this translation accurately captured the fundamental distinction between slavery and the servitude that Paul speaks of in the epistles. As they had done in their interpretation of Hebrew servitude, antislavery commentators on the New Testament maintained that the servitude Paul referred to more closely resembled hired labor than slavery. "Doulos," wrote the antislavery Presbyterian John Rankin, "answers to the English word servant, which is as applicable to the subject of a Prince, to the common hireling, or even to the apprentice, as it is to the slave."

Antislavery interpretations of the New Testament, like those of the Old, frequently appealed to the spirit of a text over its literal wording. Rankin, citing Matthew 7: 12—"Therefore all things whatsoever ye would that men should do to you, do ye even so to them"—concluded that "hence, no man can hold an innocent person to involuntary servitude without violating the Savior's law of love." Countless British and American opponents of slavery appealed to the golden rule, arguing that Jesus's "law of love" made slavery antithetical to Christianity. As Rankin put it, "The whole Bible is opposed to slavery. The sacred volume is one grand scheme of benevolence—beams of love and mercy emanate from every page, while the voice of justice denounces the oppressor, and speaks his awful doom!" Such appeals had little effect on proslavery Christians, who steadfastly held to a literal interpretation of both the Old and New Testament, an interpretation that convinced them that slavery was ordained by God. They tellingly pointed out that a thorough application of the abolitionists' understanding of the golden rule would destroy all nonegalitarian social relations, including those of employer and employee and husband and wife. The immense differences in the interpretations of scripture demonstrated forcefully the irreconcilable differences between antislavery and proslavery forces, both of whom believed that God was on their side.

See also ABOLITION AND ANTISLAVERY MOVEMENTS; CHATTEL SLAVERY; CHRISTIANITY; JUDAISM; LAW; PERSPECTIVES ON SLAVERY; THORNWELL, JAMES HENLEY.

BIBLIOGRAPHY

BARTOUR, RON. "'Cursed Be Canaan, a Servant of Servants Shall He Be unto His Brethren': American Views on 'Biblical Slavery,' 1835–1865. A Comparative Study." *Slavery and Abolition* 4 (1983): 41–55.
DAVIS, DAVID BRION. *Slavery and Human Progress.* 1984.

GENOVESE, EUGENE. *"Slavery Ordained of God": The Southern Slaveholders' View of Biblical History and Modern Politics.* (1985).

ISAAC, EPHRAIM. "Genesis, Judaism, and the 'Sons of Ham.'" *Slavery and Abolition* 1 (1980): 3–17.

MAIMONIDES, MOSES. *The Code of Maimonides.* Book 12, *The Book of Acquisition.* 1951.

RANKIN, JOHN. *Letters on American Slavery.* 1833.

RAPHALL, MORRIS J. *The Bible View of Slavery.* 1861.

Douglas Ambrose

Biblical Law

The Bible so takes for granted the institution of slavery that no rule lists such a fundamental matter as how one becomes a slave. Everyone at the time would know. Only incidentally do we learn that the grounds of slavery are capture in war, inability to pay a debt, and compensation when a thief is unable to pay for his theft. It is an open question whether biblical laws on slavery come in part from Near Eastern laws or are entirely homegrown. The three major rules regulating slavery in the Bible are Exodus 21: 2–6, Leviticus 25: 39–43, and Deuteronomy 15: 12–18.

The Exodus and the Deuteronomic rules have much in common. Each limits to six years the period of time in which an Israelite slave serves an Israelite master. Each outlines the circumstances in which the slave might choose to remain permanently with the master. There are also differences. What happens to any wife the master gives the slave and any children born to her is a concern of the Exodus rule, and the penurious state of a slave at the end of his service is a concern of the Deuteronomic rule. The Levitical rule wishes an Israelite master to think of an Israelite slave not as a slave, but rather as a resident alien or as a hired hand. The rule has the slave and his family maximally serve forty-nine years, after which they resume their ancestral way of life. The Levitical rule permits Israelites to make permanent slaves of foreigners and of resident aliens, and even of the latter's children if they were born within the land of Israel.

Other rules concerning slavery are sensitive to the need to treat slaves with some degree of humaneness. A rule in Exodus seeks to ensure that a woman purchased as a concubine is treated not as a slave, but as if she had the status of a wife. Another rule in Exodus requires that a master set free a slave whom he has injured to such as extent that the slave loses an eye or even a tooth. A Deuteronomic rule forbids an Israelite warrior who acquires a foreign captive in war, and then marries her, from treating her as a slave to be sold should he end his marriage to her. In another Deuteronomic rule a fugitive slave is to be well treated in his homeland when he escapes from a foreign master.

However much we might wish to pursue a social and historical analysis of Near Eastern and biblical sources, the nature of the material does not readily lend itself to it. The biblical provisions are not a response, at least not in any direct sense, to issues in the unknown time of the unknown lawgiver. They are attempts to reproduce ancient laws for an audience living many centuries after the time of Moses, who supposedly gave the laws to his people in his time. Like the laws in Hammurabi's code, they are hypothetical in character. They are also ideal constructions inspired by the intention, common in most legal systems, to invent a past. The biblical writers create a fictional lawgiver, Moses. He gives the Exodus and Leviticus laws shortly after the people of Israel flee from their enslavement in Egypt. When the people anticipate entry into the land of Canaan, he, about to die, gives the law in Deuteronomy.

Moses takes up problems the responses to which are directions for the future life of his people. In giving his Exodus law about a slave's length of service, Moses looks back to Jacob's problems, as described in the Book of Genesis, when serving the Aramean Laban. In giving his Leviticus law, he takes stock of the experience of the economic situation in Egypt, again in the Book of Genesis, before the Israelites become enslaved there. For his Deuteronomic law about a slave's period of service, he considers Israel's experience of slavery during his own lifetime, as recounted in the book of Exodus. The narratives that describe these developments also contain the law codes. In the person of Moses, the real lawgiver treats the stories as foundational ones from which he can extract the distinctive rules of his nation. He does so by translating into rules the deity's actions and judgments in the stories.

The first experience of some form of slavery in Israel's history is that of the nation's eponymous ancestor Jacob/Israel. As a member of Laban's household, his status proves ambiguous when he gets Laban's daughters, Rachel and Leah, as wives in return for fourteen years' service. Laban in effect gets seven years unpaid labor out of Jacob because Laban tricks Jacob into taking Leah instead of Rachel after seven years' service. Laban then serves an additional seven years for Rachel. Jacob works as a slave for his first seven years with Laban.

After this period of service, Jacob requests that, to continue serving in Laban's household, he should receive provision for his own house. Jacob labors for six more years and obtains considerable wealth from his employment. But this service involves major acts of deceptive maneuvering by both parties. Laban seeks to have Jacob work for nothing, and Jacob, in turn, has to manipulate the breeding stock to get some ani-

After Jacob meets Rachel at the well, he agrees with her father, Laban, to exchange seven years of servitude for the right to marry Rachel. [Historical Picture Archive/Corbis]

mals by way of payment for his labor. Jacob views his status more in terms of a hired servant, whereas Laban views him more as a slave, as emerges clearly when Laban tracks Jacob down after Jacob has run off with his wives and children.

At the end of six years God, representing a universal standard of fairness in such matters, intervenes and directs Jacob to leave his oppressive service under Laban. The Exodus law lays down a period of six years for a slave's service—not three, as in a rule for a debt slave in Hammurabi, nor a variable number, as in Roman law. Jacob wants his two wives and children to leave Laban's household with him, but Laban claims that Jacob's wives and children are his possessions. Moses solves the comparable problem for a Hebrew slave where, unlike the situation in the narrative, there is no ambiguity about his status as a slave. If the master gives a wife to the slave and children are born of the union, the woman and the children remain with the master.

The slave can become permanently attached to the master's household should a bond of affection prevail between them. The story suggests the issue. Jacob wants to quit his attachment because he notices that Laban is no longer well disposed to him. Presumably, if there had not been such a turn of events, Jacob might have opted to remain. The rule speaks first of the slave's loving his master. The idiosyncratic circum-

stances of the story account for a stipulation that is unique to the biblical legal material.

Should the slave opt for permanent attachment, the master "brings him to the gods" (the reference is to such household gods as Laban possesses). A contrary development takes place in the story. Rachel steals the household gods from her father's house just after declaring that he no longer treats her sister and herself as his daughters but as strangers whom he has sold. By agreeing with Jacob that they should sever their attachment to Laban's household, she acknowledges that there should be an end to the servitude Laban imposes on Jacob. In the rule the ceremony with the gods signifies that the slave is content to continue his servitude.

As a nation the Israelites first come upon the problem of slavery in Egypt when, owing to conditions of famine, the vizier Joseph has the Egyptian population become slaves to Pharaoh. In exchange for food the Egyptians give all their money and then their animals and then finally sell themselves and their lands. The Israelites appear to escape this fate because they "gain possessions" in a geographically separate part of Egypt. A future pharaoh, however, enslaves a later generation of Israelites and has them serve with "rigor."

In the Levitical law Moses requires that the Israelites do not do "what they do in the land of Egypt where you dwelt . . . [nor] . . . walk in their statutes" (Lv 18:3).

He lays down a rule in light of the events that occurred in Egypt: the Israelites are to be slaves, not to an earthly ruler like Pharaoh, but to their own ruler, God. This means that if an Israelite has to sell himself to another Israelite, he should not become a slave to him. He should serve him as a hired servant or as a sojourner, without "rigor," until the year of Jubilee. That is the year when he will return to his family and "the possession of his fathers." The contrast is with what happened to the Egyptians because of Joseph's statute. They had to sell themselves to the pharaoh and lost their possessions for all time.

The Deuteronomic rule shares features with the Exodus rule: a six-year term of service, a permanent attachment to a master if the slave so wishes, and a ceremony (without household gods) to mark such an attachment. It differs from the Exodus rule in that it takes up the issue of a Hebrew female slave's release from service as well as a Hebrew male's, does not discuss any marital arrangements for the slave, and calls for generous provision to a departing slave. The Exodus rule focused on Jacob's situation in Laban's household and the marital arrangements there. The Deuteronomic rule, in turn, focused on the situation of the Hebrew males and females enslaved in Egypt when the issue of the pharaoh's giving wives to the Hebrew male slaves does not arise.

Each rule has similar concerns because the two relevant narratives raise similar issues. Laban does not wish to have Jacob depart, nor Pharaoh the Israelites. Jacob's continuing in Laban's household is an issue, as is the Israelites' desire after their departure from Egypt to return permanently (Ex 16: 3). Each story raises the matter of provisions for the departing Israelite. Jacob leaves with many possessions, and the Israelites, oddly, depart with Egyptian jewelry. Attracted to the issue in each legend, the Deuteronomic rule requires a master "to make [as having jewels] a necklace" of produce from winepress, field, and flock for the departing slave.

The narrators of biblical history characteristically set down recurring developments over successive generations, and the lawgivers range over them. The audience was to identify with the history and imbibe the ethical spirit of the laws that are commentary on it. The authors probably did not intend that one law should be reconciled with another. Each law is Moses's response to a different experience of enslavement in the nation's history. Who the audience was and when and where it lived are unknown, but a post-exile Babylonian community is the likeliest possibility. The humanitarian character of the biblical slave laws stands out when set down alongside the slave laws of the surrounding cultures. The impressive standard is attributable to the unique process of their composition.

See also ANCIENT MIDDLE EAST; EXODUS; JEWS; JUDAISM; LAW.

BIBLIOGRAPHY

CARMICHAEL, CALUM. *The Origins of Biblical Law.* 1992.
CHIRICHIGNO, G. C. *Debt-Slavery in Israel and the Ancient Near East*. 1993.
DE VAUX, ROLAND. *Ancient Israel.* Vol. 1. 1965; pp. 80–90.
PAUL, S. M. *Studies in the Book of the Covenant in the Light of Cuneiform and Biblical Law.* 1970.
VAN SETERS, J. "The Law of the Hebrew Slave." *Zeitschrift für die Alttestamentliche Wissenschaft* 108 (1996): 534–546.

Calum Carmichael

Birney, James G.   [1792–1857]

Southern politician and prominent abolitionist.

James Gillespie Birney was the most important southern-born white abolitionist of the antebellum period. Born in Danville, Kentucky, the son of a Scots-Irish immigrant and manufacturer, Birney graduated from the College of New Jersey (Princeton) in 1810, studied law in Philadelphia, and then returned to Lexington, where he practiced law and married Agatha MacDowell, the daughter of a prominent judge and cousin of President James Madison. In 1818, Birney relocated his family and fifteen slaves to a cotton plantation he had acquired in northern Alabama. However, because of financial difficulties, Birney eventually sold the plantation and a large number of slaves and resumed his law practice. Between 1814 and 1829 he held various political offices in Kentucky and Alabama. He was a presidential elector for Andrew Jackson in 1828 and was elected mayor of Huntsville, Alabama, in 1829.

During the 1820s, Birney became active in the temperance movement. After reading a tract from the American Colonization Society, Birney began to advocate the colonization of free blacks in Liberia and began to speak publicly about the "slave question" in the South. In 1832, Birney accepted the offer of the Society to become a traveling agent to raise funds and to recruit free blacks for transport to Liberia.

Within a few years Birney had been converted to abolitionism. He formally repudiated his colonizationist leanings in an essay entitled *Letter on Colonization* (1834). By the late 1830s, Birney became a vocal proponent of manumission for all slaves, raising the ire of his fellow southerners.

After this he became a prominent and vocal opponent of slavery, traveling tirelessly in the North to recruit new followers. He edited *The Philanthropists,* an antislavery newspaper in Cincinnati, in 1836–1837 before moving the publication to New York. While in

James G. Birney. [*Dictionary of American Portraits*]

Cincinnati Birney was sued for harboring a fugitive slave and was defended by the young abolitionist attorney Salem P. Chase. In 1840 Birney's name appeared on ballots as the presidential candidate for the Liberty Party. In 1844 he actively ran for president as a candidate of that party, winning over 60,000 popular votes. Whigs blamed him for the defeat of Henry Clay that year because if all of Birney's supporters in New York had voted for Clay, he would have carried that state and with it the election. It is unlikely that Birney's supporters would have voted for Clay, who was a slaveholder—even over Polk, who was more aggressively proslavery—but the election did indicate the growing strength of abolitionism.

Birney was the Liberty Party's candidate for governor of Michigan in 1843 and 1845, but after that he left politics. In 1850 he partially reversed himself on colonization. He still believed that the American Colonization Society was a racist organization, designed to deny blacks their legitimate and hard-earned place in America. But, discouraged by the U.S. Supreme Court decision in *Strader v. Graham* (1850), he argued that blacks could never expect full legal protection in the United States and might be better off leaving the country. His dire prediction of the direction of the Supreme Court came true shortly before his death, when the Court ruled in *Dred Scott v. Sandford* that blacks had no rights under the Constitution.

See also ABOLITION AND ANTISLAVERY MOVEMENTS; AMERICAN COLONIZATION SOCIETY; LAW; LIBERIA; REPATRIATION TO AFRICA.

BIBLIOGRAPHY

BARNES, GILBERT HOBBS. *The Antislavery Impulse: 1830–1844.* 1934.
DUMOND, DWIGHT LOWELL, ed. *Letters of James Gillespie Birney, 1831–1857,* 2 vols. 1938.
FLADELAND, BETTY. *James Gillespie Birney: Slaveholder to Abolitionist.* 1955.

David A. Reichard
Paul Finkelman

Blackbirding in the Pacific Islands

When European ships began to explore and trade in the Pacific in the 1500s, they sometimes kidnapped indigenous islanders as guides or crew, and in the nineteenth century a plantation labor trade incorporated thousands of these islanders into the emerging world economy. By the 1870s regulation by the British colony in Australia and by the Kingdom of Hawai'i promoted enlistment on a more voluntary basis, but episodes of "blackbirding" (kidnapping) persisted.

As early as the thirteenth century, Indonesians were capturing dark-skinned Melanesians from the southwestern Pacific and selling them into slavery on Java, but the first incident of kidnapping by Europeans occurred in 1522. One of Ferdinand Magellan's ships captured a Chamorro from Guam for a few days to serve as a guide in the Marianas, then let him go. In 1526 another Spanish crew kidnapped eleven Chamorros to man the pumps on their leaking ship. In their quests for the spice islands and for King Solomon's mythic mines, Spanish vessels took away men, women, and children from Melanesia to convert into Christians, train as interpreters, or serve the crew. Spain also incorporated both the Philippines (1565) and Guam (1668) into a transpacific galleon trade with Mexico; the crews included some Asians and Pacific islanders, whose voyages were often less than voluntary. In 1690 privateer William Dampier purchased a castaway called "Jeoly," who had been enslaved in the Philippines. Dampier took the tattooed man to England and sold him as a "painted prince" to a traveling carnival. Jeoly later died of smallpox in Oxford, demonstrating the dangers for such captive "specimens" in an age of conquistadores and pirates.

After 1763, when the British and French made peace, their navies began more scientific exploration of the Pacific. The idealization of "noble savages" by Enlightenment philosophers such as Jean-Jacques Rousseau inspired commanders to seek out islanders to guide them around the region. The first was a Mapian islander nicknamed Joseph Freewill, who in 1767 climbed up the mast of a British exploring vessel and insisted on staying aboard; he died in Indonesia. In 1768 Louis Antoine de Bougainville took Ahutoru, at a chief's request, from Tahiti to Paris, where he caused a sensation, but the young man died during the return voyage because Pacific islanders, like Native Americans, were vulnerable to Eurasian diseases. In 1769 James Cook took a Society Islander named Tupaia (and his Tahitian servant) across the South Pacific. Tupaia was an experienced navigator, knew the locations of many islands, and translated for Cook in New Zealand, but he too died in Indonesia. On his second exploring expedition in 1772, Cook took Omai from Tahiti to London and vaccinated the islander against smallpox, so that he survived to return home again as a would-be ambassador. Despite this rising trend toward voluntarism among peoples with an ancient seafaring tradition, kidnapping continued in Pacific recruiting.

As European and U.S. merchant vessels entered the China trade and whalers and sealers began plying Pacific waters, they recruited islanders to replace lost crewmen. Some ships simply kidnapped healthy young men (or women) and deposited them on any convenient island when they had no more use for their services. In 1795 a seal-hunting vessel took away several Hawaiian captives but later returned them home with written recommendations as sailors, which they used to get jobs on other ships. Whaling and sealing vessels based in Sydney, Australia, took on Maori from New Zealand as crew, at times by force, and Australian trade-ships hired Tahitians. In 1793 the New South Wales government kidnapped two Maori to teach British convicts how to make cloth from flax, but a decade later it was issuing regulations requiring repatriation of the many Pacific islander seamen arriving in Sydney.

Ambitious chiefs like Kamehameha I of Hawai'i encouraged young men to ship out and learn foreign nautical skills so that they could man the Western-style schooners the islanders were acquiring. By 1800 hundreds of Hawaiians were working in the fur trade in northwest America, and by the 1840s an estimated three thousand were serving on whalers—about one-fifth of the sailors in the U.S. whaling fleet. As whaling ships developed regular seasonal circuits between the Japan grounds and the Line (equator), nearly every island sent young men to sea, with varying degrees of voluntarism and good treatment. Pacific islanders excelled as boat handlers, divers, and harpooners, as Herman Melville suggested in his portrayal of Queequeg in *Moby Dick*. So many shipped out of Hawai'i every year that in the 1840s the kingdom required captains to post bonds against the safe return of recruits; later it required departing seamen to post bonds to support their families while they were away. Honolulu newspapers debated the degree to which maritime "conscription" was contributing to native depopulation, but the government argued that it could not stop the process lest ships take their business elsewhere.

Between 1829 and the 1850s, sandalwood vessels used gangs of Polynesians to penetrate malarial Melanesia. Conflicts developed between the woodcutters and the native islanders, however, and many Polynesian workers died of fever. Sandalwooder James Paddon of Australia began to take Melanesian laborers away from one island for use on another, thereby rendering the workers, even if mistreated, dependent on him to get home again. During the U.S. Civil War, British cotton speculators started plantations in Fiji and Australia that required cheap labor, thereby accelerating the blackbirding process. Between the 1860s and the early 1900s, an estimated 120,000 Pacific islanders (mainly Melanesian) left their islands on three-year indenture contracts to work in places like Queensland, Australia, where sugar became the main crop.

Kidnapping prevailed in the early years of plantation labor recruiting and persisted despite attempts at formal regulation. The most notorious episode was the Peruvian slave raids across the South Pacific in the years 1862 to 1864. Chartered ships took thirty-six

James Cook interacts with Pacific Islanders. [Gianni Dagli Orti/Corbis]

hundred captives from islands as far away as the Gilbert Islands for work on Peruvian sugar and cotton plantations. Because of harsh work conditions and smallpox, only 148 slaves returned home alive, many carrying the disease. The entire chiefly class of the Tokelau Islands was wiped out, and Easter Island lost 58 percent of its small population. In 1871 the Australian labor recruiting vessel *Carl* lured Solomon Islanders alongside, then dropped weights to sink their canoes and seized the survivors. After filling the hold with captives, the crew suppressed a revolt by the prisoners, massacring seventy of them. The captain was later prosecuted in Sydney, and the British government began to enact laws to eliminate such abuses.

In 1877 the British Western Pacific High Commission, based in Fiji, began to send naval patrols through the islands and to require labor recruiting vessels to carry government agents, who were to make sure that recruits understood the terms of their indenture contracts and were well treated. Voluntarism predominated thereafter, as native passage-masters assembled passengers for ships and returnees displayed their trade boxes of foreign goods. But abuses would continue, and as late as the 1880s, some labor recruiters were still taking Melanesians and Micronesians by force. Most recruits worked on sugar and copra plantations in Australia, Fiji, Samoa, Hawai'i and Tahiti, but many died, and the survivors usually repatriated after their contracts ended.

Increasingly, Asians would provide the bulk of plantation labor in the Pacific. Fewer islander workers went abroad after 1900, when Australia banned nonwhite immigration and colonialists in the islands wanted cheap (often forced) labor for local economic production.

See also PACIFIC ISLAND SOCIETIES.

BIBLIOGRAPHY

CHAPPELL, DAVID A. *Double Ghosts: Oceanian Voyaging on Euroamerican Ships.* 1997.

CORRIS, PETER. *Port, Passage, and Plantation: A History of the Solomon Islands Labour Trade.* 1973.

DOCKER, E. W. *The Blackbirders: The Recruiting of South Seas Labour for Queensland.* 1970.

MAUDE, H. E. *Slavers in Paradise: The Peruvian Labour Trade in Polynesia, 1862–64.* 1981.

David A. Chappell

Bledsoe, Albert Taylor   [1809–1877]

Author, educator, proslavery theorist.

The son of Moses Ousley and Sophia Childress Taylor Bledsoe, Albert Taylor Bledsoe was educated at West Point (class of 1830) and Kenyon College, Ohio, where he studied theology and philosophy. After teaching at Kenyon College (1833–1834) and Miami University in Ohio (1835–1836), Bledsoe practiced law in Springfield, Illinois, from 1838 to 1848. He returned to teaching as a professor of mathematics at the University of Mississippi from 1848 to 1854, and at the University of Virginia, from 1854 to 1861. While teaching math at Virginia, Bledsoe tapped his interest in theology and philosophy to join the proslavery counterattack with his *Essay on Liberty and Slavery; or, Slavery in the Light of Moral and Political Philosophy,* published in 1856. Bledsoe contended that slavery was of divine appointment and had biblical sanction. He also asserted that people of African origin lacked the ability to participate in modern society, and so the protection of liberty and social order for whites demanded the enslavement of blacks. Jefferson Davis appointed Bledsoe assistant secretary of war, and sent him to London in 1863 to influence public opinion there about the Confederate cause. He returned in 1865 and used his collected arguments to write *Is Davis a Traitor? or, Was Secession a Constitutional Right Previous to the War of 1861?* (1866), a volume used by lawyers to defend Davis against charges of treason and among the earliest statements of the

Albert Taylor Bledsoe. [*Dictionary of American Portraits*]

postwar "Lost Cause." In his willingness "to be a slave for the South," in 1867 Bledsoe founded the *Southern Review* in Baltimore and edited it until his death.

See also CONFEDERATE STATES OF AMERICA; LAW; PERSPECTIVES ON SLAVERY.

BIBLIOGRAPHY

BENNETT, JON B. "Albert Taylor Bledsoe: Social and Religious Controversialist of the Old South." Ph.D. diss., Duke University, 1942.
COOKE, J. W. "Albert Taylor Bledsoe: An American Philosopher and Theologian of Liberty." *Southern Humanities Review* 8 (1974): 215–227.

Eric H. Walther

Branding and Branding Irons

See Badges of Slavery.

Brazil

This entry includes the following articles: An Overview; Northeastern Brazil; Dutch Brazil; Central and Southern Brazil. *Related articles may be found at the entries* Caribbean Region; Plantations.

An Overview

The date of the introduction of Portuguese slavery into Brazil is uncertain, but those who were first enslaved in Brazil were the coastal Indians. In 1511, a Portuguese ship, the *Bertoa,* loaded a cargo of logs and thirty-five Indian slaves for transport back to Portugal. The use of Africans in sixteenth-century Brazil drew on ports established by the Portuguese in Africa in the fifteenth century. The Portuguese fort of São Jorge da Mina opened on the Gold Coast in 1482; and African slaves were taken first to Portugal and the African islands. By the 1530s, the Portuguese were using enslaved Africans in Pernambuco in the Northeast and at São Vicente in the Southeast. The direct slave trade with Africa began by 1550 and lasted until the 1850s, introducing an estimated 3.5 to 4.5 million Africans to Brazil over three centuries. Of the Africans exported to all the Americas, Brazil received about one-third; and it now has the world's largest population of African descent outside of Africa.

The institution of slavery was integral to the historical evolution of Brazil and its economy. No region or period was untouched by Amerindian or African slavery, which constituted the base of all the regional economies of Brazil. African slavery predominated because the Portuguese were few in number and were unwilling, or sometimes unable, to labor in a malarial region; and the indigenous population fell to epidemics of smallpox and measles or retreated to the interior to escape slavery and death. Anyone who aspired to riches and status had to possess slaves, who provided most of the labor for plantations and mines. Even slaves, freedpersons, and free people of color owned slaves, as did women and priests. Control over people—that is, slaves—was more important than land ownership because Brazil was land-rich. It was larger than the continental United States of America and had only to be wrested from the Indian nations with the help of slave soldiers.

Although historians have good estimates for the African slave trade, there are no well-documented demographic studies to establish the total number of Afro-Brazilian slaves from the 1530s to the present. Various censuses of the eighteenth and nineteenth centuries, however, reveal that black and *pardo* (brown) slaves were at least 40 percent of the population; in mining regions, the proportion was over 80 percent. Brazilians preferred to buy male slaves, and plantation records document a ratio of three male slaves to every female slave. Mining gangs were almost all male. Thus, one feature of slavery in Brazil was the preponderance of male slaves. However, Amerindian captives were females and children. Hence African men and Indian women often labored in the fields together and raised their "mixed" (*cafuzo*) children as part of a slave family.

The Africans brought to Brazil on slave ships came from many parts of West and West Central Africa. Those that were bought on the Costa da Mina (modern Ghana, Bénin, and Togo) in particular at São Jorge da Mina, were known as Minas in Brazil; and by extension a Mina also indicated anyone from the entire region of West Africa. Another designation for West African slaves in Brazil was Guiné. The second major region of export was the present country of Angola, and many Africans from there were identified as Angolas, Benguelas, or Congos, including those from the Kingdom of Kongo in northern Angola. Proportionately fewer Africans originated in Mozambique, although they became more common in the nineteenth century. Even some people from the island of Madagascar were enslaved in Brazil. Amerindian captives came from all regions of Brazil and Paraguay. Hence, Brazil's slave population was extraordinarily complex, with many gradations of color, from those defined as black (*negro, preto,* or *crioulo*) to those who were racially mixed (*mulato, pardo, cafuzo,* and *cabra*) and to white slaves. In the colonial period, Indian captives were termed *negros da terra* ("blacks of the land" or "black natives"); this indicator that *negro* was synonymous with slave.

Individuals were enslaved in Brazil through various methods. In law, one became a slave by being purchased or being born of an enslaved mother. Thus,

Sixteenth-century slave miners lay their loads at the feet of their European masters. [Library of Congress/Corbis]

some newly arrived Africans were auctioned off or sold in retail stores in coastal slave markets, while others were acquired directly through ships' captains, who had bought them in Africa and transported them to Brazil on the commission of slaveowners. Slave markets were located in Belém do Pará, São Luis de Maranhão, Olinda in Pernambuco, Salvador da Bahia, and Rio de Janeiro. In the eighteenth century, the small coastal town of Paratí received many new Africans destined for the mines of Minas Gerais. Slaves were bought with notes of credit in money (*mil-réis*), Spanish silver, or gold. In the nineteenth century, payment of the *meia-siza* tax established legal ownership of a slave. Once African women and girls were imported, Portuguese slaveowners followed Roman law in defining the babies born of enslaved mothers as slaves; thus, slave status was inherited from the mother. Another method of defining persons as slaves was to list newborns as slaves in Catholic baptismal registries.

Other than running away, the only way to escape slave status was to undergo the legal process of manumission, in which a notary public recorded a person's letter of liberty (*carta de alforria*). The slave then kept a copy of the letter of liberty, which identified his or her new status as a *forro* (also, *liberto*). Henceforth, he or she was free, as if "born of the free womb." In general, two-thirds of those freed were female, although in the mining regions male slaves were able to purchase their freedom in installments by paying in gold. Such freedom was not absolute, however, since former owners could reenslave *forros* for "ingratitude."

There were (and are) other methods of becoming enslaved. From the sixteenth century on, Amerindians were captured in raids and wars and taken as slaves to coastal towns or the plateau of São Paulo. In São Paulo, their children inherited their slave status. In the interior of Brazil, slaves were called "*cativos*"—(war) "captives"—a term which provides an important insight into the legal and ethical justifications for Brazilian slavery, past and present. Amerindians and other ethnic groups have been enslaved over the centuries by "right of conquest"; the victors enslaved the losers, even when that was contrary to law. There were, however, legal exceptions. In 1570 the Portuguese crown authorized the seizure of slaves in the following cases: the prosecution of "just wars" against those who rejected Christianity or to ransom captives destined to be eaten by "cannibals." Although reforms in Portugal abolished forced Indian labor in 1755, a royal letter of 1811 reestablished the temporary bondage of war captives in São Paulo, Minas Gerais, Espírito Santo, Goiás, and Maranhão. Thus, Amerindian slavery experienced periods of legality under Luso-Brazilian law, although most Indian slavery has been customary and illegal.

Men and women of African ancestry were also enslaved as captives. Free men and women or even people recently manumitted were enslaved as *bens do vento*, which translates as "property of the wind" or "a windfall." In other words, people of color who had no protector or legal document establishing their legal status as *livre* (free) or *forro* could become the property of anyone who "found" them.

Finally, over the centuries Brazilians evolved customs that approximated unfree and unpaid labor in which the individual was not legally enslaved for a lifetime. In colonial Sabará, Minas Gerais, a person could sell himself into servitude for one year in exchange for gold. On the frontiers many "free" individuals, often Amerindians, were *agregados* (household dependents), who worked for a family without wages. Others were poor or abandoned children serving the families who sheltered them. Women and girls were forced into prostitution, a practice that persisted into the late 1990s. Debt peonage, sharecropping, and other systems of coerced labor, including indentured servitude, also accompanied slavery in Brazil.

In general, Amerindians were enslaved when no African slaves were available and there were no profitable export crops or rich mines. The captaincy of São Paulo built its wealth on Indian rather than African labor in the sixteenth and seventeenth centuries. The men of São Paulo were also notable slave raiders who explored Brazil's hinterland, searching for Indian slaves and emeralds. During their expeditions (*bandeiras*), they acquired captives by waging war on Indian nations or kidnapping individuals by stealth. In particular, they raided the Guarani populations of the Jesuit missions of Paraguay, returning to São Paulo with Christian captives and forcing them to labor on their farms, raising foodstuffs. Although the colonists called them *forros*, these Indians were treated as slaves, and Paulista families inherited them as property. Since periodic epidemics ravaged the Amerindians, the *bandeirantes* sought new captives throughout the seventeenth century. After the discovery of gold in Minas Gerais, Indian slavery in São Paulo gradually gave way to African slavery, as the Paulistas used the gold to buy Africans, and the population of São Paulo gradually darkened in color. The *bandeira* tradition of raiding for Indian captives, however, continued on the frontiers of Goiás and Mato Grosso into the nineteenth century.

To the north, in the Amazon region (Pará and Tocantins) and the state of Maranhão, the regional economies were also based on Indian agricultural laborers, porters, and riverboatmen. Great slave-raiding expeditions, here known as *tropas de resgate* (redemption expeditions), pursued Indian captives along the rivers of the Amazon system. Large canoes bearing armed men captured Indian slaves along the Rio Negro and as far west as the Rio Madeira. The Jesuit missions of the Amazon region were also raided, and Christianized Indians living there were enslaved.

In the early nineteenth century, Indian slavery was legalized once again in the province of Goiás, where settlers were authorized to enslave Indians temporarily in order to encourage the agricultural development of the Tocantins River valley. Indian slavery also grew on the cattle frontier of southern Maranhão and among the Botocudo of Minas Gerais and Espírito Santo. The Kaingang of São Paulo were also enslaved as captives in "just wars." Because these war captives were often abused, Indian slavery was once more declared illegal in 1835. This customary practice did not die out, however, and Indians were commonly enslaved during the rubber boom of the late nineteenth and early twentieth centuries and again during the opening of the Amazon region and the Center West after 1960.

The centers of African slavery in Brazil developed first in the Northeast in the sixteenth and seventeenth centuries; the richest captaincies, where slaveowners grew wealthy on profits from sugar plantations, were Pernambuco and Bahia. Gold was discovered in the 1690s, and throughout the eighteenth century Africans mined for gold in Minas Gerais and the Center West (Goiás and Mato Grosso). African slavery remained common in the nineteenth century on the coffee plantations of Rio de Janeiro, São Paulo, and Minas Gerais until the abolition of slavery in 1888.

The conquest and peopling of the coast and mining regions was thus a joint Luso-African project. The Portuguese brought their African slaves with them from Portugal to help subjugate the Indian nations. Lacking a sufficient number of Portuguese soldiers, they adopted the practice of arming these slaves to fight off attacks by the coastal Indians and to wage offensive wars against them. During the colonial period, black militias—named *Henriques* in honor of Henrique Dias, the black hero of the wars against the Dutch in the seventeenth century—were essential to the defense of colonial Brazil. Mulattoes had their own separate militia regiments commanded by *pardo* officers. In the nineteenth century, black troops were freed because of their service in numerous conflicts, including the Paraguayan War. One important characteristic of the Brazilian slave system was its custom of permitting slaves and ex-slaves to own slaves, thus giving them a vested interest in protecting their property rights and status as slaveowners. Hence, black and *pardo* troops even participated in the repressing of slave revolts and attacking *quilombos*—settlements of escaped slaves. On the other hand, slaves forbidden to carry weapons created their own paramilitary organization (the *maltas*), composed of those adept at weaponless martial art of *capoeira*, to defend themselves and protect other slaves.

In the sixteenth century, the sugar plantation was introduced from the African island of São Tomé. Africans and some Amerindians worked in the fields or the sugar mill (*engenho*) for an individual who came to be called the *senhor de engenho,* "lord of the sugar mill" and, by extension, the plantation—also called the *engenho.* Other slaves raised foodstuffs, such as manioc, herded cattle, or transported sugar on oxcarts to the ports of Salvador and Olinda. The first *engenhos* were established in São Vicente and Pernambuco in the 1530s and 1540s, and by 1570 perhaps 2,000 to 3,000 Africans were working on Brazilian *engenhos*. As sugar became the dominant export, Africans slaves replaced Indian slaves, who were dying out. In the last decades of the sixteenth century, Bahia and Pernambuco imported 30,000 Africans from the coast of Guiné, but sugar production reached its apogee in the seventeenth century, when half a million Africans were imported, most of them before 1640. These slaves planted and harvested sugar cane for the great *senhores de engenho,* who possessed extensive plantations with hundreds of slaves and sugar mills; or for the *lavradores de cana* (sugar sharecroppers), who owned or rented smaller plots of land, employed fewer slaves, and sent their cane to the planter's mill for processing. Because of the high mortality among slaves, sugar planters relied on the African slave trade to replenish their workers year after year.

Although sugar was the major export during the seventeenth century, some Africans and Indians escaped the hard labor it involved by working on the great livestock *fazendas* (estates) of the interior. Once horses, burros, cattle, and goats had been introduced into Brazil, Africans who were familiar with such animals in their homelands took quickly to animal husbandry. Their masters set them to work as cowboys raising cattle, horses, and goats in the backlands of the Northeast and on the pastures of the extreme south of Brazil. From the interior of Pernambuco and Bahia along the São Francisco River or in Piauí and Maranhão, black and mulatto cowboys herded the cattle to the towns and cities of the coast to be slaughtered by urban slaves and processed as dried beef (a staple of the slave diet) or as leather and tallow. In the far south of Brazil, slave cowboys rounded up cattle and delivered them for slaughter as the *charqueadas* for the export market in dried beef. Wherever mule teams and oxcarts transported goods, slaves drove the animals between urban centers and the *fazendas* and *engenhos.* Other slaves raised goats for milk, cheese, and leather; pigs for *toucinho* (pork fat); and chickens and turkeys.

Skilled hunters, in particular Amerindians, brought home the delicacies of the forest, such as anteaters, lizards, and monkeys. Slaves who had been skilled at fishing in Africa transferred their skills to Brazil's great rivers, such as the Amazon and São Francisco, or they fished from *jangadas* (rafts with sails) on the ocean. They also worked as whalers in the bays of Rio de Janeiro and Bahia, returning to the warehouses, where they cut up the whales and extracted their oil for the lamps of the cities. Africans' familiarity with the sea meant that masters also employed slaves as sailors, canoe paddlers, oarsmen, pilots, and riverboatmen. In the Amazon basin, they joined Indians as oarsmen and canoers. Both Amerindian and African slave men were essential in providing the power for Brazil's coastal and riverine trades, but black slave mariners also served as rented sailors on ships that sailed throughout the Americas and back to Africa.

Another African skill, head porterage, was also important in Brazil. Although Indian slaves preferred to carry burdens on their backs, black slaves in Brazil, both male and female, toted heavy loads on their heads, especially each household's daily supply of water. They were also the stevedores on the docks, loading Brazil's exports onto ships and unloading imports, including new Africans. In the city of Salvador, they carried merchandise from the docks of the lower city to businesses and residences of the upper city. Porters also had to carry their owners in hammocks or sedan chairs. Until the advent of European carts, wagons, and carriages in coastal cities in the nineteenth century, Africans were essential to the transportation infrastructure of Brazil. Indian "servants" also did head porterage in the absence of black slaves.

Thus slaves were important to every area of the agricultural economy. They did not just produce sugar; they also raised foodstuffs—such as corn and manioc (staples of the slave diet), rice, wheat, and tropical fruits—besides the commercial crops: indigo, tobacco,

Slaves gather at a fountain (probably in Rio) to obtain water for their masters. [Library of Congress/Corbis]

coffee, and cotton. Slaves even labored on cacao plantations in the Amazon region in the eighteenth century. Every town and city had gardens (*chácaras*) or small farms (*sítios*) on the outskirts, where property owners employed their slaves in cultivating fruits and vegetables and raising small animals and birds—frequently for sale in the urban markets. Other foodstuff producers owned, rented, or squatted on small plots of land (*roças*) on large plantations, where they raised manioc for sale to the planters. Beans, corn, bananas, oranges, and other tropical fruits were also produced by these *roceiros* (small farmers) and their three or four slaves. Small property owners also cultivated tobacco in Bahia and Pernambuco for export to Europe and Africa. Tobacco raised in the captaincy of Goiás was shipped north to Belém via the Tocantins River. Brazil also had an internal market for tobacco raised by slaves, and much tobacco cultivation was on smallholdings rather than large plantations.

Coffee was first raised in the Amazon region, but its intensive cultivation began on *chácaras* in the suburbs of Rio de Janeiro at the beginning of the nineteenth century and spread from there to the Paraíba River

valley of the provinces of Rio de Janeiro and São Paulo, as well as into Minas Gerais. Because of the great demand for labor on the large coffee plantations, there was a rapid expansion of the African slave trade even after it was declared illegal in 1830; at least one million slaves were destined for this region in the nineteenth century. Individual coffee plantations, especially those in São Paulo, employed hundreds or even thousands of slaves in the second half of the nineteenth century. At the time of abolition in 1888, slavery was still profitable on the coffee plantations of the province of São Paulo.

Brazil had yet another plantation crop whose cultivation and export surged during the North American Civil War—cotton. Slaves raised cotton in the Northeast, Goiás, and Minas Gerais during the late colonial period. From the 1780s to the 1820s, Brazilian cotton was exported to Portugal and Great Britain; but thereafter competition from the American South limited production to the internal market, until the 1860s, when international demand led masters in the Northeast to shift their slaves into cotton production for export. Otherwise, most cotton grown by slaves supplied the internal market; Indian and African slave women spun the raw fiber into thread that was then woven into cloth and coverlets. They also made fine lace to decorate clothing and homes.

Finally, a plantation crop that flourished in Maranhão at the end of the eighteenth century was rice. Rice was first introduced to Salvador in the 1550s, with African varieties from the Cape Verde Islands. Africans from the Upper Guinea coast were significant in the diffusion of rice cultivation and technology. By the mid-seventeenth century, slaves cultivated rice on marginal plantation lands in the Northeast. A century later the Portuguese had introduced "Carolina rice" seed to the Amazon region (Maranhão and Pará). They also raised rice near Rio de Janeiro, but rice did not find an international market in the nineteenth century, so most slaves cultivated it in addition to other crops for the Brazilian market.

In addition to plantation labor, Brazil's slaves were also employed in the mining sector of the colonial economy. Gold was discovered in Minas Gerais in the 1690s, and then in the captaincies of Mato Grosso (1718) and Goiás (the 1720s). Thereafter, Africans were imported to work on the gold strikes and, after the 1720s, also in the diamond mines in Minas Gerais. Miners purchased new Africans in the cities of Rio de Janeiro and Salvador and led them hundreds of miles inland to pan for gold in the rivers or to excavate mountains of soil to uncover more gold in deep mines. During the early eighteenth century, Amerindian and Afro-Brazilian slaves in São Paulo, Bahia, and Rio de Janeiro were separated from their families and force-marched to the mining region, in a massive transferral of slave labor.

Most slaves introduced into the mining region were males; but when mining camps had evolved into towns, slaveowners bought Mina and Angolan women and girls to work as cooks, household servants, and *quitandeiras* (street vendors). Such women acquired gold by exchanging prepared foods and *aguardente* (sugarcane rum) for gold dust. Since slave miners could keep a day's wage of one *pataca*, they were expected to buy their own food and rum, thus enriching enslaved black women and their owners. With access to gold dust, African market women were able to purchase their own and their children's freedom.

In the eighteenth century, the Minas Gerais mining district was Brazil's largest slave society, but as the placer mines declined in output, more and more slaves were transferred into agricultural and pastoral work. By the end of the century, slaves were raising cattle and pigs and producing food crops for the internal market in Brazil. Only a minority continued to work in mining. When planting coffee trees proved to be profitable in the early nineteenth century, large-scale plantation slavery developed in the province. The neighboring province, Goiás, also saw the evolution of a more diverse slave labor force when placer mining declined and slaves began to work on coffee, quince, and cotton plantations; raise cattle on immense *fazendas;* and produce tobacco, leather, and cotton textiles to sell to other provinces. After the effective abolition of the African slave trade in 1850, Goiás, along with the Northeast, added yet another export, young boys and girls sold to Minas Gerais and São Paulo.

Throughout Brazilian history, one of the constant uses of slaves—even to the present—was as household workers. Because of the shortage of female slaves, especially in the mining regions and on the plantations, even male slaves had to do "woman's work." The same slave woman was often required to do both domestic work and street vending. Thus, a woman who cooked the household's meals might also be ordered to sell the dishes and sweets she made to customers. Urban slaveowners also sent their domestic servants into the streets on an *ao ganho* basis—to earn a stipulated sum of money or face daily punishments. In many cases, such threats forced women into prostitution, and even some "good families" and respectable women lived off the earnings of slave prostitutes. Other household slaves, including men, earned money for their owners by doing laundry in the cities; but in the countryside, washing and laying out clothes to dry on the grass was a communal activity of groups of slave women.

Female slaves in poor and middle-income households were required to do the most labor—cook, clean, get water, care for babies and children, sew, spin, weave, make lace, wait on members of the family, and provide sexual services to the male head of the household. However, in the households of the wealthy in cities such as Salvador and Rio de Janeiro, where up to fifty slaves were housed, there was more specialization. The elite among these household workers were the elegantly dressed ladies in waiting (the *mucamas*), who were often related to wealthy families as *mulata* children or grandchildren of the male head of the household. Also prominent was the housekeeper, who commanded the other women servants. In middle- or lower-income families, the housekeeper might owe her position to being the "wife" of the male head. *Amas de leite* (nursemaids) nursed newborns in the family and sometimes stayed on to raise the family's children. In old age, a nursemaid might become the favored *mai preta* (black mother) of the master she had raised. Other household slaves labored as cooks and vendors, buyers of foodstuffs, sewers, spinners, weavers, and laundrymen and -women. Male slaves served as majordomos (butlers), pages, coachmen, footmen, stablemen, and sedan-chair carriers.

Other slaves of urban households were sent into the street as *negros de ganho* (blacks for hire), earning salaries for their owners as skilled craftsmen and artisans, such as tailors, shoemakers, and barber-surgeons. Throughout Brazilian history, male slaves were notable for their mastery of crafts—acquiring the skills, although not the legal prerogatives, of master craftsmen. They were especially talented in metallurgy, working in iron, gold, and silver and making jewelry. Other crafts especially associated with slave men were carpentry, the building trades, and all aspects of sugar technology. Female artisans were weavers, seamstresses, cigar makers, and rum distillers. Because of Brazil's long history of employing slaves as artisans and craftsmen, slaveowners who opened factories in the nineteenth century saw no incompatibility between slavery and industrialization and sent their slaves of both sexes into industrial labor.

Unique to Brazil was the employment of slave musicians to perform European classical and religious music before the royal family and to build, paint, and decorate the baroque masterpieces of the colonial period. Talented artists and craftsmen earned the price of their letter of liberty and thereafter pursued their crafts as freedmen. At least two Afro-Brazilians had an international reputation in music and the arts: the mulatto classical musician José Maurício Nunes Garcia, who composed and performed his music in Portugal; and the architect, painter, and sculptor known as Aleijadinho, who was the son of a Mina slave woman.

But these accomplished artists and artisans were exceptional; most African and Indian slaves did not work as elegantly dressed household servants in the "big houses" of the wealthy or as skilled urban craftsmen. The vast majority of slaves labored in the fields from sunup to sundown, and even at night. Twelve- to eighteen-hour days were the norm, a killing pace that contributed to the high mortality rates on the sugar plantations. In urban areas slaves who did hard labor lasted only twelve to fourteen years on the job, if new Africans survived the initial three years of "seasoning" in their new environment—a different culture, different diseases, and, of course, abuse. The continual deaths of enslaved Africans and Indians led slaveowners to believe that slavery in Brazil could continue only through constant replenishment by new Africans imported in the slave trade. Conversely, because Africans were so readily available (except during the Dutch invasion of the seventeenth century and after 1850), slaveowners did not encourage

A Brazilian plantation owner discusses a purchase with a slave trader (ca. 1850). [Corbis-Bettmann]

women to bear children and did not take special care of slave infants and children. Low fertility rates and high infant and child mortality were characteristic of sugar and coffee plantations.

The ratio of three male slaves to every female slave on large plantations means that many slaves in Brazil had great difficulty in forming stable families and raising children to adulthood in an intact family. Either death intervened or families were divided to settle an inheritance or pay debts. One powerful motive for seeking manumission, followed by marriage in the Catholic church, was to secure family stability. Thus, while matrifocal families appear in colonial inventories and complete families up to the third generation occur in nineteenth-century registries of slaves—and a few even succeeded in buying their passage back to Africa—such families were the exception in plantation and gold-mining areas.

Another characteristic of the Brazilian system was the incorporation of a few slaves, in particular Amerindian and African women, into the slaveowning families of the plantation and mining regions. Where white women were few, single men established long-term relationships with slave women, who bore their children. Affective ties led some fathers to manumit their wives and recognize their mulatto children as heirs. More common, however, was the concubinage of slave women. The children of slave concubines were also raised in the household but did not always obtain their freedom.

Foreigners visiting wealthy households observed that some slave women were treated as family members and concluded that Brazilian slavery was remarkably mild in contrast to slavery elsewhere in the Americas. Gilberto Freyre incorporated this idea in *The Masters and the Slaves,* but historians in Brazil now reject his thesis. Recent research has found that the treatment of slaves varied greatly from family to family and region to region.

However, some defining characteristics of the treatment and punishment of slaves were distinctive to Brazilian slavery. First, the master's will was dominant, unfettered by a slave code, especially in regions located far from the centers of Luso-Brazilian justice. A slaveowner was lord (*senhor*) or lady (*senhora*) in his or her own realm. The master could treat his slaves as benevolently or cruelly as he pleased; so too could the lady of the house, who had similar power over slaves she acquired by dowry rights or widowhood. In fact, some women had such an infamous reputation for sadistic treatment of their slaves that they scandalized other slaveowners. State bureaucrats frequently failed to intercede. That illegally held slaves are still whipped in the 1990s reflects the inability of the modern nation-state to enforce its laws against slavery.

Two other Brazilian institutions could intervene on behalf of slaves, however. As long as the Portuguese royal family ruled Brazil (until 1889), slaves could appeal to them for protection against owners. Royal decrees freed slaves who won an appeal to the throne. Property rights, therefore, could be annulled by royal fiat. As a consequence, Afro-Brazilians were among the loyal supporters of the monarchy, and especially of Princess Isabel after she signed the Golden Law of 13 May 1888, which abolished slavery. Afro-Brazilians also elected kings and queens of their own, who reigned over their "nations" of slaves and freed people as vassals of the Portuguese royal family.

A second mitigating influence was the Catholic church and its representatives. The church received slaves as baptized Christians, encouraged slave marriages, and permitted Afro-Brazilians to form their own religious brotherhoods (*irmandades*), with female associates; these brotherhoods built their own churches dedicated to Our Lady of the Rosary and the black saint, Benedict. Although slaves could not become priests, mulatto sons of slave women were ordained. The slaves of priests were miners, plantation workers, urban craftsmen, and servants. They often earned money to give the priests a decent living. Even the Jesuits, who struggled to protect Amerindians from enslavement, staffed their own plantations with enslaved Africans; and other religious orders, such as the Benedictines, also owned slaves. Because the clergy were deeply involved in the institution of slavery, only occasional priests spoke out against it, but many priests manumitted their own slaves and protected the slaves of other owners from mistreatment. Portuguese lay brotherhoods, including the prestigious Santa Casa da Misericórdia, intervened upon behalf of slaves and collected alms to free slaves who were being badly treated.

As emancipation approached, the Benedictines took the initiative by freeing all of their slaves in the 1860s. However, the church as an institution did not lead the abolitionist movement, although individual Catholic priests and laypeople participated in abolitionist clubs. This indifference stands in sharp contrast to the active role of Catholic bishops and priests against modern forms of slavery in Brazil since the 1960s. In Amazonia and the Center West, where illegal enslavement has appeared, clergymen and nuns have tenaciously opposed it, sometimes at the cost of their lives. They collaborate with journalists, union leaders, and lawyers to rescue people held as slaves and bring national and international attention to the renewal of forced labor on the frontier.

Those concerned about modern slavery oppose it not only on principle but also because they have personally witnessed historic types of disciplining slaves.

Brazil—like every slave society—evolved its own system of control and punishment. Not all types of discipline were unique to Brazil, but some forms symbolized the master's authority and the slave's unwilling submission. The first, and to the Portuguese the most important, was the tall stone pillory (the *pelourinho*), which once stood as a symbol of Portuguese authority in the public squares of Brazilian cities. Here slave criminals and runaways were tied up and whipped with hundreds of lashes. Municipal authorities also provided jails where masters sent disobedient and fugitive slaves to be punished. Obviously, the whip in its various forms was the usual instrument, but others were also used. The *palmatória,* a round wooden paddle with holes, raised painful welts on the hands and other sensitive parts of the body. There were iron instruments, such as heavy chains and shackles. The iron mask, thumbscrews, and iron collars with tridents and bells were also common. Among the most powerful symbols of slave punishment—still in use today—were wooden stocks (the *tronco*), which confined victim's legs. Crueler, even sadistic, tortures were limited only by the owner's imagination unless a neighbor, priest, or judge intervened.

Another powerful symbol of Brazilian slavery, past and present, is the *senzala,* the locked barracks where male slaves were confined for the night. On large sugar and coffee plantations many men did not have the "luxury" of a separate cabin for their families; instead, they slept apart from the women and children. In other cases, men, women, and children lived together in the *senzala*. Although intended as a form of control the *senzala* now evokes the Afro-Brazilian community, for here Afro-Brazilians forged the communal ties that enabled them to survive slavery.

Cruel treatment led slaves to run away and resist slavery in many ways. New Africans fled so commonly that slaveowners regarded this as part of the "seasoning" process. The fugitive was often recaptured by the bush captain (*capitão do mato*) and his men, was punished, and learned, in the master's view, that a recaptured runaway would always be punished. Severe penalties, however, did not stop slaves from fleeing. In the past and today, flight has been one of the most characteristic features of resistance, in part because Brazil, has many environments where fugitives can hide—swamps, tropical rain forests, mountains, islands, and rivers.

The most common refuges for groups who ran away together were hidden settlements known as *quilombos* or *mocambos;* their inhabitants were *quilombolas* or *calhambolas*. These settlements were found throughout Brazil and ranged in size from small camps to the seventeenth-century "kingdom" of Palmares. Most *quilombos* existed on the fringes of plantations or in the forested mountains around coastal cities and mining towns. Others, including those that survived into the twentieth century, were located in remote provinces such as Amazonia, Goiás, and Mato Grosso. The largest continuously occupied *quilombo* in Brazil, which probably dates from the eighteenth century, is Kalunga near Cavalcante, Goiás.

Because *quilombos* were so numerous—there were more than 100 in Minas Gerais alone—they affected slave revolts. Most rebel slaves on the plantations or in mines wanted not to overthrow the entire slave system but rather to escape to an area where they could form their own community or join an already existing *quilombo.*

Nonetheless, uprisings became more common among urban slaves after 1850. Although some conspiracies and revolts had disturbed the mining regions of eighteenth-century Minas Gerais and Goiás, most revolts erupted in the Northeast in the first half of the nineteenth century or in the Southeast during the final years of slavery. Bahia experienced a series of revolts in the early nineteenth century, culminating in the Malê revolt of 1835, in which Muslim clerics led Yoruba and Hausa slaves in street fighting in Salvador. Brutal repression followed this revolt, since slaveowners were determined to quench all future attempts at rebellion. In spite of further nineteenth-century revolts, they succeeded until the final years of slavery, when more than two dozen uprisings took place in São Paulo between 1885 and 1888, hastening abolition. With the passage of the Golden Law on 13 May 1888, Brazil abolished slavery—the last country in the Americas to do so.

Customary slavery, however, has continued to the present in Brazil. Thousands of men, women, and children are still "captured" by labor recruiters and transported by truck to work at charcoal kilns in Minas Gerais or on the hugh *fazendas* of the Center West and Amazonia. Young women and girls are coerced into prostitution in the mining regions of Amazonia. As of the 1990s religious leaders, lay Catholics, lawyers, union leaders, journalists, and political reformers are working to end customary enslavement. By the year 2,000, the five-hundredth anniversary of the discovery of Brazil, the Brazilian state may finally end five centuries of slavery in reality as well as in law.

See also MAROONS; MILITARY SLAVES; NATIVE AMERICANS; PLANTATIONS; RELIGIOUS GROUPS, SLAVE OWNERSHIP BY.

BIBLIOGRAPHY

BARCELOS, LUIZ CLAUDIO, OLIVIA MARIA GOMES DA CUNHA, and TEREZA CHRISTINA NASCIMENTO ARAUJO. *Escravidão e Relações Raciais no Brasil: Cadastro da Produção Intelectual (1970–1990)* 1991.

BARICKMAN, BERT J. *A Bahian Counterpoint: Sugar, Tobacco, Cassava, and Slavery in the Recôncavo, 1780–1860.* 1998.

CARDOSO, GERALD. *Negro Slavery in the Sugar Plantations of Veracruz and Pernambuco, 1550–1680: A Comparative Study.* 1983.

CASTRO, HEBE MARIA MATTOS DE. *Ao Sul da História.* 1987.

———. *Das cores do silêncio: Os significados da liberdade no sudeste escravista, Brasil século XIX.* 1995.

CHALHOUB, SIDNEY. *Visões da Liberdade: Uma história das últimas décadas da escravidão na Corte.* 1990.

CONRAD, ROBERT E. *Brazilian Slavery: An Annotated Research Bibliography.* 1977.

———. *Children of God's Fire.* 1984.

COSTA, EMILIA VIOTTI DA. *Da senzala à colônia.* 1966.

DALLA VECCHIA, AGOSTINHO MARIO. *Os filhos da escravidão: Memórias de descendentes de escravos da região meridional do Rio Grande do Sul.* 1994.

DEAN, WARREN. *Rio Claro: A Brazilian Plantation System, 1820–1920.* 1976.

EISENBERG, PETER L. *The Sugar Industry in Pernambuco: Modernization without Change, 1840–1910.* 1974.

ESTERCI, NEIDE. *Escravos da desigualdade: Estudo sobre o uso repressivo da força de trabalho hoje.* 1994.

FREYRE, GILBERTO. *The Mansions and the Shanties.* Translated by Harriet de Onis. 1986.

———. *The Masters and the Slaves.* Translated by Samuel Putnam. 1946.

GORENDER, JACOB. *A Escravidão Reabilitada.* 1990.

———. *O Escravismo Colonial.* 1978.

GUIMARÃES, CARLOS MAGNO. *Uma Negação da Ordem Escravista; Quilombos em Minas Gerais no Século XVIII.* 1988.

HEMMING, JOHN. *Red Gold: The Conquest of the Brazilian Indians.* 1978.

HIGGINS, KATHLEEN J. *Slavery and "Licentious Liberty" in Brazil's Gold Mines.* Forthcoming.

KARASCH, MARY C. *Slave Life in Rio de Janeiro, 1808–1850.* 1987.

———. "Suppliers, Sellers, Servants, and Slaves." In *Cities and Society in Colonial Latin America,* edited by Louisa Schell Hoberman and Susan Migden Socolow. 1986.

LARA, SILVIA HUNOLD. *Campos da Violência: Escravos e Senhores na Capitania do Rio de Janeiro, 1750–1808.* 1988.

LUGAR, CATHERINE. "Rice Industry." In *Encyclopedia of Latin American History and Culture,* edited by Barabara A. Tenenbaum, vol. 4. 1996.

MAESTRI FILHO, MÁRIO JOSÉ. *Depoimentos de escravos brasileiros.* 1988.

MATTOSO, KATIA M. DE QUEIRÓS. *To Be a Slave in Brazil, 1550–1888.* Translated by Arthur Goldhammer. 1986.

METCALF, ALIDA C. *Family and Frontier in Colonial Brazil: Santana de Parnaíba, 1580–1822.* 1992.

MONTEIRO, JOHN. *Negros da terra: Índios e Bandeirantes nas origens de São Paulo.* 1994.

PIRATININGA JÚNIOR, LUIZ GONZAGA. *Dietário dos escravos de São Bento.* 1991.

REIS, JOÃO JOSÉ, ed. *Slave Rebellion in Brazil: The Muslim Uprising of 1835 in Bahia.* Translated by Arthur Brakel. 1995.

REIS, JOÃO JOSÉ, and FLÁVIO DOS SANTOS GOMES. *Liberdade por um fio: História dos quilombos no Brasil.* 1996.

RUSSELL-WOOD, A. J. R. *The Black Man in Slavery and Freedom in Colonial Brazil.* 1982.

SCHWARTZ, STUART B. *Slaves, Peasants, and Rebels: Reconsidering Brazilian Slavery.* 1992.

———. *Sugar Plantations in the Formation of Brazilian Society: Bahia, 1550–1835.* 1985.

SILVA, JAIME ANTUNES DA, et al. *Guia Brasileiro de fontes para a história da África, da escravidão negra e do negro na sociedade atual.* 2 vols. 1988.

STEIN, STANLEY J. *Vassouras: A Brazilian Coffee County, 1850–1890.* 1970.

SUTTON, ALISON. *Slavery in Brazil: A Link in the Chain of Modernization: The Case of Amazonia.* 1994.

VOLPATO, LUIZA RIOS RICCI. *Cativos do sertão: Vida cotidiana e escravidão em Cuiabá, 1850–1888.* 1993.

Mary Karasch

Northeastern Brazil

Northeastern Brazil (Bahia and Pernambuco) became a slave society in the late sixteenth century. Sugar cultivation demanded intensive plantation labor, which indigenous populations could not possibly supply. In order to fill the keen labor shortage, African slaves were imported to Bahia en masse as early as the 1570s. In response to the rapid expansion of the Brazilian sugar industry, the slave population, which was 13,000 to 14,000 in 1600, rose to 150,000 in eighty years despite massive mortality. As in other New World plantation societies, men outnumbered women by a ratio of two to one among African-born slaves, who were also predominantly adult; more than 20 percent of the slave labor force was under fourteen years of age.

Sugar plantations (*engenhos*) in northeastern Brazil developed as centers of colonial life, and by 1629, 150 *engenhos* were operating in Pernambuco and 80 in Bahia. The average sugar plantation owned 120 slaves, who worked as field hands, mill workers, house slaves, artisans, boatmen, carters, and drivers, and sugar masters. The sugar plantation also employed a small number of free workers: cane farmers (*lavradores de cana*), agricultural dependents (*agregados* and *moradores*), and artisans. Gilberto Freyre, in *Casa grande e senzala* (1933), greatly romanticized plantation life in the northeast. His book, translated into English as *Masters and Slaves* (1959), was employed by Frank Tannenbaum and Stanley Elkins as a major source to support their thesis that Latin American slavery was more humane and less harsh than its Anglo-American counterpart.

Urban slavery developed in major port cities (such as Recife and Salvador) as well as in smaller interior towns. Urban slave owning existed on a much smaller scale (usually ranging from one to ten slaves per household), and the urban slave population was balanced by gender because of the high demand for fe-

Members of a northeastern Brazilian candomblé await the religious ceremony, one of the remaining cultural symbols of the slave trade. [Stephanie Maze/Corbis]

male domestic slaves. Slaves were used in a wide range of urban occupations; they were also hired out on the street as *escravos de ganho* (slaves for hire), whereby they were obliged to return a mutually agreed sum on a daily or weekly basis to their owners. Many slaves were able to accumulate extra cash in this way for the purchase of their freedom. The manumission rate was much higher in the cities than on the plantations.

Angola was the major slave source for northern Brazil until the end of the seventeenth century when West Africa, particularly the Fon- and Yoruba-speaking Slave Coast, replaced it. The overwhelming number of incoming enslaved Africans, many of whom shared the same ethnic origins, resulted in the creation of an African-Brazilian culture, most prominently in the form of a religion called *candomblé*. Slaves fled frequently, and fugitive-slave communities (*quilombos* or *mucambos*) were constantly formed near plantations, cities, and towns. Palmares in Pernambuco was home to nearly 2,000 slaves and Indians in the period from 1605 to 1696. Bahia witnessed a series of slave revolts (1807–1835), which ended with the Malê revolt in Salvador. Participants in these uprisings were predominantly African-born males.

See also PALMARES; PLANTATIONS; SLAVE SOCIETIES.

BIBLIOGRAPHY

CURTIN, PHILIP D. *The Rise and Fall of the Plantation Complex: Essays in Atlantic History.* 1990.

FREYRE, GILBERTO. *The Masters and the Slaves: A Study in the Development of Brazilian Civilizatio.* Translated by Samuel Putman. 1946.

NISHIDA, MIEKO. "Manumission and Ethnicity in Urban Slavery: Salvador, Brazil, 1808–1888." *Hispanic American Historical Review* 73:3 (1993): 361–391.

REIS, JOÃO JOSÉ. *Slave Rebellion in Brazil: The Muslim Uprising of 1835 in Bahia.* Translated by Arthur Brakel. 1993.

SCHWARTZ, STUART B. *Slaves, Peasants, and Rebels: Reconsidering Brazilian Slavery.* 1992.

Mieko Nishida

Dutch Brazil

In the sixteenth century Dutch ships distributed sugar, salt, and spices assembled in Viana, Lisbon, and Setúbal (Portugal) to northern Europe. In the period between 1580 and 1648 Spain ruled Portugal. Spain, while fighting with the Dutch, ended this trade in 1595 by confiscating hundreds of Dutch ships in Spanish and Portuguese harbors. From that moment the Dutch began a hunt for the sources of the tropical commodities in the East and West Indies. The profitable sugarcane plantations in northeastern Brazil attracted their attention. An armistice with Spain (1609–1621), however, prevented direct expansion in the West.

The end of the armistice with Spain, in 1621, marked the beginning of a battle in the Atlantic. The Dutch West India Company was established in the same year with the motto "trading and pirating in the West." In 1624 an attempt to capture Portuguese Brazil failed. The Dutch had more success in 1630, taking Portugal's rich sugar-producing captaincy of Pernambuco.

The Dutch had their first large-scale experience with African-Americans in northeast Brazil, where there were approximately 45,000 slave laborers. Soon afterward they discovered that the lucrative sugar production was impossible without a continuous supply of African slaves. The supply from Africa resumed in 1636, after the Dutch West India Company captured São Jorge da Mina, the main Portuguese outpost in West Africa, followed by São Paulo de Luanda, the main slave port in Central Africa, in 1641. During the period between 1636 and 1645 the Dutch shipped a total of 23,163 slaves from Elmina and Luanda.

According to de Mello, not necessarily a neutral observer, the Dutch in general took little interest in the life of the slaves. Vincent Joachim Soler (1639), who described (among other things) burial rituals, was an exception to the rule. De Mello also suggests that the slaves had a much more difficult time under Dutch rule than under the Portuguese, who he claimed, always gave the slaves Sundays and other holy days off. The Dutch, much more than the Portuguese, enforced segregation. The Reformed Church, for example, opposed marriage between blacks and whites.

The Portuguese planters in Brazil rebelled against the Dutch in 1645, steadily driving them back during the fighting. The Dutch surrendered in 1654. The Dutch invasion of Pernambuco and the ensuing wars allowed a great many slaves to capitalize on the general disorder by escaping inland. These fugitive slaves built a number of maroon villages in an area called Palmares, which was frequently invaded during the period of Dutch dominion. The most famous expedition was under Jan Blaer's leadership, resulting in the destruction of numerous settlements.

The Dutch West India Company shifted its activities to the Caribbean after losing Brazil, focusing its attention on the two most important colonies, Curaçao, captured from the Spanish in 1634; and Suriname, seized from the English in 1667.

See also CARIBBEAN REGION; MAROONS; NETHERLANDS AND THE DUTCH EMPIRE; PORTUGAL; SPAIN; SURINAME.

BIBLIOGRAPHY

ALVES FILHO, IVAN. *Memorial dos Palmares.* 1988.
BARLAEUS, CASPAR. *Rerum per octennium in Brazilia.* 1647.
BOXER, C. R. *The Dutch in Brazil, 1624–1654.* 1957.
MELLO, JOSÉ A. GONSALVES DE. *Tempo dos Flamengos. Influência da ocupação holandesa na vida e na cultura do norte do Brasil.* 1947.
SOLER, VINCENT JOACHIM. *Cort ende Sonderlingh Verhael van een Brief van Monsieur . . . in de welcke hij . . . verhaelt verscheyden singularieteyten van 't Landt.* 1639.
WÄTJEN, HERMANN. *Das Holländische Kolonialreich in Brasilien.* 1921.

Wim Hoogbergen

Central and Southern Brazil

In the sixteenth century Portugal set the stage for the establishment of black slavery in the Americas, including a massive system of human bondage in Brazil that lasted nearly four hundred years. Among the circumstances foreshadowing these developments were Portugal's prolonged exploration of the west coast of Africa; its building forts and trading centers from Mauritania to Angola to promote the acquisition of slaves; its founding Atlantic sugar colonies dependent in part on African labor in Madeira, the Azores, and São Tomé; and its introducing tens of thousands of Africans into Portugal itself.

The date of the first arrival of blacks in Brazil is unknown. Some, however, were almost certainly present as servants or in other capacities in the early years of Portuguese contact, though too few to contribute significantly to the work of collecting brazilwood or other local products. This early labor was performed by Brazil's indigenous population, either as volunteers or as slaves, a condition imposed on them soon after the Portuguese arrived. Subjugation of Indians was often opposed by members of Roman Catholic orders and prohibited by papal bulls and royal decrees, but enslavement of Indians and expeditions organized for their capture and enslavement persisted well into the nineteenth century.

To strengthen its feeble grip on the new colony, in the 1530s the Portuguese government bestowed huge land grants or captaincies on favored members of the Portuguese aristocracy, with the expectation that they would use their private resources to develop a sugar industry. By the second half of the sixteenth century, sugar was in production at numerous coastal points, notably São Vicente and Rio de Janeiro in the south and Bahia and Pernambuco in the northeast. This activity, of course, increased labor demands, and consequently a large and constant influx of Africans began in the 1670s and lasted until 1851, when the traffic was at last suppressed.

Over the centuries sugar was always a major crop, but cotton, tobacco, cacao, and other commodities were also abundantly produced by slave labor. In the eighteenth century, with the discovery of gold and diamond deposits in the interior, multitudes of acculturated slaves from the economically depressed sugar captaincies of the northeast and newly imported Africans from Angola were transported to the mining districts of Minas Gerais, Goiás, and Mato Grosso. In the early years of the nineteenth century, coffee became Brazil's most profitable crop, and thus newly imported Africans were increasingly destined for coffee districts, first in the province of Rio de Janeiro and later in Minas Gerais and São Paulo. With the suppression of the African slave trade in the mid-nineteenth century, hundreds of thousands of slaves, particularly those from northeastern sugar- and cotton-producing regions, were shipped and sold to coffee planters, thus concentrating captive workers in coffee-producing regions and slowly undermining the commitment to slavery in other parts of the country. Over the centuries enslaved men and women worked in towns and cities as servants, peddlers, factory workers, wet nurses, prostitutes, coachmen, porters, and in many other capacities, skilled and unskilled. As in the United States, a class of slaves, known in Brazil as *negros de ganho,* were allowed to work out or sell their services independently, with an obligation to pay stipulated sums of money to their owners.

The exact number of slaves who entered Brazil over the centuries is unknown, but many estimates exist. In *The Atlantic Slave Trade: A Census* (1969), Philip Curtin put the number at 3,646,800. In contrast, in

Slave Life in Rio de Janeiro, 1808–1850 (1987), Mary Karasch estimated that in the first half of the nineteenth century a million or more slaves entered Brazil in the vicinity of Rio de Janeiro alone. Similarly, in "The Nineteenth-Century Transatlantic Slave Trade," David Eltis put the number of Africans entering all of Brazil from 1811 to 1860 at 1,478,200 (*Hispanic American Historical Review*, 1987).

Despite this hefty forced migration, by 1872, the year of the first national census, Brazil's slave population stood at only 1,509,403, perhaps a third or less of those who had entered the country from Africa. In contrast, by 1860 the U.S. slave population had grown to nearly 4,000,000, an impressive number compared to the roughly 600,000 slaves estimated to have entered what is now the United States from abroad (combined calculations of Curtin, Robert Fogel, Stanley Engerman, and Roger Anstey). If we accept their figures, the slave population of the United States grew to perhaps six or seven times the number of Africans arriving over nearly two centuries, whereas Brazil's slave population appears to have suffered heavy and permanent losses as long as slavery lasted.

It has sometimes been suggested that Brazil's comparatively small slave population in the decades prior to abolition was in part the result of frequent manumissions. Most slaves in Brazil, however, particularly those living and working in rural areas, had little prospect of acquiring their freedom, even in the final years of slavery. Before the nineteenth century, Brazil's free black and mulatto populations, like their North American counterparts, developed slowly at best. As late as 1817 the Brazilian slave population was estimated at 1,930,000 and its free colored population, excluding Indians, at only 586,500. If these figures are accurate, only about one in four surviving blacks and mulattoes was free after about three centuries of development of that population. This slow growth occurred despite an approximately equal number of females and males among the free and their greater opportunities to live independently, to acquire marriage partners, and to raise children in relative safety. Brazil's free black and mulatto population grew significantly during the nineteenth century (partly the result of an already substantial population base), but, despite a surge of liberations in the last years of slavery, most free colored persons were born free and did not attain that status through manumission.

The harsh conditions endured by slaves in Brazil as a result of the policies and aspirations of slave traders and slaveholding entrepreneurs would appear to explain Brazil's population deficit, just as similar goals and policies in the Caribbean colonies of Spain, France, Holland, and Britain account for similarly catastrophic results. One probable reason, among many others, for the inability of the Brazilian slave population to grow or even to maintain itself was an inordinate emphasis on the production of export crops at the expense of food crops, which raised the prices of basic foods and resulted in high levels of malnutrition among not only slaves but also the free. Related to this basic deficiency was a consistently low ratio of females to males not only on slave ships, where the typical apportionment was perhaps one female to two males, but also among slaves living and working in the nation's cities, mines, and plantations. As a result of this permanent sexual imbalance and other factors, marriage and stable families were exceptional among slaves. In the last year of slavery, little more than 10 percent of slaves over sixteen years of age were registered as married or widowed, despite the Roman Catholic Church's traditional advocacy of slave marriages, and, remarkably, in three provinces only slightly more than 1 percent of adult slaves were recorded as married or widowed.

A related cause of Brazil's population deficit was slaveholders' routine neglect of slave progeny, based on the principle that it was cheaper to acquire full-grown slaves from Africa than to raise infants to maturity. Both slaveholders and abolitionists maintained that most children born into slavery died in infancy or early childhood, and only a minority reached an age at which they could begin to produce a profit for their masters. Even after suppression of the African traffic, observers of conditions in Brazil doubted that slave owners would be willing to provide the nourishment, clothing, housing, care of the young, and communication between the sexes that made natural reproduction and even the breeding of slaves profitable in the United States. Although conditions among slaves probably improved somewhat after the African traffic ended, slaveholders continued to satisfy their labor needs more through purchase than through serious attempts to conserve and expand the workforces they already possessed. Conspicuous waste and abuse continued on many plantations in the form of excessive labor, poor clothing and housing, and severe punishment often designed more to set examples than to penalize or discipline the guilty.

The victims of slavery resisted in many ways, the most dramatic of which were violent rebellions and flight to cities or to mountain and jungle havens, where they created settlements called *quilombos,* a word derived from the Kimbundu language of Angola. Others shirked their duties or performed them badly, destroyed crops or equipment, murdered masters and overseers, and even took their own lives or those of their children as a way to end their misery or deprive their masters of valuable assets. Many slaves, of course, sought accommodation or compromise with

Working in sugar-producing mill, slave laborers perform a variety of tasks under the constant threat of the whip. [Corbis-Bettmann]

their owners, at times perhaps significantly improving their living and working conditions.

See also ABOLITION AND ANTISLAVERY MOVEMENTS; BRAZILIAN ANTISLAVERY SOCIETY; PALMARES; PORTUGAL; SLAVE TRADE.

BIBLIOGRAPHY

CONRAD, ROBERT EDGAR. *Children of God's Fire: A Documentary History of Black Slavery in Brazil.* 1983.
———. *World of Sorrow: The African Slave Trade to Brazil.* 1986.
GORENDER, JACOB, *O escravismo colonial.* 5th ed. 1988.
HEMMING, JOHN. *Red Gold: The Conquest of the Brazilian Indians.* 1978.
KARASCH, MARY C. *Slave Life in Rio de Janeiro, 1808–1850.* 1987.
MILLER, JOSEPH C. *The Way of Death: Merchant Capitalism and the Angolan Slave Trade, 1730–1830.* 1988.
PRADO, JÚNIOR CAIO. *The Colonial Background of Modern Brazil.* 1967.
STEIN, STANLEY J. *Vassouras: A Brazilian Coffee County, 1850–1900.* 1957.
VIOTTI DA COSTA, EMÍLIA. *Da senzala à colônia.* 1966.

Robert E. Conrad

Brazilian Antislavery Society

In 1880 a small group of abolitionists met in Rio de Janeiro at the home of the prominent liberal politician Joaquim Nabuco to organize the Brazilian Antislavery Society. Its members, including the African-Brazilian André Rebouças, agreed to combat slavery by every peaceful means, to publish an antislavery newspaper, and to communicate with similar organizations in Europe and the Americas. A powerful manifesto, written by Nabuco, was published in Portuguese, English, and French, and on 1 November 1880 the first issue of their monthly newsletter, *O Abolicionista*, appeared. Many actual slaves in Brazil, Nabuco correctly argued in this first issue, were held unlawfully, since hundreds of thousands of Africans had been smuggled into the country after 1831, the year in which the slave trade became illegal, and so were legally free along with their offspring.

The first wave of abolitionism led by Nabuco was followed by a powerful proslavery reaction. Having strongly revealed their presence in 1880, antislavery clubs in Rio de Janeiro were forced either to close their doors or to become less active. Like most abolitionist candidates, Nabuco was defeated in parliamentary elections in 1881, and so he resigned the presidency of the Brazilian Antislavery Society and sailed for Europe in search of assistance. The organization briefly survived Nabuco's absence, but by 1883, with a sudden surge of antislavery activity in the province of Ceará, abolitionists in Rio, led by Rebouças and the African-Brazilian journalist José do Patrocinio, united numerous regional societies into an Abolitionist Confederation. This organization thus replaced the Brazilian Antislavery Society as Brazil entered the last tumultuous years of the abolitionist struggle, which ended when the General Assembly voted to end slavery 13 May 1888.

In the last five to six years of the campaign against slavery, the Brazilian Antislavery Society accomplished very little. Whether the antislavery movement was a success is a question whose answer is unclear. It ended slavery; otherwise it was not a success. Abolition was a tremendous accomplishment, but as Eric Foner put it, "Nothing but freedom."

See also ABOLITION AND ANTISLAVERY MOVEMENTS; BRAZIL.

BIBLIOGRAPHY

CONRAD, ROBERT. *The Destruction of Brazilian Slavery, 1850–1888.* 1972.
TOPLIN, ROBERT BRENT. *The Abolition of Slavery in Brazil.* 1972.

Robert E. Conrad

Breeding of Slaves

See United States.

British and Foreign Anti-Slavery Society (1839–1909)

This London-based organization was founded largely on the initiative of Joseph Sturge, a Quaker veteran of earlier antislavery struggles. Its aim was to capitalize on the movement's recent success in securing the abolition of slavery in the British Empire by launching a crusade for the eradication of slavery throughout the world at large. With this in mind it set about organizing world antislavery conventions, the first of which, held in London in 1840, attracted delegates from many countries including over thirty from the United States. Before long, however, it came to realize that leading such a crusade was impractical in view of the hostility with which other nations regarded foreign interference in their domestic affairs. Nevertheless,

the society continued to collect and disseminate information and provide advice and even modest material assistance when circumstances allowed.

It was also concerned to safeguard the interests of the West Indian freedmen, which involved monitoring developments and making representations through its spokesmen in Parliament. This led to the society's becoming embroiled, from 1841 onward, in a struggle to prevent the admission of foreign, slave-grown sugar into the country to compete with the free-grown—and now increasingly expensive—colonial variety. In 1846 it had to concede defeat when Parliament agreed to equalize the duties on all sugars. Being Quaker-led, the society opposed the Government's attempts to suppress the Atlantic slave trade by means of British naval power, partly on pacifist principles but also because it was deemed ineffective. For pacifist reasons the society similarly failed to capitalize on British support for the Union cause in the American Civil War.

From the 1850s onward the British antislavery movement was clearly in decline. Nevertheless, the society survived and found a new niche for itself advising the government and Parliament on slavery matters as they affected British colonial policy. It was instrumental in drawing public attention to such international scandals as the Congo horrors of 1897–1906. In 1909 it amalgamated with the Aborigines Protection Society, eventually becoming, after further changes of name, the present-day Anti-Slavery International.

See also ABOLITION AND ANTISLAVERY MOVEMENTS; ANTI-SLAVERY INTERNATIONAL; QUAKERS.

BIBLIOGRAPHY

HARRIS, JOHN. *A Century of Emancipation.* 1933.
TEMPERLEY, HOWARD. *British Antislavery, 1833–1870.* 1972.

Howard R. Temperley

British Colonies, Western Hemisphere

See Caribbean Region; Plantations; United States.

Brown, John   [1800–1859]

Radical U.S. abolitionist (often called "Osawatomie" Brown of Kansas).

Perhaps no single event did more to spur the United States toward civil war than John Brown's October 1859 raid on Harpers Ferry, Virginia (now West Virginia). Despite Brown's swift capture, trial, and execution, the presence of his novice abolitionist "army" caused panic throughout the South. Southern Cassandras prophesying Northern aggression gained influ-

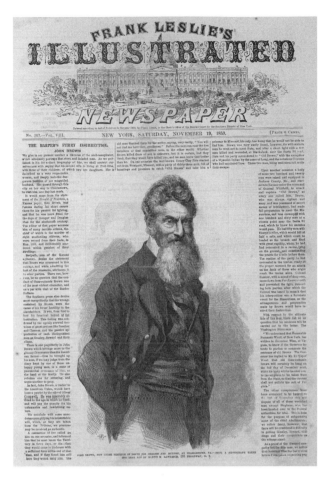

John Brown. [*Frank Leslie's Illustrated Newspaper/* Corbis]

ence as New England intellectuals canonized Brown and public meetings throughout the North memorialized his sacrifice to the cause of freedom. Because Brown had fought against Missouri "border ruffians" in Kansas, his raid helped to discredit the policy of popular sovereignty and encouraged Southerners to make demands for southern rights in the 1860 Democratic platform, thus splitting the party and ensuring the election of Abraham Lincoln, who was pledged to stop the spread of slavery.

Descended from six generations of pious Connecticut Congregationalists, Brown grew to manhood in Hudson, Ohio, where his pioneer father had become a prominent landholder and community elder. A first son, Brown embraced not only his duty to family but also his father's evangelical faith and sense of moral stewardship. The father of twenty children by two wives, Brown prospered periodically as a tanner, livestock grower, land speculator, and surveyor, but in 1842 he was forced into bankruptcy. A ten-year business partnership to market Ohio wools in the East also failed, and in 1854 Brown retired to a modest

farm in upstate New York to be a "kind of father" to a colony of African-Americans.

History beckoned when Brown received an appeal for weapons from his eldest sons, homesteaders in Kansas. At age fifty-five, Brown soon found a calling in a "war" against slavery. In May 1856 he triggered months of guerrilla fighting by directing the massacre of five proslavery neighbors on Pottawatomie Creek. Although Brown never publicly admitted responsibility for the killings, his sons later defended the murders as a retaliatory blow designed to terrorize the enemies of Free State settlers. Two years later, with peace restored to Kansas, Brown liberated eleven Missouri slaves and guided them safely to Canada. By then he had created a provisional government at a convention of blacks in Chatham, Ontario, as a vehicle to carry his war into the slave states.

Brown's war collapsed swiftly at Harpers Ferry, where local militia companies and ninety U.S. marines sent from Washington trapped Brown's raiders on the grounds of the federal armory. Brown retreated with his hostages into a small fire engine house, where at dawn on October 18, a storming party bayoneted two of his men and captured Brown himself. In all, ten of Brown's men (including two of his own sons) were killed, seven were eventually captured, and the remaining five managed to make their way through the mountains to safety in the North. Two slaves, who seem to have sided with Brown, died during or soon after the raid. Brown's men killed three residents of Harpers Ferry, a local slave owner and a marine.

Brown's sabre wounds proving superficial, he promptly determined to wield the "sword of the spirit." At his six-day trial he declared that he was ready to "mingle my blood further with the blood of . . . millions in this slave country whose rights are disregarded by wicked, cruel, and unjust enactments." As he was taken to the scaffold, the defiant Brown prophesied that "the crimes of this *guilty land will* never be purged *away;* but with Blood."

Brown's strategy in seizing Harpers Ferry remains unclear. Whether his raid was a call for slaves to rebel, the opening sally of a guerrilla war gone awry, a scheme to make slavery economically insecure, or, as his sons later claimed, a deliberate effort to provoke civil war, it was above all a warning of God's approaching justice. To Brown, slavery was the "sum of all villainies," spawning soulless masters and afflicted slave children, destroying families, perverting republican institutions, corrupting law itself. To him, the nation's tolerance for slavery even threatened the promised return of Christ to earth.

A partisan biographical literature long pictured Brown variously as a martyr to racial brotherhood or the personification of fanaticism, monomania, and criminality. To African-Americans Brown has long remained a symbol of white America's possible redemption from its history of racial oppression. Thus both Brown's fanaticism and his passion for freedom make him an enduring icon.

See also ABOLITION AND ANTISLAVERY MOVEMENTS; KANSAS.

BIBLIOGRAPHY

FINKELMAN, PAUL, ed. *His Soul Goes Marching On: Responses to John Brown and the Harpers Ferry Raid.* 1995.
OATES, STEPHEN B. *To Purge This Land with Blood: A Biography of John Brown.* 1970.
ROSSBACH, JEFFERY. *Ambivalent Conspirators: John Brown, the Secret Six, and a Theory of Slave Violence.* 1982.

Robert E. McGlone

Brussels Act (1890)

The General Act for the Repression of the African Slave Trade, subsequently the Brussels Act, was signed on 2 July 1890 and remained in force until abrogated by the St. Germain-en-Laye Convention at the end of World War I. The preamble of this convention states that, as the territories to which the Brussels and Berlin acts applied were "now under the control of recognized authorities" the parties wished to change some of the agreements—including the enforcement provisions in the Brussels Act—while retaining the principles embodied in the two acts. The states that did not ratify the convention remained bound by the Brussels and Berlin acts. The Brussels Act was the result of a conference held in Brussels that was attended by representatives from Austria, Belgium, Denmark, Great Britain, Germany, France, Turkey, Russia, Portugal, Spain, the Congo, Italy, the Netherlands, Persia, Sweden, the United States, and Zanzibar. The conference was convened at the instigation of the British government, which sought an agreement providing for enforcement procedures to eradicate the trade in African slaves that continued to exist in Africa and the Middle East. In 1885, the European nations had signed the Berlin Act, which, while denouncing slavery and the slave trade in Africa, did not contain any enforcement provisions.

The parties to the Brussels Act agreed to undertake economic, legislative, and military measures towards the eradication of the slave trade on the African continent. It established military stations in the interior to prevent the capture of slaves and provided for the interception of slave caravans. Significantly, it also established a maritime zone that included the Red Sea and the Indian Ocean, where much slave trading was taking place, within which the parties had mutual rights to board ships under five hundred tons that were suspected of slave trading.

See also BERLIN CONFERENCE; SLAVE TRADE.

BIBLIOGRAPHY

MIERS, SUZANNE. "The Brussels Conference of 1889–1890." In *Britain and Germany in Africa,* edited by Prosser Gifford and William Rogers Louis. 1967.
PAKENHAM, THOMAS. *The Scramble for Africa: White Man's Conquest of the Dark Continent from 1876 to 1912.* 1991.

Renee C. Redman

Buddhism

Siddhartha Gautama, the historical Buddha, lived and taught in an India where slavery had long existed. The Buddhist approach to slavery is therefore perhaps best understood in the context of Indian beliefs about *karma*—the notion that one's station, situation, or condition in life is predetermined by a balance of the good or ill accumulated over one's previous lives. Thus, the doctrine of karma validated the institution of slavery by explaining a slave's low station as a function of wrongs committed in previous lives. The specific Buddhist belief that all life is suffering also gives Buddhism a tolerant approach to slavery. Given this worldview, it is not surprising that the Buddha did not condemn slavery outright. In fact, he admonished slaves not to envy the wealth of their masters.

Buddhist texts use the term *dasa* to refer to various types of servitude ranging from debt bondage to chattel slavery. The texts, specifically the *Jataka,* reaffirmed previously established categories of servitude but also included a new type of slave—one who voluntarily entered into servitude to escape poverty. Thus, Buddhist literature from the sixth to the third century B.C.E. describes the development of large landholdings, revealing an India marked by extremes of wealth and poverty. And while the Buddha rejected the inequality, poverty, and exploitation born of the shifting patterns of land ownership, he conceded the existence of economic and social inequities and tried to moderate the harshness of slavery by forbidding his lay followers from engaging in the slave trade and admonishing them to treat their *dasa* with compassion.

As Buddhism spread into Southeast Asia, it encountered societies with preestablished patterns of slavery. In what historians call Pagan Burma (ninth to thirteenth centuries), where Buddhism dominated education, three types of bondage existed: to the state, to the church, and to individuals. Bondage could be voluntary or involuntary, temporary or permanent. In

Burma, as elsewhere in the world, war was a source of involuntary bondsmen, who when captured became property of the crown. The king in turn could enhance his legitimacy as a royal patron of Buddhism by donating war captives to Buddhist monasteries. Bondage to these temples was commonly a hereditary status, but being bonded to the religious establishment was not necessarily a position of inferiority, because a temple bondsperson gained spiritual merit by serving the Buddha and his monk-disciples.

The Burmese word commonly translated as "slave" is *kyun,* but this term can also mean "subject" or "servant." Those bonded to temples were known as *hpaya-kyun,* literally, "servants of the Buddha/monks/temples/monasteries." In the fifteenth century a distinction was made, in terms of the sources of such slaves, between bondspeople coming from private sources and those donated by the crown. This distinction had disappeared by the nineteenth century, by which time temple bondsmen were divided into three functional groups: those who maintained the temples and other religious buildings; those who maintained the monastic libraries, kept the religious and secular records of the temple, and copied scriptures; and those who assisted the monks by performing such duties as cooking their meals and washing their clothes. Each of these three categories was further divided into four ranks. Those of the highest rank behaved as monks did and could include past members of royalty or high-ranking political exiles. Next came those who had been high officials, followed by skilled craftsmen and others who belonged in neither the higher ranks nor the lowest. The lowest rank, which was further subdivided into five ranks, was made up of servants with inferior status. Servants in the lowest of these dealt with matters concerning the dead. The complex hierarchy indicates that the station of a *hpaya-kyun* was not necessarily one of inferiority.

Buddhist Thailand also had patterns of temple slavery similar to those in Burma. Thai temple slaves were typically prisoners of war or criminals convicted of serious crimes or slaves donated by their owners as an act of merit. Still others voluntarily became temple slaves as a sign of piety or to escape poverty or the law. Records also make numerous references to kings and princes making large donations of slaves and land to monasteries. Such philanthropy was considered meritorious, but these grants also had the important state-building function of having a preestablished community open up new lands. Furthermore, this patronage also allowed the rulers of Thailand to establish a broad political base in rural areas through patronage of the religious institution and to use the labor of temple slaves to build new communities and clear forest lands to make way for rice.

See also CAMBODIA; INDIAN SUBCONTINENT; SOUTHEAST ASIA; THAILAND.

BIBLIOGRAPHY

AUNG THWIN, M. "Athi, Kyun-Taw, Hpaya-Kyun: Varieties of Commendation and Dependence in Pre-Colonial Burma." In *Slavery, Bondage and Dependency in Southeast Asia,* edited by Anthony Reid. 1983.

CHAKRAVARTI, UMA. "Of Dasas and Karmakaras: Servile Labour in Ancient India." In *Chains of Servitude: Bondage and Slavery in India,* edited by Utsa Patnaik and Manjari Dingwaney. 1985.

KLEIN, MARTIN A., ed. *Breaking the Chains: Slavery, Bondage, and Emancipation in Modern Africa and Asia.* 1993.

TURTON, ANDREW. "Thai Institutions of Slavery." In *Asian and African Systems of Slavery,* edited by James L. Watson. 1980.

Al McDermid

Burma (Myanmar)

See Southeast Asia.

Burns, Anthony   [1834–1862]

U.S. fugitive slave.

Burns was born into slavery in Stafford County, Virginia. He lived there until 1853, when he was "hired out" to a mill in Richmond. In February of 1854, a seaman friend secreted Burns aboard his ship, which was bound from Richmond for Boston, Massachusetts. There, Burns took refuge. In the following May, Burns's master had him arrested in accordance with the Fugitive Slave Act of 1850. After his arrest the police officials held Burns incommunicado overnight. The next day Judge Edward G. Loring attempted to hold a proforma hearing, but was interrupted when the abolitionist attorney Richard Henry Dana, Jr. noticed the proceedings and volunteered to defend Burns. This led to a six day courtroom drama that riveted Boston and much of the nation. Finally, Loring ordered Burns returned to Virginia.

Outraged delegates to an abolitionist convention, as well as a number of black Bostonians held a mass meeting two days later to discuss ways to prevent Burns's extradition, the meeting degenerated into a mob, which stormed the Court House where Burns was being held, and killed a deputy marshal. The attempt to rescue Burns failed and the state militia and federal troops were dispatched to Boston to prevent further rescue attempts. Boston's black community raised enough money to purchase Burns's freedom, but the sale was blocked for political reasons by the U.S. district attorney. More than fifteen thousand soldiers were required to escort Burns through the howling crowds to the U.S. revenue cutter that returned him to Virginia.

Later that year Burns was bought by a slave trader, who resold him in 1855 to the congregation of Boston's black Twelfth Baptist Church, which immediately set him free. His remaining years were spent lecturing against slavery, getting an education, and serving as pastor of a congregation of runaway slaves in Canada.

Burns' predicament as a fugitive slave had galvanized antislavery sentiment in Boston and strengthened Northern opposition to the Fugitive Slave Act.

THE
BOSTON SLAVE RIOT,
AND
TRIAL
OF
Anthony Burns,

CONTAINING THE
REPORT OF THE FANEUIL HALL MEETING; THE MURDER OF
BACHELDER; THEODORE PARKER'S LESSON FOR THE DAY;
SPEECHES OF COUNSEL ON BOTH SIDES, CORRECTED
BY THEMSELVES; VERBATIM REPORT OF JUDGE
LORING'S DECISION; AND, A DETAILED AC-
COUNT OF THE EMBARKATION.

BOSTON:
FETRIDGE AND COMPANY.
1854.

The title page from a publication concerning the 1854 trial that resulted in Anthony Burns's return from Boston to slavery in Virginia. [Library of Congress]

He was the last slave extradited from Massachusetts under its provisions.

See also ABOLITION AND ANTISLAVERY MOVEMENTS; ESCAPE; FUGITIVE SLAVE LAWS, U.S.; MASSACHUSETTS.

BIBLIOGRAPHY

FINKELMAN, PAUL. "Legal Ethics and Fugitive Slaves: The Anthony Burns Case, Judge Loring, and Abolitionist Attorneys." *Cardozo Law Review* 17 (1996): 1793–1858.
PEASE, JANE H., and WILLIAM H. PEASE. *The Fugitive Slave Law and Anthony Burns: A Problem in Law Enforcement.* 1975.
VON FRANK, ALBERT J. *The Trials of Anthony Burns: Freedom and Slavery in Emerson's Boston.* 1998.

Charles W. Carey Jr.

Butler, Benjamin   [1818–1893]

Major general, U.S. congressman, Massachusetts governor.

Born in New Hampshire and raised in Massachusetts, Benjamin Franklin Butler, Esq., was a lifelong Democrat, except for several years during Reconstruction. Though he believed that slave property should be protected, events early in the Civil War conspired to whittle away that view. In May 1861 General Butler became commander at Fortress Monroe, Virginia, where he dealt with fugitive slaves from Hampton Roads. Because rebel owners had used their slaves in support of the Confederacy, Butler claimed them as contraband of war and put them to work. In August 1861 Congress passed the First Confiscation Act, thus giving legal sanction to his policy.

Several months before Abraham Lincoln's massive recruitment of black soldiers through the Emancipation Proclamation, Butler set another precedent as commander of the Department of the Gulf at New Orleans, when he called Louisiana's Native Guards, an all-black unit, into the service of the Union Army. Though supposedly free men, probably half were fugitive slaves. Butler was reluctant at first to use blacks as soldiers, but he needed manpower. When the First Regiment of the Native Guards was mustered in the fall of 1862, it became the first officially recognized regiment of black soldiers in the Union Army.

Elected to Congress in 1866 as a Republican, Butler became a leading radical and a House leader during the impeachment proceedings against Andrew Johnson. He supported equal rights for blacks and, after the death of Thaddeus Stevens, became their most ardent defender in the House. He served one term as Democratic governor of Massachusetts.

See also CONTRABAND; LAW.

Benjamin Franklin Butler. [Medford Historical Society Collection/Corbis]

BIBLIOGRAPHY

HOLLANDSWORTH, JAMES G., JR. *The Louisiana Native Guards: The Black Military Experience during the Civil War.* 1995.
TREFOUSSE, HANS. *Ben Butler: The South Called Him Beast.* 1957.

Michael L. Lanza

Butler, Pierce Mease   [1810–1867]

Georgia plantation owner.

A native Philadelphian, Pierce Mease changed his last name to Butler in 1826 to inherit his grandfather's two plantations on Georgia's Altamaha River and upwards of seven hundred slaves. His grandfather, Major Pierce Butler, was a South Carolina delegate to the Constitutional Convention, where he championed the slavery he practiced. No man did more to fit the slave into the Constitution he helped forge.

Pierce M. Butler married and divorced the English actress Frances Anne Kemble. Her *Journal of a Residence on a Georgian Plantation in 1838–1839* was derived from copious notes made on a visit to the plantations. The hard lives of the Butler slaves fortified the aversion to slavery she already possessed. The *Journal* was not published until 1863, late in the Civil War, as an attempt to reverse the direction of the proslavery British. The book is a graphic documentation of the wrongs of slavery.

Butler was a weak and irresponsible man, and in 1859 his huge debts forced a sale of the slaves he owned, together with his brother John's estate. Advertisements told of "A Gang of 460 Negroes" to be auctioned at a Savannah racecourse. The sale averaged slightly over seven hundred dollars per slave. The event, called "the weeping time" by the slaves, was attended incognito by the *New York Tribune*'s star reporter Mortimer Thomson (known as Doesticks), a favorite of newspaper editors across the country. His story was a devastating revelation of inhumanity.

In a futile effort to make its productivity comparable to what it was before emancipation, Pierce Butler was struck down by malaria on his rice plantation in late summer 1867. He died a slave's death.

See also KEMBLE, FRANCES ANNE; SLAVES, SALE OF.

BIBLIOGRAPHY

BELL, MALCOLM, JR. *Major Butler's Legacy—Five Generations of a Slaveholding Family.* 1987.
FURNAS, J. C. *Fanny Kemble.* 1982.
KEMBLE, FRANCES ANNE. *Journal of a Residence on a Georgian Plantation in 1838–1839.* Edited by John Anthony Scott. 1863. Reprint, 1961.
THOMSON, MORTIMER. "The Sale of the Butler Slaves." *New York Daily Tribune*, 9 March 1859.

Malcolm Bell, Jr.

Buxton, Thomas Fowell   [1786–1845]

British abolitionist writer and parliamentary leader; member of Parliament for Weymouth 1818–1837.

Thomas Buxton's religious orientation, partly Quaker and partly Evangelical, fostered his antipathy to slavery and his interest in Africa. In 1821 the aging William Wilberforce asked him to take over the leadership of the parliamentary campaign for the emancipation of slaves. Under Buxton the campaign mirrored that against the slave trade: research and documentation were brought forward to maintain public concern, and varied strategies were devised to keep slavery issues before a legislature for which they were not a priority. While the Caribbean sugar colonies were

Thomas Fowell Buxton. [Corbis-Bettmann]

most in view, Buxton highlighted the particular brutality of conditions in Mauritius. In 1833 he presented to Parliament a huge public petition for emancipation and piloted through Parliament the bill that ended slavery in the British dominions. To secure its passage he accepted—wrongly, he afterwards believed—an amendment to apprentice the former slaves to their masters for a transitional period. In his remaining time in Parliament, he sought to reduce or remove this qualification, which was abandoned in 1838.

After leaving Parliament, Buxton directed his attention to the continuing Atlantic slave trade. In *The Africa Slave Trade and Its Remedy* he argued that the miseries of Africa were due principally to European exploitation through slavery; that Africa's huge agricultural potential offered hope of extinguishing the slave trade and making Africa a free partner in the comity of trading nations; and that the Christian populations of Sierra Leone and the Caribbean proved Africa had the human as well as the economic resources for its own redemption. The interests of Christianity, commerce, and civilization (that is, African participation in the literary and technological spheres) were all interrelated in Africa.

Widespread public support greeted a British government expedition to the Niger to test these ideas in 1841. Its speedy withdrawal, with the loss of forty lives, extinguished Buxton's public career and broke him physically. The official abandonment of Buxton's New Africa Policy has obscured the extent to which mid-nineteenth century missions maintained and implemented his idea.

See also ABOLITION AND ANTISLAVERY MOVEMENTS; LAW; WILBERFORCE, WILLIAM.

BIBLIOGRAPHY

BARKER, ANTHONY J. *Slavery and Anti-Slavery in Mauritius, 1810–1833.* 1996.
BUXTON, CHARLES, ed. *Memoirs of Sir Thomas Fowell Buxton, Baronet.* 1848.
BUXTON, THOMAS FOWELL. *The African Slave Trade and Its Remedy.* 1839–1840.
Buxton Papers. Rhodes House, Oxford.
DRESCHER, SEYMOUR. *Econocide: British Slavery and the Slave Trade in the Era of Abolition.* 1977.

Andrew F. Walls

Byzantium

Byzantium, also known as the eastern Roman Empire (A.D. 325–1453), inherited the western Roman Empire's well-developed institution of slavery. The Byzantine terms for slaves, primarily, were *doulos* and then *oiketes.* There were also other categories of dependent people, including *therapos* and *hyperetes,* who were household servants. The difference between such servants and slaves was often marginal.

Byzantium's slaves were procured mainly by capturing barbarians and retaining their offspring in bondage until the third generation, when typically they were manumitted. When barbarians were near at hand and plentiful, their enslavement may have meant that as much as one-third of the population was servile. As the barbarians receded, pickings from them as slaves also declined. Perhaps the major "reservoir" of slaves was in what is now Russia and Ukraine; they were shipped into Byzantium across the Black Sea. Others came via the Mediterranean, from Europe north of the Danube, and from Arab lands. Tenth-century military campaigns produced enormous numbers of slaves, but after that Byzantium was less successful militarily and the numbers of slaves diminished. Certainly no more than 10 percent of the population of fifteenth-century Byzantium was enslaved. Slaves were also obtained by purchase abroad. Self-sale into slavery was illegal and could be severely punished. Constantine, however, in 329 permitted parents to sell children they could not feed. Later, under Manuel I Comnenus (1143–1180), in a search for protection from the extortions of tax collectors and other oppressors, many in cities sold themselves to a powerful lord. Someone who did not have slaves or needed more slaves could rent (hire) them from their owners.

The spread of Christianity in Byzantium presented problems for the institution of slavery. One issue was whether a slave's conversion to Christianity would confer manumission, and the answer was negative. Another issue was whether slaves could become monks, priests, or deacons, something to which slave owners objected because entry into the clergy cost them their chattel. The law forbade the practice without the owner's permission. Some religious writers condemned slavery; others regarded it as a necessary evil. Some monasteries forbade slave ownership, others themselves owned slaves. Jews were forbidden to own slaves.

In the early centuries, Byzantine slavery may have been primarily of the productive type. Slaves could be found working in nearly every occupation, including as merchants either on their own account or as agents of their owners. As time went on, however, household slavery became more prevalent while the importance of slavery in the economy declined. Serfs tended to replace slaves in agriculture; free people replaced slaves in urban areas as workers. In the army, slaves typically did not have combat roles but served in the baggage train and as their owners' body servants. No data are available about the gender composition of Byzantine slaves, and any claims about sex ratios would be only rough estimates.

Much of this problem has to do with sources. Byzantine sources are excellent on the legal conditions of slaves but much sparser on other issues. Legally, especially, early Byzantine slavery was much harsher than most systems, perhaps under Asian influence. Roman law was codified by Constantine (r. 330–337) and Justinian (r. 527–564) and became the basis of Byzantine law. Any free person who married a slave was automatically enslaved, and under certain circumstances free women might be put to death for having sexual relations with slaves. The offending slave was to be burned alive. For most of the time slave marriage was not recognized, but canon law in 1335 held that it was inviolable. The breaking up of the nuclear family was forbidden. Slave women who were raped by their owners were to be freed. The Byzantine norm for children was that in legal marriages their status followed that of the father, but in nonlegalized unions children's status was determined by the mother's.

At law, slaves were held responsible for criminal acts but could be neither plaintiffs nor defendants in suits; nor could they be witnesses. Premeditated killing of a slave by an owner was held to be a prosecutable homicide, although the extent to which this law was enforced is unknown. The Ecloga (A.D. 741) forbade brutalizing returned fugitive slaves. Vicious owners were deprived of their slaves and forbidden to own slaves in the future. Slaves' relation to property remained what it had been in Rome (legally they could not own it), although a slave could keep a peculium, property which would become fully his upon manumission and whose existence was rationalized as preparation for self-support in freedom. When a slave was sold, the value of his peculium was included in the price. A slave could own other slaves.

Early in Byzantine history slaves tended to evolve into a serflike dependent colonus; later they evolved into the serfs of the high Middle Ages. Household slavery remained a viable institution until the fall of Byzantium, the conquest by the Turks, in 1453.

After the fall of Byzantium in 1453, the Byzantine mantle passed to Russia. This has proved to be the case for scholarship about Byzantium as well, much of which has been done in Russia and the Soviet Union.

See also ANCIENT ROME; CHRISTIANITY; ENSLAVEMENT, METHODS OF; LAW; PECULIUM; PERSPECTIVES ON SLAVERY; RUSSIA.

BIBLIOGRAPHY

BRAUNING, R. "Rabstvo v Vizantiiskoi Imperii (600–1200 gg.)." *Vizantiiskii vremennik* 14 (1958): 38–55.

HADJINICOULAOU-MARAVA, A. J. *Recherches sur la vie des esclaves dans le monde byzantin.* 1950.

UDAL'TSOVA, Z. V. "Polozhenie rabov v Vizantii VI v." *Vizantiiskii vremennik* 24 (1963): 3–4.

WESTERMANN, WILLIAM L. *The Slave Systems of Greek and Roman Antiquity.* 1955.

Richard Hellie

C

California

When California became U.S. territory after the Mexican-American war, slavery was already illegal under the Mexican law of 1829, but prewar American settlers had covertly introduced it there.

In the census of 1850, there were 962 blacks in California; by 1852, there were more than 2,200. The exact number of slaves is impossible to ascertain, but scholars estimate between 500 and 600.

In 1849 a convention in California produced a free-state constitution, which was accepted by Congress as the first state constitution under the Compromise of 1850. Between 1852 and 1857, there were several unsuccessful proposals for a convention to divide California into a northern free state and a southern slave state.

The pervasive racism of this frontier state may help to explain why slavery was so readily tolerated where it was technically illegal. The subordination of all blacks and Asians seemed a goal of much official policy.

In 1852, the legislature passed an act supporting the federal Fugitive Slave Law of 1850. The California act also required the removal of all black slaves from California by their masters within one year's time, a deadline twice extended for a total of three years.

In *In re Perkins* (1852), Chief Justice Hugh C. Murray had to rule on the constitutionality of the 1852 act. This case involved the seizure of three blacks who had been brought from Mississippi in 1850 but were now in business on their own.

Murray maintained the fiction that the Mississippi courts would determine the slave status of the blacks, but he had to explain why the territorial constitution (before statehood) did not free slaves who were introduced into California in defiance of it. In anticipation of *Dred Scott*, Murray held that the Fifth Amendment prevented territories from banning a species of property recognized and protected by the U.S. Constitution.

In 1857, *Ex parte Archy* considered the status of a black man named Archy, who had been brought into the state from Mississippi by his owner, Charles A. Stovall, who temporarily settled in California for his health, purchased land, established a school, and hired Archy out. Archy had escaped while being transported to San Francisco for return to Mississippi.

In *Archy*, the California Supreme Court—in an opinion written by a former governor, Peter H. Burnett—ruled, contrary to the *Perkins* precedent, that the antislavery clause of the state constitution would have freed Archy, but the court held that the earlier decision would have caused the owner to assume that his slave property was safe.

The decision in *Archy* was widely attacked, and demands for the impeachment of Burnett and Chief Justice David F. Terry were common.

The struggle for Archy's freedom did not end there, however. When Archy's master tried to remove him from the state aboard the *Orizaba*, Archy was arrested for safekeeping and his master was served with a legal writ for holding a slave illegally. A hearing was held in California district court in San Francisco before Judge T. W. Freelon, where Archy's attorney, Edward D.

Baker, denounced the California Supreme Court decision in *Ex Parte Archy* and asked for Archy's immediate freedom. Judge Freelon asked James J. Hardy, the attorney for the master, if he objected, and to the surprise of all present, Hardy raised no objections.

Freed by the court, Archy was immediately rearrested by a U.S. marshal and brought before U.S. Commissioner William Penn Johnson, who, after a series of hearings, decided that he lacked jurisdiction. Archy was not covered by the Fugitive Slave Law of 1850, Johnson reasoned, because his flight had not been across state lines but entirely within California. Archy was freed.

See also COMPROMISE OF 1850; FUGITIVE SLAVE LAWS, U.S.

BIBLIOGRAPHY

Ex parte Archy, 9 Cal. 147 (1858).
FINKELMAN, PAUL. "The Law of Slavery and Freedom in California, 1848–1860." In *The Law of American Slavery,* edited by Kermit L. Hall. 1987.
In re Perkins, 2 Cal. 425 (1852).

Patrick M. O'Neil

Cambodia

Slavery in Cambodia flourished chiefly during the period of Angkor, the powerful empire that united the Khmer people and lasted from about the ninth to the fifteenth centuries A.D. Captured tribesmen from the minority populations of upland non-Khmer and prisoners of war from defeated neighbors were the main sources of slaves. Slaves were possibly the greater part of the workforce and the basis of the state economy.

The thirteenth-century Chinese visitor Chou Takuan (Zhou Daguan) described the abject condition of domestic slaves, who were reduced to performing menial tasks and who were despised as captured aliens. Only the poor lacked slaves; the prosperous had many.

Scholars have debated whether "slave" accurately designates the class of temple servants. These, of whom many thousands are listed in temple inscriptions, were donated to Hindu and Buddhist religious foundations as an act of religious piety. Such endowments had social and spiritual significance: they displayed the donors' wealth, attracted royal favors, and in Hindu and Buddhist belief generated good *karma,* thus ensuring future blessings. The inscriptions record names of men and women in approximately equal numbers. Many worked in the fields, partly for the religious foundations and perhaps partly for the households that had donated them. They were often treated as chattel property and were subject to cruel punishment if they escaped.

Other temple servants, however, worked in the temple establishments, sometimes performing important ritual or artistic functions, and some appear to have been well-born individuals who accepted temple service as a merit-making religious activity. Such people,

Relief sculpture at Bayon, Cambodia, depicts prisoners being brought back from war to become slaves. [Kevin R. Morris/ Corbis]

working under the eyes of the gods, could have high status, since these gods were seen as guardians of the country's welfare. The largest temples administered the produce and labor of thousands of villages; temple functionaries were at the center of far-reaching economic redistributive systems. Elite families had members in the temples as senior incumbents, linking secular with religious bases of power.

In most periods enslavement was commonly by capture of enemies or non-Khmer tribesmen, whose descendants remained hereditary slaves. In the Angkor period it is unclear whether people could sell themselves into slavery or be enslaved as a judicial penalty. Slaves could be donated, given in payment, sold, mortgaged, or inherited.

Household slaves could be punished at will by their masters. They lived in family groups but may not have had formal marriages. Women took their children with them from one master to another. Slaves were totally dependent on their masters.

Debt slavery is not attested to until after the Angkor period, when it became a regular institution practiced alongside the enslavement of criminals and war prisoners. Perhaps in the hierarchical society of the Angkorian empire, servile status was reserved for the easily exploited non-Khmer; in the more fluid and commercialized society of later centuries the social barrier dissolved. An elaborate system developed in which there were private slaves and state slaves. The latter class, however it originated, was built into a cumbersome administrative system that divided state resources (including slaves) into four appanages, each under different members of the royal family. The state slaves, called *pol*, were war prisoners or convicted felons or their descendants living in villages throughout the country and owing goods, payments, or spells of corvée labor to the state.

Slavery was the foundation of the power held by the great families and thus died out only slowly. Although in the fifteenth and sixteenth centuries many slave owners ceremonially emancipated slaves to gain a public reputation for meritorious conduct, the institution itself expired only under French pressure at the end of the nineteenth century.

See also SLAVE TRADE; SOUTHEAST ASIA.

BIBLIOGRAPHY

CHOU TA-KUAN. *Mémoires sur les coutumes du Cambodge.* 1951.

JACQUES, D. "À propos de l'esclavage dans l'ancien Cambodge." *XXXIXe Congrès International des Orientalistes: Asie du Sud-Est Continentale.* 1973.

MABBETT, I. W. "Some Remarks on the Present State of Knowledge about Slavery in Angkor." In *Slavery, Bondage, and Dependency in Southeast Asia,* edited by A. Reid. 1983.

Ian W. Mabbett

Canada

Slavery existed within aboriginal communities in present-day Canada long before the arrival of European-based explorers, and African slavery may have been introduced as early as the founding of Quebec in 1608. The first recorded sale of a slave occurred in 1629. While slavery received legal foundation after New France became a royal colony in 1663, the fur trade's reliance on the skills of interior aboriginal peoples proscribed the use of slaves except as agricultural laborers and domestics. By 1685 the Code Noir (Black Code) came to govern the status of slaves in New France, although it did so without being officially proclaimed. Both free blacks and slaves lived in Acadia before the English conquest and continued to do so after the British assumed control of the renamed Nova Scotia in 1713.

After the conquest of New France in 1763 the English accorded slavery stronger legal footing, and the practice spread rapidly with the Loyalist arrival after 1775. The presence of a significant number of free blacks amid the Loyalist ranks and the inclination to view slavery as a fundamental flaw within the new republic to the south served, however, to eventually undercut the practice. The contributions provided by black immigrants in these burgeoning communities engendered a variety of responses from white residents, ranging from indifference to tolerance to outright hostility. The lot of most blacks in British North America could be, given their immediate circumstances, no worse and possibly better than that experienced in the United States.

The official toleration of slavery in British North America began to unravel, in part, because of the efforts of individuals such as Upper Canadian Lieutenant Governor John Graves Simcoe, Chief Justice James Monk in Lower Canada, and Chief Justices Thomas Andrews Strange and Sampson Salter Blowers in the Maritimes. Simcoe, for example, led a direct attack on slavery by instigating the Act for the Gradual Abolition of Slavery, passed through the Upper Canadian House of Assembly in the spring of 1793. By undermining the legal foundation for slavery in British North America, Simcoe, Monk, Strange, and Blowers set an important early context for the antislavery movement. When combined with a pragmatism fueled by economic reality and anti-Americanism, slaveholding lost acceptability, and by 1821 it had effectively disappeared. The Imperial Abolition Act of 1833 put an official end to slavery, and after a one-year period of transition, the practice became illegal in the British colonies on 1 August 1834.

Even before slavery was ended officially in British North America, the region attracted fugitives fleeing conditions in the American republic. While many may have hoped for freedom and equality in the British colonies, changing circumstances produced disparate responses to the increasing number of African-Americans. As long as anti-Americanism remained vibrant and the reception of a trickle of fugitives could be construed as an indication of moral superiority, escaping slaves were usually accorded a polite if not necessarily enthusiastic welcome. For others, however, the prosperity of the fugitive slaves settling in British North America was of immense significance, for it potentially demonstrated that blacks were ready for freedom and were capable of competing on equal terms with whites.

The decades of the 1840s and 1850s were pivotal for the antislavery movement in British North America. Energized by the presence of abolitionist leaders such as English immigrants Thomas Rolph and Robert Graham Dunlop and Scotsman Peter Brown with his sons Gordon and George, the movement assumed greater vitality. Further, the proximity to the United States and the passage of the Fugitive Slave Law by the U.S. Congress ensured for Canada increasing stature as a terminus for the Underground Railroad, which brought thousands of fugitive slaves into the Canadian west. This era revealed the subtle complexities of abolitionist thought in British North America. While the colonials managed to either precede or lag behind the mother country at any one time after 1760, the geographic closeness to the United States and the presence of genuine antislavery sentiment motivated by religious and humanitarian concerns compelled many to confront the demands of putting ideals into action.

One of the greatest challenges involved the question of whether fugitive slaves could lawfully and morally be extradited back to the United States. The English view was that fugitive slaves were not returnable under the Webster-Ashburton Treaty, but such a policy was easily articulated for the Colonial Office because it was far removed from the geographic realities of North America. When it appeared in 1860–1861, therefore, that former slave John Anderson might be extradited back to Missouri to answer for killing one Seneca T. P. Digges, the case became a cause célèbre. Public and political pressure were brought to bear upon the case and, despite an initial willingness by the Court of Queen's Bench in Upper Canada to order Anderson's extradition, the Court of Common Pleas eventually denied that sufficient ground existed. By the time the decision was rendered on 16 February 1861, circumstances had overtaken the matter, for the American union had begun to fracture on the eve of the Civil War.

See also ABOLITION AND ANTISLAVERY MOVEMENTS; CODE NOIR; FUGITIVE SLAVE LAWS, U.S.; UNDERGROUND RAILROAD.

BIBLIOGRAPHY

BRODE, PATRICK. *The Odyssey of John Anderson.* 1989.
FINKLEMAN, PAUL. "The Anderson Case and Rights in Canada and England." In *Law, Society and the State: Essays in Modern Legal History,* edited by Louis A. Knafla and Susan W. S. Binnie. 1995.
STOUFFER, ALLEN P. *The Light of Nature and the Law of God: Antislavery in Ontario, 1833–1877.* 1992.
WINKS, ROBIN W. *Blacks in Canada: A History.* 1971.

Jonathan Swainger

Canary Islands

See Portugal.

Cape Verde Islands

See Spain.

Capitalism and Slavery

Since the institution of slavery spans so many centuries and continents and takes so many different forms, it is self-evident that slavery is compatible with many different economic systems. Here we shall consider only modern slavery—enslavement of Africans as it was conducted by Europeans, mainly in the Western Hemisphere. The discussion focuses on four questions: (1) Was modern slavery organized as capitalistic from its inception? (2) What contribution did slavery make to capitalist economic development? (3) What are the advantages and disadvantages of analyzing slavery in the context of a modern market economy? (4) How do capitalist societies with slave labor differ from those with free labor?

Origins of Modern Slavery

The roots of modern slavery go back to sugar production in Palestine in the late Middle Ages; when the institution eventually reached the New World, it had in many ways the same organizational form as the slavery that had developed in that earlier period. The internal economy of the sugar plantation, the organization of the industry, and even the economic production that slaves carried out on their own time outside of plantation discipline were all conducted in a system of profits and markets. Aside from bullion, slaves in the

Western Hemisphere were principally responsible for production of the commodities, services, and capital that flowed through the Atlantic world from the second half of the seventeenth century to the beginning of the nineteenth. These commodities imparted a strong impetus to capitalist development (for better or for worse) in all the regions—European and African, as well as American—involved in the Atlantic system. The political, legal, and social systems associated with capitalism in Europe were not replicated in slave societies, which developed their own distinctive institutions and ideologies, but all existed within the capitalist economic framework.

Slavery can exist with almost any economic order. Slavery had virtually ceased in Europe by the year 1000, except around the Mediterranean, where small-scale domestic and artisanal slavery persisted. Such use of slaves, as servants, guards, workshop assistants, or sexual partners, is often independent of the general mode of labor in a society. Modern capitalist slavery originated not from marginal uses of this kind, which eventually atrophied over time, but rather from use of slaves in large-scale productive enterprises characterized by capitalist forms from their inception.

The preference for slave labor over free labor, where returns must cover investment, is strengthened if the use of slaves brings advantages in cost. Slave labor is cheaper than free where the work is onerous and free labor would require very high wages before even considering such work. Slaves would also have an aversion for such work and would be motivated to perform badly, commit sabotage, and in the extreme case run away. Thus the onerous crop is a good candidate for slave labor because slavery makes tight control of the labor force neither impractical nor too costly. The crop will have to bring returns in the world economy high enough to cover these costs of labor discipline for slavery to become significant. From both the supply side and the demand side, sugar met these capitalist requirements for use of slave labor. To a lesser extent, slave labor had cost advantages in tobacco, rice, indigo, and later cotton. But sugar and slavery were nearly inseparable from the end of the Middle Ages to the nineteenth century, and the introduction, adoption, and spread of modern slavery closely followed the spread of sugar production around the tropical Atlantic.

Some scholars believe that slaves were at least part of the labor force from the earliest cultivation of sugar in southwestern Asia. Slaves may have been used in growing cane in Mesopotamia before the Arab Muslim invasion of the seventh century, although Arab traders may have introduced it there only after the expansion of Islam. In any case, Europeans encountered the crop when the Crusaders conquered Syria and Palestine at the end of the eleventh century. Sugar also reached the Iberian peninsula at about the same time with the Muslim invasions from North Africa. The Venetians took over the Levantine sugar industry, expanded it to Crete, and introduced sugar to the European market. After Saladin expelled the Christians from Syria and Palestine at the end of the thirteenth century, the Venetians and Genoese transferred the growing industry to Cyprus. The Venetians operated markets for buying and selling slaves on Crete in the fourteenth century and used some of them to produce sugar. Venetians and Genoese had slave markets on Cyprus, and slaves from Arabia and Syria worked there alongside indigenous serfs and immigrants from Palestine.

From there, the Italians took sugar to Sicily, and although Sicilian production apparently did not use slaves, slavery became more prominent as the centers of sugar production moved west from there. Production in the Iberian peninsula increased and extended to the Atlantic islands in the fifteenth century. By 1500, Madeira was the world's largest producer of sugar, and the Canary Islands grew sugar as well. The labor force on Madeira and the Canaries included enslaved Berbers, Muslims, Moriscoes, and Africans, all working with nonslave laborers.

From these islands, sugar production on large plantations spread in the sixteenth century to São Tomé, off the coast of equatorial Africa, and then across the Atlantic to Brazil, to the Caribbean, and to mainland tropical America. In the Western Hemisphere, plantation agriculture came to be associated exclusively with slaves. Sugar's association with coerced labor grew so strong in time that until the mid-nineteenth century, sugar was grown by free labor only rarely anywhere in the world: sugar was grown by slaves, and many of the world's slaves were occupied in growing sugar.

The Capitalistic Nature of Modern Slavery

If by capitalism we mean an economic system where privately owned factors of production (land, labor, and capital) are combined by profit-seeking individuals and firms to produce commodities for sale on a market, this slave-sugar industry was capitalist from its inception. On Cyprus, Venetian and Catalan families and the Hospitalers and the Catholic church all had plantations, imported capital, assembled a labor force, and produced and processed the cane for export to the European market. Prince Henry the Navigator of Portugal (active 1418–1460) initiated a similar industry on Madeira with a charter of partnership in which there is no trace of feudal forms. Since Madeira was uninhabited, all the labor had to be imported, as did all the capital and supplies. Investors in Canarian plantations came from Iberia, Italy, and Germany; labor came from Iberia and Africa; and supplies came from England and the Low Countries. The product was sold on the European market.

The sugar-slave complex was not only an example of capitalism but a pioneer of that system. While its complicated international network of capital, credit, labor, and commodity markets was in full operation, the rest of Western Europe was emerging only slowly from feudalism. Manorial society of the period was based on the labor of serfs who provided for their own consumption with inputs generated from their own holdings. Serfs rendered a traditionally set level of tribute to their lords; their tenure was determined by a system of mutual rights and obligations, and there were communal limits on decision making. There was thus no land market, no labor market, and no capital market in the modern sense in the earliest feudal society. There were some commodity markets for traded goods—mostly though not exclusively luxuries—but production was not determined by a capitalistic system of private ownership of resources that facilitated management of them in response to prices and markets.

Slavery integrated the Western Hemisphere into the international economy. Once slavery was introduced into the Americas, Europe's external trade turned in that direction. By the eighteenth century, European ships plied the Atlantic carrying slaves and supplies to slave colonies in the Caribbean, Brazil, and North America. They carried the products of slave labor to Europe, and then they carried back to the Americas European manufactures bought with the proceeds of sales to the plantation economies. Slavery made possible the exchange of European manufactures for American foodstuffs and raw materials. The eighteenth-century colonial wars between England and France were in part fought over control of the slave trade and for possession of the regions of slave-grown crops, especially sugar.

All growing economies must import or generate capital to get started; new economies must import it. The new economies in the American colonies had to develop exports to pay for the equipment and consumption goods they did not themselves produce and to remit a return on their foreign investment. To a very large extent, slave production provided the exports essential to development in the Western Hemisphere during the colonial period. Regions without slavery or without trade links to slave economies lagged behind in income and wealth. Britain's North American colonies without slavery benefited indirectly from those that used slaves. For example, the British West Indies provided the market for nearly all of New England's agricultural products in the second half of the eighteenth century, and the rise of the New England merchant class was thus tied to West Indian slavery.

The Old World also benefited from the labor of American slaves. Slavery added significant amounts of labor to the international economy, labor that was elastically supplied and very productive, beyond what the indigenous peoples of the New World or immigrants were able or willing to provide. This labor was combined with an abundant, fertile soil to produce crops that Europeans wanted. Colonial slave production thus raised the rate of return on invested capital and thus income levels in the investors' home countries. These returns accrued no matter what the investors did with their increased income; however, if they invested it further in their home economies, as many did, the increase in European income multiplied. This multiplied effect was felt especially in England and France. In both, trade with the slave colonies was a leading sector of growth and an important impetus to industrialization in the eighteenth century.

Economic Analysis of Modern Slavery

In older traditions of historical writing, slavery was attributed to geography and climate and to the racial characteristics of blacks. Recognizing modern slavery as embedded in a capitalist system allowed use of economic analysis to illuminate its history. Since owners treated slaves as factors of production, the economic analysis of production and distribution becomes relevant. From an economic viewpoint the difference between free and slave labor is that free labor is rented for a price (wage), while slave labor is purchased outright by a buyer who then enjoys the stream of the slave's services. The market price of a slave measures the difference between the present value of the services the slave is expected to provide and the present value of maintenance costs and depreciation. If this difference is positive, owning slaves is profitable to the owner. A profit-maximizing planter will compare this anticipated profit to what he could receive from alternative investments. The rate of return on a slave, as on a capital good, thus depends upon the purchase price and the value of the gross product less maintenance and depreciation. These concepts allow logical analysis of slave prices, interest rates, profitability, and maintenance and depreciation.

While classical economists applied economic concepts when writing about slavery, Conrad and Meyer harvested the first fruits of analysis of this sort. They measured the return on investment in a slave in a rigorous way, thus clearing up vague and impressionistic notions about the profitability of slavery in the antebellum American South. The best-known treatment of slavery using neoclassical economics is Fogel and Engerman's pioneering work *Time on the Cross*, which influenced much subsequent scholarship in the field. Their quantitative methods and econometric techniques have led to wider use of archival sources and to a systematic evaluation of new issues in the field.

There are limitations to the economic approach. Even if scholars agree that modern slave agriculture was operated by private decision-makers in a market economy and was a formative contributor to the Atlantic trading system, economics do not answer all questions about slavery. Not all slave owners acted as profit-maximizing entrepreneurs. Numerous slaves in the antebellum United States were not engaged in plantation agriculture at all. But planters who deviated from profit-maximizing were constrained within the limits of a capitalist economy. To pay interest on mortgages and loans, they had to be able to sell their crops at market prices. If they elected not to pursue profit-maximization, their costs rose beyond levels the market would support. Unless they were content with a lower return on their investment, such planters would face the choice of liquidating their estates, drawing on other financial resources, or adopting auxiliary occupations. Certainly such cases existed, although entire economies could not operate in that way.

Owners kept some slaves, regardless of profitability, for prestige or ostentation or sexual services, and aged or ailing slaves were sometimes retained on humanitarian grounds. A small farmer might have bought a slave when free labor would have been cheaper, although such behavior was more likely to be associated with the rich than with the poor. Such slaves are to be regarded as consumption goods, not productive factors, a kind of "consumer slavery." In addition, since legal recognition of slavery depended upon legislative decisions determined by political strategies as well as economic motives, slave systems did not disappear when they became unprofitable.

Culture and Capitalism

Obviously, as many historians of the American South have pointed out, capitalistic slave societies have legal, social, and political cultures different from societies based on free capitalist labor. Indeed their ideology, attitudes, customs, and social behavior bear some resemblance to precapitalist feudalism, where state sovereignty has passed into the hands of a hierarchy of individuals and families who exercise nearly paramount authority within personal domains, but very little outside it. Within a framework of capitalist slavery, a culture of plantation owners, a slave culture, a culture of yeomen farmers, and a culture of persons of mixed ancestry coexisted. These did not replicate the structure of urban bourgeois societies based on wage labor. Not only noneconomic characteristics but also economic characteristics—for example, income distribution, investment in human capital, and development of infrastructure—differed. Few scholars today would deny that capitalism formed the economic basis of modern slave societies, but fewer still would argue for a simple economic determinism of other areas of life.

Eugene Genovese (1967) pioneered work describing the world the slaveholders made. He has seen the antebellum South as a precapitalist form of social organization, with a hierarchical social order based on the assumption that some are fit to rule and others to obey. This ideology he identifies as paternalist, but this culture of slavery does not imply that the economic system itself was other than capitalist.

James Oakes's (1982) history of American slaveholders also shows how the culture of the American South grew out of many sorts of historical experiences other than the phenomenon of slave ownership. This observation has a wider application: the slave societies of Brazil, the British and French West Indies, Cuba, and the American South were all capitalist, and each had a culture of slavery different from those of free-labor societies, having some elements in common but differing from one another because of their particular histories.

When conflict arises in countries where free and slave labor coexist (such as the antebellum United States), instead of viewing the conflict as arising between a capitalist and a precapitalist sector, it seems more useful to see it as occurring between two capitalist sectors with different labor systems and to stress the profound and pervasive effects on ideology, identity, and culture resulting from this difference in labor systems. The mere fact of capitalism may be central to answering questions about long-term economic growth, but it is less basic to understanding the human relationships of those who achieve it.

See also ECONOMIC INTERPRETATION OF SLAVERY; ECONOMICS OF SLAVERY; HISTORIOGRAPHY OF SLAVERY; PERSPECTIVES ON SLAVERY.

BIBLIOGRAPHY

CONRAD, ALFRED H., and JOHN R. MEYER. "The Economics of Slavery in the Antebellum South." *Journal of Political Economy*. 1958.
DAVIS, DAVID BRION. *The Problem of Slavery in the Age of Revolution: 1770–1823.* 1975.

DRESCHER, SEYMOUR. *Capitalism and Antislavery: British Mobilization in Comparative Perspective.* 1987.

FOGEL, ROBERT W., and STANLEY L. ENGERMAN. *Time on the Cross.* 1974.

FOX-GENOVESE, ELIZABETH, and EUGENE GENOVESE. *Fruits of Merchant Capital: Slavery and Bourgeois Property in the Rise and Expansion of Capitalism.* 1983.

GENOVESE, EUGENE. *Political Economy of Slavery.* 1967.

———. *The World the Slaveholders Made.* 1988.

MINTZ, SIDNEY. *Sweetness and Power: The Place of Sugar in Modern History.* 1985.

OAKES, JAMES. *The Ruling Race: A History of American Slaveholders.* 1982.

PHILLIPS, WILLIAM D. *Slavery from Roman Times to the Early Transatlantic Trade.* 1985.

SHERIDAN, RICHARD B. *Slavery and Sugar: An Economic History of the British West Indies.* 1974.

SOLOW, BARBARA L., and STANLEY L. ENGERMAN, eds. *British Capitalism and Caribbean Slavery: The Legacy of Eric Williams.* 1987.

VERLINDEN, CHARLES. *The Beginnings of Modern Colonization: Eleven Essays with Introduction.* 1970.

WILLIAMS, ERIC. *Capitalism and Slavery.* 1944.

Barbara L. Solow

Capture of Slaves

See Enslavement, Methods of.

Caribbean Region

This entry includes the following articles: An Overview; English Colonies; French Colonies; Spanish Colonies; Dutch Colonies; Danish Colonies. *Related articles may be found at the entries* Brazil; Cuba; Plantations.

An Overview

No part of the Americas has been more marked by slavery than the Caribbean, which modern scholars define as the West Indies and Bahamas islands, together with the mainland enclaves of Belize and the Guianas. This definition itself derives from the historical prominence of black slavery in this area, and its extended experience of European colonialism. Spanish colonists brought the first black slaves to the West Indies probably in 1502; the last slaves in the Caribbean—in Cuba—were freed in 1886. Close to half of the more than ten million Africans transported to the New World as slaves were sold in Caribbean colonies. Because of the early and almost total elimination of the native Amerindian population following first contact with Europeans, enslaved African labor became the basis of the region's economy by the 1520s. By the late eighteenth century slaves made up more than 80 percent of the populations of most Caribbean colonies. Few "slave societies" so fully merited the term.

The Introduction of Slavery

African slavery came to the Caribbean in two phases, both associated with sugar cultivation. The first was in the early sixteenth century, when Spain was the only colonizing power in the area, and Hispaniola, Cuba, Jamaica, and Puerto Rico were its only colonies. The second was the "sugar revolution" of the mid-seventeenth century, launched in the Lesser Antilles by Britain, France, and the Netherlands. If the first phase was something of a false dawn, the second definitively transformed the region.

Within twenty-five years of Columbus's arrival in the New World, Spain's Caribbean colonies faced an economic crisis, as their gold reserves and their Amerindian inhabitants neared extinction and as the colonies' pioneer settlers looked westward for new lands. The solution that the Spanish adopted was the sugar plantation worked by African labor. The Spanish and Portuguese had already been developing this model in their earliest colonies in the eastern Atlantic, the Canaries, Madeira, and São Tomé. Sugar was then a high-priced luxury, and slavery in the Iberian peninsula had an unbroken history going back to ancient times. The seaborne slave trade from West Africa had brought Africans back to Iberia since the 1440s. The Africans were accustomed to sustained agricultural labor and occasionally had experience with livestock, but their greatest advantage in the Caribbean was that they were much less vulnerable to European diseases than were Amerindians, who lacked any immunity to them and suffered catastrophic losses from contact with Spaniards. Initially, this contrast was all the more marked because the first black slaves sent to the region had been acclimatized in Europe. Spaniards were not willing to migrate to perform manual labor themselves, because wage rates at home were then relatively high. Direct shipments of slaves from Africa to the West Indies began before 1520.

The sugar economy prospered for several decades, and by midcentury the black population of the Greater Antilles may have numbered 25,000 or more. Indian slavery was abolished in 1542, and although colonists continued to raid villages all around the Caribbean to capture Indians, Africans and their descendants numerically dominated the colonial population. Slaves were employed on ranches, in building trades, and in domestic service as well as on plantations. The sugar export economy collapsed in the late sixteenth century under the combined pressures of French and English raids, Brazilian competition, and

Spain's inability to supply enough shipping and slave labor. The Spanish West Indies stagnated economically for nearly two centuries afterward, but in relative poverty their societies achieved a degree of racial intermixture and cultural homogeneity (a socioracial continuum) that would become typical of Latin America but remained unusual in the Caribbean.

The first British and French colonies in the region were established in the 1620s and 1630s. They initially grew tobacco, cotton, and indigo and used indentured European laborers who contracted to work, usually for three or four years. Saturated markets for these crops in Europe and disruption in the Brazilian sugar regions led to the planting of sugarcane in the 1640s and 1650s. This in turn caused a switch, following the Iberian precedent, to enslaved African labor. The supply of European servants proved insufficient to meet the increased demand associated with the boom in sugar cultivation, which was highly labor-intensive. Also, planters liked the lifelong control over labor that slavery provided, and fugitive African slaves were more easily identified than runaway British servants. However, David Galenson in *White Servitude* (1982) argues that at the outset, Africans were not preferred to servants. Although maintenance costs were lower for slaves, Africans proved more expensive overall than servants until the mid-1660s, when increasing competition in the slave trade lowered prices. The price of indentured servants simultaneously rose, as higher wages in Europe made the poor less willing to migrate to the Caribbean. Other key factors underlying this change included aversion to the gang labor of sugar estates and the spread of yellow fever and falciparum malaria from Africa. Moreover, as sugar estates expanded, opportunities declined for servants to prosper as smallholders after they had worked off their contracts. Slaves replaced servants in two stages: first as fieldworkers, and then as craftsmen. The latter stage followed the emergence of a creole (meaning locally born) generation of slaves who were more easily trained by Europeans than African-born people could be. By the early eighteenth century, three-quarters of the population of the North European Caribbean colonies consisted of black slaves.

The "sugar revolution" not only changed the colonial population from mostly European to mostly African but also degraded the physical environment, stimulated the regional economy, and made the region politically significant for Europe. The high profits from sugar cultivation caused land values to skyrocket and led, on the small islands, to a rapid clearing of lowland forests. There arose out of this process a colonial elite of sugar planters—a plantocracy—who dominated their island communities, although in the eighteenth century many would use their wealth to retire to Europe as absentee proprietors. Additionally, the burgeoning volume of trade in a valuable commodity caused the English and French governments in the 1660s and 1670s to bring the colonies under their direct control; till then, they had been privately owned. Competition to dominate Caribbean commerce sharpened European rivalries and ushered in an era of "wars of trade" that lasted a century.

Figure 1. Slave Population, in Thousands.

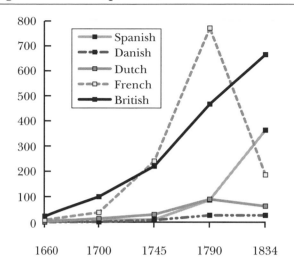

The Growth of Slavery

Stimulated especially by the popularity of tea, coffee, and cocoa in seventeenth-century Europe, the consumption of cane sugar increased steadily, and with it the relentless spread of slavery in the Caribbean. By 1700 there were about 160,000 slaves in the region, of whom three-fifths lived on British islands. Their numbers grew eightfold in the next ninety years. Barbados was the first sugar colony, but after 1700 it was eclipsed by the much larger island of Jamaica. In the Leeward Islands, the other British colonies made a slower transition to sugar and slavery. These British islands outstripped Brazilian production of sugar at the turn of the century, but they were soon overtaken by the French colonies of Martinique, Guadeloupe, and Saint Domingue (modern Haiti). By the 1740s, Saint Domingue produced more sugar than all the British islands combined, and it remained the leading producer until the Haitian revolution (1791–1803). The Windward Isles of Grenada, Dominica, Saint Lucia, and Saint Vincent, where the Amerindian population survived longest, were developed mainly after 1750 and never became major sugar producers. The Dutch grew modest quantities of sugar in the Guianas starting in the seventeenth century, but the main expansion in that area took place after 1796,

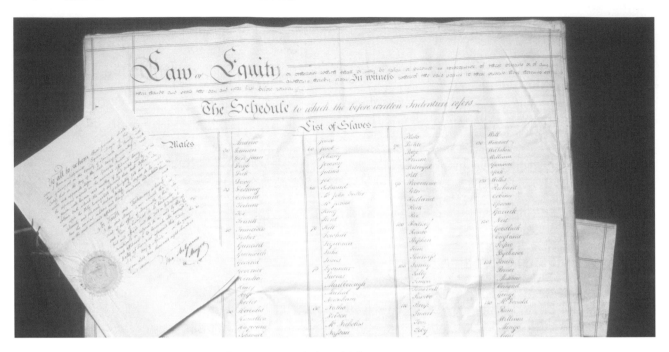

A list of slaves being shipped to Jamaica. [Bojan Brecelj/Corbis]

when much of it came under British rule. The same was true of Spanish Trinidad, seized by the British in 1797. In the late eighteenth century, the most rapid development was in Cuba, the largest island of the West Indies. Cuba became the main beneficiary of Saint Domingue's demise, and from the late 1820s the world's major exporter of sugar.

Sugar would remain the Caribbean's principal crop throughout the period of slavery, but it was not the region's only slave-grown export. In the mid-seventeenth century, only the high profits of sugar cultivation could finance the large-scale importation of enslaved African labor. In the years preceding 1690, however, a decline in the price of slaves permitted their use in other activities. In many places, indigo, a valuable dyestuff that required an intermediate amount of capital investment, played a transitional role in the shift from minor crops to capital-intensive sugar cultivation. Like sugar estates, indigo plantations involved manufacturing as well as agricultural processes. Indigo production responded to the demands of Europe's textile manufacturers, who in the late seventeenth century switched from India to the Americas as their main source of indigo. Around the middle of the eighteenth century, Saint Domingue was the largest exporter, outproducing Guatemala, South Carolina, and Venezuela. But because indigo was difficult to grow and manufacture, few regions continued to grow it for very long, and India resumed dominance of the world market after 1800.

Caribbean cotton production also declined at this time, because of the expansion of cultivation in the United States. Until then, cotton had been grown in most parts of the region from the Guianas to the Bahamas, where after 1780 it briefly became the basis of the island's economy. Cacao was also widely grown, notably on Martinique, Grenada, Saint Domingue, and Trinidad. Coffee did not arrive until it was introduced by the Dutch into Surinam in the 1690s. It spread to the French islands in the 1720s, and it stimulated frantic activity by pioneers in the mountains of Saint Domingue during the period 1763–1790. Saint Domingue dominated the world market for coffee, even more than for sugar or indigo, and accounted for more than half of world production in the 1780s. Saint Domingue's demise caused coffee booms in Jamaica and eastern Cuba that lasted through the early decades of the nineteenth century. Where tobacco survived in the Caribbean—chiefly Cuba and Santo Domingo—it remained associated with free labor.

In the Caribbean's small urban sector, slaves generally constituted half to two-thirds of the population. Spanish colonial towns, which served important administrative, ecclesiastical, and military functions, had more Europeans, however. Slaves represented little more than one-third of Havana's inhabitants, who numbered about 40,000 in 1800. This was easily the region's largest city—Kingston (Jamaica) and Cap Français (Saint Domingue) were scarcely half its size. After 1800, females formed a majority of urban slaves.

Apart from Havana's shipyards, industrial activities were invariably located outside towns, owing to the risk of fire. Rum distilleries, tanneries, lime-kilns, and small factories for making sugar-pots and bricks employed a small but overwhelmingly slave workforce.

European governments valued their Caribbean possessions for economic, fiscal, and strategic reasons. The British colonies were most important to Great Britain around 1800, when they accounted for one-quarter of British overseas trade. The claim advanced by Eric Williams, in *Capitalism and Slavery* (1944), that the profits of Caribbean slavery financed the Industrial Revolution is no longer generally accepted, but it is still debated. Import taxes on Caribbean produce represented a substantial portion of British government revenue from the end of the seventeenth century; sugar was the most important British import until about 1830. Caribbean commerce was also valued in England for its contribution to national defense, as a "nursery of seamen." As for France, by the late 1780s about seventy percent of its overseas trade consisted of the import and reexport of Caribbean produce. As the only dynamic sector of France's stagnant economy in the late eighteenth century, this trade created fewer domestic linkages than it did in the British case. But the sugar and coffee the French sold in northern Europe did let them purchase naval stores critical to national defense. Before the nineteenth century, Spanish West Indian exports ranked far below the precious metals and dyestuffs of Spain's mainland colonies. However, after losing its mainland empire in the early 1820s, Spain had an extremely unbalanced relationship with Cuba. It depended heavily on tax revenue repatriated from the island, even though the introduction of free trade allowed the United States, progressively, to become Cuba's main trading partner. Britain's North American colonies had begun supplying lumber, livestock, and foodstuffs to its Caribbean colonies in the mid-seventeenth century. In the eighteenth century they became important suppliers to the French and Spanish islands as well. Caribbean slavery thus played a major role in the economic development of the ports of the northeastern United States and their agricultural hinterlands.

Demography

In the eighteenth century, the largest concentration of slaves was in Saint Domingue, where the enslaved population passed half a million in 1790. During the period from 1855 to 1870, the number of slaves in Cuba exceeded 350,000. In Jamaica, the slave population peaked in 1811, at close to 350,000. At its apogee, only one-third of Saint Domingue's slaves lived on sugar estates, perhaps another third on indigo plantations, and one-quarter on coffee plantations. In the early nineteenth century, between 50 and 60 percent of Jamaican slaves worked on sugar estates. In Cuba in the mid-nineteenth century, the proportion was just under half; around 1790, the proportion had been between half and three-quarters. Urban dwellers constituted only 5 percent of Saint Domingue's slaves in 1790, and 10 percent of British Caribbean slaves in 1810. In nineteenth-century Cuba, the urban segment accounted for at least one-fifth of the slave population. In the tiny logging settlement of British Honduras, and on the Dutch island of Curaçao and the Danish island of Saint Thomas, which were trading entrepôts with few plantations, the urban sector was exceptionally large.

In 1790, some 45 percent of the slave population in the New World lived in the Caribbean, at least half in French colonies. By 1830, the distribution of slaves had shifted considerably, though the total number in the Caribbean declined only slightly. This resulted from the combined effect of the Haitian revolution, which ended slavery (and sugar cultivation) in Saint Domingue, the transfer of several slave-owning colonies to British rule, and the ending of the slave trade to most colonies except Cuba and Puerto Rico

Table 1.   Approximate Population of the Caribbean around 1790, in Thousands.

Colonies	Slaves	Free Coloreds	Whites	Total	Percentage
French	722	42	60	824	41
British	467	15	60	542	27
Dutch	90	4	11	105	5
Danish	27	2	7	36	2
Spanish	87	182	230	499	25
Total	1,393	245	368	2,006	
Percentage	69	12	18		

by 1808. Meanwhile, the Caribbean share of the total slave population in the New World shrank, because of continued imports to Brazil and the reproduction of the slave population in the United States.

Slave populations in the Caribbean, unlike North America, almost never grew naturally. As in mainland Latin America, the death rates of slaves exceeded their birthrates, and populations increased only because of the arrival of Africans through the slave trade. As the demographic data available before 1810 are extremely inadequate, and even thereafter the deaths of slave infants frequently went unrecorded, there is some uncertainty whether low fertility or high mortality was the main obstacle to growth. Perspectives also shift according to the point of comparison chosen. Fertility rates were clearly lower in the Caribbean than in North American slave populations, but the fertility of slaves in North America was exceptionally high. Compared with other world populations, the estimated fertility rates of Caribbean slaves look quite normal.

Paradoxically, the import of enslaved Africans that expanded slave societies also hindered their natural growth. This was because roughly two males were imported for every female (somewhat more by the Spanish, fewer by other Europeans), and because African slaves had higher mortality rates and lower fertility rates than locally born creoles. Newly arrived Africans, who were immigrants in a new disease environment and had been weakened by their brutal transplantation, suffered particularly high death rates. Creoles had greater immunity to local diseases, and they also had the advantage of being preferred for domestic service and artisan posts, occupations associated with lower mortality. Given these advantages, and fewer cultural barriers, creoles found it easier to choose partners, form households, and have healthy children. In time creoles came to make up the majority of populations of fully settled regions where new migrants were no longer needed to clear new land. In Barbados and some other highly creolized colonies, natural growth was achieved shortly after the ending of the slave trade in 1808.

High mortality was associated with sugar cultivation and with male slaves, even more than with African origin. Nonsugar islands like the Bahamas and the Caymans achieved natural growth before the slave trade ended. In all the European colonies, the harsh work and the unhealthy location of sugar estates led to lower growth rates for sugar plantations than for coffee, cotton, and other crops. Cotton and indigo, for example, were often grown in drier areas than sugar, and the upland location of coffee plantations made coffee workers vulnerable to pulmonary disease but lowered the incidence of insect-borne infections. In

the Guianas, however, all these crops were grown in the same ecological space, and the experience there suggests that the work itself was the critical factor that made sugar estates deadly.

Although women were the majority of field laborers in creolized populations and were excluded from the low-mortality artisan posts, male slaves still died more rapidly than females. Men were more prone to accidents and suicide, and enslavement arguably entailed greater adjustment, and therefore stress, for African males than for females. The high ratio of males among incoming Africans was thus steadily reduced in the maturing resident populations. Sex imbalance was at its most extreme on the sugar estates of nineteenth-century Cuba and lowest in the British colonies.

Like high mortality, low fertility was also associated with sugar estates and African slaves. In the Caribbean, as compared with the United States, a larger proportion of women slaves never gave birth, and those who did bear children spaced the births out more, following African lactation practices. Their childbearing years were also shorter in the Caribbean. Historians debate the relative impact on fertility of various material and cultural factors—from diet and workload to abortion and unstable sexual relations to drinking lead-laden rum. One important influence was the ability of slave couples to form coresidential households, which was easiest on the largest plantations. These, however, were sugar estates, where the harsh labor conditions for women led to miscarriages and lowered newborns' chances of survival. Robert Dirks, in *The Black Saturnalia* (1987), claims that inadequate diet was the main force shaping slave demography, whereas Barry Higman, in *Slave Populations* (1984), argues that workload was the more significant variable.

Work Regimens and Quality of Life

Historians of the 1990s agree that the main influences on slaves' quality of life were the type of work they did and the disease environment in which they lived, rather than the nationality of the colonizing power or the laws it passed. Though the custodial provisions of slave laws made in France and Spain distinguish them from the harsher laws of the British colonies—made by planters—the French and Spanish protections were rarely enforced. Before the nineteenth century there were certainly significant differences between Catholic and Protestant societies regarding exposure to Christianity. Only in the former were church marriages generally recognized as legal. Only under Spanish and Dutch law did slaves have a right to personal property. But accumulation of property and formation of families by slaves depended little on formal legal codes. Access to freedom was facilitated for Spanish slaves by the custom, later codified, of *coartación,* by which the government assisted slaves in setting a price for self-purchase. More significant, perhaps, was the importance in the Spanish colonies of the urban sector, where slaves had most chance to accumulate funds. The manumission of slaves in the Spanish West Indies was also related to economic stagnation—manumission decreased during the sugar boom of the nineteenth century. Finally, the free colored population of the Spanish islands was so large partly because it was a century older than any other.

The culture of the slave owners had little bearing on the demography of slave society, which in turn did much to shape the nature of the slave community. The basic divisions in Caribbean slave society were between urban and rural environments, and between different types of crop production. Urban employment itself exhibited strong contrasts. Domestic slaves, predominantly female, lived with their owners and worked long hours. Male craft specialists and waterfront and building workers might lead fairly independent lives (as was also true of female vendors and washer-

women). Many found their own lodgings and hired their own labor, paying their masters a monthly sum.

In the countryside, sugar estates were similarly distinctive for the varied occupations they offered but also for the unique severity of labor conditions. Sugar cultivation was exceptionally hard on workers because of the frenetic pace of the harvest season, with its night shifts in the boiling house, and because of the heavy labor required to plant cane. Lifting the heavy sugar barrels caused frequent hernias. (Indigo was a less demanding crop, although planting and harvesting indigo also involved stooping under the tropical sun. Its growing season was shorter, but it needed more frequent weeding. Its processing, if not mechanized, involved some intensive labor, but for only a few workers. Coffee and cacao were rarely replanted, and they could be harvested without bending. They often grew in the shade of larger trees, and coffee grew at cooler altitudes. It was sometimes claimed that cotton was the cash crop that made least demands on Caribbean slaves.) Another factor contributing to the harshness of labor on sugar estates was the

Slaves on a Caribbean plantation around 1835 receive "domestic chastisement." [Historical Picture Archive/Corbis]

fact that most were run by managers installed by absentee owners who had returned to Europe. Paid a percentage of revenue, such managers were encouraged to maximize output without concern for costs. They also had little incentive to develop the paternalist ethos sometimes associated with resident planters and farmers.

Sugar estates varied greatly in size but were always the largest plantations in any colony. Early in the eighteenth century, and in Cuba as late as 1790, few had more than one hundred slaves, but by the end of slavery the workforce on the average sugar estate in Saint Domingue, Jamaica, or British Guiana exceeded two hundred. Most Caribbean slaves lived in units very much larger than those of North or South America. The great majority of women invariably were field hands. They usually outnumbered male slaves in the canefields, as one-third or more of the men belonged to the occupational elite of drivers, artisan craftsmen, domestics, and other specialists—an elite that was overwhelmingly male and increasingly dominated by creoles. Skilled slaves frequently received extra food and clothing, and sometimes better housing. They tended to have better health than field slaves. The closely supervised lifestyles of domestics, however, restricted opportunities for recreation and the formation of families. The proportion of slaves in domestic service was higher when the plantation owner was resident, but the number of skilled slaves overall, and thus the prospects for social mobility, were much greater on sugar plantations than other plantations.

Caribbean slaves produced most of their food. Except on the smallest sugar islands, slaves received small provision grounds on marginal land that they worked on Sundays, and they kept pigs and poultry next to their huts. "Proto-peasants," they sold any surplus in urban markets or to their owners. Because provision grounds and markets were often distant, the extra work apparently raised mortality rates. Growing and marketing their own food, however, gave slaves a degree of autonomy, some exposure to new environments and ideas, and an opportunity to accumulate wealth. Through feeding the towns, slaves came to control much of the coinage circulating in a colony.

Culture and Resistance

Because slave imports into the Spanish West Indies were low before 1800 and white immigration was high, slaves almost always formed a minority of the population. Spanish became their lingua franca and, encouraged by state policy, most creole slaves became Catholics. Baptism was obligatory, though often perfunctory, and rural estates sometimes had resident priests. Elsewhere in the Caribbean, the high ratios of

blacks to whites and the constant inflow of Africans impeded the slaves' learning the colonists' language and facilitated the preservation of aspects of African cultures. Numerous creole languages that mixed European vocabulary and African phonology and syntax became the main means of communication. Most Protestant churches showed no interest in evangelizing slaves before the 1790s, and the Roman Catholic church in Saint Domingue was weak. Outside the Spanish colonies, therefore, slaves retained greater control of their spiritual lives. Cosmology, styles of worship, sorcery, witchcraft beliefs, and burial practices retained a strong African imprint. Most easily retained were items that did not impede plantation routine, such as music and dance, body language, and folklore. Mintz and Price's *Birth of African-American Culture* (1992) emphasizes linkages with Africa at the level of basic values but warns against seeking specific continuities in the fashion of R. F. Thompson's *Flash of the Spirit* (1983). Creole culture was dynamic and inevitably syncretic. No ethnic group predominated in the slave imports of any colony. The Aja-Fon influence on Haitian voodoo suggests that the earliest African arrivals in a colony could have disproportionate cultural impact, but in the case of Cuban *santería*, it is the impact of the late-arriving Yoruba that is salient. In both places, Central Africans were the most numerous African migrants, but their cultural contributions went unnoticed until recently.

How far African values, rather than the exigencies of slavery, shaped slave families and gender relations is uncertain. Different African cultures expressed differing attitudes toward premarital sex or divorce, and the Caribbean evidence is problematic. Polygynous families were rare and could be formed only by elite males, who were usually creoles. Eighteenth-century commentators frequently depict unstable sexual relations among slaves and sexual exploitation of slave women by whites. Family formation was undermined by sex imbalance in the slave and white populations. In the more pious seventeenth century, when sex ratios were lower, it seems that many slaves lived in nuclear families; so, too, in the nineteenth-century British and French colonies, when slave communities were creolized and the sex ratio was balanced. Even then, households headed by the mother were frequently the norm, because spouses often belonged to different owners and women were widowed early.

The paucity of whites that weakened the European cultural impact in the Caribbean also favored resistance by slaves. Fugitive slaves were first recorded in 1503; the first recorded revolt took place in 1521. The great majority of runaway slaves, called maroons, were young men; newly arrived Africans formed a substantial minority. Three patterns appear among fugitives: attempts to escape slavery permanently; individual short-term absenteeism, frequently for visiting relatives; and work strikes in the form of collective disappearances. Africans tended to flee to mountains and forests; creoles, particularly women, fled to the towns, where they might blend in with the free colored population, especially if they had marketable skills. Slaves familiar with the waterfront might escape to another island as seamen. Maroon communities located in jungles or mountains raided outlying plantations for female slaves, food, and manufactured goods. On the large islands and in the Guianas some of these communities achieved permanence. After the failure of military expeditions sent against them, colonial authorities made treaties with maroons in Jamaica (1739–1740), Surinam (1760–1767), and Santo Domingo (1784). The treaties recognized the maroons' freedom but coopted them as collaborators in the capture of future fugitives. Several maroon societies, with their own distinctive cultures, still exist.

Historians disagree about whether the maroons functioned more as a stimulus or an alternative to slave rebellions, whose character changed through time. Early revolts often aimed at escape from colonial society. When the expansion of settlement or maroon treaties "closed" the frontier, however, rebels had to attempt to overthrow the colonial regime. During the abolitionist agitation of the period from 1789 to 1831, many rebels apparently thought they could negotiate an end to slavery. Several revolts of those years involved thousands of slaves. African-led uprisings tended to be localized; those led by creoles were more likely to show the influence of external developments, such as abolitionism or the French and Haitian revolutions. Jamaica experienced more than a half-dozen revolts involving hundreds of slaves. The frequent betrayal or discovery of conspiracies shows the difficulty of organizing insurrections, most of which were rapidly and brutally suppressed. However, Africans took over Berbice for about a year in 1763, and slaves on Saint John drove out the white population for several months in 1733. Free coloreds and slaves fought British forces on Grenada for two years in the mid-1790s. In terms of magnitude, duration, and results, no rebellion compared with the Saint Domingue rising of 1791, which forced the French, in the throes of their own revolutionary war, to abolish slavery and eventually led to the independence of Haiti.

Ending Slavery

Although Haiti represents the only case in which slaves (with the assistance of free colored people) won their own freedom, war and slave resistance were often con-tributory factors in ending slavery elsewhere. Emancipation came to the British Caribbean in 1834, mainly because of mounting pressure from abolitionists and the region's decreasing economic importance for British politicians. Even so, Jamaica's "Christmas rebellion" of 1831 probably catalyzed the process by weakening the support for the planters that had previously existed in England. Similarly, the ending of slavery in the French colonies in 1848 resulted from political change in France, but its precise timing depended on mass demonstrations by slaves. The French example, and a rebellion on Saint Croix, ended Danish colonial slavery the same year, though gradual emancipation had already been decreed in 1847. The Dutch followed suit in 1863, in imitation of the United States. Diplomatic repercussions of the American Civil War finally closed the slave trade to Spain's colonies, whose slave populations thereafter could no longer grow. Cuba's abortive Ten Years' War (1868–1878) then sealed their fate. Competing to win the support of slaves and international opinion, secessionists and the government were forced to promise eventual emancipation. Puerto Rico abandoned slavery immediately in 1873. Wartime destruction, runaways, the emancipation of newborns, and recruitment of slaves as soldiers had already cut Cuba's slave population by one-quarter when Spain abolished slavery there in 1880. As had happened earlier in the British empire, a transitional "apprenticeship" system was instituted, which had to be terminated early in 1886. The disruptive impact of emancipation was lessened by the fact that Puerto Rican and Cuban planters had extensively used free and indentured workers alongside slaves. However, until its eradication slavery remained economically viable everywhere in the Caribbean. It would not have vanished without political intervention.

Slavery's legacy to the Caribbean, as elsewhere, has been one of social cleavage and poverty—the latter accentuated by the absentee ownership of the largest estates, whose profits were spent in Europe. At the same time, slavery made the Caribbean a crucible of cultural creation, whose blurring of boundaries has prefigured the postmodern world much as the economics of sugar foreshadowed the modern world.

See also ABOLITION AND ANTISLAVERY MOVEMENTS; COARTACIÓN; CODE NOIR; CONCUBINAGE; MAROONS; PLANTATIONS; SLAVE TRADE; TOUSSAINT-LOUVERTURE.

BIBLIOGRAPHY

BARNET, MIGUEL, ed. *The Autobiography of a Runaway Slave: Esteban Montejo.* 1968.
BERGAD, LAIRD. *Cuban Rural Society in the Nineteenth Century: The Social and Economic History of Monoculture in Matanzas.* 1990.

BLACKBURN, ROBIN. *The Overthrow of Colonial Slavery, 1776–1848*. 1988.

CRATON, MICHAEL. *Empire, Enslavement, and Freedom in the Caribbean*. 1997.

———. *Testing the Chains: Resistance to Slavery in the British West Indies*. 1982.

DEBIEN, GABRIEL. *Les esclaves aux Antilles françaises aux XVIIe et XVIIIe siècles*. 1974.

DEERR, NOEL. *The History of Sugar*. 1949–1950.

DEIVE, CARLOS E. *La esclavitud del negro en Santo Domingo (1492–1844)*. 1980.

DRESCHER, SEYMOUR. *Econocide: British Slavery in the Era of Abolition*. 1977.

DUNN, RICHARD. *Sugar and Slaves: The Rise of the Planter Class in the English West Indies, 1623–1713*. 1972.

GASPAR, D. B., and D. P. GEGGUS. *A Turbulent Time: The French Revolution and the Greater Caribbean*. 1997.

GOSLINGA, CORNELIS. *The Dutch in the Caribbean and in the Guianas*. 1985.

HALL, DOUGLAS, ed. *In Miserable Slavery: Thomas Thistlewood in Jamaica, 1750–1786*. 1989.

HALL, NEVILLE. *Slave Society in the Danish West Indies: St. Thomas, St. John and St. Croix*. 1992.

HIGMAN, B. W. *Slave Populations of the British Caribbean, 1807–1834*. 1984.

KIPLE, KENNETH F. *The Caribbean Slave: A Biological History*. 1984.

KLEIN, HERBERT. *African Slavery in Latin America*. 1986.

MINTZ, SIDNEY, and RICHARD PRICE. The *Birth of African-American Culture: An Anthropological Perspective*. 1992.

PÉREZ, LOUIS, A. *Cuba: Between Reform and Revolution*. 1995.

PRICE, RICHARD. *Maroon Societies: Rebel Slave Communities in the Americas*. 1973.

SCARANO, FRANCISCO. *Sugar and Slavery in Puerto Rico: The Plantation Economy of Ponce, 1800–1850*. 1984.

SCOTT, REBECCA J. *Slave Emancipation in Cuba: The Transition to Free Labor, 1860–1899*. 1985.

SHERIDAN, RICHARD. *Sugar and Slavery: An Economic History of the British West Indies, 1623–1775*. 1974.

VAN STIPRIAAN, ALEX. *Surinaams contrast: Roofbouw en overleven in een Caraïbische plantagekolonie 1750–1863*. 1993.

WARD, J. R. *British West Indian Slavery, 1750–1834: The Process of Amelioration*. 1988.

David Geggus

English Colonies

The English established their first Caribbean settlement colonies at Saint Christopher in 1624, Barbados in 1627, Nevis in 1628, and Montserrat and Antigua in 1632. Before the 1655–1656 military campaign against the Spanish, when Oliver Cromwell added Jamaica to the list of English possessions, these small islands were the backbone of England's early seaborne empire. By 1660 the English had gained with these colonies a demographic advantage in the Caribbean over other European nations. Up to the Restoration, the islands attracted more settlers from Europe than the

mainland colonies, which suggests that they were perceived by emigrants as the destinations that held the best prospects for material and social advancement.

Following the acquisition of Jamaica, the white population grew even more rapidly until 1680, when it reached about 47,000, constituting some 40 percent of all whites in Britain's transatlantic colonies. It has been estimated, furthermore, that of the total of 378,000 white emigrants to America between 1630 and 1700, 223,000 (about 60 percent) went first to the colonies in the wider Caribbean.

Barbados developed the largest market for African slaves in the Caribbean during the seventeenth century. This labor demand was important because it led the way into large-scale sugar production. The opportunity to switch from tobacco and cotton production was open to planters in the Caribbean because sugar prices on the European market rose in the 1640s as a result of production dislocations caused by war against the Dutch in Portuguese Brazil, previously the principal supplier. The more venturesome of the British planters in Barbados, with considerable financial and technological support from the Dutch, moved in and captured a significant market share. By the early 1650s Barbados produced an annual crop valued at over £3 million, replaced Hispaniola as the "sugar center" of the Caribbean, and was described as the richest place in the New World. In fact, the island's value, in terms of trade and capital generation,

Slaves perform various duties, including baling and removing seeds, on a cotton plantation during harvest time. [Library of Congress/Corbis]

Table 1.   Population of the English West Indies, 1635–1715.

	Barbados			Jamaica			Leeward Islands	
Year	White	Black	Year	White	Black	Year	White	Black
1655	23,000	20,000	1660	3,000	500	1660	8,000	2,000
1673	21,309	33,184	1661	2,956	3,479	1670	8,000	3,000
1684	19,568	46,502	1673	7,768	9,504	1678	10,408	8,449
1696	—	42,000	1690	10,000	30,000	1690	10,000	15,000
1715	16,888	—	1713	7,000	55,000	1708	7,311	23,500

Sources: Vincent T. Harlow, *History of Barbados 1625–1685; Calendar of State Papers, Colonial Series (CSPC), 1669–1674*, no. 1101; Sloane MSS, 24441 British Library; Richard Dunn, *Sugar and Slaves; Journal of the House of Assembly of Jamaica, 1663–1826;* David Galenson, *Traders, Planters and Slaves: Market Behaviour in Early English America;* Robert V. Wells, *The Population of the British Colonies in America before 1776: A Survey of Census Data.*

was greater than that of all the other English colonies put together. French islands lagged behind the English, even though their production of sugar rose steadily over the century.

Sugar cultivation advanced throughout the British Caribbean during the second half of the seventeenth century, with concomitant import of slaves, although sugar monoculture was never the case in these islands. Competition between sugar farmers, cash-crop producers, and cattlemen for the best lands in Jamaica remained intense, as did the battle between all mere agriculturalists and traders in contraband to mainland Spanish domains for control of official policy with respect to the colony's development. Piracy and smuggling slaves to the Spaniards remained particularly attractive in Jamaica as a way to accumulate wealth, even though mercantilist intellectuals in England considered agriculture to be the only sustainable source of wealth. Cacao, which the Spaniards had cultivated on Jamaica, also attracted some English planters, and profits from cacao made it possible for some of them to invest in sugar production.

Efforts were also made to cultivate sugar on the four Leeward islands of Antigua, Montserrat, Nevis, and Saint Christopher, but none of these became a major producer of slave-grown sugar in the seventeenth century, despite the fact that planters in all these areas were inspired by the success of slavery in Barbados. Less suitable agricultural terrain and the high cost of constructing the mill, the boiling house, and the curing house that were necessary on every sugar plantation help to explain the limited advance of sugar production into the Lesser Antilles. The more weighty disincentive, however, was the near proximity of these islands to the Caribbean settlements of other European powers. Instead of the monocrop production

of sugar that came to characterize Barbados after the 1650s, the Lesser Antilles persisted with mixed economic activity that included production of indigo, tobacco, ginger, cotton, domesticated cattle, and fish, in addition to sugar—all produced by slave labor.

The late-seventeenth-century organization of slave plantations in Barbados, and to a lesser extent in the Leewards and Jamaica, is generally referred to as the "sugar revolution." Cultivation of sugarcane on large plantations steadily displaced cultivation of tobacco, cotton, and indigo on smaller farms worked by family members and indentured servants. Sugar, with its greater need for labor and capital equipment, stimulated the consolidation of larger agricultural units. Landowners foreclosed on tenants and bought out and pushed off small freeholders. As a result, land prices escalated, and there was a rapid reduction in the size and output of nonsugar producers. Although some small-scale farmers continued to occupy prime lands on most islands, maintaining a cash-crop culture on the margins of plantations, they found it difficult to compete as tobacco and cotton prices fell, and their operations often proved unprofitable. By the 1680s the "sugar islands" had lost the reputation as hospitable places for propertyless European migrants that had made them early favorites of British settlers overseas.

This economic transformation brought about the emergence of a slave-owning planter elite—considered the richest colonists in America—which became a distinguishing characteristic of the "sugar islands." In most colonies, successive generations of men from these elite families dominated legislatures and judiciaries. On the negative side, the more successful planters, especially on Barbados and Jamaica, used property qualifications, membership in professional bodies, and possession of university degrees to dominate colonial society at the expense of middling and smaller planters, as well as a growing nonwhite population born of their sexual relations with enslaved women from Africa.

Sugar thus meant slaves, and in the Lesser Antilles, as in Hispaniola and Brazil, slaves meant Africans. Those acquainted with sugar production in Brazil would have known that the work was so severe that no free labor force would endure it and that planters there had resorted to slaves imported mostly from Africa. The work associated with sugar production was unusually burdensome because it involved a considerable manufacturing input on the plantation as well as harsh agricultural labor. Workers were required not only to clear the ground of heavy vegetation and to sow, tend, and harvest heavy, sharp-leaved cane in the tropical sun but also immediately to crush the juice from the cane in a sugar mill and then to boil the juice in cauldrons before it had time to ferment. Work on sugar plantation was arduous and labor-intensive throughout the year; but it became particularly onerous at harvesttime, when field hands had to cut the cane at the moment of maximum yield, and the sugar works operated around the clock, with the workers organized in shifts to keep the fires high and the mills turning.

Large profits in sugar during midcentury meant that the more successful sugar planters could absorb the high labor cost associated with purchased African slaves, and as they rapidly dispensed with white indentured servitude as unsuitable for long-term economic growth, they established the islands as the greatest British slave market. The capital and credit needed to finance this buildup of unfree labor were available from English as well as Dutch merchants and financiers eager to do business with sugar planters. By 1660 the African slave trade was described as the lifeline of the Caribbean economy. In 1645, some two years after the beginning of sugar production, Barbados had only 5,680 slaves; by 1698 it had 42,000 slaves. Jamaica followed Barbados into "sugar and slavery" toward the end of the century; in 1656 the colony had 1,410 slaves; in 1698 it had over 41,000. Mortality among these slaves was high from overwork, malnutrition, and resistance. The planters therefore needed large, continuing inputs of fresh slaves to keep up their labor force. In 1688 it was estimated that Jamaica needed 10,000 slaves each year, the Leewards 6,000, and Barbados 4,000 simply to maintain existing stocks. The combination of sugar exports and slave imports represents the dual economic system into which the British led the Caribbean by the early eighteenth century.

All sugar planters experienced a pressing need to regularize their control over the growing crowd of

Figure 2. Blacks as a Percentage of the Total Population in Four Regions.

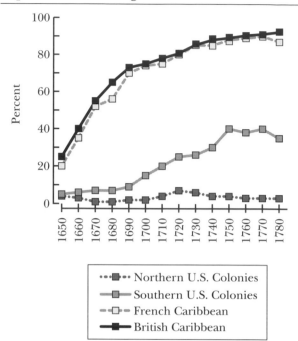

Source: Robert W. Fogel and Stanley L. Engerman, *Time on the Cross,* 1974, p. 21.

immigrant Africans. In 1661 legislators in Barbados took the lead and attempted to settle the matter with a comprehensive code entitled An Act for the Better Ordering and Governing of Negroes. The code provided for rigid racial segregation, formed the legal framework of relations between slave and owner, and represented an attempt to constitute legally a social order rigidly stratified by origin—Europeans over Africans. Under the code, masters were responsible for feeding, sheltering, and clothing slaves, who were described as "heathenish," "brutish," and "dangerous." By the end of the century, the principles of this Barbados code had been adopted throughout most English jurisdictions in the Caribbean.

Slave codes restricted almost every area of the slave's social existence. They provided that no planter should give a slave permission to leave his owner's property, the sugar estate, without a signed ticket stating a set time for return. Any white person who found a slave on his property without such a ticket and did not make an apprehension was liable to forfeit a sum of money to the colonial treasurer, some of which was paid to the informant. Codes also stated that slaves were not allowed to "beat drums, blow horns, or use other loud instruments," and their houses were to be "diligently searched" from time to time. A series of punishments was provided for slaves who traded in stolen goods, struck Christians, ran away, burned sugarcane, or stole provisions. In addition, whites were liable to fines for improper policing of their slaves, assisting the slaves of others to escape, murdering slaves, or exposing slaves to seditious doctrines. On the other hand, slaves received some legal protection, as the law recognized the need to "guard them from the cruelties and insolence of themselves, and other ill-tempered people or owners."

Since slaves were considered real estate, they could not themselves own property—the basis of social mobility—they could not even own themselves. Blacks were not permitted to give evidence in court against whites until the early nineteenth century, and whites rarely came to the legal assistance of blacks. It was not until the nineteenth century that the murder of a slave by a white became a capital felony, but slaves could be punished by death for striking or threatening a white person or for stealing property. These laws established the essential nature of English social control over slaves in Barbados, Jamaica, and the Leeward Islands as plantation owners sought to discipline their African labor forces to produce sugar cheaply in the early eighteenth century.

At the end of the Seven Years' War in 1763, the English captured the Windward Islands of Grenada, Saint Lucia, Dominica, and Saint Vincent from France, adding southerly territories to the northern Leewards and Jamaica. Imperial conflict continued during the second half of the eighteenth century, and by 1797 England added Trinidad and Tobago and Guiana to its colonial world. In the Windward Islands, however, defeat of the French did not settle the battle for control. The native Kalinago (Carib) peoples there continued their war of resistance, holding on to a significant portion of territory. Their attacks on English plantation settlements in the Leewards fueled the settlers' determination to destroy them. English merchants, settlers, and colonial officials argued that the Kalingos were "a barbarous and cruel set of savages beyond reason or persuasion and must therefore be eliminated." It was also clear that the slave-based economic system demanded an absolute monopoly of the Caribbean, and Kalingo independence and self-reliance contradicted the internal logic of capitalist accumulation.

Slaves worked in a variety of physical environments and engaged in a wide range of economic activities as the island economies became more complex. While most slaves remained confined to the agricultural sector, some worked at industrial crafts, in mercantile and social services sectors, or in fishing and domestic economies. On sugar plantations, slaves—particularly "creoles" born in the islands—came to dominate skilled technological occupations. In addition, these slaves assumed lower-level plantation management roles, as drivers, overseers, and rangers. They worked with sugar, coffee, tobacco, indigo, and cotton, and they tended cattle in the "pens" of the established husbandry sector. Even elderly people and children worked, and women toiled just as hard as men. By the end of the eighteenth century, women were in the majority in the gangs of English sugar plantations, since many men held artisan and other skilled positions. Full employment was the objective of slave economies, and the work slaves performed determined to a considerable degree the nature of their life experiences, mortality, fertility, and domestic life.

Racism emerged in the eighteenth century in response to the growth of a small group of free blacks and underpinned a proslavery ideology. Some colonialists inveighed against miscegenation, but wherever blacks labored as slaves and whites were masters—in the Caribbean and indeed throughout the Americas—a prominent feature of society was the existence of people of mixed racial ancestry, their numbers and rate of growth varying according to specific demographic, ideological, and economic factors. Since legal codes for governing the enslaved blacks provided that all juveniles should at birth take the sociolegal status of their mothers, most people of mixed racial origins, particularly those born of slave mothers, were at birth designated slaves.

However, partly because some free white males could not comfortably enslave their own progeny, and partly because the practical application of white supremacist ideology required some socioeconomic adjustment, masters who were also husbands and fathers tended to manumit some mixed-race offspring, as well as black sexual partners. Consequently, a group of "free colored" people emerged in most Caribbean societies. In general, they cherished their legal freedom, the commodity most highly valued in a slave society, but they were rejected by whites on the basis of their color—the accepted mark of servitude and inferiority. Living within and between these conflicting psychological worlds, the world of legal freedom and that of social discrimination, the free colored community developed a unique creole perspective. Patriarchy, as well as cultural and racial denomination, underpinned the white supremacist ideology of the male slaveholders.

Slave owners were caught in a trade-off between seeking profit and spending on maintenance of the slaves who produced it. As rational entrepreneurs they sought to lower the cost of productive inputs and so reduced expenditures on slaves to subsistence levels. At the same time, however, the protection of property rights in slaves meant that the daily management of subsistence and health care could not be left to chance. Slaves had to be minimally nourished and medically assisted if they were to be productive workers. At the same time class and race prejudice affected economic thinking; as a result, provisions and other care were often set below what was required to maintain general health.

Slaves so poorly fed consequently suffered a range of diseases related to malnutrition. Not only did the availability of food fluctuate seasonally, but slaves experienced long periods of hunger after hurricanes and during droughts and the recurrent major wars in the region. Crop cycles in Europe and North America also affected the availability of food. Poor health and poor nutrition contributed to the general inability of Caribbean slave populations to reproduce themselves naturally until the closing years of the eighteenth century.

In reaction to such inadequacies slaves pursued autonomous economic strategies of their own, as part of "leisure" times they claimed for themselves. Growing and selling food and other produce allowed them to improve the quality and quantity of their diets in the context of general malnutrition and to own and possess property in a system that also defined them as property. It offered them opportunity to travel and to attempt to "normalize" their social lives as much as possible under generally restrictive circumstances. They defended these benefits militantly, and it was there that women in particular displayed great tenacity. Marketing symbolized a spirit of independence and was central to the nonviolent protest and resistance that characterized day-to-day antislavery activity.

Slaves pursued their freedom by other means— including violent ones—in a virtual war against the restraints of the slave codes and the racial denigration that repeatedly broke out in bloody battles. The English colonies in the Caribbean maintained the pervasive controls of slavery only by employing against the slaves the military forces stationed there to defend the islands against European rivals. After periods of massive imports, the new Africans often organized, sometimes drawing on their military training and experience at home, to attack the plantations, or they fled individually to the hills in the mountainous islands and formed refugee, or "maroon," settlements, from which they attacked English property and recruited from among the slaves. In the late-eighteenth-century "age of revolution," creole plantation slaves organized revolts inspired by ideals of freedom, often drawing on networks of communication rooted in marketing and other systems that had grown up beyond the confines of individual plantations. In one form or another, hardly a generation of slaves in the English Caribbean failed to take their antislavery actions to the level of violent confrontation.

These large-scale, violent revolts and long-term marronage have been considered the most "advanced" acts of rebellion, but hidden, spontaneous, day-to-day acts of individuals sustained an equally costly war against domination. Although this war was difficult to perceive beneath the slaves' veneer of secrecy, female slaves, as wives and mothers, overcame slave owners' attempts to divide slave communities culturally and morally and thus provided the organizational strength necessary for more open resistance. The extreme patriarchal domination that slavery allowed masters over the women they owned forced female slaves to resist personally as well, with redoubled determination. As the prices of imported Africans rose steadily through the eighteenth century, masters moved to encourage fertility and maternity as strategies of providing labor for their plantations. The creole children that slave women bore in those late generations of slavery became the leaders of the nineteenth-century antislavery activity on the plantations that contributed much to the demoralization of slave owners and British policymakers by the 1820s.

Emancipation from above confirmed the slaves' quest for liberty in the nineteenth century and produced legislated freedom in 1834, with full autonomy

A woodcut from the 1850s depicts the moment in 1838 when a plantation owner in the West Indies announces the freeing of his slaves. [Corbis-Bettmann]

delayed until 1838 by a period of continued "apprenticeship" to the former masters. Though slaves had sustained a relentless, multifaceted assault on their bondage for more than a century in the English Caribbean, the slave owners held sufficient wealth and power in England to delay the legislative process there, which had gathered momentum in the 1770s, for several decades. Slaves and abolitionists alike drew inspiration from the revolution in French Saint Domingue, where slaves violently attacked their masters, fought French imperial forces and an army sent by Britain, abolished slavery, and succeeded in establishing the Republic of Haiti by 1804. In the British islands, slaves on Barbados, Demerara, and Jamaica revolted in 1816, 1823, and 1831, respectively, thus advancing the significance of the parliamentary discussions of emancipation under way in England. Such violent opposition to slavery illustrates the slaves' clear vision of their own freedom.

By the early nineteenth century, as Britain's slave-worked sugar economies matured, the costs of maintaining discipline over rebellious slaves rose and exacerbated other economic contradictions besetting the sugar islands of the Caribbean. The growing industrial capacity in England prompted a political struggle for free trade to open export markets, and the tariffs and other mercantilist restrictions on trade that sustained slave-worked sugar threatened the planters with a severe squeeze on profits. Historians have not agreed on how antislavery pressures in Parliament, the economics of industrial capitalism, philosophical and moral sentiments favoring freedom as an ideal, and the actions of the slaves themselves combined to produce emancipation in the 1830s, but the slaves' pursuit of their own freedom in the English Caribbean contributed to subsequent notions of progress and modernity around the world.

See also LAW; MAROONS; PLANTATIONS; REBELLIONS AND VIOLENT RESISTANCE; SLAVE TRADE.

BIBLIOGRAPHY

CARRINGTON, S. H. H. *The West Indies during the American Revolution.* 1987.

COX, EDWARD. *Free Coloureds in the Slave Societies of St. Kitts and Grenada, 1763–1833.* 1984.

CRATON, M. *Searching for the Invisible Man: Slaves and Plantation Life in Jamaica.* 1978.

CURTIN, P. D. *The Atlantic Slave Trade: A Census.* 1969.

DRESCHER, S. *Econocide: British Slavery in the Era of Abolition.* 1977.

HIGMAN, B. W. *Slave Populations of the British Caribbean 1807–1834.* 1984.

SHERIDAN, RICHARD. *Doctors and Slaves: A Medical and Demographic History of Slavery in the B.W.I. 1680–1834.* 1985.

————. *Sugar and Slavery: An Economic History of the B.W.I., 1624–1775.* 1974.

WARD, J. R. *British West Indian Slavery 1750–1834: The Process of Amelioration.* 1988.

WILLIAMS, E. *Capitalism and Slavery.* 1944.

Hilary McD. Beckles

French Colonies

In comparative studies of race and slavery in the American tropics, France's colonies often appear in an intermediate position between Iberian and Anglo-Saxon extremes. Though most scholars give little credence to the supposed influence of "Latin" or "Protestant" personality traits, it is true that the institutions of French colonies exhibited in attenuated form the Catholic absolutism of the Iberians, while in their social structure they closely resembled the North Europeans' colonies. The economic diversity of French slave society also places it somewhere between the heavily sugar-oriented British Caribbean colonies and the Hispanic societies with their larger non-plantation sector. In geographical extent, too, France's tropical settlements generally ranked between Spain's extensive Caribbean holdings and the smaller islands of Britain, as they did in the number (and sex ratio) of slaves they imported, and, it seems, in their propensity to free slaves, or at least in the size of their free nonwhite populations.

Beginnings (1623–1713)

Although French ships raided and traded in the Caribbean from the early 1500s, the first French colonies were founded only after Spanish power in the region had collapsed. The French settled Saint-Christophe (Saint Kitts) jointly with the British in 1623, and Martinique and Guadeloupe in 1635, followed by tiny Saint Barthélemy and Saint Martin. A growing French presence in western Hispaniola led to the creation of the colony of Saint Domingue (modern Haiti) in 1665. Cayenne received its first governor in 1643, though most French colonizing schemes for the mainland Guianas between the 1590s and 1790s met with failure. Dominica, Saint Croix, Tobago, and Saint Lucia were briefly French colonies, as was Grenada from 1650 to 1763.

As in the British Caribbean, the early French settlements used indentured European labor to grow tobacco but were transformed into slave societies by the introduction of sugar cultivation. Though stimulated by the migration of Jewish refugees from Brazil to Guadeloupe in the 1650s, the sugar revolution developed more slowly in the French than the British colonies. French settlement in general was hindered by the relative weakness of France's maritime bourgeoisie, by aristocratic mores, and by restrictive state

Table 1.   French Caribbean Population in the 1788 Census.

	Whites	Free Coloreds	Slaves	Total
Saint Domingue	27,717	21,808	405,564	455,089
Martinique	10,603	4,851	73,416	88,870
Guadeloupe	13,466	3,044	85,461	101,971
Sainte-Lucie	2,159	1,588	17,221	20,961
Guyane	1,307	394	10,748	12,549
Tobago	425	231	13,295	13,951
Total	55,677	31,916	605,705	693,391

commercial and religious policy. The French were also reluctant to emigrate. Although France had Europe's largest population, it experienced less of the social distress and dynamism caused in England by inequitable inheritance and land-tenure laws. Following the British example, the French government took over direct rule of its colonies in 1664, monopolized their trade, and encouraged the creation of slave-trading companies. Headed by an absolute monarchy, the French state played an active role in colonial development, albeit less encompassing than that which occurred in the Iberian case. One manifestation of this was the Code Noir (Black Code) of 1685, which sought to regulate relations between slaves and slaveowners. It had very little success, as did legislation of the 1780s that also attempted to limit slaveowners' abuses.

In the seventeenth century, the French colonies imported slightly more than 150,000 enslaved Africans, less than two-thirds as many as their British Caribbean rivals. While Guadeloupe stagnated after its early growth, Martinique emerged as the most important colony. In 1671, two-thirds of its cultivated area was given over to sugar, although tobacco farmers still outnumbered sugar planters two to one. In Saint Domingue, whites remained a majority until the 1690s, when suddenly the small slave population more than quadrupled to 9,500. The sack of Cartagena in 1697, swan song of the buccaneers, infused capital into the colony, and the war of 1702–1713 provided access to free trade. By 1713 Saint Domingue had 138 sugar estates and 1,182 indigo plantations. With the advantages of lower taxes and large reserves of virgin soil, the French colonies were poised to capture the European market for tropical produce.

Apogee (1713–1789)

The inefficient French slave trade, which provided labor only at considerably greater cost than British planters paid, was the main disadvantage the French colonies suffered. During the eighteenth century they purchased more than one million Africans from French merchants, and an unknown number from foreign smugglers. Saint Domingue must have imported close to 800,000 overall. By 1720, it had overtaken Martinique, and around 1740 the French islands overtook the British in population and sugar production. Underpricing their competitors, French sugar planters dominated the international market down to the Haitian Revolution of 1791, accounting for about 40 percent of production in the Atlantic world. Whereas most British colonies produced crude muscovado sugar, on average one-third of Saint Domingue's exports and almost all those of the French Windward Isles consisted of semirefined sugar, which was much more valuable. Sugar production declined in the Windwards after 1763 but continued to increase in Saint Domingue with the construction of irrigation systems in its dry western plains that led to very high yields per acre. Dominguan sugar estates had an average of about seventy-five slaves in 1720 and two hundred slaves in 1790; plantations in the Windward Isles were only half as big.

Not only was Saint Domingue the world's leading sugar producer for half a century, but for much of that time it was the main exporter of indigo and coffee as well. Indigo cultivation was often a stepping-stone to sugar production in the French islands. In Martinique and Guadeloupe it was largely abandoned by the early eighteenth century. In Saint Domingue, however, as old plantations converted to sugar, the crop was introduced into new frontier zones. The colony's output continued to expand and exceeded one thousand tons annually before it declined in the late 1770s. The first West Indian island to grow coffee was Martinique, where it was smuggled from Dutch Surinam in the 1720s. There and in Guadeloupe coffee cultivation spread throughout the century. Yet it was in the mountains of Saint Domingue that the crop had its greatest success. First introduced in the 1740s, coffee cultivation underwent booms in the 1760s and 1780s, when smallholders cleared much of the highland forests. Coffee and indigo workforces came to average about thirty to sixty slaves. Steadily increasing their dominance in world coffee markets, the French controlled at least 80 percent of New World production by the late 1780s. Saint Domingue alone produced more than 60 percent, five or six times as much as Surinam, its closest rival. At the same time, the colony briefly became the Americas' major cotton grower and supplied one-sixth of the booming British market. Saint Domingue's cotton was high-grade, whereas its coffee, sugar, and indigo were mass-market rather than premium quality. Finally, the French islands were the West Indies' main cacao producers, though they ranked a long way behind mainland Guayaquil and Venezuela.

Estimates of the value of this phenomenal quantity of commodity production vary. According to official customs evaluations, which understated true market value, French Caribbean exports to France in the period from 1787 to 1790 were worth annually thirty-five to forty-five million U.S. dollars, up from three million in 1716. The total value of Franco-Caribbean commerce, including the slave trade, peaked at nearly sixty million dollars. In addition, the value of Caribbean produce reexported from France reached thirty million dollars. French colonial trade, legal and contraband, with the United States and other colonies amounted to around seven million dollars. In 1790, 10 percent of U.S. exports went to the French islands, whose trade in 1778 was carried in 770 French ships and 2,500 much smaller, foreign vessels. Caribbean slavery generated some 70 percent of France's foreign trade, according to Pierre Pluchon's figures—though other authorities say 40 percent—and produced critical tax revenue while providing employment for hundreds of thousands in France. Caribbean trade was also the foundation of French seapower.

In social structure, the French Windwards, where whites made up around 12 percent of the population in the 1780s, were fairly typical of the non-Hispanic Caribbean. Saint Domingue's white community, some 6 percent of its population, was proportionately one of the Caribbean's smallest. Martinique's settlers were rather stable by West Indian standards. Many of its whites were locally born and married. It had relatively few absentee proprietors and poor whites. Most of Saint Domingue's sugar estates were owned by absentees in Europe and run by staffs of bachelor employees. Its smaller plantations had resident owners, but marriage was not common among them. As the main colony of Europe's most populous state, Saint Domingue also attracted large numbers of indigent young men seeking employment. Male colonists thus heavily outnumbered females. One thing most French colonies had in common was a "free colored" middle sector that was small by Hispanic standards but somewhat larger than that found in the British colonies. Here, too, however, Saint Domingue was exceptional. Whereas most Caribbean free coloreds were craftsmen, petty traders, or smallholders, Saint Domingue had a large number who were prosperous middling planters. They profited from the coffee and indigo booms, formed the backbone of the militia, and grew rapidly in numbers and wealth despite increasing discrimination against them after 1760. As the only sector of colonial society "native" to the Caribbean, some evolved a sense of "American" identity.

By the end of the eighteenth century, the slave populations of Martinique and Guadeloupe were fairly balanced between the sexes and consisted primarily of locally born creoles; a sizable minority was of mixed racial descent. In Saint Domingue, Africans always constituted the majority of the slaves. Most Africans in the French Caribbean came from West Central Africa and the Bight of Benin hinterland. People from the latter region formed the largest element in Martinique; "Congo" slaves were the most numerous in Saint Domingue. The sources of Guadeloupe's African population were more evenly distributed between these two regions, as well as Sierra Leone and Biafra. While slave imports slowed in the French Windward Isles, in Saint Domingue they rose from around twelve thousand per year in the 1760s to more than thirty thousand in the 1780s.

A creolized French, quite distinct from the metropolitan language, became the lingua franca of the colonies. Missionaries were active in the Windward Isles, at least until the expulsion of the Jesuits in the 1760s, but Christianization was only superficial in Saint Domingue. Even there, however, communal prayers were said daily on many plantations, and elements of Christianity were incorporated into the clandestine ceremonies of the slaves, which Europeans called "Vaudoux." Small revolts, poisoning scares, and

Table 2. Numbers and Types of Plantations, Late 1780s.			
	Saint Domingue	Martinique	Guadeloupe
Sugar	793	324	367
Indigo	3,171	—	—
Coffee	3,117	949	787
Cotton	787	652	251
Cacao	182	100	41

maroonage to the mountain forests dotted the history of the islands. Saint Domingue's long land frontier with sparsely settled Spanish Santo Domingo particularly favored fugitive slaves (maroons), as did Guyane's vast jungle. Modern Haitian historians such as Jean Fouchard have claimed for maroonage a political significance usually denied by European historians like Gabriel Debien. The latter argue that maroonage was generally motivated by individual, ad hoc causes, such as food shortages or avoidance of punishment, rather than an abstract pursuit of liberty, and that its most characteristic form was short-term absenteeism. Such historians also emphasize friction, rather than solidarity, between maroons and plantation slaves. These scholarly disagreements form part of a wider debate on the contribution to the Haitian Revolution (1791–1803) of internal factors (maroonage, voodoo, demographic imbalance) and external factors (disruption caused by the French Revolution).

Revolutionary Period (1789–1815)

The French Revolution of 1789 enflamed aspirations at all levels of colonial society while weakening the forces that had held them in check. The words "liberty and equality" in the revolutionary slogan were peculiarly dangerous to societies built on bondage and prejudice. Still more so was the revolution's weakening of colonial governments and fracturing of the white communities into warring factions. During the period from 1789 to 1791, French colonists were divided over the issues of self-government and democracy, while suppressing military mutinies, localized slave unrest, and free coloreds' demands for political rights. The Windward Isles' small size and the weakness of their free colored communities helped their white population remain dominant, but in the northern plain of Saint Domingue there broke out in August 1791 the largest and most destructive of all New World slave revolts. Coinciding with risings by free coloreds in other parts of the colony, the revolt proved unstoppable. Most insurgents were Africans, but the main leaders were locally born creoles, often slave drivers or coachmen. Troops sent from France were decimated by fever epidemics and proved ineffective against the insurgents' guerrilla tactics. The French government was forced to concede racial equality in the colonies in order to gain the free coloreds' assistance against the slaves. However, the outbreak of war with England and Spain in 1793 further complicated the situation. French planters rallied to foreign invaders, and the Spanish recruited rebel slaves to drive out the French. Fearing it would lose Saint Domingue,

the French Republic responded by abolishing slavery throughout its empire. During the mid-1790s, it built a radical, multiracial coalition in the Caribbean that spread slave and free colored rebellion in enemy colonies.

Martinique was occupied by British troops before its slaves could be emancipated, but Guadeloupe became a center of revolutionary activity organized by the French radical Victor Hugues. Blacks in Saint Lucia fought an intermittent guerrilla war against British invaders for four years. Meanwhile, the former slave Toussaint-Louverture drove the Spanish and British out of Saint Domingue and established an autonomous dictatorship, while maintaining nominal loyalty to France. Overriding the aspirations of the mass of ex-slaves to become peasant freeholders, Toussaint and his black generals established a forced labor regime to preserve the export economy that financed their armies. Victor Hugues did likewise.

The rise of Napoleon Bonaparte ended the alliance between French radicalism and black revolutionaries. Napoleon's desire to reassert French control and reestablish slavery and white supremacy precipitated an apocalyptic war of independence in Saint Domingue (1802–1803) that ended in the creation of Haiti. Amid terrible carnage, slavery and racial discrimination were restored in Guadeloupe, though the abolition of night work on sugar estates proved a durable gain of the revolutionary years.

Restoration and Abolition (1815–1848)

The French royalist government that was restored in 1815 returned its remaining colonies to the prerevolutionary status quo. After losing Saint Domingue, Saint Lucia, and Tobago, France ceased to be a major colonial power. To build up its naval strength, it fostered a considerable increase in sugar production in the Windward Isles and Guyane. Despite Napoleon's belated ending of the slave trade, slave imports were revived and continued on a clandestine basis until the revolution of 1830. Far from dominating the world market, as in the eighteenth century, French Caribbean sugar production could now survive only within the protected home market, where it faced increasing competition from beet sugar. Coffee and other secondary crops declined sharply. Slave revolts, poisoning scares, and conspiracies continued.

In 1833, the new government, following the British example, accorded civil equality to the rapidly growing free colored population and began debate on how to end slavery safely. Through the 1830s and 1840s, legislation was passed to ameliorate the conditions of slaves. Owing to the weakness of the antislavery move-

MOREAU DE SAINT-MÉRY, M. L. E. *Description topographique, physique, civile, politique et hisorique de la partie française de l'isle Saint-Domingue.* 1958.

PETITJEAN ROGET, JACQUES. *La société d'habitation de la Martinique: Un demisiècle de formation, 1635–1685.* 1980.

———. *Vaudou, sorciers, empoisonneurs: De Saint-Domingue à Haïti.* 1987.

PLUCHON, PIERRE. *Histoire de la colonisation française.* 1991.

TOMICH, DALE. *Slavery in the Circuit of Sugar: Martinique and the World Economy, 1830–1848.* 1990.

David Geggus

Spanish Colonies

The Caribbean islands conquered and settled by Spaniards—Cuba, Hispaniola, and Puerto Rico—were among the longest-running slave societies in the New World. For nearly four hundred years, slaves and slave labor were a permanent part of these islands' social and economic landscape. There, as elsewhere in the Americas, slaves performed the most strenuous labor, which Europeans disdained. Slaves grew crops for local consumption and for export; they mined for gold, copper, and other metals; they built the massive fortifications that permitted Spain to keep control of strategically valuable possessions, in the face of mounting challenges by its enemies; and they performed a range of personal and domestic services for which no other workers were available.

These slaves and their descendants constituted one of the most significant population groups in the Hispanic Caribbean, and their presence often provoked apprehension and fear among the dominant whites. For as long as bondage was permitted by law, they took part in all the main social and cultural activities in the colonies. Interacting with other ethnic elements of the population, they helped create vibrant cultures blending African, European, and Amerindian traditions. Yet, although slaves made their presence felt in just about every sphere, on a daily basis, only for relatively short periods did slavery stand out as the most important social institution and did slaves constitute the largest single element in the population. In the Spanish Caribbean, therefore, the presence of slaves almost always harbored a contradiction: they were a key ingredient in colonial society but rarely, and then only for limited periods of time, did they make up more than a small minority of the population.

The long history of Spanish Caribbean slavery may be broken up into three cycles, each corresponding to a distinct mode of appropriating slave labor. The first was a period of institutional experimentation spanning the years 1493 to 1575; the second, an era of decline and involution, covered the years 1575 to 1763; and the third, a phase of marked resurgence and

A monument on Guadeloupe commemorates the 1848 abolition of slavery in all the French colonies. [Marc Garanger/Corbis]

ment and government indecisiveness, it required the creation of the Second Republic in 1848 to bring slavery to a sudden end.

See also CODE NOIR; MAROONS; PLANTATIONS; REBELLIONS AND VIOLENT RESISTANCE; SLAVE REPUBLICS; TOUSSAINT-LOUVERTURE.

BIBLIOGRAPHY

ADÉLAÏDE-MERLANDE, JACQUES. *La Caraïbe et al Guyane au temps de la Révolution et de l'Empire.* 1992.

CAUNA, JACQUES. *Au temps des isles à sucre: Histoire d'une plantation de Saint-Domingue au XVIIIe siècle.* 1987.

DEBIEN, GABRIEL. *Les esclaves aux Antilles française aux XVIIe et XVIIIe siècles.* 1974.

FICK, CAROLYN E. *The Making of Haiti: The Saint Domingue Revolution from Below.* 1990.

FORSTER, ROBERT. *Sugar and Slavery, Family and Race: The Letters and Diary of Pierre Dessalles, Planter in Martinque, 1808–1856.* 1996.

GEGGUS, DAVID. *Slavery, War and Revolution: The British Occupation of Saint Domingue, 1793–1798.* 1982.

HALL, GWENDOLYN M. *Social Control in Slave Plantation Societies: A Comparison of St. Domingue and Cuba.* 1971.

JAMES, C. L. R. *The Black Jacobins: Toussaint l'Ouverture and the San Domingo Revolution.* 1980.

heightened exploitation of slave labor, primarily in the plantation sector, lasted from 1763 to 1886.

The first period (1493–1575) witnessed flexible experimentation with various modes of forced labor. African chattel slavery, initially one among several alternatives, gradually overshadowed all the rest in magnitude, convenience of exploitation, and cost. In this phase of the era of conquest and colonization, the Spanish enslaved some of the Amerindian inhabitants and subjected others to repartimiento, a feudal institution carried over from medieval Castile that involved exaction of labor and tribute but no ownership of people. Thus, the sedentary Tainos of Hispaniola and Puerto Rico, and the Ciboneys of Cuba, were among the first whose persons the conquerors appropriated on the presumption, expressed for the first time by Columbus himself in one of his letters to King Ferdinand and Queen Isabella, that the wealth of the islands he encountered in his first voyage included "so many slaves that they are innumerable, and they will come from the idolaters." Later, when humanitarian legislation forbade the enslavement of peaceful Indians, idolaters or not, Spanish settlers applied this principle of enslavability only to the allegedly fierce Caribs and other groups from the Lesser Antilles and northern South America, that is, to those groups who resisted Spanish advances most vehemently.

The experiments with Indian slavery did not last long, however. Not only did the crown give limited protection to a rapidly dwindling aboriginal population; it found a better way to supply its colonies with needed labor—bringing captives from Africa. With the pacified Indians dying off in huge numbers and the supply from so-called hostile tribes dwindling, a trade in slaves from western Africa came to replace unreliable Indian laborers. This decision gave impetus to a transatlantic traffic that would shape the social and cultural outlines of vast portions of the New World.

For a couple of decades, enslaved Africans worked alongside repartimiento Indians in gold mining, the original mainstay of the islands' economy. With gold deposits rapidly nearing depletion after 1530, the colonists placed many of them in sugar production. By the time the shift from mining to agriculture occurred, it had become abundantly clear that the future labor force in export activities would involve Africans almost exclusively. The rise of sugarcane farming and sugar manufacture, especially in Hispaniola and Puerto Rico, thus marked the first example in the New World of what Philip Curtin has called the "plantation complex": a series of interconnected trades in commodities and people that spanned the Atlantic and whose cornerstone was the institution of African chattel slavery. It was in the Spanish Caribbean that this complex was tested for the first time on the western shores of the Atlantic. At its peak in the 1560s and 1570s, the sugar industry of the Spanish Caribbean was entirely dependent on imported African slave labor, introduced by Portuguese traders under contract with the Spanish crown and by English privateers, of whom the most famous was Sir John Hawkins.

The second cycle of Spanish Caribbean slavery, which spanned almost two centuries (1575–1763), witnessed a diminution in the use of slave labor and in the percentage of slaves in the overall population. The rise of Brazilian sugar production put an end to the Hispaniolan and Puerto Rican slave plantation economy in the late sixteenth century, and urban centers then became the main focus of life in this part of the Caribbean. This was especially so in Cuba, whose capital city, Havana, became one of the main port cities in the Americas after the last third of the sixteenth century. Historians concur that the severity of exploitation diminished, partly because of the shift away from a rural concentration of slaves. In comparison with rural areas, cities provided better opportunities for all people, including slaves, to exercise some autonomy in life and labor. As a result, in the period under consideration a growing percentage of slaves attained their freedom, either by self-purchase (a practice known as coartación) or through manumission initiated by the master. Also, intermarriage between people of different racial backgrounds occurred more frequently, with a consequent increase in the population of mixed parentage. Spanish Caribbean societies thus became slave societies that included a substantial segment of people of mixed (European and African) descent. These people were called *morenos libres* (free blacks), *mulatos,* and *pardos,* each of these categories indicating a range of visible combinations of European and African phenotypic features, with pardos at the lighter-skinned end of the spectrum.

In sharp contrast to the relative autarky of the second cycle, the third (1763–1886) witnessed the conversion of Cuba and Puerto Rico into two of the world's most important sugar producers. Of the two, Cuba was by far the biggest—after about 1840 it produced more cane sugar than any other country in the world—and the most important slave society in all of the Caribbean once emancipation had taken place in Britain (1834). It also received the greatest number of slaves imported from Africa (about 780,000 between 1791 and 1870, second only to Brazil in the nineteenth-century Americas). In contrast to these remaining Spanish colonies, Santo Domingo, which obtained its independence from Spain in 1821 only to lose it to neighboring Haiti almost immediately afterward, ceased being a slave society when the new rulers abolished slavery in 1822. The Haitians, who controlled the entire island of Hispaniola for the next twenty-two years, were themselves the product of a violent revolution (the Haitian Revolution, 1791–1804) which had begun as a rebellion by slaves against their French masters.

Plantations in Cuba and Puerto Rico, even at this relatively late date in the history of New World slavery, helped establish social patterns resembling the eighteenth-century slave societies of the French and British Caribbean, like St. Domingue, Barbados, and Jamaica. Among these patterns were an exploitation of slave labor much more intense than in the previous period, a sharp rise in slaves imported from Africa, noticeable—and to whites, worrisome—increases in the colored population, heightened social tension and racism, and severe repression of conspiracies and rebellions. This final cycle of Spanish Caribbean slavery was also marked by intense struggles by slaves, and by others on their behalf, to achieve emancipation. This epochal event finally occurred when the last *emancipados* or "apprentices" were freed in Cuba in 1886.

While they came to resemble the classic "sugar colonies" of Britain and France in key ways, the Cuban and Puerto Rican slave regimes of the nineteenth cen-

A Puerto Rican slave takes care of a child. [Leonard de Selva/Corbis]

tury were also peculiar by Caribbean standards. For one thing, slaves never attained the absolute majority of the population to which they had risen in the sugar islands at comparable stages of development. In Cuba at the peak of slave importations from Africa during the 1840s, slaves accounted for 43 percent of the total population, whites made up 42 percent, and free people of African descent 15 percent. These categories in Puerto Rico were 12 percent, 48 percent, and 40 percent, respectively. The high proportion of people of mixed descent in Puerto Rico indicates that miscegenation had occurred on a very large scale in this society during the preceding centuries. Such social and racial breakdowns contrasted with the proportion of slaves—80 percent or more—typical in the other sugar islands, where the free coloreds were therefore a much smaller fraction of the total than in the Hispanic colonies. A second demographic difference was that slaves who lived and worked in cities in the Spanish colonies (particularly in Cuba) were a larger share of the total than their counterparts in the non-Hispanic colonies. Though most Hispanic slaves lived and worked on rural estates, as many as one-sixth lived in cities, where they worked as common laborers, peddlers, craftsmen, domestic servants, prostitutes, and the like.

Nineteenth-century Spanish Caribbean slavery was exceptional in several other ways. First, slaves had greater opportunities for manumission. Whether by the masters' initiative or by the slaves' own actions through coartación, manumissions continued to be more common in Cuba and Puerto Rico, even at the height of the plantation cycle, than they had been in surrounding territories at comparable stages. Second, contrary to the British and French experience, most slaves introduced after 1820—the vast majority of the total for the entire cycle—were illegal, as Spain had formally agreed with Great Britain in 1817 to end its involvement in the transatlantic slave trade, beginning three years later. The illegality of slave imports had measurable consequences. The danger of capture by British anti–slave trade patrols inflated the price of captives, and it also distorted the demographic composition of the slaves because it predisposed traders to bring as many women as possible to the colonies in order to enhance opportunities for reproduction. At the same time, the illegal trafficking attracted different groups of participants, drew on new sources of financing, and possibly increased the overall profitability of the nefarious trade. Still another way in which Caribbean slavery was exceptional is the fact that planters were able to influence the transition from slave labor to free labor. A protracted emancipation allowed slaveholders and officials time to plan and prepare for a deliberate, gradual transition to free labor. Owners took effective measures to replace the slave workforce in the long run. Beginning in the 1840s, for example, Cuban planters introduced Chinese coolies to supplement the declining slave population. At about the same time Puerto Rican planters devised a system of compulsory labor to force that island's large free peasantry into waged work. Although, in the final analysis, the slave system collapsed faster than most of its supporters had hoped, thanks to these cautionary measures Cuba and Puerto Rico experienced less economic disruption during and after the emancipatory process than did their neighbors.

Although these conditions ensured that the last century of Spanish Caribbean slavery had exceptional features, the slaves' own resistance showed that brutal exploitation and fierce resistance—the fundamental formula of all slave societies—remained in force. Numerous rebellions and conspiracies kept the master classes unsettled and helped ensure their continued allegiance to Spain at a time when other colonies less dependent on slavery had declared their independence. Slave resistance, even at the risk of capital punishment, seemed to prove in Cuba and Puerto Rico that the slave system had always remained unstable, a powder keg no less explosive than some of their neighbors had been a generation or two earlier. As might be expected, slave rebellions and conspiracies grew more frequent during the period of largest African importations (ca. 1790–1850). In Cuba, the Escalera conspiracy of 1843–1844 brought the unwelcome revelation that slaves could conspire with free people of color and with British abolitionists, in an array of converging plots, to bring about a sudden and violent end to the slave system. It took swift action by Spanish authorities to prevent a conflagration. But as thousands of accused conspirators were put to death in 1844, Cuba's fate as a slave society was sealed. Its dominant groups would henceforth measure the country's sugar wealth against the terror and violence sparked by racial hatred and class feuds. Over the next four decades, the uncertain prospect of emancipation—its implications for the economy, politics, and society—would be the central issue occupying the people of both Cuba and Puerto Rico.

In Puerto Rico, where slaves had been very important to the sugar industry but not at all to the large coffee sector or the small-scale peasant sector, final liberation came in 1876, after a three-year period of apprenticeship. In Cuba the last slaves attained freedom in 1886, after a similar but longer (six-year) transition. Emancipation was the result of a complex interaction of factors; local, imperial, and international. Pressure from British abolitionists and other forces helped put an end to the Cuban slave trade in 1867, yet despite the loss of the vital source of new slaves (the slave population could not reproduce itself), plantation slavery as a system of labor procurement did not immediately deteriorate. The larger planters of western and central Cuba continued to rely heavily on slave labor even as the 1870s advanced, as did most of the wealthiest sugar barons of Puerto Rico. Two interconnected events, however, helped speed up the liberation process: Cuba's Ten Years' War (1868–1878), a struggle for independence waged primarily by planters and other farmers from the eastern provinces; and the Moret Law (1870), a Spanish statute that freed slaves born after September 1868 and those aged sixty and over. Each helped undermine Cuban slavery, not least by giving the slaves themselves legal and military weapons to further their long struggle for freedom. When, in March 1873, the Spanish Cortes (parliament) decreed the emancipation of Puerto Rico's 30,000 bondsmen, Cuba's slave population, ten times larger than that, was already on a path of gradual, steady liberation.

Thus through the Moret Law, Puerto Rican emancipation, and freedom decreed by the rebels in the east of Cuba, the slave system of the Spanish Caribbean came tumbling down during the 1870s. By 1877, more than half of the 400,000 slaves counted in the 1867 census of Cuba and Puerto Rico had been liberated. The remainder, still confined to some of Cuba's most productive estates, would be freed gradually by a Spanish law of 1880 that created an apprenticeship system called the *patronato*, intended to last eight years. But numerous freedmen's challenges against their *patronos* led Spain in 1886 to put a premature end to this system, and with it, to the longest-running chapter in the history of slavery in the New World.

See also BRAZIL; CHATTEL SLAVERY; COARTACIÓN; CUBA; LABOR SYSTEMS; MANUMISSION; PLANTATIONS; REBELLIONS AND VIOLENT RESISTANCE; SLAVE TRADE.

BIBLIOGRAPHY

ANDREWS, K. R. *The Spanish Caribbean: Trade and Plunder, 1530–1560.* 1978.

BERGAD, L. W., F. IGLESIAS GARCÍA, and M. D. C. BARCIA "The Cuban Slave Market, 1790–1880." *Cambridge Latin American Studies* 79 (1995).

CURTIN, P. D. *The Rise and Fall of the Plantation Complex: Essays in Atlantic History.* 1980.

DÍAZ SOLER, L. M. *Historia de la esclavitud negra en Puerto Rico.* 1953, 1970.

KNIGHT, F. W. *Slave Society in Cuba during the Nineteenth Century.* 1969.

LARRAZABAL BLANCO, C. *Los negros y la esclavitud en Santo Domingo.* 1975.

MORENO FRAGINALS, M. *El ingenio: Complejo socioeconómico cubano del azúcar.* 1964, 1978.

MURRAY, D. R. *Odious Commerce: Britain, Spain, and the Abolition of the Cuban Slave Trade.* 1980.

PAQUETTE, R. L. *Sugar Is Made with Blood: The Conspiracy of "La Escalera" and the Conflict between Empires over Slavery in Cuba.* 1988.

SCARANO, F. A. *Sugar and Slavery in Puerto Rico: The Plantation Economy of Ponce, 1800–1850.* 1984.

SCOTT, R. J. *Slave Emancipation in Cuba: The Transition to Free Labor, 1860–1899.* 1985.

ZAMORA, M. "Reading Columbus" In *Latin American Literature and Culture,* edited by R. González Echeverría. 1993.

Francisco A. Scarano

Dutch Colonies

In 1634 Johannes van Walbeeck seized the island Curaçao, off the coast of Venezuela, for the Dutch West India Company. In the period between 1634 and 1648, the Dutch also captured two Leeward islands—Bonaire and Aruba—and three Windward islands: Saba, Saint Eustatius, and Saint Martin.

After establishing peace with the Spanish in 1648, Curaçao became an important transit harbor for slaves destined to be sold for silver in Spain's mainland colonies. Between 1651 and 1675 the Dutch transported 63,000 slaves from Africa to the New World, most often via Curaçao. In 1668 Curaçao was the most important slave depot in the West Indies. At that time there was a permanent stock of 3,000 slaves on the island. Overall, until around 1780, the Dutch shipped 457,000 slaves to the Americas, of which 31 percent landed in Spanish America, most often through Curaçao.

Plantations were established on a small scale in the Dutch Antilles, mostly for the production of food crops and livestock to support this trade. The Leeward islands were too dry for the cultivation of market crops. Curaçao, the only island with a considerable population, accounted for 13,000 slaves around 1780, 70 percent of the total population. In 1816 the island had 14,000 inhabitants, of whom approximately 11,000 were coloreds and blacks. The number of slaves had dwindled to around 7,000.

In 1721 only a few hundred black slaves worked on Bonaire, and slavery was even less prevalent on Aruba. Aruba's population of 1,700 included 564 Indians and 336 slaves; Bonaire had 700 free inhabitants and 430 slaves.

In 1660 around 600 whites lived on Saint Martin, owning ten sugar enterprises. Saint Eustatius, with a population of 1,000 free inhabitants and 600 slaves in 1665, concentrated on producing tobacco. Almost no one lived on Saba in the seventeenth century except 125 Europeans, 85 slaves, and here and there a few Indians. Around 1750 the population on these three Windward islands totaled 7,300, most of them slaves, except on Saba, where there were more free people than slaves.

Most of the whites and later also the colored proprietors of the Antilles islands owned slaves, if only a few each. In 1736, 376 inhabitants of Curaçao possessed slaves, although most (227) had only one or two. Willem van Uytrecht's widow owned the most: 120. Most slave proprietors owned fewer than five slaves at the time of abolition in 1863.

The number manumitted in the Dutch Antilles grew substantially. In the period 1816 to 1863 more than 2,100 slaves were emancipated. Between 1817 and 1833 the free population became larger than the slave population, and in the last year of slavery the number of free coloreds equaled 6,531, as compared with 5,894 slaves.

Two recorded slave rebellions occurred on Curaçao, a small one in 1750 and a larger one in 1795. The rebellion in 1795 was clearly influenced by the incidents on Haiti. Two thousand slaves participated at its high point. The rebellion came to an end when slaves captured the two most important leaders and extradited them to the authorities.

During the seventeenth century, the black population gradually converted to Christianity. The majority of blacks and coloreds (both free and slaves) on the Leeward islands were Catholic in 1816. The inhabitants of the Windward islands were converted by English Methodists, followers of John Wesley. When Wesleyans arrived on Saint Eustatius in 1787, they encountered an already established black Methodist community, founded by a slave, with at least 250 members.

See also BRAZIL; PLANTATIONS; REBELLIONS AND VIOLENT RESISTANCE; SLAVE TRADE.

BIBLIOGRAPHY

GOSLINGA, CORNELIS C. *The Dutch in the Caribbean and in the Guianas, 1680-1791.* 1985.

———. *The Dutch in the Caribbean and on the Wild Coast, 1580–1680.* 1971.

HOETINK, HARRY. *Het patroon van de oude Curaçaose samenleving: Een sociologische studie.* 1958.

HOOG, LEVINA DE. *Van rebellie tot revolutie: Oorzaken en achtergronden van de Curaçaose slavenopstanden in 1750 en 1795.* 1983.

POSTMA, JOHANNES M. *The Dutch in the Atlantic Slave Trade 1600–1815.* 1990.

RENKEMA, W. E. *Het Curaçaose plantagebedrijf in de negentiende eeuw.* 1981.

Wim Hoogbergen

Danish Colonies

Danish rule over Saint Thomas, Saint John, and Saint Croix (the Virgin Islands) was established during the period from 1672 to 1733 and lasted until 1917.

Occupation was motivated by shipping interests and plans to develop plantation agriculture. Slave imports from West Africa escalated when sugar cultivation on Saint Croix expanded after 1733. Total slave imports are estimated at approximately 96,000. Importation was partly on Danish ships, which could operate from Danish trade forts on the Gold Coast (Ghana). Slaves constituted nearly 90 percent of the total population from the 1750s to the 1830s. Their number peaked at 35,000 in 1802 and then declined to earlier levels of about 20,000. High imports, compared with the actual slave population, reflect a vicious exploitation of the plantation slaves, resulting in high mortality and low birthrates. Escalating prices of land and a high turnover of land ownership placed a premium on short-term profits, which explain the extreme exploitation. The powerful political influence of planters and the weak colonial administration perpetuated these harsh conditions. The severity of planter discipline was also influenced by a long history of slave resistance: *marronage* and revolt. To justify the draconian slave laws, the planters cited an uprising on Saint John in 1732, when newly arrived (*bosal*) slaves from the kingdom of Akwamu on the Gold Coast (war captives after a devastating defeat of the Akwamu army in 1730) took temporary control, and an aborted conspiracy on Saint Croix in 1759. More humane policies in the early nineteenth century could not restrain resistance. A massive revolt forced Governor Peter von Scholten to accept emancipation in 1848.

See also SCANDINAVIA; SLAVE TRADE.

BIBLIOGRAPHY

GREEN-PEDERSEN, SVEND ERIK. "The Danish Negro Slave Trade: Some New Archival Findings in particular with Reference to the Danish West Indies." In *De la traîte l'esclavage*, edited by Serge Daget. Vol. 1. 1988.

HALL, NEVILLE A. T. *Slave Society in the Danish West Indies.* 1992.

HERNÆS, PER. *Slaves, Danes and African Coast Society.* 1995.

JOHANSEN, HANS C. "Slave Demography of the Danish West Indian Islands." *Scandinavian Economic History Review* 29: 1 (1981): 1–20.

OLWIG, KAREN FOG. *Cultural Adaptation and Resistance on St. John: Three Centuries of Afro-Caribbean Life.* 1987.

Per Hernæs

Carving

See Arts.

Casas, Bartolomé de Las

See Las Casas, Bartolomé de.

Caste Systems

Castes are most commonly associated with India, but castelike systems have existed in a number of historical settings including Japan, Korea, Somalia, Guatemala, and the United States. These castelike systems usually have one or more outcast groups rather than socially segregating all strata from one another, as is the case in a fully developed caste system.

Caste systems are structures of social inequality in which the different strata are ranked and segregated primarily in terms of relative status rather than in terms of wealth or political power per se. Status is the accumulated expression of approval and disapproval of other people. The structural characteristics of caste systems—ranked and segmented social strata, status ascribed at birth on the basis of kinship, highly restricted mobility, stability, endogamy, commensality, and elaborate norms and rituals—are rooted in the nature of status and its centrality in these stratification systems.

These are important differences among these various systems, produced by the particular economic and cultural contexts in which they emerge. For example, Hinduism profoundly shaped the Indian caste system by providing religious justifications for the social inequality and elaborate rituals that reinforce these inequalities. In contrast, slavery was contradictory to the basic ideology of the United States, and when it was abolished, the continuing inequalities became justified primarily in terms of the racist ideologies of the Jim Crow South. Some analyses of caste systems place less emphasis on the importance of status differences per se and stress the importance of ritual purity, kinship, or bodily substances.

In most caste systems status differences are closely correlated with other forms of economic and political inequality, but they are not reducible to such differences. No matter how rich lower-caste Indians or blacks in the Jim Crow South became, they did not receive high levels of respect and deference. Conversely, no matter how poor the Brahmins, they typically received a deference not available to the low castes. This is not to say that higher levels of wealth or political power have no effect on improving caste status.

There are slave systems that have castelike features and caste systems in which slavery is practiced, but the two features can vary independently of one another. Orlando Patterson analyzed the data from *The Ethnographic Atlas* and found that most slave systems did not have castes of any kind. Nonetheless, it was common for societies with castelike systems to have slavery. In India, slavery is mentioned in some of the earliest texts. While most slaves have come from the lowest castes, not all members of these castes were slaves, and in many historical periods members of even the highest castes could be enslaved through war or debt.

In caste systems the fundamental mechanism of domination is dishonor, while in slavery it is physical force. Though it is common for both types of systems to use both means of dominance, the raison d'être of each system is different. Hence, the fundamental problem of social control in slave systems is to keep those who are enslaved incorporated into the system, that is, to keep them from absconding. In contrast, the fundamental concern in caste systems is to keep those who have lower levels of status and honor at an appropriate distance—to exclude them as respectable members of the community. Hence the archetypical subordinate groups are outcasts, not slaves.

See also INDIAN SUBCONTINENT; PATTERSON THESIS.

BIBLIOGRAPHY

DUMONT, LOUIS. *Homo Hierarchicus: The Caste System and Its Implications.* 1980.
KOLENDA, PAULINE. *Caste in Contemporary India.* 1984.
MARRIOTT, MCKIM. "Hindu Transactions: Diversity without Dualism." In *Transaction and Meaning*, edited by Bruce Kapferer. 1976.
MILNER, MURRAY, JR. *Status and Sacredness: A General Theory of Status Relations and an Analysis of Indian Culture.* 1994.
PATTERSON, ORLANDO. *Slavery and Social Death: A Comparative Study.* 1982.

Murray Milner, Jr.

Catchers, Slave

See Escape.

Celtic Cultures

See Ancient Rome; Ireland; Irish Anti-Slavery Society.

Central Africa

Related articles may be found at the entries Africa; East Africa; North Africa; Northeast Africa; Slave Trade; Southern Africa; West Africa. *See also the note accompanying the entry* Africa *for further information about the organization of these entries.*

Central Africa—as historians divide the continent before the advent of twentieth-century colonial and national boundaries—included the great equatorial forest drained by the Zaire (or Congo) River system (as far east as the chain of deep lakes extending southward to Lake Malawi) and the savanna grasslands south and north of it. The northern savannas extended eastward from the Cameroons Mountains in the northwest, well to the south of Lake Chad, to Lake Albert and the upper Nile River. The southern grasslands covered the upper Zaire and Zambezi tributaries from Lake Malawi west to the Atlantic near the mouth of the Kunene River.

Within this region transactions in human beings, glossed by historians as "slavery," developed out of strongly communal values inherited from a shared ancestral Bantu-language culture. This culture viewed wealth, prestige, and power primarily in terms of debts and dependency claimed from others, and it treated material assets—that is, goods fabricated or purchased for purposes other than consumption—as investments in control over other people.

Ambitious men sought to command as wide a range of human abilities as they could manage, which made sense in a productive economy based more on knowledge (both spiritual and practical), on the fertility of the land and of women, on technique and artisanry, and on collaboration than on mechanical, powered technologies. To achieve such power, they assembled the most varied possible retinues of people subordinated to them: wives and their children (in patrilineal societies) or nieces and nephews (in matrilineal ones) and other junior kin; unrelated male clients (political as well as personal); hostages (often termed "pawns") held as human security against loans of material wealth they had made to others; and isolated individuals taken in under terms of helpless degradation that approached the humiliation and impotence of slavery in modern Western cultures. Most of these slaves would have been women, who suffered sexual exploitation that—along with polygynous marriage—made concubinage meaningless. Such women were valued also for their reproductive capabilities, since children born to them "belonged" to the father in the sense that the children lacked both relatives and in-laws on the slave mother's side who might protect them. As such, they could be driven to perform physical labor in the master's (father's) compound or in his fields.

Such "slavery" of kinless individuals in Central Africa (as, in fact, in many other parts of the continent and elsewhere in the non-Western world) did not contrast with "freedom," in the sense of an individual's personal autonomy in relation to her or his fellows or to civil rights guaranteed by a state. Rather, it set slaves off as *not belonging* to any of the local communities of people—kin, or the following of a powerful "big man," or an enduring polity—that might guarantee personal security, respect, dignity, or honor and secure access to the necessities of life. Since individuals in these intensely local, intimate social environments prospered only by establishing multiple linkages with everyone around them, abandonment by one's kin or patron or ruler exposed an individual to death or to the whims, vicious or benign, of anyone who would provide for him or her. Patrons or senior male relatives held rights over the people dependent on them that they might transfer, but recognized limits—enforced by relatives in the case of wives and pawns, or claimed for themselves by voluntary clients who simply threatened to leave—exposed such people to far fewer risks than the total abandonment of slavery. In this array of interdependent and dependent relationships characteristic of nearly every culture in Central Africa, slavery was the extreme form, distinct in the dislocation, dishonor, and dependency that such slaves endured.

African slavery of this sort has often been characterized as "assimilative" and contrasted with the castelike exclusion of modern Western (especially North American) slaves from the societies of the masters in which they found themselves held. It has also been distinguished as "mild" or "benign" compared with the "harshness" seen in bondage of more familiar types. Scholars have recently tended to diminish these dichotomies as they have discovered the moral, personal, and cultural autonomy that enslaved Americans created for themselves and as historians have grasped the vulnerability of abandonment and isolation within communal societies, the often severe treatment of such orphaned people in Africa, and the shame of their dependency. Still other observers of African slavery of this type continue to sharpen the contrast, sometimes to emphasize the injustice of slavery in American cultures claiming dedication to human equality and rights and sometimes out of a romantic attachment to an imagined Eden-like Africa unburdened by the postslavery racial trauma of the late-twentieth-century Americas. In fact, in Central Africa as in every other part of the continent, hundreds of different practices of slavery arose out of as many distinctive cultural heritages and historical circumstances.

A few slaves must have figured among the dependents accumulated by ambitious, successful men in Central Africa from the first settlement of the region by Bantu-speaking farmers three thousand or more years ago. These settlers seem generally to have collaborated with the hunters and gatherers whose lands they entered, but conflicts would sometimes have generated individual captives taken in as rightless slavelike dependents. Occasionally women from the foraging population must have entered Bantu farmers' villages in such "slavery," as well as through marriage alliances with recognized hunting groups, as the indigenous bands collapsed. As the farmers formed communities of their own, they must have expelled recalcitrant youths and relatives accused as witches, thieves, or adulterers; so long as the settlement frontier remained open—that is, until about the sixth century C.E.—these banished troublemakers could set off on their own or find recognized places in neighboring groups eager to attract followers to populate new, still-open lands.

In the following millennium, from about 500 to 1500 C.E., communities grew increasingly pressed for living space for their own members and would have worked out judicial procedures for expelling (or killing) uncontrollable criminals. Neighboring communities would have accepted such exiles only under terms of extreme degradation and tight, slavelike discipline. Wars between crowded neighbors competing for territory would have produced captives, especially women valued for their ability to reproduce and increase their numbers and hence increase the power of the captors; such captivity met the immediate challenge of winning hostilities, of course, only at the cost of intensifying the long-term population pressures behind such conflicts. For want of direct evidence other than semantic and historical-linguistic analysis of the hundreds of Bantu languages that Central African farmers developed as they settled, it is impossible to specify the numbers of such slaves in Central Africa beyond guessing that they increased over time from "occasional" to "a few" and were more significant to the individuals who controlled (not "owned" in any modern proprietary sense) them than prominent in local institutions or productive activities or determinative of relations among groups. They would have started their enslavement in humble, perhaps abused positions, but most remained long enough to gain a measure of protection from a patron or spouse, sometimes improving their personal circumstances significantly. Their children, having one local parent, were correspondingly more integrated, though even a single slave ancestor was seldom totally forgotten.

The arrival of European explorers along the Atlantic coast of central Africa at the end of the fifteenth century, then traders and missionaries in the sixteenth-century Kongo kingdom and regions to the south, and eventually military authorities in the small Portuguese colony of Angola after about 1575 gradually embedded capture and enslavement in political and economic institutions throughout the region. The Europeans bought Africans as slaves in small numbers at first and then in quantities that rose from ten thousand or so each year in the 1590s to as many as thirty thousand annually through the 1840s. Africans able to get their hands on the goods they provided used them to convert local political rivalries into sustained wars and systematic raiding for captives and to take advantage of dispersals of farming populations during recurrent severe droughts in the southwestern part of the region to seize refugees. When they could, they retained the people they seized, or bought, and settled them in novel communities composed predominantly (though rarely exclusively) of captives and refugees, selling only some of them to Europeans for more imported goods. Through this fundamental conversion of social, political, and ultimately economic arrangements to revolve around these new kinds of slaves, rather than engaging them in the older kinds of dependency and alliance, as well as by selling others enslaved to Europeans, Central Africa entered the expanding Atlantic merchant capitalist economy of the time.

Thus, each succeeding generation poured new commercial wine into political and economic bottles formed from inherited habits. The first to profit were mid-sixteenth-century political authorities (known as *ngola*) living in the hills above the lower Kwanza River, the core of the later Portuguese colony of Angola there that took its name from their title; by the time of the first Portuguese reports from the area in the 1560s, they were warlords with significant retinues of slaves. Others became professional bandits during a violent period of prolonged drought at the end of the century, seizing refugees and others, training and keeping the most promising youths as warriors, and selling the rest of their captives to the Portuguese, just then carving out their colony of Angola along the lower Kwanza River. The successors of these bandit gangs settled after 1650 in a ring of slave-raiding, slave-staffed, slave-selling states east and south of the Portuguese domains.

To the north, an early-sixteenth-century ruler—known as Alfonso I—south of the mouth of the great river (Zaire) consolidated a kingdom of Kongo around missionary Christian religious ideology; but his heirs, in competition with one another, destroyed it in the later 1600s, using retinues of slaves taken from the caravans of captives from the Angolan wars passing through their domains. Everywhere that rough, remote terrain offered some measure of protection from the violence spreading throughout the region—by 1700, as far as two hundred miles from the coast—warlords harbored other communities of refugees and bought slaves. Many of the modern ethnic identities of Central Africa derive from such resettlement as slaves.

Africans, competing for captives, both to replace their own followers and to sell to Europeans at the coast, advanced eastward through the southern savannas throughout the eighteenth century. Dutch merchants, then English and French traders, financed these new commercial networks with ample quantities of trade goods, often sold on credit. In the forest,

where communities could grow in size only through laborious clearing of the trees for agriculture, river peoples took advantage of inexpensive canoe transportation to employ male clients and other nonslave labor in local production and exchange—dyewoods, textiles, ivory, food—rather than sending them toward the coast. On the high plateau above the great bends of the Kwanza and Kunene Rivers, warlords known as Ovimbundu had built states by 1750, using slaves they had captured in the Angolan wars. East of the Kwango and Kasai Rivers, militarist leaders of communities scattered through the river valleys had joined in a slave-trading alliance known later to the Portuguese as the Lunda. Ovimbundu raiding and trading parties ranged through this region, scouring the populous valleys of the upper Zambezi River system for captives, while Lunda raiding parties preyed on the inhabitants of the moist, densely settled grasslands just south of the forest.

The violence of their wars eventually dissipated locally, as once-vulnerable victims united to defend themselves. It would then flare anew farther to the east, as the expanding commercial networks touched populations not prepared to resist. Nearer the Atlantic, African merchant princes in the older states prospered by organizing caravans to carry imports inland, driving the coffles of slaves to the coast, and repopulating their own lands by retaining slave women from them—in effect taking their profits in people. These traders owned their slaves in a more commercial, and surely often more brutal, sense than had earlier Africans, since such slaves could be sold at any time for imports. The traders became the dominant figures in a steadily growing part of the region.

By the 1840s and 1850s, when British abolitionists suppressed maritime slaving from Central African ports, the successors of these traders had refined their methods of acquiring and making profitable use of these slaves sufficiently that they were able to employ them in producing the commodities—beeswax, ivory, will "red" rubber—that then replaced people as the region's principal sources of the imports which had become essential to recruiting followings in much of Central Africa. Commodity producers in the forests thrived as exports rose in the nineteenth century, accumulating male slaves in communities so dedicated to trading that some gave up trying to reproduce biologically—since rampant venereal diseases had sterilized many women—and became business firms recruiting members exclusively by purchasing slaves.

The inhabitants of the relatively small settlements in the northern savannas remained isolated from the Atlantic trade's transformation of most Central African communities into slave societies, but they suffered

A certain Dr. Jameson, a friend of Cecil Rhodes, is shown negotiating with the Arab trader Tippu Tib. [Corbis-Bettmann]

brutally from raids mounted by the cavalry states of the central Sudan: Bornu, Wadai, Dar Fur, and others. They dispersed to survive the onslaught and lost too many of their members to the raiders to develop states or significant production or transportation systems based on slaves. Ivory hunters and slave raiders from Egypt and the Upper Nile brought modern weapons into the region in the 1860s and all but destroyed the surviving communities, gathering their survivors as slaves in war camps (*ribats*) and in a few military states along the upper tributaries of the Ubangi River (the Azande). Other traders-turned-raiders, so-called Swahili Arabs from Zanzibar, established similar slave-based war camps in the eastern forests along the Lualaba (upper Zaire) River at about the same time. The history of slavery for these people lay mainly in the fates of daughters and sons sold to Muslim masters in the Sudan, the Sahara, and North Africa; along the East African coast; and beyond.

A distinctive characteristic of early colonial rule in Central Africa (French, Belgian, Portuguese, or British, depending on the territory) was its reliance on forced recruitment of labor under conditions of mistreatment and helplessness that more than approximated slavery. Former slaves and their descendants were the first pursued by private companies to tap rubber in the forests, to dig gold and diamonds from the sandy soils, to cultivate cotton in the grasslands, to toil in fields awarded to European settler farmers, or to participate in government "development" projects. In this environment of overwhelming European governmental violence and control, the challenge of ending "slavery" did not acquire the notoriety that the issue assumed in early-colonial West Africa, where African merchants, planters, aristocrats, and cattle-raisers widely employed slave dependents in conditions less onerous than those the Europeans imposed in Central Africa in the name of "freedom." Rather, the early colonial regimes smoothly transformed nineteenth-century Africans' pervasive reliance on slaves into violent removals of men from their families to labor for the benefit of their new rulers in forced-labor schemes rationalized as "teaching the native the value, and virtue, of work." Few nations in Central Africa, independent since 1960, have enjoyed a prosperity that would allow wages to replace compulsion in the relationship between those who toil and those who consume, and so force often continues to compel cooperation. Although slavery is seldom mentioned as such, farmers now escape heavily authoritarian, often military, exploitative governments only by retreating into self-sufficient isolation, and city-dwellers retreat into so-called second, informal economies of their own to evade the high costs of government-dominated trade.

See also SEXUAL EXPLOITATION.

BIBLIOGRAPHY

BIRMINGHAM, DAVID, and PHYLLIS MARTIN, eds. *History of Central Africa.* 3 vols. 1983, 1997.
CHEM-LANGHËË, BONGFEN, ed. "Slavery and Slave-Dealing in Cameroon in the Nineteenth and Early Twentieth Centuries." *Paideuma* 41 (1995).
CLARENCE-SMITH, W. GERVASE. "Slaves, Commoners, and Landlords in Bulozi." *Journal of African History* 20, no. 2 (1979): 219–234.
CORDELL, DENNIS D. *Dar al-Kuti and the Last Years of the Trans-Saharan Slave Trade.* 1985.
HARMS, ROBERT W. *River of Wealth, River of Sorrow.* 1981.
LOVEJOY, PAUL E., ed. *The Ideology of Slavery in Africa.* 1981.
MIERS, SUZANNE, and IGOR KOPYTOFF, eds. *Slavery in Africa: Historical and Anthropological Perspectives.* 1977.
MIERS, SUZANNE, and RICHARD L. ROBERTS, eds. *The End of Slavery in Africa.* 1988.
MILLER, JOSEPH C. *Way of Death: Merchant Capitalism and the Angolan Slave Trade, 1730–1830.* 1988.
NORTHRUP, DAVID. *Beyond the Bend in the River: African Labor in Eastern Zaire, 1865–1940.* 1988.
WRIGHT, MARCIA. *Strategies of Slaves and Women: Life-Stories from East/Central Africa.* 1993.

Joseph C. Miller

Central America

See Amerindian Societies.

Central and Eastern Europe

See Medieval Europe, Slavery and Serfdom in.

Central Asia

Central Asia is the area located between Iran in the south, the Caspian Sea in the west, and the steppes of Kazakhstan in the north. In the east it extends into Sinkian (Chinese Turkestan) in northwestern China. Geographic conditions of central Asia allowed only irrigated oasis agriculture, while the vast steppes and deserts of the region supported, at some points, considerable groups of nomads. The geographical make-up heavily influenced central Asian political and economic institutions, including slavery.

Some interpretations of the archaeological evidence suggest that slavery existed in central Asia as early as the beginning of the first millennium B.C. More data point to the presence of slavery in central Asian provinces of the Achaemenid (550–331 B.C.), Macedonian and Seleucid (331–246 B.C.), Kushan (first through fourth centuries A.D.), and Sassanian (A.D. 208–651) empires. In the mid-nineteenth century the number of slaves in the region was estimated at one hundred thousand people, or two percent of the total population.

Throughout these times the roles and uses of slaves varied. In the early period slaves were used to construct and maintain large-scale irrigation systems, which formed the basis of the local agricultural economies, since most or all arable lands required expensive artificial irrigation. Evidence from later periods shows only a marginal role for slave labor in the agricultural economy, as the labor of free, motivated peasants was preferred. However, nomads, who cultivated inferior lands on the periphery of agricultural oases, found slaves useful as laborers and as symbols of their own self-image as nomadic peoples, rather than as settled workers of the land. Among the sedentary population slaves were domestic servants and concubines.

The Samanid emirs (874–999) controlled routes into northeastern Iran and profited greatly from the trade in Turkic slaves. Later, when the Turkic nomads established themselves in central Asia, nomadic raids into territories of the neighboring centralized states of Iran and Russia became a major source of slaves. The nomads sold most of the people they kidnapped in the markets of Bukhara, Samarkand, and other cities.

The state was the major owner of slaves. The heterogeneous free population of the central Asian states was not a reliable source of support to the rulers. It was particularly unreliable in the case of the Samanids. They belonged to the sedentary aristocracy of the local Iranian stock and—in contrast to all subsequent nomadic Turkic dynasties of central Asia—could not mobilize support along tribal lines. Slaves, whose loyalty was undivided, were trained to be military and bureaucratic leaders. This was a trend that persisted until the abolition of slavery in the region.

State interests shaped the character of slavery. Iranian slavery practices, as outlined in the Pahlavi law book *Madayan i hazar dadestan,* had a significant influence throughout this area. Members of the mainstream religious community—Zoroastrians and, later, Muslims—could not be enslaved. A notable exception to this prohibition was the enslavement of Shi'i Muslims, which was allowed in a sixteenth-century Sunni *fatwa* issued in reaction to the rise of the Safavid Shi'i dynasty in Iran. Later sources of influence include the Abbasid caliphate and Ottoman Turkey. Although state interference with private slave ownership was typical in central Asia, administrative and military slavery never reached the same degree of organization that it achieved elsewhere in the Muslim world. While the impact of Islam was considerable, the flexible Hanbali legal system, adopted in the central Asia region, allowed the accommodation of local peculiarities. State-owned slaves could possess private property and enjoyed substantial vertical mobility. The legal status of slaves was relatively high, but even after manumission, significant restrictions on a slave's freedom still remained. In a particular fourteenth-century arrangement in Bukhara, slaves donated to religious foundations (*waqfs*) were subsequently manumitted but remained under control of the *waqf*.

The influence that state slaves held was affected by changes in the political makeup of the region as introduced by subsequent nomadic conquests and a growing overall nomadic presence. Under the Samanids, the local sedentary dynasty, state slaves—known as people of *zergah* (palace)—formed an influential bureaucratic group. The influence of *ghulams* (the slave guard), many of whom were enslaved Turkic nomads, rose so high they could stage palace coups and compete for state control with the *wazir*, the prime minister and leader of the freeborn bureaucracy.

Under subsequent dynasties of the nomadic conquerors, the influence of the slave guard and bureaucracy decreased. *Ghulams* disappeared for a long time after the Mongol conquest in 1231. Nomads united under a charismatic and uncontested leader were an overwhelming military force, and *ghulams* therefore were not needed. Within a generation or two after the conquest, however, the nomads usually became disunited, though they continued to maintain their military strength. Slave guards, whose loyalty could be counted on, gave an advantage in the tribal conflicts and protected rulers from conspiracies. Meanwhile, slave bureaucrats supervised such important areas as taxation and irrigation, providing a more stable administrative basis. Slave soldiers and bureaucrats thus became an overall stabilizing factor in the complex and volatile relations among the ruler, the nomads, and influential religious intelligentsia.

The fortunes of the rulers and the slaves were interrelated. Under a strong ruler the influence of the slave bureaucracy usually rose. The history of nineteenth-century Bukhara, the most significant central Asian emirate of the time, exemplifies this trend. As the leaders of the strong Manghyt Uzbek tribe consolidated their power there and established themselves as supreme rulers—emirs in the middle of the nineteenth century—the Bukharan *kush-begi* (falcon hunting master), initially a palace official and usually a Persian slave, emerged as a strong prime minister. He was in charge of state security, state lands and other property, foreign relations, and the collection of most taxes. The archive of the *kush-begi* was

the biggest repository of historical manuscripts in Bukhara.

Abolition immediately followed the Russian conquest of the region, which was accomplished in the 1880s. Persian slaves, the majority of the slave population, returned to their own country. Nomads suffered serious hardships, having lost their agricultural manpower and their profits from the slave trade. The sedentary population was less affected, and there was no visible cost to the Bukharan administration. The last slave *kush-begi*, Astanakul, continued to appoint his own Persian slaves to administrative positions and dominated the Uzbek military aristocracy—descendants of the Uzbek nomadic tribal conquerors—until his death in 1910. An anti-Shi'i uprising in Bukhara removed the last Iranian Shi'ite slaves from the administration in the same year.

See also ISLAM.

BIBLIOGRAPHY

BARTOLD, VASILII VLADIMIROVICH. *Turkestan Down to the Mongol Invasion*. 1968.
DANDAMAEV, M. A., M. MAUCH, C. E. BOSWORTH, and W. FLOOR. "Barda and Bardadari." In *Encyclopedia Iranica*, vol. 3. 1989.
FAIZIEV, T. *Bukhoro feodal zhamiiatida qullardan foidalanishga doir huzhzhatlar (XIX asr)*. 1990.
"Russian Slaves in the Khanates of Central Asia." *Oriental Church Magazine*. (Sept. 1880): 196–211.

O. Semikhnenko

Chains and Restraints

Chains and restraints are ubiquitous in the history of slavery, although their use was most prevalent in societies where the scale of slave trading and the use of forced labor heightened security concerns among masters. Chains, ropes, wooden yokes, leg shackles and irons, handcuffs, and collars with bells or "horns" are just some of the restraints employed by slave masters and traders. Generally, such devices were used to prevent flight or resistance, especially during transportation, or as punishment.

Classical sources and monuments give glimpses of the use of restraints on slaves, especially within the Roman Empire. The stele of the Black Sea slave trader A. Kapreilius Timotheus, dated to early imperial Rome, represents eight chained figures walking in line and no doubt reflects the slave coffles that were brought to Rome from imperial conquests throughout the ancient world. Slaves involved in gang labor and in large-scale enterprises such as mining were also frequently chained, and on large Roman estates some rural slaves slept chained in a prison-house (*er-*

gastula). Masters disgraced rebellious slaves by chaining them—in the case of runaways, by making them wear an iron collar inscribed with their name and address.

The best information on the use of chains and restraints derives from the transatlantic slave trade and slavery in the New World. Examples of these grim artifacts are preserved in numerous museums and private collections and are described in the testimony of slaves and observers of slavery. Illustrations of captured slaves being led from the African interior to coastal trading centers show the use of wooden yokes around the neck, which often linked pairs of slaves together, and the binding of the hands. On slave ships bound for the Americas, Africans were shackled in pairs at the ankles; neck collars and chains might also be used below deck while a ship was in sight of land. Almost a hundred pairs of the most typical style of shackle, an iron rod with two iron loops attached, were found in the wreckage of a 1699 English slave ship near Key West, Florida.

Traders in the United States' domestic slave market used various restraints to inhibit resistance or flight.

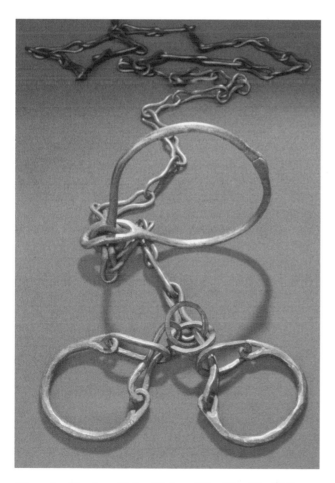

Slave shackles from Zaire. [Adam Woolfitt/Corbis]

White observers and slaves described the coffles of slaves that walked from the point of sale to faraway plantations, noting the frequency of men chained together in pairs at the ankles, who were also sometimes linked together by longer chains connected to iron collars. Rope, handcuffs, and other restraints also came into play, especially at night.

Slaves throughout the West Indies and Americas drew special punishments for acts of resistance, especially for attempting to run away. Resisters worked in leg irons and chains attached to balls, logs, and other heavy objects for months at a time and were securely chained at night. Collars with "horns" or spikes protruding from them prevented slaves from sleeping in a natural position and discouraged running through brush and forest. Masters also employed iron and wooden harnesses and collars supporting a bell or bells above the head of recalcitrant slaves—these devices served to create discomfort and reveal the slave's location.

Chains became a dominant icon of slavery's injustice in the eighteenth and nineteenth centuries. Hiram Powers's sculpture *The Greek Slave,* portraying a nude captive woman with her hands bound, was based on accounts from the Greek War of Independence against the Turks. The critically acclaimed sculpture toured the largest American cities in the late 1840s and was displayed at the Crystal Palace in New York in 1854–1855. In the same era, the chained bondsman became the defining image of the abolitionist movement, and the breaking of slavery's chains served as the ultimate symbol of emancipation.

See also DISCIPLINE AND PUNISHMENT; REBELLIONS AND VIOLENT RESISTANCE.

BIBLIOGRAPHY

The American Slave: A Composite Autobiography. 1972–1981.
BLASSINGAME, JOHN W. *Slave Testimony: Two Centuries of Letters, Speeches, Interviews, and Autobiographies.* 1977.
BRADLEY, KEITH. *Slavery and Society at Rome.* 1994.
BURNSIDE, MADELINE. *Spirits of the Passage: The Transatlantic Slave Trade in the Seventeenth Century.* 1997.
CAMPBELL, EDWARD D. C., and KYM RICE, eds. *Before Freedom Came: African-American Life in the Antebellum South.* 1991.
TIBBLES, ANTHONY, ed. *Transatlantic Slavery: Against Human Dignity.* 1994.

Gregg D. Kimball

Chattel Slavery

Chattel slavery is the condition under which one person is owned by another and deprived of most rights. Like other chattels, slaves and their offspring can typically be bought, sold, hired, exchanged, given, bequeathed, seized for debts, and put up as collateral. Unlike other property, however, slaves sometimes bear responsibility for their behavior, receive an education, and buy their own freedom.

"Chattel" meant movable wealth during feudal times. In Elizabethan England, the term increasingly became associated with livestock. Eventually, the word "cattle" was coined for this narrower usage, and "chattel" now refers to any article of property. The word "slave" derived from the most numerous ethnic group in the medieval slave trade—Slavs. The law generally considers slaves as personal chattels, although late Roman law (and Louisiana law) sometimes classified slaves as chattels real, precluding their sale separate from land.

Throughout history, people have enslaved others in war, as punishment for crimes, as payment for debt, or through purchase from parents or other authorities. Slavery has features in common with other forms of coerced labor, such as debt bondage, indenture, peonage, serfdom, and corveé (statute) labor. Yet slavery is a species of servitude set apart: slaves typically have been aliens with minimal freedom of action, permanently deprived of the title to their human capital and, if female, to their children, and often with no higher authority than their masters. Orlando Patterson put it starkly: the slave is a socially dead person.

Slavery probably developed after civilization turned from hunting to pastoral societies: agriculture brought the specialization of tasks and opportunities for exploiting another's labor. Ancient Sumerian, Phoenician, Hebrew, Babylonian, and Egyptian societies used slaves to tend flocks, work fields and mines, and help with domestic chores. The historian Moses Finley has made the provocative argument, however, that the preclassical world was one without free men: just as the Greeks invented individual freedom, so too did they invent chattel slavery.

Slavery flourished in the classical period, predominantly in cities open to commercial exchange. Rarely was the Greek a slave in his own city. Greek slaves worked in mines, quarries, or fields, produced handicrafts; or performed domestic, police, or secretarial work. Skilled slaves often lived apart from their masters. A unique feature of Greek society was benefit clubs that lent slaves money to buy their freedom.

Rome inherited the slave trade and expanded it by allowing field commanders to dispose of prisoners as they wished. Consequently, slave dealers traveled with the armies and conducted on-the-spot auctions. Slaves accounted for about 30 percent of the population in Rome's heyday. Roman slaves enjoyed limited freedoms—they could acquire property and schooling and, unlike Greek slaves, citizenship upon manumission.

Slavery declined—but did not end—with the decline of Rome. The Germanic tribes held slaves, sometimes using long hair as an identifying mark of slave status. Although the Church tried to prohibit the slave trade in the early ninth century, it failed: the trade was one of the West's few sources of the foreign exchange necessary to purchase Eastern goods. Charlemagne's efforts to reunify Western Europe finally sparked the transition from slavery to serfdom there.

Elsewhere, slavery persisted. With the emergence of Islam along the Arabian peninsula, religious wars generated large slave populations, mostly used for domestic and military service. William the Conqueror ended the export of English slaves, but serfdom did not replace domestic slavery until about 1200. Scandinavians held and traded thralls until the Swedish king declared all offspring of Christian slaves free in 1335. Slavery continued unabated in Italy and the Iberian peninsula: Genoa and Venice had active slave markets in the thirteenth century, Seville and Lisbon two centuries later. Captains of Prince Henry the Navigator brought the first black slaves to Portugal in the 1440s.

In modern times, perhaps the most notorious episode of slavery pertained to the Americas. One feature particularly distinguished New World slavery: its association with race. Early Spanish settlers enslaved Native Americans, who soon died off from diseases, especially smallpox, and hard work. In 1517, Charles I began to import Africans, first to the West Indies, then to the Spanish-controlled mainland. Brazil began the legal importation of black slaves in 1549. The first Africans in North America arrived in Virginia in 1619 on a Dutch ship, although slavery did not develop there until the 1640s and 1650s. Elizabethan-era captain Sir John Hawkins trafficked in slaves, but England did not figure large in the African trade until the seventeenth century, when the Royal African Company became the biggest slaver in the world.

The Atlantic slave trade created an infamous triangle. British and Dutch ships took liquor, guns, cotton goods, and trinkets to the West African coast to exchange for slaves. These unfortunates then embarked on the deadly Middle Passage. Over 40 percent went to Brazil. Slaves worked on sugar plantations in the West Indies, grew coffee and sugar and mined precious metals in Brazil, and grew tobacco, sugar, rice, indigo, and eventually cotton in North America. These goods, along with molasses and rum, went back to England.

Rising British sentiment against slavery culminated in the Somerset case, which outlawed slavery in England in 1772. Britain and the U.S. abolished the international slave trade in 1807 and 1808. Britain freed slaves in its colonies (except India) in 1833, with full emancipation in 1838. Abolition came later elsewhere, often accompanied by a rise in other forms of servitude. Eastern Europe and Russia kept slavery alive into the late nineteenth century. In 1890, all major European countries, the United States, Turkey, Persia, and Zanzibar signed the General Act of Brussels in an attempt to suppress slavery. Forty years later, an international labor convention acted to outlaw forced labor in the former Ottoman and German colonies. In 1948, the U.N. General Assembly declared that all forms of slavery in servitude should be abolished.

Yet slavery in Southeast Asia, the Arabian peninsula, and parts of Africa has continued well into the twentieth century. Perhaps the saddest legacy of American slavery is that the system established to supply the New World with slaves shaped society in Africa as well. Some scholars believe that slavery was endemic to Africa; others date its origins to medieval Muslim society or the later European infiltration. Regardless of beginnings, slavery within Africa burgeoned along with the Atlantic trade—in 1600 Africa had a minority of the world's slaves, in 1800 the overwhelming majority. The great scramble for Africa spread slavery further. Regrettably, the tragedy continues: Angolan slaves fought bloodily for freedom in 1961, Mauritania kept slavery legal until 1980, Nigeria still had slave concubinage in the late 1980s, and numerous other regions actively practiced slavery in the late 1990s.

See also AFRICA; ANCIENT GREECE; ANCIENT ROME; BRUSSELS ACT; LAWS; PATTERSON THESIS; SELF-PURCHASE; SLAVE TRADE; SOMERSET V. STEWART.

BIBLIOGRAPHY

BLOCH, MARC. *Slavery and Serfdom in the Middle Ages.* 1975.
BUSH, MICHAEL, ed. *Serfdom and Slavery: Studies in Legal Bondage.* 1996.
FINLEY, MOSES, ed. *Classical Slavery.* 1987.
FOGEL, ROBERT. *Without Consent or Contract.* 1989.
KLEIN, MARTIN. *Breaking the Chains: Slavery, Bondage, and Emancipation in Modern Africa and Asia.* 1993.
KOLCHIN, PETER. *Unfree Labor: American Slavery and Russian Serfdom.* 1987.
PHILLIPS, WILLIAM, JR. *Slavery from Roman Times to the Early Transatlantic Trade.* 1985.
WATSON, JAMES. *Black Ivory: A History of British Slavery.* 1992.
———, ed. *Asian and African Systems of Slavery.* 1980.

Jenny Bourne Wahl

Cheng Ho [1371–1433]

Chinese admiral.

Born Ma He, Cheng Ho was taken as a child from interior China to the coast, where he became a palace eunuch. He fought alongside the new emperor, Zhu Di, and at that time acquired the name Cheng Ho. Between 1405 and 1433 he became admiral of the treasure fleets that sailed in seven great voyages to Southeast Asia, South Asia, Aden, and the Persian Gulf, and even Mogadishu and points south in East Africa. Slavery then was widespread in China—many of the slaves were Chinese and others were people who came from elsewhere in Asia. For at least four centuries by Cheng Ho's time, there had also been slaves of African origin in China, apparently introduced through Southwest Asia by Arab slave traders.

What did not happen in the aftermath of Cheng Ho's voyages is as interesting as what did happen during them. His fleet ruled the seas only briefly. A new Chinese emperor halted the voyages and ended China's time as the leading maritime force, at least in the Indian Ocean. Later Chinese admirals never followed up on his voyages, so Cheng Ho never had the impact that his contemporary, Portugal's Prince Henry the Navigator, had on the other side of Africa. Whatever other trade might have developed, or at least been maintained had China not chosen to retreat to its own shores, the Chinese displayed no insatiable demand for exogenous labor. They never developed and expanded the African slave trade to the east as European nations soon would to the west.

See also CHINA; EUNUCHS.

BIBLIOGRAPHY

CHANG, KUEI-SHENG. "Cheng Ho." In *Dictionary of Ming Biography, 1368–1644,* edited by L. Carrington Goodrich and Chaoying Fang, 2 vols. 1976.
LEVATHES, LOUISE E. *When China Ruled the Seas: The Treasure Fleet of the Dragon Throne, 1405–1433.* 1994.

Peter Wallenstein

Chesnut, Mary [1823–1886]

Diarist; abolitionist sympathizer.

Mary Boykin Chesnut was the daughter of Senator Stephen D. Miller of South Carolina and became the wife of James Chesnut Jr., who was elected to the same office in 1858. Well taught in a Charleston school, Mary read and spoke French fluently and read German, many classics, and current literature avidly all her life. A keen observer and a gifted writer, she left perhaps the most brilliant personal account of the Civil War experience. It was based on a wartime diary that she elaborated and expanded but never published. Apart from the two prewar years in Washington and two war years in Richmond, she spent most of her adult life near Camden, at Mulberry plantation, one of several owned by her father-in-law, who was among the wealthiest planters and largest slave owners in the state (he had some five hundred slaves).

Mary Chesnut's loathing for slavery seems to have begun with her friendship toward two black servants and a mulatto ward of the headmistress of the Charleston school. At nineteen, in 1842, she wrote her husband what she called "the most fervid abolitionist document I have ever read." And a month before the war began, she declared that Charles Sumner had "said not one word of this hated institution that is not true." One of the most noted rebukes of Senator Sumner was delivered by Senator Chesnut of South Carolina. His wife remained unshaken. "God forgive us but ours is a *monstrous* institution," she declared. She did not make these views public, however, and of the slaves of her own family she wrote, "Ours are so well behaved and affectionate."

See also CIVIL WAR, U.S.; PLANTATIONS.

BIBLIOGRAPHY

MUHLENFELD, ELISABETH. *Mary Boykin Chesnut: A Bibliography.* 1981.
WOODWARD, C. VANN. *Mary Chesnut's Civil War.* 1981.
WOODWARD, C. VANN, and ELISABETH MUHLENFELD. *The Private Mary Chesnut: The Unpublished Civil War Diaries.* 1984.

C. Vann Woodward

Child, Lydia Maria [1802–1880]

Abolitionist author and antislavery activist.

Born in Medford, Massachusetts, and descended from an old New England family, Lydia Maria (née Francis) was educated in local schools. She made her mark first as a novelist, publishing *Hobomok* (1824), a sympathetic portrayal of Native Americans. In the late 1820s she began writing a series of domestic-advice books that dispensed cost-cutting recommendations based her experiences as the wife of an idealistic but impecunious reformer. These publications and her literary magazine for children, *Juvenile Miscellany,* earned Child a substantial income.

Child was drawn into the abolitionist movement through the encouragement of her husband, David Lee Child, a founding member of the New England Anti-Slavery Society, and William Lloyd Garrison. She quickly surpassed her husband's prominence as an abolitionist when in 1833 she wrote *An Appeal in Favor of That Class of Americans Called Africans.* By placing American slavery within a global perspective, she refuted notions about the economic collapse that some southerners predicted would result from emancipation, and she repudiated the idea of African colonization. Although the publication of this work cost Child her popular audience, especially in the South,

Lydia Maria Child. [Library of Congress/Corbis]

her persuasive arguments helped bring new converts to the antislavery movement.

Child served a stint as editor of the New York–based *National Anti-Slavery Standard* (1841–1843). In 1859 she gained notoriety by offering to act as nurse to the wounded John Brown. This offer led to a spirited exchange of letters with Margaretta Mason, wife of the Virginia senator James Mason, over female benevolence and the morality of slavery. Many newspapers reprinted the exchange, and the American Anti-Slavery Society printed 300,000 copies in pamphlet form. Child continued to write about reform issues until her death in 1880.

See also ABOLITION AND ANTISLAVERY MOVEMENTS; AMERICAN ANTI-SLAVERY SOCIETY; BROWN, JOHN; GARRISON, WILLIAM LLOYD; WOMEN IN THE ANTISLAVERY MOVEMENT.

BIBLIOGRAPHY

HOLLAND, PATRICIA, and MILTON MELTZER, eds. *The Collected Correspondence of Lydia Maria Child, 1817–1880* (microfiche series). 1979.

KARSHER, CAROLYN L. *The First Woman in the Republic: A Cultural Biography of Lydia Maria Child.* 1994.

Wendy Hamand Venet

Children

See Family, U.S.; Slavery and Childhood.

China

Evidence suggests that the practice of chattel slavery had existed before China was unified by the state of Qin in 221 B.C. Historians have debated whether the pre-Qin Chinese society was a slave society, but it has been generally agreed that the implementation of Qin's harsh penal code greatly contributed to the beginning of the Chinese system of perpetual human bondage. To stabilize his control of the newly unified china, Qin's first emperor ordered banishment and enslavement for life for his former enemies, as well as for anyone who attempted to challenge his authority. Such punishment began the legal institution of government enslavement in China, which lasted until the beginning of the twentieth century.

Although the use of forced labor and the buying and selling of human beings were recorded during the Qin period (221–206 B.C.), it was during the following four centuries of the Han Dynasties (206 B.C. to A.D. 25 for the Former Han and A.D. 25 to 220 for the Later Han) that the institution of Chinese slavery had matured and assumed its distinctive characteristics—the parallel existence of both state and private slavery, the principal use of slaves for domestic servitude rather than for agricultural or manufacturing production, the lack of a permanent and uniform state code regarding the treatment of slaves, the cultural inclusion of slaves juxtaposed with their social degradation, and the restrained growth of private slavery.

The Former Han Dynasty witnessed the consolidation of two major patterns of slavery: state (government) and private slavery. State slavery was largely a practice of using state power to penalize criminals for high offenses. State slaves were principally convicts, family members or relatives of major criminals (who were themselves executed in some cases), prisoners of war, and the offspring of state slaves (since state slavery was hereditary). The Chinese word for slave, *nu,* originally meant persons (especially women and children) who had been enslaved because of the crimes committed by their immediate relatives. The sources for private slavery—wherein one individual owned another—were more diverse, and included self-sale owing to financial difficulties and natural calamities; the sale of one's wife and children; kidnapping and slave raiding by professional traders; and, occasionally, a gift from the government, which sometimes rewarded individuals with state slaves.

Private slaves were traded in the market and involved middlemen or brokers. Owners of private slaves ranged from government officials and landlords to rich merchants. Although there were some cases that involved the enslavement of foreign-born peoples, the main stock of the traditional Chinese slave market was native-born Chinese. Record shows that wealthy families could own as many as several hundred slaves. The total number of those in bondage, however, has always been small. According to the historian C. Martin Wilbur, even during the expansive Han period, the slave population, state and private combined, was no more than one percent of the total Chinese population.

The limited growth of slavery in China had to do with the particular characteristics of the agricultural economy of traditional China, which featured a worship of self-sufficiency; high prestige associated with landownership; the suppression of commercial incentives; and, most important, an ample supply of cheap free labor.

Under this economic system, slaves were not used primarily for profit-making production. Neither state nor private slaves were used on large-scale plantations, or in mining or manufacturing. Although state slaves were used in building irrigation systems and other construction works, they were mostly, as a punishment, sent to live in remote, sparsely populated regions. Because it was mainly used as an instrument of punishment, state slavery never became an extensive practice after Qin. In fact, in the later dynasties, as soon as the new imperial rulers secured control of the government, they would limit their use of state slavery. Private slaves were primarily used for household services; they were employed as personal servants, cooks, tomb watchers, bodyguards, private soldiers, doorkeepers, trade assistants, and entertainers for the farm hands. Perhaps because of this particular domestic nature of Chinese slavery, those who were in bondage as servants were mostly referred as *nu-bi* (male or female servants), not as *nu-li,* which is the precise translation of the term *slave* as commonly used in the Western cultures. Thus, private ownership of slaves (*nu-bi*) in traditional China was not necessarily intended to create wealth on a large scale but rather to obtain general comfort in life, as well as to demonstrate the wealth and social status of the slaveowning family.

Partly because of the domestic nature of servitude and partly because of the absence of the concept of positive rights in Chinese culture, few laws in traditional China prescribed clear legal limits regulating slavery or the treatment of household slaves. Instead the management of slaves was largely determined by the practice of family and clan customs and tradition. Still, Chinese slavery shared many of the features of slavery found in other civilizations. A member from the *nu-bi* class, as defined by China's first comprehensive criminal code implemented in the Tang Dynasty (A.D. 618–907), was the legal equivalent of property or domestic animals. Slavery was hereditary for both state and private slaves. Ownership of a slave could be transferred from one master to another in a market or, on many occasions, through a middleman or broker. Absolute obedience to the master was expected. A slave could neither sue nor testify against the master in a court, except in the case of a master attempting to stage a rebellion or conduct treason against the state. Although both state and customary laws prohibited excessive physical abuse or the killing of slaves, enforcement of these laws was questionable. The master had the right to arrange a slave's marriage, but marriage between a slave and a commoner was prohibited. Offspring of an illicit union between a slave woman and a person of free birth belonged to the master. Severe punishment, as prescribed in several of the Qing government's fugitive laws from 1626 to 1685, was imposed against those who tried to escape from bondage and those who provided assistance for such fugitives.

Socially, *nu-bi* were placed at the bottom of the social hierarchy and were commonly referred to as degraded persons. But they were also bound by the laws of filial piety in their relationships to one another and were required to observe the rules of ancestor worship as practiced in the owner's family. Although opportunities were quite limited, a slave was, at times, able to receive an education, purchase freedom or be released from bondage, accumulate wealth, or even acquire an official title. Manumission of state slaves was possible mostly during the time of dynastic change, in which a new ruler might free those who had been enslaved by previous rulers.

From the beginning of the Han Dynasty (206 B.C.) to the end of the Qing Dynasty (1912), imperial governments had attempted to restrain the growth of private slavery. Ironically, imperial rulers saw private slavery as a waste of useful resources (both in human and monetary terms) and as a personal extravagance—an obvious contradiction to the indoctrinated values that emphasized hierarchical order and self-sufficiency. Correlated was the concern of the moral leadership of the ruling elites, whose ownerships of slaves led to the expansion of private slavery among commoners. There was also deep fear about possible slave rebellion, which in fact took place when the Manchus invaded China around the 1630s and 1640s. A law during the Ming dynasty (1368–1644) went so far as to set up a quota system for household slaves owned by the bureaucrats, with the highest-ranking officials owning no more than twenty slaves per family. The law further prohibited commoners from slave-owning. In an attempt to reduce the state-owned slave population, the ensuing Qing government limited the imposition of state slavery to cases of high treason and a few other serious offenses. In 1685 Emperor Kangxi freed all the hereditary slaves belonging to the Manchu families, and a century later, his grandson Qianlong freed all the private slaves that had served Manchu and Chinese officials for three generations. The final abolition of chattel slavery (or, to be exact, the selling and buying of *nu-bi*) came in 1909—three years before the collapse of the Qing Dynasty—when an imperial decree issued in the name of Qing's last emperor, Xuantong, ordered all slaves be released, regardless of their origins, and given the status of commoners.

See also DEBT SLAVERY; SLAVE TRADE.

BIBLIOGRAPHY

EDITORIAL BOARD OF THE STUDY OF HISTORY JOURNAL, eds. 1962. *Zhong Guo de Nu Li Zhi Yu Feng Jian Zhi Fen Oi de Wen Ti Lun Wen Xuan Ji* (*Selected Papers on Periodization on China's Slave System and Feudal System*).

GUO, MOROU. *Nu Li Zhi Shi Dai* (*The Period of the Slavery System*). 1954.

JIN, JUNJIAN. *Qing Dai She Hui de Jian Min Deng Ji* (*The Degraded-Person Class in Qing Society*). 1993.

LIU, WEIMIN. *Zhong Guo Gu Dai Nu Bi Zhi Du Shi* (*History of Ancient Chinese Slavery System*). 1975.

MEIJER, MARINUS J. "Slavery at the End of the Ch'ing Dynasty." In *Essays on China's Legal Tradition,* edited by Jerome Alan Cohen, R. Randle Edwards, and Fumei Chang Chen. 1980.

PULLEYBLANK, E. G. "The Origins and Nature of Chattel Slavery in China." *Journal of Economic and Social History of the Orient* 1 (1958): 185–220.

WATSON, JAMES L. "Transactions in People: The Chinese Market in Slaves, Servants, and Heirs." In *Asian and African System of Slavery,* edited by James L. Watson. 1980.

WEI, QINGYUAN, WU QIHENG, and LU SHU. *Qin Dai Nu Pei Zhi Du* (*The Nu-Pei System during the Qing China*). 1982.

WILBUR, C. MARTIN. *Slavery in China during the Former Han Dynasty: 206 B.C.–A.D. 25.* 1943.

Xi Wang

Christiana Slave Revolt (1851)

Perhaps better called the "Christiana Slave Riot," this incident occurred on 11 September, 1851, at Christiana, Pennsylvania. There, a violent shoot-out took place between a raiding party of slave catchers, led by Edward Gorsuch, a Maryland slave owner, and a group of blacks determined to prevent the rendition of William Parker, a runaway slave.

The event occurred at the house of Parker, as Gorsuch, leading a group consisting of his son, a nephew, a cousin, two neighbors, and U.S. Deputy marshal Henry H. Kline, attempted to take him into custody. A group of fugitives, reinforced by local blacks, had assembled to prevent Parker's capture. Two local whites who arrived at the scene, Castner Hanway and Elijah Lewis, rebuffed attempts by Kline to deputize them. In the ensuing struggle, Gorsuch was killed, his son was seriously wounded, and other members of the party fled or were wounded. Parker fled; he took a train to Rochester, New York, where he met Frederick Douglass before going on to Canada. In the aftermath of the violence, Hanway and forty other men—four whites and thirty-six blacks—were indicted for treason. The severity of the charge reflected President Millard Fillmor's search for Southern political support, as well as his desire to end resistance to the Fugitive Slave Law of 1850.

The prosecution team of seven attorneys, including the U.S. Attorney for Eastern Pennsylvania, John W. Ashmead, and the Maryland Attorney General, Robert Brent, were assembled for *U.S. v. Hanway*. A defense team of five was led by U.S. Representative Thaddeus Stevens. U.S. Supreme Court Associate Justice Robert C. Grier presided at the trial, assisted by U.S. District Judge John K. Kane. The trial, which lasted from 24 November to 8 December, 1851, ended in a verdict of not guilty after Judge Grier instructed the jury that refusal to aid in rendition under the Fugitive Slave Act of 1850 could not constitute the crime of treason. All the other indictments were ultimately dropped.

The trial and the sensational publicity surrounding it were largely the product of the public furor over the Fugitive Slave Act of 1850 and over the increasing lawlessness which ensued after attempts to seize blacks and attempts to prevent rendition. The incident also demonstrated the increasing militancy of blacks, who were no longer prepared to submit meekly to their forcible return to slavery. It also indicated the greater hostility of northern whites to attempts at rendition. The prosecution had claimed that Hanway had encouraged the blacks to resist and had given them forms of leadership, but the only fact not in dispute was the refusal of deputization.

See also REBELLIONS AND VIOLENT RESISTANCE.

BIBLIOGRAPHY

FINKELMAN, PAUL. *Slavery in the Courtroom: An Annotated Bibliography of American Cases.* 1985.
———. "The Treason Trial of Castner Hanway." In *American Political Trials*, edited by Michael Belknap. Rev. ed. 1994: pp. 77–96.
KATZ, JONATHAN. *Resistance at Christiana.* 1974.
United States v. Hanway, 26 F. Cas. 105 (C.C.E.D. Pa. 1851) (No. 15, 299).

Patrick M. O'Neil

Christianity

This entry includes the following articles: An Overview; Early Church; Medieval West; Roman Catholicism; Protestantism. *Related articles may be found at the entries* Bible; Judaism; Law.

An Overview

Christianity—the religion of those who believe that Jesus of Nazareth is the only son of the one true God—has been the most influential religion in Western and, arguably, world history. From its origins as a small Jewish sect, Christianity has grown into a worldwide religion of more than 30,000 separate churches and denominations. The differences among these varieties of Christianity, however, have not negated the essential core belief of Christian faith: Jesus, the son of God, became man, died, was resurrected, and ascended into heaven; eternal salvation comes only through Jesus, the Christ or savior of fallen and sinful humanity.

Early Developments

The first Christians, like Jesus himself, were Jews. As such, they retained many Jewish beliefs regarding the nature of God and his creation while introducing significant changes as well. Jewish monotheism, worked out over the course of centuries, emphasized the covenant that existed between God and his chosen people. Although early Christianity did not dispense with the idea of a relation between God and the collective, it stressed the notion of personal responsibility and salvation. Early Christians, especially Paul, rejected the tribal character of Judaism and preached instead the catholicity and universality of Christianity. In doing so, Paul minimized social differences, including differences between slave and free, and promoted the equality of all Christian believers: "There is neither Jew nor Greek, there is neither bond nor free, there is neither male nor female: for ye are all one in Christ Jesus" (Galatians 3: 28). Paul's decision that Gentile converts to the religion of Jesus need not undergo Jewish rituals such as circumcision encouraged the spread of Christianity to non-Jews everywhere. And the Jewish hope for the restoration of an earthly kingdom through the intervention of God's chosen servant, or messiah, was, for Christians, realized in Jesus, whose kingdom, however, was not of this world.

Christians, like Jews, continued the tradition of a sacred text and signaled their belief in the continuity of the Jewish and Christian faiths by naming the books of the Hebrew Bible the Old Testament and their own texts regarding the lives and teachings of Jesus and his disciples the New Testament. But the central idea of the New Testament, that Jesus was not merely a prophet but the son of God, the messiah foretold by the Jewish prophets, forever separated Christianity from Judaism. Since the Greek word for messiah was "Christ," those who accepted Jesus as the messiah became known as Christians.

Doctrinal and Organizational Developments
and Disagreements

From the earliest days of the sect, conflicts have surrounded the development of doctrine and practice. Questions about the virgin birth of Jesus, his divine nature, and the status of Jewish practices such as circumcision produced some conflict in the first century of Christianity, and the second century witnessed a series of theological and doctrinal struggles that decisively shaped the development of the New Testament canon. Building upon the writings and works of the first-century apostolic fathers, a new generation of Christian apologists, which included Justin Martyr and Irenaeus of Lyons, worked to clarify Christian beliefs in the face of both external and internal challenges. Gnostics, a diverse group that never formed an organized movement, maintained that human beings contained both the principle of good, the soul, and the principle of evil, the body; and some denied that Jesus was truly human, since that would require him to be both evil and good. Some Gnostics also rejected the Hebrew Bible and many of the writings, including three of the four gospels, that were becoming associated with the emerging Christian tradition. Irenaeus and others countered the Gnostics by insisting on the validity of all four gospels and many of the writings attributed to Paul and the other apostles. For another two hundred years, scholars and church leaders, most notably the third-century scholars Clement of Alexandria and Origen, would continue this effort to distinguish authentic, divinely inspired apostolic writings from nonauthentic ones. Although the final determination of the complete New Testament came only with a series of church councils in the late fourth century, its composition has remained one of the few constants in Christian history; nearly all Christians have always acknowledged the books of the New Testament as the definitive source of Christian faith. This era also witnessed the development of creeds or professions of faith, which summarized the essentials of belief contained in the scriptures.

The Gnostic controversy also raised an issue that has continued to plague Christianity throughout much of its history. Gnostic, Greek for "one who knows," derives from the word *gnosis,* the Greek word for "knowledge" or "truth." Some Gnostics maintained that gnosis came neither from the study of the law or scripture nor from participating in rituals or other actions. Gnosis, they claimed, was a gift from God that profoundly reshaped the individual, separating him from those who lacked gnosis and freeing him from unnecessary obedience to earthy observances such as the law. Although the Gnostics failed to capture the early church, the notion that the saved individual need not be bound to what mere humans or human institutions demanded has remained a persistent source of tension within Christianity. Christianity has never been entirely able to eliminate the tendency of those who are reborn, who believe themselves saved, to reject what they believe to be the corrupt or erroneous claims of unregenerate people and institutions.

The spread of Christianity throughout the Mediterranean world in the centuries after the death of Jesus resulted in a proliferation of practices and church organizations. The movement to standardize the writings of the New Testament was accompanied by attempts to develop a uniform ecclesiastical structure. Most early Christians worshiped in secret, oftentimes in private residences, away from the threat of Roman persecution. These clandestine communities usually had their own governing body of elders, some apparently appointed by the original apostles and others chosen by the members of the congregations. But the New Testament is not consistent in the terms applied to these leaders. Paul refers to "bishops and deacons" (Philippians, 1: 1), whereas Luke simply mentions "elders" (Acts 11: 30).

By the middle of the third century, however, a pattern of church government had emerged. Bishops, acting as chief ministers and increasingly assisted by priests or presbyters, and deacons, who oversaw alms collection and other worldly concerns, prevailed in nearly all churches. These offices, with various titles and names, characterized most Christian churches until the Reformation. Some of the sixteenth-century reformers rejected the notion that scripture prescribed one specific form of church government. This rejection has allowed for an increasingly diverse pattern of ecclesiastical structures, with some Christians, such as Roman Catholics, Anglicans, and some Lutherans, maintaining a hierarchical, episcopal order; and others, including most evangelical denominations, favoring congregational polities in which officers, whether deacons, ministers, or elders, are subordinate to the laity.

Christianity and Slavery

Throughout most of its history, Christianity has accepted slavery as a social institution, even as it has elevated slaves, as human beings with eternal souls, to spiritual equality with nonslaves. Indeed, until the eighteenth century Christians understood slavery as more of a spiritual than a temporal concept. Revealingly, slavery denoted both the highest form of faith, "slaves of Jesus Christ," and the worse state of sinfulness, "slaves of sin." Temporal bondage paled in comparison with the slavery of sin, and true liberty consisted of living in Christ and acknowledging him as one's only master. Historically, Christianity emphasized the meaninglessness of one's earthly station; the important distinction was between the saved and the unsaved. Only in the past two hundred years have Christians insisted that physical freedom is a necessary precondition of spiritual salvation.

Caesar and God

From its earliest days, Christianity has had a complex relation to secular authority. Jesus's famous entreaty to "render unto Caesar the things which are Caesar's; and unto God the things that are God's," (Matthew 22: 21), like many of his sayings, has left an ambiguous legacy. Slavery, at least until the eighteenth century, did not prove to be a contentious aspect of secular society for most Christians, although some medieval popes did protest holding fellow Christians as slaves. For the most part, Christianity accepted slavery as part of the earthly order. For the early Christians, Paul's admonitions in Colossians 3: 22–24, Timothy 6: 1–2, Titus 2: 9–10, and especially Ephesians 6: 5–9 strengthened the belief that slavery was divinely ordained and that the Christian's duty was to accept his earthly station. "Servants, be obedient to them that are your masters according to the flesh, with fear and trembling, in singleness of your heart, as unto Christ; Not with eyeservice, as menpleasers, but as the servants of Christ, doing the will of God from the heart" (Ephesians 6: 5–6). Later, Augustine, in Book 19 of *City of God,* reaffirmed the divine sanction of slavery, declaring, "The first cause of slavery is sin, whereby man was subjected to man in the condition of bondage; and this can only happen by the judgment of God, with whom there is no injustice, and who knows how to allot different punishments according to the deserts of the offenders." For Augustine, as for most Christians until the modern era, slavery was not simply part of "Caesar's" law but also part of God's law: "But it remains true that slavery as a punishment is also ordained by that law which enjoins the preservation of the order of nature, and forbids its disturbance; in

Saint Augustine (undated engraving). [Corbis-Bettmann]

fact, if nothing had been done to contravene that law, there would have been nothing to require the discipline of slavery as a punishment." Thus the fall of humanity produced slavery, and nothing short of the eradication of original sin could render that punishment no longer necessary or just.

From Persecution to Establishment

The early church was persecuted and consequently developed in opposition to established authority. But Christianity's attitude toward slavery, which was a fundamental institution of the Roman Empire, was not a source of that persecution. With Constantine's grant of official toleration in 313, Christianity entered into an era of cooperation with the state, culminating in its becoming the official religion of the empire by the end of the fourth century. Christianity's growth and official sanction meant that its health affected the health of society; the empire's fate was increasingly bound up with the Christian faith, making that faith an object of political concern. Theological and doctrinal problems thus assumed political importance, as emperors and other secular leaders recognized that divisions within the church threatened the stability of the empire. Slavery never became such a divisive problem. Instead, the great ecumenical councils that preoccupied both church and political leaders focused on the far more pressing matters of defining and refining the emerging faith.

Slavery, Salvation, and Scripture

The Christian religion is ultimately a religion of salvation, as opposed to a religion of enlightenment or earthly happiness or contentment, and this, historically, has been one of the primary reasons why slavery has not posed a fundamental problem to it. Christianity posits a separation or estrangement between God and man, one that began with Adam and Eve and, through original sin, persists with each individual human. Mankind was and is incapable of freeing itself from sin; but the merciful and just God, by sending his son to atone for man's sins, has permitted humans to be redeemed. Thus only the suffering and sacrifice of Christ himself have enabled man to reconcile with God. And only a being who was both God and man could provide both the sacrifice necessary to save fallen humanity and the suffering that made this sacrifice real. Humans' sins were so great that only the death of the son of God could pay for them. This atonement is the heart of Christian faith. But while nearly all Christians agree that salvation comes only through Christ, they differ widely in how one attains the forgiveness that the atonement makes possible. The question of what must one do to save oneself now that Christ has sacrificed himself for humanity has proved one of the most divisive in the history of Christianity.

Like other divisive issues, this one also has its roots in scripture. The New Testament contains ambiguous passages regarding the reception of God's saving grace. Certain passages suggest that God freely imparts his grace to those he chooses, regardless of the actions of the one chosen. Paul's famous passage in Romans 3: 28, which heavily influenced Luther, asserts that "a man is justified by faith without the deeds of the law"; this seemingly renders actions irrelevant to the work of grace. Yet James 2: 24 states, "See then that by works a man is justified, and not by faith only," suggesting that certain actions are necessary for salvation. Although Christians, especially during and subsequent to the Protestant Reformation, have differed over the emphasis to be placed on the efficacy of human will, these differences should not obscure the significant area of agreement that unites all Christians. No one can, through his own efforts, attain salvation. God's grace, a grace that is never justly earned or merited, allows humans to be reconciled with God and with one another. In this continuing recognition of man's need for divine assistance, made possible

through the redemptive power of Christ's sacrifice as revealed in the scriptures, Christianity, notwithstanding its divisions and internal disagreements, has maintained its historical cohesiveness.

Christianity and the Emergence of Opposition to Slavery

Although many have argued that Christianity played a central role in the decline of slavery in medieval Europe, no serious attack on slavery as anti-Christian emerged before the modern era. The growth of Christian opposition to slavery in the eighteenth century did not result from any significant break in the faith's essential cohesiveness. Rather, antislavery attitudes (which eventually affected all Christian churches) first developed among people—Quakers, then evangelicals—who continued to identify strongly with the essential elements of the Christian tradition even as they rejected that tradition's acceptance of slavery. Some antislavery Christians defied nearly all previous biblical interpretations and maintained that God's word did not sanction slavery. Many more adopted the less difficult strategy of appealing to what they considered the spirit of the New Testament, which they insisted was incompatible with slavery. Relying less on chapter and verse and more on emerging notions of natural law and moral sensibility, which to their minds coincided with true Christianity, these antislavery Christians throughout the West elevated morality—as they defined it—above the literal words of scripture. In doing so, they contributed to the separation of morality from the specifics of the Christian tradition laid out in the great ecumenical councils. Christian morality, they contended, required that one freely choose the good. To hold another person in bondage prevented that individual from exercising the freedom necessary to be a moral being. Slavery thus contradicted Christianity not because it violated the Old Testament law or any of Jesus's express teachings or the principles of the councils, but because, per se, it prohibited individual slaves from being morally accountable Christians.

Defenders of Slavery

Christian defenders of slavery countered all of these arguments. Appealing to centuries of biblical interpretation and church teachings, they claimed that slavery was divinely ordained and in no way incompatible with Christianity. Citing Ephesians and Colossians, they reminded their antislavery opponents that Paul himself declared that a slave could be a faithful follower of Christ. And Paul's letter to Philemon proved that a slaveowner could be a good Christian.

Furthermore, to argue that all individuals required freedom from external restraints in order to be human threatened not only slavery, but, in the words of the Presbyterian minister James Henley Thornwell of South Carolina, "every arrangement of society which did not secure to all its members an absolute equality of position." More forcefully, they asserted that severing morality from the Bible threatened Christianity itself: to rely on individual conscience, rather than the transcendent authority of scripture—to determine for oneself what was and was not moral—could only lead to the end of the Christian religion.

As some abolitionists abandoned Christianity in favor of deism or even atheism, proslavery Christians became ever more convinced that slavery in one form or another was necessary to the survival of Christianity. For many of them, slavery was but one of a series of hierarchical, unequal relations—which also included husband and wife and parent and child—that constituted society. Christianity taught its followers to recognize these human relations and the duties and obligations that followed from them. The Christian master's duty was not to free his slaves but to treat them as fellow, if unequal, Christians. Ministers, priests, and other Christians in the nineteenth century implored slaves to "obey in all things your masters" and masters to "give unto your servants that which is just and equal; knowing that ye also have a Master in heaven: (Colossians 3: 22; 4: 1). The hierarchical Christian household of masters and slaves, husbands and wives, and parents and children reflected and reinforced the traditional Christian notions of human imperfection, submissiveness to God, and the freedom that comes only through obedience to God's law as revealed in scripture.

Conflict and Resolution

On the eve of the end of slavery, both antislavery and proslavery Christians pursued their incompatible ends as inheritors of a faith produced, in large part, by the great ecumenical councils of the early church. But the conflicts that led to those councils did not involve slavery, and the fragmentation that marked Christianity since the Reformation prevented a single council from resolving the conflict between those opposed to slavery and those who supported it. Even specific denominations, such as the Methodists and Baptists, proved incapable of preventing themselves from being torn apart by slavery. Christianity, notwithstanding the common beliefs that united its followers, could not provide a singular, unequivocal answer to the question of slavery's compatibility with the faith. It was left to individual Christian men and women to determine, through force as well as argument, what exactly the relation between slavery and Christianity was to be. In 1700 no organized body of Christians believed that slavery was contrary to Christian doctrine; by 1900, however, every denomination did. Thus did unanimity among Christians regarding slavery's relation to the faith return.

See also ABOLITION AND ANTISLAVERY MOVEMENTS; BAPTIST CHRISTIANITY; BIBLE; JUDAISM; METHODISM; QUAKERS; THORNWELL, JAMES HENLEY.

BIBLIOGRAPHY

AUGUSTINE. *City of God.* 1972.
BARTOUR, RON. "'Cursed Be Canaan, a Servant of Servants Shall He Be unto His Brethren': American Views on Biblical Slavery, 1835–1865. A Comparative Study." *Slavery and Abolition* 4 (1983): 41–55.
COLEMAN-NORTON, P. R. "The Apostle Paul and the Roman Law of Slavery." In *Studies in Roman Economic and Social History in Honor of Allan Chester Johnson.* 1951.
DAVIS, DAVID BRION. *The Problem of Slavery in the Age of Revolution.* 1975.
———. *The Problem of Slavery in Western Culture.* 1967.
GENOVESE, EUGENE. *"Slavery Ordained of God": The Southern Slaveholders' View of Biblical History and Modern Politics.* 1985.
RUPPRECHT, ARTHUR A. "Attitudes on Slavery among the Church Fathers," In *New Dimensions in New Testament Study,* edited by Richard N. Longenecker and Merrill C. Tenney.
ST. CROIX, G. E. M. DE. "Early Christian Attitudes to Property and Slavery," In *Church Society, and Politics,* edited by Derek Baker. 1975.
URBAN, LINWOOD. *A Short History of Christian Thought,* 2nd ed. 1995.

Douglas Ambrose

Early Church

The institution of slavery was so embedded in the society of 100 B.C.E. to 500 C.E. that Christianity had no actual impact on it. Paul—the apostle to the Gentiles and the man to whom the New Testament Pauline epistles are traditionally attributed—required slaves who were Christians to be obedient to their masters. That he so exhorts Christian slaves, however, points to a background of ideas that may have suggested otherwise, and we do indeed find radical thinking on the subject. The fundamentally influencing idea, taken over by Paul from the Judaism of his time, is that of re-creation. According to this concept, someone who chooses to believe that Jesus is the Messiah becomes, by an event of supernatural significance, newly born in such a real sense that the past is wiped out. He or she is no longer the same person after conversion. In principle, all biological, legal, and social ties have been broken.

So powerful was the idea of re-creation that, for example, unions previously judged to be incestuous would no longer be so considered. To be sure, the then common practice of breeding slaves like cattle or dogs may have contributed to this attitude toward incest, but there is no documentary evidence that this was the case. A slave who became Christian was no longer a slave but was free. The problem was that the outside world could not be expected to appreciate the doctrine. In his writings, Paul duly anticipates such a response and in regard to the slave Onesimus in the *Letter to Philemon* he lays out the position in which the Christian slave finds himself. An actual, serious new birth has come about through conversion. Although his new status confronts the this-worldly social reality in which he lives, the converted slave should view that reality as of no account, and, therefore, he should regard his juristic lack of freedom as of no importance. If he is enslaved to a non-Christian he has to do what is expected of him, while if he is a slave to a Christian such as Philemon, the master may, even should, renounce his power over him. If the Christian master chooses not to renounce his hold, the slave should continue to serve. In heaven's eyes he remains free. Paul sought to ensure that in its practical applications the new dogma caused no trouble.

Paul's ideas about re-creation continued to dominate early Christian writings, but institutionalized practices inevitably weakened their impact. Church fathers like Augustine and John Chrysostom viewed the institution of slavery as a concession to human sinfulness. In accepting its practice, they nonetheless could protest some of its manifestations, such as the kidnapping of children. Although there was never an authoritative demand by the church to have masters liberate their slaves, some Christian groups used their common funds to pay for manumissions. A practice whereby members of a church redeemed slaves by substituting themselves (1 Clem 55: 2) neither grew nor was encouraged. The Christian emperors made virtually no change in the institution of slavery.

See also BIBLE; FREEDOM; ONESIMUS.

BIBLIOGRAPHY

DAUBE, DAVID. "Onesimus." In *Christians Among Jews and Gentiles: Essays in Honor of Krister Stendahl,* edited by G. W. E. Micklesburg and G. W. MacRae. 1986.
HARRILL, J. A. *The Manumission of Slaves in Early Christianity.* 1995.

Calum Carmichael

Medieval West

Medieval Christian theology did not spring into existence on its own but arose from deep roots, which stretched back to Old and New Testament times and through the patristic age of the church.

Most of the fathers of the church—including men such as Gregory Nazianzen (329–390), John Chrysostom (ca. 347–407), Augustine of Hippo (354–430)—saw sin as the true source of slavery and the original sin of Adam and Eve as its fountainhead. Original sin was seen as creating the postlapsarian (that is, the fallen) human condition that made slavery possible; but every instance of slavery was also, either directly or by inheritance through the enslavement of an ancestor, a result of actual sin—a sin actually committed by some human being after the fall of man. In each instance of unjust slavery, the sin was the act of a master who enslaved the innocent. And each instance of justifiable slavery could be traced to a sin by the slave or ancestor of the slave, such as crime or participation in an unjust war.

Patristic and scholastic Catholic theologians had to reconcile the recognition of slavery in the Old and New Testaments with the requirements of justice. The divine sanction of slavery in scripture was generally interpreted as an acknowledgment that in certain situations, slavery might be the lesser of evils.

Contrary to Roman law, as expressed in the *Digest* (530) and the *Code of Justinian* (534), the later fathers and doctors of the church, like Saint Basil the Great (ca. 330–397), upheld the validity of marriage between slaves, asserted the conjugal and paternal authority of the slave over his wife and children, and considered extramarital intercourse with a slave as fornication or adultery (depending on marital status), as it would be with a free person.

The fall of the Roman Empire in the West in 476 under the onslaught of the barbarian invasions brought new challenges to the church and its theologians regarding slavery. The Germanic tribes that overran Europe ended many of the protections slaves had come to enjoy in the Christianized empire; these tribes instituted new, more severe laws and customs of slavery and greatly increased the number of slaves by enslaving free tillers of the soil. In the centuries following the fall of Rome, the church struggled to raise the status of the agricultural workers of Europe from chattel slaves to bound serfs, with reciprocal rights and duties to their feudal overlords.

For those who remained slaves, lacking the benefits of enserfment, and for those who became slaves in the newly developing international slave trade, the reintroduction of Roman civil law in the High Middle Ages throughout much of Europe, under the tutelage of the church, was significant. It unified and codified slave law and extended some protections to those in bondage.

Canon law itself imposed slavery as an ecclesiastical penalty for some offences from 633 to 1535. The Council of Pavia (1012) decreed the enslavement of the children of clerics who had violated the vows of celibacy, and at the Synod of Melfi in 1089, Pope Urban II granted secular rulers the right to order perpetual servitude for the wives of clerics.

In the ninth century, Saint Agobard of Lyon declared that God created all men equal, although the mysterious workings of divine providence permitted some to be reduced to slavery. He also repeated the doctrine of the interior freedom of slaves, which had originated with the ancient Stoic philosophers and which would be incorporated into the moral philosophy of most scholastic theologians, including Thomas Aquinas (ca. 1224–1274). Slaves were subject to the will of the master only in their external activities; their souls and minds were naturally free and beyond the potential control of the master.

Slaves, furthermore, had the right to disobey a master who attempted to prevent their procreation, to work them to an unreasonable degree, or to deny them proper sustenance. If a tyrannical master attempted to make a slave commit a great moral evil, or if a master intended to kill a slave unjustly, the slave might be morally justified in fleeing from bondage. But just as the right to rebel against a tyrannical ruler of a state was strictly circumscribed—on account of the danger to justice and public order that revolutions entail—so too any violent resistance to a master could be justified only *in extremis.*

Thomas Aquinas introduced the Aristotelian notion of a symbiotic relationship between master and slave, beneficial to both, and he recognized the Roman legal rule that slave status was imparted through the mother—*partus sequitur ventrem.* This constituted a deviation from the idea of sin as the origin of slavery, for children were innocent of any wrongdoing alleged against their ancestors, but Aquinas justified this rule in terms of the pragmatic need to get masters to allow procreation and to provide sustenance for the children of slaves. Saint Bonaventure (ca. 1217–1274) also defended the Roman law, comparing it to the hereditary succession of royalty and nobility through paternal descent.

On some points regarding slavery, John Duns Scotus (ca. 1266–1308) challenged the consensus of the major scholastic theologians. Although Scotus accepted crime and self-enslavement as legitimate causes of slavery, he held that perpetual servitude for prisoners of war was inhumanly severe. Also, although Scotus did accept Aristotle's notion that some people may be suited by their nature to the position of slaves, he restricted such natural servitude to domestic ser-

A fifteenth-century portrait of John Duns Scotus by Joos van Gent. [Gianni Dagli Orti/Corbis]

vice; chattel slavery was only to be a punishment for crime.

Scotus's final contribution to medieval Christianity's understanding of the moral implications of slavery was his biblical interpretation. He argued that the apostolic teaching that slaves ought to obey their masters did not express a recognition of slavery as moral or just.

During the Protestant Reformation in Europe, Catholicism was forced to take up new issues in the moral analysis of slavery. Portuguese exploration of the coasts of Africa was opening up wide-scale exploitation of native blacks through the international slave trade, and Spain's exploration and conquest of the New World raised issues about the humanity, rights, and liability to enslavement of the Amerindian populations—peoples of whose existence the Europeans had been entirely ignorant.

In some ways, of course, the theologians of the Reformation and Counter-Reformation would continue ancient and medieval traditions, but new ground also would have to be broken as the ancient evil of slavery appeared in new incarnations.

See also ARISTOTLE; BIBLE; LAW; PHILOSOPHY; THOMAS AQUINAS.

BIBLIOGRAPHY

MAXWELL, JOHN FRANCIS. *Slavery and the Catholic Church: The History of Catholic Teaching Concerning the Moral Legitimacy of the Institution of Slavery.* 1975.
THOMAS AQUINAS. *The Political Ideas of St. Thomas Aquinas,* edited by Dino Bigongiari. 1953.

Patrick M. O'Neil

Roman Catholicism

Slavery was an integral part of the world in which the Christian church was born. Christ and his early followers did not oppose the practice but seemingly accepted it as a given of the social order. Paul exhorted the slaves of the Christian community in Corinth to obey their masters. Traditional church teaching held that slavery, though a consequence of sin, was not inherently evil, so long as the acquisition of the slave had been just (i.e., by war or self-sale) and the mutual rights and duties of slaveholder and slave were maintained. Christians—both free and slave—were equal. As Paul put it, in Christ there is neither slave nor free person, but both have become one in faith.

Papal and Church Teachings in the Early Modern Period

Seventeenth-century Roman Catholic theologians such as the Jesuit Francisco Suárez and Jacques Bossuet viewed slavery as a condition incompatible with the ideal moral order but legitimated by the universal practice of nations since the dawn of civilization. However, the possible subjects for enslavement were limited. By the age of discovery the church had come to regard Christians as improper subjects for permanent bondage. On the other hand, slavery was considered a fitting instrument for the extension of Christianity and a natural fate for pagans and heretics. As Europe intensified its enslavement and trading of Africans in the fifteenth and sixteenth centuries, several popes condemned the practice of enslaving Christian converts and excommunicated their captors. Thus in 1462 Pope Pius II imposed ecclesiastical censures on Christian slavers in Portuguese Guinea for capturing recent African converts. By the same thinking the popes, assuming that West Africans were Muslims and hence traditional enemies of Christendom, approved their capture and permanent enslavement. In 1452, Pope Nicholas V extended the King Alfonso V of Portugal permission to subjugate "saracens and pagans and any other unbelievers and enemies of Christ where they may be" and to make permanent slaves of them.

Initially, when the Spanish and Portuguese began the wholesale enslavement of natives in their new empires in America, church authorities approved it by remaining silent. In 1537 Pope Paul III did forbid any enslavement of Amerindians by Spaniards, but this was a late ecclesiastical enforcement of a royal order of 1530 prohibiting the reduction of Indians to slaves. When the king, Charles V, who had rescinded his own order in 1534, urged the pontiff to annual his brief, Paul did so.

Protests against Indian and African Slavery

Early on, missionaries in the new realms, witnessing the disastrous effects of the enslavement of natives that resulted from unjustified seizure by the Spanish and Portuguese, questioned the legitimacy of enslaving Indians and protested the scandals that had ensued. In 1511, from his pulpit in Hispaniola, the Dominican Antonio de Montesinos denounced the enslavement of Indians as a grievous sin. Five years later ten Dominicans and thirteen Franciscan missionaries in Hispaniola protested to the royal regent in Spain, Cardinal Jimenez de Cisneros, the crimes and cruelties they had witnessed being inflicted upon the Indians in bondage. Moreover, the theologian Matías de Paz argued that the Indians were unfit subjects for slavery, since they, unlike the Jews and Saracens, had not rejected the faith but were embracing it when offered the opportunity.

The most influential of the Spanish missionaries to oppose the enslavement of Indians was the Dominican Bartolomé de Las Casas. He had been a slaveholder himself, in Hispaniola, but after a conversion experience he had come to believe that Indian slavery was evil. Through his writings, particularly *El Indio Esclavo* (1552), and his personal advocacy in Spain and the Spanish colonies he decried the enslavement of innocent Indians and their cruel treatment. When he was named bishop of Chiapas (in what is now southern Mexico), Las Casas forbade his priests to absolve slaveholders who refused to emancipate their Indian slaves. Subsequent rioting forced him to flee to Spain and resign his see.

Despite Las Casas's failure, the Spanish and Portuguese crowns, out of experience as well as for legal reasons, eventually forebade the enslavement of natives. Africans became the new source of bonded labor in the colonies. Las Casas, who owned African slaves until 1544, had proposed to the Spanish crown before 1520 that blacks replace Indians as slave laborers in the New World. By 1550, the year that Las Casas en-

Bartolomé de Las Casas is depicted praying over the dead body of a man while a grieving woman clasps the legs of the missionary. [Library of Congress]

gaged in a famous debate with Juan Ginés de Súlpeda about the morality of Indian enslavement, African bondage in the Spanish realms had become widespread. Only a few protested this new form of slavery in the New World. In 1560 the archbishop of México pleaded with the king that he knew no more justification for enslaving Africans than Indians, since Africans neither rejected the gospel nor made war on Christians. A decade later the Sevillian theologican Tomás de Mercado, in a published treatise (1571), contended that many, if not most, of the African slaves had been procured through violence and deceit. Mercado, while not questioning the morality of slavery, concluded that the features of African enslavement made it a mortal sin for any Christian to be party to it. A professor of law at the University of Mexico, Bartolomé de Albornoz, argued in a book that the presumption of the natural law was always in favor of liberty, even for Africans. These pleas went unheeded. Rome even placed Albornoz's work on its Index of condemned books. Between 1595 and 1773 approximately 1.5 million Africans were imported into

the Spanish and Portuguese colonies. All told, from 1519 to 1867 about 5.5 million slaves were delivered alive to Spanish and Portuguese America.

By the seventeenth century the Roman Catholic church universally condemned Indian enslavement. Typical was Pope Urban VIII's brief *Commissum Nobi* (1639) which condemned the unjust enslavement of Indians by the Portuguese who, the pope charged, were alienating the Indians from Christianity by their barbaric behavior. But the morality of African slavery went unchallenged from Rome or beyond in the Catholic world. An exceptional voice was that of the Jesuit theologian Alonso Sandoval, who, while not condemning the enslavement of Africans in itself, excoriated their treatment by the Spanish. More than a century later, in 1794, a Capuchin friar, José de Bolonha, was expelled from a Spanish colony when he insisted that the African trade was unlawful because slaves had been acquired without regard to how they had been captured. Typical of seventeenth-century thought about race and slavery was the Dominican Jean-Baptiste Du Tertre, a missionary in the French West Indians, who strongly opposed Indian enslavement in the region but regarded Africans as natural slaves.

Everywhere in the Spanish and Portuguese colonies, laws required that slaves be baptized and be given religious instruction, the opportunity to worship, and the right to marry. Aside from the perfunctory baptism of slaves, the laws were largely honored in the breach—that is, ignored—despite periodic efforts by prelates and priests to make practice conform to law. In the French colonies the Code Noir of 1685 defined the blacks there as chattels but established their religious rights (baptism, instruction, freedom from work to attend worship on Sundays and holy days) and set down minimum requirements regarding food, clothing, and the care of the sick and aged. This law too was largely ignored. Indeed the treatment of slaves in the French colonies was among the most brutal in the western world.

Yet early on, a distinct form of Christianity formed in the slave communities in the French, Portuguese, and Spanish colonies, a syncretic blend of African religions and Christianity, in which African traditions of worship, ritual, and belief were incorporated into a Catholic framework. Thus veneration of *orisha*, or secondary gods, became associated with that the veneration of saints; and Yemoja, mother of African gods, was conflated in Afro-Christianity with the Virgin Mary. Ancestor worship, magical practices, and a kinetic liturgical style were other African influences on the Roman Catholicism the slaves embraced. This syncretism was epitomized in distinctive cults that developed among the enslaved Africans, such as *santería* in Cuba, *candomblé* in Brazil, and *vaudou* in Haiti.

The Church and Slavery in the Nineteenth Century

At the beginning of the seventeenth century a French canonist, Pierre Charron, had characterized New World slavery—which gave the master absolute power—as something that shamed human nature. Later, in 1633, Vincent Filliucius formally introduced a distinction between chattel slavery, in which the master's absolute power reduced the slave to personal property, and a limited slavery in which the master had a perpetual right to use the slave's labor but had to respect the slave's basic right to marry, exercise religious beliefs, and live humanely. Not until the end of the eighteenth century did a Catholic theologican attack—with official approval—the common Catholic teaching on slavery. In 1790 Nichlas Bergier denied the notion that slavery was a natural consequence of original sin. Even if it was, Bergier noted, Europeans had no right to presume that God had given them the charge to enslave Africans to fulfil the divine dispensation. In the next generation, the Swiss theologican Johann Sailer taught that slavery was to be condemned precisely because it converted persons into "mere things" and robbed them of their individuality. But in Spain in 1823, the authorities had put on the Index a theological handbook for confessors that condemned slavery.

Only when the church began missionary efforts in Africa in the early nineteenth century and confronted the slave trade directly did the papacy address African slavery. In 1815 Pope Pius VII, in response to appeals from European statesmen, agreed to support the efforts to abolish the international slave trade. A quarter-century later, Pope Gregory XVI—who, as a former head of the church's department of missions, had a deep interest in the African missions and knew intimately the evils of the slave trade—issued an encyclical, *In Supremo Apostolatus,* which, reflecting Sailer's argument, condemned "that inhuman trade by which Negroes, as if they were not men, but mere animals, . . . are . . . contrary to the laws of justice and humanity, bought, sold, and doomed."

The Irish reformer Daniel O'Connell and the French bishop Félix-Antoine-Philibert Dupanloup were two Europeans who condemned both slavery and racism in the mid-nineteenth century. O'Connell rejected slavery for making one person the property of another. Dupanloup reasoned that Christians had for too long failed to practice the reverse of the golden rule: "not to do to another that which you would not he should do to you."

Roman Catholicism and Slavery in the United States

In the United States which by the second quarter of the nineteenth century had become one of the last bastions of slavery in the western world, Roman Catholics were deeply involved with the institution. Until 1840 the majority of American Catholics lived in the South, and many were slaveholders, including religious orders such as the Jesuits, Vincentians, Ursulines, and Carmelites. However, many disapproved of slavery. Before 1820 many Catholics tended to view it as a social and economic affliction. In 1785, John Carroll, the first bishop of the United States, admitted to Rome his qualms about slavery. "I do the best I can to correct the evils I see," he reported. Roger Taney, a future Chief Justice of the U.S. Supreme Court (it was during his term that the Court rendered the Dred Scott decision), characterized slavery as "a blot on our national character." In 1832 William Gaston, a justice of the supreme court of North Carolina, called slavery "the worst evil that afflicts the Southern part of our confederacy." Still, few Catholics, whether laypeople or clerics, spoke openly against slavery. At the beginning of the century Bishop Carroll had removed a priest, John Thayer, from Kentucky, where he was preaching antislavery sermons to his congregation. In the 1850s, two Catholic antislavery spokesmen were David Broderick, a Democratic senator from California, and James Shields of Illinois; but they were exceptional. More typical was the Catholic editor and intellectual Orestes Brownson; he regarded slavery as a moral, social, and political evil but at the same time opposed abolition as a violation of private property that would bring disaster to the freed blacks, whom Brownson judged to be "the most degenerate branch of our race."

American Catholic leaders tended to maintain silence on the issue of slavery. Francis Kenrick, bishop of Philadelphia and the leading moral theologican in the American church, while deploring the deteriorating condition of bonded Africans by the 1840s, held that slavery was essentially a political matter that the state alone could resolve. Bishop John England of Charleston, in a series of articles in 1840–1841 occasioned by *In Supremo Apostolatus,* argued that Gregory had condemned only the slave trade practiced by the Spanish and Portuguese, not its form within the United States, much less the institution itself. After effectively legitimizing American slavery, England admitted that he was personally opposed to it but said its abolition was "a question for the legislature and not for me." When Daniel O'Connell appealed to Irish-Americans to oppose slavery, to only England but northern prelates such as John Hughes of New

York criticized him for interfering in America's internal affairs. Hughes, for his part, viewed slavery as a "comparative evil," far better than the state Africans knew in their homeland. On the matter of slavery the American bishops effected a rigid separation of the private and public orders. As a result the prelates kept their peace about even the worst evils of the system. (This separation might also explain how Roger Taney could free his own slaves and treat blacks as equals within the church, yet still write the opinion in *Dred Scott* that slavery had a special protection under the Constitution and hence that blacks had no civil rights which whites need respect.)

Ironically, the first American prelate to speak out publicly on the evils of slavery did so in the context of a pastoral in which he defended the institution. Bishop Augustin Verot of St. Augustine contended in January 1861 that the Bible, church tradition, and civil society had all approved slavery through the ages. A "man may sell his labor," Verot observed, "and work for a day, a week, a month, or a year. Why may he not sell it for all his life?" But if the Confederacy, which was then forming, was to perdure, Verot warned, the grave abuses afflicting slavery in the South, from the lack of provisions and decent housing to the sexual exploitation of slave women, had to be addressed. In that same year another southern bishop, Augustus Martin of Louisiana, gave the most radical public defense of slavery any American Catholic had ever uttered. The enslavement of Africans, Martin argued, was divinely ordained for the conversion of the black race and their rescue from Ham's curse. Thus slavery was a disguised blessing through which slaves received material care, moral enlightenment, and spiritual salvation.

During the Civil War one American bishop, John Baptist Purcell of Cincinnati, became an outspoken abolitionist. One of his suffragan bishops, Martin Spalding of Louisville, appealed to Rome in 1863 to silence Purcell. Slavery in the United States, Spalding informed the Holy See, was a tragic inherited social evil whose elimination would bring only greater evils in its wake. Indeed, he regarded Lincoln's emancipation policy as a state-sanctioned insurrection of slaves. But Spalding's attempt to muzzle Purcell failed. At that very time, the Papal States' consul in New York, Louis B. Binsse, was urging his superiors in Rome to put pressure on the American hierarchy to support abolition. American slavery, Binsse informed them, was a clear violation of natural rights. Slavery, he warned, was "the question of the day for the United States."

Throughout the century, Rome had addressed American slavery on a passive, ad hoc basis, respond-ing to requests for solutions to problems regarding slavery such as the sale of slaves (Propaganda had ruled in 1816 that this was not to be allowed, but nothing came of the decision). By chance, Martin's pastoral had by 1863 found its way to Rome, where it became the occasion for a change in papal teaching regarding slavery. A papal examiner, the Dominican Martin Gatti, found Martin's argument completely untenable. Gatti pointed out that even the blessing of Christianity was no "justification for the iniquity" which slavery and its trading in persons entailed. Slavery, Gatti said, was a violation of the natural right of liberty. Original sin was shared by all and was no excuse for perpetuating injustice. In effect Gatti's report condemned chattel slavery as well as slave trading, and Pope Pius IX accepted its recommendation to condemn Augustus Martin's pastoral and place it on the Index of Forbidden Books, should he not retract it. As Maria Caravaglios has observed in *The American Catholic Church and the Negro Problem in the XVIII–XIX Centuries*, in this byzantine way a small revolution in papal teaching was effected. But the condemnation was not promulgated.

Pius IX's successor, Leo XIII, became the first pontiff to publicly condemn not only slave trading but the institution itself, in his encyclical *Catholicae Ecclesiae* (1890). Seventy-five years later, at the Second Vatican Council, in the document *Gaudium et Spes*, the assembled bishops condemned any violence to the dignity of the human person, including slavery. They taught that any human institution must serve human needs and be a bulwark against any form of political or social slavery. *Gaudium et Spes* represented the culmination of the church's long development of its teaching on slavery.

See also BIBLE; CHATTEL SLAVERY; CODE NOIR; DRED SCOTT V. SANDFORD; NATIVE AMERICANS; PERSPECTIVES ON SLAVERY; RELIGIOUS GROUPS, SLAVE OWNERSHIP BY; SLAVE RELIGION.

BIBLIOGRAPHY

CARAVAGLIOS, MARIA GENOINO. *The American Catholic Church and the Negro Problem in the XVIII–XIX Centuries*, edited by Ernest L. Unterkoefler. 1974.

CURRAN, ROBERT EMMETT. "Rome, the American Church, and Slavery." In *Building the Catholic Church*, edited by Joseph C. Linck and Raymond Kupke. 1999.

CUSHNER, NICHOLAS P. *Lords of the Land: Sugar, Wine, and Jesuit Estates of Coastal Peru, 1600–1767.* 1980.

DAVIS, CYPRIAN, O. S. B. *The History of Black Catholics in the United States.* 1990.

DAVIS, DAVID BRION. *The Problem of Slavery in Western Culture.* 1966

FINN, PETER. "The Slaves of the Jesuits in Maryland." Master's thesis, Georgetown University. 1974.

MAXWELL, JOHN FRANCIS. *Slavery and the Catholic Church: the History of Catholic Teaching concerning the Moral Legitimacy of the Institution of Slavery.* 1975.

MICELI, MARY VERONICA. "Influence of the Roman Catholic Church on Slavery in Colonial Louisiana." Ph.D. diss., Tulane University. 1979.

MILLER, RANDALL M., and JON L. WAKELYN, eds. *Catholics in the Old South: Essays on Church and Culture.* 1983.

RABOTEAU, ALBERT J. *Slave Religion: The "Invisible Institution" in the Antebellum South.* 1978.

RICE, MADELEINE HOOKE. *American Catholic Opinion in the Slavery Controversy.* 1944.

SHARROW, WALTER G. "John Hughes and a Catholic Response to Slavery in Antebellum America." *Journal of Negro History* (1972): 252–269.

TRUDEL, MARCEL. *L'Esclavage au Canada français: Histoire et conditions de l'esclavage.* 1960.

ZANCE, KENNETH J., ed. *American Catholics and Slavery, 1789–1866.* 1994.

R. Emmett Curran

Protestantism

Responding to their Catholic critics, the great Protestant reformers of the sixteenth century adamantly denied that they sought to level all earthly distinctions among men. As early as the Peasants' War of 1524, in which the potential socially subversive aspects of the challenge to Rome and its church became real, Protestantism has provided a rationale to those who have challenged hierarchical social orders. But Martin Luther's commentary, *Against the Robbing and Murdering Hordes of Peasants*, published in the midst of the Peasants' War, unequivocally reminded his followers that the priesthood of all believers—perhaps the most fundamental of all Protestant tenets—did not mean the end of social hierarchy. Following a long Christian tradition, Luther maintained that even if one was a slave on earth, one was free in Christ Jesus.

John Calvin, Huldrych Zwingli, Martin Bucer, and the other continental reformers concurred with Luther about the social meaning of Protestantism, especially in light of an episode in Munster in 1534–1535, when the residents, much like the peasants a decade earlier, tried to put into practice the radical egalitarianism they had found in Protestant thought by establishing a communistic society. For many, the concept of a priesthood of all believers continued to challenge not only the special status of the clergy but any practice that altered the equal standing all humans had in relation to God; any distinction among men thus appeared foreign to true Christianity. Although few, if any, reformers applied this notion to slavery, including the slavery rapidly taking root in the New World, by the eighteenth century Protestants were leading the way in questioning the morality of slavery and its compatibility with Christianity. Both the movement to end the transatlantic slave trade and the abolitionist movement in Britain and the United States to end slavery itself owed an incalculable debt to Protestantism, especially evangelical Protestantism. Yet the rise of antislavery Protestantism did not signal the transformation of all Protestants into opponents of slavery. Quite the contrary: well into the nineteenth century Protestants easily reconciled their faith with slaveholding, and Protestant ministers were among the most effective and committed proslavery ideologues. Thus, historically, Protestantism proved to be a source of both antislavery and proslavery thought. This testifies to the complexity and ambiguity of the Protestant tradition.

One of the central pillars of Protestantism, *sola scriptura*, proved in the late eighteenth and nineteenth centuries to be a chief source of disagreement regarding the relationship between Christianity and slavery. Proslavery Protestants, such as the American Presbyterian James Henley Thornwell and the Baptist Richard Furman, repeatedly appealed to the Bible to support their claim that God's word sanctioned slaveholding. Citing numerous passages from the Old and New Testaments, including Genesis 9:25, Leviticus 24:44–46, and I Corinthians 12:13–26, proslavery Protestants constructed a powerful defense of slavery. But Protestantism emphasized that individuals needed to read and interpret the Bible for themselves; and antislavery Protestants—including the British evangelical William Wilberforce and the American revivalist Charles Grandison Finney—interpreted the Bible differently, finding grounds for opposing slavery. These antislavery Protestants, not bound by any authoritative mediating institution that could pronounce a "correct" interpretation of scripture, insisted that the spirit if not always the letter of the Bible condemned slavery. Antislavery Protestants generally advocated theological liberalism and individualism and a few, such as Finney, even tended toward perfectionism. Proslavery Protestants, in contradistinction, continued to emphasize original sin and viewed slavery as part of God's plan for fallen humanity. While antislavery Protestants objected to any institution or relationship that prevented individuals from pursuing their own understanding of God's word—and of God himself— proslavery Protestants maintained that the Bible required people to recognize their "station in life" and fulfill the duties and obligations imposed by that station. Antislavery Protestants increasingly distanced themselves from Luther's notion that the status of the body did not affect the relationship of the soul to Christ. Every individual, they claimed, had to be able to exercise free will in order to choose to live a Christian, sanctified life. To allow one creature to control another would inevitably and irreparably retard the subordinate's ability to live a Christian life. Therefore, slavery and Christianity were incompatible. Proslavery Protestants, in contrast, denied that physical domination necessarily interfered with the work of conversion. In fact, slaveholders and their allies argued that slavery helped spread the Gospel, and they urged masters to use their power to bring their slaves to Christ. Slavery, for them, became an efficient and divinely ordained means of Christianizing a hitherto pagan people. Thus different readings of scripture pointed to vastly different understandings of what social practices a Christian society could legitimately permit.

The extent to which slaves in the Americas embraced Protestantism depended on a number of factors, the most important being the religion of their masters. In Catholic areas, Protestantism won over few slaves, at least before emancipation. In predominantly Protestant areas, most notably the British West Indies and the area that became the United States, nearly all Christian slaves were Protestant. The great Protestant revivals, especially in North America, led to the conversion of many slaves to evangelical denominations, particularly the Baptists and, to a lesser extent, the Methodists. Part of the appeal of Protestantism was the evangelicals' emphasis on the experience of conversion, which in some respects resonated with African traditions. More important, Baptists and Methodists aggressively reached out to slaves and actively brought them to Christ. The conversion experience, and evangelical Protestantism in general, enabled slaves to feel a sense of worthiness and equality in the eyes of God. The Protestantism of the slaves stressed two themes: earthly deliverance and eternal salvation, symbolized by the figures of Moses and Jesus. Although slaves were generally denied literacy, as good Protestants they demonstrated a strong knowledge of scripture and repeatedly returned to passages and books that enabled them to see themselves as God's chosen, despite, or perhaps because of, their enslavement. Protestant slaves thus imparted to Protestantism a renewed emphasis on the redemption that follows suffering—if not in this world, then in the next.

See also BAPTIST CHRISTIANITY; THORNWELL, JAMES HENLEY; WILBERFORCE, WILLIAM.

BIBLIOGRAPHY

DAVIS, DAVID BRION. *The Problem of Slavery in the Age of Revolution.* 1975.
MCKIVIGAN, JOHN R. *The War against Proslavery Religion: Abolitionism and the Northern Churches, 1830–1865.* 1984.
SNAY, MITCHELL. *Gospel of Disunion: Religion and Separatism in the Antebellum South.* 1993.
TURLEY, DAVID. *The Culture of English Antislavery, 1780–1860.* 1991.

Douglas Ambrose

Churches, African-American

The Great Awakening of the 1740s, the first Protestant evangelical revival in British America, marked the beginning of Afro-Christianity in what was to become the United States. Africans almost certainly worshiped in slave settlements before 1740, although little evidence is available from the thirteen colonies. After the 1740s, African-Americans touched by the Great Awakening and subsequent revivals most often attended religious services in the presence of whites. Baptist and Methodist churches, often with black majorities in the South, and biracial revival meetings dominated the religious landscape.

The era directly after the American Revolution witnessed the development of African-American churches as separate institutions. The African Methodist Episcopal (AME) church in Philadelphia and the African Methodist Episcopal Zion (AMEZ) church in New York grew quickly between 1787 and 1820 from independent black congregations into independent black denominations. African-American Baptists moved more slowly to develop separate church associations, but independent congregations—with and without oversight and approval by whites—emerged not just in the North but also in the South, where slavery still prevailed.

Black-led churches derived from the spirit of evangelicalism, from the desire of blacks to worship as equals, and from a desire to establish certain religious beliefs rituals as orthodox—beliefs and rituals that African-Americans considered essential to authentic communities of faith. Though independent black churches were much more common in regions where slavery had withered, a remarkable number flourished within slave states, tolerated grudgingly by slaves masters, at least until Denmark Vesey's conspiracy in South Carolina in 1822 and Nat Turner's revolt in Virginia in 1831 proved that black churches and preachers posed a dire threat to slave society. The development of black churches in the South after 1831 was often slowed by the combined forces of slaveowners, white churches, and the state.

Undaunted, slaves barred from independent worship in their own churches often held services in the woods. Not satisfied with segregated worship in white-run plantation chapels, slaves gathered in "brush arbors" or "hush arbors" in the woods, to hear their own preachers and be transported by their own rituals.

The fundamental problem with "integrated" Christianity in a society ordered by racial slavery was that whites were generally incapable of separating their secular ideology from their religious beliefs. White supremacy as a sociopolitical ideology fatally corrupted a professed spiritual equality of all believers, creating a set of churches hobbled by a form of idolatry, the narcissism of whiteness. African-Americans withdrew from such churches, not only because they were denied equally in ritual and theology, but because they sensed a heresy that betrayed the promise of the Great Awakening. So powerful was this repulsion that black churches remained bulwarks of resistance to black as well as white chauvinism well into the twentieth century.

There is every reason to believe that the order of worship in freedpeople churches derived directly from that developed in slaves' churches. Services consisted of two contrasting frames within a single meeting. De-

votion, the first frame, consisted of alternating hymn singing and prayers led by deacons, in archaic but near-standard English; the rhythm was slow, almost dirge-like. "Shouting," the outward manifestation of spiritual possession, was discouraged. An upbeat hymn announced the appearance of the preacher, the closing of the first frame, and the start of the second. The church rocked as the music soared. The pastor rose and moved to stage center to offer the centerpiece of the worship drama—the sermon, a spiritual poem. The sermon was delivered in the vernacular called Black English. Its rhythms and tones invited and compelled spiritual possession. The sermon was often interrupted by the congregation: one type of interruption was a rhythmic counterpoint to the pastor, releasing creative energy; the other type was the cries of the possessed. This ritual structure, augmented by "ring shouts," "holy dances," and a range of other spiritual practices, was the lifeblood of a distinct black Christianity.

The African-American church, partly visible but mainly invisible during slavery, constituted one of the most important creations by any immigrants to the Western Hemisphere. It was nothing less than a challenge from a non-European tradition of spirituality and metaphysics, embedded in the structure of the most powerful European settler society in the Americas. A perpetual moral and spiritual challenger of the dominant society, black churches undermined slavery, provided sites and sources of leadership for the emancipated, and remained a center of ethnic and moral cohesion for people of African descent.

See also CHRISTIANITY; SLAVE RELIGION; TURNER, NAT; VESEY REBELLION.

BIBLIOGRAPHY

HOPKINS, DWIGHT N., and GEORGE CUMMINGS. *Cut Loose Your Stammering Tongue: Black Theology in the Slave Narratives.* 1991.

JOHNSON, CLIFTON H., ed. *God Struck Me Dead: Religious Conversion Experiences and Autobiographies of Ex-Slaves.* 1969.

RABOTEAU, ALBERT J. *Slave Religion: The "Invisible Institution" in the Antebellum South.* 1978.

SOBEL, MECHAL. *Trabelin' On: The Slave Journey to an Afro-Baptist Faith.* 1979.

Harold S. Forsythe

A nineteenth-century sketch of an African-American preacher addressing his congregation. [Corbis-Bettmann]

Church of England

See Anglicanism.

Cimarron

See Maroons.

Cinqué   [ca. 1814–ca. 1879]

Black leader of mutiny on Amistad *in 1839.*

Joseph Cinqué was born Sengbeh Pieh in Mende, located in Sierra Leone in West Africa. He was captured by slave traders in early 1839 and taken to the coast, where he and hundreds of other Africans were loaded onto the Portuguese slaver *Tecora* in preparation for the long Middle Passage to Cuba. An Anglo-Spanish treaty in 1817 had outlawed the African slave trade, but slavery was legal in Cuba and the captain of the *Tecora* disembarked the blacks onto the island secretly, at night.

In Havana, Cinqué and fifty-two other Africans were purchased by two Spanish merchants, José Ruiz and Pedro Montes, who chartered the *Amistad* to transport their slaves to two plantations three hundred miles away, in Puerto Principe. On the night of 1–2 July 1839, Cinqué led a revolt, killing the captain and the cook. Two other crew members jumped overboard and probably drowned. The mutineers took control of the vessel and ordered the two Spaniards to navigate the *Amistad* to Africa. Ruiz and Montes tried to trick the blacks by sailing back and forth in Cuban waters, hoping for rescue by a British antislave trade patrol. Instead, however, the *Amistad* inched northward until, after a sixty-day trek, it entered the waters off Long Island. An American naval captain captured the vessel and took his prize to an admiralty court in New London, Connecticut.

Cinqué attracted popular attention after a group of abolitionists, led by the New York financier Lewis Tappan, seized upon the event as a way to publicize the horrors of the slave trade and slavery itself by defending the captives in court as "kidnapped Africans." The two Spaniards sought the blacks' return as "property," and the government in Madrid wanted them tried for murder. After circuit and district court proceedings in Connecticut, the climax came in 1841, before the U.S. Supreme Court. There, former president John Quincy Adams defended the captives, accusing President Martin Van Buren of illegally interfering in the case. Adams argued for the blacks' freedom on the basis of the natural rights outlined in the Declaration of Independence. On 9 March Justice Joseph Story freed the blacks ruling that they were kidnapped Africans who had exercised their inherent right of self-defense in breaking their bonds.

In January 1842, Cinqué and thirty-four other survivors of the mutiny made it back to Africa. This was the only time in history that any blacks, captured and forced into slavery in the New Word, returned home. As a result, Cinqué's image in history is that of a successful slave rebel. No evidence has appeared regarding whether or not he was reunited with his wife and children in Africa. Like other parts of this story, Cinqué's life afterward remains a mystery.

See also AMISTAD; SLAVE TRADE; TAPPAN BROTHERS.

BIBLIOGRAPHY

JONES, HOWARD. *Mutiny on the Amistad: The Saga of a Slave Revolt and Its Impact on American Abolition, Law, and Diplomacy.* 1987; revised and expanded, 1997.
WYATT-BROWN, BERTRAM. *Lewis Tappan and the Evangelical War against Slavery.* 1969.

Howard Jones

Civil Rights Act of 1866 (U.S.)

In 1865 the Thirteenth Amendment abolished slavery in the United States. However, it did not prevent the states of the former Confederacy from passing the so-called Black Codes. Although these laws varied from one state to another, most of them forbade or restricted the rights of freedpersons to hold certain jobs, live outside rural areas, own weapons, and dictate the terms by which their children could be apprenticed. Because these codes perpetuated the legal inferiority of blacks, in 1866 Congress passed "An Act to Protect All Persons in the United States in Their Civil Rights, and Furnish Means of Their Vindication." This act conferred citizenship upon freedpersons; affirmed their right to make contracts, sue and testify in a court of law, and buy and sell property; guaranteed equal treatment for blacks in legal proceedings; and empowered federal commissioners to enforce these provisions by using federal troops and local militia.

President Andrew Johnson vetoed the bill on the ground that it also granted citizenship to American-born Chinese, taxpaying Indians, and Gypsies, and that its provisions, while pretending to promote color-blindness, actually operated to the detriment of the white majority. Shortly thereafter Congress overrode Johnson's veto, thus making the act law. Because some question existed concerning the act's constitutionality, Congress also passed the Fourteenth Amendment, the first constitutional definition of American citizenship. In 1870, following the ratification of this and the Fifteenth Amendment, which specifically gave blacks the right to vote, Congress reenacted the Civil Rights Act of 1866.

See also CIVIL RIGHTS ACT OF 1875.

BIBLIOGRAPHY

HALL, KERMIT L., WILLIAM M. WIECEK, and PAUL FINKELMAN. *American Legal History: Cases and Materials.* 2nd ed. 1996.

Charles W. Carey Jr.

Civil Rights Act of 1875 (U.S.)

The Civil Rights Act of 1866 established the legal equality of freedmen; however, it did not address the question of social equality between blacks and whites. In 1870 Senator Charles Sumner of Massachusetts introduced a bill designed to overturn the laws passed by the states of the former Confederacy that restricted the right of freedpersons to work and live where they chose. Sumner's bill, entitled "An Act to Protect All Citizens in Their Civil and Legal Rights," established the rights of blacks to sit on juries; to be admitted to all businesses that accommodated the general public, such as railway cars, steamboats, taverns, hotels, theaters, "and other places of public amusement"; and to attend public schools. This last provision was struck from the bill because white northerners objected to sending their children to integrated schools almost as much as did white southerners. After five years of acrimonious debate, the bill became law.

The Civil Rights Act of 1875 was the last piece of Reconstruction legislation. Because it confronted white racist attitudes in the North as well as the South, the support it received from federal officials was lukewarm at best. In 1883 the act was overturned by the U.S. Supreme Court in the *Civil Rights Cases,* five proceedings involving public establishments in California, Kansas, Missouri, New York, and Tennessee that refused admission to blacks. The court ruled that, although the Fourteenth Amendment prohibited racial discrimination by the states, it did not prohibit racial discrimination by private individuals or businesses.

See also CIVIL RIGHTS ACT OF 1866.

BIBLIOGRAPHY

HALL, KERMIT L., WILLIAM M. WIECEK, and PAUL FINKELMAN. *American Legal History: Cases and Materials.* 2nd ed. 1996.

Charles W. Carey Jr.

Civil War, U.S.

At the outbreak of the Civil War the expectations of northern ideologues skyrocketed. The black abolitionist Frederick Douglass exulted, "For fifty years the country has taken the law from the lips of an exacting, haughty and imperious slave oligarchy. . . . Lincoln's election has vitiated their authority, and broken their power. . . ." Many white abolitionists enjoyed a fantasy that the southern states' secession would rally the North around their cause. Few northern blacks suffered such illusions.

Most Union politicians were reluctant to tackle slavery at the outset of the war. President Abraham Lincoln insisted that the purpose of the war was to preserve the Union and not to attack slavery where it was already in place. Until he issued the preliminary Emancipation Proclamation in September 1862, Lincoln refused to tie abolition to his wartime goal of holding the nation together. Thus, on 3 December 1861, Lincoln proposed colonization of emancipated blacks. The president hoped this proposal would encourage voluntary manumission in the loyal slave states. He was convinced that those slaves from the Confederate states who sought refuge behind Union lines should be encouraged to emigrate, and that the government should assist them. Lincoln's appropriation of $600,000 for this purpose was perhaps meant to capitalize on Haitian migration schemes sponsored by black abolitionists such as Henry Highland Garnet. However, with the outbreak of war, most emigrationists shifted their efforts toward improving the status of black within the Union. In 1862 Lincoln appointed Senator Samuel Clark Pomeroy of Kansas as the "United States Colonization Agent," and authorized him to explore a scheme whereby coal would be supplied to the U.S. Navy at half-price if "colonists" would be shipped to Chiriqui (part of present-day Panama) to work in the coal mines. Free blacks throughout the North protested.

President Lincoln consistently attempted to appease the slaveholders in loyal and border states, a policy that delayed the enlistment of both slave and free black soldiers. Some did not just despair over bureaucratic foot-dragging but seized the initiative and organized on their own—knowing that progressive Union reforms would follow only if military expedience required a shift in policy.

Within weeks of the first Battle of Bull Run in July 1861—a battle in which the Confederates humiliated federal troops—Union commanders faced a perplexing problem. Slaves were escaping by the hundreds and soon by the thousands behind Union lines. Union camps overflowed with slaves who had "stolen themselves" from rebel masters. The problem was handled ad hoc during the first chaotic months of war—causing bitterness and confusion, especially for slaves seeking safety. The Reverend Sella Martin of the Joy Street Baptist Church in Boston, a former slave who had made his way to freedom in 1855, railed against Union commanders who returned runaways to their masters. On the other hand, blacks and abolitionists cheered the creative solution of General Benjamin F. Butler of Massachusetts. An attorney before the war, Butler concluded that slaves owned by Confederates were legally "contraband of war," and thus he provided safe haven for any who reached his lines.

By midsummer federal authorities realized that they were contributing to the chaos and moved to impose order. On 6 August 1861 Congress passed the First Confiscation Act, which called for the seizure of all property in aid of rebellion, including human property—slaves. The term "contraband," appropriate perhaps during the first few weeks of war, unfortunately stuck. Rapidly, quartermasters and engineers, treating ex-slaves like indentured labor, put African-American refugees to work as manual laborers—ditchdiggers and dike builders—and slave women were put to work as cooks and washerwomen. The war was less than six months old, but a growing and potent labor force of freed blacks was demonstrating its importance to the Union.

Several Union commanders interpreted the law to suit their own need for manpower. In his jurisdiction in Missouri, General John C. Fremont advocated radical change. On 30 August 1861, Fremont declared marital law and abolished slavery. After Lincoln objected, the policy was modified on 11 September to emancipate only those slaves who "aided Confederate military forces."

Another trailblazing Union commander, General David Hunter, was in charge of Union troops along the coast of South Carolina, Georgia, and Florida. As early as April 1861, Hunter had requested muskets and uniforms for 50,000 ex-slaves he planned to recruit. On 9 May 1862, recognizing the strategic impact black soldiers could have, Hunter declared slaves in the three states "forever free." Lincoln, again concerned about balancing competing northern interests, countermanded Hunter's orders on 19 May.

But by this time the War Department shifted policy, acknowledging that armed ex-slaves could be effective in defeating the Confederacy. General Rufus Saxton in South Carolina drafted five thousand black men as laborers and enlisted five thousand additional African-Americans as soldiers to "receive the same pay and rations as are allowed by law to the volunteers in the service."

The shifting winds of war had their effect. Abolitionists took this as an opportunity to demand and achieve certain victories; in April 1862 Congress abolished slavery in the District of Columbia. With this legislative stroke, the tide seemed to turn and the rest of the year saw revolutionary advances.

In July 1862 the Second Confiscation Act and the Militia Act clarified the status of former slaves. The Union, committed to crippling the enemy, declared that all captured and fugitive slaves belonging to rebel masters were "forever free." Further, they could be enlisted "in any military or naval service for which they may be found competent."

General Daniel Ullmann in Louisiana raided the cane and cotton fields in the Gulf to fill his ranks. The black troops enlisted by General Edward A. Wild in North Carolina came to be known as Wild's African Brigade. Congressional support for massive confiscation of slaves and the endorsement of black enlistment paved the way for the preliminary Emancipation Proclamation in September 1862, signaling a radicalization of Union policy.

The arguments spewing forth from Confederates—reviling former slaves, proclaiming white superiority, and other racist dogma—could well have come from the mouths of most northern statesmen and all but a handful of white Union soldiers. In reality, moral outrage against slavery in the North emanated from free labor's resentment of slave labor. Although abolitionists saw the battle as a contest between the liberating North and the despotic South, most northern whites viewed the liberation of slaves as a sacrifice on the chessboard of war, and perhaps many thought of it as a "necessary evil."

The rising dissatisfaction with the war among an increasingly alienated civilian population fostered a movement to enlist slaves to fight the war. General Ulysses S. Grant confided optimistically to Abraham Lincoln in August 1863, "By arming the negro we have added a powerful ally. They will make good soldiers and taking them from the enemy weakens him in the same proportion they strengthen us." African-Americans in the military, especially armed former slaves fighting alongside whites and against their former masters ushered in a new era.

By the time Lincoln issued the final Emancipation Proclamation on 1 January 1863, the demands for manpower exceeded the supply. As white recruits dwindled dramatically, "press gangs" roamed the countryside. The impressment of many African-Americans into Union military service by these means was akin to kidnapping. Ben Butler warned, "I found a most disgraceful trade being carried on here [Virginia] in comparison to which the slave trade was commendable." A brisk "black market" emerged as northerners paid ex-slaves $50 to $100 to go North and enlist, while unscrupulous agents collected $500 to $1,000 as fees for finding substitutes.

By the end of the War, over 186,000 blacks served as soldiers in the U.S. Army. Black army recruits were drawn from all over, but the border states of Delaware, Maryland, Missouri, and Kentucky contributed about 42,000—nearly a quarter of all blacks in the army. About 94,000 black soldiers came from the Confederate states, and with the exception of contingents of "free men of color" from Louisiana, these soldiers had been slaves before they donned blue uniforms. The numbers of black soldiers from the Confederate states were divided roughly as follows: Tennessee, 20,000; Louisiana, 24,000; Mississippi, 18,000; Virginia 6,000; North Carolina, 5,000; South Carolina, 5,500; Geor-

Black troops under the leadership of General Edward A. Wild liberate the slaves on a North Carolina plantation. [Library of Congress/Corbis]

gia, 3,500; Florida, 1,000; Alabama, 5,000; Arkansas, 5,500; Texas, 500; About 50,000 black soldiers came from the North or Canada, and they included free-born blacks and fugitive slaves. In addition to those in the army, more than 20,000 blacks served in the navy and many others numbering in the tens of thousands worked for the military as laborers, cooks, teamsters, grave diggers, and hospital attendants,

Over time, Congress was forced to face up to its responsibilities to black southerners, desperate for Union support. Congress promised to emancipate families of soldiers. In March 1865, Congress funded a "Bureau of Refugees, Freedmen, and Abandoned Lands," which came to be known as the Freedmen's Bureau, headed by an imaginative and indomitable one-armed war hero from Maine, General Oliver O. Howard. This bureau, in its short life, became not just the court of last resort but the only resource for legal, political, or moral support for freedpeople, caught up in throes of slavery's unwilling demise.

Many of the white federal officers who came into contact with black soldiers were taught volumes about race relations, lessons more valuable than mere book-learning. Surgeon Humphrey H. Hood examined re-

cruits for Third U.S. Colored Heavy Artillery and concluded, "I have occasion to see the backs of these men and anyone inspired to read might there read corroborative evidence of all that Mrs. Stowe ever wrote of the cruelty of slavery." Hood estimated that over one-half of those examined were scarred by the lash. Colonel Thomas Wentworth Higginson, commanding South Carolina Volunteers, confided, "The whole command was attacked on the return by a rebel force, which turned out to be what was called in those regions a 'dog-company,' consisting of mounted riflemen with half a dozen trained bloodhounds. The men met these dogs with their bayonets, killed four of five of their old tormentors with great relish and brought away the carcass of one."

An army superintendent near Camp Nelson, Kentucky, described a sorrowful scene: "Only this day a colored woman walked from Nicholasville six miles, bringing in her arms the body of her dead child because the Chivalry in Nicholasville, through prejidice [sic] refused its burial!" Beaufort, South Carolina was a memorable place for many Union troops, a region almost wholly abandoned by slave owners, where several thousand freedpeople started schools, farmed

Company E, Fourth Colored Infantry, 1865. [Corbis-Bettmann]

their own land, and pioneered black autonomy, under Union protection. Charlotte Forten, a black writer and teacher of freedpeople, described a moving scene on Emancipation Day, when Higginson "still stood holding the flags in his hand, some of the colored people, of their own accord, commensed singing, 'My Country 'tis of thee.' It was a touching and beautiful incident, and sent a thrill through all our hearts."

African-American families left behind on slave-owning plantations sent plaintive cries for help to black soldiers away in battle. One wife in Missouri wrote to her husband, "they are treating me worse and worse every day. Our child cries for you. Send me some money as soon as you can for me and my child are almost naked." Masters frequently retaliated against the families of men who had enlisted with the enemy. A Union provost marshal reported in March 1864, "The wife of a colored recruit came into my Office tonight and says she has been severely beaten and driven from home by her master and owner. She has a child some two years old with her, and says she left two larger ones at home." Notes and cash could

be smuggled back to loved ones behind Confederate lines only with the help of sympathetic whites as go-betweens.

Many slave women risked life and limb to escape worsening conditions. At one point, the South Carolina Volunteers rescued a soldier's wife who "had escaped from the main-land in a boat, with that child and another. Her baby was shot dead in her arms, and she reached our lines with one child safe on earth and the other in heaven." Another slave mother who tried to take advantage of a law emancipating soldiers' families was accosted by her master's son-in-law, "who told me that if I did not go back with him he would shoot me." He took her seven-year-old child as a hostage, and the woman returned to slavery with her other children. Provost marshals' reports and the Freedmen's Bureau's records overflow with complaints—kidnappings, beatings, and other abuses.

Nearly 4 million slaves lived in the Confederate states at the outbreak of war. Conspiracies and plots seemed to break out spontaneously in the weeks after war was declared. On 14 May 1861 a planter in Jefferson County, Mississippi, confided his fears to the governor: "A plot has been discovered and [alrea]dy three Negroes have gone the way of all flesh or rather paid with forfeiture of their lives." The conspirators, he went on to warn, had "diabolical plans," as "white males were all to be destroyed—such of the females as suited their fancy were to be preserved as Wives and they were to march up the river to meet 'Mr. Linkin' bearing off booty such things as they could carry." This tone of hysteria typified wartime fears in the deep South, where blacks might outnumber whites twenty to one—especially along the Mississippi River, where Union gunboats would inevitably converge.

By the end of the first long hot summer of war, slave owners isolated on their vast plantations were exhausted with worry. Another plot was uncovered in northern Mississippi, this time in Adams County. In the autumn of 1861 a Mississippi woman reported the rumor "that a miserable, sneaking abolitionist has been at the bottom of this whole affair. I hope that he will be caught and burned alive." Local investigators later decided that the affair was a homegrown conspiracy, with slaves planning to rise up against their masters when federal troops invaded. Reportedly, twenty-seven black men were hanged by secret kangaroo courts stemming from the investigation. A plantation woman confided to her niece, "it is kept very still, not to be in the papers." Slave owners feared the publicity surrounding such events almost as much as the conspiracies themselves. During wartime they hoped to quell conspiracies with swift retaliation and ominous silence.

By the second year of the war, desertion, relocations, and migration meant that the slaves remaining on plantations were disproportionately women and children. Major bloody battles had drained the states, both North and South, of able-bodied men.

Materially, day-to-day conditions on plantations behind Confederate lines declined steadily. Yet, many black young people on the land initially found the whole idea of war exotic and intriguing. Rachel Harris recalled, "I went with the white children and watched the soldiers marchin'. The drums was playing and next thing I heerd, the war was gwine on. You could hear the guns just as plain. The soldiers went by just in droves from soon of a mornin' till sundown." But soon the depletion of adult labor increased the burden on slave children. Henry Nelson, only ten years old when the war broke out, remembered, "You know chillun them days, they made em do a man's work." Eliza Scantling, fifteen in 1865, remembered that she "plowed a mule an' a wild un at dat. Sometimes me hands get so cold I jes' cry." War brought other consequences: James Goings, only three when war broke

out, recalled that by the end of the war, "it wuzn't nuthin' to fin' a dead man in de woods."

As slave men fled the plantations, leaving wives and children behind, thousands were fatherless and hundreds were orphaned. Annie Lumpkin of South Carolina recalled her wartime loss: "My daddy go 'way to de war 'bout dis time, and my mammy and me stay in our cabin alone. She cry and wonder where he be, if he is well or he be killed, and one day we hear he is dead. My mammy, too, pass in a short time." Slave children, like their white counterparts, made unwilling sacrifices.

Recalcitrant and at times rebellious slaves often thwarted the plans of rebel masters. In eastern Tennessee locals complained that women in the fields were negotiating terms by striking. During the fall of 1863, when over 20,000 slaves were recruited off plantations in the Mississippi Valley alone, Jane Pickett, a planter's wife and a refugee, exclaimed, "The negroes in most instances refused to leave with their masters, and in some cases have left the plantations in a perfect stampede. Mississippi is almost depopulated of its black population." Emma LeConte in South Carolina lamented, "The field negroes are in a dreadful state; they will not work, but either roam the country or sit in their houses." Black resistance, on top of so many other disadvantages, presented the Confederates with a massive and increasing problem.

The slave grapevine became a powerful part of Union intelligence. Robert Russa Moton recalled that "if a slave coming back from town greeted a fellow-servant with the declaration, 'Good morning' Sam, yo look mighty greasy this mornin', that meant that he had picked up some fresh information about the prospects of freedom." Blacks used other code words, such as "Old Ride-up" to refer to Abraham Lincoln.

The loss of slave labor and the effects of slave intelligence were so devastating to the Confederacy that it finally authorized impressment of slaves for noncombatant roles in its military. Eventually, in November 1864, Jefferson Davis reluctantly agreed to both gradual emancipation and the military use of African-Americans. However, the Confederate president had assumed wrongly that slave owners would do anything to win the war. He discovered that his people would rather risk defeat than give up their mastery over slaves. Slaveholders stuck to their guns—for whites only—and this doomed the Confederacy.

In 1864 the Confederacy was reeling from a final onslaught of Union victories—the Red River campaign in the early spring; the "battle of the wilderness" in May; the victory at Cold Harbor in June; the fall of Atlanta in September, the battle of Franklin, Tennessee, in November; and finally, Lincoln's Christmas present from Sherman, the surrender of Savannah in December. On 9 April 1865, as the fourth anniversary of war approached, Lee surrendered to Grant as Appomattox.

The war's end was celebrated in intense, dramatic fashion. Mathilda Dunbar, the mother of poet Paul Laurence Dunbar, recalled, "I was in the kitchen getting breakfast. The word came—'All darkies are free.' I never finished that breakfast! . . . Oh, how we sang and shouted that day!" Thousands of similar jubilees echoed throughout the South. Black soldiers could return home, but what those homes might be remained contested. For all the valor and glory garnered by African-Americans in the war, and despite the death blow dealt to slavery, the battle would continue.

See also ABOLITION AND ANTISLAVERY MOVEMENTS; BUTLER, BENJAMIN; CONTRABAND; DOUGLASS, FREDERICK; FREEDMEN'S BUREAU; GARNET, HENRY; LAW; LINCOLN, ABRAHAM; MILITARY SLAVES; REPATRIATION TO AFRICA; SLAVE NARRATIVES.

BIBLIOGRAPHY

CORNISH, DUDLEY T. *The Sable Arm: Black Troops in the Union Army, 1861–1865.* 1987.
GLATTHAAR, JOSEPH T. *Forged in Battle: The Civil War Alliance of Black Soldiers and White Officers.* 1989.
MCPHERSON, JAMES M. *Battle Cry of Freedom.* 1989.
———. *The Negro Civil War: How American Blacks Felt and Acted during the War for the Union.* 1991.

Catherine Clinton

Clarkson, Thomas   [1760–1846]

British antislavery activist.

Thomas Clarkson was a longtime associate of William Wilberforce in the campaign to end the African slave trade to the West Indies and then to abolish West Indies slavery. Educated at Cambridge, he was author of a prizewinning graduate essay on the slave trade that was translated from Latin into English and published in London and Philadelphia in 1786. Winning Wilberforce's attention, he was among the founders of a predominantly Quaker antislavetrade committee established the following year.

Clarkson's own Anglican and establishment background gave him entry to circles that Quakers had difficulty reaching. An early achievement was the enactment in 1788 by Parliament of a law regulating conditions on slaving ships. Clarkson traveled to Paris the next year with the hope that the revolutionary government would take a stronger stance. Continuing the pattern he set in England, he consorted there with such figures as Lafayette and Mirabeau. Much later, after the French Revolution's final defeat, he would try to rally the Russian czar to the antislavery cause.

Thomas Clarkson. [Corbis-Bettmann]

Clarkson was a prolific writer, both privately and publicly, on the evils of slavery and on many other causes. His enormous correspondence, preserved at the Huntington Library, is very revealing about the inner workings of the British antislavery movement. He moved from endorsing amelioration of the slaves' condition, as a first step, to a recognition that even outright abolition of the slave trade would not be enough to bring slavery down. He also produced the two-volume *History of the Abolition of the African Slave Trade.*

See also ABOLITION AND ANTISLAVERY MOVEMENTS; SLAVE TRADE; WILBERFORCE, WILLIAM.

BIBLIOGRAPHY

WILSON, ELLEN GIBSON. *Thomas Clarkson: A Biography.* 1990.

Edward Countryman

Claver, Pedro   [1580–1654]

Roman Catholic missionary to African slaves in South America.

Born in Verdú, Catalonia, near Barcelona, Pedro Claver entered the Society of Jesus (Jesuits) in 1602.

He studied in Majorca and was sent to New Granada (now Colombia) in 1616, where his Jesuit superiors assigned him to minister to the African slaves who were landed at Cartagena.

Claver considered his most important work to be the conversion of Africans and signed himself "*Aethiopum semper servus*" (forever slave of the Africans). He learned Angolan languages in order to evangelize, boarding slave ships to tend to the sick and injured and preaching the gospel with the aid of illustrations, rewards, and punishments. Slaves belonging to the Jesuit community acted as interpreters and godparents to the slaves Claver converted. He claimed to have baptized 300,000 slaves over the course of his thirty-five-year ministry. He also tended to the sick, to victims of the plague, to people in prison, and to those condemned to death.

Claver toured the hinterland to observe conditions on plantations and in mines, staying in slave quarters. He protested the inhumane treatment of slaves and struggled throughout his life for proper treatment in accord with Spanish slave law. He did not challenge the institution of slavery, although he welcomed the condemnation of the slave trade by Pope Urban VIII in 1639.

Claver fell ill with the plague in 1650 and died at Cartagena in 1654. He was canonized in 1888 by Pope Leo XIII, who named him patron saint of missions to Africans in 1896.

See also MISSIONARIES.

BIBLIOGRAPHY

LUNN, ARNOLD. *A Saint in the Slave Trade: Peter Claver, 1581–1654.* 1947.
VALTIERRA, ANGEL. *Peter Canisius: Saint of the Slaves.* Translated by Janet H. Perry and L. J. Woodward. 1960.

Stephen Wagley

A statue in Cartagena, Colombia, commemorates the works of Pedro Claver. [Jeremy Horner/Corbis]

Clothing, U.S.

Clothing was a badge of servitude for slave men and women in the antebellum United States. Slaveowners recognized this potential for clothing and legislated in eighteenth-century slave codes specific regulations for slaves' clothing. South Carolina was typical. While requiring that slaveowners provide adequate clothing for their slaves or be fined, laws passed in 1740 stipulated that slaves wear only the coarsest of fabrics—what some termed "negro cloth"—rather than the finery worn by their owners. Even when such slave codes disappeared from the law books, this distinction between the clothing of the powerless and that of the powerful continued in custom. On individual plantations, owners strictly enforced what a slave could wear. Twice a year the master distributed clothing to his servants: usually two cotton outfits for spring and summer and two woolen suits for winter. On the largest plantations, this clothing might have been manufactured by the slaves themselves, under the supervision of the plantation mistress.

The slaves' clothing reflected their work. House servants and carriage drivers who came into contact with the white family could expect clothing of a finer quality than that which was made available to field slaves. Lace, silks, and petticoats were occasionally worn by the men and women who served the master's household, although their garments were still inferior in quality to those worn by the white family. Field slaves were given the simplest of clothing, and had little opportunity to wash or change their clothing more often than once a week. Slaves' clothing also tended to reflect the status of their owners. Wealthier masters expected their slaves to look more presentable. A well-dressed slave would indicate wealth and prestige on the part of a master.

At the same time, clothing also served as an expression of a slave's individuality. Narratives of ex-slaves indicate that these men and women modified their given clothing with dyes, buttons, and other forms of decoration. Some altered their dress according to African tradition, by dying their clothes red, a color representing life and fertility in West Africa, or by wearing headwraps or jewelry. Field slaves actually enjoyed greater latitude in altering their clothing, as white families paid less attention to their dress. Slaves who hired out and were allowed to keep some payment for their work also could afford to purchase clothing of their choice. In slave quarters, it was also not uncommon for slaves to greet special occasions such as weddings, funerals, and church services with finer clothes. Yet at times the slaves came under fiery criticism from their masters for this indulgence, for finer types of clothing could serve as a disguise for slaves who ran away to freedom.

Despite their best efforts, however, slaves could hardly compensate for the poor quality that generally characterized their clothing. The fabrics were generally too rough and uncomfortable for everyday use, and some slaves became ill from being exposed to winter weather in flimsy clothing. Shoes were perhaps the most inadequate article of clothing issued to slaves. It was not uncommon for a field slave to go barefoot, and even those who received shoes often found them too stiff or too small. By the late antebellum years, ministers and other writers spoke out against the general indifference of masters to the quality of slave clothing. Despite a noticeable improvement in these decades, new clothing was still among the first items that slaves sought when they ran away to freedom during the Civil War.

See also BADGES OF SLAVERY; MATERIAL CULTURE IN THE UNITED STATES.

BIBLIOGRAPHY

FOSTER, HELEN BRADLEY. *"New Raiments of Self": African American Clothing in the Antebellum South.* 1997.
GENOVESE, EUGENE D. *Roll Jordan Roll: The World the Slaves Made.* 1972.
RAWICK, GEORGE P., ed. *The American Slave: A Composite Autobiography.* 1972.

Amy E. Murrell

Coartación

Spanish law drew on Roman precedents that allowed slaves to own property and buy freedom. In Havana and elsewhere in the Caribbean, owners commonly permitted a slave's self-purchase. If an owner refused or an agreement broke down, slaves were quick to initiate a legal action, called *coartación,* by which the court determined a slave's "just price." Slave and owner each named an assessor, but if estimates varied greatly, the court solicited a third evaluation to help make its decision. The court also appointed special advocates to protect the rights of enslaved children.

Once the court established a just price, an owner's rights were *coartado,* "restricted." The slave could live and work independently and make installment payments on his or her freedom. When the slave had paid the mandated sum, the court issued a notarized document detailing his or her citizenship rights.

In the eighteenth century adult slaves usually paid between two hundred and five hundred pesos for freedom. Highly skilled slaves paid as much as eight hundred to one thousand pesos, with pesos valued at roughly the equivalent number of contemporary U.S. dollars. A child's freedom usually cost less than one hundred pesos.

An owner might challenge an evaluation, but even influential slaveowners had difficulty impeding *coartación* when the law presumed liberty was mankind's natural state. Although the judicial system was sympathetic, even urban slaves would have found it an arduous process to save several hundred pesos when the average day's pay for a man was a half peso and for a woman, half that.

See also CARIBBEAN REGION; SELF-PURCHASE.

BIBLIOGRAPHY

AIMES, HUBERT H. S. "Coartación: A Spanish Institution for the Advancement of Slaves into Freedmen." *Yale Review* 17 (1909): 412–31.
LANDERS, JANE. "Traditions of African American Freedom and Community in Spanish Colonial Florida." In *The African American Heritage of Florida,* edited by David R. Colburn and Jane Landers.

Jane G. Landers

Cobb, Thomas R. R.   [1823–1862]

Legal scholar and Confederate officer.

Born on a Virginia plantation, Thomas R. R. Cobb grew up in Athens, Georgia, where he attended the University of Georgia and took up the study of law. After establishing a legal practice in 1849, Cobb became reporter of Georgia Supreme Court decisions and later published a digest of Georgia laws. An evangelical Christian, Cobb also participated in the temperance movement.

By the late 1850s Cobb was a leading figure in Georgia's legal community, and in 1858 he published *An Inquiry into the Law of Negro Slavery in the United States to which is prefixed, An Historical Sketch of Slavery.* The product of eight years' labor, Cobb's book drew upon science, economics, moral philosophy, history, and religion in an attempt to prove that, contrary to abolitionists' claims, positive law was not essential to the establishment of slavery. Rather, an examination of world history proved slavery to be a natural state, "more universal than marriage and more permanent than liberty." Drawing upon the ideas of contemporary ethnologists, Cobb concluded that blacks needed white guidance and protection in order to progress and were thus perfectly suited for servitude. Although he admitted the need for laws to ameliorate abuses, Cobb viewed slavery as humane and beneficial to both races. Cobb intended his work for a national audience, but his book met with a generally negative reaction in the North.

Upon Abraham Lincoln's election, Cobb emerged as Georgia's most ardent secessionist. After leading his state out of the Union, he helped write the Confederate Constitution and later attained the rank of brigadier general in the Confederate army. Cobb was killed at the Battle of Fredericksburg. He was the younger brother of U.S. Senator Howell Cobb and son-in-law of the Georgia chief justice, Joseph Henry Lumpkin.

See also CONFEDERATE STATE OF AMERICA; GEORGIA; LAW; PERSPECTIVES ON SLAVERY.

BIBLIOGRAPHY

McCASH, WILLIAM B. *Thomas R. R. Cobb (1823–1862): The Making of a Southern Nationalist.* 1983.

Timothy S. Huebner

Code Noir

Promulgated in 1685 when France's main Caribbean colonies were a half-century old and increasingly dependent on slavery, the Code Noir, or Black Code, was drawn up by Louis XIV's naval minister, Jean-Baptiste Colbert. The code coincided with increased French persecution of Protestants and was partly intended to ensure religious orthodoxy in the colonies. The first eight of its sixty clauses concern religion. They banned Sunday markets and mandated the baptism and instruction in Roman Catholicism of all slaves. The code, however, innovated little. It was based on reports solicited from colonial administrators and on existing regulations of the colonial administrations. According to Vernon Palmer, it was not influenced by Roman

law, as claimed in Alan Watson's *Slave Law in the Americas* (1989).

The detail and extent of its protective provisions distinguish the code from planter-made British slave laws and the more abstract early Spanish laws. Its prohibition of separating families was unique. Slaves could protest ill treatment to the attorney-general. They received the same form of trial as free persons and could appeal sentence, though their testimony was valid only against other slaves. The code mandated small allowances of food and clothing and care for the old and disabled. Freed slaves enjoyed the rights of other free persons. In its brutal police regulations and definition of slaves as property, however, the code differed little from other slave law.

The code remained largely a dead letter; its protective and some of its punitive provisions were rarely enforced. Several clauses were soon modified by the crown, or contradicted by legislation of local superior councils and governors. It was extended to all of France's slave colonies and remained in force until the abolition of slavery in 1848. In Louisiana the code was retained under Spanish rule (1768–1803), and French slave law continued to influence legislation in the nineteenth century.

See also CARIBBEAN REGION; LAW; LOUISIANNA.

BIBLIOGRAPHY

PALMER, VERNON V. "The Origins and Authors of the Code Noir." In *An Uncommon Experience: Law and Judicial Institutions in Louisiana, 1803–2003,* edited by Judith K. Schafer and Warren M. Billings. 1997.
PEYTRAUD, LUCIEN. *Histoire de l'esclavage aux Antilles françaises avant 1789.* 1897.
SALA-MOLINS, LOUIS. *Le Code noir ou le calvaire de Canaan.* 1987.

David Geggus

Coles, Edward   [1786–1868]

Politician and abolitionist.

Edward Coles was born twenty miles from Monticello to a large and wealthy family on a Virginia plantation that was worked by more than one hundred black slaves. His father was a cousin of Patrick Henry and his own cousin, Dolley Payne, married James Madison, whom Coles served for a few years as private secretary before and during the War of 1812. Thus he was heir to a privileged place in Virginia slave society and had prospects of serving in the highest circles of government under his friends and mentors, Thomas Jefferson, Madison, and James Monroe.

As a youth at the College of William and Mary, however, in a "political course of studies" under Bishop James Madison (second cousin to the future president) examining the Lockean and Jeffersonian ideals of natural law and human rights, he asked his teacher "in the simplicity of youth and under the new light first shed on me—if this be true how can you hold a slave—how can man be made the property of man?" Adhering to this conviction of conscience for the rest of his life, Coles resolved to free any slaves that he might inherit from his father's estate as soon as he could. In the meantime he served as President Madison's private secretary and undertook a diplomatic mission to the court of the Russian czar in St. Petersburg, where he observed "the vassalage and treatment of the serfs of Russia." He found it "an essentially different form of servitude to that of our Negroes, and indefinitely of a milder and less oppressive character." (All quotations are from an autobiographical letter Coles wrote in 1844; cited in Ketcham, 1960.)

Coles was more determined than ever to free the approximately twenty slaves he had inherited from his father. He knew, given Virginia laws requiring freed slaves to leave the state within one year, that to truly provide for their emancipation, he would have to settle them, preferably on farms, in free territory. To do this he explored and purchased frontier land in southern Illinois, across the Mississippi River from St. Louis. Finally, with all preparations made, he carried his slaves on wagons to Pittsburgh where he loaded them, together with the gear needed to start life on a farm, on two large flatboats for the trip down the Ohio River. To lessen the trauma of departure from their home and relations in Virginia, Coles had not yet told his slaves they were to be freed. He did this, dramatically, one spring morning as the party floated down the river, telling the slaves they were as free as he was, and could at any moment simply leave the barges and enter the free states of the Old Northwest. Unprepared for that, the now-freed slaves agreed to stay with Coles and with each other to reach the lands Coles had purchased for them in southern Illinois. The details of the settlement of Coles' freed slaves in Illinois, and their subsequent history, are little known; Coles reported simply that many of them became good farmers and honest citizens.

The proslavery sentiments so strong in southern Illinois, however, caused harassment to both Coles and his freed slaves as they attempted to begin their life there. Coles fought and eventually defeated lawsuits that attempted on technicalities either to void the emancipation of his slaves or to question their title to the deeded lands. Coles entered politics to resist strong efforts to rescind Illinois' antislavery constitution. He became the state's second governor in 1823 and helped defeat the move to make Illinois a slave state. Seeing the difficulties his freed slaves often faced in the hostile environment of "copperhead" Illinois, Coles urged them to seek resettlement in Liberia and offered to provide financial support but they refused, claiming themselves satisfied, overall, with their lives as freemen in Illinois.

Meanwhile, perhaps weary of the hostility and harassment faced by abolitionists in Illinois, Coles returned East, where he met and married Sally Logan Roberts, a wealthy Philadelphian, whose dowry provided a comfortable living for the couple there for the rest of their lives. Coles continued his antislavery efforts by urging the aged ex-President James Madison to fulfill his desire to free his slaves (Madison did not do so), by writing and corresponding to resist arguments of southern nullificationists and secessionists; by counseling Free Soilers, Republicans, and other opponents of slavery; and by supporting the work of the American Colonization Society. Coles was convinced, after his difficult experiences in Illinois, that even freed blacks would have oppressed and unjust lives amid white Americans, who were still prejudiced against them. Before Coles died he learned of the death on the battlefield of his eldest son, Roberts, who, partially raised on ancestral lands in Virginia, had chosen the Confederate side in the Civil War.

See also AMERICAN COLONIZATION SOCIETY; ILLINOIS; LOCKE, JOHN; RUSSIA, SERFDOM IN.

BIBLIOGRAPHY

ALVORD, CLARENCE W., ed. *Governor Edward Coles.* 1920.
KETCHAM, RALPH. "The Dictates of Conscience: Edward Coles and Slavery." *The Virginia Quarterly Review* 36, no. 1 (Winter 1960): 246–262.
MCCOY, DREW R. *The Last of the Founders: James Madison and the Republican Legacy.* 1989.

Ralph Ketcham

Collars

See Chains and Restraints.

Colombia

See Caribbean Region; Plantations.

Colonization

See Repatriation to Africa.

Columbus, Christopher   [ca. 1451–1506]

Genoese explorer, mariner, and discoverer.

Before 1492 Christopher Columbus was familiar with slavery in the Mediterranean, in Portugal, in Africa, and in the Atlantic islands, and some of his business associates traded in Canarian slaves. On his first voyage he distinguished between peaceful native islanders who accepted Spanish rule and the warlike Caribs, who resisted and could thus be legally enslaved. In this Columbus followed medieval patterns that were then being used to justify enslavement of Canary Islanders. After 1492 indigenous peoples in the Canaries and the Caribbean were considered subjects of the Spanish crown and thus were protected against enslavement in ordinary circumstances. Only if they warred against the Europeans could they be seized and enslaved.

During Columbus's second voyage, he began to conquer Española and enslave those who resisted. He suggested to the Spanish monarchs, Ferdinand and Isabella, that a regular transatlantic trade in Indian slaves be established. Meanwhile, however, they im-

An eighteenth-century etching depicts the arrival of Christopher Columbus in the West Indies. [Library of Congress/Corbis]

posed a moratorium on Indian slavery and were angered when Columbus sent more than 500 Indian slaves to Spain in 1495. Columbus contravened the moratorium on other occasions, and Ferdinand and Isabella later agreed to allow enslavement of those who resisted conquest, thus giving rise to slave trading in the colonial areas that lasted legally for several decades and illegally for much longer. Though some native American slaves ended up in the Canaries or Europe, no regular eastward traffic in slaves from the Americas ever developed. Columbus's disregard for the regulations limiting slavery was one of the reasons why the Spanish monarchs relieved him of authority in the new colonies.

Columbus was also involved in the beginning of the westward transatlantic trade in sub-Saharan Africans, who went to the new colonial possessions, as slaves and as free individuals, almost from the start. Tradition, perhaps apocryphal, holds that at least one black was on Columbus's initial voyage. It is more likely that Spaniards on the second voyage took slaves with them.

Columbus lost his positions as governor general and viceroy in 1500. Thereafter, the Spanish crown limited the trade to Christian slaves, and in 1501 it prohibited Jews, Muslims, and converted Jews or Muslims from going to the Americas. Spain had recently completed a campaign to make the kingdom almost totally Christian by forcing Spanish Jews and most Spanish Muslims to convert to Christianity or leave. Ferdinand and Isabella also wanted to prevent Judaism and Islam from developing in the newly conquered lands overseas. As part of the effort, in 1503 Isabella prohibited the slave trade altogether. Such a prohibition could not stop the growing demand for additional labor in the colonies. Some slaves continued to slip through after 1503, usually in special shipments authorized by Ferdinand. This trickle grew after 1513, when the licensing system (*asiento*) was introduced. Those who secured a license and paid a fee could ship slaves legally to the Indies. The crown in this fashion satisfied part of the colonial demand for labor and at the same time provided itself with another source of income.

See also ASIENTO; CARIBBEAN REGION; NATIVE AMERICANS; SLAVE TRADE; SPAIN.

BIBLIOGRAPHY

PHILLIPS, WILLIAM D., JR. *Slavery from Roman Times to the Early Transatlantic Trade.* 1985.

PHILLIPS, WILLIAM D., JR., and CARLA RAHN PHILLIPS. *The Worlds of Christopher Columbus.* 1992.

William D. Phillips Jr.

Comfort Women in World War II

Kazuko Watanabe has defined the term "comfort woman" as a "euphemism for enforced military sexual laborer or slave" in the service of the Japanese military forces before and during World War II. According to Yuki Tanaka, this coercion "could well be historically unprecedented as an instance of state-controlled criminal activity involving the sexual exploitation of women." Estimates of the number of women involved range from about 139,000, according to George Hicks based on a presumed ratio of women to overall troop numbers; to 200,000 or more according to Watanabe who unfortunately does not indicate how she arrived at this figure; to one comfort woman for every thirty-five soldiers according to Tanaka. Actual numbers are difficult to establish with any degree of certainty because the Japanese also took women for daytime factory work, some of whom were expected to provide sexual services at night, and because personal and documentary evidence started to emerge only in the late 1980s.

Although the ethnic mix of the women involved was varied and included Japanese, Korean, Taiwanese, Chinese, Indonesians, Dutch, Burmese, Eurasians, Filipinos, and White Russians, most surveys have concluded that around 80 percent of them were Korean and around 10 percent were Japanese. Of all the ethnic groups that came under Japanese control during the war, only Malay and Indian women do not seem to have been used as comfort women, perhaps because the Japanese feared alienating these two groups more than any other. The vast majority of the women who were involved appear to have been between fourteen and eighteen years old at the time of their "recruitment."

As with the overall numbers involved, it is not clear when the Japanese military began seizing women for sexual services. While Hicks claims that Japanese policymakers adopted the practice following the decimation of entire divisions by venereal disease during the Siberian Intervention of 1918–1922, Watanabe notes that the army was, even at this early stage, already taking prostitutes from Japan with them and that they had begun to recruit poor Korean women after Japan's annexation of Korea in 1910. However, Korean women who were recruited immediately after annexation do not seem to have been used by the military until the 1920s, and military use only became predominant following the Japanese invasion of China in 1932. Although Hicks and Watanabe appear to be at odds on this point, the differences probably lie more in each scholar's definition of "comfort women" and the extent of the system in Siberia. The use of Japan-ese women on this campaign suggests that they were all recruited from the domestic prostitution industry in Japan.

Even the date of the institutionalization of the system is subject to debate among scholars, though most seem to accept that the first comfort station, or comfort center, was established in Shanghai either following clashes between Japanese and Chinese troops in 1932, or in 1938 after the Nanking Massacre of 1937. Although the first military brothels were under the direct control of the Japanese Imperial Army's Recreation Division this was soon considered an inappropriate business for the army and, except in some areas close to the fighting, management was soon passed on to civilian contractors.

The Japanese authorities had a number of ideological justifications for developing the system. To limit the spread of sexually transmitted diseases among their troops they, in effect, extended the system of licensed, and therefore controlled, prostitution that already existed in Japan. To this end they issued condoms to front-line troops and posted rules within comfort stations insisting on their use. Apart from this desire to control disease, it seems the Japanese believed that sexual deprivation would make soldiers accident-prone while carnal gratification would make them fierce. They also argued, ignoring the relentless daily rapes of comfort women, that by providing these services they would lessen the incidence of rape of the conquered populations which, if it were allowed to occur, would alienate the very Asians that they were claiming to liberate.

While the Japanese women involved, on the whole, seem previously to have been prostitutes in Japan, women from other countries were not. Initially, economics seems to have been the deciding factor for Korean cooperation because the women were drawn from the poorer strata of society. As the numbers involved rose, however, the Japanese used increasingly sophisticated methods of deception to attract women; these ranged from such trickery as offering the women high-paying restaurant or factory work away from home or positions in important-sounding organizations such as the Women's Voluntary Corps, to coercing village headmen to provide women, to seizing girls from Korean schools. In other areas that the Japanese forces occupied, local women seem often to have been kidnapped, raped, and confined. The main exception to this were Dutch women, who were already interned as prisoners of war in camps in Indonesia. There are a few remarkable stories of successful resistance, but the majority of women did not have this option, and they were beaten until they complied with the wishes of their Japanese masters.

As far as can be ascertained, the Japanese ranked comfort women by the color of their skin, showing a distinct preference for Japanese women despite the fact that these women were often older and more likely to be diseased because they often had previously been prostitutes in Japan. They accepted Koreans, Chinese, and Southeast Asians, in that order though, as is clear from the film *Senso Daughters,* they also used Melanesians. Because officers could monopolize the coveted Japanese women, some of them presumably had an easier time than the other women.

Circumstances external to the comfort station depended on where the women were located. For example, women close to the front lines often shared the dangers of battle with the soldiers whom they were to serve, while those in the officer's comfort stations in Rangoon were in opulent surroundings. Although it is not clear how many officers a woman had to satisfy each day, those made available to common soldiers were expected to service between thirty and forty men, with these demands becoming even heavier when troops were in transit. There was also a cost per visit, half of which was meant to be for the woman, which ranged from 1.5 yen for a private, to 3 yen for a senior officer. Very few of the sources mention how this fee was to be paid but those that do claim that it would be done "mostly by tickets issued by the army." In theory at least some women could earn large amounts of money, but in practice they were often cheated out of this by management grossly overcharging for such expenses as soap. Those few women who did manage the difficult feat of accumulating some savings seem to have lost their funds very quickly at the end of the war.

The end of the war did not bring freedom for many of the women. Notwithstanding the conversion of the Singapore comfort women to "nurses," Japanese women were often expected to help in last-ditch defenses and then to kill themselves rather than be captured. Attempts were made to kill Korean women who did not sacrifice their lives as well as lend their bodies for the war efforts. In Manchuria nurses were ordered to accede to any demands from the Russians for the sake of the safety of the remaining Japanese troops. Others were simply abandoned.

In Japan itself the authorities quickly resurrected the system in the form of the Recreation and Amusement Association, this time to service the Occupation forces and to act as a "shield for all Japanese womanhood." However, they were unable to enforce the wearing of condoms, and disease soon became so rampant that officials closed the system down. Many of the non-Japanese women who went back to their own communities were victimized yet again, this time by male compatriots who rejected them because of the offensive nature of their sexual "service" to the Japanese.

A number of factors may explain why this abuse remained hidden until recently, ranging from reluctance on the part of the victims, women from traditional Confucian societies that placed a high value on their "chastity," to come forward, to a concerted effort by Japanese military administrations to destroy all evidence of the existence of comfort women by, for example, reclassifying them as nurses in Singapore when defeat was inevitable. However, when in 1992 it became public knowledge that the Japanese foreign minister Togo Shigenori in January 1942 had ordered that all comfort women be issued military travel documents, further denials became increasingly difficult. Meanwhile, international opinion became less tolerant of sexual abuse, feminists publicized the issue, and the surviving victims gained confidence as they aged. Several groups began to emerge, demanding compensation from the Japanese government, which in August 1993 admitted its predecessors' complicity in recruiting these women. However, the Japanese government's assertion that they had already settled all war claims in a series of bilateral treaties and that any compensation for the victims had to come from private sources led many to doubt the sincerity of this admission.

Many English-language sources have, understandably, adopted a strongly subjective stance on this topic. In the first book-length study of this subject, Hicks attempts a tone of scholarly objectivity, but unfortunately, lacking references (though he does include a bibliography), he leaves his more academic stance open to question. However, it is still the most comprehensive history available. On the other hand, Keith Howard's edited collection of Korean recollections makes no claim to objectivity or comprehensiveness but does include a surprisingly wide range of individual experiences. Both Kazuko Watanabe and Alice Yun Chai present a brief historical overview of the war-time experiences of comfort women, but their main strength lies in their analysis of the more recent protest movements against Japanese use of comfort women and their linkage of these abuses to more recent examples of the sexual exploitation of women. Finally, Ustina Dolgopol and Snehal Paranjape's *Comfort Women* presents "factual" information on Korean and Filipino women in a prosecutorial manner.

See also GENDER RELATIONS; SEXUAL EXPLOITATION; SLAVERY, CONTEMPORARY FORMS OF.

BIBLIOGRAPHY

BOLING, DAVID. "Mass Rape, Enforced Prostitution, and the Japanese Army: Japan Eschews International Legal Responsibility?" *The Columbia Journal of Transnational Law* 32, no. 3 (1995).

CALICA, DAN, and NELIA SANCHO, eds. *War Crimes on Asian Women: Military Sexual Slavery by Japan During World War II: The Case of the Filipino Comfort Women.* 1993.

CHAI, ALICE YUN. "Asian-Pacific Feminist Coalition Politics: The Chongshindae/Jugunianfu ('Comfort Women') Movement." *Korean Studies* 17 (1993): 67–91.

DOLGOPOL, USTINA, and SNEHAL PARANJAPE. *Comfort Women, an Unfinished Ordeal: Report of a Mission.* 1994.

Fifty Years of Silence: The Story of Jan Ruff-O'Herne (film). Directed by Ned Lander. 1994.

HICKS, GEORGE. *The Comfort Women Sex Slaves of the Japanese Imperial Forces.* 1995.

HOWARD, KEITH, ed. *True Stories of the Korean Comfort Women.* 1995.

International Public Hearing Report. *War Victimization and Japan.* 1993.

RUFF-O'HERNE, JAN. *Fifty Years of Silence.* 1994.

Senso Daughters (film). Directed by Noriko Sekiguchi. 1990.

TANAKA, YUKI. *Hidden Horrors: Japanese War Crimes in World War II.* 1996.

WATANABE, KAZUKO. "Militarism, Colonialism, and the Trafficking of Women: 'Comfort Women' Forced into Sexual Labor for Japanese Soldiers." *Bulletin of Concerned Asian Scholars* 26, N 4 October-December 1994: 3–17.

David Booth

Henry Clay. [Library of Congress]

Compromise of 1850

In 1848 the Mexican Cession gave the United States a vast expanse of western land, but its organization became embroiled in the controversy over the expansion of slavery. In 1849 California applied for statehood as a free state, thus threatening the delicate balance between slave and free states in the Senate; and in 1850 Senator Henry Clay of Kentucky introduced an omnibus bill to settle several questions related to slavery. Clay proposed to admit California as a free state, establish popular sovereignty in the territories of Utah and New Mexico so that they could determine their own alignment, settle a boundary dispute between Texas and New Mexico, outlaw the slave trade in the District of Columbia, and enact a stronger fugitive-slave law. After months of debate, during which the bill's supporters appealed to common national ideals, the bill was defeated, largely because its all-inclusive nature required each senator to vote in favor of at least one provision that he and his constituents abhorred. Shortly thereafter Clay's provisions were reintroduced as separate bills, thus permitting senators and congressmen to avoid voting for provisions to which they objected. Several Congressmen were also swayed by promises to issue government bonds and build railroads in their districts.

The passage of the five provisions, known collectively as the Compromise of 1850, only worsened the intersectional conflict over slavery. Popular sovereignty resulted in "Bleeding Kansas," while the Fugitive Slave Act of 1850 outraged northerners by requiring them to participate actively in the slave system; both helped to bring on the Civil War.

See also FUGITIVE SLAVE LAWS, U.S.

BIBLIOGRAPHY

FEHRENBACHER, DON E. *Sectional Crisis and Southern Constitutionalism.* 1995.

Charles W. Carey Jr.

Comte, Auguste   [1798–1857]

French intellectual and father of nineteenth-century positivism.

In his best-known work, the six-volume *Cours de la philosophie positive,* Auguste Comte stated that human intellectual development passed through three historical stages. During the first, or theological, state humans attributed all observed phenomena to supernatural forces. Abstractions rooted in the real world replaced supernatural explanations during the next stage, the metaphysical state. Finally, in the positive state, humans would recognize the impossibility of absolute truth and instead would concentrate on empirical knowledge to formulate laws of phenomena. Positivist scientists, including social scientists, were to play prominent roles in the final stage of human development. Each stage, however, possessed its own appropriate social laws. Thus, Comte felt that slavery had a proper place in the first two stages but would be obsolete in the final one. Comte's comments on slavery's obsolescence had special relevance in late-nineteenth-century Brazil where final abolition did not occur until 1888. Positivist intellectuals, such as Benjamin Constant, a professor at the Brazilian military academy, helped convince military officers and civic leaders that slavery was an archaic institution that hindered national progress. The Positivist Church of Brazil in Rio de Janeiro, whose tenets derived from Comte and not Roman Catholicism, added to abolitionist propaganda with claims that the final stage of human development would be unattainable as long as slavery existed. Although its influence was largely confined to the urban middle class, Comtean positivism contributed significantly to final abolition in Brazil.

See also ABOLITION AND ANTISLAVERY MOVEMENTS; PHILOSOPHY.

BIBLIOGRAPHY

BURNS, E. BRADFORD. *A History of Brazil.* 2nd ed. 1980.
COMTE, AUGUSTE. *Auguste Comte and Positivism: The Essential Writings.* Edited and with an introduction by Gertrud Lenzer. 1975.
STANDLEY, ARLINE REILEIN. *Auguste Comte.* 1981.

John J. Crocitti

Concubinage

This entry includes the following articles: Ancient Rome; Islamic World; China; United States; Caribbean Region; Latin America.

Ancient Rome

Long-term monogamous relations with *concubinae* were one of a wide range of sexual relationships between slaveholders and slaves or ex-slaves in Rome. These included the casual exploitation of prostitutes and domestic slaves and, at the other extreme, relationships ending in the liberation of the slave and legal marriage.

Relationships between married women and their slaves were strongly condemned. Eventually the emperor Septimius Severus (A.D. 193–211) banned marriages, never socially acceptable, between any woman and her ex-slave. Most of our information concerns the relationships of male owners with female slaves, considered a less serious matter and probably more common.

Neither concern about racial mixture nor sympathy for unwilling slaves played any part in Roman morality concerning sex with slaves. Moralists censured loss of self-control; wives and relatives would resent any threat to a marriage. Men's extramarital affairs were judged by a lenient standard, but freeborn partners or permanent relationships evoked censure or legal sanctions. Before marriage, men's casual or even long-term liaisons with their own domestic slaves—or someone else's slaves, with the owner's connivance—and the use of prostitutes, often slaves or ex-slaves, evoked lukewarm condemnation or a "boys will be boys" attitude. After marriage, casual affairs with slave women and boys, sometimes purchased for their attractiveness, still seem to have been common and were judged variously. Any illegitimate children took the status of their mother and would thus be slaves. The manumission of a master's natural children was exempted from the *lex Aelia Sentia*, which prohibited the manumission of slaves under thirty years of age. Such manumissions, however, were not required.

Any affair of a married man invited jealousy, but to set up a concubine was an outrage. Seneca says, "To keep a mistress is the gravest injustice to a wife" (*Epistle* 95.37). Some aristocrats may have committed this offense, but social pressure probably kept it rare; the *concubinae* who appear on epitaphs appear not to have been contemporaneous with wives. Legal texts indicate that Roman concubinage was favored when the differing social status of the partners made marriage illegal or unacceptable—in almost all cases the *concubina* was a slave or ex-slave and her partner a man of substance. Such relations were particularly attractive during two periods in the life of wealthy men. Young men might take up with *concubinae* from puberty until marriage, typically in their late twenties. A *concubina* would also prove convenient for an older man who did not want further legitimate children after a wife's death or divorce; similar concerns about the imperial succession probably contributed to the decision of several of the most responsible emperors to take up with freedwomen *concubinae* late in life.

Manumission for the sake of marriage was also exempted from the restrictions of the *lex Aelia Sentia*. Many epitaphs commemorate the apparently happy marriages of owners, both men and women, and ex-slaves. Two complications should be noted. First, many of these epitaphs probably record relationships that began between slaves, one of whom was freed and subsequently bought and freed the other. Second, if a freedwoman divorced her husband and former owner, he could prevent her from marrying anybody else.

See also ANCIENT ROME; SEXUAL EXPLOITATION.

BIBLIOGRAPHY

RAWSON, BERYL. "Roman Concubinage and Other *De Facto* Marriages." *Transactions of the American Philological Association* 104 (1974): 279–305.

SALLER, RICHARD. "Slavery and the Roman Family." In *Classical Slavery*, edited by M. I. Finley. 1987.

TREGGIARI, SUSAN M. "Concubinae." *Papers of the British School at Rome* 49 (1981): 59–81.

———. *Roman Marriage: Iusti Conjuges from the Time of Cicero to the Time of Ulpian.* 1991.

Peter Hunt

Islamic World

The practice of slave concubinage in southwestern Asia dates back to twelfth century B.C.E. Assyria, and it was noted among the Persian Sassanids (224–640 C.E.) prior to the rise of Islam. Slave concubinage as a Byzantine custom was transformed into an Islamic practice. It was recognized during the second dynasty of Islam (750–1258) under the Abbasid caliphs and was firmly established by the fifteenth-century reign of the Ottoman ruler Sultan Mehmed II.

Slave concubinage allowed for controlled reproduction that reinforced patriarchal political power without the imposition of legal marriage costs. Because a concubine was by definition a slave, and not legally married to her master, she carried no competing lineage affiliations and required no dowry, which a legal wife was entitled to keep as her own wealth. The benefit of having concubines in a large household was that they provided both an increased labor pool and a greater number of progeny than the limit of four wives would allow. As property, slave women frequently were exchanged between men of high status to be used as concubines. Such a gift underlined the high status of the benefactor and reinforced the affiliation between the men. There was no limit to the number of concubines a Muslim could have, provided that the women were non-Muslim slaves, and hence of foreign origin.

Slave owners controlled the rights to sell or give away a slave as a concubine unless she had borne her master's child. Motherhood raised the concubine's social position to one equivalent to a wife, with legal protection against sale and mandatory manumission upon her master's death. If a slave master wished to marry a concubine, he had to manumit her prior to the marriage and was required to pay dowry to her. Alternatively, freeing a concubine could also free the slave master of legal and economic responsibility for her. Although she would be allowed to remain a free woman in the slave master's household, she also was able to marry outside that home, thus becoming someone else's dependent.

The concubine's role was the only slave role that carried with it potential for transformation to free status, which was accomplished through childbearing. Thus, concubinage benefited a woman slave in a significant way, allowing her to move directly to free status upon conceiving a child. A concubine acquired the social status of her master; the concubine to a king, for example, assumed royal status. Furthermore, concubinage functioned as a means of guaranteeing free status to a slave woman's descendants. Agnatic descent patterns means that a woman's children inherited the social status of their fathers regardless of their mother's position. Therefore, a concubine's children shared a status equal to that of the children of legal wives. Thus, concubinage offered freedom for a woman and her children, and in the case of royal concubines it provided royal status and the prospect of a position as queen mother.

Depending on the affluence and size of the harem in which concubines found themselves, they were

In this late-nineteenth-century photo, a servant brings drinks to the women of an Islamic harem in Turkey. [Hulton-Deutsch Collection/Corbis]

expected to contribute to the daily operations of the household in ways suited to their position as nonlegal "wives." If the household had only a few concubines, they were likely to participate equally with female slave domestics in the tasks related to food preparation, cleaning, and the maintenance of order in the home. A household with many concubines would also have many more slave women to help with the quotidian work. In this case, concubines would be trained in more refined domestic and cultural skills, such as those relating to literacy, the arts, and politics. Concubines, along with legal wives, would be most actively involved with the enculturation of the children of the household, preparing them for appropriate social roles.

Concubinage in the Ottoman Empire

During the Ottoman Empire concubines were selected from among slaves from Circassia, Africa, Asia, and sometimes Europe, with lighter-skinned concubines in highest demand. By the mid-fourteenth century the Ottomans had come to prefer concubinage over legal marriage for reproduction in a royal context in order to guarantee patriarchy and to avoid incurring the political alliances inherent in legal marriages. A royal concubine in the Topkapi imperial palace was allowed to bear only one son, and her subsequent career was spent promoting his accession. This required political and social training that prepared a woman to act as tutor to her son in his future position as emperor. Slave women fulfilled domestic tasks, freeing the concubines to concern themselves with the education of a prince and the advising of a sultan.

A concubine sought to rise through the harem hierarchy to the position of favorite concubine (*haseki*), in which role she could amass both material assets and political power that would serve her well should she become the queen mother, or *valide* sultan, of a son who succeeded to the throne. The tremendous wealth amassed by both the *haseki* and the *valide* was expended on philanthropic endeavors such as the building of mosques, libraries, monasteries, and schools. Such activities in turn raised the benefactor's credibility and authority within and beyond the palace.

Islam reveres motherhood, and in the context of imperial concubinage, that reverence was intensified, facilitating a concubine's acquisition of both high status and authority that extended beyond the family. Originally a slave valued for her lack of lineage, the concubine who became the *valide* gained high status by association with her ruling son. The *valide* could wield significant authority over a sultan and his associates, who were compelled by their own roles as moral exemplars to respect her because she was the quintessential mother in a culture that revered maternal status. The *valide* used the respect afforded her to further reinforce her authority with the sultan and his political associates. In the fifteenth and sixteenth centuries the queen mother often was a concubine whose role as *valide* developed into one with authority that rivaled the sultan's own power. Such an evolution of the role results logically from the inwardly directed nature of Islam, which valued the family over public affiliations. In the esteemed family unit the maternal figure is the principal player: "paradise lies at the feet of the mother."

In an Islamic context only non-Muslims could be enslaved, and slave women were the only women available as concubines. Nevertheless, by virtue of the maternal role they played and the esteem with which that role was regarded in Islam, concubines shed the stigma of slave status by playing out their role to its fullest—becoming unofficial wives, revered as mothers if not respected as highly as spouses. Such a transformation of status was confirmed by a concubine's automatic conversion to free status in motherhood.

Late Twentieth Century

In the last years of the twentieth century, the practice of concubinage continued, most actively in the palace communities of Muslim emirs, who followed the Ottoman example. In the emir's palace in Kano, Nigeria, concubines functioned as special attendants to royal wives; thus they were positioned in a stratum between slave domestics and royal wives. The sons of concubines inherited the emir's royal status and were eligible to succeed him. It was common to find a concubine who was an emir's mother, in which case she assumed a royal title and lived in a special residence outside the palace. Thus, concubinage continued to elevate a woman's standing from that of slave to that of royal status in the space of one generation. The advantage of such a liaison to the woman was the honor it accorded her as mother of a child of royal status and the security it provided in a large, wealthy household. The advantage of concubinage to the patron was the potential it provided to increase the pool of offspring eligible as successors to the throne. At the same time, these conditions could lead to destructive competition; the Ottoman Empire is famous for its harem intrigues in the Topkapi palace, in which wives and concubines struggled to promote their own sons' precedence over the others.

See also ANCIENT NEAR EAST; AFRICA; EGYPT; EUNUCHS; HAREM; ISLAM; OTTOMAN EMPIRE; PALACE SLAVES; WEST AFRICA.

BIBLIOGRAPHY

AHMED, LEILA. *Women and Gender in Islam* 1992.
ALDERSON, A. D. *Structure of the Ottoman Dynasty.* 1956.
ALLOULA, MALEK. *The Colonial Harem.* 1986.
BEHR, EDWARD. *The Last Emperor.* 1987.
CARDASHIAN, VAHAN. *Actual Life in the Turkish Harem.* 1914
CROUTIER, ALEV LYTLE. *Harem: The World behind the Veil.* 1989.
DJAVIDAN, HANUM. *Harem Life.* 1931.
MILLER, BARNETTE. *Beyond the Sublime Porte: The Grand Seraglio of Stambul.* 1931.
PENZER, N. M. *The Harem.* 1937.
PIERCE, LESLIE PENN. *The Imperial Harem: Women and Sovereignty in the Ottoman Empire.* 1993.
TARNAR, YESIM. *The Book and the Veil: Escape from an Istanbul Harem.* 1994.

Beverly B. Mack

China

Chinese and international scholarship on this complex and still underresearched area of Chinese women's history may be examined under three major headings: definition of female servitude, concubinage, and slavery; family systems and concubinage; and economics of slavery and concubinage.

Cixi entered the Forbidden City as a low-ranking concubine in the 1850s but eventually rose to the position of dowager empress of China. [Underwood & Underwood/Corbis-Bettmann]

Definitions

By situating the "female domestic slave" (*yatou, yahuan*; its Cantonese equivalent is *muitsai*) together with the "concubine" (*qie*) in a context of family (seen here as central to the reproduction of gender inequality and female servitude), I am contextualizing low-class concubines in a market of female slaves. The well-connected imperial consorts whose personal fate as politically influential women shaped the national fate and Chinese collective memory are relatively well-documented; they include Empress Wu, Empress Cixi, Xishi, and Yang Guifei.

Were *yatou* "slaves"? James Lee Watson's "Slavery as an Institution: Open and Closed Systems" (in J. L. Watson, ed., 1980) defines a slave as having been purchased or captured, coerced into labor, and excluded from the kinship group. But, according to Watson, all Chinese women "belonged to" the patriline (either through bride price or through purchase), and never "belonged in" it. Thus domestic slaves could attain concubine status, and concubines could achieve a degree of power without threatening the patriline. They

could not become wives, however. Rubin S. Watson, in "Wives, Concubines, and Maids: Servitude and Kinship in the Hong Kong Region, 1900–1940," (in R. S. Watson and Patricia Buckley Ebrey, eds., 1991) analyzes the case to be made for using the term "female servitude" (instead of slavery) to represent one, if extreme, end of the spectrum of female servile statuses. Somewhat different is Ebrey's position, in "Concubines in Sung China," (*Journal of Family History.* 1986. 11: 1–24) that all household women—significantly, excluding primary wives—should be categorized as "menials." A more revisionist school within Chinese women's history inclines to the viewpoint that women inside families negotiated, and defended, exclusionist and hierarchial spheres of female experience (delineated by access to dowry, ritual participation, and kinship nexus) from wife as mistress of the home (*neizhu*) to the tenuous dependency and social invisibility of *yatou*. It was precisely this domestic stratification, Maria Jaschok contends in *Concubines and Bondservants* (1988), which distinguished the ex-slave concubine from the first wife and from other concubines of nonslave origin, positioning her in a border zone between *yatou* and lowly concubine status (etymologically carrying echoes of the origin of *qie* in the dual meaning of "slave" and the generic term for "female").

Family Systems and Concubinage

Within the context of the Confucian marriage system, which placed family interests (economic, political, social) over personal preference, concubinage performed a liberalizing function for male sexuality by institutionalizing a double morality that granted to men romantic outlet—conditional on a disempowered, servile female body—without compromising ancestral obligations.

Legal provisions gave owners nearly unconditional power over slaves as family property; the owners' prerogatives, included resale and transfer, though not murder. Clearly, ethical masters rather than legal provisions were the source of protection in what Sybille van der Sprenkel (*Legal Systems in Manchu China*, 1962) considers to have been a benign institution. The legal status of a concubine was less clearly defined than (but distinctly inferior to) that of a wife. Embedded instead in customary law, the concubine's security and prospects depended on her relationship with husband and wife and the family's need of her reproductive or sexual contribution. Unlike wives, concubines (like *yatou*) were given an often demeaning name upon entry into a household: they lost their family name.

The birth of a son could give a concubine greater security or could give a slave the prospect of elevation to concubine status. But the wife always remained the legal mother of the concubine's child—her rights over the child overroad the birth mother's claims—and she often powerless to protect her son's inheritance. The mourning code of the father's family (*wufu*) excluded the concubine mother, obliging only her children to mourn for her. Even in afterlife she suffered discrimination; only the wife had a place in ancestral worship. A widowed concubine was vulnerable to rejection or neglect; if she was childless, resale was not uncommon.

Economics of Slavery and Concubinage

Two major suppliers of children in prerevolutionary China's extensive slave market were destitute families and professional traffickers. Historical sources suggest that female slaves and concubines were a feature of even humble households. While statistics are unavailable, we know that males, because precious, were not sold in large numbers. The transaction of females without dowry served multiple uses: for example, to finance a brother's betrothal; to pay for funerals or repay debts; to be pawned out, temporarily or indefinitely; to be used as a gift or a bribe; or to support a man's whoring, gambling, or an opium habit.

A *yatou*'s work was structured by such variables as age, sex, appearance, skills, and talent, but also by her owner's socioeconomic standing. Males slaves were entrusted with security, family businesses, and outdoor labor; *yatou* more commonly performed domestic duties to support mistresses (many of whom had bound feet) and to supply entertainment and companionship. Their gender rendered female slaves more vulnerable to sexual abuse and commercial transactions but also provided them opportunities to escape menial labor.

R. S. Watson's review of relevant literature leads her to conclude that although concubinage was intimately linked to urban wealth and social prestige, this was not exclusively the case. No single set of economic or social factors can account for its ubiquity. Many paths led to concubinage: as part of a sister's or mistress's dowry; as a gift or reward; as promotion from *yatou* to concubine status; as an outright purchase from a brothel or a trader, or from the natal family; on temporary loan or as payment in kind; as a victim of forceful abduction; as a prize won in a contest.

Body prices fluctuated with supply, which in turn depended on the economic state of the rural poor and frequency of natural and human-made catastrophes. Female slaves were cheap, sometimes acquired for a few catties of rice, sometimes for nothing. The purchase price of concubines varied with their age, appearance, talents, and value to a current owner; with the status of the buyer; and with the nature of the transaction.

Official and private slavery were abolished in 1906, but women's customary lives were little affected. Concubinage was made illegal in 1936 under nationlist law, and abolished in 1950 by the Communist Party as part of a comprehensive reform of the marriage laws. Hong Kong outlawed concubinage in 1971.

See also CHINA; GENDER RELATIONS; HOUSEHOLD SLAVES; SEXUAL EXPLOITATION.

BIBLIOGRAPHY

CHENG, LUCIE, et al. *Women in China: Bibliography of Available English Language Materials.* 1984.

GRONEWORLD, SUE. *Beautiful Merchandise: Prostitution in China, 1860–1936.* 1982.

HERSHATTER, GAIL. *Dangerous Pleasures: Prostitution and Modernity in Twentieth-Century Shanghai.* 1997.

JASCHOK, MARIA, and SUZANNE MIERS, eds. *Women and Chinese Patriarchy: Submission, Servitude and Escape.* 1994.

LIM, JANET. *Sold for Silver.* 1958.

MEIJER, MARINUS J. "Slavery at the End of the Ch'ing Dynasty." In *China's Legal Tradition*, edited by J. A. Cohen, F. M. Ch'en, and R. Edwards. 1979.

WATSON, JAMES LEE, ed. *Asian and African Systems of Slavery.* 1980.

WATSON, R. S., and PATRICIA BUCKLEY EBREY, eds. *Marriage and Inequality in Chinese Society.* 1991.

WOLF, MARGERY. *Women and the Family in Rural Taiwan.* 1972.

M. H. A. Jaschok

United States

Concubinage is a legal term that describes the cohabitation of individuals who participate in informal, unsanctioned, or natural marriage. The legal concept can be traced back to Roman law and has been in use throughout Western history. It establishes and protects the rights of concubines to inherit. The law of inheritance, while certainly important to all women who lived in informal liaisons, was central to the transfer of property, and thus power, in all slave societies.

In the United States concubinage was a legal state only in Louisiana and reflected the evolution of slavery there. The earliest laws, established by Louisiana's French settlers, forbade whites to donate property, whether during life or after death, to women of color. When the Spanish took control of the colony in 1769 and implemented their own law, they allowed white men to donate property to their concubines and their children. Legislation passed after Louisiana was ceded to the United States allowed a woman defined as a concubine to inherit up to 10 percent of her cohabitant's estate.

Even though the language of concubinage is not and never was race specific, the term in Louisiana has been most commonly directed, both legally and popularly, to the practice of cohabitation between white men and women of color, both slave and free. In eighteenth- and nineteenth-century Louisiana, white men regularly cohabited with slave women and free women of color. This is evident not only in the region's sacramental records, but also in the many complaints that were levied against the practice by the region's religious and secular officials.

Officials throughout the eighteenth, nineteenth, and twentieth centuries were especially concerned about interracial liaisons because the racially mixed free population in the region grew rapidly during the colonial period, and continued to grow during the antebellum period. White men who cohabited with women of color blurred the color line, and many officials feared that miscegenation threatened the dominance of the master class. Despite the threats voiced by officials, however, the practice continued, and many racially mixed free people of color became influential and wealthy.

Cohabitation, defined as concubinage in Louisiana, was perhaps not as common in the other southern colonies or states as it was in the Gulf South region. Yet, neither was it extraordinary. Lawmakers in the colonial and antebellum South passed laws that forbade marriage across racial lines, and they passed and re-passed laws forbidding interracial liaisons. Despite these repeated attempts to separate the races, the practice of cohabitation continued and the population of free people of color, mostly racially mixed, grew.

See also MISCEGENATION.

BIBLIOGRAPHY

BLASSINGAME, JOHN W. *The Slave Community: Plantation Life in the Antebellum South.* 1972.

GASPAR, DAVID BARRY, and DARLENE CLARK HINE, eds. *More Than Chattel: Black Women and Slavery in the Americas.* 1996.

SCHAEFER, JUDITH KELLEHER. *Slavery, the Civil Law, and the Supreme Court of Louisiana.* 1992.

STERLING, DOROTHY, ed. *We Are Your Sisters: Black Women in the Nineteenth Century.* 1984.

Virginia Meacham Gould

Caribbean Region

Church-solemnized marriage was never common among Caribbean slaves, and it was extremely rare at the height of the slave system in the eighteenth century, when missionary activity was weakest. Those slaves and free coloreds who did marry tended to do so late in life and to come from the upper economic strata of their communities. Slaves married somewhat more frequently in Catholic than Protestant colonies; in most British colonies slave marriage had no legal standing before the nineteenth century. French and Spanish law encouraged Christian marriage, but for slaveowners it was an obstacle to the future sale of a slave, and for slaves it was an unwelcome restriction, according to some commentators. In the Spanish colonies, exceptionally unbalanced sex ratios and sex-segregated plantation housing were impediments to any sort of conjugal union, and interracial marriages between a slave and a free person required state permission. Interracial marriage in Cuba was generally restricted to lower-class whites and women of mixed racial descent. In French Saint Domingue, where such marriages were usually confined to frontier regions, one source estimated the ratio of married women to concubines and prostitutes in the 1770s at 3 to 2 among whites and 3 to 7 among free coloreds. Concubinage was the normative form of gender relations among Caribbean slaves and free coloreds, and—with the exception of prostitution, which was common in the seaports—between both groups and Euro-Americans.

The slaves most likely to form households were creoles and those slaves on large plantations. When slavery ended in the British colonies, the proportion of slaves living in nuclear households varied from about twenty-five per cent (in Jamaica) to seventy-five per cent (in the Bahamas), probably less overall than in Brazil or the United States. Though historians debate the accuracy of contemporary depictions of extreme promiscuity, the stability of concubinal relations was undermined by several factors. Traditions of premarital sexual freedom, polygyny, and easy divorce in some African cultures perhaps contributed to the pattern of shifting or multiple relationships many observers described. Only elite male slaves, however, could afford polygynous families, a form perpetuated in the modern Haitian *plasaj*. Couples who belonged to different owners could not live together, and early death separated many who did. Above all, the heavy male majorities in both the slave and Euro-American populations created competition for women, worsened by the imbalance of power between the two groups.

Some scholars argue the scarcity of men merely added to the oppression of enslaved women, but others claim it also brought empowerment and advantages comparable to those skilled male slaves enjoyed. Women slaves were freed far more often than slave men. As the Jamaican diary of Thomas Thistlewood suggests, relations between white men and slave women on plantations were usually predatory and ephemeral, albeit remunerated, but they also included stable consensual unions, a few of which resulted in emancipation for the concubine and her children by the master and the granting of a property endowment. Female servants might be expected indiscriminately to provide sexual services, but slave and free "housekeepers" enjoyed a higher status commonly assumed to include the more stable, quasi-recognized role of concubine to the owner or manager. The tendency for sugar estates to be owned by absentees and run by staffs of European bachelors encouraged interracial concubinage. So, too, perhaps did French and Spanish legal traditions of recognition of illegitimate offspring. Interracial unions of all sorts appear to have been least common where white women were most numerous, as in Barbados.

See also GENDER RELATIONS; SEXUAL EXPLOITATION.

BIBLIOGRAPHY

GASPAR, DAVID BARRY, and DARLENE C. HINE, eds. *More Than Chattel: Black Women and Slavery in the Americas.* 1996.
HALL, DOUGLAS. *In Miserable Slavery: Thomas Thistlewood in Jamaica, 1750–1786.* 1989.
MARTINEZ-ALIER, VERENA. *Marriage, Class, and Color in Nineteenth Century Cuba: A Study of Racial Attitudes and Sexual Values in a Slave Society.* 1989.

David Geggus

Latin America

Although technically forbidden by church and state, concubinage was common and accepted in many areas of colonial Latin America and still is today. During the initial conquests large numbers of Iberian men formed sometimes enduring and often affectionate relationships with Indian women whom they either received as "gifts" from Indian allies—as in the case of Doña Marina, the famous concubine of Hernando Cortés—or took as spoils of conquest.

Enslaved African women also became concubines of Iberian men in Latin America, as they had in Spain and Portugal. Men often made concubines of their own slaves, but Iberian men might also develop relationships with slaves belonging to others and with free women of African descent. While quantification of such illicit arrangements is impossible, the seventeenth-century decline in Indian populations, combined with new African imports and the rapid growth of a racially mixed population, diversified concubinage. During a pastoral visit through Venezuela in the late eighteenth century, one bishop recorded 300 incidences of fornication and concubinage, 174 of which involved white males and women of color (including women of Indian and African descent). Even elite Spanish or Brazilian women might become

Doña Marina (center), the concubine of Hernando Cortés, serves as interpreter for the Spaniard's interactions with her people. In Mexican folklore, she is known as the witch Malinche, betrayer of the Aztecs. [Corbis-Bettmann]

concubines if, for some reason, they were unable to wed the man of their choice. More common, however, were informal alliances between Iberian men and free and enslaved women of Indian or African descent.

As Gilberto Freyre and others have noted, Brazilians, in particular, lauded black and mulatto women for their alleged sensuality and prized them as concubines. While Freyre described concubinage on the plantation, many Brazilian men maintained their concubines in townhouses in Salvador de Bahia, Recife, and Rio de Janeiro and left their wives on isolated rural estates. Social prejudice, the right of family members to lodge legal objections to marriages they opposed, and widespread acceptance of concubinage all made legitimate unions between partners considered to be socially unequal much less common. Nevertheless, studies of parish registers from a number of colonial cities show that interracial marriages occurred much more frequently in Latin America than in British America and were more common in Spanish than in Portuguese America.

Latin Americans viewed society as an extension of family structures. Owners might regard minor female slaves as dependents or wards and elderly slaves as fictive grandmothers or aunts, but the same men often considered young slave women sexual objects. As such, the women might have to endure harassment by men in the household and vindictive, sometimes sadistic, mistreatment by jealous wives. Although Iberian law recognized a master's property rights, it also held the master accountable for the good treatment of slaves. Slaves could pursue legal suits against a cruel or sexually abusive master, and the courts carefully investigated the most notorious cases of rape and sexual violence. It is almost certain, however, that most cases of sexual abuse, then as now, went unreported and unpunished.

Enslaved women did not always resist the sexual advances of their owners. In fact, they frequently used concubinage and Iberian understandings of the extended family to win advantages in Latin American society. A sexual relationship with the owner might result in better material conditions for women and their children, as well as gifts of personal or real property. Another prize enslaved women often sought, and sometimes gained, from their sexual connections was either their freedom or that of their children. It was even possible, although extremely rare, for a free white man to marry an enslaved concubine, and in such cases he would usually also arrange her freedom.

Wealthy ranchers, planters, government officials, and merchants sometimes raised large mulatto families, often while they were also raising legitimate white families. In some cases, men kept concubines in rural or urban estates equal to that they provided for a legal wife; if the concubines lived circumspect lives, the community did not object. And, much as earlier generations of conquistadors had done for their mestizo children, Iberian men often recognized and freed their mulatto children, educated them, and provided for them in their wills. Law and community consensus generally protected the children's inheritance rights. In Brazil it was more common for white fathers to recognize and support their mixed-race children but keep them enslaved in their households.

Freed concubines of African descent enjoyed the full legal and customary rights held by Iberian women. The privileged few managed plantations, operated small businesses, litigated in the courts, and bought and sold property, including slaves. If concubines lived circumspect lives, the wife and the community generally looked the other way, especially if the involved man were elite or powerful. If, however, the man flaunted the relationship by publicly escorting his concubine, the situation became "notorious" and actionable by the wife or church authorities. Wives' petitions for legal separation often described enduring years of public humiliation as their husbands pampered and cherished their concubines to the detriment of their legal families. Few concubines, however, were lucky enough to be plantation mistresses, and there was always the possibility that their illegal and unsecured relationship might end abruptly and that they might be abandoned by their lover. Such women joined the ever-growing ranks of unmarried and poor freedwomen, some of whom turned to prostitution to support themselves and their children.

Like concubinage, prostitution was both common and illegal, but since its casual, public nature threatened rather than emulated the privacy and bonds of family life, church and state officials in major colonial cities condemned prostitutes to "houses of correction." One such institution established in Caracas in the 1790s was designated for nonwhite women, many of whom were former slaves, who "without known profession live in the most luxurious style . . . without other means than the prostitution of their persons." Officials worried about the spread of venereal disease and about the bad example such women set for young girls "of their own class." In smaller venues lacking correctional institutions, authorities often drove prostitutes out of town. Although prostitution was always a dangerous and unstable life, it could sometimes be lucrative, and enslaved women sometimes earned enough to buy freedom and support lavish lifestyles. Despite public opprobrium, in some cases slave prostitution involved the complicity of owners, who put slave women on the street on the *jornal* system. This self-hire arrangement allowed slaves to keep any earnings surpassing an amount set by the owner, but the slave was normally expected to engage in legal occupations such as laundering or huckstering.

The rapid growth of the largely illegitimate mulatto population in colonial Latin America testifies to the frequency of sexual activity, legal or illicit, between Iberians and enslaved and free women of color. Illegitimacy was common among all races in Latin America and did not carry the stigma it would in other places and times. If occupational advancement demanded it, however, illegitimacy could be "corrected" post facto. If parents married after the birth of a child, that child became legitimate. Later in the eighteenth century the "taint" of illegitimacy might also be erased legally through the purchase of a legal document called *gracias al sacar*. Money not only "whitened" in Latin America, it "legitimated."

See also GENDER RELATIONS; MANUMISSION; PROSTITUTION; SEXUAL EXPLOITATION.

BIBLIOGRAPHY

CLINTON, CATHERINE, and MICHELE GILLESPIE, eds. *The Devil's Lane: Sex and Race in the Early South.* 1997.
LANDERS, JANE G. *Against the Odds: Free Blacks in the Slave Societies of the Americas.* 1996.
LAVRIN, ASUNCIÓN. *Sexuality and Marriage in Colonial Latin America.* 1989.

Jane G. Landers

Condorcet, Marquis de

See Franklin, Benjamin, and the Marquis de Condorcet.

Confederate States of America

In March 1861, delegates from seven states of the lower South (South Carolina, Mississippi, Florida, Alabama, Georgia, Louisiana, and Texas) drafted the constitution of the Confederate States of America. The establishment of the Confederacy was the culmination of years of constitutional debate over the status of states in the Union and the future of slavery in the republic. Nationalists argued that the Union was perpetual and indivisible, while champions of state sovereignty claimed that the states had created the Union and could secede at any time. Acting on the theory of state sovereignty, these seven slaveholding states seceded from the United States after Abraham Lincoln's election as president. Many Southerners, particularly wealthy slaveholding planters, feared that Lincoln's election would end the expansion of slav-

ery to new western territories and threaten slavery where it already existed.

After writing the Confederate constitution, the delegates elected Jefferson Davis of Mississippi as president and Alexander Stephens of Georgia as vice president. Although Davis would have preferred to avoid war, as head of the new Confederacy he wanted to establish its independence by asserting control over all its territory, including all the forts along the southern coast. In April 1861, when President Lincoln sent a supply ship to the besieged Fort Sumter in Charleston harbor, Confederate forces opened fire and the Civil War began. In the months to follow, four more slave states (North Carolina, Virginia, Arkansas, and Tennessee) joined the Confederacy, which eventually established its capital at Richmond, Virginia. Four other slave states—Maryland, Delaware, Missouri, and Kentucky: those on the border between the North and the South—remained loyal to the United States.

The Confederacy rested upon the institution of black slavery. Although only 25 percent of all white Southerners owned slaves in 1860, the Confederacy embodied the ideals and interests of the planter class. In a famous speech delivered in Savannah just after the completion of the Confederate constitution, Vice President Stephens clearly articulated the reasoning behind secession: "Our new government is founded . . . its foundations are laid, its cornerstone rests, upon the great truth that the Negro is not equal to the white man; that slavery, subordination to the superior race, is his natural and normal condition." The Confederate constitution affirmed Stephen's declaration. Although in other respects it was modeled after the Constitution of the United States, it overtly supported slaveholders' rights. It guaranteed the return of fugitive slaves and upheld masters' "right of transit and sojourn in any State of this Confederacy, with their slaves and other property." Moreover, should the Confederacy acquire new territory, the Confederate Congress and the territorial government would protect "the institution of Negro slavery, as it now exists in the Confederate States." The constitution also explicitly prohibited the passage of any "law denying or impairing the right of property in Negro slaves." Such language stood in sharp contrast to the words of the framers of the United States Constitution, who, though they sanctioned the institution of slavery, had carefully avoided using the term *slavery* or *slave.*

Internal conflict undermined the development of the sense of nationalism required to sustain the Confederacy. Much controversy stemmed from the government's attempts to centralize its power in order to mobilize the Southern people for war. The Confeder-

REBEL ENLISTMENT IN VIRGINIA. ——A "WILLING VOLUNTEER."

A political cartoon illustrates the resistance to the draft enacted by the Confederacy in 1862. [Library of Congress/ Corbis]

atc Congress imposed a tax-in-kind, under which citizens gave one-tenth of all agricultural produce and livestock to the government, and it also implemented a policy of "impressment" whereby military authorities could seize private property (including slaves) necessary to sustain the army—two measures that proved particularly unpopular. But the most divisive policy in the war-torn Confederacy was the draft.

In 1862, the Confederate Congress passed the first conscription law in American history, which mandated military service for men between the ages of eighteen and thirty-five. The law permitted draftees to hire substitutes to serve in their places, and one provision exempted a white man if he had at least twenty slaves under his control. This "twenty-Negro" rule engendered much resentment on the part of common white Southerners, who viewed the draft as favoring the interests of wealthy planters, and the Congress later repealed it. Such disputes over the constitutional authority of the central government and the fairness of its wartime policies undermined the unity of the South.

Ultimately, of course, defeat on the battlefield led to the death of the Confederacy. The Confederate army won a number of key victories in 1861 and 1862, but its losses at Gettysburg and Vicksburg in the summer of 1863 proved to be major turning points in the war. Such defeats lowered morale at home and led to desertion from the army. After the fall of Atlanta and the reelection of Lincoln at the end of 1864, President Davis startled many by proposing the enlistment of black soldiers. Under his plan, slaves who fought faithfully for the Confederacy would receive emancipation and the right of residence in the South. The Confederate government had long employed slaves as noncombatants—building fortifications, working in factories, and serving in hospitals. Slaves made up more than half the labor force in Confederate iron, salt, and lead mines and nearly half of all the nurses in Confederate military hospitals. Yet, the proposal to outfit and arm black troops angered most Southern slaveholders, who believed that it went against the foundations of the Confederacy. Still, the plan earned the support of the Confederate general Robert E. Lee, and the Congress eventually approved the use of black soldiers, though it did not agree to emancipation. Recruiting the training of blacks went ahead, but the war ended before any of these recruits saw combat.

On 9 April 1965, General Lee surrendered to the Union general Ulysses S. Grant, and the Confederate States of America died. A month later, President Davis, who had hoped to continue the fight for Southern independence through guerrilla warfare, was captured in Georgia by United States troops.

See also CIVIL WAR, U.S.; CONSTITUTION, U.S.; EMANCIPATION IN THE UNITED STATES; LINCOLN, ABRAHAM.

BIBLIOGRAPHY

CLEVELAND, HENRY. *Alexander H. Stephens in Public and Private.* 1866.
ESCOTT, PAUL. *After Secession: Jefferson Davis and the Failure of Confederate Nationalism.* 1978.
FAUST, DREW. *The Creation of Confederate Nationalism: Ideology and Identity in the Civil War South.* 1988.
ROARK, JAMES L. *Masters without Slaves: Southern Planters in the Civil War and Reconstruction.* 1977.
THOMAS, EMORY. *The Confederate Nation: 1861–1865.* 1979.

Timothy S. Huebner

Confiscation Acts, U.S.

During the first year of the American Civil War, Congress adopted the first Confiscation Act on August 6, 1861, giving the federal government the right to take control of any property intended for hostile use against the United States. As this property included slaves, the act provided for limited emancipation, which Republicans in Congress believed would create havoc in the South. President Abraham Lincoln may also have favored emancipation at this time but feared that making slavery the central issue of the war would cost him the loyalty of the four slave states still in the Union. Lincoln also thought that emancipation might trigger desertions from the army, as many soldiers believed that the aim of the war was the preservation of the Union.

This first Confiscation Act provided only for the seizure of property, including slaves, used to assist the Confederate cause. In July 1862 Congress passed a second, more far-reaching Confiscation Act that made the property of all Confederate supporters subject to seizure, although at Lincoln's insistence the bill allowed heirs to recover confiscated property. This second bill did not altogether supersede the first Confiscation Act, and property seized under the authority of the first act was not recoverable. Furthermore, recovery did not extend to confiscated slaves, whose freedom was confirmed by the second Confiscation Act. Lincoln objected to this provision because he believed that Congress had no authority over slavery in the states and that the only federal power over slavery arose from powers he insisted he possessed as commander in chief in areas of actual rebellion. Rather than quarrel with Congress, however, Lincoln seized the initiative by issuing his preliminary Emancipation Proclamation in September 1862. Thus although the Confiscation Acts had little real effect on the institu-

tion of slavery, these acts nonetheless constituted a first step toward emancipation.

See also EMANCIPATION IN THE UNITED STATES.

BIBLIOGRAPHY

DONALD, DAVID HERBERT. *Lincoln.* 1995.
HYMAN, HAROLD M. *A More Perfect Union: The Impact of the Civil War and Reconstruction on the Constitution.* 1973.
RANDALL, JAMES G. *Constitutional Problems under Lincoln.* Rev. ed. 1951.

Al McDermid

Conflict of Laws

In Europe and the American colonies and counties the status of "slave" was created by local or national laws. A "conflict of laws" arose when a person enslaved under the laws of one jurisdiction was found in another, "foreign" jurisdiction, particularly one that did not recognize slavery. With regard to the status of slaves, a "foreign" jurisdiction could also be another state within the United States, since some American states allowed slavery and others did not. Slaves entered foreign jurisdictions as runaways, as travelers, or through some misadventure at sea. The courts where these slaves were found then had to decide their status.

Conflict-of-laws theory is based on three principles articulated by the seventeenth-century Dutch theorist Ulrich Huber. First, Huber asserted, "The laws of each sovereign authority have force within the boundaries of its states, and bind all subject to it, but not beyond." Next, he noted that people "found within" the boundaries of a state are "subject to" the "sovereign authority" of that state, "whether they are there permanently or temporarily." Thus the laws passed by a jurisdiction apply to everyone in that jurisdiction but are not enforceable by that jurisdiction once people leave it. However, to avoid conflicts between nations, Huber articulated a third principle: that laws, court decrees, contracts, legal obligations, and statuses created by legal actions (such as marriage) cling to individuals when they leave the place where the legal event took place, unless such legal events "prejudice the power or rights" of people where the individual travels. The recognition of the foreign law was done as a matter of "comity"—that is, one state or nation granted comity to another by recognizing the civil statuses it created.

Slavery tested these principles, and in the United States it overwhelmed them. But long before American politics began to disintegrate over slavery, the institution posed problems for jurists on both sides of the Atlantic.

As early as 1552 a French military commander in Metz refused to return a fugitive slave to Spanish authorities. The commander declared that under "l'ancienne et bonne coutume de France" the slave became free the moment he touched French soil. Similarly, in 1571 authorities in Bordeaux ordered the release of slaves brought into that city. In 1716 French authorities declared that slaves brought into France would be immediately free, unless registered in Paris within eight days after their arrival. In *Boucaut v. Verdelin* (1738) a French court ruled that slaves brought to France from the American colonies were free because they had escaped after they arrived in France but before their master could register them in Paris. These rules applied to slaves brought from other nations as well. While serving as ambassador to France, Thomas Jefferson warned an American master that his slaves would become free if he took them to France, although Jefferson also noted that if the master kept his slaves away from meddling Frenchmen, it would be possible to retain them there. This suggests that the French authorities were not vigilant about emancipating foreign slaves but that the French courts and perhaps French government officials would recognize as free any slaves who sought their protection.

England also had a long history of freeing foreign slaves. In *Cartwright's Case* (1569) an English court declared a "Slave from Russia" to be free, because "England was too pure an Air for Slaves to breathe in." The English colonies, however, did not have such "pure" air and by the early eighteenth century slavery had become an important source of labor in the West Indies and on the British North American mainland. In *Chamberline v. Harvey* (1696) the Court of King's Bench ruled that a slave brought to England ceased to be property. In *Smith v. Browne and Cooper* (1702?), Chief Justice John Holt again ruled in favor of a slave brought to England, declaring: "as soon as a negro comes into England, he becomes free." In 1729 Attorney General Philip Yorke and Solicitor General Charles Talbot issued a joint opinion, asserting that "a slave coming from the West Indies, either with or without his master, to Great Britain or Ireland, doth not become free" and that the master might "legally compel him to return to the plantations." This statement, from crown officials, was useful to masters but not binding on the courts. In *Somerset v. Stewart* (1772) the Court of King's Bench specifically rejected the claims of Yorke and Talbot. Chief Justice, Lord Mansfield ruled that a master could not compel a slave to leave England—that the laws of the colonies did not apply in England, and thus the moment a slave entered England there was no law that allowed a master to exert dominion over a slave.

In *The Slave, Grace* (1827) the High Court of Admiralty ruled that this denial of comity within the empire was partially reciprocal, and that the colonies were free to ignore a residence in England when determining whether a slave was entitled to be free. Grace had lived in England but had returned to Antigua with her master, who then treated her as a slave. In his opinion Lord Stowell acknowledged that Grace had had a claim to freedom while in England because England did not enforce colonial slave law. But once she left England and returned to slave jurisdiction, she lost her claim to freedom.

In its foreign policy Great Britain also refused to give comity to the laws of slavery created by other nations. Thus after the Revolution, Great Britain refused to return American slaves who had left the United States with the departing British Army. Similarly, almost all fugitive slaves who reached Canada, the British West Indies, or England gained their liberty under the Union Jack. In 1860 England refused to allow the extradition of John Anderson, a fugitive slave who had killed a white while escaping from Missouri. More contentious was the "*Creole* incident." In 1841 the *Creole* sailed from Virginia toward New Orleans with 135 slaves. The slaves mutinied and sailed the ship to Nassau, where British officials in the Bahamas declared that under English law all the slaves were free. In 1853 an Anglo-American claims commission ruled against Britain, which paid compensation to the owners of the slaves. The slaves, however, remained free under the protective paw of the British lion.

The most intense, recurrent, and ultimately disruptive conflict of laws questions arose within the United States, between slave and free jurisdictions. The Constitution provided that "No Person held to Service of Labour in one State, under the Laws thereof, escaping into another, shall, in Consequence of any Law or Regulation therein, be discharged from such Service or Labour." Instead, the person who escaped would "be delivered up on Claim of the Party to whom such Service or Labour may be due." This provision, known as the "fugitive slave clause," incorporated concepts of conflict of laws, acknowledging that without this clause the laws in states not recognizing slavery could be used to free runaways. In essence, the fugitive slave clause, mandated that free states grant comity to the owners of fugitive slaves and likewise prohibited the free states from using their own laws to emancipate runaways.

However, the fugitive slave clause did not protect masters who visited in or traveled through free states with their slaves. During and after the Revolution the northern states acknowledged the need for interstate comity on the issue by passing laws granting temporary recognition of slave property owned by visiting masters from other states. Thus, the Pennsylvania Gradual Emancipation Act of 1780 allowed visiting masters to keep their slaves in the state for up to six months. Slaves kept in Pennsylvania longer than six months would become free. New York adopted a similar rule, but allowed visitors to keep slaves in the state for nine months. Before the 1830s there is no evidence that any northern state attempted to free slaves accompanying their visiting masters.

Northern law changed dramatically with the decision in *Commonwealth v. Aves* (1836). In that case the highest court in Massachusetts declared free a Louisiana slave because the law creating her status did not follow her to Massachusetts. The decision, written by the distinguished chief justice of Massachusetts, Lemuel Shaw, carried great weight throughout the North. Connecticut adopted a similar rule in 1837, and in the 1840s New York and Pennsylvania repealed their exemptions. By 1861 almost all the northern states freed slaves in transit. In *Lemmon v. New York* (1860) that state's highest court held that all slaves (except fugitives) became free the moment they set foot in New York.

The breakdown in interstate comity also affected criminal extradition. Starting in the late 1830s, northern states also refused to give force to southern criminal law that affected slavery. Thus, governors in New York, Maine, Illinois, and Ohio refused to allow the extradition of men indicated in southern states for helping slaves escape. In these cases the northern governors asserted that their states did not recognize property in slaves and therefore could not recognize that a crime was committed by helping a slave escape. In *Kentucky v. Dennison* (1861) Chief Justice Roger B. Taney of the U.S. Supreme Court chastised Governor William Dennison of Ohio for refusing to send a free black back to Kentucky to stand trial for theft, for helping a slave woman escape to Ohio. However, deciding the case after a number of southern states had seceded, Taney declared that the national government could not force state governors to act in such a situation.

Southern states also faced conflict-of-law issues involving slavery. Before the 1830s most southern states held that a slave who resided in a free state became free and, once free, remained free. Courts in Kentucky, Missouri, Louisiana, and Mississippi all reached this conclusion before 1824. Mississippi began to reject this rule in the 1830s but did not completely abandon it until the late 1850s. Louisiana rejected the rule in the 1850s, but Kentucky kept it until the abolition of slavery itself. Missouri continued to recognize the rule until 1852, when the Missouri Supreme Court held, in *Scott v. Emerson*, that the slave Dred Scott did

not gain his freedom by residence in Illinois and the free federal territory that later became the state of Minnesota. The U.S. Supreme Court later upheld this result in *Dred Scott v. Sandford* (1857).

Some southern states refused to recognize the status of free blacks from the North. Every coastal slave state (except Mississippi, which had no coastal ports) had laws requiring the arrest of free black sailors entering its jurisdiction. These hapless seamen were kept in jail until their ships left the state. Most of the southern states also had laws requiring the expulsion, incarceration, or enslavement of free blacks who entered their jurisdictions. No southern state recognized the citizenship of free blacks from northern states.

The U.S. Supreme Court sided with the South on all issues of conflict of law, except in interstate criminal extradition, as noted in the discussion of *Kentucky v. Dennison*. In *Strader v. Graham* (1850) the Court held that a slave state did not have to recognize the free status that a slave might have acquired while living in or visiting the North. In *Dred Scott v. Sandford* (1857) the Supreme Court affirmed this ruling and also held that free blacks had no legal rights under the Constitution, thus implicitly recognizing that the slave states could ignore the rights of northern free blacks. The Supreme Court never ruled on whether the free states could emancipate visiting slaves, but Justice Samuel Nelson, in his concurrence in *Dred Scott*, noted, "A question has been alluded to, . . . namely: the right of the master with his slave of transit into or through a free State, on business or commercial pursuits, or in the exercise of a Federal right, or the discharge of a Federal duty, being a citizen of the United States." Nelson asserted that this question "turns upon the rights and privileges secured to a common citizen of the republic under the Constitution of the United States." He declared, "When that question arises, we shall be prepared to answer it." Most observers believed that this "answer" would in fact support the right of a master to travel with his slave into a free state. Abraham Lincoln in fact predicted that Americans would "*lie down* pleasantly dreaming that the people of *Missouri* are on the verge of making their state *free;* and we shall awake to the *reality, instead,* that the *Supreme Court* had made *Illinois* a *slave* sate."

Lincoln's fears illustrate the way in which slavery challenged the legal theories surrounding conflicts of law and comity. Nations could deny comity to the citizens of other nations and risk retaliation or even war. European nations eventually denied claims of comity involving slavery, and no retaliations or wars resulted. In America a tribunal existed—the United States Supreme Court—which could in fact resolve interstate conflicts of law cases. Chief Justice Taney and his brethren on the Court tried to do this in *Dred Scott v. Sandford,* with disastrous results. Ironically, in the United States the conflict-of-law issues helped push the nation toward civil war.

See also FUGITIVE SLAVE LAWS, U.S.; DRED SCOTT V. SANDFORD; LAW; SOMERSET V. STEWART; TANEY, ROGER B.

BIBLIOGRAPHY

FINKELMAN, PAUL *An Imperfect Union: Slavery, Federalism, and Comity.* 1981.

WATSON, ALAN. *Joseph Story and the Comity of Errors: A Study in the Conflict of Laws.* 1992.

Paul Finkelman

Conjurers

See Slave Religion.

Connecticut

The bondage of Native Americans and African-Americans was an early and accepted practice in colonial Connecticut. After bloody victories in the Pequot War (1637) and King Philip's War (1675–1676), Puritan settlers enslaved Indian prisoners of war. During the same time New England merchants in the Atlantic trade sold black slaves to planters in the West Indies and South, but some were brought to the ports of New Haven, Hartford, and New London. Geography and small-scale agriculture precluded the plantation slavery that flourished where tobacco, rice, indigo, and sugarcane were staple crops. Instead, a Connecticut master, who usually owned no more than a few slaves, employed them in the house, in the fields, or sometimes as artisans. In 1715 about 1,500 slaves existed among a white population of 46,000.

Connecticut's slave laws enacted between 1690 and 1730 regulated African-Americans and Native Americans. The codification of white supremacy required slaves and free blacks to carry written passes when traveling. They prohibited whites from harboring fugitives, trading with slaves, and selling alcoholic beverages to them. Inflammatory speech, stealing, striking a white person, or being about at night without the master's permission warranted as many as forty lashes in some cases. No restrictions existed on manumission, but owners were financially liable for their freed slaves. No distinction between slaves and whites existed in the application of the death penalty. Slaves were tried in the same courts as citizens, could testify against whites, and had the right of appeal. In brief, the slave had the same right to life and the

ownership of property as an apprentice, except that the former served for life and the latter for a fixed term of usually four to seven years.

During the agitation of the American Revolution the clergy first indicted slavery. Ebenezer Baldwin, Jonathan Edwards Jr., and Levi Hart argued that slavery violated natural law and social equity. They contended that the contradiction between the colonies' demand for liberty and the practice of slavery was untenable. The Connecticut Assembly in 1774 banned the importation of slaves. A law in 1777 facilitated the manumission of slaves who served in the army; masters of such slaves met their military obligation and were absolved of any financial obligation for the freed slaves. As many as 400 slaves gained their freedom in this way. In the aftermath of the War of Independence the state passed a gradual emancipation law providing that no child born after 1 March 1784 should be held in bondage after reaching the age of twenty-five.

The Connecticut Society for the Promotion of Freedom and for the Relief of Persons Holden in Bondage was organized in 1790 and included such prominent people as Ezra Stiles, Simeon Baldwin, Zephaniah Swift, Jonathan Edwards Jr., and Noah Webster. In 1792 the society argued for the immediate abolition of slavery in the state, with masters required to support their needy former slaves and a provision for the education of black children. The legislature in 1795 failed to enact this farsighted plan, but in 1797 it did reduce the age for manumission to twenty-one. The number of slaves significantly diminished over time, until in 1848, amid the sectional antagonism over the Mexican War, Connecticut declared the unequivocal abolition of slavery. It was, however, not until 1869, when Connecticut ratified

Table 1. Decline in Slave Population in Connecticut, 1790 to 1860.			
Year	Free	Slave	Blacks as % of Total Population
1790	2,771	2,648	2.3
1800	5,330	951	2.5
1810	6,435	310	2.6
1820	7,870	97	2.9
1830	8,064	23	2.7
1840	8,105	54	2.6
1850	7,693	0	2.1
1860	8,627	0	1.9

the Fifteenth Amendment, that an 1814, statute restricting suffrage to white men was repealed.

See also LAW; MANUMISSION.

BIBLIOGRAPHY

CATTERALL, HELEN T. *Judicial Cases Concerning American Slavery and the Negro,* vol. 4. 1936.
MARS, JAMES. *Life of James Mars: A Slave Born and Sold in Connecticut.* 1866.
STEINER, BERNARD C. *History of Slavery in Connecticut.* 1893.
WARNER, ROBERT AUSTIN. *New Haven Negroes: A Social History.* 1940. Reprint 1969.
WHITE, DAVID O. *Connecticut's Black Soldiers, 1775–1783.* 1973.
ZILVERSMIT, ARTHUR. *The First Emancipation: The Abolition of Slavery in the North.* 1967.

Lawrence B. Goodheart

Constitution, U.S.

The word *slavery* does not appear in the main body of the Constitution of the United States. It is found only in the Thirteenth Amendment, adopted in 1865, which prohibited slavery and involuntary servitude. Yet, despite the absence of the word, the Constitution protected the institution of slavery, which existed in most of the nation at the time of the Constitutional Convention.

Slavery affected how Congress implemented the Constitution and how the Supreme Court interpreted it. During the Constitutional Convention, James Madison asserted that the great division in the nation was not between the large and the small states but along sectional lines, and that it came "principally from their having or not having slaves." The intensity of the debates on questions involving slavery bears out this insight.

Most delegates to the Convention accepted that representation in Congress ought to be based on the population of each state. This idea led to heated debates over whether to count slaves when determining how many members of Congress each state would get. In one of these debates Gouverneur Morris of Pennsylvania argued against counting slaves because "when fairly explained [it] comes to this that the inhabitant of Georgia and S.C. who goes to the Coast of Africa, and in defiance of the most sacred laws of humanity tears away his fellow creatures from their dearest connections [and] damns them to the most cruel bondages, shall have more votes in a Govt. instituted for the protections of the rights of mankind, than the Citizen of Pa or N. Jersey, who views with a laudable horror, so nefarious a practice" (quoted in Max Farrand, ed., *The Records of the Federal Convention of 1787,* rev. ed., 1966, 2:220–223). On the other hand, Charles Pinckney of South Carolina declared that slavery was "justified by the example of all the world." Pierce Butler, also of South Carolina, declared that "the security the [southern] States want is that their negroes may not be taken from them which some gentlemen within or without doors, have a very good mind to do" (both quoted in Farrand, 2:371–375 and 1:605). In the end, the South managed to get each counted as three-fifths of a free person toward the allocation of seats in the House of Representatives. This would give the South extra voting power in Congress. The "three-fifths clause" also increased southern influence over the election of the president, because the votes of each state in the Electoral College were based on the number of representatives it had in Congress.

There were also angry debates over the continuation of the African slave trade. A majority of the delegates—on both moral and economic grounds—wanted to give Congress power to ban the importation of slaves. Even some slave owners, such as George Mason of Virginia, believed that whatever the morality of owning slaves, the African trade was immoral. Some opponents of the African trade also saw newly imported slaves as a threat to the security of the nation. They feared that in time of war, a large population of African-born slaves would become an internal enemy. South Carolina's delegates, however, argued that they would not support the Constitution if it did not protect the foreign trade. In the end, the deep South prevailed upon the New England states to support a provision allowing the African trade to continue until at least 1808. In return for this concession, South Carolina's delegates voted to support a clause allowing Congress to regulate all commerce on a simple majority vote.

The protection of slavery under the Constitution of 1787, as finally written, would shape American politics and law in far-reaching ways. The three-fifths clause (Art. I, Sec. 2) gave masters extra representation in Congress because of their slaves. This clause and the capitation tax clause (Art. I, Sec. 9, Par. 4) limited the potential taxation of slaves. The presidential election provision (Art. II, Sec. 1), as noted above, based a state's electoral votes on the number of members of Congress it had. The migration and importation clause (Art. I, Sec. 9, Par. 1) prohibited Congress from ending the African slave trade before 1808. The "fugitives from labor" clause (Art. IV, Sec. 2, Par. 3) provided for the return of fugitive slaves. The amendment provision (Art. V) gave added protection to the slave trade by prohibiting any amendment of the migration and importation clause before 1808. Other clauses strengthened slavery by guaranteeing that federal troops would be used to suppress slave rebellions and by prohibiting export taxes, which would have allowed for indirect taxation of slaves. The requirement that three-fourths of the states must assent to any constitutional amendment guaranteed that the South could always block proposed amendments.

Finally, and most important, under the Constitution the national government had no power to interfere with slavery in states where it existed. In the 1840s William Lloyd Garrison, America's most famous abolitionist, examined these clauses and concluded that the Constitution was proslavery—a "covenant with death" and an "agreement in Hell." Southerners agreed that the document protected their special institution. Shortly after returning from the Constitutional Convention in Philadelphia, General Charles Cotesworth Pinckney told the South Carolina legislature: "We have a security that the general government can never emancipate them, for no such authority is granted, and it is admitted on all hands, that the general government has no powers but what are expressly granted by the constitution and that all rights not expressed were reserved by the several states" (quoted in Jonathan Elliot, ed., *The Debates in the Several State Conventions on the Adoption of the Federal Constitution*, 5 vols., 1888, reprinted 1987, 4:286).

Charles Cotesworth Pinckney. [Library of Congress/ Corbis]

During the struggle over ratification, a number of northern Antifederalists complained about the three-fifths provision and the continuation of the slave trade for at least twenty more years. These two clauses have often been misunderstood. Despite claims to the contrary, the three-fifths clause did not assert that a black was three-fifths of a person. It simply allocated representation in Congress by adding to the free population three-fifths of the total number of slaves. It counted free blacks the same as whites; and in a number of states—including Massachusetts, New York, and North Carolina—free blacks voted under the same conditions as whites. The three-fifths rule was a compromise over the allocation of political power in the House of Representatives, not a racial calculation of human worth. Southerners at the Convention wanted to count slaves fully for purposes of representation, while northerners did not want to count slaves at all.

Often overlooked is the extent to which the three-fifths clause also affected the election of the president. Southerners at the Convention opposed direct election of the president, because it would favor the North, where there were few slaves. The Electoral College, since it was based on the states' representation in Congress, gave the South extra votes in presidential elections. These extra votes proved crucial in 1800. If no electoral votes had come from counting slaves, Thomas Jefferson (who owned about two hundred slaves) would not have been elected president.

The slave-trade clause has been misunderstood as requiring the end of the trade in 1808. It in fact only prohibited Congress from ending the importation of slaves before 1808. The Constitution did not require Congress to ban the trade after 1808, and if the deep South had had the political clout, Congress might not have done so. The compromises over slavery led to Supreme Court decisions on the African slave trade, slaves in interstate commerce, fugitive slaves, federal regulation of slavery in the territories, and the rights of free blacks under the Constitution. With the exception of the African slave trade cases, the Supreme Court invariably sided with slave owners.

After 1808 the federal courts heard numerous cases involving the importation of slaves from Africa. In the *Antelope* case (1825), the Supreme Court dealt with a ship attempting to import slaves illegally into the United States. The *Antelope*, originally a Cuban ship, had itself been seized illegally by Americans. When an American Coast Guard cutter captured the ship off the coast of Georgia, it was carrying over 280 slaves. Some had belonged to the Cubans who owned the *Antelope;* others had been seized illegally by the Americans and brought onboard. At the time of this case the African slave trade was legal in Cuba. In his opinion, Chief Justice John Marshall asserted that the African slave trade was "contrary to the law of nature" but that it was "consistent with the law of nations" and "cannot in itself be piracy." The Court recognized the right of foreigners to engage in the slave trade if their own nations allowed them to do so. Thus, although the Court freed most of the slaves and ordered them returned to Africa, it ordered that some of them be turned over to Cuban claimants.

Similar issues arose in a more famous case, *United States v. Amistad* (1841). The slaves on the *Amistad* had been born in African but illegally imported to Cuba. While on a voyage from one part of Cuba to another these Africans, led by a man named Cinqué, revolted, killed some of the crew, and forced the captain to sail to Africa. During the day the ship sailed east, but at night the captain turned north and west, hoping to reach a southern port of the United States. Eventually the ship reached Long Island Sound, and in 1839 a U.S. Coast Guard cutter took it to a port in Connecticut. This led to protracted litigation over the status of the blacks on the ship. The U.S. district court in Connecticut and then the U.S. Supreme Court determined that the Africans were illegally enslaved and could not be returned to Cuba or prosecuted for the mutiny in Cuba. The Court sided with the captured Africans, not out of antislavery sentiment but because the Africans on the *Amistad* had been taken to Cuba and illegally enslaved.

Soon after the Constitution was adopted, the nation reached an unstated political agreement on federal authority over interstate commerce and slavery. Although most lawyers would have conceded that after 1808 Congress had the power to regulate the interstate slave trade—on which the expanding cotton economy of the deep South depended—the consensus was that such regulation would be impossible to get through Congress, but that if it did, it would threaten the Union. Indeed, arguments of counsel and the opinions of the justices in cases involving the commerce clause but having nothing to do with slavery per se often recognized the special status of slaves in the general regulation of commerce.

Groves v. Slaughter (1841) was the only major case to come before the Supreme Court that involved slavery and also directly raised commerce-clause issues. The Mississippi Constitution of 1832 prohibited the importation of slaves for sale—not as an antislavery provision but as an attempt to reduce the flow of capital out of the state. In violation of this provision, Slaughter sold slaves in Mississippi and received notes signed by Groves, who later defaulted on the notes, arguing that sales of slaves in Mississippi were void. The Court ruled that the notes were not void because Missis-

sippi's constitutional prohibition on the importation of slaves could not go into effect without enabling legislation. Absent legislation implementing the prohibition, Mississippi's clause was inoperative. In other cases, northern and southern justices agreed that a state might legally ban the importation of slaves. This principle heartened northerners who wanted to keep slaves out of their states, but it also encouraged southerners who wanted to ensure that the federal courts could not interfere with slavery on the local level.

During the ratification debates of 1787–1788, no northern opponents of the Constitution complained about the fugitive-slave clause (Art. IV, Sec. 2, Par. 3), perhaps because the language of the clause was obscure and the problem of returning runaways was not obvious to the public. However, the jurisprudence surrounding fugitive slaves became the most divisive constitutional issue in antebellum America. Federal and state courts heard numerous cases involving fugitive slaves. While these cases settled legal issues, none of them dealt satisfactorily with the moral and political questions raised when human beings escaped to freedom. In fact, such cases only exacerbated the sectional crisis. Ultimately, the issues were decided not by constitutional arguments and ballots but on the battlefield.

The wording of the fugitive-slave clause suggests that the Constitutional Convention did not anticipate any federal enforcement of the law. However, in 1793 Congress passed the first fugitive-slave law, which spelled out procedures for the return of runaway slaves. In *Prigg v. Pennsylvania* (1842), Justice Joseph Story upheld the 1793 act and struck down state laws passed to protect free blacks from kidnapping if those laws interfered with the return of fugitive slaves. Story urged state officials to continue to enforce the 1793 law, but he concluded that they could not be required to do so. In response to this decision, a number of states passed new personal liberty laws that prohibited state officials from participating in the return of fugitive slaves and barred the use of state jails and other facilities for such returns.

In *Jones v. Zandt* (1847), the Supreme Court interpreted the 1793 law to favor slavery over liberty. This case was a civil suit brought by Jones for the value of one slave who was never captured and the cost of recovering other fugitive slaves who had escaped from Kentucky to Ohio, where Van Zandt offered them a ride in his wagon. Van Zandt's attorneys, Salmon P. Chase and William H. Seward, argued that in Ohio all people were presumed free, and thus Van Zandt had no reason to believe he was transporting runaway slaves. In a harsh interpretation of the 1793 law, the Court rejected this argument and concluded that

Van Zandt should have known that the blacks he assisted were slaves. In essence, this decision meant that all blacks in the North were presumptively slaves.

The refusal of northern judges and state legislatures to implement the Fugitive Slave Law of 1793 led to the adoption of the Fugitive Slave Law of 1850, which provided for federal commissioners to enforce the law throughout the United States. These commissioners could call on federal marshals, the military, and "bystanders, or posse comitatus" as necessary. The law provided long prison sentences and large fines for people interfering with its enforcement, and it did not allow seized blacks to testify on their own behalf or to have a trial by jury.

In *Ableman v. Booth* (1859) the Supreme Court upheld the constitutionality of this law. In two monumental acts—the Northwest Ordinance (1787; reenacted in 1789) and the Missouri Compromise (1820)—Congress prohibited slavery in most of the territories owned by the United States. Congress passed these laws under its constitutional power to make all "needful Rules and Regulations respecting the Territory" of the United States (Art. IV, Sec. 3, Par. 2). These acts led to some of the most important, controversial, and complicated cases that ever reached the Supreme Court. From 1820 until 1850, the Missouri Compromise excluded slavery in most of the western territories. Some southerners argued that this law unconstitutionally deprived them of the right to bring their property into the federal territories, but before 1846 this claim had few adherents. The acquisition of new lands in the Mexican War (1846–1847), and the acceptance throughout the South of a "positive good" theory of slavery, led southerners to demand access to all the western territories.

In 1854 Congress repealed some of the Missouri Compromise, by opening Kansas and Nebraska to slavery, under a theory of popular sovereignty. According to this theory, the settlers of a territory would decide for themselves whether or not to have slavery. Rather than democratizing the West, popular sovereignty led to a small-scale civil war known as "bleeding Kansas," in which free-state and slave-state settlers fought for control of the territorial government. In Kansas the struggle over slavery thoroughly undermined the constitutional process of turning territories into states. Meanwhile, in the North the newly organized Republican Party achieved enormous success campaigning against the spread of slavery into any of the western territories. In 1856 this party, which was less than two years old, carried all but five northern states in the presidential election.

This set the stage for *Dred Scott v. Sandford* (1857), the most famous—or infamous—legal case of the antebellum period, if not of the entire history of the Supreme Court. Chief Justice Roger B. Taney used *Dred Scott* to decide pressing political issues in favor of the South. In his two most controversial points, Taney ruled that the Missouri Compromise unconstitutionally prohibited citizens from bringing their slaves into federal territories and that under the Constitution free blacks could never be citizens of the United States or sue in federal courts as citizens of the states in which they lived.

As a result of this aggressively proslavery decision, the constitutionality of slavery became the central political issue of the decade. In 1860 Lincoln ran successfully for president, in part by attacking Taney and the Dred Scott decision. Lincoln argued that Taney had interpreted the Constitution incorrectly. Lincoln held that Congress could ban slavery in the territories and that free blacks had at least some basic constitutional rights. Lincoln's election led to secession and civil war. A key argument in favor of secession was that the North had failed to live up to the proslavery constitutional bargains of 1787. In particular, southern states complained that northern states did not adequately enforce the fugitive-slave law.

During the Civil War President Lincoln used his constitutional powers as commander in chief of the army to undermine slavery. The constitutional structure created in 1787 gave Lincoln no power to end slavery in the loyal slave states, like Maryland. But he used his wartime powers to issue the Emancipation Proclamation (1863), freeing slaves in those states that were at war against the United States. In 1865 Congress passed a new amendment, the Thirteenth, ending slavery throughout the nation. The states ratified this amendment on 6 December 1865.

The Fourteenth Amendment (1868) made blacks citizens of the United States, and the Fifteenth (1870) prohibited discrimination in voting rights on the basis of race. The events of the Civil War and these three amendments effectively repealed the proslavery compact of 1787, and created, in Lincoln's words, "a new birth of freedom."

See also AMISTAD; LAW.

BIBLIOGRAPHY

FEHRENBACHER, DON E. *The Dred Scott Case: Its Significance in American Law and Politics.* 1978.
FINKELMAN, PAUL *Dred Scott v. Sandford: A Brief History with Documents.* 1997.
———. *An Imperfect Union: Slavery, Federalism, and Comity.* 1981.
———. *Slavery and the Founders.* 1996.
MORRIS, THOMAS D. *Free Men All: The Personal Liberty Laws of the North, 1780–1861.* 1974.

ROBINSON, DONALD L. *Slavery in the Structure of American Politics, 1765–1820*. 1971.

WIECEK, WILLIAM M. *The Sources of Antislavery Constitutionalism in America, 1760–1848*. 1977.

Paul Finkelman

Contraband

In the first year of the U.S. Civil War (1861–1865), President Abraham Lincoln prohibited the freeing of slaves by the United States Army. Nevertheless, wherever federal troops occupied southern territory the institution of slavery crumbled and collapsed. Northern commanders followed the example set by General Benjamin F. Butler at Fortress Monroe, Virginia. There, on 23 May 1861, three black men offered their services to Butler's forces. The next morning a Virginian dressed in a militia uniform claimed the three men as his property and demanded their return under the terms of the federal Fugitive Slave Law. Butler responded by observing that military forces in Virginia used the labor of slaves to erect fortifications in support of a rebellion against the United States. Butler then declared the slaves under his control contraband and, therefore, liable to confiscation by the laws of war. Meeting with his cabinet on 30 May, Lincoln jokingly referred to "Butler's fugitive slave law" and let the contraband decision stand. Early in July 1861, a House Resolution added support by expressing the opinion that "it is no part of the duty of the soldiers of the United States to capture and return fugitive slaves." Later in the same month, Congress provided explicit legal sanction for Butler's contraband policy: the first Confiscation Act declared all property (including slaves) used to aid the rebellion subject to confiscation.

The contraband policy maintained the antebellum definition of slave property but it effectively nullified the Fugitive Slave Law. Rather than return slaves to their masters, federal forces in the South encouraged slaves to enter union lines. For the first two years of the war, before the Emancipation Proclamation freed some slaves and the union army began recruiting black soldiers, tens of thousands of black men, women, and children fled from their masters to enter contraband camps, where their labor contributed to the defeat of the Southern rebellion.

See also BUTLER, BENJAMIN; CONFISCATION ACTS, U.S.; FUGITIVE SLAVE LAWS, U.S.

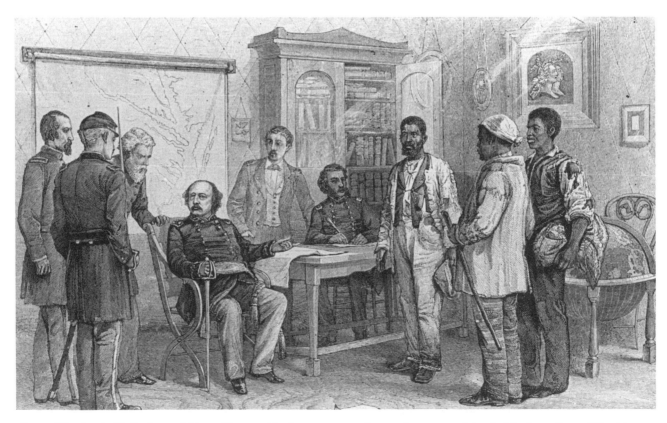

General Benjamin F. Butler and his staff meet with three runaway slaves who want to join the Northern forces. [Corbis-Bettmann]

BIBLIOGRAPHY

BERLIN, IRA, BARBARA J. FIELDS, THAVOLIA GLYMPH, JOSEPH P. REIDY, and LESLIE S. ROWLAND, eds. *Freedom: A Documentary History of Emancipation, 1861–1867*. Series 1, vol. 1. *The Destruction of Slavery*. 1985.

GERTEIS, LOUIS S. *From Contraband to Freedman: Federal Policy toward Southern Blacks, 1861–1865*. 1973.

Louis S. Gerteis

Convict Labor

See Labor Systems.

Coolies

See China; Labor Systems; Slave Trade.

Corvée

See Labor Systems.

Cotton

See Plantations; Whitney, Eli.

Creole Incident (1841)

On 7 November 1841, 19 slaves of 135 on the American brig *Creole* led a revolt near the Bahamas as the vessel, then engaged in the domestic slave trade, passed from Virginia to Louisiana. The leader of the mutiny, Madison Washington, opted to sail for Nassau, a British possession where slavery was illegal. The British attorney general freed, first, those blacks who had not participated in the rebellion and then even the mutineers, once approval arrived from London.

Southern slaveholders demanded compensation for the loss of property resulting from Britain's violation of freedom of the seas. President John Tyler, a slaveholder from Virginia, could not seek extradition of the slaves because the Jay Treaty of 1795 had expired. Secretary of State Daniel Webster requested their return on the basis of "comity," or hospitality, between nations, but this effort likewise proved fruitless. British prime minister Sir Robert Peel feared trouble with abolitionists at home.

Anglo-American relations were already raw owing to a series of grievances held by Americans against the mother country, so the result of the incident was a negotiated settlement initiated by the Peel ministry's decision to send Lord Ashburton (Alexander Baring) to Washington with instructions to resolve all differences between the Atlantic nations. The Webster-Ashburton Treaty, signed on 9 August 1842, assured against "officious interference" with American vessels entering British ports for reasons beyond their control. It also authorized extradition for seven nonpolitical crimes that, because of abolitionist pressure in England, did not include mutiny. Not until 1853 did an Anglo-American claims commission award compensation to those southerners who had lost their slaves on the *Creole*.

See also GREAT BRITAIN, AFRICAN SLAVERY IN; REBELLIONS AND VIOLENT RESISTANCE; WEBSTER-ASHBURTON TREATY.

BIBLIOGRAPHY

JONES, HOWARD. "The Peculiar Institution and National Honor: The Case of the *Creole* Slave Revolt." *Civil War History* 21 (1975): 28–50.

———. *To the Webster-Ashburton Treaty: A Study in Anglo-American Relations, 1783–1843*. 1977.

JONES, HOWARD, and DONALD A. RAKESTRAW. *Prologue to Manifest Destiny: Anglo-American Relations in the 1840s*. 1997.

Howard Jones

Crusades

The Crusades were a series of religious military campaigns that western Europeans mounted from the late eleventh century to the late thirteenth century against the Seljuk Turks, who had occupied Asia Minor (at the expense of the eastern Roman Empire) and gained control of the Abbasid Muslim caliphate in western Asia and Egypt. These religious campaigns were undertaken at the urging of the papacy, but the enthusiastic response of western Europeans was based on more than religious fervor and the desire to free the Holy Land from the infidel Turk, or to help the Byzantine Empire regain its lost possessions in Anatolia, or to heal the schism between the Eastern and Roman churches.

Europe's economy was expanding. An agricultural revolution supported an increased population, a movement from rural to urban environments, a growing interest in travel in the form of pilgrimages and international trade, greater economic resources, and land hunger. So numbers of Europeans on four major and many minor expeditions made the journey east to participate in efforts that resulted in the establishment of four small crusader states along the Syrian coastline: Edessa, Antioch, Tripoli, and Jerusalem. These states would last only until the late thirteenth century, but in the meantime Muslims and Christians had come into close contact with one another, with important implications for slavery. European traders, primarily Italians, had opened wide the doors between east and west.

The eastern Crusades, combined with a simultaneous series of western movements of Christians against Muslim power in Spain, provided conflicts in which prisoners could be taken and held for ransom or offered to slave traders. Perhaps of most importance, the religious difference between Christians and Muslims became more exaggerated, with Christians increasingly ready to enslave Muslims and Muslims ready to enslave Christians. So Christian slave traders (primarily Italian) and somewhat fewer Muslim slave traders provided more recruits to the slave markets.

So far as Europe was concerned, late medieval slavery was confined primarily to the layer of states along the northern shore of the Mediterranean Sea, and even there slavery was confined to artisanal and domestic occupations—there was very little use of slaves for agriculture by this time (except in a few Mediterranean islands, especially Sicily and Majorca). So far as the Muslim world was concerned, slavery was a significant institution; but also without much agricultural use of slaves—slaves were used mostly in domestic service and to a lesser extent as business agents. In both worlds, the preferred slaves were strangers from outside the community, youths and females were preferred. Again in both worlds, the slave came to be integrated into the household, manumission was frequent, and lasting ties between freed slaves and former master's household were frequently preserved. Thus contact between Christians and Muslims during the Crusades had little immediate effect on the institution of slavery itself, since in that regard the two cultures were similar. The main immediate effect was to increase the slave trade, especially after the middle of the fourteenth century, when the ravages of the black death—bubonic plague—reduced the labor supply and increased the demand for slaves.

The most important effect of the Crusades was their stimulation of European tastes for imported luxuries. Europeans had known sugar and cotton before the Crusades, but supplying these items was difficult and they were available only in tiny amounts, so no widespread taste for them had developed. But during the Crusades, many Europeans became acquainted with them while in the East and returned to Europe with an almost insatiable desire for sugar (demand for cotton would not soar for some time). European traders rose to the demand, and sugar (as well as other products, such as citrus fruits, spices, and domestic slaves) became common in the houses of the wealthy. Sugar plantations moved westward, primarily in the Mediterranean islands. A rapidly increasing demand for sugar would be a legacy of the Crusades and would contribute to the desire for colonial empires to produce it with slaves from Africa.

BIBLIOGRAPHY

PHILLIPS, WILLIAM D. JR. *Slavery from Roman Times to the Early Transatlantic Trade.* 1985
VERLINDEN, CHARLES. *L'esclavage dans l'Europe médiévale,* vol. 1: *Peninsule iberique—France;* vol. 2: *Italie—Colonies italiennes du Levant—Empire Byzantin.* 1955, 1977.

Katherine Fischer Drew

Cuba

Enslaved Africans and persons of African descent labored in Cuba for more than four centuries. One or more black slaves may have accompanied Diego Velásquez from Hispaniola on his settlement expedition of 1511, and before midcentury African slaves were mining gold—and rebelling—in eastern Cuba. The numbers of slaves grew from perhaps a thousand (excluding Indians) in 1534 to 5,000 by the mid-seventeenth century and to 30,000 by the mid-eighteenth century. Not until the late eighteenth century did Cuba begin to experience the kind of plantation boom that had transformed the British and French islands generations before. By 1840, however, Cuba had ascended to leadership in global sugar production and was the world's wealthiest slave-based colony. The island's slave population had then peaked at around 400,000. Cuba's slave trade had also changed, from both African and interisland to almost exclusively African. Record numbers of African slaves entered Cuba in the 1830s and 1850s, despite Anglo-Spanish treaties in 1817 and 1835 that prohibited the trade. From 1800 to the early 1870s, when the island became the last country in the Americas to end the Atlantic slave trade, Cuba imported more African slaves (700,000) than the United States during its entire colonial and national history. In the hemisphere, only Brazil maintained slavery longer. Slavery died an anticlimactic death in Cuba in 1886, unraveling in a protracted rebellion against Spanish colonial rule.

During the early colonial period the number of black and mulatto slaves reached about half of the total population. They worked in ranching, construction, petty trading, and domestic service as well as agriculture, often by hiring themselves out. The ordinances of Alonso de Cáceres (1574) marked the first systematic legal attempt in Cuba to regulate slavery. Provisions restricted the ability of slaves to move about, trade, assemble, and carry arms and also set standards of treatment and procedures for the apprehension of runaways. Copper mining and sugar cultivation concentrated slaves in small gangs in the seventeenth century, but slavery on this strategic insular frontier retained a diverse, urban flavor. Before 1700, demand seldom led to annual imports of more than a few hundred Africans. So-called Angolas and Congos from West-Central Africa predominated among the arrivals. In the hands of nonslaveholders and small slaveholders, tobacco cultivation gradually expanded in scattered regional zones, then boomed during the first decades of the eighteenth century. When production eventually slumped under statist controls, sugar cultivation returned to importance by the mid-eighteenth century.

Almost one hundred estates milled sugar in the Havana region in 1761, the larger ones employing around twenty slaves. In response, annual imports had risen in the previous decades to several thousand slaves, drawing heavily from the Gold Coast region as well as from West-Central Africa. Cuban planters enjoyed a windfall of at least 1,700 slaves during Britain's ten-month occupation of Havana (1762–1763) near the end of the Seven Years' War and—with their eyes now widened to economic opportunity—succeeded subsequently in lobbying for more liberal Spanish commercial policies. Thus, after 1791, when slave revolution precipitated the collapse of Saint Domingue's front-running coffee and sugar producers, Cuban elites stood ready with their own capital to respond to rising prices by expanding production with slave labor.

French refugees from Saint Domingue proved crucial to the genesis of Cuba's coffee industry, which thrived in the east near Santiago and for about a half century alongside sugar plantations on the fertile clay soils in the dynamic western region. An official census of 1826 that embraced most of the western districts identified 437 sugar plantations (*ingenios*) that averaged 105 slaves, and 1,180 coffee plantations (*cafetales*) that averaged 43 slaves, although a few districts had coffee estates with larger average slaveholdings than the sugar estates. Perhaps one-quarter of Cuba's slaves at this time worked on sugar estates, one-quarter on coffee estates, one-quarter in ranching and farming, and one-quarter in urban occupations. As late as 1846, coffee estates outnumbered sugar estates (1,670 to 1,442), but Brazilian competition and the lure of higher profits resulted in massive shifting of resources into sugar. In good times, slaves that worked on sugar plantations could generate income that would pay back their cost of purchase within three years. By midcentury a rising proportion of about 40 percent of all Cuban slaves were living on sugar plantations, and more than half of all Cuban slaves were living in the prime western sugar zones. Those districts tied to the ports of Havana, Matanzas, and Cárdenas boasted railroads that serviced a dense black belt of sugar plantations of great size and technological sophistication whose average workforce was approaching 200 slaves.

Sugar cultivation made such notorious exactions on slave labor that it begat a popular Cuban saying, "Sugar is made with blood." Fourteen- to sixteen-hour work days expanded to as many as twenty hours, seven days a week, during a five-month harvest (December-January to May-June). Gang labor prevailed; its factorylike rhythms were set by the operational capacity of mechanized mills. Gender preferences directed members of the male majority into the roles of drivers, artisans, carters, and boilers, although women planted and cut cane side by side with men. After 1820 prime female field hands closed a price differential of less than 10 percent with prime male field hands to virtual equality as the mounting transatlantic campaign against the Atlantic slave trade forced Cuban planters

Table 1.   Population of Colonial Cuba, Official Censuses, 1774–1877 (%).

	Slave	Free Colored	White	Total
1774	44,333 (26)	30,847 (18)	96,440 (56)	171,620
1792	84,590 (31)	54,152 (20)	133,559 (49)	272,301
1817	199,145 (36)	114,058 (21)	239,830 (43)	553,033
1827	286,942 (41)	106,494 (15)	311,051 (44)	704,487
1841	436,495 (43)	152,838 (15)	418,291 (42)	1,007,624
1846	323,759 (36)	149,226 (17)	425, 767 (47)	898,752
1862	370,553 (27)	232,493 (17)	793,484 (57)	1,396,530
1877	199,094 (14)	272,478 (19)	963,394 (67)*	1,434,747

*Includes Asians.

Table 2. Decadal Imports of Cuban Slaves, 1790–1870, in Thousands.

Decade	Slaves
1791–1800	69.5
1801–1810	74.0
1811–1820	168.6
1821–1830	83.1
1831–1840	181.6
1841–1850	50.8
1851–1860	121.0
1861–1870	31.6
Total	780.2

to value more equal sex ratios and the natural reproduction of their enslaved laborers. African-born field hands generally sold for about 10 percent less than similar creole slaves.

At the end of a long day, field slaves returned to quarters that varied from arranged rows of *bohios*—crude, palm-thatched huts—to imposing *barracoons*, rectangular barracks-like compounds designed to maximize slave control. Basic provisions consisted of three to eight ounces of jerked beef or an equivalent amount of salt fish, supplemented by polished rice and cornmeal or some other grain or tuber. Throughout colonial Cuba's history, masters allowed slaves the conditional use of property to cultivate provisions and earn income, but these plots (*conucos*) receded on some estates during the sugar boom.

Hard work and poor diet left Cuban slaves vulnerable to epidemic diseases, which spread rapidly in densely packed quarters on big estates. Tuberculosis and beriberi hit Cuban slaves particularly hard; and cholera epidemics in 1833 and 1853 killed tens of thousands of slaves. Slave suicides, by the hundreds annually, actually compelled a government inquiry in 1847. Cuba's slaves failed to reproduce themselves naturally and decreased on sugar plantations at a rate of perhaps 2 to 3 percent per year. Infant mortality probably ranged between 300 and 500 deaths per 1,000 live births. The continued operation of the Atlantic slave trade during the nineteenth century resulted in imports, almost 70 percent of which were male. The sex ratio of slaves—males per hundred females—in the sugar sectors remained much higher than that for the entire island, which declined from 166 in 1817 to 130 in 1877. Demographic factors, plantation regimentation, and forced separations threw grievous obstacles in the way of the formation of stable Cuban slave families.

Treatment of slaves varied widely in Cuba according to time, place, crop, age, gender, and occupation, and the personality of the master. The surviving part of Juan Francisco Manzano's extraordinary autobiography, written in the 1830s, about his life as a Cuban slave documents wild swings in his individual case between patriarchal generosity and capricious brutalization. (Manzano was the author of one of the very few autobiographies ever written without an amanuensis and one of the very few slave narratives from Latin America.) On paper, Cuba's slave laws looked relatively humane in their attempts to balance treatment and control. Detailed articles in the Spanish slave code of 1789 and the Cuban ordinances of 1842 set standards for religious instruction, punishment, provisioning, leisure, and manumission. But these celebrated laws became dead letters as masters protested and officials looked the other way. Unwritten laws and customs, shaped by a dialectic of resistance and accommodation between masters (or their surrogates) and slaves, had much more to do with the daily realities of slave life.

Wealthy Cuban planters often owned multiple estates and tended to abdicate their managerial responsibilities to hired subordinates in order to escape the drabness of rural life for urban attractions. An elaborate hierarchy of administrators, white overseers (*mayorales*), and slave drivers (*contramayorales*) kept the big plantations running, using an imaginative assortment of stocks, whips, dogs, and chains to discipline recalcitrant slaves. *Bocabajo*, a common punishment, entailed tying a slave face downward, often on a ladder, then applying stripes, which the law tried to limit to twenty-five. Salve drivers frequently applied the lash; but, in their ambivalent position, they also assumed vital leadership roles, as evidenced by their conspicuous presence in major Cuban slave revolts.

Catholic priests were never present in sufficient numbers to minister to the needs of Cuba's rural masses. For 323,759 slaves in 1846, an official census counted only 481 priests, and for every one priest in the leading sugar districts there were thousands of slaves. Planters and officials debated whether conversion to Catholicism would improve slave discipline. Unenforced laws and the planters' active resistance to their mandated religious obligations left a space for slave initiatives, informed by an African past, to satisfy their own spiritual needs.

The Cuban bishop Pedro Agustín Morell de Santa Cruz tried to speed the conversion of Africans to Catholicism in 1755 by legitimating their urban confraternities, known as *cabildos*. These mutual-support societies usually had a distinctive African regional or ethnic content, embraced slaves and free coloreds, and developed branches that extended into the coun-

Slave labor, under the scrutiny of the overseer, brings in the tobacco harvest on a Cuban plantation around 1840. [Corbis-Bettmann]

tryside. A *cabildo* of Mende-speaking Mandingas existed in Havana as early as 1598, and the official number had increased to twenty-one in 1755. Yoruba-based (Lucumf) *cabildos* flourished in the nineteenth century, consistent with the growing importance of the contraband slave trade in the Bight of Benin as a source of Cuban supply. *Cabildos* raised money for manumissions, hosted recreational activities, and acted generally as mediating institutions with white society. Only nominally did they serve to speed conversion to Catholicism; instead, they functioned more like hothouses for regenerate African cultures. In 1812 José Antonio Aponte, who was a talented woodworker, a former officer in the free black (*moreno*) militia, and the head of a Lucumf *cabildo* was executed for plotting an islandwide conspiracy that attempted to unite slaves and free coloreds in rebellion.

Colonial Cuba acquired a reputation for a liberal manumission policy, and, indeed, a Cuban institution known as *coartación* evolved early in the colonial period into a process by which slaves could have their value fixed by a third party, then purchase their freedom by installments. Official documents for the period 1858–1862 record 9,462 manumissions, a minimum figure, of which almost 60 percent were women; *pardos*, persons of partial African ancestry, obtained freedom in numbers disproportionate to their presence in the total slave population. The price of slaves, which tended to follow the price of sugar, affected the percentage of slave manumissions, and during the sugar boom a legal debate ensued as to whether *coartación* was a slave's legal right or a privilege granted by the master. African-born slaves impounded in rural barracoons had far fewer opportunities to avail themselves of *coartación* than did urban creole slaves, especially adult females, who were disproportionately employed in Cuba's bloated domestic service sector. Manumission contributed less than natural reproduction in producing Cuba's sizable but internally divided free-colored class. This class dominated many skilled crafts and trades and served admirably in the militia, although its very success provoked spasms of official repression.

Colonial Cuba has a rich and lengthy history of slave rebellion. Small groups of fugitive African slaves, at times allied with Indians, plagued white communities east and west in the sixteenth century. A handful of enslaved African miners revolted in eastern Cuba in 1533. Royal slaves in an eastern copper-mining zone not only gained renown for two centuries of episodic resistance to challenges to their semiautonomous existence but actually won their freedom in 1799. The number of runaway slaves mounted with the intensification of the plantation regime, and prompted the whites to undertake more systematic efforts at control. In 1796 elaborate regulations on fugitive slaves distinguished between *cimarrones simples*, fugitive slaves who fled an estate individually or in groups of less than seven, and *apalencados*, runaways in larger and more organized communities. For the former, special lock-ups were created, first in Havana and then in other urban areas, where fugitives, more than 90 percent men, were taken from rural districts, held for reclamation, and, while unclaimed, used in public works. Mountains in eastern and western Cuba and swamps to the south concealed numerous maroon communities. The larger ones had fifteen to fifty members, and eastern Cuba gave rise to several with more than a hundred fugitives. The number of documented *palenques* seems to have peaked at about fifteen in the early 1840s. Professional slave hunters (*rancheadores*) roamed the Cuban hinterland, but even if they found the fugitives' fortified enclaves (palengues) the typical confrontation ended indecisively, with dead bloodhounds and few if any captures.

Cuba's sugar boom precipitated one of the most intense periods of collective slave resistance in the history of Latin America from 1825 to 1845. The western districts experienced a revolt (in 1825) of hundreds of African and creole slaves that killed fifteen whites and destroyed dozens of plantations; several essentially ethnic slave revolts (in the 1830s and early 1840s) mostly by Yoruba-speakers; and the so-called Conspiracy of La Escalera (1843–1844), a complicated revolutionary movement with distinctive but overlapping cores of slaves and free coloreds. Its discovery culminated in horrific repression by government officials that cost the lives of hundreds of people of color. The arrival of Chinese coolies, a few years after La Escalera, addressed planters' concerns about the labor supply in light of Britain's antislavery campaign without necessarily resolving problems of insular security. Between 1847 and 1874 legal imports of coolies totaled 124,813; only about eighty of these were women.

Slave rebellion merged into a larger anticolonial struggle during the Ten Years' War (1868–1878), delivering blows that helped to end Cuban slavery. Former slaves and free people of color came to form the majority of the liberation army; many rose to prominence as field commanders; and 16,000 slaves on both sides attained legal freedom in the Pact of Zanjón at the war's end. Under British pressure, the contraband slave trade had slumped sharply from 25,000 imports in 1859 to near extinction before the outbreak of the Ten Years' War. Internal trading had by then weakened slavery in the eastern region, where the anticolonial rebellion began, by moving slaves to more productive western sugar plantations. Near the end of the war the western sugar provinces of Havana, Matanzas, and Santa Clara had 78 percent of Cuba's slaves; the eastern province of Santiago had less than 7 percent.

The separatist leader Carlos Manuel de Céspedes prefaced his call to arms by freeing his own slaves, but in the beginning the rebellion had little to do with slavery per se. White rebels called for the gradual abolition of slavery but moved cautiously until the exigencies of war quickened the pace. A declaration of freedom, despite reluctant implementation, acted with the disruption of war to disintegrate slavery in the east. Spanish efforts to preempt domestic and foreign support for the rebels resulted in the passage of the Moret Law of 1870, which emancipated all slaves born after 1868 and all slaves more than sixty years old. Cuban slaveholders, unlike their counterparts in the United States, never seriously considered a death struggle to maintain slavery but sought a gradual process of emancipation that would spare them losses, keep order, and allow them to substitute alternative sources of cheap labor, although the western sugar planters proved to be the most grudging of gradualists.

Subsequent legislation in 1880 replaced slavery with a patronage system whereby slaves, now called *patrocinados,* worked for a stipend to be used for self-purchase. If the plan had worked as intended, all *patrocinados* would have become free in 1888. But the authorities could not fully control the pace of change as slaves initiated their own liberation. The law of 1886 recognized that fact and freed the remaining *patrocinados.* Emancipation hastened the diffusion of the independence movement east to west and brought on a crisis in sugar production that led to centralization of mill operations and to reformulated class and labor relations. Cuban whites had long harbored fears of a replay in Cuba of the Saint Domingue Revolution and of the cultural Africanization of the island. Contrary to the dream of Cuba's revered patriot, José Martí, emancipation and independence failed to quell them.

See also CARIBBEAN REGION.

BIBLIOGRAPHY

BERGAD, LAIRD W. *Cuban Rural Society in the Nineteenth Century: The Social and Economic History of Monoculture in Matanzas.* 1990.

BERGAD, LAIRD W., FE IGLESIAS GARCÍA, and MARÍA DEL CARMEN BARCIA. *The Cuban Slave Market, 1790–1880.* 1995.

ELTIS, DAVID. *Economic Growth and the Ending of the Transatlantic Slave Trade.* 1987.

HELG, ALINE. *Our Rightful Share: The Afro-Cuban Struggle for Equality, 1886–1912.* 1995.

KIPLE, KENNETH F. *Blacks in Colonial Cuba, 1774–1899.* 1976.

KNIGHT, FRANKLIN W. *Slave Society in Cuba during the Nineteenth Century.* 1970.

MARRERO, LEVÍ. *Cuba: Economía y sociedad.* 15 vols. 1972–1992.

MORENO FRAGINAL, MANUEL. *El ingenio: complejo económico social cubano del azúcar.* 3 vols. 1978.

PAQUETTE, ROBERT L. *Sugar Is Made with Blood: The Conspiracy of La Escalera and the Conflict between Empires over Slavery in Cuba.* 1988.

SCOTT, REBECCA J. *Slave Emancipation in Cuba: The Transition to Free Labor, 1860–1899.* 1985.

Robert L. Paquette

Dance

In spite of the considerable temporal distance between present-day social conditions and those of the centuries in which slaveholding existed, dances produced by, and treating the subject matter of, slaves continue to attract attention the world over, especially in those societies identified with the institution. This is especially evident in North, Central, and South America, the Antilles, and elsewhere in the world where a slave past is commemorated in ritual terms, such as in South Africa. As is true in music and verbal arts, slave dance existed in conversation with other genres, and routines which have developed over time wholly independently of the circumstances that pertained during slavery have often shown signs of influence from previous, largely lost styles.

Slave dance may be talked about in three ways: (1) in terms of its influence on slave society; (2) in terms of the manner in which it assimilated forms and elements from the slaveholder society; and (3) in terms of how slave imagery, narrative, and movements continue to provide dance themes.

Influence on Slave Society

Like other cultural motifs, the evolution of dance in slave society mixed traits, gestures, and movements either directly remembered by slaves from the days before slavery or passed along by their peers and relatives, and new techniques observed or taught after they had been deculturated, reculturated, and acculturated to lives under the authority of others. The particular combinations which led to these forms were shaped by the nature of the collective memory of certain types of movements, the localities from which the majority of slaves and their forebears sprang, the rules pertaining in the new societies around slaves' physical expression and recreation, and the persistence of secret societies in which old techniques had ritualized resilience.

In general, the larger the holding and the greater the proportion of salves to slaveholders, the greater the likelihood of African survivals. This was true of the large plantations in the U.S. South, and in Jamaica, Barbados, Haiti, Brazil, Cuba, Guadeloupe, and Martinique. Another key variable was the regularity of fresh imports of slaves from Africa to a given locality, the so-called *bozal,* or "saltwater," slaves who were in their initial stages of socialization, or "seasoning." Such recent arrivals would have had a clearer and more tenacious awareness of indigenous dance styles. It was through the interplay of these forces that the characteristic slave dances emerged—the "ring shout" in the American South, and the quadrille throughout the New World, as well as vernacular variants associated with the "feeder" societies of the Kongo, Akan, Yoruba, Ibgo, Fon, Manding, Wolof, or Fulbe, to cite prominent West African ethnic groups whose dance styles predominated. If slaveholders, their wives, or especially their children took an interest in these movements, they could have been passed on, as was true across racial lines in Brazil, Cuba, and Latin America.

235

Influence from Slaveholder Society

The encounter between Africans and non-Africans in the New World and between slaves and nonslaves of every description elsewhere typically led to various levels of exchange of cultural information. Christianity, whether Catholic or Protestant, usually brought with it rules and restrictions on artistic and cultural expression, if these were deemed as not being in accord with the mores of the slaveholder society. At the same time, slaves were keenly interested in the genres that their free counterparts revered, most notably the jigs and reels of the British Isles, especially Ireland and the Highlands of Scotland. Aspects of these were often integrated into the ensemble improvisations of slave dancers. Indeed, so adept did some become at these new forms that terms like "jigging" were applied not only to their fancy footwork but also to the performers, often with pejorative connotations. And a wholly new genre grew in the early nineteenth century, when white dancers in blackface both imitated and insulted slaves and free blacks by reducing them and their innovations to tragicomic, stereotypical cultural icons.

Persistence of Slavery as a Theme

Well after the end of slavery, late-nineteenth-century and twentieth-century students of African-American dance writ large, that is in a hemispheric sense, continued to draw upon imagery identified with slavery. Such scholar-choreographers and master practitioners as Katherine Dunham, Pearl Primus, Alvin Ailey, Talley Beatty, Eleo Pomare, and Rod Rodgers have all used movements and situations associated with slavery as narrative subjects. Alvin Ailey's "Revelations" continued in the repertoire of his Dance Theater under the direction of Judith Jamison, once Ailey's principal dancer and then director of the company, to great effect.

Together with postslavery genres that nonetheless remain linked with it in the popular imagination, such as the cakewalk and the cotillion once identified with the haughty *gens de couleur* of New Orleans (where percentages of "Negroness" retained both literal and figurative meanings, as in "mulatto," "quadroon," "octoroon," and so on), the recovery of these movements in the United States, and in the West India, Brazil, and

Members of the Alvin Ailey American Dance Theater rehearse a scene for a 1973 production of Revelations. [Hulton-Deutsch Collection/Corbis]

Cuba, has become a special priority for national dance theater companies.

See also ARTS; LITERATURE OF SLAVERY.

BIBLIOGRAPHY

AILEY, ALVIN, with A. PETER BAILEY. *Revelations: The Autobiography of Alvin Ailey.* 1993.

DUNHAM, KATHERINE. *A Touch of Innocence: A Memoir of Childhood.* 1994.

LOTT, ERIC. *Love and Theft: Blackface Minstrelsy and the American Working Class.* 1993.

NATHAN, HANS. *Dan Emmett and the Rise of Early Negro Minstrelsy.* 1962.

PRIMUS, PEARL. *Dance among Black People in America.* 1980.

STEARNS, JEAN, and MARSHALL STEARNS. *Jazz Dance: The Story of American Vernacular Dance.* 1979.

David H. Anthony III

Danish Colonics

See Caribbean Region; Scandinavia; Slave Trade.

De Bow, James D. B.   [1820–1867]

Proslavery editor and southern nationalist.

Born on 10 July 1820, James D. B. De Bow graduated first in his class from the College of Charleston and, in 1845, moved to New Orleans, where he founded the monthly journal *De Bow's Review* (1846–1880). Though originally intended to be nonpartisan, the magazine quickly became an influential forum for defending slavery and instilling southern nationalism. Alongside contributors such as Samuel Cartwright and Josiah Nott, who espoused a doctrine of white racial superiority, De Bow employed his impressive knowledge of statistical data, largely drawn from his work as superintendent of the seventh U.S. census, to expose the harsh realities of free labor and to promote southern commercial independence. Slaves, he insisted, not only were ideal cultivators of cotton but were also suitable for industrial work on railroads and in factories.

In April 1860 De Bow openly advocated secession in the columns of his *Review.* That December, in a pamphlet entitled *The Interest in Slavery of the Southern Non-Slaveholder,* he called on even the poorest white farmer to "look down upon those who are beneath him" and to "die in the last trenches in defense of . . . slave property." Forced to suspend publishing his magazine during the war, in 1865 De Bow rededicated it "to the Restoration of the Southern States, and the Development of the Wealth and Resources of the Country." Far from apologizing for slavery or disunion, he remained firmly convinced that the South should resolve its own "negro question." "The North

may be sure that . . . [blacks] will in time get every right and privilege," he wrote shortly before his death in February 1867. "That day cannot be hurried."

See also INDUSTRIAL SLAVES; NOTT, JOSIAH CLARK; PERSPECTIVES ON SLAVERY.

BIBLIOGRAPHY

MCMILLEN, JAMES A. *The Works of James D. B. De Bow: A Bibliography.* 1940.

PASKOFF, PAUL F., and DANIEL J. WILSON, eds. *The Cause of the South: Selections from De Bow's Review, 1846–1867.* 1982.

SKIPPER, OTIS C. *J. D. B. De Bow, Magazinist of the Old South.* 1958.

Eric Robert Papenfuse

Debt Peonage

"Debt peonage" is the term used to describe the status of debtors compelled to labor for creditors to repay debts. "Peonage" derives from the Spanish, and defines the relations of landless agricultural workers in Latin America to landowners. Debt peonage, or debt servitude, has figured as a prominent labor institution in Chinese, Indian, Hebrew, and ancient Greek societies. Solon's legal reforms eliminated peonage for Athenian citizens. Many African societies featured a version of peonage, called pawnship, in which debtors pledged the labor of relatives, typically children, as sureties for debts. Free persons in early America and elsewhere could also be sold into debt servitude by courts for failure to pay taxes, fines, or legal fees.

Debt peons resembled slaves in that they had no choice in offering or withdrawing their services. As with slaves, their labor could be sold to a third party without their consent. If a debt peon's living expenses and debt interest outpaced his or her earnings, the term of service, like that of a slave, could be lifelong.

Peons differed from slaves in retaining some socially recognized kin ties. Family members could mitigate their sufferings or redeem them from captivity by repaying their debt. Similarly, the status of a debt peon was not heritable in most societies, although some children of peons could be thrust into their parents' status for debts accrued by masters for their upbringing. Finally, while slaves typically possessed no status or honor recognized by society, peons retained the status of their birth, generally that of a "good," if unfortunate, member of society.

See also PEONAGE; SLAVERY, CONTEMPORARY FORMS OF.

BIBLIOGRAPHY

PATTERSON, ORLANDO. *Slavery and Social Death.* 1982.

T. Stephen Whitman

In this bas relief from an Old Kingdom tomb (ca. 2400 B.C.), a debtor in ancient Egypt is brought before the scribes to account for his debt or be placed in servitude. [Gianni Dagli Orti/Corbis]

Debt Slavery

Although peonage is often referred to as a form of debt slavery, in many historical cultures and civilizations full-scale debt slavery has arisen and flourished.

The ancient laws of India as envisioned in the Hindu epics and in the Hindu and Buddhist sacred writings recognized a voluntary slavery into which persons might enter on account of severe poverty, debt, or other exigent circumstances. In some cases debts may have already been contracted, with the perpetual servitude of the debtor the surety to guarantee the loan, but in other cases slavery directly paid for some services, eliminating the role of money in the exchange.

During an epidemic, some people offered themselves as slaves to the famous physician Jivaka, in exchange for a cure, according to the *Vinaya Pitaka.* The *Milinda-panho,* furthermore, tells of fathers who give their children into slavery when they have had too many offspring to provide properly for them, and husbands had been known to do the same with wives they could no longer afford to sustain.

Narada, the ancient Hindu lawgiver, had the most elaborate categories of slaves (by origin), listing fifteen types—which superseded Kantilya's ninefold and Manu's sevenfold classification. Of Narada's categories, five could clearly be seen as essentially involving debt slavery: (1) one saved in a famine, (2) one enslaved for debt, 93) one enslaved through a wager, (4) one who becomes a slave for his maintenance, and (5) one who sells himself into slavery. The only restriction on these causes of enslavement was the dictum that a member of the Brahman caste could not become a slave.

In ancient Israel, the Bible presented the possibility that a man might give himself into bondage to satisfy a debt (Leviticus, 25: 39; Isaiah, 50: 1; Amos, 2: 6, 8: 6). Such a person, usually a Hebrew, had to be freed in the seventh year of his captivity (Exodus, 21: 2; Deuteronomy, 15: 12) or in the jubilee year (Leviticus, 25: 40), but he could voluntarily remain a slave if he chose. If he so chose, his ear was to be pierced to symbolize his perpetual servitude. A slave who was abused had to be freed (Exodus, 21: 26–27). He could be chastised but not wounded (Exodus, 21: 26–27), and the killing of a slave was punishable, like the killing of a freeman (Exodus, 21: 20).

A slave was to be treated as a hireling (Leviticus, 25: 40, 53), was not to be oppressed (Leviticus, 25: 43, 46, 53), and was to suffer no ill treatment (Deuteronomy, 23: 17). The abduction of a freeman into slavery was a capital offense (Exodus, 21: 16; Deuteronomy, 24: 7).

Early Roman law recognized that a judgment debtor might ultimately be sold into slavery as an *iudicatus* (i.e., one condemned to slavery by a civil rather than by a criminal judgment, as opposed to *servi poenae*). Closely connected to the concept of Roman debt slavery was the status of *liberi expositi.* An exposed child left to die by his father could be claimed by one who rescued him, and he could be claimed as a son or as a slave.

In early Babylonian law, a man could be condemned to slavery for debt, but this practice ended in the early second millennium B.C. Under section 117 of the code of Hammurabi (1700 B.C.) debt slavery was limited to three years, but that code and the laws of Eshnunna allowed a husband to pledge his wife as a security for a loan. Self-sale and the sale of children were permitted in Babylonian law, but such sales were rare—usually undertaken only by those in abject poverty—and the contracts could provide conditions for redemption.

In Greece, the laws of slavery varied from polis to polis, but Athens can serve as an exemplar for the whole. In the code of Draco (621 B.C.) and in the unwritten laws which preceded it, debtors could be enslaved; but in the laws of Solon (early sixth century) debt slavery for the free residents of Attica was abolished.

In the sultanates of Malaya well into the twentieth century, a person borrowing from a raja (or chief) was obliged, upon defaulting on the loan, to go to work for the raja and continue in his service until the debt was paid, and his labor for the raja did not itself count against his indebtedness.

Most systems of slavery have permitted some kind of slavery for debt, and many have required a somewhat different status for those so enslaved.

See also: ANCIENT GREECE; ANCIENT MIDDLE EAST; ANCIENT ROME; ENSLAVEMENT, METHODS OF; INDIAN SUBCONTINENT; LAW; MALAYA.

BIBLIOGRAPHY

BUCKLAND, W. W. *The Roman Law of Slavery: The Condition of the Slave in Private Law from Augustus to Justinian.* 1969.

CHANANA, DEV RAJ. *Slavery in Ancient India As Depicted in Pali and Sanskrit Texts.* 1960.

COHEN, B. *Jewish and Roman Law.* 1966.

DANDANAEV, MUHAMMAD A. *Slavery in Babylonia: From Nabopolassar to Alexander the Great (626–331 B.C.).* 2nd ed. Translated by Victoria A. Powell and edited by Marvin A. Powell and David B. Weisberg. 1984.

DINGWANEY, MANJARI. "Unredeemed Promises: The Law and Servitude." In *Chains of Servitude: Bondage and Slavery in India,* edited by Utsa Patnaik and Manjari Dingwaney. 1985.

GARNSEY, PETER. *Ideas of Slavery from Aristotle to Augustine.* 1996.

GULLICK, JOHN M. "Debt-Bondage in Malaya." In *Slavery: A Comparative Perspective—Readings on Slavery from Ancient Times to the Present,* edited by Robin S. Winks. 1972.

URBACK, E. E. *The Law Regarding Slavery as a Source for the Social History of the Period of the Second Temple, the Mishnah and Talmud.* 1964.

Patrick M. O'Neil

Declaration of Human Rights

See Universal Declaration of Human Rights.

Defenses of Slavery

See Perspectives on Slavery.

Definitions of Slavery

See Perspectives on Slavery.

Delaware

African slavery began in Delaware in 1639, when a Swedish privateering expedition brought "Black Anthony" to Fort Christina in New Sweden, in what is now northern Delaware. After the Dutch conquest of New Sweden in 1655, the Dutch West India Company brought a few more slaves to Delaware, either from West African trading stations or from Curaçao. When the English took Delaware from the Dutch in 1664, it had an estimated 125 slaves—20 percent of the colony's population. In the early 1700s, tobacco planters from Maryland's eastern shore began taking up land in Delaware, bringing slaves with them. By 1726, the colony had enacted slave codes that stipulated lifelong slavery for children of slave mothers and denied slaves' claim to freedom as a consequence of baptism as Christians.

From the 1720s onward, Delaware obtained more slaves from Philadelphia and various Chesapeake Bay ports. When tobacco cultivation declined in Delaware after 1750, the slaves' work was diversified to include growing corn and wheat, tending cattle and sheep, logging cypress and cedar, and working in crafts such as carpentry, shoemaking, tanning, ironmaking, spinning, and weaving. In 1770, roughly a thousand slaveholders owned about seven thousand slaves, who still made up about 20 percent of Delaware's population. A majority of slave owners held one to three slaves. Only a few hundred blacks were free.

The Decline of Slavery in Delaware, 1775–1865

Over 90 percent of Delaware's blacks became free before the Civil War—far more than in any other slave state. This was due to a unique combination of political, religious, and economic circumstances. In the 1770s and 1780s, as a matter of religious principle, Quaker and Methodist slaveholders began to manumit slaves, usually following a term of service akin to apprenticeship, or by allowing them to purchase their freedom. In 1787 Delaware, alone among southern slaveholding states, banned the sale of slaves to other slave states. This restriction on sales to areas where slavery was more profitable led to a drop in the value of slaves in Delaware. One by-product of this law was a rise in the kidnapping of slaves, as well as free blacks, in order to sell them out of state. The larger impact of the law, however, was to make the purchase of freedom more feasible for slaves and more eco-

Table 1. Slavery and Emancipation in Delaware, 1790–1860.

Year	Slaves	Free Blacks	Blacks Enslaved (%)	Whites	Total
1790	8,887	3,899	70	46,310	59,096
1800	6,153	8,268	43	49,852	64,273
1810	4,177	13,136	24	55,361	72,674
1820	4,509	12,958	26	55,282	72,749
1830	3,292	15,855	17	57,601	76,748
1840	2,605	16,919	13	58,561	78,085
1850	2,290	18,073	11	71,169	91,532
1860	1,798	19,829	8	90,589	112,216

nomically attractive for masters in Delaware than elsewhere. The proximity of free Pennsylvania and the relative ease of fleeing from slavery also induced slaveholders to grant manumission after a period of loyal and productive labor. By 1810, three-quarters of Delaware's blacks were free; by 1860, fewer than two thousand people, only 8 percent of the state's blacks, remained enslaved.

In 1782, 1803, and 1847 Delaware considered legislative proposals to end slavery gradually, but resistance from slaveholders, coupled with widespread white prejudice against free blacks, resulted in the rejection of these proposals. In 1862, President Lincoln urged federal legislation to compensate Delaware slaveholders in return for the emancipation of all remaining slaves by 1872, but Delaware also rejected this proposal, and in 1865 it unsuccessfully opposed the ratification of the Thirteenth Amendment, which finally brought an end to slavery in the state.

See also EMANCIPATION IN THE UNITED STATES; GRADUAL EMANCIPATION STATUTES; LAW; MANUMISSION.

BIBLIOGRAPHY

ESSAH, PATIENCE. *A House Divided: Slavery and Emancipation in Delaware, 1638–1865.* 1996.

WILLIAMS, WILLIAM H. *Slavery and Freedom in Delaware, 1639–1865.* 1996.

T. Stephen Whitman

Demerara Slave Revolt (1823)

The Demerara slave revolt, which took place in 1823 in the British colony of Guyana, was one of the latest and largest slave revolts in New World history. It started out on a plantation named Success, which belonged to John Gladstone (father of the future British prime minister), and it eventually involved some ten thousand slaves who labored on more than sixty sugar plantations. These enslaved people rose up in the name of their rights when they heard rumors that slavery had been abolished in England but that the Demerara planters were withholding this informa-

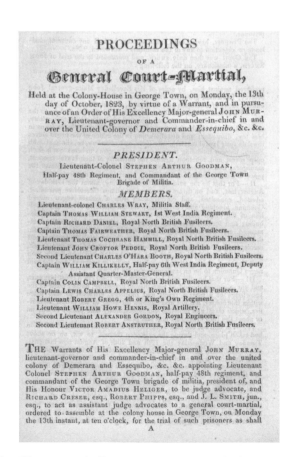

A military court in Demerara convicted Methodist missionary John Smith of treason for allegedly fomenting a slave rebellion. Though undoubtedly innocent, he died in prison while appealing his conviction to Parliament. [Law Library, Library of Congress]

tion in order to keep them enslaved. Emília Viotti da Costa, in her *Crowns of Glory, Tears of Blood* (1994), successfully delineates various historical factors that shaped the Demerara slave revolt and reconstructs a wide range of dynamic interactions among several groups of actors: slaves, planters and colonists, free people of color, and evangelical missionaries from England. This slave revolt took place in a unique local and international context.

First, the sugar-producing Demerara region, originally a Dutch colony, had changed hands six times from 1780 to 1803, when it was finally integrated into the British Empire, although most of the plantations had been owned by British citizens for the entire time. Second, as in the case of Saint Domingue (Haiti), whites constituted an extreme minority: slaves amounted to 75,000 out of a total population of 80,000 in the Demerara and neighboring Essequibo regions. Furthermore, by the 1820s, planter-slave relations had become very uneasy. The planters who had borrowed money to invest in their plantations and slaves because of high sugar prices could not get out of debt once the sugar prices dropped, while the price of the slaves needed to produce the sugar remained high. The slaves, forced to work even harder to make profits for their owners, became increasingly frustrated and hostile toward the colonial power.

The abolitionist movements in England during the 1820s also had a critical impact on the enslaved people in Demerara, though the teachings of the evangelical missionaries sent by the London Missionary Society between 1803 and 1823. These missionaries became agents of Methodism and introduced liberal ideas to the Demerara slave population. In fact, a missionary named John Smith was assuredly the instigator of the Demerara revolt. Smith, his wife Jane, and his fellow missionary John Wray perceived slaves as innocent victims of oppression at the whim of "sinful and godless" planters. As a result of this missionary point of view, the slaves, as well as the free people of color, were made well aware that the colonial power was critically divided between the planters, who intended to retain slavery, and the missionaries, who opposed it. Under the guidance of Smith, slaves gathered at the chapel of Success, created a new social and moral space, and forged new bonds of community. The slaves were even able to take initiatives to organize their meetings at the chapel. These religious opportunities gave them new pretexts by which to challenge the power of their owners and managers in the name of God and human rights.

See also ABOLITION AND ANTISLAVERY MOVEMENTS; MISSIONARIES; PLANTATIONS; REBELLIONS AND VIOLENT RESISTANCE.

BIBLIOGRAPHY

GENOVESE, EUGENE D. *From Rebellion to Revolution: Afro-American Slave Revolts in the Making of the New Modern World.* 1979.

VIOTTI DA COSTA, EMÍLIA. *Crowns of Glory, Tears of Blood: The Demerara Slave Rebellion of 1823.* 1994.

Mieko Nishida

Demographic Analysis of Slaves and Slavery

The academic study of demography began with a focus on those most basic of events, birth and death. Thus, the early and lasting strength of the discipline has been in noting the differences in rates of fertility and mortality within populations and between populations. Early demographers sought out populations with little migration and little social differentiation, or they neglected these movements and distinctions where they existed. "Life tables" (based on death rates) and birthrates were the core of demographic analysis.

Slavery did not fit easily into these basic studies of demography. The very act of enslavement, for instance, involves both a change in status and usually a migration for the victim. Demographers long declined to address these complexities, leaving other social scientists to analyze and quantify slavery and the slave trade. The result was the development of a literature on the demographic history of slavery which, while substantial, has not generally measured up well in demographic rigor.

Fortunately, the analytical and computational tools of demographers have become increasingly sophisticated, and their interests have turned to more complex issues. Migration and changes in social status—two socially distinct but analytically linked issues—are now the subject of active demographic analysis. As a result, slavery can now be seen as an issue that is appropriate for developing and testing techniques at the frontiers of demographic analysis and for which there exist significant historical data.

If academic demographers have shown little interest in slavery until recent times, the record-keepers of society gave a much higher priority to slavery and other complexities of society. Thus, Spanish censuses of their eighteenth-century colonial territories broke down the population by sex, age group, free and slave status, color, and sometimes ethnicity, occupation, and birthplace. Such records, numerous though of course incomplete, provide a substantial basis for reconstructing the demography of slavery.

Typology for the Demography of Slavery

Since terminology in the demography of slavery is not yet standardized, this discussion must begin with definitions and typologies at two levels. At the first level, the field of demography itself may be divided into four arenas—biological, physical, social, and economic—each with a characteristic set of variables. By biological demography I mean numbers and rates of birth and death, and aggregates of these. The rates of birth and death vary systematically with the age and sex of the individual. By physical demography I mean in addition the enumeration of populations, the numbers and rates of migration, and aggregates of these which yield estimates of total populations, growth rates, and migratory flows. The facts of physical migration are thus less basic and less final than those of biological migration, but the two types of analysis are commonly combined. At the biological and physical level, demography focuses simply on *persons* and on their biological characteristics of age and sex.

Social demography involves demographic analysis not only of populations but of subpopulations defined within society according to a variety of criteria. For the demography of slavery, the key criterion is that distinguishing the categories of free persons, captives, slaves, and ex-slaves. Other criteria determining subpopulations are those of gender, marriage, family relations, race, ethnicity, occupation, and state authority, where each of these variables may have several values or specific configurations. Social demography must take account of the interactions of these subpopulations. For instance, a slave population overlaps significantly with populations of captives entering it, the ex-slaves leaving it, the free persons who exploit or coexist with the slaves, and the children born from unions of free and slave persons. Economic demography represents a subset of social demography for which the criteria and variables are primarily economic. The main variables in economic demography are the currency values of slaves, as represented in their prices, and their productivity—the quantity and money value of their output.

The second level of typology introduces processual stages of the slave experience. It begins with a social distinction between "captive" and "slave." This distinction is appropriate and indeed necessary in order to address the recruitment stage of the slave experience. The term "captive" may be applied to people who have been wrenched out of their status as free persons yet are in transition, not yet integrated or resigned to servile status. The term "slave" then applies to persons who recognize their subordinated status and work (perhaps reluctantly but dependably) within its bounds. Captive populations, created by enslave-

ment, are dissolved rapidly, as the captors transfer them to a long-term existence as slaves.

Recruitment, or enslavement, is the addition of persons to a slave population. Its main demographic stages are seizure, partition, transportation, and seasoning. For captives, recruitment is their transformation from free persons into slaves. In the seizure of captives, the issues in biological and physical demography are the age and sex composition of the captives, and the rates of mortality, fertility, and escape of those captured. The issues in social demography include such mechanisms for seizure of the captives as war, kidnapping, court decisions, religious proceedings, taxation, debt, and famine.

Transportation of captives typically takes place in various stages—by land and by sea, by various owners and merchants. In this arena are addressed the biological issues of births and deaths for migrant captives (including epidemiology), the physical issues of the distance and pace of their migration, the social issues of their family relations, and economic decisions

Men, women, and children in Zanzibar are shown yoked and driven into slavery in this undated lithograph.
[Corbis-Bettmann]

on whether to transport or abandon captives. Another migratory issue is posed by the partition of captives among various markets and destinations. For instance, partition occurs in the choice made by African captors as to which captives would be held in Africa and which sold across the Atlantic, or in the allocation of captives after the Saharan crossing.

The main social issue in seasoning is the preparation of captives for their new role as slaves. The biological issues are the rates of mortality and fertility during seasoning. The economic issues in seasoning are the cost of training and socialization of captives, as compared with the potential benefits of their later exploitation as slaves.

For slaves, in contrast to captives, recruitment is their movement from one slave role to another—by capture, by sale, or by migration under a single owner. Seizure may not be the start of the process of recruitment, since they have already been enslaved. But since slave raiding includes the capture of any available persons, some of those seized must have already been enslaved. Transportation of slaves involves the same elements as the transportation of captives, though slaves generally did not require being restrained and guarded to the same degree as captives. Seasoning of slaves into new roles was, similarly, analogous to that for captives, but seasoning was required only into the specifics of the task at hand rather than involving a general socialization into the role of slave.

The term "exploitation" refers to the work of slaves under the direction of their masters, but also to work done under their own direction. The rates of birth, death, and migration for slaves provide the basic facts of slave demography. These differ with the age and sex of the slaves and by the occupations and industries in which they work. The social organization of exploitation includes these conditions, and the accompanying systems of law and status. One may seek to generalize, and to identify various models or regimes of slave exploitation. For instance, plantation or chattel slavery is often thought to provide a general model for slavery in the Americas, while family or domestic slavery is often thought to provide a general model for slavery in Africa. Slaves also work for themselves, in time left to them after working for their masters. The time and conditions allowed for this work vary significantly, but the regime of self-exploitation is generally a significant part of the social system of slavery.

The reproduction of slave populations takes place on both biological and social levels. In biological terms, this is the fertility of slave men and women. In physical terms, reproduction of slave populations is accomplished not only through births but also by recruiting new captives or slaves. In social terms, it is a question of determining whether the child of a slave is a slave, and if so to whom that slave child belongs. In a given social situation, it may be that the child of a slave woman is always a slave; it may be that the child of a free man and a slave woman may be free; the children of the rare unions of slave men and free women may be free. The child of a slave woman or a slave couple may not belong socially or economically to the parents.

Termination of servile status may take place at the biological level, through mortality; or at the social level, through liberation. Biological mortality includes the deaths of captives or slaves, with their variations by age and sex. Mortality rates may be calculated for various subpopulations by ancestry, occupation, etc.

Social liberation takes place through a variety of processes, and at both individual (manumission) and group (emancipation) levels. Rates of the various categories of liberation may be noted by age and sex, and at various stages of the course of a slave's life. At the individual level, manumission is the release of individual slaves by their owners, either voluntarily or through purchase by the slaves themselves or by others. For captives, ransoming by family or friends is the equivalent of purchase. Escape is the individual evasion of captivity by slaves, which may result in the individual regaining the status of freedom. Rebellion is the equivalent effort by slaves to eliminate the category of slavery, or to escape it as a group. Emancipation is the elimination of the category of slave, and hence the collective liberation of slaves by owners or by the state.

Biological Fertility and Social Reproduction of Servile Populations

Captive women, in the time between their seizure and their settlement as slaves, generally had low fertility. The disruption of enslavement and transportation made conception difficult and carrying children to term even more unlikely. For the populations left behind after enslavement, there has been speculation in the literature that women increased their fertility to replace lost family members. This is unlikely for two reasons. Populations facing enslavement were generally "natural fertility" populations—that is, there were no calculated restraints on births, and by that logic there was no way consciously to increase the number of births. The second reason is even stronger: if captives averaged between 10 and 25 years of age, it would be all the more difficult for their (older) mothers to replace them with another child.

Once women became settled as slaves, they were more likely to enter into regular sexual relations, whether voluntarily or involuntarily, and their fertility increased. Child-woman ratios and other ratios of fertility for the Americas have shown the number of children for women born in Africa to be lower than for women born in the Americas. This difference was likely a result of two factors. First, African women had some of their children before enslavement, so that the record of their births in slavery was less than their total fertility. Second, immigrant slave women had a lower rate of fertility than native-born slave women because of their newness to the disease environment. In addition, slave women may often have had lower rates of fertility than free women, to the degree that their levels of nutrition and health care were inferior. Similar distinctions may have held force for slave populations within Africa.

Measures of fertility understandably focus on motherhood rather than fatherhood. It is, however, important not to forget the male role in biological and social reproduction: a two-sex model of fertility in slave society permits observations that might otherwise remain unnoted. For heuristic purposes, one may imagine polar opposites in slave communities. In one case, the slave community is biologically autonomous, and slave men and women have children among themselves. In that case, the average fertility of the men and of the women is similar. In the other case, sexual access to slave women is monopolized by the masters and other free men, so that the fertility of slave men is far lower than that of slave women. The long-term biological and social consequences of this difference are significant.

Analysis of the social reproduction of slaves adds issues distinct from questions of biological reproduction. Slave parents of slave children did not generally own or control their children. Slave families may have been recognized or not—in the latter case, children were considered to be part of the family of the master. According to the law of many African societies, children of slave mothers by free men were born free. To this degree, the biological reproduction of slaves did not bring about the social reproduction of the slave population, leading therefore to a demand for more slave recruitment to replace those exiting to other statuses.

Biological Mortality and Social Termination of Servile Status

Death rates may be calculated not only by the age and sex of the individual, but by the stage of the slave life course. For instance, the death rates of infants and young children, which are relatively high in all populations, were raised even higher by the hardships of seizure, transportation, and seasoning. Death rates for captives were elevated by several aspects of their experience: violence and trauma in capture, exhaustion and exposure to new disease environments in the course of long voyages, changes and reductions in nutrition, and reinforcement of contagious disease through crowding. Thus, the small numbers of young children who survived to enter slave populations may have been a remnant of much larger numbers of children initially captured.

Estimates of mortality during transportation must account for the various stages in transportation. To take the example of the Atlantic slave trade, captives suffered mortality during transportation in Africa (including those captives destined for African rather than overseas sale), holding at the coast, the Middle Passage, and the subsequent stages of transportation to final destination—as from Jamaica to Cartagena to Lima.

The calculation of death rates among captives during transportation leads to statistical difficulty and confusion because of the tendency to calculate them as crude rates by voyage, without accounting for the varying length of voyages. Systematic comparison of death rates during voyages requires accounting in a standard fashion, usually deaths per year. Calculations of death rates for the Atlantic slave trade show an overall decline in the mortality rate over time.

African slaves in the Americas were utilized partly because of their relatively high resistance to tropical disease, yet their mortality rates were high when they were settled in tropical lowlands where malaria and other diseases took a heavy toll. Mortality of first-generation slaves exceeded that of second-generation or creole slaves. Slaves working in the most laborious trades and dangerous occupations, notably mining and sugar production, had relatively high death rates.

Aside from biological death, the alternative end of servile status was through liberation. For individual slaves, rates of liberation differed sharply by age and sex and by the specific mechanism of liberation. Males dominated among runaways; females dominated among those manumitted; manumission of children at birth was usually done without respect to sex. Other patterns included manumission of young adult female favorites or of aged slaves by masters, manumission of slaves at the death of the master, and self-purchase by adult slaves with access to cash earnings. In the purchase of family members, children purchased the freedom of parents or siblings, and parents purchased the freedom of children. Individual escape for a short time did not end slave status, but permanent marronage changed that status to free as long as the maroons were able to maintain their independence. Among captives, slave status could be ended by ransoming, by escape, or by rebellion.

For the liberation of slaves in groups, there is need for more clarity in the literature on the various types of group liberation, and the relative significance of

An 1855 engraving by Henry Howe depicts deckhands stowing slaves in the hold of a ship (probably a coastal-trade vessel). [Library of Congress/Corbis]

each in history. Abolition of a slave trade does not bring liberation to those already in slavery but interdicts the change in status of free persons to captives, and from captives to slaves. It may bring about the liberation of small numbers of captives, as was achieved by the British antislavery squadron. Full and direct emancipation from slavery, liberating slaves in one step, took place under French rule (abortively in 1794 and successfully in 1848), in the United States in the period from 1863 to 1865, and in Brazil in 1888. Emancipation in stages was more common: some northern states of the United states emancipated slaves by stages in the early national period; in British colonies (including the Cape of Good Hope) slaves became apprentices in 1834 before being freed in 1838; in Cuba and Brazil, the newborn children of slaves were emancipated some years before the adults.

Quite different again is legal-status abolition, the device by which states ceased to recognize the legal status of slavery, without actually emancipating the slaves. Legal-status abolition, formally adopted in British India in 1843 but also applied at much the same time in areas of South America, was widely applied by colonial and national authorities in Africa, the Mediterranean, and Southwest Asia. In all of the

Old World areas with slave populations, the end of slavery came through a complex mix of mechanisms. Occasionally there was simple emancipation of slaves, as in Madagascar in 1897; much more commonly there was legal-status abolition, followed by the emancipation of children born after a given date.

Physical Migration and Social Flows of Servile Populations

Physical migration centers on the migration of captives—the slave trade—though it includes the migration of persons already enslaved. Young adults were prime targets of enslavement, but people of all ages were taken; the old and the young died disproportionately in recruitment. For those left behind after enslavement, there was accordingly a relative shortage of young adults. The data are unclear on whether or not capture was sex-specific: it seems likely that capture by kidnapping and court proceedings allowed for selection of the least desirable as captives, while warfare and raiding were relatively unselective. In addition, the composition of captive populations varied according to whether captivity resulted from occasional large-scale enslavement or an ongoing process.

The partition of captives among various destinations allowed for selectivity in the composition of flows. Senegambia in western Africa sent some captives (mostly male) to the Americas, sent others (mostly female) to North Africa, and settled still others (mostly female) within the region.

Estimated rates of flow of captives must account properly for dimensions. Rates of delivery (the inverse of mortality in transit) can be calculated per trip or per unit time period (commonly, per year), and results may differ significantly according to the standard selected. The number of participants and proportion of survivors will differ significantly according to whether the basis selected is the number of persons at the beginning of a voyage or at the end.

The totals on which major debates center are cumulative totals—for the Atlantic trade, the trans-Saharan trade, etc.—but the meaning and utility of these calculations are limited by the scarcity of dimensions, comparisons, and well defined scope presented with such aggregates. Summaries of the volume of slave trade would be more usefully presented—for purposes of comparison or for understanding of the demographic dynamics—as rates per time period (per year, per decade, per century), or as proportions of some relevant population (in region of origin, region of destination, or globally). Within these parameters, flows of captives may usefully be estimated by region of origin, by destination, or globally). Within these parameters, flows of captives may usefully be estimated by region of origin, by destination, or by national grouping of captives and of captors.

For those already enslaved, there have been some great migrations—notably migrations of slaves from the Upper South to the Lower South and Southwest in the nineteenth-century United States, and the migrations of slaves from Bahia to southern Brazil at much the same time. Over a million slaves were displaced in each of these migrations, many of them changing owners, terrain, and occupation. Social migration is virtually the same as the social recruitment to and termination of slave status. Examples include birth into slave status, birth out of slave status, liberation by emancipation, and sentencing to slavery for social transgression.

Size, Composition, and Growth Rate of Slave and Related Populations

The physical census of a slave population addresses the magnitude, composition, and growth rate for a slave population itself, but also the total population in source areas from which slaves are recruited, and the total population in slaveholding areas. In absolute magnitude, the three largest slave populations were those of the United States in the 1850s, Brazil from the 1860s to the 1870s, and northern Nigeria in the early twentieth century. These three large populations, each surviving for decades after the end of large-scale slave trade, had a relatively even sex ratio and numbers of children which approximated or even exceeded the numbers of young adults: they achieved natural growth without the import of new slaves. Slaves became the largest proportion of the total population in such Caribbean territories as Saint Domingue and Jamaica, though portions of the western Sudan in Africa also reached very high proportions of slaves to total population.

For the sending areas—western and eastern Africa, the Caucasus, Brazil—recent work suggests that the substantial export of captives from a region brought moderate population decline and a transformation in the age and sex structure. A crude ratio of losses to a regional population of as little as two per thousand per year was sufficient to cause a general decline in population if most captives were young adults and at least one-third of them were female. The unbalanced sex ratio among exported slaves was sufficient to transform the overall sex ratio in the sending areas. That is, the significant excess of adult males over adult females in the Americas had its reflex in a shortage of adult males in Africa. Similarly, the excess of adult females in the Mediterranean areas of large slave populations had its reflex in the shortage of adult females in the African and Caucasian regions that supplied the slaves.

Populations in areas receiving large numbers of slave imports tended to be naturally declining populations—that is, these populations grew, but through imports rather than natural increase. Where recruitment was cut off but slavery continued, slave populations were sometimes able to grow. This resulted as the proportion of females in the population grew amidst restrictions against emancipation, and especially from improved treatment of mothers and children.

Economic Demography

The focus of the economic demography of slavery is on relative prices of males and females, adults and children, and on the ups and downs of prices and productivity with time. Issues in recruitment provide the supply side of captive prices: prices rise as captives become scarce and as costs of sustenance and transportation rise, including rents collected by merchants and officials. Prices may also be affected by demand from competing markets. Economic calculations become important in questions of reproduction. When productive slaves can be purchased cheaply, owners

TO Be fold, — a likely Negro Wench, about 37 Years of Age, fit for all forts of Houfe Work, and is a tolerable good Cook; fhe can be well recommended,   mii

TO BE SOLD,
A LIKELY young fturdy Negro Wench, about 19 years of Age, fit for Town or Country; She is a trufty Wench, and, with a little Inftruction, being young, may be of great fervice to any Family in Town. Enquire of Weyman, in Broad-Street.

An undated newspaper advertisement (probably eighteenth century, perhaps Charleston, SC) offering slaves for sale includes much personal detail. [Corbis-Bettmann]

give little emphasis to raising slaves from birth; in contrast, when productive slaves are scarce or expensive, slave owners become more willing to pay the cost of raising slave infants to adulthood.

Issues in exploitation provide the demand side of prices for newly recruited captives and for those already enslaved. These include the slaves' forced productivity in agricultural and artisanal output, and the physical productivity and social value of their domestic work. Purchasers assessed such productivity for each enslaved individual, but the viability of a system of slavery depended on the aggregate productivity of the slave population.

The distinction between slavery with and without a slave trade elicits the difference between slave trade and slave dealing: Slave dealing is commerce in persons already enslaved. In most cases in the Americas and in Africa it was legal to continue slave dealing even after the purchase or recruitment of new captives had been legally abolished.

Details of the rise and fall of slave prices with time, and of the relative price of slaves (by age, sex, occupation, and personal characteristics), provide indices of social valuations, economic changes, and demographic shifts. Slave prices, being relatively common in the historical record, provide important evidence on social and demographic structures.

Demography of Slavery by Historical Era

During the past seven centuries, five interacting systems of slavery and slave trade have succeeded each other. Here are some characteristics of each.

Mediterranean cycle, 1200–1450. Late-medieval slavery, centered on the Mediterranean basin, brought captives to the regimes of the Mamluks in Egypt and the Ottomans in Anatolia, and included slaves forced to produce sugar on Mediterranean islands. The slaves were mostly female. While some of these slaves came across the Sahara, most of them came from areas ad-

joining the Black Sea. The latter trade died down as Ottoman influence expanded in the sixteenth century.

Early modern cycle, 1450–1660. The cycle of maritime expansion in slavery arose with Portuguese and Spanish seizure of lands along the shores of the Atlantic and Indian Oceans and in the Americas. African slaves, predominantly from Senegambia, Upper Guinea, and Angola, went first to the islands of the Atlantic and the Caribbean, and then to northeast Brazil and the highlands of Mexico and the Andes. The Portuguese carried smaller numbers of slaves to their Indian and other Asian territories. These slaves were mostly male. In the same era, Ottoman and Russian societies expanded their slaveholdings, the Ottomans drawing slaves from the fringes of their lands, and the Russians enslaving unfortunates within their own society. This cycle of slave trade peaked in the seventeenth century and declined in the eighteenth century. Enslavement of the native populations in Brazil declined in the eighteenth century, as did the delivery of African slaves to Mexico, Peru, and Colombia.

Mercantile cycle, 1660–1800. A third and larger cycle of slavery developed with the expansion of commercial capitalism during the seventeenth and eighteenth centuries under the leadership of Dutch, English, French, and Brazilian merchants. This cycle focused heavily on western Africa: captives came in largest numbers from the Bight of Benin, Angola, the Bight of Biafra, and the Congo coast, with smaller but significant numbers coming from Gold Coast, Upper Guinea, and Senegambia. In the Americas, slaves were delivered primarily to the British and French Caribbean, but also to Bahia and Minas Gerais in Brazil and secondarily to British North America. The losses in Africa led to a significant disruption and decline in population, to a relative shortage of adult males, and, it appears, to enslavement of many of the women remaining in western Africa. The smaller slave trades across the Sahara and the Red Sea may have declined somewhat during this cycle. The Indian Ocean slave trade, led by Dutch and French merchants, expanded somewhat: the French drew slaves from Madagascar and Mozambique to send to the Mascarene Islands, while the Dutch collected slaves there, in Malaya, and in India to settle in Java and South Africa. In this era the slaves in the Americas were mostly male; those in Africa were mostly female. The sharp decline in this cycle of slavery, at the turn of the nineteenth century, resulted from democratic revolutions, the Napoleonic wars, and humanitarian abolitionism.

Industrial cycle, 1800–1900. A fourth cycle of slavery expanded along with industrial capitalism. As slavery declined in some areas, it expanded in others. Great numbers captives were brought to Cuba and southern Brazil in the nineteenth century; through internal migration, many slaves moved from the Upper South to the cotton-producing areas of the United States. Most of those carried across the Atlantic in this phase came from Angola, Congo, and the Bights of Benin and Biafra. As compared with earlier times, these captives included larger proportions of people from Africa's far interior (these almost entirely male) and larger proportions of children. In the same period, demand for slaves expanded sharply in the Indian Ocean and in the Muslim Mediterranean, apparently in response to expanded opportunities for global commerce. Captives went from the Nile Valley and the Central Sudan to Saharan oases, to Egypt, the Ottoman heartland, and the Arabian peninsula. Captives from East Africa went to Indian Ocean islands and to the Persian Gulf. Linked to this expanded export of slaves was a great expansion of the slave trade and slavery on the African continent. A similar expansion of the slave trade, in a context of expanding commerce, took place in areas of Southeast Asia. For most of these populations, the sex ratio was fairly balanced; several of them sustained slavery without a slave trade.

Slavery in the corporate economy, since 1990. Slavery ended in all centers of corporate and industrial economic structure, but it survived in some poorer regions for production of raw materials and for domestic service, though without state support. Large slave populations disappeared in the 1930s, but smaller groups were reproduced thereafter in Africa and western Asia. These vestigial slave populations were reproduced more through birth than through capture, and were roughly equal in their sex ratio.

This discussion has given little explicit attention to slavery in civilizations before the modern period: the ancient Near East, Greece, and Rome; the early Middle Ages; and the premodern Muslim world. It is likely that many of the issues and principles addressed here were of similar importance in these societies, but the social and economic conditions of earlier times may also have led to important differences. These potentially significant institutional differences and the relative absence of demographic data on slavery suggest that it would be wise to refrain from attempting to extend the argument explicitly to premodern times.

See also DEMOGRAPHY OF SLAVES IN THE UNITED STATES; SLAVE TRADE; UNITED STATES.

BIBLIOGRAPHY

BUXTON, THOMAS FOWELL. *The African Slave-Trade.* 1839.
CONRAD, ALFRED H., and JOHN R. MEYER. *The Economics of Slavery, and Other Studies in Econometric History.* 1964.
CURTIN, PHILIP D. *The Atlantic Slave Trade: A Census.* 1969.
FOGEL, ROBERT WILLIAM, and STANLEY L. ENGERMAN. *Time on the Cross.* 2 vols. 1974.
HIGMAN, B. W. *Slave Populations of the British Caribbean, 1807–1834.* 1984.
LOVEJOY, PAUL E., and JAN S. HOGENDORN. *Slow Death for Slavery: The Course of Abolition in Northern Nigeria, 1897–1936.* 1993.
MANNING, PATRICK. *Slavery and African Life: Occidental, Oriental, and African Slave Trades.* 1990.
MEILLASSOUX, CLAUDE. *Anthropology of Slavery: The Womb of Iron and Gold.* 1991.
MILLER, JOSEPH C. "Mortality in the Atlantic Slave Trade: Statistical Evidence on Causality." *Journal of Interdisciplinary History* 11 (1981): 385–423.
MINTZ, SIDNEY. "Slavery and the Rise of Peasantries." *Roots and Branches: Current Directions in Slave Studies,* edited by Michael Craton. 1979.
PATTERSON, ORLANDO. *Slavery and Social Death: A Comparative Study.* 1982.

Patrick Manning

Demography of Slaves in the United States

The U.S. slave population can be compared with the other slave populations in the Western Hemisphere. As in the slave societies in South America and in the Caribbean, blacks in the United States originated overwhelmingly in western Africa. Prior to 1840 the total number of slaves imported was so large that the Western Hemisphere as a whole became more a demographic outpost of Africa than of Europe. Although British North America imported relatively few Africans, the birthrate was sufficient to establish the United States as the possessor of the largest slave population in the hemisphere by 1825.

Table 1 shows that the slave population of the United States increased more than fivefold between 1790 and 1860, doubling on average every twenty-eight years. The rapid increase between 1790 and 1810 was boosted by the importation of over 200,000 slaves prior to the official close of the African slave trade in 1808. Thereafter, the overall growth rate declined owing to manumissions and a diminishing rate of births. As a result of the decline in births, along with a significant rise in immigration from Europe, the proportion of blacks in the total U.S. population declined from about 19.3 percent in 1790 in 14.1 percent in 1860.

Because slave importation was negligible after 1808, the most important aspects of demographics were geographic distribution, fertility rate, and health. Westward migration was the most far-reaching of the demographic changes in the antebellum period. Slaves participated heavily in this westward movement but were essentially confined to the South for reasons of climate, soil, and the politics of admitting slave states to the Union.

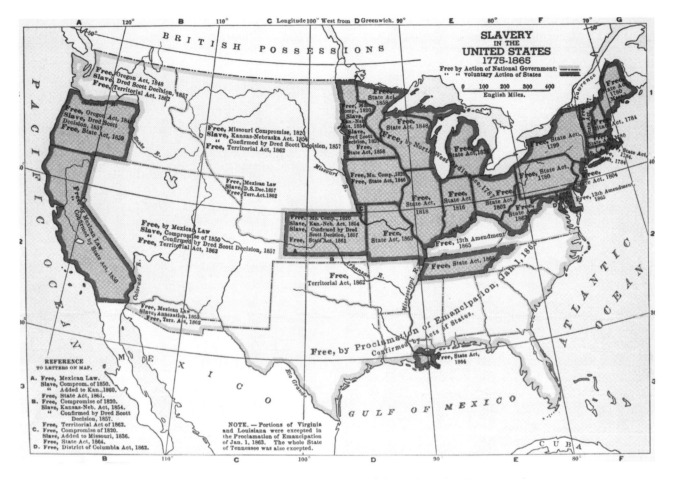

Post–Civil War map showing dates of emancipation within the United States. [Corbis-Bettmann]

Although slavery was legal in most northern states in the late 1700s, the region had relatively few slaves, especially after emancipation laws took effect between 1780 and 1804. Some historians have explained the geographic distribution by cropping patterns, suggesting that the "peculiar institution" flourished only where a staple such as tobacco, cotton, sugar, or rice could be grown. More recently, some scholars have suggested that slavery failed in the North but succeeded in the South because blacks had very high mortality rates in the northern but not in the southern climate.

Like most large-scale migrations, the westward movement of slaves was based on selection by age, gender, and family status. In the late antebellum period a majority of slave migrants (51.7 percent) were males, 59.2 percent of whom were between the ages of fifteen and thirty-nine in 1860. While all historians recognize that this movement was stressful for slave families, no consensus on its magnitude has emerged.

Given the paucity of vital registration records prior to the twentieth century, studies of fertility rates often use the ratio of children to women of childbearing age, which can be calculated from the census for slaves beginning in 1820. Within the South the child-woman ratio declined by 11 percent from 1820 to 1860; for blacks, in contrast to whites, the ratio was higher in the eastern states.

Study of demographic evidence on age at menarche, age at first birth, child spacing, age at last birth, and the proportion of women who ever had children indicates that slave fertility was high but significantly below a biological maximum. Large plantations adversely affected the number of births by restricting marriage opportunities to those who lived on the farm. The growth of plantation size and the existence of large farms in the West were important factors affecting time trends and geographic patterns of fertility.

The debate over slave health has a long tradition that dates from the abolitionist movement. The most recent work establishes that children's health was comparable to that in the poorest populations ever studied, while working-age slaves were substantially better off. These conclusions rest on plantation records of births and deaths and on stature statistics recorded

Table 1.   Growth of the Black Population in the United States, 1790–1860.

Year	Slaves	Free Black Population	Total Black Population	Annual Growth (%)	Blacks as % of Total Population
1790	697,897	59,466	757,363		19.27
1800	893,041	108,395	1,001,436	2.79	18.87
1810	1,191,364	186,446	1,377,810	3.19	19.03
1820	1,538,038	233,524	1,771,562	2.51	18.38
1830	2,009,043	319,599	2,328,642	2.73	18.10
1840	2,487,455	386,303	2,873,758	2.10	16.84
1850	3,204,313	434,495	3,638,808	2.36	15.69
1860	3,953,760	488,070	4,441,830	1.99	14.13

Source: U.S. Bureau of the Census, *Historical Statistics of the United States*, 1976.

on manifests of slaves shipped in the coastwise trade, since stature measures nutritional status.

Slave mortality rates were approximately 350 deaths per 1,000 among infants and 200 per 1,000 at ages one to four. These childhood rates were roughly double those of the entire free population in the United States, but the rates of slave and free adults were approximately equal. Low birth weight, attenuated breast-feeding, and a poor diet contributed to poor child health, but catch-up growth occurred and health improved when young slaves entered the labor force and received the better rations of working slaves.

See also DEMOGRAPHIC ANALYSIS OF SLAVES AND SLAVERY; HEALTH; UNITED STATES.

BIBLIOGRAPHY

FOGEL, ROBERT WILLIAM. *Without Consent or Contract.* 1989.
STECKEL, RICHARD H. "The Black Population of the United States, 1790–1920." In *A Population History of North America,* edited by Michael R. Haines and Richard H. Steckel. 1999.
———. *The Economics of U.S. Slave and Southern White Fertility.* 1985.

Richard H. Steckel

Denmark

See Caribbean Region; Scandinavia; Slave Trade.

Dew, Thomas Roderick   [1802–1846]

College professor and proslavery theorist.

One of ten children of Thomas and Mary E. Gatewood Dew of King and Queen County, Virginia, Thomas R. Dew graduated from the College of William and Mary in Williamsburg in 1820. Dew received an appoint-

ment as chair of Political Economy at William and Mary in 1827. In this capacity Dew published his *Review of the Debate in the Virginia Legislature of 1831 and 1832*, which arose in response to the Nat Turner uprising of 1832 and centered upon the question of abolishing slavery. Dew used a combination of historical, biblical, social, and political arguments to bolster his case that slavery benefited both master and slave. Many historians consider this the first major work of the antebellum "proslavery argument," a movement away from defensive apology for the institution and toward a stance asserting that slavery was entirely good. Dew's contribution to proslavery ideology spread through his influence both on faculty members at William and Mary, especially law professor Nathaniel Beverley Tucker, and on academicians across the South. In 1836 he became president of William and Mary and helped restore the institution to a vitality and level of student enrollment that it had not enjoyed in decades. In 1845 Dew married Natilia Hay of Clarke County, Virginia; he died in Paris while on his honeymoon trip, probably of pleurisy or pneumonia. Dew's impact on the southern mind, however, remained powerful, especially through the inclusion of his *Debates* in the seminal collection of essays *The Pro-Slavery Argument*, published in 1852.

See also PERSPECTIVES ON SLAVERY; TURNER, NAT.

BIBLIOGRAPHY

MANSFIELD, STEPHEN. "Thomas Roderick Dew at William and Mary: A Main Prop of That Venerable Institution." *Virginia Magazine of History and Biography* 75 (1967): 429–442.
———. "Thomas Roderick Dew: Defender of the Southern Faith." Ph.D. Diss., University of Virginia, 1968.

Eric H. Walther

Diet

See Food and Cooking.

Disability, Legal

Legal disabilities of slaves centered on the fact that slaves derived all legal protection from their masters, who in turn owned all property claims against their slaves' labor, production, and possessions. These sweeping claims derived from three chief sources: slaves were, or were descended from, persons who had lost all legal protections by capture in war, by condemnation at law as criminals, or by selling themselves to another.

As persons who could be only the object, not the author, of property claims, slaves were excluded from due process of the law of property. Slaves could not buy, sell, own, inherit, or bequeath property. Thus slaves could not make contracts, sue to protect property rights, or be sued for actions that damaged another's property. All such actions had to be brought by or against the slave's master.

Slaveholders in nearly all slave societies did find it in their interest to allow slaves to enjoy the use of property and of income generated from that property's use. The Romans called such property, and the practices governing its disposition, the slaves' *peculium*. In Rome and many other societies, slaves were allowed by masters to engage in business and trade as part of amassing a *peculium*. Slaves even purchased or sold other slaves. A slave might use his *peculium* to purchase his own freedom, sometimes by purchasing a replacement slave for the master. Upon the slave's death, possession of the *peculium* might be passed on to his child. But none of these actions could take place without the approval of the master, who retained legal ownership of the property in question.

Because marriage partners can make property claims upon each other, slaves' sexual unions were generally not legally recognized as marriages. Nor could a slave marry a free person: this would have violated the master's sole ownership of such property claims in the slave. An exception that demonstrates the rule is that masters could legally marry their own slaves, in Middle Eastern and African societies, because this act created no new property claims. Many societies did accord a limited recognition of marriage between slaves, by passing laws that forbade the separation of slave families or the sexual abuse of a slave wife by someone other than her master. Examples include the general practice of Islamic law and a fourth-century edict of the Roman emperor Constantine. The Ashanti allowed male slaves to pay a bride price

and to claim damages against adulterers. In most cases such marriages gained legitimacy only if entered into with the master's permission.

Closely related to marriage is the question of how parental power over children was exercised. Virtually no societies allowed slaves to exercise custodial power over their children. Masters could dispose of slave children without regard for the parent's wishes.

An enslaved person could act as a legal agent in actions to gain freedom: manumission, self-purchase, or petitioning to show that he was wrongfully held as a slave. Masters could rarely be compelled to offer manumission to a slave, but they could enter into legally binding contracts to free slaves, and courts protected the prospective freedperson's property rights in himself. Petitions for freedom generally sought to prove that a person had been kidnapped, was descended from a freeborn mother, or was otherwise wrongfully being held as a slave. In some jurisdictions slaves could file these petitions on their own behalf; more commonly, someone with full legal personality acted for the slave.

Slaves could sometimes act for themselves with regard to seeking a change of masters. In Islamic societies of Africa, the Middle East, and Asia, a dissatisfied slave could ritually damage the property of an intended new master, in the hope that a court would compel his current master to give him to the new master as compensation. Roman law permitted slaves to claim sanctuary from an oppressive master in the shadow of the emperor's statue in a city square. A slave claiming sanctuary could also request a court-ordered sale to a new master, a concept also incorporated in Spanish slave law. Slave masters in the United States sometimes provided their slaves with written authorization to seek a new master, but the contract of sale remained the master's sole province.

Despite these exceptions, slaves had little legal personality under civil law. But the same could not be said of criminal law. Slaves could be held responsible for both property crimes and acts of violence, especially when committed against free persons, although they commonly were not tried under the same procedures as free persons and might be subject to different, often harsher, penalties when found guilty. In the United States state laws provided jury trials for a narrower range of offenses when committed by slaves than was the case for free people, and courts allowed convictions on less evidence or lower standards of proof. By the same token, slave crimes against other slaves frequently carried lighter penalties than the norm or were resolved out of court by the master or masters of the slaves.

Most legal systems forbade slaves to bring criminal accusations and circumscribed their ability to give testimony, as slaves were persons presumed to have no stake in telling the truth. Roman law admitted slave testimony only if it was obtained under torture, a method that was deemed to produce reliable evidence. Many jurisdictions permitted slave testimony only respecting the crimes of other slaves. Where slavery was racially based, as in the United States, slaves might be permitted to testify against free blacks.

Finally, most legal systems did recognize a slave's right to self-defense against assaults by persons other than the master: by defending himself, a slave also defended his master's property interests. This construct could extend to allowing a husband to defend a female slave from sexual abuse. But slaves who did resist still could not testify on their own behalf against a free assailant; their actions had to be validated by the testimony of another free person.

See also LAW; PECULIUM.

BIBLIOGRAPHY

PATTERSON, ORLANDO. *Slavery and Social Death: A Comparative Study.* 1982.
WATSON, ALAN. *Slave Law in the Americas.* 1989.

T. Stephen Whitman

Discipline and Punishment

Juan Francisco Manzano, the Cuban-born author of one of the very few autobiographies written without an amanuensis by a slave, penetrated to the core of slavery in an 1835 letter to a white patron. He recalled how in his youth brutal lashings had seared into his consciousness for the first time an awareness of his dishonorable condition and how during maturity repeated punishment had forced him into desperate flight, albeit still fettered with a profound sense of unworthiness that left him reluctant to even record on paper the mortifications of his flesh. He pleaded to his patron for understanding: "Remember, sir, when you read this that I am a slave and that a slave is a dead being before his master."

As quintessentially deracinated, dishonored, and dominated bodies, slaves throughout history have endured methods of discipline and punishment that have stretched the boundaries of the perverse mind. Yet precisely because slaves resisted their enslavement and persistently sought to redeem themselves from social death, masters had to administer discipline and punishment, often of an elaborate and ritualized kind. Slaves extracted concessions to their humanity from masters in a tense, conflicted relation that invariably extended the battle for control from the slave's body to his mind, from reliance on brute force to the cul-

tivation of the master's authority in a quest for the slave's consent. An example from a mining region in colonial Brazil has parallels in other slave societies. To deal with a runaway problem Portuguese officials mandated in 1741 that fugitive slaves bear a branded F on their shoulder. But the mark quickly became a badge of honor to uncaptured repeat offenders, who were attracting increasing numbers of adherents. To put an end to this inversion, officials changed the punishment from branding to slicing the Achilles tendon. As the whip, the common instrument of slave punishment in virtually every slave society, expressed the master's power, the trophied scars on the back of slaves expressed their own claim to honor.

The leading penal reformers of the Enlightenment observed that the Greeks and Romans had tortured their slaves. So too did Muslims, Africans, and most other slaveholding peoples. Status-laden concepts of discipline and punishment that for centuries remained central to law and jurisprudence in the Western tradition emerged from the antinomy of slavery and freedom in the slave societies of ancient Greece and ancient Rome. In Book VI of the *Laws,* Plato has the Athenian stranger advise, "Slaves ought to be punished as they deserve, and not admonished as if they

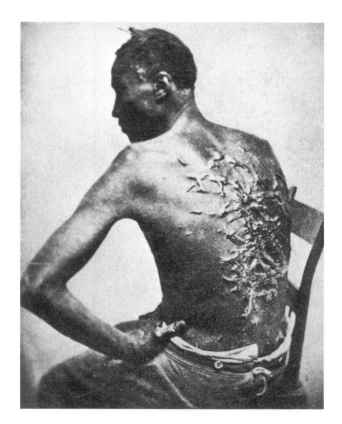

This 1863 photo shows a former slave scarred by whippings from his master, John Lyon, a cotton planter from Washington, LA. [Corbis-Bettmann]

were freemen." Under certain conditions, slaves deserved torture, which was legitimated by state after state as a kind of drama of persuasion in a judicial process that aimed at extracting the truth from slave witnesses (usually in private) and at aggravating the punishment for those found guilty of serious crimes (in a public spectacle). Aristotle, who doubted the efficacy of torture in yielding the truth, provided future generations with a justification for the corporal punishment of slaves and other lesser sorts by making justice proportional to status. The soul (master) ruled the body (slave). Torture functioned as a touchstone, compelling the body of slaves, barbarians, and outsiders—one and the same in many cases—to disgorge the truth, since slaves and other inferiors lacked the "deliberative faculty." As dead beings they existed, in a sense, outside of justice. Oaths had no meaning for slaves, since they lacked honor and reason. Slaves could come to apprehend truth, but the investigators could make them tell it only by inflicting bodily pain to overcome the master's control of their voices. As a living tool, slaves had only the body to surrender in retribution for crimes committed. Two millennia after Aristotle, while Brazilian officials were still applying the thumbscrew to extract confessions from slaves, Thomas R. R. Cobb, one of the antebellum South's preeminent legal theorists, defended ancient wisdom: "The condition of the slave renders it impossible to inflict upon him the ordinary punishments, by pecuniary fine, by imprisonment, or by banishment. He can be reached only through his body." Manzano, however, spoke for the tortured: "I said a thousand different things because they were commanding me to tell the truth, and I did not know which truth they wanted."

Both Plato and Aristotle acknowledged that slaves could be a particularly troublesome form of property and, in words that echoed throughout the plantation economies of the Americas, they counseled masters to implement divide-and-rule techniques by recruiting slaves from mixed language and cultural groups. In addition, masters should always dangle freedom as a reward for good behavior. They should treat their slaves well; punishment should be certain and firm, not abusive—if for no other reason than that the slave's condition reflected on the master's virtue. Xenophon, Plato's contemporary, compared the proper disciplining of slaves to the training of wild beasts, yet he urged masters to encourage status differentiation on the basis of merit.

Roman law mirrored the Greek understanding of punishment as both retribution and deterrence, which in extreme cases translated into incapacitation or elimination. Romans and Greeks had to secure households that were considered incomplete without slaves. During the Roman Republic, the *paterfamilias* enjoyed virtually absolute power over his slaves, although during the Empire the state narrowed the ground on which masters could kill their slaves and reserved to itself punishment for insurrection and other major crimes by slaves. Slaves could be tortured and executed for failing to prevent a master's suicide. If a master died by violence in his own house, domestic slaves "within earshot" of the crime could be tortured and executed. Whipping was a slave punishment appropriate for wrongdoing and small crimes. Mutilation and branded foreheads identified runaway slaves. Many Roman estates had a place of detention (*ergastulum*) for unruly slaves. More serious troublemakers suffered death by burning, by being thrown to wild beasts, or, more frequently, by having the head and neck immobilized with a wooden fork (*furca*). Until Constantine abolished crucifixion, it ranked as the most common form of slave execution. To inspire a salutary terror, more than six thousand crucified followers of Spartacus were lined along the Appian Way from Capua (where the slave revolt began) to the gates of Rome.

To some extent, every Western European country looked to the Roman past for guidance and broadly wrote slave law for its American colonies. In the beginning European masters enjoyed practical immunity from state interference in disciplining and punishing their slaves except in conspicuous cases in which they wantonly butchered or murdered their own or, more likely, someone else's slave. Both *Las Siete Partidas,* the landmark legal code of thirteenth-century Castile, which shaped legal theory in Spanish America, and Portugal's *Ordenações Filipinas* (1603), which structured Brazilian law, repeated Roman words in attending to the security of the patriarchal household and in prescribing torture for slaves under certain conditions. *Las Siete Partidas* explained that unless deterred by punishment slaves would "naturally" commit offenses against their masters. Many of the most important slave codes that set local standards for slave discipline and punishment in the Americas (for example, the Danish West Indian code of 1733, South Carolina's Negro Act of 1740, and the Cuban ordinances of 1842) grew out of confrontations between the ruling class and rebellious slaves, although legal enforcement tended to correlate with the seasonal temperature of slaveholders' anxieties.

For centuries customary punishment of slave conspirators and insurrectionaries in the Americas entailed a horrifying process of torture, mutilation, prolonged execution, and desecration of the corpse. Dutch authorities in Curacao, for example, indulged in an array of familiar methods after uncovering a plot in 1750, when they publicly executed more than thirty slaves, including thirteen women. They pulled

In this lithograph (ca. 1835) slaves receive public punishment in Rio de Janeiro as other slaves and townspeople watch. [Historical Picture Archive/Corbis]

limbs from joints with the rack, broke bones on the wheel, and tore flesh from the body with red-hot pincers. Convicted slaves were also burned to death, and the decapitated heads of mutilated corpses topped stakes planted in strategic locations for public viewing until they rotted away. In January 1811, after authorities in the Territory of Orleans crushed what turned out to be the largest slave revolt in the history of the United States, they executed captured rebels, cut off their heads, and piked them at intervals along the east bank of the Mississippi River for more than thirty miles, from the sugar plantation where the revolt began to one of the walled entrances to New Orleans. Although by the time of Nat Turner's revolt (1831), hanging had widely replaced the more excruciating forms of slave execution in the Americas, white Virginians appear to have dishonored Turner's hanged body by decapitating, dissecting, and perhaps even skinning it. Similarly, after John Brown's raid on Harpers Ferry in 1859, Virginia authorities turned bodies of the black raiders—but not the white raiders—over to a medical school for dissection.

Beginning in 1825 a special military tribunal handled cases of slave rebellion in colonial Cuba. State magistrates judged slaves accused of capital crimes in the French Caribbean. Justices of the peace filled a similar role in the British Caribbean, imperial Brazil, and at various times in the antebellum South. In most slaveholding countries convicted slaves had rights of appeal to higher tribunals. In the United States, where slaves came to hold procedural rights similar to white defendants, country courts, which seated a combination of justices and freeholders, judged most capital cases involving slaves. To prevent masters from concealing evidence in capital cases, most state governments legislated compensation for owners of executed slaves.

Most slaves crimes, however, never reached a court. Frontier isolation and official recognition of the necessity for subordinating slaves gave masters a wide sway in disciplining slaves. Centralizing states, metropolitan reformers, and abolitionist crusaders succeeded in ending the absolute dominion of masters, but community pressure and sentiment, feelings of

Christian charity, and the slave's own market value acted as a more efficient brake than government statutes on the gross abuse of slaves. A typical New World plantation existed as "imperium in imperio" or, as Frederick Douglass said of the Maryland estate on which he was kept as a slave, as "a little nation of its own, having its own language, its own rules, regulations and customs. The laws and institutions of the state, apparently touch it nowhere."

Agricultural manuals attempted to guide slaveholders on plantations to distinguish coercion from cruelty. They advocated punishment proportional to the crime, the minimum force necessary for correction. Masters were advised to punish quickly, with certainty, but without threats, passion, revenge, or favoritism. Common methods of punishing slaves acquired regional flavor: *kargo*-tree switches in the Sokoto Caliphate, rhinoceros-hide lashes in South Africa, hippopotamus-hide lashes in East Africa, manatee-skin whips in Cuba, tamarind rods in Surinam, wooden paddles (*palmatórias*) in Brazil, cowskin scourges in Barbados. The Spanish slave code of 1789 set a whipping limit of twenty-five lashes; the British Caribbean and states of the antebellum South tended to heed the biblical injunction (Deuteronomy 25:3) and limit stripes to thirty-nine. One of the few verses in the Koran to mention slave punishment (4:25) says that an adulterous female slave should suffer half the mandatory hundred stripes given to her free counterpart.

Despite legal limits, slaves in every slave society died from receiving well beyond a hundred stripes. Sexual crimes and physical challenges to authority earned far more stripes on average than theft. A detailed diary kept from 1839 to 1841 by Bennet Barrow, an unusually harsh owner of a sexually balanced Louisiana plantation with more than one hundred slaves, gives one rare example of the frequency of whippings. Each of his field hands averaged about one whipping per year, and whippings occurred every four days, though Barrow's female slaves, almost as unruly as the men, were whipped half as frequently. Barrow whipped about 70 percent of his field hands. In contrast, the proportion of whipped slaves in the British Caribbean colonies of Berbice, Saint Lucia, and Trinidad in the 1820s ranged between 7 and 50 percent, according to statistics compiled by officials during a metropolitan program of amelioration.

Stocks and pillories confined some slaves on most plantations, and respected manuals valued them more than the whip in reducing salves' misbehavior. Profit-minded slaveholders in the United States found a term of confinement that ran during the slave's time off, from Saturday afternoon until Sunday evening, especially instructive. Some explicitly discouraged overseers from whipping slaves because a damaged body lowered a slave's price. A remarkably detailed record of slave punishment from 1836 to 1847 for a mine in Brazil shows that the *palmatória* and stocks were much preferred to the lash for minor wrongs. The typical paddling exceeded a dozen whacks; the typical stay in the stocks lasted more than a day. Masters in East and West Africa fastened slaves with an iron collar to which a log or beam was attached by a chain—the infamous *kongo,* as it was called in Zanzibar.

Branding endured for centuries as a means of identifying slaves and punishing runaways. It declined in the Americas only in the late eighteenth century, under pressure from humanitarians. South Carolina and the French Caribbean waited until 1833 to abolish it. For labor in the fields, disobedient slaves wore collars and chains, the worst ones with bells, spikes, hooks, wood blocks, and other aggravating features. In the British Caribbean "putting a man to die" meant hanging a slave from a tree and letting him starve to death. Thomas Thistlewood, an eighteenth-century Jamaican arriviste, named a plantation punishment "Derby's dose" after a persistent slave offender who was regularly subjected to having another slave defecate in his mouth.

The French Code Noir (1685), the Spanish Código Negro (1789), and state law in the antebellum South explicitly frowned on mutilating slaves, but though the practice declined, it continued in the Americas well into the nineteenth century. Slaves lost a leg for desertion, a hand or nose for theft, and genitals for sexual crimes. Florida's slave code of 1828 allowed as punishment cropping a slave's ear or nailing a slave by the ear to a post. In Surinam Indians collected bounties by delivering the hands of runaway slaves. In China the frequent mutilation and branding of slaves bespoke the major role of the criminal justice system as a means of enslavement. Whereas mutilation might mean permanent shaming for a free person, mutilation recorded an offense on a dishonored slave's body while rendering the body less fit to repeat the offense.

Many large plantations in Africa and the Americas boasted houses of detention for slaves. Rehabilitative state prisons and penitentiaries of the nineteenth century rarely took slave wrongdoers, who could not readily be punished by denying them the rights and freedom that, in law, they never possessed. Jails largely served to hold runaways who awaited reclamation or slaves who awaited trial for such capital crimes as murder, rape, arson, poisoning, and insurrection. By the late eighteenth century urban workhouses offered wealthier masters a popular option for professional correction of disobedient (usually male) slaves. Treadmills made their appearance in British Caribbean towns in the 1820s. Long before then, public squares had whipping posts or trees to which slaves were taken for a spectacle of stripes, commonly administered by another slave or a free person of color. During the eighteenth century, Cape Town, South Africa, averaged one public hanging of a slave per month. Many masters concluded that exemplary punishment must be given where the crime had been committed and in the presence of the criminal's fellow slaves.

Slave housing on American plantations also exacted discipline. Cluster patterns reflecting the slaves' initiative and their African past gave way to more standard linear forms with the house of the overseer or driver in a commanding position. Wealthy nineteenth-century Cuban sugar planters perfected the barracoon, a barracks-like masonry compound with a locked central iron gate, grated windows, dogs, and watchmen to keep slaves in line. Slave quarters everywhere re-

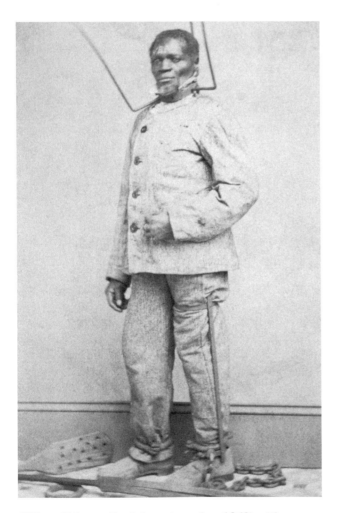

Wilson Chinn, a freed slave, poses (ca. 1863) with a variety of equipment used to control slaves. [U.S. Army Military History Institute/Corbis]

ceived unannounced visits and periodic searches. Vigilantes, patrols, and militia roamed the countryside to curb slaves' night rambles and assemblages. The authorities required slaves who traveled off the estate to carry a pass, license, tag, or ticket. Cities imposed curfews on slaves. Like the *fugitivarii* of ancient Rome, professional slave hunters, drawn from the ranks of Indians, free people of color, and poor whites, tracked down fugitives. Imported Cuban bloodhounds served whites in Jamaica against maroons, in Saint Domingue against slave revolutionaries, and in Florida to track down black deserters among the Seminoles. To insulate themselves from the punitive act and make a display of paternalistic intervention, masters often delegated punishment to overseers and drivers. Slave drivers, however, learned to choreograph the assigned punishment of their fellow slaves, and the drivers' conspicuous roles in slave revolts throughout the Americas suggest that they played more than the role of the master's henchmen. For this and other reasons, slave codes mandated proportional representation of white supervisors to black slaves on American plantations.

The master's arsenal contained numerous alternatives to corporal punishment. Privileged urban or domestic slaves feared a return to field work. Cotton slaves in the United States were threatened with sale to Caribbean sugar plantations. For insubordination, masters cut rations, abridged privileges and leisure time, assigned more rigorous tasks, canceled holiday celebrations, and dressed male slaves in female clothing. The slaves themselves regarded separation of families as one of the worst punishments. Planters and courts sold incorrigible slaves off the estate to mines, galleys, and other provinces or colonies. Crimes by individual slaves on a plantation often precipitated collective punishment in order to break, as one South Carolina master conceded, the "deep sympathy of feeling which binds them so closely together." Where the Atlantic slave trade continued, masters consciously resorted to divide-and-rule by buying an ethnic mix of Africans, although some masters thought ethnic homogeneity led to greater order on the plantation.

Resident masters tried to break slave solidarity, dispensing rewards as well as punishments. They paid slave informers, promoted family ties, and promised manumission as a reward for loyal service. Obedient slaves received choice tasks; better food, housing, and clothing; more leisure time; permission to travel off the estate; land for the cultivation of garden crops; and cash payments. The manipulation of religion as a tool of obedience engendered considerable debate among masters. Many would have agreed with a leading Cuban planter who called it the "cement of the social edifice." In the nineteenth-century Caribbean, however, missionaries fell under suspicion as abolitionist agitators. In the antebellum South the trend was to support slaves' conversion and their religious practices, under the master's watchful eye, with a method of oral instruction by a white preacher.

Masters and their surrogates regularly complained that slave women were harder to manage than slave men. At law, slave punishment did not discriminate by sex, although in reality slave women tended to receive lighter sentences than slave men for the same time. Of all the slaves in the Americas executed for capital crimes, women counted for much less than 10 percent; they appeared in court mainly to answer charges of poisoning. In nineteenth-century Jamaica slave women were branded less frequently than slave men. Still, even pregnant women felt the sting of the whip. Spanish-American Jesuits ruled on their well-run estates that, in the name of decency, only women were to whip other women. Muslim masters in the Sokoto Caliphate whipped their female slaves in isolation from the males. Throughout the British Caribbean, slave women were stripped and tied to a pole or tree before being flogged. This practice and notorious cases of slave brutalization by Arthur Hodge in Tortola (1811) and Edward Huggins in Nevis (1817) supplied abolitionists with powerful ammunition against slavery. Their efforts at amelioration before the Emancipation Bill of 1833 moved the British government to outlaw the flogging of slave women. Some colonies did, but Barbados resisted, insisting only that the female slave's body not be indecently exposed.

See also ANCIENT GREECE; ANCIENT ROME; BARRACOONS; CHAINS AND RESTRAINTS; CODE NOIR; DOUGLASS, FREDERICK; LAW; PATTERSON THESIS; SPARTACUS; TURNER, NAT.

BIBLIOGRAPHY

AKINOLA, G. A. "Slavery and Slave Revolts in the Sultanate of Zanzibar in the Nineteenth Century." *Journal of the Historical Society of Nigeria* 6 (1972): 215–228.

BREEDEN, JAMES O., ed. *Advice among Masters: The Ideal in Slave Management in the Old South.* 1980.

COBB, THOMAS R. R. *An Inquiry into the Law of Slavery in the United States of America.* 1858.

DOUGLASS, FREDERICK. *My Bondage and My Freedom.* 1855.

GENOVESE, EUGENE D. *Roll, Jordan, Roll: The World the Slaves Made.* 1974.

GOULART, JOSÉ ALIPIO. *Da palmatória ao patíbulo (castigos de escravos no Brasil).* 1971.

HINDUS, MICHAEL STEPHAN. *Prison and Plantation: Crime, Justice, and Authority in Massachusetts and South Carolina, 1767–1878.* 1980.

MANZANO, JUAN FRANCISCO. *Autobiografía, cartas y versos.* 1937.

MORRIS, THOMAS D. *Southern Slavery and the Law, 1619–1860.* 1996.

PATTERSON, ORLANDO. *Slavery and Social Death: A Comparative Study.* 1982.

SELLIN, J. THORSTEN. *Slavery and the Penal System.* 1976.

SCHWARZ, PHILIP J. *Twice Condemned: Slaves and the Criminal Laws of Virginia, 1705–1865.* 1988.

Robert L. Paquette

Dort, Synod of

The Synod of Dort gathered Calvinist theologians chiefly from the Netherlands but also from England, Switzerland, and the Palatinate to define Reformed Church doctrine. Meeting for six months in 1618 and 1619, the synod dealt primarily with the Arminian controversy over the nature and meaning of election, atonement, and grace. The canons of the synod asserted that God's election of the saved is unconditional, that Christ's atonement for human sin applies only to the elect, that man is naturally depraved, that the gift of grace is irresistible, and that the elect do not fall away from grace.

The synod also discussed slavery. It debated whether children born to slaves owned by Reformed masters should be baptized, and whether baptism should free a slave. The synod's proceedings stated that

> baptized slaves should enjoy equal right of liberty with other Christians and ought never to be handed over again to the powers of the heathens by their Christian masters either by sale or by any other transfer of possession.

The Swiss theologian Giovanni Deodatus went so far as to urge that baptized slaves be treated in all respects like Christian servants.

But the synod stopped short of requiring masters to baptize their slaves, choosing instead to leave this matter to the discretion of heads of household. As a result of this finding, many seventeenth-century Dutch slaveholders in Brazil and Suriname resolutely opposed preaching to or baptizing their slaves, fearing that baptism would require the slave's manumission.

See also CHRISTIANITY; NETHERLANDS AND THE DUTCH EMPIRE.

BIBLIOGRAPHY

BLACKBURN, ROBIN. *The Making of New World Slavery, 1492–1800.* 1997.

MCNEILL, JOHN T. *The History and Character of Calvinism.* 1967.

T. Stephen Whitman

Douglas, Stephen A. [1813–1861]

Attorney and U.S. politician.

Stephen A. Douglas might be called the last "dough-face" politician, a "northern man with southern principles." He illustrates the complexities of northern expansion as the sectional crisis built toward the Civil War.

Although he was not formally educated, Douglas became a lawyer and professional politician. He narrowly lost a congressional race in 1837, despite the fact that he was too young, constitutionally, to serve. In 1843 he went to Congress, and in 1847 he went to the U.S. Senate, where he became chair of the Committee on Territories. In 1847 he also married an heiress from North Carolina who owned land in Mississippi and 150 slaves. The committee chairmanship gave him the power to influence a crucial national issue; his marriage suggests his indifference to the question of slavery.

Douglas did not vote on the Fugitive Slave Act of 1850, a key element in the North-South "compromise" of that year, even though he put the compromise together. Four years later he offered his own solution to the issue of expansion of slavery, the Kansas-Nebraska Act. Douglas proposed to end federal involvement by invoking "popular sovereignty" when territories sought statehood. But he disapproved of the so-called Lecompton Constitution adopted by Kansas, a proslavery state, on the grounds that its adoption had been fraudulent.

His senatorial opponent in 1858, Abraham Lincoln, also forced him to admit that his doctrine of popular sovereignty on slavery was incompatible with the Dred Scott decision, which he supported. He was the official presidential candidate of a divided Democratic Party in 1860, in a four-way contest. When Lincoln's victory provoked secession, Douglas gave full support to the Union, and he continued to support it until his death.

See also DRED SCOTT V. SANDFORD; KANSAS-NEBRASKA ACT; LINCOLN, ABRAHAM.

BIBLIOGRAPHY

JOHANNSEN, ROBERT W. *Stephen A. Douglas.* 1973.
NICHOLS, ROY FRANKLIN. *The Disruption of American Democracy.* 1948.

Edward Countryman

Stephen A. Douglas (ca. 1859). [*Frank Leslie's Illustrated Newspaper*/Corbis]

Douglass, Frederick [1818–1895]

American slave and political activist.

Born Frederick Augustus Washington Bailey in Talbot County on Maryland's eastern shore in February 1818, Douglass was a slave in a region where many considered the face of slavery to be relatively mild. Nevertheless, the range of possible experiences was broad and Douglass experienced some of the worst as well as the better features of the system. He recalled often being hungry as a child. As with other slave children, his only clothing was a knee-length sackcloth shirt; and at one point during his life, he had to crawl into a feedbag and sleep in a closet during the winter months to keep warm. Yet his earliest years, up to the age of seven, were almost idyllic, since he had a carefree existence and no notion of his circumscribed status. He was brought up by his grandmother, also a slave, and his grandfather, a free black, in a cabin along Tuckahoe Creek. His father was an unknown white man and his mother, Harriet Bailey, belonged to Aaron Anthony, a middling farmer who claimed about thirty slaves in his own right and managed the thousand-slave workforce of Colonel Edward Lloyd, one of the largest slaveholders in the state. Douglass saw his mother only a few times in his life. She worked at locations some miles distant and died when he was young, and his memory of her was vague. Commenting on the fact that she walked as many as twelve miles to see him, he stated that "a true mother's heart was hers." But he also said that he felt little at her death and blamed slavery for his own lack of filial attachment and her inability to see him.

His grandmother, Betsey Bailey, was the only mother he knew. She cared for him and her other grandchildren while their parents worked. She had attained a privileged status in the slave community and her owner allowed her to go pretty much her own way, as long as she cared for the children, his property. (Douglass later complained bitterly that she was left to die alone in her cabin once she had outlived her usefulness.) One of Douglass's earliest and most painful experiences, marking his introduction to slave life, occurred when she was commanded to bring the child to his master's house, twelve miles away, where she introduced him to relatives. She left quietly while he was playing, without saying good-bye, thinking, perhaps, that that was the easiest way to handle an unfortunate situation. But one biographer thinks that this incident scarred Douglass for life and that thereafter he never completely trusted anyone.

Despite a difficult adjustment to his new condition, Douglass was fortunate. His owner's daughter took a liking to him and shielded him from some mistreatment, and eventually he was dispatched to Baltimore, where the wife of his owner's brother found him equally attractive. He was to act as playmate and protector of her young son, but she treated him as a member of the family and began teaching him to read. Although her husband interrupted the lessons when he discovered them, saying that education ruined a slave, she had already planted the seeds of a quest for literacy and laid the groundwork for Douglass's success in attaining it. The urban environment also provided an opportunity for cultural interchange between black and white youngsters, slave and free, as they played in the streets and alleys of the city, and Douglass was able to devise games that permitted his white playmates to impart their school learning to him. With the first money he earned in his spare time he bought *The Columbian Orator,* a primer that taught elocution along with democratic values. He mastered it, and its teachings would have a profound influence on his later development.

An important event in Douglass's life as a slave was his struggle with Edward Covey, a man who had a reputation as a "slave breaker," when he was hired out after he returned to his master's rural environment. He was whipped weekly for six months, but he finally resisted and got the best of Covey in a wrestling match. This event he called a "turning point": "It rekindled the few expiring embers of freedom, and revived within me a sense of my own manhood. . . . I now resolved that however long I might remain a slave in form, the day had passed forever when I could be a slave in fact."

In 1838 Douglass escaped from Maryland, going by train and ferry to New York City. He married Anna, a free black woman who followed him from Baltimore, and he soon became involved in the abolitionist movement, becoming one of its most powerful speakers. He came under the sway of William Lloyd Garrison, the foremost white abolitionist of the era, who for a time served as a surrogate father until Douglass outgrew his mentor. The break between them proved to be bitter and deeply felt. Douglass had initially adopted Garrison's belief in the efficacy of moral persuasion alone in altering the public consciousness and causing Americans to demand an end to slavery; but he later came to believe that political action was also useful—a position Garrison rejected. Behind this dispute were philosophical differences over the nature of the Constitution and the American political system and strategic differences over how to prioritize other reform efforts, including temperance and women's rights.

Douglass went on to become the foremost black abolitionist and statesman of the nineteenth century, always actively opposing segregation and discrimination. He published two antislavery newspapers, *The North Star* in 1847 and *Frederick Douglass' Paper* in 1851. He also published three autobiographies, the first two of which—*Narrative of the Life of Frederick Douglass, an American Slave* (1845) and *My Bondage and My Freedom* (1855)—were important in the antislavery movement. *The Life and Times of Frederick Douglass* (1881; revised 1892), also detailing incidents of slavery, was a mature reflection on his life and career.

Douglass strongly supported military participation by blacks during the Civil War, arguing that this course was necessary to vindicate black manhood and to establish the irrefutable claim of blacks to citizenship. He recruited enthusiastically and successfully for Massachusetts's all-black fifty-fourth regiment, in which two of his sons served. Despite promises of fair play, however, black soldiers received unequal treatment in almost every feature of military life, including pay, accommodations, commissions, and promotion, inequities that provoked Douglass to cease his recruiting efforts and to seek an audience with President Abraham Lincoln. The meeting in August 1863 marked the first ever between a former slave—in a formal capacity—and the nation's chief executive. But it yielded nothing. Although Lincoln gave Douglass his

Frederick Douglass (ca. 1850). [UPI/Corbis-Bettmann]

earnest attention, he made no concessions. Douglass had more reason for satisfaction a year later, when Lincoln sought his advice in a second meeting. As a result of his active support of the Republican Party after the war, he was appointed marshall of the District of Columbia by President Rutherford B. Hayes in 1877, recorder of deeds for the District of Columbia in 1881, and minister to Haiti in 1889. His wife of forty-four years died in 1882, and seventeen months later, in 1884, he incurred controversy by marrying a much younger white woman, but they appear to have been extremely happy together. He died in February 1895.

See also ABOLITION AND ANTISLAVERY MOVEMENTS; GARRISON, WILLIAM LLOYD; SLAVE NARRATIVES.

BIBLIOGRAPHY

DOUGLASS, FREDERICK. *Life and Times of Frederick Douglass.* 1892. Reprint, 1962.
———. *My Bondage and My Freedom.* 1855. Reprint, 1987.
HUGGINS, NATHAN I. *Slave and Citizen: The Life of Frederick Douglass.* 1980.
MCFEELEY, WILLIAM S. *Frederick Douglass.* 1991.
MARTIN, WALDO E., JR. *The Mind of Frederick Douglass.* 1984.
QUARLES, BENJAMIN. *Frederick Douglass.* 1971.

Daniel C. Littlefield

Draco, Code of

In 621–620 B.C. the Athenian lawgiver Draco (also Dracon or Drakon) set down the law code of the city in written form, where previously it had existed only in an oral tradition. Very little is known about the specific laws of Draco, for only the law on homicides from this code has survived, having been carried over into the laws of Solon. Modern scholarship is unable to discover what penalties, if any, were visited upon the murderers of slaves or what special provisions the laws made for the punishment of crimes by slaves. One major aspect of Draco's code, which was eliminated under Solon, involved the enslavement of Athenian citizens for debt, which not only was regarded as inhumane but threatened to destabilize Athenian society.

Solon's revision of the Code of Draco was necessary not only to reduce the severity of many provisions of the criminal statutes but also to reduce through constitutional innovations the inordinate power the wealthy had come to possess in Athens. Aristotle in his classic study *The Constitution of Athens* implied that the civil disorder that preceded Solon's temporary assumption of plentipotentiary powers in order to establish a new constitutional order was in large part the result of two social realities: the securing of debt with the person of the debtor, under the laws of Draco, and the concentration of land in the hands of the wealthy.

Although most scholars believe Draco to have been a real historical person, not merely a legendary figure, there is limited agreement concerning how much innovation Draco put into the laws he set down. The Code of Draco was seen as beneficial to the lower classes in that the laws, by virtue of being written down, could be known by all citizens and not be subject to easy manipulation by aristocratic archons. On the other hand, Draco's laws were noted for their severity, with the vast majority of crimes punishable by death—hence the term *draconian.* This legendary severity—some ancients claimed that the laws were "written in blood, not ink"—may be exaggerated, since exile was a penalty permitted for many of these crimes, with death the punishment for willful return from exile.

Draco's law of homicide was extremely sophisticated, with various categories recognized from premeditated to intentional but unpremeditated to involuntary. This law of homicide was the sole portion of the Code of Draco that was retained as a part of the new laws of Solon in Athens in the fifth century B.C.

See also ANCIENT GREECE; LAW.

BIBLIOGRAPHY

Aristotle's Constitution of Athens and Other Texts. Edited and
    translated by Kurt von Fritz and Ernst Kapp. 1950.
GAGARIN, MICHAEL. *Drakon and Early Athenian Homicide
    Law.* 1981.
OSTWALD, MARTIN. *From Popular Sovereignty to the Sovereignty of
    Law: Law, Society, and Politics in Fifth-Century Athens.* 1986.
STROUD, RONALD S. *Drakon's Law on Homicide.* 1968.

Patrick M. O'Neil

Dred Scott v. Sandford (1857)

Dred Scott was the slave of John Emerson, a U.S. Army
surgeon who lived in St. Louis, Missouri. From 1833
to 1840 Scott attended Emerson as his personal servant at military outposts in Illinois, a free state, and in
the Wisconsin and Iowa territories, in which slavery
was prohibited by the Missouri Compromise. In 1843,
three years after Scott returned to St. Louis, Emerson
died; the terms of his will left Scott to Mrs. Emerson
and appointed John Sanford, her brother and a St.
Louis resident, as one of the executors of the will. In
1846 Scott sued for his freedom in a Missouri court
on the grounds that his having set foot on free soil
made him free. Scott's case was supported by Missouri
precedents dating back to 1824, most notably *Rachel
v. Walker* (1836). That case led to the freedom of a
slave who had accompanied her master, a military
officer ordered to report to a post in free territory.
After several delays and three trials, in 1850 a Missouri court declared Scott a free man.

Mrs. Emerson immediately appealed the decision to
the Missouri Supreme Court, a body which had just become elective rather than appointive. Because two of
the three justices were staunch supporters of slavery, in
1852 the court refused to apply *Rachel v. Walker* to *Dred
Scott v. Emerson* on the grounds that Scott's case was an
attack on slavery and therefore an attempt to overthrow the state government. Instead, it overturned the
lower court's decision and denied Scott his freedom.

Scott did not appeal to the Supreme Court because
his lawyers did not believe the Court had jurisdiction over the case. Had he appealed, however, the
Court would probably have rejected his claim, under
the precedent of *Strader v. Graham* (1851). In that case
one side argued that slaves from Kentucky had become
free when their master carried them briefly to Ohio
before returning them to Kentucky. However, Chief
Justice Roger B. Taney denied that the Supreme Court
had jurisdiction in the matter on the grounds that one
state's laws had no effect on residents of another state.
In 1853 Scott was evidently bought by Sanford, who

Frank Leslie's Illustrated Newspaper *displays a story
on the Dred Scott decision, including illustrations of Dred
Scott and his family.* [Library of Congress/Corbis]

had moved to New York City. Because the case now
involved residents of two different states, Scott could
pursue his freedom in a lower federal court.

In 1854 Scott sued Sanford in federal court in Missouri. The basis of the court's jurisdiction was the diversity of the citizenship of the parties. Sanford argued
that Scott could not sue in federal courts because as
a Negro he could not be a citizen of the United States
or of Missouri. Sanford based his claim not on
Scott's status as a slave, but on his race. Judge Robert
Wells, a native of Virginia, ruled that *if* Scott were free,
then he could sue as a citizen of Missouri in federal
courts. However, after a trial Wells concluded that
under Missouri law Scott was still a slave, and that the
federal courts were obligated to follow Missouri law.
Scott then appealed to the Supreme Court. Sanford
hired new attorneys, one of whom was Maryland senator Reverdy Johnson, a former U.S. attorney general
and a personal friend of Taney's. In addition to citing
the *Strader* decision, Sanford's attorneys argued that

Congress had no power to prohibit slavery in a territory. In a 7-to-2 decision, the Supreme Court accepted both arguments. Furthermore, although neither side had appealed the decision of Judge Wells on the right of a black to sue in federal court, Chief Justice Taney ruled on that issue as well. Taney's majority opinion declared that by virtue of their race blacks were not citizens of the United States and therefore could not sue in federal court; that visiting a free state did not make a slave free if he subsequently returned with his owner to a slave state; and that visiting a free territory did not make a slave free because the Constitution guaranteed a property owner's right to carry his property, including a slave, with him wherever he went. Consequently, ruled Taney, the Missouri Compromise, the congressional action by which certain territories had been declared off-limits to slavery since 1820, was unconstitutional; the power to permit or prohibit slavery could be exercised only by a state and not by the federal government. Shortly after the decision, Scott was sold to Taylor Blow, a Missouri acquaintance who set him free.

The court's decision in *Dred Scott v. Sandford* (a Supreme Court clerk misspelled Sanford's name in the official report) delighted southerners, who saw it as vindication of their claim that the Constitution endorsed and protected slavery. But it outraged northerners, who refused to accept that the federal government could regulate territorial affairs in all matters except slavery. More ominously, it raised the possibility that a future Supreme Court decision would deny the free states' right to ban slavery within their own borders. Although the ruling threatened to work against the nascent Republican Party, which had formed to restrict slavery's expansion, it served instead to recruit many new party members, thus contributing to Abraham Lincoln's election to the presidency in 1860 and the outbreak of the Civil War.

See also LAW.

BIBLIOGRAPHY

EHRLICH, WALTER. *They Have No Rights.* 1979.
FEHRENBACHER, DON E. *The Dred Scott Case: Its Significance in American Law and Politics.* 1978.
FINKELMAN, PAUL. *Dred Scott v. Sandford: A Brief History with Documents.* 1997.
———. *An Imperfect Union: Slavery, Federalism, and Comity.* 1981.

Charles W. Carey Jr.

Drivers

Aptly conceptualized as "the men in the middle" by historians of the United States South, black drivers occupied a tenuous position within the managerial hierarchy of plantation agriculture. Also referred to by contemporaries as foremen, head men, overlookers, or whipping bosses, drivers possessed varying degrees of supervisory or police authority over the field hands and served as intermediaries between slaveholders and members of the slave community. Like modern-day factory foremen, they frequently were torn between enforcing the dictates of their superiors and representing the interests of fellow laborers. Although there was no generalized response to this tension-producing problem, the vast majority of those who held such privileged positions remained close to their communal roots. As a result, most were able to avoid becoming traitorous sychophants or unfeeling, dehumanized tyrants. Capable drivers often knew more about agricultural affairs than white planters, stewards, or overseers and could barter this practical wisdom for both personal and group gain. The field hands' refusal to be bullied beyond acceptable limits ensured that the supervisory elite could not become overly dependent upon brute force as a motivational tool. Typically, a planter's code of conduct was interpreted and applied within this context of informally mediated relationships.

A driver's duties were numerous and varied. Black foremen awakened the field hands before dawn, led them to the job site, and assigned daily tasks. Often, they set the pace of the day's work through their own labors. At midday, they directed the feeding of the workers and draft animals, checked the condition of agricultural implements, and, if necessary, mediated disputes and meted out punishments. Some drivers also kept basic accounts, weighed and distributed weekly rations, and served as their master's representative in dealings with merchants, tradesmen, and suppliers. After turning in a nightly oral report of work accomplished, they were responsible for policing the quarters.

Typical perquisites accruing to drivers included extra allotments of food and clothing, superior housing, and bonuses of tobacco, whiskey, or cash. Equally desirable privileges were the ability to move about the countryside on errands, to acquire the use of a larger-than-normal garden plot, and to "hire out" during the winter months in order to earn extra money. This system of rewards might serve to enhance elite slaves' standing within the quarters, but it also could erode drivers' authority if their special indulgences or conspicuous consumption alienated envious field hands.

Over time, growth in the scale and complexity of plantation agriculture created numerous supervisory positions for trustworthy and resourceful slaves. Foreman-to-field-hand ratios for slave societies in the Western Hemisphere are highly impressionistic. How-

In this undated engraving a driver orders a young female slave with a child back to work. [Library of Congress/Corbis]

ever, it is estimated that at least two-thirds of the slaves in the antebellum South worked under black leaders who assumed responsibility for the pace and quality of work. As "men in the middle," drivers provided both black and white Southerners with iconclastic images of enslaved African-Americans who were possessed of decision-making authority and recognized managerial talent.

See also FIELD LABOR; OVERSEERS; PLANTATIONS.

BIBLIOGRAPHY

MILLER, RANDALL M. "The Man in the Middle: The Black Slave Driver." *American Heritage* 30 (1979): 40–49.
VAN DEBURG, WILLIAM L. *The Slave Drivers: Black Agricultural Labor Supervisors in the Antebellum South.* 1979.

William L. Van Deburg

Du Bois, W. E. B.   [1868–1963]

Pioneer African-American historian of slavery.

Born in Massachusetts and trained at Fisk University (A.B., 1888), the University of Berlin (1892–1894), and Harvard (A.B., 1890; Ph.D., 1895), William Edward Burghardt Du Bois wrote influential studies on the Atlantic slave trade, slave culture and religion, the African origins of America's slaves, and black life during Reconstruction. He also was one of the most articulate critics of the post–Civil War era proslavery argument and of racism in American life.

In his *Suppression of the African-Slave-Trade to the United States of America, 1638–1870* (1896), Du Bois argued that after the 1808 congressional prohibition on slave imports, Southerners smuggled over 250,000 African slaves into the South. Northern capitalists and Southern slaveholders, Du Bois said, profited from slavery and were uncommitted to enforcing the slave trade laws. Though late-1990s scholars have lowered Du Bois's estimate considerably—to as low as 54,000 for the period from 1808 to 1861—his book remains influential. In *The Souls of Black Folk* (1903) Du Bois probed deeply into the minds of the slaves. The bondsmen, Du Bois explained, employed exorcism and witchcraft to resist their enslavement. The slave preacher connected the slaves to their African roots, comforted them in their sorrows, and helped direct their future. In their music, slaves sang of hope for ultimate justice. In *The Negro* (1915) and other studies, Du Bois celebrated the African background of America's slaves. He proudly summarized past African achievements in art, industry, political organization, and religion. Transplanted in America, the African-Americans drew upon this heritage to form churches, to plan revolts, to run away, and to resist slavery in various forms. Du Bois also identified Africanisms in slave housing and family life. The bondsmen, he concluded, employed African traditions to withstand slavery's dehumanizing and destructive effects.

Eloquent and outspoken in his condemnation of slavery, Du Bois also exposed racism in twentieth-century America in many articles, book reviews, and editorials. In 1918, for example, he criticized historian Ulrich B. Phillips's *American Negro Slavery* (1918) as incomplete and biased. Phillips, Du Bois said, like proslavery ideologues of old, refused to treat blacks as human beings and failed to recognize the progress achieved by the race over time. As historian, sociologist, and activist, Du Bois dedicated himself to explaining the "double consciousness" of African-American life, "this sense of always looking at one-self through the eyes of others, of measuring one's soul by the tape of a world that looks on in amused contempt and pity."

See also HISTORIOGRAPHY OF SLAVERY; PERSPECTIVES ON SLAVERY.

BIBLIOGRAPHY

LEWIS, DAVID LEVERING. *W. E. B. Du Bois: Biography of a Race.* 1993.

SMITH, JOHN DAVID. "Du Bois and Phillips—Symbolic Antagonists of the Progressive Era." *Centennial Review* 24 (Winter 1980): 88–102.

———. *An Old Creed for the New South: Proslavery Ideology and Historiography, 1865–1920* (1985).

———. "The Unveiling of Slave Folk Culture, 1865–1920." *Journal of Folklore Research* 21 (April 1984): 47–62.

ZAMIR, SHAMOON. *Dark Voices: W.E.B. Du Bois and American Thought, 1888–1903.* 1995.

John David Smith

Dutch Trading Companies

See Brazil; Caribbean Region; Netherlands and the Dutch Empire; Plantations; Slave Trade; Southeast Asia; Suriname.

E

East Africa

This entry includes the following articles: Swahili Region; Madagascar. *Related articles may be found at the entries* Africa; Central Africa; North Africa; Northeast Africa; Slave Trade; Southern Africa; West Africa. *See also the note accompanying the entry* Africa *for further information about the organization of these entries.*

Swahili Region

Slaves were present in the Swahili towns that emerged after the seventh century and for centuries were exported in small numbers to many parts of the Indian Ocean littoral. After 1800 slave trading became big business, and coastal slave traders helped extend Swahili influence into the East African interior.

In the early Swahili region, which stretched from present-day southern Somalia to the Tanzania-Mozambique border and to the islands of Zanzibar, Pemba, and Mafia, slaves were used as domestics. The Swahili (or Zanj) ports were ruled by Muslim families with African, Shirazi (Persian), and Arab connections and were visited by merchants trading slaves and other African goods to the Hadramaut, Oman, the Persian Gulf, and northwestern India. Kiswahili, a Bantu trade language with infusions of Arabic vocabulary, emerged as early as the ninth century. The most important towns were Pate (Kenya), known for ivory and skins; and Kilwa (Tanzania), known for gold dust and slaves.

Early estimates of slave exports before A.D. 1500 range from 200 to 1,000 per year, and sizable num-

bers at least at one point are indicated by the large "Zanilj" slave revolt in ninth-century Basra, but these guesses are often based on scattered references to African slaves of indistinct progeny in Mesopotamia, India, and China. Kilwa and several other towns prospered, though in cycles that fluctuated with such exports as gold and ivory, rather than slaves. During the Portuguese period (1500–1729) economic activity was modest to miserable; although trade in slaves at the time has been estimated as high as 4,000 per year, that figure is well in excess of available evidence; only ivory and mangrove poles were likely regular exports.

Beginning in the late eighteenth century, sugar and clove plantations created an unprecedented demand for slaves. In the 1780s Kilwa began supplying slaves to French sugar planters in Mauritius and Reunion. Soon afterward, the Busaidi family (Oman) colonized the Swahili coast, took control of Kilwa in 1819, and imported slaves to Zanzibar and Pemba islands to develop clove plantations. The Busaidi seyyid (sultan) used his relatives and Arab mercenaries to control the main coastal ports as far north as southern Somalia, employ slave labor on the mainland to raise grain to feed the slaves on the island plantations, and establish coastal staging points for long-distance ivory and slave caravans into the interior. British Indian merchants helped finance this expansion and served as the seyyid's custom agents.

In 1840, when the seyyid made Zanzibar his permanent capital, the port had become an international city with consulates representing several European nations engaged in trade in cloves, ivory, copra, and other

Tippu Tib, also known as Hamed bin Mohammed, was the most successful Swahili-Arab slave trader in Zanzibar, owning more than ten thousand slaves at the height of his career. [Bojan Brecelj/Corbis]

commodities. Zanzibar was also the region's central slave market. Approximately half of the slaves sold there remained in the Swahili region. Zanzibar maintained a large slave population (estimated at 250,000 in 1860), as did Pemba, mostly engaged in clove production. Slaves were also transshipped to the Kenya coast, where thousands were employed raising millet, sesame, and other food products for consumption in Zanzibar. The balance of slaves were shipped to the Hadramaut, Persian Gulf, and India, mainly by small Arab merchants. All together, the nineteenth-century trade totaled from 750,000 to 1 million slaves.

The nineteenth-century slavery boom increasingly stratified coastal society. Busaidi power and coastal economic ties to the Hadramaut and gulf elevated the status of recent Arab settlers, lowered the position of old Swahili families, and implanted a large, despised, servile element of slaves used as domestic servants, concubines, porters, and laborers in the towns. Slaves lived in the homes of their owners, participated

in the social and religious life of the larger community, and had some opportunities to acquire property and semifree status. The vast majority of slaves was located in the countryside where they worked on plantations, lived in nearby villages, and labored under overseers (usually also slaves) all year. Their lives were difficult, and on the islands escape was next to impossible. Slaves on the mainland often absconded. Maroon settlements there date back to the 1840s, and in times of coastal conflict, slaves often seized the opportunity to bolt for the interior.

Slavery outlived the slave trade. The British pressured the Busaidi to abolish slave trading in 1873, though clandestine exports continued into the 1890s. Legal slavery was abolished in Zanzibar and Pemba in 1897, but not until 1907 in Kenya. Until abolition, Europeans commonly hired their laborers from large slave owners. Slaves made up most of the caravans supplying interior mission and administrative stations, and ex-slaves were conspicuous among the early colonial employees. Ex-slaves, especially those who remained dependent on coastal Muslim households, retained the social stigma of slavery in the twentieth century.

See also AFRICA; ISLAM; MAROONS; SLAVE TRADE.

BIBLIOGRAPHY

COOPER, FREDERICK. *Plantation Slavery on the East Coast of Africa.* 1977.
MORTON, FRED. *Children of Ham: Freed Slaves and Fugitive Slaves on the Kenya Coast, 1873 to 1907.* 1990.
NURSE, DEREK, and THOMAS SPEAR, *The Swahili: Reconstructing the History and Language of an African Society, 800–1500.* 1985.
SHERIFF, ABDUL. *Slaves, Spices, and Ivory in Zanzibar.* 1987.

Fred Morton

Madagascar

Slavery in Madagascar was unique in Africa for two reasons: the institution was imported, and it was inextricably linked to a two-way trade in which slaves were both exported from and imported onto the island.

Madagascar was colonized sometime in the first millennium A.D., probably by Indonesian traders and their African slaves. These traders shipped slaves and other valuable East African commodities such as gold and ivory to markets around the Indian Ocean and possibly as far east as China. By 1500, when European powers first directly entered the Indian Ocean trading network, Madagascar was an established, albeit relatively minor, slave export and reexport center, and slavery was a ubiquitous domestic institution supported by internecine slave raiding. The European sea route around the Cape of Good Hope, which passed Madagascar, integrated the island into the mainstream of Indian Ocean trade. European demand for Malagasy provisions and slaves supplemented the traditional demand from Islamic markets to the north and stimulated the rise of the first Malagasy kingdoms on the west coast in the sixteenth and seventeenth centuries. Political consolidation in turn resulted in an increased demand for servile labor to produce food for, and service the personal needs of, the ruling elites. From about 1750 the French development of a plantation economy on Réunion and Mauritius stimulated a larger demand for slaves from eastern Madagascar, which laid the basis for the rise first of the Betsimisaraka polity of the northeast coast and subsequently of the Merina polity of central Madagascar.

The Britanno-Merina treaty of 1820 ended slave exports from Merina territory, but domestic slavery expanded as the Merina in 1825–1826 rejected the British alliance and subjected non-Merina regions of the island to a series of raids; from 1820 to 1853 an estimated one million slaves entered Imerina. However, demand for labor for industrial and agricultural projects continued to grow, as the free population was increasingly subject both to military service and to attack by coastal peoples, notably the Sakalava, who enslaved plateau peoples to retain as agricultural workers and for export. In consequence, there developed a two-way slave trade possibly unique in Africa: highland slaves were exported into the Islamic and European slave-trading systems operating in the western Indian Ocean, and East Africans, predominantly from the Malawi-Mozambique region, were imported to meet Merina demand and for reexport to the French plantation islands (Réunion, Nosy Be, and the Comoros). From 1820 to 1880 possibly ten to eleven thousand African slaves were imported into Madagascar annually, signifying the emergence of Madagascar as a major center in the East African slave-trade network.

Despite this influx, owing to low birth and high mortality rates, the slave population of Imerina remained stable. The preponderance of female slaves following the 1820 decision to kill male captives, combined with a sharp sexual division of slave labor and a rigid caste prohibition against sexual relations between slaves and the "free" population, limited Malagasy slave reproduction. Non-Merina slaves were frequently accused of witchcraft and sorcery and in consequence bore the brunt of the Malagasy *tangena* nut poison ordeal, approximately one-third of whose victims died. Also, porters—all slaves from the 1830s on—proved highly vulnerable to imported illnesses; such was the case with the influenza epidemic of 1893.

Slavery was traditional in most Malagasy societies, slaves comprising in the main kidnap and battle victims from neighboring communities of the same eth-

nic group, and from other Malagasy peoples. However, increased demand for slaves in Imerina, where from about 1817 to 1895 an estimated 33 percent of the population were slaves, rising to two-thirds in the capital of Antananarivo, led to an elaboration of the structure of slavery. The *mainty* (literally, "black"), or slave, was ordered in a hierarchy of three endogamous groups. Those of lowest status comprised "Mozambiques" or "Makua," recently imported Africans. Ranked above them were the *andevo*, non-Merina Malagasy peoples enslaved in Merina slave raids or battle. The highest ranking group, from which the monarch drew to fulfill important ritual tasks, was the *zazahova* ("children of the *hova*"—the lower of the two free Merina castes), divided into two groups: *olomainty* ("black people"), hereditary slaves—possibly descendants of slaves imported into the island by the first settlers—who, like the "Mozambiques," could not purchase liberty; and a second group comprising Merina enslaved mainly for indebtedness or crime—although in periods of famine some parents would sell their children into slavery.

Slaves were traditionally employed in agriculture and in domestic service. From about 1810 their influx into Imerina was so great that they largely replaced free agricultural labor. However, economic stagnation from 1830 on forced most ordinary Merina to sell their slaves. The resulting shortage of slave labor in agriculture encouraged polygamy, and led to the development of "wife markets"; by midcentury wives sold for twenty to thirty dollars less than single female slaves, who could command prices of up to one hundred dollars. Slave ownership became increasingly concentrated in the hands of the court elite, who used them alongside *fanompoana*, or forced and unremunerated labor, in large-scale state agricultural and industrial projects, and to cater to their private agricultural and domestic needs—performed mostly by males and females, respectively. Surplus male slaves were hired out to foreigners, most as porters, notably on the chief commercial routes between Antananarivo and the main ports of Toamasina and Mahajanga. Slave porters were estimated to have numbered sixty thousand by 1896.

Few *zazahova* redeemed themselves even when they had access to the requisite fund. First, slaves represented the chief capital resource in precolonial Madagascar and in consequence were generally well treated. This was particularly the case for *zazahova*, who shared the same cultural attributes and values as their owners. Second, slaves could gain status, notably through religion; some male slaves achieved high office in the Christian church from the 1820s on, while female slaves played important roles, notably as mediums, in traditional ancestral religion. Slaves for hire consti-

In this mid-nineteenth-century engraving, slaves are shackled at the Shaka slave market before being sent to locations in the trading network of the western Indian Ocean. [Library of Congress/Corbis]

tuted the only sizable salaried workforce in Madagascar and, as they generally retained between one-third and two-thirds of their earnings, had the opportunity to accumulate capital. By contrast, redemption was an unattractive option, as it entailed subjection to *fanompoana,* which was both unsalaried and increasingly extortionate.

However, *zazahova* convicted of treason and non-*zazahova* slaves were not as well treated, often being subjected to the poison ordeal and employed in more arduous work, such as in industrial projects and on the east coast plantations. Slaves of this category were more liable to rebel. Slaves were involved in the destruction of the industrial center of Mantasoa in the 1850s and in plantation revolts. Many fled to form "slave republics," which also attracted free Merina deserters from *fanompoana.* It was a vicious circle, for such refugees lived by slave raiding, thus accentuat-

ing the misery of ordinary subjects and encouraging a greater exodus from the land.

Depopulation in a labor-intensive economy rendered the Merina state desperate for additional sources of labor. In 1877 the state "liberated" into *fanompoana* an estimated 150,000 Mozambiques, without compensation to their owners, and imports of African slaves increased, rising in the 1880s to about ten thousand per annum. However, the 1883–1885 Franco-Merina war undermined what little authority the Merina possessed on the west and southwest coasts and led to a dramatic increase in raids into the imperial Merina heartland for slaves whom French merchants purchased in exchange for arms. Thus the labor shortage in Imerina continued. This was reflected in the average price of a slave, which rose, with fluctuations, from three dollars in 1820, to around thirty-six dollars by 1850, to sixty dollars by 1870. Although the price fell following the 1877 emancipation and during the 1883–1885 war, it subsequently recovered to again reach sixty dollars by 1895. However, slave imports failed to stem the flight from the land of the "free" population subjected to *fanompoana*. As a result, agricultural production plummeted, and famine and disease became prevalent.

Disenchantment with the Merina regime grew to crisis proportions, and when the French attacked the island in 1895, resistance was minimal. In 1896 the French officially abolished slavery; an estimated 500,000 slaves were liberated, some 200,000 of whom lived in Imerina. Many chose to remain as servants with their former owners, and all became subject to forced labor imposed by the French colonial regime.

See also MAURITIUS AND RÉUNION.

BIBLIOGRAPHY

CAMPBELL, GWYN. "The East African Slave Trade, 1861–1895: The 'Southern' Complex." *International Journal of African Historical Studies* 22 (1) (1989): 1–27.

———. "Labour and the Transport Problem in Imperial Madagascar, 1810–1895." *Journal of African History* 21 (1980): 341–356.

———. "Madagascar and Mozambique in the Slave Trade of the Western Indian Ocean, 1800–1861." In *The Economics of the Indian Ocean Slave Trade in the Nineteenth Century,* edited by W. G. Clarence-Smith. 1989; pp. 166–193.

———. "Slavery and Fanompoana: The Structure of Forced Labour in Imerina (Madagascar), 1790–1861." *Journal of African History* 29, no. 2 (1988): 463–486.

———. "The State and Precolonial Demographic History: The Case of Nineteenth-Century Madagascar." *Journal of African History* 31, no. 3 (1991): 415–445.

ELLIS, WILLIAM. *History of Madagascar.* 1838.

FILLIOT, J. M. *La traite des esclaves vers les Mascareignes au XVIIIe siècle.* 1974.

FREEMAN, J. J., and D. JOHNS. *A Narrative of the Persecution of the Christians in Madagascar.* 1840.

SHAW, GEORGE A. "The Betsileo: Country and People." *Antananarivo Annual and Madagascar Magazine* 11 (1877).

SIBREE, JAMES. "Origin and Division of the Malagasy People." In *The Great African Island.* 1880. Reprint, 1969; pp. 109–182.

Gwyn Campbell

Economic Interpretation of Slavery

The economic interpretation of slavery grapples with issues such as the profitability of slavery to individual slaveowners, the efficiency of slavery relative to other production methods, the behavioral incentives used by masters to increase output, and the contribution of slavery to economic growth. Economic analyses of slavery focus primarily on measurable variables, including prices, wages, and quantities of inputs and outputs. Cultural, legal, moral, and political aspects of slavery are not typically analyzed for their own sake but rather are viewed as institutional factors that may have affected quantifiable variables. By centering upon the pecuniary features of slavery, economics therefore helps explain why this evil institution persisted in the antebellum U.S. South—because it profited those whom it served.

Perhaps the most controversial book ever written about American slavery is *Time on the Cross,* published in 1974 by Robert Fogel and Stanley Engerman. These scholars were among the first to use modern statistical methods, high-speed computers, and masses of data to answer a series of questions about the economics of slavery. Their research led them to conclude that investments in slaves generated high rates of return, that masters held slaves for profit motives rather than for prestige, and that slavery thrived in cities and rural areas alike. They also found that antebellum southern farms were 35 percent more efficient than northern ones and that slave farms in the Cotton South were 28.5 percent more efficient than free farms. On the eve of the Civil War, slavery flourished in the South and generated a rate of economic growth comparable to that of many European countries, according to Fogel and Engerman. They also

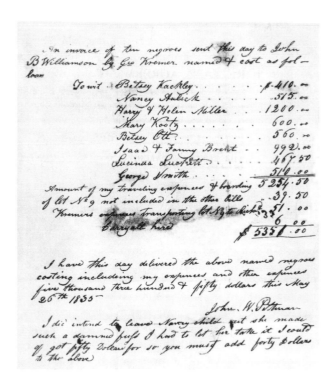

An 1835 invoice for the sale of ten U.S. slaves. [Corbis-Bettmann]

discovered that, because slaves constituted a considerable portion of individual wealth, masters fed and treated their slaves reasonably well. Their findings about profitability and efficiency clashed with those of earlier scholars such as Ulrich Phillips and Charles Ramsdell, as well as with the opinions of many antebellum abolitionists.

Fogel and Engerman, like others who interpret slavery from an economic viewpoint, stressed the similarity between slave markets and markets for other sorts of capital. To find profit levels and rates of return, they built upon the work of Alfred Conrad and John Meyer, who in 1958 had calculated similar measures from data on cotton prices, physical yield per slave, demographic characteristics of slaves (including expected lifespan), maintenance and supervisory costs, and (in the case of females) number of children. To estimate the relative efficiency of farms, Fogel and Engerman devised an index of "total factor productivity," which measured the output per average unit of input on each type of farm. They included in this index controls for quality of livestock and land and for the age and sex composition of the workforce, as well as amounts of output, labor, land, and capital. The authors used data from probate and plantation records, invoices from the New Orleans slave-sale market, coastwise manifests for shipped slaves, and manuscript schedules for the U.S. censuses of agriculture, population, slaves, mortality, and manufacturing.

Time on the Cross generated praise—and considerable criticism. A major critique appeared in 1976 as a collection of articles entitled *Reckoning with Slavery*. While some critics took umbrage at the tone of the book and denied that it broke new ground, others focused on flawed and insufficient data and inappropriate inferences. Despite its shortcomings, *Time on the Cross* unarguably brought people's attention to a new way of viewing slavery. The book also served as a catalyst for much subsequent research, including a collection of essays edited by Hugh Aitken called *Did Slavery Pay?*, Roger Ransom's and Richard Sutch's assessment of the costs of emancipation (*One Kind of Freedom*), Claudia Goldin's *Urban Slavery in the American South*, and Gavin Wright's *The Political Economy of the Cotton South*. Kenneth Stampp's 1956 book *The Peculiar Institution* and Yasukichi Yasuba's 1961 article "The Profitability and Viability of Slavery in the U.S." provided important precursors to *Time on the Cross* and also helped shape the debate on the economics of slavery. Even Eugene Genovese, long an ardent proponent of the belief that southern planters had held slaves for their prestige value, finally acknowledged that slavery was probably a profitable enterprise (see his introduction to the 1989 edition of *The Political Economy of Slavery*). Fogel himself refined and expanded his views in a 1989 book, *Without Consent or Contract*. Two accompanying volumes contain helpful technical papers written by Fogel's fellow researchers.

See also CAPITALISM AND SLAVERY; ECONOMICS OF SLAVERY; HISTORICAL APPROACHES TO SLAVERY.

BIBLIOGRAPHY

AITKEN, HUGH G. J. *Did Slavery Pay? Readings in the Economics of Black Slavery in the United States.* 1971.

CONRAD, ALFRED H., and JOHN R. MEYER. "The Economics of Slavery in the Antebellum South." *Journal of Political Economy* 66 (1958): 95–130.

DAVID, PAUL A., HERBERT G. GUTMAN, RICHARD SUTCH, PETER TEMIN, and GAVIN WRIGHT. *Reckoning with Slavery: A Critical Study in the Quantitative History of American Negro Slavery.* 1976.

FOGEL, ROBERT W., and STANLEY L. ENGERMAN. *Time on the Cross: The Economics of American Negro Slavery.* 1974.

GENOVESE, EUGENE. *The Political Economy of Slavery: Studies in the Economy and Society of the Slave South.* 1989.

GOLDIN, CLAUDIA D. *Urban Slavery in the American South, 1820–1860.* 1976.

PHILLIPS, ULRICH B. *American Negro Slavery: A Survey of the Supply, Employment, and Control of Negro Labor as Determined by the Plantation Regime.* 1918.

RAMSDELL, CHARLES W. "The Natural Limits of Slavery Expansion." *Mississippi Valley Historical Review* 16 (1929): 151–171.

RANSOM, ROGER L., and RICHARD SUTCH. *One Kind of Freedom: The Economic Consequences of Emancipation.* 1977.

STAMPP, KENNETH M. *The Peculiar Institution: Slavery in the Antebellum South.* 1956.

WAHL, JENNY B. *The Bondsman's Burden: An Economic Analysis of the Common Law of Southern Slavery.* 1997.

WRIGHT, GAVIN. *The Political Economy of the Cotton South: Households, Markets, and Wealth in the Nineteenth Century.* 1978.

YASUBA, YASUKICHI. "The Profitability and Viability of Slavery in the U.S." *Economic Studies Quarterly* 12 (1961): 60–67.

Jenny Bourne Wahl

Economics of Slavery

Slavery is fundamentally an economic phenomenon. Throughout history, slavery has existed where it has been economically worthwhile to those in power—that is, where masters have derived either market profits or other sorts of net benefits from having slaves supply services that masters otherwise would have had to provide for themselves. Certain conditions enhance the probability that any given society might hold slaves—cheaply obtainable supplies of foreigners (especially those with physical, linguistic, or cultural features distinct from those of the reigning class), a division of production processes into series of simple and easily monitored tasks, and well-developed markets that sell specialized commodities for specie. But slavery has flourished in many places, regardless of religion, climate, or cultural attainments.

Economic Features of Slavery

Central to the economic success of slavery are political and legal institutions that validate the ownership of other persons. Some slave societies have considered slavery a part of the natural order of things; others have viewed slavery as established only by positive law. Regardless of underlying philosophy, slave societies often craft finely nuanced legal rules that govern the private ownership of slaves. In many instances, these laws reveal economic principles at work. Consider manumission rules. Allowing masters to free their slaves at will would create incentives to free only unproductive slaves, those for whom no one would pay a positive price. Consequently, the community at large would bear the costs of young, old, and disabled former slaves. The public might also run the risk of having rebellious former slaves in its midst. Roman emperor Augustus worried considerably about this adverse selection problem and eventually enacted restrictions on the age at which slaves could be free, the number freed by any one master, and the number manumitted by last will. Antebellum U.S. southern states passed similar laws.

Aside from these sorts of restrictions, societies that permit private ownership of slaves typically confer upon masters the usual rights of property ownership, particularly the right to transfer title. The exchange prices for slaves—often substantial—reflect their economic value. In Sumeria in 2000 B.C. the price of a healthy male slave could be a date plantation grove. In early Athens, slaves cost about a year's keep; prices soon rose significantly as slaves went to work as managers, secretaries, and civil servants, in addition to performing chores in fields, quarries, mines, and kitchens. Eight oxen bought a slave among the Anglo-Saxon tribes in the mid-400s. Prime field hands went for four to six hundred dollars in the United States in 1800, thirteen to fifteen hundred dollars in 1850, and highly skilled slaves sold for up to three thousand dollars on the eve of the Civil War. Even controlling for inflation, the prices of U.S. slaves rose significantly in the six decades before South Carolina seceded from the Union.

Prices also serve as sophisticated signals of overall market conditions and characteristics of particular slaves. As supply expands, prices fall. The price of Egyptian slaves in the fourth century dropped dramatically, for example, when the sale of babies became legal. Conversely, the price of U.S. slaves rose upon the close of the international slave trade, as did slave prices after the ravages of the Black Death. Studies of ancient Rome, fifteenth-century Spain and Portugal, and the antebellum U.S. South all reveal that the prices of slaves varied by their sex, age, skill levels, and physical condition. One pricing variant appeared in the West Indian "scramble." Here, owners and agents devised a fixed-price system, dividing slaves into four categories, penning them up accordingly, and assigning a single price per pen. Potential buyers then jumped into the pens, attempting to pick off the best prospects for the price. One review of slave prices in the Spanish colonies uses economic theory to explain the steeper price profile for unskilled slaves: because the human capital associated with physical strength depreciates more quickly than that related to skills and training, so too do prices of unskilled labor fall relatively faster as such workers age. One interesting influence on prices has to do with childbearing. Fertile female slaves sold for a premium in the U.S. South. In contrast, men who impregnated female slaves in medieval Italy had to compensate the slaves' masters—because childbirth deaths were so common, Genoan men could even buy indemnification insurance against this possibility.

Slave Markets

Throughout history, slaves have suffered not only the travails of enslavement itself but also the humiliation of public sale. Several early societies set up thriving markets for trade in slaves. Greek slaves sold like other commodities, in the agora. Many Roman slaves started out as prisoners of war: because field commanders could dispose of prisoners as they wished, Roman slave dealers simply began traveling along with the army to snap up likely specimens. Judging from the distribution of Italian wine jars in Gaul, wine was evidently exchanged for Gallic slaves in the first and second centuries B.C. The slave trade generated so much gold for Western Europe—gold that was necessary for trade with the East—that the early ninth-century Church made little headway in its abolition campaign. In his writings, Hernando Cortés left a description of the large number of slaves brought to auction at the great marketplace near Tenochtítlan (present-day Mexico City).

Slave markets also existed across the antebellum U.S. South. Even today, one can find stone markers like the one next to the Antietam battlefield, which reads: "From 1800 to 1865 This Stone Was Used as a Slave Auction Block. It has been a famous landmark at this original location for over 150 years." Private auctions, estate sales, and professional traders facilitated easy exchange. Established dealers like Franklin and Armfield in Virginia, Woolfolk, Saunders, and Overly in Maryland, and Nathan Bedford Forrest in Tennessee prospered alongside itinerant traders who operated in a few counties, buying slaves for cash from their owners, then moving them overland in coffles to the lower South. In his monumental study, the economic historian Michael Tadman found that slaves who lived in the upper South faced a very real chance of being sold by their owners for speculative profits. Along with the U.S. slave-sale markets came far-seeing methods for coping with risk, such as explicit—and even implicit—warranties of title, fitness, and merchantability.

Perhaps the most highly developed market of its time, however, was the lucrative African slave trade. From 1500 to 1900, an estimated twelve to eighteen million Africans left their homes to go west to the New World, with about ten to thirteen million of them completing the journey. Africans were sold east as well as west: millions of them made the long trek across their own continent to Arab, Asian, and even some European countries. Some six million African slaves were sent from sub-Saharan Africa eastward;

another eight million remained enslaved on their own soil.

The Atlantic Trade

Public and private documents have yielded up a wealth of information about the economics of the Atlantic trade. Via licensing arrangements, Portugal and Spain began importing African slaves into their colonies in the early 1500s to replace the dying native population. Traders could acquire slaves in specific African zones, then sell them in America—up to 120 per year per Brazilian planter, for example. Because prices for Brazilian licenses were cheaper, traders applied for these, then rerouted their vessels in search of extra profits.

The evils of the trade expanded when Britain replaced Spain and Portugal as the major trafficker in African slaves. Many profited from the infamous "trading triangle": European captains plied the chieftains of West Africa with liquor, guns, cotton goods, and trinkets. In exchange, Africans supplied slaves to suffer through the arduous Middle Passage to the

Slaves are examined at the mouth of the Gambia River before being loaded for transport. [Library of Congress/Corbis]

West Indies and the Americas. The New World in turn sent molasses, rum, sugar, tobacco, rice, indigo, and cotton back to the Old. One innovative study even links the rise in tooth decay in Britain to the slave trade. It suggests that sugar in one's tea increasingly signified respectability, so even the working class could enjoy rotting teeth in their quest for social standing as sugar flowed freely and cheaply back to England.

Commanders of slave vessels and their financial backers made fortunes from the Atlantic trade. Transporting slaves was a major industry in the seventeenth and eighteenth centuries, with the Royal African Company a principal player for at least five decades. The economic historian David Galenson, in his study of the company, uncovered a picture of closely connected competitive economic markets in Africa and America that responded quickly to economic incentives. Despite its size, the company was hardly a monopoly—hordes of small ship captains found the trade worthwhile, with the principal costs being those associated with purchasing and transporting Africans, and the prospective profits at least comparable to returns on other sorts of ventures. Many researchers have devoted themselves to ascertaining the exact rate of return that these captain-traders earned, with the most plausible estimates being about 9 to 10 percent. Among these scholars are David Eltis, Seymour Drescher, David Richardson, William Darity, Joseph Inikori, Roger Anstey, and E. W. Evans.

Yet other interests also profited greatly from the Atlantic trade. European banks and merchant houses helped develop the New World plantation system through complicated credit and insurance mechanisms, enjoying substantial returns as part of the bargain. Well-placed African dealers also benefited. In sickening cycles, Sudanic tribes of the fifteenth and sixteenth centuries sold slaves for horses, then used the horses to obtain more slaves. Tribes of the seventeenth and eighteenth centuries similarly traded slaves for guns, then used guns to hunt down more slaves.

But of all who reaped rewards from the Atlantic trade, England and the United States stand out. In the 1940s, West Indian scholar Eric Williams went so far as to suggest that British industrialization was intimately linked to slavery. Without the slave trade to fuel growth in the colonies, Williams claimed, Great Britain could not have become the industrial superpower of the eighteenth and nineteenth centuries that it was. Although Williams's thesis has since largely been discarded, other scholars nevertheless agree that the slave trade benefited the British. Even Elizabeth I made money by investing in slaving ships and captains. David Eltis speculates, in fact, that Britain would have enjoyed higher living standards by

continuing as a slave trader rather than becoming an abolitionist power. Early industry in New England—cotton textiles, shipbuilding, and the like—also had strong connections to the slave trade and slavery. Among those who benefited were the New England families of the Browns, Cabots, and Faneuils.

The Profitability of Slavery

Not only has trading in slaves been profitable through the centuries, so has slavery itself, at least in antiquity and in the New World. As the classical scholar Moses Finley put it, Greek and Roman slave owners went on for centuries believing they were making profits—and spending them. Americans and West Indians found slave owning lucrative as well. In fact, among those who supported the closing of the transatlantic slave trade were several southern slave owners. Why this apparent anomaly? Because the resulting reduction in supply drove up the prices of slaves already living in the United States and, hence, increased their masters' wealth. U.S. slaves had high enough fertility rates and low enough mortality rates to reproduce themselves, so southern slave owners did not worry about having too few slaves to go around.

That slavery was profitable seems almost obvious. Yet scholars have argued furiously about this matter. On one side stand antebellum writers such as Hinton Rowan Helper and Frederick Law Olmstead, and contemporary scholars like Eugene Genovese (at least in his early writings), who speculated that American slavery was unprofitable, inefficient, and incompatible with urban life. On the other side are scholars—particularly economists Alfred Conrad, John Meyers, Stanley Engerman, and Robert Fogel—who marshaled legions of data to support their contention that southern slavery was profitable and efficient relative to free labor. Fogel and Engerman pioneered the use of an index they called "total factor productivity," which measures the ratio of output per average unit of all inputs. They and their students have devoted considerable time and energy to calculating these indices and have concluded that southern slaves, particularly in agriculture, were far more productive than northern free laborers. In this camp of researchers are also those like Claudia Goldin who have found that slavery worked well in urban areas.

This scholarly battle has been won largely by those who claim that New World slavery was profitable. Much like any other businessmen, New World slave owners responded to market signals—adjusting crop mixes, reallocating slaves to more profitable tasks, hiring out idle slaves, and sometimes selling slaves for profit. One instance well-known to labor historians shows that contemporaneous free labor thought that urban slavery may even have worked too well: workers at the Tredegar Iron Works in Richmond, Virginia, went out on their first strike in 1847 to protest the use of slave labor at the works.

A large proportion of the reward to owning and working slaves results from innovative labor practices. Certainly, the use of the "gang" system in agriculture contributed to profits in Roman times as well as in the antebellum period. Treating people like machines pays off handsomely. In the West Indies, for instance, sugar slaves worked in three separate gangs: one harvesting the crop, a second cleaning up after the first, and a third bringing water and food to the others. Planters in the U.S. South also used the gang system to their advantage.

Integral to many gang-oriented operations across the Americas were plantation overseers, who served as agents for often absent plantation owners. Overseers had some authority so they could elicit work from their charges. Yet law and custom alike circumscribed overseers' abilities to administer correction, because slaves represented such a large chunk of their masters' wealth. This balance between authority and accountability worked well enough to turn handsome profits for many planters, particularly those who entrusted reliable slave drivers as liaisons. By the mid-1820s, slave managers actually took over much of the day-to-day operations of plantations in the West Indies.

Antebellum slave owners experimented with a variety of other methods to increase productivity. Masters developed an elaborate system of "hand ratings" in order to improve the match between the slave worker and the job. Slaves could sometimes earn bonuses in cash or in kind, or quit early if they finished tasks quickly. Slaves—in contrast to free workers—often had Sundays off. Some masters allowed slaves to keep part of the harvest or to work their own small plots. In places, slaves could even sell their own crops and produce. To prevent stealing, however, many masters limited the crops that slaves could raise and sell, confining them to corn or brown cotton, for example. Masters capitalized on the native intelligence of slaves by using them as agents to receive goods, keep books, and the like. In some societies—for example, ancient Rome and her offspring, antebellum Louisiana—slaves even had under their control a sum of money called a peculium. This served as a sort of working capital, enabling slaves to establish thriving businesses that often benefited their masters as well. Yet these practices may have helped lead to the downfall of slavery, for they gave slaves a taste of freedom that left them longing for more.

In the United States masters profited from reproduction as well as production. Southern planters encouraged slaves to have large families because U.S. slaves lived long enough (past about age 27) to generate more revenue than cost over their lifetimes. In contrast, the average West Indian slave did not live past his or her mid-twenties. Masters in Jamaica, Haiti, Barbados, and Trinidad therefore behaved differently, establishing much longer periods of breast-feeding (which helped provide a natural protection against subsequent pregnancy). As a result, birth rates among West Indian slaves were relatively much lower.

All of these actions paid off: the great sugar plantations in the eighteenth century and cotton plantations in the nineteenth were the largest privately owned enterprises of their time, and their owners among the richest men in the world. During the three centuries of New World slavery, slave-produced goods—especially sugar—dominated world trade. Accordingly, slaveowners were not the only ones to reap rewards. French, Spanish, Portuguese, Dutch, and Danish citizens also thrived on buying from or selling to slave colonies. So too did cotton consumers, who enjoyed low prices, and northern entrepreneurs, who helped finance plantation operations. As James De Bow put it, without slavery "ships would rot at [the New York] docks; grass would grow in Wall Street and Broadway, and the glory of New York . . . would be numbered with the things of the past."

Society at large shared in maintaining the machinery of slavery as well as in enjoying its yields. All southern states save Delaware passed laws to establish citizen slave patrols that had the authority to round up suspicious-looking or escaped slaves, for example. Patrollers were a necessary enforcement mechanism in a time before standing police forces were customary. Essentially, southern citizens agreed to take it upon themselves to protect their neighbors' interests as well as their own so as to preserve slavery as an institution. Northern citizens often worked hand in hand with their southern counterparts, returning fugitive slaves to masters either with or without the prompting of national and state law. Yet not everyone was so civic-minded. As a result, the profession of "slave-catching" evolved—often highly risky (enough so that insurance companies denied such men life insurance coverage) and just as often highly lucrative.

One potent piece of evidence supporting the notion that slavery provides pecuniary benefits is this: slavery often gives way to other forms of organizing the labor force when the costs and risks of maintaining it become too large. In Europe, for example, serfdom evolved in part as a way of shifting some of the risks of poor crop yields away from masters. A similar system arose within Africa in the nineteenth century. Slaves paid their masters for the right to work on their own; in exchange, masters no longer paid for the slaves' upkeep. The Spanish Crown for a time favored a system of forced labor called *encomienda*, whereby the indigenous population could not be bought, sold, rented, bequeathed, or removed from the area. Scholars have speculated that this form of coercion, relative to outright slavery, reduced threats to the security of the crown's interest. Thus, other types of labor take the place of slaves when slavery costs too much.

In like fashion, slavery replaces other labor when it becomes relatively cheaper. In the early U.S. colonies, for example, indentured servitude was common. As the demand for skilled servants (and therefore their wages) rose in England, the cost of indentured servants went up in the colonies. At the same time, second-generation slaves became more productive than their forebears because they spoke English and did not have to adjust to life in a strange new world. Consequently, the balance of labor shifted away from indentured servitude and toward slavery.

One element that contributed to the profitability of New World slavery was, for several reasons, the African heritage of the slaves. Africans, more than native people, were accustomed to the discipline of agricultural practices and knew metalworking. Some scholars surmise that Africans, relative to Europeans, could better withstand tropical diseases and, unlike Native Americans, also had some exposure to the European disease pool. Perhaps the most distinctive feature of Africans, however, was their skin color. Because they looked different from their masters, their movements were easy to monitor. Denying slaves education, property ownership, contractual rights, and other things enjoyed by those in power was simple: one need only look at people to ascertain their likely status. Using color was a low-cost way of distinguishing slaves from free persons. For this reason, perhaps, early colonial practices that freed slaves who converted to Christianity quickly faded away. Deciphering true religious beliefs is far more difficult than establishing skin color. Other slave societies have used distinguishing marks like brands or long hair to denote slaves, yet color is far more immutable and therefore better as a cheap way of keeping slaves separate from the free population.

The Economic Efficiency of Slavery

So New World slavery was profitable; was it efficient? Roughly speaking, was output per average unit of input higher with slaves than with free workers if one corrects for differences among laborers in benefits received? On this question, controversy remains. Slavery might well profit masters, but only because they exploit their chattel. Fogel and Engerman claim that slaves kept about 90 percent of what they produced.

Inventions such as the cotton gin helped to increase the economic efficiency of the slave system. [Library of Congress/Corbis]

Because these scholars also found that agricultural slavery was 35 percent more efficient than family farming in the North, they argue that slaves actually may have shared in the overall benefits resulting from the gang system. Other scholars contend that slaves in fact kept less than half of what they produced and that slavery, while profitable, certainly was not efficient. Gavin Wright calls attention as well to the difference between the short run and the long run. He notes that slaves accounted for a very large proportion of most masters' portfolios of assets. Although slavery might seem an efficient means of production at a point in time, it ties masters to a certain system of labor that may not adapt quickly to changed economic circumstances. This argument has some merit. Yet many sugar plantations used the most advanced technologies of the day. In Cuba, planters were behind the move to construct railroads. Slave owners were the first to use a variety of new inventions, such as the circular saw. It is true, of course, that different inventions might have arisen had slavery not existed.

What of the profitability and efficiency of slavery in places other than the ancient world and the antebellum Americas? Much less empirical economic work exists on slavery elsewhere, although Orlando Patterson and Eugene Genovese portray slavery in Islamic societies as nonproductive. Yet to the extent that slaves in these regions performed domestic and other chores, they freed masters from drudgery and therefore conferred some benefits, though not necessarily market profits. Even slaves who appear merely ornamental must provide some pleasure to the masters, or else they would go free. One suspects that slavery generally confers monetary benefits upon masters. Still, one can consider slavery an economic entity merely because it provides more benefits—pecuniary or otherwise—than costs.

Slavery in the Twentieth Century

Some of the harshest forms of slavery have come, regrettably, in the twentieth century. Modern weaponry, increased population density, and mass communication and transportation technology have made it that much easier to capture and move purported enemies as well as to incite one's allies to do the same. The classic mechanism of modern slavery, patterned after practices of Nazi Germany and the Soviet Union, is this: those in power arrest suspected opponents of the current political regime, or those considered to be racially or nationally unfit, and throw them into forced labor camps to work under terrible conditions. Unlike slaves in earlier societies, the unfortunates who landed in Nazi and Soviet concentration camps were not privately owned and traded in open markets. Rather, they served as property of the state, sometimes to be rented out to private interests. As such, these slaves represented something far different than their historic counterparts.

From preclassical times through the nineteenth century, masters—including public entities—have typically viewed their slaves as productive investments, as bookkeeping entries in their wealth portfolios, as forms of valuable capital. Slaves in these circumstances could often count on minimal food, shelter, and clothing, and time for rest and sleep. This was true even for government-owned slaves, because these slaves were typically used in money-making enterprises that just happened to be government-run, and they could potentially be sold to private owners. Not so for the "publicly owned" slaves of the twentieth centuries. Because these people were "acquired" at very low cost with public dollars and served primarily as political symbols, their masters had little incentive to care for them as assets. To be sure, when Nazi Germany needed labor to fuel production of its war machinery, the country turned to the inmates of concentration camps. Likewise, the Soviets rounded up peasants to work on public projects and mineral extraction. Various regions across Africa, Asia, America, and Europe have done the same. Yet these sorts of "slaves" are often worth more dead than alive. Killing one's political adversaries makes the state that much easier to run. Exterminating those labeled as unfit "cleanses" society—in a truly twisted sense of the word—and binds together the "chosen." Accordingly, modern forms of mass slavery seem far different institutions than those of earlier times.

Conclusion

Slavery in any time and place cannot be thought of as benign. In terms of material conditions, diet, and treatment, slaves in some societies may have fared as well in many ways as the poorest class of free citizens. Yet, the root of slavery is coercion. By its very nature, slavery involves involuntary transactions. Slaves are property, whereas free laborers are persons who make choices (at times constrained, of course) about the sort of work they do and the number of hours they work. The behavior of former slaves after abolition clearly reveals that they cared strongly about the manner of their work and valued their nonwork time more highly than masters did. Even the most benevolent former masters in the U.S. South, for instance, found it impossible to entice their former chattels back into gang work, even with large wage premiums. Nor could they persuade women back into the labor force: many female ex-slaves simply chose to stay at home. In the end, slavery is an economic phenomenon only because slave societies fail to account for the incalculable costs borne by the slaves themselves.

See also CAPITALISM AND SLAVERY; ECONOMIC INTERPRETATION OF SLAVERY; LAW; OVERSEERS; PECULIUM; PLANTATIONS; PRICES OF SLAVES; ROYAL AFRICAN COMPANY; SLAVE SOCIETIES; SLAVE TRADE.

BIBLIOGRAPHY

AITKEN, HUGH, ed. *Did Slavery Pay? Readings in the Economics of Black Slavery in the United States.* 1971.

ANSTEY, ROGER. *The Atlantic Slave Trade and British Abolition, 1760–1810.* 1975.

BLACKBURN, ROBIN. *The Making of New World Slavery: From the Baroque to the Modern.* 1997.

CONRAD, ALFRED H., and JOHN R. MEYER. *Economics of Slavery in the Ante-bellum South.* 1964.

DUNN, RICHARD S. *Sugar and Slaves: The Rise of the Planter Class in the English West Indies, 1624–1713.* 1972.

ELTIS, DAVID. *Economic Growth and the Ending of the Transatlantic Slave Trade.* 1987.

EVANS, E. W., and DAVID RICHARDSON. "The Economics of Slaving in Pre-colonial Africa," *Economic History Review* 48 (1995): 665–686.

FINLEY, MOSES. *Slavery in Classical Antiquity.* 1961.

FOGEL, ROBERT W. *Without Consent or Contract.* 1989.

FOGEL, ROBERT W., and STANLEY L. ENGERMAN. *Time on the Cross.* 1974.

GALENSON, DAVID W. *Traders, Planters, and Slaves: Market Behavior in Early English America.* 1986.

———. *White Servitude in Colonial America: An Economic Analysis.* 1981.

GENOVESE, EUGENE D., *The Political Economy of Slavery: Studies in the Economy and Society of the Slave South.* 1989.

GOLDIN, CLAUDIA D. *Urban Slavery in the American South, 1820–1860: A Quantitative History.* 1976.

HIGMAN, BARRY. *Slave Population and Economy in Jamaica, 1807–1834.* 1976.

RICHARDSON, DAVID. "The Costs of Survival: The Transport of Slaves in the Middle Passage and the Profitability of the Eighteenth Century British Slave Trade." *Explorations in Economic History* 24 (1987): 178–196.

SHERIDAN, RICHARD B. *Sugar and Slavery: An Economic History of the British West Indies, 1607–1776.* 1947.

SOLOW, BARBARA, and STANLEY ENGERMAN. *British Capitalism and Caribbean Slavery: The Legacy of Eric Williams.* 1987.

STAMPP, KENNETH M. *The Peculiar Institution: Slavery in the Antebellum South.* 1956.

WRIGHT, GAVIN, *Political Economy of the Cotton South: Households, Markets, and Wealth in the Nineteenth Century.* 1978.

Jenny Bourne Wahl

Education of Slaves

This entry includes the following articles: Ancient Rome; United States.

Ancient Rome

Despite the considerable amount that has been written on Roman education, we do not in fact know very much about it as a process. Still less do we know about the education of slaves. Traditionally, Roman children were educated at home in their early years by their mother as well as their father. Fee-paying schools were, however, open to the public as early as the third century B.C. There was no training for crafts in schools; craftsmanship was something to be learned on the job, as an apprentice, after basic literacy and numeracy had been acquired at school. Practical skills were not part of the Roman understanding of "liberal" education, that is, education fit for a free man. We hear of such practical instruction, and the discipline that went with it, in the legal sources such as the *Digest.*

We know that there were ordinary elementary schools open to any member of the public who could pay the teacher, usually a pittance. Such schools taught reading, writing, and simple calculating, including the use of an abacus. It seems likely that quite a high proportion of the population attended them, at least for a couple of years; both graffiti and the prevalence of written notices of all sorts suggest basic literacy, at least in Rome itself. At secondary schools a *grammaticus* taught grammar and literature, both Greek and Latin. Discussion of the texts seems to have provided some instruction in history, philosophy, law, music, and the natural sciences as well as grammar and prosody. It is clear that only a relatively tiny number attended secondary schools, since Suetonius says that sometimes there were as many as twenty of them in Rome, a city of roughly a million. Rhetoric was taught at the tertiary stage, suitable only for the upper classes, and it is inevitably this that we know most about.

It seems probable that the brighter boy slaves raised within the households of all but the poor, at Rome and presumably in the Italian towns, would be sent to elementary school; it would make them much more useful, and therefore more valuable. Owners of all ranks might often take a personal interest in the education of their young slaves; Crassus did, for example, and his household was very profitable for him. We know that both Varro and Cicero thought it desirable for slaves such as farm managers to have not only practical knowledge but also some more general education. In commercial employment some education must have been essential. Doctors often, and architects sometimes, were freedmen; in the Republic they may often have been Greek captives, but later there was no source of civilized prisoners and they must have been slave-born. It is probable that promising slaves were trained and then freed (manumitted) soon after qualification. Their patron, the former owner, could do well from them under the terms that could be imposed on them as the price of manumission. Best known, particularly from Cicero, Pliny the Younger, and Marcus Aurelius, are the slaves or freedmen who read to their owners (*lectores*), who copied books for them or organized their libraries (*librarii*), who were their secretaries (*notarii*), and who acted as their companions when free friends were absent. These slaves and freedmen must have been well educated.

The majority of the grammarians whose schools and teaching were described by Suetonius were freedmen. In Rome teaching was not a liberal profession, any more than medicine was until the later Roman Empire. Certainly the elementary teachers would have been freedmen, perhaps slaves. The nurse, who in practice was the child's first teacher, would always have been a slave; Quintilian remarked that it was important for her to speak properly. Some grammarians, such as Gnipho and Hyginus, taught in the households of great men, even of the emperors. Imperial slave children seem to have been educated within the palace in their own school. Inscriptions record slave pupils between the ages of twelve and eighteen and also staff for the school, including at least one doctor.

Most of the famous teachers seem to have been pupils of other leading teachers, but some were self-taught—such as Remmius, who learned along with the boy to whom he was *paedagogus*. A *paedagogus* was primarily the slave who escorted a boy—or sometimes girl—to school, but some pedagogues must also have taught, for Quintilian held that they too should be educated persons. It is often not easy to make out if someone was a teacher or merely an attendant. What is clear is that the relationship was often affectionate, as is revealed in memorial inscriptions from former pupils, slave as well as free, to their pedagogues, and in some cases from pedagogues to their pupils.

See also ANCIENT ROME.

BIBLIOGRAPHY

BONNER, S. *Education in Ancient Rome.* 1977.
BRADLEY, K. *Slavery and Society at Rome.* 1994.
MOHLER, S. L. "Slave Education in the Roman Empire." *Transactions of the American Philological Association* 71 (1940): 262–280.

O. F. Robinson

United States

While fewer than one in ten slaves in the United States South learned to read and write, slaves widely understood that literacy could be a useful tool for gaining freedom, and education was among the most highly prized symbols of freedom. Slaves saw in literacy a promising strategy for redemption—either earthly redemption, in the case of those who could forge passes and escaped to freedom, or spiritual redemption, in the case of those who could read the Bible. During and after slavery, black and white reformers emphasized the centrality of education in the drive for racial uplift, urging African-Americans to acquire social standing and their own culture through reading.

The education of slaves posed a vexing problem for masters. Even as elite whites created a self-consciously highbrow literacy culture for themselves, their desire for safety and control demanded that they eliminate slaves' access to reading and writing. The popular opinion among whites was that Africans were brutish and ignorant, but at the same time masters who advertised for runaways frequently described them as artful or cunning, and southern legislatures instituted elaborate legal codes to keep slaves separate from the written word. Paternalism toward slaves, perhaps best captured in the historian U. B. Phillip's infamous and influential metaphor of plantations as "the best schools yet invented," further complicated whites' attitudes toward the education of slaves.

Colonial legislatures passed laws prohibiting whites from teaching slaves to read, and while offenders were rarely prosecuted, masters were wary of slaves forging passes or reading newspapers and letters intended for whites' eyes. The publication of abolitionist literature, especially David Walker's insurrectionary pamphlet *Appeal to the Colored Citizen of the World* (1829), alarmed slaveholders and stirred rumors of revolt. Two years later Nat Turner, a literate preacher, led a bloody rebellion against whites in Southampton County, Virginia. Beginning in 1829, a wave of restrictive statutes swept the South, statutes whose language was more specific and whose scope was more inclusive than before, thus at once broadening the scope and sharpening the focus of earlier laws. In addition to the old injunctions against teaching slaves and free blacks, new laws banned the circulation of abolitionist literature in the mails; made it illegal to sell paper, pens, and ink to slaves; and forbade the employment of slaves in print shops.

Despite these legal restrictions, it was impractical and probably impossible to keep the slave population entirely illiterate. Some slaves learned to read secretly; others learned with the aid of sympathetic whites. Many masters, motivated by paternalism (or by paternity), felt that they could best prepare their slave children for freedom by teaching them to read. Christians who believed in the Protestant doctrine of *sola scriptura*—that the scriptures alone could offer salvation for each individual—could not justify withholding the Bible. However, oral instruction, promoted by the Georgia planter Charles Colcock Jones, offered a solution: this involved teaching slaves to memorize the catechism and the scriptures.

Many masters chafed against state laws that limited their control over their property, and they reserved the right either to educate their slaves or to punish them for learning. A number of former slaves interviewed in the 1930s recalled seeing thumbs cut off slaves found in possession of reading material, while others recalled painful whippings and beatings. Octavia Rogers Albert's book *House of Bonding* (1892) suggests the range of whites' responses to slave education in the story of a slave named Stephen who, when caught forging passes, was first threatened with death and then sold to a storekeeper who prized his ability to keep books.

Literacy among slaves and free blacks was highest in urban centers. Cities offered comparatively fluid social relations, and the presence of newspapers, books, and street signs provided both an opportunity and a motive for slaves to learn to read. "It is not unusual to see slaves reading newspapers, and familiar with the current news of the day," a woman visiting Augusta, Georgia, noted in 1860 (Lillian Foster, *Wayside Glimpses, North and South,* 1860; quoted in Wade, 1964). In the mid-1840s, all the churches in Charleston, South Carolina, supported Sunday schools for black children. Slave and free black women are known to have secretly operated schools for slaves in

After the Civil War the literacy rate among blacks in the United States increased significantly, as schools were established during Reconstruction to educate the freed slaves. [Corbis-Bettmann]

Savannah, Georgia; Charleston, South Carolina; and Natchez, Mississippi. In rural areas opportunities for learning to read were fewer, but slave narratives abound with stories of slaves secretly learning to read using Webster's *Elementary Spelling Book*, commonly known as the "blue-back speller."

Perhaps the most famous account of a slave learning to read appears in the *Narrative of the Life of Frederick Douglass* (1845). Douglass found a copy of an antislavery publication, *The Columbian Orator*, which gave him words to describe his enslavement and helped him formulate his own arguments for freedom. He discovered that the fruit of the tree of knowledge left a bitter aftertaste: "I would at times feel that learning to read had been a curse rather than a blessing. It had given me a view of my wretched condition, without a remedy."

Literacy rates among slaves are impossible to know with certainty, but the census of 1870 suggested that literacy rates of African-Americans in the United States South were between 5 to 10 percent. Scarcely a generation later, by the end of the nineteenth century, literacy among African-Americans had jumped almost tenfold, to more than 50 percent.

See also DOUGLASS, FREDERICK; SLAVE CODES; TURNER, NAT; WALKER, DAVID.

BIBLIOGRAPHY

ANDERSON, JAMES D. *The Education of Blacks in the South, 1860–1935.* 1988.

CORNELIUS, JANET DUITSMAN. *When I Can Read My Title Clear: Literacy, Slavery, and Religion in the Antebellum South.* 1991.

JONES, CHARLES COLCOCK. *The Religious Instruction of the Negroes in the United States.* 1842. Reprint, 1969.

WADE, RICHARD C. *Slavery in the Cities: The South, 1820–1860.* 1964

WOODSON, CARTER G. *The Education of the Negro Prior to 1861.* 1919. Reprint, 1968.

Bruce Fort

Egypt

This entry includes the following articles: Ancient Egypt; Greco-Roman Egypt; Medieval Egypt; Ottoman Egypt; Modern Egypt.

Ancient Egypt

There is considerable debate in the scholarly world regarding the existence of slavery in ancient Egypt. The chief difficulty is finding one word in ancient Egyptian that can actually be translated as "slave." The most common term rendered as "slave" in older translations is the word *hem*. This is actually the word for "person" and could be used to refer to the king himself, as in the expression "His Majesty" (literally, person). A secondary meaning of the word is "servant." Thus the high priest was called "the first servant of the god." Hence, the use of the term *hem* in a text referring to service of any kind implies no more than a servant and does not necessarily denote servitude. Similarly, the word *bak*, which has also been translated as "slave," is etymologically speaking the word for "laborer" and thus again has no connotation of bondage. Other words, like *merit*, "dependent," or *hesbu*, "conscript laborer," also have their well-defined place within the ancient Egyptian social structure and in no way indicate any kind of slavery.

Another fundamental problem lies in imposing one country's social structure—imperial Rome's, for example—upon that of another. Much of the agrarian population in ancient Egypt was attached to property owned by a major institution, such as the royal palace or a temple. Such occupants were often recorded as being part of that institution's possessions and owed the fruit of their labor to the institution. Given this situation, it would perhaps be best to speak of serfdom rather than slavery, although that term is also reserved for a particular social institution from another era. Thus when a text mentions the "acquisition" (literally, the bringing) of an individual and some oxen along with a piece of property, the reference here is to the acquisition of the labor value of that individual, that is, what he can produce in a given amount of time, and not the individual himself.

Old Kingdom

In the Old Kingdom (twenty-seventh to twenty-second century B.C.E.), the so-called pyramid age, the basic

Conscripted workers (probably indentured servants) labor in the building of the pyramids. [Corbis-Bettmann]

social structure was twofold: the officials (*ser*), who profited from the population's labor, and the dependents (*merit*), the majority of whom were engaged in agricultural work, but who could also be engaged in specialized crafts. All of these dependents can be considered to have been working for the crown, since in these earlier periods the king essentially owned all of the land in Egypt. The labor for massive construction projects such as the pyramids was gathered through conscription. Workers were brought to the capital city, where they were housed, clothed, and fed by the state. This distribution of food rations in exchange for work came as close as possible to what we call "wages" today. Workmen in the quarries and the men engaged in transporting the stone to the construction site were also levied through a corvée. So-called royal decrees of exemption show that individuals exempted from corvée duty worked for religious foundations. The wages for those workers came out of the temple's revenues.

Middle Kingdom

By the time of the Middle Kingdom (twentieth to seventeenth century B.C.E.), this social structure had not changed significantly, save for a certain amount of freedom granted by the palace to provincial rulers. New terms for the working class emerged in the language, as *baku* (workers) but mostly *hesbu* (conscripts), appear in administrative documents. In these documents the wages were reckoned through intricate calculations using ratios of the number of men necessary for the project multiplied by the cubic content of the material to be moved or erected, which produced figures of man-days needed for a given task. As in the Old Kingdom, the institution of the corvée was the major source of manpower for the state. Although the evidence is scant, it appears that a conscripted laborer worked for a period of two months, after which the individual presumably returned to the agricultural estate whence he had come.

Thus, as Loprieno (1997) succinctly put it, we are once again dealing with service rather than servitude. The only hint at anything resembling slavery at this time comes from notations in administrative documents, which state that desertion from the corvée resulted in forced labor for life. Such individuals were placed in the *khenret*—a term that used to be rendered as "prison" but was more likely the state-run department of labor—and made to work on the *khebsu*, or state-owned farmland. Also relevant for this period is a literary text, the so-called *Satire on the Trades*. This is a catalogue of comparisons between various occupations and the profession of scribe, in which the latter is inevitably said to be a more advantageous under-taking. What is noteworthy is that a "slave" is never mentioned among any of the people derided. This suggests that slavery was not considered part of the social fabric of the time.

New Kingdom

The period of the New Kingdom (sixteenth to eleventh century B.C.E.), with its militaristic and imperialistic outlook, brought a number of foreigners into the social fabric described above. The settling of prisoners of war in Egypt was not a new custom, but there were now enough captives to warrant description in royal texts. As one king recounts, they were "... settled in strongholds ... branded and made into slaves (*hem*), (marked with) a cartouche with my name." At times the king allowed veterans to keep the captured as slaves. What is not clear in such cases, however, is whether the king retained ownership of these slaves and simply gave the veteran their services, that is, their labor value, or whether the captives became outright possessions of the soldiers. These captive foreigners made up the bulk of what could be called slaves in New Kingdom Egypt although the extant contemporary sources do not allow us to define more precisely the legal status of these prisoners of war.

Native Egyptians, however, could also be categorized as such by this time. Some documents show individuals falling into self-imposed servitude as a result of debt, although such cases only appear very late in the New Kingdom, a time of rampant inflation and an uncertain economy. These were called *bak* (laborers), even though their legal status resembled that of the foreign *hem* (slaves). Another instance in which people could be enslaved was as punishment for a crime, recalling the earlier settling of such perpetrators on state-run farmlands in perpetuity.

The legal status of the slaves in this period was no different than that of freemen. Save for the cases in which they were branded, no singularly ill treatment befell them. They could own property; request—and actually expect to receive—emancipation; marry into a free citizen's family, and request that treatment equal to that accorded to a freeman be given to them in a court of law. There is no evidence of the breaking up of families of slaves.

Indeed, as in the earlier periods, the significant social distinction still remained between the class of officials (*ser*) and those obligated to perform labor on their behalf. The latter group could include dependents, cultivators, the staff of a temple or of a royal enterprise, and laborers, as well as slaves. Legally speaking, none of the members of these groups could be distinguished. Rather, what was more important was the function they performed and the institution to which they belonged, be it the royal domains, a temple, large privately owned agricultural holdings, or the like.

Late Period

During the Late Period (the first millennium B.C.E.), documentary evidence for slavery is less frequent than in the New Kingdom. As Egypt's imperial power waned, so did the number of prisoners of war brought into the country. At this time, the terms *hem* and *bak* can now be said to refer to "slaves," although once again it is difficult to ascertain whether the monetary values attached to these individuals referred to their price or to the value of their work, as the wording of an administrative document from the mid-tenth century B.C.E. seems to indicate. In a description of a newly established religious foundation, among the personnel is one field-worker responsible for four *hem* slaves. The document concludes with the following summation: "In total: five men, for an overall value of four *deben* (around 1,000 grams) and one *kite* (nine to ten grams) of silver." In other words, both the free citizen and the slaves are accounted for in the final tally of the labor force in terms of value.

The period introduced new terminology but little else in terms of the composition and status of the labor force. The social distinction between free subjects and slaves appears to have been between the *hem* or the *bak* slaves, and the *nemeh*. *Nemeh*—the word literally meant "orphan"—can be rendered as "freeman," and it referred to individuals who were directly responsible to the royal treasury. The slaves' legal status had changed very little from that of earlier periods, and the circumstances already described still applied.

Noteworthy for this period is the fact that Herodotus (fifth century B.C.E.) did not mention slaves among the seven classes of Egyptians he enumerated, nor did Diodorus Siculus, a Greek historian writing during the first century B.C.E. From the absence of such remarks, we can gather that slaves appear to have been generally low in numbers at this time, and that, in fact, slavery seems to have had little impact on the economy of Egypt in any period.

See also ARCHAEOLOGY OF SLAVERY; LABOR SYSTEMS.

BIBLIOGRAPHY

BAKIR, ABD EL-MOHSEN. *Slavery in Pharaonic Egypt.* 1952.
CRUZ-URIBE, EUGENE. "Slavery in Egypt during the Saite and Persian Periods." *Revue internationale des droits de l'antiquité* 29 (1982): 47–71.
EYRE, CHRISTOPHER. "Work and the Organisation of Work in the New Kingdom." In *Labor in the Ancient Near East*, edited by M. A. Powell. 1987.

HELCK, WOLFGANG. "Sklaven." In *Lexikon der Ägyptologie*, vol. 5. 1984; pp. 982–987.
LOPRIENO, ANTONIO. "Slaves." In *The Egyptians*, edited by Sergio Donadoni. 1997.
MENU, BERNADETTE. "Le régime juridique des terres en Égypte pharaonique: Moyen Empire et Nouvel Empire." *Revue historique de droit française et étranger* 49 (1971): 555–585.
WESTERMANN, W. L. *Upon Slavery in Ptolemaic Egypt.* 1929.

Ronald J. Leprohon

Greco-Roman Egypt

Although slavery existed in Greek (332–30 B.C.), Roman (30 B.C.–A.D. 284) and Byzantine Egypt (A.D. 284–642), it certainly did not play a preponderant part in economic and social life. Greek settlers developed slavery in Egypt, but it seems that the number of slaves in the population, except in Alexandria, was lower than in some cities of the Greek world and the towns and country of Roman Italy. Thanks to census declarations of the Roman period, it can be assessed that slaves represented about 13.5 percent of the population in the cities and 9 to 10 percent in the villages. Soil exploitation relied on a free and very cheap workforce instead of on extensive use of slaves as was the case in Italian *latifundia* and in the mines of Roman Spain. During the Byzantine period large Egyptian estates were exploited by free *coloni*. Although it cannot be denied that slaves were employed in agriculture and artisan workshops, the large majority of the enslaved population was employed in domestic tasks. These household slaves could also sometimes work in the fields and workshops when needed. Indeed, the fewer the number of slaves there were within a *familia*, the less specialized they were. Masters who possessed few slaves, as was often the case in the Egyptian countryside, would use them in various employments, not only in domestic tasks.

It seems that the servile population was renewed or increased through natural reproduction. Some cases of enslaving war prisoners are known. Slavery through debt is attested in the Byzantine period. Under Greek domination the state alone would have had the right to enslave the insolvent debtors. During the Roman period rearing of abandoned children as slaves is well attested. Slave trade existed, but nearly nothing is known about its structure. Foreign slaves imported into Egypt mainly came from the eastern part of the Mediterranean basin and from sub-Saharan Africa. In the Greek and Roman periods export of Egyptian slaves was under close control and sometimes forbidden.

It is impossible to generalize on the social condition of slaves in Greco-Roman Egypt. Some slaves escaped, perhaps because they were ill-treated. However, fugitive slaves had sometimes robbed their masters.

Slave manumission existed in Greek Egypt but is better attested for in the Roman period and the beginning of the Byzantine period. Every slave could hope to be freed at some time or other, provided that he or she reached maturity. According to census declarations of the Roman period, it seems that men were manumitted by their early thirties and women towards the end of their childbearing years.

In conclusion, slavery in Greco-Roman Egypt was very similar to that in other parts of the Greco-Roman world. The main difference was that no large gangs of slaves were to be found in the Egyptian fields.

See also ANCIENT GREECE; ANCIENT ROME; MANUMISSION.

BIBLIOGRAPHY

BAGNALL, ROGER S. *Egypt in Late Antiquity.* 1993; pp. 123–127, 208–214.
BIEŻUŃSKA-MAŁOWIST, IZA. *L'esclavage dans l'Egypte gréco-romaine.* 2 vols. 1974 and 1977. Italian edition 1984.
SCHOLL, REINHOLD. *Corpus der ptolemäischen Sklaventexte,* 3 vol. 1990.
STRAUS, JEAN A. "L'esclavage dans l'Egypte romaine." *Aufstieg und Niedergang der römischen Welt* (2nd ser.) 10, no. 1 (1988): 841–911.

Jean A. Straus

Medieval Egypt

Two distinct institutions of slavery existed in Islamic Egypt from the Arab invasion of 641 C.E. to the Ottoman conquest in 1517. The most ancient form, chattel slavery (in Arabic, *ubudiyya*), had been legally in force for many centuries prior to Muslim rule and was sanctioned under Islamic law, with specific limits placed upon who could be subjugated. Chattel slaves were the personal property of their owners, and as such enjoyed no formal political power or social mobility. But if chattel slaves adopted Islam, they received the prerogatives and accepted the responsibilities of membership in the religious community. Owners performed a meritorious act by freeing such converts. Chattel slavery did not assume economic significance in Egypt owing to the efficient productivity of indigenous peasants who worked the land either as freeholders or as tenants on the estates of absentee landlords. No latifundia or plantation-style systems of agrarian labor, with farmers legally tied to plots of land, existed in Egypt during the Middle Ages, despite the allotment of proceeds from most arable land to members of successive military ruling elites. Since peasants were vulnerable to state intervention and

dependent upon the state for protection from nomadic marauders, they were in no position to dispute a regime's formal ownership of their land or to resist its demands for a majority share of their crops. Nonetheless, under the law, most of Egypt's agrarian laborers were personally free. While in practice their mobility was limited and political opportunities were minimal, under law they were not the property of either their landowners or agents of the government. Chattel slaves (*'abd*, pl. *'abid*; *raqiq*, pl. *ariqqa'*), as personal property, were largely confined to urban households as domestic servants or intimate companions of their owners. Many of these slaves were of Sudanese origin, but female slaves (*jariya*; pl. *jariyat*) were frequently imported from districts of the Caucasus or Central Asia throughout the Islamic period.

The second institution involved the status of military slaves (*Mamluk*; pl. *Mamalik*; literally, one owned). The English term "slave" does not adequately connote either the considerable authority or elevated social station of this category of persons during the Middle Ages in Egypt. When the cadres of free Bedouin soldiers assimilated into the regions they had conquered after approximately 700 C.E., governments attempted to replace the resultant loss of reliable troops with slaves that were loyal to their patron and showed prowess in battle. These military slaves were the Mamluk. In the Abbasid caliphate during the ninth and tenth centuries C.E., military slaves were initially purchased or collected as war booty, primarily from Turkish Central Asia. These pagan youths were trained, and ultimately converted to Islam, to serve as elite troops or praetorian defenders of the ruling dynasty. Mamluks first appeared in Egypt during the autonomous rule of Ahmad ibn Tulun (868–884), himself the son of a Turkish slave officer in Samarra, Iraq. Successive regimes of Ikhshidids (935–969), Fatimids (969–1171), and Ayyubids (1171–1250) employed military slaves, mainly from Central Asia or Circassia but with a prominent representation of Sudanese troops, in conjunction with their freeborn soldiers. But when the last Ayyubid sultan, al-Salih Ayyub, was enthroned in Cairo, he established a large corps of Mamluks to defend against possible rivals from among his Syrian relatives. Following Ayyub's death in 1249, the officers of this corps assassinated the Ayyubid claimant from Damascus and founded an independent regime of Mamluk soldiers that would last until the Ottoman conquest in 1517.

Following its consolidation under Sultan Baybars (r. 1260–1277), this regime became the great power of the central Islamic lands for two and a half centuries. The Mamluk elite monopolized executive and military authority, the upper ranks of which were recruited exclusively from imported slaves. Their offspring and descendants were relegated to the subordinate status of auxiliaries and were denied revenues generated by land allotments (*iqta's*) reserved exclusively for Mamluk soldiers. Following a hierarchy designed by Baybars and his associates, these soldiers were promoted and salaried according to four officer-grades, based on the number of their retainer. Officers (*amirs*) commanded (and equipped) ten, twenty, forty, or one hundred retainers. The latter group of grand amirs led battalions of one thousand soldiers. Numbering between twenty and twenty-five at a given time, these senior officers elected the sultan from among themselves; the rest constituted an advisory council to their designee.

Although the Mamluk sultanate in Egypt never transcended the conspirational political tradition that determined its formation, it successfully administered a vast state extending from Aswan in southern Egypt to the Iraqi frontier on the Euphrates. Until the advent of the bubonic plague (the black death) around 1340, which decimated the population of both Egypt and Syria, the Mamluk sultanate prospered owing to high agrarian yields and lucrative foreign trade linking southern Asia with the Mediterranean through the Red Sea and Isthmus of Suez. Despite the slave origins of the sultan, he was recognized as the paramount monarch of Sunni Islam because of his dominion over all four holy cities: Mecca, Medina, Jerusalem, and Hebron. No foreign competitor in Europe or Southwest Asia posed a tangible threat to Mamluk suzerainty until the final years of the fifteenth century, when the international balance of power shifted radically with the arrival of the Turks, and of gunpowder weaponry. Because Mamluks confined their factional quarrels to themselves, the mass of the civil population and its productive sectors remained largely unscathed until insurmountable fiscal crises compelled the regime to stave off insolvency with predatory measures. Cairo, Damascus, and Aleppo flourished as luminous cultural centers while the literary arts experienced a renaissance of refinement. The Mamluk elite invested heavily in charitable endowments (*waqfs*) that supported a sophisticated scholarly class in these cities. Since the sultanate's economy never surmounted the famines and plagues of the fifteenth century, it devised no effective means of coping with the threats of invasion from Asia Minor and encroachment on sea routes by European cursairs and navigators that became formidable after 1500. It therefore succumbed to the Ottoman Turks in 1516–1517. Yet, despite its factional turbulence, this regime of military slaves left an indelible mark on administration of Egypt that carried over into modern times. Its bureaucracy, cultural tradition, and social order assumed their contemporary character during the Mamluk period. The Mamluk sultanate imparted to this country a legacy of security that later governments have sought to emulate, though with less success.

See also CHATTEL SLAVERY; ISLAM; MILITARY SLAVES.

BIBLIOGRAPHY

AYALON, DAVID. "Aspects of the Mamluk Phenomenon, A & B." *Der Islam* 53 (1976): 196–225; 55 (1977): 1–32.
———. "Mamluk." In *Encyclopaedia of Islam*, 2nd ed., vol. 6, pp. 314–321.
———. "Studies on the Structure of the Mamluk Army: I, II, III." *Bulletin of the School of Oriental and African Studies* 15 (1953): 203–228, 448–476; 16 (1954): 57–90.
BRUNSCHVIG, R. "'Abd." In *Encyclopaedia of Islam*, 2nd ed., vol. 1, pp. 24–40.
HOLT, P. M. "Mamluks." In *Encyclopaedia of Islam*, 2nd ed., vol. 6, pp. 321–331.
HUMPHREYS, R. STEPHEN. "The Emergence of the Mamluk Army." *Studia Islamica* 45, 47 (1977): 67–99, 147–182.
RABIE, HASSANEIN M. *The Financial System of Egypt, A. H. 564–741/A.D. 1169–1341.* 1972.

Carl F. Petry

Ottoman Egypt

Slavery, both black and white, has a long history in Egypt—Alexandria and Cairo having served as a crossroads between Central Asia and Africa, especially for the black slave trade, centuries before the arrival of the Ottomans in 1517. The conquest of Egypt gave the Ottomans control over the two holy cities of Mecca and Medina, making them nominal leaders of the Muslim world and reducing Egypt to a province.

To enter Cairo, the Ottomans had to defeat the Mamluks (1250–1517), a unique dynasty based on slaves recruited from the Caucasus area, initially Kipchaks and then Circassians, but generally denoted Turks. Mamluks (Arabic, "enslaved"), essentially a military caste, were manumitted upon entrance into the private armies of the grand households of their patrons and maintained fierce loyalty against rival households. After the conquest, they clashed continually with the seven regiments of the Ottoman Janissary guard, who served the newly appointed Ottoman governor (*pasha*) of the province. Mamluk households continued to hold numerous important local offices and participated in street rivalries as Ottoman control waxed and waned, especially in the middle decades of the eighteenth century when the Qazdağlı faction dominated city politics. The Mamluks were defeated by Napoleon at the Battle of the Pyramids in 1798 and were finally eliminated in 1812 by Muhammad Ali

Depiction of the massacre of the Mamluks by Muhammad Ali and his troops. [Corbis-Bettmann]

(1769–1841), initially appointed as governor by the Ottomans.

Egyptian caste rule meant that slavery, military and household, was a means of independence from local landholding elites, making the Cairo context different from the rest of the Ottoman Empire. The regimental officers and teachers of new Mamluk recruits were frequently eunuchs, black and white, who represented a second kind of slave trade in Egypt. Eunuchs (*khadīm*, "servants") were prized for use in harems as well and were distributed from the Cairo market all over the Muslim world. Black eunuchs served in the mosques of Mecca and elsewhere, accompanied their masters on caravans, and were often their owners' confidants and agents. Many acquired great power, notably the chief black eunuch of the imperial harem in Istanbul, who was enormously influential in the mid-seventeenth century, largely because of his control over the annual Meccan tribute that Cairo sent to Istanbul. Eunuchs in Cairo were predominantly from black Africa and were castrated upon being captured.

Mortality rates must have been tremendously high, perhaps as high as ten deaths, if not more, for each survivor (Gordon, p. 96)

Black and white domestic slaves were ubiquitous in Egypt, as elsewhere in the Ottoman Empire, a practice embedded in all Middle Eastern societies before 1900. While Islamic law does not forbid slavery, it goes a long distance to ameliorate the condition of the slave, insisting on certain protections, especially of female slaves, and also promoting the virtues of manumission. Manumission became a pious act, but this had the effect of encouraging a continual trade in slaves, to replenish the ranks. In the Egyptian slave market slave traders and owners included merchants of all ethnic and religious groups. Female slaves predominated—they were generally valued more highly than men for domestic use and as concubines—although use of slaves on plantations was historically less widespread. It is estimated that the trade in slaves to the Muslim world from Africa ran at 8,000 a year in the sixteenth century to as high 10,000 to 12,000 per year by the early decades of the nineteenth century (Gordon, pp. 148–149, 159). Probably half to two-thirds ended up in the market in Cairo. One rare census of slaves, in 1850, listed 11,481 in Cairo, at a ratio of three females to one male (Gordon, p. 58).

The black slave trade in Egypt was stimulated by Muhammad Ali's challenge to Ottoman rule. In an effort to raise an army, Muhammad Ali invaded the Sudan in 1820 to round up as many as twenty thousand black slaves for his new army. Only after the black troops failed as soldiers did he resort to mass conscription of the peasantry. This campaign, coupled with increased cotton cultivation and other kinds of plantation crops in East Africa, as well as a decline in the Caucasus slave trade owning to Russian colonization, led to a stimulation of the black slave trade just as Western pressure for its abolition intensified. The trade in black slaves was legally abolished by the Ottoman government in 1846, but enforcement in Egypt was difficult. This prohibition was renewed by Sultan Abdülhamit II (1842–1918). In 1877 the Convention for the Suppression of the Slave Trade between Britain and Egypt attempted to stem the flow of slaves from the Sudan. This effort was repeated in 1895, after the British occupation of Egypt in 1882, and effectively ended the trade. Manumission was officially undertaken in Egypt throughout the last three decades of the nineteenth century; perhaps as many as 18,000 slaves were freed (Gordon, p. 180; Erdem, p. 171) Growing social awareness, coupled with frequent admonitions from Western and Ottoman governments alike, eliminated most slavery in Egypt by 1900.

See also EUNUCHS; JANISSARIES; OTTOMAN EMPIRE.

BIBLIOGRAPHY

BRUNSCHVIG, R. "'Abd." In *Encyclopedia of Islam*, 2nd ed., vol. 1, pp. 24–40. 1960.
ERDEM. Y. HAKAN. *Slavery in the Ottoman Empire and Its Demise, 1800–1909*. 1996.
GORDON, MURRAY. *Slavery in the Arab World*. 1989.
HATHAWAY, JANE. *The Politics of Households in Ottoman Egypt: The Rise of the Qazdağlı*. 1997.
TOLEDANO, EHUD. *Slavery and Abolition in the Ottoman Middle East*. 1997.

Virginia H. Aksan

Modern Egypt

When Napoleon's troops landed in Egypt in 1798, slavery there was already as old as the pyramids. French scholars accompanying Napoleon described slavery in Egypt and the thousands of slaves imported annually across the Sahara from Sinnar and Dar Fur (in the Sudan). Until 1820, trans-Saharan slave dealers openly sold slaves in a market (*wakālat al-jallāba*) in Cairo, as well as in other major Egyptian towns. Although most slaves in Egypt were from black Africa, more than one in five were from other ethnic groups, mostly Circassians from the Black Sea region. Three-quarters of the slaves were females, and several thousand were eunuchs.

Slaves in Egypt worked in homes, in the military, and in agriculture. Slaves most commonly worked in wealthy Egyptian homes as cooks, doormen, maids, pageboys, or concubines. Slave soldiers were common in Muslim states, and the Mamluk dynasty in Egypt had begun with slaves (*mamluks*) brought from the Balkans by the Ottomans to serve as soldiers in their Egyptian province. The Mamluks gradually took control of Egypt, yet remained loyal to the Ottoman Empire.

Muhammad Alī, viceroy of Egypt from 1805 to 1849, extended slavery from urban homes and the military barracks into the fields of the lower Nile Valley. In 1821 Egyptian forces invaded Sudan with instructions to bring back black slaves suitable for agricultural work. Some of the captives served in the Egyptian army as slave soldiers in increasing numbers from 1821. Imports of these slaves to Egypt grew as Muhammad Alī modernized the Egyptian economy, emphasizing production of cotton, indigo and sugar. In Egypt, each of these crops required irrigation, and on the large estates of the wealthy, slaves did this work. They also worked in new sugar mills and in the fields of Upper Egypt. Because Egyptian armies in the Sudan captured and enslaved thousands of Sudanese each year, slaves were plentiful and inexpensive in Egypt until 1838. Between 1838 and 1840, conservative estimates of the slave population of Cairo range from 22,000 to 30,000, less than one percent of a total Egyptian population of just over four million.

In 1854 under diplomatic pressure from the British government, Egypt banned further import of Sudanese slaves. Despite this prohibition, slaves were smuggled into Egypt along the Nile in boats, and across the Sahara via the Forty-Day Route. This route connected Asyut in Upper Egypt to the Dar Fur sultanate, which raided for and purchased slaves from central and southern Sudan. During the U.S. Civil War (1861–1865), the federal government's blockade of cotton exports from Southern ports stimulated a cotton boom in Egypt. As Egyptians scrambled to produce more cotton, they put more slaves to work, especially to irrigate cotton fields. Newly prosperous Egyptian cotton growers used some of their profits to buy slaves to serve in their homes.

In principle, Islam regulated slavery in modern Egypt. The buying and selling of slaves was legal until 1854 and covered under commercial law. Slaves could be returned to their sellers if found defective (i.e., ill or pregnant) within a certain time period. Masters were not allowed to physically abuse their slaves. Any child of a free father and a slave mother was free, and the birth of the child freed the mother. The manumission of slaves was a meritorious act in Islam, even though it often occurred only on the master's death.

The lives of Egyptian slaves varied enormously. Eunuchs, concubines, and servants who served in the viceroy's court lived well compared with girls in rural households or men working on sugar plantations. In reality, not all masters followed the regulations of Islam. Some frequently beat their slaves; children born to slave mothers were not always acknowledged by their free fathers; and the mothers remained in slavery. Slaves often died of epidemic disease such as cholera and malaria. Newly imported Sudanese slaves were the most likely to become ill and die, until they adjusted to the changes in diet and the new climate and disease environments.

The end of slavery in Egypt was not accomplished easily. The 1877 Convention between the British and Egyptian Governments for the Suppression of the Slave Trade formalized the earlier ban and set up manumission bureaus to register freed slaves and to aid them in finding work or enrolling in schools. In 1880 the Egyptian government created its own Service for the Abolition of Slavery. These measures led to about 18,000 registered manumissions by 1889. In 1895 a further treaty between Great Britain and Egypt led to the more effective prosecution of slave dealers. By 1900 slavery had virtually ended in Egypt itself, although it continued in its Sudanic dependencies along the upper Nile.

See also ISLAM; LAW; SLAVE TRADE.

A slave tends to his master and the master's harem in the late 1800s. [Corbis-Bettmann]

BIBLIOGRAPHY

BAER, GABRIEL. "Slavery in Nineteenth Century Egypt." *Journal of African History* 8 (1967): 417–441.

WALZ, TERENCE. *The Trade between Egypt and Bilād as-Sudān, 1700–1820.* 1978.

George Michael La Rue

Elite Slaves

In Roman legal theory there was no such thing as an elite slave. "There are many classes of free men but men are either free or slave," as Justinian said (*Institutes* 1.3.5). There were in fact certain legal differences, even among slaves. The chief of these differences was that public slaves, *servi publici populi romani,* known from the second century B.C. through the first century A.D., had some rights. So too, in the Empire, did *servi Caesaris,* imperial slaves, and also *servi fisci,* slaves belonging to the fisc or imperial treasury. Further, some slaves (*statuliberi*) were guaranteed to gain their freedom at some future date.

Servi publici populi romani were not simply slaves who were the property of the Roman people; nobody was born to the status of *servus publicus.* They were slaves taken into public service, to act on behalf of the *res publica* with a general administrative function; this public function is why we hear only of males having this status. Such slaves received an annual stipend; further, they seem to have had power to dispose by will of half of their personal fund (*peculium*). From the evidence of the inscriptions *servi publici* seem often to have cohabited with, or even "married," free women (whether freeborn or freed). Their children were free or slave, depending on the status of the mother. While forbidden to wear the toga, the badge of the citizen, these elite slaves seem to have had some special dress. When the Republic gave way to the Empire, the importance of the concept of the *populus romanus* declined.

Wider administrative functions then came to be carried out by those described as *servi Caesaris;* this term was limited to those slaves of the emperor who performed civil service duties. Their cohabitation, in contrast to *servi publici,* was servile, but any children were born as slaves of Caesar. (In this context we occasionally hear also of female slaves, *ancillae Caesaris,* as housekeepers in charge of small imperial properties.) But a slave within the personal fund of a slave of Caesar was not also a slave of Caesar, but of the emperor as an individual. Slaves owned by municipalities were functionally in much the same position as *servi Caesaris;* they too could be born as such, but they probably had no power of testation. However, in the course of the Principate, probably by the beginning of the third century A.D., slaves were excluded from the civil service, even from fiscal administration, and thus this legally distinct category of elite slaves disappeared.

The satirists moralized about the overweening attitude of some slaves. Slaves could be rich—rich in the amount of property they had under their immediate control, rich in the sense of being well-fed, well-dressed, and able to indulge their desires in a way not possible for proletarian free persons—but such slaves were very much in the minority. "Ordinary" elite slaves functioned as managers, land-agents, and normal tenant farmers; we find one reference to a slave acting as a banker without supervision. Others, with whom their owners might have affectionate relations—as Cicero did with Tiro—were secretaries, teachers, philosophers, and physicians; these slaves were closer to members of the modern middle classes.

In social and economic practice, de facto, the status of slaves ranged almost as widely as that of free persons, with a major concentration in the servants' hall. In early Rome slaves had been predominantly farmhands, living almost with the family along with free employees and distant relations. In the period of conquest, in the last two centuries B.C., huge numbers of slaves were forced workers in the latifundia—this was the age of slave revolts. In the earlier Empire free labor gradually returned to the countryside; by the later empire slaves were concentrated in the servants' hall. Elite slaves came into prominence, in contrast with the chained masses, after the conquests of civilized Greek and Hellenistic states. In the Empire they seem to have been a significant top stratum of slave society. But, however arrogantly they might act, all slaves, even slaves of this sort, could find themselves through the death—or the whim—of their owner exposed for sale in the market. They had no security. They did have, however, a high chance of manumission, as did skilled slaves in Greece in managerial positions.

See also ANCIENT GREECE; ANCIENT ROME; LAW; MANUMISSION; PECULIUM.

BIBLIOGRAPHY

BUCKLAND, W. W. *The Roman Law of Slavery.* Chap. 14. 1908

KIRSCHENBAUM, A. *Sons, Slaves, and Freedmen in Roman Commerce.* 1982

WEAVER, P. R. C. *Familia Caesaris.* 1972

O. F. Robinson

Elkins Thesis

In 1959 Stanley M. Elkins published *Slavery: A Problem in American Institutional and Intellectual Life.* At that time scholars had hardly progressed past discussing the morality of slavery as an institution. Wanting to redirect the debate, Elkins used the techniques of social psychology in order to consider the effect of the institution on the slaves themselves. He compared slavery in the United States to slave systems in the Caribbean and Brazil and concluded that U.S. slavery was harsher than that practiced elsewhere in the New World.

Even more controversial was Elkins' contention that slavery in the United States bred among slaves a unique and pervasive personality type, which he called "Sambo." Owing to the plantation's insular nature and the master's paternalistic manner (which Elkins compared to conditions in concentration camps in Nazi Germany), Sambo rarely progressed past infantilism and so he remained loyal, docile, cheerful, playful, lazy, untruthful, and thievish.

Elkins' thesis occasioned a major shift in the debate concerning slavery in the United States. Over the next twenty years a number of historians, many of them profoundly disturbed by his conclusions, generated hundreds of studies concerning the community, family, folk culture, and religion of slaves. These works demonstrated that slaves in the United States succeeded in creating lives for themselves beyond the purview of their masters, and that U.S. slavery was not as debilitating to their psychological development as Elkins claimed. Nevertheless, his work influenced scholars of slavery to use interdisciplinary techniques and forced them to consider the social and cultural aspects of slavery.

See also HISTORICAL APPROACHES TO SLAVERY; HISTORIOGRAPHY OF SLAVERY; STEREOTYPES, SLAVISH.

BIBLIOGRAPHY

DEW, CHARLES B. "The Slavery Experience." In *Interpreting Southern History: Historiographical Essays in Honor of Sanford W. Higginbotham,* edited by John B. Boles and Evelyn Thomas Nolen. 1987.

Charles W. Carey Jr.

Ellison, William   [1790–1861]

Prosperous free African-American cotton gin maker and slaveholding planter in Stateburg, South Carolina.

Born a slave in Fairfield District, South Carolina, William Ellison was a mulatto who was given the name April. The identities of April's parents remain uncertain; his mother was a slave woman and his father was probably a white planter and slave holder, Robert Ellison, or his white son, William. Apprenticed to a white cotton gin maker between 1802 and 1816, April learned how to build and repair the South's most important machine. He also became adept at reading, writing, arithmetic, and all the social skills required to do business with southern white men and women. April purchased his freedom in 1816, moved to Statesburg, and opened a cotton gin shop, the foundation for the life of freedom he crafted for himself and his family. By 1820 he had changed his name from April to William, bought the freedom of his wife Matilda and their daughter, and begun his acquisition of slaves. They first were purchased to work in his cotton gin shop, later, as he prospered and became a landowner, he acquired more to labor in his cotton fields. Aided by help from his three free-born sons, Ellison came to own thirty slaves and more than three hundred acres of land in 1840; by 1860 he had amassed sixty-three slaves and nine hundred acres. Owning more slaves than the ninety-nine percent of the South's white slaveholders on the eve of the Civil War, Ellison was probably the richest African-American in the South who had begun life as a slave. He never allowed any of his slaves to become free and follow his example. Although his economic success vaulted him far beyond his slave origins and won him the respect of his white neighbors, his freedom remained hostage to the contempt most southern whites had for all African-Americans, slave or free.

See also FREE PEOPLE OF COLOR; SELF-PURCHASE.

BIBLIOGRAPHY

JOHNSON, MICHAEL P., and JAMES L. ROARK. *Black Masters: A Free Family of Color in the Old South.* 1984.

———, eds. *No Chariot Let Down: Charleston's Free People of Color on the Eve of the Civil War.* 1984.

Michael P. Johnson
James L. Roark

Emancipation

Scores of nations and empires have undergone the processes of legal emancipation. Three of these—the British Empire, Russia, and Brazil—provide instances of diverse forms of servitude ended by variegated political processes within quite different socioeconomic contexts.

British Empire and Europe

During the eighteenth century, while Britain became the greatest slave trading power, a number of factors

combined to undermine the ideology of slavery. Adam Smith, in his *The Wealth of Nations* (1776) found free labor more profitable than slave. Negrophile literature, such as Samuel Johnson's *Rasselas, Prince of Ethiopia* (1759), challenged racist preconceptions. Methodism and Quakerism combined with evangelical movements within the established churches, and spokesman like Granville Sharp, Thomas Scott, and William Wilberforce, denounced slavery as anti-Christian.

The judicial climate too began to change, with cases such as *Somerset v. Stewart* (1772). Amelioration of conditions of slavery was a halfway house to full emancipation. As early as 1787, Sierra Leone was established as a colony for freed slaves. Reformers began to concentrate on the abolition of the slave trade because that trade was regarded as the most barbarous part of slavery. The goal seemed achievable, and ending the trade would, theoretically, improve the treatment of those already enslaved as their value would grow.

A bill to end the trade was presented to Parliament in 1776 by David Hartley. In 1789 the Dolben Act regulated the trade, while in 1791 a Privy Council inquiry was initiated. A ban on the slave trade was passed in 1807, and the Foreign Office sought cooperation from others in its suppression efforts. A Royal Navy squadron eventually was assigned to West African waters to interdict slavers, and a slave registry system was established.

Detail of a sculpted portrait of Granville Sharp, the noted English scholar, philanthropist, and abolitionist. The portrait was made from a wax model by M. C. Andras. [Corbis-Bettman]

In 1823 the Anti-Slavery Society was formed. Following the Napoleonic Wars, the influence of the West Indies planters began to wane. The tremendous wealth that had obtained seats for them in the Commons and peerages in the Lords was soon overmatched by the growing wealth of the industrialists and the commercial classes.

In 1831 an Order-in-Council set minimum protections for slaves. In December of that year, the bloody suppression of a rising by Jamaican blacks increased British public revulsion.

Parliamentary reform was instrumental in allowing emancipation to pass in 1833. The act, which received Royal Assent on 28 August, provided immediate freedom for children under six, with conversion from slavery to apprenticeship for all others. Agricultural laborers were to serve as apprentices for six years, with all others serving for four. Twenty million pounds was provided for owners' compensation, but India and Ceylon were excluded from the effects of the bill.

In the aftermath of emancipation, the British West Indies went into economic and social decline, although problems with the world price of sugar may have also played a significant role. In response to the chronic shortage of labor following emancipation, immigration from the eastern empire, especially India, was encouraged in those colonies such as the islands of the West Indies where slave labor had played a crucial commercial role.

In 1834 Boer *vortrekkers* left Cape Colony to establish independent Dutch republics in Transorangia and the Transvaal in reaction to emancipation. In the Indian Raj, slavery was banned in Act Five of 1843 and by the Indian Penal Code of 1860.

In France the *Société des Amis des Noirs* was founded in 1788. During the Revolution the National Convention abolished slavery in 1794, but this was merely recognition that slaves on Martinique and St. Domingue had seized their freedom. Napoleon Bonaparte, however, reestablished both slavery and the slave trade in 1802. By this time France's most important slave colony, St. Domingue, had become the independent Republic of Haiti, where slavery no longer existed.

In 1839, under British pressure, Pope Gregory XVI issued an apostolic letter hostile to slavery. When emancipation came in 1848, however, it was through Parisian revolutionaries acting by decree.

In Holland abolition was never as contentious an issue as it was elsewhere. During the Batavian Republic, Dutch revolutionaries refused to abolish slavery, fearing planters would deliberately surrender their colonies to the British. Mild abolitionist activity, assisted by British organizations, operated from the 1830s to the 1860s. In 1844 the Dutch Colonial Minister informed the king that abolition was inevitable, and after

1852, the planters' lobby ceased opposing emancipation and concentrated on compensation for former owners. Emancipation, with immediate freedom in the Antilles and a ten-year apprenticeship elsewhere, with generous planter compensation, became law in 1862.

Russia

While Western Europe moved toward the complete elimination of serfdom after 1600, a "new serfdom," with conditions like those of chattel slavery, arose east of the Elbe. In the mid-nineteenth century, European Russia held forty-seven million serfs.

Enlightenment ideas, including those of Adam Smith, which influenced elites in the Russia of Catherine the Great, together with massive peasant uprisings, turned many against serfdom. Ideas of German Romanticism and the Slavophile Movement intensified opposition to the condition of the peasants, but Russia's defeat in the Crimean War provided the first real impetus for emancipation. In the wake of that war, the imperial government forbade the public sale of serfs or the break-up of families, and in 1817–1818, the Baltic serfs were emancipated.

Nicholas I established a Secret Committee to examine approaches to emancipation and stopped the spread of serfdom. In 1857 under Alexander II, the Nazimov Rescript, an imperial decree, announced the intention to free all serfs. This involved a transition period during which they would remain bound to the soil, after which they were to receive allotments of land, which they were to pay for over a period of years. The April Program (1858) envisioned provincial assemblies of gentry developing reform proposals.

In 1858 and 1859–1860, a Main Committee, composed of two representatives from each province, met to consider those proposals. An Editing Committee drafted a law for all Russia, with refinements for each province, and on 19 February 1861, emancipation was proclaimed. Effects were profound: censorship had been relaxed to allow discussions of the "peasant question," discontentment with "bureaucratized autocracy" spread, and the economic plight of the gentry was exacerbated.

Brazil and Portugal

Portugal outlawed slavery in 1836, although implementation of the law required several years. Brazil's Golden Law of 13 May 1888, abolished slavery without qualification and without indemnification. That law was the culmination of a long process starting with an 1831 treaty with Britain against slave trading. However, more than five hundred thousand slaves were illegally imported after 1831, and many suits by abolitionists were aimed at freeing illegally imported slaves or their descendants. In 1850, Brazil passed an effective domestic law to enforce the ban.

In 1869 the imperial government outlawed the public sale of slaves and the break-up of families. The Rio Branco Law (1871) declared free all children born to slave mothers after the enactment of the law, but such children were to be held in semibondage until twenty-one, unless the slaveholder chose to redeem them with the government at age six.

The War of the Triple Alliance, in which the combined forces of Brazil, Argentina, and Uruguay battled Paraguay, helped delegitimize slavery. Twenty thousand Brazilian slaves fought honorably, thereby winning their freedom. Fear of servile insurrection and the poor performance by Brazilian forces caused many to see slavery as an impediment to modernization. In addition, the crown was tepid in its opposition to slavery, and the Catholic church in Brazil was ambivalent, with some religious orders owning slaves.

An abolitionist press developed, and abolitionist orators and authors, such as Joaquin Nabuco, were highly active after 1870. 1880 saw a major emancipation conference in Rio de Janeiro, which proposed liberation for all slaves over fifty years of age and a term of four to six years during which all others would "earn" emancipation. Outlawing of the interprovincial slave trade was proposed, and an "underground railroad" was arranged by militant abolitionists.

Antiabolitionist mobs attacked abolitionist speakers and organs, while abolitionist mobs prevented the rendition of fugitives, and assassination and servile insurrection increased in the countryside.

Individual provinces, such as Amazonas and Ceara, and cities such as Rio Grande do Sul, instituted local emancipation. The Saraiva-Cotegipe Law of 1885, which freed slaves at the age of sixty but required three more years of service for indemnification of the former owner, split society. Fugitive slave provisions were equally controversial.

The abolition of Cuban slavery in 1886 left Brazil alone as a slave society in the Americas, and mass desertions by slaves and mass manumissions by planters reduced slavery to a hollow shell, as did the law of that year which outlawed even moderate chastisement of slaves. In 1888, amid anarchic conditions, parliament adopted universal emancipation. In the next years, the agricultural economy faltered badly over problems of labor supply, and in 1889, republican agitation and a military revolt ended the monarchy.

Hispanic America

In the chaos following Napoleon's imprisonment of Ferdinand VII, the triumvirate—one of a succession of three-man committees of colonial military and administrative officers who ruled in Argentina while Spain was in the hands of the Napoleonic usurper—decreed the end of the slave trade in the United Provinces (Argentina) in 1812. Although many slaves were freed as a result of military service in the War of Independence, slavery was only abolished in 1853.

The new nation of Uruguay in its constitution of 1830 ended both slavery and the slave trade. Paraguay, poor and isolated, did not end slavery until 1842.

In Chile, under the revolutionary government of Bernardo O'Higgins, the slave trade was abolished in 1811, and all children of slaves were freed. Complete emancipation arrived with the constitution of 1823. When Jose San Martin occupied Lima, Peru, he decreed that all slave children born from 28 July 1821 were free, and this so-called free womb law continued in effect until all the existing slave population of Peru had died off or been manumitted by private charity. In the 1830s and 1840s, Peru resumed participation in the slave trade, but the freedom guaranteed to all the children of slave mothers more than overbalanced the effects of this policy, and slavery continued on a path to extinction.

In the struggle for Venezuelan independence, slaves fought on whichever side they thought promised the best prospects for freedom. Simon Bolivar was an abolitionist who had freed his own slaves, but he had difficulty converting the Creole aristocracy to his position on the issue. The slave trade was proscribed in 1811, but only limited manumission was adopted in 1821 and 1839. In his Bolivian Constitution of 1826, Bolivar had declared slavery ended, but the legislature turned the slaves into peons, bound to the land. Full emancipation was decreed in 1854.

In 1821 the Congress of Cucuta established a slave law for Columbia which freed those born after that date, although they had to serve their masters until age eighteen. Other slaves might be purchased for emancipation if taxes from death duties permitted for the purchases of slaves were to be financed by a fund generated by estate taxes.

Miguel Hidalgo y Costilla and José Morelos, Mexican revolutionaries, attempted to abolish slavery by imposing the penalty of death on slave owners. The slave trade was effectively abolished in 1824 under President Guerro, and slavery was ended in 1829.

In the United Provinces of Central America, slavery was abolished as part of the general Liberal Party's reform program of 1823, which saw not only emancipation but also abolition of noble titles, generous immigration laws, limitations on monopolies, and the adoption of a new constitution in 1824.

In 1870 the Spanish minister for colonies Segismundo Moret prevailed upon the Cortes (legislative assembly of Spain) to pass Moret's Law, which introduced gradual emancipation to Cuba. The children of slave mothers would henceforward be free, and all slaves reaching sixty years of age were also emancipated. The freed children would be raised under the master's "patronage" until arriving at eighteen years of age, and the elderly slaves were entitled to stay with the master if they could not support themselves. All slaves who had served under the Spanish flag in the rebellions would also be freed by government purchase. For those who remained in slavery, whipping was forbidden as was the break-up of families, and the government promised to end all slavery at the earliest possible date.

In November 1879 the Spanish prime minister General Martinez Campos decreed the end of Cuban slavery beginning in 1888. No compensation was offered, but an eight-year *patronato*, or apprenticeship, was established for liberated slaves. Slavery in Puerto Rico had been abolished with compensation in 1873.

In the Danish West Indies the slave trade was abolished by the king in 1792, partly out of humanitarian considerations and partly out of the desire of the slaveholders to stabilize prices within those islands. In 1848, with slave unrest on St. Croix and revolutionary political activity at home, the Danish government freed the 75,000 slaves held on the islands.

Slavery was never extensive in Canada, but some small slaveholding existed in the colony of Ontario (Upper Canada). In 1793 Lieutenant Governor John Graves Simcoe signed a law banning any transportation of slaves into Ontario—from the international

Montage showing Abraham Lincoln with congressmen who signed a resolution supporting the Emancipation Proclamation. [Michael Maslan Historic Photographs/Corbis]

slave trade or otherwise—and emancipating all slaves over twenty-five years of age at the passage of the law or who attain that age subsequently. This made Ontario the first British colony to undertake emancipation as well as the banning of the slave trade. Complete emancipation occurred in 1834 by virtue of a British law passed in 1833, which ended slavery throughout the empire.

United States

The first abolitionist legislation in the United States was the Pennsylvania Gradual Abolition Act of 1780, which freed all children born after March 1, 1780. Connecticut (1784), Rhode Island (1784), New York (1799), and New Jersey (1804) passed similar laws. The Northwest Ordinance (1787) which forbade slavery in the territories north of the Ohio River. Vermont, the fourteenth state, outlawed slavery under its first constitution, and over the next several decades many northern and western states followed suit.

The slave trade was outlawed in 1808, the first permissible date under the U.S. Constitution, and a Colonization Society was established to resettle freed slaves in Africa.

Once the Confederate states seceded, the first congressional act abolishing slavery, with compensation, affected the District of Columbia and the territories. Executive orders and two congressional confiscatory acts allowed Union forces to free slaves used in rebel activities and to refuse rendition of fugitives from rebel areas. Finally, after the Battle of Antietem, President Abraham Lincoln issued the Emancipation Proclamation, freeing slaves owned by masters who were still in rebellion as of 1 January 1863.

The Thirteenth Amendment to the U.S. Constitution was ratified on 15 December 1865, abolishing slavery without compensation.

See also LAW; SOCIÉTÉ DES AMIS DES NOIRS; SOMERSET V. STEWART.

BIBLIOGRAPHY

BOLT, CHRISTINE, and SEYMOUR DRESCHER, eds. *Anti-Slavery, Religion, and Reform: Essays in Memory of Roger Anstez.* 1980.
EMMONS, TERENCE. *The Russian Landed Gentry and the Peasant Emancipation of 1861.* 1968.
KLEIN, MARTIN A., ed. *Breaking the Chains: Slavery, Bondage, and Emancipation in Modern Africa and Asia.* 1993.
MELLOR, G. R. *British Imperial Trusteeship, 1783–1850.* 1951.
RICHARDSON, RONALD KENT. *Moral Imperium: Afro-Caribbeans and the Transformation of British Rule, 1776–1838.* 1987.
TOPLIN, ROBERT BRENT. *The Abolition of Slavery in Brazil.* 1972.

Patrick M. O'Neil

Emancipation Act, British (1833)

The British Emancipation Act of 1833, which passed into law on 29 August, provided that as of 1 August 1834 slavery would cease throughout the empire. As a result, some 700,000 West Indian, 60,000 Mauritian, and 40,000 South African slaves became, theoretically at least, free. In practice, however, they were required, under the terms of the act, to serve a six-year term of apprenticeship (four years in the case of domestic servants) during which they would be required to work for a specified number of hours daily in return for wages. This was to ensure a smooth period of transition during which, under the supervision of special magistrates appointed by the government, both employers and workers would adapt to their new conditions. These provisions also helped to mollify those opponents of the measure who had argued that, given the opportunity, the freedmen would immediately withdraw their labor. A more significant palliative, however, was the £20,000,000 compensation paid to the planters. This was, by the standards of the day, a truly enormous sum, approximately equivalent to a third of the nation's annual budget.

The act marked the culmination of a decade of antislavery agitation. Conscious of Parliament's sensitivity regarding rights to property, abolitionists had initially argued for amelioration followed by gradual emancipation but, finding the planters intransigent, had in 1831 converted to a more radical approach. In the event, riding the tide of Parliamentary reform, victory came sooner than had been foreseen. Nevertheless, many regretted the concessions regarding apprenticeship and the £20,000,000 compensation, which, it was argued, should have gone to the freedmen rather than the planters.

Despite dire predictions, the transition from slavery to freedom passed uneventfully. There were no major disturbances, and the freedmen went on working much as before. This was a great relief to those who supported the act although it soon occurred to some that the peacefulness of the transition period merely reflected the fact that nothing had really changed. These suspicions were strengthened by stories from the colonies to the effect that apprenticeship was actually worse than slavery. Because apprenticeships lasted only for a limited time, it was said, masters had become more grasping. Instead of being whipped, recalcitrant workers were now consigned to the treadmill.

These stories were not without foundation. Persuaded of their truthfulness, abolitionists launched a new agitation. The reality, however, was more varied. What the Emancipation Act had done was to create an entirely new category of person, the apprentice, whose status and rights were not always easy to define. Employers and workers found the system confusing. So too did the special magistrates responsible for its implementation, who found themselves continually open to the charge of favoring one party over another. It was for these reasons, rather than on account of the mounting political storm in England, that the West Indian assemblies resolved to end the system on 1 August 1838 rather than wait until it automatically expired.

In a sense, therefore, British slavery really ended on 1 August 1838. The former slaves were at last free to leave their employers, as many now chose to do. The results, however, differed from colony to colony. In Antigua, where most of the land was already cultivated and alternative employment was unavailable, former slaves continued to work on the plantations, whereas in Jamaica they left in droves to establish free villages in the mountains. Overall, sugar production fell by a third. This falloff was at a time of rising consumer demand, with the result that prices soared. Abolitionists fought a prolonged rearguard action to prevent the admission of foreign slave-grown sugar into Britain, but their efforts were overridden when Parliament in 1846 resolved to equalize the duties on all imported sugars.

The results of the 1833 Act were thus mixed. Many were disappointed by the fall in sugar production that followed its passage. Others drew consolation from the peacefulness of the transition and the way the freedmen had adapted to a more self-sufficient style of living. In both the East and West Indies planters took to importing indentured coolie laborers to fill the places of the departing freedmen. In Cape Colony discontented Boers, tired of British meddling, trekked off to establish independent republics of their own. American observers, North and South, drew from the British experience such lessons as suited them. The British themselves came to see the 1833 act as a validation of their commitment to freedom and of their right to pursue their national interests as an expanding world power.

See also ABOLITION AND ANTISLAVERY MOVEMENTS; EMANCIPATION ACT, BRITISH; LAW.

BIBLIOGRAPHY

BURN, W. L. *Emancipation and Apprenticeship in the British West Indies.* 1937.
GREEN, WILLIAM A. *British Slave Emancipation: The Sugar Colonies and the Great Experiment 1830–1865.* 1976.
TEMPERLEY, HOWARD. *British Antislavery, 1833–1870.* 1971.

Howard R. Temperley

Emancipation in the United States

This entry includes the following articles: The Northern Experience; Civil War.

The Northern Experience

In the antebellum South, planters often referred to slavery as their "peculiar institution." At the time of the American Revolution, slavery had been firmly established in the northern as well as the southern colonies. But as a result of a series of legislative acts, constitutional clauses, and judicial interpretations in the northern states during and after the Revolution, slavery increasingly became an institution peculiar to the South.

The impetus behind the emancipation movement in the North came from diverse sources—religious principles, political ideology, and economic concerns. Of these, the religious impulse was the oldest and most deeply embedded. The religious revival of the middle of the eighteenth century—the "great awakening"—played an important role, through its radically egalitarian principle of a priesthood of all believers. Especially in the middle colonies, the Society of Friends (Quakers), became increasingly outspoken in criticizing slavery as an institution that violated the Quaker doctrine of the "inner light"—the idea that all humans have direct access to God and are therefore spiritually equal. Opposition to slavery also was an important aspect of John Wesley's Methodist movement, and of the Baptist denomination. In New England, the New Lights, a group within the Congregationalist movement, often took an antislavery position.

The political ideology that developed during the Revolution, summed up eloquently in the Declaration of Independence, made an important contribution to the movement for emancipation. These principles influenced not only slaveowners, judges, and legislators but also a number of African-Americans, who recognized that the ideology of the Revolution had particular relevance to their condition. They pointed out in their appeal to the Massachusetts General Court (its legislature) in 1777: "Your Petitioners apprehend that they have in Common with all other men a Natural and Unaliable Right to that freedom which the Grat Parent of the Unavers hath Bestowed equalley on all menkind and which they have Never forfeited by any Compact."

Economics played a less important role in the antislavery movement, but it did make emancipation easier to achieve in the North. Despite the fact that slaves were engaged in important economic activities, the institution of slavery was not seen as vital to the economy. The influx of immigrants into northern ports provided an important alternative source of labor for tradespeople and farmers.

In a number of states the process of emancipation began before the Revolutionary War was over. Vermont, which became the fourteenth state, had very few slaves and outlawed slavery in its constitution of 1777. In Massachusetts, legislative efforts to end slavery were unsuccessful, but a series of judicial decisions held that slavery was incompatible with the state's newly adopted bill of rights. As a result, slavery had disappeared in Massachusetts by the time of the first federal census in 1790. The abolition of slavery in New Hampshire was probably similar to that in Massachusetts, though as late as 1792 there were still almost 150 slaves in New Hampshire. By 1800 there were no slaves in the state, and in 1857 New Hampshire outlawed slavery.

African-Americans did not wait for the courts or legislatures to free them. Many slaves took advantage of wartime confusion to escape. In addition, a large number of blacks secured their freedom by serving in the Revolutionary armies.

Between 1780 and 1804 Connecticut, Rhode Island, Pennsylvania, New York, and New Jersey provided for emancipation through legislation. The gradual abolition laws devised by these states attempted to reconcile the competing claims of property and liberty (which were equally important in Revolutionary ideology). They provided for the eventual end of slavery, but they recognized slaveowners' property rights by freeing only slaves born after the law was enacted and requiring the freed children of slaves to serve their mothers' masters for a period of years as compensation for the expense of raising them. Although the Quakers were no longer in power when Pennsylvania passed its Gradual Abolition Act of 1780, the antislavery activities of the members of the Society of Friends, especially John Woolman and Anthony Benezet, helped to prepare public opinion. Quakers, led by Moses Brown, were also an important influence in Rhode Island's decision to adopt a gradual abolition law in 1784. Gradual abolition was defeated in Connecticut in 1779 and 1780, but when the state revised its laws in 1784, it adopted a gradual abolition plan.

Shortly after the end of the Revolutionary War, emancipation through judicial interpretation or legislation had begun in all of the New England states and in Pennsylvania. But in New York and New Jersey, both of which had large concentrations of slaves in some areas, emancipation proved to be much more difficult. There was antislavery sentiment in New York, but the primarily Dutch counties of the Hudson River area and Long Island long opposed abolition. In New Jersey there was a similar division between the Quaker-influenced areas near Philadelphia and the proslavery counties of east Jersey.

New York finally began the gradual abolition of slavery in 1799, but its laws—unlike previous gradual abolition laws—provided some compensation to slaveowners. The law allowed the owners of the mothers of the newly freed slave children to "abandon" these children, who would then be considered paupers and would be supported by the state. Since it was likely that these children would be reassigned to their mothers' masters, slaveowners could receive a monthly stipend for each child. In 1804 New Jersey followed the example of New York and adopted a gradual abolition program that also allowed masters to "abandon" the freed children of their slaves (even though New York's experience had demonstrated how expensive this aspect of the law could become). In 1817 New York went beyond gradual abolition, providing for the emancipation of all slaves born before the gradual abolition act after ten years of additional service. In New Jersey slavery was converted to a form of apprenticeship in 1846. The last of these "apprentices" were freed from their involuntary servitude by the Thirteenth Amendment.

In the North, slavery rapidly diminished in the first decades of the nineteenth century. (This was not entirely a direct result of antislavery activities. Despite laws making the export of northern slaves illegal, some masters undoubtedly sold their slaves out of state to evade the abolition laws.) By 1830, when a new aboli-

As late as February 1861, when this cartoon was published in Vanity Fair, *individuals in the North who advocated the abolition of slavery were often the subject of contemptuous satire.* [Corbis-Bettmann]

tionist movement began, there were fewer than three thousand slaves in the northern states.

The formal abolition of slavery did not rescue northern African-Americans from discrimination, poverty, or disease. They were restricted to the most menial occupations, housed in wretched conditions, and subject to periodic episodes of brutal violence.

See also ABOLITION AND ANTISLAVERY MOVEMENTS; AMERICAN REVOLUTION; METHODISM; QUAKERS. *See also entries on specific northern states.*

BIBLIOGRAPHY

DAVIS, DAVID B. *The Problem of Slavery in the Age of Revolution, 1770–1823.* 1975.

———. *The Problem of Slavery in Western Culture.* 1966.

FOGEL, ROBERT, and STANLEY ENGERMAN. "Philanthropy at Bargain Prices: Notes on the Economics of Gradual Emancipation." *Journal of Legal Studies* 3 (June 1974): 377–389.

HODGES, GRAHAM RUSSELL. *Slavery and Freedom in the Rural North: African Americans in Monmouth County, New Jersey, 1665–1865.* 1997.

NASH, GARY B. "Forging Freedom: The Emancipation Experience in the Northern Seaport Cities, 1775–1820. In *Slavery and Freedom in the Age of the American Revolution,* edited by Ira Berlin and Ronald Hoffman. 1983; pp. 3–48.

NASH, GARY B., and JEAN R. SODERLUND. *Freedom by Degrees: Emancipation in Pennsylvania and Its Aftermath.* 1991.

WHITE, SHANE. *Somewhat More Independent: The End of Slavery in New York City, 1770–1810.* 1991.

ZILVERSMIT, ARTHUR. *The First Emancipation: The Abolition of Slavery in the North.* 1967.

Arthur Zilversmit

Civil War

The South's attack on Fort Sumter began the process that freed the slaves. When Edmund Ruffin, "white haired and mad" in the words of W. E. B. Du Bois, fired the first shot and thereby began a war that culminated in emancipation, neither he nor his northern opponents intended this result. The North, responding to the southern attack, intended to preserve the Union, not to abolish slavery. President Abraham Lincoln clearly stated his position in his inaugural address: "I have no purpose to interfere with the institution of slavery in the States where it exists." Lincoln went further; he pledged his support for an amendment that Congress had just accepted and sent to the states for ratification. This amendment (which would have been the thirteenth, and unamendable) would have forever protected slavery from federal interference.

Lincoln and the Congress eventually changed their war aims and enacted emancipation. Equally significant, however, is the story of how slaves emancipated themselves. The slaves recognized that the war offered an opportunity for freedom and from the beginning of hostilities they sought safety and liberation within the Union lines. Thus, a year before Lincoln issued the Emancipation Proclamation a fugitive slave from Maryland proudly wrote his wife from a Union army camp in Virginia, "this day i can Address you thank god as a freeman." He was now, he told her, "in Safety in the 14th Regiment of Brooklyn." Like thousands of other African-Americans, John Boston had seized the opportunity brought by war to free himself.

Large numbers of refugees from slavery came to Union Army camps. At first commanders not only refused to aid escaped slaves but even returned them to their Confederate owners. When it became clear that the Confederacy was using slave labor to build fortifications, however, northern generals began to treat fugitives as "contraband of war" and used them as laborers. In many cases these fugitives brought valuable military intelligence, and they were willing to do much of the camps' work, relieving soldiers of these duties. Anxious to placate the loyal slave states and the border states, Lincoln countermanded the orders of northern generals who went further and declared fugitive slaves to be free. But the irony of Union soldiers acting as slave catchers for their enemies soon became intolerable. In August 1861 Congress passed a Confiscation Act, which declared that slaveowners lost their ownership rights when they allowed their

A group of slaves seeks protection from federal troops and becomes "contraband of war." [Illustrated London News/ Corbis]

slaves to be used for military service. In March 1862 Congress formally prohibited the use of Union troops to return fugitive slaves.

In some areas emancipation came relatively easily. When Union troops landed on the Sea Islands off the coast of South Carolina in 1861, they found that most of the resident planters had fled, leaving their slaves behind. Some of these slaves were used as laborers by Union forces, but many were left free to cultivate individual patches of land on their former owners' plantations. While they were not legally emancipated, they lived the lives of freeman.

As in the Sea Islands, the circumstances of war forced the Union to move toward emancipation. Less than a year after the war began, Lincoln urged Congress to aid any state that sought to gradually abolish slavery by providing funds to compensate slaveowners and to pay for the colonization of freedmen outside of the United States. Congress, increasingly recognizing that slavery was the basis for the rebellion, became more radical. In March of 1862 it emancipated the slaves of the District of Columbia. At Lincoln's insistence, Congress provided funds to compensate slaveowners and also to provide for the colonization of freedmen. A few months later, Congress abolished slavery in the territories. This time, however, it did not provide for compensation. In the summer of 1862 progress toward emancipation accelerated. As the Union armies under General George McClellan proved unable to make any progress against the Confederacy, Congress passed the Second Confiscation Act, which declared the fugitive slaves of any person aiding the rebellion to be "forever free of their servitude." The act permitted the voluntary colonization of freedmen; it also allowed the president to use African-Americans as soldiers. Although he had grave reservations about its constitutionality, Lincoln signed the bill.

After a year of fighting, more and more people in the North realized that the destruction of slavery was a way of striking at the heart of the Confederacy. By July Lincoln had joined them and announced to his cabinet his intention to issue an Emancipation Proclamation. On 22 September 1862, after the victory of the United States Army at the Battle of Antietam, he issued the Preliminary Emancipation Proclamation, which warned the South that all slaves in any states still in rebellion on 1 January 1863 would be freed. On New Year's Day, when Lincoln issued the Final Emancipation Proclamation, Frederick Douglass, the great African-American abolitionist, publicly congratulated Lincoln "upon what may be called the greatest event of our nation's history."

One of the most radical provisions of the proclamation was the call for the enrollment of African-American troops. Lincoln sent General Lorenzo Thomas to the Mississippi Valley to recruit thousands of former slaves. In the border states, the recruitment of African-American soldiers, with a promise of freedom for them and their families, destroyed the institution even before legal emancipation had been enacted. By the end of the war over 200,000 African-Americans had served in the United States Army and Navy, forcing most white Americans to recognize the role of the slaves in their own liberation. As Lincoln pointed out to critics of his emancipation policy: "You say you will not fight to free negroes. Some of them seem willing to fight for you . . . . If they stake their lives for us, they must be prompted by the strongest motive—even the promise of freedom. And the promise being made, must be kept."

Since it was a military measure, the proclamation applied only to those areas that were still in rebellion and did not apply to areas under Union control. Yet it meant that as United States troops advanced, so did the cause of freedom. Federal troops now welcomed fugitive slaves, and more and more of them came to the "contraband" camps set up within Union lines. The Civil War had become what neither Edmund Ruffin nor Abraham Lincoln had intended: a war for emancipation.

Although there was strong opposition to Lincoln's radical shift, for the most part northern public opinion supported emancipation. In reply to those who urged him to reverse direction, Lincoln clearly insisted that as long as he was president he would not "retract or modify the emancipation proclamation nor return to slavery any person" who had been emancipated by it.

There was still the question of what to do about those slaves who were owned by masters who were exempted from the proclamation. Lincoln's appeal to the border states to begin a process of gradual, compensated abolition had been of no avail. At the same time, however, slavery was rapidly being undermined as more and more slaves became fugitives, and more and more former slaves were recruited as Union soldiers. Slavery had collapsed in Maryland by 1864, a fact that was recognized in that state's new constitution. By the end of 1864, the new Unionist governments of Arkansas and Louisiana had ended slavery, as had the new state of West Virginia. Missouri slaveholders tried to avoid immediate abolition by enacting a gradual abolition law in July 1863, but here, too, slaves liberated themselves and Missouri's immediate emancipation act of January 1865 only gave legal recognition to an accomplished fact. In Kentucky and Delaware, unlike the other loyal slave states, slaveholders resisted emancipation to the very end. It was the Thirteenth Amendment that finally ended slavery in those states.

An illustration originally published in January 1867 in Harper's Weekly *expresses doubt about the ability of various pieces of federal legislation to end slavery in the United States.* [Library of Congress/Corbis]

Although, in the words of its vice president, Alexander Stephens, slavery was the "cornerstone" of the Confederacy, the war undermined the institution even in the South. In late 1864 and early 1865 the Confederacy seriously debated the use of African-American soldiers, even if this meant that they and their families would earn their freedom. Robert E. Lee endorsed the idea of arming African-Americans, and a bill authorizing the president to requisition black troops failed by only a single vote in the Confederate Congress. At the same time, President Jefferson Davis sent an envoy to Europe to explore the possibility of securing foreign recognition for the Confederacy if it were to adopt emancipation.

But even without formal action by the Confederate government, slavery was collapsing. As United States troops came closer, slaveowners found themselves bargaining with their slaves in an effort to persuade them not to leave. In the sugar country of Louisiana, for example, slaves were now demanding salaries for their work.

In the North, Abolitionists enjoyed a new popularity. Pleased by the Confiscation Acts and the Emancipation Proclamation, they worried about the fate of an emancipation policy based on "military necessity" once peace was restored. They therefore launched a massive petition campaign to procure a constitutional amendment ending slavery. In April 1864, a vote for the amendment failed to get the required two-thirds majority in Congress. After Lincoln's reelection on a platform that had endorsed the amendment, several Democrats succumbed to heavy pressure from the Administration. Accordingly, the lame duck session of Congress approved the abolition amendment and sent it to the states. On 18 December 1865 Secretary of State William H. Seward announced that the required three-quarters of the states had ratified the Thirteenth Amendment and slavery was formally abolished.

With the ratification of the Thirteenth Amendment the process of legal emancipation was completed; it was not clear, however, how freedom for the former slaves would be defined. Lincoln's plan for Reconstruction would have allowed the southern states to adopt temporary measures for the freedmen, "consistent . . . with their present condition as a laboring, landless, and homeless class." For a number of years, the freedmen could have been placed in an intermediate category between slavery and full citizenship, but Lincoln was flexible on this. Shortly before his assassination, Lincoln suggested that the reconstructed government of Louisiana give at least some of the freedmen the right to vote. However, under the new state governments established with the approval of President Andrew Johnson, African-Americans were subject to "Black Codes," which to varying degrees denied them the benefits of full citizenship. For a brief period, after Congress took over the process of Reconstruction, the freedmen began to exercise political and civil rights, but they were never given permanent possession of the land, which would have allowed them true independence. Within a few decades, they lost their political and civil rights and were subject to a rigid system of segregation, sharecropping, and racial violence. In light of the decades of oppression that succeeded slavery, the celebrations that heralded emancipation were premature.

Contrary to legend, emancipation, like the war itself, was not the product of a hero's vision. In telling the story of how he came to issue the Emancipation Proclamation, Lincoln acknowledged: "I claim not to have controlled events, but confess plainly the events have controlled me." Individual African-Americans played a crucial role in those "events."

See also CIVIL WAR, U.S.; CONFEDERATE STATES OF AMERICA; LINCOLN, ABRAHAM; RECONSTRUCTION, U.S.

BIBLIOGRAPHY

BASLER, ROY B., MARION DOLORES PRATT, and LLOYD DUNLAP, eds. *The Collected Works of Abraham Lincoln.* Vols. 4–8. 1953.

BERLIN, IRA, BARBARA J. FIELDS, STEVEN MILLER, JOSEPH P. REIDY, and LESLIE S. ROWLAND, eds. *Freedom: A Documentary History of Emancipation, 1861–1867.* Series 1, vols. 1–3. 1985–1993.

COX, LAWANDA. *Lincoln and Black Freedom: A Study in Presidential Leadership.* 1981.

DU BOIS, W. E. BURGHARDT. *Black Reconstruction in America.* 1935.

FONER, ERIC. *Reconstruction: America's Unfinished Revolution, 1863–1877.* 1988.

FRANKLIN, JOHN HOPE. *The Emancipation Proclamation.* 1963.

GERTEIS, LOUIS S. *From Contraband to Freedman: Federal Policies toward Southern Blacks.* 1973.

LITWACK, LEON F. *Been in the Storm So Long.* 1979.

MCPHERSON, JAMES M. *Battle Cry of Freedom: The Civil War Era.* 1988.

————. *The Struggle for Equality: Abolitionists and the Negro in the Civil War and Reconstruction.* 1964.

Arthur Zilversmit

Encyclopédie

The *Encyclopédie,* the French Enlightenment's most famous reference work, was published in seventeen volumes of articles and eleven of illustrations, between 1750 and 1772 under the editorship of Denis Diderot and Jean Le Rond d'Alembert. Having begun as a French translation of Ephraim Chamber's *Cyclopedia,* it covered the broad range of human knowledge, with articles on the liberal arts, the sciences, and technological subjects.

Among the numerous contributors, besides Diderot and d'Alembert, were such leading figures as the Baron d'Holbach, Claude-Adrien Helvétius, François Quesnay, Jean-Jacques Rousseau, and Voltaire. Many of the views expressed were regarded as subversive, and French authorities banned publication of the *Encyclopédie* several times (1752, 1755, 1759).

Louis, chevalier de Jaucourt, contributed an especially large number of articles to the *Encyclopédie* (24 percent of the total), including several with an antislavery theme: "Slavery" (1755), "Natural Liberty" (1765), "Maroons" (1765), "Negroes" (1765), and "Trade in Negroes" (1765). In these articles, he attacked the role of Europeans and European institutions, including the church, in sponsoring or condoning slavery and the slave trade. In the last, he argued that, because freedom is an inalienable natural right of every man, no man can literally dispossess himself of it, he can only contract out the use of his freedom. Moreover, no society can legislate slavery, because slavery is a crime against the laws of nature. Jaucourt also argued that freeing the slaves would eventually result in the greater prosperity of the lands where they were held, because free labor was more productive than slave labor.

See also ENLIGHTENMENT; PERSPECTIVES ON SLAVERY.

BIBLIOGRAPHY

DAVIS, DAVID BRION. *The Problem of Slavery in Western Culture.* 1966.

DIDEROT, DENIS, and JEAN D'ALEMBERT, eds. *Encyclopédie, ou Dictionnaire raisonné des sciences, des arts et des métiers.* 1750–1772.

DONATO, CLORINDA, and ROBERT M. MANIQUIS, eds. *The Encyclopedia and the Age of Reason.* 1992.

LOUGH, JOHN. *The Contributors to the "Encyclopédie."* 1973.

———. *The "Encyclopédie."* 1971.
PROUST, JACQUES. *Diderot et l'Encyclopédie.* 1967.

Charles E. Williams

Enforcement Acts, U.S.

Enforcement Acts, also known as "Force Acts," were a series of federal laws—principally, the Enforcement Act of 31 May 1870, the Enforcement Act of 28 February 1871, and the Ku Klux Force Act of 20 April 1871—enacted by the then Republican-controlled United States Congress between 1870 and 1872 to enforce the Fourteenth and Fifteenth Amendments and the Civil Rights Act of 1866. Representing the Republican Party's efforts to ensure that the recently enfranchised black males in the South participated in Reconstruction, these statutes were chiefly formulated to penalize any state or individual that, for racial reasons, prevented a qualified voter from exercising the right to vote and from enjoying his civil rights. To guarantee the federal protection of citizens' rights, these laws established an extensive federal machinery for supervising elections, designated federal courts to handle the cases arising under these laws, and empowered the president to use federal troops to keep peace at the polls if necessary.

The vigorous implementation of these laws helped the Republicans to deter the then rampant Ku Klux Klan violence and acts of intimidation against black and Republican voters in the South. In 1873 alone, more than a thousand cases were brought into the federal courts from the South, and nearly half of them resulted in convictions. Although the legality of the first act was questioned by the Supreme Court in *U.S. v. Reese* (1876) and *U.S. v. Cruikshank* (1876), the statutes remained valid and continued to be used by the federal judiciary to punish election frauds in the post-Reconstruction period, although much less effectively. It was not until 1894, when the Democrats—who had long regarded these laws as intrusions on states rights—regained the control of Congress, that many of the provisions of the enforcement laws were repealed.

See also LAW; RECONSTRUCTION, U.S.

BIBLIOGRAPHY

GILLETTE, WILLIAM. *Retreat from Reconstruction, 1869–1879.* 1979.
GOLDMAN, ROBERT MICHAEL. *"A Free Ballot and a Fair Count": The Department of Justice and the Enforcement of Voting Rights in the South, 1877–1893.* 1990.
SWINNEY, EVERETTE. *Suppressing the Ku Klux Klan: The Enforcement of the Reconstruction Amendments, 1870–1877.* 1987.
WANG, XI. *The Trial of Democracy: Black Suffrage and Northern Republicans, 1860–1910.* 1997.
WILLIAMS, LOU FALKNER. *The Great South Carolina Ku Klux Klan Trials, 1871–1872.* 1997.

Xi Wang

An undated political cartoon depicts masked Ku Klux Klan members killing blacks as a way of "reforming colored voters in the South." [Corbis-Bettmann]

Engels, Friedrich   [1820–1895]

Socialist philosopher and associate of Karl Marx.

For Friedrich Engels, the first genuine classes to arise in primitive society were master and slave, and these further intensified the division of labor that had begun with differentiation of the sexes.

Although medieval serfs and modern proletarians must sell their labor as a commodity, the slave was an object of commerce in his or her own person. Thus, while the alienation of the serf and the wage laborer and the expropriation of the surplus value of their labor was enormous, for slaves expropriation was total.

Slavery began with prisoners of war but was quickly extended to members of one's own tribe. Settled agriculture, cattle raising, weaving, and other means of producing wealth were required before a primitive economy could support slavery. The vast enhancement of wealth and it appropriation into private property called forth the institution of the state.

With the fall of the Roman empire, slavery became insignificant in Europe, because smallhold farming, which came with the Germanic invasions, was unsuitable for it. But the effects of slavery were long-lived, for it degraded the labor of free people.

In modern society, the categories of slave and master were disappearing—along with all the other categories of the old order—as the two great classes, proletariat and bourgeoisie, began their struggle for domination.

Much of Engel's thought on slavery is contained in his *Origin of the Family, Private Property and the State.* His ideas, together with those of Karl Marx, dominated much of the ideology of the communist world and influenced socialist thought everywhere.

See also ECONOMICS OF SLAVERY; MARXISM.

BIBLIOGRAPHY

ENGELS, FRIEDRICH. *The Origin of the Family, Private Property and the State—In Light of the Researches of Lewis H. Morgan.* Edited by Eleanor Burke Leacock. 1972.

MARX, KARL, and FRIEDRICH ENGELS. *Basic Writings on Politics and Philosophy.* Edited by Lewis S. Feuer. 1959.

Patrick M. O'Neil

England

See Great Britain, African Slavery in.

Enlightenment

The libertarian and anticlerical intellectual movement known as the Enlightenment focused political discourse on human happiness rather than social order, and fostered from the 1720s to 1780s an enquiring and critical cultural climate. Its ideas were disseminated through local academies, essay competitions, and a flood of publications for an expanding reading public. In establishing secularism, rationality, and universal human rights as central features of Western culture, it did much to undermine traditional defenses of slavery based on biblical sanction, Aristotelian philosophy, and the concept of just war. Few Enlightenment thinkers (or philosophes) were abolitionists, however, and antislavery sentiments were a peripheral feature of enlightened thought until the 1770s. The movement, moreover, also developed a scientific basis for racist ideas, which complicated its impact on slavery. Scholars debate its importance relative to an older free-soil juridical tradition and eighteenth century developments in Protestantism in bringing about the antislavery campaigns launched in the 1780s.

Long after slavery had ended in medieval northern Europe, and as late as the libertarian writings of John Locke (1632–1704), political theorists and theologians continued, as in ancient times, to construct justifications for human bondage. The Enlightenment broke this age-old continuity. Slavery gradually was condemned as illegitimate under all circumstances, not just for co-religionists or fellow Europeans. Employing satire alongside the solemn treatise, a new generation of intellectuals critical of established authority argued that individual liberty was a constant principle of natural law, and that moral precepts should not be bounded by geography or culture. Individuals could not alienate their own freedom or appropriate another's. The new trend began somewhat ambivalently with the Baron de Montesquieu (1689–1755). He mocked prejudices against blacks and found all slavery morally pernicious, but his theory of climate's influence on culture suggested that there was a role for slavery in the tropics. Montesquieu's comparative study of political systems *L'Esprit des lois* (Spirit of the Laws; 1748) was more concerned with ancient than contemporary slavery and included advice on how to make slave societies more stable. He was cited as an authority by slavery's critics and apologists alike.

Whereas Montesquieu believed Christianity had caused slavery's demise in medieval Europe, it was Voltaire (1694–1778) who exposed the Catholic Church's long tolerance of the institution and ridiculed scriptural sanction of it. Voltaire's humorous *Candide* (1759) raised consciousness of the cruelties of Caribbean and South American slavery and helped bring home to its readers the social cost of using sugar. Yet Voltaire was interested far less in the slave colonies than in oppression and injustice in Europe, for which slavery often served as a metaphor. This attitude was even more true of the radical libertarian Jean-Jacques Rousseau (1712–1778). His *Contrat Social* (1762) is entirely uncompromising in denying slavery any legal basis but avoids the issues of black slavery and the slave trade altogether.

A different type of critique emerged in the 1750s. It opposed slavery not, or not only, on humanitarian grounds but as an obstacle to economic and demographic growth. It was first associated with the sceptic David Hume (1711–1776) in Scotland, Benjamin Franklin (1706–1790) in America, and the physiocratic school in France, which included Mirabeau senior, Pierre Samuel Dupont de Nemours, and Anne-Robert-Jacques-Turgot. This view depicted slave labor as expensive and slaveowners as motivated by the desire to dominate rather than by economic rationality. Moral and utilitarian arguments against slavery were combined in the posthumous *System of Moral Philosophy* (1755) by Glasgow professor Francis Hutcheson (1694–1746), in whose teachings Enlightenment and

David Hume. [Library of Congress/Corbis]

latitudinarian Protestantism intersected. Hutcheson's student Adam Smith (1723–1790) pursued both ethical and economic indictments in his *Theory of Moral Sentiments* (1759) and his influential *Wealth of Nations* (1776). As Britain entered the industrial age, Smith's student John Millar elaborated the depiction of slavery as a retrograde obstacle to progress. Millar remained uncertain, however, how far his argument applied to tropical plantations. In France, the journal *Ephémérides du Citoyen* (1765–1772) showcased physiocratic ideas such as a project to encourage the cultivation of sugar in Africa by free workers. Optimistic that self-interest would ultimately prevail, and respectful of private property, the economists generally proved no more likely than the philosophes to take up the cause of antislavery.

Some scholars, like Louis Sala-Molins, attribute the philosophes' hesitations and silences regarding black slavery to their racial prejudices. All thought that the degrading effects of slavery rendered slaves unfit for immediate freedom. A few, like Voltaire, considered blacks a separate species, though this view was frequently attacked. As living experiments, a handful of Africans were given university educations by wealthy European patrons. Despite their successes, the Enlightenment became the seedbed of nineteenth century "scientific racism," partly because it undermined

Christian traditions of the unity of mankind and reinforcing older heterodox ideas about racial hierarchy, and partly because of the growth of biological science and its attempt to classify all living things. Thinking about race came to be dominated by the biologist Comte de Buffon (1707–1788). He accepted the oneness of humankind but, echoing the environmentalism made respectable by Montesquieu, he conceived of racial characteristics in terms of degeneracy from a European norm.

The multi-authored, 35-volume *Encyclopédie* (1751–1780), the Enlightenment's central text, reflects these tensions and changing attitudes. Between the articles written in the 1750s and those authored in the 1760s one sees a shift toward a more forthright denunciation of slavery, alongside an image of Africans that remained very negative. Also multi-authored and multi-volume, the very popular *Histoire des deux Indes* (History of the Two Indies) of Abbé Guillaume-Thomas Raynal (1713–1796) similarly contains contradictory views of colonization and slavery. Published in three editions between 1770 and 1780 and frequently reprinted, it is best remembered for its calls for a slave revolt that would bring about emancipation. These passages were authored not by Raynal but Denis Diderot (1713–1784) and Jean de Pechméja (1741–1785), who were inspired by Louis-Sébastien Mercier's futurist novel *L'An 2440* (Year 2440) (1772) and by actual resistance in the Caribbean. Such recognition of the slave's right to violent

Georges-Louis Leclerc, Comte de Buffon. [Leonard de Selva/Corbis]

self-liberation had earlier appeared in Montesquieu's unpublished *Pensées* (at least as regards European slaves). Some see the call for revolt as a shallow rhetorical flourish or device for selling books; others, as a sign of genuine despair at a time when no other alternative seemed feasible.

Raynal's *Histoire* marks a notable turning point in including a concrete plan for gradually ending slavery. Under an ameliorated regime, Raynal proposed, slaves might be given their freedom and a plot of land at age 25. The Marquis de Condorcet's *Réflexions sur l'esclavage* (Reflections on Slavery) (1781, 1788) contained a similar plan, in which slaves would be freed after age 40 and slavery ended within seventy years. Future luminary of the abolitionist society Société des Amis des Noirs (1788–1792), Condorcet (1743–1794) bridged the Enlightenment and antislavery movements. With Franklin, he was one of the rare philosophes to become a committed abolitionist. In contrast, Raynal, Voltaire, Locke, and some say, Montesquieu, all invested in the Atlantic slave trade that continued to expand dramatically. Raynal went on to collaborate with Pierre-Victor Malouet on a proslavery work, and during the colonial crisis of the French Revolution he publicly recanted all his former radicalism.

Despite the limitations of its leading thinkers, the Enlightenment undoubtedly prepared the way for more direct abolitionist action. By destroying the traditional arguments that slavery was divinely ordained or natural to human society, and by questioning its efficiency, it irrevocably narrowed the grounds on which slavery could be defended. More generally, its iconoclastic challenge to tradition and its criticism of authoritarian government, often using slavery as a metaphor, created a climate that helped undermine the institution. If it was not responsible for the mass mobilization of the antislavery movement, its arguments influenced the statesmen who had to respond to antislavery pressure. In the late 1780s the French government, assisted by Condorcet, conducted secret experiments with remunerated slave and free black labor in Guiana and Saint Domingue. British prime minister William Pitt admired Adam Smith. One should note that antislavery views were never subject to censorship; although writers from Montesquieu to Raynal commonly had their books banned by church or state, this was never because of what they wrote about slavery.

Critics of the philosophes see their engagement with black slavery as shallow, abstract, and ambiguous. They stress the Enlightenment's tendency to strengthen racial prejudice, and the way its elevation of utility sometimes weakened its defense of human liberty. The critics additionally question how much

the intellectual movement added to the religious factors that stimulated antislavery, and how radical a break with earlier thought it really represented. Jean Bodin had anticipated much of the Enlightenment critique of human bondage (as well as its racism) in the 1570s. Instead of seeing him as an isolated figure, Seymour Drescher argues that he formed part of a libertarian juridical traditional that had established a free-soil ideology in France, England, and the Netherlands by the late sixteenth century. Although Bodin's opposition to slavery overseas does seem most unusual, Drescher's *Capitalism and Antislavery* (1986) downplays the change in ideas that took place in the eighteenth century in favor of emphasizing the geographical uniqueness of northwest Europe and its libertarian traditions.

See also ABOLITION AND ANTISLAVERY MOVEMENTS; FRANKLIN, BENJAMIN, AND THE MARQUIS DE CONDORCET; PERSPECTIVES ON SLAVERY; ROUSSEAU, JEAN-JACQUES; SOCIÉTÉ DES AMIS DES NOIRS.

BIBLIOGRAPHY

BENOT, YVES. *Diderot, de l'athéisme à l'anticolonialisme.* 1981.

DAVIS, DAVID BRION. *The Problem of Slavery in Western Culture.* 1966.

DRESCHER, SEYMOUR. "Esclavage." In *Dictionnaire d'éthique et de philosophie morale*, edited by Monique Canto-Sperber. 1996.

DUCHET, MICHÈLE. *Anthropologie et histoire au siècle des Lumières.* 1971.

PEABODY, SUE. *"There Are No Slaves in France": The Political Culture of Race and Slavery in the Ancien Régime.* 1996.

PLUCHON, PIERRE. *Nègres et Juifs au XVIIIe siècle: Le racisme au siècle des Lumières.* 1984.

SALA-MOLINS, LOUIS. *Les Misères des Lumières: Sous la raison, l'outrage.* 1992.

David Geggus

Enslavement, Methods of

Human nature produced war, and war produced slaves. Slaveholding peoples did not have to agree with Aristotle that slavery was a natural condition to concede that it was a fact of life, something that had always existed and always would exist. Indeed, respected ancient and modern thinkers defended enslavement as a leap forward in human progress, for while the alleged barbarians of the world had put prisoners of war to the sword, civilized people had put them to work. Enslavement had replaced a worse fate, death. War supplied millions of such enslaved outsiders to the Roman Empire, the Muslim world, and the plantation economies of the Americas. War decisively shaped the meaning of slavery itself.

In cuneiform, the world's oldest written language, the Sumerians expressed the concept "slave" with an ideograph that combined the sign for man or woman with the sign for foreignness. In ancient Babylon a common word for slave literally meant "booty of the bow." Justinian's celebrated sixth-century codification of Roman law explains that slaves were called *servi* "because generals have a custom of selling their prisoners and thereby preserving rather than killing them: indeed they are said to be *mancipia,* because they are captives in the hand (*manus*) of their enemies." To most of the world's slaveholding peoples, the theoretical slave lived as a peculiarly dishonored body, breathing yet naked and isolated, having been forcibly disembedded from society, dispossessed of its protective bundling of claims, rights, and conventions, and confined within a highly personalized and individuated relation of despotical domination with a triumphant, omnipotent other.

Although mass enslavement stands out in history as a harrowing conclusion to wars between states, other methods have supplemented or even replaced war in replenishing slave populations made unsustainable not only by high mortality and low fertility but also by manumission. A concise compilation of the leading methods of enslavement appears in Book 1 of *Les six livres de la république* (1576), the most famous work of the French philosopher Jean Bodin. He distinguishes war from such lesser methods of violent enslavement as brigandage, kidnapping, and piracy. In some places vulnerable insiders chose self-enslavement or the sale of family members into slavery as an alternative preferable to starvation. Bodin also recognized enslavement by debt, observing that Germans had fallen into slavery by gambling and that the Twelve Tables (451 B.C.), one of the earliest compilations of Roman law, had allowed creditors to enslave debtors. The Roman *servi poenae,* he noted, became slaves as punishment for crimes. Bodin called those who were born into slavery "natural slaves."

In truth, the drama of war may have obscured the more persistent process of birth as the single most important method of enslavement in history, but slaveholding peoples sometimes devised elaborate rules to govern the inheritance of the status. In a global study of slavery, Orlando Patterson has identified seven broad patterns of status inheritance and named each one after a people who were prominent practitioners. In the Ashanti pattern, named after the slave-exporting state in eighteenth-century West Africa, status follows the mother for the offspring whether neither parent, either parent, or both parents are enslaved. Thus, the children of a union between two slaves owned by different masters belong to the owner of the mother. A free woman in union with a male

slave begets free children. The Somali pattern, named for the pastoralists of northeast Africa, differs from the Ashanti pattern in that the rule of inheritance follows the father, also regardless of the nature of the union. The children from a union between two slaves owned by different masters belong to the owner of the father. A free woman in union with a male slave begets enslaved children.

The Sherbro people of the West African forests proved unusual in having no fixed pattern of inheritance. The Saharan Muslim Tuaregs, as Patterson points out, differed from other Islamic people in following a matrilineal pattern of status inheritance for the children of free parents. But they determined inheritance patrilineally for children from mixed unions. Given the prevalence of concubinage in Tuareg society, these rules meant that many enslaved women bore free children.

The Roman inheritance pattern influenced all European systems of slavery in the Americas. Roman slaves, like their counterparts in the United States, could not contract legal marriage (*connubium*), which guaranteed patrilineal descent and was confined to free people. Unions (*contubernia*) between Roman slaves or between Roman slaves and free persons followed matrilineal rules of descent. By a senate decree of A.D. 52, however, a free Roman woman in *contubernium* with a slave could be punished with enslavement herself, and the master of the male slave could claim as slaves any children from their union.

In the Chinese pattern, children of mixed unions inherited the status of the inferior parent of either sex. In contrast, the slaveholding peoples of the ancient Near East had a less confining pattern: the children of a mixed union took the status of the free (usually male) parent. The children of free parents, however, inherited status from the father.

Slaveholding countries and major slave societies relied on more than one method to maintain slavery, and the relative importance of various methods varied over time. In the ancient Near East, indebtedness ranked with birth and war as a leading method of enslavement. Creditors could seize debtors or members of their families and sell them into permanent bondage, although the code of Hammurabi (ca. 1750 B.C.) in Babylon and such Old Testament passages as Exodus 21: 2–8 and Deuteronomy 15: 12 suggest a concerted effort by some rulers to roll back debt slavery into debt servitude, at least for indebted insiders. The apparent decline in debt slavery in Persia during the Achaeminid Empire (ca. 550–331 B.C.) coincided with a rising number of mass enslavements by warfare. Exodus 21:5–6 speaks of debt servitude becoming voluntary self-enslavement. If a servant chooses to stay with his master in the seventh year, he becomes a slave

In this seventeenth-century German engraving illuminating 2 Kings 4, the prophet Elisha miraculously increases the widow's supply of oil to save her sons from debt bondage. [Historical Pictures Archive/Corbis]

who is then marked by having his ear pierced with an awl. In 2 Kings 4:1 a widow of Israel cries to Elisha for help against a creditor who has come to lay claim to her two sons by placing them in bondage. Since all premodern populations experienced Malthusian cycles of growth and catastrophic recession, the most vulnerable members of a society frequently staved off starvation by selling themselves or their children, especially their young daughters, into slavery. Documents on self-enslavement for money, with the status inherited by the current and future children of the enslaved man, exist from Egypt in the sixth century B.C.

Chronic warfare and the marketing of captives obtained in warfare clearly brought a substantial portion of slaves into ancient households, but concern about security and a lack of resources probably limited mass enslavements by victors from weak, nonexistent, or incipient states. When the losers were not massacred or sacrificed, they could end up as ransomed captives, not necessarily as slaves. Victorious chieftains frequently spared themselves and their homeland future trouble by killing defeated men and enslaving only women and children. In ancient wars between city-states residents of a fallen city might escape mass enslavement on site only to be selectively scattered as slaves by sale or by being extracted at regular intervals in the form of tribute. Ancient Egypt had slaves, but apparently not in large numbers until the expansionist New Kingdom (ca. 1550–1075 B.C.) pushed east across the Red Sea and south up the Nile and enslaved

the adversaries it conquered. One subjected people to the south, the darker-skinned Nubians, eventually agreed to surrender slaves as annual tribute, an arrangement that continued for long periods and that resume by treaty (the *baqt*) after the Muslim conquest of Egypt in the seventh century after Christ. Herodotus mentions similar Persian exactions from ancient Babylon, which agreed to send five hundred enslaved and castrated boys as annual tribute to Persian kings.

If the Homeric epics and other sources are any indication, victorious Greeks who lived before the transition of Athens and other Greek city-states into full-fledged slave societies preferred to execute male warriors they defeated and to enslave the women and children they captured. Aristotle's listing of piracy and hunting (a legitimate subset of which was people-hunting) among the five "natural" ways of making a living suggests the long-standing importance of these methods of enslavement to the ancient Greeks and neighboring peoples. Mass enslavements became more conspicuous products of war at the end of the Archaic period (ca. 500 B.C.). One scholar has counted 120 pitched battles in ancient Greece, 28 of which ended in mass enslavement and 24 of which ended in massacre; seizures of among one hundred cities, 34 resulted in mass enslavement and 26 ended in massacre.

Throughout the ancient world, merchants elbowed ahead of prostitutes in bringing up the rear of advancing armies to get at the vendible harvest of humans reaped by the victors. No one knows in what precise proportions the various methods of enslavement were represented in ancient or modern marketplaces, but the significance of collective violence in global history as an indirect and regular supplier of slaves to traders can scarcely be underestimated. Expanding empires, rival city-states, and volatile frontiers yielded slaves who were directed into any number of thriving urban markets dotting the eastern half of the ancient Mediterranean. Such roving seafarers as the Phoenicians, Cretans, and Cilecians earned their reputations as pirates by raiding and plundering for slaves. Their sale of human game helped to turn such places as the Aegean island of Delos into renowned slave markets. A revealing strand of Greek memory attributes the initial acquisition of enslaved outsiders by Greeks to the inhabitants of the Aegean island of Chios, one such ancient entrepôt.

Xenophon, among other Greeks, advise his fellow householders on how to foster the natural reproduction of their slaves, and from the Homeric to the classical period, birth seems to have assumed increasing importance in ancient Greek societies as a method of enslavement, as more enslaved males were recruited in war and as inheritance patterns in most—though not all—Greek states shifted from patrilineal to matrilineal descent of the children of enslaved mothers. People could also be enslaved for debt in ancient Greece (less commonly, however, than in ancient Mesopotamia), but usually for sale abroad. About 590 B.C. Solon passed laws for Athens, which of all the classical Greek city-states acquired the largest slave population; these laws virtually eliminated debt as a method of enslaving fellow Greeks. The Persian wars of the fifth century B.C. seem to have furthered a pan-Hellenic loathing of Greeks who enslaved Greeks. Nor did many classical Greek citizens enslave themselves, although Athenian fathers had the right to sell promiscuous daughters into slavery. The selling of children into slavery appears to have occurred far more frequently outside of Athens in the Aegean rimland. A more important Greek source of enslaved children was abandonment, a practice prohibited in Thebes but otherwise commonplace in antiquity, in Asia, and in precolonial and colonial Africa. Although overlooked by Jean Bodin as a method of enslavement, abandonment continued to be a minor source of slaves in Europe through the Middle Ages.

The city of Rome, at its height, had a slave population that may have been more than one-third of the population, which approached 1 million. During the expansionist Republic, the numbers of slaves rose from infusions of enslaved prisoners of war. From 262 to 142 B.C., according to one study, seventeen major victories resulted in mass enslavements that produced from 2,500 to 150,000 victims. Prisoners of war continued to stream into the Roman slave population, indirectly through merchants as well as directly from soldiers bringing home the spoils of victory, after the ascension of Augustus to imperium in 27 B.C. But fewer campaigns and stronger rule over firming boundaries in the first two centuries of the Empire and beyond probably meant that slave births later outpaced conquest as the leading Roman method of enslavement. Roman writers at this time certainly paid more attention to slave births and applauded masters who had learned the value of rewarding procreative female slaves.

Urban slave markets in the wider Mediterranean world disposed of slaves obtained by kidnappers and brigands, although the victory of Sextus Pompeius in 67 B.C. over a fleet of Mediterranean pirates precipitated a brief shortage in some places. Classical Romans, almost as much as classical Greeks, condemned self-enslavement by free citizens. Slavery actually spared many abandoned freeborn (mostly female) Roman children death. Yet this practice became a growing concern to Roman officials, prompting inquiries and eventually legal prohibition in A.D. 374. Penal slaves (servi poenae) were usually removed from Rome to spend their lives at hard labor in the imperial mines. All criminals sentenced to death, according to Roman law, became penal slaves until their execution. The empire also permitted freedmen and freedwomen to be reenslaved for certain crimes, including an affront to their former masters' status.

As serfdom advanced in rural Western Europe after the fall of the Roman Empire, slavery receded. But slavery retained considerable strength in certain urban areas, in Scandinavia, among Germanic peoples, and in the lands that bordered the Mediterranean basin. Centuries of back-and-forth warfare between Christians and Muslims kept long-distance trade routes coursing with enslaved infidels. Various Western European kingdoms obtained enslaved outsiders during the Middle Ages, but the sale of children, self-enslavement, debt, and penal slavery probably increased the proportion of enslaved locals in generally diminishing slave populations. Las Siete Partidas, the great thirteenth-century Spanish legal code informed by Roman law and Christian theology, acknowledged three types of slaves: "the first are those taken captive in war who are enemies of the faith; the second, those born of female slaves; the third, when a person is free and allows himself to be sold." For the last to happen, however, five conditions had to be met. The person had to give his consent to be sold; he had to receive at least a portion of the price; he had to be aware of his free status at the moment of sale; the prospective buyer had to believe he was buying a slave;

and the prospective slave had to be more than twenty years of age.

Slavery in the Byzantine Empire remains a neglected subject, despite perennial scholarly fascination with the court eunuchs. Among the methods of enslavement, tribute payments, unlike war and birth, accounted for only a small portion of slaves there—as in Byzantium's Roman antecedent. Justinian outlawed both penal slavery and the enslavement of children by abandonment; Emperor Leo VI (A.D. 886–912) outlawed self-enslavement. Emperor Alexios I Komnenos (A.D. 1081–1118) may have stimulated enslavement by birth by sanctioning slave marriages, although the proportion of slaves obtained in warfare appears to have risen during the tenth century as a result of successful eastward expansion into Islamic domains. In this and the previous century Italian merchants prospered by carrying on a brisk trade in enslaved captives of Byzantiums wars as well as other commodities.

The Vikings established a fearsome reputation as seaborne marauders and slave traders during their heyday from the ninth to the mid-eleventh century. They may even have created a genuine slave society in Iceland. Elsewhere, slave populations formed a small minority of the whole among Scandinavian peoples, but the prevalence of raiding, which often looked indistinguishable from war, maintained a high proportion of enslaved outsiders. Among insiders, punishment for such crimes as theft, witchcraft, and sexual transgressions generated more slaves than did debt, which tended to be punished by servitude rather than by enslavement. With the decline of the Vikings, birth probably became more important as a method of enslavement. All medieval Scandinavian peoples accepted hereditary slavery, but they had no common pattern of inheritance: For mixed unions, the Swedes followed the Near Eastern rule of favoring freedom; the Danes followed the Roman pattern of matrilineal inheritance. Many freeborn Scandinavian children found themselves enslaved when their parents sold or abandoned them.

When English colonists settled in the Americas in the seventeenth century, they reveled in their distinctive liberties and in the absence of a homegrown model of slavery. They had faulty memories, however. In Anglo-Saxon England before the Norman conquest of 1066, slaves were about 10 percent of the total population, and 20 percent in some counties. Slavery lasted as much more than an oddity in English life from the sixth to the twelfth centuries. The numbers fluctuated with the intensity of violence: invasions, warfare, raiding, and kidnapping. Anglo-Saxon invaders enslaved Celts; Viking invaders enslaved Anglo-Saxons; warring Anglo-Saxon kingdoms enslaved Anglo-Saxons. Self-enslavement in Anglo-Saxon England be-

Alfred the Great. [Michael Nicholson/Corbis]

came as familiar as the dislocation, poverty, and debt generated by the chronic warfare and raiding. King Alfred the Great (A.D. 871–899) tried to restrict the sale of freeborn daughters into slavery; King Canute (A.D. 1014–1035) tried to limit the sale of children into slavery. Sunday labor, theft, and incest ranked high among the causes of penal enslavement. A paucity of evidence prohibits confident generalizations about birth as a method of enslavement, and legal and religious documents conflict in their positions on the status children of mixed unions inherited.

Asia gave rise to many slaveholding peoples but few slave societies. China possessed a bewildering array of dependent statuses, and methods of enslavement varied by region and time. Several Chinese dynasties developed criminal punishment as a major strategy. Under Chinese law, not only the perpetrator but the perpetrator's relatives could be enslaved for certain crimes. Over millennia, poverty and famine drove unknown numbers of Chinese to enslave themselves and to sell their children into slavery. In some cases entire lineages surrendered themselves as slaves. Like the ancient Nubians and the Aztecs, the Shang dynasty (1766–1122 B.C.) appears to have used warfare as a means of mass enslavement to achieve the end of ritual sacrifice.

A true slave society emerged in medieval Korea during the Koryo dynasty (A.D. 918–1392), which was exceptional in its reliance on enslaved insiders. Birth, criminal punishment, and the self-enslavement of desperate peasant supplied the overwhelming majority of slaves, who, at their peak, may have approached one-third of the total population. Enslavement by war, a commonplace in ancient Korea, served as a minor method during this period and later. Korean law contradictorily recognized slave marriages as well as the master's right to separate slave families. The rules of inheritance for the children of mixed unions seem to have changed over time; evidence exists of the application of both the Chinese preference for slavery and the Roman transmission of the mother's status, neither of which was particularly conducive to natal escape from slavery.

Russian slavery resembled Korean slavery in its enslavement of insiders. During the expansion of the Muscovite state from the fifteenth century to the early seventeenth century, slaves came to be about 10 percent of the total population, and they accounted for a higher proportion when combined with certain categories of Russian serfs who either inherited their condition or enslaved themselves by sale or by debt. Free Russians frequently entered into contracts for loans that, if not repaid, allowed enslavement of the delinquent borrower. Any free person who cohabited with a slave became enslaved, thus resolving the question of inheritance. Slaves had a legal right to marry, even though masters inclined toward arranging the partners. The children of free parents who became enslaved became slaves also.

Irresistible internal pressures to recruit enslaved outsiders attended the explosive growth of Islam during the Middle Ages. Islam permits the enslavement of infidels captured in a holy war (*jihād*), but it prohibits Muslims from enslaving fellow Muslims and even from enslaving nonbelieving "people of the book" (i.e., Jews and Christians, or *dhimmīs*) who accept Muslim rule. Muslims cannot punish Muslims with enslavement for debt or for crimes. Muslim fathers cannot sell their children or other family members into slavery. Abandoned Muslim children cannot be reared by Muslims as slaves.

Islamic law and precepts also facilitated the slave's quest for freedom by promoting manumission. Conversion to Islam did not automatically free an enslaved outsider, but a female slave who gave birth to her master's children became free upon his death. Inheritance followed the Near Eastern pattern. Children of

masters and enslaved concubines inherited the free status of the father, if he acknowledged parentage. As a result, birth became less important as a method of enslavement in the Muslim world than in, say, imperial Rome or the antebellum southern United States, even though Muslim slaves, unlike their Roman and southern counterparts, could, with their masters' consent, legally marry—free persons as well as slaves. The Muslim predilection for eunuchs to tend harems and perform administrative duties obviously limited natural reproduction among slaves.

To meet the demand for domestic, administrative, and agricultural slaves, Muslims thus had to look for sources of supply beyond their frontiers, which within several centuries of Muhammad's death reached into Central Asia, across North Africa, and into Western Europe. With vital help from the camel for commercial transportation, Muslims originated the long-distance trade in West African slaves along the routes opened. One specialist has estimated trans-Saharan imports into the Islamic world from the seventh to the twentieth century at more than 7 million slaves, the majority of them female, with peak volume during the nineteenth century of about fourteen thousand slaves per year. When combined with an estimated 5 million slaves extracted from East Africa and transported by way of the Red Sea and the Indian Ocean from the ninth to the twentieth century, imports of enslaved Africans into the Muslim world by merchants approximate the most credible estimates of imports of enslaved Africans into the Americas during the entire history of the Atlantic slave trade.

Muslims recruited slaves by violence, purchase, and tribute. Sectarian disputes about the purity of believers—not to mention greed—occasioned wars and the capture and enslavement of avowed Muslim by avowed Muslim, contrary to Islamic law. An impressive class of Muslim merchants spread the faith as they negotiated purchases for slaves and other commodities with a multicultural array of vendors throughout much of the Old World. During the European Middle Ages, Muslims obtained large numbers of Christians and pagan slaves from Danish Vikings, who raided and subjugated the Anglo-Saxons; and from Swedish Vikings, who penetrated into Russia and reduced many Slavs to slavery. Jewish merchants acquired slaves for Muslim consumers throughout the Mediterranean and beyond, and in Verdun (northern France) apparently set up a notorious house of castration to produce valuable eunuchs who, according to Islamic law, could not be mutilated on Islamic ground. Genoese and Venetian merchants earned fortunes in trading slaves and other goods to Muslims as well as incurring the outrage of Catholic officials for including enslaved Christians in their cargos. Various Christian rulers at the urging of various popes tried to stop Christians from selling Christians to Muslim buyers. The eastern bias in the resulting slave trade showed up by the ninth century after Christ: the word for Slav in Arabic had by then become synonymous with the condition of slavery in Europe.

The Muslims' conquest of most of the Iberian Peninsula in the eighth century opened a major market and redistribution point for enslaved Europeans in southern Spain. The Visigoths had presided over a sizable slave population noteworthy for its proportion of penal slaves during the previous three centuries, then became targets of enslavement themselves in a Muslim holy war. Having been pushed back to the Cantabrian Mountains, the Visigoths regrouped and initiated the Christian Reconquest, an erratic process that took more than seven centuries to complete. Shifting alliances, periodic campaigns, and endemic raiding dumped slaves into the hands of Christian, Muslim, and Jewish traders, who generally refrained from selling their coreligionists. Comely women and castrated males (many of them, until the end of the tenth century, of Slavic origin) fetched high prices in Muslim domains. The ruling elite must have bid them up, for one caliph of Cordoba, it was said, had accumulated a harem of more than 6,000 women. The Umayyad caliphs in Spain also instituted a practice that would remain a curious feature of Muslim slavery for years to come: the recruitment and training of slaves for military service.

Muslim rulers used war, raids (*razzias*), kidnapping, and tribute to acquire their slave soldiers. The Spanish Umayyads began purchasing large numbers of Slavs for military purposes in the eighth century, and at about the same time in the Middle East, the Abassids were molding enslaved Turkish nomads into a disciplined fighting force. The fabled mamluks, who included enslaved Turks, black Africans, and Caucasian peoples in the ranks of the Fatamid military in Egypt, became so powerful that in the mid-thirteenth century they overthrew the Ayubbids and established a dynasty of former slaves sustained by the ongoing purchase of successors. Ottoman invaders could not have ended the rule of the Mamluks in 1517 without the janissaries, an elite corps of soldiers derived from a levy of enslaved boys (*devshirme*) imposed on subjugated Christians.

Perennial border skirmishing and kidnapping between the Ottoman Turks and Slavic peoples yielded large number of slaves for the empire. Turkish slave traders also benefited from tribal rivalries to the north and purchased captive Caucasian women and children from Caucasians. The Turks claimed with some exaggeration that the Circassians sold their children into Turkish slavery in order to provide them with an escape from poverty. Some Circassian girls actually saw life in a harem as an opportunity and enslaved themselves to take advantage of it.

The Ottoman Empire stands out for its use of tribute as a method of enslavement. Besides the *devshirme*, annual contributions of enslaved men and women arrived from dependencies that ranged from Africa to the Crimea, although the numbers enslaved in this way were a small part of the whole. Ottoman expansion, beginning in the fourteenth century, led to enslavements of a magnitude similar to the Roman conquests during the republic. Even the failed campaign against Vienna in 1683 netted more than 75,000 slaves, the overwhelming majority women and children. The Ottomans gave up mass enslavement of captives by the early nineteenth century, but slavery itself lingered on for more than a century, supported more and more by trade. As in other Muslim domains, Ottoman slavery had a predominantly urban character and for centuries Istanbul's slave markets, like those in other Muslim cities, did a brisk business in harem girls and eunuchs. The Ottomans acquired far more slaves by trade than by birth.

Ottoman authority, at its apogee in the sixteenth century, stretched across North Africa, but the community of Islam at that time extended much farther, embracing the Sahara and much of the Sudan as well as a narrow strip of coastal East Africa as far south as the Swahili Bantus. East and west, Muslim traders continued to push out, elaborating intricate networks of exchange that included slaves. From the time of Muhammad to the ending (actually, submersion) of slavery in Africa under colonial rule in the twentieth century, Muslim slave traders benefited from scores of holy wars that swept the land like firestorms. Holy war contributed to the rise of Songhai and Borno in the sixteenth century and to the Sokoto caliphate in the nineteenth, three of the greatest empires in the history of the Sudan. Largely by war, raiding, and tribute, each of these polities, over decades, acquire slaves in numbers that exceeded one third of the total population. The *jihād* headed by Usuman dan Fodio, which began in 1804 and led to the creation of the Sokoto caliphate, was only one of many during the nineteenth century that together caused the enslavement of millions of Africans.

Portuguese maritime explorations of the fifteenth century down the coast of West Africa began more than four centuries of slave trading in the Atlantic by cutting into long-established Muslim commercial sources of slaves. At the time of European contact, non-Muslim areas of West Africa appear to have had substantial slave populations, since communal ownership of land enhanced the desirability of slaves as a form of private property. Africanists generally agree on the primacy of war and raiding as methods of enslavement in West Africa, and, indeed, throughout the continent. Kidnapping probably ranked close behind. Given the hundreds of small states and stateless societies defined by vague or changing borders, lesser methods of violence probably predominated over war in West Africa for certain periods in certain places. Raids could encompass anything from an organized expedition by military units at the behest of a central authority to freelancing by stateless individuals or warrior bands.

Non-Muslim as well as Muslim states also exacted tributary slaves from dependencies in Africa. Among the lesser methods, flexible juridical proceedings sentenced many Africans convicted of sorcery, theft, adultery, and other crimes to enslavement. Warlike Aro traders, who operated in the region of the Bight of Biafra, took slaves by brigandage and used their famous oracle to condemn the losing parties in local disputes to enslavement. Self-enslavement and the barter or sale of children and other dependents into slavery also played significant roles, particularly during the recurring droughts, famines, and other natural disasters. Inheritance patterns with Africa tended to favor escape from slavery by birth to an enslaved parent through lineage systems that assimilated children into the group of the master.

Scholars continue to debate the impact of the Atlantic slave trade on these African processes of enslavement, and without question, Europeans' demand for slaves intensified the search by Africans for new methods to supply it. But millions of West African slaves also embarked on slave ships because of war and violence that had intrinsically African causes. What one investigator has concluded about Afonso I, king of Congo (1506–1545), based on a careful reading of his detailed correspondence, could be applied to many other African rulers before the twentieth century: "He has the conviction . . . that one man may be property of another and may be forced to submit to this state by birth, poverty, punishment for a crime, or the laws of war . . . . A slave, like any other property, may be passed on by the habitual methods of transmission: sale, trade, gift, inheritance."

For West Central Africa, the region that supplied more slaves to the Americas than any other, methods of enslavement show stages linked to the European trade. Whereas civil war and statist expansion first provided the largest number of slaves, overextension and indebtedness later forced African elites to drop accumulated dependents into slavery when Europeans came to collect. Thus, as Joseph Miller has pointed out for the Congo-Angola region, "Debts for trade goods the mercantile kings had received, or credits the people of their states owed in people, enforced by the

institutions of law and coercion, thus produced a significant proportion of the slaves handed over to European merchants."

At one time or another in the early history of the Atlantic slave trade, all participating European powers took comfort from the fiction that their purchased slaves had originated in Africa in just wars—just, that is, by the standards of Christian theology. And although the Spanish and Portuguese have been praised for their "abolition" of Indian slavery in the Americas during the sixteenth century, the loophole of the just war, amply stretched by white colonists, continued the enslavement of Indians in Latin America by capture for centuries. Frontier raiding in Brazil, most notably, enslaved Indians in such numbers that they, not enslaved Africans, became the basis of an agricultural economy in the southern captaincy of São Vincente well into the eighteenth century. Still, in Brazil and other American colonies, metropolitan restraint and the decline of Indian populations through exposure to European and African diseases gradually confined enslavement almost exclusively to the purchase of Africans and retention of people of African descent in slavery.

Violence in Africa thus predominated as the original means of enslavement for the 11 million or so Africans who arrived in the Americas by way of the Atlantic slave trade; birth predominated as the later means of enslavement for every slave society in the Americas. To be sure, everywhere from the mining regions of Minas Gerais in Brazil to the Mason-Dixon line, some free people of color fell victim to kidnapping and were enslaved. In a few instances free people of color enslaved themselves, and before the U.S. Civil War the majority of the slaveholding states passed laws to permit this choice, albeit very few people exercised it.

With marginal qualifications, every slave society in the Americas adopted the Roman principle of *partus sequitur ventrem* (the status of the child derives from the mother) in determining whether a child was born free or enslaved. No slave society in the Americas had more prolific slave mothers than did the United States. Although a relatively minor participant in the Atlantic slave trade, the United States, by 1860, had the largest slave population in the hemisphere, almost 4 million slaves. After considerable debate over the reasons for this growth demographic analysis has shown that female slaves in the United States had a longer span of childbearing years and a narrower interval between births than other slave populations in the Americas. Abolitionists charged slaveholders with breeding slaves, and scattered evidence reveals a few masters throughout the hemisphere who went beyond improving the material conditions and domesticity of

An 1830 U.S. woodcut depicting the interstate sale of slaves. [Corbis-Bettmann]

slave life to attempting to coerce their slaves into procreating. For the United States, however, the argument for slave breeding for commercial purposes is weakened by the absence of any strong correlation between the movement of prices for plantation staples and rates of slave fertility. Some writers have pointed to differences between a young female slave population in the slave-exporting states of the Atlantic seaboard and the older male slaves in the slave-importing states of the Southwest as evidence of breeding strategies, but the same differences exist for the white populations of the two regions as well.

Similar confusion reigns about the contribution of birth as a method of enslavement in other regions of the Americas, especially in the sugar colonies, where crude growth rates show naturally decreasing slave populations. The United States, unlike most other slave societies in the Americas, had a relatively stable slave population, for slaves entered or left the country in insignificant numbers after the legal abolition of the Atlantic slave trade in 1808. The slave trade continued to supply large number of Africans to places like Cuba and Brazil until 1850 and later. By subjecting existing slave populations to these substantial in-migrations of adults, the Atlantic slave trade grossly distorted age and sex composition toward a clustering in the upper age brackets, thereby including disproportionately large numbers of slaves at higher risk of dying. Meaningful comparisons of demographic growth, however, can be made only between stable populations. With migration factored out, slave pop-

ulations, even in the notoriously lethal sugar zones, have shown rates of natural increase and impressive age-specific fertility under the hardships of labor and life under slavery. Thus, even though slaves in the United States had higher fertility rates than their Caribbean and Brazilian counterparts, birth remained far and away the single most important method of enslavement throughout the hemisphere.

See also ANCIENT GREECE; ANCIENT NEAR EAST; ANCIENT ROME; BIBLE; BYZANTIUM; ISLAM; JANISSARIES; JEWS; LABOR SYSTEMS; LAW; OTTOMAN EMPIRE; PATTERSON THESIS; SIETE PARTIDAS; SLAVE TRADE; SLAVS.

BIBLIOGRAPHY

ARCHER, LÉONIE, ed. *Slavery and Other Forms of Unfree Labour.* 1988.

BALANDIER, GEORGES. *Daily Life in the Kingdom of the Kongo: From the Sixteenth to the Eighteenth Century.* 1968.

BOSWELL, JOHN. *The Kindness of Strangers: The Abandonment of Children in Western Europe from Late Antiquity to the Renaissance.* 1988.

BONNASSIE, PIERRE. *From Slavery to Feudalism in South-Western Europe.* 1991.

BRADLEY, K. R. "On the Roman Slave Supply and Slave-breeding." *Slavery and Abolition* 8 (1987): 42–64.

DANDAMAEV, MUHAMMAD A. *Slavery in Babylonia: From Nabopolassar to Alexander the Great (626–331 B.C.).* 1984.

ERDEM, Y. HAKAN. *Slavery in the Ottoman Empire and Its Demise, 1800–1909.* 1996.

FOGEL, ROBERT WILLIAM. *Without Consent or Contract: The Rise and Fall of American Slavery.* 1989.

FOGEL, ROBERT WILLIAM, and STANLEY ENGERMAN. *Time on the Cross: The Economics of American Negro Slavery.* 1974.

GARLAN, YVON. *Slavery in Ancient Greece.* 1988.

GEMERY, HENRY A., and JAN S. HOGENDORN. *The Uncommon Market: Essays in the Economic History of the Atlantic Slave Trade.* 1979.

HELLIE, RICHARD. *Slavery in Russia, 1450–1725.* 1982.

HIGMAN, B. W. *Slave Populations of the British Caribbean, 1807–1834.* 1984.

KARRAS, RUTH MAZO. *Slavery and Society in Medieval Scandinavia.* 1988.

LEWIS, BERNARD. *Race and Slavery in the Middle East: An Historical Enquiry.* 1990.

LOVEJOY, PAUL E. *Transformations in Slavery: A History of Slavery in Africa.* 1983.

MANNING, PATRICK. *Slavery and African Life: Occidental, Oriental, and African Slave Trades.* 1990.

MENDELSOHN, ISAAC. *Slavery in the Ancient Near East.* 1949.

MILLER, JOSEPH C. *Way of Death: Merchant Capitalism and the Angolan Slave Trade, 1730–1830.* 1988.

PATTERSON, ORLANDO. *Slavery and Social Death: A Comparative Study.* 1982.

PELTERET, DAVID A. E. *Slavery in Early Mediaeval England: From the Reign of Alfred until the Twelfth Century.* 1995.

PHILLIPS, WILLIAM D., JR. *Slavery from Roman Times to the Early Transatlantic Trade.* 1985.

THORNTON, JOHN. *Africa and Africans in the Making of the Atlantic World, 1400–1680.* 1992.

VERLINDEN, CHARLES. *L'esclavage dans l'Europe médiévale.* 2 vols. 1955, 1977.

Robert L. Paquette

Épaone, Council of

The Council of Épaone met in 517 under the auspices of King Sigismond of Burgundy, a recent convert to Christianity. Convened by Bishops Avitus of Vienne and Viventiolus of Lyons, this regional church council was attended by twenty-four Frankish and Burgundian bishops.

The canons of the council dealt with matters of clerical and monastic discipline and with protecting the property of the Roman church from appropriation by clerics or lay persons. Priests and deacons were forbidden to keep hunting dogs or falcons; priests who married and their spouses were to be forbidden communion until they separated; and, the consecration of women as deacons was barred. Several canons dealt with the Arians, defining them as heretics and forbidding Catholic clergy to associate in any way with them.

Two canons dealt with slavery. The eighth canon forbade abbots to manumit slaves owned by their monasteries, suggesting that slaveholding by the church was not uncommon. The thirty-fourth canon prescribed two years of excommunication and penance for a churchman who killed his slave, unless authorized by a judge to do so as a punishment. This canon represented a departure from Burgundian law, with its tendency to punish violent crime by exacting fines.

See also CHRISTIANITY.

BIBLIOGRAPHY

CROSS, F. L., ed. *The Oxford Dictionary of the Christian Church.* 1997.

La grande encyclopédie. 1893.

T. Stephen Whitman

Éphémérides du Citoyen

In 1765 the Abbé Nicolas Baudeau (1730–1792) founded the publication *Éphémérides du citoyen, ou chronique de l'esprit national* (The Citizen's Almanac, or Chronicle of the National Spirit), to propound Physiocratic doctrines. Baudeau, a follower of Mirabeau and Quesnay, supported free trade, agrarianism, and ideas of natural rights. In 1766 Baudeau argued that Spain and France should jointly develop the Louisiana Territory, which had been transferred to Spain in 1763. Accepting a need for African labor in Louisiana, Baudeau nonetheless had scruples against slavery, which he regarded as unprofitable in the long run. He called for transporting slaves to Louisiana, where they would be freed, with profit to be recouped by charging the freedmen a permanent rent on all goods they produced. This scheme drew an angry response from a proslavery colonist, who insisted on the natural inferiority of blacks and who saw slavery as a good institution.

In 1767 *Éphémérides du citoyen* carried a piece by Benjamin Franklin that backed up Baudeau with calculations purporting to show the unprofitability of slavery. The next year Pierre Du Pont de Nemours succeeded Baudeau as editor. Du Pont also questioned slavery's profits, contending in 1771 that humane treatment of slaves would eliminate profits for slave traders. Du Pont applauded the rise of antislavery sentiment among Pennsylvania Quakers, as reported in the *Éphémérides* by Benjamin Rush, and hoped their example might influence other slaveholders, as well as Europeans whose lands were worked by serfs. Finally, the *Éphémérides* lent its imprimatur to replacing American slave-grown tropical produce with staples cultivated by free workers in Africa, an idea that would eventually be realized in the colonies of Sierra Leone and Liberia.

See also ECONOMICS OF SLAVERY; ECONOMIC INTERPRETATION OF SLAVERY; QUAKERS.

BIBLIOGRAPHY

DAVIS, DAVID BRION. *The Problem of Slavery in Western Culture.* 1966.
Grand Larousse Encyclopédique. 1960.

T. *Stephen Whitman*

Epictetus   [ca. A.D. 50–ca. 130]

Stoic philosopher.

Epictetus was a Greek inhabitant of the Roman Empire who became a prominent Stoic philosopher. He was born to a slave woman in Hierapolis, in the province of Phrygia in Asia Minor.

Epictetus remained the slave of a master named Epaphroditus, until he was freed sometime after A.D. 68. Even while a slave, Epictetus was allowed to study under C. Musonius Rufus, a Stoic philosopher renowned in the first century after Christ.

Exiled from Rome sometime between A.D. 89 and 93 by a decree of the emperor Domitian (who exiled all the philosophers from the city), Epictetus set up a school in Epirus, where he taught Stoic logic, ethics, and physics to students gathered from all parts of the empire.

His chief works include the *Discourses* and the *Manual* (or *Enchiridion*), both of which were assembled from lecture notes by Arrianus, the Roman historian of Alexander the Great. More than any other Stoic, Epictetus emphasized the virtue of submission to the inevitable. Some commentators have seen his own lameness and his long years of servitude as having influenced his notion of submissiveness—he saw all events as God's will and as gifts from God.

Freedom was the central concept of Epictetus's philosophy, but freedom conceived as self-restraint and grounded in the fundamental distinction between what an individual may change in the world and what must be accepted as it is. For Epictetus, the mind is always free to determine itself regardless of our material limitations or the perceptions imposed by others, and the basis of liberty is the power of each to exercise rational control over one's own *prohairesis,* that is, one's moral purpose in life.

This vigorous separation of external conditions from the internal freedom to make rational decisions under all circumstances led Epictetus to a certain condescension toward the flesh, even to the point of deprecating any emotional attachment to the pleasures of the world. Thus he endorsed the traditional Stoic ideal of tolerance toward the divine order of nature, with his own original emphasis on the ascetic implications of complete forbearance. Epictetus urged: "Do not admire your wife's beauty and you will not be angry if she is unfaithful" (*Discourses* 1. 18).

In this political philosophy, he preached that, since Zeus had created men free, a tyrant could enslave only their bodies; their spirits remained free to pursue righteousness. The tyrant or the brutal master believes that he is powerful because of his ability to carry out excesses, but in reality, he is the greatest of slaves—a slave to his own passions and whims.

Whether one had the status of slave or freeman, Epictetus required continued moral instruction and self-examination. The faculty of choice and refusal in regard to giving assent to one's external circumstances, Epictetus reasoned, made each person entirely responsible for his actions.

Lecturing at about the same time that the New Testament was written, Epictetus shared with the Apostles an emphasis on the existence of a universal, living God, reflected in the human community. He argued that however much individuals were corrupted by their participation in the world, they all possessed a rational capacity to act for the common good in accordance with a higher order in nature. To underscore human equality before the divine law, he advised that a slaveholder accept the behavior of his slave as he would a brother "born of the same seed as you begotten like you from above" (*Discourses* 1. 13).

Epictetus stressed *prosopon*—the concept of proper character in a man—and he saw an individual's duty to produce this, but also to display it to others in order to lead others to the virtuous life.

Unlike Cynicism and early Christianity, the later Stoicism accommodated more easily to the successors of Domitian. Marcus Aurelius adapted the cosmopolitan doctrine of human community propagated by Epictetus as the basis of Roman law, extending judicial protections to citizens throughout the empire regardless of their social standing. However briefly, Epictetus's agenda entered the philosophy of an enlightened state, with the emperor reflecting the ideal of universal reason and governing for the common good.

Epictetus seems to have been influenced by the doctrines of the Cynics as well as by his Stoic predecessors, and his influence affected Christian philosophy as well as neo-Stoicism.

See also ANCIENT ROME; PHILOSOPHY.

BIBLIOGRAPHY

ARNOLD, E. V. *Roman Stoicism.* 1958.
Epictetus. 2 vols. Translated by W. A. Oldfather. 1926–1928.

Robert Fahs
Patrick M. O'Neil

Epidemiology

See Health.

Equiano, Olaudah   [1745–1797]

Former slave and African abolitionist.

Olaudah Equiano ("Gustavus Vassa"), kidnapped with his sister from their Ibo village (Isseke) in 1756, was traded through southern Nigeria and ultimately sold to Europeans. He never saw his sister or family again. Bought by a British sea captain who gave him the name Gustavus Vassa, he was taken to England just as the Seven Years's War began and served in the British navy during the war. Expecting his freedom at war's end, he was instead returned to slavery in the West Indies. Equiano worked for three years trading between the West Indies and the North American mainland before buying his freedom on 11 July 1766. Moving to London, he served on expeditions to the Arctic, the Mediterranean, and Central America. His Christian religious faith deepened, and he considered the date of his conversion (6 October 1774) as important as the date of his emancipation. He joined other Africans in London in the Sons of Africa, an organization founded to improve their position in English society. In 1783 he brought the massacre of African slaves on the ship *Zong* to the attention of the British public, instigating a move in England to ban the slave trade. In 1788 he wrote *Interesting Narrative of the Life of Olaudah Equiano,* vividly describing his African childhood, the brutal Middle Passage, and his life as a slave and as a free African in the West Indies and England. U.S., German, Dutch, French, and Russian editions appeared by 1791. He married Susan Cullen, of Cambridgeshire, on 7 April 1792; they had two daughters: Anna Marie (1793–1797) and Joanna (b. 1795). Susan Vassa died in 1795. Olaudah Equiano spent his last years lecturing on the evils of the slave trade and slavery and died 30 April 1797; his book remains a powerful indictment of slavery.

See also ABOLITION AND ANTISLAVERY MOVEMENTS; LITERATURE OF SLAVERY; SELF-PURCHASE.

BIBLIOGRAPHY

ACHOLONU, CATHERINE OBIANUJU. *The Igbo Roots of Olaudah Equiano: An Anthropological Research.* 1989.

EQUIANO, OLAUDAH. *Interesting Narrative of the Life of Olaudah Equiano, or Gustavus Vassa, the African. [1791].* Edited by Robert J. Allison. 1995.

INIKORI, JOSEPH E., and STANLEY L. ENGERMAN, eds. *The Atlantic Slave Trade: Effects on Economies, Societies, and Peoples in Africa, the Americas, and Europe.* 1992.

SHYLLON, FOLARIN. *Black People in Britain. 1555–1833.* 1977.

Robert J. Allison

Olaudah Equiano. [Library of Congress]

Escape

Slaves ran away from masters in every society that practiced slavery. They escaped in order to obtain freedom, to improve their well-being within slavery, or to avert a worsening of their lives as slaves. The objectives of escapees could range from the grand, such as joining an army to make war upon and destroy a slaveholding society, to the purely personal, as when a slave took temporary flight from an enraged master to avoid physical abuse. Escapees in most societies were predominantly male and were disproportionately likely to be between the ages of fifteen and thirty. Modes of escape included flight by individuals and large groups of slaves, with or without the assistance of free persons or other slaves.

Escaping to Freedom

Slaves could gain freedom by escaping from a society that legally recognized a master's claim to own them, to a society that denied the legitimacy of slavery either in toto or as applied to a particular individual.

For persons enslaved and removed from the land of their birth, liberty could be attained by returning to one's native land. Returning home was the hope of escaped slaves taken to ancient Rome and Greece, or captured in African wars. Africans attempted to flee while being marched from the interior to slave-trading ports, or mutinied and seized control of slave-trading ships in the Atlantic. Desperate individuals even leaped overboard, escaping slavery through death. The goal of return also drove free persons of color kidnapped and illicitly sold into slavery in the nineteenth-century United States, and Christian Europeans or Americans enslaved by Algerian corsairs of the fifteenth to nineteenth centuries.

Slaves could also hope to become free by escaping from one slaveholding society to another, when the latter offered freedom to escapees as a military measure. Thus, slaves fled from British South Carolina to Georgia to Spanish Florida from 1738 onward when the Spanish offered to free and arm escapees in order to strengthen Florida's defenses from northern incursions. The British sought black allies during the American Revolution by offering to free slaves of rebel masters who reached their army's lines. This strategy was later employed successfully by the United States against the Confederacy from late 1862 to the end of the American Civil War. In Latin America, both Spanish authorities and colonial rebels made selective grants of freedom to slaves willing to fight for them.

Another escape alternative would be to flee to a society that accorded no legitimacy to slavery whatsoever. This alternative appealed to people born as slaves as well as those enslaved during their lifetimes. Examples would include blacks from the United States going to Mexico or British Canada after the abolition of slavery in those areas in 1829 and 1838, respectively, or from West Indian colonies to Britain or France once those countries adopted the doctrine that no residents could be slaves.

A variation would be flight within a slaveholding society to an area where slavery enjoyed little public support, rendering recapture difficult or impossible. Slaves who ran from the U.S. South to the North after 1800 fit this category, as do Brazilian fugitives of the 1870s or 1880s, who fled the last strongholds of slavery in that country's southern coffee-growing regions.

Slaves also ran to maroon societies, that is, communities wherein ex-slaves and their descendants controlled territory within a slaveholding society, generally without official sanction. Maroon societies operated throughout the Atlantic plantation world; evidence of them has also been adduced in the ancient Mediterranean and in Iraq under the Abbasid Caliphate. Some communities had thousands of members and lasted for decades, such as Palmares in seventeenth-century Brazil. Most numbered in the dozens or hundreds and lasted for shorter periods. A few maroon societies, such as those in eighteenth-century Dutch Suriname and British Jamaica, attained official recognition of their free status. Perhaps the most extensive maroon community in the United States existed in the Great Dismal Swamp on the border of eastern Virginia and North Carolina, where as many as two thousand black people lived in quasi-freedom for much of the nineteenth century. Finally, runaways might seek to reach a public place of sanctuary within a slaveholding society, in order to advance legal claims to freedom or to seek mercy from harsh treatment. In the Roman Empire, for example, sanctuary could be sought in the shadow of an emperor's statue in a public square. Persons born into slavery in African societies may have been less likely to attempt escape than their counterparts elsewhere, because those societies often afforded slaves or their descendants greater opportunity to rise in status or attain freedom. Where African slavery more nearly resembled the plantation slavery of the Americas, as in nineteenth-century Zanzibar, escapes were more frequent.

Almost all escapes to freedom could be combined with insurrection against slaveholders, either to gain control of resources permitting escape, or more rarely, to overthrow the slave society entirely. The Stono rebellion of Angolan slaves in South Carolina in 1739, for example, featured an armed rebellion as prelude to an attempted march to Spanish Florida. Gabriel's Rebellion in Virginia in 1800 may have had as its ultimate goal escape to Haiti. Outright revolts to end slavery by taking control of society have been comparatively less common, the best known cases being the failed revolts in Roman Sicily and Italy and the successful revolution in Saint Domingue (now Haiti).

Escaping within Slavery

Many slave escapes, perhaps a majority, aimed not at complete freedom, but either at improving the quality of life within slavery or at securing a temporary relaxation of its harshness. Slaves ran away to forestall sales that would separate family members, or to reunite after such a sale. Events that portended sale, such as the death of a master and impending distribution of the slaves as bequests to heirs or to settle debts, often led to slave flight. So did the appearance of a slave trader on a plantation, and in antebellum cities in the United States runaway rates moved up or down in tandem with the scale of slave trading. It should be noted that a slave also might run away in the hope of generating a sale, if he or she was extremely dissatisfied with a master.

Slaves escaped to avoid physical punishment and sexual abuse, or to prevent being assigned or hired to onerous, dangerous, or distasteful jobs, such as mining, canal digging, ironmaking, chimney sweeping, or removing night soil from privies. Rural slaves' escape patterns showed a seasonality, occurring more frequently during harvest seasons, when work was hardest, and in warmer weather, when living in the open air as a fugitive was easiest. For urban slaves, escape was a year-round proposition. The moment of escape could be timed to allow the longest possible period before absence would be detected. Slaves hired by the calendar year often ran off in the week between Christmas and New Year's Day, because this was a time allotted for them to return from their place of hire to visit their masters. Field hands, therefore might decamp on a Saturday evening, knowing that they would not be missed until work resumed on Monday morning.

Modes of Escape and Obstacles

Persons escaping from slavery hoped to shed a slave identity and acquire or resume that of a free person. To do so, runaways sought both to alter their appearance and to get away from areas where they were known as slaves. Cutting hair, changing clothes, or hiding brand marks or whipping scars that identified one as a slave were typical runaway strategies. In Africa, the presence or absence of body marks connoting membership in a tribe or nation could betray one's slave status, as could a shorn head. In societies where slavery was based on race, such as the United States, black escapees often traveled at night to avoid detection. But an unusually light-skinned slave could hope to "pass" as white, and travel openly. Ellen Craft used this subterfuge, posing as a young white man traveling with a black servant, who was in fact her husband. Both successfully left the South in 1850 via railroad and became free in Great Britain. Alternatively, runaway slaves might obtain or forge legal documents authorizing them to travel, such as certificates

A reward poster offers $100 for the apprehension of a fugitive slave, but according to the fine print, the actual amount to be paid out depends on the location of the slave's capture. [Corbis-Bettmann]

of freedom for a free person of color or sailors' protection papers or a pass allowing a slave to move about in pursuit of a master's business. Frederick Douglass used a free black sailor's identification papers to present himself as a free person while en route from slave Maryland to free Pennsylvania in 1838. Born a slave in the United States, Henry Brown left slavery behind by posing as cargo, having himself nailed up in a packing crate and shipped to Philadelphia, earning him the sobriquet "Box" Brown.

Slaves could avail themselves of help in escaping. Maroon societies frequently raided plantations to liberate slaves and acquire new recruits. During the American Civil War, advances by United States troops afforded thousands of southern slaves an opportunity to gain freedom by reaching the Union lines. In the antebellum period, slaves gained help from black and white abolitionists via the Underground Railroad, a loosely organized group that provided guides, hiding places, and food to runaways. Perhaps the best known "conductor" on the Underground Railroad was Harriet Tubman, who led over three hundred black persons from slavery on Maryland's Eastern Shore to freedom.

Slaveholders sought to counter escape in a number of ways. Most slaveholding societies passed laws requiring the surrender of runaways and the punishment of free persons who employed or harbored fugitives, or who enticed them to run away. Slave patrols might roam the roads at night, and public officials and facilities, such as jails, could be used to recapture and hold runaways. Slaveholders could also call on assistance from slave catchers, private individuals who earned rewards for capturing fugitives: every slave society from Rome to the United States had such persons. To summarize, escape from slavery was ubiquitous but dangerous, much contested but never thoroughly suppressed.

See also AMISTAD; CIVIL WAR, U.S.; DOUGLASS, FREDERICK; FUGITIVE SLAVE LAWS, U.S.; GABRIEL'S REBELLION; INSURRECTIONS; MAROONS; MILITARY SLAVES; REBELLIONS AND VIOLENT RESISTANCE; STONO REBELLION; UNDERGROUND RAILROAD.

BIBLIOGRAPHY

BERLIN, IRA. *Free at Last: A Documentary History of Slavery, Freedom, and the Civil War.* 1912.
KOLCHIN, PETER. *American Slavery, 1619–1877.* 1993.
MULLIN, GERALD W. *Flight and Resistance: Slave Resistance in Eighteenth-Century Virginia.* 1972.
PATTERSON, ORLANDO. *Slavery and Social Death: A Comparative Study.* 1982.
PRICE, RICHARD, ed. *Maroon Societies: Rebel Slave Communities in the Americas.* 1996.

T. Stephen Whitman

Ethiopia

See Northeast Africa.

Eunuchs

The term *eunuch* (*khasi* in Arabic) usually designates a male slave whose testicles have been ablated by one of several methods; some eunuchs were subjected to the complete removal of all sexual organs (*madjbub*). The practice is ancient and universal. Earliest accounts of eunuch slaves predate the first millennium, having been recorded in the historical accounts of China's Chou dynasty. There is also evidence of eunuchism in the records of Mesopotamia, the classical world, Syria, Asia Minor, Africa, India, and Europe. Historians note that eunuchs are mentioned in both the East and the West in the eighth century B.C., so the custom may have been established simultaneously in both regions. The practice has nearly always been associated with slave status.

In China eunuchs have been common for nearly all known history. From the Chou dynasty (1122–250 B.C.) until the collapse of Imperial China in 1911, China's rulers employed eunuchs in the imperial palace as servants and as harem chamberlains. Enslaved war captives from throughout inner Asia were castrated for service as menial workers in palaces, while others chose self-castration as a means to secure a position in the imperial palace, which carried the potential for attaining wealth and power.

Eunuchs were common in ancient Greece and Rome. They were outlawed in the first century A.D. by the Roman emperor Domitian, but eunuchism continued during the Byzantine Empire. Herodotus (fifth century B.C.) reported that the Persians castrated Ionians and took them to their king. The poet Claudian describes Eutropius, a eunuch castrated by an Armenian, who controlled Arcadia from A.D. 383 to 408.

Around the Mediterranean, slaves to fill the ranks of eunuchs as well as concubines came from defeated groups in Egypt, Iran, Syria, Asia Minor, Bulgaria, and Croatia. The Persians began the practice of castrating slaves for service as palace eunuchs. In Turkey the custom was established only with Ottoman adoption of this Byzantine Greek custom. In the early fifteenth century the custom of employing white eunuchs was adopted, along with the seclusion of women in harems and the keeping of concubines. Initially white eunuchs for the Ottoman Empire were drawn from the European conquest of Hungarian, Slavonian, and German communities. Later, white slaves for eunuchism came from Central Asian conquests in Armenia, Georgia, and Circassia. Boys enslaved in this way were castrated upon arrival in Turkey.

Late in the nineteenth century, black eunuchs were brought from sub-Saharan Africa and shared equally in both status and the potential for acquiring power. African boys were transported to North Africa (Morocco, Tripoli, and Tunis) from throughout West Africa through the trans-Saharan slave trade and then sold across the Mediterranean into the Ottoman heartland. Alternatively, slaves from the upper Nile, Kordofan, Darfur, and the Lake Chad region came through Ethiopia and Egypt to Beirut, India, Istanbul, Jeddah, Mecca, Medina, and Smyrna. From ancient times Ethiopia was one of the major suppliers of slave eunuchs to the Mediterranean.

Once captured, these boys were castrated along the way to the foreign markets; often the operation was performed in the Sahara with only sand as a styptic. The resultant high mortality rate guaranteed high prices to slave dealers for those boys who survived. Whether Africans or Asians, the enslaved survivors of the operation were destined for a life as members of an elite corps, where they could acquire power and wealth.

Slave and Nonslave Eunuchs as Religious Servants

Although the prophet Muhammad objected to the practice of creating eunuchs and Islam recommended manumitting one's slaves, eunuchs rapidly became powerful figures at the center of Islamic empires. In these contexts, eunuchs guarded not only large domestic harems but also holy tombs. During the twelfth century a sacred society of eunuchs associated with the tomb of the prophet Muhammed evolved in Mecca. In the thirteenth and fourteenth centuries, the roles of eunuchs as sexually ambiguous guardians of sanctity (*baraka*, blessedness) at tombs in Mecca, Medina, Cairo, Jerusalem, and Hebron led to their emergence as powerful, wealthy figures in Muslim society. These sacred societies continued to exist at the end of the twentieth century and are still associated with the sanctuaries in Mecca and Medina. Originally of slave lineage, these eunuchs were called "servant" (*khadim*). The meaning of the term implied servitude to both God and a human master.

One form of eunuchism not directly associated with a legal status as a slave is that derived from self-castration for membership in a religious cult, arguably constituting metaphorical enslavement to the pre-Christian and early Christian religious groups that required it. The best known of ancient self-castrates were the Galli of Cybele and Atargatis, wandering mendicants and temple attendants in the cult of the Anatolian mother-goddess. Other such eunuchs of the period were the temple attendants of Hecate in Lagina and the earliest chief priests of Artemis at Ephesus. Eunuchs in these circumstances were slaves to God.

Although some historians argue that eunuchism was outlawed in incipient Christian cultures, eunuchs made for religious purposes are mentioned throughout the Old Testament and were common in the early years of the faith. Origen and Tertullian advocated castration as a means to salvation, and the writings of Athanasius, St. Jerome, and Gregory of Nyssa support this practice. Castration was used much later to insure a supply of boys' soprano voices for the papal choir in the Sistine Chapel. An orthodox religious sect practiced castration in Russia from 1772 through the late twentieth century in the Belev and Alexin districts. Beyond the confines of the church in modern times, eunuchs also were commonly used as male sopranos in Italian opera until the end of the nineteenth century.

Slave Eunuchs as Servants to Monarchs

From earliest times, the castration of captives was both a powerful confirmation of conquest and an expression of revenge. The captivity of the castrated slaves soon evolved into the role of eunuchs as retainers who could preserve an emperor's power while remaining impotent to threaten it. Castration extended slave status by eliminating any chance of the slave's assimilation into society. Thus isolated himself, the eunuch was ideally positioned to preserve the monarch's insulation from society and to perpetuate the ruler's mystique, which was central to his power. The eunuch became at once the opposite and the surrogate of the monarch; he was impotent and therefore powerless in the wider world, but his impotence made him a powerful intimate of the ruler. Thus the relationship of eunuch and ruler was symbiotic and founded on mutual dependence.

Attendant to the eunuch's role as guardian of the monarch's privacy and assets was his role as guardian to the harem—the arena of an emperor's greatest wealth. The wives and concubines who populated the harem not only constituted a ruler's currency but also reproduced the children who were at once a monarch's assets and also his potential liabilities. The eunuch was entrusted as guardian of the royal harem owing to his presumed inability to function sexually. But beyond this, a eunuch's absolute dependence on and loyalty to the monarch required that he guard against the political threat of successors, which was the focus of activity in the harem community.

The highest ranking eunuch in the sixteenth and seventeenth century Ottoman Empire—the chief

The chief white eunuch guarding the harem's bath (J.-L. Gérome). [Corbis-Bettmann]

eunuch—was initially a white eunuch, replaced in later years by a black eunuch. His duties included acting as head of the inner service, confidant to the sultan, head of the palace school, chief gatekeeper, head of the infirmary, and general master of ceremonies for the harem. The chief eunuch acted as mediator between the sultan and the outside world and between the *valide* (queen mother) and the rest of the women. Other titled eunuchs subordinate to the chief eunuch headed the treasury, the palace food and kitchen staff, and the entire palace in the sultan's absence. Each titled eunuch had many untitled eunuchs in his charge.

The eunuch was trusted and powerful because he was the ultimate slave, incapable of affiliating himself with anyone but his master. Devoid of sexual, familial, and social bonds, eunuchs used the liminal nature imposed by their impotence to gain power through wealth, the only avenue open to them for establishing identity beyond slave status.

See also CONCUBINAGE; HAREM.

BIBLIOGRAPHY

ANDERSON, MARY M. *Hidden Power: The Palace Eunuchs of Imperial China.* 1990.

BAER, G. "Slavery in Nineteenth Century Egypt." *Journal of African History* 8 (1967): 417–441.

BEHR, EDWARD. *The Last Emperor.* 1987.

BENNETT, N. R. "Christian and Negro Slavery in Eighteenth Century North Africa." *Journal of African History* 1 (1960): 65–82.

BURCKHARDT, J. L. *Travels in Nubia.* 1822. Reprint, 1968.

FISHER, A. G. B., and J. J. FISHER. *Slavery and Muslim Society in Africa.* 1970.

GULIK, ROBERT VAN. *Sexual Life in Ancient China.* 1974.

JAFFREY, ZIA. *The Invisibles: A Tale of the Eunuchs of India.* 1996.

MARMON, SHAUN ELIZABETH. *Eunuchs and Sacred Boundaries in Islamic Societies.* 1995.

MITAMURA, TAISUKE. *Chinese Eunuchs: The Structure of Intimate Politics.* 1970.

NANDA, SERENA. *Neither Man nor Woman: The Hijras of India.* 1990.

PATTERSON, ORLANDO. *Slavery and Social Death.* 1982.

PIERCE, LESLIE PENN. *The Imperial Harem: Women and Sovereignty in the Ottoman Empire.* 1993.

PENZER, N. M. *The Harem.* 1937.

STENT, G. C. "Chinese Eunuchs." *Journal of the Royal Society* II (1887).

TSAI, SHIH-SHAN HENRY. *The Eunuchs in the Ming Dynasty.* 1996.

WATSON, JAMES L. *Asian and African Systems of Slavery.* 1980.

Beverly B. Mack

Europe, Medieval

See Medieval Europe, Slavery and Serfdom in.

Exodus

The book of Exodus in the Bible tells how, some three thousand years ago, the Hebrews living in Egypt because of famine in the neighboring land of Canaan end up as slaves under an especially harsh pharaoh. The story describes their prolonged sufferings and how deliverance comes to them from their god, who inspires their leader Moses.

In political terms the story is about an oppressed people who seek independence. They achieve it not in a way typical of independence movements in history, by resorting to illegality that usually involves violence, but rather by violence emanating from a supernatural source. For groups whose circumstances are such that earthly means are not available to them to escape their oppressors, the story offers some hope for deliverance.

Throughout the centuries the Jews have recalled the story in their annual service of redemption, the Passover seder. Shortly after the death of Jesus, the seder current in first-century-C.E. Palestine inspired those who believed in his messiahship to view him as a second Moses bringing deliverance to his people.

The Roma (Gypsies) who turned up in Europe in the sixteenth century tell versions of the story. In the seventeenth century, English Puritans and Prussian Lutherans identified with the story, for they saw themselves as escaping hardship from their European oppressors, going to a new land of destiny (New England or Australia), and living under the authority of the God of the Bible. In the nineteenth century, African-Americans in the United States adopted the story to express their hope for deliverance from slavery. Similarly, the Mormons, identifying themselves as God's people Israel, undertook their journey to the American West. In this century, especially in a Latin-American context, the story is a major source of reflection and inspiration for liberation theology, a Christian movement whose goals are economic, social, and political reforms. In this theology, the church is an "Exodus community," a collective that cannot be assimilated or conquered but must cast off the constraints imposed on it by society.

See also ANCIENT MIDDLE EAST; BIBLE; LAW.

BIBLIOGRAPHY

VAN IERSEL, BAS, and ANTON WEILER, eds. *Exodus: A Lasting Paradigm.* 1987.

Calum Carmichael

Familia Caesaris

The *Familia Caesaris* in imperial Rome, in its broadest sense, included all the emperor's slaves and ex-slaves. Literary sources and even epitaphs represent only the upper tiers of this group. The life of a slave working on an imperial farm differed little from that of a slave on a senator's farm; imperial slaves would rarely identify themselves as members of the *Familia Caesaris* on their epitaphs. Accordingly scholars use *Familia Caesaris* to denote the members of the *familia* in domestic or civil service.

Some members of the *Familia Caesaris* acquired informal power and wealth from their access to the emperor. The chamberlain, who had some control over access to the emperor, first rose to prominence in the early empire. A wider range of slaves and ex-slaves were able to sell "smoke" about the emperor's plans or even his moods. By the late empire, imperial eunuchs owed their power to proximity to the emperor, who was increasingly regarded as sacred and consequently unable to associate directly with the aristocracy.

In the early empire, most notoriously under Claudius (A.D. 41–54), ex-slaves such as Narcissus, Pallas, and Callistus gained power not only from personal access to the emperor but also because they served him as able administrators. Even during the republic, officials had used domestic staff to compensate for the lack of a regular bureaucracy. Implementing the incomparable powers of the emperor required competent administrators. The dignity of a senator was incompatible with taking orders, especially orders from early emperors who wished to disguise and soften the absolute control they exercised. The emperor's use of personal slaves and freedmen for public business was an obvious recourse.

Slaves in the imperial "civil service" were typically freed after age thirty, so the highest ranks tended to contain freedmen. The three most important department heads were the *a libellis*, the *ab epistulis*, and the *a rationibus*. The *a libellis* dealt with petitions to the emperor. The *ab epistulis* controlled the imperial correspondence with governors, with foreign powers, and concerning military campaigns and commands. The *a rationibus*, the emperor's chief financial agent, was in charge of all revenue from imperial provinces, from the emperor's domains, and from certain taxes along with an equally broad range of expenditures.

The ex-slaves in charge of these bureaucracies gained substantial wealth and independent power—much to the chagrin of senators, who, when not forced to fawn on ex-slaves, insisted that "great freedmen are the sign of a mediocre emperor" (Pliny, *Panegyricus* 88). From the late first century on, many of the top positions were filled by men from the nonsenatorial elite as imperial service lost its stigma.

The éclat associated with membership in the imperial household extended down through the ranks of minor bureaucrats and domestic slaves. The epitaphs of four thousand individuals declare membership in the *Familia Caesaris,* a source of pride. In addition, male members of the *Familia Caesaris* were able to contract alliances with free women while still slaves; imperial freedmen married freeborn women far more often than freedmen in general did. Legally, imperial slaves were able to dispose by will of half of their *peculium* as if it were their legal property.

See also ANCIENT ROME; PECULIUM.

BIBLIOGRAPHY

HOPKINS, KEITH. "The Political Power of Eunuchs." In *Conquerors and Slaves.* 1978.

TREGGIARI, SUSAN. "Domestic Staff at Rome in the Julio-Claudian Period, 27 B.C. to A.D. 68." *Histoire Sociale* 6 (1973): 241–255.

WEAVER, P. R. C. *Familia Caesaris: A Social Study of the Emperor's Freedmen and Slaves.* 1972.

Peter Hunt

Family, U.S.

Families made up the fabric of life for enslaved African-Americans. Threaded together to form broad patterns of kinship and community, they were also pieced uncomfortably into the larger scheme of patriarchal plantation society. Families provided strength and a crucial sense of belonging but also functioned to reproduce the slave system. All children born to enslaved mothers after 1662 became legal chattels. Slaves' birthrates outstripped their death rates by the mid-eighteenth century, and by 1800 their number had increased from a total of 500,000 African immigrants to 1 million, mostly American-born. After the Revolution and the 1808 ban on African imports, planters improved physical treatment and living conditions; this allowed slaves to multiply to 4 million by the time of general emancipation in 1865. This "domestication" of the "domestic institution," as Willie Lee Rose outlined it in *Slavery and Freedom* (1982), put family at the center of the lives of both slaves and masters, entangling them in local webs of power and powerlessness, aspiration and oppression.

Creolization

Kinship lay at the foundation of social relations in western Africa and formed the primary bond between individuals. Through a rich variety of lineage strategies, rites of passage, marriage practices, toboos, and domestic arrangements, people in western Africa constructed extended clans and multiclan polities to organize labor; to create, conserve, and distribute wealth; and to produce and pass on religion and culture. The Atlantic slave trade severed countless kinship bonds from the seventeenth to the early nineteenth century. Once on North American soil, enslaved Africans found that living conditions and their masters' choices con-

spired against their attempts to re-create familiar kinship and cultural structures. In the seventeenth century a two-to-one ratio of men to women and death rates of 25 percent loomed large. The diversity of Africans' linguistic backgrounds, complicated by the scattered nature and small size of early slaveholdings, further hampered their efforts to coherently reproduce kinship systems.

In this unknown world, Africans worked to create new networks of known kin. Despite differences in their practices, West Africans shared a flexible set of underlying notions and assumptions about kinship— explored by Sidney Mintz and Richard Price in *The Birth of African-American Culture* (1992)—which allowed slaves to build new kinship structures that resonated with their old ones. Drawing from both patrilineal and matrilineal descent, slaves fashioned new, broader families that encompassed the relatives of both parents. They adopted the concept of nuclear two-parent households but also embraced single mothers, stepchildren, half-siblings, and extended, adopted, and fictive kin. Over time, they created distinctly African-American kinship and household systems, circum-

A lithograph of a diagram for a family tree depicts the contrast between life before and after the Civil War.
[Library of Congress/Corbis]

scribed by their masters' designs but also asserting their own desires and values.

Households

Robert "King" Carter's 1733 plantation inventory provides a snapshot of the process of household creolization that immigrants underwent: while newly arrived Africans lived in single-sex barracks, "seasoned" slaves had married, and American-born slaves lived with spouses and children. Planters and slaves alike seem to have preferred two-parent nuclear households whenever possible. On larger Chesapeake tidewater plantations in the late eighteenth century, about 45 percent of slaves lived in such arrangements, with another 20 percent in households headed by one parent, usually the mother. Another 16 percent, including one-fourth of children aged ten to fourteen, lived with siblings or other kin. About 18 percent remained apart from any apparent kin. On smaller farms, in stark contrast, 40 percent lived apart from any discernible kin. Over a third lived in mother-headed households. Fewer than 20 percent lived with both parents.

Slaves and masters reproduced these patterns throughout the territorial and temporal span of slavery in North America, gradually increasing the density of kin in their communities. Generally, the larger the plantation, the more likely it was that fathers and mothers were housed together with children, and the less likely that any slaves lived only with nonrelatives. In nineteenth-century Louisiana, on expansive plantations with over 200 slaves, about 60 percent lived in two-parent households. On plantations and farms with fewer than 100 slaves, about 45 percent did. Households, however, served only as the building blocks of family, as slaves linked them together within and between plantations to form extended kin-based communities.

Kinship

Slaves' families stretched far beyond individual households. Various siblings, cousins, aunts, uncles, and grandparents shared in the daily routines of work and pleasure within a plantation's quarters. Local sale, hire, and inheritance distributed other kin throughout the neighborhood. While separating family members spatially, such short-distance migration also expanded slaves' world of kin. Men often had to marry "abroad" and would travel miles to visit their families weekly, or whenever they could. Countless other such family visitations—either with or without the masters' permission—created broad interplantation networks of kinship and friendship among slaves.

Friends stepped in to become adoptive or fictive kin, adding yet more strands to the network of family. Masters often failed to recognize extended kinship as family, but such ties provided an individual slave with a web of significant others resilient enough to help sustain the loss of a spouse, child, sibling, or parent.

Over time, slaves nurtured family trees with deep roots and wide branches, keeping account of those connections by oral tradition. Applying and extending their genealogical knowledge, mothers and fathers named their own children, especially sons, after themselves and their parents, siblings, aunts, uncles, and grandparents. When masters assigned unwanted names, slaves often kept their own "basket" (clandestine) names, including surnames. Whether derived from African, Biblical, classical, or local sources, African-Americans' names served to locate them among their peers in the genealogical present.

Family served as a powerful and lasting metaphor in African-American life. "Brother," "sister," "aunt," "uncle," "granny," and "cousin" encompassed the entire slave community, and by extension, all of "our people." African-Americans used familial terms to unite themselves and distinguish themselves from their masters, in the same way a religious community might. When white people called slaves and freedpeople "uncle" and "aunt," it implied a disrespectful intimacy, an infringement of the black community.

Cycles

A frustrating cycle of family destruction and reconstitution dogged slaves throughout the eighteenth and nineteenth centuries. As masters built up their slaveholdings and expanded production, slaves wove an increasingly complex kin-based community. But when the masters overextended themselves, ran short of cash, or died, they scattered the slave community among heirs, creditors, or buyers. Slaves had to transplant truncated families and graft them onto new communities.

These communities had to deal with systemwide disruptions as slaveholders expanded their political and agricultural boundaries. In the 1750s–1780s, just as family roots began to take hold in the Chesapeake tidewater, second-generation planters removed to the piedmont, forcing the migration of one-fourth (26,000) of their slaves, importing more Africans—especially men—and starting the creolization process over again. In the nineteenth century, as planters abandoned depleted upper-South tobacco soil and brought deep-South cotton and sugar lands under cultivation, they forced more than 1 million slaves to move. As Michael Tadman concludes, at least half were carried singly and in family fragments by commercial traders, not by planters migrating with relatively intact communities. Sellers and traders in the upper South broke up perhaps one-third of slave marriages and separated as many children from one or both parents, despite legal restrictions on separating mothers from children under age ten. Slave communities in the Mississippi Delta and Gulf Coast regions rebuilt from the fragments of families scattered by the boom and bust of "Alabama fever," the panic of 1837, and the ascension of king cotton.

Marriage

African-Americans developed their own rules and taboos concerning marriage. They condoned premarital sex; but once pregnant, a young woman was generally expected to find a suitable husband, in her own community or in the neighborhood. Slaves seem to have married outside the family, holding first-cousin marriage taboo, though it was common among whites. Only seldom do men appear to have taken several wives at the same time.

Masters' control of key resources—property, shelter, and basic provisions—meant that slave husbands and wives entered unions on roughly equal terms. Up through the nineteenth century both spouses often did "men's" agricultural work, and both spent their spare time providing extra food, clothing, or other amenities and completing household chores. African-derived notions of gender allowed spouses some flexibility in fulfilling their roles. Each complemented the other, both sharing authority over private family decisions.

Churches, black and white, held enslaved spouses to vows of fidelity but recognized separation by sale as grounds for remarriage. Although no law protected their marriages, slaves often sought official validation by employing a minister or reasonable proxy, or by having masters record the event in their daybooks. Some masters worked to keep spouses together, but others separated them through work assignments, punishment, hiring, migration, inheritance, mortgage, and sale. Enforced serial monogamy meant that even two-parent households often encompassed children of different fathers, introducing potential conflict but also encouraging further expansions of African-Americans' notions of kin.

Child Rearing

While about half of enslaved children lived with both a mother and a father, slaves deployed a wide variety of parenting strategies, drawing on entire kinship networks to accommodate the many kinds of households.

Fathers, when present, fished, trapped, and gardened, often at night, supplying extra food. Together with other adult men, they taught children to build furniture and to carve utensils and drinking vessels. They made and played banjos, drums, and fiddles, passing along these skills. Artisans with expertise in carpentry or ironworking proved especially keen to train their sons, giving them some leverage with masters.

Mothers were separated from young children far less often than fathers were, so they more frequently played the central role in the lives of children. In addition to field work, housework, or nursing for their masters' families, they sewed, cleaned, cooked, hauled water, chopped wood, did laundry, and gardened for their own spouses and children, teaching sons and daughters these skills. Mothers sometimes tended their nursing infants while at work in the fields, but more often they relied, reluctantly, on elderly slave women or young girls in plantation nurseries. The network of female kin and community provided mothers with important child-rearing resources.

Adults taught enslaved children important skills for enduring and surviving slavery. Unable fully to protect their children from masters' and mistresses' punishments, parents taught them discipline, obedience, and deference to those with power. Parents also tried to instill in their children a sense of individual self-worth and a Christian sense of justice. Ex-slaves recalled learning from their elders that they would one day be free, either in this world or in the next.

Masters

By the mid-eighteenth century, slaveholders understood the conservative potential of nurturing slave kinship, reasoning that slaves with deep-rooted local family ties would have more to lose than to gain by revolting or running away. Threats to separate families through sale proved effective in maintaining discipline. Masters also saw families as an especially useful means of reproducing the labor force and increasing their own capital. Abolitionists' accusations notwithstanding, "stud farms" seem to have been rare. Most masters did, however, express an active interest in their "breeding wenches," usually by encouragement or reward, but sometimes by force.

Planters recognized slave families, but more important to them was the fictive "family, black and white," encompassing the entire patriarchal plantation household, especially house servants, wetnurses, and drivers. In many cases, planters's families proved more black-and-white than they wished to admit. Many enslaved women found themselves tangled in an array of sexual relations with masters or their sons, cousins, nephews, or other male-relatives, ranging from quasi-consensual to violently abusive. The conflicts resulting from such unions resonated through both the big house and the slave quarters. Slave families worked to integrate their light-skinned offspring, while white patriarchs struggled with their wives over recognizing or ridding themselves of their progeny.

Reunions

Reunion always remained a crucial though elusive goal. Fugitives and free people raised money to buy their spouses and children out of slavery. Even long after the Civil War, newspapers continued to carry advertisements by people seeking family members who had been sold away decades before. African-American kinship ties remained rooted in the soil of their birth but extended into heaven. Some insisted on burial among their predecessors, and many had faith in a divine reassembly of families long gone.

Debate

Enslaved families have long stood in the limelight of historical, sociological, and policy debates in the United States. Proslavery ideologues portrayed orderly, static slave families under patriarchal protection, while abolitionists described family chaos—breakups and sexual immorality. After the collapse of Reconstruction, in its broad and lingering wake, reactionary policy makers and scholars argued that emancipated blacks had retrogressed into African barbarity. In the 1930s, the sociologist E. Franklin Frazier countered that African practices, having been largely lost, were irrelevant. Black families, shunted away from the white mainstream, had created numerous configurations, including "matriarchal" households built on the natural mother-child bond. Social thinkers in the mid-twentieth century, culminating with Daniel P. Moynihan's government report of 1965, saw matrifocal structure as "disorganization" and found a "tangle of pathology" in black families, rooted in slavery.

Beginning with Herbert Gutman, social historians and anthropologists have undertaken the empirical and theoretical task of unearthing and tracing the variety and meaning of black family strategies, including matrifocal, nuclear, and extended kin. As Nell Painter suggests in *Soul Murder and Slavery* (1995), we have only begun to explore more deeply the psychological complexities African-Americans faced in creating enslaved families within the larger patriarchal household.

See also DEMOGRAPHY OF SLAVES IN THE UNITED STATES; EDUCATION OF SLAVES; NAMES AND NAMING; UNITED STATES.

All of the members of this multigenerational family photographed around 1890 were born on the plantation of J. J. Smith in Beaufort, South Carolina. [Corbis-Bettmann]

BIBLIOGRAPHY

ALSTON, MACKY, director. *Family Name.* Opelika Pictures, 1997. A documentary film.

BALL, EDWARD. *Slaves in the Family,* 1998.

BERLIN, IRA, and LESLIE S. ROWLAND, eds. *Families and Freedom: A Documentary History of African-American Kinship in the Civil War Era.* 1997.

DEW, CHARLES B. *Bond of Iron: Master and Slave at Buffalo Forge.* 1994.

GUTMAN, HERBERT G. *The Black Family in Slavery and Freedom, 1750–1925.* 1976

KULIKOFF, ALLAN. *Tobacco and Slaves: The Development of Southern Cultures in the Chesapeake, 1680–1800.* 1986.

MALONE, ANN PATTON. *Sweet Chariot: Slave Family and Household Structure in Nineteenth-Century Louisiana.* 1992. Malone provides the most comprehensive and up-to-date bibliography of slave family studies.

STEVENSON, BRENDA E. *Life in Black and White: Family and Community in the Slave South.* 1996.

TADMAN, MICHAEL. *Speculators and Slaves: Masters, Traders, and Slaves in the Old South.* 1989.

WEBBER, THOMAS L. *Deep Like the Rivers: Education in the Slave Quarter Community, 1831–1865.* 1978.

WHITE, DEBORAH GRAY. *Ar'n't I a Woman? Female Slaves in the Plantation South.* 1985.

Phillip D. Troutman

Fantasy

See Science Fiction and Fantasy, Slavery in.

Fear of Slaves

See Panics.

Field Labor

Field labor drove the emergence of slavery in the New World and its long history there. Indentured servants played critical early roles—in the Caribbean and in the Chesapeake—but black slavery soon supplanted white servitude. Whether in Brazil, the Caribbean, or the colonies that became the United States, the demand for agricultural workers could not be met with the supply of Europeans or Native Americans. Thus people from Africa supplied the labor that made possible the enormous growth of plantation agriculture in Europe's New World colonies.

Slaves also worked in transport, mining, manufacturing, cattle raising, naval stores, and domestic service, but field labor remained the central focus of slave labor, whether in the Spanish Caribbean in 1650, the French Caribbean in 1750, or the U.S. South in 1850. The shortfall in free labor was far more critical in areas that produced staple crops, particularly in the hottest climates, and in such places slavery dominated field labor.

The main crops varied by time and place. Sugar was the mainstay of the slave economies of the greater Caribbean, including Louisiana (until the nineteenth century); tobacco of the Chesapeake; rice, indigo, and sea island cotton of eighteenth-century coastal South Carolina and Georgia; and short-staple cotton across much of the nineteenth-century Deep South. At some times and in some places, other crops were the economic mainstays or at least played important secondary roles, among them hemp, cocoa, and coffee. Sugar was the major plantation crop across the New World in the era of slavery, though in the area that became the United States the dominant crop was tobacco in the early years and cotton in the later period.

Though the core requirement of field workers was to produce cash crops—the labor emphasized in this essay—there were always other jobs to do as well. Many of the tobacco farms and plantations of the Chesapeake area, for example, produced wheat and other cash crops as well as tobacco, and in fact some shifted away from tobacco to concentrate on other agricultural production. Across the upper South, and to a lesser extent in the Cotton South, slaves produced much of the food for local consumption by humans and livestock alike. Thus, they worked in the fields to produce grains, vegetables, and hay. In addition, after working usually five and a half or six days a week for their masters, slave men, women, and children often spent time and effort in garden plots growing vegetables and other crops for themselves and their families.

The work lives of field laborers varied by crop and by time and place, but in every case the fields had to be prepared before planting, then came the planting and tending of the growing crops, and finally came harvest and the many subsequent steps to prepare the crop for market. Men generally did the bulk of the field work, while women and children often worked at other occupations. Yet at critical points in the season, especially at harvest, nearly all hands might be pressed into service in the fields, though women sometimes worked in separate gangs or at separate tasks. And young slaves gradually learned everything from the etiquette of slavery to the specific skills required of adult slaves in the fields.

One of the more important recent conceptual breakthroughs in the study of New World slave societies relates to Philip D. Morgan's distinction between "task" and "gang" systems of organizing labor. Either could be found on plantations in most times and places, and they were combined in various ways. Yet in the New World the sugar plantation was the characteristic home of the gang system—closely supervised, carefully orchestrated, highly regimented—though cotton and coffee plantations often also used it. The task system—whether tasks were calibrated in terms of daily or weekly work quotas—often ruled elsewhere, especially by the nineteenth century.

Slaves worked, and masters directed that work. The masters who owned (or hired) the slaves might personally direct their laborers' work in the fields and, especially on the smaller holdings, even work alongside them. Yet other managers, in one pattern or another, often directed the day-to-day labor on a plantation. To meet the demand for supervisors on the larger plantations, overseers—usually white men, whether sons or other relatives of the owner, poor white neighbors, or professionals, any of whom might hope themselves someday to possess and run their own operations—hired themselves out to masters, often for a year at a time. An overseer played the role of intermediary, translating the master's strategy into production tactics. Particularly in the largest operations, drivers—slaves themselves, but men who had worked their way into lower management—directed their fellow slaves, sometimes mitigating the harshness of slavery but as often compelled to resort to its physical punishments and other coercive features.

Slaves, both men and women, work in the fields picking cotton (undated engraving). [Corbis-Bettmann]

Both slaves and their masters (or overseers), though not in equal measure, had a role in shaping expectations regarding an acceptable pace for work and persistence in work. How much should be accomplished in a day? How much time off should a slave have on weekends or at Christmas? These were central questions regarding the field work that slaves were intended to accomplish, and they were central areas of conflict as slaves and masters in effect negotiated the specifics of slaves' daily, weekly, and seasonal work lives.

In the seventeenth century tobacco became a plantation crop in the Chesapeake area—Virginia and Maryland—and it so remained through the long history of slavery in the United States. Workers, both men and women, set the tobacco plants out in the spring and harvested the leaves in the summer. In between, while the plants were growing, workers had to remove the lower leaves, and children were usually assigned the daily chore of removing worms from the maturing leaves—many would later remember and report that if they were seen to have missed a worm, they might be forced to eat it. Much of the work was by hand. Though tedious, working tobacco was not exhausting or life-threatening—unlike working with rice and, especially, sugar.

Rice plantations were typically larger than tobacco plantations, in part because of the greater capital improvements required to flood and drain the growing crop, and rice operations therefore generally used more hands. Rice workers labored by the task system—a certain amount of work was assigned for the day, and then the day was done. Workers' tools included hoes to tend the crops, sickles to harvest them, flails for threshing, and mortars and pestles for pounding. The planting year took the entire twelve months; preparing the fields in winter; planting in the spring; flooding and draining the fields during summer; and harvesting, threshing, pounding, and shipping the crop to market in the fall.

Planting sugar took from January through April, as sequential gangs of workers cut off the tops of cane stalks, planted those stalks, and covered the plants with several inches of soil. Hoeing continued until the harvest, first of the seed cane in August, then of the ripe tops and the rest of the stalks for molasses and sugar. Even in Louisiana, but particularly in the West Indies, young men supplied most of the labor force, but children, too, often played crucial support roles at the sugarhouse, unloading the harvested stalks and placing them on the conveyor belts that took them through the processing plant.

In the antebellum deep South, cotton ranked first in labor input and production output. Cotton—like tobacco, but unlike sugar and rice—could readily be grown on small or large production units. Most North

American slaveholdings were relatively small, but a majority of workers in cotton lived on plantations that had at least twenty slaves (as did a majority of those in sugar and rice). Planting, weeding, and picking all were hard work, and then came men's work at the cotton gin as they prepared the fluff for market.

In short, slave labor played a critical role in the fields of plantations in the U.S. South and throughout much of the New World. It also played a significant economic role during the colonial period even in some northern colonies and in the southern backcountry, just as it did among small holders in plantation areas and in parts of the mountainous South until slavery was abolished. Many northern slaves lived and worked in an urban environment, but slaves in rural Connecticut, New York, New Jersey, and Pennsylvania did farm labor. Northern holdings were typically small, and slaves—like free workers usually alongside them—plowed the land and mowed the hay or wheat. Slave ownership and slave hiring provided critical supplements to a rural labor force where, because land was cheap, free laborers who were willing to work in the employ of others proved to be scarce and expensive.

Rivaling the United States as a huge slave society in the Americas was Brazil. The types of field labor performed by slaves in the South, the Caribbean, and much of the rest of the New World in the seventeenth, eighteenth, and nineteenth centuries appeared, too, in other times and places. Centuries before the system shifted its geographical focus to the New World, slaves performed field labor (growing grapes and olives, for example, which would be made into wine and olive oil) on estates throughout the Roman Empire—Iberia, North Africa, Sicily, Italy, Greece, and Turkey. On the eve of the shift of agricultural slavery to the Americas, slaves were working sugar plantations in such Portuguese-controlled places as Cape Verde, off the west coast of Africa. Unfree workers labored in the fields of Russia as late as the 1860s; the abolition of serfdom there came at about the same time as the abolition of slavery in the United States. Even later, for a time, slaves labored in the fields of the Americas, Africa, and Asia producing coffee, cocoa, cloves, and other commercial crops in such extensive areas as Brazil, West Africa, East Africa, and the Dutch East Indies.

When systems of unfree labor ended, field labor persisted, though the dominant patterns of field labor could prove very different after emancipation. In the U.S. South, freedpeople typically worked family plots even though the land was usually still owned by white people. Concentrated housing quarters did not long persist in the postslavery era in the South, nor did either gang labor or daily task labor in the fields.

See also CARIBBEAN REGION; ECONOMICS OF SLAVERY; OVERSEERS; PLANTATIONS.

BIBLIOGRAPHY

BERLIN, IRA, and PHILIP D. MORGAN, eds. *Cultivation and Culture: Labor and the Shaping of Slave Life in the Americas.* 1993.

BREEDEN, JAMES O., ed. *Advice among Masters: The Ideal in Slave Management in the Old South.* 1980.

COOPER, FREDERICK. *Plantation Slavery on the East Coast of Africa.* 1977.

GRAY, LEWIS CECIL. *History of Agriculture in the Southern United States to 1860.* 2 vols. 1933.

HUDSON, LARRY E., JR. *To Have and to Hold: Slave Work and Family Life in Antebellum South Carolina.* 1997.

INNES, STEPHEN, ed. *Work and Labor in Early America.* 1988.

KLEIN, MARTIN A. *Breaking the Chains: Slavery, Bondage, and Emancipation in Modern Africa and Asia.* 1993.

MULLIN, MICHAEL. *Africa in America: Slave Acculturation and Resistance in the American South and the British Caribbean, 1736–1831.* 1992.

PHILLIPS, ULRICH B. *American Negro Slavery: A Survey of the Supply, Employment and Control of Negro Labor As Determined by the Plantation Regime.* 1918.

SCARBOROUGH, WILLIAM KAUFFMAN. *The Overseer: Plantation Management in the Old South.* 1966.

SMITH, MARK M. *Mastered by the Clock: Time, Slavery, and Freedom in the American South.* 1997.

VAN DEBURG, WILLIAM L. *The Slave Drivers: Black Agricultural Labor Supervisors in the Antebellum South.* 1979.

Peter Wallenstein

Film and Television, Slavery in

For more than a century, Hollywood has made use of images and stories of slavery. The first silent films in the late 1890s often included representations of the workaday world—ordinary images that lasted for only a moment but that viewers nevertheless found fascinating because the medium itself was so new. African-Americans appeared in various guises in these brief glimpses of "moving images," whether as a young mother bathing her child, a laborer harvesting crops, or a street dancer performing along a city thoroughfare. More detailed images of African-American life, and slavery in particular, did not appear until the early 1900s, when companies began presenting motion pictures of sufficient length to include a story line.

It was in 1903 that the inventor and film pioneer Thomas Edison and the director Edwin S. Porter presented the first film version of *Uncle Tom's Cabin*. Three months later, the Sigmund Lubin Company presented a second. Together, the two established a cinematic interpretation of slavery that persisted for the next forty years. Both motion pictures relied heavily on an already well established and highly romantic image of the South. By then, for example, the illustrations of Currier and Ives, *Harper's Weekly,* and such southern artists as John Elder and William Ludwell Sheppard; the regional writings of Thomas Nelson Page, John Esten Cooke, and Joel Chandler Harris; and especially the late-nineteenth-century conventions of blackface minstrelsy had significantly refashioned the public perception of the South and slavery. The quickly recognizable milieu of contented, well-treated laborers within a rural Eden was ideal for early films—films that relied on elements of romance to attract audiences yet were so brief that they required settings needing little time for explanation. Thus by 1903 *Uncle Tom's Cabin* had steadily evolved from an abolitionist novel into a film celebration of an idealized plantation world.

So successful were the first two versions of *Uncle Tom's Cabin* that filmmakers followed with a dozen more adaptations between 1909 and 1927. As was traditional in stage productions, white actors in blackface usually performed the African-American parts. It was not until 1914 that a black finally played the role of Uncle Tom, and even as late as 1927 whites still played the slaves in the comedy *Topsy and Eva.* The characterization of slaves also became increasingly stereotyped. In many of the silent films produced between 1903 and 1927, for instance, African-Americans vigorously supported the Confederate cause. Three pictures in 1911 alone—*Mammy's Ghost, A Special Messenger,* and *Uncle Peter's Ruse*—involved slaves' efforts to protect wounded southern soldiers. Loyalty to the system took several other forms as well. In *For Massa's Sake* (1911), a slave sells himself to help pay off his master's debts; in *Old Mammy's Charge* (1913), blacks return south, to a world they know best; and in *The Old Oak's Secret* (1914), a faithful slave hides a master's will rather than accept his own freedom and leave the plantation. D. W. Griffith's epic *Birth of a Nation* (1915) remains the best-known of the silent films depicting the slave-master relationship as beneficial, but it is only one of more than a hundred motion pictures that presented the same message. Griffith himself had turned to the theme repeatedly with *In Old Kentucky* (1909), *His Trust,* and *His Trust Fulfilled* (both 1911).

By 1930, the advent of sound motion pictures, the heightened need for escapist films in the midst of the Great Depression, and the growing commercialization of the studio system increased the demand for films—and further exaggerated the slave characters. At first, however, the movie industry hesitated to use the expensive and still new technology of sound except for brief "fillers" presented before the main feature. In "short subjects" such as *Dixie Days* (1928), *Slave Days* (1929), and *Cotton Pickin' Days* (1930), the Hall Johnson Choir, the Forbes Randolph Kentucky Jubilee Singers, and other well-known African-American choral groups stood in front of studio plantation sets singing spirituals and folksongs from the days of slavery. These and similar films presaged many of the song-and-dance roles to follow throughout the 1930s.

For example, black actors, comics, and dancers such as Willie Best, Stepin Fetchit, and Clarence Muse played secondary roles in a series of musicals and light drama such as *Dixiana* (1930), *Mississippi* (1935), *Can This Be Dixie?* (1936), and *Way Down South* (1939). One of the decade's most popular black actors, Bill "Bojangles" Robinson, was famous among white audiences for his dance performances with Shirley Temple in *The Littlest Rebel* (1935). More serious roles were few and permitted little deviation from the narrow interpretation of slavery as a benign institution.

Paramount Pictures in 1935, for instance, did include a scene of black rebellion in the film adaptation of Stark Young's novel *So Red the Rose,* but considerably tempered it by depicting the leader (played by Clarence Muse) as motivated more by plunder than by freedom. In contrast, the loyal butler (played by Daniel Haynes) exuded dignity and a sense of his special position in the plantation household. Similarly, Eddie "Rochester" Anderson in *Jezebel* (1938) and Hattie McDaniel in *Gone with the Wind* (1939) adopted the class-consciousness of their owners.

The year after *Gone with the Wind,* Warner Brothers released *The Santa Fe Trail* (1940). Half-fact, half-fiction, the story line followed the prewar careers of two of the Civil War's most dashing cavalry leaders, J. E. B. Stuart (played by Errol Flynn) and George Armstrong Custer (played by Ronald Reagan). The story is dominated, however, by the violent rise and fall of the abolitionist John Brown, played by Raymond Massey as a dark, overpowering, vicious fanatic. The film ends in 1859 with Brown's capture during his ill-fated raid on the federal arsenal at Harpers Ferry, and his subsequent execution. Neither western nor "southern," this motion picture nevertheless said more about the evils of slavery—and much more about the passions it aroused—than any other sound film to that time. The Warner Brothers studio was famous for its unsettling biographical films, such as *I Am a Fugitive from a Chain Gang* (1930), which often left audiences with an uneasy feeling—in the case of *The Santa Fe Trail,* that a madman had received his due but that his cause was just. This movie stood, then, as something of a harbinger of a shifting perspective.

The entry of the United States into World War II brought even more significant changes to the film industry. The Office of War Information's Motion Picture Section, for example, repeatedly pressured Hollywood studios to make numerous changes in plots, dialogue, and especially characterizations that might affect morale and hurt the war effort. And, since the nation was waging a war for freedom and democracy, it was particularly inappropriate for movies to persist in presenting the same forty-year-old image of slavery. As a result, the industry released few films with a southern setting, and even those were perceptively different. In one of them, a light comedy, *The Flame of New Orleans* (1941), Teresa Harris portrayed a slave who was more a friend and confidante than a servant to her mistress. In another, the popular musical *Dixie* (1943), Paramount Pictures carefully obscured any references to slavery.

Other forces were at work as well. The National Association for the Advancement of Colored People was one of several groups during the 1940s that steadily lobbied the studios for better scripts. The effort was not always successful. Amid considerable protest from numerous black newspapers and organizations, Walt Disney in 1946 released *Song of the South*—based on African-American folktales collected by Joel Chandler Harris as the "Uncle Remus" stories. Although the setting was Georgia in the years after the Civil War,

much of the studio publicity, and Disney himself, advertised the film as a "musical drama of the romantic Old South." In striking contrast, the opening scene of *The Foxes of Harrow* one year later (1947) made it clear that a significant change had at last occurred. This motion picture, adapted from a novel by the African-American writer Frank Yerby, opened with a black mother drowning her newborn son, and herself, rather than raise the child in slavery.

The Foxes of Harrow was the first of many films produced between 1945 and 1965 that reflected the sweeping changes in postwar race relations. Between 1945 and 1955, for example, the federal government integrated the armed services, enacted fair-hiring guidelines, and ruled against the long-standing segregationist policy of providing "separate but equal" facilities for black citizens. By 1960, twenty states had enacted fair-employment laws, and Congress passed civil rights legislation in 1957, 1960, and 1964. By 1947, the Congress of Racial Equality had staged its first protests to raise public awareness of racial injustices; the 1960s were a period of yet more "sit-ins," "freedom rides," marches, and other demonstrations.

Vivien Leigh (left) and Hattie McDaniel won Academy Awards for their performances as a plantation owner's daughter and her slave in the film Gone with the Wind. *[Corbis-Bettmann]*

Despite some white backlash against the fight for African-American civil rights, the motion picture industry realized that films had to change as well.

For example, *The Mississippi Gambler* (1953) and *The Gambler from Natchez* (1954) had avoided more than a glimpse of slave society, but two films of 1956, both set outside the South, featured brief but pointed criticism. In *Friendly Persuasion,* adapted from Jessamyn West's stories about Quakers, a black Indiana farmhand (played by Joel Fluellen) mourned his wife and children left behind in the South, their fate and whereabouts unknown. Even farther afield, the film version of the musical *The King and I,* by Richard Rodgers and Oscar Hammerstein II, set around 1862, included an imaginative presentation of *Uncle Tom's Cabin,* with actors in Siamese stage masks colored black rather than in blackface.

Taking a bolder direction, Warner Brothers' *Band of Angels* (1957), from the novel by Robert Penn Warren, explored the subject of miscegenation, as did *Raintree County,* released the same year. In 1958, a re-release of a silent version of *Uncle Tom's Cabin* (1927) drew respectable attention, particularly—as the publicity stated—"since integration is a major issue in the current news." The change in perspective was especially evident in *Shenandoah* (1965). Produced in time to profit from the national observance of the Civil War centennial, the film included a farmer's daughter encouraging a neighbor's slave to escape to freedom.

During the same period, Hollywood presented a view of slavery within a very different context. By 1946, ticket sales had peaked. Thereafter, the film industry had to contend with the rise of suburban communities, the accompanying fall in receipts at downtown movie theaters the changing tastes of former moviegoers, and the breakup of the studios' longtime monopoly on the production, distribution, and exhibition of motion pictures. Production companies thus turned to "prestige" pictures—pictures with extravagant plots and settings—to attract traditional ticket buyers and new audiences as well. Stories associated with the Bible proved especially appropriate. *The Robe* (1953) and its sequel, *Demetrius and the Gladiators* (1954), followed the religious awakening of a slave (Victor Mature) at the time of the Crucifixion. *The Land of the Pharaohs* (1955) dramatized the construction, by slaves, of the Great Pyramid. Two major films, *Ben Hur* (1959) and *Spartacus* (1960), included extensive scenes of Roman slavery, with the latter based on an actual slave revolt in 73 B.C.

While the Hollywood studio system continued to decline and television audiences grew, the film industry also explored newer, harsher story lines—or "message pictures"—that reflected difficult contemporary issues and attracted a new generation of moviegoers. In the 1960s and 1970s, for example, several independent producers turned to themes of racial violence and revenge. A European production of *Uncle Tom's Cabin* (1965) was a conscious effort to shock audiences. *Slaves* (1969), *The Quadroon* (1971), and *Passion Plantation* (1978) afforded audiences the chance to "see, feel the bloody whip of truth." For *Mandingo* (1975) and its sequel *Drum* (1976), the Italian producer Dino DeLaurentis pointedly adopted the poster design of *Gone with the Wind* but featured two interracial couples instead of the expected pairing of Rhett and Scarlett. Known as "blaxploitation" films, these productions rarely played outside the inner-city and drive-in circuits. Among the few to succeed as mainstream films was *The Skin Game* (1971), a comedy starring Louis Gossett Jr. as a black confidence trickster who is "sold" from town to town by his white partner. (In stark contrast, audiences that same year saw *One Day in the Life of Ivan Denisovich,* a horrific view of slavery in the Soviet gulag, based on a novel by Alexander Solzhenitsyn.)

By the 1970s, television presented the most palatable examinations of slavery for general audiences. Although the medium occasionally misjudged its viewers' tolerance, as in productions such as *Beulah Land* (1980), other made-for-television dramas proved popular as introductions to African-American history. *The Autobiography of Miss Jane Pittman* (1974) and *Freedom Road* (1979), for example, traced the struggles of former slaves to survive in the postwar South. By far the most influential, however, were the twelve-hour *Roots* (1977) and its fourteen-hour sequel, *Roots: The Next Generation* (1979), based on Alex Haley's best-selling account of his family's descent from the African Kunta Kinte.

Since then, however, television has not addressed the topic of slavery in a major production. Few films have either. In one film, slavery is but a momentary though nevertheless significant backdrop. A "John Henry," or runaway, found near the battlefield in *Gettysburg* (1993) prompts an extraordinary dialogue on race between a well-read colonel, who is a former college professor, and one of his soldiers, a rough-hewn Irish immigrant with a firsthand knowledge of prejudice and subjugation.

Four other recent films have taken slavery as a more primary theme. One of them, *The Mission* (1986), set in eighteenth-century Brazil, pitted a Jesuit missionary against the Portuguese slave trade (which was then still legal) and the often blind eye of the church. Another, the Academy Award–winning *Glory* (1989), recounted the story of the black Fifty-fourth Massachusetts Regiment. Free blacks composed the overwhelming majority of the real unit. However, for

In Roots, *the 1977 dramatization of Alex Haley's novel, LeVar Burton (right) portrayed the slave Kunta Kinte, and Edward Asner the conscience-stricken Captain Davies.* [Photographs and Prints Division, Schomburg Center for Research in Black Culture, The New York Public Library, Astor, Lenox and Tilden Foundation]

dramatic purposes, the regiment in the film is made up primarily of former slaves. Three of the principal black characters—Trip (played by Denzel Washington), Sergeant Major Rawlins (Morgan Freeman), and Jupiter Sharts (Jihmi Kennedy)—are all runaways. In contrast, the freeborn, well-educated Thomas Searles (Andre Braugher) is not nearly so physically intense or emotionally motivated as his tentmates. In reshaping the regiment's character, however, the film created a far more effective and poignant symbolic representation of the Union army's hundreds of regiments of United States Colored Troops.

Most recently, *Amistad* (1997)—based on the actual mutiny in 1839 of fifty-three Africans taken as slaves, their subsequent trial in the United States, and the eventual repatriation of thirty-five survivors to Africa in 1841—has attracted considerable popular attention. It has also been the focus of several attacks on how filmmakers refashion actual events. Critics and audiences alike made much the same criticism of the Merchant-Ivory production *Jefferson in Paris* (1994). The film explored several of Thomas Jefferson's rela-

tionships during his service as ambassador to France, especially his association with Sally Hemings (played by Thandie Newton), one of his Monticello slaves brought to France by his daughter.

Films, and particularly films involving historical events, have long relied on various advisers. However, motion pictures, as entertainment and sometimes as art, traditionally fail to present any current interpretive consensus. Instead, far more is invested in the dramatic verisimilitude of the details—the tenor of a time, the cut of jacket, the look of a period room, all those ingredients that led credibility without impinging upon the dramatic, fictionalized story. Thus D. W. Griffith, David O. Selznick, Dino De Laurentiis, Steven Spielberg, and numerous others have devoted their efforts first to the story line and second to their own view of events, but seldom to the strict precepts of the historical record. Still, the nearly century-long interpretive evolution of the cinematic view of slavery—from Thomas Edison's *Uncle Tom's Cabin* in 1903 to Steven Spielberg's *Amistad* in 1997—bears witness to a changing industry and, more important, a changing audience.

See also: AMISTAD; ARTS; JEFFERSON, THOMAS; SPARTACUS; STOWE, HARRIET BEACHER.

BIBLIOGRAPHY

BOGLE, DONALD. *Toms, Coons, Mulattoes, Mammies, and Bucks: An Interpretive History of Blacks in American Films.* 1973.

CAMPBELL, EDWARD D. C., JR. *The Celluloid South: Hollywood and the Southern Myth.* 1981.

CRIPPS, THOMAS J. *Making Movies Black: The Hollywood Message Movie from World War II to the Civil Rights Era.* 1993.

———. *Slow Fade to Black: The Negro in American Film, 1900–1942.* 1977.

KIRBY, JACK T. *Media-Made Dixie: The South in the American Imagination.* 1978.

PINES, JIM. *Blacks in Films: A Survey of Racial Themes and Images in American Film.* 1977.

WOLL, ALLEN, and RANDALL M. MILLER. *Ethnic and Racial Images in American Film and Television.* 1987.

Edward D. C. Campbell Jr.

Finley, Moses I.   [1912–1986]

Leading authority on ancient Greek and Roman social and economic history.

Born in New York City under the name of Finkelstein, Moses Finley was trained in law and history. In the 1930s and 1940s, he worked at the Frankfurt Institute of Social Research (then affiliated with Columbia University), familiarizing himself with Marxist thought and modern sociology, and taught history at the City College of New York and, from 1948 to 1952, at

Rutgers University. Appearing before a one-man subcommittee of the Senate Committee on Internal Security in March 1952, Finley pleaded constitutional privilege in declining to answer questions about his alleged membership in the Communist Party prior to 1941. He was consequently dismissed from his job by the board of trustees of Rutgers, against majority votes of the faculty, at the end of the same year. Offered positions in Cambridge and Oxford, he moved to the University of Cambridge where he taught as Lecturer in Classics (1955–1964), Reader in Ancient Social and Economic History (1964–1970), and Professor of Ancient History (1970–1979). Naturalized as a British citizen in 1962 and knighted in 1979, he served as Master of Darwin College, Cambridge, from 1976 to 1982 and was made an honorary member of the American Academy of Arts and Sciences in 1979. His highly influential studies on the social background of the Homeric epics, the ancient economy, democracy and politics, and the methodology of ancient history have shaped modern approaches to and perceptions of classical antiquity.

Finley explored ancient slavery in a series of seminal papers now collected in *Economy and Society,* in a chapter of *The Ancient Economy* (1973; 2nd ed., 1985), and in a more systematic way in *Ancient Slavery and Modern Ideology* (1980). He also edited two important collections of pertinent essays: *Slavery in Classical Antiquity* (1960) and *Classical Slavery* (1987).

Preoccupied with classical Greece and Rome as two of the few genuine slave societies in history, Finley urged scholars to examine the function of slavery within given times and places rather than trace the contradictions that supposedly rendered slavery unstable. In order to avoid the pitfalls of quantification lacking a solid evidential base, he focused on the location of slavery within ancient societies. Preferring Max Weber's sociological concepts of status and order to the Marxist category of class, he located slavery and various other categories of dependence on a spectrum of statuses according to the rights and duties these conditions entailed.

Finley argued that in Greece and Rome, slavery and freedom advanced hand in hand: shades of dependence between chattel slavery and freedom that were characteristic of archaic societies (and persisted in the Near East) faded together with the replacement of debt bondage by a chattel slavery that drew on outsiders and developed pari passu with the emancipation of insiders and their conversion into free members of self-governing communities. Greek and Roman society thus moved from a situation in which status ran along a continuum toward one in which statuses were bunched at two ends, the slave and the free, a movement that was reversed from the Roman empire into the Middle Ages. Finley deliberately set the study of ancient slavery in the context of broader contemporary intellectual traditions. In *Ancient Slavery and Modern Ideology,* he turned a wide-ranging review of previous scholarship into a critique of antiquarian, positivistic, and humanistic approaches, attacking what he considered modern myths, propounded by German scholars, that posited a humanitarian softening of ancient slavery.

See also ANCIENT GREECE; ANCIENT ROME.

BIBLIOGRAPHY

FINLEY, MOSES I. *Ancient Slavery and Modern Ideology.* 1980.
———. *Economy and Society in Ancient Greece,* edited by Brent D. Shaw and Richard P. Saller. 1981.
MOMIGLIANO, ARNALDO. "Moses Finley on Slavery: A Personal Note." In *Classical Slavery,* edited by Moses I. Finley. 1987.
WHITTAKER, CHARLES R. "Moses Finley 1912–1986." *Proceedings of the British Academy* 94 (1997): 458–472.

Walter Scheidel

Fitzhugh, George   [1806–1881]

Proslavery polemicist and editor.

Born on 4 November 1806, George Fitzhugh was a self-educated struggling lawyer, virtually unknown outside Port Royal, Virginia, until in his early forties he began writing and lecturing widely on slavery. The author of two significant treatises, *Sociology for the South; or the Failure of Free Society* (1854) and *Cannibals All! or, Slaves without Masters* (1857), as well as numerous pamphlets and articles, including more than one hundred essays for *De Bow's Review* and scores of editorials for the Richmond *Examiner* and Richmond *Enquirer,* Fitzhugh was a prolific and influential author. Yet, despite the extraordinary amount of modern scholarship devoted to his work, most mid-nineteenth-century intellectuals dismissed the Virginian as a reckless, self-interested extremist.

In the 1850s Fitzhugh gained widespread notoriety from his shocking assertions that white free laborers or "wage slaves" would be better off if placed under the paternalistic care of southern plantation owners. "Domestic slavery must be vindicated in the abstract," he wrote, ". . . without regard to race or color." In Fitzhugh's judgment, a "state of dependence" was a natural and necessary temporal condition. Not only were "universal liberty and equality . . . absurd and impracticable" values, but human bondage protected the "weakest members" of society from the devouring forces of capitalism. Slaves, he confidently proclaimed, were "all well fed, well clad, [and] . . . happy" with "no dread of the future" nor "fear of want." In the

George Fitzhugh. [*Dictionary of American Portraits*]

aftermath of the Civil War, Fitzhugh's opinions on slavery and emancipation grew increasingly racist in their underlying assumptions, and in 1881 he died impoverished, all but forgotten by his contemporaries.

See also CAPITALISM AND SLAVERY; PERSPECTIVES ON SLAVERY; STEREOTYPES, SLAVISH.

BIBLIOGRAPHY

FITZHUGH, GEORGE. *Cannibals All! or, Slaves without Masters.* Edited by C. Vann Woodward. 1960.
GENOVESE, EUGENE D. *The World the Slaveholder's Made: Two Essays in Interpretation.* 1969.
WISH, HARVEY. *George Fitzhugh, Propagandist of the Old South.* 1943.
———, ed. *Ante-bellum Writings of George Fitzhugh and Hinton Rowan Helper on Slavery.* 1960.

Eric Robert Papenfuse

Florida

The diversity of Florida's white rulers, the distinctiveness of the territory's subregions, and the convolutions of its history all combine to make the history of African slavery in Florida a complex and diffuse narrative. By 1565 enslaved Africans were present at the creation of the town of St. Augustine. For almost two centuries, the northeastern coast was the main site of European settlement in the colony. The Spanish relied upon the labor of black slaves, but the characteristic fluidity of race relations in Iberian colonies permitted the growth of a substantial free black community around St. Augustine. During the eighteenth century most of the inhabitants of the nearby town of Gracia Real de Santa Teresa de Mose, or "Fort Mose," were fugitives from South Carolina. They drilled as a free black militia that helped to defend the area from British invasion.

Between 1763 and 1784, Great Britain controlled Florida. During this period, entrepreneurs developed substantial sugar plantations and cattle-raising operations, all staffed by slaves. The second Spanish period (1784–1821) saw the continuation of such ventures. American planters settled in East Florida, taking advantage of the legal African slave trade to Florida that continued until the colony's cession to the United States in 1821. In part, Seminole Indians' ability to destabilize black bondage had encouraged the United States' designs on the territory. Although some Seminoles claimed to own Africans as slaves, in reality the latter were client communities of maroons existing alongside patron villages of Native Americans. During the First Seminole War (1817–1818), blacks in East Florida revolted en masse, burning plantations and fleeing to the maroons and Seminoles. In the Second Seminole War (1835–1842), American whites sought to remove all Native Americans in order to protect plantation slavery. Florida's new masters also restricted the rights of free black communities around St. Augustine and Pensacola.

Table 1.   Slavery in Florida, 1830–1860.

Year	Slave Population	Free Blacks	Total Population	Bales of Cotton
1830[1]	15,501	844	34,730	—
1840	25,717	817	54,477	—
1850[2]	39,310	932	87,445	45,131
1860	61,745	932	140,425	65,153

[1] There was no U.S. census for Florida before 1830.

[2] In 1850, 3,520 out of 9,107 free families in Florida (roughly 38.7 percent) owned slaves. These households owned a mean of 11.2 slaves apiece. This is the only year for which the U.S. census provides such information.

Source: U.S. Bureau of the Census.

The old slave market, still nestled behind a church in St. Augustine, Florida, in 1896. [Library of Congress/Corbis]

Soon after the United States acquired Florida in 1821, white planters from the Chesapeake and the Carolinas began to settle the area around present-day Tallahassee. Slaves soon cleared hundreds of large cotton plantations from live oak and saw palmetto. Migrant whites moved African-Americans whom they already owned (often separating them from family members left behind in the old states) and bought others through the interstate slave trade. Small numbers of Africans continued to enter the peninsula via the illegal international trade. The experiences of family separation, disease, and overwork shaped a frontier generation of bondspeople. And cotton's boom-and-bust cycle encouraged masters short of cash to sell slaves to the New Orleans market, further disrupting black life in plantation Florida.

By the 1850s, a rising demand for cotton brought stability to the panhandle counties, and African-Americans could form families and communities. In southern Florida, still a sparsely settled frontier, slaves served as cattle herders and turpentine workers. During the Civil War, the heart of plantation Florida remained in Confederate hands until June 1865, over a month after Lee's surrender at Appomattox. Thus Florida, the first area of what became the present-day United States to profit from slavery, was among the last to experience freedom.

See also NATIVE AMERICANS; PLANTATIONS; SPAIN; UNITED STATES.

BIBLIOGRAPHY

COLBURN, DAVID R., and JANE L. LANDERS, eds. *The African-American Heritage of Florida.* 1995.
GANNON, MICHAEL, ed. *The New History of Florida.* 1996.

Edward E. Baptist

Food and Cooking

As a rule, the diets of slaves throughout the Western Hemisphere focused on a single vegetable food and some kind of animal protein. The manioc and dried beef of Brazil's northeast, the "hog and hominy" of the American South, and the salt fish and rice of many of the Caribbean islands serve as classic examples. These examples, however, can be misleading. Much rice and pickled or salted fish were also consumed by the slaves of northeast Brazil; in the far south, around Rio Grande do Sul, slave menus featured fresh beef, a variety of cereals, and vegetables; cornmeal figured into the diets of the coffee slaves of São Paulo; and in Minas Gerais diets like the "hog and hominy" fare served in the southern United States were not uncommon.

Even in the southern United States, the famous combination of pork and cornmeal was not invariably the core diet. In Louisiana, in South Carolina, and along the Georgia coast, rice often replaced corn; wherever slaves were located in the wheat belt, such as in Virginia, wheat bread supplemented the diet; and although most planters seemed to be of the opinion that pork (especially fat pork) was the best fuel for those engaged in hard labor, there were some who argued for the efficacy of beef—not fresh, but properly pickled and cured.

It was in the Caribbean, however, that diets probably varied most from place to place. Fish rations—pickled herring and salted cod—were most common in the English islands that imported much of their foodstuffs, such as Barbados and, to a lesser extent, Jamaica. But in the case of Jamaica, many planters imported little else for their slaves, who were compelled to grow their own substitutes for corn or rice. These include yams, plantains, sorghum (guinea corn), and cassava (yucca, manioc), as well as other starchy roots like taro—the dasheen and eddo of Jamaica and the *malanga* and *yautia* of Puerto Rico and Cuba. In the island of Cuba, slaves ate beef imported from Argentina along with cornmeal or rice, whereas slaves in Puerto Rico frequently were issued beans (the poor man's meat) such as kidney beans (*habichuelas coloradas*) and pigeon peas (*gandules*).

Depending on location, core diets were routinely supplemented by other, lesser staples, such as molasses, flour, pumpkins, turnips, squashes, sweet potatoes, salt, sugar, and a variety of legumes. Dried horsebeans (favas), for example, were issued regularly to slaves on many of the Windward Islands plantations; cowpeas (field peas, or black-eyed peas, or crowder peas) were familiar ingredients in slave dishes of the American South; in Brazil, however, beans were said to be only a part of the slave diet on rich plantations. Finally, diets were supplemented seasonally with greens and other vegetables and fruit, in addition to fish, oysters, crabs, wild birds, and game acquired through foraging.

These foods—those of the core diet and the supplements—were generally cooked together, at least for the evening meal, in pots that blended them into a kind of stew often enlivened by the addition of chili peppers. In the Caribbean and Brazil and on the larger plantations of the southern United States, women (particularly those in charge of the children during the day) did the cooking for everyone. In part this was for reasons of economy, but it was also because of concern that the slaves would not have the energy to cook for themselves after a long day in the fields. Yet, planters frequently complained that many who had families preferred to cook for themselves "in their own peculiar way." Slaves who did cook for themselves were generally issued a skillet, and it was said that in many a slave cabin there was also a worn-out cornfield or tobacco hoe on whose blade hoecake was turned out. Breakfast frequently consisted of grits, mashed vegetables, or manioc porridge, although often it was a matter of dipping into the communal pot for the first of three times that day. The noon meal was sometimes cold, but generally it was hot and carried to the fields, or even prepared there. If the fields were close to the slaves' quarters, the workers returned to their communal pots at noon for whatever they held and used breads made from corn meal, farinha (manioc flour), or even wheat to mop up the pot liquor.

The most important beverage of the slaves was water, and many planters maintained cisterns, fearing the contamination of well water, let alone that of rivers and ponds. Milk was sometimes provided to slave children, but it was seldom consumed by older slaves, whose African ancestry meant that they were almost uniformly lactose-intolerant by the time they reached adulthood. In coffee-growing regions slaves enjoyed the real thing. Elsewhere coffee was an expenditure planters thought necessary only seldom, in which case the coffee was ersatz, the result of roasting corn, bran, okra, or potato peelings. In sugar-growing regions slaves seem to have regularly procured cheap rum (cachaça in Brazil), and corn whiskey was abundant in slave states of North America.

Planter records indicate, and laws regulating slavery suggest, that adults each week were allotted about three to four pounds of meat or fish, seven to eight pints of cornmeal or rice, and perhaps twenty pounds of vegetable supplements (yams, plantains, sweet potatoes, turnips, etc.), along with salt, sugar, and molasses. The young and the old often received proportionally less of this allowance, depending on their age and level of physical activity. For an adult this allotment would have provided between three and four thousand calories a day—probably enough to satisfy the daily energy requirements of hard physical labor.

In addition, most slaves also produced some of their own foodstuffs. They tended garden plots, and many raised chickens and pigs. However, the extent to which such enterprise was a matter of nutritional supplementation is in doubt. Often, at least the pigs and chickens were sent to market or sold to masters so the slaves could procure tobacco, alcohol, fabrics, and other luxury goods.

In balance, it would seem that, barring wars which prevented supplies from getting through (wars were especially devastating for the diets of slaves in the West Indies), and hard times resulting from low sugar or cotton prices, slaves (at least the adults) usually received sufficient calories on a daily basis. Unfortunately, however, the diets of slaves were deficient qualitatively, and, therefore, many suffered severely from nutritional deficiencies ranging from beriberi to scurvy, and slave children were plagued with protein-energy malnutrition.

See also HEALTH.

BIBLIOGRAPHY

BREEDEN, JAMES, O., ed. *Advice among Masters: The Ideal in Slave Management in the Old South.* 1980.

COLLINS, ROBERT. *Practical Rules for the Management and Medical Treatment of Negro Slaves in the Sugar Colonies.* 1811.

FREYRE, GILBERTO. *The Masters and the Slaves.* 1944.

KIPLE, KENNETH F. *The Caribbean Slave: A Biological History.* 1984.

KIPLE, KENNETH F., and VIRGINIA H. KING. *Another Dimension to the Black Diaspora: Diet, Disease, and Racism.* 1981.

Kenneth F. Kiple

Forced Labor

See Labor Systems.

Forty Acres and a Mule

See Reconstruction, U.S.

France

See Abolition and Antislavery Movements; Caribbean Region; Literature of Slavery; Medieval Europe, Slavery and Serfdom in.

Franklin, Benjamin, and the Marquis de Condorcet

When the American statesman Benjamin Franklin (1706–1790) eventually joined the antislavery cause, his attitude toward slavery had been evolving over several decades. He had owned slaves for thirty years, and early in his career he also sold slaves in his general store. But in 1756 he was approached by an English group called the Associates of Doctor Bray who wanted to establish Negro schools in America—a project that appealed to Franklin. He sent a detailed proposal for such a school in Philadelphia, hoping that the idea might spread to other colonies, and with his help and advice black schools were opened in Williamsburg, New York, and Newport; his wife, Deborah, was also enthusiastic. Franklin's first visit to one of these schools gave him, as he wrote, "a higher Opinion of the Natural Capacities of the black race."

When Franklin, now a widower in his seventies, went to France during the American Revolution, his change of heart deepened, in part as a result of his relationship with the French philosopher and politician Marie-Jean-Antoine Nicolas de Caritat, marquis de Condorcet (1743–1794). Condorcet, an important mathematician, was secretary of the Académie Royale des Sciences, which became one of two anchors of Franklin's life in Paris—the other being the Masonic Lodge of the Nine Sisters, a hotbed of antislavery sentiment. Condorcet and Franklin became close friends. Condorcet was a man of passionate convictions, decidedly antislavery, and a champion of the oppressed, be they Jews, women, Protestants, or blacks.

Condorcet began his campaign in defense of slaves in 1777 by writing articles that brought down on his head the wrath of the powerful French sugar planters, who argued that France's economy (and its gastronomy) depended on slavery. But Condorcet forged ahead, publishing *Réflexions sur l'esclavage des nègres* (Reflections on the Enslavement of the Blacks) in 1781, by which time Franklin was familiar enough with French to follow his friend's reasoning. Condorcet argued against slavery on grounds of morality, economics, and politics. He held that buying and selling human beings and keeping them in servitude was morally worse than theft. Economically, he said, slavery was not in the best interest of commerce, and the sugar and indigo plantations could just as well be cultivated by whites. He pointed out that according to calculations made in the United States, it took five slaves to do the work of three free persons—an estimate that was probably given to him by Franklin. And Franklin would later echo Condorcet's argument that slavery corrupted white society.

Franklin cannot have failed to grasp that, like it or not, this issue was of huge importance. Still, though he hated slavery, Franklin could not bring himself to like the slave; furthermore, as long as he was in France representing his country—which desperately needed help from the French—he could not afford to antagonize the planters. Thus it was not until he returned to Philadelphia in 1785 that he became fully committed to an antislavery position.

After his return home, Franklin kept in touch with Condorcet's Société des Amis des Noirs (Society of Friends of Black People) and became president of the Pennsylvania Abolition Society. He did not petition the Constitutional Convention against the slave trade (fearing that South Carolina and Georgia would refuse to join the Union), but he drafted and signed a plan for the integration of freed slaves into white society, a thorny problem. The plan proposed to counsel free blacks, place young people in trade, provide schools for promising children, and offer employment to

Benjamin Franklin. [Corbis-Bettmann]

adults. Franklin sent it to the Société des Amis des Noirs for comments, and on 20 January 1790 he received a warm reply from its current president, the liberal philosopher Jean-Pierre Brissot de Warville, who said that the plan had been translated and sent to all the French newspapers. There seems to have been a friendly race between Paris and Philadelphia as to who would abolish slavery first: the French National Assembly or the American Congress.

In the end, Franklin did sign a memorandum to Congress asking for an end to slavery in the United States. The blessings of liberty, he said, should be granted to all people regardless of color, since all had been created by the same Almighty Being. Not surprisingly, this drew an intensely hostile reaction from some quarters, especially from Representative James Jackson of Georgia. Franklin had less than a month to live, but he rallied his energy and his sense of humor to produce a satirical hoax: a speech supposedly delivered by a Muslim in support of enslaving white Christians. How can we raise food without Christian slaves? the Muslim asks, and—just as Jackson justified slavery by appealing to the Bible—the Muslim defends it by invoking the Koran.

Condorcet, meanwhile, fought for his ideals with such rage that during the French Revolution he ran afoul of Robespierre's Reign of Terror and had to go into hiding. One can only hope that in the little room where he had found refuge he learned that on 7 February 1794 the French Republic abolished slavery in its colonies (in practice, though, only in Guadeloupe and Guyana). A month later Condorcet was arrested. He died in jail the following morning, probably by his own hand.

Brissot de Warville was executed along with other members of the Girondist party. In 1802 Napoleon reestablished both slavery and the slave trade. The antislavery crusade, for the time being, had been lost on both sides of the Atlantic.

See also ABOLITION AND ANTISLAVERY MOVEMENTS; ENLIGHTENMENT; PERSPECTIVES ON SLAVERY; SOCIÉTÉ DES AMIS DES NOIRS.

BIBLIOGRAPHY

BAKER, K. M. *Condorcet: From Natural Philosophy to Social Mathematics.* 1975.

LEMAY, J. A. LEO, ed. *Reappraising Benjamin Franklin: A Bicentennial Perspective.* 1993.

LOPEZ, CLAUDE-ANNE, and EUGENIA W. HERBERT. *The Private Franklin: The Man and His Family.* 1976.

The Papers of Benjamin Franklin. 1956.

SMYTH, ALBERT H., ed. *The Writings of Benjamin Franklin.* 1836–1840.

Claude-Anne Lopez

Freedmen

This entry includes the following articles: Ancient Rome; Brazil and the United States.

Ancient Rome

The ex-slaves of Roman citizens were citizens themselves. This high status for former slaves, combined with potential economic and educational advantages, made them a major force in the urban economy and culture of Rome and, to a lesser extent, the empire. Although ex-slaves encountered strong prejudice, their children, unmarked by any racial difference, were generally assimilated at appropriate levels in the social hierarchy. Only among the elite would any stigma attach to the grandchildren of a freedperson.

Ex-slaves are remarkably conspicuous in the literary, epigraphic, and legal sources: senatorial authors focused resentful attention on the most powerful freedmen; lower on the social scale, ex-slaves of both genders often had the means and desire to commemorate their lives and families on epitaphs; and the relations of ex-slaves and their former owners required revealing legal clarification.

Relations with Masters

Even after manumission, ex-slaves remained legally and often economically connected to their former owners, (called their patrons). The tone of such relationships ranged from affection and mutual respect to resentment and hostility. Given this variation, the "typical" case is unrecoverable. Laws and conventional practices, however, allow some insight into minimum obligations as well as social expectations.

Ex-slaves owed to their patron the vague and probably unenforceable *obsequium,* "dutiful respect." In addition, at the time of manumission, slaves often contracted to do a certain amount of work, *operae,* for their ex-masters. Legal texts discuss the limits of the work that could be demanded of a former slave: for example, slave prostitutes could not be required to continue in their profession; freedpersons had to have adequate time to support themselves. From the end of the second century B.C., patrons held claims against the estates of former slaves. These rights varied over time and depended on the wealth and gender of the ex-slave, the gender of the master, and whether the ex-slave had natural children. For example, a wealthy freedman in the early empire could disinherit a male patron only if the freedman had three descendants. The *lex Aelia Sentia* (A.D. 4) allowed patrons to accuse their former slaves of ingratitude. Punishments ranged up to condemnation to the mines or later reenslavement, depending on the particular case. The harsher punishments were invoked only when an offense more concrete than mere disrespect was involved.

Legal texts deal with requirements and abuses. In epitaphs, patrons are the "kindest," the "most honorable and deserving," while freedmen are the "best" and a freedwomen "never caused me [her patron] grief but by her death." Literary sources reveal moral expectations. They dwell on the courage and loyalty of ex-slaves in their patrons' hour of need, or complain of their arrogance and ungratefulness when their own power and wealth eclipsed that of their master's. Patrons were expected to treat their ex-slaves with paternalistic care and protection. Bequests of land or regular subsidies to ex-slaves are attested. In the early and middle republic, ex-slaves may have had the right to be buried in the same tomb as their patrons. By the late republic the standard epitaph formula giving burial rights to "descendants, freedmen, and freedwomen" was an empty display of paternalism without legal force.

Acceptance and Assimilation

Although ex-slaves became citizens, their legal rights were inferior to those of the freeborn. Freedpersons who committed crimes were subject to torture, like slaves. From the middle of the second century B.C., the political influence of ex-slaves was minimized by confining them to certain voting units in the tribal and plebian assemblies. Freedmen almost never became senators and were barred from wearing the gold ring that marked equestrian status—although emperors could bestow the "right of the gold ring" and "free birth" on freedmen. Freedmen were generally excluded from town senates. From the time of Augustus on, senators and certain of their descendants were penalized for marrying freedwomen. Freedmen were not allowed to serve in the army except during emergencies; they provided marines for the navy. The descendants of ex-slaves suffered none of these disabilities. The supposition that the sons of ex-slaves were prohibited from entering the senate is based on doubtful evidence.

Freedmen also encountered social obstacles. In Satire 1.6, Horace mentions the hostility in the highest ranks of society that attached even to the son of a freedmen. But even at this level, the power and support of patrons and their own abilities and wealth could help former slaves overcome most barriers, if never all resentment. Less fortunate freed slaves quickly merged with an urban plebs, partially composed of descendants of previous generations of ex-slaves. Slave, freed,

and freeborn mixed indiscriminately in the *collegia,* which were social and burial clubs for followers of a specific trade. Epitaphs reveal many mixed marriages, not only between freedpersons and slaves—marriages with no legal validity, since one partner was a slave— but also between freeborn and freed partners. In the latter case, the inferior status of the ex-slave can be seen in the rarity of marriages between a freedman and a freeborn woman. Only high-status freedmen, such as those of the *Familia Caesaris,* were able to "marry up" in this way. In general, the effective families of ex-slaves tended to be small: family ties among slaves were insecure, and only children born after a mother's manumission were free.

Former slaves generally adopted Roman culture. For them to own slaves was standard practice and rarely evoked comment. When rich ex-slaves tried to flaunt their new wealth in the Roman style, they were criticized if they misjudged the nuances of aristocratic display. Barred from many public careers, freedmen dominated the *Seviri Augustales* in the imperial period. This annual priesthood involved considerable expense, but it allowed freedmen to display their wealth and civic spirit. Some freedmen changed their names to avoid revealing their prior enslavement; they tended not to give their children Greek names, which were associated with slavery. Nevertheless, many ex-slaves included their status on their epitaphs and referred to their friends and spouses as "fellow freedpersons." In a striking passage in Petronius's Satyricon (57), an angry freedman contrasts his hard work and accomplishments with the indolence of the freeborn, for whom everything is easy.

Economic and Cultural Role

Freedmen played a large, if not a central, role in the urban economy of Rome and the other great cities of the empire. They were present even in smaller towns. Of epitaphs at Rome which unequivocally mark the status of the deceased, far more record ex-slaves than freeborn Romans. Since even those who died as freedpersons may have been slaves for most of their lives, status at death is likely to exaggerate the size of the ex-slave population and underestimate the number of slaves. In addition, freedpersons seemed to dominate the class of small shopkeepers and craftsmen, numerous and with money enough to put up simple epitaphs; the freeborn urban poor, lacking the connections and skills of ex-slaves, were probably poorer and ended up buried in lime-pits with no commemoration. Although the evidence from epitaphs may inaccurately suggest a large preponderance of ex-slaves, that they were numerous is undeniable.

The columbarium tomb is an underground burial chamber lined with niches that contain urns with the ashes of the dead. Inscriptions found in Rome point to their being associated mainly with slaves and freedmen. [Mimmo Jodice/Corbis]

The wealth and social standing of their patrons played a large role in the prospects of ex-slaves. Domestic slaves in large households often continued in their previous line of work. Large productive enterprises, such as the Arretine potteries, tended to have freeborn, or occasionally freed, owners; the most important craftsmen were freed, and the great mass of the workers were slaves. Most production was on a small scale: skilled slaves could set up shop independently upon liberation. In occupations that required little capital, such slaves probably tended to run their own businesses. In cases when a large investment was needed, ex-slaves probably managed businesses still owned by their ex-masters.

Domestic slaves of less wealthy households often had neither the requisite skills nor access to enough capital to start a business. They either continued to serve their masters after manumission or joined the free poor in competition for casual labor. Many of the followers of the radical politician Clodius in the late republic were ex-slaves. Their political and economic discontent helps adjust the rosy picture of ex-slaves' success we get from the epitaphs, a record skewed toward those who could afford them.

During the late republic, the conquest of the Greek eastern Mediterranean brought many highly trained and educated slaves whose culture and talents were highly esteemed by Romans. A large proportion of writers, artists, entertainers, teachers, doctors, and intellectuals during this period began their Roman careers as slaves. Even later, during the empire, their training and origins often gave former slaves an edge in these fields, although freeborn immigrants played an increasing role.

Rural slaves were less likely to gain their freedom. Independence without money or land was not desirable in the countryside; some ex-slaves were given small plots, and old slaves were perhaps allowed a free retirement on the farm. Freedmen who had made their fortunes elsewhere might invest in land: Pliny the elder records several striking cases of land improvement by ex-slaves.

See also ANCIENT ROME; FAMILIA CAESARIS; LAW; MANUMISSION; PECULIUM.

BIBLIOGRAPHY

DUFF, A. M. *Freedmen in the Early Roman Empire.* 1928.
FABRE, GEORGE. *Libertus.* 2 vols. 1981–1982.
HOPKINS, KEITH. *Conquerors and Slaves.* 1978.
PATTERSON, ORLANDO. *Freedom in the Making of Western Culture.* Vol 1. 1991.
RAWSON, BERYL. "Family Life among the Lower Classes at Rome in the First Two Centuries of the Empire." *Classical Philology* 61 (1966): 71–83.
TREGGIARI, SUSAN. "Family Life among the Staff of the Volusii." *Transactions of the American Philological Association* 105 (1975): 393–401.
———. *Roman Freedmen during the Late Republic.* 1969.

Peter Hunt

Brazil and the United States

The scale and consequences of slaveholding in Brazil and the United States make comparisons of the terms by which the institution was ended in each logical and useful. In Brazil it is customary to date the existence of legal slavery within the span of years from 1550 to 1888, while in the United States this is typically considered to date from about 1619 to 1865. Each of these estimates is to some extent misleading. In the former case, while slavery followed the formation of the Brazilian state after 1549, Portugal and its rival Holland, who vied for control of Brazil, were deeply involved in slaving well before the mid-sixteenth century. Portuguese West African voyages for slaves and other commodities, well established by the late fifteenth century, led others to follow suit. Similarly, while Anglo-American society coalesced in the seventeenth century, its Spanish, Dutch, and French forebears and competitors had all carved out North American spheres of influence where slaves were bought, sold, and used. This is clear in Spanish Florida, the Southwest, and Alta and Baja California, the latter serving as extensions of Spain's Mexican presence. Dutch settlers in New Netherlands brought slavery to what English colonists later called New York.

It is true, however, that from the perspective of American law and custom, slavery's evolution is generally taken to lie within these chronological boundaries of 1619 and 1865. In fact, the present consensus suggests that the "twenty Negars" whom John Rolfe described as having landed in Virginia in August 1619 after being sold by a Dutch man-of-war were indentured servants rather than slaves. This is in some ways a semantic distinction, but it does speak to the varieties of "unfreedom" that characterized early North American migration. Documentation of African slavery in Virginia begins after 1640. While enslaved Native Americans and Africans might have existed in Virginia earlier (as may also have been true in New Netherlands and Massachusetts), they were not the norm.

There are two ways to conceptualize the experience of freed slaves in Brazil and the United States. One concerns the privileges and restrictions they faced during the era of slavery, while the other situates them within the broader context of the new postslave society. In each setting former slaves represent visible but circumscribed minorities in largely anomalous social and juridical positions. As a class they are also very much stepchildren of the mid- to late-nineteenth-century post-Enlightenment. While Brazil and the United States each produced elites capable of presenting articulate and rational critiques stressing the immorality and enormity of man-stealing and bondage, these were insufficient to persuade the planter and mercantile classes in the latter, or planters, merchants, and mine owners in the former, to dispense with the proverbial goose that laid the golden egg. In spite of the powerful example set by Britain's disengagement from slaveholding in a spate of parliamentary measures climaxing in the Act of 1833, issues like compensation of owners and the effect of having former slaves living and working alongside free whites complicated matters. Both North American and Brazilian economies were largely monocultural, depending upon cash crops like tobacco, sugar, and cotton, while Brazil was also economically dependent upon minerals like gold and diamonds. Ending slavery would thus require political, social, and financial realignments.

While manumissions had been a fact throughout slavery in Brazil and the United States, it was simultaneously rare and evident. Slaves were aware of freedmen who had been able to buy themselves out of bondage, or whose fathers had acknowledged them, whose lovers had manumitted them, or who had fled to freedom. A large number of early free blacks were women manumitted as a result of relationships with their masters. In North America former slaves were in evidence not only in the North but also in the slaveholding South and border states even in the darkest days of slavery. They tended to congregate in larger urban areas like Charleston or New Orleans, where they had more latitude to pursue artisanal or skilled occupations. Law and custom designated the rights and limits for former slaves on a state-by-state basis.

The status of free blacks in the United States was severely circumscribed before 1865. In the South they were denied freedom of assembly and movement, prohibited from voting, and frequently blocked from testifying or otherwise making use of the court system; they were generally discouraged from, and often legally proscribed from, attending school or learning to read. They were denied the right to bear arms, and were required to carry "free papers" verifying their nonslave status (even then risking reenslavement for trivial offenses). They were commonly required to leave their natal state upon emancipation. As Chief Justice Roger B. Taney said of Dred Scott in *Dred Scott v. Sandford*, as a class blacks "had no rights" that whites were bound to respect.

Even in the Northern states, while legally allowed to acquire an education, freedmen could be subjected to discriminatory treatment on a customary basis, forcing them to attend separate schools; in general, even though they could own weapons, pursue a wide range of professions, and enjoy relative freedom of movement (though some states, like Indiana, Illinois, and Oregon, sought to restrict their migration, albeit with little success), they still tended to exist in largely separate worlds. They relied to a considerable degree upon their own groups, such as burial societies, churches, fraternal and sororal orders, and mutual-aid societies. Free blacks could exercise the franchise throughout New England (with the exception of Connecticut) and, upon owning property, in the state of New York.

In Brazil elaborate manumission laws passed after the 1824 constitution, in 1832, 1843, 1850, 1855, and 1860, and later acts, ranging from the "law of the free womb" of 28 September 1871, providing for children to follow their mother's status, to the sexagenarian law of 28 September 1885, entitling slaves over the age of sixty to freedom if they could indemnify their masters, were both fraught with loopholes and fairly unknown to the slave population; until 1865 this status could easily be revoked. Former Brazilian slaves held property without full civil rights until 1917. Rights varied with locality, the northeast being preferable to São Paulo. Despite a constitution granting freeborns citizenship, African-born *emancipados* required long nationalization processes. Voting was tied to income. Rural free laborers worked as sharecroppers. Manu-

Students and teachers pose outside the Freedmen's Bureau school in Beaufort, South Carolina, around 1865. [U.S. Army Military History Institute/Corbis]

mission, typically protracted, frequently left beneficiaries with a stigma persisting for generations.

The legal rights and status of former slaves in the United States after 1865 and in Brazil following 1888 were both tenuous and contradictory. Stateside, freedmen faced discrimination in employment and housing in all regions, but especially in the former rebel states. For brief moments refugee slaves benefited by pursuing the line of march of Union troops, several receiving plots of land, notably in the "Port Royal Experiment" of 1861 to 1865 in South Carolina's Sea Islands, until the practice was overturned by President Andrew Johnson's restoration of former confederate lands from 1865 to 1868, by Ku Klux Klan terror, and by Reconstruction's end in 1877. The fate of four million former slaves, inspired by Lincoln's 1863 Emancipation Proclamation but freed only by war and three key constitutional amendments—the Thirteenth Amendment (1865), ending slavery; the Fourteenth Amendment (1868), granting citizenship; and the Fifteenth Amendment (1870), outlawing denial of the right to adult male suffrage—hinged upon federal enforcement. The rights and status of freedpeople depended upon the Union Army. With the withdrawal of troops after the 1876 election, Southern conservatives, using legal and extralegal means, "redeemed" state and local governments, nullifying black gains without federal opposition. In each case slavery's end spurred other forms of repression and restriction.

See also EMANCIPATION; MANUMISSION.

BIBLIOGRAPHY

BENNETT, LERONE. *Black Power, U.S.A.: The Human Side of Reconstruction, 1867–1877.* 1967.
COX, JOHN H., and LAWANDA COX. *Reconstruction, the Negro, and the New South.* 1973.
ELTIS, DAVID. *Economic Growth and the Ending of the Transatlantic Slave Trade.* 1987.
FINKELMAN, PAUL. *Dred Scott v. Sandford: A Brief History with Documents.* 1997.
FRANKLIN, JOHN HOPE. *Reconstruction after the Civil War.* 1961.
HIGGINBOTHAM, A. LEON, JR. *In the Matter of Color: Race and the American Legal Process—the Colonial Period.* 1978.
MATTOSO, KATIA M. DE QUEIROS. *To Be a Slave in Brazil.* 1986.
ROSE, WILLIAM LEE. *Rehearsal for Reconstruction: The Port Royal Experiment.* 1964.

David H. Anthony III

Freedmen's Bureau

Known as the Freedmen's Bureau, the Bureau of Refugees, Freedmen, and Abandoned Land (BRFAL), created under the executive's warmaking authority, became the first federal social service agency. It was signed into law on 3 March 1865, for a term of one year, but its life was extended and its powers were enhanced by a bill passed over President Andrew Johnson's veto on 16 July 1866. The Freedmen's Bureau continued to function throughout most of the former slave states until 1869, with agents in almost every locality.

The bureau's location within the War Department pointed up the link between the war, emancipation, and Reconstruction. The selection of Major General O. O. Howard, the "Christian general," as commissioner reflected the lofty reformist goals contemplated upon the founding of the agency. The bureau set agents, chiefly former Union officers, to administer the delicate and complicated processes of emancipation and Reconstruction. Their responsibilities consisted of adjudicating disputes among freedpeople and between freedpeople and whites, until state judicial systems were properly reconstituted, and monitoring local courts afterward to see that justice was done. Agents also witnessed and adjudicated work contracts, investigated incidents of violence, and reported on the moral, physical, and even temperance conditions of freedpeople. In addition, agents cooperated with missionary associations and freedpeople in providing building materials, sites, and teachers' salaries to commence a black primary school system. They also administered distribution of food, clothing, and travel vouchers to white refugees and freedpeople in need. The task of each agent was a combination of serving as a conduit for policy directives flowing from the national government to the freedpeople, and of information, petitions, and protests flowing in the opposite direction. Each agent, depending on character, politics, and disposition, modeled a different mix of these two functions.

The unification under Howard of administrative powers over freedpeople and land within the bureau was important; the central challenge for the bureau was the relationship between four million emancipated African-Americans and the immense acreage under federal control. Section 4 of the enabling legislation (1865) empowered the commissioner to set aside confiscated land, distribute plots of no more than forty acres to freedmen and loyal whites, and, finally, to sell with full title the land so occupied to the clients of the bureau.

This central function of the bureau was quickly undermined by President Johnson, who asserted that his general amnesty and individual pardons negated wartime confiscation. Johnson ordered bureau-occupied land vacated and returned to its antebellum owners. Freedpeople across the South protested and resisted this policy, claiming a right to the land based on the value of their labor, the blood they had spilled, and the idea of spoils of conquest, as well as a "divine right" to the land. All this was to no avail. Howard accepted his orders and led the bureau away from fulfillment of its major purpose as conceived by those who had framed the enabling legislation.

President Andrew Johnson's vetoing of the Freedmen's Bureau is caricatured as he kicks a bureau full of people down the steps. [Corbis-Bettmann]

The closure of the bureau in the field in 1869 marked the end of an era in the relationship between the U.S. government and freedpeople. Small units of the U.S. Army remained in the South until withdrawn in 1877, but the government's administrative contact with the rank and file of freedpeople was terminated with the bureau.

The failure to distribute the promised land, the cessation of oversight over local tribunals, and the termination of the third-party audits of labor contracts—all consequences of the closure of the bureau in the field—highlighted the failure of the Freedmen's Bureau as the administrator of emancipation and marked the first step in the retreat from Reconstruction.

See also: FREEDMEN; RECONSTRUCTION, U.S.

BIBLIOGRAPHY

MCFEELY, WILLIAM S. *Yankee Stepfather: General O. O. Howard and the Freedmen.* 1968.

NIEMAN, DONALD G. *To Set the Law in Motion: The Freedmen's Bureau and the Legal Rights of Blacks, 1865–1868.* 1979.

Harold S. Forsythe

Freedom

Freedom, as the principal civic virtue and principal means of personal fulfillment stands in modern popular culture, much modern law, and most academic conceptualizations as the polar opposite of enslavement. The nineteenth-century struggle to eliminate slavery in Europe and the Americas drew on a deep heritage in Western culture to give this contrast an emotional and political edge in the minds of American slaves and their descendants and in the writings of many activists that made freedom an axiomatic, idealized goal, a future utopian relief from the burdens of life. This dichotomy explains a tendency in the middle and late twentieth century to castigate many infringements of civil and human rights, and even personal injustices, as slavery in a metaphorical sense that could not have met a rigorous definition of the term. These rhetorical, even polemical uses of the term "freedom" distinguished it from such related but more precise concepts as "manumission" (the legal act of terminating slavery for a given individual) or "emancipation" (governmental elimination of the status of slavery from formal legal codes) and invited critical scrutiny of the ambiguities that lay behind the historical experience of freedom thus attained.

Against this background of idealization, intensified by the cold war–era opposition of "Western freedoms" to "communist slavery," it came as something of a surprise when critical historians in the 1950s and 1960s highlighted a paradox: moments in world history conventionally identified as the birthplaces of the ideal of personal freedoms were also precisely the times and places where slavery had thrived most vigorously. The historian Moses I. Finley first punctured the prevailing idealization of the civic freedoms attributed to the ancient Greek *polis* by wondering whether Greek civilization was based on slave labor and answering his own rhetorical question affirmatively (1959). Finley went on to explore the origins of the modern mythology of freedom in nineteenth-century European romantic nationalisms, which had obscured the prominence of slavery throughout the ancient Mediterranean, in Rome as well as Greece. Slavery has become a less sensitive topic in classical studies, since the enslavement of many is generally accepted to have underpinned limited "freedom" for a minority in both democratic Greece and republican Rome. However, a characteristically late-twentieth-century preoccupation with race has replaced freedom in the enduring modern search for analogs of contemporary issues in the classical world. The question has become the extent of ancient Egyptian influence on the early Greeks, and the "African" character of pharaonic Egypt, through a chain of largely nominal associations extending from culture to geographical location to somatic type.

Some scholars have questioned the obviousness of "freedom" as a personal and civic virtue, and therefore also question it as the quintessential contrast with the denigration of slavery, largely as a result of their growing understanding of non-Western cultures. They contemplated alternative conceptual bases for social hierarchy and other possible scales of human ranking. Drawing on Finley, who had emphasized a slave's alienness to the community in which she or he lived as the defining source of the degradation of enslavement, social anthropologists—Africanists in particular—have emphasized the principle of kinship in defining cohesive, enduring "lineages" as basic elements of social structure, and held that slavery in such primary communities was opposed to the notion of "belonging." They also blurred the totality of the contrast between slavery and its theoretical opposite by discerning degrees of belonging, whether by social assimilation of individual slaves, who found a welcome, if not full legitimacy, in communities constantly trying to increase their numbers by recruiting outsiders or by incorporation of descendants of slaves through generations of marrying into the group.

Orlando Patterson—whose comprehensive world sociology of slavery (1982) had generalized, dramatized, and personalized Finley's socially alien slave as a condition of being powerless, dishonored, and uprooted—drew on these and many other intellectual currents to reflect on the social construction of freedom as a central cultural value, from very small communities of hunters and gatherers through its distinctive elaboration in Western culture from classical Greece and Rome to the dawn of the modern era. For Patterson, outsiders—slaves themselves, and also women in strongly patriarchal contexts—generated the ideal of personal freedom as individual autonomy, distinct from the older and more widespread valuation of membership in the community, out of their suffering from the isolation of individuated alienness. Only through possession of women and slaves could men in such positions break free from obligations to the collectivity in such communalist environments to achieve a different kind of personal autonomy. But the prevailing ethos of loyalty to the group limited the power thus gained and made it a private vice rather than a public virtue. Where male honor was a fundamental social value, as was commonly the case, men sought power by gaining respect rather than winning freedom.

According to Patterson, in preclassical times Greek women, who had no hope of claiming honor, instead asserted freedom of a personal sort. At the dawn of the classical era, nonaristocratic men appropriated the concept for themselves, in the interests of patriarchy and to protect themselves against aristocrats who had escaped the social restraints of agrarian communalism by using the profits of commerce to surround themselves with imported slave retainers. These men's freedom grew as a principle of participation in public life in the emerging towns, an ironic political "democracy" in the classical polis: the civic privilege of a domestic minority of elite males, limited in turn by the ability of the most powerful to maintain control through their monopoly of the spoils of foreign wars—especially captured slaves. Women survived the accompanying patriarchal restraints by redefining freedom as the spiritual liberty of heart and mind, soaring even in death far above the corresponding male emphasis on "freedom" as the ability to inhibit physical domination, or—conversely—as competitive freedom to limit others' autonomy. The dilemmas arising from these alternative meanings of freedom became central preoccupations in classical and Hellenistic Greek philosophy, poetry, and theater.

The vast military power gained under the republic made the Roman Empire, for Patterson, an even more rapaciously competitive regime of aristocrats surrounded by retinues of slaves, with popular freedom meaning merely the limited relief from absolute subjugation to such tyrants afforded by elaborately codified civil law. Aristocratic Roman masters manipulated these increasingly legalistic notions of freedom as opportunities to do anything they wanted that was not prohibited by the code. Slave majorities, particularly in rural areas, transformed the Palestinian sect of Jesus into a Christian religion of religious liberation and left their descendants—freedmen and serfs denied civic freedom—with a love of personal and spiritual freedom that would sustain the underclasses of Christian Europe for a millennium to come.

Historical ironies reappeared behind the ideals of modern slaves' struggles for "freedom" and behind the legal "emancipation" that they won in the eighteenth and nineteenth centuries. The "rights of individuals" celebrated by the Virginia planters who proclaimed the world's first modern republic in the United States in 1776 included the freedom to own Africans as slaves. Protestant currents of religious freedom flowing through northern Europe and North America brought a guilty sense of personal responsibility for human destinies that imbued the latent ethical contradiction inherent in European notions of slavery with the fervor of a secular crusade. Emerging democratic politics made the elimination of slavery by government decree an accessible means of freeing abolitionists' consciences, although slaveholders viewed emancipation as a confiscatory violation of their freedom to own property, whether human or otherwise. The British impulse to end slavery in the early nineteenth-century empire also arose from aristocrats at home, who wished to protect their authority from libertarian Protestant politics and the egalitarian ideals of revolutionary France by diverting popular enthusiasm for personal freedom to remote colonial possessions in the Americas. After emancipation, ambiguities like these allowed some abolitionists to abandon ex-slaves to survive with only their own inadequate resources.

According to Eltis (*Economic Growth and the Ending of the Transatlantic Slave Trade,* 1982) the promotion of "freedom" for slaves remaining in the nonanglophone nations of the Americas after emancipation in British territories in 1834 became a rationale for British economic penetration and political pressure in Brazil, Cuba, and elsewhere. Aggressive military expansion in nearly all of Africa and much of the Muslim world at the end of the nineteenth century promoted the same cause as a leading justification for imperialist conquest of regimes that could be depicted, with only moderate exaggeration, as slave owners or slave traders. Modern capitalism in Europe and the United States thus extended the meaning of freedom from the spiritual liberty of European Christianity and the individual political rights of eighteenth-century liberalism in Britain and North America to aggressive economic expansionism throughout the world.

The slow consolidation of European rule in early-twentieth-century Africa and Asia created profound contradictions for the weak colonial governments of that era. The colonizers distracted attention from their profoundly authoritarian character by claiming to free populations from enslavement by previous rulers. But colonial officials on the scene often could not avoid dependence on local politicians, whose utility as collaborators derived from their control of the slaves they continued to own. In this colonial predicament, economic progress and political order replaced individual freedom for slaves as the rhetoric of the realm, and European governments nursed colonial slavery to a slow, quiet death in most places only by the 1930s.

Despite the contradictory meanings given to freedom in modern times, the slaves themselves consis-

A portrait of Abraham Lincoln appears at the bottom of an engraving that celebrates the emancipation of slaves by contrasting the free family in the center with scenes of the cruelty and hardship characteristic of the life of a slave. [Library of Congress/Corbis]

tently seized on the growing powers of governments to identify emancipation, or state protection of individual civil rights, as an effective way to escape the intensely personal domination of their masters. In the Americas, slaves from Rio to Richmond drew on the spiritual liberation of Christianity, the political liberalism of the "age of revolution" in Europe and the Americas, and their own notions of peasant economic independence, to tailor "freedom" to their own preferences during the lapse in social control that often followed decrees of emancipation, or—in the unique case of Haiti—through the violent overthrow of the slave regime. For the generation of men and women freed, freedom also meant land to farm, families to work it, and time to enjoy the fruits of their labors.

Freedom experienced as the negation of slavery thus acquired subtle cultural and historical resonances far beyond legal and philosophical abstractions, as a social ideology of absolute individualism largely distinctive to Western culture, with a corresponding slow growth of awareness among Europeans and their intellectual heirs of slavery as a "problem" in relation to it. The slaves consistently redefined the concept to overcome recurrent obstacles to the self-fulfillment they sought, against the barriers raised by the powerful and wealthy who were defending their own conflicting, similarly unhindered freedoms. To the extent that, at the end of the twentieth century, worldwide commitment to freedom as a universal human right applicable to many spheres of life far beyond its origins in slavery, is their legacy, the paradox of the close association of freedom and progress with slavery seems resolved.

See also ABOLITION AND ANTISLAVERY MOVEMENTS; EMANCIPATION; MANUMISSION.

BIBLIOGRAPHY

BERLIN, IRA, and RONALD HOFFMAN, eds. *Slavery and Freedom in the Age of the American Revolution.* 1983.

BERLIN, IRA, JOSEPH P. REIDY, and LESLIE S. ROWLAND, eds. *Freedom: A Documentary History of Emancipation, 1861–1867.* 1982.

BLACKBURN, ROBIN. *The Overthrow of Colonial Slavery, 1776–1848.* 1988.

BONNASSIE, PIERRE. *From Slavery to Freedom in South-Western Europe.* Translated by Jean Birrell. 1991.

DAVIS, DAVID BRION. "American Slavery and the American Revolution." In *Slavery and Freedom in the Age of the American Revolution,* edited by Ira Berlin and Ronald Hoffman. 1983.

———. *The Problem of Slavery in the Age of Revolution, 1770–1823.* 1975.

———. *The Problem of Slavery in Western Culture.* 1966. Reprint, 1989.

———. *Slavery and Human Progress.* 1984.

ELTIS, DAVID. *Economic Growth and the Ending of the Transatlantic Slave Trade.* 1987.

FIELDS, BARBARA JEANNE. *Slavery and Freedom on the Middle Ground: Maryland during the Nineteenth Century.* 1985.

FINKELMAN, PAUL. *Slavery and the Founders: Race and Liberty in the Age of Jefferson.* 1996.

FINLEY, MOSES I. *Ancient Slavery and Modern Ideology.* 1980.

———. "Was Greek Civilization Based on Slave Labour?" *Historia* 8, no. 2 (1959): 145–164.

FONER, ERIC. *Nothing but Freedom: Emancipation and Its Legacy.* 1983.

GENOVESE, EUGENE D. *From Rebellion to Revolution.* 1979.

JAMES C. L. R. *The Black Jacobins: Toussaint l'Ouverture and the San Domingo Revolution.* 2d rev. ed. 1963.

LOVEJOY, PAUL E., and JAN S. HOGENDORN. *Slow Death for Slavery: The Course of Abolition in Northern Nigeria, 1897–1936.* 1993.

MEILLASSOUX, CLAUDE. *Anthropologie de l'esclavage: le ventre de fer et d'argent.* 1986. Translated as *The Anthropology of Slavery: The Womb of Iron and Gold.* 1991.

MIERS, SUZANNE, and IGOR KOPYTOFF, eds. *Slavery in Africa: Historical and Anthropological Perspectives.* 1977.

MIERS, SUZANNE, and RICHARD ROBERTS, eds. *The End of Slavery in Africa.* 1988.

MILLER, JOSEPH C. "The Abolition of the Slave Trade and Slavery: Historical Foundations." In Proceedings of the International Conference on "The Slave Route." 1994.

MORGAN, EDMUND S. *American Slavery–American Freedom: The Ordeal of Colonial Virginia.* 1975.

———. "Slavery and Freedom: The American Paradox." *Journal of American History* 59, no. 1 (1972): 5–29.

NASH, GARY B. *Forging Freedom: The Formation of Philadelphia's Black Community, 1720–1840.* 1988.

OAKES, JAMES. *Slavery and Freedom: An Interpretation of the Old South.* 1990.

PATTERSON, ORLANDO. *Freedom in the Making of Western Culture.* 1991.

———. "Freedom, Slavery, and the Modern Construction of Rights," In *Historical Change and Human Rights,* edited by Olwen Hufton. 1995.

———. *Slavery and Social Death: A Comparative Study.* 1982.

———. "The Unholy Trinity: Freedom, Slavery, and the American Constitution." *Social Research* 54, no. 3 (1987): 543–577.

SCOTT, REBECCA J. *Slave Emancipation in Cuba: The Transition to Free Labor, 1860–1899.* 1985.

Joseph C. Miller

Free People of Color

Free people of color were individuals of African descent, who were born free or who were born into slavery and subsequently obtained their freedom. The term, often abbreviated f.p.c. or p.c. in contemporary documents, grew from the common presumption in slaveholding regions that people of African appearance were slaves. Being identified as a free person of color marked one as an exception—not just as an individual of African ancestry who was free rather than enslaved but as a free person who was black rather than white, like the vast majority of the free population.

In reality, black-white nomenclature did not accurately describe the skin color of persons of either African or European ancestry. Just as the skin tones of European Americans ranged from swarthy to pale, the complexions of free persons of color covered a spectrum from black through various shades of brown to a color indistinguishable from that of "white" people. Although individuals of unmixed African descent possessed a range of skin hues, the major reason the complexions of many free persons of color tended to be lighter than slaves was that they were often descendants of both African and European ancestors. In many cases they were the children of their own masters, who were then manumitted. The term *mulatto* was often used to describe a light-skinned free person of color and generally indicated mixed racial ancestry. More precise terminology of the degree of racial mixture (for example, quadroons were supposed to be one-fourth African; octoroons, one-eighth) was common in the Caribbean and Brazil, but less so in the United States, except for Louisiana and especially New Orleans. In the United States any visible hint of African ancestry in a person's hair, facial features, or skin color led whites to regard the individual as a person of color. This use of the color of one's features for racial designation was less rigidly observed in Brazil and the Caribbean, but even there African ancestry tended to be stigmatized.

Ancestry determined not just appearance but also status. A child born to a free mother was free even if the father was a slave. Likewise, the child of a slave mother was a slave even if the father was free. Since one or both parents of many free persons of color were slaves, strong personal ties often linked free persons of color to slaves. In addition to free birth, individuals obtained their freedom principally by manumission or self-purchase. Masters sometimes freed one or more of their slaves as a reward for long and faithful service, in recognition of affection growing out of relations of concubinage or parentage, to honor religious or political convictions of human equality, or to adjust their labor force to a changing economy. In the United States manumission peaked in the two decades immediately following the American Revolution, then declined when states restricted or prohibited manumission except in special cases. Although a few masters manumitted all their slaves—usually following the master's death—masters typically manumitted only slaves with whom they had a special relationship: a house servant, a person of unusual skill or responsibility, or a concubine or child. Consequently, those free persons of color who had been manumitted often had comparatively privileged experiences as slaves.

Slaves who managed to purchase their own freedom also tended to be relatively privileged. Their masters permitted them opportunities denied to most slaves, namely to save money earned by doing extra work or by marketing such items as their own eggs, poultry, or vegetables. Self-purchase was more available to slave men than to slave women because carpenters, blacksmiths, coopers, and other skilled laborers who could earn money for extra work were nearly all men.

Free persons of color were a privileged caste of individuals of African descent in slave societies, and they strove to defend and expand their privileges. Although

A group of freedwomen works together at meal preparations. [Corbis-Bettmann]

many sympathized with the plight of slaves and maintained close personal ties to individual slaves, as a group they tended to distance themselves from slaves, in large measure to protect their own status from the degradations of slavery.

Out of economic necessity, free people of color tried to cultivate good relations with the dominant free population that was not of African descent. Both men and women worked at a variety of skilled trades, but most were either common laborers or domestic servants. In New Orleans, Charleston, Baltimore, and to a lesser extent in smaller cities such as Richmond, Savannah, and Mobile, free people of color formed self-conscious communities that intermarried and participated in religious, educational, and mutual aid societies. In these places and more frequently in the Caribbean and Brazil, the dominant free population valued free people of color as a convenient buffer between themselves and the slaves. But most white people in the American South despised free people of color—as uppity individuals of African descent who were trying to escape their racial identity and become like whites, as bad examples to the masses of people of African ancestry who were slaves, or as dangerous incendiaries who awaited an opportune moment to ignite a slave rebellion.

Such views lay behind the laws that discriminated against free people of color and restricted their freedom. Legally, their freedom meant the ability to make contracts, to defend themselves in court, to get married, and to pass the legacy of freedom to the next generation. In virtually all other ways, freedom was circumscribed: they could not vote, for example, or serve on juries. In effect, their freedom was subject to the sufferance of the dominant free population. The terrain they inhabited between free and slave and between black and white was treacherous and politically vulnerable. Yet thousands in this difficult position managed to survive and raise families, and some even to prosper.

See also: FREEDOM; SELF-PURCHASE; STEREOTYPES, SLAVISH.

BIBLIOGRAPHY

BERLIN, IRA. *Slaves without Masters: The Free Negro in the Antebellum South.* 1974.

COHEN, DAVID W., and JACK P. GREENE, eds. *Neither Slave nor Free: The Freedmen of African Descent in the Slave Societies of the New World.* 1972.

CURRY, LEONARD P. *The Free Black in Urban America, 1800–1850: The Shadow of a Dream.* 1981.

DEGLER, CARL N. *Neither Black nor White: Slavery and Race Relations in Brazil and the United States.* 1971.

HEUMAN, GAD J. *Between Black and White: Race, Politics, and the Free Coloreds in Jamaica, 1792–1865.* 1981.

HOGAN, WILLIAM RANSOM, and EDWIN ADAMS DAVIS, eds. *William Johnson's Natchez: The Antebellum Diary of a Free Negro.* 1951.

JOHNSON, MICHAEL P., and JAMES L. ROARK. *Black Masters: A Free Family of Color in the Old South.* 1984.

——, eds. *No Chariot Let Down: Charleston's Free People of Color on the Eve of the Civil War.* 1984.

LITWACK, LEON F. *North of Slavery: The Negro in the Free States, 1790–1860.* 1961.

MILLS, GARY B. *The Forgotten People: Cane River's Creoles of Color.* 1977.

WILLIAMSON, JOEL. *New People: Miscegenation and Mulattoes in the United States.* 1980.

ZILVERSMIT, ARTHUR. *The First Emancipation: The Abolition of Slavery in the North.* 1967.

Michael P. Johnson

French Antislavery Society

See Société des Amis des Noirs.

Freyre, Gilberto   [1900–1987]

Brazilian anthropologist.

A prolific writer, Gilberto Freyre promoted new attitudes about race, miscegenation, and his nation's cultural heritage. Descended from elite planters, Freyre grew up in Recife, a provincial city in northeastern Brazil, a region long identified with sugar plantations. During the 1920s he studied at Columbia University under Franz Boas, the noted anthropologist who stressed the contribution of culture rather than race to human differences. Returning home from a brief exile after Brazil's Revolution of 1930, Freyre challenged prevailing opinions that denigrated Brazil's African, Indian, and European racial mixture. Clearly breaking with the scientific racism espoused by leading intellectuals such as Oliveira Viana, he championed racial fusion as a unique and positive feature of Brazilian society rather than a necessary step toward "whitening" the population. As the basis for his claims, Freyre studied Brazilian plantation history, emphasizing child development, intimate if not benign master-slave relations, and interracial sexual liaisons. Two seminal works resulted in 1933 and 1936. The first, *Casa grande e senzala (The Masters and the Slaves)*, presented the plantation as the foundation of Brazilian society and the source of racial harmony. In contrast, *Sobrados e mucambos (The Mansions and the Shanties)* described the urban, middle-class mulatto as a corruption of Brazil's fundamental values. Numerous other works followed, including two in 1959, *Ordem e progresso (Order and Progress)* and *New World in the Tropics.* Modern studies of North American slavery—Frank Tannenbaum's *Slave and Citizen* (1945)

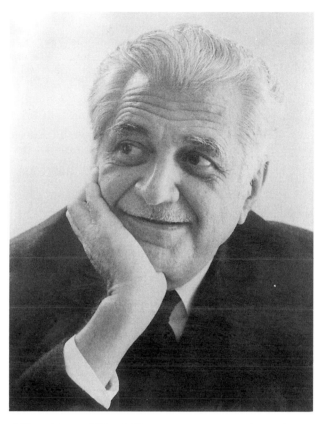

Gilberto Freyre. [The Gilberto Freyre Foundation]

and Stanley Elkins's *Slavery* (1959)—gathered momentum through pessimistic assessments of Freyre's image of Brazil as less racist and, by extension, Brazilian slavery as less harsh than the comparable aspects found in the United States. Although Freyre's works are today criticized as romanticized accounts of plantation life and as apologia for slavery, the myth of racial democracy that they invented remains an important element in Brazilian national identity.

See also ANTHROPOLOGY OF SLAVERY; BRAZIL; ELKINS THESIS; TANNENBAUM, FRANK.

BIBLIOGRAPHY

NEEDELL, JEFFREY D. "Identity, Race, Gender, and Modernity in the Origins of Gilberto Freyre's *Oeuvre.*" *American Historical Review* 100 (February 1995): 51–77.

SKIDMORE, THOMAS E. *Black into White: Race and Nationality in Brazilian Thought.* 1993.

VIOTTI DA COSTA, EMILIA. "The Myth of Racial Democracy: A Legacy of the Empire." In *The Brazilian Empire: Myths and Histories.* 1985.

John J. Crocitti

Friends, Society of

See Quakers.

Fugitive Slave Laws, U.S.

As early as 1643 the New England Confederation agreed to return runaway slaves. Similarly, in the 1640s Maryland and Virginia cooperated in the return of runaways. This cooperation continued during the Revolution. Pennsylvania's Gradual Abolition Act of 1780, for example, while setting into the motion the process of ending slavery in that state also guaranteed that masters could recover runaways there. In July 1787 Congress prohibited slavery in the Northwest Territories, but the same clause also provided that "any person escaping into the same, from whom labour or service is lawfully claimed in any one of the original states, such fugitive may be lawfully reclaimed, and conveyed to the person claiming his or her labour or service as aforesaid." This was the first enactment of a national fugitive slave law.

In August 1787, without serious discussion, the Constitutional Convention meeting in Philadelphia added a fugitive slave clause to the draft of the U.S. Constitution. Broadening its terms beyond slavery itself to lessen the suspicions of Northern opponents of slavery, the clause declared "No Person held to Service or Labour in one State, under the Laws thereof, escaping into another, shall, in Consequence of any Law or Regulation therein, be discharged from such Service or Labour, but shall be delivered up on Claim of the Party to whom such Service or Labour may be due." No Northerners debated this provision during the struggle over ratification, but in the South supporters of the Constitution argued that it was one of the important reasons for adopting the Constitution.

The Fugitive Slave Clause in the Constitution seemed to assume that the states would enforce the clause themselves. Nevertheless, in 1793 Congress passed a statute that covered both interstate criminal extradition and the return of fugitive slaves. The law of 1793 empowered all federal and state judicial authorities to give certificates of removal to allow masters to bring fugitive slaves back to the jurisdiction from which they had fled. The law provided fines for those who interfered with the return of runaways and also allowed masters to sue for damages anyone who helped their slaves escape. Many states responded to this act with "personal liberty laws" that gave alleged fugitive slaves jury trials and required that state officials supervise the return of fugitive slaves to prevent the kidnapping of free blacks. In *Prigg v. Pennsylvania* (1842) the Supreme Court struck down these state personal liberty laws, while upholding the constitutionality of the federal law of 1793. In response to *Prigg* a number of Northern states passed new personal liberty laws, to prohibit their officials from enforcing the

federal law and denied the use of state jails and courtrooms to hold or to try alleged runaway slaves.

In 1850 Congress responded to these state evasions by amending the 1793 law to provide for direct federal enforcement through the appointment of commissioners in every county in the nation. The 1850 law marked the first time in United States history that Congress had mandated a federal law enforcement presence at the local level. The statute allowed for $1,000 fines and up to a year in jail for anyone who helped rescue a fugitive slave from custody. The law also allowed the use of the army, state militias, and federal marshals to remove fugitive slaves. The law provided

A handbill urges the reader to examine the text of the Fugitive Slave Law of 1850 and consider the implications of the law as it affects the constitutional rights of the individual. [Library of Congress]

for a summary hearing, without a jury, to determine whether a captured black was a fugitive and prohibited alleged fugitive slaves from testifying at their own hearings. Federal commissioners received $5 if they found that the black before them was not a fugitive slave, but they got $10 if they found in favor of the master.

Between 1850 and 1864, when the law was finally repealed, fewer than 400 slaves were returned to their owners. The law led to resistance, and sometimes violence, by fugitive slaves, free blacks, and white abolitionists. Famous rescues, riots, and legal cases included the Shadrach case in Boston (1851); the riot in Christiana, Pennsylvania (1851); the Jerry rescue in Syracuse (1851); the Anthony Burns case in Boston (1854); the Ableman-Booth Case in Milwaukee (1854–1859); and the Oberlin-Wellington rescue (1858). These cases and incidents made the law a constant source of sectional conflict. They also provided the antislavery movement with dramatic examples of the dangers to liberty in the North. During the trial of Anthony Burns the federal government ringed the Boston courthouse with a heavy anchor chain and surrounded the building with soldiers and cannon, spending perhaps as much as $100,000 to remove one slave from Boston. In 1860–1861 a number of Southern states cited federal failure to enforce the law as one reason for secession.

See also BURNS, ANTHONY; COMPROMISE OF 1850; CONSTITUTION, U.S.; PRIGG V. PENNSYLVANIA.

BIBLIOGRAPHY

CAMPBELL, STANLEY. *The Slave Catchers.* 1968.

FINKELMAN, PAUL. *Slavery in the Courtroom.* 1984.

MORRIS, THOMAS D. *Free Men All: The Personal Liberty Laws of the North.* 1974.

Paul Finkelman

G

Gabriel [1776–1800]

Slave in Virginia who became a revolutionary leader.

The black revolutionary known as Gabriel was born near Richmond, Virginia, at Brookfield, the Henrico County Plantation of Thomas Prosser. The identity of Gabriel's parents is lost to history, but he had two older brothers, Martin and Solomon. Most likely, Gabriel's father was a blacksmith, the craft chosen for Gabriel and Solomon; in Virginia, the offspring of skilled bondpersons frequently inherited the parent's profession.

Gabriel's status as an apprentice artisan provided the young craftsman with considerable standing in the slave community, as did his ability to read and write (a skill said to have been taught to him by the mistress of the plantation, Ann Prosser). As Gabriel developed into an unusually tall young man, even older slaves looked to him for leadership. By the mid-1790s, as he approached the age of twenty, Gabriel stood "six feet two or three inches high," and the muscles in his arms and chest betrayed nearly a decade in Brookfield's forge. A long and "bony face, well made," was marred by the loss of the two front teeth and "two or three scars on his head." His hair was cut short and was as dark as his complexion. According to journalist James T. Callender, blacks and whites alike regarded him as "a fellow of courage and intellect above his rank in life."

During his apprenticeship as plantation smith, Gabriel married a young slave named Nanny. Much is unknown about her, including the identity of her owner and whether she had any children with Gabriel. Most likely she lived on a nearby farm or tobacco plantation.

In the fall of 1798 Gabriel's old master died, and the ownership of Brookfield fell to twenty-two-year-old Thomas Henry Prosser. An ambitious young man with a townhouse in Richmond and a lucrative auction business, Prosser increasingly maximized his profits by hiring out his surplus slaves. Even the most efficient planters could not find tasks enough to keep their slave artisans occupied year-round, and many masters routinely hired out their craftsmen to neighboring farms and urban businessmen. Despite all of the work to be done at Brookfield, Gabriel spent a considerable part of each month smithing in and around Richmond. Though no less a slave under Virginia law, Gabriel enjoyed a rough form of freedom as his ties to young Prosser became ever more tenuous.

Emboldened by this quasi liberty, in September 1799 Gabriel moved toward overt rebellion. Caught in the act of stealing a pig, a delicacy slaves used to supply their families with protein, Gabriel refused to suffer the verbal abuse of its owner, a white neighbor. Instead, he wrestled his tormentor to the ground and bit off the better "part of his left Ear." Under Virginia law, slaves were not tried as whites; they were prosecuted under a colonial statute of 1692 that established special segregated county tribunals known as courts of oyer and terminer, composed of five justices of the peace. There was no jury and no appeal except to the governor. On 7 October Gabriel was formally charged with attacking a white man, a capital crime in Virginia.

Although he was found guilty, Gabriel escaped the gallows through an antiquated clause that since the Revolution had been denied to white defendants. Slaves possessed the right to "benefit of clergy," which allowed them to escape hanging in favor of being branded on the thumb with a small cross if they were able to recite or read a verse from the Bible. This option was available to Gabriel, thanks to the Afro-Baptist faith of his parents and his own literacy. (There is no truth, however, to a myth of the later "gilded age" that Gabriel was a messianic figure who wore his hair long in imitation of his hero, Samson.)

Gabriel's branding and incarceration were the final indignity. By the spring of 1800, his fury began to develop into a carefully considered plan to bring both his own freedom and the end of slavery in Virginia. As he revealed to his brothers Solomon and Martin, slaves from Henrico County would gather at the blacksmith shop at Brookfield on the evening of 30 August and march on the capital city of Richmond. But the planned uprising collapsed just before sunset on the appointed day when a severe thunderstorm hit southern Henrico. The storm frightened two slaves into informing their master of the conspiracy. As the militia closed in, Gabriel escaped south by way of the swampy Chickahominy River. After hiding along the James River for nearly two weeks, Gabriel decided to risk boarding the schooner *Mary*. Captain Richardson Taylor, a former overseer who had recently converted to Methodism, willingly spirited Gabriel downriver to Norfolk. There Gabriel was betrayed by Billy, a slave crewman who had heard that Governor James Monroe was offering a $300 reward for Gabriel's capture. Returned to Richmond under heavy guard, Gabriel was found guilty of "conspiracy and insurrection." On 10 October 1800 the slave general died with quiet composure at the town gallows near Fifteenth and Broad. He was twenty-four.

See also GABRIEL'S REBELLION; INSURRECTIONS.

BIBLIOGRAPHY

EGERTON, DOUGLAS R. *Gabriel's Rebellion: The Virginia Slave Conspiracies of 1800 and 1802*. 1993.

MULLIN, GERALD W. *Flight and Rebellion: Slave Resistance in Eighteenth-Century Virginia*. 1972.

SCHWARZ, PHILIP J. *Twice Condemned: Slaves and the Criminal Law of Virginia, 1705–1865*. 1988.

Douglas R. Egerton

Gabriel's Rebellion (1800)

The most sophisticated and politicized of all North American slave conspiracies, the Virginia plot of 1800, was organized by a literate slave blacksmith known

The plans for Gabriel's Rebellion included making a hostage of James Monroe (above), the governor of Virginia at the time. [U.S. Treasury/Corbis]

only as Gabriel. Inspired by the egalitarian promise of the revolutions in the United States and Saint Domingue, Gabriel and his chief lieutenants—all of whom lived in or around Richmond—conspired to end not only their own bondage but slavery in Virginia as well. Armed with crude swords fashioned from scythes, Gabriel's army intended to rise up in concert with slaves in other Tidewater towns. The main force, led by Gabriel, planned to approach Richmond in three units. The first group proposed to swarm into Capitol Square and seize the guns stored in the building. Governor James Monroe, slumbering in the adjacent executive mansion, would be taken hostage. The other columns would set fire to Rocketts Landing, the warehouse district, as a diversion and then fortify the town. A small number of city leaders were to die, but most would live as hostages in order to force the Virginia elite to grant the slaves' demands, which included their freedom and an equitable division of city property. If Monroe agreed to Gabriel's demands, the slave general intended to "hoist a white flag" and drink a toast "with the merchants of the city."

Using their ability to hire their time away from their owners, Gabriel and his key lieutenants—Sam Byrd, Jack Ditcher, and Gabriel's brother Solomon—contacted only those slaves whose talents and skills meant they had little contact with their owners. Recruiter Ben Woolfolk moved north into Hanover, Goochland, and Caroline counties, while black mariners ferried word of the uprising down the James River to Petersburg, Norfolk, and Gloucester County.

The uprising, set to begin on the night of Saturday, August 30, collapsed just before sunset on the appointed day when a severe thunderstorm hit southern Henrico County. Perhaps only a dozen slaves reached the rendezvous point on Brookfield plantation. The chaos of the storm convinced two Henrico house slaves, Tom and Pharoah, that the revolt could not succeed. They informed their owner of the conspiracy, and he hurried word to Governor Monroe. In all, twenty-six slaves, including Gabriel, were hanged for complicity in the conspiracy. Another bondman allegedly hanged himself while in custody. Eight more rebels, including Jack Ditcher, were transported to Spanish New Orleans; at least thirty-two others were found guilty. Reliable sources placed the number of slaves who knew of the plot to be between five hundred and six hundred.

Although the abortive uprising failed in its goals, Southern whites were painfully aware that it was the most extensive slave plot yet devised in North America. In the aftermath, Virginia legislators labored to ensure that it would not be repeated. Intent on crushing black autonomy, the General Assembly passed a number of laws abolishing black liberties, including the right to congregate on Sunday for religious services. After 1806 all manumitted slaves had twelve months to leave the state or be "apprehended and sold" back into bondage. However, this law was almost never enforced, and local authorities regularly granted exemptions to recently manumitted slaves, allowing them to remain in Virginia.

See also GABRIEL; INSURRECTIONS; MANUMISSION.

BIBLIOGRAPHY

APTHEKER, HERBERT. *American Negro Slave Revolts.* 1943.

EGERTON, DOUGLAS R. *Gabriel's Rebellion: The Virginia Slave Conspiracies of 1800 and 1802.* 1993.

MULLIN, GERALD W. *Flight and Rebellion: Slave Resistance in Eighteenth-Century Virginia.* 1972.

Douglas R. Egerton

Galley Slaves

Throughout the preindustrial era, slaves were employed to propel galleys. The term "galley" is used generically for a ship which relied on oar power and used sail only when wind and circumstances were favorable. In classical Athens of the fifth and fourth centuries B.C., oar-driven fighting ships were mostly manned by poor free citizens whereas slaves served as oarsmen only in emergencies during the wars against the Persians and Sparta. Other Greek city states, such as Kerkyra (Corfu), Corinth, Chios, and Syracuse, also used galley slaves in times of crisis. The crews of merchant ships commonly consisted of slaves and freedmen, but only a small number of oarsmen (from under twenty to fifty) were required for the launch and navigation in coastal waters of these sailing-vessels.

The Romans may have used slave oarsmen on their large war fleets during the First Punic War (264–241 B.C.) but later on usually relied on poor free citizens, allies, and freedmen. Slaves were drafted only in rare military emergencies. (Thus, the picture of slave-manned galleys popularized by the novel *Ben Hur* is largely fictitious.) Again, Roman merchant ships were sailing ships and manned by few slave oarsmen.

The use of galley slaves was relatively uncommon throughout the Middle Ages. Some oarsmen in tenth-century Muslim Andalusia may have been slaves, and Genoa, Morocco, Tunis, and the Turks occasionally employed galley slaves during the late Middle Ages (twelfth to fifteenth centuries). In the major medieval navies, oarsmen were mostly free men who were hired or pressed into service. In the early modern period, the use of convicts as oarsmen, known as *forcats,* became the predominant form of involuntary service on military galleys.

It is important to distinguish between penal servitude and slavery proper, which coexisted on galleys from the sixteenth to the eighteenth century. Most of the galley slaves used by European maritime powers (such as Genoa, Venice, Leghorn, the Grand-Duchy, the Pontifical State, Spain, and France) were Muslims who were generically referred to as "Turks," even though most of them originated in North Africa. They were either purchased in Mediterranean slave markets or captured at sea or in operations against Muslim states on the North African coast. Galley slaves acquired in this fashion also included orthodox Christians, mainly from Russia but also from Greece and Central Eastern Europe, as well as Muslims who had been converted to Christianity. In the 1680s, France briefly but unsuccessfully experimented with blacks from Senegal and Iroquois from French Canada.

The average number of oarsmen per galley increased over time and varied from around 150 to 250 and over. The proportion of slaves in the crews fluctuated considerably over time and place: from ten to thirty percent in Italian navies of the seventeenth century, twenty-five to fifty percent in sixteenth- and seventeenth-century Spain, or twenty and ten percent in France in the seventeenth and eighteenth century, respectively. Galley slaves were all male and mostly fifteen to thirty-five years old. When not at sea, slaves were put to work in the ports. Their market price remained stable during the sixteenth and seventeenth centuries but rose in the eighteenth.

Although galley slaves were expensive and the aggregate value of a crew would often exceed the value of the vessel, their diet was poor and monotonous. Dehydration was a common problem, and medical care was absent or inadequate. Most died from natural causes, while death in battle or in flight was rare. Convicts and slaves served side by side and were subject to the same harsh treatment. Whipping and mutilations as disciplinary measures are attested to for both Christian and Muslim galleys, though in Europe some care was taken not to disable slaves, who were chosen for their physical suitability and whose performance was considered superior to that of convicts.

A sixteenth-century engraving of a Venetian galley slave with ankle chains. [Christel Gerstenberg/Corbis]

In the Ottoman Empire of the Turks, most oarsmen were subjects of the sultan, drafted through corvée and supplemented by convicts. In the seventeenth century, the Turks used galley slaves more frequently. Most came from Russia and some from Italy. Blacks, though common as domestic slaves, do not seem to have been used widely on Turkish galleys. For reasons of security, slaves of common origin and language were dispersed across different crews. In the sixteenth and above all the seventeenth centuries, galley slaves were exceptionally common on the ships of the Barbary corsairs based in Tunis, Algiers, and Morocco. Many of them were Christian captives from the western Mediterranean; they were the property of captains or were rented from merchants. The use of slaves as oarsmen generally came to an end with the demise of the galley in the mid-eighteenth century.

See also ANCIENT GREECE; ANCIENT ROME.

BIBLIOGRAPHY

BAMFORD, PAUL W. *Fighting Ships and Prisons: The Mediterranean Galleys of France in the Age of Louis XIV.* 1973.
CASSON, LIONEL. "Galley Slaves." *Transactions and Proceedings of the American Philological Association* 97 (1966): 35–44.
PIKE, RUTH. "Penal Servitude in Early Modern Spain: The Galleys." *Journal of European Economic History* 11 (1982): 197–217.
RAGOSTA, ROSALBA, ed. *Le Genti del Mare Mediterraneo.* Vols. 1 and 2. 1981.

Walter Scheidel

Garnet, Henry   [1815–1882]

Black nationalist, abolitionist, and diplomat.

Henry Highland Garnet was born on 23 December 1815 to slave parents on a tobacco plantation in New Market, Maryland. In 1824 he escaped with his family to New York City with the help of Thomas Garrett, a Quaker; the family assumed the surname Garnet, which may be linked to Garrett. At age thirteen Garnet left school to work at sea. He returned home crippled in 1829 to find that his family had narrowly escaped slave catchers.

Unfit for physical labor, Garnet pursued theological studies with Reverend Theodore Wright as his mentor. An honors graduate of Oneida Institute in 1840, he spoke before the American Anti-Slavery Society. Unwilling to accept the strategy of "moral suasion," he left that society for the American and Foreign Anti-Slavery Society and became the Liberty Party's first black member. Ordained in 1842, he became First Pastor of Liberty Street Presbyterian Church in Troy, New York, and relied on monies from Gerrit Smith, his lifelong benefactor. In 1843 he mar-

Henry Highland Garnet. [Library of Congress]

ried Julia Ward Williams. When he founded the *Clarion* in 1843, he tried to establish an all-black weekly. He also cofounded the National Convention of Colored Citizens and Their Friends. At its convention in Buffalo, on 17 August 1843, he delivered his "Address to Slaves," a call for slave insurrection that sharply divided blacks and alienated most whites, except radicals such as John Brown, who published the speech in 1848. Another speech, "The Past and Present Condition and the Destiny of the Colored Race," pleaded for black unity and the end of American slavery.

In the late 1850s he used his prominent European contacts, the African Civilization Society, and his pastorate at Shiloh Presbyterian Church to promote African culture, voluntary emigration, and aid for fugitive slaves. During the Civil War, he was a recruiter and chaplain for several black regiments. A leading black American orator, he became the first black to address Congress at an 1865 ceremony honoring passage of the Thirteenth Amendment. After the war he supported education, land ownership, and voluntary emigration for blacks. Garnet died of "tropical fevers" in Monrovia while serving as First Counsel and Minister to Liberia, the highest diplomatic office awarded to an African-American in his time.

See also ABOLITION AND ANTISLAVERY MOVEMENTS; AMERICAN AND FOREIGN ANTI-SLAVERY SOCIETY; AMERICAN ANTI-SLAVERY SOCIETY; LIBERIA.

BIBLIOGRAPHY

O'FARI, EARL. *"Let Your Motto Be Resistance": The Life and Thought of Henry Highland Garnet.* 1972.
PASTERNAK, MARTIN B. *Rise Now and Fly to Arms: The Life of Henry Highland Garnet.* 1995.
SCHOR, JOEL. *Henry Highland Garnet: A Voice of Black Radicalism in the Nineteenth Century.* 1977.

Sharleen N. Nakamoto

Garrison, William Lloyd [1805–1879]

Abolitionist and editor.

William Lloyd Garrison was born in Newburyport, Massachusetts, to a seaman father and a pious Baptist mother. His childhood was marred by poverty after his alcoholic father abandoned the family. He had little formal education. At the age of ten he was apprenticed to a shoemaker, a trade he despised. From 1818 to 1825 he apprenticed as a printer with the editor of the *Newburyport Herald,* mastered the trade, and fell in love with journalism. His attempt to publish his own newspaper in Newburyport ended in financial failure.

In the late 1820s Garrison met Benjamin Lundy, a proponent of African-American colonization and the editor of *The Genius of Universal Emancipation.* Lundy's concern for slave welfare touched Garrison deeply and introduced him to a cause he would find more compelling than the temperance or peace movements with which he had been associated previously. Garrison joined the newspaper's Baltimore-based staff as a junior editor. A devout Christian, Garrison had religious convictions that quickly caused him to move to the political left of Lundy. When, in 1829, he wrote a fiery article condemning a New England ship captain who was lawfully transporting slaves, he was convicted of libel, fined, and jailed.

Garrison broke with the colonizationists and began to publish his own newspaper in Boston, *The Liberator.* In its inaugural issue, he set the tone for the paper's thirty-five-year run, from 1831 to 1865: "I am in earnest—I will not equivocate—I will not excuse—I will not retreat a single inch—AND I WILL BE HEARD." Denouncing slavery as a sin, he rejected gradual, compensated emancipation and demanded an immediate end to slavery. More than any other individual, he discredited colonization and placed the antislavery movement on a more radical course. His pamphlet, *Thoughts on African Colonization* (1832), completed the break with Lundy.

The front page of the 23 April 1831 issue of The Liberator. [Corbis-Bettmann]

Garrison's compassion and fervor soon attracted both a readership for his publications and activists who began founding local antislavery societies, which then affiliated with his American Anti-Slavery Society. His ideas inspired controversy as well. On more than one occasion Northern mobs threatened his life. Southern states offered rewards for his capture.

In 1840 the American Anti-Slavery Society divided over the question of female participation in the movement (which Garrison encouraged) and whether to seek political solutions to slavery. Because the U.S. Constitution sanctioned slavery, Garrison believed the American political system was morally corrupt. He hoped to persuade Americans of the immorality of slavery by using what he called "moral suasion." By the 1850s he was advocating separation of the Northern states from the slaveowning South, believing that without the support of the U.S. Army and under the weight of slave insurrection and international condemnation, slavery could not be sustained.

During the Civil War he complained of the Lincoln administration's slow steps toward emancipation, but this skepticism regarding the president and the Republican Party gave way to admiration, and he endorsed Lincoln's reelection in 1864. Unlike other abolitionists such as Wendell Phillips, Garrison was unable to look beyond the need for emancipation toward winning legal and political rights for the former slaves. *The Liberator* ceased publication in 1865, and Garrison's public activism slowed.

See also ABOLITION AND ANTISLAVERY MOVEMENTS; AMERICAN ANTI-SLAVERY SOCIETY; LUNDY, BENJAMIN; WOMEN IN THE ANTISLAVERY MOVEMENT.

BIBLIOGRAPHY

KRADITOR, AILEEN S. *Means and Ends in American Abolitionism: Garrison and His Critics on Strategy and Tactics, 1834–1850.* 1969.

MERRILL, WALTER M., and LOUIS RUCHAMES, eds. *The Letters of William Lloyd Garrison.* 6 vols. 1971–1981.

STEWART, JAMES BREWER. *Holy Warriors: The Abolitionists and American Slavery.* 1977.

——. *William Lloyd Garrison and the Challenge of Emancipation.* 1992.

THOMAS, JOHN L. *The Liberator: William Lloyd Garrison.* 1963.

Wendy Hamand Venet

Gender Relations

The gender relationship between slave men and women in the American South was constantly overshadowed by the presence of white owners. The slave system throughout the Americas gave slaveholders the power of separation or sale over their slaves. To those powers must be added control over slaves' marital status. While slave women did not escape the rigors of field labor by virtue of their gender, a significant part of their value to their owner lay in their reproductive capacity. A bondswoman in her early twenties could potentially add ten slaves to her owner's workforce. Therefore, in order to realize fully the childbearing potential of female slaves, owners encouraged slave pair-bonding.

All social relations between the sexes are influenced by choice. A loving, stable relationship between men and women arises more frequently if the partners have chosen each other freely. Yet most slaves were not given that right. As slaves' marriage arrangements were informal, usually having no legal status, owners sometimes simply assigned a particular male and female slave to be partners, without a marriage ceremony and ignoring the wishes of either slave. These relationships were often temporary; and if a union proved to be unproductive, the owner could always substitute another bondsman in the attempt to make the woman pregnant. However, by the nineteenth century it was increasingly common for slaves in the United States to seek permission from their owner to marry the person of their choice, even if such unions were not formally recognized by state legal codes. The pervasive influence of evangelical Protestantism in the South ensured that these requests were increasingly granted, and a service of sorts might be conducted by a fellow slave, by the master, or even by an ordained minister. The couple would then begin their life together.

The degree of independence and autonomy that slave couples enjoyed depended on several factors: whether they resided on a small or large plantation, whether they lived in a town, and above all the character of their owner. On large plantations slaves may well have been able to escape the owner's interference in their domestic relations. On smaller plantations such autonomy was less likely, owing to the close proximity of slaves and owners. Urban slaves often had the freedom to live more normal family lives than their plantation counterparts, especially if one or both partners were permitted to hire out their own labor, paying their owner a set weekly fee from their earnings in return for this privilege. Regardless of the location, if the owner of a slave couple was willing to let them live in peace, this greatly facilitated the formation of a normal, stable family life.

Gender relations within slave marriages varied enormously. Some male slaves may well have refused to assist with domestic chores, believing—like most white men—that such work was the exclusive preserve of women. Consequently, some bondswomen would have had to spend what little time they had away from the fields doing washing, cooking, and cleaning. Child care also generally fell to slave women. A woman with a newborn infant was sometimes given as little as three weeks away from the fields to nurse the child, and after that time the child would be entrusted to the care of an elderly female slave during working hours. The peculiar position of slave women thus denied them many of the normal joys of motherhood.

In some slave societies, most notably in the Caribbean and the coastal states in the southern United States, bondsmen and bondswomen were encouraged to work in their spare time growing crops and making handicrafts. On plantations that used a task system, slaves who completed their work early were given free time to spend how they pleased. Bondswomen took it upon themselves to tend garden patches and to weave baskets, while bondsmen often went hunting. This efficient division of labor provided extra food for the family, while also producing items for immediate use or for trade. Surplus goods would be sold or bartered at a store for items unobtainable on the plantation. By working in family units, some slaves were able to improve their material standard of living.

While slaves were sometimes able to build strong families on plantations where they were permitted to live together, many slave couples were at some time forcible separated. Not all enslaved married couples were owned by the same person; sometimes one partner was owned by a neighboring planter, who permitted weekly visits to the spouse. Although the resilience of bondspeople in this situation is remarkable, these couples lived under the constant fear of separation, through relocation or sale. In the nineteenth century there was a continual flow of American slaves from the coastal states of Virginia, Maryland, and North Carolina to new slave states such as Mississippi, Arkansas, and Texas. If an owner believed that relocation was a good idea, then the slaves had little

An engraving depicts a father bidding good-bye to his wife and children after being sold away from them. [Library of Congress/Corbis]

option but to follow. Similarly, an owner might choose, or be forced, to sell one half of a married couple. If an owner was indebted, or had become angered by the behavior of a particular slave, that slave would be sold. On too many occasions, the wishes and pleas of bondsmen and -women to remain together were ignored.

Enslaved couples, therefore, had to contend with the central role of an outside agency in their domestic affairs, and this is a principal difference between slave and free couples. Whereas gender relations between white couples throughout anglophone America reflected male dominance, slave men and women were equally subordinate to the power of slaveholders. Slave men did not have the same power over their wives that white men had. A white man in the American South was legally his wife's guardian, able to conduct business and make contracts on her behalf, confident in the knowledge that divorce was unlikely or even—in states such as South Carolina—illegal. Bondsmen, by contrast, knew that the only power they effectively had over their wives was what the slaveholder tolerated. A bondsman could not direct his spouse's labor, nor was he able to curtail her movements or provide much in the way of home comforts. Aside from what the partners could produce through informal economic activity (and in some areas of the South, that was very little), they were totally reliant on what was provided for them by their owner. This effectively stripped black men of a normal southern gender role, that of provider. No matter how hard they worked, slave men were unable to change their family's social

situation. Another gender role, that of protector, was also denied to slave men. White men went to great lengths to protect their own honor as well as that of their families, and especially their women's. Dueling, brawling, and even murder were common ways of avenging insults to the family. Black men, on the other hand, were almost totally powerless to prevent assaults upon traditional gender prerogatives. When white men raped black women or took them as unwilling concubines (and they did so, in the United States particularly frequently in the pre-Revolutionary period), little regard was given to the fact that the slave women might already be married, and most slave men knew that protest was pointless. Killing, harming, or even striking a white man was a capital crime for slaves throughout the Americas. In contrast, white men who killed slaves while administering punishment were rarely prosecuted. If bondsmen wished to avoid making a bad situation worse, they simply had to ignore such activities and, if necessary, include children fathered by a white owner or overseer within their own household.

Slave men also had no control over the work their wives had to do on the plantation. They had no power to ask that workloads be changed and, with few exceptions, a man was unable to help his wife complete her work. The man could not prevent whippings meted out by overseers for offences such as failure to complete a task in the specified time, or completing it poorly. Thus the normative gender relations in the American South—where a man was the king of his own little castle—did not apply to African-Americans.

Still, it is certainly possible that the horrors of slavery helped to foster gender relations that were significantly more equal than those of white couples. Slave men and women may well have been brought together by the shared ignominy of slavery, their inability to decide basic issues concerning their lives, and the constant threat of separation. The strength and support they drew from each other and the united front they often presented to whites suggest that gender relations were in some ways far more modern in the slave quarters than among whites. In this sense, strong gender relations helped slaves to survive slavery.

See also FAMILY, U.S.; SLAVES, SALE OF.

BIBLIOGRAPHY

BLASSINGAME, JOHN W. *The Slave Community: Plantation Life in the Antebellum South.* 1972.

CLINTON, CATHERINE. *Plantation Mistress: Woman's World in the Old South.* 1984.

JONES, JACQUELINE. *Labor of Love, Labor of Sorrow: Black Women, Work and the Family from Slavery to the Present.* 1985.

MCMILLEN, SALLY G. *Southern Women: Black and White in the Old South.* 1992.

WHITE, DEBORAH. *Ar'n't I a Woman? Female Slaves in the Plantation South.* 1985.

WOOD, BETTY. *Women's Work, Men's Work: The Informal Slave Economies of Lowcountry Georgia, 1750–1830.* 1995.

Timothy J. Lockley

Genocide, Slavery as

In the twentieth century, totalitarian systems have used forced labor (or slave labor, as it is sometimes called) as part of their programs to eliminate racial or religious minorities, political opponents, class enemies, etc. In such cases, slavery is an incidental tool used to make such genocidal campaigns pay a part of their costs and to assist as a means of killing when the conditions of slave labor are sufficiently brutal. The best-known example of mass extermination was the Holocaust perpetuated against Jews by the Nazi government of Germany during World War II. As part of their overall plan to kill all the Jews that Germany came into contact with, the Nazis used hundreds of thousands of Jews as forced laborers in concentration camps or leased them or assigned them to privately owned factories.

When the voyages of Christopher Columbus revealed to Europe the existence of a New World of vast continents and rich islands blocking the hoped-for water routes to Asia, the European mind was unprepared to fit the inhabitants of these lands into prevailing conceptual models of humanity. Were they children of Adam? If they were not Christians, did they have souls? Could they be said to have rights? Did their condition as unbelievers affect their rights? In the earliest dealings of the Spanish with the indigenous peoples of the Caribbean, no fixed ideas prevailed, except the notion that the Europeans as Christians and as the possessors of superior knowledge and technology had a natural right to rule the Indians.

Enslavement of Indians could be justified, in the minds of some, by the fact that the Amerindians were infidels who had not accepted the Catholic faith. This was particularly telling for the Spanish, who had seen their homeland conquered by Muslims and who had fought a 600-year civil war of religion, called the Reconquista. Although some theologians such as Enrico da Susa (d. 1271), a Catholic, and John Wycliffe (1324–1384), a proto-Protestant, held that an infidel could not hold dominion, the Council of Constance (1415–1415) and Pope Innocent IV (d. 1254) repudiated this position. Nevertheless, despite the attempts of many theologians to defend the human rights of the Amerindians and despite the attempts of the royal government in Spain to assist in this protection, colonial administrators, European settlers, and the glory-

and profit-seeking conquistadors ignored or perverted regulations designed to extend basic protections.

A canonist of the Spanish court, Juan Lopez de Palacios Rubios, wrote a treatise on the supremacy of papal authority in temporal as well as spiritual matters and drew up an injunction (*requerimiento*) to be read to villages of Indians, calling on them to submit peacefully. If they did so, they were to be secure in their freedom and property. If they refused, one could make "just" war on them; and once conquered, they, their wives, and their children could then be legitimately reduced to slavery.

The effects of the application of this doctrine were thoroughly and graphically described by Bartolomé de las Casas (1484–1566), a cleric assigned to the New World. Because of the abundance of Indians in the islands of the Caribbean, those enslaved were treated with outrageous cruelty. In addition to mistreatment, which often involved atrocious torture and overwork, despair over enslavement took its toll. Disease too decimated the Indian slaves, for the indigenous populations of the New World had no immunity to many of the diseases of the Old World—such as smallpox—and millions died.

Las Casas wrote *Historia de las Indias* (1527) and *Brevisima relación de la destrucción de las Indias* (A Brief Account of the Destruction of the Indies; 1542), which described the genocidal consequences of contact with Europeans; and in 1542 a code of "new laws" was promulgated for Spanish colonial possessions. The Indian population of the Indies dropped throughout the remainder of the century, and the labor force for the cities of the empire was obtained by the importation of Negro slaves from Africa.

Some modern commentators have compared the enslavement of Africans in the New World to genocide, for two reasons. First, there was the high rate of deaths among Africans brought to the sugar-producing regions of the New World, especially Brazil and the Caribbean. However, other scholars see the term *genocide* as inappropriate because the goal of slavery was to realize profits, and the rising cost of new slaves gave owners an incentive to keep slaves alive, as laborers, rather than exterminate them; and also because slaves in North America did in fact survive and procreate from the 1730s, and later on in the tropical regions of the New World. A second reason why some commentators compare slavery to genocide has to do with the context of "cultural genocide." Some scholars argue that the enslavement of millions of Africans in the New World denied these enslaved peoples their natal cultures. Other scholars, however, note the survival of all sorts of African cultural forms in the Americas; still others reject a priori the reified notion of a "culture" inherent to a "people," a notion implicit in and supportive of these usually rhetorical assertions of cultural genocide.

See also: LAS CASAS, BARTOLOMÉ DE; NAZI SLAVE LABOR; SPAIN.

BIBLIOGRAPHY

GUTIERREZ, GUSTAVO. *Las Casas: In Search of the Poor of Jesus Christ.* Translated by Robert R. Barr. 1993.

LAS CASAS, BARTOLOMÉ DE. *History of the Indies.* Translated and edited by Andrée Collard. 1971.

ZAVALA, SILVA. *The Defense of Human Rights in Latin America—Sixteenth to Eighteenth Centuries.* 1964.

Patrick M. O'Neil

Georgia

Georgia, a southern slave state, was unique in the New World in that it was settled, in 1733, expressly without slaves. It was established as a military outpost, a nursery for independence for poor white immigrants, and a buffer between its neighbor across the Savannah River, South Carolina, and the powerful Indians and Spanish to the south and west. By the 1740s, however, would-be planters in Georgia insisted on imitating South Carolina, and in 1750 the colony's trustees reversed themselves and permitted slavery. In a strip of territory along the Atlantic coast and up the Savannah, a plantation society quickly developed. Many slaves were brought south across the river, and many others were brought from Africa or the West Indies. Before the mid-1760s, South Carolina supplied most of the slaves in Georgia. For the next few years and again after the American Revolution—which interrupted the rapid growth of a plantation society in Georgia—direct importation from Africa supplied large numbers of slaves.

In the Constitutional Convention of 1787, Georgia, like South Carolina, insisted that the slave trade be left unregulated by the proposed new federal government for the next twenty years. When this agreement was reached, Georgia quickly ratified the Constitution. In the new state constitution of 1799, Georgia declared an end to the foreign slave trade into the state. By that time planters could rely on natural increase, supplemented by the interstate slave trade south from Virginia and Maryland. Before midcentury, Georgia had become a net exporter of slaves, as a new generation of slaves and their owners moved west to new lands in the Gulf coast states.

Slavery remained a central feature of Georgia's social, economic, and political scene through the Civil War, with slaves constituting a large minority—usually more than 40 percent—of all residents. The percentage of white families owning slaves kept pace with this percentage of slaves. Among all white families in Georgia in the 1850s, about 40 percent owned at least one slave, and one in five owners held at least twenty slaves. A majority of slaves lived on plantations with at least twenty slaves.

The number of slaves varied from one region of the state to another. Most slaves in the coastal counties continued to cultivate rice and sea island cotton, but a vast interior region, a wide band across the middle of the state, was opened up to the cultivation of short-staple cotton. There, a majority of all white families owned slaves, and slaves often outnumbered whites. By contrast, much of south Georgia, together with mountainous north Georgia, had relatively few slaves or slaveowners. Some slaves made their way to freedom in Florida, at least before the Spanish Cession in 1819 and the Second Seminole War in the 1830s, after which Florida increasingly resembled Georgia.

Until the 1860s, few black residents of Georgia—less than 1 percent—were free, and black freedom was more sharply distinguished from white freedom than from black slavery. For example, a state law made it a felony to teach any black, slave or free, to read or write. Only 3,500 free blacks lived in Georgia in 1860, out of more than a million residents in all, and most of them lived in two small cities: Savannah and Augusta. Elsewhere in the state, whatever the proportions of black and white, there was almost a perfect identity between "black" and "slave."

Politicians in Georgia embraced what the historian William Cooper Jr. has termed the "politics of slavery," particularly from the 1830s into the 1860s, and for a time between the 1810s and 1830s they also embraced the politics of Indian removal. These two racial

The slave market in Louisville, Georgia, was built in 1758. [Corbis-Bettmann]

Table 1. Population of Georgia, 1790–1860.

Year	White	Slave	Free Nonwhite	Total
1790	52,886	29,264	398	82,548
1800	101,678	59,404	1,019	162,101
1810	145,414	105,218	1,801	252,433
1820	189,566	149,656	1,767	340,989
1830	296,806	217,531	2,486	516,823
1840	407,695	280,944	2,753	691,392
1850	521,572	381,682	2,931	906,185
1860	591,550	462,198	3,538	1,057,286

policies converged in the seizure of vast territory into which the plantation system could be expanded. Politicians sought federal support for their racial agenda and challenged the legitimacy of federal actions that threatened their interests at home. That was true both in Governor George M. Troup's time, the 1820s, and in Alexander H. Stephens's time, 1861, when he became vice president of the Confederate States of America and declared that slavery was the "cornerstone" of the Confederacy.

Early in the Civil War, Georgia moved to first place among all states in slave population. According to the census of 1860, Virginia—always the state with the most slaves, despite its slow growth in the antebellum years—still retained its lead, but Georgia was on course to overtake Virginia even before West Virginia split off and went its separate way.

The best that could be said about slavery for most slaves in nineteenth-century Georgia was that the climate was less deadly than that of the Caribbean, short-staple cotton was a less demanding crop than sugar or rice, and a sex ratio at parity meant that slaves could more readily create families and communities. Much as in the black societies that had emerged in the Chesapeake a generation or two earlier, people of African ancestry living in antebellum Georgia were largely Protestant Christians and American natives. Among them were people who, in the aftermath of the Civil War and emancipation, became teachers, preachers, and lawmakers.

See also CONFEDERATE STATES OF AMERICA; DEMOGRAPHY OF SLAVES IN THE UNITED STATES.

BIBLIOGRAPHY

FLANDERS, RALPH B. *Plantation Slavery in Georgia.* 1933.

LANE, MILLS, ed. *"Neither More nor Less Than Men": Slavery in Georgia, a Documentary History.* 1993.

MOHR, CLARENCE L. *On the Threshold of Freedom: Masters and Slaves in Civil War Georgia.* 1986.

REIDY, JOSEPH P. *From Slavery to Agrarian Capitalism in the Cotton Plantation South: Central Georgia, 1800–1880.* 1992.

SMITH, JULIA FLOYD. *Slavery and Rice Culture in Low Country Georgia, 1750–1860.* 1985.

WALLENSTEIN, PETER. *From Slave South to New South: Public Policy in Nineteenth-Century Georgia.* 1987.

WOOD, BETTY. *Slavery in Colonial Georgia, 1730–1775.* 1984.

Peter Wallenstein

Germany, Medieval

See Law; Medieval Europe, Slavery and Serfdom in.

Gladiators

Gladiators were both disreputable and glamorous, perhaps more akin to rock stars than football players. Cicero, who disliked gladiatorial games, saw honor in the courage of gladiators—an example to citizens, even from such debased persons. The satirists, such as Juvenal, deplored the gladiators' attraction to women of the respectable classes. They were trained, fit young men; the term properly describes those skilled in fighting, not those simply flung into the arena. After Spartacus's rebellion (in the mid-70s B.C.) legal controls were imposed, for the sake of public safety, on the keeping of gladiators and their arms near Rome. In the Empire there were four gladiatorial schools, all near the Colosseum. There were different names for different specialities, such as the trident-and-net man (*retiarius*) and the heavily armed Samnite (*secutor*). (Of course, it was slaves too who cleared up after gladiators, removing the corpses from the sand, etc.)

Early gladiatorial combat was a religious ritual to appease the dead, a ritual the Romans had probably borrowed from the Campanians. In the early days of public gladiatorial shows (*munera*), in the late republic, gladiators would predominantly have been prisoners of war—ex-soldiers, one could say—with an admixture of convicted criminals. Gladiators were largely slaves, at first slaves by capture or by condemnation. Later, when the supply of prisoners of war had diminished, private persons trained suitable slaves and rented them out to the managers of the games. However, there seem always to have been free gladiators, occasionally men (or even women) from the upper classes, seeking celebrity or fleeing from ruin, as well as former soldiers or freed gladiators and social outcasts of various kinds—all prepared to gamble with their lives.

Nevertheless, most gladiators were slaves, and most of them would have been there as a result of condemnation in a criminal court. Indeed the cost of specially trained gladiators, whether slave or free, made

A victorious gladiator, as imagined by the French painter Jean-Léon Gérôme. [Corbis-Bettmann]

the use of convicts normal, as we see from the *2*(resolution of the senate) from Larinum under Marcus Aurelius. We find governors being ordered to reserve suitable convicts for their purpose. However, gladiators were required to put on a good show for the crowd, so some preparation must have been accepted as necessary. Tertullian, somewhat later, tells of sacrifices made of captives and of slaves of poor quality; others, with some training, became suitable material for gladiatorial combats.

Gladiatorial games had lost most of their religious element and become predominantly entertainment fairly early in the Empire. Under Constantine there was an attempt to abolish them, but it was not effective; they did not disappear until the fifth century. Although these games were held regularly only on some ten, or fewer, days in December, probably they were dependent on the availability of slaves, and by then slavery was much reduced.

See also ANCIENT ROME; SPARTACUS.

BIBLIOGRAPHY

GRANT, M. *Gladiators.* 1967.
ROBINSON, O. F. *Ancient Rome.* Chap. 11. 1994.

VILLE, G. *La gladiature.* 1981.
WIEDEMANN, T. *Emperors and Gladiators.* 1992.

O. F. Robinson

Godwyn, Morgan   [ca. 1640–?]

Early English commentator on slavery.

Born at Bicknor in Gloucestershire, England, Morgan Godwyn was the son of an Anglican minister and grandson of a bishop. After graduating from Christ Church College at Oxford University in 1664, he took Anglican orders and served as a minister in Virginia during the governorship of the controversial Sir William Berkeley. Godwyn also visited Barbados, where the Quaker George Fox gave him a pamphlet attacking the Anglican church for failing to minister to slaves. On returning to England, Godwyn wrote two short books and preached sermons on slavery in the American colonies. Godwyn defended the compatibility of slavery and Christianity but also advocated a large-scale Anglican missionary effort to the slaves. He contended that the baptism of a slave did not necessitate emancipation and that conversion made slaves more efficient and loyal workers. A social as well as religious conservative, Godwyn was offended by both the materialism and the infidelity he saw as being unleashed by slavery and the African slave trade. He attacked the West Indian planters for the heretical belief that everything profitable was legal. He also blamed the planters for encouraging the belief in a separate creation for Africans in order to justify their exploitation. Anglican ministers in the colonies should remain financially independent of the planters, he argued, so that they could protect slaves from overwork or forced breeding. Ironically, since he was a defender of slaveholding, many of Godwyn's ideas would be adopted by a later generation of religious abolitionists.

See also ANGLICANISM; CHRISTIANITY.

BIBLIOGRAPHY

DAVIS, DAVID BRION. *The Problem of Slavery in Western Culture.* 1966.
KLINGBERG, FRANK J. *The Antislavery Movement in England: A Study in English Humanitarianism.* 1926.
RICE, C. DUNCAN. *The Rise and Fall of Black Slavery.* 1975.

John R. McKivigan

Gone with the Wind

See Film and Television, Slavery in; Literature of Slavery.

Gradual Emancipation Statutes

A gradual emancipation statute freed no slaves immediately but instead declared that the children of all slaves born after its passage would be free, subject to an indenture. In 1780 Pennsylvania became the first state to adopt such a law, which was copied by Connecticut (1784), Rhode Island (1784), New York (1799), New Jersey (1804), and Upper Canada (1793). Delaware briefly considered such a law in the 1790s. In 1796 the Virginia jurist St. George Tucker published *A Dissertation on Slavery: With a Proposal for the Gradual Abolition of It, in the State of Virginia.* As proposed, this "gradual" emancipation scheme would have taken nearly a century to fully end bondage there. In 1803 Tucker reprinted this pamphlet in the five-volume edition of William Blackstone's *Commentaries on the Laws of England.* In 1831–1832 Virginia debated gradual abolition in the wake of Nat Turner's rebellion, but this debate led to no legislation.

The Pennsylvania act of 1780, the model for all other gradual emancipation laws, provided that after its enactment all children of slaves born in the state would be free at birth but would be required to serve the mother's master as indentured servants until age twenty-eight. At the end of the indenture they would be unconditionally free. Under this law slavery would gradually die out in the state.

The 1780 law and a substantial amendment passed in 1788 gave some protection to indentured blacks and required their masters to give them a minimal education. The law prohibited the importation of new slaves, and under the 1788 amendment all slaves of immigrants were immediately free upon entering the state. However, visitors were allowed to keep slaves in the state for up to six months at a time, and members of Congress and foreign ambassadors could retain their slaves in Pennsylvania as long as they held office. The law provided for the return of runaway slaves. The initial draft of the law prohibited interracial marriage, but the legislature removed this provision. The law allowed children of slaves to testify in court against their masters and any other whites. Under this act all blacks, including slaves, were to be subject to the same criminal punishments as all "other inhabitants." After 1788 anyone removing an indentured black with the intention of enslaving him or her could be severely punished. The law required that masters register all slaves, and any black not registered was presumptively free. Significantly, the preamble to the 1780 law asserted the fundamental equality of all people and specifically condemned the "unnatural separation of husband and wife."

The other states adopting gradual abolition acts followed the form used by Pennsylvania, although not always the details. New York, for example, allowed masters to bring their slaves into the state for up to nine months, while Connecticut and Rhode Island had no specific limitations on how long visitors could keep slaves. The other states all had shorter indenture periods, ranging from age eighteen to age twenty-five.

The gradual abolition acts led to a rapid decline of slaveholding in most of the North. In 1827 New York accelerated the process by freeing all its remaining slaves. New Jersey, on the other hand, had slaves into the 1840s, when all remaining bondsmen and bondswomen had their status converted to indentured servants.

The gradual abolition acts allowed some states to end slavery during the Revolutionary era while not actually depriving masters of existing property rights. Thus, these laws can be seen as an attempt to balance two ideological underpinnings of the Revolution: the commitment to liberty and the commitment to property.

See also EMANCIPATION; LAW.

BIBLIOGRAPHY

FINKELMAN, PAUL. *An Imperfect Union: Slavery, Federalism, and Comity.* 1981.

ZILVERSMIT, ARTHUR. *The First Emancipation: The Abolition of Slavery in the North.* 1967.

Paul Finkelman

Gray, Simon [ca. 1810–1870]

Mississippi quasi-slave and businessman.

Simon Gray was a riverman who achieved many elements of freedom, including the operation of his own business, yet remained a slave until freed by Union armies in 1863. Beginning in 1835, Gray worked for Andrew Brown and Company, a Natchez lumber firm. Initially hired as a laborer, he became a raft crew chief by 1838. As such he placed orders and collected debts for his company. From 1845 to 1862, as chief boatman for Brown and Company, Gray supervised white workers, paid their wages, and kept business records.

In 1853 Gray became all but free. He was not formally manumitted; state law required a legislative act to do so. But his master ceased to collect hiring fees, suggesting that Gray purchased himself in a private transaction. He obtained the money from his boatman's salary and from profitable enterprises as an independent flatboat operator, hauling sand to New Orleans. In this capacity Gray owned boats and hired slaves.

Gray also purchased one of his sons, who, along with the rest of his family, were legally owned by Brown and Company. In 1863 with the fall of Vicksburg, Gray and his family gained their freedom. Gray's life demonstrated that there were situations in which blacks could stretch the boundaries of race, thereby redefining what were "acceptable activities" for slaves. Skilled work, work in urban settings, and work among watermen, with its less racially charged work ethos, became such newly acceptable activities. Still, Gray's desire to keep his family together, combined with high slave prices in the 1850s, made full freedom within his slave society unattainable.

See also SELF-PURCHASE.

BIBLIOGRAPHY

MOORE, JOHN HEBRON. "Simon Gray, Riverman: A Slave Who Was Almost Free." *Mississippi Valley Historical Review* 49 (1962).

T. Stephen Whitman

Great Britain, African Slavery in

Though Africans had arrived in Britain from early times (we know of Africans in Britain's Roman legions), their numbers were insignificant. Africans found their way to Britain through early maritime contacts with West Africa and via trading links with other Europeans maritime peoples. An Elizabethan proclamation of 1601 ordered the expulsion of black settlers. But the subsequent development of trade to, and settlement of, the Caribbean ensured that their numbers would grow. Their arrival posed legal problems (which mounted as their numbers increased), for slavery had long ago died out in England, though not in Scotland. What was the legality of slavery in a country which, after the political upheavals of the seventeenth-century revolution, prided itself on its political liberties? The issue was not fully resolved until the abolition of the slave trade in 1807.

Some Africans were imported directly to England from Africa by the Royal African Company and other traders, but most came via the Americas. Some were brought to England for sale, but most, as far as we can tell, traveled to England with their owners: visiting or retiring planters, military and colonial officials. Crews of slave ships occasionally imported slaves for personal use or for sale. Though the numbers were always small, the growth of the Atlantic trade in the late seventeenth and eighteenth centuries increased the movement of Africans and of blacks born in the Americas. The largest single settlement came in the wake of the American Revolution and the departure of the British military, colonial officials, and American loyalists. Even then, the number remains imprecise. It was unlikely to have been more than ten thousand in the 1780s. But from first to last, the size of the black community became a major political controversy in the 1770s and 1780s. Those opposing black settlement (led by exiled Caribbean planters) sought to inflate the numbers to illustrate the dangers that, they claimed, lay in the continuing process of black settlement.

Most blacks in Britain were male, perhaps reflecting the overall sexual imbalance in the Atlantic slave trade itself. Naturally enough, those men sought female company among women of their own humble social class. That too created friction, or at least gave grounds for complaint from critics who were unhappy to contemplate the development of a black community in England. Yet it is not clear even if the term *community* is appropriate for what emerged. The evidence suggests that only in London were blacks able to cohere in a community with any meaningful structure. Most were isolated one from another, living with their owners or employers, like other domestics, and rarely able to meet other blacks. But in London—home to the largest number—there were periodic gatherings, social occasions and, eventually, political activity.

Domestic service provided the most obvious form of employment for blacks in Britain. There were also substantial numbers who, like Olaudah Equiano, made a living at sea on Royal Navy and commercial vessels. Some emerged from domestic work to secure a different, improved status. Ignatius Sancho, for example, became a shopkeeper in Westminster; his letters (1782) are now perhaps the best remembered and earliest examples of black writing in England. Similarly, Olaudah Equaino's autobiography (1789) established his unique place both in contemporary black society and in black history. These two men were unusual; both were also literate and devout—qualities which doubtless helped them to rise, impressing whites who met them. But in addition both men also illustrate a generally neglected (though important) aspect of local black life: each had contact with other blacks.

Equiano in particular had black friends and associates across London, in North America, and in the West Indies, visiting them on his voyages and receiving messages from them. Blacks in Britain were part of a broader black community that reached from the slave barracoons of the African coast, to the slave colonies of the Americas, and to Europe.

Many blacks were imported into Britain as slaves of white owners and employers and remained enslaved. But the freedoms in England and the encouragement of free blacks led many to run away. Advertisements for blacks in English newspapers are as much directed at securing runaways as at selling slaves. Try as they might, slaveowners could not maintain the bondage of their black domestics in a society marked not by slavery but by freedom. There was, inevitably, a string of legal cases and judgments on the legality of slav-

Marriage à la Mode *by William Hogarth was created as a satire of the English society of the 1740s; Plate IV of the engravings includes a black manservant (center) and a young black page (lower left).* [Historical Picture Archive/Corbis]

ery. This series culminated in the famous—though often misunderstood—Somerset case of 1772. The lord chief justice, Lord Mansfield, determined that blacks could not be forcibly removed from England against their wishes and shipped back to the slave colonies. He effectively determined that slavery was illegal in England. Both law and social custom were changing.

For a start, there was a small band of English reformers, led in the 1760s and 1770s by Granville Sharp, who were eager to secure a legal decision against slavery in England and active in securing the rights of blacks wherever they were violated. Blacks joined the campaign, and together they formed an important pressure group in defence of blacks' interests. Their case was strengthened after 1783 by the arrival of American blacks, and by a growing concern in London about the emergence of what was called the *black poor*. The subsequent efforts to relieve blacks' poverty, and a scheme (1787) to resolve it by encouraging migration to Sierra Leone, were a turning point. These efforts attracted the Quakers (already committed to antislavery), generated political self-help among the black community, and laid the foundations for the first effective attack on the slave trade itself. However, the migration scheme ended in disaster for the small number of blacks who volunteered to settle in Sierra Leone.

By the last years of the eighteenth century, the social climate had changed. Slavery could no longer be easily sustained in Britain. Slaves ran away or were targeted by free blacks and their white friends. Moreover, the rapid rise of abolitionism had put pressure on the Atlantic slave trade (which ultimately sustained the flow on blacks to Britain). Even as early as 1789, it was clear that the slave trade was doomed. Moreover, slaves were too valuable in the West Indies to be carried to Britain to be displayed by the wealthy as exotic domestic possessions. The decline in black migration was compounded by the seismic impact of the French Revolution and the subsequent wars.

Slavery in British colonies was abolished partially in 1833, completely in 1838. But it had little effect on black migration to Britain. That did not revive until later in the century. Without fresh arrivals from Africa or the Americas, the black population in Britain inevitably declined in the early nineteenth century, melting into the wider (and rapidly expanding) British population. Not until the late nineteenth century was black settlement effectively renewed—again via new maritime routes—with the development of steam shipping lines to West Africa and the West Indies. Yet, for the best part of two centuries black slavery had existed in Britain, however small the numbers involved. It was just one more variant of that massive system which sustained the development of the Atlantic world in the seventeenth and eighteenth centuries.

See also EQUIANO, OLAUDAH; SHARP, GRANVILLE; SLAVE TRADE; SOMERSET V. STEWART.

BIBLIOGRAPHY

BRAIDWOOD, STEPHEN J. *Black Poor and White Philanthropists.* 1984.
MYERS, NORMAL *Reconstructing the Past: Blacks in Britain, 1780–1830.* 1996.
WALVIN, JAMES. *An African's Life: Olaudah Equiano, 1745–1797.* 1998.

James Walvin

Greece, Ancient

See Ancient Greece; Draco, Code of; Law; Miners; Philosophy.

Grégoire, Henri, Bishop   [1750–1831]

Bishop of Blois, France, and prominent abolitionist.

Early in his career as a theologian and polemicist, Henri Grégoire espoused equality for Jews. With the advent of the French Revolution and stirrings of rebellion in Saint-Domingue, a French West India colony, Grégoire turned his attention to the rights of blacks. His initial involvement with the rights of blacks came in 1787, when he became a member of the Société des Amis des Noirs (Society of Friends of Blacks), the French version of the better-known English Slave Trade Committee. As an elected representative from the District of Nancy to the First Estate, Grégoire argued for representation for mulattos. In 1791 he penned a pamphlet, *Lettre aux citoyens de coleur* (Letter to Citizens of Color), which many in France blamed for fomenting the rebellion in Saint-Domingue. Angry West Indian planters burned Grégoire in effigy. Even he, however, was surprised when civil commissioners, sent by the French revolutionary government to Saint-Domingue to investigate, suddenly emancipated all slaves in the island. Over the next few years, Grégoire corresponded regularly with Toussaint-Louverture and advised him to restore the Catholic Church to a key role in Haitian society. In 1802 Grégoire opposed Napoleon Bonaparte's attempt to reenslave Haitian blacks.

In 1808 Grégoire composed *De la Litterature des negres* (Of the Literature of Negroes), a book intended to rebuff philosophers and statesmen such as Thomas

Henri Grégoire, Bishop of Blois. [Corbis-Bettmann]

Jefferson, who argued for the intellectual inferiority of blacks. Translated into English as *An Enquiry Concerning the Intellectual and Moral Faculties and Literature of Negroes, with an Account of the Life and Works of Fifteen Negroes and Mulattos, Distinguished in Science, Literature, and the Arts*, the book infuriated Jefferson but delighted African-Americans, who found solace in its sympathetic portraits. The book influenced such black American writers as James W. C. Pennington, William Wells Brown, and Russel Parrott and white abolitionists, such as Lydia Maria Child. In 1820 Grégoire published a manual for the conversion of blacks to Catholicism, in which he included much antislavery commentary. He spent the remainder of his life assisting the Haitians in a variety of causes while emphasizing the role of the Catholic Church.

See also CARIBBEAN REGION; CHILD, LYDIA MARIA; SOCIÉTÉ DES AMIS DES NOIRS.

BIBLIOGRAPHY

GRÉGOIRE, HENRI. *An Enquiry concerning the Intellectual and Moral Faculties, and Literature of Negroes.* Edited by Graham Russell Hodges. 1997.

NESCHELES, RUTH F. *The Abbé Grégoire, 1787–1831: Odyssey of an Egalitarian.* 1971.

Graham Hodges

Grimké, Angelina and Sarah

Politically prominent abolitionists.

The Grimké sisters, Angelina Emily (1805–1879) and Sarah Moore (1792–1873), born in Charleston, South Carolina, were members of a wealthy, politically connected family. As pampered daughters of the plantation elite, they enjoyed the benefits of private tutors and personal servants. After Sarah Grimké visited Philadelphia in 1819 she felt an immediate attraction to the Quaker faith, with its emphasis on simplicity and religious commitment. Ultimately, she rejected the Episcopal faith of her youth and embraced a new life in Philadelphia as a member of the Society of Friends. The Quakers' rejection of slavery as immoral also appealed to her. Angelina later underwent a similar conversion and joined Sarah in 1829.

Realizing the potential these daughters of the plantation South might hold as abolitionists, William Lloyd Garrison printed a letter Angelina had written praising his newspaper, *The Liberator.* The positive response to this publication encouraged Angelina to write an *Appeal to the Christian Women of the Southern States* (1836), in which she grounded her argument for emancipation in the natural rights philosophy of the Declaration of Independence. An outpouring of public interest followed, though southern postmasters destroyed many copies and Angelina was no longer welcome in the city of her birth. The same year, Sarah wrote an *Epistle to the Clergy of the Southern States* in which she denied a biblical justification for slavery in the American South.

The Grimkés became agents of the American Anti-Slavery Society, with the charge of speaking to groups of women. Their family's prominence and the novelty of women as public speakers made the sisters subjects of a great deal of curiosity, and soon men began to attend their lectures. As part of a New England lecture tour in 1837, Angelina addressed the Massachusetts legislature, the first woman ever to address a state legislature. Arguing that women were citizens of the American republic, she alienated many by claiming a role for women that went beyond that of moral and religious teacher. Congregational ministers formalized their opposition in a pastoral letter. Angelina, in letters to the *Liberator,* and Sarah, in *Letters on the Equality of the Sexes and the Condition of Woman* (1838), staunchly defended women's right to participate in the antislavery movement and to have a voice in American legal and political life.

Public furor over the sisters subsided after Angelina married abolitionist Theodore Dwight Weld in 1838. Motherhood and recurrent illnesses limited her activism. Sarah lived with the Welds for the rest of her life. The sisters signed and disseminated antislavery

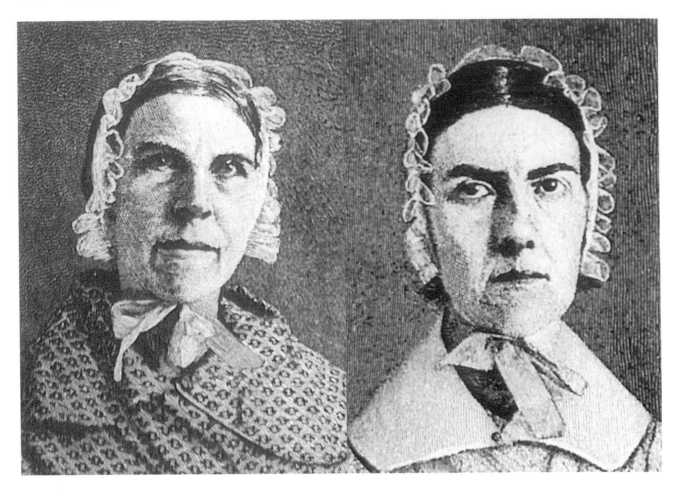

Sarah Grimké (left) and Angelina Grimké Weld. [Library of Congress]

petitions, wrote occasional articles, taught school, and dabbled in a variety of reform movements.

See also ABOLITION AND ANTISLAVERY MOVEMENTS; GARRISON, WILLIAM LLOYD; QUAKERS; WOMEN IN THE ANTISLAVERY MOVEMENT.

BIBLIOGRAPHY

CEPLAIR, LARRY, ed. *The Public Years of Sarah and Angelina Grimké: Selected Writings, 1835–1839.* 1989.
LERNER, GERDA. *The Grimké Sisters from South Carolina.* 1967.

Wendy Hamand Venet

Gulag

"Gulag" is an acronym from the Russian *glavnoe upravlenie lagerei,* meaning "main administration of camps." It became widely known as a term through the three-volume account of its history and workings. *The Gulag Archipelago,* written by former prisoner Aleksandr Solzhenitsyn and published in 1973.

The gulag network of labor camps existed in the Soviet Union from the late 1920s onwards. Shortly after the death of Soviet leader Josef Stalin in 1953, an amnesty saw the gulag population decrease rapidly. However, gulag labor camps containing political prisoners remained in existence up until the end of the Soviet era, although not on the scale of the Stalin era.

Soviet archives show that between 1936 and 1953 the annual figure for forced laborers in the gulag camps was always between one million and two and a half million. In total, around eighteen to twenty million people were in the gulag at some point during these years, although there has been considerable academic debate surrounding the precise number of prisoners and the Soviet figures are considered by many to be incomplete.

Prisoners were engaged in forced labor for the state. This differed from slavery in that imprisonment was a judicial sentence, of a specific period, imposed for a criminal offence, albeit the supposed offence may have been political in nature. Furthermore, forced labor was theoretically intended to be corrective, for the benefit of the criminal. The gulag did indeed see a large turnover of prisoners. However, it is also the case that many prisoners died in the gulag due to the extremity of the conditions of work. Many were arbitrarily resentenced at the end of their stated terms of imprisonment, and Soviet judicial processes themselves were similarly arbitrary. Furthermore, it is arguably the case that economic factors as much as political and legal factors lay behind arrest rates. Forced labor outputs were written into the national economic plan assigned to the secret police, and sufficient numbers of "criminals" had to be found to meet plan targets.

See also RUSSIA; RUSSIA, SERFDOM IN.

BIBLIOGRAPHY

BACON, EDWIN. *The Gulag at War: Stalin's Forced Labour System in the Light of the Archives.* 1994.
CONQUEST, ROBERT. *The Great Terror: A Reassessment.* 1990.

Edwin T. Bacon

Gypsies

See Roma.

Haiti

See Abolition and Antislavery Movements; Caribbean Region; Plantations; Slave Religion.

Haley, Alex

See Film and Television, Slavery in; Literature of Slavery.

Hammond, James Henry   [1807–1864]

Prominent South Carolina slaveholder, politician, and intellectual.

James Henry Hammond aspired to be recognized by his peers as the preeminent statesman and leader of the antebellum South. The eldest child of Elisha Hammond, a poor schoolmaster originally from Massachusetts, and his wife, Catherine Fox Spann Hammond, of Edgefield, South Carolina, he graduated from South Carolina College in 1825, fourth in a class of thirty-one. Admitted to the South Carolina bar in 1828 at the age of twenty-one, Hammond in 1829 met Catherine Fitzsimons, the sister-in-law of Wade Hampton II, at the Columbia, South Carolina, home of Catherine's sister, Ann Fitzsimons Hampton. Hammond married the Charleston heiress in June 1831 and took control of Catherine's dowry, which consisted of 147 slaves and 10,800 acres at Beech Island, South Carolina, near the Savannah River.

Although Hammond at first knew little about large-scale planting, he threw himself energetically into learning to become an agriculturist and eventually achieved great success at it. Many slaves died in the early years of his marriage, and their sufferings are documented in the pages of Hammond's diary.

Despite his success as a planter, he yearned for public office. He won a seat in Congress for the fall term of 1835. Hammond said on the floor of the U.S. House of Representatives on 1 February 1836 that slavery was a positive good, "the greatest of all the great blessings which a kind Providence has bestowed upon our favored region," and the cornerstone of the Republic. In the spring of 1836, he resigned from the House of Representatives owing to ill health. In 1842 he was chosen governor of the state of South Carolina; he served for two years. Elected a U.S. senator in 1857, Hammond coined the phrase "Cotton is King." In his maiden speech before the Senate on 4 March 1858, he touched upon the importance of the South's production of cotton in world commerce, concluding, "No, you dare not make war on cotton. No power on earth dares to make war on it. Cotton is King." In making his second point, he said in the defense of slavery that

in all social systems there must be a class to do the menial duties, to perform the drudgery of life. That is, a class requiring but a low order of intellect and but little skill. Its requisites are vigor, docility, fidelity. Such a class you must have, or you would not have the other class which leads progress, civilization, and refinement. It constitutes the very mudsill of society and of political government; and you might as well attempt to build a house in the air, as

James Henry Hammond. [*Dictionary of American Portraits*]

to build either the one or the other, except on this mud-sill. Fortunately for the South, she found a race adapted to that purpose to her hand. . . . We use them for our purpose, and call them slaves.

Hammond achieved national prominence with this speech.

By the time of the Civil War, he held over fourteen thousand acres and owned over three hundred slaves. Dedicated to the defense of slavery, Hammond resigned from the U.S. Senate in November 1860 upon learning of Lincoln's presidential victory. When the war came in April 1861, he gave the Confederacy his full financial support; by 1864 one-half of his estate consisted of Confederate bonds. Hammond died on 13 November 1864 at his plantation home, Redcliffe, survived by his wife and five children.

See also PERSPECTIVES ON SLAVERY; SOUTH CAROLINA.

BIBLIOGRAPHY

BLESER, CAROL. *The Hammonds of Redcliffe.* 1981.
———. *Secret and Sacred: The Diaries of James Henry Hammond, a Southern Slaveholder.* 1988.
FAUST, DREW GILPIN. *James Henry Hammond and the Old South: A Design for Mastery.* 1982.
———. *A Sacred Circle: The Dilemma of the Intellectual of the Old South, 1840–1860.* 1977.
MERRITT, ELIZABETH. *James Henry Hammond, 1807–1864.* 1923.

Carol Bleser

Hammurabi's Code

A seven-foot high, black stone slab discovered in Susa in Iran in 1902 is the most extensive existing text of what has been dubbed Hammurabi's Code. It contains, by modern count, 282 legal instances and a prologue and epilogue, and is the most important source for understanding the function of law in Mesopotamian society, although it may have recorded unusual and interesting cases and not normal procedures.

Though some scholars would see Hammurabi's effort to codify legal practice in 1752 B.C.E. as an attempt to unify his realm legally, he appears to have viewed the code as a series of legal examples through which one might come to understand the nature of justice. It is an open question what the code might have had to do with practice since it was rarely referred to in texts reflecting the actual exercise of law, but its dictates paralleled legal actions in some areas.

In the code, known also from excerpts that have survived through the ages, slaves represented the lowest of the three categories of society. Slaves ranked below the "men," that is, the free, and the "commoners," who were lower-status free persons. Of the lists of legal penalties, the harshest punishments were always applied to slaves, and their losses were compensated for most lightly.

Hammurabi assumed that slaves would wear a slave haircut, and habitual runaways might be marked with other, less effaceable signs. Persons who harbored runaways were to be severely punished, but the punishment of runaways themselves was not discussed in the code. A captured runaway was probably returned to the owner for private punishment.

See also ANCIENT MIDDLE EAST; DRACO, CODE OF; LAW.

BIBLIOGRAPHY

DRIVER, GODFREY R., and JOHN C. MILES. *The Babylonian Laws.* 2 vols. 1960.
ROTH, MARTHA T. *Law Collections from Mesopotamia and Asia Minor.* 1995.

Daniel C. Snell

Harem

In Middle and Far Eastern cultures the harem is a protected, inviolate section within a large household or imperial residence. The term refers to both the physical space and the women who reside there. It also signifies a religious sanctuary, like the holy cities of Mecca and Medina. The term *harem* derives from several variants of the Arabic root *h-r-m*. *Harim* describes the characteristic of being sacred to adherents, forbidden to outsiders; *haram* indicates sanctuary. In non-Arabic languages other terms also describe the harem: *zenana* (Hindi and Urdu) is the term for the private women's quarters of a residence; *seraglio* (Italian) is the word, borrowed from Persia, often used in relation to women's quarters, although it actually refers to the entire palace community.

In large households the harem was the center of domestic operations and was therefore the site of a large concentration of slaves whose service was essential to the vitality of the home. In the harem, slaves were servants and concubines; in imperial settings it also contained an elite corp of guardian slaves, the eunuchs. This significant cadre of slaves—as well as the legal wives and children who resided within the harem—was overseen by the senior woman in the household, either the senior wife or, in the case of a royal household, often the mother of the sultan.

The best-known example of the harem may be that of the Ottoman Empire's Topkapi Palace in what is now Istanbul, where the harem evolved late in the fifteenth century and lasted until 1909. The Topkapi harem consisted of a kingdom within a kingdom, with its own rules, regulations, productivity, and politics. It was the home, the focus of socialization and education of the sultan's large extended family. The harem housed women and all children until puberty, at which time the boys moved elsewhere for training and the girls gradually moved to their marriage homes. The harem was also close to the nexus of government activity, which was conducted within the royal family compound, not in public venues.

The Topkapi harem was ruled by the sultan's mother, the *sultana*, or *valide* sultan. The *valide*, usually a concubine herself, wielded tremendous power, influencing the affairs of state through her son and mediating conflict between wives and concubines, each of whom sought to elevate her own position to the level of *valide* by promoting her own son's accession to the throne. As the most private arena of imperial affairs, the harem was the forum for the empire's most significant political decisions. It was not separate

The throne room in the harem section of the Topkapi Palace. [Richard T. Nowitz/Corbis]

from decision-making forums, but was the locus of authority, the heart of the palace. The *valide*'s position as head of the harem, along with the roles of slave women there, indicates that the harem housed the entire range of statuses within the social spectrum, from that of domestic servant to *valide* as de facto ruler of the empire.

In addition to being a political center of the palace, the harem also regulated its lifeblood: the *valide* oversaw the daily operations of the royal kitchens, hospitals, schools, mosques, monasteries, gardens, and burial grounds. In the harem slave-status servant women produced, processed, and served food; they also cleaned the area, washed and prepared clothing, ran errands, and transmitted messages between the harem and the world outside. In addition to overseeing all these operations, the *valide* also supervised the education and enculturation of the harem's inhabitants, including the training of concubines in the arts, literacy, and politics.

Contemporary harems housing slave-status women as servants and concubines continue to operate in sub-Saharan and North Africa and around the Mediterranean. In Muslim northern Nigeria, emirate harems resemble those of legendary Topkapi in function, albeit not in size. In Kano, Nigeria, the queen mother, often a concubine, has a royal title, but her residence is outside the palace. Royal wives and concubines reside in the harem, where the servant women still identify themselves as being of slave status, despite slavery having been outlawed in 1901.

See also CONCUBINAGE; EUNUCHS; ISLAM.

BIBLIOGRAPHY

ALDERSON, A. D. *Structure of the Ottoman Dynasty.* 1956.
ALLOULA, MALEK. *The Colonial Harem.* 1986.
BEHR, EDWARD. *The Last Emperor.* 1987.
CARDASHIAN, VAHAN. *Actual Life in the Turkish Harem.* 1914.
CROUTIER, ALEV LYTLE. *Harem: The World behind the Veil.* 1989.
DJAVIDAN, HANUM. *Harem Life.* 1931.
LEWIS, BERNARD. *The Political Language of Islam.* 1988.
MILLER, BARNETTE. *Beyond the Sublime Porte: The Grand Seraglio of Stambul.* 1931.
PENZER, N. M. *The Harem.* 1937.
PIERCE, LESLIE PENN. *The Imperial Harem: Women and Sovereignty in the Ottoman Empire.* 1993.
TARNAR, YESIM. *The Book and the Veil: Escape from an Istanbul Harem.* 1994.

Beverly B. Mack

Harper, Robert Goodloe   [1765–1825]

Lawyer and southern U.S. congressman.

Deeply affected by the egalitarian promise of the American Revolution, and inspired by the moral phi-

Robert Goodloe Harper. [*Dictionary of American Portraits*]

losophy of his Princeton mentor, John Witherspoon, Robert Goodloe Harper rose to prominence among backcountry South Carolinians in the early 1790s as an outspoken advocate of innate racial equality and the gradual end to slavery's western expansion. Confronted with the mounting atrocities in France and Saint Domingue, he grew increasingly apprehensive of an American slave rebellion, renounced his youthful radicalism, and worked relentlessly as a Federalist Congressman from 1794 until 1801 to prevent the "good intentions" of antislavery reformers from undermining the nation's fragile stability and igniting a bloody civil war.

Though greatly troubled by the moral and political evils of slavery, Harper accepted the system as a temporary necessity. Moving his law practice to the "middle ground" of Maryland, he played a critical role in foiling the efforts of hundreds of slaves to win their freedom in *Mahoney v. Ashton* (1802). Over the next decade, Harper turned his efforts to achieving social progress through the education of lower-class white Americans and the "emancipation" of European peasants from Napoleonic tyranny. The founding of the American Colonization Society in 1816 renewed his commitment to resolving the problems of slavery by educating blacks and transporting them to an environment free from white racial prejudice, where they might one day become a "great nation." It was he who proposed the names Liberia and Monrovia, and by the time of his death in 1825, few had done more to earn popular support for colonization or to establish the possibility of its future success.

See also AMERICAN COLONIZATION SOCIETY; LIBERIA; PERSPECTIVES ON SLAVERY; REPATRIATION TO AFRICA.

BIBLIOGRAPHY

PAPENFUSE, ERIC ROBERT. *The Evils of Necessity: Robert Goodloe Harper and the Moral Dilemma of Slavery.* 1997.
———. "From Recompense to Revolution: *Mahoney v. Ashton* and the Transfiguration of Maryland Culture, 1791–1802." *Slavery and Abolition* 15 (1994): 38–62.

Eric Robert Papenfuse

Hawaii

In the Hawaiian Kingdom (1795–1893) Hawaiians despised the institution of slavery. Ancient Hawaiian society had two classes: the chiefs (*ali'i*) and the common folk (*maka'ainana*), who were obligated to serve the chiefs. Both classes were bound by the strict rules of a religious, or *kapu*, system.

A slave class, the *kauwa*, were outcastes living apart, godless, and sometimes identified by a black tattoo on the forehead. They were used for degrading work and also as human sacrifices to the god *Ku*. During a period of wars of conquest before 1778 and continuing to 1795, many *kauwa* were lost in the dislocation of the population. The wars ended in a unified kingdom under King Kamehameha I.

In 1819, after forty years of contact with the Western world, powerful women chiefs led by Ka'ahumanu, convinced the monarch, Kamehameha II, to revoke the *kapu* system. Under the influence of westerners, especially Protestant missionaries from the United States, Hawaiians became Christians and grew familiar with the ideas of liberty and equality. In 1839 Kamehameha III released Hawaiians from obligations to their chiefs. In the first constitution, in 1840, he confirmed the freedom of all people in this kingdom. These developments effectively abolished the *kauwa* class. However, *kauwa* was still used as a term of contempt and scorn.

Hawaiians learned of the issue of slavery in the Western world through contact with people from the United States and Europe who made Hawaii their home. Many residents became naturalized citizens and served in the government as advisors to the king and as elected officials. Hawaiians were aware that many residents of the United States considered them to be a people of color, as despised as Negro slaves. Hawaiians also knew that Indians in the United States had been degraded, deprived of their land, and killed in wars.

In 1854 Kamehameha III initiated negotiations for a treaty of annexation with the United States. As news of these negotiations became public, Hawaiians responded with fury. In Hawaiian-language newspapers, in speeches in the legislature, in petitions to their leaders, and in public meetings, Hawaiians objected to annexation to a slave nation. Hawaiian leaders quieted the storm of protest by assuring the people that any treaty would include provisions against slavery. The treaty was written, but it was never signed; the negotiations ended.

If Hawaiians rejected any suggestion of *kauwa* status, they did not reject the concept of indentured servitude when members of the legislature passed the Masters and Servants Act of 1850 without objection. Both Hawaiians and Euro-Americans accepted the contract labor system with harsh legal penalties placed on the worker. Hawaiians themselves worked under such contracts, as did the large number of contract laborers who came from China, Japan, Portugal, Germany, Norway, and Pacific islands.

The modern clothing worn by King Kamehameha III at a meeting with his council is a visual symbol of the struggles taking place during the nineteenth century between the traditional and the modern points of view in Hawaii. [*Illustrated London News*/Corbis]

In the 1860s Hawaiians generally did join in criticism of the contract labor system. Along with Caucasian newsmen, ministers, attorneys, workingmen, and Chinese merchants, they asked the legislature to eliminate the penal sanctions. But the only changes accomplished between 1865 and 1898 were amendments in favor of the worker.

Hawaiians were more concerned with the number of immigrants from any one nation than with these people's condition of servitude. As their own numbers declined through depopulation, Hawaiians reacted in racist ways. By the 1870s they began to criticize the Chinese, then the most numerous of the immigrants.

A similar attitude existed in the kingdom among residents of any ethnicity: an objection to chattel slavery and a general acceptance of indenture in contract labor. Many Euro-Americans were ardent abolitionists in the period before the Civil War in the United States. But the production of sugar cane demanded large numbers of relatively unskilled workers. Thus, those men in charge of the sugar industry found no conflict in being abolitionists toward African slavery while at the same time accepting contract labor with penal sanctions.

A similar economic interest prompted the Hawaiian kingdom to declare neutrality during the United States Civil War. Two southern confederate warships in the Pacific threatened the safety of whalers from the northeastern ports of the United States. Both President Lincoln's administration in the United States and the leaders of the Hawaiian kingdom wished to protect the whaling industry.

The penal contract system became illegal only after annexation to the United States in 1898, when U.S. law was extended to the Islands. Then all forms of indenture were made illegal and passed from Hawaii's history, as had the *kauwa* class long before.

See also CHATTEL SLAVERY; LABOR SYSTEMS.

BIBLIOGRAPHY

DAWS, GAVAN. *Shoal of Time: A History of the Hawaiian Islands.* 1968.

KING, PAULINE N., ed. *The Diaries of David Lawrence Gregg: An American Diplomat in Hawaii, 1853–1858.* 1982.

KUYKENDALL, RALPH S. *The Hawaiian Kingdom.* 3 vols. 1938–1967.

Pauline N. King

Headright System

The headright system encouraged immigration by rewarding with land those who settled in the southern colonies, or who paid the transportation expenses of others. During the colonial period, the system was used in Maryland, Virginia, North Carolina, South Carolina, and Georgia.

Practices varied from one colony to another. In North Carolina, headrights were earned for different amounts of land, according to the type of head (male, female, child, free, bonded, or slave) brought into the colony. In Virginia, planters received fifty acres for each individual whose passage they paid. In Maryland, records were carefully kept; elsewhere, the system was often abused, causing some to complain that, instead of acting as "a lasting Encouragement to Adventurers," headrights were the reason that the country was "so badly peopled."

Entrepreneurs bringing individuals (slave or free) to the southern colonies grew rich in land, like Edmund Scarborough, who purchased large numbers of slaves in New Amsterdam in the 1650s and transported them to Northampton County, Virginia. Listed in land office records, "Negroes" like Antonio, Domingo, and Calentia (all 1657 arrivals in Virginia) made their masters wealthy in property.

By the end of the seventeenth century, the transition from indentured labor to slave labor in the colonies was underway. The headright system began to lapse as the importation of slaves increased; by the time the trade peaked in the late eighteenth century, the slaves themselves, and not the land to which they entitled their owners, had become the key to wealth in the southern colonies.

See also CAPITALISM AND SLAVERY; DEMOGRAPHY OF SLAVES IN THE UNITED STATES; UNITED STATES.

BIBLIOGRAPHY

BREEN, T. H., and STEPHEN INNES. *"Myne Owne Ground": Race and Freedom on Virginia's Eastern Shore, 1640–1676.* 1980.

HENING, WILLIAM WALLER. *Statutes at Large* 3 (1823): 304–329. Reprint, 1969.

WOOD, PETER H. *Black Majority: Negroes in Colonial South Carolina from 1670 through the Stono Rebellion.* 1974.

Jennifer Davis McDaid

Health

This entry includes the following articles: Diseases and Epidemiology; Medicine and Medical Care; Nutrition.

Diseases and Epidemiology

The influence of slavery on the history of disease, physical suffering, sexual exploitation, and preventable mortality is one of the most intricate aspects of global slave studies. On one hand, slavery rested on the power of masters to impose their will over the physical being of the slave. On the other hand, in most slave societies the system required that the health of slaves be guarded so that slaves could perform their functions—labor, reproduction, or sex. Thus, slave systems were frequently a blend: physical coercion and harsh working and living conditions were tempered by minimally sufficient food and housing and some adjustment of demands to prevent slaves from perishing.

Historians have confronted great difficulties in documenting the complex health picture that emerged out of these contradictory relationships between masters and slaves. There are only limited historical records of the physical and psychological damage caused by capture, transport, settlement, and slave life for specific age groups. Moreover, enslaved populations were normally denied the literacy and professional expertise they would have needed to leave their own written evidence of their health concerns. This lack of historical documents stymies the broad-scale application of current epidemiological techniques to assess slaves' health over broad spans of geography and time. However, there is now a growing area in Western scholarship: microstudies of specific plantations. This newer research uses current medical and epidemiological concepts, economics, demography, and social history and has begun to reveal patterns of health and disease in the transatlantic and trans-Saharan slave trade and societies.

Mortality from Capture and Forced Relocation

The imprisonment and transport of slaves in the transatlantic and African slave trade frequently started with the capture of populations dislocated by brutal fighting between warring ethnic groups, or with an ecological catastrophe such as a famine. Disease, malnutrition, and exposure killed many of the new captives en route to ports and other centers of slave trading.

Historians estimate that between the years 1500 and 1870 about 11 million Africans were sent across the Atlantic in the infamous Middle Passage. Death from disease and overexertion afflicted these slave populations in significant yet widely varying degrees. Overall, one of every seven or eight slaves died during the Middle Passage.

Roughly four-tenths of the slaves in the Atlantic trade were distributed in South America, another four-tenths in the Caribbean Islands, about one-tenth in Central America (including Mexico), and less than one-tenth in British North America. Slaves were distributed throughout the New World according to the labor needs of each region's plantation economy. The health and the birth and death rates of enslaved Africans differed according to the size of the plantation, the harshness of the work and social conditions, and the geographical environment.

An advertisement announcing the arrival of new slaves in the colonies emphasizes the fact that they were free of smallpox, with one-half of them already having had the disease in their own country. [Corbis-Bettmann]

The trans-Saharan slave trade in Africa during the nineteenth and early twentieth centuries also generated mass population shifts and increases in morbidity and mortality attributable to violent capture, exposure of the newly enslaved population to deadly diseases, and material deprivation. In fact, some historians argue that mortality en route was higher by up to 7 percent for the trans-Saharan and East Africa slave trades than for the transatlantic.

During the third quarter of the nineteenth century approximately 35,000 slaves were taken each year from the northern half of East Africa, most to the Middle and Near East. Throughout the nineteenth century, more than 10,000 slaves annually were sent across the Saharan Desert. While the transatlantic trade favored male captives, the trans-Saharan trade favored women and children. In one incident during the 1850s, a slave raid took place in the Muslim area of Bornu (modern Nigeria) in which women and children were captured, but some 170 men were left behind with their legs severed to bleed to death.

Even in the absence of such horrific incidents, death rates both before and during embarkation were also substantial for the transatlantic trade. The acquisition or roundup of captives by transatlantic traders was conducted more rapidly and involved opening slaving frontier zones deep in the African interior among

Table 1.   Crude Birth and Death Rates in Various Slave-Based Societies in the Americas, 1633–1861.

Place	Date	Population	Crude Birthrate (per 1000 population)	Crude Death Rate (per 1000 population)
Brazil				
1. Salvador				
S. Antonio parish	1775	All		35.1
Penha parish	1775	All		33.9
Passo parish	1798	All		34.5
2. São Paulo	1765	Males	64.2	59.2
		Females	56.6	51.5
3. São Paulo	1798	All free		54.4
4. Pernambuco	1775	All	41.4	32.8
5. Maranhão	1798	Whites	16.3	27.9
		Pardo slaves	38	26.7
		Black slaves	24	26.7
		All slaves	26.5	26.7
6. Minas Gerais	1815	Whites	36.6	27.4
		Free colored	41.7	34.3
		Slaves	33.4	32.9
7. Minas Gerais	1821	Whites	40	28
		Free colored	41.5	39.6
		Pardo slaves	38	60
		Black slaves	29	65
		All slaves	33.7	62.8
8. Espirito Santo	1817	All	44.2	33.5
9. Brazil	1873	All slaves	30	
10. Jamaica	1817–1832	All slaves	23	26
11. Jamaica	1844–1861	All	40	32
12. Suriname	1826–1848	All slaves	27.5	50
13. Suriname (Caterina-Sophia plantation)	1852–1861	All slaves	26.8	43.4
14. U.S. South	1850	Whites	46–50	
15. U.S. South	1820–1860	Slaves	60	
16. Cuba	1791–1792	All blacks	52.5	34.0
	1816–1817	All blacks	50	34.2
17. Danish West Indies	1840s	All slaves	40	50
18. Bahia				
S. Amaro Parish	1817	Slaves		47
Engenho Sergipe	1633–1636	Slaves		75
Engenho Santana	1730–1731	Slaves		39
Engenho Santana	1748–1752	Slaves	28	27
Engenho Petinga	1744–1745	Slaves		115 (plague)
Fazenda Saubara	1750–1760	Slaves	17–26	
		Adult male slaves		115
		Adult female slaves		81

Stuart B. Schwartz, *Sugar Plantations in the Formation of Brazilian Society* (1986).

peoples in the midst of social breakdown. For example, about 40 percent of the slaves purchased in interior Angola (usually bound for Brazil) perished during their six months en route to embarkation ports. Also, congestion of slaves being prepared for shipment at African ports, longer voyages, and overcrowding on ships were factors behind the high death rate of slaves bound for the New World.

Violence, Whippings, and Atrocities

Physical punishment detrimental to health was probably typical of almost all slave societies. But once again, the nature and extent of this practice varied widely according to historical period, local laws and practices, and related social practices involving war and religious sacrifice. Ritual murders or forms of killing slaves with impunity were common among certain social segments of early civilizations in locations and societies as diverse as Native American or "Indian" North America (groups along the northwest coast), Japan, China, Arab regions, Mexico, and West Africa.

Whipping was frequently the primary means of coercing slaves on the larger plantations throughout North and South America and the Caribbean. Laws protecting slaves from mutilation and wanton murder developed in New World slave societies as slavery became more formalized. But evidence of significant numbers of incidents in which slaves were victims of homicides and atrocities perpetrated with impunity by their masters have been uncovered by legal historians.

Infectious Diseases

Historical sources such as plantation journals, shipping logs, ledgers of slave sales, and legal documents are fragmentary; hence, as noted above, there is a lack of reliable, age-specific medical data. This has made it extraordinarily difficult to identify direct links between mortality rates and specific infectious, chronic, and deficiency diseases in large slaveholding regimes. However, interdisciplinary research involving social history, demography, economics, and medical science, such as that of Nobel laureate Robert William Fogel, has verified associations between certain crops and death rates in Western slave regions such as the United States, Jamaica, Trinidad, and Brazil.

In the United States death rates were higher among slaves on rice plantations relative to cotton plantations. In the Americas overall, the sugar plantation and its ancillary production activities were the work environment in which slaves' health fared worse. In Trinidad, adult slaves on sugar plantations died at a rate three times higher than slaves on cotton plantations. In Jamaica, the mortality rate was 50 percent higher among slaves on sugar plantations than among slaves on coffee plantations. In the United States, births among the slave population occurred about twice as frequently as deaths. But in the sugar plantation region of Bahia (Brazil), the death rate for slaves (while exceeding births by about one-third) was over four times higher than the rate for slaves in the United States. Intensity of work was one key factor underlying the higher rates of disease and death rates for slaves in the same region who worked on different crops. Also pivotal were malnutrition and the unsanitary and unsafe living and work environments typical for field and mining slaves.

As enslaved African populations were resettled throughout the Western world, biological protections and susceptibilities they had accumulated from generations of prior exposure to or isolation from classic diseases such as malaria, yellow fever, and tuberculosis influenced the morbidity of these populations. Malaria was endemic to the lower South of the United States and the tropical zones of the New World. Since transplanted African populations possessed sickle-cell genes, they and many in subsequent generations were largely protected against malaria. Yellow fever was another mosquito-borne disease to which slave populations tended to have relatively less susceptibility than Europeans transported to the tropics. By contrast, respiratory diseases, such as pneumonia, influenza, and especially tuberculosis, probably took the highest toll of lives among slaves in the southern United States. These and other bacterial and viral infections killed slaves at the highest rates because of heavy work demands and environmental and dietary deficiencies that tended to accelerate the onset and severity of infection.

Cholera and diseases spread by domestic animals such as anthrax and brucellosis broke out sporadically in the southern slave region of the United States. Cholera is usually spread through personal contact and communal water and food supplies. It can spread rapidly from a few families or households to whole counties. In the New World cholera killed many more blacks than whites. In Brazil a cholera epidemic broke out in 1855–1856, killing as many as 200,000 people, at least two-thirds of whom were blacks.

Housing of slaves has been linked to their higher rates of childhood illness. In the United States, slave cabins typically had dirt floors and were damp and poorly ventilated. Hence, childhood diseases such as chicken pox, measles, and mumps struck slave children much more harshly than whites. Two other leading causes of death among U.S. plantation slaves were dysentery and tetanus. These are linked to poor hygiene and unsanitary conditions.

An 1864 drawing of the interior of a slave cabin in Spotsylvania Courthouse, Virginia. [Library of Congress/Corbis]

Malnutrition and Infant Mortality

Inadequate nutrition was a problem that impaired the physical health of slaves of all regions. Studies have found that nutritional deficiencies, including anemia, were widespread among slave populations in Maryland, Virginia, and North and South Carolina (United States). Throughout the Caribbean, it is likely that poor nutrition contributed most to slave mortality. In this region, malnutrition increased the slaves' risk of infectious diseases and other ailments. According to Kenneth Kiple, poor nutrition also caused specific deficiency diseases such as frank beriberi (linked to thiamine deficiency) and pellagra (linked to niacin deficiency). Moreover, in the case of slave mothers, inadequate nutrition eroded their children's health as well as their own. With regard to beriberi, for example mothers passed thiamine-deficient milk to nursing infants, who almost inevitably would then die.

Indeed, demographers, historians, and medical researchers have uncovered excess infant mortality in slave populations throughout the Americas. In many cases, slaves on large plantations—in Cuba, for instance—had higher rates of infant and child mortality. Data available for North American slave regions indicate that slave women lost over half of their pregnancies to stillbirths and to infant and early childhood mortality. These slave infants and children died frequently from respiratory diseases, whooping cough, and sudden infant death syndrome, as well as from diarrhea and digestive problems. In slave regions in which pregnant and lactating women were allowed to work less and breast-feeding was permitted, some of the causes of mortality were lessened.

Current Issues

Historians and other social and medical scientists have added important pieces to the puzzle of health and disease of slaves in the New World. Recently, among scholars involved in the global study of slavery, there has been growing interest in health in nonwestern slave societies. Also, in both western and nonwestern slave studies, new research looking at continental and diaspora subsocieties will reveal how enslaved populations used their own cultural mechanisms, indigenous knowledge, and informal social institutions to promote their health and well-being. Evidence of resistance and revolts by slaves in the New World against the dehumanization and risk of death that slavery entailed is now well established. More research is required on the anthropology and sociology of the internal slave community itself, applied comparatively across regions, nations, and continents. It may reveal much larger roles for the slave population's own independent religious institutions and cultures, female and family resources and practical scientific knowledge. These institutions and resources—which were developed both despite and because of enslavement—promoted well-being in the face of disease and social disdain.

See also: DISCIPLINE AND PUNISHMENT; FOOD AND CLOTHING; HOUSING; MIDDLE PASSAGE; PLANTATIONS; SLAVE TRADE.

BIBLIOGRAPHY

ELTIS, DAVID, and DAVID RICHARDSON, eds. *Routes to Slavery: Direction, Ethnicity and Mortality in the Transatlantic Slave Trade.* Special Issue, *Slavery and Abolition* 18, no. 1 (April 1997).

FINKELMAN, PAUL, ed. "Symposium on the Law of Slavery." *Chicago-Kent Law Review* 68, no. 3 (1993).

FOGEL, ROBERT W. *Without Consent or Contract: The Rise and Fall of American Slavery.* 1989.

GIBBS, TYSON, KATHLEEN CARGILL, LESLIE SUE LIEBERMAN, and ELIZABETH REITZ. "Nutrition in a Slave Population: An Anthropological Examination." *Medical Anthropology* 4 (1980): 175–262.

GORDON, MURRAY. *Slavery in the Arab World.* 1987.

KIPLE, KENNETH F., ed. *The Cambridge World History of Human Diseases.* 1993.

———. *The African Exchange.* 1987.

MCBRIDE, DAVID. *From TB to AIDS: Epidemics among Urban Blacks since 1900.* 1991.

MILLER, JOSEPH C. *Way of Death: Merchant Capitalism and the Angolan Slave Trade, 1730–1830.* 1988.

PATTERSON, ORLANDO. *Slavery and Social Death: A Comparative Study.* 1982.

SAVAGE, ELIZABETH, ed. *The Human Commodity: Perspectives on the Trans-Saharan Slave Trade.* 1992.

SCHWARTZ, STUART B. *Sugar Plantations in the Formation of Brazilian Society.* 1985.

SIMPSON, GEORGE E. *Black Religions in the New World.* 1978.

David McBride

Medicine and Medical Care

The role of medicine and medical care in world slavery evolved from two intertwining historical currents: (1) the evolution of medical institutions, physicians, and other formal and traditional healers generally; and (2) the unique shapes these medical-care agencies took within the contexts of the vastly different slave societies that have appeared throughout world history. Historians such as Timothy Miller have documented institutions that can be defined as hospitals as far back as the twelfth-century eastern Roman or Byzantine Empire. Just where, when, and how such institutions functioned outside of Europe and the Byzantine Empire is an issue that Western scholars have barely opened, and so this entry highlights some of what is known about hospital and medical care only in American slave societies.

Slave Masters and Medical Necessities

At the heart of Western slave systems is the process of extracting physical exertion from dominated people to a limit just short of disability or death. Driving Africans and native American Indians by the thousands and millions into plantations where working and living conditions were usually harsh caused abrupt death or grinding physical wear and tear. The slaves' physical condition deteriorated from frequent work injuries, inadequate living quarters, and an inadequate diet, which left them vulnerable to disease and maternal and infant deaths. From the earliest stages of slavery, the desire to limit such losses in productivity and human capital caused most owners to view providing some form of medical treatment for their slaves as an unavoidable necessity. In each New World slave society, owners developed a broad array of hospitals or "sick houses," infirmaries, and lying-in-rooms and turned to doctors, pharmacists or apothecaries, midwives, nurses, and lay healers.

First and foremost, slave owners found it in their economic interest to promote their slaves' capacity to perform continuous and vigorous labor, as well as for females to bear and raise healthy children. Furthermore, slaves were always potentially rebellious against conditions that provoked suffering they perceived as avoidable. So masters were prone to furnish at the least basic food, housing, and health assistance, the minimal accommodations slaves expected. Second, by the early nineteenth century slaveowners in the New World came increasingly under pressure from humanitarians—abolitionists, clerics, and sometimes official authorities—to provide better living conditions and health services for their slaves.

Finally, in urban areas whites interacted daily with resident slave populations. Although knowledge about the specific causes, prevention, and treatment of infectious diseases (or "fevers" or "febrile illnesses") was still prescientific and generally inaccurate during most of the years of slavery in the New World, understanding of the communicability of some diseases—especially smallpox, cholera and yaws—improved by the mid-nineteenth century. Increasingly, public health authorities viewed black city districts as unhealthy environments, with "miasmas" dangerous to whites who lived, worked, or traveled in those sections; thus the authorities tried to control unsanitary conditions and diseases rampant in the slave districts, to protect the health of city-dwelling whites.

Medical Thought

From the colonial period through the early nineteenth century, physicians, surgeons, and apothecaries in North America and the British West Indies were a largely informal profession. The only professional physicians were those who had trained in European medical schools; most physicians had learned through apprenticeships or were self-taught. Lacking any diagnostic instruments or understanding of bacteriological disease processes—medical understanding that did not emerge until the latter nineteenth century—physicians in slave societies used a hodgepodge of Old World and New World therapies.

Iron-instrument surgery, originally adopted in Spain from Muslim medicine, was used in territories of the Spanish Americas. Anglo-American doctors in North America and the Caribbean, especially prior to the nineteenth century, imported medical theories and pharmacopoeia from Europe. They relied largely on a version of Galen's theories that attempted to restore health by balancing the body's four "humours": heat, cold, dryness, and moistness. Bleeding, purging, and blistering by heat were the fundamental therapies, since they appeared to help restore the sick person's body to balance and thus to health. These "treatments" by doctors and apothecaries "worked" in the eyes of their employers—the planters—since they sometimes appeared to alleviate visible symptoms. But more often than not, such care was probably ineffective or detrimental to the patient's health. White physicians of the planter class from the United States to Brazil were shocked by the slaves' dark skin, different facial features, and strange cultures and attempted to create a separate medical discipline for Africans, based on the premise that blacks and whites were anatomically distinct races.

Physician Care

Despite the superficial ideas about therapy and the largely harmful techniques of Euro-American medicine during the colonial period and the early republic, care by physicians or physician-supervised care was

integral to Western slave societies. Owners hired doctors either part-time or full-time to treat slaves. In Barbados, for example, one visitor to a large plantation wrote in 1789: "There is not a single estate in Barbados that does not pay a doctor . . . annually for each Negroe [sic], sick or well. The doctors either attend themselves, or send their journeymen, at least once a week, at all times." (cited in Handler and Lange, 1978). In rural Brazil during the 1850s, in a less well-tended slave population, one doctor was responsible for approximately 900 slaves living on five separate coffee plantations (Conrad, 1994).

When viewed in a global historical context, the numbers of physicians available to treat slaves in both the U.S. South and the British West Indies was substantial. Doctor-population ratios are crude but still suggestive indicators of how much health care is being provided. In 1800 Georgia, in a state of 102,000 whites and 60,000 blacks, had about 100 physicians, that is, a physician-to-population ratio of 1 to 1,620. According to B. V. Higman, in Barbados during 1820 the ratio was 1 doctor to every 1,300 slaves and 1 to 1,600 for the population overall. In Trinidad in 1830, the ratio was 1 doctor to 780 slaves and 1 to 1,450 for the total population. In Jamaica in 1833 ratio was about 1 doctor to 1,500 slaves and 1 doctor to 1,800 Jamaicans overall.

American slave societies were thus more populated with doctors than are today's developing nations. For example, in 1977 Bangladesh and Nigeria each had less than 1 doctor for 10,000 residents. By contrast, the United States had a ratio of about 1 to 500. Despite the inefficacy of medicine in the time of slavery, the relatively large supply of doctors in slave regions suggests that masters were willing to pay to have them on hand, if only for psychological comfort and for maintaining social order in an inherently cruel situation.

Hospital and Emergency Care

Next in importance to physicians for medical treatment of slaves were specific places for ongoing care, such as the small hospitals or sick-houses established on the plantations and the public or charitable health facilities that sometimes offered their services to slaves. Territories in the Americas colonized by Spain became the sites of the first hospitals in the Western world. By the early 1600s, "New Spain," encompassing much of modern Mexico and Central America, had nearly 130 such hospitals, while Spain's colonies in South America had an additional 20 or so similar institutions. Many black slaves, skilled and unskilled, helped construct Peru's earliest hospitals, churches, monasteries, and schools beginning as far back as the sixteenth century. In some instances, slaves worked at hospitals of religious or charitable bodies to which their masters had bequeathed them.

The availability of the early Spanish American hospitals to Indian and African slaves, either as patients or as health workers, varied throughout the course of these institutions' long history. In Lima by 1607, for example, the hospital of Santa Ana cared for the city's Indians and employed twenty-seven African slaves. These Afro-Peruvians worked as practical nurses, laundresses, bookkeepers, cooks, and other menial employees. Also in Lima, the Hospital of San Andrés provided slaveholders with care for their slaves, but it ended this practice in 1640 because impoverished, ill Spaniards overcrowded its facilities. In other cases, masters paid hospitals or physicians to provide care for their slaves, or Jesuits donated medical care to slaves.

In the slave regions of North America and the West Indies plantations operated a wide variety of hospitals or other special places for the care of sick slaves. In Virginia, according to Todd Savitt, these facilities ranged from separate hospitals or infirmaries with several beds to simple rooms in farm buildings or in the large house belonging to the master. Slaves in Richmond and Norfolk, Virginia, frequently could obtain treatment at hospitals owned privately or by planters or the city. In New Orleans slaves were rarely treated at Charity Hospital (founded 1736), the oldest hospital operating in what became U.S. territory. But other hospitals in that city did attend to slaves. Hospitals throughout Hispanic America included special institutions for smallpox, venereal disease, and leprosy. However, according to available English language sources, it is not clear to what extent they admitted African or Indian slaves.

Hospitals and other physician-care facilities on plantations in the British West Indies also varied in structure and size of staff. In addition to general hospitals and lying-in rooms, some British West Indian plantations operated special houses to isolate slaves with yaws, a highly infectious disease. Many Caribbean hospitals differed from those in North America in that their daily administration was in the hands of slave "sick nurses," who were frequently elderly men. On large plantations, an apothecary, attendants, and sick nurses assisted slave doctors. These health workers were supervised only loosely by white physicians and were often permitted to use herbal remedies of their own. Whites endorsed these unconventional therapies because their black slaves were frequently reluctant to take medicine prescribed by whites.

On large plantations, where fieldwork was especially harsh and dangerous, transporting injured slaves quickly to nearby hospitals was not feasible. There-

fore, conscientious overseers had primitive first-aid kits—thread, rags, and oil of turpentine—to deal with emergencies in the fields. Both planters and abolitionists agreed, according to the historian Robert Paquette (1988), that "sugar cultivation took a terrible toll on slave life. . . . Long hours of intense work caused accidents. Arms and legs were slashed, crushed, and dismembered along with the cane. Cuts and punctures from work in and around the fields easily led to serious infections like tetanus." Credible estimates reported about 15 to 20 percent of the slaves from the work gangs in the sick bay during the sugar harvest on Cuban plantations in the 1840s, and 40 percent by the end of the harvest.

African-American Medical Caregivers: Slave and Free

Throughout the slave societies of the Americas, slave doctors and informal slave practitioners or "designated healers," drawing on a rich body of traditional folk medicine (or *curanderismo* in Latin America), were also important sources of medical care among slaves. Their African and Indian knowledge of plants, herbs, and minerals, as well as their active religious beliefs, provided important psychological and physical support for their slave brothers and sisters. The various types of slave doctors (male and female) and midwives not only treated slave communities on large plantations but occasionally served local whites as well.

The traditional remedies of American Indians and Africans sometimes crept into the medical practices of white doctors. Most notable was the use of inoculation to prevent smallpox. The prominent early American medical leader, Reverend Cotton Mather, was renowned for having popularized this technique throughout the colonies during the early 1700s. Less recognized is the fact that he learned of smallpox inoculation on large plantations and from his slave Onesimus, as well as from European journals.

Freeborn and freed African-American doctors, midwives, and nurses also contributed to health care during the era of slavery in the United States. Most notable was James Derham, who was born a slave. Derham became one of the most prominent physicians in New Orleans. Benjamin Rush, the leading physician in early America, praised Derham in 1788: "I have conversed with him upon most of the acute and epidemic diseases of the country where he lives. . . . I expected to have suggested some new medicines to him, but he suggested many more to me" (cited in Morais, 1967).

Childbirth was another area of health care in which African-Americans played a vital role. In Jamaica and Barbados, especially as momentum built toward abolition of the slave trade, planters paid incentives to both slave mothers and their medical attendants for delivering healthy infants, or, as they said, "for bringing out their children." An attorney on a large plantation in Barbados emphasized the practice of paying incentives to childbearing women in a letter he wrote in the late 1780s: "To encourage the Midwives to perform their duty with attention and ability, every Child she brings me one Month old, as a reward, I give her 6/8 and the Mother of the infant 3/4 to buy the stranger a Fowl to commence its little stock in life," (cited in McDonald, 1993).

Some African-American healers were so effective they received their freedom in appreciation of their work. The historian Herbert Morais found accounts of such healers in colonial America and the nineteenth-century United States. For example, in 1729 Virginia's lieutenant-governor, William Gooch, reported" "[I] met with a negro, a very old man, who has performed many wonderful cures of diseases. For the sake of his freedom, he has revealed the medicine, a concoction of roots and bark. . . . There is no room to doubt of its being a certain remedy here" (cited in Morais, 1968). The successes of African-American medical attendants continued until the eve of emancipation. In his account of early U.S. medicine Daniel Boorstin noted that in Virginia prior to 1860, crude mortality rates for puerperal sepsis (an infection associated with childbirth) were much higher among whites attended by doctors than among blacks cared for by black midwives.

Proslavery Medicine

In the United States scientists and physicians developed medical theories and treatments based on their racism and their proslavery ideologies. Thomas Jefferson, who was well known as a man of science as well as a man of politics and letters, suggested in the 1780s that the blackness of his slaves came from "the colour of the blood." He also asserted that blacks were "inferior to whites in the endowments of body and mind and that they gave off a "disagreeable odour," needed "less sleep" than whites, and in other ways were anatomically different than whites.

Throughout the first half of the nineteenth century, southerners interpreted slave behavior in medical and biological terms. Slaves who ran away were often diagnosed as being "addicted to running away." In other cases, records describe slaves as "addicted to madness." The Louisiana code referred to an "addition" to theft that some slaves had.

By the 1850s southern scientists and physicians had developed an entire theory of proslavery medicine. The physicians Samuel Cartwright of New Orleans

and Josiah Nott of Mobile argued that blacks and whites were anatomically different and that the internal organs of blacks were darker. Cartwright wrote that the Negro's brain and blood were "a shade of the pervading darkness," that the ankle was "planted in the middle of the foot," that blacks had fewer nerves to the brain than whites, that their brains were 10 percent smaller than those of whites and that "the negro approximates the monkey anatomically more than he does the true Caucasian." He argued that blacks had a digestive system closer to that of primates and could thus be fed coarse grains and fatty foods. He also argued that blacks suffered from various diseases that whites did not contract. He identified the disease "Dysthesia Ethiopica, or Hebetude of Mind," which, he noted, "overseers call Rascality." He believed black slaves "caught" this disease when they were allowed to eat, drink, and behave like free blacks. The cure included whipping the slave to increase his blood circulation. Another disease he discovered was "Synaesthesia Aethiopis," which led to "stupidness of the mind" and rendered them needful of the care and protection of whites. In an 1851 article in *De Bow's Review*, Cartwright discussed "Drapetomania," better known as the "running-away disease." This disease made slaves run away from their masters. Cartwright thought it could be cured with "proper medical advice." He warned planters that slaves who had a "sulky and dissatisfied" attitude were susceptible to the disease, which he advised could be cured by "whipping the devil out of them."

Josiah Nott, who practiced medicine in Mobile, Alabama, argued that blacks and whites were actually separate species. In *Indigenous Races of the Earth, or, New Chapters of Ethnological Inquiry* (1857), Nott argued that blacks had a different physiology from whites, had smaller brains, and therefore needed different medical care. He claimed this assessment was "unquestionably true," based on his years of treating slaves in Mobile.

Slaveholders and apologists for slavery used such medical theories to justify harsh treatment of slaves. Masters could take comfort in feeding them the poor-quality food because the doctors said such a diet was good for them. Similarly, masters could whip slaves because physicians like Cartwright and Nott explained that a slave's nervous system was not well developed, and hence a slave did not feel as much pain as whites. Moreover, whipping was actually good for slaves, according to the proslavery doctors, because it helped their blood circulation and made them exercise their lungs.

These same theories were responsible for poor medical treatment for slaves as well as overwork. If blacks, all blacks, were naturally lazy—as many scientists from

Jefferson's time to Nott's claimed—then it would be legitimate to ignore the symptoms when they appeared tired or overworked.

Conclusion

Medical care provided by physicians, health institutions, and African-American healers was essential to the functioning of the Western slave system. This medical care was vital not just because of the physical suffering it may have alleviated but also because these health practitioners and places for care were important for the social and psychological relief they provided. The broad spectrum of medical care for slaves helped to hold together the tense, dangerous social world of slave societies.

See also CARIBBEAN REGION; FOOD AND COOKING; PLANTATIONS.

BIBLIOGRAPHY

CONRAD, ROBERT E. *Children of God's Fire: A Documentary History of Black Slavery in Brazil.* 1994.

FINKELMAN, PAUL, ed. *Medicine, Nutrition, Demography, and Slavery.* 1989.

HIGMAN, B. W. *Slave Populations of the British Caribbean, 1807–1834.* 1984.

MCDONALD, RODERICK A. *The Economy and Material Culture of Slaves: Goods and Chattels on the Sugar Plantations of Jamaica and Louisiana.* 1993.

MCKITRICK, ERIC L. *Slavery Defended: The View of the Old South.* 1963.

MILLER, TIMOTHY S. *The Birth of the Hospital in the Byzantine Empire.* 1985.

MORAIS, HERBERT M. *The History of the Negro in Medicine.* 1968.

NUMBERS, RONALD L., ed. *Medicine in the New World: New Spain, New France, and New England.* 1987.

PAQUETTE, ROBERT L. *Sugar Is Made with Blood: The Conspiracy of La Escalera and the Conflict between Empires over Slavery in Cuba.* 1988.

SAVITT, TODD L. *Medicine and Slavery: The Diseases and Health Care of Blacks in Antebellum Virginia.* 1979.

SHERIDAN, RICHARD B. *Doctors and Slaves: A Medical and Demographic History of Slavery in the British West Indies, 1680–1834.* 1985.

STANTON, WILLIAM. *The Leopard's Spots: Scientific Attitudes toward Race in America, 1815–1859.* 1960.

David McBride

Nutrition

Whether in Brazil, the West Indies, or the southern United States, the diets of slaves in the Western Hemisphere were similar in that they centered on rations of meat or fish and cereals. These core diets, when buttressed by vegetable supplements, seem to have provided slaves with the daily three to four thousand calories needed for hard physical labor. But although the diets generally satisfied energy requirements, there is abundant evidence that they were qualitatively deficient and lacking (sometimes significantly) in one or more of the chief nutrients.

Slave laws and planter records suggest that meat or fish rations amounted to three or four pounds weekly. Although hardly generous, this should have provided enough high-quality protein (one containing all of the essential amino acids) to maintain bodies and immune systems. That slaves did in fact generally, if unevenly, receive these rations is indicated by their heights, with stature serving as something of an indicator of protein intake. For example, that slaves born in the American South were taller than their Caribbean creole-born counterparts (such data for Brazil remain to be published) suggests that the slaves in the South were more likely to receive their ration of pork on a regular basis than the creoles their pickled fish (in the British islands) or dried beef (in Cuba).

Geographical circumstances, in turn, can explain much of the variance. In the United States pork was homegrown and plentiful, whereas in the Caribbean fish and dried beef had to be imported and, consequently, their availability was subject to interruption by war, weather, planters' whim, and the price of sugar. But because the islands had to rely on the slave trade to redress an annual excess of deaths over births, which the United States, with a rapidly growing slave population, did not, we have the opportunity to compare the heights of African-born slaves and of those who were creole-born. Because the Africans were significantly shorter, we can surmise that although slaves in the Caribbean did not consume as much good-quality protein as their counterparts to the north, they did better in this regard than free people in Africa.

The next point to be noted, however, is that among the slaves in the United States only the adults were taller and more robust than slaves elsewhere. Their children, by contrast, were stunted as badly as children in the poorest of today's underdeveloped countries. One might expect such findings in the Caribbean, where the rule of thumb was that it was cheaper to import a slave than to raise one, and where, in fact, there seems no question that the young slaves suffered greatly from malnutrition. In Barbados, for example, an examination of teeth from a slave burial site on the Newton plantation revealed pervasive hypoplasia. These growth-arrest lines, which can be dated to the age of weaning, suggest strongly that this event confronted the island's slave youngsters with a real challenge to their very existence.

Although an indifference to the slave children in the West Indies is not surprising, widespread hypoplasia also characterized the teeth of slaves in the United

States. Such a condition, in turn, hints strongly at equally widespread protein-energy malnutrition (PEM) that occurs when a child is weaned from the protein in mother's milk to a pap made from corn, rice, plantains, or manioc flour, all practically devoid of the good-quality protein desperately needed by rapidly developing toddlers. Sometimes it takes the synergistic effect of PEM and parasitism or disease to produce kwashiorkor—one of the symptomatic poles of PEM—recognizable by the swollen bellies that its young victims develop. Evidence that the slave young in the United States and Brazil did indeed suffer from kwashiorkor can be found in the potbellies revealed in photographs taken of them, as well as its frequent mention in the accounts of planters and physicians.

Slave children in the United States, then, (and probably all slave children in the hemisphere), grew up in a malnourished state that did not end until they reached their teens. At that point, however, they began a biological process of "catching up" in terms of growth—after years of stunting—and by the time of adulthood, they had caught up. Clearly, it is difficult to know what to make of this poor treatment of the young. One explanation is that planters begrudged food to those who were still unable to give them a good day's work. Another is that children did not fare well in competition with adults at the communal pot where slaves got most of their food. A third is that children were fed separately and differently from adults and got little or none of the pork thought so important for laborers. Probably all of these factors had something to do with the problem. But it is worth repeating that the slave young were protein-deprived until they reached an age where they were large enough to work the day through and large enough to take care of themselves.

Old advertisements for runaway slaves also reinforce the contention that slaves, when young, were frequently victims of poor nutrition. Identifying features such as bowlegs, bandylegs, knock-knees, jaundiced complexions, and rotten or missing teeth suggest primary nutritional deficiencies. One of the consequences seems to have been rather severe bouts of rickets, probably caused (in these cases) by a lack of calcium and phosphorus in the diet rather than inadequate exposure to sunlight, although it is true that darker pigment significantly reduces the synthesis of vitamin D by the skin.

The poor nutritional status of children is without question the most significant indictment of slave diets. But the occurrence of the classic deficiency diseases throughout the slave societies of the hemisphere comes in a close second. The diseases in question are scurvy, pellagra, and beriberi, resulting from a lack of

vitamin C and the B vitamins niacin and thiamine respectively.

Livid and spongy gums resulting from scurvy were not uncommon among slaves of the southern United States and were a function of a diet heavy in cornmeal and salt pork but light in vegetables. More surprisingly—given the availability of fruit in the tropics—was the presence of scurvy among slaves in the West Indies. Probably the use of communal pots for cooking vegetables and fruits caused much of the problem because the pots boiled for hours, and heat destroys vitamin C. But the suspicion that in many instances supplements to the monotonous core diets were not as forthcoming as the records suggest is probably justified.

A lack of supplemental foods must have been at the root of the problem in the United States whenever pellagra occurred in the slave quarters. This disease has traditionally afflicted those whose diets have centered heavily on corn, because the niacin contained in corn is in a chemically bound form not available to consumers (at least not unless treated with lime, as

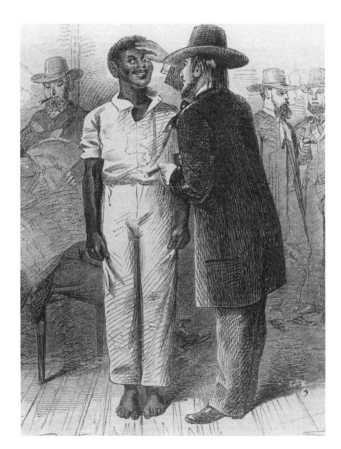

A potential buyer examines the slave's eyes and teeth for signs of any diseases resulting from nutritional deficits. [Corbis-Bettmann]

Native Americans had learned to do). However, even heavy consumers of corn do not develop pellagra unless there are so few items in the diet that niacin cannot be obtained from other sources. Moreover, tryptophan (an amino acid) can help to keep pellagra at bay even when niacin is absent in the diet because tryptophan in foods encourages the body to synthesize niacin. Beef, poultry, and dairy products—to mention just a few foods—are all excellent sources of tryptophan. Thus, the fact that slaves developed pellagra (most often in the winter months) and suffered the symptoms—its four Ds, diarrhea, dermatitis, dementia, and death—speaks loudly about the extraordinarily limited nature of some slave diets.

Pellagra was also present from time to time in some of the West Indian islands. But there, and in Brazil, beriberi was the most frequent deficiency disease. Beriberi has a reputation for striking those whose diets center on rice because it is triggered by a thiamine deficiency, and the practice of milling rice—stripping away its husk to prevent spoilage—also strips away most of the grain's thiamine. The vitamin is also present in other cereals, as well as in vegetables, and usually abounds in meats. Thus, as in the case of pellagra, a diet has to be incredibly limited to produce beriberi.

The disease appeared in the islands of the French Antilles, in Cuba, and in Brazil in both its wet and dry forms. In Brazil, however, it was not rice that was to blame but cassava (or manioc) meal—which is even more devoid of thiamine than milled rice—and the dried beef that, together, constituted the core diet in the northeast. Ordinarily, beef is rich in thiamine, but the beef in Brazil was sun-dried, and irradiation destroys thiamine. So does the soaking (thiamine is water-soluble) and prolonged cooking (heat also destroys thiamine) that the beef in question was subjected to.

However, the swellings and cardiac symptoms developed by those who developed wet beriberi and the peripheral nerve lesions of dry beriberi, which often caused paralysis, were probably less of a health problem for the slaves than a third form of the disease—infantile beriberi. Thiamine deficiency (unlike niacin deficiency) can be transmitted to infants through a mother's milk, and when this occurs, it is generally fatal. It is also important to note that a mother does not have to be so thiamine-deficient as to have beriberi symptoms. Thus, in those areas of the hemisphere where the slave diet focused too narrowly on cassava or rice, thiamine deficiency was doubtless responsible for a portion of the high mortality rates suffered by slave infants and children.

Vitamin A deficiency lay at the root of the sore eyes and, especially, the night blindness that seems to have reached epidemic proportions on some plantations. Dirt eating, a compulsion that was regularly reported among slaves throughout the hemisphere, was symptomatic of nutritional deficiencies. When the practice occurred among pregnant and lactating women, it almost certainly represented an effort to take from clay soils the iron, calcium, and magnesium in which they were deficient from their diets and pregnancy. Finally, speaking of iron—the lack of it—it should be noted that examinations of slave skulls have produced evidence of widespread anemia.

In brief summary, slave diets probably delivered enough calories for daily energy requirements. But any diet that centers on little meat and a lot of cereal will lead to poor health unless there are sufficient supplemental foods to deliver the chief nutrients that are missing from or insufficiently supplied by the core. It seems clear that often in the case of slaves there were too few supplements.

See also DEMOGRAPHY OF SLAVES IN THE UNITED STATES; FOOD AND COOKING.

BIBLIOGRAPHY

HANDLER, JEROME S., and ROBERT S. CORRUCCINI. "Plantation Life in Barbados: A Physical Anthropological Analysis." *Journal of Interdisciplinary History* 14 (1983): 65–90.

KIPLE, KENNETH F. *The Caribbean Slave: A Biological History.* 1984.

——— "The Nutritional Link with Slave Infant and Child Mortality in Brazil." *Hispanic American Historical Review* 69 (1989): 677–690.

KIPLE, KENNETH F., and VIRGINIA H. KING. *Another Dimension to the Black Diaspora: Diet, Disease, and Racism.* 1981.

STECKEL, RICHARD H. "A Dreadful Childhood: The Excess Mortality of American Slaves." In *The African Exchange: Toward a Biological History of Black People,* edited by Kenneth F. Kiple. 1988.

Kenneth F. Kiple

Hebrews

See Ancient Middle East; Bible; Jews; Judaism; Law.

Hegel, G. W. F.   [1770–1831]

Idealist philosopher and dialectician.

Much of Hegel's thought on slavery can be found in his *Encyclopaedia of the Philosophical Sciences* (1817), *The Philosophy of Right* (1821), and *The Phenomenology of Mind* (1807).

Hegel saw slavery not simply in terms of right and wrong but in terms of its necessary role in the development of human civilization.

Slavery arose not merely from force but also from the desire of the conqueror for recognition. The simple triumph of force produced the death of the defeated. Slavery arose when one combatant (the master) was prepared to risk his life, while another (the slave) was not.

The master had made an advance over simple animality in his triumph over the fear of death, but the slave who labored for the benefit of the master overcame the negativity of nature by shaping the material world, objectifying reason in the product of his labor, and thereby learning invaluable skills.

The slave rose above egoism because he had to work for the benefit of another. A discipline breaking the hold of self-will arose, so that slavery and tyranny were relatively justified in preparing men for freedom. The struggle of the slave for freedom helped to free the master from his own narrow particularity, forcing him to recognize the slave's personhood.

Finally, in history, Christianity led to the end of slavery and serfdom because its emphasis upon interior freedom eventually achieved its fullest expression in liberty within the social order.

Hegel's influence has been most marked in the approaches of the social sciences to historical development and through his influence on Marx and Marxist thought.

See also CHRISTIANITY; MARXISM; PHILOSOPHY.

BIBLIOGRAPHY

HEGEL, G. W. F. *The Encyclopaedia of the Philosophical Sciences.* Translated by William Wallace and A. V. Miller. 1971.
———. *Hegel's Philosophy of Right.* Edited and translated by T. M. Knox. 1975.
———. *The Phenomenology of Mind.* Translated by J. B. Bailie. 1967.
———. *The Philosophy of History.* Translated by J. Sibree. 1956.

Patrick M. O'Neil

Helots

See Ancient Greece.

Hemings, Sally   [1773–1835]

Domestic slave of Thomas Jefferson.

Born on a plantation in eastern Virginia, Sarah Hemings was the daughter of Elizabeth ("Betty") Hemings, an enslaved domestic servant of a wealthy planter, lawyer, and merchant engaged in the slave trade, John Wayles. According to her son Madison, Sally (as she was called) and five of her siblings were Wayles's children. After Wayles's death in 1773, Betty Hemings and her children became the property of his son-in-law Thomas Jefferson and were moved to Monticello, in Albemarle County.

At the age of fourteen Sally Hemings accompanied Jefferson's daughter Mary from Virginia to Paris, where Jefferson was minister to the court of Louis XVI. Here she was reunited with her brother James, who was Jefferson's chef, and began her training as lady's-maid to Jefferson's daughters. She was acting in this capacity when the family returned to Virginia late in 1789.

Sally Hemings lived at Monticello until Jefferson's death in 1826, a member of an enslaved domestic staff that was largely composed of her own relatives. Her duties, known only from the recollections of her son, included needlework and the care of Jefferson's room and wardrobe. Jefferson's records reveal the names and birthdates of four of her children who survived infancy. Hemings's son Beverly, a carpenter, and her daughter Harriet, a textile worker, left Monticello in 1821 or 1822, evidently with Jefferson's blessing and financial support. Her sons Madison and Eston Hemings, both carpenters and musicians, were freed by the terms of Jefferson's will. After Jefferson's death they lived with their mother, who was never legally freed, in the neighboring town of Charlottesville. Sally Hemings, who was listed as a free person of color in an Albemarle County census in 1833, had probably been "given her time" (unofficially freed) by Jefferson's daughter Martha Randolph, so that she would not be subject to the Virginia law prohibiting freed slaves from remaining in the state more than a year.

For the last thirty years of her life, Hemings was perhaps the best known slave in the United States. From the beginning of Jefferson's presidency, newspapers hinted at a master-slave liaison. In September 1802, private rumor became public allegation when the political writer James Thomson Callender published in the Richmond *Recorder* the specific claim that Sally Hemings was Jefferson's mistress and the mother of his children. She immediately became subject to the distortions of notoriety. According to the few surviving accounts, she was a beautiful woman with long straight hair and a very light complexion, but in the partisan Federalist press she became an object of extreme racial stereotyping.

Callender's story rippled through the publications of Jefferson's political enemies and was kept alive by nineteenth-century critics of both slavery and the United States. Abolitionists pointed to the liaison between Hemings and Jefferson to highlight their own holy cause. Foreign commentators cited Jefferson as a personification of the profound contradictions in the American political system. This view of a hypocritical nation espousing liberty and enslaving one-sixth of its inhabitants was memorably expressed by the Irish poet Thomas Moore, whose verse portrayed a president "who dreams of freedom in his slave's embrace" (1806).

Those closest to the issue took no part in the public discussion. Jefferson maintained his customary silence when under personal attack, and there is no known direct testimony from Sally Hemings. Jefferson's daughter and grandchildren strenuously, though privately, denied such a relationship. A grandson, who admitted that Hemings's children bore a striking resemblance to Jefferson, assigned blame to Jefferson's Carr nephews. Madison Hemings's assertion that he was the son of Jefferson appeared in a newspaper in Ohio in 1873. His brother Eston made a more private statement by changing his surname to Jefferson when he moved into white society in Wisconsin in the 1850s. Descendants of Sally Hemings's sons (including those of Thomas C. Woodson, who state that their ancestor was Hemings's oldest child) carry a strong and enduring family tradition of Jefferson ancestry.

For all her celebrity, Sally Hemings is one of the least known members of a remarkable family. Over eighty of Betty Hemings's descendants lived in slavery at Monticello, and they occupied most of the important domestic and artisans' positions. Sally Hemings and her relatives have been eclipsed by the issue of her connection with Jefferson, which captured the public imagination in the late twentieth century, particularly after the publication of Fawn Brodie's biography of Jefferson in 1974 and Barbara Chase-Riboud's novel *Sally Hemings* (1979). Linked with Jefferson in popular and scholarly debate, Sally Hemings has been implicated in discussions of Jefferson's character, the validity of African American oral tradition, and the legacy of slavery and miscegenation. Over two centuries, she has had a striking symbolic importance that reflects changing attitudes toward American society and the American past.

See also JEFFERSON, THOMAS; MISCEGENATION.

BIBLIOGRAPHY

BEAR, JAMES A., JR. "The Hemings Family of Monticello." *Virginia Cavalcade* 29 (1979): 84–85.
BRODIE, FAWN M. *Thomas Jefferson: An Intimate History*. 1974.
GORDON-REED, ANNETTE. *Thomas Jefferson and Sally Hemings: An American Controversy*. 1997.
STANTON, LUCIA. *The African-American Families at Monticello*. 1998.

Lucia C. Stanton

Henson, Josiah   [1789–1883]

Ex-slave, minister, author.

The talented Josiah Henson was born a slave in Maryland in 1789. Later he was made the manager, or overseer, of a plantation in Maryland. In 1825 he led a coffle of slaves from his master's plantation in Maryland to the plantation of his master's brother, in Kentucky. On the way through free territory in Ohio he refused to help the slaves under his charge escape in Cincinnati. Henson's deep religious views and own sense of integrity prevented him from "stealing" property, even human property, from his master. Eventually, however, Henson stole himself, escaping to Canada with his wife in 1830. There he became a minister, learned to read, served as a captain in the Essex Company of Colored Volunteers during the Canadian Rebellion (1837–1838), and started a manual training school that mostly served blacks who had escaped from the United States. In the 1840s Henson went back to Kentucky to help slaves escape to Canada.

Henson published his autobiography, *The Life of Josiah Henson, Formerly a Slave, Now and Inhabitant of Canada as Narrated by Himself*, in 1849. He later expanded versions of his autobiography in 1858, 1876, and 1878. On two trips to England he met Queen Victoria, as well as various English leaders, including

Josiah Henson. [Corbis-Bettmann]

Lord John Russell and the Archbishop of Canterbury. On a trip to the United States he was the guest of President Rutherford B. Hayes. Henson became the model for Uncle Tom in Harriet Beecher Stowe's *Uncle Tom's Cabin.* Like the fictional Tom, Henson was religious and carried out his tasks, even when unpleasant. But the differences between the two are significant. The fictional Tom allowed himself to be sold South, where he was ultimately beaten to death by the evil Simon Legree. Tom, however, stands firmly in defense of his own people. Henson, on the other hand, refused to help his fellow slaves but eventually escaped from slavery and returned to help others escape. Henson's life illustrated the complexities of slavery for its victims, as well as demonstrating the ability of some slaves to escape bondage and rise to prominence.

See also STOWE, HARRIET BEECHER.

BIBLIOGRAPHY

BEATTIE, LOUISE. *Black Moses: The Real Uncle Tom.* 1857.
HENSON, JOSIAH. *The Autobiography of Josiah Henson (Harriet Beecher Stowe's "Uncle Tom").* 1876.

Paul Finkelman

Hepburn, John   [ca. 1667–ca. 1763]

Quaker abolitionist.

John Hepburn immigrated in 1684 to eastern North America, where he was bound for four years as an indentured servant to the Scots Proprietors of the colony of East Jersey (roughly, the northern part of present-day New Jersey). Evidence about his life and witness against slavery is sketchy beyond his ninety-four-page book, *The American Defence of the Christian Golden Rule* (1715). Hepburn was a tailor and owned land in several East Jersey locations, including Perth Amboy, a port through which Africans were imported into the colony. He considered himself a Quaker, but he may have been a follower of the schismatic George Keith, whose Christian Quakers in 1693 issued an antislavery tract.

In *American Defence,* one of the earliest published abolitionist works by a North American, Hepburn decried the growth of slavery in East Jersey as it swung markedly upward in the 1710s. He rebuked slave owners on a number of counts, blaming Quakers as well as members of other denominations for violating basic Christian principles. Like other abolitionist Quakers, Hepburn emphasized the effects of slavery on owners and their children: it bred laziness, vanity, and ostentation. His description of the conditions that New Jersey slaves endured—inadequate clothing and shelter,

harsh beatings, separation of families—undermines the notion that, at this time, northern slavery was milder than the developing institution in the Chesapeake Bay area and the Carolinas. While Hepburn's book elicited no direct response in the Quaker Philadelphia Yearly Meeting, he may have influenced members of Shrewsbury Monthly Meeting in East Jersey to free their slaves in their wills during the 1720s and 1730s, the first known emancipation movement among Quakers.

See also ABOLITION AND ANTISLAVERY MOVEMENTS; QUAKERS.

BIBLIOGRAPHY

CADBURY, HENRY J. "John Hepburn and His Book against Slavery, 1715." *Proceedings of the American Antiquarian Society,* n.s., 59 (1949): 89–160.
HEPBURN, JOHN. *The American Defence of the Christian Golden Rule; or, An Essay to Prove the Unlawfulness of Making Slaves of Men.* 1715.

Jean R. Soderlund

Hinduism

The Sanskrit term *dāsa* means, at various times and in various contexts, slave, demon, enemy, infidel, barbarian, and servant. It is etymologically related to the term *dasyu,* which also means demon and was the early term used by the Aryans for the indigenous people of South Asia. The institution of slavery in ancient India (before 600 B.C.) was both widely known and widely practiced. In later times (600 B.C.–A.D. 1776) the slave was so pervasive an element of Indian society that the Sanskrit legal literature has extensive provisions for the institution of slavery and the place of slaves in everyday life. For example, the *Nāradasmṛti* (ca. A.D. 200), describes fifteen categories of slaves. These range from individuals born into slavery as the children of slaves to those captured in battle and forced into slavery, those pledged as security for a loan, or those who had to sell themselves into slavery from financial exigency.

Gifts of slaves are mentioned frequently in the great Indian epic the *Mahābhārata* (ca. A.D. 200). Slaves were clearly participants in the commercial and legal life of ancient India, as evidenced by the number of provisions cautioning that slaves were not legally competent to enter into contracts or to make sales. The one exception was that a slave could enter into a debt if that debt was for the good of the family he served. Under these circumstances, the debt was the obligation of the slave owner. There was debate over the question whether or not a *brāhmaṇa* (the highest caste) woman could be sold into slavery, but some held the view that under no circumstances could a *brāhmaṇa* man become a slave. However, if a man willingly sold himself into slavery, we are told that such a person was the most evil wretch in society. The status of slave precluded an individual (i.e., a man) from performing prescribed religious rituals, and failure to perform these rituals had, in the Hindu view, dire consequences for the individual, for his family, and for society as a whole. Thus, to voluntarily give up one's right to perform these rituals was a terrible thing. Slaves generally fell outside of the discussions of dharma (righteousness) since these discussions prescribed the appropriate behavior for righteous people. The status of slave was either temporary—and therefore one's behavior should conform to the permanent status one held in society—or permanent, in which case the slave's dharma was simply to fulfill the wishes of the owner and thus needed no further elaboration.

The lot of a slave varied a great deal. Megasthenes, a fourth-century B.C. Greek emissary to India, could not identify slaves in the circles in which he traveled, and so we might deduce that the treatment of slaves was so similar to that accorded to the lowest castes of society that he could not make the distinction. Both the Hindu legal texts and the dictates of the Buddha provided some measure of protection for slaves. Slaves could be beaten, for example, but only with a rope or a thin piece of bamboo, and then only on the back, never on the head. A slave owner violating these rules was liable to confiscation of the slave, prosecution as a thief, or both. Enforcement of this rule fell to the king.

It would seem that marriage between slaves and freemen occurred. There is a specific provision in the *Katyāyanasmṛti* (A.D. 725) that stipulates that a woman who marries a slave becomes a slave herself, since her husband is her master and he is himself subject to another master. In the reverse case, a man who married a slave would in effect "own" her and was free to liberate her.

See also CASTE SYSTEMS; INDIAN SUBCONTINENT.

BIBLIOGRAPHY

CHANANA, D. R. *Slavery in Ancient India As Depicted in Pali and Sanskrit Texts.* 1960.

CHOUDHURY, R. K. "Visti (Forced Labour) in Ancient India." *Indian Historical Quarterly* 38 (1962): 44–59.

RAI, G. K. "Forced Labor in Ancient and Early Medieval India." *Indian Historical Review* 3 (1976): 16–42.

REUBEN, WALTER. *Die Lage der Sklaven in der altindischen Gesellschaft.* 1957.

Richard W. Lariviere

Historical Approaches to Slavery

This entry, prepared by the editors of this encyclopedia in close consultation, includes the following articles: An Overview; United States; Bibliography of Slavery. Paul Finkelman made important substantive contributions to Joseph C. Miller's two articles, as Professor Miller did to Professor Finkelman's article.

In addition, the reader should note that the bibliography that follows An Overview also usefully supplements the works cited in United States. The full titles of the works cited in Bibliography of Slavery, however, will be found in A Select Bibliography of Slavery, in the Appendix near the end of Volume 2.

Articles related to those in this entry may be found at the entry Historiography of Slavery.

An Overview

Because nineteenth-century abolition and emancipation had ended legal enforcement of slavery nearly everywhere in the world, the institution entered twentieth-century scholarship already in a vaguely "historical" mode—an arrangement from the past that was deemed best forgotten in academic circles, so long as those circles reflected the dominant culture of shamed former masters. In the Americas, freed former slaves and their descendants retained vivid memories of slavery, but these were private souvenirs of a troubled past; few blacks had the standing to write publicly or as scholars. In the 1950s, as slavery and the struggles that had ended it faded from living memory, recollection fell to professional historians trained to consult the evidence left by others who had experienced it directly. In Europe nineteenth-century abolitionism stimulated a parallel struggle over memories of slavery, but it was located in a more distant past. European polemicists who diminished slavery in an idealized ancient Mediterranean as a moral exemplar for an abolitionist present debated more dispassionate analysts who hoped to discern why the Greeks and Romans had become masters and how they had conducted themselves in that role.

Debates between moralists and technicians, ranging through subtle shadings from deliberate propagandists to curious antiquarians, have framed most subsequent approaches to a subject that has been rendered persistently emotional by continuing racism and other violations of human rights, and thus has remained very much present even as slavery itself has receded in time and became accessible only through the methodology of professional historians. These methods of the historical discipline and how they have

An author writes down the stories of several freeborn African-Americans who had been kidnapped into slavery in 1822.
[Library of Congress/Corbis]

influenced recent understandings of slavery are the focus of this essay. An imagined past may be appropriated for polemical purposes by directing historians' techniques selectively toward the private ends of the polemicist; but historians—always within limits set by questions derived from their personal inclinations and cultural background—apply formal methods comprehensively to all available sources and reach rigorous conclusions regardless of their personal beliefs. Historians—though no longer aspiring to the higher standard of a "pursuit of truth"—distinguish their own quest for understanding from the creative arts by anchoring it in empirical research; they distinguish themselves from the empirical social sciences by narrating their understanding through changes produced by human agency (rather than by delineating the logical coherence of equilibrium states or timeless structures), against a background of the time and place in which the actors lived. By this standard, slavery, isolated from its historical context as an "institution" or a "relationship" of transcendent essence is understood in terms of other than historical.

The first generation of professional historians of slavery in the United States approached the subject in the 1950s though laws enacted by masters to define property rights in human beings and to secure profits from their slaves' labors, and because of this (or as a result) they understood it largely in terms of masters' expectations. Slaves' voices were heard in the positivist academic circles of that time only through disciplines regarded as less rigorous and thus less reputable: folklore and, occasionally in Brazil and the Caribbean, cultural anthropology. In the 1960s, to examine the witness of the slaves themselves, "social" historians appropriated folklore and anthropology as part of a very broad movement throughout the discipline to hear the testimony of the otherwise inarticulate—peasants, workers, women, colonized subjects. So-called quantitative methods served this end by drawing an outline of aggregate behavior from vast numbers of quasi-anonymous, social-science-like observations in census counts, legal documents, fiscal records, baptismal registers, and new readings of narrative sources. Historians then speculated on what the statistical parameters calculated from aggregates they created from them might reveal. One example of the insights gained in this way was the now axiomatic distinctive ability of United States slaves to reproduce themselves since early in the eighteenth century. The categories highlighted by social history methods, often demographic, appeared unproblematic against the structural background of nearly all scholarship of that era, whether the "classes" of Marxism or the "institutions" of Weberian sociology.

But the extensive records that quantitative methods revealed as evidence bearing on slaves' lives also exposed underappreciated slave initiatives, even under oppressive laws; the profit-driven domination of their masters; and the confines of apparently rigid institutions. Historians first noticed that slaves had been active in resistance and revolt, the initiatives that most concerned—indeed, threatened—the masters. But they pushed on at once to the structure of the lives the slaves created among themselves and sought the personal motivations, for masters and slaves alike, behind the collective behavior observed through the methodology of social science. John Blassingame's "slave community" and Eugene Genovese's "paternalist" masters and enslaved Christians marked the emergence of this trend in the United States in the early 1970s.

The search thus launched for meaning, particularly for how people living under slavery experienced it, has led to rereadings of familiar narrative sources through the fresh eyes of literary critical theory, to consultation of the maturing field of African history to sense who the people arriving as slaves in the Americas may have been, and to a historicized cultural anthropology to explore the slaves' own mental worlds. With the slaves' and masters' intimately interlinked worlds thus sketched in, historians in the 1990s have applied the historicizing tendencies under way throughout the academic disciplines to integrate their relationships in the broader changing historical contexts that they must also have reflected. Such cultural history is leading, in turn, to a dynamic understanding of slavery's structural aspects—its laws and economic "institutions"—as creations changing in response to the tensions in the lives of actors on both sides; thus individual voices are being heard against the background chorus. The most recent work has begun to detect individuals within the groups to which historians previously felt themselves limited by their evidence. Advances in these directions foretell interest in the psychology of domination and in how mental processes produced the abstracted models of slavery that perpetuated it.

Historians of the United States led the way, largely because of two special circumstances: They were favored with access to records of unparalleled richness, and further, they were spurred on to what may fairly be called a historiographical rivalry by the civil rights movement and various other racially based aspects of 1960s' and 1970s' politics. Meanwhile, scholars elsewhere were discovering that slavery had been a worldwide phenomenon. Historians in Africa and Asia and throughout the Caribbean and Latin America—influenced by the revolution in social history that had focused primary attention on the search for the "invisible man" (i.e., ordinary people)—explored the lives of slaves in detail. A lack of adequate resources, however, forced these scholars to argue more often by analogy and inference than from hard evidence. The field of ancient history, on the other hand, already possessed rigorous, tried-and-true methods for extracting meaning from the scarce and difficult-to-interpret sources available to it—epigraphs, theatrical evidence, archaeological data, and the like. When ancient historians applied these methods to slaves and masters, they produced analyses rich in detail, nuance, and specificity. These analyses easily dislodged the view of slavery as an "institution," a view that textual descriptions and Roman law had previously seemed to support.

Historians now see slavery itself as a fast-moving process that each generation experienced in characteristic ways, indeed a process that each slave and master experienced uniquely—though both slave and master nonetheless imagined themselves living in an enduring, even universal "institution" that served their own interests in surviving or imposing it. Thus historians have brought within a more classical framework of historical style and method a subject that had originated in political contention and that had long been seen through approaches derived from other academic disciplines.

See also AFRICA; ANCIENT GREECE; ANCIENT MIDDLE EAST; ANCIENT ROME; BRAZIL; CARIBBEAN REGION; SLAVE NARRATIVES.

BIBLIOGRAPHY

BLASSINGAME, JOHN W. *The Slave Community: Plantation Life in the Antebellum South*. Rev. ed. 1979.

CRATON, MICHAEL M. *Searching for the Invisible Man: Slaves and Plantation Life in Jamaica*. 1977.

DAVID, PAUL A., HERBERT G. GUTMAN, RICHARD SUTCH, PETER TEMIN, and GAVIN WRIGHT. *Reckoning with Slavery: A Critical Study in the Quantitative History of American Negro Slavery*. Introduction by Kenneth Stampp. 1976.

DU BOIS, W. E. B. *The Negro*. Introduction by Herbert Aptheker. 1915. Reprint, 1975.

EGYPT, OPHELIA SETTLE, J. MASUOKA, and CHARLES S. JOHNSON, eds. *Unwritten History of Slaves: Autobiographical Accounts of Negro Ex-Slaves*. 2nd ed. 1968.

FINLEY, MOSES I. *Ancient Slavery and Modern Ideology*. 1980.

FOGEL, ROBERT W., and STANLEY L. ENGERMAN. *Time on the Cross: The Economics of American Negro Slavery*. 2 vols. 1974. Reissued with new afterword by Fogel, 1989.

GENOVESE, EUGENE D. *Roll, Jordan, Roll: The World the Slaves Made*. 1974.

MEIER, AUGUST, and ELLIOT RUDWICK. *Black History and the Historical Profession, 1950–1990*. 1986.

PALMIÉ, STEPHAN, ed. *Slave Cultures and the Cultures of Slavery*. 1995.

RAWICK, GEORGE P., ed. *The American Slave: A Composite Autobiography.* 19 vols. 1972.

———. *The American Slave: A Composite Autobiography.* Supplement, Series 2. 1979.

SMITH, JOHN DAVID. *An Old Creed for the New South: Proslavery Ideology and Historiography, 1865–1910.* 1985.

Joseph C. Miller

United States

Even before the American Civil War, histories of slavery appeared as part of the debate over the institution. Most of the early histories in the United States were by proslavery writers. The most comprehensive was Thomas R. R. Cobb's "An Historical Sketch of Slavery," which formed an eighteen-chapter, 228-page preface to his book *An Inquiry into the Law of Negro Slavery in the United States of America* (1858). Cobb tried to prove that slavery had always been part of human culture, that southerners were not responsible for slavery in the United States, and that on the whole, slavery, and particularly the enslavement of Africans, was a good thing. Although not academically trained, Cobb was a scholar and a cofounder of the institution that eventually became the University of Georgia School of Law.

The first generation of professional historians in the United States emerged just as Reconstruction was ending in the South. These scholars, nationalist in their vision and antislavery in their sentiments, rarely wrote about slaves but did write sympathetically about abolitionists, while condemning slavery as a political, social, and economic institution. Hermann Eduard Von Holst (*Constitutional and Political History of the United States,* 7 vol., 1876–1892) and John Bach McMaster (*A History of the People of the United States,* 8 vols., 1883–1913) blamed slavery for the American Civil War. James Ford Rhodes, although a racist (and not professionally trained), nevertheless offered blistering attacks on slavery and the treatment of slaves in his enormously influential *History of the United States from the Compromise of 1850* (9 vols., 1892–1922). Albert Bushnell Hart, the premier historian of the antebellum United States, a Harvard professor and president of the American Historical Association, also took a neoabolitionist position on slavery. Hart was the mentor of the first African-American to earn a Ph.D. in history, W. E. B. Du Bois. Starting in the 1890s a new generation of historians, such as James C. Ballagh, Jeffrey R. Brackett, John Spencer Bassett, and Howell M. Henry, produced detailed institutional monographs about slavery, focusing on specific states, legal developments, or economic issues. Although many of these studies were racist in tone and analysis, they were nevertheless pioneering forays into the archives, manuscript collections, and newspaper holdings of the newly emerging graduate research institutions, including Columbia, Johns Hopkins, Michigan, Yale, and Vanderbilt. They were generally descriptive and accepted that slavery was wrong but assumed that blacks were inferior to whites. These set the stage for the first single-volume history of the subject, *American Negro Slavery,* published by Ulrich B. Phillips in 1918.

Phillips was the grandson of a Georgia planter who had owned 1,500 acres and twenty-four slaves on the eve of the Civil War. Phillips eared a Ph.D. at Columbia and eventually taught at Wisconsin, Tulane, Michigan, and Yale. *American Negro Slavery* made extensive use of primary sources, including plantation records and other manuscripts. While thoroughly scholarly, it was nevertheless racist in its overall approach. Phillips talked about plantations as "schools for civilization" and argued that slaves were treated better than workers in the North. He claimed that only a southern white, "intimately acquainted with the negro character and with the mild nature of his servitude," could write validly about slavery.

Generations of black scholars, and a few whites, who had never accepted the racism of Phillips and his predecessors established a second, less apologetic stream of scholarship. Before the Civil War some black abolitionists, such as William C. Nell and J. W. C. Pennington, had used history as part of their attack on slavery. In his two-volume work, *History of the Negro Race from 1619 to 1880* (1882), George Washington Williams condemned slavery for its cruelties and challenged proslavery defenses of the institution. In 1896 W. E. B. Du Bois, published *The Suppression of the African Slave Trade to the United States of America, 1638–1870,* the first of a long series of scholarly works by blacks on the history of slavery. Later, in *The Souls of Black Folk* (1903), Du Bois began using folktales, songs, and other nonarchival sources to get at the heart of slavery and the experience of blacks under slavery.

The *Journal of Negro History,* begun in 1916 under the editorship of Carter G. Woodson, published documents relating to slavery, often from the perspective of slaves, along with numerous articles on slavery by black and white scholars alike. These perspectives were almost always sympathetic to the slave and hostile to the institution. In the 1920s the Carnegie Institution in Washington, D.C., funded two massive projects that gave scholars access to many primary sources about slavery: Elizabeth Donnan's *Documents Illustrative of the History of the Slave Trade to America* (1930–1935) and Helen T. Catterall's *Judicial Cases concerning American Slavery and the Negro* (1926–1937). From World War I until the end of World War II a cadre of black scholars, including Benjamin Quarles, John Hope Franklin, Charles Wesley, Charles S. Johnson, E. Franklin Frazier, Lorenzo Greene, John G. Van Deusen, Rayford Logan, and Carter Woodson, created a small library of monographic studies and more sweeping histories of African-American life under slavery. Some white scholars, notably Frank L. Klingberg and Herbert Aptheker, added to this literature. In 1948 John Hope Franklin's *From Slavery to Freedom: A History of American Negroes* gave legitimacy to African-American history among mainstream white historians and gave all readers of the book an understanding of American bondage through the eyes of the slaves, rather than from the perspective of the masters.

Otherwise, as a result of Phillips's impeccable scholarly credentials and his extensive research, *American Negro Slavery* dominated academic understanding of slavery in the United States until the publication of Kenneth Stampp's *The Peculiar Institution* in 1956. Stampp, like Phillips, made extensive use of plantation records. He was able to refute Phillips's contentions about the mildness of the law of slavery in part because Catterall's collection gave him access to all the published legal opinions on slavery. Where Phillips had seen blacks as inferior, Stampp argued that race did not matter at all. Phillips had blamed blacks' incompetence and criminality for broken tools, poor maintenance of the plantation, or food and animals stolen from the master, but Stampp understood these as calculated day-to-day resistance resulting from the slaves' sense that they were entitled to get enough to eat. Phillips had argued that slavery was mild and that harsh laws were rarely enforced; Stampp detailed the legal decisions implementing an overall policy designed "to make them stand in fear." Much of Stampp's work was based on the pioneering work of earlier scholars who published in the *Journal of Negro History*, as well as on Catterall's important compilation of legal cases.

Almost simultaneously, Stanley Elkins, in *Slavery; A Problem in American Institutional and Intellectual Life* (1959), consolidated Stampp's neoabolitionist approach. However, a controversial chapter on "Sambo" as a stereotypical slave personality had overtones of Phillips's proslavery approach and Phillips's notion of slaves as incapable. Drawing an analogy between plantation slaves and prisoners in concentration camps, Elkins argued that slavery "infantilized" Africans throughout the New World, especially in Protestant, Anglo-Saxon regions like the United States, though much less in the Catholic colonies and nations of South America and the Caribbean. A small cottage industry of articles and books appeared at once to refute most of Elkins's arguments, logic, and history by

documenting the resilience and creativity of the people living under slavery. By the 1970s and 1980s the field was dominated by works of this genre, such as Charles Joyner's *Down by the Riverside: A South Carolina Slave Community* (1984), Herbert Gutmann's *The Black Family in Slavery and Freedom, 1750–1925* (1976), and—perhaps most important of all—John Blassingame's *The Slave Community: Plantation Life in the American South* (1972). Works on slave rebellions, including Gerald W. Mullin's *Flight and Rebellion* (1970), Peter Wood's *Black Majority; Negroes in Colonial South Carolina from 1670 through the Stono Rebellion* (1974), Douglas Edgerton's *Gabriel's Rebellion: The Virginia Slave Conspiracies of 1800 and 1802* (1993), and Thomas J. Davis's *A Rumor of Revolt* (1985) set the scholarship of slavery firmly in the direction of black resistance and the creation of African-American cultures under slavery. Other books on slave religion, education among slaves, and slave women, for example, fleshed out the diversity of slave culture, exemplified by Lawrence Levine's massive *Black Culture and Black Consciousness: Afro-American Folk Thought from Slavery to Freedom* (1977).

A field of "abolitionist" history studying the opponents of slavery developed in the 1960s, led by David Brion Davis's *The Problem of Slavery in Western Culture* (1966) and *The Problem of Slavery in the Age of Revolution* (1975), which placed antislavery in a broad international context. Studies of antislavery movements in the United States, such as James B. Stewart's *Holy Warriors* (rev. ed., 1997), as well as a multitude of biographies and case studies, have sharpened our understanding of opposition to slavery. Economic historians, feeding massive amounts of data into computers in attempts to quantify everything from how much slaves ate to how often they were whipped, added to the body of knowledge about how slaves lived and made slavery part of the general economic history of the United States. Political historians debate the issue of slavery as part of American national party politics, local elections, and of course, the coming of the Civil War. Social historians provide detailed information about the day-to-day life of slaves, and demographic historians have examined births, death, and other intimate details of the lives of large numbers of slaves. Medical historians have studied the health of slaves. Legal and constitutional historians have offered detailed accounts of how law affected slavery and how slavery in turn affected general legal developments in the United States.

These studies of slavery and slaves' lives underscored the centrality of slavery to American life from the early eighteenth century until abolition of the institution in 1865. How Americans have thought about slavery has affected how they have thought about race relations in each generation. In the period before and just after World War I, Phillips and his generation supported the development of statutory segregation throughout the South, and in much of the rest of the nation as well. This was true also in the 1950s and 1960s, when "neoabolitionists" like Stampp provided intellectual support for the civil rights movement. It remains so at the end of the twentieth century, as a presidentially appointed commission on race relations struggles to offer guidance to the nation on this troubling issue. The chairman of that commission is the distinguished historian John Hope Franklin, who began his career studying the free blacks in the slave South before writing his magisterial history of African-Americans, *From Slavery to Freedom.*

See also ABOLITIONISM AND ANTISLAVERY MOVEMENTS; COBB, THOMAS R. R.; DEMOGRAPHY AND DEMOGRAPHIC THEORIES OF SLAVERY; DU BOIS, W. E. B.; ELKINS THESIS; GABRIEL'S REBELLION; HEALTH; HISTORIOGRAPHY OF SLAVERY; LAW; PERSPECTIVES ON SLAVERY; REBELLIONS AND VIOLENT RESISTANCE.

BIBLIOGRAPHY

See the bibliography for the preceding article, An Overview.

Paul Finkelman

Bibliography of Slavery

As of 1997 some fifteen thousand scholarly publications featuring slavery as their primary focus had appeared in western European languages in this century (Miller 1993, 1998). This outpouring of academic energy—much of it historical, but also works in economics and law, as well as sociology and anthropology, folklore, demography and (in recent years) also literary criticism and archaeology—represents only the tip of a massive iceberg of postemancipation preoccupation with the sins of the slaving fathers and the sufferings of their human property. Hierarchy fascinates modern egalitarian liberals, and antipathy toward it has inspired scholars to include slavery in an even broader range of other studies on colonialism, early Christian theology, agricultural history, Marxism, macroeconomics, and all forms of power and domination.

The bulk of this work—aside from an independent debate among European classicists, Marxists and non-Marxists, on Greek and Roman slavery (Finley 1980)—originated with African and African-American slaves' quest for freedom in the Americas, the modern world's "promised land." Scholars of the freedom generations—George Washington Williams (1882), W. E. B. Du Bois (1896), Booker T. Washington (1904), Eric Williams (1944), and C. L. R. James (1963)—drew inspiration from the oppression that their parents and grandparents had overcome, and the subject flowered in the hothouse of twentieth-century liberal defense of human rights. The resulting rich, often moving academic literature has helped transform the racist, paternalist premises of most scholarship early in the century, often exemplified by U. B. Phillips' (1918) interpretation of plantation slavery in the U.S. South as a "school constantly training and controlling pupils . . . in a backward state of civilization" (p. 342). But slavery, seen through the prisms of ideological struggles over its heritage in the immediate postemancipation era, appeared "peculiar," not only in a United States otherwise nominally dedicated to freedom, but also as a deviation from an otherwise steady, broadly European progress toward human perfection and as a noncapitalist drag in an age of enterprising wage-earning workers. This self-centered emphasis on slavery as an anomaly ignored the significance of slavery elsewhere in the world (beyond the Caribbean and Brazil), sometimes vigorously denying its very existence (Finley 1980).

The narrow focus has since widened to emphasize the ubiquity of slavery throughout world history before the nineteenth century, in tones ranging from resentment as to its injustice to coldly objective calculations of its material, social, and political causes and effects, to tragico-ironic acceptance of its human costs. In the ironic mode, it is now clear that enslaved people contributed most to the very fonts of prized democratic/republican values and institutions, even the ideal of human freedom: ancient Greece and Rome, liberal Britain, the foundational era of the United States, and prerevolutionary France (Davis 1984; Patterson 1991). African-American outrage at the continuing injustices of twentieth-century racial discrimination was so intimately linked with the slavery under which their ancestors had labored—sentiments mirrored by white liberals' corresponding guilt about the past as well as the present—that the first modern historiography of the subject after World War II often mixed slavery indistinguishably with race (Tannenbaum 1947; Handlin and Handlin 1950; Mellafe 1964; Jordan 1968; Mörner 1970; Lewis 1971/1990; Degler 1971; Engerman and Genovese, eds. 1975). Only slowly, with growing awareness of the nonracial justification for most slavery throughout world history (Evans 1980; Finley 1980; Patterson 1982), has scholarship clearly differentiated the discrimination of race from the domination of slavery.

In academic terms, scholars of slavery rode the developing wave of 1960s and 1970s inclusive social history from studying the institution as masters conceived it to exploring how slaves experienced it. They exploited untapped sources that echoed the voices of people who had left few articulate records of their own, emphasizing—distinctively in the United States—narratives of former slaves (*Slave Narratives* 1941, Egypt 1945, Bontemps 1969, Yetman 1970, Starobin 1971, 1974, Rawick 1972/1979, Escott 1979). Methodological inventiveness remained a hallmark of the field, as historians plumbed American plantation records, local government archives, economic data, records of slave sales and auctions, census counts, and legal materials (including judicial opinions, trial-court records, and statutes) as indicators of slaves' behavior, perceptions, and motivations. The technical challenge posed by scattered and incomplete data and its often oblique bearing on slaves' experiences, against the subjects' background of strong racial stereotypes, occasionally pushed historians beyond inspired creativity to dubious inventiveness (Fogel and Engerman 1974; per critics, e.g., Gutman 1975; David et al. 1976; Kolchin 1992).

The first attempts to discover the slaves' world reinterpreted the masters' patronizing images of their wards as helpless victims of a plantation oppression as total as nineteenth-century antislavery propaganda had depicted it (Elkins 1959). Only slowly did mainstream historians discover the slaves' enduring resilience, the overt and covert resistance to their bondage that they mounted (following Aptheker 1943), the communities they created to support themselves (Blassingame 1972; Gutman 1976), and their own ideas, integrity, and pride (Genovese 1974; Stuckey 1987). Extending the inseparable poles of the individual "master-slave dyad" (Patterson 1982) to sense the interdependence of the interacting groups, studies revealed intimately linked *Slave Cultures and the Culture of Slavery* (Palmié, ed. 1995; also Sobel 1987).

Political economists had begun by depicting slavery as an entity unto itself, as an anachronism in a modern capitalist economy, isolated and doomed to failure; in this separatist depiction resonated triumphalist moral justifications for the then-still-recent suppression of the institution (but not reflected in the classic Nieboer 1900). Marxist theory in the 1950s and 1960s, which sharply distinguished slavery from other modes of production like capitalism (Meillassoux 1986/1991), implicitly confirmed this sense that slavery was a world apart—particularly in the ancient Mediterranean (Padgug 1976; Ste. Croix 1981, 1988; Konstan 1986) but also in early China—and posed inevitable, revolutionary conflicts between two incompatible ways of life. Among non-Marxist political economists (see Moses I. Finley's influential 1968 equivalent notion of a "slave system"), background Cold War polarization of freedom and totalitarianism invited a one-dimensional classification of slavery with all other labor systems viewed as deviations from normative free-market economics: serfdom, debt bondage, Indian caste, corvée and other forms of government-forced labor, brainwashing of prisoners, even incarceration of criminals (e.g., Dovring 1965; Reuck and Knight, eds. 1967; Domar 1970; Engerman 1995, 1996; M. Bush, 1996; Lovejoy and Rogers 1994). The conglomerated abstractly negative class of coercive strategies resulting from this scholarly attitude was defined more by its violation of idealized individual autonomy than by similarities in the circumstances in which these systems arose, the methods of compulsion employed to establish the control attained, their frequently unforced disappearance, or the understandings of the people involved on either side.

This isolating view, because it reified slavery as a principle of control operating independent of time or space, invited a search for its essence by identifying—and then discounting—its variant aspects in specific historical contexts, typically, at first, the accompanying degree of its racial exclusiveness. But the comparative strategy subverted the intention of identifying a single essence by calling attention to the infinite historical particularity of the slave experiences it revealed society by society. Scholars active in the fields of non-Western area studies proliferating during the 1970s—particularly Africa (Miers and Kopytoff, eds. 1977; Meillassoux 1981; Robertson and Klein, eds. 1983), but also the Islamic world (Lewis 1971) and southeastern Asia (Reid 1983)—discovered unsuspected histories of slavery in the world regions they studied (culminating in Patterson 1982). They gradually showed how laws of slavery, employments of slaves, even the premises of their inequality, expressed the values of the cultures in which they occurred. The opposition presumed between slavery and capitalist wage employment blurred, and a thoroughly capitalist interpretation of American slave systems gradually emerged (Stampp 1956; Conrad and Meyer 1958; Fogel and Engerman 1974; Craton 1974, 1977; Fox-Genovese and Genovese 1983; Schwartz 1986; Miller 1988). Capitalist slavery, in fact, turned out to have shown considerable economic vitality and little prospect of ending without the force that abolitionists mustered against it (Drescher 1977, 1986; Eltis 1987).

Scholars thus historicized slavery, previously seen mostly in terms of its static internal structures of domination, by integrating its practice into the economic, demographic, and intellectual contexts in which people had claimed dominion over other human beings through the centuries. A previously relatively obscure critique of European capitalism, which attributed eighteenth-century acceleration in economic growth in Europe to profits made from slavery in the Americas (Williams 1944), gained attention in the light of world-systems theories, which became prominent in the 1970s. According to these, large regions of the world—and eventually the entire globe—diverged in complementary ways as European trade brought them into contact. Capital accumulated within a wealthy, industrialized, wage-paying western European core, and poorer peasant, share- and tenant-farming regions supplied its urban populations with foodstuffs and basic industrial raw materials. Slavery and other coerced labor systems intensified in a periphery to produce precious metals and raw materials for luxury consumption goods (Wallerstein 1974–1989; Wolf 1982; Solow, ed. 1991). Wars among populations not otherwise integrated into the system—notably Africa—generated slaves, whom trading networks within the system transported to toil in the mines and plantations of the periphery.

Within the microscale of these slave-worked producing units of the periphery, historians sought more intimate portraits of the slaves themselves. The stereotype of the implicitly male slave fieldhand (originally differentiated only according to plantation mistresses' associations with domestic servants in the "big house") began to break down to distinguish among women (Morrissey 1989; B. Bush 1990; Morton, ed. 1996; Gaspar and Hine, eds. 1996), mothers, children, conjugal units, conjure artists, escape artists, artisans, entrepreneurs, and many other members of vital and complex communities of the enslaved. The image of totally dominated labor softened with evidence of independent economic lives that slaves built for themselves (Cardoso 1988; Berlin and Morgan, eds. 1991). Aggregative, inherently anonymous quantitative methods—often demographic, or inspired by economic behavior—opened the windows onto these scenes, but their intricacy and the increasingly human qualities that historians thus found in the slaves led to a search for the meanings of slavery to the slaves, which literary critics pursued by examining narratives and poetry by and about slaves (Miller, current bibliographies in *Slavery and Abolition*).

Most scholars treated slavery within essentially national frameworks (though not Du Bois 1915), particularly in the comparative studies popular in the 1960s and 1970s (Tannenbaum 1947; M. Harris 1964; Genovese 1969; Degler 1971; see also Kolchin 1987; Watson 1989), and so the studies of intercontinental slave trades, integral to every significant concentration of slaves, developed as subjects largely separate from studies of the same people once they had been driven off the ships. For the Atlantic trade (see Mannix and Cowley 1962), Philip Curtin's *Census* (1969) defined the field in quantitative economic and demographic terms that nearly all subsequent studies have followed. It is accordingly known primarily in aggregates of volume, direction, mortality of slaves, and profitability for the slavers (H. Klein 1978; Lovejoy 1982, 1989). A definitive database that includes all the information on slaving voyages in the Atlantic collected during this quantitative phase of research (Eltis et al. 1998) provides analytical possibilities to link the movements of Africans to the regional histories of their origins in Africa and their destinations in the Americas. Broader work on the trade has set it in the context of its effects on African economies and societies (Inikori, ed. 1981; Inikori 1994) and accelerating European economic growth, limited and then eliminated by increasingly humanistic sensibilities (Anstey 1975; Rawley 1981; Eltis 1987; Miller 1988; Solow, ed. 1991; Inikori and Engerman, eds. 1992; Thomas 1997; see also Northrup 1994 for an anthology).

Mortality was the most accessible aspect of the experience of the people in the holds of the ships studied. Most scholars assumed that the Middle Passage so isolated and disabled its victims that they could contribute little to the process beyond occasional, futile revolts and survived it only to have to build lives in the New World essentially from scratch [Mintz and Price 1976/1992]. Studies of the Atlantic as a diaspora of African emigrants, enslaved but creating meaningful histories of their own have recently begun to give a sense that the slaves made much more significant contributions to the creation of new American societies (Thornton 1992/1998; Gilroy 1993; Berlin 1998; Gomez 1998; Morgan 1998; Palmer 1998).

Other trades, carrying slaves from Africa across the Sahara and the Red Sea and throughout the Indian Ocean, have received less attention, owing to the absence of quantitative data on them comparable to those available for the Atlantic (Toledano 1982; Clarence-Smith, ed. 1988; Savage, ed. 1992). Comprehensive histories of slavery in Africa have taken account of these export trades (Lovejoy 1983; Manning 1990), but scholars have yet to understand them as aspects of the distinctive—mostly Muslim—societies and economies that produced them (but see Toledano 1998). Even less is known about trading in the ancient Mediterranean (Bradley 1992), the often linked trades of medieval Europe and the contemporaneous expanding Islamic world (Phillips 1985; Constable 1996), the Renaissance Mediterranean (Phillips 1985), southern and southeastern Asia (Mukherjee 1967; Needham 1983), or the Pacific Ocean (Munro 1993; Luengo 1996).

Regional studies of slavery itself now cover virtually every area of the world (e.g., Central Asia: Paul 1994), though still often in implicit—and sometimes explicit—comparison with familiar modern Western forms of the institution. For classical Greece and

Rome, slavery is now accepted as prominent at least in Athens by the fifth century B.C. (Garlan 1988) and to have virtually repopulated Italy as Roman legions sent back war captives during two centuries of imperial conquests far beyond the Mediterranean (Bradley 1994), and as manumission filled the city of Rome with freed men and women and their descendants. Preoccupation with features of ancient Mediterranean slavery apparently anomalous compared to the U.S. South—opportunities for manumission provided under Roman law (Watson 1987), the comfort and responsibility that some urban, elite slaves enjoyed, and early Christianity's tolerance of the institution—have limited efforts to present slavery there on terms derived from the context of the times (recent survey interpretations in English: Patterson 1991; Wiedemann 1992; Garnsey 1996). Its medieval and Renaissance European sequels, long ignored, are being recognized as significant (in English: Bloch 1975; Dockès 1979; Saunders 1982; Hancock 1987; Karras 1988; Bonnassie 1991; Frantzen and Moffat, eds. 1994; Pelteret 1995; M. Bush, ed. 1996), as well as its counterpart in Russia (Hellie 1982).

As the history of Africa—the source of most of the slaves dispersed in modern times—has become clearer, slaves—especially women (Robertson and Klein, eds. 1983)—have been emphasized as contributing to larger-scale political and economic developments there, particularly as capitalist goods and credit obtained for the exported labor armed and financed developments in the eighteenth and nineteenth centuries (Lovejoy 1983; Manning 1990). Scholarship on seventeenth- and eighteenth-century Dutch slavery at the Cape of Good Hope has flourished separately, less in relation to the quite distinct patterns in tropical Africa than in comparison within the Americas plantation slavery (Worden 1985; Eldredge and Morton, eds. 1994).

For slavery in the Islamic world, attention has focused once again on qualities exotic by the standard of the Cotton Kingdom (Willis, ed. 1985; Gordon 1989), particularly the prominence of women as concubines, use of eunuchs, and deployment of military slave guards in the larger polities, and the tendency of the slave soldiers to seize power for themselves at moments of dynastic weakness (Crone 1980; Pipes 1981; Ayalon 1994; Toledano 1998). Slavery in Asia is accessible only through collections of small studies by specialists (Watson, ed. 1980; Warren 1981; Reid, ed. 1983; M. Klein, ed. 1993), except for India, where longstanding attention to inequality has moved beyond formal rankings of caste to illuminate ubiquitous and varied forms of slavery, Hindu as well as Muslim (J. Harris 1971; Patnaik and Dingwaney, eds. 1985; Prakash 1989; Lal 1994; Chauhan 1995). Studies of

Native Americans, both before and after contact with Europeans, are also taking account of slavery (e.g., Leland 1997).

Approaches to modern slavery in the tropical Americas have suffered less from continuing implicit comparison with the once-archetypal model of slavery in the nineteenth-century United States. Scholars in the Caribbean, in Hispanic America, and in Brazil have taken up the subject in the context of its legacies for their own national, and sometimes personal, experiences. The first generation to confront slavery in Brazil, in the 1920s, sought to overcome its postabolitionist image as responsible for a mulatto population deemed inferior by the pseudoscientific racism of the time. They interpreted Brazilian slavery as distinctively integrative rather than exclusionary and exploitative and saw Africans as contributing a distinctive vibrancy and diversity to the emergent national culture (Freyre 1933/1946). Subsequent generations of Brazilians rediscovered the harshness of the slaves' experiences in Brazil (Conrad 1994), the ways in which slavery and the slave trade subordinated the colony in the economic and political web of Portuguese imperial control ("Colonial Brazil" 1984; Graham, ed. 1991; Worden 1991), and its many regional variants: on sugar plantations (especially Schwartz 1986), in a booming, brutal eighteenth-century gold mining economy, in coastal cities (e.g., Karasch 1987), on cattle ranches, on nineteenth-century coffee estates (Stein 1957), and elsewhere (in English, in general: Mattoso 1986; Schwartz 1992). Given the cruelties thus revealed, a corresponding emphasis developed on slaves' resistance to their bondage (Reis 1993) and their resilience and cultural creativity under duress (Russell-Wood 1982). Recently, political concerns over current exploitation of Brazil's Amerindians has turned attention to Portuguese enslavement of Native American populations in colonial times (Monteiro 1988).

A primary focus on slavery had always marked studies of the plantation islands of the eighteenth- and nineteenth-century Caribbean, where thoroughly commercial sugar-exporting economies and transient communities of Europeans rested on the overwhelming presence of enslaved Africans, more so than at any other time or place in world history. This scholarship began as a secondary aspect of British imperial history (Ragatz 1928, with Williams 1944 as a counterpoint), and updated strains of colonial and imperial political economy have continued productively (Sheridan 1974; Drescher 1977; Tomich 1990). The French-speaking islands have remained most firmly in the orbit of metropolitan concerns, oriented toward *la Révolution française* and abolition. Elsewhere, local scholars have uncovered the lives of the people enslaved (e.g., for the English islands: Goveia 1965;

Patterson 1967; Craton 1974; Higman 1976, 1984), with an accent on resistance (Craton 1977; Beckles 1984, 1989a; Costa 1994). The emphasis on people has proliferated into studies of distinguishable categories of slaves (especially women: Morrissey 1989; B. Bush 1990; Shepherd et al., eds. 1995). Histories specific to other colonizing powers—France (R. Stein 1988), the Netherlands (Lamur 1987), and Spain (Knight 1970; Moreno Fraginals et al. 1985; Paquette 1988)—have proliferated to include individual islands (e.g., Puerto Rico: Scarano 1984; Antigua: Gaspar 1985; Barbados: Beckles 1989b; Martinique: Tomich 1990; Danish Virgin Islands: N. Hall 1992).

Spain sent relatively few Africans to its mainland colonies, except as domestic servants and artisans who continued renaissance Mediterranean styles of urban slavery into the sixteenth- and seventeenth-century cities of the Spanish Main ("Africans in Spanish American Colonial Society," Mellafe 1964; Bowser 1974; Rout 1976; Palmer 1976; Sharp 1976). In the 1990s attention expanded to colonies peripheral to the imperial focus on Peruvian and Mexican precious metals (e.g., Bolland 1994), to scattered plantation sectors (Carroll 1991), and to later periods (Blanchard 1992; Hünefeldt 1994; Johnson 1995); most of this work was written in Spanish by a corps of local scholars.

Studies of slavery in the United States are much more numerous than for any other part of the world—nearly a third of all titles published during the 1990s—and correspondingly varied. Delineating distinctions in North American slavery by period and by region, in fact, has been the principal direction in which these studies have developed from their initial paradigmatic reliance on antebellum plantation slavery in the cotton South. The seventeenth century defined institutions and attitudes, among English and Africans alike, that structured the integration of subsequent enslaved immigrants, most of whom arrived during the following century, down to 1807. Appreciation of the profound uniqueness of North American slaves' success in bearing and raising children has grown, so that many of their descendants shared in the idealism of the revolutionary era as African-Americans. Their heirs, in turn, adapted their masters' Christian religion to their yearnings as slaves in what they well understood as a land of promised freedom, even as an interstate slave trade (Tadman 1989/1996) broke up the families and communities they had created in the Chesapeake and the Carolina low country to support the nineteenth-century rise of cotton production in the lower South (surveys: Fogel 1989, Kolchin 1993; historiographical essays: Parish 1989; Smith and Inscoe, eds. 1990; Littlefield 1993). Histories of slavery in Louisiana (G. Hall 1992) and in northern colonies (e.g., Essah 1996), as well as a new generation of stud-

ies of the law of slavery (Wiecek 1977; Fehrenbacher 1978; Tushnet 1981; Finkelman 1981, 1986, 1988, 1997a, 1997b; "Bondage, Freedom, and the Constitution" 1996; Morris 1974, 1996; Schafer 1994) have extended the sense of the institution's profound presence in U.S. history. And the formative years of North American history are being seen increasingly in their full Atlantic context, including Africa as well as Britain's West Indian colonies (Morgan 1975; Thornton 1992/1998; Berlin 1996, 1998; Morgan 1997).

The bibliography of slavery thus moved far beyond its origins in studies carrying the preemancipation polemics of its opponents and its apologists forward into academic-styled debate, beyond the first efforts to recover the lost worlds of anonymous victims or compulsive resisters, beyond still-anonymous quantified behavior, to real people who suffered indignities and hardships but who also constructed meaningful lives they could control. In other times and places, where masters and slaves accepted authority and duty as axiomatic, if also morally conditioned, studies have begun to abandon projections of modern Western preoccupations with freedom (especially Patterson 1991) and property (e.g., Kopytoff 1982, 1988)—obsessions deriving from the eighteenth- and nineteenth-century challenge of converting ancient human dependencies into human security for the financial credit that sustained capitalist economic growth—and abolitionist defenses of collateral Africans as "men, and brothers." A productive recognition of slavery as itself a historical process, rather than a static institution, a labor-intensive method of economic or political expansion at rates faster than local populations could grow to support it, were also starting to appear.

With the humanization of the slaves, integration of them as participants in histories no longer understood exclusively in their masters' terms, and the growing acknowledgment of slavery's legacies for modern life, the subject is, finally, moving in from the academic peripheries to the heart of popular culture. During the 1990s, national monuments ("Slavery in the Age of Washington" 1994; Stanton 1996) and museums around the world expanded permanent exhibits and mounted special exhibitions featuring slavery. Best-selling, prize-winning novels (Unsworth 1992), studies of the Founding Fathers in the United States as slaveholders (Bailyn 1993; Finkelman 1996; Gordon-Reed 1996), and sweeping histories (Blackburn 1988, 1996; Thomas 1997) and films (*Amistad* 1997) gripped the imaginations of the public. UNESCO, the cultural agency of the United Nations, launched a multi-year, international "Slave Route" project, with prominent components of public representation and even tourism (UNESCO 1994/1998). By the late 1990s human rights abuses were stigmatized by invoking slavery as a metaphor to characterize their involuntary qualities, although slavery's other defining features—origins alien to the locale, violence, a property aspect—were not prominent. Schoolchildren in the United States read Equiano's *Narrative* and Frederick Douglass's *Life* as foundational documents of their nation's freedoms. This encyclopedia, and at least two other works for the general reader devoted to slavery, appeared in 1998. In academic thinking, slavery has become so expectable a means of achieving power and so elemental an aspect of communities' definitions of themselves, in every part of the world, that it no longer stands alone as a subject separate from the histories of which it is a vital aspect. Four decades of diligent, often inspired scholarship have changed the meaning of slavery from a discomfiting, anomalous peculiarity to an accepted consequence of human ambition everywhere before the modern age of Enlightenment and industrial capitalism, when control of technology and information replaced personal domination of other human beings.

See also ECONOMIC INTERPRETATION OF SLAVERY.

Joseph C. Miller

Historiography of Slavery

This entry includes the following articles: Slavery in North America, 1865–1920; Slavery in North America, 1920–1997; World Slavery; China and the Ancient Mediterranean. *Related articles may be found at the entry* Historical Approaches to Slavery.

Slavery in North America, 1865–1920

Though northern victory in the Civil War and passage of the Thirteenth Amendment in 1865 ended decades of debate over legalized slavery in the United States, during the postwar years the conflict over African-American slavery continued to rage among politicians, sectional polemicists, and the first generation of professional historians. From 1865 to 1920, a broad range of writers, from the North and the South, white and black, revived both the old proslavery and antislavery arguments. In the years from 1865 to 1889 alone, more than six hundred books and articles on slavery appeared. Slavery also served as a common theme and comparative model in the large volume of postbellum writings devoted to race and the "Negro problem."

When writing about slavery, most whites, especially white Southerners, restated the old proslavery argument almost point by point. They depicted slavery as a patriarchal, "civilizing" labor system and remained convinced that some variant of the "peculiar institution" was necessary for racial order in the New South. While few whites openly advocated returning the freedmen and women to chattel slavery, scores of writers nevertheless glorified slavery, crediting it with rendering the Old South a land where the races lived harmoniously. Though whites admitted that the slaves worked hard and toiled for long hours, they insisted that under slavery the blacks had received fair compensation in the form of food, clothing, housing, and training in the ways of "civilization." According to this new proslavery argument, slaves generally received humane and just treatment from their paternalistic masters. Cruel, abusive masters were considered to be the exception and the interstate trade in slaves was thought to have had only a minimal negative impact on slave families. The new defense of slavery accomplished three things. It eased white Southerners' pain in losing the war. It justified their treatment of the freedpeople and their descendants as quasi-slaves. And it united late nineteenth-century Americans, Northerners and Southerners, who viewed foreigners and people of color as threats. This proslavery interpretation, closely linked to the tenets of white supremacy, remained very much alive in the New South. Slavery as metaphor helped to fuel the racist reaction by whites toward blacks that engulfed the nation in the 1890s.

Despite the pervasiveness of the new proslavery argument, Northerners, especially former abolitionists, blacks, and reformers, challenged this rhetoric. These "neo-abolitionists," like the abolitionists of old, condemned slavery as un-Christian and a black mark on American civilization. Under slavery, they said, African-Americans were chained like animals, brutalized, and exploited in innumerable ways. Masters cruelly divided slave families, sexually abused slave females, and humiliated slave males. The new abolitionists also recognized the direful legacy of slavery in the impositions visited upon blacks following Appomattox, including the black codes of early Reconstruction years, sharecropping, convict labor, peonage, and later, the Jim Crow laws. Like the white neoabolitionists, during the postwar years former bondsmen like Frederick Douglass condemned slavery and identified the racial discrimination and proscription that surrounded it as painful reminders of the old system of bondage. In 1882 George Washington Williams, a black politician and amateur historian, published his two-volume *History of the Negro Race in America, 1619–1818.* This work challenged the new proslavery argument head-on, arguing that masters meted out cruel and thoughtless treatment to their slaves. Though theirs was the minority voice, the neoabolitionists loudly denounced

George Washington Williams. [Corbis-Bettmann]

slavery and underscored its deleterious influence on contemporary race relations.

While polemicists revived the old pro- and antislavery arguments, the first generation of professional American historians focused intently on slavery as a subject of historical inquiry. More than two thousand items related to slavery, including many theses and dissertations, appeared in the period from 1890 to 1920. Influenced strongly by the forces of nationalism, scientism, and the development of graduate training in history, scholars were determined to examine slavery—a subject previously interpreted with passion—impartially and objectively. The nationalist historians—Hermann E. von Holst, James Schouler, John Bach McMaster, James Ford Rhodes, and Albert Bushnell Hart—dominated historians of slavery at the turn of the century. They were transitionary figures between the postwar polemicists and the "scientific" historians of slavery educated in this period at Johns Hopkins University and other graduate schools.

The nationalist historians, especially Rhodes and Hart, popularized the scholarly study of slavery and identified institutional features of slavery that generations of later historians examined in more detail. Determined to chart a genuinely national history, they interpreted slavery and the Civil War as American tragedies. While restrained in blaming the South

for slavery and the Civil War, the nationalist historians nonetheless criticized slavery with the moral fervor of the abolitionists. They emphasized the evils of the domestic slave trade, the severity of field labor, and the inadequate conditions of slave life. Their outrage with slavery, though expressed in moral terms, was largely constitutional and theoretical in nature. Sharing the pervasive white racism of their day, these historians distanced themselves from the plight of slaves as persons. The nationalist historians' obvious antislavery bias conflicted with the ideal of objective "scientific" history. In the end, their histories served polemical ends: to counter the pro-Southern and proslavery arguments of their day. These historians therefore were no more impartial, dispassionate, or "scientific" than the old antebellum abolitionists or the postbellum neo-abolitionists.

Johns Hopkins University led the way in training the earliest "scientific" historian of slavery. Under Herbert Baxter Adams's tutelage, students wrote legalistic, detailed, factual monographs that shunned emotion, partisanship, and sectional bias. Students at Johns Hopkins employed previously unused primary sources—government records, manuscripts, and newspapers—to trace the evolution of slavery as an institution over time. From 1889 to 1914 Johns Hopkins doctoral students completed fifteen monographs on slavery, seven treating slavery in the antebellum South. In pathbreaking studies, Jeffrey R. Brackett, John Spencer Bassett, James C. Ballagh, John H. Russell, and Harrison A. Trexler, evaluated slavery systematically on the colonial and state levels. Their foremost contribution was in posing fresh questions about the origins of slavery and race in North America. Unlike earlier writers, the Johns Hopkins authors described, but did not judge, the development of slavery's various institutional features. In sheer volume and in detail, the Johns Hopkins studies on slavery brought a new scholarly dimension to the study of slavery. Graduate students at other institutions modeled state and local studies of slavery on the Johns Hopkins prototype.

At Harvard, for example, the pioneer black scholar William Edward Burghardt Du Bois cast his net more broadly. In his *Suppression of the African-Slave-Trade to the United States of America, 1638–1870* (1896), Du Bois argued that following the 1808 congressional ban on slave imports, Southerners smuggled over 250,000 African slaves into the South. Though recent scholars have lowered Du Bois's estimate considerably, his book was considered pathbreaking in its day and remains influential today.

But Du Bois—ever sensitive to slavery's barbarities and painful legacy—was atypical among his generation's historians of slavery. The students trained at Johns Hopkins in fact retained elements of the old proslavery argument and contributed to the lingering image of slavery as a patriarchal, benign institution. Like the vast majority of whites of their generation, the Johns Hopkins authors concurred that blacks benefited from slavery's tutelage. Legalistic in emphasis, and "dry as dust" in style, these monographs generally interpreted slave laws as humane and failed to determine the degree to which the statutes were enforced. They also uniformly ignored the human qualities of the bondsmen and women. Though less moralistic in tone than the nationalist historians, the Johns Hopkins graduate students nonetheless felt obliged to assess slavery, almost always portraying the masters as magnanimous in their treatment of the bondsmen. Significantly, the Johns Hopkins students virtually excluded economic questions from their consideration. In short, for all their attempts at producing "scientific" analyses of slavery, the Johns Hopkins authors, like the nationalist historians before them, failed in their quest of an objective history of slavery.

Among those influenced by the early Johns Hopkins studies was Ulrich Bonnell Phillips, who dominated North American slavery studies until the mid-1950s. In the first two decades of the century Phillips, a Georgia native who earned his doctorate at Columbia University in 1902, published many pioneering articles on slavery, especially its economic aspects. Like

W. E. B. Du Bois. [Corbis-Bettmann]

the Johns Hopkins authors, Phillips objected to the neoabolitionism of Rhodes and Hart and defended the South from what he deemed unfair attacks by Northern polemicists and historians. But while Phillips found little fault with the proslavery bias of the Johns Hopkins studies on slavery, he nevertheless judged their legal orientation too narrow and lifeless. Phillips was the lone scholar of his generation to interpret slavery for the Old South as a whole. He conceived it as an organic, well-ordered society with black slavery at its core.

Slavery, Phillips said repeatedly, enabled white Southerners to employ the profitable plantation system. In his opinion, the plantation was the agricultural equivalent of the factory of the industrial age. But slavery also provided whites with a crucial system of police control over blacks, a race that Phillips deemed backward and inert—culturally, genetically, and intellectually inferior to whites. Phillips argued that slavery served as a positive force on African-Americans, schooling and civilizing them. He described black-white relations on the plantation as harmonious, and he praised slaveholders for their firm but indulgent treatment of their bondsmen. Phillips was quick to note, however, that for all its advantages for blacks, slavery proved disadvantageous for whites. It encumbered his beloved region with long-term economic liabilities.

In 1918 in *American Negro Slavery*, Phillips summarized his ideas regarding slavery. Drawing upon twenty years of original research in previously unmined source material—plantation records—Phillips depicted slavery as a benign, yet dynamic, evolving institution, one shaped largely by social and economic influences. Surpassing the work of any previous investigator, Phillips focused on the daily world of master, overseer, and slave. He emphasized changes in the "peculiar institution" over time and recognized local and regional variations in slavery within the South. Unlike his contemporaries, Phillips deemphasized the importance of slave law as a force in the plantation community. Blacks and whites lived together in a plantation community, he said, that reflected mutual understandings of dependency by slaves and responsibility by their masters. Slavery, Phillips explained, proved unprofitable as a labor system but succeeded admirably as a social system.

In *Life and Labor in the Old South* (1929), his gracefully written social history, Phillips added texture to his portrait of slavery as a humane and civilizing labor system for blacks. In both of his books Phillips espoused a decidedly pro-Southern, proslavery interpretation. Although his works faced strident criticisms from blacks, including historians W. E. B. Du Bois and Carter G. Woodson, whites greeted Phillips's books with almost universal applause. This is not surprising,

Ulrich Phillips. [Hargrett Rare Book and Manuscript Library/University of Georgia Libraries]

because Phillips wrote during an age of rigid de jure segregation in the South and de facto segregation and anti-immigrant sentiment in the North.

Despite his dogged research, innovative method, and brilliant insights into the social and economic life of the South, Phillips's contributions were circumscribed by his racism and class bias. Unable to accept blacks as persons with human needs and feelings, Phillips failed to understand that they suffered from slavery's harmful effects and that they sought freedom and resisted their bondage overtly and covertly. Like the proslavery writers, Phillips overlooked slavery's cruelties and ignored the significant accomplishments of the bondsmen and women. Though he raised important questions about slave economics and the Old South's social relations, Phillips miscalculated slavery's profitability and virtually ignored slavery on small farms. Despite these weaknesses, Phillips reigned over North American slavery studies until he was dethroned by historians of the civil rights era.

See also ECONOMIC INTERPRETATION OF SLAVERY; HISTORICAL APPROACHES TO SLAVERY; LITERATURE OF SLAVERY; PERSPECTIVES ON SLAVERY.

BIBLIOGRAPHY

DILLON, MERTON L. *Ulrich Bonnell Phillips: Historian of the Old South.* 1985.

ELKINS, STANLEY M. *Slavery: A Problem in American Intellectual and Institutional Life.* 1959.

ROPER, JOHN HERBERT. *U. B. Phillips: A Southern Mind.* 1984.

SMITH, JOHN DAVID. "The Formative Period of American Slave Historiography, 1890–1920." Ph.D. diss., University of Kentucky. 1977.

———. "'Keep 'em in a Fire-Proof Vault': Pioneer Southern Historians Discover Plantation Records." *South Atlantic Quarterly* 78 (1979): 376–391.

———. *An Old Creed for the New South: Proslavery Ideology and Historiography, 1890–1920.* 1985.

———. "Ulrich Bonnell Phillips' *Plantation and Frontier:* The Historian as Documentary Editor." *Georgia Historical Quarterly* 77 (1993): 123–143.

SMITH, JOHN DAVID, and JOHN C. INSCOE, eds. *Ulrich Bonnell Phillips: A Southern Historian and His Critics.* 1990.

John David Smith

Slavery in North America, 1920–1997

From World War I to the Korean War, white scholars, despite the protests of black historians, considered Ulrich B. Phillips's *American Negro Slavery* the definitive account of the "peculiar institution." His interpretation of slavery as a benign, paternalistic, but unprofitable institution dominated the field. From the 1920s through the 1940s, the works of a number of historians referred to collectively as "the Phillips school," applied Phillips's perspective, method, and racial assumptions to studies of slavery on the state level. These included works by V. Alton Moody (Louisiana, 1924), Rosser H. Taylor (North Carolina, 1926), Charles S. Sydnor (Mississippi, 1933), Ralph B. Flanders (Georgia, 1933), Charles S. Davis (Alabama, 1939), and James B. Sellers (Alabama, 1950). J. Winston Coleman Jr.'s study of slavery in Kentucky (1940) adopted Phillips's approach, but the author sympathized more with the blacks than other contemporary white scholars. In the 1930s, however, scholars began a major reassessment of slavery that overturned Phillips and viewed slavery not from the perspective of the big house but from the slave quarters.

1930s through 1950s

In *Slave Trading in the Old South* (1931) Frederic Bancroft openly attacked slavery and its apologists, including Phillips. Revising previous interpretations of the domestic slave trade, Bancroft exposed its severity, its volume, and its importance to the South's antebellum economy. Relegating Phillips's work on slavery to the realm of "propaganda," in *Black Reconstruction in America* (1935) W. E. B. Du Bois presented a Marxist interpretation of slavery. According to Du Bois, American slaves ranked among the most degraded workers in world history. Their bondage was a system of institutionalized cruelty, part of the larger capitalistic exploitation of laborers throughout the United States. Like Bancroft and Du Bois, Herbert Aptheker emphasized slavery's barbarities and interpreted slaves as victims. In *American Negro Slave Revolts* (1943) Aptheker described the bondsmen and women as restless, discontented, and rebellious. He argued, disagreeing both with Phillips and white moderates, that slave militancy was rampant throughout the Old South.

Kenneth M. Stampp's landmark *The Peculiar Institution* (1956) signaled the end of Phillips's influence and the start of a major redirection in slave studies. Writing during the early years of the civil rights movement, Stampp assumed that blacks were human beings, not inferior to whites, and described the "peculiar institution" as dehumanizing and exploitative for the slaves but highly profitable for their masters. Slavery, Stampp wrote, required rigid discipline and demanded unconditional submission by blacks to whites. Blacks routinely were overworked and treated harshly. Challenging Phillips's paternalism thesis, Stampp defined slavery as a social system that continually impressed upon slaves their alleged innate inferiority, one that sought to inculcate in them fear of and dependence upon whites. In his opinion, the slaves craved their freedom, resisted within the bounds of their enslavement, and endured.

Though Stampp repudiated Phillips, according to Stanley M. Elkins he essentially updated the antislavery and neoabolitionist arguments and paid too little attention to the impact of enslavement on the slaves. In his provocative *Slavery: A Problem in American Institutional and Intellectual Life* (1959), Elkins employed comparative history, role psychology, and interpersonal theory to argue that North American slavery was more oppressive than slavery elsewhere. It so was brutal that it reduced many of the South's slaves to childlike, dependent "Sambos." Elkins asserted that the behavior of the "Sambo" personality type was comparable to the behavior of Nazi concentration victims of World War II.

1960s through 1970s

Elkins's controversial thesis, the civil rights movement, and an increased interest in the lives of the obscure and oppressed worldwide, redirected North American slavery studies in the 1960s and 1970s. No longer did scholars feel obliged to convince readers of the essential equality of the races and slavery's barbarities. These were commonly held assumptions. White, mainstream historians increasingly emphasized new issues—the importance of Africanisms, slave rebelliousness, and subtle forms of day-to-day resistance. They utilized sources—ex-slave autobiographies, interviews with former slaves, black folklore—that placed the bondsmen, not their masters, at center stage. The new slavery scholarship examined all aspects of slave life, including communal behavior, familial patterns, religious beliefs, folklore, and overt and covert resistance.

For example, in *The Slave Community: Plantation Life in the Antebellum South* (1972), John W. Blassingame drew heavily on black testimony to explain the psychology of the slave quarters. Blassingame argued that instead of just "Sambo," slaves displayed a full range of personality types. Typical bondsmen were resourceful, complex human beings, skilled at masking their true feelings and strong enough to withstand slavery's oppression. In *Roll, Jordan, Roll: The World the Slaves Made* (1974), Eugene D. Genovese argued that slaves used the planters' paternalism and Christianity to fashion a meaningful world for themselves under the extreme adversity of enslavement. Slaves and masters accepted paternalism as a system of reciprocal duties and rights. Throughout their captivity the slaves asserted their rights and maintained their self-respect.

Kenneth Stampp. [The Bancroft Library/University of California, Berkeley]

Stanley Elkins. [Jim Gipe]

Guided by their preachers, the bondsmen resisted slavery's assault and learned to value themselves, to love their fellows, and to have faith in their deliverance. Herbert G. Gutman, in *The Black Family in Slavery and Freedom, 1750–1925* (1976), credited the slave family's adaptability with enabling it to survive the rigors of enslavement. Gutman concluded that nuclear family units enforced dominant patterns of courtship, sexual behavior, and marital obligations.

Though 1970s scholarship emphasized the slaves' creativity, resistance, and survival, Robert W. Fogel and Stanley L. Engerman, in their controversial *Time on the Cross: The Economics of American Negro Slavery* (2 vols., 1974), concluded that the conditions of slave life compared favorably with those of contemporary free industrial workers. Typical slaves, they said, were efficient laborers who received approximately 90 percent of the income they produced. Fogel and Engerman also concluded that the South's slave-based economy grew at a faster rate than the North's free labor economy.

1980s through 1990s

While scholars in the 1970s and 1980s challenged Fogel and Engerman's econometric model and con-

clusions, the most influential works on slavery that appeared in these years were detailed state and local studies. For example, Charles Joyner's *Down by the Riverside: A South Carolina Slave Community* (1984) and Orville Vernon Burton's *In My Father's House Are Many Mansions: Family and Community in Edgefield, South Carolina* (1985) underscored the diverse ways that bondspeople retained their humanity despite slavery's cruelties. Joyner argued that slaves in Georgetown District, South Carolina, adapted African crafts, foodways, housing, language, and work and leisure patterns to New World conditions. To an important degree, they used their cultural heritage as a weapon against total enslavement. In his heavily quantified study, Burton, like Gutman, credited the slave family with providing blacks with the strength both to withstand slavery and to forge new lives as freedmen and women.

Scholarship on slavery of the 1990s continued to focus minutely on the slaves and their world. Slave familial and communal structure, religious beliefs and practices, culture and "style," forms of resistance, daily routines and behavior—these and other topics remain subjects of intense scholarly interest among contemporary historians. Modern studies have examined closely the lives of slave women and children. While the slaves remain central to contemporary analyses of the "peculiar institution," recent historians also have revived interest in their masters, especially slave mistresses. In *Mothers of Invention: Women of the Slaveholding South in the American Civil War* (1996), Drew Gilpin Faust analyzed the inner conflicts white women faced in managing their slaves as the Confederacy crumbled.

In the 1990s most scholars interpreted slavery as a complex, contradictory, intensely human institution. On the one hand, they credited slaves with maintaining a degree of autonomy over themselves and their community. On the other hand, they emphasized slavery's cold reality. Despite elements of "paternalism" in the master-slave relation, masters remained masters and slaves remained slaves. For over two centuries whites bought, sold, raped, and abused blacks.

For example, in *Life in Black and White: Family and Community in the Slave South* (1996), Brenda E. Stevenson underscored slavery's severity in a minute study of life in Loudoun County, Virginia. In doing so she challenged scholars who, while recognizing slavery's oppression, credited blacks with maintaining traditional "nuclear" families. Like Stevenson, in *Them Dark Days: Slavery in the American Rice Swamps* (1996), William Dusinberre stressed the antagonistic interests of extremely callous low country South Carolina and Georgia planters and their rebellious slaves. The work of these historians signals a move back toward the school of slavery studies that rejects plantation "paternalism," emphasizes that the slaves labored under extraordinary hardships, adapted to shape their families and communities, and endured.

The overriding theme of contemporary slave studies is that the blacks were active, not passive, in trying to shape their own destinies. Modern scholarship identifies a broad and influential African-American cultural nexus and recognizes the importance of variations within the slave experience—differences based on personality, character, changes in time and place, on varying size of slaveholdings, and on slave occupation patterns. Much 1990s scholarship is informed by comparative analysis, interdisciplinary methodology, and the use of slave-generated sources, including oral history testimony, folklore, historical photographs, material culture, and the archaeological remains of slave cabins, plantation outbuildings, yards, and cemeteries.

Future research must examine ecological aspects of slavery, relationships between black slaves and Native Americans, and variations of the slave experience within the South. More nuanced interpretations await such recurrent themes as the various forms of slave resistance, skin color differentiations within the slave and free black communities, and contrasts between North American slavery and other systems of legal bondage.

See also ANTHROPOLOGY OF SLAVERY; DEMOGRAPHY OF SLAVES IN THE UNITED STATES; ECONOMIC INTERPRETATION OF SLAVERY; ELKINS THESIS; HISTORICAL APPROACHES TO SLAVERY; LITERATURE OF SLAVERY; PERSPECTIVES ON SLAVERY.

BIBLIOGRAPHY

DEW, CHARLES B. "The Slavery Experience." In *Interpreting Southern History: Historiographical Essays in Honor of Sanford W. Higginbotham*, edited by John B. Boles and Evelyn Thomas Nolen. 1987.

DUNN, RICHARD S. "Of Human Bondage." *Times Literary Supplement* (17–23 June 1988).

ELKINS, STANLEY M. "The Slavery Debate." *Commentary* 60 (1975): 40–54.

FINKELMAN, PAUL, ed. *Articles on American Slavery*. Vol. 1, *Slavery and Historiography*. 1989.

LACHANCE, PAUL. "Use and Misuse of the Slave Community Paradigm." *Canadian Review of American Studies* 17 (1986): 449–458.

PARISH, PETER J. *Slavery: History and Historians*. 1989.

SMITH, JOHN DAVID. "Historical or Personal Criticism? Frederic Bancroft vs. Ulrich B. Phillips." *Washington State University Research Studies* 49 (1981): 73–86.

———. *An Old Creed for the New South: Proslavery Ideology and Historiography, 1865–1920*. 1985.

VAN DEBURG, WILLIAM L. *Slavery and Race in American Popular Culture*. 1984.

John David Smith

World Slavery

History before the middle of the twentieth century was largely concerned with political and military events, and early historians did not study broad phenomena like slavery. The great empires of antiquity and the universal religions nonetheless provide source material on the subject, because they recognized the humanity of slaves and created law, jurisprudence, philosophical inquiry, and literature for historical study. Critical inquiry on the history of slavery, however, dates to eighteenth-century philosophical and social thought on social evolution and the movement to abolish slavery. Eighteenth-century social thinkers like Montesquieu and the Scottish theorist John Millar believed that slavery made it possible for ancient societies to evolve more complex forms of social organization but were convinced that the institution had outlived its utility in their own, more progressive times. Political economists like Adam Smith believed that slave labor was inefficient. In general, evolutionists sought to understand why slavery had been useful in much of earlier history, but they identified progress in their own times with liberty. The most influential evolutionary theory was Marxism, which stressed the exploitation of slave labor as a source for the primitive accumulation of capital. Friedrich Engels described the evolution of Western society in stages that ran from primitive communism through ancient slavery to feudalism to capitalism. Communist scholars subsequently often tried to impose this framework on other world civilizations.

While philosophes criticized slavery, abolitionists attacked it, in the process building up a literature on the subject. In 1808, the year that British abolition of the trade went into effect, Thomas Clarkson published a two-volume history of the antislavery movement. The question of slavery in antiquity was addressed most comprehensively by another abolitionist, Henri Wallon, in *Histoire de l'esclavage dans l'antiquité* (1847). Some classicists saw ancient slavery as a peripheral institution that did not detract from the timeless accomplishments of classical Greece and Rome, but others saw it as a source of their eventual decadence and decline. If the humanists had difficulty justifying Greek and Roman slavery, Christian thinkers were uncomfortable with the biblical acceptance for slavery. Abolitionists rarely turned to the scriptures for antislavery material. From the mid-nineteenth century, a body of literature, which was generally ahistorical, also explored slavery in various nonwestern societies.

With the abolition of slavery in Brazil in 1888, slavery no longer existed within the Western world. Within a generation, most colonial regimes had also legislated against slavery in Africa and Asia, though they were often lax in enforcing antislavery decrees. The result was a decline of academic interest in slavery, reinforced in the United States by a desire to soothe the wounds of the Civil War. The most impressive work on American slavery produced in this period, that of Ulrich Phillips, presented a benign view of the South's slave past. Though Phillips was challenged by a small group of African-American historians led by Carter G. Woodson, his argument was widely accepted. Similarly in Brazil, Gilberto Freyre presented a romanticized view of that country's recent slavery. At the same time, rapid successes in abolishing a profitable labor system challenged economic historians concerned to demonstrate the economic rationality underlying human history. Reginald Coupland saw abolition as a triumph of altruism over economic interest, but the Trinidadian Eric Williams challenged that idea in *Capitalism and Slavery* (1944). Williams argued that West Indian slavery had contributed to the economic growth of Britain and mainland North America before the 1790s and that abolition came only when the West Indies were declining and Britain was increasingly dominated by industrialists with no interest in slavery. The "Williams thesis" provoked a half-century of attempts to refute it. Seymour Drescher challenged the notion of a West Indian decline, and Roger Anstey argued that profits from the slave trade were insignificant for British industrialization. Howard Temperley and David Brion Davis argued that abolition had more to do with the ideology of free labor than with the ascendancy of industrialists.

Capitalism and Slavery was written on the eve of a period of dramatic change marked by the end of colonial rule in Asia and Africa and the rise of the African-American civil rights movement. The emergence of these new political interests inspired a reevaluation of African-American history and of the slave experience in terms less rosy than Phillips's image of the plantation as a civilizing "school" for untutored slaves. Kenneth Stampp, in *The Peculiar Institution* (1956), replaced Phillips's plantation with an image of a hard-driving agrobusiness. Stanley Elkins, in *Slavery* (1959), broadened the harsh image of slaves' lives and speculated about the damage that the plantation as a "total institution" might have done to the slave's personality. While Elkins saw the slave as victim, John Blassingame, George Rawick, Lawrence Levine, Albert Raboteau, Sterling Stuckey, and Herbert Gutman depicted a struggle by slaves to define their culture, to maintain social relationships, and to defend a small social space of their own. Robert Fogel and Stanley Engerman, in *Time on the Cross* (1974), used the new methodology of cliometrics to argue that slavery was productive and that slaves often lived in better mate-

rial conditions than free workers in northern cities; this economic analysis was taken as a defence of slavery and provoked controversy as a host of critics disputed Fogel and Engerman's quantitative techniques and their view of slavery.

While some focused on slaves, others studied masters. Winthrop Jordan and George Frederickson explored racial thought; James Oakes, Bertram Wyatt-Brown, and Drew Gilpin Faust focused on the slave owners' paternalistic culture and their concern with honor. Slave studies were also influenced by the new social history's interest in the lower classes and by a renaissance of Marxist thought stimulated by publication of Marx's early writings. One major school, led by the British labor historian E. P. Thompson (*The Making of the English Working Class*), described social classes not in terms of social theory but in terms of how they created class interests and culture for themselves. The prime example of this style in works on slavery was Eugene Genovese's *Roll, Jordan, Roll* (1974), subtitled *The World the Slaves Made*. It is still the most richly textured study of American slavery available.

These debates found echoes in other American societies, which also knew slavery and the racial divide

Eric Williams. [Eric Williams Memorial Collection]

that was its inheritance. Thus, for almost every part of Latin America and the Caribbean, the work of North American historians has been paralleled by efforts of local scholars to understand their own slave heritages. In Brazil, Freyre's picture of a benign, racially mixed, distinctively Brazilian form of slavery has yielded, in the works of Brazilian historians like Katia Mattoso and Jacob Gorender and Americans like Stuart Schwartz, to a fuller portrayal of economic exploitation and personal brutality. Numerous studies of the plantation economy in the Caribbean make similar points: Richard Dunn on Barbados, Elsa Goveia on the Leeward Islands, Edward Brathwaite on Jamaica, Franklin Knight on Cuba, Hilary Beckles on Barbados, and Gabriel Debien on the French islands. Barry Higman studied slave demography; Barry Gaspar, Michael Craton, and Hilary Beckles focused on slave behavior as resistance.

In Africa, as in the West Indies, decolonization stimulated historical scholarship on slavery, and both foreign and African scholars discovered its importance there. Two collective works—Claude Meillassoux (ed.), *L'esclavage en Afrique précoloniale* (1975) and Suzanne Miers and Igor Kopytoff (eds.), *Slavery in Africa* (1977)—gave modern intellectual form to an old debate about whether African slavery had the harsh characteristics of slavery elsewhere in the world. Miers and Kopytoff depicted an essentially assimilative institution, while Meillassoux and his collaborators depicted a more exclusionary and exploitative institution. A second concern in the historiography of African slavery has been the destructive effect of the export slave trade, particularly that of the Atlantic, on societies within Africa. Walter Rodney, writing about the upper Guinea Coast, attributed "slavery and other forms of social oppression" in Africa to trade with Europeans. Martin Klein and Claire Robertson elaborated on this theme, stressing the importance of female slavery in Africa. Frederick Cooper showed commercial plantations on Zanzibar operating within a Muslim culture. Richard Roberts and Jean-Pierre Olivier de Sardan, writing about the western Sudan, and Paul Lovejoy, writing about the Hausa, emphasized the ubiquity of slavery there by the nineteenth century, and these societies' dependence on it.

Although slavery was also important in the Mediterranean and across Asia, its heritage has been less significant in these areas. Neither slavery nor the slave trade left clearly defined groups of slave descent or the attendant social conflict. Slavery has accordingly not been a major subject of historical inquiry in Asian countries. This is particularly true in Islamic countries sensitive to Western stereotypes of Muslims as inveterate slavers. Except for the Turkish scholar Hilal Inalcik and the Moroccan Mohammed Ennaji, research on Muslim slavery has been done mostly by outsiders. The Muslim slave institution that has attracted most interest among westerners is the slave soldier (or *mamluk*), studied by David Ayalon, Daniel Pipes, and Patricia Crone. Bernard Lewis projected the Western preoccupation with race onto the Middle East, and Ehud Toledano provided comprehensive accounts of slavery under the Ottomans. For China, James Watson and C. Martin Wilbur describe a slavery that provided not productive labor but services to the elite. Antony Reid's collection on Southeast Asia depicts a range of servile institutions, with the common thread being the transfer of people from poorer societies to wealthier ones and the importance of hierarchical relations in those wealthier societies. Scholars working on India have written more on caste than slavery, but the collection edited by Utsa Patnaik and Manjari Dingwaney makes it clear that various forms of servitude, including agricultural slavery, were common there. The most suggestive monograph on South Asia, however, is Gyan Prakash, *Bonded Histories* (1990), which shows how colonial rulers projected their own categories of analysis onto Indian institutions of unequal, but reciprocal, rank and thus saw very different forms of bondage as something equivalent to Western slavery.

Some scholars have systematically compared slavery among world regions: George Fredrickson on race and slavery in the United States and South Africa and Peter Kolchin on American slavery and Russian serfdom. Other studies see the movements of slaves and other workers across the Indian Ocean and the South Atlantic as integrated intercontinental systems. Philip Curtin's studies on the history of the plantation system, on epidemiology, and, most important, on slave demography have been based on such a concept. Curtin's work has also provoked continuing discussion of the numbers of people transported and the factors contributing to the high mortality they suffered. The most important development of the idea of pan-Atlantic structures has been Joseph Miller's *Way of Death* (1988), which studies the Angolan slave trade from its sources in the African interior to the Brazilian plantation and its financial backing in Europe.

What is missing in the literature on slavery is systematic cross-cultural theorization, with two exceptions. In 1910, the Dutch ethnographer H. J. Nieboer argued in *Slavery as an Industrial System* that slavery was likely to develop where land was freely available, labor in short supply, and technology simple. His argument, with refinements, still influences attempts to explain why slavery has been important in some areas but not in others. The only work of similar scope is Orlando Patterson, *Slavery and Social Death* (1982), which replaces economic interpretations of slavery with its psychological and social dynamics and stresses natal alienation (removal from society of birth) and lack of honor as making possible the total control of the slave. Patterson's emphasis on the origins of the slaves' vulnerability draws on insights of Moses Finley, the most influential modern student of classical slavery. Finley, Patterson, and Miers and Kopytoff define the slave essentially as an "outsider." In describing the emergence of a slave society in ancient Athens, Finley also outlined a distinction between societies based on slave labor (or "slave societies"), which have been rare in world history (only Greece, Rome, the colonial Americas, and the United States), and societies where slaves, though numerous, have more circumscribed roles. Claude Meillassoux's *Anthropology of Slavery* (1986) is an important, highly theoretical neo-Marxist work based exclusively on African data. It stresses that slavery originated in violence and depicts tension between two kinds of slavery: that of the warrior-aristocrats, who live off war, sell their slave booty and exploit slaves as soldiers and producers of subsistence; and that of merchants, who handle the slave trade but also use slave labor to produce commodities for exchange. While historians have read each of these works, none of these theorizers is a historian, with the exception of Finley, who tries to see patterns of change in the rise and decline of slave systems.

See also DEMOGRAPHY AND DEMOGRAPHIC THEORIES OF SLAVERY; ELKINS THESIS; ENLIGHTENMENT; MARXISM; PATTERSON THESIS; WILLIAMS THESIS.

BIBLIOGRAPHY

ELKINS, STANLEY M. *Slavery: A Problem in American Institutional and Intellectual Life.* 1959; 2nd ed., 1968; 3rd ed., 1976.
FINLEY, MOSES I. *Ancient Slavery and Modern Ideology.* 1980.
FOGEL, ROBERT W., and STANLEY L. ENGERMAN. *Time on the Cross: The Economics of American Negro Slavery.* 2 vols. 1974.
GENOVESE, EUGENE D. *Roll, Jordan, Roll: The World the Slaves Made.* 1974.
MEILLASSOUX, CLAUDE. *Anthropologie de l'esclavage: Le ventre de fer et d'argent.* 1986. *The Anthropology of Slavery: The Womb of Iron and Gold.* Translated by Alide Dasnois, with a foreword by Paul E. Lovejoy. 1991.
———, ed. *L'esclavage en Afrique précoloniale.* 1975.
MIERS, SUZANNE, and IGOR KOPYTOFF, eds. *Slavery in Africa: Historical and Anthropological Perspectives.* 1977.
MILLER, JOSEPH C. *Way of Death: Merchant Capitalism and the Angolan Slave Trade, 1730–1830.* 1988.
NIEBOER, H. J. *Slavery as an Industrial System: Ethnological Researches.* 1900; 2nd rev. ed., 1910.
PATTERSON, ORLANDO. *Slavery and Social Death: A Comparative Study.* 1982.
PRAKASH, GYAN. *Bonded Histories.* 1990.
STAMPP, KENNETH M. *The Peculiar Institution: Slavery in the Ante-Bellum South.* 1956.
WALLON, HENRI. *Histoire de l'esclavage dans l'antiquité.* With preface, bibliography, chronology, and index by Jean-Christian Dumont. 1879, 1988.
WILLIAMS, ERIC. *Capitalism and Slavery.* 1944.

Martin A. Klein

China and the Ancient Mediterranean

Historians generally agree that slaves or people with a social-political status similar to that of slaves formed part of the Chinese population from the Shang dynasty (sixteenth to eleventh centuries B.C.) to the Qing dynasty (1644–1912), although the number and kind of slaves under different dynasties varied greatly. However, there has never been much agreement among historians about whether China was ever actually a slave society. That question was first seriously raised in the late 1920s and 1930s, in China, with regard to a debate about Chinese social history and the nature of Chinese society. The debate was conducted by various groups of young Chinese revolutionary intellectuals, including the Chinese Communist Party, the Trotskyites, and the leftist Nationalists who, after the failure of the so-called Great Revolution between 1925 and 1927, strove to come to terms with that failure and to seek a theoretical foundation for their respective programs for a new revolution.

Unlike the traditional Chinese, who interpreted social-political changes in terms of a "mandate of heaven," these modern revolutionary intellectuals tried to adopt laws of society to legitimate and guide their revolutions. In China at that time, "laws of society" meant Marxist historical materialism, which argues that all human societies must go through five successive stages of development—primitive commune, slavery, feudalism, capitalism, and socialism—and that societies at different stages of development require a different kind of revolution. Therefore, whether or not China had experienced a stage of slavery became not only an academic issue but also a political issue, because the answer was directly related to whether Marxist historical materialism could be fully applied to Chinese society and indirectly related to whether China should have a revolution and, if so, what kind of revolution it should have.

Few non-Marxist scholars believed that China had gone through the stage of being a slave society. Most held that from the end of the Shang dynasty to the Qin unification in 221 B.C., China was a feudal society. After that China became a unique society that was neither feudal nor capitalistic. Most of these scholars also denied that there were any drastic class differences in China and argued, accordingly, that there was no social basis for a class revolution in China. And the Marxists themselves—who had different interpretations of both Marxist classics and Chinese historical sources—could not agree with each other about whether there had been a stage of slavery in Chinese history. Some Chinese Trotskyites and other nonorthodox Marxists argued that slavery was not a necessary stage in the Marxist social-evolutionary scheme and that China had never gone through a stage of slavery mainly because slaves had never been the dominant force in production. The theoreticians of the Chinese Communist Party, however, all agreed that a stage of slavery had existed in ancient China, because they believed that the five-stage social evolutionary scheme was universal and that China should not be an exception. Some of them emphasized the similarities between ancient Chinese society and the ancient Mediterranean world and considered ancient China a typical slave society, while others stressed the differences between ancient Chinese society and the classic Mediterranean slave system. The latter argued that the Chinese system of slavery was a special type and called it "incipient slavery" or simply "oriental slavery." Some believed that slavery in ancient China was unique and that it fit well with Marx's concept of the "Asiatic mode of production."

The duration of slavery in China was also controversial for Marxist historians, who argued for the existence of slavery in ancient China, although this controversy was more technical than political. Three debates about the issue took place in China—in the late 1920s and 1930s, then in the 1950s, and finally in the 1980s. Many prominent Chinese Marxist historians, such as Guo Moruo, Fan Wenlan, Lu Zhenyu, and Jian Bozan, joined the debates. Historians of the Soviet Union and Japan also paid much attention to the issue. The great majority of Chinese historians now agree that China entered a stage of slavery at the beginning of the Shang dynasty, but a few still argue for an earlier or later date. Moreover, there is still no agreement about who the slaves were or how large the slave population was during the Shang dynasty.

There is even more controversy about when slavery ended and the feudal age began. Using different definitions of slavery and feudalism and a different selection and interpretation of historical sources, Chinese historians have proposed that the stage of slavery ended at any one of the following times: the beginning of the Zhou dynasty (eleventh century B.C.), the beginning of the eastern Zhou period (eighth century B.C.), the beginning of the "warring states" period (fifth century B.C.), the beginning of the united Qin dynasty (221 B.C.), the beginning of the Han dynasty (206 B.C.), the beginning of the eastern Han dynasty (A.D. 25), or during the Wei and Jin dynasties (third to fifth centuries after Christ). The issue has attracted so much attention from Marxist historians because

it forms an important part of their effort to periodize Chinese history according to the Marxist social-evolutionary scheme.

In the 1950s, Chinese ethnologists who joined a state-sponsored investigation of the social history of China's ethnic minorities found that a slave system, believed to be similar to that in ancient China, still exists among the Yi people in the Cool Mountains in southwestern China.

See also CHINA; MARXISM; MEDITERRANEAN BASIN.

BIBLIOGRAPHY

Editorial Board, Historical Studies, ed. *Selected Essays on the Issue of Periodization of Slavery and Feudalism in China.* 1962.
JIAN-FU, QIAN. *The Issue of Slavery in Chinese Social-Economic History.* 1948.
WEI-MIN, LIU. *Servitude in Ancient China.* 1975.
WINNINGTON, ALAN. *The Slaves of the Cool Mountains: The Ancient Social Conditions and Changes Now in Progress on the Remote South-Western Borders of China.* 1959.

Han Xiaorong

Hobbes, Thomas [1588–1679]

British philosopher and ethicist who laid the theoretical foundations for Utilitarianism.

Most of Hobbe's political thought is contained in *Leviathan, De Cive [On the State], De Corpore Politico [Concerning the Body Politic],* and *Behemoth,* a history which concentrated on the political origins of the English Civil War. Hobbes theorized a "state of nature," wherein men lived in perfect liberty, owing obedience to no other. In that state, due to the absence of law and morality, the life of man was "solitary, poor, nasty, brutish, and short." Hobbes held that, rejecting this "war of all against all," men entered a covenant with a sovereign whereby they pledged to obey him in exchange for his protection. No limitation could be placed upon the sovereign's power, since the sovereign was necessarily the judge of all contracts, including the covenant.

The practical limits, which Hobbes did admit, were that no man could be expected to submit to death voluntarily, because that violated the purpose for entering the covenant, and that, although no legal right to revolt exists, any sovereign who is overthrown deserves it for failing in his primary duty—to keep power.

Hobbes said that those in jail or in fetters were slaves, and that they labored not from duty, but to avoid the master's cruelty. Given the absence of consent, slaves violate no law of nature if they use any means to escape, even deadly violence. Hobbes dealt with slavery in the abstract only, and in spite of his interest in the ancient world and despite the prevalence

The title page from Leviathan *by Thomas Hobbes.*
[Corbis-Bettmann]

of slavery in the overseas European empires of his day, he had little to say concerning the particularities of ancient or modern slavery as they actually developed historically.

Hobbes's influence is difficult to exaggerate. He ranks with Machiavelli as a founder of modern political thought, and virtually every subsequent theorist has written in reaction to his doctrines.

See also LAW; PHILOSOPHY.

BIBLIOGRAPHY

HOBBES, THOMAS. *The English Works of Thomas Hobbes of Malmesbury.* 11 vols. Edited by William Molesworth. 1845.
SORELL, TOM, ed. *The Cambridge Companion to Hobbes.* 1996.

Patrick M. O'Neil

Holidays

The practice of allowing slaves some free time has often been mentioned by historians, and we have numerous accounts of these "big times," controlled by the masters, that took place in or around the big house. Besides the usual holidays, Christmas, or Sundays, there were many festive occasions in which slaves participated—weddings, burials, dances, or seasonal events like cornshuckings. More than a break from work, these official feasts provided slaves with an opportunity to interact with whites, to observe their customs, meet slaves from neighboring plantations, and learn news from the outer world. Other festivities took place in the quarters where slaves gathered, told stories and tales, played music, entertained their own visitors, and created multiple rituals. Still others were staged in more secret places, near the water or in the hush arbors where slaves held baptism and worship ceremonies, played the forbidden drum, and performed dances very different from those the masters requested. These events enabled slaves to renew links with their African heritage and were part of a range of New World performances, which started with the slave ship dance that the captives were forced to perform.

In some parts of the South, slaves developed distinctive traditions, like the Congo Square dances that started near New Orleans at a marketplace where slaves and Indians met. Too troublesome for white citizens, less respectable than those held by the colored creoles, these dances were restricted and finally canceled. Scholars have argued that they reappeared under different forms, in the voodoo ceremonies or in carnival parades when, in the mid-nineteenth century, blacks started to organize their own societies and had their own float, known to this day as Zulu. But it is probably on the fringes of the carnival that the early slave tradition is best kept, among the Mardi Gras Indians who bear Indian names, wear Indian costumes, and march in the streets of their neighborhood to meet other tribes in a very ritualized way, reminiscent of Capoiera dance contests in Brazil.

In Key West, Florida, or in North Carolina, slaves chose the Christmas season, propitious for larger gatherings, to organize a JonKonnu festival, which, though akin to the Christmas mumming, was closer to the more carnivalesque festivities that developed in the Bahamas or in Jamaica where it was first observed. Whatever its origins—it is supposed to have honored the first African king who defended a Prussian fort on the Guinea coast against the attacks of other colonial powers—JonKonnu was one of the most striking slave celebrations because of its fanciful headgear and exuberant music.

In the North, slaves and free blacks established in colonial times a tradition of festivals that varied slightly from one region to another and honored an African King elected among their peers. Negro Elec-

TWELFTH DAY CUSTOM AT HAVANA.

A group of Africans brought to Cuba as slaves participate in Twelfth Day festivities, bringing an end to the 1851 Christmas season. [*Gleason's Pictorial Drawing Room Companion*/Corbis]

tion Day in New England, and Pinkster in New York and New Jersey, grew from two distinct white traditions: the elections held by the masters and a Dutch Pentecostal seasonal feast, but developed into all-black celebrations, watched by motley crowds. These feasts often assumed a more civic character than the southern festivals: slaves not only displayed rhetorical and artistic skills and showed that they could march in style, but also demonstrated their ability to elect an authority figure and conduct some sort of self-government.

With the abolition of the slave trade, which was first celebrated in 1808, and the passing of Emancipation Acts in the Northern states, a string of new "Freedom" celebrations gradually replaced the earlier festivals. The newly freed African-Americans organized parades and marches through the cities and towns, gave speeches, and created a calendar of events commemorating the various steps toward freedom: January 1 for the end of the slave trade in 1808, July 4 in New York for the emancipation of the slaves in 1827, August 1 to celebrate the abolition of slavery in the British West Indies. African-Americans seized these occasions to make their appearance in the public sphere, where societies and organizations would march

and display their emblems—the black Masonic Lodges figured prominently among them. As the abolitionist movement grew, so did concern for those held in slavery. Commemorative celebrations became occasions to frame petitions, thus creating a tradition of black jeremiad and assertiveness. The choice of date and place and the appropriateness of parades and marches became much-debated issues, especially in the emerging black press, but these Emancipation Days continued to be observed, in anticipation of general Emancipation, and featured famous speakers such as Frederick Douglass.

The years from 1862 to 1865 saw the creation of more "Jubilees": May 9, when a measure was introduced in 1862 to free the slaves of all masters disloyal to the United States; September 22, for Lincoln's preliminary proclamation; 1 January 1863, for the actual Emancipation; and finally 19 June 1865, when slaves in Texas heard about their freedom. This last celebration, called Juneteenth, is still observed today in Texas and other states.

All these ritual events summoned an impressive range of skills and fulfilled multiple functions. Reflecting or shaping the changes that occurred through slavery times, they provided an opportunity to socialize, to build up a community. In the North, where they became more civic ceremonies, they contributed to the creation of a political culture. In the South and in the islands, where fanciful costuming, music, song, and dance prevailed, the idea of freedom was also very much present, although in disguise. This festive culture, sustained for so many years, helped African-Americans to come to terms with their history and paved the way for a future when freedom would no longer be a dream deferred.

See also DANCE; EMANCIPATION; ENTERTAINERS, SLAVES AS; FREEDOM; MUSIC BY SLAVES.

BIBLIOGRAPHY

ABRAHAMS, ROGER D. *Singing the Master: The Emergence of African American Culture in the Plantation South.* 1992.

FABRE, GENEVIÈVE. "African American Commemorative Celebrations in the Nineteenth Century." In *History and Memory in African-American Culture,* edited by Geneviève Fabre and Robert O'Meally. 1994.

SWEET, LEONARD I. "The Fourth of July and Black Americans in the Nineteenth Century." *Journal of Negro History* 61, no. 3 (1976): 256–275.

WHITE, SHANE. "'It Was a Proud Day': African Americans, Festivals, and Parades in the North, 1741–1834." *Journal of American History* (June 1994): 13–50.

WIGGINS, WILLIAM H., JR. *O Freedom! Afro-American Emancipation Celebrations.* 1987.

Geneviève Fabre

Holmes, George Frederick   [1820–1897]

Proslavery southern educator.

Born in British Guiana on 2 August 1820, George Frederick Holmes studied briefly at the University of Durham in England before emigrating to the United States as a penniless teenager. Admitted to the South Carolina bar in 1842, he gained widespread acclaim as a writer and intellectual through his prolific contributions to such journals as *De Bow's Review,* the *Southern Literary Messenger,* and the *Southern Quarterly Review.* In 1857 Holmes was appointed professor of history and general literature at the University of Virginia, where he remained until his death on 4 November 1897.

Though admitting that slavery's merits could be debated "in the abstract," Holmes argued that the institution as it existed in the United States was "ineradicable without the subversion of the whole fabric of government and society," and "any persons who agitate[d] the question of emancipation, or in any way endeavor[ed] to bring it about," were "guilty of the wildest and most wicked incendiarism." In his judgment, a "calm and philosophic investigation" would not only convince reasonable men of the "vital truth" to the numerous biblical, historical, and scientific justifications for slavery but also inspire them to reform the system's occasional abuses. Nevertheless, Holmes feared that such moderate reflection was actively discouraged by "dangerous" extremist publications, from Harriet Beecher Stowe's abolitionist *Uncle Tom's Cabin* (1852) to George Fitzhugh's proslavery *Sociology for the South* (1854). Holmes criticized both of these authors for passionately advocating the same "fatal" proposition: that "any social institution"—whether slave or free—which resulted in "instances of individual misery" was "criminal . . . and ought to be universally condemned."

See also FITZHUGH, GEORGE; PERSPECTIVES ON SLAVERY; STOWE, HARRIET BEECHER.

BIBLIOGRAPHY

FAUST, DREW GILPIN. *A Sacred Circle: The Dilemma of the Intellectual in the Old South, 1840–1860.* 1977.

GILLESPIE, NEAL C. *The Collapse of Orthodoxy: The Intellectual Ordeal of George Frederick Holmes.* 1972.

HOLMES, GEORGE FREDERICK. "On Slavery and Christianity." *Southern Quarterly Review* 3 (January 1843): 252–256.

MCKITRICK, ERIC L., ed. *Slavery Defended: The Views of the Old South.* 1963.

Eric Robert Papenfuse

Honor

Every large-scale slaveholding society has placed a great deal of importance on honor as a code of behavior and as a way of ordering society in a highly hierarchical fashion. Slaveholders commanded, at the top of the hierarchy; slaves occupied the lowest level; nonslaveholders assumed the middling positions. In honorific societies, honor and power are virtually synonymous. Honor flows from power, and the quest for honor causes men to gather the tools of power. Power made men independent and autonomous of others, because one does not have to obey one's subordinate. Slaves were ruled by the whim of their masters, and their total dependence marked them as dishonorable.

The relationship between power and honor can best be seen in primitive slaveholding societies, where the slave's primary purpose was to enhance the master's reputation. For the slaveholders of Anglo-Saxon, Germanic, and many African tribes, a slave was an economic burden, but they kept slaves to increase their standing within the community. Similarly, the Tlingit Indians of the northwest coast used the potlatch ceremony to demonstrate their honor: during the ceremony the host destroyed or gave away large amounts of wealth, including slaves, to prove his worth. Later, in the U.S. South, planters utilized slave labor primarily for economic reasons, but although economics fueled slavery, the master gained great prestige through slaveholding.

Men who made a claim to honor looked to the community for confirmation or rejection of that claim. The community judged worthiness by assessing the individual's outward appearance. This emphasis on appearance led men, whether in public or private, by word or deed, to project an image of themselves calculated to enhance their reputation. Kenneth Greenberg, in *Honor and Slavery* (1996), aptly uses masks as a metaphor for the preoccupation with appearances in the U.S. South. Free men, he says, wore masks of honor, but they could be unmasked by anyone powerful enough to assault their honor with slurs, insults, or violence. Men faced an additional worry: protecting their dependents—women, children, and slaves—who lacked power and honor. The patriarch's personal honor extended over his dependents, and he was responsible for their protection. An attack directed at the weakest family member also struck at the strongest. Men were touchy about their honor and responded to insult or injury with immediate and often violent retaliation. Failure to respond implicitly validated the insult and was equated with weakness, dishonor, and slavishness. For the planter class of the U.S. South, dueling became a ritualistic way of settling grievances with honor.

Nonslaveholding freemen generally accepted the concept of honor and lived by its dictates because they were proud not to be slaves. The need to feel superior motivated poor freemen to associate themselves with wealthy slaveholders rather than slaves. By participating in a society based on honor, nonslaveholders implicitly acknowledged and deferred to the superiority of the slaveholding class. Those who refused, or were unable, to compete for honor were considered outside of society and treated with contempt. Nonslaveholders were as touchy about their honor as the planters, but they settled disputes in a less dignified manner—with their fists.

Many cultures adhere to a belief system that values honor over life. By reason of birth, defeat, kidnapping, indebtedness, or punishment, slaves, or their ancestors, accepted enslavement and life as an alternative to honor—an arrangement that Orlando Patterson called social death. Masters saw in their slaves everything that was the opposite of themselves. They believed their slaves to be lazy, ignorant, and dishonest, traits that reinforced the master's sense of superiority. Owners used violence, or the threat of violence, to enforce the slave's continued dependence. A slave who asserted independence or honor might be bru-

tally repressed, because that threatened the master's authority. Day-to-day survival demanded that slaves behave in a servile manner. "Sambo" was one term used to describe the infantile personality that some slaves adopted in the U.S. South. Furthermore, slavery undermined the male slave's authority over his family by denying his right to protect them. Some owners emasculated male slaves by selling families apart, raping wives and daughters, and beating family members. Out of anger and frustration male slaves sometimes fought in the quarters or abused family members.

Although adopting a servile personality had serious ramifications for slaves, it did help them maintain a certain autonomy within the slave system. Slaves successfully hid behind the mask of slavery, which planters often found to be disturbingly inscrutable. Masters seldom knew what a slave was thinking, and this kept them from enquiring too deeply into the slaves' lives. Slaves retained a degree of autonomy and independence because planters never saw beyond the mask of dishonor.

See also PATTERSON THESIS; STEREOTYPES, SLAVISH.

BIBLIOGRAPHY

AYERS, EDWARD L. *Vengeance and Justice: Crime and Punishment in the Nineteenth-Century American South.* 1984.
FRANKLIN, JOHN HOPE. *The Militant South.* 1956.
GREENBERG, KENNETH. *Honor and Slavery.* 1996.
PATTERSON, ORLANDO. *Slavery and Social Death.* 1982.
PERISTIANY, J. D., ed. *Honor and Shame: The Values of Mediterranean Society.* 1965.
PITT-RIVERS, JULIAN. "Honor." In *International Encyclopedia of the Social Sciences,* edited by David L. Sills. 1968.
WYATT-BROWN, BERTRAM. "The Mask of Obedience: Male Slave Psychology in the Old South." *American Historical Review* 93 (December 1988): 1228–1252.
———. *Southern Honor.* 1982.

James W. Paxton

Household Slaves

In most slaveholding societies, masters have commonly employed a few slaves as household servants. In many important respects household slaves everywhere have shared similar experiences. Domestic servants worked in and around the main house, performing such tasks as cleaning, cooking, laundering, making and mending clothes, gardening, running errands, driving coaches, and tending the master's children. While slaveholders on farms and plantations usually kept at least one house slave, and some maintained a large staff, by far the greatest proportion of household slaves lived in towns and cities. In particular, slaveholders in the port towns of the Dutch West Indies and French-controlled Martinique kept large numbers of house slaves. In some cases each family member had his or her own personal servant in addition to the general household help.

Historians have traditionally viewed the house servant as a privileged member of the slave workforce, who was spared the harsh conditions of field labor and who identified more closely with the master's interests than with the field hands'. This may have been true in the wealthy households of ancient Rome, where loyal experienced slaves gained promotions to more prestigious jobs and the occupational hierarchy greatly favored household slaves (*familia urbana*) over field slaves (*familia rustica*). Over the past twenty-five years, however, historians have modified this interpretation. Compared with field laborers, domestic servants generally did have better food, clothing, and shelter, but because of their close and constant contact with their owners, they had less independence. Unlike field hands, who enjoyed some leisure time,

the camaraderie of working with family and friends, and separate living quarters, house servants were always on call and seldom escaped from their owners' direct supervision. Some slaves preferred the relative independence of the fields over confinement to the house. Although many house slaves had close relationships with their owners, others became targets of their masters' fits of anger, systematic abuse, and unwanted sexual advances. Also, when a master took an interest in a female slave, the jealous wife frequently took her anger out on the slave woman.

There is little evidence to support the contention that house slaves allied themselves more closely with their masters than with the field hands. Rather than distancing themselves from other slaves, many house servants had husbands, wives, and children among the field hands. Domestics used their positions within the main house to aid the rest of the slave community. They commonly passed information, food, and stolen items from the house to the quarters. On the largest, most aristocratic plantations a caste system of

Family Amalgamation among the Men-stealers.   Page 91.

In this U.S. antislavery cartoon from the 1830s, children working as domestic slaves serve at table for a white southern family. [Library of Congress/Corbis]

sorts may have divided the slaves, but most plantations simply did not have enough slaves for the house servants to remain aloof.

Still the genuine affection many masters felt for their domestics gave house slaves some important advantages over field hands. In urban settings masters allowed their slaves a degree of independence not found on plantations. Often, slaves hired themselves out for money, and in Rio de Janeiro masters permitted slaves to earn money by peddling goods in the streets. Only with reluctance did masters sell their house servants apart from their families. In the Dutch West Indies, household slaves who had to be sold were given a slip marked with their price and allowed to seek a new master on their own. Occasionally, masters freed their favorite house slaves who had given years of faithful service. Almost universally, household slaves were manumitted more often than field slaves, who had less personal contact with their masters.

Despite these similarities, there were some notable differences from place to place in the experiences of household slaves. In many regions, masters preferred female slaves as domestics; but in the Dutch West Indies, Jamaica, and the U.S. South a significant number of males worked in the main house, and in the French Caribbean men composed the bulk of house slaves. When males and females served together, the division of labor was often based on gender. Men usually served as coachmen, valets, and gardeners, while women were cooks, laundresses, and nannies. Latin American and Caribbean slaveholders showed a distinct preference for light-skinned mulatto or quadroon servants; planters in the U.S. South, with some exceptions, had servants of every color.

In some regions a household slave was highly specialized, performing only one task such as cooking, sewing, or child rearing. Specialization among slaves was probably most pronounced in ancient Rome, where the slaves of wealthy masters were given only one job, thus making them more accountable for their work. Although slaves were less specialized in the Dutch West Indies, Rio de Janeiro, and Martinique, if one slave became sick, the master might have difficulty coaxing another to take over. During the eighteenth century in the Dutch colony at Cape of Good Hope, wet nurses and nannies were the most common domestic servants. In the U.S. South, masters expected their house slaves to perform a number of duties. During peak times, planters sent their household slaves into the fields to harvest crops or shuck corn.

See also ANCIENT ROME; URBAN SLAVERY.

BIBLIOGRAPHY

GENOVESE, EUGENE D. *Roll Jordan Roll: The World the Slaves Made.* 1974.

KARASCH, MARY C. *Slave Life in Rio de Janeiro, 1808–1850.* 1987.

MORRISSEY, MARRIETTA. *Slave Women in the New World: Gender Stratification in the Caribbean.* 1989.

SHELL, ROBERT C.-H. *Children of Bondage: A Social History of the Slave Society at the Cape of Good Hope, 1652–1838.* 1994.

James W. Paxton

Housing

Slave houses are usually described in historical assessments as little more than rude hovels, but housing actually demonstrates considerable regional variation in plantation conduct, and it provides intimate evidence of African-Americans' attempts to shape their fate even though they were held captive.

Lacking a consistent form, slave housing was determined essentially by function and location; it consisted of commonplace houses (often identical to those of whites!) intended to shelter captive African-Americans, mainly on plantation estates. Plans and building techniques for slave houses closely followed the patterns used by "plain folk." Since their customs varied markedly from place to place, so did the forms of slave housing. For example, slave dwellings in southern Louisiana, with their distinctive built-in porches—a feature acquired from the French Caribbean—would never be confused with the slave houses of South Carolina and Georgia, which were based on English plans. The upper South was strongly influenced by farming practices derived from nearby Pennsylvania; but what proved particularly appealing to planters in Maryland and Virginia was the Pennsylvanians' preference for stone masonry over wood frame construction, and so these planters used stone, when appropriate, even in the construction of slave quarters. In the nineteenth century the Georgia planter Thomas Spalding experimented with "tabby," a crude type of concrete made of sand, lime, and oyster shells, which led to a tradition of building concrete slave cabins throughout the coastal regions of Georgia and Florida, but nowhere else.

Slave houses were generally small—most consisted of only one or two rooms, although plans with as many as eight rooms were becoming more common by the mid-nineteenth century. Most were expediently constructed and were meant to provide nothing more than a place to eat and sleep. Yet former slaves frequently testify that they often found ways to add comforting domestic touches. They describe their efforts to keep their quarters neat and tidy; one woman recalls that even a dirt floor could be swept "clean and white." Men with carpentry skills built stools and cupboards and diligently attended to necessary repairs.

A row of brick slave quarters on the Hermitage Plantation, Savannah, Georgia. [Library of Congress/Corbis]

Gifted needleworkers sewed quilts with interesting designs; since the cabins were filled mainly with beds and mattress ticks, these quilts could powerfully brighten a room. On occasion, slaves who had managed to earn a little of their own money by working overtime in the garden patches designated for their personal use purchased color lithographs to decorate the rough cabin walls. As a result of these efforts, hovels were converted into an approximation of homes—an achievement that reflects both the slaves' will to endure and their desire to sustain a sense of home and family, two social institutions that were as precious as they were vulnerable.

Planters, when they looked out over their slave cabins, saw devices for social control. The quarters, rows of identical buildings set at regular intervals and all facing in the same direction, were intended as a statement of discipline. But from the slaves' perspective another interpretation was possible. Held there together but apart and often a considerable distance away from the plantation owner, slaves felt keenly the spatial coherence of their own community. It was within the quarters that they began to stitch together an alternative culture marked by repeated expression of the hope for liberation. Seen in this light, the quarters were also a site of resistance.

See also CLOTHING, U.S.; MATERIAL CULTURE IN THE UNITED STATES; PLANTATIONS.

BIBLIOGRAPHY

VLACH, JOHN MICHAEL. *Back of the Big House: The Architecture of Plantation Slavery.* 1993.
———. "Not Mansions . . . But Good Enough": Slave Quarters as Bi-Cultural Expression." In *Black and White Cultural Interaction in the Antebellum South,* edited by Ted Ownby. 1993.

John Michael Vlach

Hughes, Henry   [1829–1862]

Southern sociologist and politician.

Born in the small town of Port Gibson, Mississippi, on 17 April 1829, Henry Hughes lost his father when he was thirteen, graduated from a local Presbyterian college in 1847, studied law in New Orleans, and at the age of twenty-one gained admission to the Louisiana bar. In 1853–1854 he toured Europe and upon his return published *Treatise on Sociology, Theoretical and Practical* (1854). Boldly proclaiming that there were "no slaves" in the South, Hughes argued that unfree labor, as it existed in the United States, was best understood as a "form of mutual insurance or warranteeism" dedicated to "the subsistence and progress of all." Unlike the North's free-labor economy, which he believed should "be abolished," the South's progressive "systemic organization" seemed to him a "necessity of justice, humanity, purity, and order."

An active Democratic politician in late-1850s Mississippi, Hughes railed against the "atrocities" of "racial amalgamation," bitterly opposed the "unnatural" and "unwarranted" extension of political rights to women, and zealously campaigned for the reopening of the African slave trade as a means of restoring southern honor and facilitating the region's expansion. According to Hughes, "sagacious and benevolent extermination" of the mixed-blooded populations in "all Mexico, all Central and South America" was "a certainty and perhaps an ethnical duty." Moreover, "since the pure blooded Indians" could never "be civilized," they would have to be "directly or indirectly . . . benignly slaughtered." During the Civil War, Hughes served as colonel for the Twelfth Regiment of Mississippi Guards, and on 3 October 1862 he died of inflammatory rheumatism while recruiting "Partizan Rangers" for the Confederate cause.

See also MISCEGENATION; PERSPECTIVES ON SLAVERY.

BIBLIOGRAPHY

AMBROSE, DOUGLAS. *Henry Hughes and Proslavery Thought in the Old South.* 1996.
LYMAN, STANFORD M., ed. *Selected Writings of Henry Hughes, Antebellum Southerner, Slavocrat, Sociologist.* 1985.

TAKAKI, RONALD T. *A Pro-Slavery Crusade: The Agitation to Reopen the African Slave Trade.* 1971.

Eric Robert Papenfuse

Human Sacrifice

This entry includes the following articles: The New World and Pacific Cultures; The Old World.

The New World and Pacific Cultures

Where slave owning cultures in pre-Columbian America and the precontact Pacific Islands practiced human sacrifice, they often made slaves the victims. The Tlingit and Nootka, who inhabited the northwestern part of North America (present-day British Columbia, Washington, and Oregon), sacrificed slaves at potlatches, funerals, and other ceremonies. The Tlingit would throw bound slaves on funeral pyres of deceased relatives, burning the slaves alive with the body. The Aleuts in Alaska often killed slaves in mourning ceremonies and in other tribal or family celebrations.

Human sacrifice, often of slaves, was particularly common in the large, often warlike states of Mexico, Central America, and South America. The Aztec state in Mexico held elaborate political rituals, which included sacrifice of as many as twenty thousand people a year. The Aztecs frequently ate parts of their victims' bodies. The main sources of humans for these ceremonies were captured enemy warriors and purchased slaves. Captured enemies were much like slaves in that they were denied liberty and access to their own people and were forced to serve the interests of their captors, even by dying. The Maya and Inca also sent slaves to their death for the politico-religious purposes of the rulers.

Uncentralized peoples of the Americas and the Pacific atolls also sacrificed slaves. The Tupinamba, hunters and gatherers of present-day Brazil, turned captured enemies, including women and children, into slaves, whom they later sacrificed and sometimes ate. In the central Celebes the Toradjas often sacrificed a slave—bought from neighboring tribes or captured in raids mounted for the purpose—at the death

A human sacrifice among the Inca of Peru. [Leonard de Selva/Corbis]

of an important member of the community. The Maori of New Zealand sometimes enslaved and later sacrificed enemy captives in religious ceremonies. In Hawaii lower-caste members of the community were sometimes enslaved, to be sacrificed later when priests required such gifts to the gods.

See also AMERINDIAN SOCIETIES.

BIBLIOGRAPHY

BRUNDAGE, BURR C. *The Fifth Sun: Aztec Gods, Aztec World.* 1979.
PATTERSON, ORLANDO. *Slavery and Social Death: A Comparative Study.* 1982.

Paul Finkelman

The Old World

Societies throughout the world have sacrificed human beings at the climactic moments of their most sacred community ceremonies, and they have often concentrated this sacramental shedding of blood on the killing of slaves. Examples range from ancient Egyptian interment of servants with deceased royalty in a cult of the dead, through ritualized Roman confrontations of slave gladiators against savage lions and the regular immolation of large numbers of war captives in the "annual customs" in the nineteenth-century West African kingdom of Dahomey, to the formal slaughter of single slaves by small communities of Native American hunters and gatherers. Collective, symbolically intense killings of captives did not survive as political ritual in cultures of slavery based on universalistic ethics—Christian or Muslim monotheism, or capitalist economic environments—except faintly, as exemplary public punishments for threatened revolt under racialized slavery or as brutal perversions of individual masters.

Sacrifice in this ritualized, socially legitimate (or legitimizing) sense must thus be distinguished from occasional individual killings deriving from the personal abuse of the unbridled power that slavery accords masters. Public, collective rituals of this sort concentrate on killing slaves for reasons that go beyond even the economic cost of a human life valued as property, since the slaves sacrificed primarily represent "outsiders," symbolically charged "others" who negatively define the boundaries and meaning of any community. In cultures that accent communal social identities, the collective murder of a human token of the aliens excluded from sharing in the deed intensely confirms the benefits of belonging. The sacrifice of slaves lies at the controlled, internal end of a symbolic continuum of shared ritual violence that extends outward from the center of a society, through ceremonial warfare, to the genocidal slaughter of uncaptured outsiders perceived as "enemies."

See also AMERINDIAN SOCIETIES; WEST AFRICA.

BIBLIOGRAPHY

BAY, EDNA G. *Wives of the Leopard.* 1998.
PATTERSON, ORLANDO. *Slavery and Social Death: A Comparative Study.* 1982.

Joseph C. Miller

Hurd, John Codman   [1816–1892]

U.S. legal theorist and author.

John Codman Hurd was raised in Boston, Massachusetts, and New York City. A trained lawyer and member of the bar, he preferred to study law rather than practice it. He was particularly interested in the legal theories associated with slavery because the debate on this issue in the United States prior to the Civil War made little distinction between principles of law and matters of conscience. His books, *Topics of Jurisprudence Connected with Conditions of Freedom and Bondage* (1856) and *The Law of Freedom and Bondage in the United States* (2 vols., 1858–1862), present a dispassionate exposition of U.S. juridical thinking regarding slavery. These works examine the articles of the Constitution and the Federal, state, and local laws dealing with slavery, as well as hundreds of judicial decisions that interpreted those statutes.

The most interesting aspect of Hurd's work concerns slavery's role as a cause of the Civil War. Approaching slavery from a juridical rather than an ethical perspective, he regarded the war as a constitutional crisis arising over the slavery question. He contended that, while states' rights underlay southern court decisions in favor of slavery, it also informed northern court decisions against slavery. He concluded that, on this question at least, the Constitution failed to operate as a point of positive law and functioned instead as if it were an international treaty, a failure he blamed on the legal profession and the judiciary. In any event, Hurd's work was published too late to have much effect on the events of his day.

See also LAW; CONSTITUTION, U.S.

BIBLIOGRAPHY

HURD, JOHN CODMAN. *The Law of Freedom and Bondage in the United States.* 2 vols. 1858–1862. Reprint, 1968.

Charles W. Carey Jr.

I

Iceland

See Scandinavia.

Illinois

In the mid-eighteenth century French settlers, who often owned slaves, moved into what is today Illinois. After the Seven Years' War (1763) the region became part of the British empire, and at the time of the American Revolution it was claimed by Virginia. In 1787, Congress, operating under the Articles of Confederation, passed the Northwest Ordinance, which among other things provided that

> There shall be neither slavery nor involuntary servitude in the said territory, otherwise than in the punishment of crimes whereof the party shall have been duly convicted: *Provided always,* that any person escaping into the same, from whom labor or service is lawfully claimed in any one of the original States, such fugitive may be lawfully reclaimed and conveyed to the person claiming his or her labor or service as aforesaid.

The slave owners in the "Illinois country" of the Indiana territory, some from Virginia and others "old French" settlers, resisted the ordinance, and as early as 1788 began petitioning Congress to either repeal it or grant them an exemption from it. They claimed that the ordinance illegally deprived them of their property. In 1800 over 365 residents of the region petitioned Congress to allow them to bring an unlimited number of new slaves into the territory, with the proviso that the children of these slaves would be freed, the sons at age thirty-one and the daughters at age twenty-eight. When Congress did not act, the settlers took matters into their own hands, often holding blacks in servitude as "indentured servants" or "apprentices" for terms as long as ninety-nine years. In addition, various territorial legislatures adopted laws to protect the property of slave owners already in Illinois and to encourage new masters to settle there.

Unlike the constitutions of other northern states, Illinois' constitution of 1818 did not end slavery. Rather, it declared that slavery could not "hereafter be introduced into this State." It also confirmed the status of slaves and black servants under long-term indenture who were already in the state. Finally, it allowed operators of salt mines to import rented slaves for one-year periods up to 1825. In 1819 the new state legislature enacted a law to regulate "Free Negroes, Mulattoes, Servants, and Slaves." At the time, there were over eleven hundred slaves and indentured blacks in Illinois. In 1822–1823 proslavery forces in Illinois attempted to call a constitutional convention to legalize bondage in the state. They were defeated in part because of heroic campaigning by Governor Edward Coles, a former slave owner who had come from Virginia to free his slaves in Illinois. Nevertheless, more than one thousand people remained in bondage in Illinois. Eventually, in 1848, a new state constitution banned slavery, freeing the last slaves owned by the settlers of the territorial era.

423

OUR POLITICAL SNAKE-CHARMER.

DOUGLAS.—You perceive, ladies and gentlemen, that the creatures are entirely under my control.   (Aside) Say, Forney, hope these bruits won't bite!

A political cartoon from Vanity Fair *depicts Senator Stephen Douglas as a charmer of snakes, referring to his attempt to placate differing factions just before the Civil War.* [Library of Congress/Corbis]

Illinois remained hostile to black immigrants and prohibited them in the 1850s, but this had little or no effect: the state's black population continued to grow throughout the decade. There were a few notable instances of whites helping runaways, but for most southern owners Illinois was one of the best "free" states in which to recover fugitive slaves.

Settlement patterns in Illinois were responsible for the state's ambivalent attitude toward slavery and race. Southern Illinois, especially the "little Egypt" region near Cairo, had many of the "old French" settlers as well as former Virginians and Kentuckians. Hostility to blacks was high; sympathy for slaves was low. Northern Illinois had many former New Englanders and New Yorkers, who tended to oppose slavery and to support the Free Soil Party in 1848 and the Republicans after 1854. The two most famous politicians from Illinois, Stephen A. Douglas and Abraham Lincoln, personified the divided nature of the state. Douglas, its most popular politician throughout the 1850s, claimed that he did not care if slavery was "voted up or down" in the territories; Lincoln did care, and his unswerving opposition to the spread of slavery helped catapult him to the White House.

See also COLES, EDWARD; DOUGLAS, STEPHEN A.; LINCOLN, ABRAHAM; NORTHWEST ORDINANCE.

BIBLIOGRAPHY

FINKELMAN, PAUL. *Slavery and the Founders: Race and Liberty in the Age of Jefferson.* 1996.
HARRIS, N. DWIGHT. *The History of Negro Servitude in Illinois.* 1904.

Paul Finkelman

Inca

See Amerindian Societies; Human Sacrifice.

Indiana

At the end of the Revolution, Virginia claimed the sparsely populated area that now makes up Indiana. A few slaveholding "old French" settlers lived there, mostly around Vincennes, as well as a few slave-owning Virginians who moved there after the Revolutionary War. In 1787 Congress, operating under the Articles of Confederation, passed the Northwest Ordinance, which among other things provided that

> There shall be neither slavery nor involuntary servitude in the said territory, otherwise than in the punishment of crimes whereof the party shall have been duly convicted: *Provided always,* that any person escaping into the same, from whom labor or service is lawfully claimed in any one of the original States, such fugitive may be lawfully reclaimed and conveyed to the person claiming his or her labor or service as aforesaid.

The slave owners in the territory, some from Virginia and others "old French" settlers, resisted the ordinance and petitioned Congress either to repeal it or to grant them an exemption from it. In 1802 the territorial governor William Henry Harrison, who was a slave owner from Virginia, chaired a convention in Vincennes that petitioned Congress to allow slave imports into Indiana for a ten-year period. When Congress did not act, the Indiana territorial legislature adopted laws allowing for the long-term indenture of blacks. Throughout its territorial period these settlers held blacks in servitude, often as "indentured servants" or "apprentices," for terms as long as ninety-nine years. In addition, various territorial legislatures adopted laws to protect the property of slave owners already in Indiana, to encourage new masters to settle there, and to limit the rights of free blacks.

In 1809 Congress separated Indiana Territory from Illinois Territory. After that, Indiana prohibited the introduction of new slaves or indentured servants. Indiana's constitution of 1816 flatly prohibited slavery and also prohibited importing blacks held to long indentures. It also asserted that slavery could "only originate in usurpation and tyranny." In 1816 the supreme court of Indiana declared that any slaves remaining in the state were free, and in 1830 the state census recorded only a handful of slaves—who were in fact legally entitled to be free.

Indiana remained hostile to free blacks until after the Civil War. Nevertheless, many Indianians were also strongly antislavery. In 1849 virtually the entire town of South Bend turned out to rescue fugitive slaves being taken back to Kentucky by their master. Quaker communities throughout the state were also known as being antislavery and for their willingness to aid fugitive slaves. In 1860 Indiana, like the rest of the North, supported Lincoln, who, for all his contradictions, was unalterably opposed to the spread of slavery and was dedicated to somehow putting slavery on the road of "ultimate extinction."

See also ILLINOIS; NORTHWEST ORDINANCE.

BIBLIOGRAPHY

DUNN, JACOB P. *Indiana: A Redemption from Slavery.* 1900.
FINKELMAN, PAUL. *Slavery and the Founders: Race and Liberty in the Age of Jefferson.* 1996.
THORNBROUGH, EMMA LOU. *The Negro in Indiana: A Study of a Minority.* 1957.

Paul Finkelman

Indians, American

See Native Americans.

Indian Subcontinent

The earliest Sanskrit texts outline several modes of enslavement, such as capture and purchase, birth to a domestic slave, and judicial decree. In later texts it is clear that enslavement could also result from debt, apostasy, and defilement by cohabitation with a slave. The characteristic social alienation of the individual slave was more pronounced when she or he came from outside the owner's region. In those instances where a community had surrendered some of its members or individuals assented to their own enslavement, for reasons such as poverty and misbehavior, such people were ostracized and became absolutely dependent on one household, but they were rarely absolute aliens in cultural terms.

Although slaves have existed in all periods for which there are historical records, their characteristic features, patterns of acquisition, location, labor, and manumission have varied enormously in time and across regions within the subcontinent. For instance, while capture appears to have been a major source of slaves in Upper India between about 700 and 1100 C.E. a more dependable supply through markets and trade routes was assured from the thirteenth century onward. We know this from documents that speak of rulers attempting to regulate slave prices. Nonetheless, many issues remain either unresolved or unstudied. For instance, although some historians of medieval India have argued for the disappearance of internal slave markets in the fifteenth century, European traders who arrived after 1498 (Portuguese, Dutch, French, and English) reported the prices of slaves at specific ports in the Indian Ocean. It is possible that these were not mutually contradictory observations: it is also possible that the reduced visibility of the public market from the fifteenth century onward may have expanded direct, private modes of slave transfers such as distress mortgages and sales, postmortem legacies, and ritual gifting. The intensification of taxation within each region starting in the late seventeenth and early eighteenth centuries under the regional ruling houses that broke away from the Mughal Empire may well have created a network of indebtedness along which younger, poorer, and female sections of each population were transferred into slavery. While we know of regular but small-scale slave trades between the major regions from the seventeenth century through to the nineteenth century, the trade routes between different regions and localities within the subcontinent have yet to be mapped. The numbers of slaves might have expanded over time, but the numbers that the British administration in the 1830s recorded are unreliable because of confusion regarding the categories enumerated.

Slavery and Caste

Typologies of labor (such as agrarian and domestic and waged and wageless) and the conditions of its performance—coerced or free—led both early English observers and twentieth-century historians to merge the concepts of slavery and caste in much of India. Thus, officials of the English East India Company recorded large numbers of agricultural and laboring *jatis* (formally endogamous, commensal groups), particularly in Hindu South India, as slave castes. However, the indigenous records reveal that within each *jati* there were slaves, those born into slavery, and nonslaves alike. The social and legal destinies of each section depended on a host of intersecting factors. Since social and ritual rank depended on the observance of ancestor-feeding rituals, observance of proscriptions on food and commensality, normative connubiality, and the power of local authorities to maintain or lower the ranks of individuals and families, slaves within a lower *jati* might be either segmented off (as in Maharashtra) or assimilated with the nonslave sections of a higher *jati* (as in Bengal). Before the establishment of colonial rule and census operations in the mid-nineteenth century, the predominance of certain lower *jatis* among slaves was the consequence of their inability to pay taxes or judicial fine: in short, poverty. However, famine or warfare could entrap the poorer sections of any *jati* and force higher *jatis* to violate all written injunctions meant to protect them from enslavement. Hence, in the thirteenth century, female slaves of the higher *rajaputra* status were held by lower-*jati* masters in Gujarat, while high-status Brahmin boys sold by their parents in times of famine eventually became viceroys and military commanders of regional ruling houses in northern and eastern India in the eighteenth century.

The two major questions regarding *jati* status and jural status that have concerned historians of slavery have been the stability of instability of *jati* rank regardless of slave status and the location and labor of slaves commensurate with *jati* prescriptions on pollution and purity. The answers vary according to time, gender, and the nature of the acquiring household. In the early and later medieval period, male slaves worked as artisans, traders, agents, soldiers, personal attendants, and grooms in both Islamic and non-Islamic households. Fourteenth-century records of Hindu households speak of slave girls performing "pure" (such as threshing grain and gathering fuel) and "polluting" (sweeping and cleaning) labor in both house and field, evidence that some households did not restrict high-status slaves to indoor tasks, and lower-*jati* slaves to outdoor tasks. By the eighteenth century, however, the demand for higher-*jati* slaves for domestic purposes led to some lower-*jati* females (including Muslims) "passing" into the households of highborn Hindus. The consequences of discovery varied according to the region and class of the acquiring household;

in Maharashtra, for example, a large household had to undergo ritual purification after such an unwitting contamination, while in Bengal a poorer Brahmin household evaded such expiation. Those enslaved as infants would have found it hard to remember and reenact their originary *jati* identities because the very process of acculturation in a slaveholder's household ensured the obliteration of origins and the inability to maintain prescriptive norms, such as those associated with food. Thus by the early nineteenth century, some first-person accounts by female slaves in the households of British military officers spoke of having "lost caste." The inability of female slaves to avoid the sexual predation of male members of their master's or mistress's household might have enhanced their own sense of having infringed given codes of conduct. Both male and female slaves could be "married off" to others by their owners. Since few extant records delineate the *jati* status of the slave's spouse, it may be inferred that the matter of conforming to the endogamous norms governing nonslave members of a *jati* depended on the will of their masters and mistresses.

Slavery and Law

The onset of English East India Company rule in large parts of the subcontinent in the nineteenth century brought a legal makeover of older modes of enslavement, status reckoning, and the judicial and fiscal exemptions enjoyed by some slaves. For instance, the diminished liability of slaves for public taxes (like the

Nineteenth-century Indian slaves transport an official in a sedan chair. [Christel Gerstenberg/Corbis]

jaziya paid by non-Islamic subjects under the Mughals in the seventeenth century) and public labor (as in the Assamese militia) and the diminished responsibility of minor slaves for offenses punishable by the ruler were eroded by a European legal system that imposed a uniform punishment for all offenders. From the 1830s particularly, landed households that had allotted plots to some male slaves at reduced rents faced government demands for the standard tax from all lands. Contemporary (1800–1850) legislative efforts to curb the slave trade of other European powers in India strengthened the growing abolitionist lobby in England. However, when the charter of the English East India Company was renewed in 1833, the abolition of slavery in India was left to the initiative of the governor-general. The law commission, under Thomas Babington Macaulay, was divided on the issue of abolition. Finally, under pressure from Parliament, the brief Act 5 of 1843 was passed. Since this act stipulated that no government officials would sell slaves to realize taxes, that no slave could be disinherited on the ground of his or her slave status, and that offences committed by masters against slaves were as culpable as those against freemen, it is believed to have delegalized slavery. However, there was no emancipation of slaves, and very little publicity was given to the act. Furthermore, since many of the officials who interpreted and implemented the act supported slavery, the law gave slaves little relief. Socioeconomic change in the course of the late nineteenth and early twentieth centuries led to the transformation of slave-master relations into other asymmetrical forms.

See also CASTE SYSTEMS.

BIBLIOGRAPHY

ANDERSON, MICHAEL R. "Work Construed: Ideological Origins of Labour Law in British India to 1918." In *Dalit Movements and the Meanings of Labour in India*, edited by Peter Robb. 1993.

BANAJI, DINSHAW. *Slavery in British India*. 1933.

CHAKRAVARTI, UMA. "Conceptualising Brahmanical Patriarchy in Early India: Gender, Caste, Class and State." *Economic and Political Weekly* 28, no. 14 (1993): 579–585.

CHANANA, DEV RAJ. *Slavery in Ancient India*. 1960.

CHATTERJEE, INDRANI. "Slavery and the Household: Bengal 1770–1880". Ph.D. diss., University of London, 1996.

CHATTOPADHYAYA, AMAL K. *Slavery in Bengal Presidency*. 1977.

DINGWANEY, MANJARI, and UTSA PATNAIK, eds. *Chains of Servitude*. 1985.

GUHA, SUMIT. "An Indian Penal Regime: Maharashtra in the Eighteenth Century." *Past and Present* 147 (1995): 101–126.

HABIB, IRFAN. "Slavery in the Delhi Sultanate, Thirteenth and Fourteenth Centuries—Evidence from Sufic Literature." *Indian Historical Review* 15, nos. 1–2 (1988–1989): 248–256.

KUMAR, DHARMA. "Colonialism, Bondage and Caste in British India." In *Breaking the Chains: Slavery, Bondage and Emancipation in Africa and Asia*, edited by Martin A. Klein. 1993.

KUMAR, SUNIL. "When Slaves Were Nobles: The Shamsi Bandagan in the Early Delhi Sultanate." *Studies in History* 10, no. 1 (1994): 23–52.

PRAKASH, GYAN. "Terms of Servitude: The Colonial Discourse on Slavery and Bondage in India." In *Breaking the Chains: Slavery, Bondage and Emancipation in Africa and Asia*, edited by Martin A. Klein. 1993.

Indrani Chatterjee

Indonesia

Slavery was widespread in the diverse precolonial societies of archepelagic Southeast Asia, including those islands which constitute modern Indonesia. It usually involved patron-client ties resulting from debt bondage, although war captives and criminals were also sometimes enslaved.

Inscriptions found in southeast Sumatra (on the Straits of Melaka), and attributed to the maritime empire of Srivijaya (seventh through fourteenth centuries), provide evidence for the antiquity of slavery in this region. Dating from 683 C.E., these inscriptions assert the king's power over his subjects and their bondspeople. Slavery was also used in the inland Javanese kingdom of Mataram (sixth through tenth centuries). The enormous temple complex of Borobudur, dating from the late eighth century, was built by royal bondsmen, although their numbers and origins are unknown.

Chronicles from the Majapahit empire, centred in eastern Java but controlling trade and exerting suzerainty over most of modern Indonesia at its height in the fourteenth century, give specific details about social distinctions. Apart from the religious communities and nobility, the bulk of the population were free peasants and debt-slaves, although the king used *kawula*, the Javanese word for slave, for all of his subjects. The nominally free peasantry became debt-bondspeople after the disintegration of Majapahit and the rise of the inland Javanese kingdom of late Mataram in the fifteenth century. Written sources cannot confirm the existence of large numbers of war captives being enslaved or an extensive insular slave trade prior to this time.

It was not until Islamization intensified in Southeast Asia after 1400 that written legal codes provided details about the status of slaves. The fifteenth-century Melaka Law Code, Udang-undang Melaka, distinguishes between royal slaves and common slaves and those enslaved for crimes or as war captives. (Although situated on the Malay peninsula, within the history of

Sculptures of Buddha stand in niches on Borobudur Temple, which was built by royal bondsmen, in Java, Indonesia, around 800 A.D. [Charles & Josette Lenars/Corbis]

Indonesia, Melaka is considered a direct descendent of the classical empire of Srivijaya). Slaves were the main source of labor and of concubines in the city. Most were Javanese bondspeople supplied by merchants from Java. The considerable extent of slaveholding can be gauged by European travellers, who estimated that slaves were the greatest source of wealth in precolonial Melaka, and that the wealthiest merchants had as many as seven hundred slaves each.

Conversion to Islam by rulers and their subjects had a profound effect on the religious and legal organization of Indonesian societies, particularly the institution of slavery. Because Islamic law forbade the sale of Muslims and encouraged conversion of slaves by their masters, the supply of slaves shifted to external non-Muslim sources. By the sixteenth century Islamic Java was no longer exporting its own people. In the Aceh sultanate in western Sumatra, which rose to power just as the European presence in Indonesia was intensifying, Sultan Iskander Muda (1607–1636) sub-

jugated Aceh's non-Islamic neighbors, taking approximately twenty-two thousand captives into slavery.

Anthony Reid argues that accelerating commercialism in Southeast Asia from the sixteenth century hardened relationships of bondage, introducing a more rigid concept of slaves as property. Women bought as slave concubines were often traded in these commercial cities, although their children were eventually assimilated into the free population. Commercial cities, rice-growing lowland states in Sumatra, Java, and Borneo, and the Bugis people of South Sulawesi absorbed increasing numbers of slaves from microstates in Nias, Bali, eastern Indonesia, and New Guinea and from the more vulnerable stateless hills people. Both Islamic Makassar in South Sulawesi and Banten in western Java sought slaves from Maluku and the Lesser Sunda Islands, including Bali. At the height of its power the Makassarese state of Gowa cut off the export of slaves from its own domain. The Dutch conquest of Makassar in 1669 reopened the area to raiding and trade in slaves. The tiny island sultanates of Sulu, Buton, and Tidore raided eastern Indonesian islands and the southern Philippines to supply slaves for the city markets and the pepper plantations in Borneo.

After the seventeenth century some forms of slavery used by the Dutch East India Company in the region were initially similar on the surface to those of indigenous societies, particularly the use of slaves as indicators of wealth and status in cities, such as Batavia, and the use of slave women as concubines. But the Dutch instituted new forms of chattel and plantation slavery to the archipelago as well, while also extending the transportation of slaves to the Cape of Good Hope, making Batavia a major slave entrepôt for the region until the end of the eighteenth century.

See also NETHERLANDS AND THE DUTCH EMPIRE; PHILIPPINES; SLAVE TRADE; SOUTHEAST ASIA.

BIBLIOGRAPHY

REID, ANTHONY. *Southeast Asia in the Age of Commerce 1440–1680,* vol 1: *The Land below the Winds.* 1988.
———, ed. *Slavery, Bondage and Dependency in Southeast Asia.* 1983.
TARLING, NICHOLAS, ed. *The Cambridge History of Southeast Asia,* vol. 1: *From Early Times to ca. 1800.* 1992.

Kerry Ward
Nigel Worden

Industrial Slaves

In the decades between 1820 and 1860, as many as 5 percent of the 4 million enslaved African-Americans in the United States worked in industry. Slave labor was used in most industries in the South. Slaves often worked alongside free workers in the same textile mill. This could be risky for free workers because southern law and social custom allowed slaves only minimal status and capacity, which meant that industrial slaves could not be held legally responsible for their actions in the workplace. Iron manufacturing in the South depended on slaves as general laborers and as skilled ironworkers. Industrial slaves processed southern agricultural products such as tobacco, hemp, rice, and sugar. The mining of coal, iron, and even gold in the South also relied heavily on industrial slaves. Slaves worked in railroad construction and ship building, and as laborers or switchmen on railroads and steamships. Before his escape from slavery, Frederick Douglass worked alongside white workers as a ship's caulker in Baltimore.

Industrial bondspeople—men, women, and even children—worked in a number of occupations and tasks. Women and older children operated water-powered equipment in textile mills to produce yarn and cloth from carded cotton. In the tobacco manufactories of the upper South, men worked in the heavy occupations; for example, twisters fashioned the tobacco into twists which were cut for chewing, and hogsheads-men bound the leaves into heavy bundles for transport. In the same tobacco factories women worked at lighter tasks, such as preparing the tobacco leaves for processing. Most industrial bondspeople who worked in occupations that required skill received training in the workplace. Even though most of the occupations could be learned in a short period of time, a number of industrial slaves were trained as skilled artisans, completing long-term training or an apprenticeship. Industrial slaves were prominent in occupations such as blacksmithing, carpentry, and coopering (barrel making), and this work frequently brought them into competition with free laborers in urban areas.

The use of slave labor in industry was quite profitable, and most industrialists either invested directly in the purchase of bondspeople or leased agricultural slaves for their industrial enterprises. Many slaveholders involved in industrial activities in the South counted the value of their enslaved workers as investment capital. This was especially true in industries, such as textile mills, sugar refineries, and rice mills, that processed agricultural products. Not all industrialists were willing to make such a large investment in labor; about one-fifth of industrial slaves were leased to industrialists on a monthly or annual contract. Slaves were hired especially for tobacco manufacturing and mining operations. The cost of hiring slaves fluctuated with the difficulty (and danger) of the task, but it increased significantly in the latter antebellum

decades. The hiring of slaves reached its peak in the 1850s, when the cost averaged between $120 and $150 per hand annually.

For industrialists, it was less expensive to purchase or hire slave labor than to employ free wage labor. To further cut labor costs, industrial slaves were forced to work long hours, six days per week, and often were not provided with adequate food, clothing, or shelter. Unlike free laborers, who could leave an unfavorable work situation, slaves were bound to their employer against their will. Slaves' dissatisfaction was expressed occasionally through attempts to escape, but more frequently through work slowdowns, refusal to work, feigned illness, or temporary absences from the workplace.

See also MINERS; RESISTANCE, DAY-TO-DAY.

BIBLIOGRAPHY

FINKELMAN, PAUL. "Slaves as Fellow Servants: Ideology, Law, and Industrialization." *American Journal of Legal History* 31 (1987).
LEWIS, RONALD L. *Coal, Iron, and Slaves: Industrial Slavery in Maryland and Virginia, 1715–1865.* 1979.
STAROBIN, ROBERT S. *Industrial Slavery in the Old South.* 1970.
WHITMAN, T. STEPHEN. "Industrial Slavery at the Margin: The Maryland Chemical Works." *Journal of Southern History* 59 (1993): 31–62.

Diane Barnes

Insurance on Slaves and Slave Traders

See Plantations; Slave Trade.

Insurrections

Resistance was a steady product of slavery itself, but its most extreme form, insurrection, occurred relatively rarely. Violent revolt was generally a dubious tactic because of the gross imparities of power within the system and the slaveholders' vigilance and willingness to repress brutally any overt challenge to their presumed total mastery. Only one slave rebellion has been deemed lastingly successful, that in Haiti in 1791. Only about fifty slave uprisings are known worldwide in which the victims of the insurrectionists were not confined to a single property. Also recorded are about an equal number of major alleged slave conspiracies where all actual violence came from the owners. In addition, there were over fifty shipboard slave insurrections, such as that on the *Amistad* in 1839.

Some sociologists and historians of slavery have suggested that slave insurrection was likely under the following conditions: (1) economic decline; (2) divisions within or threats to the ruling society; (3) a high proportion of slaves in the population; (4) notably harsh treatment; and (5) cultural-linguistic unity among slaves. Such preconditions for slave rebellion are commonsensical, but most of the largest insurrections drew together slaves of very diverse backgrounds. And there is little evidence that such conditions were notably stronger when rebellions occurred than in many of the long stretches when they did not.

Three of the largest slave insurrections in world history occurred in a seventy-year period in the Roman Empire, two of them in Sicily (ca. 137–132 and 103–99 B.C.) and the third under Spartacus in southern Italy (73–71 B.C.). The first of these, which began with the murder of two particularly cruel slaveholders, was the largest and most nearly successful. At one time, perhaps 200,000 slaves were involved who controlled four major towns and almost half the island of Sicily. Roman tenacity, however, repressed each of these revolts, in which an estimated 60,000 rebels were killed in battles. Brutalities occurred on both sides, but the slave rebels often showed a moderation lacking in their oppressors. The thousands crucified by the Romans were matched throughout the history of slavery by hundreds burnt alive, quartered, castrated, gibbeted, or torn on wheels, or whose heads were displayed on poles by Christian slaveholders well into the nineteenth century. Ten other Roman slave revolts occurred in the second century B.C., but after 70 B.C. there were no more recorded uprisings of any size until the Zanj rebellion in the Abassid Empire 869–873 A.D. (present-day southern Iraq). Here slaves, probably from East Africa, rose up, killed thousands, and made slaves of Arab women and children before being defeated by the regime.

Subsequent slave insurrections followed the westward course of empire and capitalism to the Americas, where Europeans first enslaved native populations and then relied on slave labor from Africa to produce cash crops such as sugar, tobacco, rice, cotton, cocoa, and coffee for an international market economy. Where the new slave economy went, violence and sometimes insurrection followed, along with self-justifying bourgeois investigations and reports on incidents, which provide the basic evidence about them.

Some American insurrections, like those in the Roman era, began as a vengeful thrust, but only in Jamaica in 1760 and in Berbice in 1763 did such revolts spread over a broad area. In Jamaica slaves killed 120 people, while suffering five times that many deaths themselves. In only six other revolts of this kind did the number of victims of slaves surpass ten, and in only three did it rise above fifty: in Saint John's in 1749, in Berbice, and in Virginia, 1831.

By far the bloodiest of American insurrections occurred in Saint Domingue after 1791. Here, hostilities against and within French society, and those between whites and free coloreds on the island, led competitors to use slaves in the conflicts. This eventually allowed these 400,000 slaves to develop their own policies, military skills, and leaders, notably the freedman Toussaint-Louverture, and to gain freedom and political power. This volatile mixture of goals—independence, racial aspirations, and antislavery—underlay several subsequent revolts in Venezuela and Cuba from 1795 to 1812. The insurrectionists came nearest to success in British Grenada in 1795–1796, when French free colored forces and their slave allies controlled all but one city on the island for fifteen months, killing about two hundred before their struggle failed. Racial antagonisms among the free population also influenced the several nineteenth-century Brazilian uprisings, including the most deadly one in Bahai in 1835.

In another major American type of insurrection, slaves essentially went on strike while doing limited property damage to call attention to their cause. Slaves on Curaçao first used this tactic in 1795, and it was central in the revolt of thousands in British Barbadoes (1816), Demerara (1823), and Jamaica (1831–1832). In these three incidents slaves acted increasingly on expectations based on British antislavery sentiment and on principles derived from the Baptist and Methodist faiths. These mild insurrectionists killed a few of their attackers—twenty-two in three huge incidents—while the planters killed about one hundred times as many slaves, most of them summarily or legally executed. These revolts probably contributed to the British abolition of slavery that soon followed. Certainly the brave restraint of these slaves, symbolized by the Jamaican leader Sam Sharpe, made clear where brutal barbarism chiefly resided. More immediate results came in 1848 on Saint Croix, where eight thousand slaves converged peacefully to demand freedom, and the Danish governor decently granted it, hastening projected emancipation by a decade.

Much more common than insurrection in all slave societies was the rebellion of running away, which led in isolated settings to the formation of long-lived maroon communities of belligerent escaped slaves. Palmares in Brazil maintained a separate existence for about a hundred years before the community was crushed in 1695. In Jamaica and Suriname some maroon groups lasted as long as slavery did, at times by partly cooperating with the regime to repress other slave runaways and revolts. Some maroons contributed to the success of Haiti's insurrection.

More numerous than actual slave revolts were the conspiracies planters either nipped in the bud or conjured up themselves. Doubtless some insurrections were planned, but the evidence, usually whipped or bribed out of a few slaves, suggests at least as much fantasy on the part of whites as plotting on the part of slaves. Despite the "property" costs, planters took satisfaction in these scenarios, in which they exorcised their fears and exercised their absolute power, and which demonstrated to them how providence sided with them against their black beasts. Insurrections, real or alleged, also commonly provided an incentive or excuse for slaveholders to increase legally the harshness of their slave codes. This pattern was clear in ancient Rome, as it was in South Carolina, where the Stono Rebellion of 1739 encouraged some legal changes; and the Denmark Vesey conspiracy of 1822 even more markedly inaugurated a legal tightening of the system. In rare instances serious revolts, such as in Virginia in 1831, aroused reconsideration of a regime's commitment to slavery, but the more comforting wholly controlled conspiracies almost always led to sterner laws, as in Virginia's 1800 response to Gabriel's plot.

Hence, there may have been aspects of slaveholder calculation mixed with hysteria in slave "plots" for which all evidence seems the product of white fears

Toussaint-Louverture. [Library of Congress/Corbis]

and whips. These incidents of hysteria among slaveholders were especially common in nineteenth-century Cuba, Brazil, and the United States as most of the West turned against slavery, especially at times when there was a desire to tighten control over slaves or quell any questioning of the system. Such was the case with almost all incidents in the United States after the Nat Turner uprising in 1831. This pattern is also clear in Cuba in 1844, where a plot was "revealed" by thousands who were whipped until they said what the government wanted—except for the three hundred or so whipped to death.

Leading scholars of American insurrections like Herbert Aptheker in *American Negro Slave Revolts* (1943) and Michael Craton in *Testing the Chains: Resistance to Slavery in the British West Indies* (1982) have accepted the reality of most of these conspiracies. Two competent studies of specific slave plots that insist on their reality even when the evidence also fits a pattern of essential white hysteria are David Barry Gaspar's *Bondsmen and Rebels: A Study of Master-Slave Relations in Antigua* (1993) and Winthrop Jordan's *Tumult and Silence at Second Creek: An Inquiry into a Civil War Slave Conspiracy* (1993). These studies use slave insurrections as evidence of heroic resistance, but neither bravery nor hostility to slavery required slaves to develop insurrection conspiracies—let alone such cumbrous conspiracies—in the face of the slaveholders' power and enthusiasm for brutal repression.

See also MAROONS; PANICS; REBELLIONS AND VIOLENT RESISTANCE; RESISTANCE, DAY-TO-DAY.

BIBLIOGRAPHY

BRADLEY, KEITH. *Slavery and Rebellion in the Roman World, 140–70 B.C.* 1989.

COSTA, EMILIA VIOTTI DA. *Crowns of Glory, Tears of Blood: The Demerara Slave Revolt of 1823.* 1994.

GEGGUS, DAVID. "The Haitian Revolution." In *The Modern Caribbean,* edited by Franklin Knight and Colin Palmer. 1989; pp. 21–50.

GENOVESE, EUGENE. *From Rebellion to Revolution: Afro-American Slave Revolts in the Making of the Modern World.* 1979.

REIS, JOÃO JOSÉ, *Slave Rebellion in Brazil: The Muslim Uprising of 1835 in Bahai.* 1993.

David Grimsted

International Labor Organization

The International Labor Organization (ILO) was created in 1919 by the Treaty of Versailles as an agency of the League of Nations for purposes of ensuring social and economic justice for working people. Initially the ILO sought to abolish forced labor throughout the world but especially in the overseas possessions of Belgium, Denmark, France, Great Britain, Italy, the Netherlands, Portugal, and Spain. These powers often utilized forced labor in their colonies to complete public works projects, and they permitted its use by private businesses because it involved natives in the modern economic system. The ILO opposed forced labor because it taught natives to despise work and because it often involved flogging, involuntary migration, and slavelike living conditions, which in turn introduced high rates of alcoholism, venereal disease, and mortality among indigenous populations. The ILO's efforts on behalf of the League's Commission on Slavery resulted in the adoption in 1926 of the Slavery Convention, which called on the colonial powers to abolish forced labor for private purposes while permitting its use on public works projects.

In 1930 the ILO established the Forced Labor Convention, which abolished forced labor for private purposes and established a five-year grace period during which forced labor could be utilized only for public works projects that directly benefited natives. In 1936 this convention addressed the legal and social rights of indigenous rural peoples who worked on colonial plantations. In 1947, two years after the ILO became affiliated with the United Nations, it established a labor inspection service to guarantee those rights.

In the decade after the end of World War II, millions of political prisoners died in forced labor camps in the Soviet Union while similar numbers of peasants and city-dwellers in the People's Republic of China were relocated involuntarily as part of the Communist regime's Five-Year Plan of economic development. Consequently, in 1957 the ILO adopted the Abolition of Forced Labor Convention, which condemned compulsory labor as a means of discrimination, economic development, political coercion, education, or punishment. Although it effected no changes in China, the convention generated enough adverse international public opinion to contribute to a substantial relaxation of totalitarian control over labor in Czechoslovakia, Poland, and the Soviet Union and resulted in moderate improvements in Albania, Bulgaria, Hungary, and Romania.

In 1961 the Abolition of Forced Labor Convention addressed allegations that forced labor continued to exist throughout Africa, particularly in the Union of South Africa, Liberia, and the Portuguese colonies of Angola and Mozambique. Although South Africa refused to cooperate with the organization's investigators, ILO commissions of inquiry resulted in the abolition of practices approaching forced labor in Angola, the most serious of which involved tribal chiefs and colonial officials coercing native laborers to work for private corporations. ILO investigators also succeeded in getting Liberia to repeal or amend labor laws not in compliance with the dictates of the convention, and to establish procedures regarding labor inspection, public employment services, and grievance procedures to counteract the use by privately owned plantations of tribal chiefs as labor recruiters.

See also LEAGUE OF NATIONS; SLAVERY CONVENTION.

BIBLIOGRAPHY

ALCOCK, ANTONY. *History of the International Labour Organisation.* 1971.
JOHNSON, G. A. *The International Labour Organisation: Its Work for Social and Economic Progress.* 1970.

Charles W. Carey Jr.

Iowa

Iowa was part of the territory acquired from France in the Louisiana Purchase. Though slavery was legal in that area until 1820, few if any slaves lived there, and the Missouri Compromise of 1820 banned slavery in all the territory that eventually became Iowa. In 1838 the first territorial legislature, dominated by Southerners, passed laws restricting the immigration of free blacks. In the case of *In the Matter of Ralph* (1839), an Iowa court ruled that slaves became free if their masters brought them into the state. In the early 1840s antislavery settlers, mostly Quakers or former New Englanders, began to agitate for greater racial fairness, and the first state constitution (1846) declared that "neither slavery nor involuntary servitude, unless for punishment of crimes, shall ever be tolerated in this State." After statehood the restrictive laws remained on the books but were unenforced. Between 1850 and 1860, Iowa's black population grew from 333 to 1,069.

In June 1848, Ruel Daggs, a master from Missouri, attempted to seize about ten runaway slaves of his in Salem, Iowa, a Quaker settlement. Between fifty and one hundred residents, some of them armed, intervened, and a number of the slaves escaped or were spirited away by Quaker abolitionists in the community. Daggs eventually recovered about half of his slaves. He sued for monetary damages for the value of the other lost slaves but never collected any money. Other fugitives from slaveholding Missouri successfully eluded capture and found a safe haven and freedom in Iowa. During the Civil War Iowa was staunchly antislavery, and during Reconstruction the state was often on the side of radical reform for racial justice.

See also MISSOURI COMPROMISE; QUAKERS.

BIBLIOGRAPHY

DYKSTRA, ROBERT R. *Bright Radical Star: Black Freedom and White Supremacy on the Hawkeye Frontier.* 1993.

FINKELMAN, PAUL. "Fugitive Slaves, Midwestern Racial Tolerance, and the Value of 'Justice Delayed.'" *Iowa Law Review* 78 (1992): 89–141.

VOEGELI, V. JACQUE. *Free but Not Equal: The Midwest and the Negro during the Civil War.* 1967.

Paul Finkelman

Iraq

See Modern Middle East.

Ireland

The main sources for early Irish social institutions are the Old Irish law tracts. Although these cover practically every facet of social life, not one deals with slavery. This silence, however, may reflect the newly Christianized milieu in which Irish legal writing developed, for there are many random references suggesting that slavery was commonplace. Slavery comes into view historically in sources describing disturbed conditions on the fringes of the collapsing Roman empire in the fifth century. Saint Patrick described how he was captured, along with many thousands of others, during raids on mainland Britain. Gildas too refers to raiders coming from Ireland in coracles. According to the legends of the two new overlordships of early Ireland (the Ui Neill and the Eoganachta) the mothers of their founders were captives.

Apart from capture, an individual might be enslaved as punishment for a crime. Two sources refer to women who were given by their kin to atone for a blood debt that would otherwise have resulted in a feud. These women were assigned to hard domestic labor, one in the laundry, the other heating bath water. (This entailed heating stones in a fire and throwing them into a water-filled pit.) The Ui Neill's ancestress (Carina, mother of Niall of the Nine Hostages) was depicted slaving over a quern, grinding grain by hand. Women slaves were so strongly associated with the quern that *cumal*, Old Irish for "female slave," was etymologically linked to hand-grinding. Moreover, the *cumal* was the basic large unit of value in the Old Irish currency system, which was generally based on livestock. In the law tracts one *cumal* was usually worth three cows. The use of a female slave as a unit of value suggests that female slavery was a deep-seated phenomenon in Irish society, and that it may have stimulated the Viking slave raids of the early Middle Ages, rather than that these raids introduced slavery for the first time. Male slaves also helped with the food supply (Saint Patrick, for example, was a herdsman).

Slavery was strongly associated with royalty in early Ireland. In the "Book of Rights" regional kings are said to give male and female slaves to their chief vassals, along with a variety of other prestigious items. Elsewhere it is said that male slaves made up the bodyguard of a regional king. In elite households slaves would have enhanced the food-producing capacity of each farming unit held by an aristocrat, as well as processing clients' gifts of raw materials. (Irish clientage was a distinctive form of vassalage based on loans of cattle from a lord to his followers. Clients were often lower-ranking kinsmen within the same clan as the lord.) Food production was politically crucial to the aristocracy, since strategies and plots were developed when allies and clients met at seasonal feasts.

The demand for slave labor derived from the social structure of the highly pastoral, quasi-feudal, clan-based mode of production that prevailed in early Ireland. This could sustain only a scattered native-born population over the long term. It was socially cost-effective in this system for the elite to meet its specialized labor requirements by using a captive labor force, for during times of scarcity captives could be ejected with fewer social consequences than dependent natives. It is probable, then, that traditional clan hierarchies tended to seek captive labor, but that the level of demand varied locally and chronologically according to the development of the elite. The high points of enslavement were probably during the fourth to sixth centuries and the ninth to tenth centuries, both periods of intense international raiding and the emergence of new elite groups in Ireland.

See also ECONOMICS OF SLAVERY; GREAT BRITAIN, AFRICAN SLAVERY IN.

BIBLIOGRAPHY

KELLY, FERGUS. *A Guide to Early Irish Law.* 1988.

PATTERSON, NERYS THOMAS. *Cattle-Lords and Clansmen: The Social Structure of Early Ireland*, 2nd ed. 1994.

Nerys Thomas Patterson

Irish Anti-Slavery Society

The Dublin-based Hibernian Anti-Slavery Society was founded in 1837 to support the successful lobbying of Parliament for the overthrow of the apprenticeship system for emancipated slaves in the British West Indies. Tours by William Lloyd Garrison, Charles R. Remond, John A. Collins, and Frederick Douglass in the 1840s generated considerable support for American Garrisonianism among Irish abolitionists. As a

Daniel O'Connell. [Michael Nicholson/Corbis]

consequence, the Hibernian Anti-Slavery Society broke with the British and Foreign Anti-Slavery Society after the latter sided with Garrison's American opponents in the American and Foreign Anti-Slavery Society and the Liberty Party. The Hibernian Anti-Slavery Society's most active leaders, Richard D. Webb and James Haughton, were both Quakers who became Unitarians by the end of the 1840s. The Irish Garrisonians were urban, middle-class, dissenting Protestants and English-speakers and were never able to reach much beyond their narrow circle. For a time in the early 1840s, they cooperated with the popular Irish parliamentary leader Daniel O'Connell, who had outspoken abolitionist opinions. Irish Garrisonians, however, criticized O'Connell's close ties to the London-based British and Foreign Anti-Slavery Society. In the mid-1840s, tension over issues related to O'Connell's campaign for repeal of the Act of Union isolated the Irish Garrisonians from broader domestic political movements. By the 1850s, the Hibernian Anti-Slavery Society, composed mainly of the Webb and Houghton families, was the only remaining active antislavery society in Ireland.

See also BRITISH AND FOREIGN ANTI-SLAVERY SOCIETY; DOUGLASS, FREDERICK; GARRISON, WILLIAM LLOYD.

BIBLIOGRAPHY

RAICH, DOUGLAS C. "Daniel O'Connell and American Anti-Slavery." *Irish Historical Studies* 20 (1976): 3–25.
———. "Richard Davis Webb and Antislavery in Ireland." In *Antislavery Reconsidered: New Perspectives on the Abolitionists,* edited by Lewis Perry and Michael Fellman. 1979.
TEMPERLEY, HOWARD. *British Antislavery, 1833–1870.* 1972.

John R. McKivigan

Islam

This entry includes the following articles: An Overview; Islamic Caliphates; Muslims in America.

An Overview

Slavery is the antithesis of freedom and equality in the Judeo-Christian tradition. It acquired its sharpest definition during the era of the Atlantic slave trade to the Americas. This essentially African-American experience should not obscure other historical traditions and experiences, which neither mirror nor replicate it.

The Islamic tradition dates to the first decade of the seventh century and to the Arab prophet Muhammad of Mecca. In 622 C.E. he retreated to Medina (the Hegira) and established a state and society in accordance with Allah's laws. An idealized construct of master-slave relations lay at the heart of this community. The true believer was *'abd,* or the "slave," of Allah, construed as a loyal, obedient follower, trusting unquestioningly in the power and goodwill of his master. Equality was what united mankind: all *'abid* were equal in the eyes of Allah. But freedom had no value in an Arab society delineated by the ties of family and tribe. Status and honor were rooted in a myriad of reciprocal responsibilities and closely circumscribed behaviour. To be "free" of these obligations was to be an outsider, without access to status. Outsiders found entry only through marriage, clientship, or enslavement; only outsiders could be enslaved. To the extent that "free" had meaning, it was embedded in ethnic identity: to be Arab meant, in large part, not to be a slave. Thus, to belong to the Muslim Arab community was, from the outset, an experience defined in contradistinction to slavery.

Masters' treatment of slaves became a measurement of piety. Good Muslims had a duty to feed, clothe, and educate slaves in Islam; to grant them the right to marry or to enjoy the protection of Islamic law directly brought spiritual rewards. The Muslim family's moral obligation extended to assisting the former slave in his or her independence. But the question of manumission and its spiritual value was relevant only with respect to converts; non-Muslim slaves could hope for nothing better in terms of improving their lives than to request a new master from the local judge (*qadi*). Muslim slaves, on the other hand, in accepting Islam, were acquiescing in the inevitability of their dependent role vis-à-vis their masters.

The master-slave relationship, basic to Muslim life, was reflected in early religious law (*sharia*). While almsgiving and charity were the weightiest acts of penance, prescribed atonement for sins or public offenses frequently demanded the manumission of a stipulated number of slaves. As slaves were both people and property before the law, they were controlled by the regulations on the exchange and transfer of goods, including the distribution of inheritance.

Reforms proposed by the prophet also gave prominence to male-female social interaction. Indiscriminate polygamy and divorce were blurring distinctions between conditions of respectability, destitution, and prostitution. To restore decency and social order, the prophet limited the number of wives a man could take to four and insisted on their equitable treatment. He also secluded and veiled his wives (in the Byzantine and Persian world the veil had become a mark of status forbidden to slaves and harlots), and he proposed innumerable ways in which personal conduct between slave and master should be regulated, including restricting women's interaction with adult male slaves to the extent that they were prohibited entry to the secluded household (harem). Distinctions between wives, slaves, and prostitutes had become blurred through an abuse of concubinage. The prophet's reforms clarified the distinctions and acknowledged a carefully delineated role for female slaves. Most importantly, they turned attention to the children born of these relations and ensured those offspring incorporation into the family. The status of their mothers (*umm al-walid*) was concomitantly raised. This control over slave sexuality is often perceived as giving definition to Islamic slavery; it was, rather, an attempt to use slavery to further social reform and ensure family reproduction.

During the century following Muhammad's death, military expansion took Muslims throughout the Arabian peninsula, into the Byzantine and Persian empires, and across North Africa and the Mediterranean as far as Europe's Frankish kingdom. The incessant campaigns necessitated acquiring new troops and administering to non-Arab, non-Muslim peoples. Assimilating these strangers raised new cultural and legal issues. The incorporation of wealthy cities offer-

ing opportunities for debauchery and enrichment subtly altered the intellectual discourse and overtly challenged the prophet's rigorous morality. Between the seventh and tenth centuries the prophet's words and actions were interpreted (*hadith*), and analogous situations and local consensus were sought in response to these dilemmas (collectively, the *sharia*). The Byzantines and Persians bought slaves from the Turks, northern Slavs, and sub-Saharan and East Africans; they used eunuchs extensively.

Already by the 660s, the caliph was using these castrated slaves to guard his harem, and by the late eighth century Abbasid rulers were augmenting their armies with Mamluks—purchased slaves given military and religious training, then manumitted. In the early ninth century the creation of a Mamluk army began a Middle East tradition that soon saw Mamluks everywhere in positions of royal trust. In some regions, such as Egypt and northern India, they became a power and a class unto themselves, retaining their slave identity to reinforce their distinction from the ruled. Eunuchs also acquired privileged positions in state administration. Under the Ottomans this slave-based military and court hierarchy was perfected: the religious sense of 'abd affirmed the obedience of royal slaves, and the

Eighteenth-century Ottoman chief eunuch. [Leonard de Selva/Corbis]

harem evolved into the center of court politics. Meanwhile, state-building in the provinces (for example, West Africa's Kanem-Bornu), as well as in Islamic lands beyond the Ottomans' direct control (such as northern Nigeria and the Delhi sultanate), generated comparable systems.

The ability to keep the ruler's power base independent of the political alliances and patronage policies necessitated by expansive empire, through astute harem politics and controlled Mamluk dependency, reduced the danger of political destabilization. But it was local cultures and historical conjunctures that ultimately determined which aspects of royal slavery would take root. The Mughal conquest of India insinuated court culture and administration into Hindu systems, supplanting the earlier Turkish slave system with one promoting Indian personnel. And in the nineteenth century a northern Nigerian jihad opposed the very palace slave system that had evolved since early Ottoman times. It sought to reimpose the pure caliphate in that free nobles would reassert authority over slave rulers. What was Islamic about governance was specific to contextual politics.

Neither the definitions of the enslavable outsider nor what constituted jihad were any longer uniform throughout the Muslim world. Those in the expanding empires sought clarification of the legal position of conquered Jews and Christians, those who converted after capture, and those whose religion was unknown because they entered slavery through the marketplace. Technically, neither Muslims nor *dhimmis* (Jews and Christians who submitted to Islamic authority) were subject to enslavement or castration, but non-Muslims (even slaves from Muslim societies) and "people of the book" who neither converted nor submitted were. The international slave trade that empire encompassed posed ongoing difficulties for Muslim jurists.

So too did the complex nature of the maturing economy. The flourishing agricultural and craft-based industrial lifestyle of the Maghreb, Egypt, Byzantium, and Persia fed a far more extensive network of international trade and urban activity than the largely pastoral Arabian peninsula whose commercial sector, Mecca-Medina, had given rise to the prophet's regulation of slavery. The use of slaves as artisans, domestics, and concubines grew commensurately with city bourgeoisie. Commercial cultivation of fruits, grains, and sugar was also the work of slaves. And where slaves were exploited in large numbers, as was customary in southern Persia, the presumed intimacy of master-slave relations disappeared.

In the late ninth century masses of East African (*Zanj*) slaves in the Basra region rose in lengthy and bloody resistance. This revolt, neither led by, nor composed exclusively of, slaves, espoused what was viewed as the purified, more egalitarian Islam of the early caliphs. It reflected the fracturing of Islam, a process begun with the dispute over Muhammad's successor, intensified with the debates generated by creating a state out of a religion, and articulated initially as the competing powers of Sunni and Shiite brotherhoods. It also revealed how that religious dynamic, which continued to splinter over questions of ritual, mysticism, and law, was intersecting with the evolution of slavery. Slavery was, arguably, considered no longer truly Islamic by either slaves or noblemen in this part of the empire.

By the tenth century jurists had wished to end codification of the *sharia*, but their efforts were frustrated by the phenomenal force of Islam over the next five centuries, as the faith simultaneously attracted far-flung multicultural believers and fragmented the largely homogeneous political empire. In Africa (North, West, and East), the Middle East, and Asia (central and southern), great empires flourished embracing Islamic law. Muslim rulers, masters, and slaves wrestled with reconciling Islamic laws with local cultures, changing economies, and an increasingly integrated capitalist world system. Muslim scholars constituting an international religious elite continued to debate who was enslavable and under what circumstances, as well as what constituted proper ethics among Muslim merchants and masters: hence, the incessant Ottoman debates over forcibly enrolling Christian children in military training (*devshirme*), enslaving the Persian (*Shiite*) enemies, allowing inheritance rights to slave soldiers (janissaries) who worked in agriculture and industry, treating *dhimmis* who revolted as traitors under law (and therefore once again enslavable), and tightly controlling authorization to sell slaves to the powerful urban Slave Dealers' Guild.

In the distant Sahara issues were the same: a seventeenth-century Moroccan sultan creating his own version of a Mamluk army was opposed by scholars over the questionable slave status of his enlistments; slave traders in the oasis of Tuat questioned a sixteenth-century Timbuktu scholar about the lawfulness of purchasing slaves of uncertain religion from sub-Saharan states; and the Muslim ruler of one of these states in turn sought advice from Moroccan scholars on the correct marketing of female slaves.

In the Indian sultanate of Delhi Islamic slave regulations were adapted uneasily to Hindu castes, and the enslaving of peasants within the conquered territories (as distinct from during the conquest) was ultimately interpreted as being contrary to the legitimacy of enslavable outsider and prohibited under Mughal rule. Yet, debt defaulters were sold regularly into slavery on the grounds that failure to pay state taxes was a form of rebellion, and debt slavery emerged (especially during recurrent famines), which was questionable under the *sharia*'s prohibition of usury. Compromises were agreed to with local Hindus to limit the amount of work required to cover loans and interest payments. The role of the Muslim *'ulamma* ("learned," "jurists") in interpreting Islamic law as it might apply to slavery was an essential one in negotiating the expansion of Islam.

As the global slave trade expanded its areas of capture in sub-Saharan Africa during the eighteenth and nineteenth centuries to feed flourishing slave-based economies in the Americas, slave merchants and masters in the Islamic world responded to shifting routes, expanding opportunities, and changing prices. More systematic production and marketing of slaves stimulated exports across the Sahara, which at times may have surpassed the numbers crossing the Atlantic. Much of this commerce was in the hands of Muslims who, in addition to creating diasporic trading networks, settled many of these slaves in agricultural communities, some arguably plantations, in the West African Sahel. The Muslim Swahili of East Africa experienced a similar mercantile evolution, and their emergent plantation economy from the early 1800s derived from the initiative of the sultan of Oman and the investment of Muslim Indian financiers.

These slave trades, in reintegrating African, Middle Eastern, and Asian Muslim worlds, significantly colored slavery among Asian Muslim populations. Even taking into account the sub-Saharan eunuchs and soldiers previously found throughout these regions, slavery had been largely white: Turkish Mamluks; Christian *devshirmes;* Abyssinian and Circassian concubines; Berber, Slav, Mongol, and Persian domestics; and Indian caste slaves. Among the questions put earlier to that Timbuktu scholar was whether being black justified enslavement. Although in the sixteenth century the answer had been negative, as importations from black Africa increased and supplies from elsewhere diminished, growing price differentials precluded purchase of white slaves by anyone other than the rich and powerful. From the eighteenth through the mid-nineteenth century, white slaves in the Middle East cost from four to six times more than comparable blacks. Where this model influenced Islamic Africa, as it did the Swahili coast, Egypt, Tunisia, Morocco, Hausaland, and Kanem-Bornu, ownership of light-skinned slave women similarly delineated status. In India this coloring was seen in the rising numbers of Africans in domestic and sexual slavery, itself a reflection of the growing urban middle class and the semipermanent European presence, whose color preferences added to the impact of economics.

European abolitionist pressure and African jihads intersected in the nineteenth century to chart yet another course for slavery in Islamic societies. Suppression of Atlantic slave trading out of West Africa stimulated Muslim slave-based commerce in East Africa; Muslim raiders and traders from the upper Nile and the Indian Ocean coast shaped new political economies in the central African interior, generating slave prisoners in the process. Combined with those produced by Egypt's conquest of Sudan and facilitated by transport improvements (the Suez Canal and the steamship), the region augmented the export of African slaves in spite of abolitionist pressures. Nonetheless, during the latter part of the century, the Ottomans shifted increasingly to a reliance on naturally reproduced slaves from newly incorporated Caucasian slave populations and on the enslavement of Greeks who lost their *dhimmis* status during the wars of independence in the 1820s. In West Africa incessant jihads enslaved both nonbelievers and corrupt

Sultan Barghash, under threat of British warships invading the harbor of Zanzibar, signed a treaty abolishing slavery on 5 March 1873. [Bojan Brecelij/ Corbis]

Muslims (juridically comparable to Ottoman enslavement of Persians) and supplied growing domestic markets with slaves to produce commodities for the legitimate commerce meant to replace slave trading. Discussion over what distinguished the evils of trade in slaves originating outside dar al-Islam (land of Islam) from the cultural values of slavery within it influenced intellectual debate and artistic expression wherever Europeans made abolition an issue. From Algeria to Zanzibar to Istanbul to Delhi, the process contributed heavily to idealizing and reifying publicly held notions of a beneficent "Islamic slavery," which colonial authorities internalized and acted upon as they dealt with it into the twentieth century.

Colonial rhetoric about Western freedom did not end slavery in the Muslim communities under European rule. Europeans' fear of the political power of Islam, a response to experiences with nationalist Pan-Islamism and Muslim reformist movements in North Africa and the Middle East before World War I, further distorted their romanticized, orientalist notions of slavery in these societies. While colonial policy aimed to free slaves in the modern Western sense, administrators also sought to protect social order and collect revenue, both dependent on a continuing slave presence: they transformed rather than smashed institutions of slavery. In Muslim Africa the reproduction and circulation of slaves moved out of the marketplace and back within the household; attempts to retain control over servile women and their offspring encouraged new forms of marriage and strengthened hereditary clientage. In the Middle East the elite definition of slavery as the route to social status prevailed, especially among women, where the harem tradition continued to provide a nurturing environment. The nobility in whose bosom domestic slavery nestled continued to dominate colonial polities; the facility with which slaves (and children born of them) were rendered invisible within these families continued to frustrate abolition decrees. In India the astounding range of debt and bonded labor arrangements that had coexisted with and nourished slavery readily reabsorbed freed slaves, effectively restructuring slavery itself.

But the persistence of Islamic slavery was not attributable only to the state. Where few channels for social mobility existed and family identity provided the only access to them, slavery remained an attractive option. Because the legitimacy Islam gave to slave status was reinforced in many parts of Africa, Asia, and the Middle East by the inextricable association with wealth and power (an emir's harem, a great merchant's household, the palace administration), it remained an ideology capable of "captivating the captive."

And it remains so at the end of the twentieth century. The security of the exchange of loyalty and obligation between master and slave promised in Islam and delivered in the realization of interdependent identity carried "slavery" into late-twentieth-century capitalism. Changes in political economy have long been central to the evolution of slavery and its ideology, because they so fundamentally shape the material context in which slave masters (men and women) interact with their slaves, from production and acquisition through reproduction. The assumption that the material conditions of contemporary capitalism should perforce destroy rather than transform this social relation essential to Islam ignores history yet again. The end of the twentieth century is experiencing once more the romanticizing and orientalizing of the non-Western, as articulated in so-called fundamentalist movements. They contain within them the potential for reinforcing traditional institutions of servility. While scholars are beginning to understand how Islam and slavery intersected at given historical moments, they are far from knowing what aspects of Islam will appear attractive to future generations, especially when juxtaposed with an international capitalism whose moral and material poverty prostitutes and enslaves its women and children. The most salient indicator may be that as fewer people, even within the Judeo-Christian tradition, experience that liberty and equality which once so clearly defined slavery by opposition to it, the submission inherent in other social formations and ideologies may become more attractive than the euphoria of Western democracy and freedom predicts.

See also EGYPT; EUNUCHS; HAREM; JANISSARIES; OTTOMAN EMPIRE.

BIBLIOGRAPHY

CLARENCE-SMITH, WILLIAM GERVASE, ed. *The Economics of the Indian Ocean Slave Trade in the Nineteenth Century.* 1989.
COOPER, FREDERICK. *Plantation Slavery on the East Coast of Africa.* 1977.
ERDEM, Y. HAKAN. *Slavery in the Ottoman Empire and Its Demise, 1800–1909.* 1996.
FISHER, ALLAN G. B., and HUMPHREY J. FISHER. *Slavery and Muslim Society in Africa: The Institution in Saharan and Sudanic Africa and the Trans-Saharan Trade.* 1970.
GORDON, MURRAY. *Slavery in the Arab World.* 1989.
KIDWAI, SALIM. "Sultans, Eunuchs and Domestics: New Forms of Bondage in Medieval India." In *Chains of Servitude: Bondage and Slavery in India,* edited by Utsa Patnaik and Manjari Dingwaney. 1985.
MIERS, SUZANNE, and RICHARD ROBERTS, eds. *The End of Slavery in Africa.* 1988. See especially the chapters by Roberts, Cassanelli, McDougall, Hogendorn, and Lovejoy.
PIPES, DANIEL. *Slave Soliders and Islam: The Genesis of a Military System.* 1981.

SAVAGE, ELIZABETH, ed. *The Human Commodity: Perspectives on the Trans-Saharan Slave Trade.* 1992.

SIKAINGA, AHMAD A. *Slaves into Workers: Emancipation and Labor in Colonial Sudan.* 1996.

TOLEDANO, EHUD R. "Ottoman Concepts of Slavery in the Period of Reform, 1830s–1880s." In *Breaking the Chains: Slavery, Bondage, and Emancipation in Modern Africa and Asia,* edited by Martin A. Klein. 1993; pp. 37–63.

———. *The Ottoman Slave Trade and Its Suppression, 1840–1890.* 1982.

WILLIS, JOHN RALPH, ed. *Slaves and Slavery in Muslim Africa.* 2 vols. 1985.

E. Ann McDougall

Islamic Caliphates

Slavery was a universal practice in the Mediterranean world, modulated but not condemned by the scriptures of Judaism, Christianity, and Islam alike. Koranic and Islamic law limited slave status to non-Muslims, captives in war, or people purchased outside the boundaries of Islam. But *dhimmis,* non-Muslims with holy scriptures, such as Christians and Jews, were legally exempt from enslavement. Manumission was viewed as a pious, meritorious act, practiced as a gesture of atonement or simply as a good deed. The prophet Muhammad and his companions served as a model for the treatment of slaves, with numerous hadith—narratives—illustrating the prophet's kindness. A number of members of the early community in seventh-century Arabia were Ethiopians, including a freed slave named Bilal ibn Rabah who became a companion to the prophet and was reputedly the first Muslim *muezzin* (the person who chants the call to prayer).

In the classical period, especially during the Umayyad and Abbasid caliphates (seventh to thirteenth century), legal doctrine and local conditions established a system of slavery practiced in Muslim societies until its abolition in modern times. Expansion beyond the Arabian peninsula stimulated the slave trade, since captives were readily available and prosperous enlarged households demanded servants. The prohibition against enslaving Muslims and protected non-Muslims also led to the development of a significant long-distance slave trade. Black slaves from Africa, part of the trans-Saharan trade, and white slaves from the Caucasus region became an integral part of the Muslim community in the classical age. Slave traders came from all ethnic and religious groups, and the slave market was a feature of medieval Middle Eastern cities. The capture and transport of slaves over long distances took an appalling toll, but slaves who were established in a domestic setting were generally treated as members of the household.

Little is known about slave practices in the Umayyad period. Privileged status was originally restricted to Muslim Arabs. Confrontations with and assimilation of new groups of people created more complex hierarchies, as other ethnicities, especially Persians and Turks, came under Muslim jurisdiction. The Abbasids (750–1258) came to power by promoting a universal empire, a brotherhood with membership based on religion rather than ethnicity. This could sometimes ameliorate the status of individual slaves, but it did not alter the ascription of racial and ethnic characteristics to slaves, and such characteristics determined their value on the market. Black female slaves were considered docile and fecund; white "Slavs" (Turks and Georgians) were prized for their fortitude and bellicosity; and so on. Eunuchs, black and white, had a higher value than noncastrated males; younger slaves had a higher value than older slaves; and women, especially beautiful women, had a higher value than men.

Most of our information about this early period comes from legal texts. Recognizing that freedom was the natural condition of humans, such texts argued that the relationship between master and slave was contractual and commercial in nature (Lewis, p. 8). Relegated to the lowest status were black male laborers; the highest male rank was occupied by eunuchs and military slaves. Women were prized as concubines as well as domestics, and the earliest Muslim chronicles abound with stories of the court life of Abbasid Baghdad, where highly educated women served and entertained a sophisticated circle of patrons. The number of slaves and concubines owned became an indicator of wealth and power, and this proved to be a persistent aspect of later Muslim dynasties.

Under Abbasid rule, the legal status of slavery evolved into its institutionalized form in the *sharia* (legal code). Slaves, male and female, were considered both persons and property, to be bought and sold at the master's will. Female slaves were a distinctive group, however, because their owners were legally allowed sexual access to their bodies. Converting to Islam did not guarantee manumission, nor did bearing a master's child. Codes of conduct for slaves and masters were often at variance, and in criminal cases slaves were sometimes punished less severely. Most slaves were domestics, and many of these assumed important roles in large households as teachers and confidants. There are few instances of plantation-style slavery in the classical caliphates, though there was one notable exception: thousands of black agricultural slaves (Zanj) in ninth-century Iraq who rebelled against being forced to clear the river marshes of salt.

Military slaves (*mamluks*) became common in Muslim dynastic households under the Abbasids. These slaves were mostly of Turkish stock, although black regiments are also mentioned. The Turks' fame as horsemen, and as archers with the compound bow, made them much sought-after as warriors for the personal entourage of the caliphs. Imperial slave regiments were often manumitted after training, developing into military castes, seizing power, and establishing their own dynasties—this was a primary cause of the breakup of Abbasid unity after the tenth century.

Black slave troops were more common in Egypt and West Africa than in the eastern Mediterranean, notably under the brief reign of Ahmad ibn Tūlūn (d. 884) in Cairo, one of the first of the independent dynasties to resist Abbasid hegemony. At his death, Ahmad was said to have had 24,000 white and 45,000 black slave troops (Lewis, pp. 65–66). Black troops were also used under the Fatamids (969–1171).

See also MILITARY SLAVES; ZANJ SLAVES.

BIBLIOGRAPHY

BRUNSCHVIG, ROBERT. "Abd." In *Encyclopdia of Islam,* 2nd ed., vol. 1, pp. 24–40. 1960.
GORDON, MURRAY. *Slavery in the Arab World.* 1989.
LEWIS, BERNARD. *Race and Slavery in the Middle East.* 1990.
PIPES, DANIEL. *Slave Soldiers and Islam: The Genesis of a Military System.* 1981.

Virginia H. Aksan

Muslims in America

The presence of Muslims among the enslaved population of what would become the United States has not been a prominent theme in the secondary literature on slavery. It seems, however, that thousands of African Muslims were imported into North America via the slave trade. For various reasons, only a few achieved appreciable fame. Among those who became more or less well known are Umar b. Said (also called Prince Moro and Moreau, ca. 1770–1864); Abd al-Rahman (or Abdul Rahahman, ca. 1762–1829); Ayuba b. Sulayman (or Job Ben Solomon, ca. 1702–1773); Salih Bilali (or Tom, ca. 1765–?); and Bilali, a contemporary of Salih Bilali.

These African Muslims came from a long tradition of Islam in West Africa, in some places dating back to the ninth century C.E. There they fairly often enjoyed important social privileges and sometimes owned slaves themselves. They came from different ethnic backgrounds; the most numerous were the Fulbe (or Fula or Fulani), the Mandinka and certain other Mande speakers, the Wolof, and the Hausa-Fulani. Those enslaved by these Islamized people were invariably from other ethnic groups, which—according to Islamic law—should have been groups without an established tradition of adherence to Islam. Indeed, some African Muslims participated in the slave trade, supplying captives for both the trade across the Atlantic and that across the Sahara Desert. Ironically, a few of the prominent Muslims captured by slave traders had themselves been in the process of procuring captives when they were caught. Muslims were not alone in slave trading: a number of non-Muslim groups trafficked in slaves for export. At the same time, there were many Muslims and non-Muslims who were opposed to the slave trade and fought to end it.

While most Muslims were either farmers or cattle herders, many lived in large towns such as Jenne, Kano, and Timbuktu. Still others, the Juula, were long-distance traders who effectively linked the various subregions of West Africa. It was customary for Muslim children, both boys and girls, to receive a modicum of education in Islam and to become literate in Arabic. The discovery that certain slaves could read and write drew considerable attention and explains much of the reason for their distinction.

There is evidence that African Muslims followed the tenets of their faith in colonial and antebellum North America. To begin, a number of individuals were reported to have prayed in the prescribed Muslim fashion. Ayuba b. Sulayman, for example, was harassed by a local white youth for praying as a Muslim. Other aspects of Islamic ritual and observance were also followed; Salih Bilali fasted on Ramadan, for example, and Bilali wore a fez and kaftan. Feast days were observed, and prayers were always directed to the east. Paraphernalia such as prayer beads and prayers rugs are mentioned in the historical record. In most instances, Muslims were observed practicing their religion as individuals, so it is difficult to determine the degree to which Muslims came together as congregations for worship, prayer, or instruction.

Certain areas had a greater concentration of Muslims than others. The Georgia sea islands of Sapelo and Saint Simons, for example, had relatively sizable numbers of Muslims, who often were blood-related. It was within families that Islam was able to survive for a while, as the religion was passed on from parents to children to grandchildren. Bilali, for instance, had seven daughters, four of whom bore discernibly Muslim names (Medina, Fatima, Bintu, and Yaruba).

Slaveholders tended to view Muslim slaves more favorably than non-Muslims. Differential treatment by slaveholders, in turn, had a significant impact upon the interactions of Muslim and non-Muslim slaves. Generally speaking, whites thought that Fulbe and Mande Muslims were more intelligent and more aesthetically pleasing than others. This sometimes meant that favored slaves were given better jobs on plantations or in towns and cities, especially tasks requiring nonagricultural skills or close proximity to slaveholders in living quarters. Such advantages exacerbated religious tensions among the enslaved.

One of the most vivid illustrations involved Bilali of Sapelo Island. Bilali was a driver on a large plantation, and this meant that he wielded considerable authority over the other slaves. In 1813 he developed a sensational reputation after defending the island against a British attack, having stated a preference for using his coreligionists rather than non-Muslims to mount the defense. This distinction in Bilali's mind reflects a number of issues. One was the elevated status of Muslim slaves. Another was the fact that Muslims in West Africa often saw themselves as superior to non-Muslims, especially non-Muslims who practiced some form of indigenous religion. A third issue was ethnicity—many Muslims also distinguished themselves from other Africans on the basis of ethnic identity.

Muslims living in an isolated areas such as Sapelo may have been numerous enough to continue some semblance of an Islamic community, but throughout most of the slaveholding regions the story was very different. Elsewhere in North America, non-Muslim Africans were decidedly in the majority, either practicing their own religions or at least maintaining a perspective and philosophy of life originally shaped and fashioned in Africa. Throughout both the colonial period and the antebellum years, there would be a slow, gradual conversion to Christianity among the southern slave population. In the face of African indigenous religions and the incremental growth of Christianity, Islam as a coherent system of belief within the slave quarters would necessarily decline over time.

Even though Islam as a separate and distinct religion may have dissipated as the period of slavery progressed, there is evidence that in certain areas an Islamic legacy remains, since certain rituals found in the black church may have their origins in Islam. A great deal more research is required to elucidate these and related issues.

See also AFRICA; CHURCHES, AFRICAN-AMERICAN; DRIVERS; LAW; SOLOMON, JOB BEN.

BIBLIOGRAPHY

ALFORD, TERRY. *Prince among Slaves.* 1977.
AUSTIN, ALLAN D. *African Muslims in Antebellum America: A Sourcebook.* 1984.
CURTIN, PHILIP D., ed. *Africa Remembered: Narratives by West Africans from the Era of the Slave Trade.* 1967.
GOMEZ, MICHAEL A. "Muslims in Early America." *Journal of Southern History* 60 (1994): 671–710.

Michael A. Gomez

Israel

See Ancient Middle East; Bible; Law.

Italy

See Ancient Rome; Medieval Europe, Serfdom and Slavery in; Mediterranean Basin.

Jacobs, Harriet [1813–1897]

Ex-slave and author.

Harriet Jacobs was born a slave in Edenton, North Carolina. She was orphaned by her mother's death at the age of six. She hoped to be freed after her kindly mistress died in 1825. Instead, Jacobs found herself bequeathed to her mistress's three-year-old niece, whose father, Dr. James Norcom, became her new master. She was preyed upon by the doctor and escaped the Norcom household in 1835—and finally fled the South entirely in 1842. Jacobs lived in several northern towns and cities for ten years before she was able to secure freedom for herself and her two children in 1852. Following the success of Harriet Beecher Stowe's *Uncle Tom's Cabin,* Jacobs decided to write her own story. Her autobiographical account was published in 1861 under the title *Incidents in the Life of a Slave Girl: Written by Herself.* Jacobs employed the pseudonym Linda Brent and gave fictitious names to other individuals appearing in the book as well. Throughout most of the nineteenth century and into the twentieth century, this work was believed to be the product of a white woman's pen—until Jean Yellin's annotated edition appeared in 1987, which provided authentification of Jacob's story and included important biographical data about Jacobs's relief work during the Civil War and her reform career afterwards. Jacobs's narrative remains the most powerful indictment of slavery published by a black woman during the nineteenth century. In her first-person account Jacobs offered graphic detail about the sexual exploitation of slavery and its debilitating effects on African-Americans and white southern families as well. *Incidents* became a rediscovered classic in the 1980s and remains a central interpretive text for American slave historiography.

See also SLAVE NARRATIVES; STOWE, HARRIET BEECHER.

BIBLIOGRAPHY

FLEISCHNER, JENNIFER. *Mastering Slavery: Memory, Family, and Identity in Women's Slave Narratives.* 1996.

Catherine Clinton

Janissaries

Janissaries (Turkish, *yeniçeri,* "new troops") is the name given to the standing army of the Ottoman Empire created in the late fourteenth century. Recruits were initially war captives but were later supplemented by levies of Christian boys from newly conquered territories, largely Balkan communities, one for every forty families. This system, known as the *devşirme* (Turkish, "collection" or "roundup"), was unique to the Ottoman Empire. The janissaries were slave conscripts, generally between the ages of twelve and eighteen, unmarried, converted to Islam, and educated in special schools that graduated both fighting men and administrative officials. The best of the levy, probably 5 to 10 percent, served in the palace; the remainder were attached to the cadet corps (*acemioğlan*), where they were trained as replacements for the regular

A chief of the Janissary corps. [Historical Picture Archive/Corbis]

corps. The janissaries, crack infantry troops, constituted a part of the sultan's grand household, where everyone was a "servant slave" (*kapukulu*). Twenty thousand janissaries fought for Süleiman I, the Magnificent (1494–1566), and the number of these slave soldiers rose to as high as eighty thousand by the end of the seventeenth century.

Devşirme levies, which have been estimated at 5,000 to 8,000 boys each, were theoretically scheduled once every seven years, perhaps more frequently in the sixteenth century. The practice gradually lapsed, and the last substantial levy was the one for the vigorous campaigns of Murad IV (1623–1640). Some territories, generally those that submitted voluntarily to Ottoman rule, obtained an exemption from the *devşirme*. The legality of enslaving populations who were technically protected by Islamic law (*dhimmi* status, for Christians and Jews, considered peoples with their own scriptures and thus tolerated in Muslim territories), was debated in the sixteenth century, and various justifications were asserted. In reality, once the young men were attached to a Janissary regiment (*orta*), they acquired independence, camaraderie, and discipline that were the envy of European military observers of the sixteenth and seventeenth centuries.

Janissaries were stationed everywhere throughout the empire, on campaign, manning fortresses, guarding cities, and quelling rebellion. They were unparalleled at sustained sieges, as in 1683, when they literally came within inches of breaking through the walls of Vienna. Their significance to the spread of Ottoman power in the first two to three centuries of the empire's existence cannot be exaggerated.

By the beginning of the seventeenth century, if not before, recruits also came from the free Muslim population, increasingly from sons of the janissaries themselves. By 1800, the roll of the janissary corps was swollen to as many as some 400,000 names, but this figure was based on corrupt and marketable ration coupons. Probably 10 percent of that number could be counted upon to defend the empire. The Ottomans evolved other means of recruitment through state-funded militias, both cavalry and infantry, to defend the frontiers. Such militias were volunteer or conscripted, but not slaves, as Muslim law forbids the enslaving of fellow Muslims. Mahmud II (1808–1839) put an end to the corps in 1826 in order to create a modern western-style army.

Historians have argued about the impact of the janissary system on the development (or backwardness) of Balkan society. There is no doubt that the young men were alienated from their homelands and families, but the degree to which they were actually Islamicized is debatable. They were proud Ottomans: a number of graduates of the system became grand viziers and were known for their patronage of their former hometowns.

See also MILITARY SLAVES; OTTOMAN EMPIRE.

BIBLIOGRAPHY

GOODWIN, GODFREY. *The Janissaries.* 1997.

HUART, C. L. "Janissaries." In *Encyclopedia of Islam,* 2nd ed., vol. 4, pp. 572–574. 1987.

MÉNAGE, V. L. "Devshirme." In *Encyclopedia of Islam,* 2nd ed., vol. 2. 1965; pp. 210–214.

MIHAILOVIÇ, K. *Memoirs of a Janissary.* 1975.

Virginia H. Aksan

Japan

From a distant time known only through archaeological evidence and sporadic references in ancient Chinese records, until the mid-nineteenth century, bondage in Japan took the form of serfdom more than slavery. Beginning in the first century after Christ, contact with the culturally and technologically more sophisticated Asian mainland allowed certain tribal chiefs of the Yamato people to consolidate power in the area around Nara (in central Honshu). The clans that ruled Yamato were ranked vertically. On the top were families who owned land and justified their power by claiming divine lineage. Below them were serfs and artisans. On the bottom were slaves. The most powerful of these clans grew into the imperial house. By the seventh century they had firmly established imperial rule after the Chinese model, though powerful remnants of the clan system remained. Evidence concerning earlier periods is sketchy, but it is clear that by the fifth century Japanese society was divided between the "good people" (*ryomin*)—those, including commoners belonging to established families, who had family names—and the "base people" (*semmin*), who did not. The semmin were further divided into five groups, with the lowest two categorized as slaves, who could be bought and sold and who could not es-

tablish families. In addition, a group of "untouchables" dates from the late eighth century (and perhaps earlier); it traditionally consisted of war captives, criminals, butchers, leatherworkers, and those involved with handling the dead.

Consistent with patterns of slavery found elsewhere in the world, those enslaved in Japan were primarily war captives. They were apparently never numerous. Female slaves typically worked as washerwomen, wet nurses, or rice-chewers for imperial infants. The farmers and artisans who occupied the upper ranks of the semmin were either tied to the land or confined to hereditary occupations. In both cases they also labored in the service to the ruling classes. Although "freedom" was not a concept relevant to this society of ranked groups, the artisans gradually emerged from subordination to positions independent of the landed

An 1853 drawing depicts the members of the court of the emperor of Japan, including two royal servants, as they pay him homage and see to his needs. [Gleason's Pictorial Drawing Room Companion/Corbis]

lords. During the ninth and tenth centuries, many peasants on imperial lands sought protection from the excessive taxation and civil unrest that preceded the Kamakura period (1185–1392) by "voluntarily" placing themselves and their land under the control of a landlord. These peasants regained much of their freedom from these lords under the Kamakura shogunate. By 1200, with the exception of a few, primarily female, domestic servants, virtually all forms of slavery had disappeared.

Feudal servitude, however, did not end with slavery. Nor was slavery completely eradicated from Japanese society for all time. During the Edo period (1603–1867), the Tokugawa shogunate restructured Japanese society into rigid categories of ranks, with the peasants second behind the warriors, because of their importance as agricultural producers, and ahead of artisans and merchants. The new government tied the peasants to the land and placed on them most of the tax burden. While this new stratification did not create a class of slaves, the status of Japan's "untouchables" became hereditary and static. Their contamination was considered contagious, and they were therefore confined to segregated hamlets (*buraku*)— hence the term *burakumin*, which identifies members of this group and their descendants. Although the Meiji government (1868–1912) abolished their hereditary low status in 1871, discrimination against the descendants of the *burakumin* persists.

See also BUDDHISM; CHINA; COMFORT WOMEN IN WORLD WAR II.

BIBLIOGRAPHY

HALL, JOHN W., and JEFFREY P. MASS, eds. *Medieval Japan: Essays in Institutional History.* 1974, 1988.
SANSOM, G. B. *Japan: A Short Cultural History.* 1931, 1943, 1952, 1978.
VARLEY, H. PAUL. *Japanese Culture,* 3rd ed. 1973, 1977, 1984.

Al McDermid

Java

See Indonesia.

Jefferson, Isaac   [1775–ca. 1850]

Blacksmith.

Born at Monticello in Albemarle County, Virginia, Isaac—who later took the surname Jefferson—was the son of George and Ursula, slaves purchased by Thomas Jefferson in Powhatan County in 1773. Isaac was trained in metalworking, was apprenticed for several years to a Philadelphia tinner, and worked at Monticello as a nailmaker, a blacksmith, and a tinsmith. From 1797 until about 1822, he carried on his trade for Jefferson's neighbor and son-in-law, Thomas Mann Randolph, who leased and then purchased Isaac, his wife Iris, and their sons, Squire and Joyce. At the end of his life, Isaac Jefferson had his own blacksmith shop in Petersburg, Virginia.

In 1847, the author and teacher Charles Campbell, who had heard of Isaac Jefferson's fondness for telling stories about his life at Monticello, interviewed the former slave. Although Campbell prepared the interview for publication in 1871, it did not appear in print until 1951, as *Memoirs of a Monticello Slave,* edited by Rayford W. Logan, along with a striking daguerreotype of Jefferson in his blacksmith's apron.

Jefferson's recollections, in which boyhood memories predominate, provide vivid and authentic testimony—some available nowhere else—about Thomas Jefferson and his family, as well as dynamic evocations of the tumult of Revolutionary events in Virginia in 1781. While the harsher aspects of slavery, and how he escaped it, are omitted from his account, significant portions deal with the two occasions when he came closest to freedom: with Cornwallis's army at Yorktown and in a Quaker tinshop in Philadelphia. Since their publication, Isaac Jefferson's arresting words and portrait have given voice and features not only to the African-Americans of Monticello but also to thousands whose lives within the confines of slavery went unrecorded.

See also SLAVE NARRATIVES.

BIBLIOGRAPHY

BEAR, JAMES A., JR., ed. *Jefferson at Monticello.* 1967.
STANTON, LUCIA. *The African-American Families at Monticello.* 1998.

Lucia C. Stanton

Jefferson, Thomas   [1743–1826]

Third president of the United States (1801–1809).

Thomas Jefferson was the primary author of the American Declaration of Independence (4 July 1776), which proclaimed that "all men are created equal," and (in 1782) he was the second largest slaveowner in Albemarle County, Virginia. Despite his well-known opposition to slavery, most famously expressed in Queries XIV and XIX of his *Notes on the State of Virginia* (first English edition, 1787), Jefferson freed only eight of the several hundred slaves he owned over the course of his life. An ardent opponent of the international slave trade, banned by Congress as of 1 January 1808 in conformity with Article I, Section 9 of the

Thomas Jefferson. [Corbis-Bettmann]

U.S. Constitution, Jefferson nonetheless sold many of his own slaves in the domestic trade: from 1784 to 1794 alone, he sold eighty-five slaves and gave another seventy-six to family members. While serving in the Confederation Congress, Jefferson drafted a territorial government ordinance for the new national domain (1 March 1784), stipulating that "after the year 1800 of the Christian aera, there shall be neither slavery nor involuntary servitude in any of the said states." The provision was dropped in the adopted ordinance, but it was reinstated for the new states north of the Ohio River in the Northwest Ordinance of 13 July 1787. During the Missouri Crisis of 1819–1821, however, Jefferson's solicitude for states' rights led him to become a strong advocate for the "diffusion" of slavery in the trans-Mississippi West.

The favorite explanation for Jefferson's ambivalent record on slavery is that his progressive Enlightenment political philosophy was compromised by his class position. It is also asserted that his personal indebtedness, originating in pre-Revolutionary War debts of his father-in-law's estate, severely limited his freedom of action: at his death, Jefferson's debts exceeded a staggering $100,000. But the *Notes on Virginia* suggest that for Jefferson "natural" racial differences constituted the most "powerful obstacle to the eman-

cipation of these people." Jefferson could never envision the possibility of an integrated, biracial republic.

Jefferson conceived of slavery as a state of war between two distinct and inveterately hostile nations. As he wrote in Query XIV of the *Notes,* "Deep rooted prejudices entertained by the whites; ten thousand recollections, by the blacks, of the injuries they have sustained; new provocations; the real distinctions which nature has made; and many other circumstances, will divide us into parties, and produce convulsions which will probably never end but in the extermination of the one or the other race." In his draft of the Declaration of Independence, Jefferson blamed King George III and British slave-trading interests for waging "cruel war" against the innocent Africans. In his view, the only just and humane alternative to a continuing war that jeopardized the security and moral standing of the American republic was the emancipation, expatriation, and colonization of the captive nation of enslaved Africans. Then, having "declare[d] them a free and independant people," the United States could recognize and help secure the equal rights of Africans as a people in the family of nations. Jefferson believed that national self-determination was for enslaved Africans—as it was for revolutionary Americans—the threshold for the actual exercise of an individual's natural rights.

In Jefferson's time "nation," "people," and "race" were not clearly distinct concepts. In the *Notes,* national differences were influentially elaborated in invidious racial terms. Jefferson sought to defend the purity of the Virginian nation by asserting a natural hierarchy of beauty (and sexual attraction); he insisted on the mental inferiority and ineducability of slaves in order to demonstrate the impossibility of preparing them for citizenship in an integrated republic. "Will not a lover of natural history then, one who views the gradations in all the races of animals with the eye of philosophy, excuse an effort to keep those in the department of man as distinct as nature has formed them?"

Jefferson's aversion to race-mixing is the subject of continuing controversy, particularly in view of the strong possibility that he conducted a long-term liaison and had several children with his (probably quadroon) slave Sally Hemings, who is alleged to have been his wife's half sister. Defenders of Jefferson's "character" argue that such a relationship was inconsistent with his principles and pronouncements; proponents of the story suggest that the liaison epitomizes and illuminates the complex and contradictory positions on race and slavery characteristic not only of Jefferson but of many of his fellow slaveholding republican revolutionaries as well.

See also AMERICAN REVOLUTION; CONSTITUTION, U.S.; ENLIGHTENMENT; NORTHWEST ORDINANCE.

BIBLIOGRAPHY

FINKELMAN, PAUL. "Jefferson and Slavery: 'Treason against the Hopes of the World.' " In *Jeffersonian Legacies*, edited by Peter S. Onuf. 1993.

———. *Slavery and the Founders: Race and Liberty in the Age of Jefferson*. 1996.

GORDON-REED, ANNETTE. *Thomas Jefferson and Sally Hemings: An American Controversy*. 1997.

MILLER, JOHN CHESTER. *The Wolf by the Ears: Thomas Jefferson and Slavery*. 1977.

STANTON, LUCIA C. " 'Those Who Labor for My Happiness': Thomas Jefferson and His Slaves." In *Jefferson Legacies*, edited by Peter S. Onuf. 1993. Includes a summary of Jefferson's slave ownership and sales.

Peter S. Onuf

Jews

Jews have lived as a minority among non-Jewish populations from the second century until the founding of the state of Israel. When Jews lived in a society which had slavery, some Jews had slaves, if the law of the land allowed them. When Jews lived in a society without slavery, Jews had no slaves. In only two instances were Jews either prominent slave traders or slaveholders.

The one time when Jews were prominent as slave traders was during portions of the ninth and tenth centuries. This resulted from a combination of many factors. Following the death of Charlemagne in 814, Western Europe suffered disunion and poverty. Western Europeans wanted a return to prosperity through trade for luxuries from the East. Their most valuable commodity to sell in return was slaves available from conquests in Slavic lands and desired by Muslims. Political relations with the Muslim East, however, had deteriorated. Christians and Muslims were no longer speaking with one another. Furthermore, the Mediterranean region at the center of the trade was fraught with danger. Vikings raided from the West, Muslims from the South, and Magyars from the East. All three converged on the Mediterranean Sea.

The ninth century was a rare time of reduced anti-Semitism in Europe. Jews had good relations with Western Christians and with Byzantine Christians and Muslims in the East. Jews were living almost everywhere along the main trade routes, and a group of Jewish merchants known as Radhanites had market contacts from Portugal to China. The Radhanites originated in Iraq and spoke six languages—Arabic, Persian, Greek, French, Spanish, and Slavonic. Radhanites were willing to continue the trade—despite the Viking,

Muslim, and Magyar raiders—because they had established relatively safe routes, and if they were captured, they were most likely to be redeemed by fellow Jews. Western European merchants sold slaves to Jews, who led them across Europe to North Africa and Arabia, returning with luxuries from Muslim lands. During the tenth century, the growth of anti-Semitism, combined with Christians' refusal to let Jews have all the profits from the slave trade, ended the Jews' dominance.

Following the Jews' expulsion from Spain in 1492 and persecution in Portugal, many settled in Germany and Holland. Early in the seventeenth century the Dutch established settlements in the Caribbean and, with the use of both African and Indian slaves, took over sugar production in formerly Portugese Brazil. With the displacement of the Portugese, some of the more adventuresome of the exiles followed the Dutch to the New World. Jews were involved in slavery in places like Brazil and Curaçao. Only in Suriname, however, did a large percentage of Jewish settlers become slaveholding planters. English Jews were among the first settlers who came to the colony with Lord Willoughby. In 1658 a Jewish colony settled in Cayenne. In 1664, however, the French drove the Jews off Cayenne, and many fled to Suriname, then controlled by the Dutch. By 1700 Jews in Suriname owned 40 sugar plantations with a total of 9,000 slaves. Jewish colonists established their own village, Joden Savanne, in the area near most of the Jewish sugar plantations, about ten miles from the capital, Paramaribo. The high point of Jewish plantation ownership was around 1730, when Jews owned 110 out of a total of 400 plantations.

In *The Secret Relationship between Blacks and Jews,* volume 1 (1991), the Nation of Islam alleged that Jews played a dominant role both in the African slave trade to the Americas and as slaveholders in the Americas. But in fact, the vast amount of slave trading and slaveholding by non-Jews in the Americas, and the small number of Jews living there, makes Jewish participation in slavery unremarkable and relatively insignificant. For example, in 1820 there were fewer than 3,000 Jews living in the United States when the general population was 9,638,453 and slaves numbered 1,538,038. More than 469,000 slaves lived in Virginia alone, the vast majority on plantations. Most of the Jews lived in the North. Fewer than 300 lived in Virginia, and of those, 200 lived in the city of Richmond.

Southern Jews as a group were less actively involved in slavery than the general population. Among the Jews living in the rest of the United States, some worked actively against slavery. For example, Theodore Weiner, Jacob Benjamin, and August Bondi established a

Judah Philip Benjamin, a prominent Jewish lawyer, served as a U.S. senator from Louisiana (1853–1861), attorney general in Jefferson Davis's cabinet (1861), and Confederate secretary of war (1861–1862) and secretary of state (1862–1865). His proposal to arm slaves for Confederate service proved unpopular, and he moved to England in 1865. [Library of Congress/Corbis]

trading post in Kansas to support its entry into the Union as a free state. Despite threats to their lives and destruction of their homes, they joined with John Brown's abolitionist forces in 1855. Bondi in particular was a prominent antislavery activist until the Civil War and was one of the first to join the Fifth Kansas Cavalry in 1861. Rebecca Hart was for many years an officer of the Female Anti-Slavery Society in Philadelphia. Harmon Hendricks, one of the most successful shipping merchants in New York City, refused to become involved in the slave trade. Sabato Morais of Philadelphia, Bernhard Felsenthal of Chicago, and David Einhorn of Baltimore are examples of rabbis who gave antislavery sermons. Einhorn's antislavery stance provoked an angry mob to chase him out of Baltimore.

On the other hand, some Jews were active in the slave trade, and some owned plantations. For example, Aaron Lopez came to North America in 1752 and settled in Newport, Rhode Island. At first he was a general trader, specializing in candles made from whale spermaceti. In 1762, he entered the slave trade with his father-in-law and brother-in-law. His records show fourteen direct voyages to Africa and over fifty to the West Indies. It is likely that at least some of the West Indies voyages brought slaves to the United States. Abraham Seixas advertised slaves along with diverse other goods in the *South Carolina State Gazette* in 1794. The Davis family of Petersburg and Richmond, Virginia, has been cited as having the largest Jewish slave-trading firm in the South. This family was mentioned in Harriet Beecher Stowe's *Key to Uncle Tom's Cabin.* The treasurer of the Confederacy, Judah Benjamin, a Jew, owned a large plantation and many slaves.

Jews' attitudes toward slavery reflected those of the general population. Jews in the North generally opposed slavery; Jews in the South generally supported it. The facts would not justify a claim that Jews, as a whole, were prominent abolitionists. Just as clearly, though, the facts do not justify the allegations that Jews were more prominent as slaveholders or slave traders than any other citizens of the United States.

See also ABOLITIONISM AND ANTISLAVERY MOVEMENTS; JUDAISM.

BIBLIOGRAPHY

COBIN, DAVID M. "Jews and the Medieval Slave Trade: The Law and Its Historical Context." In *Jewish Law Association Studies IX,* edited by E. A. Goldman. 1997.

GOSLINGA, CORNELIS. *A Short History of the Netherlands Antilles and Surinam.* 1979.

HUBNER, LEON. "Some Jewish Associates of John Brown." *Publication of the Jewish Historical Society* 23 (1915): 55–78.

KORN, BERTRAM. "Jews and Negro Slavery in the Old South, 1789–1865." In *The Jewish Experience in America,* vol. 3, edited by Abraham J. Karp. 1969.

ROSENSWAIKE, IRA. "The Jewish Population of the United States as Estimated from the Census of 1820." In *The Jewish Experience in America,* vol. 2, edited by Abraham J. Karp. 1969.

THOMAS, HUGH. *The Slave Trade.* 1997.

WHITEMAN, MAXWELL. "Jews in the Anti-Slavery Movement" (introductory essay). In *The Kidnapped and the Ransomed.* 1970.

David M. Cobin

Jim Crow Laws

See Law; United States.

Judaism

The Bible provides for two kinds of slaves: the Jewish slave, in Hebrew the *eved ivri;* and the non-Jewish slave, the *eved canaani.* Since the *eved ivri* became free following a fixed six-year term of service, this status was more like indentured servitude than slavery as it is currently understood. A male *eved ivri* could free himself prior to the expiration of the six years by paying his purchase price to his master. A master could also voluntarily free a slave prior to expiration. Also, a male slave who did not want to leave his master could voluntarily lengthen his service, though extending servitude was discouraged. A female slave became free prior to the expiration of six years upon showing the first signs of puberty, or at the death of her master. A Jewish slave could serve only Jewish masters. The *eved ivri* status ceased to exist by the close of the first century. The *eved canaani* status, however, continued into the nineteenth century in those lands where observant Jews lived among slaveholders and where Jews owned slaves.

The non-Jewish slaves remained in servitude for life, unless the they were voluntarily freed by the master or had their purchase price paid by another. Leviticus 25:46 states, "They shall be your bondmen forever." This quotation from Leviticus would seem to prohibit manumission—that is, freeing a slave. In fact, in the Talmud Rabbi Akiba ruled that manumission violated a positive commandment. Jewish law, however, did not follow Rabbi Akiba in this ruling.

Talmudic law required that within the first day after being purchased by a Jew, a non-Jewish slave be converted to Judaism by immersion in a ritual bath and—for a male—by circumcision. If a male slave was reluctant to undergo circumcision, the Talmud allowed the master to defer the act for up to a year. If after a year the slave refused circumcision, the master was required to sell him to a non-Jew. Following immersion and (for a male) circumcision, the slave became an *eved canaani,* a partial member of the Jewish community subject to some of its religious commandments. Slaves could not be required to work on the Sabbath or certain holidays. Slaves were required to follow the dietary laws. They could inherit from their masters if there was no other issue. Masters were discouraged, however, from educating slaves in Jewish law. A master could not marry an unmanumitted slave. Sexual relations between a master and a slave were strictly forbidden. If a slave was manumitted, he or she became a full member of the Jewish community.

Maimonides in the Mishneh Torah listed a series of occurrences that would require a master to free an *eved canaani.* These included striking a slave and causing an apparent permanent disability, such as losing a tooth; selling a slave to a non-Jew; selling a slave outside the land of Israel if the master lived within the land of Israel; and treating a slave like a free person—for example, having him or her read from the Torah. A master who sold a slave illegally was required to repurchase the slave for up to ten times the slave's value, and set him or her free. Maimonides ruled that it was permitted to work an *eved canaani* with rigor but counseled that piety and wisdom required a master to be merciful and pursue justice, give the slave food and drink in plenty, and not impose a heavy yoke or distress a slave.

During the Middle Ages, Western Europeans were involved in an active slave trade. Slaves captured in Slavic lands were sold for luxuries in the East. The prohibition against selling a properly converted *eved canaani* to a non-Jew would have prevented observant Jews from participating in this slave trade. In the ninth century, however, a Jewish trader wrote to Rav Nahshon, Gaon of Sura, the leading rabbinic authority of his time, for permission not to convert his slaves. The trader argued that slaves of the time were not sincerely converting to Judaism. Rav Nahshon agreed and permitted the traders to sell their slaves to non-Jews. In this way Jews were legal participants in the slave trade during portions of the ninth and tenth centuries.

Pre-enlightenment rabbis did not publish criticism of the institution of slavery. The acceptance of slavery at that time resulted naturally from the rabbis' understanding that slavery was approved in the Bible and heavily regulated in Jewish law. Rabbis were very concerned that the laws of slavery be followed, especially the prohibition against sexual relations with slaves. In a case where a convert to Judaism maintained a female slave for sexual relations, Rav Amram ruled that the slave should be sold and the proceeds given to poor Jews. The owner was to be flogged, his head was to be shaved, and he was to be shunned for thirty days. Another decision characterized sexual relations between a Jewish master and his slave as prostitution and advised that a Jew who saw such a relationship could strike down the offender, even if this resulted in the offender's death, "as did Pinchas to Zimri." (The reference is to Numbers 25. Pinchas killed the Israelite Zimri while Zimri was having sexual relations with a Midianite woman—he put a spear through both of them and thereby ended a plague.)

Post-enlightenment rabbis, however, did challenge the legitimacy of modern slavery in Judaism. Among the notable opponents of slavery was the Orthodox rabbi Sabato Morais of Philadelphia. Beginning in 1856 Morais spoke against slavery from his pulpit at Mikveh Israel synagogue. He argued, "One God created us all. One sun shines over all of us." Morais would later found the Jewish Theological Seminary in New York, a stronghold of historical Judaism. The seminary is now the rabbinic training institution for the Conservative movement. Another notable opponent of slavery was the Reform rabbi David Einhorn of Har Sinai congregation in Baltimore. Although Baltimore was in a slave state, Rabbi Einhorn regularly preached against slavery from the time he arrived there in 1855. In June 1859, a Danish Reform rabbi, Moses Mielziner, published his doctoral dissertation for the University of Giessen, "Slavery Among the Ancient Hebrews." In his introduction Mielziner argued that the servant of God could not be the servant of man. With the diffusion of the knowledge of God among all nations, this principle would become accepted for all people. The restrictions on the terms of service for the *eved ivri* in biblical law should then apply to all slaves and eventually lead to "the total abolition of slavery, not only among the Israelites, but among all nations." This dissertation was immediately translated into English and distributed widely in the United States by the abolitionist movement. In 1865, Mielziner emigrated from Denmark to the United States to become rabbi of Anshei Hesed congregation in New York.

A prominent defense of slavery came from Rabbi Morris Raphall (Orthodox) of New York. On the eve of secession Rabbi Raphall published a sermon defending slavery as biblically ordained. Raphall distinguished between biblical and contemporary slavery but criticized those who attributed antislavery sentiments to the Bible. On 4 July 1861, Rabbi Einhorn, who by that time had been chased out of Baltimore by a threatening mob, responded in a sermon at Kenereth-Israel congregation in Philadelphia, attacking Raphall's position. Einhorn saw an affinity between the Jewish people and America, which he said had been founded on principles of Mosaic descent.

One of these shared principles was the equality of all humanity: "Is it possible to imagine a more distinct proclamation of the innate equality of all rational beings than the teaching that 'God created man in his image'?" Recognizing the equality of all human beings meant that slavery must not persist, for the good of both the United States and Judaism.

This rabbinic debate demonstrates the conflict within Judaism between the apparent legal acceptance of slavery and the ethical rejection of it. As the Civil War neared, those rabbis who opposed slavery resolved the conflict by elevating the ethical concerns and confining the legal acceptance to the ancient period. After reviewing the rabbis' writings, it is safe to conclude that among antebellum rabbis the antislavery view predominated.

See also BIBLE; JEWS.

BIBLIOGRAPHY

EINHORN, DAVID. *Memorial Volume—Selected Sermons and Addresses,* edited by Kaufmann Kohler. 1911.

KIRON, ARTHUR. "'Dust and Ashes': The Funeral and Forgetting of Sabato Morais." *American Jewish History* 84, no. 3 (1996): 155–188.

MANN, JACOB. *The Responsa of the Babylonian Geonim as a Source of Jewish History.* Reprinted 1970.

MOSES BEN MAIMON. *The Code of Maimonides, Book Twelve, The Book of Acquisition,* translated by Isaac Klein. 1951.

MIELZINER, ELLA M. F. *Morris Mielziner.* 1931.

NUSSENBAUM, MAX SAMUEL. *Champion of Orthodoxy: A Biography of the Reverend Sabato Morais, LLD.* 1964.

URBACH, EPHRAIM E. "The Laws Regarding Slavery as a Source for Social History of the Period of the Second Temple, the Mishnah and Talmud." In *Papers of the Institute of Jewish Studies.* 1964.

WHITEMAN, MAXWELL, "Jews in the Anti-Slavery Movement." An introductory essay to *The Kidnapped and the Ransomed.* 1970.

David M. Cobin

K

Kansas

Black slavery had a brief and feeble life in Kansas, from 1854 to 1861. The number of slaves, though not precisely known, was certainly small. Slavery proved more important in Kansas, and in national life, as a potential presence than it did in fact as a labor or social institution. The area that became Kansas Territory lay in the northern portion of the Louisiana Territory, from which slavery was banned by the Missouri Compromise of 1820. Not until 1854 was the Kansas Territory organized, and then by a tumultuous repeal of the Missouri Compromise.

Opening the territory to slavery did not result in substantial migration of slaves, but the possibility provoked turbulence that dominated politics for five years. Slaveholding Missourians, living immediately east of Kansas, fearful that a free state would be organized and intent on establishing slavery in Kansas, fraudulently and violently interfered in the formation of a territorial government. The outcome was a proslavery government that was upheld by presidents Franklin Pierce and James Buchanan. Free-state forces stoutly opposed proslavery forces, and violence flared on the Kansas frontier.

The geographical as well as the political climate was inhospitable to slavery and free blacks. A proslavery judge, Rush Elmore—who, as the owner of fourteen slaves, was one of the largest slaveholders in the territory—during a very cold winter found it necessary to haul and cut wood himself to keep his slaves warm, only to see one freeze to death and another incapacitated for life by frostbite. Free-staters drafted the Topeka constitution that prohibited entry of blacks into the territory. Sara Robinson, the wife of a territorial governor, recorded the hostility toward a free black who was brought into the territory by two white families.

John Steuart Curry's mural in the Kansas state capitol depicts John Brown at the center of the struggle over slavery. A Bible in his left hand and a rifle in his right, Brown is flanked by the contending free-soil and proslavery forces. At their feet are two figures symbolic of the Civil War dead. [Kansas State Historical Society]

453

The black belt of Kansas ran along its eastern edge. The territorial census of 1855 offers perhaps the best window through which to view slavery in the territory. Of 6,525 people in Kansas, only 186 were slaves. About two-thirds of the slaves were concentrated in two of seventeen electoral districts; not quite half of these were owned by masters and mistresses who had only one slave. The average slaveholding was 2.3 slaves, in contrast to 12.7 in the deep South. Slavery in territorial Kansas maintained a balance between males and females and adults and children. Plantation slavery, with its harsh labor system, did not develop in Kansas; observers witnessed kind treatment of slaves. Many slaves helped the owner's family work the family farm. Others worked in such capacities as cooks, ferrymen, and teamsters. Emancipation became easy to attain, and some slaves followed the Underground Railroad to freedom.

At its height slavery in territorial Kansas claimed perhaps five hundred persons. The certainty of a free Kansas that developed in late 1858, when territorial voters rejected a proposed proslavery constitution, made Kansas an inhospitable place for any future slavery. The U.S census of 1860 reported only two slaves in the territory. In early 1861 Kansas entered the Union as a free state.

See also KANSAS-NEBRASKA ACT; MISSOURI; MISSOURI COMPROMISE; UNDERGROUND RAILROAD.

BIBLIOGRAPHY

RAWLEY, JAMES A. *Race and Politics: "Bleeding Kansas" and the Coming of the Civil War.* 1969. Examines the impact of slavery in Kansas on national politics.

ROBINSON, SARA. *Kansas: Its Interior and Exterior Life.* 1856. A firsthand account that includes the story of free blacks.

SENGUPTA, GUNJA. *For God and Mammon.* 1996. Includes an excellent account of slaves in Kansas.

James A. Rawley

Kansas-Nebraska Act (1854)

The issue of the expansion of slavery had prompted the Missouri Compromise (1820), which prohibited slavery north of latitude 36° 30′ in the Louisiana Territory. For the next third of a century the northern segment of the territory remained unorganized, and this inaction maintained a truce between rival northern and southern interests. Lack of political organization worked against settlement and against building a transcontinental railroad linking the East with the Pacific coast, which had been added to the nation in 1848.

A SPEECH ON THE KANSAS QUESTION.

A vociferous congressman presents his point during a speech on the Kansas question. [*Harper's Weekly*/Corbis]

Senator Stephen A. Douglas, chairman of the Committee on Territories, taking charge of a bill to organize the huge northern segment, encountered resistance from southern congressmen opposed to adding free soil to the Union. Without southern support, passage was impossible. Intent on driving the bill to enactment, Douglas sponsored a revised version that repealed the restriction in the Missouri Compromise, substituted popular sovereignty for the prohibition, and organized not one but two territories.

Repeal provoked a storm of angry protest in the North. Hot-tempered debate characterized congressional consideration of the bill. President Franklin Pierce, who had approved introduction of the bill, exerted his influence; and the bill passed the Senate 37–14 and a reluctant House 113–100. On 30 May 1854 it became law.

The Kansas-Nebraska Act ignited a blaze that led to the conflagration of the Civil War. John Brown's execution of five proslavery settlers added fuel to the fire. A massive realignment of political parties occurred. The national pattern of two national parties broke down. The Whig Party passed out of existence; a new Republican Party, committed to nonextension of slavery and supported only in the North, swiftly rose. By

1860 four political parties were vying for the presidency, and the election culminated in the victory of the Republican Party.

See also BROWN, JOHN; CIVIL WAR, U.S.; DOUGLAS, STEPHEN A.; MISSOURI COMPROMISE.

BIBLIOGRAPHY

DOUGLAS, STEPHEN A. Papers. University of Chicago Library.
GIENAPP, WILLIAM E. *The Origins of the Republican Party, 1852–1856*. 1987. A scholarly study of great merit.
JOHANNSEN, ROBERT W. *Stephen A. Douglas*. 1973. The best biography.
RAWLEY, JAMES A. *Race and Politics: "Bleeding Kansas" and the Coming of the Civil War*. 1969. Examines the Kansas-Nebraska struggle from 1854 through 1858.

James A. Rawley

Kant, Immanuel   [1724–1804]

Philosopher and ethicist.

Immanuel Kant rejected slavery in all its forms, as well as the traditional defenses for it.

The surrender of prisoners of war could not justify slavery because international relations were a state of nature where no law existed. A war, therefore, could never be punitive, and the victor could not annex the vanquished or make slaves of its subjects. Military conquest, furthermore, could never justify slavery because its hereditary nature would still be unjust.

Surprisingly, Kant, who emphasized freedom, equality, and independence for citizens, required that citizens should endure tyranny rather than revolt against the state. Drawing upon a German intellectual tradition going back at least to Luther, Kant condemned all rebellion against the state as inherently evil. There could be no right to rebel and no power to determine what would constitute a right to rebel.

Kant did, rather inconsistently, support the French Revolution, and he clearly recognized passive resistance or passive disobedience to be a right, or even a moral duty, under certain circumstances.

Kant's thoughts about slavery are contained for the most part in *The Metaphysics of Morals,* although the roots may be found in his moral theories as expressed in his *Lectures on Ethics* and the *Critique of Practical Reason* and in his political philosophy as put forward in the "Idea for a Universal History," "Perpetual Peace," and "On the Common Saying: 'This May Be True in Theory, but It Does Not Apply in Practice.'"

Kant's influence has permeated modern philosophy in every discipline from metaphysics and theology to ethics and aesthetics.

See also HEGEL, G. W. F.; HOBBES, THOMAS.

BIBLIOGRAPHY

Kant's Political Philosophy. Edited by Hans Reiss and translated by H. B. Nisbet. 1970.
WILLIAMS, HOWARD. *Kant's Political Philosophy*. 1983.

Patrick M. O'Neil

Kemble, Frances Anne ("Fanny")
[1809–1893]

British-born antislavery activist and author.

Born in London into the most illustrious theatrical family in England, Frances Anne Kemble made her acting debut at the age of nineteen. While touring the United States, in 1832 she fell in love with and married Pierce Butler, the heir to one of the largest slave fortunes in Georgia. Kemble, an outspoken opponent of slavery before her marriage, muzzled her unpopular opinions in her husband's hometown of Philadelphia, where the couple resided and raised their two daughters. Kemble's marriage was an unhappy one, especially when the entire family spent the winter of 1838–1839 in the sea islands of Georgia on the Butler plantations, where Kemble was able to

Fanny Kemble. [Corbis-Bettmann]

see the operation of a slave plantation firsthand. Butler hoped the encounter would soften his wife's views, but this sojourn only hardened her opposition and hastened the end of the marriage. Kemble kept a diary, and this plantation journal circulated among abolitionists during the early 1840s. Butler forbade his wife to publish the journal, and even following the couple's acrimonious divorce in 1849, Kemble could not be persuaded to publish it. However, while living in England during the American Civil War, Kemble, alarmed over British sympathy for the Confederacy, released her work for publication in 1863. Her *Journal of Residence on a Georgian Plantation* (1863) has been debated by critics for generations and remains a searing and stirring indictment of slavery—an antislavery classic. Kemble wrote eleven volumes of memoirs during her lifetime, but it was her Georgia journal which secured her an enduring international reputation.

See also BUTLER, PIERCE MEASE.

BIBLIOGRAPHY

BELL, MALCOLM, JR. *Major Butler's Legacy: Five Generations of a Slaveholding Family.* 1987.
FURNAS, J. C. *Fanny Kemble.* 1982.

Catherine Clinton

Kentucky

The moderate slave state of Kentucky was situated in the upper South, where slavery was not widespread. During the nearly forty years before Kentucky became a state in 1792, some slavery had existed there among the westward migrating Virginians. Fewer than 10 percent of European immigrants to the United States entered Kentucky during the period from 1820 to 1850; most white settlers, therefore, came from the old eastern slave states. By 1860, when slaves were 19.5 percent of its population, some 38,645 (23.5 percent) of the white families owned the 225,483 slaves, with an average holding of 5.8 bondsmen. Rocky and hilly soil and a cold-to-mild climate dictated that Kentucky could support only a moderate slave population on small farms of twenty to fifty acres each. Kentucky thus annually exported thousands of surplus slaves to the deep South from 1830 to 1860. Louisville became an important slave market for the upper South.

The slaves lived mostly in the central and western counties. Only 10 percent resided in the eastern area, including just 5 percent in the mountainous counties. In Louisville, where many free blacks lived, some 30 percent of the slaves were hired out as craftsmen, laborers, and railroad and riverboat workers by their masters. Slaves cost from eight hundred to a thousand dollars or more and by 1860 could be rented for a hundred dollars a year. Slaves also labored as miners in the eastern part of the state. Kentucky, along with Missouri, produced more than three-fourths of America's hemp. The slaves produced large amounts of corn, tobacco, and grains, but hardly any cotton; and they also worked in tobacco factories, mainly in the eastern and middle parts of Kentucky.

The types of slaves included field hands (75 percent men, 80 percent women), house servants, artisans (craftsmen), and industrial and urban slaves. Slaves began work at sunup and returned to their quarters after sundown, working five to six days a week. Four to five slaves usually lived in one-room cabins of about two hundred square feet, with a central fireplace for heat and cooking. Bedding was straw or feather pallets on the floor or, in rare instances, crude post beds made by the slaves. Annual issues of clothing consisted of two hats, two pairs of shoes, and two pairs of pants and two shirts or, for the women, wool or calico dresses. Slave mortality was higher than that of whites, and children accounted for most of the deaths among the slaves, who suffered from pneumonia, whooping cough, cholera, bowel disorders, and various other diseases, mostly caused by hard work, poor housing, bad diet, and little, if any, health care. Food for slaves consisted of fat pork, corn meal, molasses, peas, potatoes, corn, and fruits from local orchards, supplemented by wild game.

Kentucky's harsh slave laws (slave codes) included a requirement of written permission to leave the farm, ten lashes as punishment for wandering away, a ban on the possession of firearms by slaves, a prohibition on selling items to other slaves, and a ban on holding assemblies for free blacks or slaves. Slaves initially attended church with their masters. But by 1860, Kentucky had nearly twenty separate black churches. Slave patrols roamed the countryside to control the blacks who engaged in various forms of resistance, such as breaking tools, slowing the work pace, making trouble in the slave quarters, pretending to be sick, attacking their masters, doing extra work to earn money to buy their own freedom and that of relatives, and running away and escaping to the North across the Ohio River. Developing their own culture through storytelling, music, dance, and religion and keeping strong family ties were also considered forms of resistance. There were several black Underground Railroad leaders from Kentucky: Josiah Henson, Elijah Anderson, and John Mason.

By 1849 the slavery issue in Kentucky had generated many debates, a movement to colonize freed slaves in Liberia, Africa, and even a statewide antislavery convention. Among Kentucky's many antislavery lead-

Table 1.   Slave and Free Population of Kentucky, 1790–1860.

	1790	1800	1810	1820	1830	1840	1850	1860
Free blacks	114	739	1,713	2,759	4,917	7,317	10,011	10,684
Slaves	12,430	40,343	80,561	126,732	165,213	182,258	210,981	225,483
Whites	61,133	179,873	324,237	434,644	517,787	590,253	761,413	919,484
Owners	–	–	–	–	–	–	38,385	38,645

Source: *The Negro in the United States, 1790–1915* (1968).

ers were Germans, Presbyterians, the Shakers at Pleasant Hill, Cassius M. Clay, William Bailey, and Calvin Fairbank.

When the Civil War began, Kentucky, a border state, remained in the Union. Kentucky furnished 23,703 black troops for the Union army. Slavery was ended by ratification of the Thirteenth Amendment to the national Constitution in December 1865.

See also the individual entries for the other states of the United States.

BIBLIOGRAPHY

BROWN, WILLIAM WELLS. *Narrative of William W. Brown: A Fugitive Slave.* 1847.
COLEMAN, J. WINSTON, JR. *Slavery Times in Kentucky.* 1940.
MCDOUGLE, IVAN E. *Slavery in Kentucky, 1792–1865.* 1970.
MURPHY, JAMES B. "Slavery and Freedom in Appalachia: Kentucky as a Demographic Case Study." *Register* (Kentucky Historical Society) 80 (1982): 151–169.
WRIGHT, GEORGE C. *Life behind a Veil: Blacks in Louisville, Kentucky, 1865–1930.* 1985.

Bobby L. Lovett

Koran

See Islam.

Korea

The first Korean state, the Old Choson, emerged during the first millennium B.C., though except for the Old Choson the region was tribal. From the first century B.C. to the second century after Christ, the Three Kingdoms were formed: Koguryo, Paekche, and Silla. Each was a centralized monarchy with an aristocracy and a strict, precise hereditary class or caste hierarchy. Silla's caste arrangement, consisting of eight layers, was known as the bone rank system (*kolp'um*). Among other functions, it established eligibility for various ranks of official positions. In ancient times Korean tribes seem to have imposed servitude on conquered peoples, prisoners of war, and criminals; according to the historical records, however, it was during the period of the Three Kingdoms that something like actual slavery developed. Commoners—the lower castes—were a source of corvée labor, and the bottom caste probably included slaves.

In A.D. 669 Silla gained control of the Korean peninsula, conquering first Paekche and then Koguryo; this period is known as Unified Silla. Just before this, the bone rank system had weakened, and slavery as an institution probably weakened also. The explanation may be that the Koreans were then beginning to adopt Confucianism. Since one tenet of this ideology was that political leaders and bureaucrats should be chosen by merit rather than heredity, it is likely to have gradually diluted class distinctions. During the 800s, Silla broke apart; and by the time it was reunited as Koryo around 935, the Korean social hierarchy was much simpler, comprising only three classes.

The pattern of caste and slavery in Korea was similar to that in China, were Confucianism and dynastic governance were influential factors. At the top of the social hierarchy were the scholar-officials, an elite consisting of less than 5 percent of the population. The main body of Confucian society consisted of commoners, who paid the bulk of the taxes and from whom—through civil service examinations—much of the bureaucracy was drawn. Slaves, at the bottom of the hierarchy, were a relatively small part of the population, normally less than 10 percent; and as hereditary outcastes they could not enter the civil service. As a dynasty neared its end, with the accompanying social disorder, these proportions could change.

Around 956, Koryo freed many of its slaves, but little is known about the ensuing period. In 1170 there was a military coup, and in 1231 Koryo was invaded by the Mongols. During the period of Mongol rule, the number of slaves increased substantially, although enslavement at this time might perhaps be more accurately described as a kind of serfdom. The increase seems to have been due to a striking feature of the period:

the vast manors owned by absentee aristocrats and cultivated by tenants. (These large farms were made possible by improved technology: fertilizers, which doubled the productivity of the land, and water management, which made more land arable. As a result, commercial agriculture for domestic markets began.) The tenant farmers were subject to forced labor, taxes, and military service; and to avoid these obligations—especially taxation—many of them became servants, that is, slaves. In addition, vagrants were sometimes caught by the aristocrats and impressed into servitude. As the number of slaves rose, numerous slave rebellions broke out.

Twentieth-century Japanese scholars, impressed by the large number of enslaved people in Korea during this period—slaves may have accounted for as much as a third of the population—were led at one point to describe traditional Korean society as a "slave state." However, that is not entirely just: it was only at this one time in Korea's history that slaves were so numerous.

Around 1368 Koryo broke free of Mongol rule, but the country then underwent internal strife; in 1392 Koryo's existing dynasty was supplanted by the new Yi dynasty (which would rule until 1910). General Yi Song-Gye, its founder, renamed the country—again—Choson.

At its inception, Choson followed the usual pattern and freed many slaves. It was then faced with determining the status of children born to one parent who was free and one who was a slave. In Confucian societies a child of a slave concubine (the mother) and a scholar-official (the father) would always be considered free. But if one parent was a slave and the other a commoner, the status of the child varied from time to time. In Choson this issue was related to the problem of achieving an appropriate ratio of commoners and slaves in the population. Liberals (to use the modern term) wanted a proportionally small slave population because this would create a stronger nation and a larger number of taxpaying commoners.

An interesting aspect of slavery in Korea from ancient times was that it could be, in a sense, public or private. The state of the slave depended on the identity of the owner. The farms could be owned either by private individuals and public agencies in combination or by a branch of government. The government rewarded certain officeholders with servants known as public slaves, and in addition some of these individuals also held private slaves as servants. Both public and private slaves were used as farm laborers and domestic servants, and some public slaves were office workers and artisans. A few slaves became important inventors and painters. Many slaves still lived as tenant farmers, and although they paid tribute to their owners, some slaves had an independent income and

A Korean woman is pulled by a male servant in a covered ricksha, with the usually drawn curtain open, as her maid walks beside her down the streets of Seoul. [Library of Congress/Corbis]

a high degree of autonomy. Actually, the law treated slaves only slightly worse than it treated commoners; the sharpest distinction, legally, was not between slaves and commoners but rather between both groups on the one hand and the scholar-officials on the other.

As the population of Choson increased during the fifteenth century, the ratio of people to land became greater. Landless people were being absorbed into the growing economy as hired laborers, and this opportunity became an inducement for slaves to run away. By the end of the sixteenth century, the institution of slavery was declining.

In 1775 a policy of gradual emancipation was established, in effect, when King Yongjo made taxes the same for slaves and commoners, so that becoming a servant was no longer a way to avoid being taxed. In 1801 the royal family and the central government freed all their agricultural slaves. In 1806 Choson abolished hereditary slavery by limiting servitude to one generation. Finally, in 1895—under the modernizing influence of Japan, which was planning to annex Korea—Choson abolished slavery altogether. This emancipation was uncompensated; it simply made slaves hired laborers.

Korean slaves and their owners were of the same race, and that made it easier for former slaves to be integrated into the mainstream population of Korea. Another factor in this integration was Korea's movement, through political and social turmoil, toward the modern era.

See also CHINA; JAPAN.

BIBLIOGRAPHY

HIRAKI, MINORU. *Choson Huki Nobiche Yonku* (A Study of Slavery in Later Choson). 1982.
HONG, SEUNG-KI. *Koryoeui Kuijoksahoewa Nobi* (Aristocratic Society of Koryo and Slaves). 1983.

KIM, HYONG-IN. "Rural Slavery in Antebellum South Carolina and Early Choson Korea." Ph.D. diss., University of New Mexico. 1990.
SALEM, ELLEN. "Slavery in Medieval Korea." Ph.D. diss., Columbia University. 1978.

Hyong-In Kim

Kuwait

See Modern Middle East.